Basic Mathematics

Preliminary Edition

Robert H. Prior

Riverside Community College

Boston San Francisco New York
London Toronto Sydney Tokyo Singapore Madrid
Mexico City Munich Paris Cape Town Hong Kong Montreal

Publisher: Greg Tobin
Editor in Chief: Maureen O'Connor
Acquisitions Editor: Jennifer Crum
Project Editor: Katie Nopper
Editorial Assistant: Emily Ragsdale
Managing Editor: Ron Hampton
Text Designer: Scott Silva
Cover Designer: Dennis Schaefer
Composition: Laura Wiegleb
Marketing Manager: Jay Jenkins
Marketing Assistant: Alexandra Waibel
Prepress Services Buyer: Caroline Fell
First Print Buyer: Evelyn Beaton

Library of Congress Cataloging-in-Publication Data available upon request.

ISBN: 0-321-37495-9

2 3 4 6 7 8 9 10 CRS 09 08 07 06

Contents

Preface

Welcome to *Basic Mathematics*

You are about to begin a course that will teach you the fundamentals of arithmetic and help you to build a solid foundation for future math courses. Thanks so much for making my book part of your learning experience. I recognize that some of you may have had less-than-favorable experiences in math while others have simply been away from a traditional math course for quite some time. I'm sure that to many of you, math is a mystery with lots of rules to be memorized. You may never have been shown that there is a "why" to the math you've been asked to learn. Now that you are in college, it's time to learn *why* math works the way it does, and that's what my *Basic Mathematics* text is all about.

I first wrote my basic math text for online community college students. I had to write it in such a way that they could learn on their own, mostly by reading the book and doing the exercises. What I found through class-testing the material was that students in a traditional classroom benefited from my extremely thorough explanations and detailed development of the content. It was my goal to create a book that is:

- easily readable for the student.
- detailed in its explanations and development of the ideas and rules of mathematics.

To aid your success in this course, it is helpful to know how my book works. Below are some suggestions on how to make the best use of this book.

Layout

Chapter Opener and Preparation Exercises: Each chapter opens with a brief introduction to what you are about to learn. Reading this introduction will help you prepare your mind for upcoming topics and skills. Following the introduction is a set of Preparation Exercises. These are a great way to check your understanding of the prerequisite skills that will be needed for the upcoming chapter. The answers to these are provided in the back so you can assess your readiness for the chapter. If you struggle with any of these exercises, section references are provided so you can refresh your skills and understanding of these topics.

Objectives and Prerequisites: Each section begins with a list of section objectives indicating "what you will learn" to help you prepare for the upcoming material. In addition, most sections include a list of the necessary prerequisite subtopics that you should already know before reading the section. These prerequisite topics are followed by section references, so if you are struggling with a prerequisite topic, you can refer back to a previous section for help.

Examples and Exercises: Following the listing of objectives and prerequisites is the written explanation of the new material (sometimes with prerequisite information), followed by an example or two, and immediately followed by **You Try It** exercises that mirror the examples. Some of these exercises are specific to the objectives, while others are intermediate steps that lead to the focal points of the section. I strongly encourage you to try these exercises when they appear within the text. The section continues in this pattern until each major focal point is fully developed. In addition to the exercises presented directly in the body of the text, I include a set of **Focus Exercises** at the end of the section to highlight those items about which the section is directed. Answers to the You Try It exercises are given at the end of the section; answers to the odd-numbered Focus Exercises and all answers for each Preparation Exercise, Review Exercise, Chapter Test question, and Cumulative Review Exercise are found at the end of the text.

Help along the Way: Within the body of the text, I have included many features to give you support and guidance along the way. As necessary, I include **Caution** boxes to keep you from making common mistakes. In addition, I include **Think about It** questions to keep you engaged in what you are learning and to force you to truly understand the concept behind the skills. The questions will require some thought, but will help you to retain the knowledge you are gaining. You are encouraged to discuss these questions with your classmates. Finally, I also include **side bar** comments that enhance what you are reading.

End-of-Chapter Material: At the end of each chapter, you will find an abundance of material to help you pull all the content you have been learning together into one cohesive chunk of knowledge. Each chapter ends with a Chapter Review that points out the key topics in the chapter, a set of Chapter Review Exercises, which provide plenty of practice leading up to a chapter test, a Chapter Test, which is excellent practice for your in-class tests, and a Cumulative Review (after every other chapter) to help prepare you for midterms and the final exam.

Again, I really appreciate being a part of your education. I hope that you find the book to be a reliable guide and resource for your learning. The last page of the book is a student questionnaire. Please take a few minutes to fill it out and let me know what you like or don't like about the book and how I might make it a better resource for future students. I truly value your feedback and look forward to hearing from you.

Best wishes in this and all future math courses.

Bob Prior

CHAPTER 1

Whole Numbers and Number Sense

Introduction

Arithmetic hasn't changed much through the years. Numbers are numbers, after all. In his arithmetic book called Complete Arithmetic, written in 1874, Daniel W. Fish writes this problem:

> "A boy bought a book for 36 cents, a slate for 20 cents, and a pencil for 4 cents. How much change should he receive from a 1 dollar bill?"

That same problem today might read,

> "A student bought the latest best-selling John Grisham novel for $24.99, a cappuccino for $4.85, and CD of Nirvana's greatest hits for $17.95. How much change should she receive from a 50 dollar bill?"

Some of the material presented in this chapter may be quite familiar to you. If that is so, that's great! Use that knowledge to build on ideas presented later in the book. If some of the material is new to you, take the time to understand why it works as well as how it works.

Above all, make a commitment to yourself, to your education, and to your goals. Set up a daily (or weekly) study routine, find a study partner, and do not be afraid to ask questions when something is unclear to you. Use this book to its fullest, make it your own so that you can use it as a reference when you move on to algebra and beyond.

Preparation Exercises

Every chapter, except this one, opens with a set of Preparation Exercises. These exercises are from previous chapter(s) in the text and are designed to help prepare you for the material in the upcoming chapter.

Because this is the first chapter of the book, the Preparation Exercises ask you, instead, to either write or discuss the following.

1. Why are you taking this course?
   a) What plans do you have for your education?
   b) What career plans do you have in mind?
   c) Where will you be in five years?

2. How do you plan to be successful in this course?
   a) Where is your favorite place to study?
   b) Do you like to study alone or in a group?
   c) How much time should be spent on math each week, including time in class?
   d) How important is it to do the assigned homework?
   e) How important is it to read the textbook?
   f) What is the best advice you can give to someone to help them succeed in this class?

SECTION 1.1 Whole Numbers

Objectives

In this section, you will learn to:

- Identify the base-10 numbers.
- Find the place value of a digit in a whole number.
- Write a whole number in expanded form and in words.
- Round whole numbers.

Introduction

Numbers have been around since the beginning of language. People first used numbers to count things, especially when items were being traded, such as five sheep for three pigs. As time progressed, numbers were used to measure things, such as the length of an ark, the distance between two cities, the amount of daylight in a day, and so on.

Eventually people started doing calculations with numbers, and it was called "arithmetic." They started drawing circles and triangles, and it was called "geometry." They started using letters for numbers, and it was called "algebra." They gave all of it a name; they called it "mathematics."

Mathematics is at the heart of every computer, every television set, and every cell phone. In short, mathematics is a hidden part of your everyday life. As complex as our world has become, even the simplest mathematics plays a role.

Most students of arithmetic—basic math—will continue their studies through algebra; some of you may even go on to study higher levels of math, such as statistics or calculus. Whatever your goal, learning basic math—the first building block—is an important step.

Numbers and Numerals

In the world of language, a number is an adjective; it describes something. Just like the color red is an adjective, as in "the *red* balloon," a **number** describes *how many* items there might be, as in "Tina has *six* balloons."

A **numeral** is a symbol that represents a number. For example, the number *six* can be expressed by any of these symbols (and there are others):

In this text we often use the word "number" in place of the word "numeral" to make the reading easier.

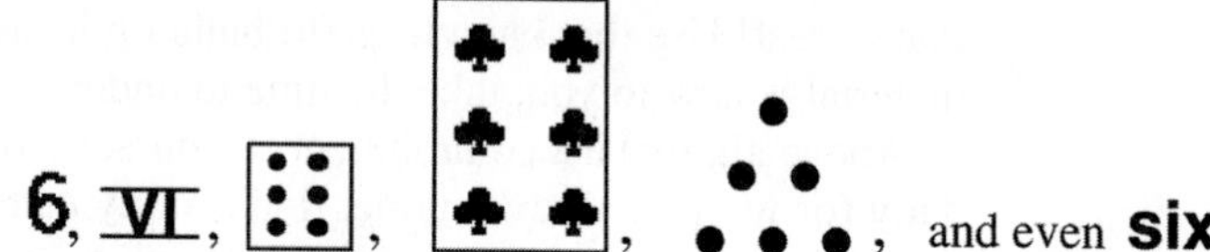

Our way of counting is built on a **base-ten numbering system** that uses ten **digits**, or numerals:

0, 1, 2, 3, 4, 5, 6, 7, 8 and 9.

These digits are the first of the **whole numbers**. When we get to 9, we have exhausted all of the single digit whole numbers, so in order to represent the next whole number, ten, we must use two digits, 10.

The whole numbers: 0, 1, 2, 3, 4, 5, 6,7, 8, 9, 10, 11, 12, 13, 14 ... and so on.

Even though 0 is written as the first whole number, it is not the first counting number.

The **counting numbers**, or **natural numbers**: 1, 2, 3, 4, 5, ..., 10, 11, 12, ... and so on.

We can represent whole numbers visually along a **number line**:

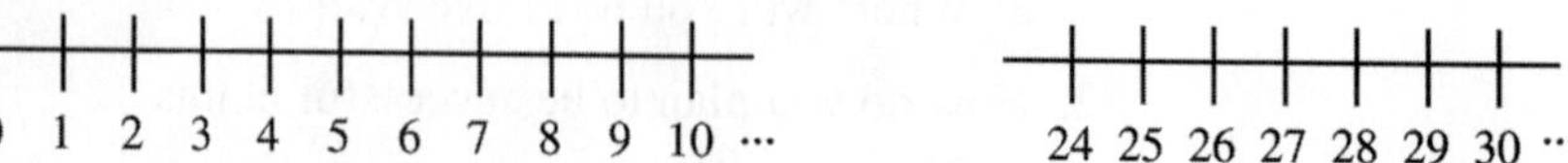

The further to the right along the number line, the higher the value of each number.

Place Value

Let's look at a simple way to think of numbers that have two or more digits. In the following illustrations, we consider dollar bill amounts of $1, $10, $100 and $1,000. These are shown without the dollar sign, $.

First, we can always add 1 to any whole number and get the next whole number:

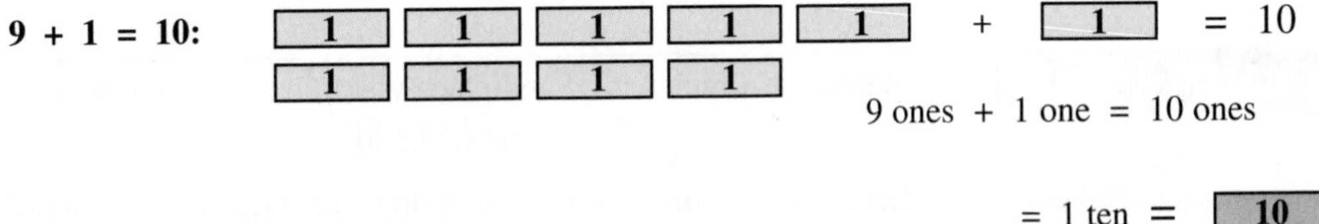

Also, we can add *more than* 1 to any number and get a larger (valued) number.
10 + 3 = 13 means **1 ten** and **3 ones**

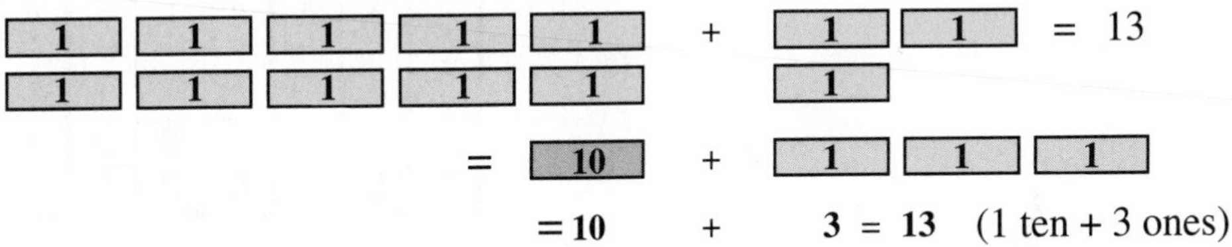

This leads us to the idea of **place value**. The far right digit is in the **ones place** and the digit on its immediate left is in the **tens place**.

For example, in the number 53, 3 is in the *ones place* and 5 is in the *tens place*; it is the place that determines the value given to each digit.

Here is a diagram of the place values (a place-value chart). Notice the groups of threes, called **periods**, and the pattern of repetition (hundreds, tens, ones) within each period.

Trillions period			**Billions period**			**Millions period**			**Thousands period**			**Ones period**		
Hundreds	Tens	Ones	Hundreds	Tens	Ones	Hundreds	Tens	Ones	Hundreds	Tens	Ones	Hundreds	Tens	Ones

Ten billions place

Hundred millions place

One thousands place

To make large numbers easier to read, we typically use a comma to separate numbers into their periods, every three digits reading from right to left. You will probably agree that the number 28930564 is too hard to read without commas. Written as 28,930,564 it can be more easily read. Let's place the number, one digit for each place, in the place-value chart:

Trillions period			**Billions period**			**Millions period**			**Thousands period**			**Ones period**		
Hundreds	Tens	Ones	Hundreds	Tens	Ones	Hundreds	Tens	Ones	Hundreds	Tens	Ones	Hundreds	Tens	Ones
							2	8	9	3	0	5	6	4

This large number can be read (and written) as:

twenty-eight *million*, nine hundred thirty *thousand*, five hundred sixty-four.

Notice that:

1. We use commas to separate the number into periods even when it is written out in words;
2. The numerical period is written before each comma. (The word *one*, for the ones period, is never written.)
3. When spelled out, two-digit numbers, such as 28, are hyphenated: *twenty-eight.*

EXAMPLE 1 Identify in which period and place you find the digit 4, then write the value the 4 represents.

a) 62,439 b) 94,023,186

PROCEDURE: Let's use a place-value chart to help us read the numbers more easily.

Millions period			Thousands period			Ones period		
Hundreds	Tens	Ones	Hundreds	Tens	Ones	Hundreds	Tens	Ones
				6	2	4	3	9
5	9	4	0	2	3	1	8	6

ANSWER: a) In 62,439 the 4 is in the ones period and in the hundreds place, so the 4 represents four hundred (400).

b) In 94,023,186 the 4 is in the millions period and in the *ones place*, so the 4 represents four million (4,000,000).

YOU TRY IT 1 *Identify in which period and place you find the 6, then write the value the 6 represents. Use Example 1 as a guide.*

Millions period			Thousands period			Ones period		
Hundreds	Tens	Ones	Hundreds	Tens	Ones	Hundreds	Tens	Ones

The **You Try It** exercises—**YTI**—are presented within the section because you are expected to do these exercises at this point, while the material is fresh in your mind. These exercises will sometimes lead to other ideas that rely on what you do here. The answer to each YTI can be found at the end of the section.

	Period	Place	Value
a) 629,418	________	________	________
b) 65,023,189	________	________	________

Writing a Number in Expanded Form

We can write a number in *expanded form* when we consider (1) the value of each digit, and (2) the place of each digit. For example, consider the digit 6 in the number 26,358. It is in the thousands place so it represents 6,000 (six thousand).

Likewise, the digit 3 is in the hundreds place and represents 300 (three hundred). In fact, we can break down the entire number into its individual digits, each according to its place, in the following manner:

Millions period			Thousands period			Ones period		
Hundreds	Tens	Ones	Hundreds	Tens	Ones	Hundreds	Tens	Ones
				2	6	3	5	8

20,000; 6,000; 300; 50; 8

= 20,000 + 6,000 + 300 + 50 + 8

This is the expanded form.

YOU TRY IT 2

Write each number in expanded form.

a) 3,075 = ______________________

b) 503,142 = ______________________

Writing Whole Numbers in Words

You saw the number 28,930,564 written in words as

twenty-eight *million*, nine hundred thirty *thousand*, five hundred sixty-four.

Again, notice that commas are used to separate each period and that the period (million and thousand) is written before each comma.

A simpler example is 307. We write this as three hundred seven.

Caution

You might be tempted to include the word *and* in three hundred seven, but this is not appropriate when writing whole numbers. We reserve the word *and* for mixed numbers that include both whole numbers along with either fractions or decimals. In this sense, the word *and* means *plus.*

For example, compare two hundred six million, which is 206,000,000
to two hundred *and* six million, which is 200 + 6,000,000 = 6,000,200.

To eliminate this confusion, we do not use the word and when writing out whole numbers.

EXAMPLE 2

Write each number in words.

a) 239 b) 8,104 c) 403,005 d) 49,023,000

PROCEDURE: Write the number, reading left to right, using a comma to indicate the conclusion of one period and the beginning of a new period.

ANSWER:

a) 239 is two hundred thirty-nine. Notice that thirty-nine is spelled with a hyphen between 'thirty' and 'nine'.

b) 8,104 is eight thousand, one hundred four. Once we write the word *thousand*, we place a comma after it and finish writing the number.

c) 403,005 is four hundred three thousand, five. After the thousands, the ones period contains only 5; it is the comma that shows us the separation.

d) 49,023,000 is forty-nine million, twenty-three thousand. Because there are no non-zero digits in the ones period, we stop at the thousands.

YOU TRY IT 3 *Write the number in words. Use Example 2 as a guide.*

a) 863 ______________________

b) 3,075 ______________________

c) 62,009 ______________________

d) 5,003,102 ______________________

EXAMPLE 3 Write the whole number in numeral form.

a) Seven thousand, five hundred nine

b) Two hundred four thousand, fifty-three

c) Six million, eighteen

PROCEDURE: Look for the numerical period and the comma.

ANSWER: a) Seven thousand, five hundred nine is 7,509. There are no tens between the five hundred and the nine. No tens is represented by 0 in the tens place.

b) Two hundred four thousand, fifty-three is 204,053 This time there are no ten thousands and no hundreds, each of which is represented by a 0.

c) Six million, eighteen is 6,000,018 Since we never see the word thousand, it must be that there are no thousands at all. We can't skip them, but represent that fact with three 0's in the thousands period.

YOU TRY IT 4 *Write the whole number in numeral form. Use Example 3 as a guide.*

a) Two thousand, forty-eight ______________

b) Seventy-five thousand, four ______________

c) One hundred four thousand, two hundred ______________

Rounding Values

Sometimes, when working with a large number, it is easier to think of the number in *rounded* terms. For example, if the price of a lawn mower is \$287.99, it is easier to think of it as, maybe, \$290, or maybe as \$300. These rounded numbers, \$290 and \$300, are called *approximations*, or *estimates*.

In a moment, you will be introduced to the rules for rounding numbers. First, though, let's take a look at how to visualize numbers in a "higher and lower" sense.

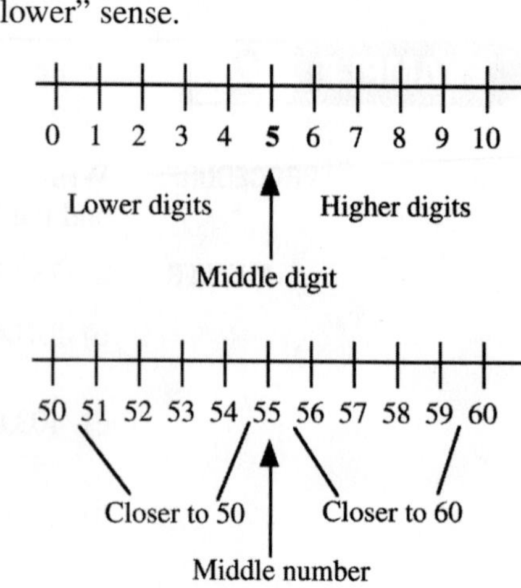

The diagram on the right shows the whole numbers 0 through 10. The digit 5 is in the middle; the digits 6, 7, 8, and 9 are higher digits (to the right of the middle); and the digits 0, 1, 2, 3 and 4 are considered lower digits.

When rounding a number to the nearest *ten*, we rewrite the number with a zero in the *ones* place.

For example, to round 57 to the nearest ten, we must either round it *down* to 50 or round it *up* to 60. In other words, it's like asking the question, "Is 57 closer to 50 or to 60?"

It's the ones digit that indicates whether we should round up or round down. In 57, the ones digit is 7, a higher digit; this means that we should round *up* to 60.

When rounding to the nearest ten we use the digit in the ones place—called the *rounding digit*—to determine whether we should round the number up or down. The diagram indicates that

- When the rounding digit is either 0, 1, 2, 3 or 4, we round *down*.
- When the rounding digit is either 6, 7, 8 or 9, we round *up*.

What happens when the rounding digit is 5? Should we round up or round down? Since there are five digits (0, 1, 2, 3 and 4) that cause a number to be rounded down, there should also be five digits that cause a number to be rounded up (5, 6, 7, 8 and 9). So,

- When the rounding digit is 5, we round *up*.

Below are the rules for rounding. We use two examples—one that rounds up and one that rounds down—to show the application of the various steps.

Rules for Rounding

1. Identify the place digit that is to be rounded.

a) "Round 28,714 to the nearest thousand" means that the 8, in the thousands place, is the place digit.

↓
28,714

b) "Round 28,714 to the nearest hundred" means that 7, in the hundreds place, is the place digit.

↓
28,714

2. Identify the number to its immediate right, called the rounding digit.

a) Rounding 28,714 to the nearest thousand means the rounding digit is the 7.

↓
28,714

b) Rounding 28,714 to the nearest hundred means the rounding digit is the 1.

↓
28,714

3. **i)** If the rounding digit is 5 or higher, round up (add 1 to the place digit).

ii) If the rounding digit is 4 or lower, round down (add 0 to the place digit).

4. All digits to the right of the place digit are written as zeros. Rewrite the number showing the appropriate approximation.

a) In rounding 28,714 to the nearest thousand, the rounding digit, 7, is more than 5, so we need to add 1 to the place digit 8, making a 9 in the thousands place, and all of the digits following it are zeros:

↓
28,714
+ 1
↓
29,000

b) In rounding 28,714 to the nearest hundred, the rounding digit, 1, is less than 5, so we need to add 0 to the place digit, meaning the hundreds place will remain a 7, and all of the digits following it are zeros:

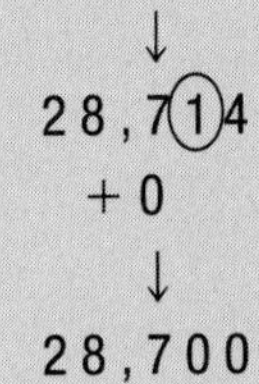

28,700

So, 28,714 can be approximated as 29,000 when rounded to the nearest thousand and can be approximated as 28,700 when rounded to the nearest hundred.

Notice that the digits to the left of the place digit remain unchanged. This is true for most rounding. As you will see in a little bit, when the place digit is 9, rounding up will change more than just the place digit.

EXAMPLE 4

For each of the following, identify the place digit and the rounding digit, decide whether the number will round up or down, and round the number.

Round	To the nearest	Place digit	Rounding digit	Round up/down	Rounded number
a) 726	ten	2	6	up	730
b) 726	hundred	7	2	down	700
c) 1,082	thousand	1	0	down	1,000
d) 235,471	ten-thousand	3	5	up	240,000

YOU TRY IT 5

For each of the following, identify the place digit and the rounding digit, decide whether the number will be rounded up or down, and round the number. Use Example 4 as a guide.

Round	To the nearest	Place digit	Rounding digit	Round up/down	Rounded number
a) 528	ten	______	______	______	______
b) 4,609	hundred	______	______	______	______
c) 4,609	thousand	______	______	______	______
d) 75,406	ten-thousand	______	______	______	______
e) 1,925,046	hundred-thousand	______	______	______	______

Rounding When the Place Digit Is 9

What happens when the place digit is 9? If the number needs to be rounded up, then it rounds up to 10. This means that more than just the place digit is affected; the digit to the left will also increase by 1. (If the number is to be rounded down, the 9 will stay a 9.)

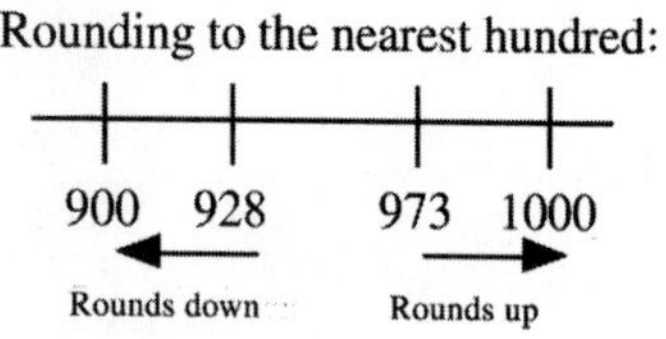

Rounding 928 to the nearest hundred means rounding down to 900.

Rounding 973 to the nearest hundred means rounding it up to "one more than 9" hundred. This means rounding it to ten hundred (1000), or 1,000.

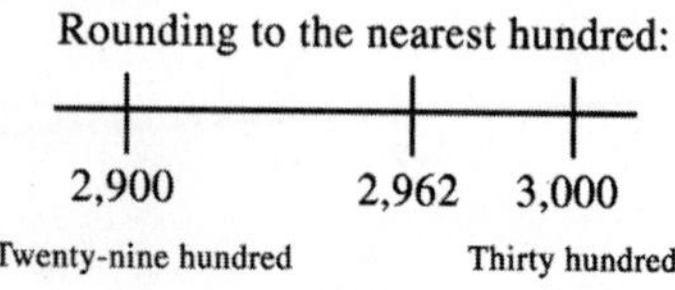

Likewise, rounding 2,962 to the nearest hundred means rounding it up to "one more than 29" hundred. This means rounding it to *thirty* hundred (3000), or 3,000.

So, when the place digit is 9, rounding up affects more than just the place digit; it affects the digit to its left, as well.

EXAMPLE 5

For each of these the place digit is 9. Think about them carefully.

Round	To the nearest	Round up/down	Rounded Number
a) 97	ten	up	100
b) 928	hundred	down	900
c) 4,951	hundred	up	5,000
d) 29,950	hundred	up	30,000
e) 9,850	thousand	up	10,000

YOU TRY IT 6

Round each of these numbers to the place shown. Use Example 5 as a guide.

Round	To the nearest	Round up/down	Rounded number
a) 597	ten	________	________
b) 987	hundred	________	________
c) 3,948	hundred	________	________
d) 691,956	ten thousand	________	________
e) 399,604	thousand	________	________

Applications

Sometimes it's helpful when working with large numbers to round them first. What follows are some statistical data involving large numbers. Your job is to round them and write a sentence that shows the approximation.

EXAMPLE 6

In April 2005, the U.S. population was believed to be 295,981,000. Round this number to the nearest million, and write a sentence indicating the approximation.
Source: www.census.gov/main/www/popclock.html

PROCEDURE: First round the number to the nearest million. It rounds to 296,000,000. Then write a sentence for the approximation. Use the word "about" in the sentence.

ANSWER: In April 2005, the U.S. population was about 296,000,000.

YOU TRY IT 

In 2003, the median (average) income of a four-person California family was $63,761. Round this number to the nearest thousand, and write a sentence indicating the approximation. Use Example 6 as a guide. Source: www.census.gov

Sentence: ____

YOU TRY IT 8 *In 2000, the United States Census Bureau counted 105,522,964 registered women voters. Round this number to the nearest* ***million****, and write a sentence indicating the approximation. Source: www.census.gov*

Sentence: ______________________________

____

Think about it Do you ever round numbers in any of your daily activities at work, while shopping, in your hobbies, or other daily routines? Write a few examples.

____

____

You Try It Answers: Section 1.1

YTI 1

	Period	Place	Value
a)	thousands	hundred	six hundred thousand
b)	millions	ten	sixty million

YTI 2 a) 3,000 + 70 + 5
b) 500,000 + 3,000 + 100 + 40 + 2

YTI 3 a) eight hundred sixty-three
b) three thousand, seventy-five
c) sixty-two thousand, nine
d) five million, three thousand, one hundred two

YTI 4 a) 2,048 b) 75,004 c) 104,200

YTI 5

	Place digit	Rounding digit	Round up/down	Rounded number
a)	2	8	up	530
b)	6	0	down	4,600
c)	4	6	up	5,000
d)	7	5	up	80,000
e)	9	2	down	1,900,000

YTI 6

	Round up/down	Rounded number
a)	up	600
b)	up	1,000
c)	down	3,900
d)	down	690,000
e)	up	400,000

YTI 7 In 2003, the median income of a four-person California family was approximately $64,000.

YTI 8 In 2000, the United States Census Bureau counted approximately 106,000,000 registered women voters.

Focus Exercises: Section 1.1

Apply what you learned in this section to answer the following.

1. In your own words, what is the difference between whole numbers and counting numbers?

2. Place each number on the number line: 30, 35, 22, 27, 38

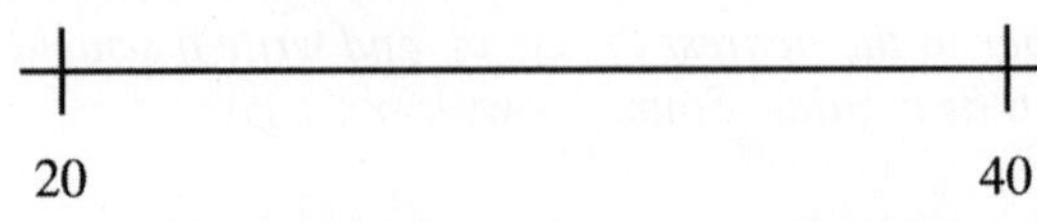

Identify in which period and place you find the digit 7, then write the value the 7 represents.

	Period	Place	Value
3. 53,278	________	________	________
4. 352,716	________	________	________
5. 6,703,214	________	________	________
6. 17,480,300	________	________	________

Write each number in expanded form.

7. 486 ________

8. 4,065 ________

9. 203,058 ________

10. 1,500,043 ________

Write each number in words.

11. 498 ________

12. 6,204 ________

13. 507,093 ________

14. 1,013,000 ________

Write the whole number.

15. Five hundred eighteen ________

16. Two thousand, three hundred six ________

17. Two hundred eighty thousand, thirty-four ________

18. Nine hundred five thousand, eight ________

19. One million, four hundred twenty-six ________

20. Three million, two thousand ________

Round each of these numbers to the nearest ten.

21. 67 ________

22. 683 ________

23. 795 ________

24. 1,941 ________

Round each of these numbers to the nearest hundred.

25. 638 ________

26. 2,049 ________

27. 1,708 ________

28. 2,350 ________

29. 6,951 ________

30. 9,962 ________

Round each of these numbers to the nearest thousand.

31. 2,906 ____________________ **32.** 8,061 ____________________

33. 36,407 ____________________ **34.** 49,513 ____________________

35. 699,850 ____________________ **36.** 3,580,416 ____________________

Round each of these numbers to the nearest ten thousand.

37. 25,408 ____________________ **38.** 324,612 ____________________

39. 650,894 ____________________ **40.** 3,996,416 ____________________

Round each of these numbers to the nearest hundred thousand.

41. 624,058 ____________________ **42.** 850,043 ____________________

43. 952,407 ____________________ **44.** 9,980,376 ____________________

Round each of these numbers to the nearest million.

45. 3,580,416 ____________________ **46.** 4,277,095 ____________________

47. 9,508,416 ____________________ **48.** 46,283,000 ____________________

Rewrite the underlined sentence or phrase with the requested approximation.

49. In 2005, the Rialto Unified School District's budget revenue was **$192,863,877**. Round this number to the nearest million. *Source: www.rialto.k12.ca.us*

50. In 2004, the population of Florida was **17,397,161**. Round this number to the nearest hundred thousand. *Source: factfinder.census.gov*

51. In 2002, gas consumption statistics for all international flights showed that the total number of gallons of gas consumed was **4,990,797,640**. Round this number to the nearest hundred million. *Source: www.bts.gov*

52. It is estimated that the world's rain forests are being destroyed at a rate of **77,893,900** acres per year. Round this yearly acreage to the nearest million. *Source: www.rain-tree.com*

53. In the 2001–2002 school year, **6,248,610** students were enrolled in grades K–12 in California. Round this number to the nearest hundred thousand. *Source: nces.ed.gov*

54. Statistics compiled by the Centers for Disease Control through December, 2003, indicate the total number of reported AIDS cases was **920,566**. Round this number to the nearest ten thousand.

SECTION 1.2 Definitions and Properties

Objectives

In this section, you will learn to:

- Identify and apply the four basic operations.
- Evaluate a mathematical expression.
- Identify and apply the Commutative Properties.
- Identify and apply the Associative Properties.
- Recognize the identities for addition and multiplication.
- Add by grouping to 10.

Introduction

There are a variety of occupations that have their own vocabulary and expressions. For example, nursing students need to learn relevant medical terminology and procedures; this is how doctors and nurses communicate with each other. A nurse must be able to understand what a doctor is saying and the doctor must understand the nurse.

The same is true of math students. As a math student, you must learn the definitions and properties of math so that you can understand your instructor—or this textbook—when those terms are discussed.

Likewise, if you have a question or a problem with math, you need to be able to effectively communicate to the instructor or a tutor. If you are unclear in your question, then the instructor may not answer it properly.

Basic Math Terminology

There are four basic **operations** in mathematics, addition (+), subtraction (−), multiplication (×), and division (÷).

The *written form* of an operation, such as **5 + 4,** is called an **expression.**

We also have words for the results of the operations. To get the result of an operation we must *apply* the operation.

The chart below shows:

(1) the name of each operation;
(2) the operation as an expression (in written form);
(3) the given names of the parts of the operation; and
(4) the result of applying the operation to the numbers given.

Operation	As an expression (written form)	Result
Addition **(plus)**	**Addend + addend** 3 + 5	**= sum** = 8
Subtraction **(minus)**	**minuend − subtrahend** 9 − 5	**= difference** = 4
Multiplication **(times)**	**multiplier × multiplicand** 2 × 3 Also, **factor** × **factor**	**= product** = 6 = **product**
Division **(divided by)**	**dividend ÷ divisor** 136 ÷ 3	**= quotient** = 2

For multiplication, the numbers in a product are called **factors.** For example, 2 and 3 are factors of 6 because 2 × 3 = 6. 1 and 6 are also factors of 6 because 1 × 6 = 6.

For division, the quotient can also be expressed using the long division symbol

$$\text{divisor}\overset{\textbf{quotient}}{\overline{)\textbf{dividend}}}\text{, as in } 3\overset{2}{\overline{)6}}$$

EXAMPLE 1 Write both the expression and the result of each of the following.

ANSWER:

	As an expression		As a result
a) the sum of 5 and 1	$5 + 1$	=	6
b) the difference between 10 and 6	$10 - 6$	=	4
c) the product of 4 and 7	4×7	=	28
d) the quotient of 20 and 4	$20 \div 4$	=	5

YOU TRY IT 1 *Write both the expression and the result of each of the following. Use Example 1 as a guide.*

	As an expression		As a result
a) the sum of 9 and 3	________	=	________
b) the difference between 12 and 4	________	=	________
c) the product of 5 and 8	________	=	________
d) the quotient of 30 and 5	________	=	________

YOU TRY IT 2 *Determine whether the expression shown is a sum, difference, product, or quotient.*

Expression	Operation	Expression	Operation
a) 10×6	________	b) $15 - 8$	________
c) $27 \div 9$	________	d) $12 + 4$	________

To **evaluate** means to "find the value of."

When we find the sum of the expression $3 + 5$, we are simply finding a different way to express the *value* of $3 + 5$; in other words, we are *evaluating* $3 + 5$.

YOU TRY IT 3 *Evaluate each expression.*

a) $5 + 3 =$ ________ b) $9 - 2 =$ ________

c) $4 \times 5 =$ ________ d) $12 \div 3 =$ ________

The Commutative Property of Addition

Evaluate $2 + 4 =$ ________ and $4 + 2 =$ ________. For each of these, the resulting sum is 6. These two sums illustrate a simple, yet important, property of mathematics, the *Commutative Property of Addition.*

The **Commutative Property of Addition** states: When adding two numbers, it doesn't matter which number is written first, the resulting sum will be the same.

To understand this property visually, let's use pieces of two separate rulers, one that is 2 inches long and another that is 3 inches long:

First, as you know, 2 inches + 3 inches = 5 inches,

and it's also true that 3 inches + 2 inches = 5 inches.

In other words, it doesn't matter which measure is written first, the sum of 2 inches and 3 inches will always be 5 inches.

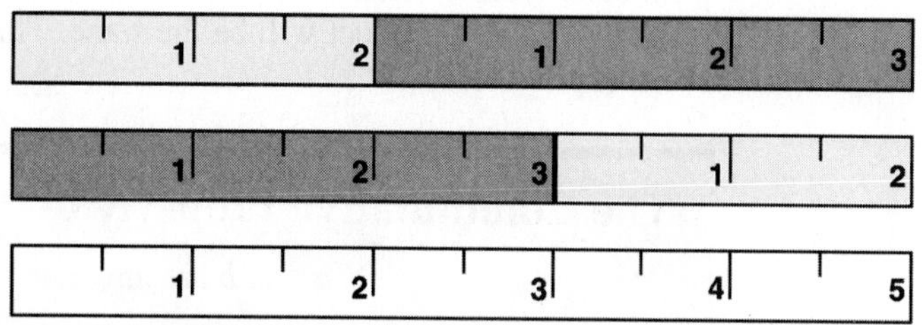

The Commutative Property of Addition is more formally written using letters, a and b, to represent any two numbers:

The Commutative Property of Addition

If a and b are any two numbers, then $a + b = b + a$.

In other words, the order in which we add two numbers doesn't affect the resulting sum.

EXAMPLE 2 Write each expression two different ways using the Commutative Property.

ANSWER: a) The sum of 7 and 3 can be written $\underline{7 + 3}$ or $\underline{3 + 7}$.

b) The sum of 5 and 4 can be written $\underline{5 + 4}$ or $\underline{4 + 5}$.

YOU TRY IT 4 *Write each expression two different ways using the Commutative Property. Use Example 2 as a guide.*

a) The sum of 2 and 8 can be written ____________ or ____________.

b) The sum of 6 and 1 can be written ____________ or ____________.

The Commutative Property of Multiplication

There is also a *Commutative Property of Multiplication.* We can use the multiplication table to see many examples of this property.

×	**1**	**2**	**3**	**4**	**5**	**6**	**7**	**8**	**9**	**10**	**11**	**12**
1	1	2	3	4	5	6	7	8	9	10	11	12
2	2	4	6	8	10	12	14	16	18	20	22	24
3	3	6	9	12	15	18	21	**24**	27	30	33	36
4	4	8	12	16	20	24	28	32	36	40	44	48
5	5	10	15	20	25	30	35	40	45	50	55	60
6	6	12	18	24	30	36	42	48	54	60	66	72
7	7	14	21	28	35	42	49	56	63	70	77	84
8	8	16	**24**	32	40	48	56	64	72	80	88	96
9	9	18	27	36	45	54	63	72	81	90	99	108
10	10	20	30	40	50	60	70	80	90	100	110	120
11	11	22	33	44	55	66	77	88	99	110	121	132
12	12	24	36	48	60	72	84	96	108	120	132	144

In the multiplication table, we can see that **3 × 8 = 24** and that **8 × 3 = 24**, and we can write this as 8 × 3 = 3 × 8.

In other words, when multiplying two numbers, it doesn't matter which number is written first, the resulting product will be the same. This is an example of the **Commutative Property of Multiplication**:

The Commutative Property of Multiplication

If *a* and *b* are any numbers, then $a \times b = b \times a$.

In other words, the order in which we multiply two numbers doesn't affect the resulting product.

EXAMPLE 3 Write each expression two different ways using the Commutative Property.

ANSWER: a) The product of 9 and 2 can be written 9 × 2 or 2 × 9.

b) The product of 4 and 6 can be written 4 × 6 or 6 × 4.

YOU TRY IT 5 *Write each expression two different ways using the Commutative Property. Use Example 3 as a guide.*

a) The product of 5 and 6 can be written ______ or ______.

b) The product of 4 and 9 can be written ______ or ______.

What could you tell a classmate to help him or her remember why the two properties above are called *commutative* properties?

______

______

Caution Division is *not* commutative. If we switch the order of the numbers in a division, then we don't get the same result. For example, 10 ÷ 5 is *not* the same as 5 ÷ 10. Here's an illustration:

At a youth car wash, if 5 youths wash a truck for $10, they get $2 each (10 ÷ 5 = 2); however, if 10 youths wash a car for $5, they get only $0.50 each (5 ÷ 10 = 0.50).

Similarly, subtraction is *not* commutative.

The Associative Properties

Another important property of mathematics is the *Associative Property*. There is an Associative Property for addition and one for multiplication. Before discussing these properties, we'll look at the role parentheses can play in an expression.

Parentheses, (and), are considered **grouping symbols**. Parentheses group different values together so that they can be treated as one *quantity*.

A **quantity** is an expression that is considered to be *one value*. For example, (6 + 2) is a quantity; it has just one value: 8.

Whenever we need to add three numbers together, such as $3 + 2 + 4$, we must always choose to add two of them first. We can use parentheses to group two of them to create a quantity, then evaluate the quantity first.

Generally, in any expression that has parentheses, the quantity within those parentheses should be evaluated *first.*

For example, with the sum $3 + 2 + 4$, we can either group the first two numbers or the last two numbers:

a) $(3 + 2) + 4$ ↑ Add 3 and 2 first. $= 5 + 4$ $= 9$

or

b) $3 + (2 + 4)$ ↑ Add 2 and 4 first. $= 3 + 6$ $= 9$

Notice that the resulting sum, 9, is the same no matter which grouping we choose. The same is true of multiplying three numbers together, such as $3 \times 2 \times 4$:

c) $(3 \times 2) \times 4$ ↑ Multiply 3 and 2 first. $= 6 \times 4$ $= 24$

or

d) $3 \times (2 \times 4)$ ↑ Multiply 2 and 4 first. $= 3 \times 8$ $= 24$

Notice that the resulting product, 24, is the same no matter which grouping we choose.

The Associative Property uses letters *a, b,* and *c* to represent any numbers we wish to put in their place.

The Associative Properties of Addition and Multiplication

If *a, b,* and *c* are any three numbers, then

Addition

$$(a + b) + c = a + (b + c)$$

If the only operation is addition, we can change the grouping of the numbers without affecting the resulting sum.

Multiplication

$$(a \times b) \times c = a \times (b \times c)$$

If the only operation is multiplication, we can change the grouping of the numbers without affecting the resulting product.

EXAMPLE 4 Write each expression two different ways using parentheses, then evaluate it.

a) $1 + 6 + 3$ b) $6 \times 2 \times 3$

PROCEDURE: Use the Associative Property; notice that the order in which the numbers are written doesn't change.

ANSWER:

a) $1 + 6 + 3 = \underbrace{(1 + 6)}_{7} + 3 = 1 + \underbrace{(6 + 3)}_{9} = \mathbf{10}$

b) $6 \times 2 \times 3 = \underbrace{(6 \times 2)}_{12} \times 3 = 6 \times \underbrace{(2 \times 3)}_{6} = \mathbf{36}$

YOU TRY IT 6

Write each expression two different ways using parentheses, then evaluate it. Use Example 4 as a guide.

a) $2 + 8 + 6$ = ________ = ________ = ________

b) $4 + 6 + 9$ = ________ = ________ = ________

c) $3 \times 2 \times 4$ = ________ = ________ = ________

d) $6 \times 5 \times 2$ = ________ = ________ = ________

What could you tell a classmate to help him or her remember why the two properties above are called *associative* properties?

____

____

The Identities

The notion of *identity* is another important property of addition and multiplication. An **identity** is a number that, when applied, won't change the value of another number or quantity. In other words, it keeps the original number's *identity*, its value.

For addition, the identity is 0 (zero), because

a) $6 + \mathbf{0} = 6$ b) $\mathbf{0} + 3 = 3$ 0 is called the **additive identity**.

Notice that adding 0 (zero) to a number doesn't change the value of the number.

For multiplication, the identity is 1 (one), because

a) $5 \times \mathbf{1} = 5$ b) $\mathbf{1} \times 8 = 8$ 1 is called the **multiplicative identity**.

Notice that multiplying a number by 1 doesn't change the value of the number.

YOU TRY IT 7

Apply the idea of identity by filling in the blank.

a) $4 + 0 =$ ________ b) $9 +$ ________ $= 9$ c) $0 +$ ________ $= 12$

d) $7 \times 1 =$ ________ e) $23 \times$ ________ $= 23$ f) $1 \times$ ________ $= 15$

What could you tell a classmate to help him or her remember why the two numbers above are called identities?

____

____

Fast Addition, Grouping to 10

The Associative and Commutative Properties allow us to rearrange the numbers in a sum (or product) without changing the value of the end result.

For example, the sum $7 + 9 + 3$ could be rearranged as and then we could group the first two numbers:

The advantage of rearranging the numbers this way is to add 7 and 3 first because they add to 10, and 10 is a good number to work with in addition (and in multiplication).

$$\begin{aligned} & 7 + 3 + 9 \\ &= (7 + 3) + 9 \\ &= \quad 10 \quad + 9 \\ &= 19 \end{aligned}$$

In rewriting $7 + 9 + 3$ as $7 + 3 + 9$ and then as $(7 + 3) + 9$, we have used both the Commutative and Associative Properties of Addition.

This idea of combining the Associative and the Commutative Properties of Addition together leads to a quick addition process called *grouping to 10.* This speedy process works well when we need to add a lot of numbers.

The idea of grouping to 10 is to find numbers that easily add to 10, such as 4 and 6. We sometimes use three numbers; for example, 2 and 3 and 5 add up to 10 as well. We can use these facts to quickly add a list of numbers.

EXAMPLE 5 Given the following list of numbers, find groups that add to 10, then find the sum of the entire list.

a) 6, 4, 8, 2, 1, and 9

b) 9, 3, 8, 1, 5, 7, 2, and 5

c) 1, 6, 3, 2, 4, and 4

d) 9, 6, 1, 2, 5, 4, and 5

PROCEDURE: Look for groups of two or three numbers that add to 10; then add the 10's. Rearrange the list if necessary.

ANSWER: a) Sometimes the list is organized nicely:

6, 4, 8, 2, 1, and 9

$(6 + 4) + (8 + 2) + (9 + 1)$

$= 10 \quad + \quad 10 \quad + \quad 10$

$=$ **30**

b) Sometimes we need to search for the numbers that add to 10, and rearrange them:

9, 3, 8, 1, 5, 7, 2 and 5

$(9 + 1) + (3 + 7) + (8 + 2) + (5 + 5)$

$= 10 \quad + \quad 10 \quad + \quad 10 \quad + \quad 10$

$=$ **40**

c) Sometimes we can get sums of 10 by grouping three numbers:

1, 6, 3, 2, 4, and 4

$(1 + 6 + 3) + (2 + 4 + 4)$

$= 10 \quad + \quad 10$

$=$ **20**

d) Sometimes there are numbers that can't be grouped to form a sum of 10; these need to be added in at the end:

9, 6, 1, 2, 5, 4 and 5

$(9 + 1) + (6 + 4) + (5 + 5) + 2$

$= 10 \quad + \quad 10 \quad + \quad 10 \quad + 2$

$=$ **32**

YOU TRY IT 8 *Given the following list of numbers, find groups that add to 10, then find the sum of the entire list. Use Example 5 as a guide.*

a) 6, 4, 9, 1, 8, 2, and 4

b) 9, 2, 5, 8, 5, and 1

c) 5, 2, 4, 3, 1, 3, and 7

Grouping to 10 and the Associative Property

Adding to 10 has its advantages. From Section 1.1 you'll remember that we can exchange ten \$1 bills for a single \$10 bill. So, we can use 10 as a "target" number when adding two digits whose sum is *greater* than 10. This technique requires the use of the Associative Property, as you'll see in Example 6.

Even though you probably already know that the sum of 6 and 7 is 13 ($6 + 7 = 13$), the method presented in Example 6 shows *why* the sum is 13.

EXAMPLE 6 Find the sum of 6 and 7 by breaking up the second number into the sum of two smaller numbers.

PROCEDURE: Keep the number 10 as a target number in the addition process.

ANSWER: Start with 6; think of the number that you can add to 6 to make 10: $6 + \mathbf{4} = 10$

		$6 + 7$
Break 7 up into a sum of two numbers, one of which is **4**.	=	$6 + (4 + 3)$
Use the Associative Property to regroup as shown.	=	$(6 + 4) + 3$
Now add within the parentheses to get 10.	=	$10 + 3$
Now complete the addition. (We get 1 ten and 3 ones.)	=	13

6 + 7 → 6 + 4 + 3 → 6 + 4 + 3

Caution For the sake of understanding this addition better than you already do, please follow the steps outlined in Example 6, using 10 as a target number.

YOU TRY IT 9 *Find the following sums using the technique outlined in Example 6.*

a) $8 + 7$
$= 8 + (\quad + \quad)$
$= (8 + \quad) +$
$= 10 +$
$=$ ______

b) $9 + 5$
$= 9 + (\quad + \quad)$
$= (9 + \quad) +$
$= 10 +$
$=$ ______

c) $6 + 9$
$= 6 + (\quad + \quad)$
$= (6 + \quad) +$
$= 10 +$
$=$ ______

You Try It Answers: Section 1.2

YTI 1 a) 9 1 3 5 12 b) 12 2 4 5 8 c) 5 3 8 5 40 d) 0 4 5 5 6

YTI 2 a) product b) difference c) quotient d) sum

YTI 3 a) 8 b) 7 c) 20 d) 4

YTI 4 a) $2 + 8$ or $8 + 2$ b) $6 + 1$ or $1 + 6$

YTI 5 a) 5×6 or 6×5 b) 4×9 or 9×4

YTI 6
a) $(2 + 8) + 6 = 2 + (8 + 6) = 16$
b) $(4 + 6) + 9 = 4 + (6 + 9) = 19$
c) $(3 \times 2) \times 4 = 3 \times (2 \times 4) = 24$
d) $(6 \times 5) \times 2 = 6 \times (5 \times 2) = 60$

YTI 7 a) 4 b) 0 c) 12 d) 7 e) 1 f) 15

YTI 8 a) 34 b) 30 c) 25

YTI 9
a) $8 + 7$
$= 8 + (2 + 5)$
$= (8 + 2) + 5$
$= 10 + 5$
$= 15$

b) $9 + 5$
$= 9 + (1 + 4)$
$= (9 + 1) + 4$
$= 10 + 4$
$= 14$

c) $6 + 9$
$= 6 + (4 + 5)$
$= (6 + 4) + 5$
$= 10 + 5$
$= 15$

Focus Exercises: Section 1.2

Which property does each represent?

1. $5 + (8 + 2) = (5 + 8) + 2$ ____________
2. $12 \times 5 = 5 \times 12$ ____________
3. $0 + 11 = 11$ ____________
4. $8 \times (5 \times 4) = (8 \times 5) \times 4$ ____________
5. $25 + 19 = 19 + 25$ ____________
6. $13 \times 1 = 13$ ____________

Given the following list of numbers, find groups that add to 10, then find the sum of the entire list.

7. 7, 3, 5, 5, 2, 8, 6
8. 3, 9, 6, 4, 5, 7, 1
9. 1, 6, 3, 4, 1, 5, 8
10. 5, 3, 4, 9, 2, 8, 1, 7, 5
11. 5, 1, 4, 7, 3, 6, 5
12. 5, 3, 2, 1, 6, 3, 2
13. 2, 7, 4, 9, 3, 8, 6
14. 1, 2, 4, 7, 1, 5, 9

Find the following sums using the technique outlined in Example 6.

15. $5 + 7$
$= 5 + (\quad + \quad)$
= ____________
= ____________

16. $9 + 8$
$= 9 + (\quad + \quad)$
= ____________
= ____________

17. $8 + 6$
$= 8 + (\quad + \quad)$
= ____________
= ____________

18. $7 + 6$
$= 7 + (\quad + \quad)$
= ____________
= ____________

19. $6 + 9$
$= 6 + (\quad + \quad)$
= ____________
= ____________

20. $4 + 8$
$= 4 + (\quad + \quad)$
= ____________
= ____________

21. $9 + 9$
$= 9 + (\quad + \quad)$
= ____________
= ____________

22. $5 + 8$
$= 5 + (\quad + \quad)$
= ____________
= ____________

23. $7 + 9$
$= 7 + (\quad + \quad)$
= ____________
= ____________

SECTION 1.3 Adding and Subtracting Whole Numbers

Objectives

In this section, you will learn to:

- Add whole numbers.
- Find the perimeter of a geometric figure.
- Subtract whole numbers.

To successfully complete this section, you need to understand:

- Place value (1.1)
- The Associative Property (1.2)
- The Commutative Property (1.2)
- Adding by grouping to 10 (1.2)

Introduction

You have been adding numbers since you were young, and it's possible you've had an easy time of it. It's also possible that there are certain facts about addition that still puzzle you.

It is the purpose of this section to explain the ideas behind addition and subtraction so that they are less of a mystery. The technique from Section 1.1 of thinking of addition in terms of money will come in handy here.

It's also important to know that to add two numbers, the numbers must represent an amount or quantity of the same item. For example,

we know that **2** feet + **3** feet = **5** feet

and that **2** *inches* + **3** *inches* = **5** inches

but **2** feet + **3** *inches* is not 5 of anything.

To add 2 feet and 3 inches as a single unit of measure, we must first rewrite one of the measures—let's choose feet—in terms of the other measure, inches. In this case, you might know that 2 feet is equivalent to 24 inches (as shown in the diagram below), so

Units of Measure
Feet and inches are called units of measure. They are standard lengths.

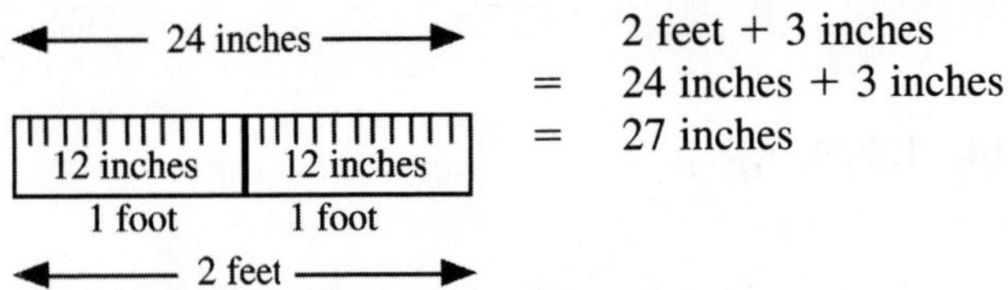

2 feet + 3 inches
= 24 inches + 3 inches
= 27 inches

If we were to add two such measures, such as 2 feet 3 inches + 6 feet 4 inches, we would be smart to add the feet together and, separately, add the inches together:

2 feet	3 inches
+ 6 feet	4 inches
8 feet	7 inches

Adding Whole Numbers

Now let's consider place value in finding the sum of two numbers. For example,

we know that 2 ones + 3 ones = 5 ones

and that 2 tens + 3 tens = 5 tens

but 2 tens + 3 ones is not 5 of anything.

Just as in adding feet and inches, we can combine tens and ones as long as they are represented by the same place value.

2 tens + 3 ones
= 20 ones + 3 ones
= 23 ones

Furthermore, we can keep the numbers in terms of both tens and ones and combine them with other two-digit numbers:

2 tens	3 ones	(or 23)
+ 6 tens	4 ones	(or 64)
8 tens	7 ones	(or 87)

This idea suggests that when adding two numbers, such as 23 and 64, we must add the tens with the tens and the ones with the ones. Typically, we write the numbers *vertically*, one number directly above the other, aligning the tens and ones places from each number. In doing so we create two columns of numbers, a ones column and a tens column:

$$\begin{array}{r} 23 \\ +\ 64 \\ \hline 87 \end{array}$$

EXAMPLE 1 Add each pair of numbers.

a) 34 + 53 b) 27 + 41 c) 175 + 304 d) 507 + 291

PROCEDURE: Align the numbers vertically so that one number is directly above the other; make sure the ones place is above the ones place, tens place above tens place, and so on.

ANSWER:

a) $\begin{array}{r} 34 \\ +\ 53 \\ \hline 87 \end{array}$ b) $\begin{array}{r} 27 \\ +\ 41 \\ \hline 68 \end{array}$ c) $\begin{array}{r} 175 \\ +\ 304 \\ \hline 479 \end{array}$ d) $\begin{array}{r} 507 \\ +\ 291 \\ \hline 798 \end{array}$

The numbers in each pair in Example 1 have the same number of digits. It's also possible to add a two-digit number to a three or four-digit number, and so on. To make sure that the place values align with each other, we can place extra zeros in front of one of the numbers to make all have the same number of places, as illustrated in Example 2.

EXAMPLE 2 Add each pair of numbers.

a) 324 + 53 b) 31 + 914 c) 2,457 + 421 d) 1,075 + 12

PROCEDURE: Although it's not necessary, it may be helpful to place one or more zeros in front of the smaller number so that it has the same number of places as the larger number.

ANSWER:

a) $\begin{array}{r} 324 \\ +\ 053 \\ \hline 377 \end{array}$ b) $\begin{array}{r} 031 \\ +\ 914 \\ \hline 945 \end{array}$ c) $\begin{array}{r} 2457 \\ +\ 0421 \\ \hline 2{,}878 \end{array}$ d) $\begin{array}{r} 1075 \\ +\ 0012 \\ \hline 1{,}087 \end{array}$

YOU TRY IT 1 *Add. Use Examples 1 and 2 as guides. (These are already aligned, but you may want to place some zeros in front of one number or the other.)*

a) $\begin{array}{r} 157 \\ +\ 230 \\ \hline \end{array}$ b) $\begin{array}{r} 2{,}754 \\ +\ 1{,}121 \\ \hline \end{array}$ c) $\begin{array}{r} 133 \\ +\ 4{,}426 \\ \hline \end{array}$ d) $\begin{array}{r} 135{,}604 \\ +\ \ \ 2{,}261 \\ \hline \end{array}$

Addition by Carrying Numbers Over

You probably noticed that none of the sums in YTI 1 was more than 9 in any place. The problems were carefully chosen so you could add directly without having to worry about *carryover*.

Let's consider what would happen if two of the digits add to 10 or more.

In Section 1.2 we saw, and explored why, 6 + 7 = 13. Written vertically, this looks like:

$$\begin{array}{rr} \text{addend} & 6 \\ +\ \text{addend} & +\ 7 \\ \hline \text{sum} & 13 \end{array} \quad \text{(13 is 1 ten and 3 ones)}$$

What's especially important to recognize is that the sum includes another place value that wasn't in either addend. In other words, though both 6 and 7 are in the ones place, we get a sum that extends itself into the tens place.

If we add, for example, 26 + 57, the extra ten that we get from 6 + 7 must be figured into the sum. Here's the long way to look at it:

$$\begin{array}{rcrcr} 26 & \rightarrow & 2 \text{ tens} & \text{and} & 6 \text{ ones} \\ +\ 57 & \rightarrow & +\ 5 \text{ tens} & \text{and} & 7 \text{ ones} \\ \hline & & 7 \text{ tens} & \text{and} & 13 \text{ ones} \end{array}$$

Because 13 ones can be rewritten as 1 ten and 3 ones, this answer becomes

$$\begin{array}{lccl} = & \underline{7 \text{ tens and } 1 \text{ ten}} & \text{and } 3 \text{ ones} & = 70 + 13 \\ = & 8 \text{ tens} & \text{and } 3 \text{ ones} & = 80 + 3 = 83 \end{array}$$

The short way to find this sum is to show that extra 10 (from the 13) in the tens column. In other words, the 13 we get from 6 and 7 needs to be recognized as being 1 ten and 3 ones. This way, the 3 ones can stay in the ones place and the 1 ten can move to the tens column. This is called **carrying over**; the 1 ten is a *carryover* into the next column of numbers, the tens column, as illustrated in Example 3.

EXAMPLE 3

Add 26 and 57. Follow the steps outlined here.

a) Starting with the ones columns, 6 + 7 = 13: Start here ↓

$$\begin{array}{r} 26 \\ +\ 57 \\ \hline 6 + 7 = 13 \end{array}$$

b) Carry the 1 ten into the tens column (1 ten and 3 ones)

1 ten → $\begin{array}{r} ^{1} \\ 26 \\ +\ 57 \\ \hline 3 \end{array}$ ← and 3 ones

c) Complete the addition by adding the tens column Finish here ↓

$$\begin{array}{r} ^{1} \\ 26 \\ +\ 57 \\ \hline 83 \end{array}$$

How would you describe carrying over to a classmate?

____

____

Let's practice adding two-digit numbers that require us to carry 1 ten.

YOU TRY IT 2

Add. Use Example 3 as a guide.

a) $\begin{array}{r} 17 \\ +\ 58 \\ \hline \end{array}$ b) $\begin{array}{r} 48 \\ +\ 36 \\ \hline \end{array}$ c) $\begin{array}{r} 64 \\ +\ 29 \\ \hline \end{array}$ d) $\begin{array}{r} 28 \\ +\ 38 \\ \hline \end{array}$

Of course, the idea of carrying can extend to other place values as well. Just as

$$6 \text{ ones} + 7 \text{ ones} = 13 \text{ ones},$$
$$6 + 7 = 13$$
$$= 1 \text{ ten and } 3 \text{ ones}$$

it's also true that

$$6 \text{ tens} + 7 \text{ tens} = 13 \text{ tens}$$
$$60 + 70 = 130$$
$$= 1 \text{ hundred and } 3 \text{ tens}$$
$$(\text{and } 0 \text{ ones})$$

EXAMPLE 4 Add 358 and 294.

PROCEDURE: Follow the steps outlined here.

a) Starting with the ones columns,

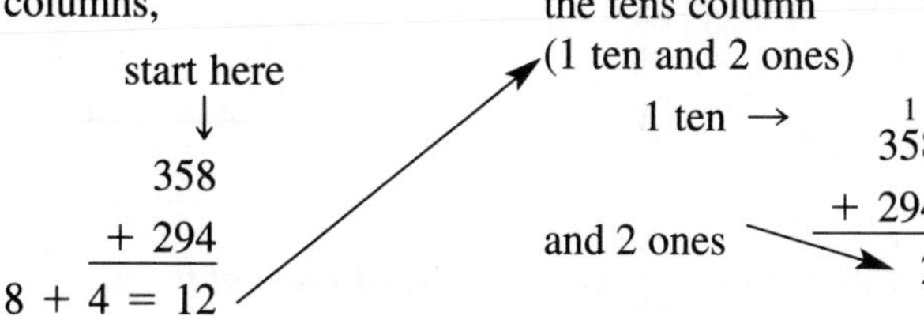

start here ↓

```
  358
+ 294
```

8 + 4 = 12

b) Carry the 1 ten into the tens column (1 ten and 2 ones)

1 ten →

```
   1
  358
+ 294
    2
```

and 2 ones

c) Adding in the tens column. 1 + 5 + 9 = 15 tens: (1 hundred and 5 tens)

1 hundred →

```
  11
  358
+ 294
   52
```

and 5 tens

d) Complete the addition by adding the hundreds column

```
  11
  358
+ 294
  652
```

ANSWER: 358 + 294 = 652

YOU TRY IT 3 *Add. Use Example 4 as a guide.*

a) 197 + 386   b) 482 + 168   c) 634 + 267   d) 525 + 387

All of the exercises in YTI 3 required carrying into both the tens place and the hundreds place. Sometimes we'll need to carry into the tens place only, or the hundreds place only, or— as we saw in YTI 1, not carry at all.

YOU TRY IT 4 *Add.*

a) 37 + 96   b) 375 + 6,925   c) 3,708 + 6,533   d) 995,213 + 4,787

Adding More Than Two Whole Numbers

There are occasions when we need to add a list of numbers, whether they be the prices of items in a grocery cart, or your scores on tests, or the weights of boxes to be shipped to your customers.

Adding more than two numbers is similar to what we've seen already, we just need to be more careful. We still:

1. align the numbers so that the ones place is above the ones place, etc., and
2. carry the tens (or hundreds) value to the next column for any sum over 9.

When adding three or more numbers, the sum in any one column could be more than 20, as shown in Example 5. In that case, we'd need to carry the 2 to the next column (or 3, if the sum is 30 or more).

EXAMPLE 5 Add 186, 395, 478 and 294. Follow the steps outlined here.

PROCEDURE: Add one column at a time, starting with the ones column.

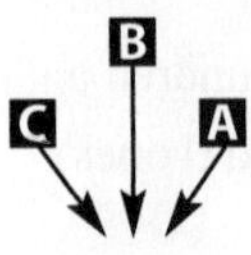

ANSWER:

```
   32
  182
  395
  478
+ 294
-----
1,353
```

A The ones column adds to 23, so place the 3 and carry the 20 (as a 2 in the tens place).

B The tens column adds to 35, so place the 5 and carry the 3 (in the hundreds place).

C The hundreds column adds to 13.

YOU TRY IT 5 *Add. Use Example 5 as a guide. (You may want to place zeros in front of some of the numbers that have fewer digits.)*

a)
```
   7
  36
+ 98
```

b)
```
    8
  346
   95
+ 673
```

c)
```
  1,634
  2,976
  9,597
+ 8,967
```

d)
```
  36,525
   7,489
  20,946
     877
+ 48,103
```

Applications of Addition

In a story problem, or word problem, the last sentence is usually in the form of a question asking us to find an amount of something. In the question, you should look for a word or phrase that indicates which operation is to be used.

In an addition problem, you will likely see words like *total*, *combined*, *sum*, and *in all*. There are many situations to which addition can apply.

EXAMPLE 6 The South Orange County Community College District has two colleges, Irvine Valley College and Saddleback College. Last summer, Irvine Valley had an enrollment of 4,569 and Saddleback had an enrollment of 9,912, and no one attended both colleges. How many total students were enrolled in the entire district last summer?

PROCEDURE: The key word in the last sentence is *total*. This indicates that we should add the student enrollments at each college:

ANSWER:

Irvine Valley	4,569
+ Saddleback	+ 9,912
Total	14,481

SENTENCE: Last summer there was a total of 14,481 students enrolled in the district.

YOU TRY IT 6

Juan's monthly salary is $3,457 and his wife Angelica's monthly salary is $2,845. What is their combined monthly salary?

Sentence: ______________________________

____

YOU TRY IT 7

Allison often travels out of state for business. On her last trip she flew from Los Angeles to Boston (2,988 miles), then from Boston to Miami (1,511 miles), and from Miami to Los Angeles (2,772 miles). How many total miles did she travel on that trip?

Sentence: ______________________________

____

YOU TRY IT 8

Enerio is out shopping for a new car for his young family. The Suzuki Aerio has caught his attention. The car has a sticker price of $16,798. To add a sunroof is an extra $1,564. Add to that sales tax, $1,377, and dealer charges of $983. What is the total cost of the car?

Sentence: ______________________________

____

Perimeter

The **perimeter** of a geometric figure—such as a triangle or rectangle—is the total measure around the figure. The perimeter is found by adding the lengths of all of the sides.

For the triangle at right,

Perimeter = 19 inches + 28 inches + 26 inches
Perimeter = 73 inches

$$\begin{array}{r} 19 \\ 28 \\ +\ 26 \\ \hline 73 \end{array}$$

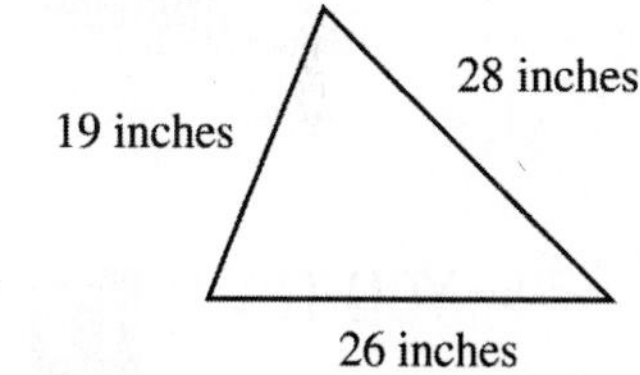

YOU TRY IT 9

Find the perimeter of each shape.

a)

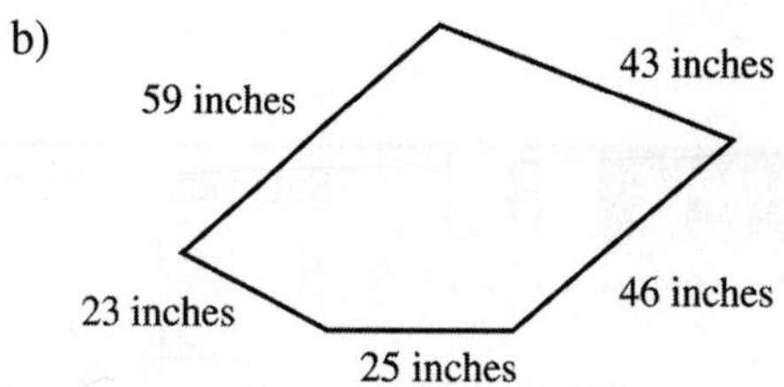

b)

Subtracting Whole Numbers

Addition and subtraction are *inverse* operations. This means, among other things, we can check our subtraction answers using addition and vice versa. Let's see how this is so by exploring the basics of subtraction.

Consider 8 – 5 = 3. This type of subtraction is usually written vertically:

$$\begin{array}{r} 8 \\ -\ 5 \\ \hline 3 \end{array}$$

Because of the inverse nature of addition and subtraction, understanding addition is key to understanding subtraction. Below is an example of how we can use addition to check whether or not our subtraction result (the difference) is correct:

$$\begin{array}{r} 8 \\ -\ 5 \\ \hline 3 \end{array} \quad \text{because} \quad \begin{array}{r} 3 \\ +\ 5 \\ \hline 8 \end{array}$$

YOU TRY IT 10

Subtract. Check each answer (on paper or mentally) by addition.

a) $\begin{array}{r} 7 \\ -\ 4 \\ \hline \end{array}$ b) $\begin{array}{r} 8 \\ -\ 6 \\ \hline \end{array}$ c) $\begin{array}{r} 8 \\ -\ 1 \\ \hline \end{array}$ d) $\begin{array}{r} 4 \\ -\ 4 \\ \hline \end{array}$

Subtraction of larger numbers follows the same process as single-digit subtraction. Just as in addition, in order to subtract vertically we must align the place values.

EXAMPLE 7 Subtract 57 – 26.

PROCEDURE: Follow the steps outlined here:

a) Start with the ones column,
Start here ↓

$$\begin{array}{r} 57 \\ -\ 26 \\ \hline 1 \end{array}$$

b) Then subtract in the tens column: 5 – 2 = 3
Finish here ↓

$$\begin{array}{r} 57 \\ -\ 26 \\ \hline 31 \end{array}$$

c) Check by addition:

$$\begin{array}{r} 31 \\ +\ 26 \\ \hline 57 \end{array} \checkmark$$

This checks out.

ANSWER: 57 – 26 = 31

YOU TRY IT 11

Subtract. Check each answer by addition. Use Example 7 as a guide.

a) $\begin{array}{r} 78 \\ -\ 41 \\ \hline \end{array}$ b) $\begin{array}{r} 83 \\ -\ 62 \\ \hline \end{array}$ c) $\begin{array}{r} 694 \\ -\ 321 \\ \hline \end{array}$ d) $\begin{array}{r} 2{,}576 \\ -\ 1{,}471 \\ \hline \end{array}$

EXAMPLE 8 Subtract.

a) $\begin{array}{r} 683 \\ -\ 31 \\ \hline \end{array}$ b) $\begin{array}{r} 759 \\ -\ 725 \\ \hline \end{array}$

PROCEDURE:

a) We can rewrite 31 as 031 so that every place is represented by a digit.

b) Notice that, in the answer, the 0 in the hundreds place is unnecessary.

ANSWER:

a) $\begin{array}{r} 683 \\ -\ 31 \\ \hline \end{array} \rightarrow \begin{array}{r} 683 \\ -\ 031 \\ \hline 652 \end{array}$ Check: $\begin{array}{r} 652 \\ +\ 31 \\ \hline \end{array}$

You supply the answer to check:

b) $\begin{array}{r} 759 \\ -\ 725 \\ \hline 034 \end{array} \rightarrow \begin{array}{r} 759 \\ -\ 725 \\ \hline 34 \end{array}$ Check: $\begin{array}{r} 34 \\ +\ 725 \\ \hline \end{array}$

YOU TRY IT 12

Subtract. Check each answer by addition. Use Example 8 as a guide.

a) $\begin{array}{r} 491 \\ -\ 61 \\ \hline \end{array}$ b) $\begin{array}{r} 2{,}156 \\ -\ 14 \\ \hline \end{array}$ c) $\begin{array}{r} 36{,}815 \\ -\ 36{,}514 \\ \hline \end{array}$ d) $\begin{array}{r} 193{,}476 \\ -\ 41{,}140 \\ \hline \end{array}$

Regrouping in Subtraction

Recall that in addition we sometimes carry a number (usually 1) from the ones to the tens column. In subtraction—the inverse of addition—we sometimes need to take from the tens place to complete the subtraction in the ones place. This is called *regrouping*.

Before we see what is behind the idea of regrouping, let's practice some mental subtraction problems.

EXAMPLE 9

Without doing any regrouping, subtract (find the difference).

a) 12 – 3 b) 15 – 7

PROCEDURE: Think about the inverse nature between addition and subtraction. Check the answers mentally, using addition.

ANSWER: a) 12 – 3 = 9 because 3 + 9 = 12 b) 15 – 7 = 8 because 7 + 8 = 15

YOU TRY IT 13

Subtract (find the difference). Notice that all of the first numbers have a 1 in the tens place. Also, all of the answers will be one-digit numbers. Use Example 9 as a guide.

a) 16 − 9 = ______ b) 14 − 5 = ______

c) 13 − 8 = ______ d) 10 − 4 = ______

Caution

Your ability to subtract numbers like these is necessary to fully understand subtraction, especially as it relates to regrouping.

Suppose, for a moment, that the only paper money that you are allowed to use is $1, $10, and $100 bills. This means that there would be no such thing as a $5, $20, or $50 bill. And suppose you have a special wallet that has a separate pocket for each type of bill.

In a sense, you could take a $10 bill from one pocket of your wallet, trade it in for ten $1 bills, and put these new bills in the $1 pocket. In this way, you'd still have the same amount of money; it would simply be reorganized, or regrouped.

Consider the following:

37 is the same as

3 tens and **7 ones**

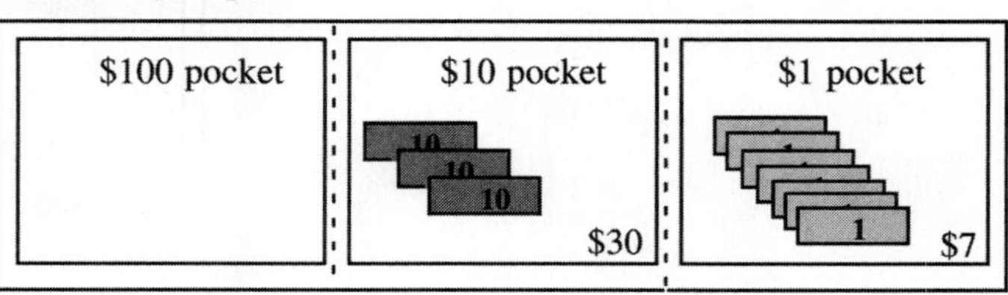

but we can take **1 ten**, trade it in for **10 ones** and get:

2 tens and **17 ones**,

which is still $37.

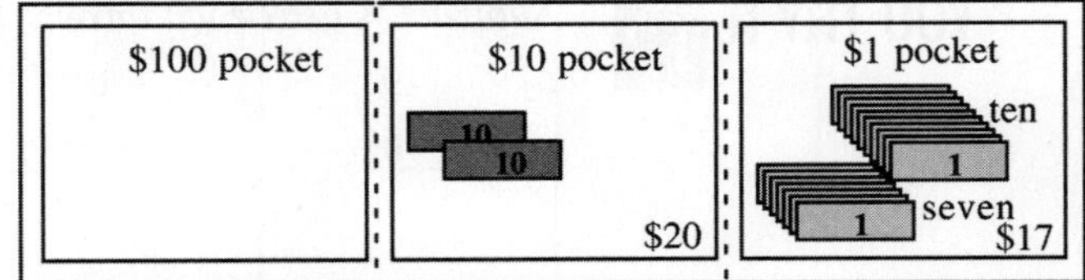

EXAMPLE 10 For each of these, regroup by taking one ten and making it into 10 ones.

ANSWER:

a) 58 = 5 tens and 8 ones = 4 tens and 18 ones

b) 90 = 9 tens and 0 ones = 8 tens and 10 ones

c) 16 = 1 tens and 6 ones = 0 tens and 16 ones

YOU TRY IT 14 *For each of these, regroup by taking one ten and making it into 10 ones. Use Example 10 as a guide.*

a) 58 = 2 tens and 4 ones = ________

b) 90 = 1 tens and 5 ones = ________

c) 16 = 6 tens and 0 ones = ________

Suppose all you have in your wallet is two $100 bills and three $1 bills. What would you do if you needed to trade a $10 bill for ten $1 bills?

First, let's look at the money in your wallet: $203 = **two $100 bills** and **three $1 bills**.

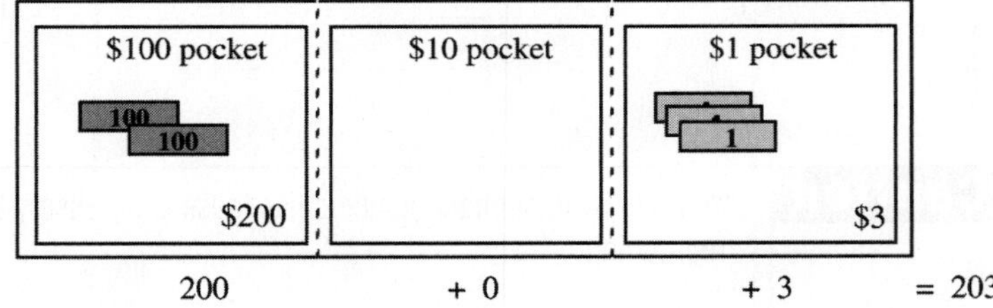

To get a $10 bill, you would first need to trade *one* of the $100 bills in for *ten* $10 bills. Now you have:

$203 = **one $100 bill**, **ten $10 bills** and **three $1 bills**.

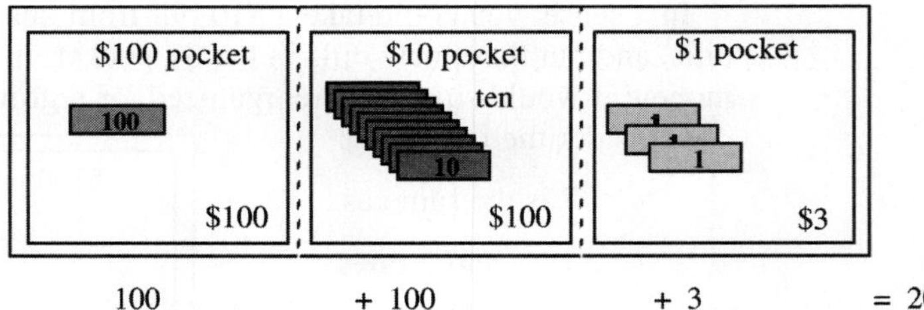

Now it's possible to take one $10 bill and trade it in for ten $1 bills. Now you have:
$203 = **one $100 bill**, **nine $10 bills** and **thirteen $1 bills**.

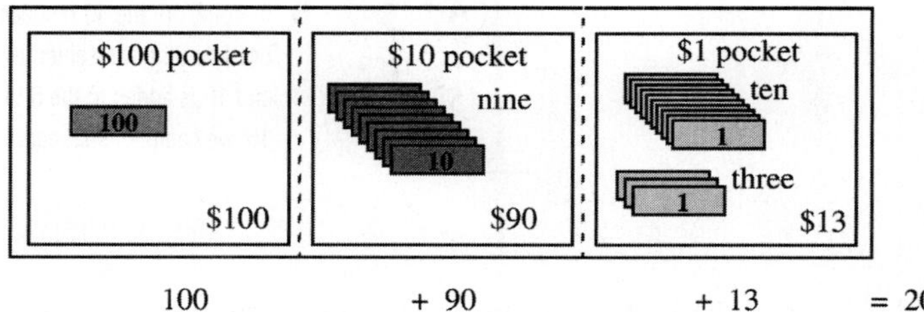

100 + 90 + 13 = 203

EXAMPLE 11 For each of these, regroup by first trading 1 hundred for 10 tens. Then trade 1 ten to make 10 ones.

a) 308 = 3 hundreds, 0 tens, 8 ones
= 2 hundreds, 10 tens, 8 ones
= 2 hundreds, 9 tens, 18 ones

b) 700 = 7 hundreds, 0 tens, 0 ones
= 6 hundreds, 10 tens, 0 ones
= 6 hundreds, 9 tens, 10 ones

YOU TRY IT 15 *For each of these, regroup first by trading 1 hundred to make 10 tens. Then take 1 ten to make 10 ones. Use Example 11 as a guide.*

a) 407 = 4 hundreds, 0 tens, 7 ones
= ____________
= ____________

b) 801 = 8 hundreds, 0 tens, 1 one
= ____________
= ____________

c) 102 = 1 hundred, 0 tens, 2 ones
= ____________
= ____________

d) 200 = 2 hundreds, 0 tens, 0 ones
= ____________
= ____________

When we subtract, just as when we add, we do so one place at a time. In subtraction, we always start in the ones place first, then go the tens place, and so on.

If we come to a place in which we can't subtract—because the first number is less than the second number—then we need to use regrouping to adjust the first number, as shown in the next example.

EXAMPLE 12 Subtract. Check using addition.

a) $\begin{array}{r} 45 \\ -\ 18 \\ \hline \end{array}$

b) $\begin{array}{r} 537 \\ -\ 275 \\ \hline \end{array}$

PROCEDURE: For each, we'll need to regroup to subtract.

ANSWER: a) **A** Because, in the ones place, 5 is less than 8, we'll need to take from the 40 (represented by the 4 tens) and regroup.

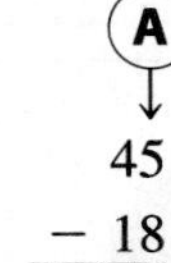

$$\begin{array}{r} 45 \\ -\ 18 \\ \hline \end{array}$$

B In doing so, the 40 reduces by 10 to become 30 (represented by just 3), and 10 is added to the 5 to become 15; we can then subtract to get 27.

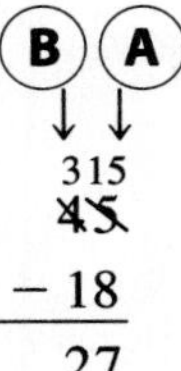

$$\begin{array}{r} {}^{3}\not{4}\,{}^{15}\not{5} \\ -\ 18 \\ \hline 27 \end{array}$$

Complete the check

$$\begin{array}{r} 27 \\ +\ 18 \\ \hline \end{array}$$

b) **A** In this case, we subtract the ones column without needing to regroup.

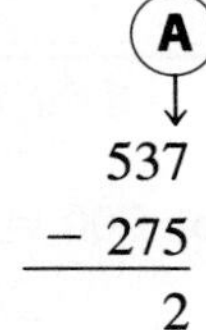

$$\begin{array}{r} 537 \\ -\ 275 \\ \hline 2 \end{array}$$

B However, we can't subtract in the tens column until we take from the hundreds place.

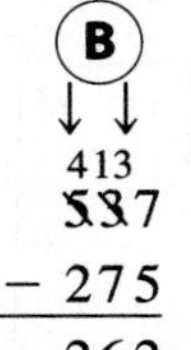

$$\begin{array}{r} {}^{4}\not{5}\,{}^{13}\not{3}\,7 \\ -\ 275 \\ \hline 262 \end{array}$$

Complete the check

$$\begin{array}{r} 262 \\ +\ 275 \\ \hline \end{array}$$

YOU TRY IT 16

Subtract. Some of these require regrouping more than once. Be careful! Use Example 12 as a guide.

a) $\begin{array}{r} 61 \\ -\ 44 \\ \hline \end{array}$ b) $\begin{array}{r} 163 \\ -\ 89 \\ \hline \end{array}$ c) $\begin{array}{r} 3{,}327 \\ -\ 2{,}046 \\ \hline \end{array}$ d) $\begin{array}{r} 1{,}429 \\ -\ 613 \\ \hline \end{array}$

Caution In regrouping, it is very important to keep the columns properly aligned.

EXAMPLE 13 Subtract 306 2 149. Be sure to align the numbers vertically. Check by addition.

PROCEDURE: **A** Here, we need to take from the tens column, but there is only 0 there, meaning no tens at all. So, we must first take from the hundreds column:

$$\begin{array}{r} 306 \\ -\ 149 \\ \hline \end{array} \qquad \begin{array}{r} {}^{2}\not{3}\,{}^{10}0\,6 \\ -\ 149 \\ \hline \end{array}$$

B Now we have 10 in the tens column so we take a ten from it:

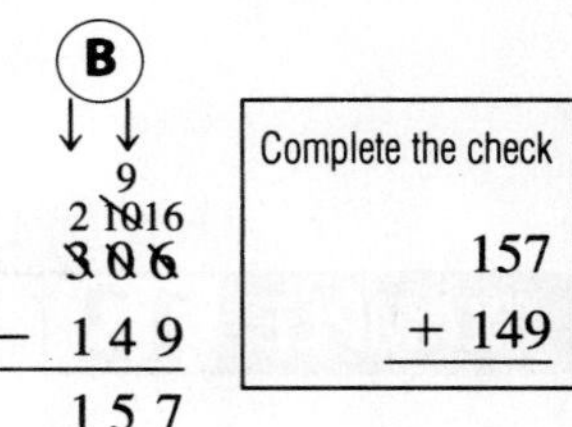

$$\begin{array}{r} {}^{2}\not{3}\,{}^{9}\not{10}\,{}^{16}\not{6} \\ -\ 1\,4\,9 \\ \hline 1\,5\,7 \end{array}$$

Complete the check

$$\begin{array}{r} 157 \\ +\ 149 \\ \hline \end{array}$$

YOU TRY IT 17

Subtract. Some of these require regrouping more than once. Be careful! Use Example 13 as a guide.

a) $\begin{array}{r} 620 \\ -\ 312 \\ \hline \end{array}$ b) $\begin{array}{r} 450 \\ -\ 256 \\ \hline \end{array}$ c) $\begin{array}{r} 2{,}000 \\ -\ 1{,}316 \\ \hline \end{array}$

Applications Involving Subtraction

Here are some applications involving subtraction. Generally, subtraction is used when we are asked to compare two numbers. Phrases like, "How much more than..." or "What is the difference between..." or "What was the change in..." almost always indicate subtraction.

For each, check the answer with addition, and write a sentence answering the question.

YOU TRY IT 18 *Tammi sold $132 worth of Girl Scout cookies and Monica sold $84 worth of them. How much more did Tammi sell than Monica?*

Sentence: ____________________

YOU TRY IT 19 *Marcus traveled 1,385 miles on business last month while Ruben traveled 859 miles. How many more miles did Marcus travel last month than Ruben?*

Sentence: ____________________

YOU TRY IT 20 *South Orange County Community College District has two colleges, Irvine Valley College and Saddleback College. Last summer Irvine Valley had an enrollment of 4,569 and Saddleback had an enrollment of 9,912, and no one attended both colleges. How many more students attended Saddleback than Irvine Valley?*

Sentence: ____________________

YOU TRY IT 21 *Last year, Sara's annual salary was $24,389. This year she got a raise and is now making $25,742. What was the amount of Sara's raise?*

Sentence: ____________________

YOU TRY IT 22 *Two years ago, Sam's Neighborhood Market had receipts totaling $1,685,417. Last year, sales were better and the market had receipts totaling $1,805,302. How much more were the market receipts last year than the year before?*

Sentence: ____________________

You Try It Answers: Section 1.3

YTI 1 a) 387 b) 3,875 c) 4,559 d) 137,865

YTI 2 a) 75 b) 84 c) 93 d) 66

YTI 3 a) 583 b) 650 c) 901 d) 912

YTI 4 a) 133 b) 7,300 c) 10,241 d) 1,000,000

YTI 5 a) 141 b) 1,122 c) 23,174 d) 113,940

YTI 6 Their combined monthly salary is $6,302.

YTI 7 Allison traveled a total of 7,271 miles.

YTI 8 The total cost of the car is $20,722.

YTI 9 a) Perimeter = 410 feet
b) Perimeter = 196 inches

YTI 10 a) 3 b) 2 c) 7 d) 0

YTI 11 a) 37 b) 21 c) 373 d) 1,105

YTI 12 a) 430 b) 2,142 c) 301 d) 152,336

YTI 13 a) 7 b) 9 c) 5 d) 6

YTI 14 a) 24 = 1 ten and 14 ones
b) 15 = 0 tens and 15 ones
c) 60 = 5 tens and 10 ones

YTI 15 a) 3 hundreds, 10 tens and 7 ones = 3 hundreds, 9 tens and 17 ones

b) 7 hundreds, 10 tens and 1 one = 7 hundreds, 9 tens and 11 ones

c) 0 hundreds, 10 tens and 2 ones = 0 hundreds, 9 tens and 12 ones

d) 1 hundred, 10 tens and 0 ones = 1 hundred, 9 tens and 10 ones

YTI 16 a) 17 b) 74 c) 1,281 d) 816

YTI 17 a) 308 b) 194 c) 684

YTI 18 Tammi sold $48 more than Monica.

YTI 19 Marcus traveled 526 miles more than Ruben.

YTI 20 5,343 more students attended Saddleback than Irvine Valley.

YTI 21 Sara's raise was $1,353.

YTI 22 Last year's receipts were $119,885 more than receipts from the year before.

Focus Exercises: Section 1.3

Add.

1. 17 + 42

2. 41 + 56

3. 425 + 132

4. 416 + 23

5. 52 + 835

6. 5,461 + 36

7. 72 + 6,803

8. 1,581 + 3,709

9. 4,706 + 58,219

10. 24,360 + 74,654

11. 15,086 + 742,511

12. 230,495 + 604,201

13. $\begin{array}{r} 41{,}580 \\ +\ 63{,}219 \\ \hline \end{array}$	**14.** $\begin{array}{r} 34{,}692 \\ +\ 81{,}050 \\ \hline \end{array}$	**15.** $\begin{array}{r} 875{,}213 \\ +\ 124{,}787 \\ \hline \end{array}$	**16.** $\begin{array}{r} 263{,}819 \\ +\ 612{,}086 \\ \hline \end{array}$
17. $\begin{array}{r} 28 \\ 35 \\ +\ 41 \\ \hline \end{array}$	**18.** $\begin{array}{r} 36 \\ 94 \\ 28 \\ +\ 50 \\ \hline \end{array}$	**19.** $\begin{array}{r} 129 \\ 214 \\ 78 \\ +\ 396 \\ \hline \end{array}$	**20.** $\begin{array}{r} 512 \\ 418 \\ 91 \\ +\ 229 \\ \hline \end{array}$
21. $\begin{array}{r} 4{,}426 \\ 9{,}508 \\ +\ 3{,}077 \\ \hline \end{array}$	**22.** $\begin{array}{r} 11{,}581 \\ 6{,}215 \\ +\ 23{,}024 \\ \hline \end{array}$	**23.** $\begin{array}{r} 52{,}681 \\ 17{,}938 \\ 33{,}075 \\ +\ 40{,}206 \\ \hline \end{array}$	**24.** $\begin{array}{r} 146{,}819 \\ 253{,}022 \\ 346{,}795 \\ +\ 361{,}364 \\ \hline \end{array}$

Subtract.

25. $\begin{array}{r} 285 \\ -\ 33 \\ \hline \end{array}$	**26.** $\begin{array}{r} 389 \\ -\ 269 \\ \hline \end{array}$	**27.** $\begin{array}{r} 147 \\ -\ 45 \\ \hline \end{array}$	**28.** $\begin{array}{r} 964 \\ -\ 920 \\ \hline \end{array}$
29. $\begin{array}{r} 3{,}452 \\ -\ 140 \\ \hline \end{array}$	**30.** $\begin{array}{r} 48{,}839 \\ -\ 614 \\ \hline \end{array}$	**31.** $\begin{array}{r} 42 \\ -\ 17 \\ \hline \end{array}$	**32.** $\begin{array}{r} 63 \\ -\ 25 \\ \hline \end{array}$
33. $\begin{array}{r} 53 \\ -\ 48 \\ \hline \end{array}$	**34.** $\begin{array}{r} 80 \\ -\ 29 \\ \hline \end{array}$	**35.** $\begin{array}{r} 100 \\ -\ 46 \\ \hline \end{array}$	**36.** $\begin{array}{r} 100 \\ -\ 73 \\ \hline \end{array}$
37. $\begin{array}{r} 156 \\ -\ 99 \\ \hline \end{array}$	**38.** $\begin{array}{r} 274 \\ -\ 93 \\ \hline \end{array}$	**39.** $\begin{array}{r} 621 \\ -\ 528 \\ \hline \end{array}$	**40.** $\begin{array}{r} 512 \\ -\ 133 \\ \hline \end{array}$
41. $\begin{array}{r} 230 \\ -\ 157 \\ \hline \end{array}$	**42.** $\begin{array}{r} 406 \\ -\ 392 \\ \hline \end{array}$	**43.** $\begin{array}{r} 316 \\ -\ 23 \\ \hline \end{array}$	**44.** $\begin{array}{r} 800 \\ -\ 352 \\ \hline \end{array}$
45. $\begin{array}{r} 5{,}461 \\ -\ 36 \\ \hline \end{array}$	**46.** $\begin{array}{r} 2{,}754 \\ -\ 1{,}121 \\ \hline \end{array}$	**47.** $\begin{array}{r} 40{,}216 \\ -\ 15{,}381 \\ \hline \end{array}$	**48.** $\begin{array}{r} 604{,}201 \\ -\ 230{,}495 \\ \hline \end{array}$
49. $\begin{array}{r} 6{,}803 \\ -\ 72 \\ \hline \end{array}$	**50.** $\begin{array}{r} 2{,}374 \\ -\ 515 \\ \hline \end{array}$	**51.** $\begin{array}{r} 4{,}426 \\ -\ 133 \\ \hline \end{array}$	**52.** $\begin{array}{r} 25{,}053 \\ -\ 624 \\ \hline \end{array}$
53. $\begin{array}{r} 135{,}604 \\ -\ 2{,}261 \\ \hline \end{array}$	**54.** $\begin{array}{r} 742{,}511 \\ -\ 5{,}086 \\ \hline \end{array}$	**55.** $\begin{array}{r} 300{,}000 \\ -\ 106{,}578 \\ \hline \end{array}$	**56.** $\begin{array}{r} 1{,}000{,}000 \\ -\ 361{,}047 \\ \hline \end{array}$

Work each application and answer with a complete sentence.

57. Throughout 2005, Dionne gave monetary donations to two charities, $1,258 to the Salvation Army and $875 to the United Way. What was Dionne's total contribution to these two charities?

58. Ron's electric bill for July was $212 but only $87 for June. How much more was Ron's electric bill for July than June?

59. Debbie has an adjustable rate mortgage that could change from year to year. In 2004, her monthly mortgage payment was $1,426. In 2005, her monthly payment was $1,347. How much less was Debbie's monthly payment in 2005 than in 2004?

60. Throughout their NBA careers, Kareem Abdul Jabbar scored a total of 38,387 points and Micheal Jordan scored a total of 29,277 points. How many more total points did Kareem Abdul Jabbar score than Micheal Jordan?
Source: sportsillustrated.cnn.com

61. The Detroit office of Globe Realty employs four agents. Mike, the owner, has 21 years of experience in real estate; Ann has 23 years of experience; Uta has 19 years; and Francisco has 17 years. How many combined years of experience in real estate do the four agents have?

62. Eugenia ordered some new furniture for her Portland, Oregon, office. The order included an executive desk, $327; a computer desk, $133; a swivel chair, $148; and a client chair, $92. Along with shipping charges of $116, what was the total amount of the order? (By the way, there is no sales tax in Oregon!)

63. Baseball attendance figures for a weekend series between the Houston Astros and the Florida Marlins were 35,403 on Friday, 41,292 on Saturday, and 28,515 on Sunday.

a) What was the total attendance for the three-game series?

b) How many more fans were in attendance on Saturday than on Sunday?

64. The elevation of Mount Everest, in Nepal, is 29,035 feet (8,850 meters). The elevation of Mount Kilimanjaro, in Tanzania, is 19,340 feet (5,895 meters). How much higher is Mount Everest than Mount Kilimanjaro...

a) in feet?

b) in meters?

65. Find the perimeter for each figure.

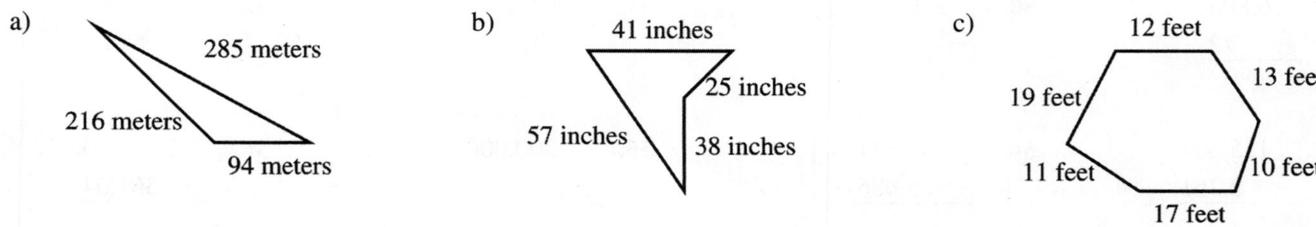

SECTION 1.4 Multiplying Whole Numbers

Objectives

In this section, you will learn to:

- Define the term *multiplication.*
- Write numbers in factored form.
- Multiply by 10's and 100's.
- Identify and apply the Distributive Property.
- Multiply two-digit numbers.
- Find the area of a geometric figure.

To successfully complete this section, you need to understand:

- The Commutative Property (1.2)
- The Associative Property (1.2)
- Adding whole numbers (1.3)

Introduction: What Is Multiplication?

For whole numbers, **multiplication** is an abbreviation for repeated addition.

For example, in the lobby of an apartment building is a rectangular mail box center, which has 4 rows of 6 mailboxes each. How many mailboxes are there altogether?

4 rows

6 mailboxes in each row

Because there are four rows of 6 mailboxes, we can answer the question by adding the number of mailboxes in each row:

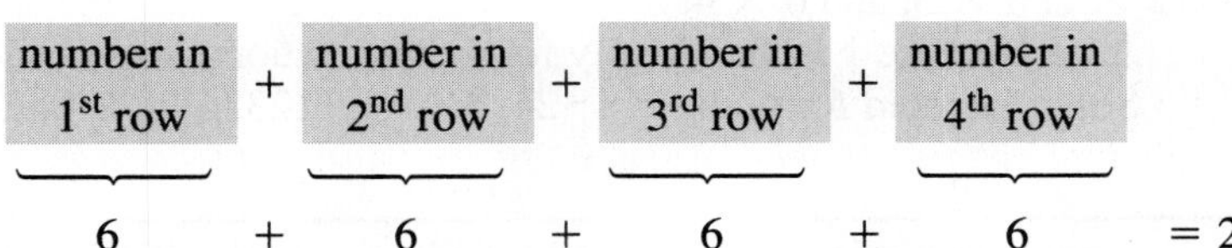

6 + 6 + 6 + 6 = 24 mailboxes

We can also think of this as *four* 6's.

This sum of four 6's is an example of *repeated* addition, and it can be abbreviated using multiplication:

$$\textit{four } 6\text{'s} = 4 \times 6 = \mathbf{24}.$$

Furthermore, there is a variety of ways that multiplication can be represented. For example, *4 times 6* can be written as

4×6	typical arithmetic
$4 \cdot 6$, $4(6)$, $4(6)$, and $(4)(6)$	typical algebra

In this text, we will often (though not always) use the raised dot for multiplication.

Caution The raised dot is not a decimal point, and when we get to multiplying decimals (in Section 5.4), we'll use the arithmetic multiplication sign, ×, to avoid confusion.

EXAMPLE 1 Write each repeating sum in words, and abbreviate it as a multiplication. Find the product.

ANSWER:

Repeating sum	In words	Multiplication		Product
a) 7 + 7 + 7	three 7's	$3 \cdot 7$	=	21
b) 11 + 11 + 11 + 11 + 11	five 11's	$5 \cdot 11$	=	55

YOU TRY IT 1 *Write each repeating sum in words and abbreviate it as a multiplication. Find the product. (You may refer to the multiplication table, if necessary.) Use Example 1 as a guide.*

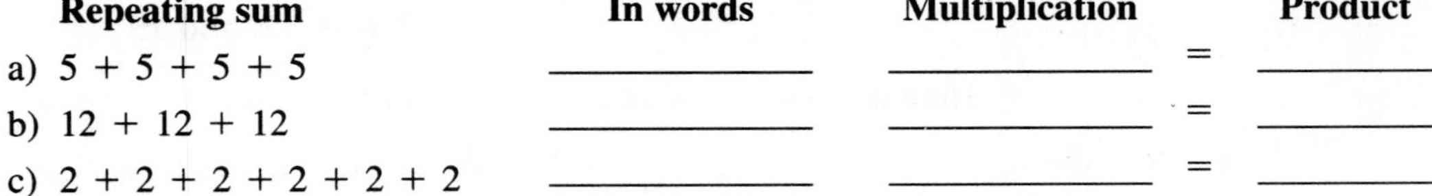

Repeating sum	In words	Multiplication		Product
a) 5 + 5 + 5 + 5	________	________	=	________
b) 12 + 12 + 12	________	________	=	________
c) 2 + 2 + 2 + 2 + 2 + 2	________	________	=	________

Numbers in Factored Form

Recall, from Section 1.2, that the numbers in a product are called *factors*:

factor × factor = product

Since we know, for example, that $4 \times 6 = 24$, we can say that 4 and 6 are factors of 24.

Also, a number is in **factored form** when it is written as a product of factors. So, we can say that

4×6 is a factored form of 24.

There are other factored forms of 24. In fact, in the multiplication table we can locate 24 as a product a total of six times: 2×12, 3×8, 4×6, and—by the Commutative Property—12×2, 8×3, and 6×4.

Also, because 1 is the identity for multiplication, $24 = 1 \cdot 24$.

So, in factored form, $24 = 1 \cdot 24$, $24 = 2 \cdot 12$, $24 = 3 \cdot 8$, $24 = 4 \cdot 6$, and so on.

EXAMPLE 2 Using the multiplication table and the identity for multiplication, find six ways to write 18 in a factored form.

ANSWER: $18 = 2 \cdot 9$ $18 = 9 \cdot 2$ $18 = 3 \cdot 6$

$18 = 6 \cdot 3$ $18 = 1 \cdot 18$ $18 = 18 \cdot 1$

YOU TRY IT 2 *Using the multiplication table, find different ways to write each number in a factored form. Use Example 2 as a guide.*

a) 12 ______ ______ ______ ______ ______ ______

b) 20 ______ ______ ______ ______ ______ ______

Multiples of a Number

The 5 × 5 Multiplication Table

×	1	2	3	4	5
1	1	2	3	4	5
2	2	4	6	8	10
3	3	6	9	12	15
4	4	8	12	16	20
5	5	10	15	20	25

In this 5×5 multiplication table, both the row and column starting with 3 are highlighted to show you the first five **multiples** of 3:

3, 6, 9, 12, and 15

Here is the same list of multiples with each number written in a factored form:

3	**6**	**9**	**12**	**15**
$1 \cdot 3$	$2 \cdot 3$	$3 \cdot 3$	$4 \cdot 3$	$5 \cdot 3$

Notice that 3 is one of the factors in each of these multiples. We can always find the next multiple of 3 by simply adding 3:

The next multiple of 3 is 18 because $15 + 3 = 18$.

In factored form, $18 = 6 \cdot 3$.

In general, if a and b are two whole numbers, then their product, $a \cdot b$, is a **multiple** of a and a **multiple** of b.

EXAMPLE 3 Use the 5 3 5 multiplication table to find the first seven multiples of 2.

PROCEDURE: We can find the first five multiples from the table, then add 2 to find the sixth, and add 2 more to find the seventh.

	First five	Sixth 10 + 2 ↓		Seventh 12 + 2 ↓
ANSWER: First seven multiples of 2:	2, 4, 6, 8, 10,	12,	and	14

YOU TRY IT 3 *Use the 5 × 5 multiplication table to find the first seven multiples of each number. Use Example 3 as a guide.*

a) First seven multiples of 4: ______________________

b) First seven multiples of 5: ______________________

YOU TRY IT 4 *Evaluate. Use the multiplication table—or your own memory—to multiply the following.*

a) $8 \times 2 =$ b) $4 \cdot 7 =$ c) $6 \times 6 =$ d) $5 \cdot 9 =$

The Multiplication Property of 0

Consider this: $4 \cdot 0 =$ four 0's $= 0 + 0 + 0 + 0 = 0$.

In other words, $4 \cdot 0 = 0$. This is true of any multiple of 0. Also, the Commutative Property allows us to say that $0 \cdot 4 = 0$.

The Multiplication Property of 0

$$\mathbf{a \cdot 0 = 0} \quad \text{and} \quad \mathbf{0 \cdot a = 0}$$

The product of 0 and any number is always 0.

Multiplication by 10 and by 100

Recall that 1 is the multiplicative identity, so multiplying by 1 is very easy: any number times 1 is itself:

$6 \cdot 1 = 6$ and $1 \cdot 19 = 19$. In general, $a \cdot 1 = a$ and $1 \cdot a = a$.

Multiplying by 10 and multiplying by 100 is just as easy. In Section 1.2, the 12 x 12 multiplication table shows the first twelve multiples of 10.

YOU TRY IT 5

Write the first twelve multiples of 10. (You may use the multiplication table.) Below each, write the number in a factored form. (The first two are given to get you started.)

10	20	___	___	___	___	___	___	___	___	___	___
$1 \cdot 10$	$2 \cdot 10$	___	___	___	___	___	___	___	___	___	___

Multiplying by 10

When one factor is 10, the product is the *other* factor with a 0 placed on the end.

For example, $3 \cdot 10$ is *three* 10's: $10 + 10 + 10 = 30$, so $\mathbf{3} \cdot 10 = \mathbf{30}$. The Commutative Property also allows us to say that $10 \cdot \mathbf{3} = \mathbf{30}$.

Think about it

In your own words, how would you explain to a classmate that numbers such as 30, 40, 110, 150, and 190 are multiples of 10?

____

____

Multiplying by 100 is similar:

Multiplying by 100

When one factor is 100, the product is the *other* factor with *two* 0's placed on the end.

Since $100 = 10 \cdot 10$, multiplying by 100 is the same as multiplying by 10 twice. That's why we place *two* 0's after the other factor.

EXAMPLE 4

Evaluate.

a) $16 \cdot 10$ b) $10 \cdot 30$ c) $9 \cdot 100$ d) $100 \cdot 58$

PROCEDURE: Multiply by placing one or two zeros at the end of the other factor, whichever is appropriate.

ANSWER:

a) $16 \cdot 10 = 160$ (16 with one 0 placed on the end = 160)

b) $10 \cdot 30 = 300$ (30 with one 0 placed on the end = 300)

c) $9 \cdot 100 = 900$ (9 with two 0's placed on the end = 900)

d) $100 \cdot 58 = 5{,}800$ (58 with two 0's placed on the end = 5800 = 5,800)

YOU TRY IT 6

Evaluate. Use Example 4 as a guide.

a) $8 \cdot 10 =$ ________ b) $10 \cdot 32 =$ ________ c) $604 \cdot 10 =$ ________

d) $100 \cdot 7 =$ ________ e) $100 \cdot 50 =$ ________ f) $298 \cdot 100 =$ ________

Using the Associative Property of Multiplication

We can use the Associative Property of Multiplication to understand more about multiplication. In particular, if a number is a multiple of 10, such as 30, 40, 80, 120, and so on, then it has 10 as a factor.

We can use this information to quickly multiply two numbers where at least one of them is a multiple of 10. Consider $30 \cdot 6$:

	$30 \cdot 6$
Because $30 = 10 \cdot 3$, we can replace 30 with $(10 \cdot 3)$	$= (10 \cdot 3) \cdot 6$
We can apply the Associative Property:	$= 10 \cdot (3 \cdot 6)$
$3 \cdot 6 = 18$, so we get	$= 10 \cdot 18$
which is, because we are now multiplying by 10, 180:	$= 180$

What is important to see here is that the end product is just $3 \cdot 6$ multiplied by 10: $18 \cdot 10 = 180$.

The point is this,

Multiplying by Multiples of 10

If one or more factors is a multiple of 10, such as 20, or 80, or 300 and so on, then you may temporarily ignore such (ending) zeros, and include them together in the final product.

Let's see this rule illustrated by some examples:

EXAMPLE 5 Evaluate each.

a) $3 \cdot 20 = 60$ Ignore the 0 after the 2, treat the problem as $3 \cdot 2$ to get 6, then place the 0 at the end, 60.

b) $40 \cdot 7 = 280$ Ignore the 0 after the 4, treat the problem as $4 \cdot 7$ to get 28, then place the 0 at the end, 280.

c) $80 \cdot 60 = 4{,}800$ Ignore both 0's after the 8 and the 6, treat the problem as $8 \cdot 6$ to get 48, then place the two 0's at the end, 4800 = 4,800.

d) $300 \cdot 90 = 27{,}000$ Ignore all of the 0's—there are three of them in all—and treat the problem as $3 \cdot 9$ to get 27; then place all three 0's at the end, 27000 = 27,000.

e) $500 \cdot 400 = 200{,}000$ Ignore all of the 0's—there are four of them in all—and treat the problem as $5 \cdot 4$ to get 20; then place all four 0's at the end. Notice that the 0 in 20 is not counted as one of the four 0's—they were all placed *after* the 20. This gives the number a total of five 0's. This will sometimes happen when 5's (as in 500) are involved.

YOU TRY IT 7 *Evaluate each. Use Example 5 as a guide.*

a) $3 \cdot 50 =$ ________ b) $90 \cdot 7 =$ ________ c) $50 \cdot 8 =$ ________

d) $300 \cdot 30 =$ ________ e) $800 \cdot 200 =$ ________ f) $6{,}000 \cdot 500 =$ ________

The Distributive Property of Multiplication over Addition

As you learned in Section 1.2, parentheses group a quantity and make it one value. For example, in the expression $3 \cdot (10 + 2)$, the parentheses suggest that $(10 + 2)$ should be treated as one value, 12.

The expression can become $3 \cdot (12)$, which is just three 12's: $12 + 12 + 12 = 36$. This means that $3 \cdot 12 = 36$.

Treating $3 \cdot (12)$, though, as $3 \cdot (10 + 2)$ suggests that we have three 10's and three 2's:

$3 \cdot (10 + 2) = (10 + 2) + (10 + 2) + (10 + 2)$ The Commutative and Associative Properties allow us to rearrange the numbers into groups of three 10's and three 2's.

$3 \cdot (10 + 2) = (10 + 10 + 10) + (2 + 2 + 2)$

$3 \cdot (10 + 2) = (\text{three 10's}) + (\text{three 2's})$

$3 \cdot (10 + 2) = 3 \cdot 10 + 3 \cdot 2$

$3 \cdot (10 + 2) = 30 + 6$

$3 \cdot (10 + 2) = 36$

We can say that the multiplier 3 is being distributed to both the 10 and the 2.

This diagram is a shortcut to the work shown above:

$$\mathbf{3} \cdot (10 + 2) = \mathbf{3} \cdot 10 + \mathbf{3} \cdot 2 = 30 + 6 = 36$$

This idea helps to introduce an important property of mathematics, the Distributive Property, formally known as the **Distributive Property of Multiplication over Addition.**

The Distributive Property of Multiplication over Addition

We can distribute a multiplier, $\boldsymbol{a}$, over a sum $(b + c)$ so that it multiplies both numbers in the sum.

$$\boldsymbol{a} \cdot (b + c) = \boldsymbol{a} \cdot b + \boldsymbol{a} \cdot c$$

In other words, $\boldsymbol{a}$ is a multiplier of both b and c.

Usually, when evaluating an expression, we evaluate within the parentheses first. However, when specifically applying the Distributive Property, we multiply first.

The notion of the Distributive Property is quite useful in multiplying by numbers with two or more digits. We'll use the fact that every two-digit number can be separated into the sum of its tens and ones.

For example, $14 = 10 + 4$ and $59 = 50 + 9$. We can use this information and the Distributive Property when multiplying horizontally, as in Example 6.

EXAMPLE 6 Multiply.

a) $6 \cdot 14$

b) $7 \cdot 59$

PROCEDURE: Treat 14 as $(10 + 4)$ and 59 as $(50 + 9)$ and use the Distributive Property:

ANSWER:

a) $6 \cdot 14 = 6 \cdot (10 + 4)$

b) $7 \cdot 59 = 7 \cdot (50 + 9)$

Apply the Distributive Property:

$$\mathbf{6} \cdot (10 + 4) = \mathbf{6} \cdot 10 + \mathbf{6} \cdot 4 = 60 + 24 = 84$$

$$\mathbf{7} \cdot (50 + 9) = \mathbf{7} \cdot 50 + \mathbf{7} \cdot 9 = 350 + 63 = 413$$

YOU TRY IT 8 *Multiply using the technique demonstrated in Example 6.*

a) $4 \cdot 18 = 4 \cdot (10 + 8)$

b) $5 \cdot 46 = 5 \cdot (40 + 6)$

c) $7 \cdot 19 = 7 \cdot (\_\_\_\_\_\_\_\_)$

d) $8 \cdot 73 = 8 \cdot (\_\_\_\_\_\_\_\_)$

Traditional Multiplication by a Single-Digit Number

Because multiplication is an abbreviation for repeated addition, multiplication and addition are really inseparable. Notice that we needed to add at the end of each multiplication problem, above.

Also, in addition, we sometimes have to carry from one column to the next, as in the sum of 24 and 38, shown as the right.

$$\begin{array}{r} {}^{+1} \\ 24 \\ +\ 38 \\ \hline 62 \end{array}$$

First, the ones column adds to 12 (more than 9), so we write the 2 in the ones place and carry a 1 into the tens column. Next, we add the tens column, including the 1 that we carried there. (The plus sign is shown with the 1 to remind us that we need to add the carried 1.)

The same idea applies when we multiply. We start by multiplying the ones column numbers together, and if the product is more than 9, then we carry the tens number to the next column.

Consider $26 \cdot 3$, set up as $\begin{array}{r} 26 \\ \times\ 3 \\ \hline \end{array}$ Remember, this is equivalent to

$$\begin{aligned} & 3 \cdot (20 + 6) \\ &= 3 \cdot 20 + 3 \cdot 6 \\ &= 60 + 18 = 78 \end{aligned}$$

The actual step-by-step process of multiplying 26×3 is ...

$$\begin{aligned} & \ldots 6 \cdot 3 + 20 \cdot 3 \\ &= 18 + 60 = 78 \end{aligned}$$

(A) Multiplying the ones, we get $6 \times 3 = 18$. Just as in addition, we can put the 8 in the ones place (in the answer) and carry the 1 to the next column.

$$\begin{array}{r} {}^{+1} \\ 26 \\ \times\ 3 \\ \hline 8 \end{array}$$

(B) We now multiply 2×3 and add the 1 that we carried:

$$(2 \times 3) + 1 = 6 + 1 = 7$$

and we put the 7 in the tens place in the answer.

$$\begin{array}{r} {}^{+1} \\ 26 \\ \times\ 3 \\ \hline 78 \end{array}$$

The reason the 7 belongs in the tens place is:

1. the 1 we carried is really **10** (from 18 = **10** + 8), and
2. the 2 we multiplied by the 3 is really **20**.

So, in part (**B**) the actual multiplication is $(\mathbf{20} \cdot 3) + \mathbf{10} = 60 + 10 = \mathbf{70}$.

YOU TRY IT 9

Multiply using the technique demonstrated above.

a) $\begin{array}{r} 23 \\ \times\ 4 \\ \hline \end{array}$ b) $\begin{array}{r} 19 \\ \times\ 5 \\ \hline \end{array}$ c) $\begin{array}{r} 37 \\ \times\ 2 \\ \hline \end{array}$

If we need to multiply a three-digit number by a one-digit number, the procedure is the same, it just continues one more place.

YOU TRY IT 10

Multiply.

a) $\begin{array}{r} 286 \\ \times\ 3 \\ \hline \end{array}$ b) $\begin{array}{r} 429 \\ \times\ 5 \\ \hline \end{array}$ c) $\begin{array}{r} 581 \\ \times\ 9 \\ \hline \end{array}$

Two-Digit by Two-Digit Multiplication

The multiplication process learned above can be extended to two-digit by two-digit multiplication. For example, if we are to multiply 57 · 63, also written as

$$\begin{array}{r} 57 \\ \times\ 63 \\ \hline \end{array}$$

then we can multiply the tens place digit, 6 (which is really 60), in the same manner as we multiply the ones place digit, 3.

This is a three-step process, giving us two partial products that we'll add to get the final product:

1. multiply 57 · 3 (this will give us the first partial product);
2. multiply 57 · 60 (this will give us the second partial product); and
3. add the two partial products together to get the final product.

Here is the step-by-step outline for 57 · 63:

(A) Multiplying the ones, we get 7 × 3 = 21.

So, place the 1 and carry the 2.

$$\begin{array}{r} {\scriptstyle +2} \\ 57 \\ \times\ 63 \\ \hline 1 \end{array}$$

(B) We now multiply 5 × 3 and add the 2:

(5 × 3) + 2 = 17

There's no more to multiply by the 3, so we place 17 into the answer.

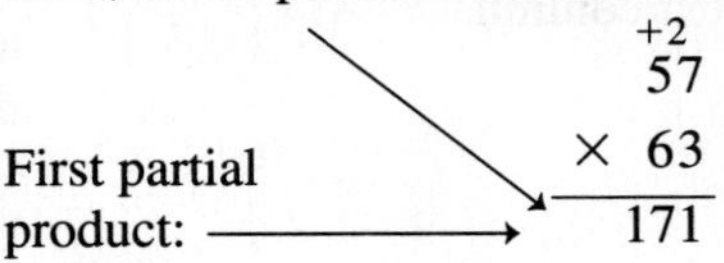

First partial product: →
$$\begin{array}{r} {\scriptstyle +2} \\ 57 \\ \times\ 63 \\ \hline 171 \end{array}$$

(C) We now multiply 7 × 60 giving us 420.

We put the 0 in the ones place, the 2 in the tens place, and carry the 4:

$$\begin{array}{r} {\scriptstyle +4\ \not{+2}} \\ 57 \\ \times\ 63 \\ \hline 171 \\ 20 \end{array}$$

(D) We now multiply 5 × 6 and add the 4 to get 34, which is placed in the second partial product:

(E) Then we add the partial products:

$$\begin{array}{r} {\scriptstyle +4\ \not{+2}} \\ 57 \\ \times\ 63 \\ \hline \times\ 171 \\ +\ 3420 \\ \hline 3591 \end{array}$$

Second partial product: → + 3420

Final product: → 3591

This is what your work probably looks like, altogether:

$$\begin{array}{r} {\scriptstyle +4\ \not{+2}} \\ 57 \\ \times\ 63 \\ \hline 171 \\ +\ 3{,}420 \\ \hline 3{,}591 \end{array}$$

YOU TRY IT 11

Multiply.

a) $\begin{array}{r} 17 \\ \times\ 25 \\ \hline \end{array}$

b) $\begin{array}{r} 41 \\ \times\ 33 \\ \hline \end{array}$

c) $\begin{array}{r} 534 \\ \times\ 46 \\ \hline \end{array}$

Applications of Multiplication

There are many situations to which multiplication can apply. Since multiplication is an abbreviation for repeated addition, we use it whenever the same number is added over and over a certain number of times.

For each of these word problems:

- Read it through carefully (maybe two or three times).
- Think about the situation (imagine yourself in the situation).
- Remember that in multiplication, there are two numbers:

1. one number that will be repeated, and
2. another number that indicates the number of times it is repeated.

- Multiply appropriately.
- Write a sentence answering the question.

EXAMPLE 7 Bindee just completed her associate's degree and is now looking for a job. Searching the Internet, she found a job as an entry level secretary that pays $1,783 per month. If she is hired for that job, how much would she earn in 12 months?

PROCEDURE: Here, the monthly wage is the same each month—and Bindee would earn that wage 12 *times*—so multiplication is the operation to use.

Multiply the monthly wage ($1,783) by the number of months (12).

ANSWER:

Bindee monthly wage: → 1783
Times 12 months: → × 12

$$\begin{array}{r} 1783 \\ \times\ 12 \\ \hline 3566 \\ 17830 \\ \hline 21{,}396 \end{array}$$

SENTENCE: If Bindee gets the job, she will earn $21,396 in 12 months.

YOU TRY IT 12 *George sells sports cards. In each Upper Deck Stars box there are 24 packs of cards. If George has 5 of these boxes, how many packs of Upper Deck Stars does he have?*

Sentence: ______________________________

YOU TRY IT 13 *At the restaurant where Leilani is a waitress, there is a buffet special for $8 per person. A group of 15 patrons came in one afternoon and they all ordered the buffet special. Before tax and tip, what was the total amount of their bill?*

Sentence: ______________________________

YOU TRY IT 14 *Sam, a truck driver, is asked to pick up 93 boxes, each weighing 38 pounds. What is the total weight of this load?*

Sentence: ______________________________

Multiplication in Geometry: Area

In geometry, **area** is the amount of surface in an enclosed region. Area is always measured in square units, such as square feet (*sq ft*) or square centimeters (*sq cm*).

We can use the area of a rectangle to illustrate the idea that multiplication is repeated addition. This illustration will also develop the formula for the area of a rectangle.

First, consider the single centimeter square, at right. (A *centimeter* is a unit of measure and is abbreviated *cm*. It takes about $2\frac{1}{2}$ centimeters to make an inch.)

It can be put together with other such centimeter squares to form a horizontal row of 4 centimeter squares:

From there, we can build a rectangle with three of these rows, one on top of the other; this is repeated addition coming together as one value:

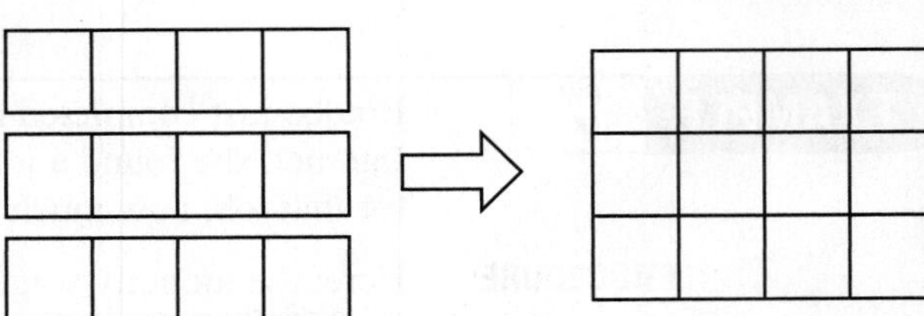

$$4 + 4 + 4 = 12 \text{ cm squares}$$
$$3 \cdot 4 = 12$$

We see the rectangle that is formed with the individual centimeter squares; we can count them to verify that there are, indeed, 12 unit squares.

The illustration below also shows the area formula for a rectangle:

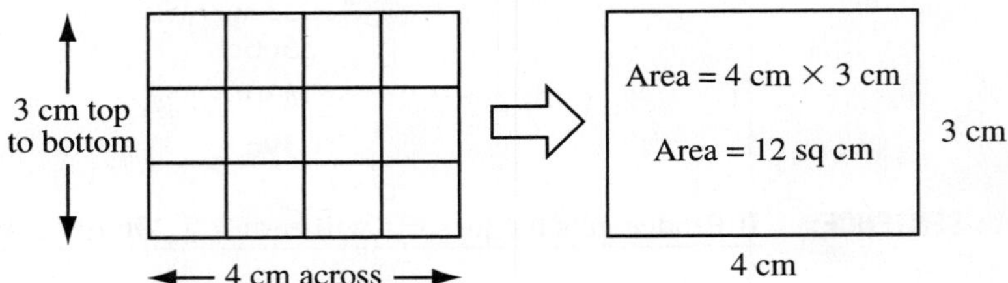

In general, **Area of a rectangle = Length × Width.**

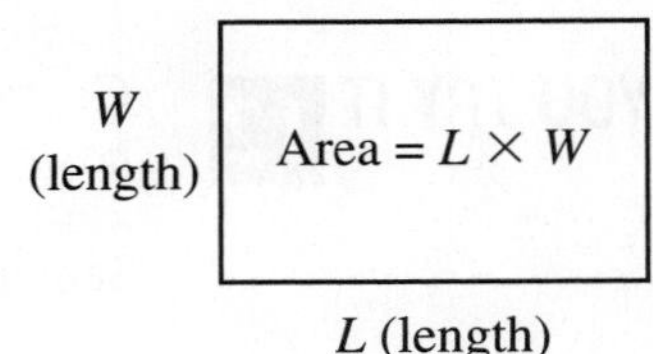

EXAMPLE 8 Find the area of the rectangle below.

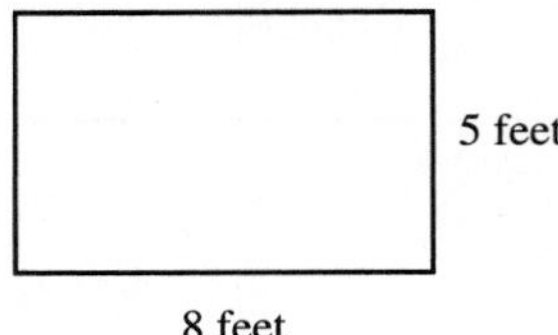

ANSWER:

$$\text{Area} = \text{Length} \times \text{Width}$$
$$\text{Area} = 8 \text{ feet} \times 5 \text{ feet}$$
$$\underline{\text{Area} = 40 \text{ sq ft}}$$

YOU TRY IT 15 *Find the area of each rectangle. Use Example 8 as a guide.*

a) b)

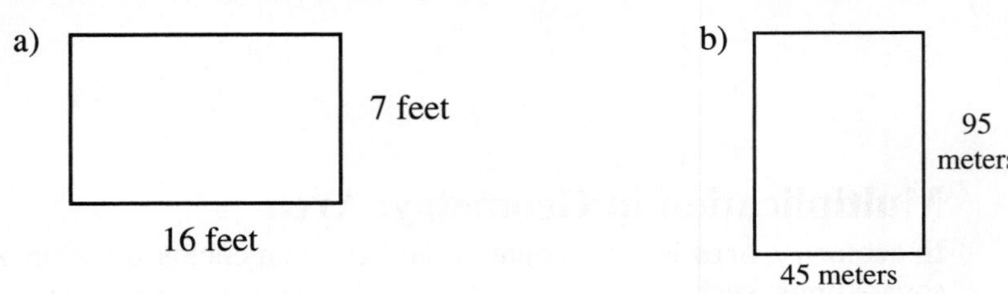

You Try It Answers: Section 1.4

YTI 1

	In words	Multiplication		Product
a)	four 5's	$4 \cdot 5$	=	20
b)	three 12's	$3 \cdot 12$	=	36
c)	six 2's	$6 \cdot 2$	=	12

YTI 2 a) $2 \cdot 6$, $6 \cdot 2$, $3 \cdot 4$, $4 \cdot 3$, $1 \cdot 12$, and $12 \cdot 1$
b) $2 \cdot 10$, $10 \cdot 2$, $4 \cdot 5$, $5 \cdot 4$, $1 \cdot 20$, and $20 \cdot 1$

YTI 3 a) 4, 8, 12, 16, 20, 24, and 28
b) 5, 10, 15, 20, 25, 30, and 35

YTI 4 a) 16 b) 28 c) 36 d) 45

YTI 5

10	20	30	40	50	60
$1 \cdot 10$	$2 \cdot 10$	$3 \cdot 10$	$4 \cdot 10$	$5 \cdot 10$	$6 \cdot 10$
70	80	90	100	110	120
$7 \cdot 10$	$8 \cdot 10$	$9 \cdot 10$	$10 \cdot 10$	$11 \cdot 10$	$12 \cdot 10$

YTI 6 a) 80 b) 320 c) 6,040 d) 700
e) 5,000 f) 29,800

YTI 7 a) 150 b) 630 c) 400 d) 9,000
e) 160,000 f) 3,000,000

YTI 8 a) $40 + 32 = 72$ b) $200 + 30 = 230$
c) $7 \cdot (10 + 9) = 70 + 63 = 133$
d) $8 \cdot (70 + 3) = 560 + 24 = 584$

YTI 9 a) 92 b) 95 c) 74

YTI 10 a) 858 b) 2,145 c) 5,229

YTI 11 a) 425 b) 1,353 c) 24,564

YTI 12 George has 120 packs of Upper Deck Stars.

YTI 13 The total amount of the bill, before tax and tip, was $120.

YTI 14 The total weight of the load is 3,534 pounds.

YTI 15 a) 112 square inches b) 4,275 square meters

Focus Exercises: Section 1.4

Multiply.

1. $5 \cdot 4$ **2.** $6 \cdot 3$ **3.** $4 \cdot 7$ **4.** $8 \cdot 5$

5. $9 \cdot 4$ **6.** $3 \cdot 8$ **7.** $9 \cdot 6$ **8.** $8 \cdot 7$

9. $9 \cdot 3$ **10.** $8 \cdot 4$ **11.** $7 \cdot 5$ **12.** $6 \cdot 8$

13. $8 \cdot 8$ **14.** $9 \cdot 8$ **15.** $7 \cdot 7$ **16.** $9 \cdot 9$

Multiply.

17. $3 \cdot 80$ **18.** $4 \cdot 90$ **19.** $60 \cdot 7$ **20.** $50 \cdot 9$

21. $6 \cdot 50$ **22.** $80 \cdot 5$ **23.** $6 \cdot 400$ **24.** $8 \cdot 200$

25. $900 \cdot 7$ **26.** $500 \cdot 5$ **27.** $30 \cdot 90$ **28.** $70 \cdot 40$

29. $600 \cdot 60$ **30.** $400 \cdot 50$ **31.** $600 \cdot 800$ **32.** $200 \cdot 900$

Multiply.

33. $\begin{array}{r} 18 \\ \times\ 19 \\ \hline \end{array}$ **34.** $\begin{array}{r} 26 \\ \times\ 15 \\ \hline \end{array}$ **35.** $\begin{array}{r} 43 \\ \times\ 43 \\ \hline \end{array}$ **36.** $\begin{array}{r} 62 \\ \times\ 62 \\ \hline \end{array}$

37. $\begin{array}{r} 218 \\ \times\ 45 \\ \hline \end{array}$ **38.** $\begin{array}{r} 307 \\ \times\ 92 \\ \hline \end{array}$ **39.** $\begin{array}{r} 425 \\ \times\ 209 \\ \hline \end{array}$ **40.** $\begin{array}{r} 528 \\ \times\ 303 \\ \hline \end{array}$

41. $\begin{array}{r} 153 \\ \times\ 112 \\ \hline \end{array}$

42. $\begin{array}{r} 216 \\ \times\ 144 \\ \hline \end{array}$

43. $\begin{array}{r} 256 \\ \times\ 128 \\ \hline \end{array}$

44. $\begin{array}{r} 1{,}153 \\ \times\ 224 \\ \hline \end{array}$

Which property is being demonstrated?

45. $6 \cdot 9 = 9 \cdot 6$

46. $3 \cdot (5 + 8) = 3 \cdot 5 + 3 \cdot 8$

47. $4 \cdot (7 \cdot 2) = (4 \cdot 7) \cdot 2$

48. $18 \cdot 0 = 0$

Work each application and answer the question with a complete sentence.

49. The parking lot at the Hillside Christmas Craft Fair has 14 rows of parking with 12 parking spaces in each row. How many cars can fit in the parking lot?

50. Monica has a one year lease on her apartment and pays a monthly rent of $835. How much rent will Monica pay for the entire year (12 months)?

51. Ignacio's truck gets 13 miles per gallon of gas. He just filled the gas tank to a total of 28 gallons. How many miles can Ignacio's truck go before it runs out of gas?

52. Sandy is counting inventory at The Office Station. In the pen and pencil section, there are 33 boxes of Script Magic gel pens. If each box holds 18 pens, how many Script Magic gel pens does The Office Station have in its inventory?

53. A jumbo jet is flying from San Francisco to Australia and is averaging 492 miles per hour. How many miles will the jet travel in 16 hours?

54. Rico spends $25 every week on lottery tickets. How much does Rico spend in a year (52 weeks) on lottery tickets?

55. Diane is a massage therapist. During her first week working for Dr. Kent's chiropractic office, she saw 23 patients. If she earns $18 for every patient, how much did Diane earn that first week?

56. Toby is preparing a 23-pound turkey for his family's Thanksgiving gathering. The recipe he's using says to roast the turkey 12 minutes per pound. For how many minutes should Toby roast the turkey?

57. There are 306 families in the Magnolia Elementary PTA. Each family must contribute $18 throughout the year to support the PTA's field trip program. What will be the total income for the PTA's field trip program for one year?

58. Soo works for the purchasing department of a mid-sized company. Last week she bought 12 computers for their new West Valley office, which opens in two months. Each computer is priced at $1,289. What is the total price for the 12 computers?

59. A youth soccer field is in the shape of a rectangle. The length is 60 yards and the width is 28 yards. What is the area of this soccer field?

60. An official college basketball court is 94 feet long and 50 feet wide. What is the area of this basketball court?

61. The state of Wyoming is in the shape of a rectangle. It is 357 miles long and 274 miles wide. Round each of these dimensions to the nearest ten. Use the rounded numbers to approximate the area of Wyoming.

SECTION 1.5 Dividing Whole Numbers

Objectives

In this section, you will learn to:

- Define the term *division.*
- Perform short division.
- Perform long division.

To successfully complete this section, you need to understand:

- Rounding whole numbers (1.1)
- Adding whole numbers (1.3)
- Subtracting whole numbers (1.3)
- Multiplying whole numbers (1.4)

Introduction

Consider the following situations:

1. Edgar brought home 72 donut holes for the 9 children at his daughter's slumber party. How many will each child receive if the donut holes are divided equally among all nine?
2. Three friends, Gloria, Jan, and Mie-Yun won a small lottery prize of $1,450. If they split it equally among all three, how much will each get?
3. Shawntee just purchased a used car. She has agreed to pay a total of $6,200 over a 36-month period. What will her monthly payments be?
4. 195 people are planning to attend an awards banquet. Ruben is in charge of the table rental. If each table seats 8, how many tables are needed so that everyone has a seat?

Each of these problems can be answered using division. As you'll recall from Section 1.2, the result of division is called the quotient. Here are the parts of a division problem:

Standard form: $\text{dividend} \div \text{divisor} = \text{quotient}$

Long division form: $\begin{array}{r}\text{quotient}\\ \text{divisor}\overline{)\text{dividend}}\end{array}$

Fraction form: $\dfrac{\text{dividend}}{\text{divisor}} = \text{quotient}$

We use these words—dividend, divisor, and quotient—throughout this section, so it's important that you become familiar with them. You'll often see this little diagram as a continual reminder of their proper placement.

$\begin{array}{r}\text{quotient}\\ \text{divisor}\overline{)\text{dividend}}\end{array}$

Here is how a division problem is read:

In the standard form: $15 \div 5$ is read "15 divided *by* 5."

In the long division form: $5\overline{)15}$ is read "5 divided *into* 15."

In the fraction form: $\dfrac{15}{5}$ is read "15 divided *by* 5."

EXAMPLE 1 In this division problem, identify the dividend, divisor and quotient.

$36 \div 4 = 9,\quad \begin{array}{r}9\\ 4\overline{)36}\end{array}\quad \text{or}\quad \dfrac{36}{4} = 9$

ANSWER: For each, the dividend is <u>36</u>, the divisor is <u>4</u>, and the quotient is <u>9</u>.

YOU TRY IT 1 *In each division problem, identify the dividend, divisor and quotient. Use Example 1 as a guide.*

a) $28 \div 7 = 4$ dividend: ________ divisor: ________ quotient: ________

b) $\dfrac{40}{8} = 5$ dividend: ________ divisor: ________ quotient: ________

c) $\begin{array}{r}6\\ 2\overline{)12}\end{array}$ dividend: ________ divisor: ________ quotient: ________

What Is Division?

Division is *the inverse operation of multiplication.* Just as multiplication is repeated addition, division can be thought of as repeated subtraction. For example, to find out how many times 3 will divide into 12, we can subtract 3 repeatedly until we get to 0:

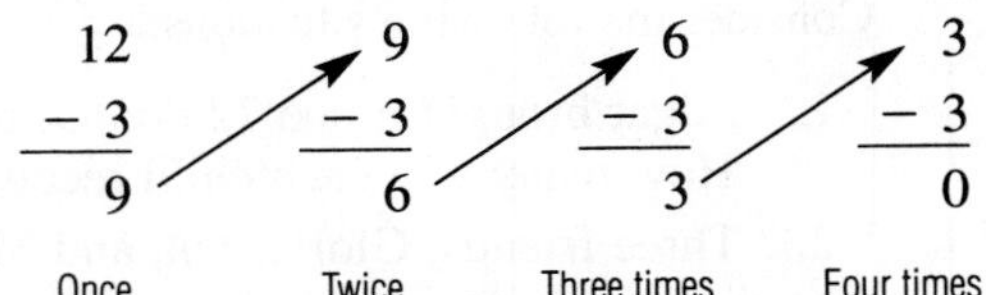

We see that 3 will divide into 12 exactly four times. In other words, $12 \div 3 = 4$ (exactly). We often use the phrase "divides evenly into" when speaking of *exact* division. In the example $12 \div 3$, we can say that "3 divides evenly into 12 four times."

Another term that means *divides evenly* is "divisible." We can say, for example, that 12 is divisible by 3.

Sometimes this repeated subtraction process will not result in 0, and we'll have a little left over, a *remainder*. For example, 3 will divide into 16 five times with 1 left over:

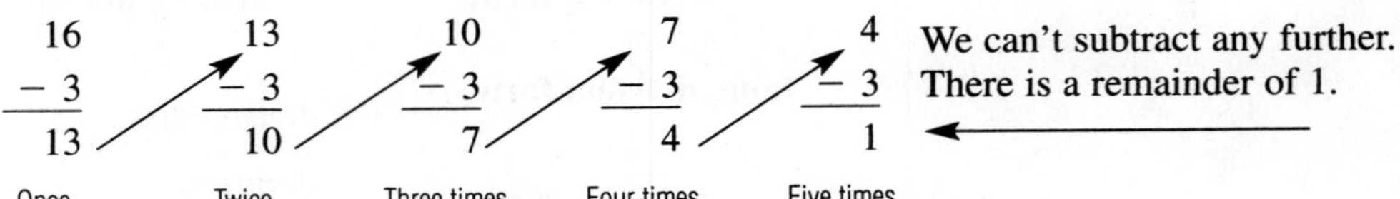

We can say that 3 does *not* divide into 16 exactly.

The remainder must be smaller than the divisor. For example, in repeatedly subtracting 3 from 16, we can't stop when we get to 13, 10, 7, or 4 because it is still possible to subtract 3 at least one more time.

For exact division, we can use a circular argument of inverses to see how multiplication and division work together:

Standard form	**Fraction form**	**Long division form**
$12 \div 3 = 4$	$\frac{12}{3} = 4$	$3\overline{)12}$ with quotient 4
$3 \times 4 = 12$	$3 \times 4 = 12$	$4 \times 3 = 12$

This circular argument says:

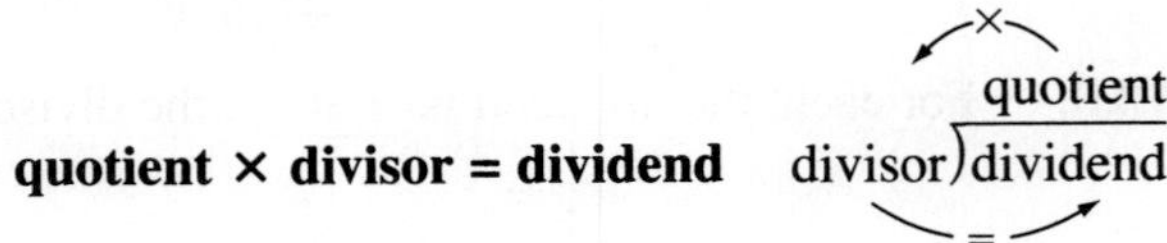

Because of the circular nature of division and multiplication, we can use multiplication to verify the accuracy of our division result, the quotient.

Short Division

When we are able to divide in one step, as demonstrated in Examples 2 and 3, we call it **short division**. When the division is not obvious (it cannot be done in just one step), we call it **long division**.

In demonstrating short division, we can use the standard form (as shown in Example 2) or the long division form (as shown in Example 3).

EXAMPLE 2 Use short division to evaluate. Verify each answer by multiplying the divisor and the quotient.

a) $35 \div 7 =$ ________ b) $5 \div 5 =$ ________ c) $0 \div 4 =$ ________

PROCEDURE: Think about what number will multiply by the divisor to get the quotient. In other words, use the circular argument for division, divisor × quotient = dividend, to find the quotient.

ANSWER:

a) $35 \div 7 = \underline{\ 5\ }$ because $7 \times \underline{\ 5\ } = 35$

b) $5 \div 5 = \underline{\ 1\ }$ because $5 \times \underline{\ 1\ } = 5$ Rule: a natural number divided by itself is 1.

c) $0 \div 4 = \underline{\ 0\ }$ because $4 \times \underline{\ 0\ } = 0$ Rule: 0 divided by a natural number is 0.

Parts b) and c) of Example 2 demonstrate two basic principles of division:

1) A natural number divided by itself is 1.
2) 0 divided by a natural number is 0.

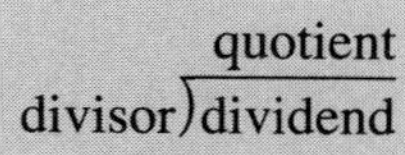

YOU TRY IT 2 *Use short division to evaluate. Verify each answer by multiplying the divisor by the quotient, as in Example 2.*

a) $50 \div 5 =$ ________ b) $18 \div 3 =$ ________ c) $4 \div 4 =$ ________

d) $40 \div 5 =$ ________ e) $0 \div 2 =$ ________ f) $7 \div 1 =$ ________

In standard form, to verify that $28 \div 4 = 7$, we might write $\underline{\text{because } 4 \times 7 = 28.}$

To verify the same division using the long division form, we can show the product of 4 and 7 *below* the dividend:

$$4\overline{)28}\ \text{(quotient 7)} \xrightarrow{\text{becomes}} 4\overline{)28}\ \text{(quotient 7)}$$
$$28 \leftarrow 7 \times 4 = 28$$

Notice that this product is identical to the dividend. This verifies that the quotient is accurate.

And, because they are the same, the result is 0 when we subtract:

$$\begin{array}{r} 7 \\ 4\overline{)28} \\ -28 \\ \hline 0 \end{array}$$

EXAMPLE 3 Use short division to evaluate. Verify each answer by multiplying the divisor and the quotient, and write that product below the dividend and subtract.

a) $2\overline{)18}$ b) $10\overline{)60}$ c) $1\overline{)3}$

PROCEDURE: To find the quotient, think about what number will multiply the divisor to get the dividend. In other words, use the circular argument for division, divisor × quotient = dividend, to find the quotient.

Answer: a) $\begin{array}{r} 9 \\ 2\overline{)18} \\ -\,18 \\ \hline 0 \end{array}$ ← This 0 indicates that 2 divides evenly into 18.

b) $\begin{array}{r} 6 \\ 10\overline{)60} \\ -\,60 \\ \hline 0 \end{array}$

c) $\begin{array}{r} 3 \\ 1\overline{)3} \\ -\,3 \\ \hline 0 \end{array}$ Rule: any number divided by 1 is itself.

YOU TRY IT 3

Use short division to evaluate. Verify each answer by multiplying the divisor by the quotient, as in Example 3.

a) $7\overline{)49}$ b) $6\overline{)54}$ c) $8\overline{)8}$ d) $1\overline{)6}$

Can the Divisor Ever Be 0?

We can *never* divide by 0 (zero). We have seen that 0 can be the dividend, but it can never be the divisor. The circular argument shows us why:

$3 \div 0 = ??$ ⟶ $0 \times ?? = 3$

There is no number that fits here because $0 \times$ any number $=$ **0**, never 3.

In general, we say that $a \div 0$, or $\frac{a}{0}$, is undefined.

As an example, you might think of division by 0 in terms of distributing equal lottery winnings among a "group" of people:

Lottery winnings	÷	# of people	=	Each person gets	
\$0	÷	3	=	\$0	$0 \div 3 = 0$
\$35	÷	0	=	??	$35 \div 0 = ??$ (impossible)

You can't distribute \$35 among 0 people. It isn't possible.

The Remainder

Earlier in this section we saw that 3 does not divide evenly into 16, that when we subtracted 3 repeatedly, we ended with a remainder of 1.

We also saw that 3 does divides evenly into 12 four times; when we subtracted 3 repeatedly, we were able to get an end result of 0.

If the divisor divides evenly into the dividend, then the remainder is 0 (there is no remainder).

Here is a simple example to illustrate how the remainder is found in the division process. Consider $17 \div 5$:

5 does not divide into 17 evenly, so we will have a remainder. Using the long division form, $5\overline{)17}$, we can start the quotient by choosing a number that, when multiplied to 5, will give a product close to 17.

The number we choose to start the quotient can't be too large—it can't give us a product more than the dividend (because then we can't subtract to find the remainder); nor can it be too small—the remainder we get must be less than the divisor. Let's try 4:

$$\begin{array}{r} 4 \\ 5\overline{)17} \\ -20 \\ \hline ?? \end{array}$$

It turns out that 4 is too large, because $4 \times 5 = 20$ and can't be subtracted from 17.

If we try to start the division process with 2, we'll get a remainder that is larger than the divisor, and that is not allowed.

$$\begin{array}{r} 2 \\ 5\overline{)17} \\ -10 \\ \hline 7 \end{array}$$

This remainder, 7, is greater than 5. This means that the quotient, 2, was too small.

Instead, if we try 3, it gives us a product that is a little less than 17, and a remainder that is smaller than the divisor:

$$\begin{array}{r} 3 \\ 5\overline{)17} \\ -15 \\ \hline 2 \end{array}$$

This remainder is just right.

$$\begin{array}{r} 3 \text{ r } 2 \\ 5\overline{)17} \\ -15 \\ \hline 2 \end{array}$$

The remainder is shown to the right of the quotient.

Notice that the remainder is shown next to the quotient—a whole number—and is abbreviated by the letter **r**. When a remainder exists, we will see the long division answer as

$$\begin{array}{r} \text{quotient r remainder} \\ \text{divisor}\overline{)\text{dividend}} \end{array}$$

EXAMPLE 4 Divide. If—after multiplying the quotient and the divisor—there is a remainder, show it next to the quotient.

a) $6\overline{)27}$ b) $7\overline{)42}$

PROCEDURE: If the divisor doesn't divide evenly into the dividend, then think about what number it will divide into evenly.

ANSWER: a)

$$\begin{array}{r} 4 \text{ r } 3 \\ 6\overline{)\ 27} \\ -\ 24 \\ \hline 3 \end{array}$$

$6 \times \mathbf{4} = 24$ is less than 27 and $6 \times \mathbf{5} = 30$ is too much.

The quotient is 4 and the remainder is 3.
(This remainder is less than the divisor, 6, so we have divided properly.)

b)

$$\begin{array}{r} 6 \\ 7\overline{)\ 42} \\ -\ 42 \\ \hline 0 \end{array}$$

$7 \times \mathbf{6} = 42$, so 42 is divisible by 7, and the remainder is 0.

YOU TRY IT 4 *Divide. Be sure to show any remainder (other than 0) next to the quotient. (Do these in pencil. Have an eraser handy in case your first try gives a quotient that is either too large or too small.) Use Example 4 as a guide.*

a) $7\overline{)60}$ b) $8\overline{)15}$ c) $4\overline{)28}$ d) $11\overline{)70}$

The Long Division Algorithm

As you might imagine, not every division problem can be done so quickly. For example, it is true that 4 divides evenly into 948 (as you'll soon see), but how many times?

$$\text{divisor}\overline{)\text{dividend}}^{\;\text{quotient}}$$

To discover the answer, we'll need to learn a process called the **Long Division Algorithm**, or just the **Division Algorithm**. (An *algorithm* is a set of repeated rules that leads to a desired result.) This algorithm works even if there is a remainder (other than 0).

The Long Division Algorithm

1. If possible, divide the divisor into the first (left-most) digit in the dividend, whether or not it divides it evenly; if the first digit of the dividend is too small, divide the divisor into the first two or more (left-most) digits. Place the quotient over the last digit used.
2. Multiply the quotient and the divisor; place this product directly under the digits used in this division and subtract.
3. "Bring down" the first unused digit in the dividend, and repeat this process (starting at step 1) until you can divide no further. Write the remainder next to the quotient.

   The division process stops when the quotient "covers" the last digit in the dividend. The **remainder** is the amount left over after the last digit in the dividend is covered by the quotient

The example that follows shows the steps one at a time. The explanation requires a lot of space, but your actual problems won't be as long.

EXAMPLE 5 Use the Long Division Algorithm to divide 948 by 4.

ANSWER: Steps

(1) Recognize that 4 will divide into 9 *two times.*

and Place the 2 above the 9 and multiply: $2 \times 4 = 8$.

(2) Subtract this product from 9.

$$\begin{array}{r} 2 \\ 4\overline{)948} \\ -\,8 \\ \hline 1 \end{array}$$

Step

(3) Bring down the first unused digit, 4. Start the division process over with a "new" dividend, 14.

$$\begin{array}{r} 2 \\ 4\overline{)948} \\ -\,8\!\downarrow \\ \hline 14 \end{array}$$

Repeat steps

(1) Recognize that 4 will divide into 14 *three times.*

and Place the 3 above 4 (the last digit used) and multiply: $3 \times 4 = 12$.

(2) Subtract this product from 14.

$$\begin{array}{r} 23 \\ 4\overline{)948} \\ -\,8 \\ \hline 14 \\ -\,12 \\ \hline 2 \end{array}$$

Step

③ Bring down the first unused digit, 8. Start the division process over with a "new" dividend, 28.

```
    23
 4)948
  - 8
    14
  - 12
    28
```

Repeat steps

① 4 divides evenly into 28 *seven times.*

and Place the 7 above the 8 (the last digit used) and multiply: $7 \times 4 = 28$.

② Subtract this product from 28 and get a remainder of 0.

Your work will show all of these steps combined into one division problem. It will look like the very last one only. ⟶

```
   237
 4)948
  - 8
    14
  - 12
    28
  - 28
     0
```

Notice that the last digit of the dividend is "covered" by the 7 in the quotient, so we know that we're finished dividing.

This next example shows all of the steps combined into one division problem. There is some explanation for each step, but please realize that the numbers shown don't appear all at the same time.

EXAMPLE 6 Use the Long Division Algorithm to divide: $863 \div 5$. (You may want to cover up part of the problem so you can see the progress step by step.)

ANSWER:

1. 5 divides into 8 one time; place the 1 above the 8 and multiply, $1 \times 5 = 5$. ⟶

   Subtract this product from 8 and bring down the 6. ⟶
2. 5 divides into 36 seven times; place the 7 above the 6 and multipy, $7 \times 5 = 35$. Subtract and bring down the 3. ⟶
3. 5 divides into 13 two times; place the 2 above the 3 and multipy, $2 \times 5 = 10$. Subtract. There is a remainder of 3. ⟶

```
   172 r 3
 5)863
  - 5
    36
  - 35
    13
  - 10
     3
```

Continue dividing until the quotient covers the last digit in the divident. Now the remainder can be included.

We know that we're finished dividing because the last digit in the dividend is covered by the quotient.

The next example shows what to do when a 0 appears in the quotient.

EXAMPLE 7 Use the Long Division Algorithm to divide: $2{,}461 \div 8$.

ANSWER:

1. 8 won't divide into 2, but it does divide evenly into 24 three times; place the 3 above the 4 and multiply, ⟶ $3 \times 8 = 24$. Subtracting gives 0, and bring down the 6. ⟶

```
     3
 8)2461
  - 24
     06
```

2. At this point, the new dividend is 6 (same as 06) but it is less than 8, and 8 can't divide into 6. So, we say that 8 divides into 6 zero times and place the 0 above the 6.
3. We can multiply the 0 and the 6, but we'll get just 0 and the remainder will still be 6. We then bring down the 1. →
4. 8 divides into 61 seven times; place the 7 above the 1 and multiply, 7 × 8 = 56. Subtract. The remainder is 5. →

```
    307 r 5
 8)2461
  - 24
     06
    - 0   ← Showing the multiplication by 0 is not necessary.
     61     Instead, once we get a 0 in the quotient, we can just
    - 56    bring down the next digit in the dividend.
       5
```

Again, in each division problem, we know that we're finished dividing when the last digit in the dividend is covered by the quotient.

Divide each using long division. Use Examples 5, 6, and 7 as guides.

a) 372 ÷ 4 b) 1,628 ÷ 7 c) 7,835 ÷ 6 d) 40,016 ÷ 8

When the Divisor Is a Two-Digit Number

So far in the long division process, all of the divisors have been single digit numbers. When the divisor contains more than one digit, then we need to do some estimation and, at times, some trial and error.

For example, when dividing 1,167 ÷ 38, we'll first set it up as 38)1167 and prepare to use long division. We know that 38 won't divide into 1, and 38 won't divide into 11. Here, we'll need to use the first *three* digits in the dividend before we can even start to divide. In other words, we'll try to divide 38 into 116.

This can prove to be a challenge by itself. But, if we round each number (the divisor 38 and the three digits 116) to the nearest ten, then we can make an educated guess as to what the first digit of the quotient will be.

We can estimate that 38 rounds up to 40 and 116 rounds up to 120, so we might think of this as 40)120. This is, when ignoring the 0's, like dividing 4)12: 12 ÷ 4 = 3.

This suggests that our choice for the first digit of the quotient should be 3.

Caution Keep an eraser handy because often you'll need to make a second educated guess. Also, the rounded numbers, 40 and 120, are used only for the purpose of making an educated guess. We do not use them in any other part of the division process (though we might need to round 38 again later on in the problem).

EXAMPLE 8 Use the Long Division Algorithm to divide 1,167 by 38.

ANSWER:

1. 38 won't divide into 1 or 11, but it does divide into 116. After rounding to the nearest ten, we'll make an educated guess that it divides in three times; place the 3 above the 6 and multiply, 3 × 38 = 114 (shown at left). Subtracting gives 2, bring down the 7.

```
  +2
  38
 × 3
 114
```

```
     30 r 27
 38)1167
  - 114
      27
```

2. At this point, the new dividend is 27, but it is less than 38. So, 38 divides into 27 zero times and place the 0 above the 7.

Caution The 0 above the 7 is necessary because without it, the quotient wouldn't cover the last digit in the dividend.

Sometimes the estimation will get us close but not quite right. If we had chosen to start this quotient...

with 4, we'd get:

$$\begin{array}{r} {}^{+3} \\ 38 \\ \times\ 4 \\ \hline 152 \end{array} \longrightarrow \begin{array}{r} 4 \\ 38\overline{)1167} \\ -\ 152 \\ \hline \end{array}$$

Clearly, 152 is too much, so we should start with a quotient value smaller than 4.

and with 2, we'd get:

$$\begin{array}{r} {}^{+1} \\ 38 \\ \times\ 4 \\ \hline 76 \end{array} \longrightarrow \begin{array}{r} 2 \\ 38\overline{)1167} \\ -\ 76 \\ \hline 40 \end{array}$$

Here the remainder, 40, is larger than the divisor, 38. This means that 38 will divide into 116 at least one more time, so we should start with a quotient value larger than 2.

YOU TRY IT 6 *Divide each using long division. Use Example 8 as a guide.*

a) 936 ÷ 18 b) 8,912 ÷ 32 c) 12,728 ÷ 43

Applications

Applications that involve division often request that a number of items be divided equally among individuals of a group. A key word meaning division is *each*. It will often be found in the last sentence.

EXAMPLE 9 Kayla is making arrangements for 93 basketball fans to attend an out-of-town high school basketball game. She needs to know how many vans to rent so that everyone has a ride. If each van seats 6, how many vans are needed so that everyone has a seat?

PROCEDURE: Here we want to divide the 93 people up into groups of 6 so that each group can fit into a van. Notice that the last sentence includes the word *each*. We will divide to find the answer.

ANSWER:

$$\begin{array}{r} 15\ \text{r}\ 3 \\ 6\overline{)93} \\ -\ 6 \\ \hline 33 \\ -\ 30 \\ \hline 3 \end{array}$$

Notice that 6 did not divide evenly into 93. What should be done with the remainder of 3?

The answer suggests that the 15 vans will be full with 6 people each and there will be one more van needed to carry the remaining 3 people, so 16 vans are needed in all.

SENTENCE: 16 vans are needed so that everyone has a seat.

YOU TRY IT 7

Edgar brought home 72 donut holes for the 9 children at his daughter's slumber party. How any will each child receive if the donut holes are divided equally among all nine?

Show work here:

Sentence: ______________________________

YOU TRY IT 8

Three friends, Gloria, Jan, and Mie-Yun, won a small lottery prize of $1,450. If they split it equally among all three, how much will each get?

Sentence: ______________________________

YOU TRY IT 9

Shawntee just purchased a used car. She has agreed to pay a total of $6,200 over a 36-month period. What will her monthly payments be?

Sentence: ______________________________

YOU TRY IT 10

195 people are planning to attend an awards banquet. Ruben is in charge of the table rental. If each table seats 8, how many tables are needed so that everyone has a seat?

Sentence: ______________________________

You Try It Answers: Section 1.5

YTI 1
a) dividend: 28 divisor: 7 quotient: 4
b) dividend: 40 divisor: 8 quotient: 5
c) dividend: 12 divisor: 2 quotient: 6

YTI 2
a) 10 b) 6 c) 1 d) 8
e) 0 f) 7

YTI 3
a) 7 b) 9 c) 1 d) 6

YTI 4
a) 8 r 4 b) 1 r 7 c) 7 d) 6 r 4

YTI 5
a) 93 b) 232 r 4 c) 1,305 r 5 d) 5,002

YTI 6
a) 52 b) 278 r 16 c) 296

YTI 7
Each child will receive 8 donut holes.

YTI 8
They will each get $483, but there will be $1 left over (remainder). Since they're friends of mine, they'll give the $1 to me.

YTI 9
Shawntee will need to pay $172 each month, with $8 left over. The dealer will ask her to pay that extra $8 in the first month.

YTI 10
Ruben will need to order 25 tables. (24 of the tables can be full, and 1 table will be needed for the extra 3 people.)

Focus Exercises: Section 1.5

Divide. Check by multiplying the divisor and the quotient.

1. 20 ÷ 4 **2.** 28 ÷ 7 **3.** 0 ÷ 6 **4.** 0 ÷ 5

5. 36 ÷ 9 **6.** 24 ÷ 8 **7.** 54 ÷ 9 **8.** 56 ÷ 7

9. 27 ÷ 3 **10.** 32 ÷ 4 **11.** 35 ÷ 5 **12.** 18 ÷ 6

13. 80 ÷ 8 **14.** 90 ÷ 9 **15.** 40 ÷ 10 **16.** 50 ÷ 10

Divide.

17. 90 ÷ 6 **18.** 85 ÷ 5 **19.** 87 ÷ 3

20. 76 ÷ 4 **21.** 74 ÷ 2 **22.** 96 ÷ 8

23. 91 ÷ 7 **24.** 68 ÷ 4 **25.** 115 ÷ 9

26. 137 ÷ 6 **27.** 166 ÷ 5 **28.** 183 ÷ 4

29. 951 ÷ 8 **30.** 966 ÷ 7 **31.** 1,218 ÷ 4

32. 2,516 ÷ 5 **33.** 18,029 ÷ 3 **34.** 16,509 ÷ 8

35. 27,036 ÷ 9 **36.** 35,042 ÷ 7 **37.** 78,300 ÷ 6

38. 90,080 ÷ 4 **39.** 345 ÷ 15 **40.** 594 ÷ 18

41. 876 ÷ 12 **42.** 2,756 ÷ 13 **43.** 24,054 ÷ 24

44. 40,016 ÷ 32 **45.** 1,386 ÷ 33 **46.** 1,431 ÷ 27

47. 6,300 ÷ 75 **48.** 8,645 ÷ 91 **49.** 258,387 ÷ 129

50. 375,250 ÷ 125 **51.** 209,100 ÷ 204 **52.** 625,770 ÷ 306

Work each application and answer it with a complete sentence.

53. 96 people attended a concert in the park. Each person paid the same amount. If the total of the receipts was $2,208, how much did each person pay to attend the concert?

54. Jorge is in charge of scheduling trash pickup in Norco, California. He has 18 trash trucks to cover 5,310 homes. If he divides the homes equally among his drivers, to how many homes will each driver be assigned?

55. Kinko's printed 1,350 booklets for a large company. It's Carrie's job to box them all. If she can fit 24 booklets into each box, how many boxes will she need for all of the booklets?

56. In planning for the next semester, Mr. Tom anticipates 900 students will want to take Elementary Algebra. If each section can contain up to 42 students, how many sections of Elementary Algebra should he schedule?

57. A running club is planning to raise money to help preserve an historic part of Yosemite National Forest. The 27 runners in the club will take turns—relay style—running the entire length of California, from Oregon to Mexico, 783 miles in all. If the distance is divided equally among all of the runners, how many miles will each run?

SECTION 1.6 Equations

Objectives

In this section, you will learn to:

- Define the term *equation.*
- Apply the Subtraction Property of Equality.
- Apply the Division Property of Equality.
- Solve simple equations.

To successfully complete this section, you need to understand:

- The identities (1.2)
- The Commutative Properties (1.2)
- Adding whole numbers (1.3)
- Subtracting whole numbers (1.3)
- Multiplying whole numbers (1.4)
- Dividing whole numbers (1.5)

Introduction

To this point we have looked at some application situations that involve only one operation, either addition, subtraction, multiplication, or division. Here is a situation that involves two operations, addition and subtraction.

> Wendy's monthly budget includes \$529 for rent, \$175 for food, \$192 for utilities and transportation, and \$125 for entertainment. If she takes home (after taxes and other deductions) \$1,238 per month, how much does she have left at the end of the month for savings?

Such situations—those that involve more than one operation—are more common than you might think. This section, and the next, will introduce you to a little algebra and some fairly consistent techniques for solving applications. First, though, you need to become familiar with the notion of *equations*.

Equations

An **equation** is a mathematical sentence in which one expression = another expression.

We use an equation when we are asked to find a number that is not yet known. In this way, we say that we are seeking an **unknown value**.

The unknown value that we seek is a number that must be represented in the equation. Since we don't yet know what the number is, we use a letter to represent it. For our purposes, we will use the letter ***n***. The letter ***n*** is called a **variable**, and it represents a number, the unknown value.

A known value, such as 8, is called a **constant**.

The word *variable* can be thought of as *vary - able*. How would you explain to a classmate the difference between the words *variable* and *constant*?

____

____

Here are some examples of equations:

$$n + 3 = 8$$
$$18 = 6 \cdot n$$
$$6 + 5 = n$$
$$28 + 38 + 65 + n = 178.$$

Notice that each equation contains an equal sign (=). This is used to indicate that the two "sides" of the equation—the left side and the right side—are **equivalent**, that is, they have equal value. Notice further that the variable, *n*, can be on either side of the equal sign.

The purpose of writing an equation is to find the value of the variable, the unknown value. Finding the value of the variable means finding a *solution* to the equation. A **solution** to an equation is a number that makes the equation true.

EXAMPLE 1 For each equation, is 6 the solution?

a) $n + 5 = 11$ b) $12 = 8 + n$ c) $n \cdot 5 = 35$ d) $24 = 4 \cdot n$

PROCEDURE: For each equation, replace *n* with 6. Evaluate one side and see if it equals the other side. If they are equal, then 6 makes the equation true, and 6 is the solution. If they are not equal, then 6 does *not* make the equation true, and 6 is *not* the solution.

ANSWER:

	Equation	Does replacing n with 6 make the equation true?
a)	$n + 5 = 11$	
	$6 + 5 = 11$	
	$11 = 11$	Yes. 6 is the solution.
b)	$12 = 8 + n$	
	$12 = 8 + 6$	
	$12 = 14$	No. 6 is not the solution.
c)	$n \cdot 5 = 35$	
	$6 \cdot 5 = 35$	
	$30 = 35$	No. 6 is not the solution.
d)	$24 = 4 \cdot n$	
	$24 = 4 \cdot 6$	
	$24 = 24$	Yes. 6 is the solution.

YOU TRY IT 1 *For each equation, is 5 the solution? Use Example 1 as a guide.*

a) $18 = n + 11$ b) $15 + n = 20$ c) $50 = n \cdot 10$ d) $8 \cdot n = 45$

To solve an equation means to find the solution, to find the number that makes the equation true.

To do so we must get the variable, n, by itself on one side of the equation and all constants on the other side. This is called **isolating the variable**. The best way to isolate the variable is to remove the constants that are on the same side of the equal sign as n.

For example, in the equation $n + 3 = 8$, we wish to isolate the variable, n, by removing 3 from the left side. This will leave n alone (isolated) on that side.

In the process of isolating the variable, we'll write a new equation based on the original equation. It is important to know that the solution to the new equation must be the same as the solution to the original equation.

Before learning how to isolate the variable, let's explore the idea of a **balanced equation**. All equations must be balanced.

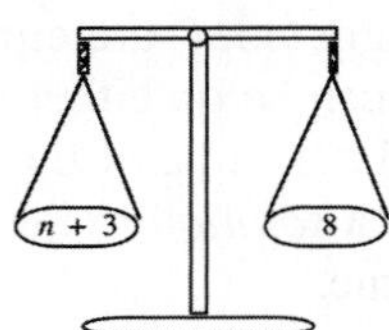

This scale is here to help you visualize a balanced equation.

The equation, $n + 3 = 8$, has a solution of 5. In other words, the equation is true when n is replaced with 5, but it isn't true for any other number.

What do you think would happen if we subtracted some "weight" from just one side of the scale?

Caution Subtracting weight from just one side of a balanced scale means that side becomes lighter and goes up. We should not write a new equation based on what we see (at left) because the sides are not in balance.

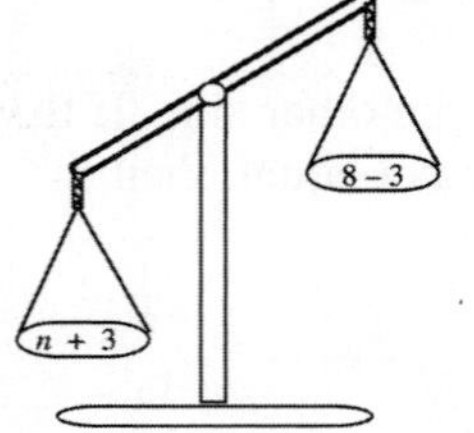

So how do we keep an equation in balance?

Whatever value is subtracted from one side must also be subtracted from the other side at the same time; this will keep the equation in balance.

So, we may remove 3, by subtraction from *each* side, to isolate the variable. Notice that, in subtracting 3 from *each* side, we get a new equation:

Original equation:	$n + 3 = 8$
New equation (subtract 3 from each side):	$n + 3 - 3 = 8 - 3$
This simplifies to:	$n + 0 = 5$
And this simplifies to just:	$n = 5$
	The solution is **5**.

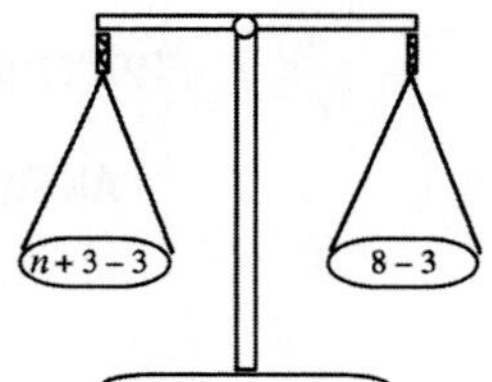

Though the solution, itself, is 5, it's often appropriate to leave it as $n = 5$.

When an equation involves addition, such as $n + 3 = 8$, we can *isolate the variable* using the Subtraction Property of Equality.

The Subtraction Property of Equality

If $n + a = b$, we can isolate the variable by subtracting the same value, a, from each side—whether the variable is written first or second—and still have a balanced equation.

	Example A:	**Example B:**
$n + a = b$	$n + 8 = 20$	$18 = 5 + n$
$n + a - \mathbf{a} = b - \mathbf{a}$	$n + 8 - \mathbf{8} = 20 - \mathbf{8}$	$18 - \mathbf{5} = 5 - \mathbf{5} + n$
↑	$n + 0 = 12$	$13 = 0 + n$
$a - a$ is 0, the identity for addition. Adding 0 helps isolate the variable.	$n = 12$	$13 = n$
		or n* = 13
	Check: $12 + 8 = 20$ True!	Check: $18 = 5 + 13$ True!

After solving, we can check the answer to show that it is the solution; replace the variable in the original equation with the answer and see if it makes the equation true.

*Notice that, in Example B, the variable is first isolated on the right side. It is customary to write the final result with n on the left side and the number on the right.

EXAMPLE 2 Solve the equation $n + 6 = 9$ by using the Subtraction Property of Equality.

ANSWER:

$n + 6 = 9$	To isolate the variable we need to subtract 6 from each side.
$n + 6 - 6 = 9 - 6$	Apply subtraction to each side.
$n + 0 = 3$	Because 0 is the identity for addition, $n + 0$ is just n.
$n = 3$	We now know the value of the variable; it is no longer unknown.

CHECK: We can show that 3 is the solution by replacing n with 3 in the original equation:

$n + 6 = 9$	becomes
$3 + 6 = 9$	which is true. So, 3 is the solution.

Whether the constant is written before or after the variable, we may place the subtraction right after the constant.

EXAMPLE 3 Solve the equation $23 = 15 + n$ by using the Subtraction Property of Equality. Check the answer to show that it is the solution.

PROCEDURE: Isolate the variable by subtracting 15 from each side.

ANSWER:

$23 = 15 + n$ — To isolate the variable we need to subtract 15 from each side.

$23 - 15 = 15 - 15 + n$ — Apply subtraction to each side.

$8 = 0 + n$ — Because 0 is the identity for addition, $0 + n$ is just n.

$8 = n$

Write n on the left: $n = 8$

> **Check:**
> Replace n with 8 in the original equation:
> $23 = 15 + 8$ which is true.
> So, the solution is 8.

YOU TRY IT 2 *Solve each equation by using the Subtraction Property of Equality. Show all steps. Use Examples 2 and 3 as guides. Check each answer to show that it is the solution.*

a) $n + 8 = 12$

b) $20 = 7 + n$

c) $45 + n = 73$

d) $51 = n + 39$

In some equations, there is more than one constant on the same side as the variable. Before subtracting a constant from each side, we must first add those constants.

EXAMPLE 4 Solve the equation $15 + 6 + n = 30$.

PROCEDURE: First, simplify the left side by adding $15 + 6$.

ANSWER:

$15 + 6 + n = 30$ — $15 + 6 = 21$. Rewrite the equation.

$21 + n = 30$ — Now we can subtract 21 from each side.

$21 - 21 + n = 30 - 21$ — Apply subtraction to each side.

$0 + n = 9$ — $0 + n$ is just n.

CHECK: Replace n with 9: $15 + 6 + 9 = 30$

The solution is 9.

> **Check:**
> $$\begin{array}{r} 15 \\ 6 \\ +\ 9 \\ \hline 30 \end{array}$$
> True!

YOU TRY IT 3 *Solve the following by isolating the variable. Use Example 4 as a guide.*

a) $29 + 61 + n = 96$

b) $113 = n + 46 + 28$

In some equations, the variable is already isolated, but one side needs to be evaluated.

EXAMPLE 5 Solve the equation $17 + 26 + 8 = n$.

PROCEDURE: Evaluate the left side. Here, the only check necessary is our addition work.

ANSWER: $17 + 26 + 58 = n$ — Since n is already isolated (on the right side)

$101 = n$ — we simply need to evaluate the left side:

Write n on the left: $n = 101$

$$\begin{array}{r} 17 \\ 26 \\ +\ 58 \\ \hline 101 \end{array}$$

YOU TRY IT 4 *Solve the equation. Use Example 5 as a guide.*

a) $49 + 57 + 38 = n$ b) $n = 559 + 467$

Solving an Equation Involving Multiplication

When a variable, n, is multiplied by a number, we call that number a **coefficient**, pronounced "co - ee - fish´ - unt."

EXAMPLE 6 In each equation, identify the coefficient.

a) $n \cdot 6 = 18$ b) $8 \cdot n = 40$ c) $12 = 4 \cdot n$

ANSWER: a) Coefficient: **6** b) Coefficient: **8** c) Coefficient: **4**

YOU TRY IT 5 *In each equation, identify the coefficient, the number multiplied by the variable. Use Example 6 as a guide.*

a) $n \cdot 5 = 30$ Coefficient: ______ b) $7 \cdot n = 28$ Coefficient: ______

c) $24 = 3 \cdot n$ Coefficient: ______ d) $18 = n \cdot 9$ Coefficient: ______

If an equation involves multiplication instead of addition, then we can isolate the variable by dividing each side by the same number, the coefficient. This rule is the Division Property of Equality.

The Division Property of Equality

If $n \cdot a = b$, then we can isolate the variable by dividing each side by the same value, a (the coefficient)—whether the variable is written first or second—and still have a balanced equation.

	Example A:	Example B:
$n \cdot a = b$	$n \cdot 8 = 40$	$36 = 4 \cdot n$
$n \cdot a \div \mathbf{a} = b \div \mathbf{a}$	$n \cdot 8 \div \mathbf{8} = 40 \div \mathbf{8}$	$36 \div \mathbf{4} = 4 \div \mathbf{4} \cdot n$
↑	$n \cdot 1 = \mathbf{5}$	$9 = 1 \cdot n$
$a \div a$ is 1, the identity for multiplication.	$n = 5$	$9 = n$
Multiplying by 1 helps isolate the variable.	Write n on the left:	$n = 9$

This time, instead of trying to subtract to get 0 (the identity for addition), we want to multiply the variable by 1 (the identity for multiplication).

EXAMPLE 7 Solve the equation $n \cdot 6 = 18$ using the Division Property of Equality.

PROCEDURE: Isolate the variable by dividing each side by the coefficient, 6.

ANSWER:

$n \cdot 6 = 18$	To isolate the variable we need to divide each side by the coefficient 6.
$n \cdot 6 \div \mathbf{6} = 18 \div \mathbf{6}$	Apply division to each side.
$n \cdot 1 = 3$	Because 1 is the identity for multiplication, $n \cdot 1$ becomes just n.
$n = 3$	We now know the value of the variable; it is no longer unknown.

CHECK: Replace n with 3 in the original equation: $3 \cdot 6 = 18$, which is true. So, 3 is the solution.

Whether the coefficient is written before or after the variable, we may place the division right after the coefficient.

EXAMPLE 8 Solve the equation $4 \times n = 156$ using the Division Property of Equality.

ANSWER:

$4 \cdot n = 156$	Divide each side by the coefficient.
$4 \div \mathbf{4} \cdot n = 156 \div \mathbf{4}$	Divide each side by 4.
$1 \cdot n = 39$	
$n = 39$	

$$\begin{array}{r} 39 \\ 4\overline{)156} \\ -\ 12 \\ \hline 36 \\ -\ 36 \\ \hline 0 \end{array}$$

CHECK: Does $4 \cdot 39 = 156$?

$$\begin{array}{r} 39 \\ \times\ 4 \\ \hline 156 \end{array}$$

So, the solution is 39.

YOU TRY IT 6 *Solve each equation by using the Division Property of Equality. Use Examples 7 and 8 as guides. Show each step.*

a) $n \cdot 5 = 30$ b) $21 = 3 \cdot n$ c) $12 \cdot n = 3{,}768$ d) $675 = 25 \cdot n$

In some equations, the variable is already isolated on one side, but the other side must be evaluated, as shown in Example 9.

EXAMPLE 9 Solve the equation $36 \cdot 5 = n$.

PROCEDURE: Evaluate the left side. Here, the only check necessary is our multiplication work.

ANSWER:

	$36 \cdot 5 = n$	Because n is already isolated (on the right side)	36
	$180 = n$	we simply evaluate the left side; apply multiplication directly.	$\times\ 5$
Write n on the left:	$n = 180$	So, the solution is 180.	180

YOU TRY IT 7 *Solve the equation. Use Example 9 as a guide.*

a) $n = 25 \cdot 32$ b) $40 \cdot 15 = n$

You Try It Answers: Section 1.6

YTI 1	a) 18 = 16 No.	b) 20 = 20 Yes.	YTI 5	a) 5	b) 7
	c) 50 = 50 Yes.	d) 40 = 45 No.		c) 3	d) 9
YTI 2	a) $n = 4$	b) $n = 13$	YTI 6	a) $n = 6$	b) $n = 7$
	c) $n = 28$	d) $n = 12$		c) $n = 314$	d) $n = 27$
YTI 3	a) $n = 6$	b) $n = 39$	YTI 7	a) $n = 800$	b) $n = 600$
YTI 4	a) $n = 144$	b) $n = 1{,}026$			

Focus Exercises: Section 1.6

For each, replace n with 16 and decide whether 16 is the solution.

1. $29 + n = 55$

2. $114 = n + 98$

3. $5 \cdot n = 80$

4. $210 = n \cdot 15$

Solve each equation. Check each answer to show that it is the solution.

5. $8 + n = 21$

6. $16 + n = 49$

7. $63 = n + 28$

8. $129 = n + 45$

9. $n = 38 + 84 + 76$

10. $925 + 110 + 640 = n$

11. $191 + 186 + n = 500$

12. $1{,}000 = 306 + 471 + n$

13. $2{,}817 + 3{,}199 = n$

14. $4{,}608 + 3{,}392 = n$

15. $5{,}208 + 3{,}691 + n = 10{,}000$

16. $8{,}156 + 7{,}519 + n = 20{,}000$

17. $n \cdot 3 = 57$

18. $52 = n \cdot 4$

19. $98 = 7 \cdot n$

20. $8 \cdot n = 96$

21. $n \cdot 12 = 156$

22. $405 = 15 \cdot n$

23. $37 \cdot 40 = n$

24. $n = 23 \cdot 30$

25. $25 \cdot n = 800$

26. $700 = 35 \cdot n$

27. $n \cdot 53 = 2{,}491$

28. $n \cdot 48 = 3{,}168$

SECTION 1.7 Solving Applications Using Equations

Objectives

In this section, you will learn to:

- Solve applications involving addition and subtraction.
- Solve applications involving multiplication and division.
- Solve applications involving averages.
- Solve applications involving perimeter and area.

To successfully complete this section, you need to understand:

- Rounding Whole Numbers (1.1)
- Adding Whole Numbers (1.3)
- Subtracting Whole Numbers (1.3)
- Multiplying Whole Numbers (1.4)
- Dividing Whole Numbers (1.5)
- Solving Equations (1.6)

Introduction

Now we are ready to apply our understanding of solving equations to applications. Here is a situation we might find in the workplace:

> Tony needs to make sure his truck isn't carrying too much weight for the road conditions ahead. His truck weighs 3,125 pounds and it is carrying a 586-pound load. What is the total weight of the truck and the load?

As you can see, an application is simply an equation written in sentence form. Approach the problem as if it were an assignment given to you by a boss or supervisor. Impressing a supervisor with your math skills makes you more valuable to the company.

One formula that we use very often is:

The sum of all of the parts equals the whole.

As you might imagine, the "whole" is always larger than any individual "part."

Some words that might help you identify the whole are "total," "combined" (as in combined weight) and "altogether." Mostly, though, you should rely less on words and more on *thinking* about the situation to identify the whole and the parts.

If an application has only two parts, say Part 1 and Part 2, and if the unknown value is the whole, then the rule could be written as:

Part 1 + Part 2 = Whole (n)

If, instead, the unknown value is one of the parts, then this formula could be written as

Part 1 + Unknown Part (n) = Whole

Key Steps for Solving Application Problems

1. Think about the application
   a) by putting yourself in the situation,
   b) by drawing a diagram,
   c) by making estimates about the answer, and
   d) by using smaller numbers and making a model of the situation.
2. Decide what is known and what is unknown.
   a) Each number is either a part or the whole. Usually, the last sentence in the problem indicates what is unknown; this is n.
   b) Write a **legend** identifying what n represents.
3. Write an equation, based on a formula.
4. Solve the equation by isolating the variable.
5. Write a complete sentence to answer the question in the application problem. Usually, it's possible to just reword the question and put it in the form of an answer.

The legend, in this regard, is like that found on a map. A legend lists symbols and explains what each symbol represents.

In the problem-solving process, it's a good idea to read the problem through once, just to get an idea of the situation. Then read it a second time and look for the important information, thinking about which might be the whole and which might be the parts.

As you read it the second time, either underline or put a [box] around important information. Also, in the last sentence underline the unknown value and write n under it; you will use this for your legend.

> Tony needs to make sure his truck isn't carrying too much weight for the road conditions ahead. His truck weighs [3,125 pounds] and it is carrying a [586-pound] load. What is the total weight of the truck and the load?
> (n written under "total weight")

Applications Involving Addition and Subtraction

Let's use the key steps for solving applications to answer the questions in Examples 1 and 2.

EXAMPLE 1

Tony needs to make sure his truck isn't carrying too much weight for the road conditions ahead. His truck weighs 3,125 pounds and it is carrying a 586-pound load. What is the total weight of the truck and the load?

PROCEDURE: First, reread the problem and put a [box] around important information. Put yourself in Tony's spot. Picture the truck and picture the load going into the truck. As you might imagine, the truck weighs more with the load than it does when empty.

In this case, the parts are

1. The weight of the truck when there is no load (3,125 pounds), and
2. the weight of the load that he is carrying (586 pounds).

From the last sentence we know the unknown value, the total weight, is the whole.

ANSWER: We start with the legend: Let n = the total weight

Part 1 + Part 2 = Whole

Write the equation: $3{,}125 + 586 = n$

Apply addition: $3{,}711 = n$

$$\begin{array}{r} 3125 \\ +\ 586 \\ \hline 3711 \end{array}$$

Since the legend says that n is the total weight, we can write a sentence based on the question, "What is the total weight of the truck and the load?"

SENTENCE: The total weight is 3,711 pounds.

EXAMPLE 2

Julia is delivering old newspapers to the recycler. The scale indicates the total weight to be 3,928 pounds. After the papers have been emptied, the scale indicates the weight to be 3,195 pounds. What was the weight of the newspaper she delivered for recycling?

PROCEDURE: First, reread the problem and put a [box] around important information. Use the outline shown below. These steps aren't necessary but are a useful aid in thinking about the situation.

a) Write down any known information.
- The total weight (whole) is 3,928 pounds.
- The empty weight is 3,195 pounds.

b) Also write what we're trying to find.
- Find the weight of the newspapers.

c) Write the legend: Let n = the weight of the newspapers. We know the whole, so the unknown value is one of the parts.

ANSWER:

d) Write the formula: Part 1 + Unknown Part = Whole

Write the equation: $3{,}195 + n = 3{,}928$

Subtract 3,195 from each side: $3{,}195 - 3{,}195 + n = 3{,}928 - 3{,}195$

$n = 733$

$$\begin{array}{r} 3928 \\ -\ 3195 \\ \hline 733 \end{array}$$

SENTENCE: The weight of the newspapers is 733 pounds.

Caution Although it's true that the whole will be larger than any of the individual parts, just because one number is larger than another doesn't make it the whole.

The You Try It exercises in this section show how you might organize the written information given in a problem. Use these exercises as guides to help you in solving the Focus Exercises at the end of the section.

YOU TRY IT 1

Mark owns a courier service and uses his small plane to make deliveries. His plane can carry cargo that has a combined weight of 1,280 pounds. One customer has asked him to deliver several large packages that total 891 pounds. How much more cargo weight can his plane carry? (*Hint:* His plane is not full, so there is space available.)

a) Write down any known information.

Whole: ______________________

Parts: ______________________

b) Legend: ______________________

c) Write the equation and solve by isolating the variable.

d) Sentence: ______________________

YOU TRY IT 2

One of Kami's customers places an order for 113 shirts. Kami already has 22 of that style in stock. How many more shirts of that style does Kami need?

a) Write down any known information. Also write what we're trying to find.

Whole: ______________________

Parts: ______________________

b) Legend: ______________________

c) Write the equation and solve by isolating the variable.

d) Sentence: ______________________

Applications Involving More Than Two Parts

There are many applications that require adding more than two numbers together. Also, some applications involve both addition and subtraction.

EXAMPLE 3

Mark owns a courier service and uses his small plane to make deliveries. One customer has asked him to deliver cargo that weighs 289 pounds. Another needs to ship 481 pounds and a third customer wishes him to deliver 340 pounds. What is the total weight of the cargo he will be carrying?

PROCEDURE: First, reread the problem and put a box around important information. This problem has three parts, a cargo weight from each customer. The unknown value is the total weight, the whole.

ANSWER: Legend: Let n = the total weight of the cargo.

$$\text{Part 1} + \text{Part 2} + \text{Part 3} = \text{Whole}$$
$$289 + 481 + 340 = n$$
$$1{,}110 = n$$
$$n = 1{,}110$$

$$\begin{array}{r} 289 \\ 481 \\ +\ 340 \\ \hline 1{,}110 \end{array}$$

SENTENCE: Mark will be carrying 1,110 pounds of cargo.

EXAMPLE 4

[This is the same situation as Example 3 with a different question to answer.] If Mark's plane can carry a maximum cargo weight of 1,280 pounds, how much more cargo weight can his plane carry?

PROCEDURE: First, reread the problem and put a box around important information. This problem has four parts, the original three cargo weights and how much more weight his plane can carry. This time the whole is the total weight that he is allowed to carry, the 1,280 pounds.

ANSWER: Legend: Let n = how much more weight his plane can carry.

EQUATION:

$$\text{Part 1} + \text{Part 2} + \text{Part 3} + \text{Part 4} = \text{Whole}$$
$$289 + 481 + 340 + n = 1{,}280$$
$$1{,}110 + n = 1{,}280$$
$$n + 1{,}110 - 1{,}110 = 1{,}280 - 1{,}110$$
$$n = 170$$

$$\begin{array}{r} 289 \\ 481 \\ +\ 340 \\ \hline 1{,}110 \end{array} \qquad \begin{array}{r} 1{,}280 \\ -\ 1{,}110 \\ \hline 170 \end{array}$$

SENTENCE: Mark's plane can carry 170 more pounds of cargo.

YOU TRY IT 3

At her bookstore this month, Gena sold 167 books the first week, 228 books the second week, and 174 books the third week. How many books must she sell during the fourth week to reach her monthly goal of 700?

a) Write down any known information.

Whole: ______________________________

Parts: ______________________________

b) Legend: ______________________

c) Write the equation and solve by isolating the variable.

d) Sentence: ______________________________________

Applications Involving Multiplication

In this section we will solve applications that involve multiplication. Just as in situations that involve addition, there are some values that are known and some that are unknown. As with addition, we use an equation to solve for the unknown value.

The formula for addition is: the sum of all of the parts equals the whole.

For multiplication, we use the same formula; the difference is that the parts are repeated parts. The formula can be shown as:

Part + <u>Same Part</u> + <u>Same Part</u> + ... + <u>Same Part</u> = Whole.

This formula can also be rewritten as a product:

(Number of Same Parts) × Part = Whole.

For example, Kahlil earns $87.00 per day working as a plumber's assistant. How much does he earn in a 5-day week?

His earnings can be looked at as $\frac{\$87}{\text{Monday}} + \frac{\$87}{\text{Tuesday}} + \frac{\$87}{\text{Wednesday}} + \frac{\$87}{\text{Thursday}} + \frac{\$87}{\text{Friday}}$

This is the same part added repeatedly, and there are 5 of them, so the equation is

$$5 \times \$87 = \text{whole}$$
$$5 \times \$87 = \$435$$

In the application where a number is added repeatedly, the unknown value will be either:

1. the part,
2. the number of parts (number of repeats), or
3. the whole.

Identifying the unknown value is relatively simple because it is usually mentioned in the question. However, determining whether the unknown is the whole or not can be a little more challenging.

Guidelines for Recognizing the Whole, the Part, and the Number of Parts

1. The whole and the part always have the same unit measure. They might both be inches, or cookies, or dollars, or miles, or many other units of measure, but they must always be the same.
2. The whole is always larger than the part.
3. The number of parts will almost always be of a different unit of measure, such as the number of days, the number of boxes, or the number of months.

Yet, with all of the helpful information you might find on these pages, it's still best to approach the problem by *thinking*, by putting yourself in the situation and by looking for key words.

The examples presented in this section will give you some insight into the best approach; however, it is still up to you to think about the situation, beyond simply reading the words.

EXAMPLE 5 Union dues are \$432 a year and are split into 12 equal monthly payments. How much must Gloria pay each month for union dues?

PROCEDURE: First, reread the problem and put a box around important information. Use the guidelines above to think about the problem and to set up the equation.

The unknown value is: n = how much (dollars) Gloria pays each month.

The whole is the total dues (also dollars) she pays for the year: \$432.

The part is how much she pays each month. The part occurs 12 times.

Notice that the whole and the part are both measured in dollars; the other measure is number of months.

ANSWER: Legend: Let n = the amount Gloria pays each month for union dues.

The equation is this: $12 \cdot n = 432$

Solve it: $12 \div 12 \cdot n = 432 \div 12$

$n = 36$

$$\begin{array}{r} 36 \\ 12\overline{)432} \\ -\ 36 \\ \hline 72 \\ -\ 72 \\ \hline 0 \end{array}$$

SENTENCE: Gloria must pay \$36 each month for union dues.

YOU TRY IT 4 *Keith works in a factory that produces 600 nails per hour, and 40 nails fit into each box. How many boxes are needed for those 600 nails?*

a) What is the unknown value? Legend: Let n = ____________________

b) What value (known or unknown) represents the whole? ____________________

c) What value (known or unknown) represents the part? ____________________

d) What value (known or unknown) represents the number of times the part occurs?

____

e) Write the equation and solve it.

f) Sentence: ____________________

EXAMPLE 6 It cost Adrian \$29 per day to rent a car. He rented the car for 7 days. How much total rent did Adrian pay for the car?

PROCEDURE: First, reread the problem and put a box around important information. The unknown value is the total paid (in dollars), the whole.

The part is \$29 per day. (Notice that it's also in dollars, same as the whole.)

The part is repeated 7 times (7 days).

ANSWER: Legend: Let n = the total rent Adrian paid for the car.

$7 \cdot 29 = n$

$203 = n$

$n = 203$

$$\begin{array}{r} 29 \\ \times\ 7 \\ \hline 203 \end{array}$$

SENTENCE: Adrian paid $203 to rent the car.

YOU TRY IT 5

Mary contributes $15 from her paycheck each month to the United Way. How much does she contribute in a year (in 12 months)?

a) What is the unknown value? ______

b) What value (known or unknown) represents the whole? ______

c) What value (known or unknown) represents the part? ______

d) What value (known or unknown) represents the number of times the part occurs?

______

e) Write the equation and solve it.

f) Sentence: ______

Applications Involving Averages

For this next situation, you see the key words "on average." An average suggests that the part was divided *evenly* among the whole. We usually also find the word "each" with the words "on average;" this indicates a part.

EXAMPLE 7

Sally, a saleswoman at an electronic appliance store, worked 20 days in February. She sold a total of 140 televisions during that month. How many televisions did she sell, on average, each day?

PROCEDURE: First, reread the problem and put a box around important information. The key words, appearing in the question, are *on average*. This means the unknown value is the part.

The measure that appears twice in the problem is televisions. The unknown value is the average number of televisions sold (the part).

The whole is 140 televisions.

The part is repeated 20 times (20 days).

ANSWER: Legend: Let n = the average number of televisions sold per day.

$20 \cdot n = 140$

$20 \div 20 \cdot n = 140 \div 20$

$n = 7$

SENTENCE: Sally sold, on average, 7 television sets each day.

Does this mean that Sally actually sold 7 TV sets each day? Probably not.
If she sold 7 sets every day, a chart of her TV sales might look like this:

Day	Feb. 1	Feb. 2	Feb. 3	Feb. 4	Feb. 5	Feb. 8	Feb. 9	etc.
TV sets	7	7	7	7	7	7	7	...

Most likely, though, Sally had some good selling days and some poor selling days. One day she may have sold as many as 15 TV sets and another day she may have sold as few as 2. But, over the course of one full month, she was able to sell an average of 7 sets per day.

YOU TRY IT 6

At her bookstore, Gena sold 165 books in one five-day period. How many books did Gena sell, on average, each day?

a) What is the unknown value? Legend: Let n = ______________________

b) What value (known or unknown) represents the whole? ______________

c) What value (known or unknown) represents the part? ______________

d) What value (known or unknown) represents the number of times the part occurs?

____

e) Write the equation and solve it.

f) Sentence: ______________________________

Applications Involving Geometry

Recall from Section 1.3 that the perimeter of a figure is the sum of the lengths of its sides. If we know the perimeter (P) of a triangle, but only two of the side measures, then we can use an equation to find the length of the third side.

We can let n be the length of the unknown side and solve for it using *the sum of the parts equals the whole*.

EXAMPLE 8

The perimeter of a triangle is 52 inches. The longest side measures 20 inches and the shortest side measures 14 inches. What is the length of the third side?

PROCEDURE: First, reread the problem and put a box around important information. If a triangle is not provided, you can draw one of your own and label the sides. The triangle (at right) can be used for this problem.

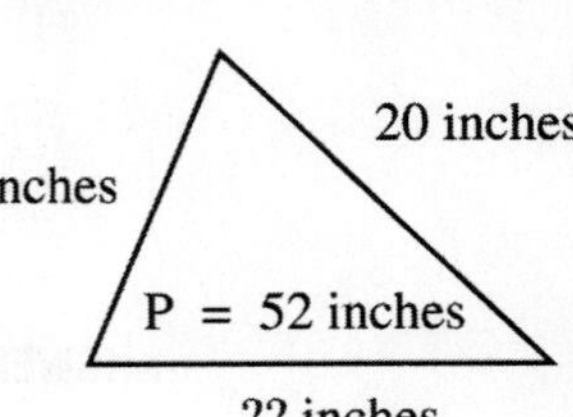

ANSWER: Legend: n = the measure of the third side.

$20 + 14 + n = 52$ Simplify the left side by combining the numbers.

$34 + n = 52$ Subtract 34 from each side.

$34 - 34 + n = 52 - 34$ Simplify.

$n = 18$

SENTENCE: The third side is 18 inches long.

YOU TRY IT 7

A park is in the shape of a triangle. The perimeter of the sidewalk around it is 168 yards. The shortest side is 42 yards and the longest side is 70 yards. What is the length of the third side? Draw a triangle and place the known measures around it.

Legend: Let n = ______________________

Sentence: ______________________

Recall from Section 1.4 that the area of a rectangle is the product of its length and width:

Area of a rectangle = Length × Width

Width

Length

If the area and the measure of one side are known, then we can find the measure of the other side using an equation.

EXAMPLE 9

The area of a rectangle is 78 square inches. The width is 6 inches. What is the length?

PROCEDURE: We can draw a rectangle and label the width as 6 and the length as L. We can even use L, instead of n, in the equation: $A = L \cdot W$.

A = 78 sq in | 6 inches

L

ANSWER: Legend: Let L = the length of the rectangle

$$78 = L \cdot 6 \quad \leftarrow \text{Divide each side by 6.}$$
$$78 \div 6 = L \cdot 6 \div 6$$
$$13 = L$$

$$\begin{array}{r} 13 \\ 6\overline{)78} \\ -\ 6 \\ \hline 18 \\ -\ 18 \\ \hline 0 \end{array}$$

SENTENCE: The length of the rectangle is 13 inches.

YOU TRY IT 8

A rectangular dance floor has an area of 255 square feet. The length is 17 feet. What is the width? Draw a rectangle and place the known measures around it.

Legend: Let n = ______________________

Sentence: ______________________

You Try It Answers: Section 1.7

YTI 1
a) Whole is 1,280 pounds; part is 891 pounds
b) Let n = how much more weight can be carried
c) $891 + n = 1{,}280$
d) Mark's plane can carry 389 pounds more.

YTI 2
a) Whole is 113 shirts; part is 22 shirts
b) Let n = the # of shirts needed
c) $22 + n = 113$
d) Kami needs to order 91 more shirts.

YTI 3
a) Whole is 700 books; parts are 167 books, 228 books, and 174 books
b) Let n = the # of books Gena must sell during the fourth week.
c) $167 + 228 + 174 + n = 700$
d) Gena must sell 131 books during the fourth week.

YTI 4
a) Let n = the # of boxes needed.
b) Whole is 600 nails
c) Part is 40 nails
d) The number of times the part occurs is n.
e) $40 \cdot n = 600$
f) Keith needs 15 boxes for the 600 nails.

YTI 5
a) Let n = the amount (in dollars) she will contribute in one year.
b) Whole is n
c) Part is $15
d) The number of times the part occurs is 12 months.
e) $12 \cdot 15 = n$
f) In one year, Mary will contribute $180 to the United Way.

YTI 6
a) Let n = the average number of books sold each day.
b) Whole is 165 books
c) Part is n
d) The number of times the part occurs is 5 days.
e) $5 \cdot n = 165$
f) Gena sold, on average, 33 books each day.

YTI 7
Let n = the length of the third side.

$42 + 70 + n = 168$
The third side is 56 yards long.

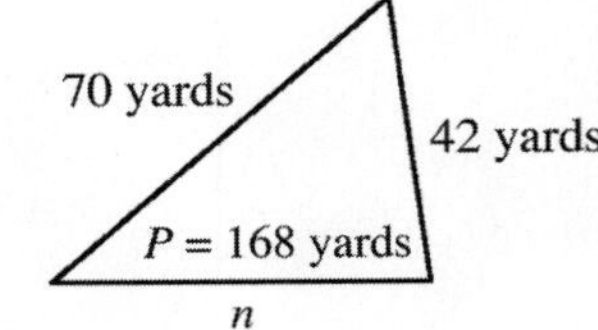

YTI 8
Let n = the width of the rectangle.

$17 \cdot n = 255$

The width is 15 feet.

A = 255 sq ft
n
17 feet

Focus Exercises: Section 1.7

Work each application. Write a legend and an equation; solve the equation, and answer the question in a complete sentence.

1. Nate is saving his money to buy an Xbox. So far he has $73 saved. The model he wants sells for $162, including tax. How much more money does Nate need to pay for the Xbox?

2. Shika needs 132 yards of material to make enough doll dresses to sell at the craft fair. She already has 58 yards of material. How many more yards of material does Shika need?

3. Adam has saved $900 for his vacation. He has figured that he'll spend $380 on the hotel room, $140 on meals, and $115 on transportation. How much will Adam have left over to spend on other things during his vacation?

4. A cab company spends $18,652 per year in insurance for its drivers. Insuring a new driver costs $1,208. How much total insurance will the company pay if it adds one more driver?

5. Sandra works for the city accounting office. She must prepare a report for the city manager listing a variety of costs that must be paid. For example, it cost the city $21,000 to operate and maintain the public pool. So far, the city has collected $19,629 from user fees. How much more must the city collect to equal the costs of operating the pool?

6. Through a regular deduction from her paycheck, Alexis paid a total of $2,867 last year for federal taxes. In filing her income tax return, she really needed to pay $3,052. How much does Alexis still owe on her federal taxes?

7. Kinko's is putting together 5,000 brochures for a company, due tomorrow at noon. Kelley has assigned the job to three different workers, each using a different photocopier. Heather's copier has produced 1,758 copies; Omar's copier has produced 1,365 copies; and Carla's copier has produced 1,259 copies. How many copies are left to produce?

8. The billing department in a large company had $15,000 in their annual supplies budget. So far this year they have purchased a computer system for $3,193, new furniture for $2,607, and various office supplies for $612. It's Rika's job to update the department's budget. How much is left in the supplies budget after these purchases?

9. Ajay belongs to the local carpenter's union. He pays $252 per year in union dues. If they are spread equally over 12 months, how much does Ajay pay each month in union dues?

10. Kami owns an embroidery business, and she just received a rush order. She has to embroider 168 caps in 7 days. How many caps, on average, must Kami embroider each day?

11. Beth is a nutritionist. She has many overweight clients. Most of her clients are referred to her by doctors who work at a nearby hospital for eating disorders.

    a) One of her heaviest clients has been put on a strict diet and exercise program by his doctor. His total weight loss, over a 6 month period, was 138 pounds. How much many pounds did he lose, on average, each month?

    b) Beth has another client, Lona, who is on a plan to lose 15 pounds a month for 12 months. Assuming that Lona stays on the plan, what will her total weight loss be?

12. Mansour owns a courier service and uses his small plane to make deliveries.

a) One customer has asked him to deliver 25 boxes, each weighing 42 pounds. How much cargo will Mansour's plane be carrying?

b) A customer has 24 boxes weighing a total of 864 pounds. What is the average weight of each box?

13. Aimee pays $375 for rent each month. How much does Aimee pay in rent for a full year?

14. Allison works at a printer. The business often receives large printing orders for pamphlets and flyers. One customer wants 3,200 flyers printed and needs them right away. Allison decides to use 5 printing machines to do the job. On average, how many flyers will each machine print?

15. The home plate in a youth sports league is shown at right. The perimeter of the plate is 48 inches. What is the length of the top side?

7 in. 7 in.
10 in. 10 in.

16. The Bermuda Triangle, famous for disappearing ships and planes, forms a triangle between three Atlantic locations: Miami, Bermuda, and San Juan. The perimeter of this triangle is 2,992 miles. The distance from Bermuda to Miami is 1,059 miles. The distance from Bermuda to San Juan is 955 miles. What is the distance from San Juan to Miami?

17. A rectangular plot of land is a full acre: 4,840 square yards. If the width is 40 yards, what is the length of the rectangle? Draw a rectangle and place the known measures around it.

18. A hotel pool is in the shape of a rectangle. The rectangle is 15 yards wide and has an area of 540 square yards. What is the length of the pool?

Chapter 1 Review

Section 1.1 Whole Numbers

CONCEPT	EXAMPLE
Counting numbers, or **natural numbers**	1, 2, 3, 4, 5, ..., 10, 11, 12, ... and so on.
Whole numbers	0, 1, 2, 3, 4, 5, 6, 7, 8, 9, 10, 11, 12, ... and so on.
Every digit in every whole number has a **place value** based on the position it holds in the number. In the pace value chart at the right, the value of the 8 is 8 hundred: 800. The value of the 9 is 9 ten thousands: 90,000. The value of the 3 is 3 one millions: 3,000,000.	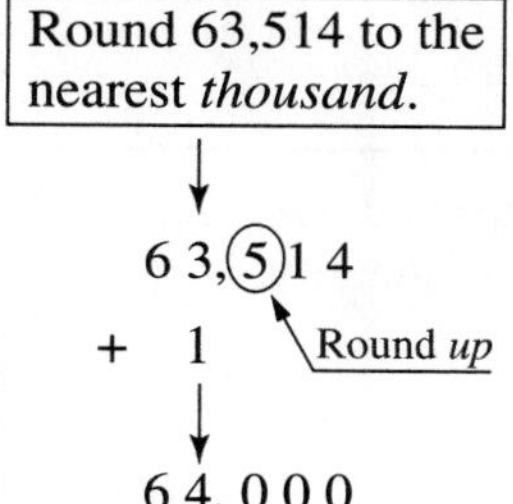
To write a whole number in words: 1. Hyphenate two-digit numbers. 2. Never use the word "and." 3. Separate the periods with commas.	1. 34 is thirty-four. 2. 306 is three hundred six, *not* three hundred and six. 3. 5,073,109 is five million, seventy-three thousand, one hundred nine.
To round a whole number: 1. Identify the place digit. 2. Identify the rounding digit. a. If the rounding digit is 5 or higher, round up. b. If the rounding digit is 4 or lower, round down. 3. Write all digits after the place digit as zeros.	Round 63,514 to the nearest *thousand*. 6 3,(5)1 4 + 1 Round *up* 6 4, 0 0 0

Section 1.2 Definitions and Properties

CONCEPT	EXAMPLE
The four basic **operations** are addition (+), subtraction (−), multiplication (×), and division (÷).	$5 + 2 = 7$ $7 - 2 = 5$ $3 \times 2 = 6$ $6 \div 2 = 3$
A **sum** is both the written addition and the result of adding.	*addend* + *addend* = *sum*
A **difference** is both the written subtraction and the result of subtracting.	*minuend* − *subtrahend* = *difference*
A **product** is both the written multiplication and the result of multiplying.	*factor* × *factor* = *product*
A **quotient** is both the written division and the result of dividing.	*dividend* ÷ *divisor* = *quotient*, $\frac{dividend}{divisor} = quotient$, and $divisor\overline{)dividend}$ with *quotient* above

CONCEPT	EXAMPLE
The written form of an operation is an **expression**.	$5 + 4$
To **evaluate** means "to find the value of."	Evaluate $5 + 4$: $5 + 4 = 9$
Parentheses group different values together so that they can be treated as one **quantity**.	$(5 + 2) \cdot 4 = 7 \cdot 4$
The **Commutative Property** allows us to change the order of a sum or product. The Commutative Property of Addition: $a + b = b + a$ The Commutative Property of Multiplication: $a \times b = b \times a$	$6 + 2 = 2 + 6$ $6 \cdot 2 = 2 \cdot 6$
The **Associative Property** allows us to change the grouping in a sum or product. The Associative Property of Addition: $(a + b) + c = a + (b + c)$ The Associative Property of Multiplication: $(a \cdot b) \cdot c = a \cdot (b \cdot c)$	$(6 + 4) + 3 = 6 + (4 + 3)$ $(5 \cdot 2) \cdot 4 = 5 \cdot (2 \cdot 4)$
An **identity** is a number that, when applied, won't change the value of another number or quantity. The **additive identity** is 0: $a + 0 = a$ and $0 + a = a$ The **multiplicative identity** is 1: $a \cdot 1 = a$ and $1 \cdot a = a$	$12 + 0 = 12$; also $0 + 12 = 12$ $15 \cdot 1 = 15$; also $15 \cdot 1 = 15$

Section 1.3 Adding and Subtracting Whole Numbers

CONCEPT	EXAMPLE
To add whole numbers: 1. Align the numbers one above the other; if they don't have the same number of digits, place zeros in front of them. 2. Add each column, starting with the ones column. 3. If any column adds to more than 9, carry over the sum's tens digit to the next column.	Add: $68 + 274$ $\begin{array}{r} {}^{1\,1} \\ 068 \\ +\ 274 \\ \hline 342 \end{array}$

CONCEPT	EXAMPLE
To subtract whole numbers: 1. Align the numbers, one above the other; if they don't have the same number of digits, place zeros in front of one of them. 2. Subtract each column, starting with the ones column. 3. If subtraction cannot be performed in a certain column, regroup the number on top. 4. Check subtraction by adding the result (the difference) to the bottom number.	$\begin{array}{r} {}^{5}\not{6}\,{}^{11}\not{2}\,\not{4}^{14} \\ -\ 0\,7\,9 \\ \hline 5\,4\,5 \end{array}$ Check: $\begin{array}{r} {}^{+1\,+1} \\ 5\,4\,5 \\ +\ 0\,7\,9 \\ \hline 6\,2\,4 \end{array}$
The **perimeter** of a geometric figure is the total measure around the figure. The perimeter is found by adding the lengths of all of the sides.	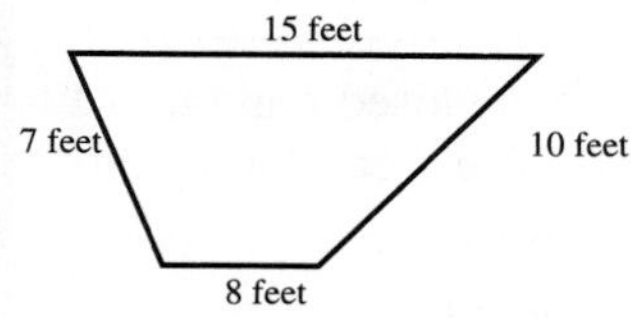 The perimeter is: 7 feet + 8 feet + 10 feet + 15 feet = 40 feet

Section 1.4 Multiplying Whole Numbers

CONCEPT	EXAMPLE
Multiplication is an abbreviation for repeated addition. Numbers in a product are called **factors**.	$5 \cdot 8 = 8 + 8 + 8 + 8 + 8 = 40$; $5 \cdot 8 = 40$ 5 and 8 are factors of 40
A number is in **factored form** when it is written as a product of factors.	Factored forms of 40: $1 \cdot 40$, $2 \cdot 20$, $4 \cdot 10$, and $5 \cdot 8$.
If a and b are two whole numbers, their product, $a \cdot b$, is a multiple of a and a multiple of b.	5, 10, 15, 20, and 25 are multiples of 5 because each has a factored form that includes 5: $\underbrace{5}_{1\cdot 5}\quad \underbrace{10}_{2\cdot 5}\quad \underbrace{15}_{3\cdot 5}\quad \underbrace{20}_{4\cdot 5}\quad \underbrace{25}_{5\cdot 5}$
The Multiplication Property of 0: $a \cdot 0 = 0$ and $0 \cdot a = 0$	$5 \cdot 0 = 0$ and $0 \cdot 5 = 0$
Multiplying by 10: When one factor is 10, the product is the other factor with a 0 placed on the end.	$15 \cdot 10 = 150$
Multiplying by 100: When one factor is 100, the product is the other factor with two 0's placed on the end.	$9 \cdot 100 = 900$

CONCEPT	EXAMPLE
Multiplying by a Multiple of 10: If one or more factors is a multiple of 10, such as 30, 60, 700 and so on, temporarily ignore such (ending) zeros, and include them in the final product.	$30 \cdot 400 = 12{,}000$
The Distributive Property of Multiplication over Addition: We can distribute a multiplier, $\boldsymbol{a}$, to a sum $(\boldsymbol{b} + \boldsymbol{c})$ so that it multiplies both numbers in the sum: $\boldsymbol{a} \cdot (b + c) = \boldsymbol{a} \cdot b + \boldsymbol{a} \cdot c$	$\mathbf{3} \cdot (6 + 4) = \mathbf{3} \cdot 6 + \mathbf{3} \cdot 4$ $= 18 + 12$ $= 30$
Area is the amount of surface in an enclosed region, and is always measured in square units. The area of a rectangle is the product of its length and width: Area = length × width	7 inches 10 inches The area is: 7 inches · 10 inches = 70 square inches

Section 1.5 Dividing Whole Numbers

CONCEPT	EXAMPLE
Division is the inverse operation of multiplication. It can be thought of as repeated subtraction. If the repeated subtraction results in 0, then the divisor divides evenly into the dividend; we also say that the dividend is **divisible** by the divisor.	$15 \div 5$: $15 - 5 = 10$ *Once* $10 - 5 = 5$ *Twice* $5 - 5 = 0$ *Three times*, 0 remainder $15 \div 5 = 3$
If the repeated subtraction doesn't result in 0, then there is a remainder.	$17 \div 5$: $17 - 5 = 12$ *Once* $12 - 5 = 7$ *Twice* $7 - 5 = 2$ *Three times*, remainder of 2 $17 \div 5 = 3$ r 2
Division by 0 is not allowed; $a \div 0$, or $\frac{a}{0}$, is undefined.	$12 \div 0$ is undefined

CONCEPT	EXAMPLE
The Long Division Algorithm: 1. If possible, divide the divisor into the first digit in the dividend, whether or not it divides in evenly; if the first digit is too small, divide into the first two or more digits. Place the quotient over the last digit used. 2. Multiply the quotient and the divisor; place this product directly under the digits used in this division and subtract. 3. "Bring down" the first unused digit in the dividend, and repeat this process (starting at step 1) until the quotient "covers" the last digit in the dividend. Write the remainder next to the quotient. The remainder is the amount left over after the last digit in the dividend is covered by the quotient.	$\begin{array}{r} 14 \text{ r } 2 \\ 5\overline{)72} \\ -5 \\ \hline 22 \\ -20 \\ \hline 2 \end{array}$

Section 1.6 Equations

CONCEPT	EXAMPLE
An **equation** is a mathematical sentence in which one expression = another expression. The letter ***n*** is a **variable**, and it represents a number, an unknown value, that is to be solved for in an equation. A known value, such as 6, is a **constant**. When a variable, *n*, is multiplied by a number, we call that number a **coefficient**.	$24 = 6 \cdot n$
The Subtraction Property of Equality: If $\boldsymbol{n + a = b}$, we can subtract the same value, $\boldsymbol{a}$, from each side: $n + a = b$ $n + a - \boldsymbol{a} + \; = b - \boldsymbol{a}$	$n + 8 = 15$ $n + 8 - 8 = 15 - 8$ $n + 0 = 7$ $n = 7$
The Division Property of Equality: If $\boldsymbol{n \cdot a = b}$, we can divide each side by the same value, $\boldsymbol{a}$: $n \cdot a = b$ $n \cdot a \div \boldsymbol{a} = b \div \boldsymbol{a}$	$24 = 6 \cdot n$ $24 \div 6 = 6 \div 6 \cdot n$ $4 = 1 \cdot n$ $4 = n$ $n = 4$

Section 1.7 Solving Applications Using Equations

CONCEPT

To solve an application problem:

1. Read the problem and think about the situation.
2. Decide what the unknown value is (usually from the last sentence in the problem), represent it by n, and write a legend.
3. Write an equation, based on a formula.
4. Solve the equation and write a complete sentence answer to the question.

EXAMPLE

A textbook salesperson drove 212 miles on Monday, 87 miles on Tuesday, and 146 miles on Wednesday. What is the total number of miles she drove in those 3 days?

Legend: Let n = total number of miles

Formula: Miles + miles + miles = total

$$212 + 87 + 146 = n$$
$$445 = n$$

Sentence: The salesperson drove 445 miles.

CONCEPT

The basic formula for addition:

The sum of all of the parts equals the whole.

Consider:

Manuel works for FedEx in the accounts receivable department. One client owes FedEx $4,328 for the month of April, but the client paid only $2,550. How much money does Manuel still need to collect from the client?

EXAMPLE

Legend: Let n = the amount to be collected from the client

Formula:

$ collected + $ still to be collected = total due

$$2550 + n = 4328$$
$$2550 - 2550 + n = 4328 - 2550$$
$$n = 1778$$

Sentence: Manuel still needs to collect $1,178 from the client.

CONCEPT

The basic formula for multiplication:

(Number of same parts) × part = whole.

Consider:

Karea works for a pool supply company. She placed an order for 6 identical pool sweepers. The total price for the 6 sweepers is $1,134. How much does each pool sweeper cost?

EXAMPLE

Legend: Let n = the cost of each pool sweeper

Formula:

Number of parts · price of each = total price

$$6 \cdot n = 1134$$
$$6 \div 6 \cdot n = 1134 \div 6$$
$$n = 189$$

Sentence: Each pool sweeper costs $189.

Chapter 1 Review Exercises

Vocabulary

For each, fill in the blank with the correct word from the Word List. Each word in the Word List will be used only once.

1. A ________________ describes how many of something there is.
2. A ________________ is a symbol that represents a number.
3. There are ten ________________ in our base-ten numbering system.
4. Addition and division are two ________________ .
5. To ________________ means "to find the value of."
6. The ________________ of a geometric figure is the sum of the lengths of the sides.
7. ________________ is the amount of surface in an enclosed region.
8. A rounded number is called an ________________ .
9. For addition, the ________________ is 0.
10. The numbers in a product are called ________________ .
11. Multiplication is an abbreviation for repeated ________________ .
12. The answer to an exact division is called the ________________ .
13. The amount left over after dividing is the ________________ .
14. A ________________ is a letter that represents a number.
15. In the expression $9 \cdot n$, the number 9 is called the ________________ .
16. In the expression $n + 7$, the number 7 is called the ________________ .
17. The ________________ of an equation makes the equation true.
18. The ________________ describes the unknown value in an application problem.
19. If a and b are two whole numbers, then their product, $a \cdot b$, is a ________________ of a.
20. The basic ________________ for addition is *the sum of all of the parts equals the whole*.

Word List

- addition
- approximation
- area
- coefficient
- constant
- digits
- evaluate
- factors
- formula
- identity
- legend
- multiple
- number
- numeral
- operations
- perimeter
- quotient
- remainder
- solution
- variable

Section 1.1

Write each number in expanded form.

21. 724
22. 6,807

Write each number in words.

23. 408
24. 9,051
25. 206,005
26. 5,470,000

Write the whole number as a numeral.

27. one hundred seven
28. two thousand, five
29. five hundred eight thousand, forty-one
30. one million, six hundred fifty-two

Round each number to the nearest ten.

31. 642 **32.** 295 **33.** 1,450 **34.** 2,996

Round each number to the nearest hundred.

35. 642 **36.** 30,295 **37.** 126,450 **38.** 4,949

Round each number to the nearest thousand.

39. 30,529 **40.** 54,067 **41.** 249,801 **42.** 812

Rewrite the underlined sentence or phrase using the requested approximation.

43. In 2003, the total number of full-time airline employees was 507,091. Round this number to the nearest ten thousand. *Source: www.bts.gov*

44. In 2004, the U.S. population, was 294,490,706. Round this number to the nearest hundred thousand. *Source: www.census.gov*

Section 1.2

Which property is being demonstrated?

45. $39 \cdot 1 = 39$

46. $4 + (3 + 7) = (4 + 3) + 7$

47. $74 + 15 = 15 + 74$

48. $0 + 26 = 26$

Section 1.3

Align the numbers, then add.

49. $7 + 9$ **50.** $4 + 8$ **51.** $16 + 44$ **52.** $319 + 211$

53. $457 + 93$ **54.** $1{,}934 + 98$ **55.** $1{,}048 + 673$ **56.** $9{,}184 + 828$

57. $36 + 51 + 14 + 9$ **58.** $435 + 943 + 25 + 1{,}462$

Work each application and answer with a complete sentence.

59. On Tuesday morning, Brian rode an exercise bike for one-half hour and burned 387 calories. After a break he rode another half hour and burned 295 calories. How many total calories did Brian burn on the exercise bike that morning?

60. Kaira added up her test scores for the first three math tests. Her scores were 89, 75, and 92. What is the total number of points Kaira received on her first three tests?

Find the perimeter of each figure.

61.

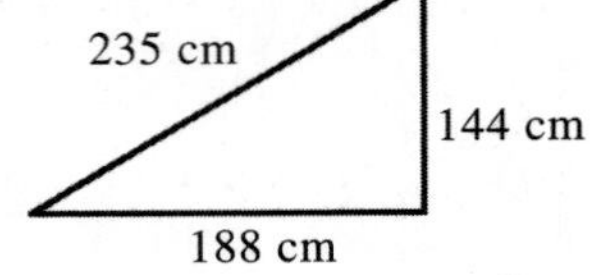

62.

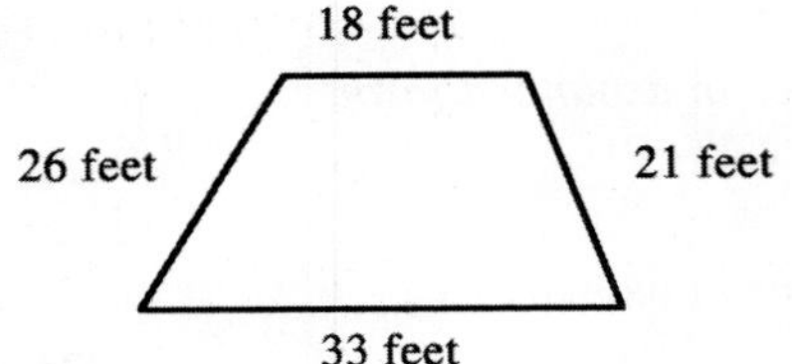

Align the numbers, then subtract. Check each answer (on paper or mentally) by addition.

63. $56 - 32$ **64.** $549 - 408$ **65.** $71 - 26$ **66.** $132 - 58$

67. $1{,}193 - 546$ **68.** $16{,}425 - 841$ **69.** $1{,}013 - 165$ **70.** $6{,}050 - 5{,}872$

71. $200{,}000 - 19{,}793$ **72.** $4{,}000{,}000 - 3{,}096{,}205$

Work each application and answer with a complete sentence.

73. In 2003, the average attendance for the Washington Redskins home games was 80,500. The average attendance for the Chicago Bears home games was 61,603. On average, how many more fans were in attendance at Washington home games than Chicago home games? *Source: www.kenn.com*

74. The total area of Nevada is 110,561 square miles, and the total area of Michigan is 96,716 square miles. How much larger (in square miles) is Nevada than Michigan? *Source: www.infoplease.com*

Section 1.4

Multiply.

75. $8 \cdot 7$ **76.** $9 \cdot 6$ **77.** $7 \cdot 4$ **78.** $2 \cdot 8$

79. $7 \cdot 5$ **80.** $6 \cdot 2$ **81.** $5 \cdot 8$ **82.** $9 \cdot 9$

Multiply.

83. $6 \cdot 20$ **84.** $7 \cdot 30$ **85.** $90 \cdot 20$ **86.** $80 \cdot 30$

87. $9 \cdot 800$ **88.** $200 \cdot 8$ **89.** $90 \cdot 700$ **90.** $20 \cdot 500$

Align the numbers, then multiply.

91. $25 \cdot 9$ **92.** $47 \cdot 8$ **93.** $91 \cdot 7$ **94.** $152 \cdot 6$

95. $28 \cdot 43$ **96.** $56 \cdot 82$ **97.** $174 \cdot 12$ **98.** $192 \cdot 306$

Which property is being demonstrated?

99. $3 \cdot (8 \cdot 5) = (3 \cdot 8) \cdot 5$ **100.** $0 \cdot 9 = 0$

101. $4 \cdot (2 + 7) = 4 \cdot 2 + 4 \cdot 7$ **102.** $15 \cdot 4 = 4 \cdot 15$

Work each application and answer the question with a complete sentence.

103. Marley drives 38 miles round trip to work and home each workday. In March, she worked 23 days. How many total miles did Marley drive to and from work in March?

104. Colin's basement floor is in the shape of a rectangle. The width is 19 feet and the length is 34 feet. What is the area of Colin's basement floor?

Section 1.5

Divide. Check the division by multiplying, mentally, the divisor and the quotient.

105. $36 \div 4$ **106.** $49 \div 7$ **107.** $0 \div 8$ **108.** $40 \div 5$

109. $72 \div 9$ **110.** $56 \div 8$ **111.** $24 \div 3$ **112.** $54 \div 6$

Use long division to divide. Be sure to write any remainder next to the quotient.

113. $60 \div 9$ **114.** $43 \div 7$ **115.** $29 \div 3$ **116.** $38 \div 6$

117. $98 \div 7$ **118.** $115 \div 5$ **119.** $168 \div 4$ **120.** $172 \div 2$

121. $2{,}268 \div 7$ **122.** $1{,}369 \div 8$ **123.** $3{,}587 \div 6$ **124.** $2{,}832 \div 9$

125. $364 \div 14$ **126.** $1{,}024 \div 16$ **127.** $9{,}100 \div 65$ **128.** $246{,}321 \div 81$

129. $916 \div 15$ **130.** $1{,}921 \div 26$ **131.** $4{,}250 \div 59$ **132.** $7{,}929 \div 73$

Work each application and answer it with a complete sentence.

133. The Jacksonville Rotary club purchased a trailer to sell food from at county fairs. Each of the 24 members had to contribute the same portion to pay for the $6,360 trailer. How much was each member's contribution?

134. 405 sixth grade students are visiting a college. The director of the event wants to divide them up into different classrooms for the variety of programs planned. If each classroom can hold 32 students, how many classrooms are needed?

Section 1.6

For each, replace n with 12 and decide whether or not 12 is the solution.

135. $41 = n + 19$ **136.** $18 + n = 30$ **137.** $6 \cdot n = 72$ **138.** $350 = n \cdot 25$

Solve the following. Check each answer to show that it is the solution.

139. $n + 7 = 15$

140. $72 = n + 39$

141. $151 + 94 + 208 = n$

142. $2{,}094 + 3{,}516 + n = 10{,}000$

143. $n \cdot 7 = 98$

144. $490 = 5 \cdot n$

145. $34 \cdot 40 = n$

146. $35 \cdot n = 1{,}260$

Section 1.7

Work each application and answer it in a complete sentence.

147. Carlotta sells bedroom furniture. Her company gives her bonus pay if she has sales of $20,000 or more during the Labor Day weekend (Saturday through Monday). On Saturday she sold $10,560 of merchandise. On Sunday, she had sales of $6,280. What do Carlotta's sales need to be on Monday to reach the $20,000 goal?

148. Rhani purchased a used car for $4,500 from her parents. She has agreed to pay them back over the next three years with 36 equal monthly payments. How much will Rhani pay her parents each month?

149. Antonio is a waiter at a pricey restaurant. Last Saturday he waited on 14 tables and earned $266 in tips. On average, how much in tips did Antonio earn from each table?

150. The carpeted children's reading room at the library is in the shape of a rectangle. The carpet is 9 yards wide and has an area of 243 square yards. What is the length of the carpet?

Chapter 1 Test

Round each number to the indicated place.

1. 749 to the nearest hundred ______________________

2. 9,524 to the nearest thousand ______________________

3. 582,907 to the nearest ten thousand ______________________

4. Write the number 300,045 in words.

____

5. Write as a numeral: twenty-three million, six hundred four thousand, fifteen

____

Evaluate each.

6. 135×64 **7.** $3{,}547 + 958$ **8.** $1{,}017 - 459$ **9.** $980 \div 35$

Identify the property shown.

10. $16 \cdot 1 = 16$ ________________

11. $4 \cdot (3 + 5) = 4 \cdot 3 + 4 \cdot 5$ ________________

12. $(14 + 6) + 18 = 14 + (6 + 18)$ ________________

13. $35 + 15 = 15 + 35$ ________________

Solve for n.

14. $24 = n + 9$ **15.** $7 \cdot n = 343$ **16.** $25 + 17 + n = 61$

Solve each application.

17. Alfre needs 500 voters' signatures to put a no-growth measure on the city's November ballot. In June, Alfre collected 126 signatures, and in July, another 248. How many more signatures does Alfre need to collect to reach 500?

18. A school's kindergarten playground has a rectangular sandbox with an area of 450 square yards. If the width of the sandbox is 18 yards, what is its length?

19. Jerry treated the 12 members of his youth basketball team to a Harlem Globetrotters game. Children's tickets were $14 each. How much did Jerry spend on his team's tickets?

20. The 17 members of the Lincoln High School Madrigal Choir raised a total of $3,655 for their annual trip to Chicago. What was the average amount of money raised by each member?

CHAPTER 2
Factors and the Order of Operations

Introduction

The topics in math are a lot like bricks in a wall. Some bricks lay next to each other, and some bricks are on top of two or more lower bricks.

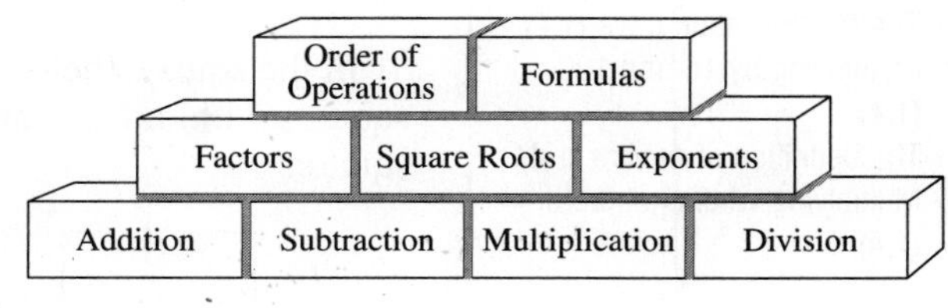

In Chapter 1, we put in place the foundation of the wall. In this chapter, we're building the next one or two layers in preparation for fractions, decimals, and percents.

As in Chapter 1, the ideas in this chapter are developed slowly and completely. Some of the topics in this chapter rely on what you learned in Chapter 1. As a preparation, you should be able to do the following exercises. You may be able to do these immediately, or you may wish to review the section each comes from.

Preparation Exercises

Section 1.4, Multiplying Whole Numbers:

Multiply.

1. $9 \cdot 6$	**2.** $4 \cdot 8$	**3.** $5 \cdot 7$	**4.** $3 \cdot 9$
5. $8 \cdot 10$	**6.** $24 \cdot 100$	**7.** $8 \cdot 70$	**8.** $20 \cdot 9$
9. $50 \cdot 80$	**10.** $300 \cdot 40$	**11.** 6×56	**12.** 17×49

Section 1.5, Dividing Whole Numbers:

Divide.

13. $36 \div 4$	**14.** $45 \div 5$	**15.** $39 \div 3$	**16.** $50 \div 2$
17. $4\overline{)96}$	**18.** $7\overline{)252}$	**19.** $8\overline{)352}$	**20.** $9\overline{)954}$

SECTION 2.1 Exponents and Square Roots

Objectives

In this section, you will learn to:

- Identify perfect squares.
- Use exponents to abbreviate repeated multiplication.
- Evaluate powers of 10.
- Find square roots of perfect squares.

To successfully complete this section, you need to understand:

- The multiplication table (1.4)
- Multiplying by 10 and 100 (1.4)
- The definition of *factors* (1.4)
- Multiplying whole numbers (1.4)

Introduction

Exponents and square roots are found in many formulas in math, chemistry, physics, economics, and statistics. The ability to perform calculations with exponents and square roots, for instance, helps astronomers provide a safe flight for the space shuttle and for the many satellites orbiting the earth.

Perfect Squares

This is a diagram of a *unit* square centimeter. It is called this because it consists of one unit. It looks square, and it is.

We call this "1 square centimeter" and abbreviate it as "1 sq cm."

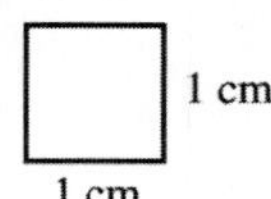

In the squares below, notice that there is a number associated with each—the number of unit squares within. Each number is called a **perfect square** because the unit squares form a perfect square.

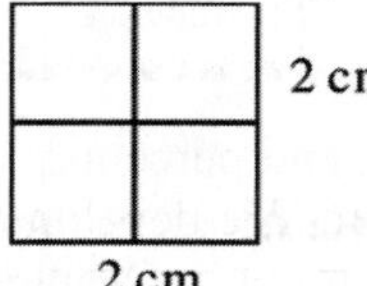

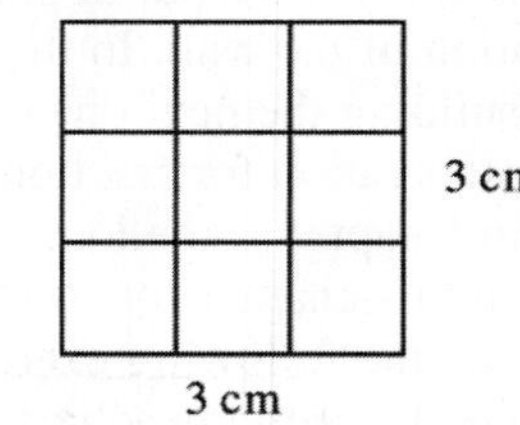

2 cm × 2 cm = 4 sq cm
4 is a perfect square.

3 cm × 3 cm = 9 sq cm
9 is a perfect square.

Whenever we create a square with a number, *n*, as the length of one side, that same number, *n*, must appear as the length of the other side. The product of these two numbers is called a perfect square number, or just a perfect square.

In other words, because $1 \cdot 1 = 1$, 1 is a perfect square
$2 \cdot 2 = 4$, 4 is a perfect square
$3 \cdot 3 = 9$, 9 is a perfect square
$4 \cdot 4 = 16$, 16 is a perfect square
$5 \cdot 5 = 25$, 25 is a perfect square

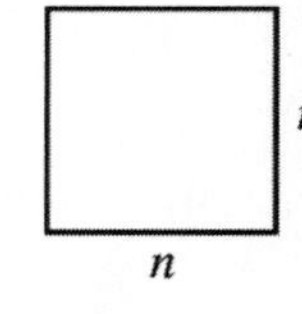

The list of perfect squares goes on and on. Any time you multiply a whole number by itself you get a result that is (automatically) a perfect square.

Notice, also, that there are a lot of numbers that are *not* perfect squares: 2, 3, 5, 6, 7, … and the list goes on and on. 2 is not a perfect square because no whole number multiplied by itself equals 2. The same is true for the other numbers in the list.

EXAMPLE 1

Is it possible to draw a square that has:

a) 81 unit squares within it?

b) 24 unit squares within it?

ANSWER:

a) Yes, a square with 9 units on each side will have 81 square units within it because $9 \cdot 9 = 81$.

b) No, there is no whole number that, when multiplied by itself, will give 24.

YOU TRY IT 1

Use Example 1 as a guide to answer the following questions. Is it possible to draw a square that has:

a) 36 unit squares within it? ______

b) 12 unit squares within it? ______

c) 49 unit squares within it? ______

EXAMPLE 2

Find the perfect square number associated with each product.

a) $7 \cdot 7$ b) $11 \cdot 11$ c) $13 \cdot 13$ d) $20 \cdot 20$

ANSWER:

a) $7 \cdot 7 = 49$

b) $11 \cdot 11 = 121$

c) $13 \cdot 13 = 169$

d) $20 \cdot 20 = 400$

YOU TRY IT 2

Find the perfect square number associated with each product. Use Example 2 as a guide.

a) $6 \cdot 6$ b) $10 \cdot 10$ c) $18 \cdot 18$

This multiplication table contains twelve perfect squares. Being familiar with the perfect squares in the table will prove helpful, in a variety of ways, in this chapter and later in this course.

The Multiplication Table

×	**1**	**2**	**3**	**4**	**5**	**6**	**7**	**8**	**9**	**10**	**11**	**12**
1	**1**	2	3	4	5	6	7	8	9	10	11	12
2		**4**	6	8	10	12	14	16	18	20	22	24
3			**9**	12	15	18	21	24	27	30	33	36
4				**16**	20	24	28	32	36	40	44	48
5					**25**	30	35	40	45	50	55	60
6						**36**	42	48	54	60	66	72
7							**49**	56	63	70	77	84
8								**64**	72	80	88	96
9									**81**	90	99	108
10										**100**	110	120
11											**121**	132
12												**144**

Exponents

Notice that all perfect squares have repeated factors:

49 is a perfect square number and $49 = 7 \cdot 7$.
7 is a repeated factor of 49.

There are also numbers with more than two repeated factors; for example, $8 = 2 \cdot 2 \cdot 2$, $81 = 3 \cdot 3 \cdot 3 \cdot 3$, and $100{,}000 = 10 \cdot 10 \cdot 10 \cdot 10 \cdot 10$.

Exponents give us a way to abbreviate repeated multiplication (repeated factors) using the powers of a whole number. 2^3 represents the repeated multiplication $2 \cdot 2 \cdot 2$ and is read "2 to the *third power*."

In the notation 2^3, 2 is the **base**, and ^{3} is the **exponent** or **power**. The whole number 2 is raised to the *third* power, or 2 to the power of 3.

It's most common to say "6 squared." The phrase "6 squared" comes from a square in which each side has a length of 6.

Let's look at some examples of this notation:

6^2 is "6 to the 2nd power," or "6 to the power of 2," or "6 ***squared***."

10^3 is "10 to the 3rd power," or "10 to the power of 3," or "10 ***cubed***."

5^4 is "5 to the 4th power," or "5 to the power of 4."

Think about it

Notice that we have special names only for bases being raised to the second power and bases being raised to the third power. Knowing how 6 *squared* (6^2) got its name, can you think of how 10 *cubed* (10^3) got its name?

It's common to write area with the power of 2 on the unit of measure. For example, 8 square feet is abbreviated as 8 ft^2.

When we write the meaning of an exponent, such as 2^4 means $2 \cdot 2 \cdot 2 \cdot 2$, we are *expanding* the expression.

EXAMPLE 3

Expand each and find its value.

a) 2^3 b) 3^4 c) 10^5

ANSWER:

a) $2^3 = 2 \cdot 2 \cdot 2 = 8$ — You can probably do this in your head.

b) $3^4 = 3 \cdot 3 \cdot 3 \cdot 3$
$= (3 \cdot 3) \cdot (3 \cdot 3)$
$= 9 \cdot 9 = 81$ — If you use the Associative Property to group two factors at a time and then multiply them, you'll get $9 \cdot 9$ which is 81.

c) $10^5 = 100{,}000$ — 10 to the 5th power is 1 followed by 5 zeros; pretty neat!

YOU TRY IT 3

Expand each and find its value. Use Example 3 as a guide.

a) 6^2 b) 2^4 c) 9^3

We can also express an exponent as "the number of repeated factors." For example, 5^3 means "three factors of 5."

EXAMPLE 4

For each, write out the expression as the number of repeated factors and then expand the expression.

a) 6^2 b) 7^4

ANSWER:

a) 6^2 is two factors of 6: $6 \cdot 6$.

b) 7^4 is four factors of 7: $7 \cdot 7 \cdot 7 \cdot 7$.

YOU TRY IT 4

Write out, as outlined in Example 4, the expression as the number of repeated factors and then expand the expression.

a) 2^3 is ______________________________

b) 3^5 is ______________________________

How should we interpret 5^1? 5^1 means "one factor of 5." In this case, there are no repeated factors of 5, there is only 5 itself. In other words, $5^1 = 5$.

This principle is true for any base: **If b represents any base, then $b^1 = b$.**

EXAMPLE 5

Rewrite each without an exponent.

a) 6^1 b) 13^1 c) 10^1

ANSWER: a) $6^1 = 6$ b) $13^1 = 13$ c) $10^1 = 10$

YOU TRY IT 5

Rewrite each without an exponent. Use Example 5 as a guide.

a) $2^1 =$ b) $9^1 =$ c) $17^1 =$ d) $1^1 =$

The Powers of 10

In Section 1.4, we discussed multiples of 10 (such as 20, 30, 40, etc.) and multiples of 100 (such as 200, 300, 400, etc.). We also learned that when multiplying by either 10 or 100, we need only place the appropriate number of zeros on the "end" of the other factor.

For example, $7 \cdot 10 = 70$ and $4 \cdot 100 = 400$.

Numbers such as 100, 1,000 and 10,000 are called **powers of 10** because

$$10^2 = 10 \cdot 10 = 100$$
$$10^3 = 10 \cdot 10 \cdot 10 = 1{,}000$$
$$10^4 = 10 \cdot 10 \cdot 10 \cdot 10 = 10{,}000$$

Think about it

What do you notice about the exponent of each 10 and the final result?

____

____

Did you write this?

The exponent of 10 indicates the number of zeros that follow the 1.

So, 10^6 will be a 1 followed by six zeros: 1,000,000; in other words, 1,000,000 is the 6th power of 10.

EXAMPLE 6

For each power of 10, write out its interpretation and the resulting value.

a) 10^2 b) 10^3 c) 10^4

PROCEDURE: Treat the exponent as the number of zeros following a 1.

ANSWER: a) 10^2 is 1 followed by two zeros = 100.
b) 10^3 is 1 followed by three zeros = 1,000.
c) 10^4 is 1 followed by four zeros = 10,000.

YOU TRY IT 6 *For each power of 10, write out the special interpretation and the resulting value. Use Example 6 as a guide.*

a) 10^5 is ______________________

b) 10^7 is ______________________

c) 10^1 is ______________________

Likewise, 1,000,000 is abbreviated as 10^6, the number of zeros indicating the power of 10.

EXAMPLE 7 For each, indicate the number of zeros and abbreviate it as a power of 10.

a) 1,000 b) 10,000,000 c) 10

PROCEDURE: Count the number of zeros. That number is the power of 10.

ANSWER: a) 1,000 is 1 followed by three zeros: 1,000 = 10^3.
b) 10,000,000 is 1 followed by seven zeros: 10,000,000 = 10^7.
c) 10 is 1 followed by one zero: 10 = 10^1.

YOU TRY IT 7 *For each, indicate the number of zeros and abbreviate it as a power of 10. Use Example 7 as a guide.*

a) 100 is ______________________

b) 10,000 is ______________________

c) 1,000,000 is ______________________

Three hundred can be written as 300 and as $3 \cdot 100$. This can be further abbreviated as $3 \cdot 10^2$. In other words, $300 = 3 \cdot 10^2$. When written this way, 3 is called the *coefficient* (just as in Section 1.6).

When a number ends in one or more zeros, it can be written as a product of a whole number (the coefficient) and a power of 10.

For example, 45,000,000 has six zeros following the 45, so the *sixth* power of 10, or 10^6, is a factor: $45{,}000{,}000 = 45 \cdot 10^6$.

EXAMPLE 8 Identify the power of 10, and rewrite the number as a product using the power of 10 as a factor.

a) 6,000 b) 290,000 c) 56,000,000 d) 80

PROCEDURE: Count the number of zeros following the non-zero digit(s); that is the power of 10. The non-zero digit(s) is the coefficient.

ANSWER: a) $6{,}000 = 6 \cdot 10^3$ 6 followed by three zeros.
b) $290{,}000 = 29 \cdot 10^4$ 29 followed by four zeros.

c) $56{,}000{,}000 = 56 \cdot 10^6$ 56 followed by six zeros.

d) $80 = 8 \cdot 10^1$ 8 followed by one zero.

YOU TRY IT 8

As outlined in Example 8, rewrite the number as a product using the power of 10 as a factor.

a) 240 = ________________ b) 5,600 = ________________

c) 380,000,000 = ________________ d) 7,260,000 = ________________

The Square Root

Consider this perfect square of 16. We know from our discussion of perfect squares, the number 4 makes the perfect square 16. For this reason, we call 4 a **square root** of 16.

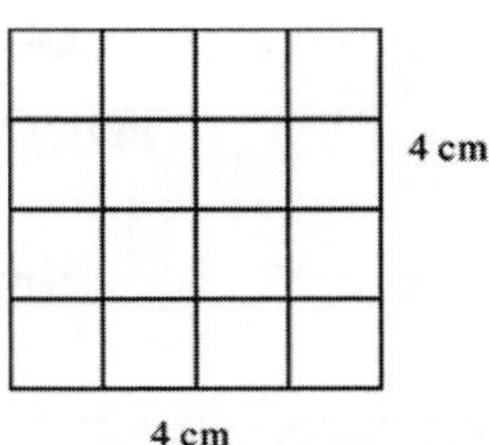

The Square Root Property

If $p = r^2$ (**p** is a **p**erfect square using **r** as one side), then **r** is a square **r**oot of **p**.

EXAMPLE 9 What is a square root of the following numbers?

a) 49 b) 36 c) 1 d) 25

PROCEDURE: What number, multiplied by itself, gives each of those above?

ANSWER: a) A square root of 49 is **7**. b) A square root of 36 is **6**.

c) A square root of 1 is **1**. d) A square root of 25 is **5**.

YOU TRY IT 9

What is a square root of the following numbers? Use Example 9 as a guide.

a) A square root of 4 is ____________. b) A square root of 9 is ____________.

c) A square root of 64 is ____________. d) A square root of 100 is ____________.

YOU TRY IT 10

Identify which of the following are perfect squares; of those that are, identify a square root. Use the multiplication table as a guide.

a) 48: ________________________________

b) 121: ________________________________

c) 144: ________________________________

The Square Root Symbol

The square root symbol, $\sqrt{\ }$, called a **radical**, makes it easier to write square roots.

So, instead of writing "A square root of 16 is 4," we can simply write $\sqrt{16} = 4$. The number within the radical, in this case 16, is called the **radicand**.

When we use the radical to find a square root of a number, like 16, the radical becomes an operation. Just like the plus sign tells us to apply addition to two numbers, the radical tells us to take the square root of a number.

EXAMPLE 10 Evaluate each square root.

ANSWER: a) $\sqrt{1}$ b) $\sqrt{25}$ c) $\sqrt{144}$

PROCEDURE: Because each radicand, here, is a perfect square, applying the radical leaves a number with no radical symbol.

ANSWER: a) $\sqrt{1} = 1$ b) $\sqrt{25} = 5$ c) $\sqrt{144} = 12$

YOU TRY IT 11 *Evaluate each square root. Use Example 10 as a guide.*

a) $\sqrt{4} =$ b) $\sqrt{9} =$ c) $\sqrt{121} =$

d) $\sqrt{36} =$ e) $\sqrt{100} =$ f) $\sqrt{81} =$

You Try It Answers: Section 2.1

YTI 1
a) Yes, a square with 6 units on each side will have 36 square units.
b) No, there is no whole number that, when multiplied by itself, equals 12.
c) Yes, a square with 7 units on each side will have 49 square units.

YTI 2 a) 36 b) 100 c) 324

YTI 3 a) 36 b) 16 c) 729

YTI 4 a) 2^3 is three factors of 2: $2 \cdot 2 \cdot 2$ b) 3^5 is five factors of 3: $3 \cdot 3 \cdot 3 \cdot 3 \cdot 3$

YTI 5 a) 2 b) 9 c) 17 d) 1

YTI 6
a) 10^5 is 1 followed by 5 zeros $= 100{,}000$
b) 10^7 is 1 followed by 7 zeros $= 10{,}000{,}000$
c) 10^1 is 1 followed by 1 zero $= 10$

YTI 7
a) 100 is 1 followed by 2 zeros: $100 = 10^2$
b) 10,000 is 1 followed by 4 zeros: $10{,}000 = 10^4$
c) 1,000,000 is 1 followed by 6 zeros: $1{,}000{,}000 = 10^6$

YTI 8 a) $24 \cdot 10^1$ b) $56 \cdot 10^2$ c) $38 \cdot 10^7$ d) $726 \cdot 10^4$

YTI 9 a) 2 b) 3 c) 8 d) 10

YTI 10
a) 48 is not a perfect square.
b) 121 is a perfect square; a square root is 11.
c) 144 is a perfect square; a square root is 12.

YTI 11 a) 2 b) 3 c) 11 d) 6 e) 10 f) 9

Focus Exercises: Section 2.1

Expand each and find its value.

1. 6^3 = ______________________ **2.** 2^5 = ______________________

3. 15^2 = ______________________ **4.** 3^3 = ______________________

5. 12^1 = ______________________ **6.** 4^3 = ______________________

7. 5^4 = ______________________ **8.** 8^1 = ______________________

9. 10^3 = ______________________ **10.** 10^5 = ______________________

Express each as a power of 10.

11. 100,000 = ______________________ **12.** 1,000,000,000 = ______________________

13. 10,000 = ______________________ **14.** 1,000,000 = ______________________

Rewrite the number as a product using the power of 10 as a factor.

15. 300 = ______________________ **16.** 5,000 = ______________________

17. 48,000 = ______________________ **18.** 710,000 = ______________________

19. 9,500,000 = ______________________ **20.** 200,000,000 = ______________________

Evaluate the following square roots.

21. $\sqrt{49}$ **22.** $\sqrt{25}$ **23.** $\sqrt{36}$ **24.** $\sqrt{1}$

25. $\sqrt{81}$ **26.** $\sqrt{16}$ **27.** $\sqrt{144}$ **28.** $\sqrt{64}$

SECTION 2.2 The Order of Operations

Objectives

In this section, you will learn to:

- Evaluate expressions by applying the order of operations.

To successfully complete this section, you need to understand:

- Adding whole numbers (1.3)
- Subtracting whole numbers (1.3)
- Multiplying whole numbers (1.4)
- Dividing whole numbers (1.5)
- Exponents (2.1)
- Square roots (2.1)

Introduction

As we learned in Chapter 1, to evaluate a mathematical expression means to find the value of the expression. Consider this expression: $3 + 4 \cdot 5$. How could it be evaluated?

If we apply the operation of addition first, and then multiplication, we get

$$3 + 4 \cdot 5$$
$$= 7 \cdot 5$$
$$= \mathbf{35}$$

If, however, we evaluate using multiplication first and then addition, we get

$$3 + 4 \cdot 5$$
$$= 3 + 20$$
$$= \mathbf{23}$$

Notice that, depending on which operation is applied first, we get two different results. Math, however, is an exact science and doesn't allow for two different values of the same expression. So we must develop a system—a set of guidelines—that will lead us to the same result every single time it is applied correctly. This system is called the **order of operations**.

Let's review the operations we've worked with so far:

OPERATION	EXAMPLE	NAME
Multiplication	$3 \cdot 5 = 15$	**product**
Division	$14 \div 2 = 7$	**quotient**
Subtraction	$12 - 9 = 3$	**difference**
Addition	$2 + 8 = 10$	**sum**
Exponent	$2^3 = 8$	**power**
Radical	$\sqrt{25} = 5$	**square root**

The order of operations asks us to explore what would happen if there is more than one operation in an expression; which operation should we apply first?

It is one of the most important rules you will learn in this course, and it is used in every math course beyond this one. In fact, whenever we use a formula—in forestry, nursing, police work (the list goes on and on)—the order of operations must be applied.

To see how the order of operations works, let's begin by looking at grouping symbols.

Grouping Symbols

There are a variety of symbols that we can use to group two or more values. The most common are parentheses ( ), but we also find use for brackets [ ] and braces { }. These grouping symbols create a quantity, suggesting that what's inside could be thought of as one value. They also act as a barrier, a protector of sorts, to outside influence until the value within is known.

> Any operation within grouping symbols must be applied first so that we can know what that one value is.

There are basically two types of grouping symbols:
- Those that form a quantity, like ( ), [ ], and { }, and
- Those that are actual operations, like $\sqrt{\ }$.

The radical is *both* a grouping symbol *and* an operation!

The radical, or the square root symbol, $\sqrt{\ }$, is also considered a grouping symbol. It groups any quantity that is within it. For example, $\sqrt{5 + 11}$ could be written as $\sqrt{(5 + 11)}$, and this would simplify to $\sqrt{16}$ before we could apply the radical.

So, what *is* the order in which the operations should be applied?

The Order of Operations

The Order of Operations

1. Evaluate within all grouping symbols (one at a time), if there are any.
2. Apply any exponents.
3. Apply multiplication and division *reading from left to right.*
4. Apply addition and subtraction *reading from left to right.*

We sometimes refer to the order of the operations by their rank. For example, we might say that an exponent has a "higher rank" than does multiplication.

Similarly, multiplication and division have the same rank; that is why we must apply them (carefully) from *left to right.* You'll see how this works in the examples.

Is it ever possible to give addition a higher rank than multiplication? Explain.

One question that might have occurred to you is, "Does the order of operations have to be that way?" To answer this question, let's take a look back at the expression presented at the beginning of this section, $3 + 4 \cdot 5$. We tried two different approaches:

(1) If we apply *addition first*, and then apply multiplication, we get

$3 + 4 \cdot 5$

$= 7 \cdot 5$ Should we add first?

$= 35$

(2) If we apply *multiplication first* and then apply addition, we get

$3 + 4 \cdot 5$

$= 7 + 20$ Should we multiply first?

$= 23$

We now know that the second approach is the accurate one because multiplication has a higher rank than addition, so we must apply multiplication first.

Why is it that way? Just because someone said so? What if we took away the order of operations and were allowed to apply only addition and nothing else? Could it be done?

Let's take a look at what the expression $3 + 4 \cdot 5$ really means. Because multiplication is an abbreviation for repeated addition, we could think of it as:

3 + four 5's	Let's expand the abbreviation.
$= 3 + (5 + 5 + 5 + 5)$	The Associative Property of Addition says we don't need parentheses if the only operation is addition.
$= 3 + 5 + 5 + 5 + 5$	
$= 23$	

Because multiplication is an abbreviation for repeated addition, we needed to expand it first to get only addition. Another way would be to recognize that four 5's equals 20 without expanding it. In other words, we can apply multiplication (it's a lot faster) directly without having to expand it first.

All in all, this just tells us why multiplication has to come before addition; it is why multiplication has a higher rank than addition.

Similarly, exponents have a higher rank than multiplication because the exponent is an abbreviation for repeated multiplication.

Applying the Order of Operations

The best way to understand these guidelines is to put them to work. We'll find that there is only one way to evaluate an expression using the rules, but we'll also find that some steps can be combined in certain situations. For now, though, let's evaluate each expression one step at a time.

Caution When looking through Example 1, be sure to notice how the steps are presented in the answer. Notice that, in each step, only one operation is applied. Please try to imitate this process so that your work is done in the same way. Also, if an operation has *not yet* been applied, then it should be shown on the next line.

EXAMPLE 1

Evaluate each according to the order of operations.

a) $14 - 6 \div 2$ b) $(14 - 6) \div 2$ c) $7 + 3^2$

d) $(7 + 3)^2$ e) $24 \div 4 \cdot 2$ f) $24 \div (4 \cdot 2)$

ANSWER: Each of these has two operations; some have grouping symbols that will affect the order in which the operations are applied.

a) $14 - 6 \div 2$ Two operations, subtraction and division: divide first.

$= 14 - 3$ Notice that the minus sign appears in the second step. That's because it hasn't been applied yet.

$= \boxed{11}$

b) $(14 - 6) \div 2$ Here are the same two operations as above, this time with grouping symbols. Evaluate the expression inside the parentheses first. Because we've already evaluated within the grouping symbols, we don't need the parentheses any more.

$= 8 \div 2$

$= \boxed{4}$

c) $7 + 3^2$ Two operations, addition and exponent: apply the exponent first, then add.

$= 7 + 9$

$= \boxed{16}$

d) $(7 + 3)^2$ The same two operations as in (c); work within the grouping symbols first.

$= (10)^2$ or 10^2; at this point, the parentheses are no longer necessary.

$= \boxed{100}$

e) $24 \div 4 \cdot 2$ Two operations: division and multiplication. Because they have the same rank, and there are no grouping symbols to tell us which to apply first, we apply them in order from left to right. That means that division is applied first.

$= 6 \cdot 2$

$= \boxed{12}$

f) $24 \div (4 \cdot 2)$ This time we do have grouping symbols, so we begin by evaluating the expression within the parentheses.

$= 24 \div 8$

$= \boxed{3}$

YOU TRY IT 1

Evaluate each according to the order of operations. First identify the two operations, then identify which is to be applied first. Show all steps! Use Example 1 as a guide.

The expression	The two operations	The first to be applied
a) $24 \div 6 + 2$	______________	______________

$=$

$=$

b) $24 \div (6 + 2)$ ____________________ ____________________

=

=

c) $10 - 3 \cdot 2$ ____________________ ____________________

=

=

d) $(10 - 3) \cdot 2$ ____________________ ____________________

=

=

e) $12 \div 2^2$ ____________________ ____________________

=

=

f) $(12 \div 2)^2$ ____________________ ____________________

=

=

Some expressions contain more than two operations. In those situations, we need to be even more careful when we apply the order of operations.

EXAMPLE 2

Evaluate each according to the order of operations.

a) $36 \div 3 \cdot 6 - 2$ b) $36 \div (3 \cdot 6) - 2$ c) $36 \div [3 \cdot (6 - 2)]$

ANSWER: Each of these has three operations. In part c there is a smaller quantity $(6 - 2)$ within the larger quantity of the brackets, [ ].

a) $36 \div 3 \cdot 6 - 2$ Because multiplication and division have the same rank, we apply them from left to right. We divide first.
$= 12 \cdot 6 - 2$ Notice that we are applying only one operation at a time and rewriting everything else. Patience is a virtue.
$= 72 - 2$
$= 70$

b) $36 \div (3 \cdot 6) - 2$ Evaluate the expression within the grouping symbols first.
$= 36 \div 18 - 2$ Divide.
$= 2 - 2$ Subtract.
$= 0$

c) $36 \div [3 \cdot (6 - 2)]$ Start with what is inside the large brackets. Inside those grouping symbols is another quantity, and we must evaluate it first: $6 - 2 = 4$. Evaluate $3 \cdot 4$.
$= 36 \div [3 \cdot 4]$
$= 36 \div 12$ Divide.
$= 3$

Example 2(c) illustrates that when one quantity is within another one, the inner quantity is to be evaluated first.

Sometimes an expression will have two sets of grouping symbols that are unrelated to each other, meaning that evaluating one does not affect the evaluation of the other. In other words, some quantities can be evaluated at the same time.

For example, in the expression $(8 - 3) \cdot (12 \div 4)$ we can evaluate within each grouping symbol regardless of the operation:

$(8 - 3) \cdot (12 \div 4)$ Here there are three operations: subtraction, multiplication and division.

$= (5) \cdot (3)$ Subtraction and division have equal rank here because the order of operations tells us to

$= 15$ begin by evaluating what is inside of the parentheses.

YOU TRY IT 2

Evaluate each according to the order of operations. Identify the order in which the operations should be applied. On each line, write the operation that should be applied and then apply it.

a) $36 \div 3 + 3 \cdot 2$ __________
$=$ __________
$=$ __________
$=$

b) $36 \div (3 + 3) \cdot 2$ __________
$=$ __________
$=$ __________
$=$

c) $36 \div (3 + 3 \cdot 2)$ __________
$=$ __________
$=$ __________
$=$

d) $11 + 4 \cdot 6 - 1$ __________
$=$ __________
$=$ __________
$=$

e) $(11 + 4) \cdot (6 - 1)$ __________
$=$ __________
$=$

f) $11 + [4 \cdot (6 - 1)]$ __________
$=$ __________
$=$ __________
$=$

g) $2 \cdot 3^2 \div (6 + 3)$ __________
$=$ __________
$=$ __________
$=$ __________
$=$

h) $(2 \cdot 3)^2 \div (6 + 3)$ __________
$=$ __________
$=$ __________
$=$

Now let's look at some examples that contain a radical.

EXAMPLE 3

Evaluate each completely. Remember, the radical is both a grouping symbol and an operation.

a) $\sqrt{5 + 11}$ b) $\sqrt{3^2 + 4^2}$ c) $13 - 2 \cdot \sqrt{9}$

PROCEDURE: Because the radical is a grouping symbol, we must evaluate within it first.

ANSWER: a) $\sqrt{5 + 11}$ First apply addition.

$= \sqrt{16}$ Now apply the square root.

$= 4$

b) $\sqrt{3^2 + 4^2}$ Apply both exponents within the same step.

$= \sqrt{9 + 16}$ Next apply addition.

$= \sqrt{25}$ Apply the square root.

$= 5$

c) $13 - 2\cdot\sqrt{9}$
$= 13 - 2\cdot 3$
$= 13 - 6$
$= 7$

The radical is the only grouping symbol, but there is nothing to evaluate inside; however, because the radical is a grouping symbol, we apply it—the square root—first.

YOU TRY IT 3

Evaluate each according to the order of operations. Identify the order in which the operations should be applied. Use Example 3 as a guide.

a) $\sqrt{4\cdot 9}$ ________
= ________
=

b) $\sqrt{25} - \sqrt{9}$ ________
= ________
=

c) $\sqrt{1 + (12\cdot 4)}$ ________
= ________
= ________
=

d) $\sqrt{(6 - 2)\cdot 5^2}$ ________
= ________
= ________
= ________
=

You Try It Answers: Section 2.2

YTI 1
a) The operations are division and addition; division is applied first; = 6
b) The operations are division and addition; addition is applied first; = 3
c) The operations are subtraction and multiplication; multiplication is applied first; = 4
d) The operations are subtraction and multiplication; subtraction is applied first; = 14
e) The operations are division and the exponent; the exponent is applied first; = 3
f) The operations are division and the exponent; division is applied first; = 36

YTI 2
a) Division, multiplication, addition; = 18
b) Addition, division, multiplication; = 12
c) Multiplication, addition, division; = 4
d) Multiplication, addition, subtraction; = 34
e) Both addition and subtraction, multiplication; = 75
f) Subtraction, multiplication, addition; = 31
g) Addition, exponent, multiplication, division; = 2
h) Both multiplication and addition, exponent, division; = 4

YTI 3
a) Multiplication, the radical; = 6
b) Both radicals, subtraction; = 2
c) Multiplication, addition, the radical; = 7
d) Subtraction, exponent, multiplication, the radical; = 10

Focus Exercises: Section 2.2

Evaluate each according to the order of operations. Simplify just one step, one operation at a time.

1. $30 \div 5 + 1$

2. $30 \div (5 + 1)$

3. $(8 + 5)\cdot 2$

4. $8 + 5\cdot 2$

5. $5\cdot 6 \div 3$

6. $5\cdot(6 \div 3)$

7. $5\cdot 3^2$

8. $2^3\cdot 2^2$

9. $2^3 \cdot 3^2$

10. $28 \div (7 \cdot 2)$

11. $28 \div 7 \cdot 2$

12. $16 \div 4 - 2$

13. $30 \div 2 \cdot 3$

14. $30 \div (2 \cdot 3)$

15. $7^2 + 5 - 3$

16. $5 \cdot 2^2 - 7$

17. $(5 \cdot 2)^2 - 7$

18. $4^2 \div 2 + 2$

19. $(5 + 3) \cdot 9$

20. $(6 + 12) \div (2 \cdot 3)$

21. $6 + [12 \div (2 \cdot 3)]$

22. $12 + [28 \div (7 - 3)]$

23. $24 \div (6 - 2) \cdot 3$

24. $(6 + 12) \div (2 \cdot 3)$

25. $(12 + 28) \div (7 - 3)$

26. $[(6 - 2) \cdot 3]^2$

27. $(6 - 2) \cdot 3^2$

28. $3 + \sqrt{16}$

29. $9 \cdot \sqrt{25}$

30. $11 - \sqrt{49}$

31. $6^2 - \sqrt{25}$

32. $\sqrt{64} - \sqrt{25}$

33. $9 + \sqrt{2 \cdot 2}$

34. $\sqrt{4 \cdot 9}$

35. $3 \cdot \sqrt{9 + 7}$

36. $\sqrt{8 \cdot 6 + 1}$

SECTION 2.3 Formulas

Objectives

In this section, you will learn to:

- Evaluate formulas by using the order of operations.

To successfully complete this section, you need to understand:

- The order of operations (2.2)

Introduction

If you've ever baked a cake, then you probably used a recipe telling you how much of each ingredient to use, what the oven temperature should be, and how long the cake needs to be in the oven. You mixed the ingredients together and poured them into the cake pan. If you followed the recipe correctly, then the result was a delicious cake for dessert.

Using a formula in math is like following a recipe. We:

1. put certain numbers into the formula, and
2. use the order of operations to evaluate the expression.

If we follow the order of operations correctly, then we will have a new value that can be applied to whatever problem we're trying to solve.

Formulas are the best application of the order of operations. Many formulas—in a variety of fields—require the order of operations for their proper evaluation.

For example, you may have seen Celsius temperatures at bank buildings. The sign out front might say that the temperature is 10° C (Celsius), but is that t-shirt or jacket weather? To convert the temperature reading from Celsius degrees to Fahrenheit degrees, we use the formula:

$$F = 9 \cdot (C \div 5) + 32, \qquad \text{where: } F = \text{Fahrenheit degrees}$$
$$C = \text{Celsius degrees}$$

Notice that the formula contains two variables, F and C. To evaluate the formula, we need to know the value of *only one* of the variables; we then use that value to find the value of the other variable.

If we substitute the known value of C (10°) into the formula, we can then evaluate the expression on the right side using—that's right—the order of operations!

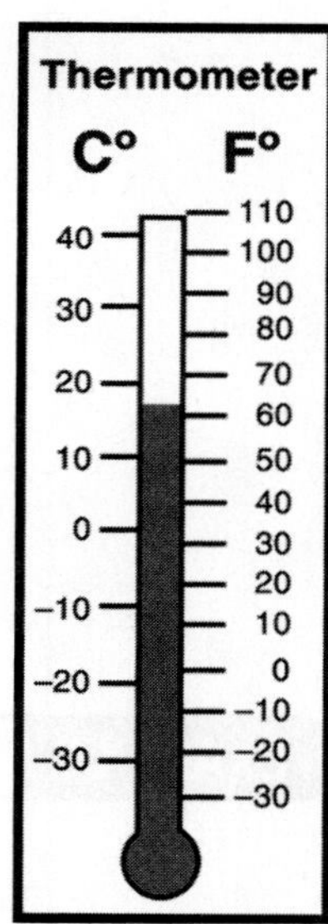

Replacement Values

To **substitute** a value into a formula means to replace the variable with a number; this number is called the **replacement value**. Whatever operation affected the variable now affects—and is applied to—the replacement value.

EXAMPLE 1 What is the Fahrenheit temperature equivalent of 10° C?

PROCEDURE: Use the formula $F = 9 \cdot (C \div 5) + 32$ and substitute 10 for C.

ANSWER:

$F = 9 \cdot (10 \div 5) + 32$

$F = 9 \cdot (2) + 32$ Apply the order of operations to complete the evaluation.

$F = 18 + 32$

$F = 50$

This means that 10° C is equivalent to 50° F. By the way, you might want to put a jacket on, it's starting to get a little chilly!

If, instead, we know the Fahrenheit degree—and we want to know the equivalent Celsius value—we use a different form of the same formula:

$$C = 5 \cdot [(F - 32) \div 9]$$

Notice that the numbers and variables are the same as in the Celsius-to-Fahrenheit formula, but they are in a different order.

EXAMPLE 2 What is the Celsius temperature equivalent of 77° F?

PROCEDURE: Use the formula $C = 5 \cdot [(F - 32) \div 9]$ and substitute 77 for F.

ANSWER:

$C = 5 \cdot [(77 - 32) \div 9]$

$C = 5 \cdot [45 \div 9]$ Apply the order of operations to complete the evaluation.

$C = 5 \cdot 5$

$C = 25$

This means that 77° F is equivalent to 25° C, a normal room temperature.

YOU TRY IT 1 *Find the equivalent temperature in either Celsius or Fahrenheit. Use Examples 1 and 2 as guides. (Be sure to use the correct formula.)*

a) The temperature is 40° C.

b) The temperature is 15° C.

c) The temperature is 86° F.

d) The temperature is 41° F.

Many formulas contain more than one variable. In this case, we substitute for all such variables—using their corresponding replacement values—at the same time.

EXAMPLE 3 Evaluate the numerical value of each formula with the given replacement values.

a) $d = r \cdot t$ $r = 50$, $t = 2$

b) $z = (x - m) \div s$ $x = 77$, $m = 63$, $s = 7$

c) $E = 9 \cdot R \div I$ $R = 10$, $I = 45$

d) $c = \sqrt{a^2 + b^2}$ $a = 3$, $b = 4$

ANSWER:

a) $d = r \cdot t$
$d = (50) \cdot (2)$
$d = 100$

b) $z = (x - m) \div s$
$z = (77 - 63) \div 7$
$z = 14 \div 7 = 2$

c) $E = 9 \cdot R \div I$
$E = 9 \cdot 10 \div 45$
$E = 90 \div 45 = 2$

d) $c = \sqrt{a^2 + b^2}$
$c = \sqrt{3^2 + 4^2}$
$c = \sqrt{9 + 16}$
$c = \sqrt{25} = 5$

YOU TRY IT 2

Evaluate the numerical value of each formula with the given replacement values. Use Example 3 as a guide.

a) $d = r \cdot t$ $\quad r = 15$, $t = 3$

b) $z = (x - m) \div s$ $\quad x = 24$, $m = 16$, $s = 2$

c) $E = 9 \cdot R \div I$ $\quad R = 20$, $I = 60$

d) $c = \sqrt{a^2 + b^2}$ $\quad a = 8$, $b = 6$

From where do we get all of these formulas, anyway? In YTI 2, we saw four formulas from a variety of disciplines and interests:

(a) $d = r \cdot t$ is from physics: distance = rate · time.

(b) $z = (x - m) \div s$ is from statistics: a conversion formula.

(c) $E = 9 \cdot R \div I$ is from baseball: a pitcher's earned run average. R = number of runs allowed; I = number of innings pitched.

(d) $c = \sqrt{a^2 + b^2}$ is from geometry: the Pythagorean Theorem; c is the length of the longest side of a right triangle and a and b are the lengths of the other two sides.

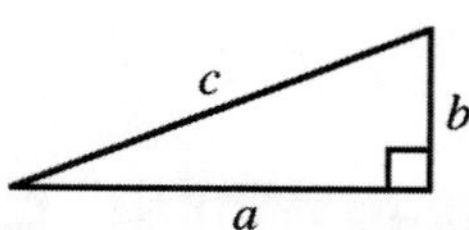

The Distance, Rate, and Time Formula

The formula $\boldsymbol{d = r \cdot t}$, read as "**d**istance equals **r**ate times **t**ime," is used in motion problems such as traveling by car, by plane, by train, by bicycle, and by foot. In each case, a certain distance is traveled at a certain rate of speed for a certain period of time.

A common use of this formula is related to driving a car where the unit of measure for distance is *miles*, for time is *hours*, and for rate is *miles per hour*. The formula is not restricted to those measures, though.

For example, we might want to measure the rate of an ant in terms of *centimeters per second* or in *feet per minute*. What must be present is a measure of length (miles, feet, centimeters) and of time (seconds, minutes, hours).

Imagine, for example, that you are driving a car at a rate of 60 miles per hour (mph). If you travel for 1 hour, you will have gone 60 miles. Traveling for 2 hours will take you 120 miles.

Using the formula $\boldsymbol{d = r \cdot t}$, we get:

a) $r = 60$ mph, $t = 1$ hour
$d = 60 \cdot 1 = 60$ miles

b) $r = 60$ mph, $t = 2$ hours
$d = 60 \cdot 2 = 120$ miles

We don't need to represent the units of measure (mph and hours) throughout the process, but we must represent one (miles) at the end.

EXAMPLE 4

Use the distance formula to determine the distance traveled at the given rate and time.

a) rate = 18 mph, time = 4 hours

b) rate = 45 mph, time = 3 hours

PROCEDURE: Use $d = r \cdot t$

ANSWER: a) $d = 18 \cdot 4 = 72$ miles

b) $d = 45 \cdot 3 = 135$ miles

We can use the distance formula to find the distance when the rate and time are known (as in Example 4). However, if we know how far Janelle traveled (say, 310 miles) and for how long she traveled (say, 5 hours), then we can use a slight variation of the distance formula to find out what her average rate of speed was for the trip:

$$\boldsymbol{r = d \div t}$$
$$r = 310 \text{ miles} \div 5 \text{ hours}$$
$$r = 62 \text{ miles per hour}$$
$$\text{or } r = 62 \text{ mph}$$

$$\begin{array}{r} 62 \\ 5\overline{)310} \\ -\ 30 \\ \hline 10 \\ -\ 10 \\ \hline 0 \end{array}$$

The formula for rate makes sense in this way: **per** means "divided by." So, "miles per hour" suggests "miles *divided* by hours." This is what we create when we use distance (miles) ÷ time (hours).

If, instead, we know how far it is to get from Des Moines, Iowa, to Detroit, Michigan (585 miles), and we have an idea how fast we might go (65 miles per hour), then how much *time* will it take to get there? The distance formula now looks like this:

$$\boldsymbol{t = d \div r}$$
$$t = 585 \text{ miles} \div 65 \text{ miles per hour}$$
$$t = 9 \text{ hours}$$

$$\begin{array}{r} 9 \\ 65\overline{)585} \\ -\ 585 \\ \hline 0 \end{array}$$

Notice that the unit is *hours*, a measure of time.

EXAMPLE 5 Use one of the distance formulas to determine the missing value, which will be either rate, distance, or time.

a) rate = 65 mph, time = 4 hr
b) distance = 48 cm, time = 12 sec
c) distance = 80 feet, rate = 5 feet per minute
d) distance = 738 mi, time = 6 hr

PROCEDURE: Use the formula for the measure that is not known: $d = r \cdot t$, $r = d \div t$, or $t = d \div r$.

ANSWER:

a) We know rate and time; we don't know distance, so we'll use $d = r \cdot t$.
$d = r \cdot t = 65 \cdot 4 = 260$ miles

b) We know distance and time; we don't know the rate, so we'll use $r = d \div t$.
Notice that the units are in centimeters and seconds, so the rate will be centimeters per second.
$r = d \div t = 48 \div 12 = 4$ centimeters per second

c) We know distance and rate; we don't know the time, so we'll use $t = d \div r$.
$t = d \div r = 80 \div 5 = 16$ minutes

d) We know distance and time; we don't know rate, so we'll use $r = d \div t$.
$r = d \div t = 738 \div 6 = 123$ mph

We say that r represents an *average* rate of speed because we don't consider the speed every second of every minute of the trip. We don't see the slowing down due to heavy traffic, the stopping at a traffic signal, the acceleration when the traffic is lighter. Instead, the formula $r = d \div t$ asks you to consider the rate of speed over the entire trip (or over a certain portion of the trip).

YOU TRY IT 3 *Ben drove from San Diego to Los Angeles, a distance of 147 miles. The traffic was so rough it took him 3 hours to get there. What was Ben's average rate (speed) for the trip?*

Sentence: ______________________________

YOU TRY IT 4 *Veronica was piloting a plane from Seattle to Cincinnati. She averaged 240 miles per hour while traveling the 1,920 miles. How many hours was the flight from Seattle to Cincinnati?*

Sentence: ______________________________

YOU TRY IT 5 *Banjo the Beagle loves to chase tennis balls. While playing at an empty football field one day, his owner timed him while he was chasing balls. On one chase, Banjo ran 162 feet in 9 seconds. What was Banjo's rate (in feet per second) on that chase?*

Sentence: ______________________________

YOU TRY IT 6 *A jet is averaging 385 miles per hour. How far will it travel in 6 hours?*

Sentence: ______________________________

You Try It Answers: Section 2.3

YTI 1
a) 40° C is equivalent to 104° F.
b) 15° C is equivalent to 59° F.
d) 86° F is equivalent to 30° C.
e) 41° F is equivalent to 5° C.

YTI 2
a) $d = 45$ b) $z = 4$
c) $E = 3$ d) $c = 10$

YTI 3 Ben averaged 49 miles per hour for the trip.

YTI 4 The flight from Seattle to Cincinnati was 8 hours.

YTI 5 Banjo's rate was 18 feet per second on that chase.

YTI 6 The jet will travel 2,310 mile in 6 hours.

Focus Exercises: Section 2.3

Find the equivalent temperature in either Celsius or Fahrenheit.

$$F = 9 \cdot (C \div 5) + 32 \qquad C = 5 \cdot [(F - 32) \div 9]$$

1. The temperature is 5° C.

2. The temperature is 30° C.

3. The temperature is 50° F.

4. The temperature is 95° F.

Evaluate the numerical value of each formula with the given replacement values.

5. $z = (x - m) \div s$ $x = 25$, $m = 16$, $s = 3$

6. $A = (a + b + c) \div 3$ $a = 13$, $b = 41$, $c = 33$

7. $a = \sqrt{c^2 - b^2}$ $c = 10$, $b = 6$

8. $A = b \cdot h \div 2$ $b = 5$, $h = 8$

9. $P = 2 \cdot L + 2 \cdot W$ $\quad L = 13$, $w = 8$

10. $r = d \div t$ $\quad d = 108$, $t = 9$

11. $A = h \cdot (b + c) \div 2$ $\quad h = 3$, $b = 5$, $c = 7$

12. $c = \sqrt{a^2 + b^2}$ $\quad a = 4$, $b = 3$

13. $W = A \div L$ $\quad A = 120$, $L = 15$

14. $C = 2 \cdot W \div E^2$ $\quad W = 18$, $E = 3$

15. $P = 2 \cdot (L + W)$ $\quad L = 9$, $W = 6$

16. $I = A \div (T - B)$ $\quad A = 60$, $T = 10$, $B = 6$

Use one of the following distance formulas to answer Focus Exercises 17–24.

$$\text{rate} = \frac{\text{distance}}{\text{time}}, \quad \text{time} = \frac{\text{distance}}{\text{rate}}, \quad \text{distance} = \text{rate} \cdot \text{time}$$

17. Mai traveled from Chicago to Cleveland by car. She was able to make the 335 mile trip in 5 hours. What was Mai's average rate of speed?

18. If Reggie averages 65 miles per hour on his trip, how far will he be able to travel in 8 hours?

19. If it took Bertie 5 hours to drive her car 295 miles, what was her average rate of speed for the trip?

20. Jorge works for a cross-town courier service in Atlanta delivering packages and mail throughout the city. One day the freeways were particularly crowded, and Jorge took 3 hours to drive 78 miles to make a delivery. What was Jorge's average rate of speed?

21. Hank, a truck driver, is trying to figure out how long it will take him to get from Baltimore to Worcester, MA. The whole trip is about 495 miles, and the load he is carrying allows him to average about 55 miles per hour. How many hours should it take Hank to complete the trip?

22. Luisa is planning to fly her small plane from Kansas City to Roanoke, VA. The trip is 925 miles and her plane averages 185 miles per hour. How many hours should it take Luisa to complete the flight?

23. Padam plans to drive from San Diego to San Francisco, 512 miles in all. What will Padam's average rate of speed need to be if he wishes to drive for 8 hours (not counting rest stops)?

24. Michael drives a bus for a touring company. This weekend he is taking a Riverside youth group on a tour to Phoenix. The distance between the cities is about 390 miles. Michael's bus is able to average 65 miles per hour. How many hours will it take the group to get to Phoenix?

SECTION 2.4 Factors

Objectives

In this section, you will learn to:

- Identify factors and factor pairs.
- Identify prime numbers and composite numbers.
- Use the divisibility tests to determine if one number is a factor of another number.

To successfully complete this section, you need to understand:

- The multiplication table (1.4).
- Dividing whole numbers (1.5).
- Square roots (2.1).

Introduction

Chemists want to know which atoms make up a particular molecule. They know, for example, that

- Water is two parts hydrogen (H) and one part oxygen (O), written H_2O.
- Ammonia is three parts hydrogen (H) and one part nitrogen (N), written NH_3.
- Methane is four parts hydrogen (H) and one part carbon (C), written CH_4.

In math, we want to understand the factors that make up a number. For example, $15 = 3 \cdot 5$, so two of the factors of 15 are 3 and 5. But what about a number such as 105? Does it have a factor of 3? Does it have a factor of 5? What other factors does 105 have? By the end of this section you will be able to answer each of these questions.

Recall from Section 1.2 that the product of any two numbers is the result when those two numbers are multiplied together. Because $6 \cdot 5 = 30$, we can say that 30 is the *product* of 6 and 5.

The **multiples** of any number, a, are all of the products involving a and some other whole number. In the multiplication table, the multiples of 3 are those numbers that are found in the column directly below the 3 at the top of the table or the row to the right of the 3 on the side of the table.

THE MULTIPLICATION TABLE

×	1	2	3	4	5	6	7	8	9	10	11	12
1	1	2	3	4	5	6	7	8	9	10	11	12
2	2	4	6	8	10	12	14	16	18	20	22	24
3	3	6	9	12	15	18	21	24	27	30	33	36
4	4	8	12	16	20	24	28	32	36	40	44	48
5	5	10	15	20	25	30	35	40	45	50	55	60
6	6	12	18	24	30	36	42	48	54	60	66	72
7	7	14	21	28	35	42	49	56	63	70	77	84
8	8	16	24	32	40	48	56	64	72	80	88	96
9	9	18	27	36	45	54	63	72	81	90	99	108
10	10	20	30	40	50	60	70	80	90	100	110	120
11	11	22	33	44	55	66	77	88	99	110	121	132
12	12	24	36	48	60	72	84	96	108	120	132	144

EXAMPLE 1 List the first twelve multiples of 3.

PROCEDURE: Look at the multiplication table under 3.

ANSWER: 3, 6, 9, 12, 15, 18, 21, 24, 27, 30, 33, 36.

The list of multiples of 3 is not restricted to the multiplication table; any whole number multiplied by 3 results in another multiple of 3.

Consider: $20 \cdot 3 = 60$, so 60 is a multiple of 3.
$45 \cdot 3 = 135$, so 135 is a multiple of 3.

So a multiple of 3 is the product of multiplying any whole number by 3.

The list of multiples of 3 is infinite: it goes on forever.

YOU TRY IT 1

List the first eight multiples of the given number. Use the multiplication table, if needed.

a) 2: __________

b) 3: __________

c) 5: __________

d) 6: __________

e) 9: __________

f) 10: __________

Based on what you just wrote, notice that:

(1) The multiples of 2 are all even (have a 0, 2, 4, 6, or 8 in the ones place).
(2) The sum of the individual digits of the multiples of 3 add up to other multiples of 3. (For example, 24 is a multiple of 3 and $2 + 4 = 6$ which is also a multiple of 3.)
(3) The multiples of 5 have 0 or 5 in the ones place.
(4) The multiples of 6 are also multiples of both 2 and 3.
(5) The sum of the individual digits of the multiples of 9 add up to other multiples of 9. (For example, 45 is a multiple of 9 and $4 + 5 = 9$ which is also a multiple of 9.)
(6) The multiples of 10 have 0 in the ones place.

We explore these ideas a little later in this section as divisibility tests.

Factors

If two whole numbers, m and n, multiply to get a product, $p(m \cdot n = p)$, then

1. p is a *multiple* of both m and n.
2. p is *divisible* by both m and n.
3. both m and n *divide* evenly into p.
4. both m and n are *factors* of p.

EXAMPLE 2

Because $6 \cdot 7 = 42$,

- 42 is a multiple of both 6 and 7.
- 42 is divisible by both 6 and 7.
- 6 and 7 divide evenly into 42.
- 6 and 7 are both factors of 42.

YOU TRY IT 2

Use example 2 as a guide to complete each of the following.

a) Because $4 \cdot 5 = 20$,

- __________
- __________
- __________
- __________

b) Because $9 \cdot 8 = 72$,

- __________
- __________
- __________
- __________

Factors can always be written in pairs. Because $3 \cdot 5 = 15$, 3 and 5 are both factors of 15, and we call 3 and 5 a **factor pair** of 15. The numbers 1 and 15 form another factor pair of 15, because $1 \cdot 15 = 15$.

EXAMPLE 3 List the factors of 24.

PROCEDURE: Think of 24 as a product of two numbers.

Consider $1 \cdot 24 = 24$,

$2 \cdot 12 = 24$,

$3 \cdot 8 = 24$,

$4 \cdot 6 = 24$.

ANSWER: The factors of 24 are 1, 2, 3, 4, 6, 8, 12, and 24.

In finding *all* of the factors of 24, notice that we have a number of factor pairs. Factor pairs can be found—and shown—using a **factor pair table**:

24	
1	24
2	12
3	8
4	6

Start with 1 on the left and write the other factor of the pair, 24, on the right. Do the same for 2, 3, and so on. Do not include 5, because 5 isn't a factor of 24.

There is a total of four factor pairs of 24.

EXAMPLE 4 Use a factor pair table to find all of the factor pairs of 30. From the table, write a list of the factors of 30.

PROCEDURE: Think of 30 as a product of two numbers. Start with 1 on the left side, then 2, then 3, etc., and decide whether those numbers are factors of 30.

ANSWER:

30	
1	30
2	15
3	10
5	6

$1 \cdot 30 = 30$

$2 \cdot 15 = 30$

$3 \cdot 10 = 30$

$5 \cdot 6 = 30$

Notice that 4 is not on this list because 4 doesn't divide evenly into 30.

So, the factors of 30 are 1, 2, 3, 5, 6, 10, 15, and 30.

YOU TRY IT 3 *Use a factor pair table to find all of the factor pairs of each number. From the factor pair table, write the list of factors of that number. Use Example 4 as a guide.*

a) 12

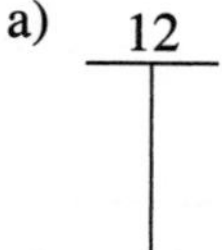

The factors of 12 are ____________

b) 16

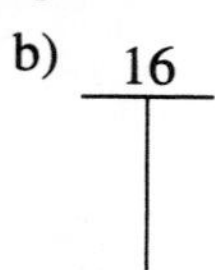

The factors of 16 are ____________

c) 18

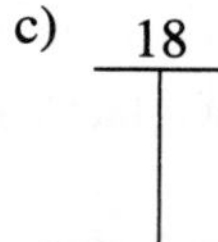

The factors of 18 are ____________

d) 20

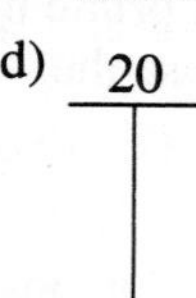

The factors of 20 are ____________

24	
1	24
2	12
3	8
4	6
6	4
8	3
12	2
24	1

Consider this list of the factor pairs of 24 (at right). There are no factor pairs missing, so it is complete. However, as it is shown here, every factor pair is written twice, and this is not necessary. In other words, if we include the factor pair 3 and 8, then we don't need to also include the factor pair 8 and 3.

It's a good idea, when creating a factor pair table, to write the left side in numerical order, starting with 1 so that we don't accidentally skip any factor pairs. But how do we know when to stop searching for factor pairs? Is there a *magic number* that tells us when to stop searching for factors?

Yes and no. Yes, there is a number that tells us when to stop, but no, it isn't magic. This number is *the square root of the first perfect square larger than the given number.*

For example, if we're trying to find all of the factor pairs of 24, the first perfect square after 24 is 25. Because $\sqrt{25} = 5$, we don't need to go beyond 5 in our search for factor pairs.

Yes, there are factors of 24 beyond 5, such as 8, but this factor is paired with a number less than 5, namely 3.

As the diagram below shows, the magic number isn't in the center of the whole number line from 0 to 24, but it is in the middle of the factor pairs of 24.

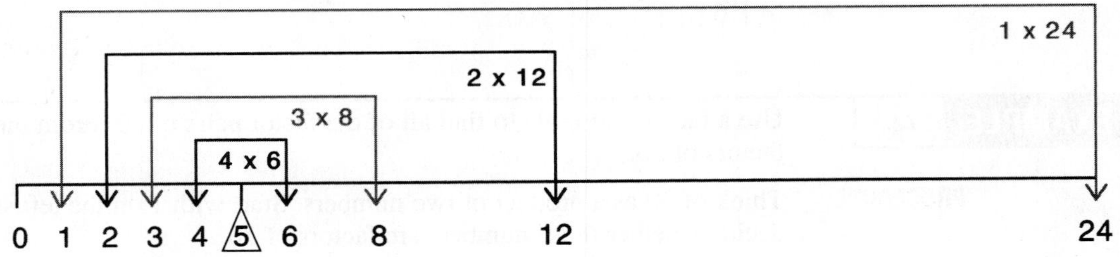

Prime and Composite Numbers

Whole numbers greater than 1 fall into one of two categories: they are either *prime* or *composite.*

A whole number is a **prime number** if it has exactly two distinct, whole number factors: 1 and itself.

A whole number that has *more* than two distinct factors is a **composite number**. A composite number is any whole number (greater than 1) that is not prime.

Caution 1 *is not a prime number* because it has only one factor.

EXAMPLE 5 For each number, determine if it is prime or composite.

a) 7 b) 12 c) 9

ANSWER:

a) 7 is a prime number because the only factors of 7 are 1 and 7; or we might say, 7 is prime because the only whole numbers that divide evenly into 7 are 1 and 7.

b) 12 is a composite number because it has more than two factors. The factors of 12 are 1, 2, 3, 4, 6, and 12.

c) 9 is a composite number because it has more than two factors. The factors of 9 are 1, 3, and 9.

YOU TRY IT 4

For each number, determine if it is prime or composite. Use Example 5 as a guide.

a) 15 b) 13 c) 1 d) 4

YOU TRY IT 5

Here is the list of prime numbers less than 100.

2, 3, 5, 7, 11, 13, 17, 19, 23, 29, 31, 37, 41, 43, 47, 53, 59, 61, 67, 71, 73, 79, 83, 89, 97.

a) What do you notice about the first prime number? ______________

b) What do you notice about all of the other prime numbers? ______________

c) Are all odd numbers prime numbers? Support your answer with some examples.

____

Refer to the list of prime numbers less than 100 in YTI 5. Notice that the only even prime number is 2 and that no *two-digit* prime number ends in 5. Also notice that there really is no pattern to the list of primes; in other words, you can't predict what the next prime number is going to be just by looking at the list.

The Divisibility Tests: 2, 3, 5, 9, and 10

This example shows us the connection between the ideas of *divisibility* and *factor.*

If 203 is ***divisible*** by 7, then 7 is a ***factor*** of 203. We can use long division to find the other factor:

$$\begin{array}{r} 29 \\ 7\overline{)203} \\ -14 \\ \hline 63 \\ -63 \\ \hline 0 \end{array}$$

This shows us that $203 = 7 \cdot 29$. Both 7 and 29 are factors of 203, and 203 is divisible by both 7 and 29.

What follows are divisibility tests for 2, 3, 5, 9, and 10. We can use these tests to find some factors of some composite numbers.

Divisibility Test for 2

2 is a factor of a whole number if and only if* the number is even (has either 0, 2, 4, 6, or 8 in the ones place).

*This means that if the number is odd—has 1, 3, 5, 7, or 9 in the ones place—then 2 is not a factor.

YOU TRY IT 6

Without trying to find any other factors or factor pairs, determine if 2 is a factor of each. Explain why or why not.

a) 52 b) 61 c) 70

______________ ______________ ______________

______________ ______________ ______________

Divisibility Test for 5

5 is a factor of a whole number if and only if the number has either 5 or 0 in the ones place.

YOU TRY IT 7

Without trying to find any other factors or factor pairs, determine if 5 is a factor of each. Explain why or why not.

a) 90 ______ ______

b) 175 ______ ______

c) 608 ______ ______

Divisibility Test for 10

10 is a factor of a whole number if and only if the number has 0 in the ones place.

10 is a factor of each of these numbers: 30, 160, 1,420 and 700 because each has 0 in the ones place.

Divisibility Test for 3

3 is a factor of a whole number if and only if the number's digits add to a multiple of 3.

EXAMPLE 6

Determine if 3 is a factor of the number. Verify each answer by dividing the number by 3.

a) 285

b) 473

PROCEDURE:

a) Add the digits: $2 + 8 + 5 = 15$; 3 is a factor of 15.

b) Add the digits: $4 + 7 + 3 = 14$; 3 is not a factor of 14.

ANSWER:

a) ***Yes***, 3 is a factor of 285.

b) ***No***, 3 is ***not*** a factor of 473.

CHECK:

a)
```
    95
 3)285
  - 27
    15
  - 15
     0
```
So, 285 is divisible by 3, and 3 is a *factor* of 285.

b)
```
   157 r 2
 3)473
  - 3
    17
  - 15
     23
   - 21
      2
```
Because the remainder is not 0, 473 is not divisible by 3. Therefore 3 is ***not*** a factor of 473.

YOU TRY IT 8

Determine if 3 is a factor of the number. Verify each answer by dividing the number by 3. Use Example 6 as a guide.

a) 87: ______

b) 671: ______

c) 8,395: ______

d) 25,074: ______

Divisibility Test for 9

9 is a factor of a whole number if and only if the number's digits add to a multiple of 9.

EXAMPLE 7

Determine if 9 is a factor of the number. Verify each answer by dividing the number by 9.

a) 675 b) 1,983

PROCEDURE: a) Add the digits: 6 + 7 + 5 = 18; 18 is a multiple of 9.

b) Add the digits: 1 + 9 + 8 + 3 = 21; 21 is not a multiple of 9.

ANSWER: *Yes*, 9 is a factor of 675. *No*, 9 is ***not*** a factor of 1,983.

CHECK:

```
  75
9)675
- 63
  45
- 45
   0
```

So, 675 is divisible by 9, and 9 is a *factor* of 675.

```
  220 r 3
9)1983
- 18
   18
 - 18
   03
 - 00
    3
```

Because the remainder is not 0, 1,983 is not divisible by 9, and 9 is ***not*** a factor of 1,983.

Determine if 9 is a factor of the number. Verify each answer by dividing the number by 9. Use Example 7 as a guide.

a) 548: ______________ b) 3,582: ______________

c) 8,511: ______________ d) 20,142: ______________

If we add the digits of 25, we get 2 + 5 = 7. Does this mean that 7 is a factor of 25?

____

____

Let's put the divisibility tests for 2, 3, and 5 together in the following example.

EXAMPLE 8

Which of the first three prime numbers—2, 3 and 5—are factors of the following?

	a) 42	b) 135	c) 570	d) 91
TEST FOR 2:	• 42 is even (2)	• 135 is not even	• 570 is even (2)	• 91 is not even
TEST FOR 3:	• 4 + 2 = 6 (3)	• 1 + 3 + 5 = 9 (3)	• 5 + 7 + 0 = 12 (3)	• 9 + 1 = 10
TEST FOR 5:	• doesn't end in 0 or 5	• ends in 5 (5)	• ends in 0 (5)	• doesn't end in 0 or 5
ANSWER:	a) 2 and 3	b) 3 and 5	c) 2 and 3 and 5	d) none of these

Which of the first three prime numbers—2, 3 and 5—are factors of the following? Use Example 8 as a guide.

a) 213 b) 390 c) 419 d) 2,835

__________ __________ __________ __________

Think about it

If a number, such as 91, doesn't have 2, 3, or 5 as one or more of its factors, is it a prime number? Explain your answer.

____

____

The Principle of Smaller Factors and the Principle of Composite Factors

The Principle of Smaller Factors

If a number, F, is a **F**actor of a **L**arger number, L, then all of the smaller factors of F are also factors of L.

Replacing the variables with sample numbers, we have:

> If a number, 6, is a Factor of a Larger number, 30, then all of the smaller factors (2 and 3) of 6 are also factors of 30. In other words, because 6 is a factor of 30, 2 and 3 are also factors 30.

EXAMPLE 9

Use the Principle of Smaller Factors to finish each sentence.

a) 14 is a factor of 42; 2 and 7 are (smaller) factors of 14; so, it must be that both 2 and 7 are *also* factors of 42.

b) 15 is a factor of 45; 3 and 5 are (smaller) factors of 15; so, it must be that both 3 and 5 are *also* factors of 45.

c) 30 is a factor of 120; 2, 3 and 5 are (smaller) factors of 30; so, it must be that 2, 3 and 5 are all *also* factors of 120.

YOU TRY IT 11

Use the Principle of Smaller Factors to finish each sentence. Use Example 9 as a guide.

a) 6 is a factor of 78; 2 and 3 are factors of 6; so it must be that ____________.

b) 10 is a factor of 90; 2 and 5 are factors of 10; so it must be that ____________.

c) 35 is a factor of 140; 5 and 7 are factors of 35; so it must be that ____________.

The Principle of Composite Factors

If two **P**rime **N**umbers, P and N, are factors of a **L**arger number L, then the product of those prime numbers, $P \cdot N$, is a composite factor of L.

This principle is also true when there are more than two prime factors.

Replacing the variables with sample numbers, we have:

> If two Prime Numbers, 2 and 7, are factors of a Larger number, 70, then the product of those prime numbers, $\mathbf{2 \cdot 7 = 14}$, is also a factor of 70. 14 is a composite factor of 70.

EXAMPLE 10

Use the Principle of Composite Factors to finish each sentence.

a) Because 2 and 7 are both prime factors of 98 (and because $2 \cdot 7 = 14$) it must be that <u>14 is also a factor of 98.</u>

b) Because 3 and 5 are both prime factors of 75 (and because $3 \cdot 5 = 15$), it must be that <u>15 is also a factor of 75.</u>

c) Because 2 and 11 are both prime factors of 264 (and because $2 \cdot 11 = 2$), it must be that <u>22 is also a factor of 264.</u>

d) Because 2, 3, and 5 are all prime factors of 240, it must be that:

<u>30 is also a factor of 240</u>, $(2 \cdot 3 \cdot 5 = 30)$

<u>6 is also a factor of 240</u>, $(2 \cdot 3 = 6)$

<u>10 is also a factor of 240</u>, $(2 \cdot 5 = 10)$

<u>15 is also a factor of 240</u>. $(3 \cdot 5 = 15)$

We can use all three known prime factors, or we can use any two of the known prime factors.

YOU TRY IT 12

Use the Principle of Composite Factors to finish each sentence. (Use Example 10 as a guide.)

a) Because 2 and 3 are both prime factors of 96, it must be that ____________________.

b) Because 2 and 5 are both prime factors of 130, it must be that ____________________.

c) Because 3 and 11 are both prime factors of 231, it must be that ____________________.

d) Because 7 and 2 are both prime factors of 434, it must be that ____________________.

e) Because 2, 3 and 7 are all prime factors of 546, it must be that ____________________ and ____________________ and ____________________ and ____________________.

Think about it

On the first page of this section, the following questions were asked about 105. Can you answer them now?

Does 105 have a factor of 3? ____________________

Does 105 have a factor of 5? ____________________

What other factors does 105 have? ____________________

Think about it

4 is a factor of 36. 6 is also a factor of 36. Does the Principle of Composite Factors say, then, that $4 \cdot 6 = 24$ is also a factor of 36? Explain your answer.

____

____

What do you need to know to determine if 21 is a factor of a number? Explain your answer.

____

____

You Try It Answers: Section 2.4

YTI 1
a) 2, 4, 6, 8, 10, 12, 14, 16
b) 3, 6, 9, 12, 15, 18, 21, 24
c) 5, 10, 15, 20, 25, 30, 35, 40
d) 6, 12, 18, 24, 30, 36, 42, 48
e) 9, 18, 27, 36, 45, 54, 63, 72
f) 10, 20, 30, 40, 50, 60, 70, 80

YTI 2
a) • 20 is a multiple of both 4 and 5.
• 20 is a divisible by both 4 and 5.
• 4 and 5 divide evenly into 20.
• 4 and 5 are both factors of 20.
b) • 72 is a multiple of both 9 and 8.
• 72 is a divisible by both 9 and 8.
• 9 and 8 divide evenly into 72.
• 9 and 8 are both factors of 72.

YTI 3

a)

12	
1	12
2	6
3	4

The factors of 12 are 1, 2, 3, 4, 6, and 12

b)

16	
1	16
2	8
4	4

The factors of 16 are 1, 2, 4, 8, and 16

c)

18	
1	18
2	9
3	6

The factors of 18 are 1, 2, 3, 6, 9, and 18

d)

20	
1	20
2	10
4	5

The factors of 20 are 1, 2, 4, 5, 10, and 20

YTI 4
a) Composite
b) Prime
c) Neither prime nor composite
d) Composite

YTI 5
a) The first prime number is even. (It is the only even prime number.)
b) All other prime numbers are odd numbers.
c) No, there are many odd numbers that are not prime. The number 9 is an example of an odd number that is not prime. Other examples of odd numbers that are not prime are 15, 21, 25, 27 and 33.

YTI 6
a) 2 is a factor of 52 (because 52 is an even number).
b) 2 is not a factor of 61 (because 61 is an odd number).
c) 2 is a factor of 70 because 70 is an even number.

YTI 7
a) 5 is a factor of 90 because 90 has a 0 in the ones place.
b) 5 is a factor of 175 because 175 has a 5 in the ones place.
c) 5 is not a factor of 608 because 608 does not have a 0 or 5 in the ones place.

YTI 8
a) Because $8 + 7 = 15$, and because 3 is a factor of 15, 3 is a factor of 87.
b) Because $6 + 7 + 1 = 14$, and because 3 is not a factor of 14, 3 is not a factor of 671.
c) Because $8 + 3 + 9 + 5 = 25$, and because 3 is not a factor of 25, 3 is not a factor of 8,395.
d) Because $2 + 5 + 0 + 7 + 4 = 18$, and because 3 is a factor of 18, 3 is a factor of 25,074.

YTI 9
a) Because $5 + 4 + 8 = 17$, and because 9 is not a factor of 17, 9 is not a factor of 548.
b) Because $3 + 5 + 8 + 2 = 18$, and because 9 is a factor of 18, 9 is a factor of 3,582.
c) Because $8 + 5 + 1 + 1 = 15$, and because 9 is not a factor of 15, 9 is not a factor of 8,511.
d) Because $2 + 0 + 1 + 4 + 2 = 9$, and because 9 is a factor of 9, 9 is a factor of 20,142.

YTI 10
a) 3 only b) 2, 3 and 5
c) none of these d) 3 and 5

YTI 11
a) … both 2 and 3 are also factors of 78.
b) … both 2 and 5 are also factors of 90.
c) … both 5 and 7 are also factors of 140.

YTI 12
a) … 6 is also a factor of 96 (because $2 \cdot 3 = 6$).
b) … 10 is also a factor of 130 (because $2 \cdot 5 = 10$).
c) … 33 is also a factor of 231 (because $3 \cdot 11 = 33$).
d) … 14 is also a factor of 434 (because $7 \cdot 2 = 14$).
e) … 42 is also a factor of 546 (because $2 \cdot 3 \cdot 7 = 42$), and 6 is a factor of 546 (because $2 \cdot 3 = 6$), and 14 is a factor of 546 (because $2 \cdot 7 = 14$), and 21 is a factor of 546 (because $3 \cdot 7 = 21$).

Focus Exercises: Section 2.4

List the first eight multiples of the given number.

1. 4 **2.** 5 **3.** 7 **4.** 9

Use a factor pair table to find all of the factor pairs of

5. 32 **6.** 40 **7.** 28 **8.** 42

Of the first three prime numbers—2, 3, and 5—which are factors of the following? Use the divisibility tests for 2, 3, and 5.

9. 32 **10.** 80 **11.** 127 **12.** 414

13. 76 **14.** 57 **15.** 125 **16.** 390

17. 315 **18.** 860 **19.** 156 **20.** 4,231

21. 7,287 **22.** 41,592 **23.** 322,980 **24.** 994,515

Determine if 9 is a factor of the number. (Verify each answer by dividing the number by 9.)

25. 372 **26.** 4,797 **27.** 7,506 **28.** 20,601

Use the Principle of Composite Factors to finish each sentence.

29. Because both 5 and 13 are prime factors of 715, it must be that

30. Because both 7 and 11 are prime factors of 1,309, it must be that

31. Because 2, 3, and 7 are all prime factors of 966, it must be that

32. Because 3, 5, and 7 are all prime factors of 1,785, it must be that

Of the following numbers, determine which are prime, which are composite, and which are neither.

33. 0, 7, 9, 23, 8, 40, 1, 15, 33, 32, 12, 41, 51, 50

SECTION 2.5 Prime Factorization

Objectives

In this section, you will learn to:

- Find the prime factorization of composite numbers.
- Build composite factors.

To successfully complete this section, you need to understand:

- The multiplication table (1.4)
- Dividing whole numbers (1.5)
- The divisibility tests of factors (2.4)

Introduction

Here is an analogy to help you think about primes and composites. In paints, we have three primary colors, red, blue, and yellow. For the purposes of this analogy, we can think of these as representing the prime numbers.

We can mix any two of these primary colors together to get other colors, called secondary colors. In particular,

mixing equal amounts of red and yellow makes orange;
mixing equal amounts of red and blue makes purple;
mixing equal amounts of blue and yellow makes green.

These secondary colors are like composite numbers. You can't get green without both blue and yellow, just as a whole number can't have 6 as a factor without also having both 2 and 3 as factors.

We can even mix all three primary colors together to form brown, so we can say that brown is composed of red, blue and yellow. Brown is like 30; 30 is a composite number. It is composed of the prime factors 2, 3 and 5: $2 \cdot 3 \cdot 5 = 30$.

Also, we can mix yellow and blue to get green, and then we can mix in more yellow for lime green. Lime green is a composite color with two amounts of yellow and one amount of blue. Similarly, 12 is a composite number with two factors of 2 and one factor of 3: $2 \cdot 2 \cdot 3 = 12$.

In this section, we discover which primes some composite numbers are composed of. We analyze composite numbers just like a paint scientist might analyze an interesting color of paint, called puce: She might first discover that puce is composed of brown and purple; then, the brown is composed of red and green, and so on.

Here is a diagram of what this breakdown into primary colors might look like. The primary colors are circled to indicate that they can't be broken down further.

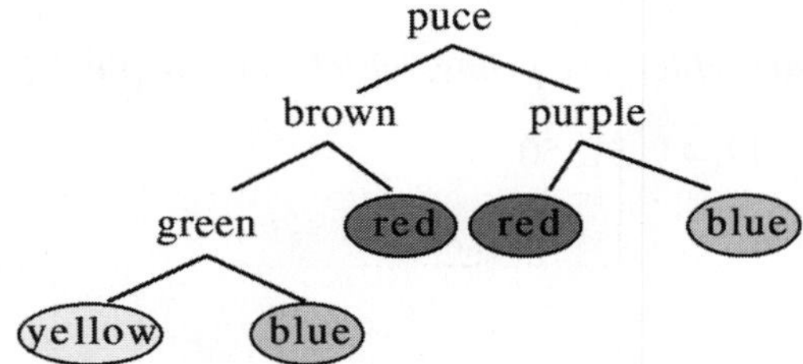

We see that puce is composed of one amount of yellow, two amounts of red, and two amounts of blue.

Prime Factorization and Factor Trees

Just as composite colors can be broken down into their primary colors, composite numbers can be broken down into a product of their prime factors, called *prime factorization*.

> The **prime factorization** of a composite number is the product of the prime factors (including repetitions) of the number.

EXAMPLE 1

Find the prime factorization of the following.

a) 6 b) 14 c) 15

ANSWERS: a) $6 = 2 \cdot 3$ b) $14 = 2 \cdot 7$ c) $15 = 3 \cdot 5$

YOU TRY IT 1

Find the prime factorization of the following. Use Example 1 as a guide.

a) 21 b) 22 c) 35 d) 77

Think about it

Though it's true that $7 = 7 \cdot 1$, we can't use this as the prime factorization. Why not?

A **factor tree** is a visual method used to look at the factors of a number. First let's look at the variety of factors of 24 using a factor tree:

a) 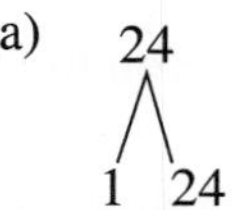
b) 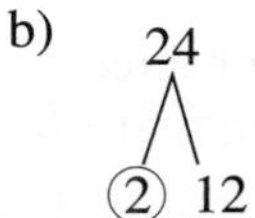
c) 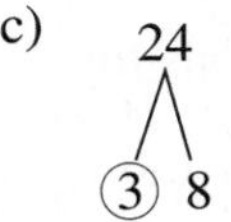
d) 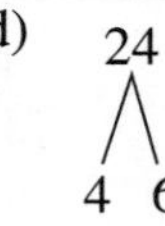

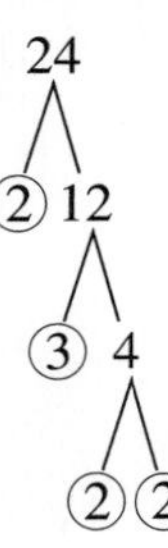

Think of the number—24 in this case—as a flower or plant. The lines leading to the factors are like *branches*. The circled numbers are prime numbers, like the fruit of the tree, and this is the purpose of a factor tree: to identify prime factors of the original number.

Each branch that leads to a prime number bears fruit, and each branch that leads to a composite number must branch again until it bears the fruit of a prime number. At right is the completed factor tree for 24. This factor tree indicates that $24 = 2 \cdot 2 \cdot 2 \cdot 3$.

Think about it

Is this factor tree a good start for the prime factorization for 36? Why or why not?

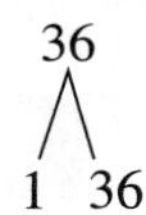

EXAMPLE 2 Find the prime factorization of 30.

PROCEDURE: We'll use a factor tree to first find any two factors of 30. We'll circle any primes that appear to indicate that the branch can't be factored further.

If we arrive at any composite numbers, we must factor them further to continue our search for prime factors.

Here are three different paths to finding the prime factors of 30:

(1) 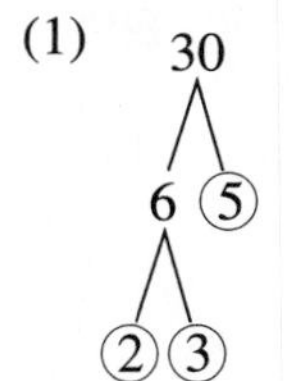
(2) 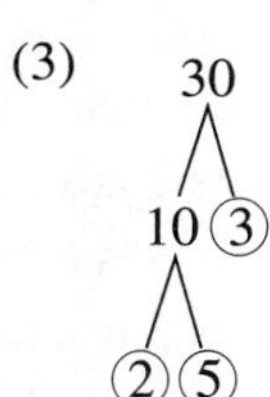
(3) 30 → 10, ③; 10 → ②, ⑤

ANSWER: $30 = 2 \cdot 3 \cdot 5$ $30 = 3 \cdot 5 \cdot 2$ $30 = 2 \cdot 5 \cdot 3$

Notice that the result (the prime factorization) is the same no matter which factor path we choose. Generally, though, we write the prime factorization in numerical order, starting with the lowest. So we'd write $30 = 2 \cdot 3 \cdot 5$.

YOU TRY IT 2

Find the prime factorization of the following. Create a factor tree and put a circle around any prime factor. Use Example 2 as a guide.

a) 42 b) 54 c) 70

42 = 54 = 70 =

EXAMPLE 3 Find the prime factorization of 24. Write the answer two ways, with and without exponents.

PROCEDURE: This time you are given one of three paths. It is up to you to find two more. Any correct path you choose will give the same prime factorization.

(1) Our path: (2) Your first path (3) Your second path

Notice this time we have repeated prime factors, and we must list them all in writing the prime factorization.

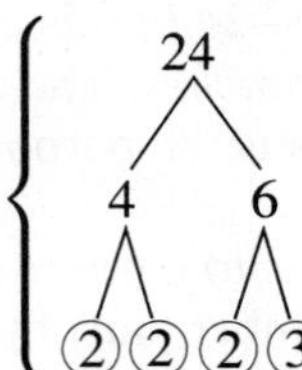

ANSWER: $24 = 2 \cdot 2 \cdot 2 \cdot 3$ or $2^3 \cdot 3$.

YOU TRY IT 3

Find the prime factorization of the following using a factor tree. Write the answer two ways: with and without exponents, as shown in Example 3. Be sure to show the factor tree and circle the prime factors as they appear.

a) 36 b) 50

36 = ________ or ________ 50 = ________ or ________

(without exponents) or (with exponents) (without exponents) or (with exponents)

EXAMPLE 4 Find the prime factorization of 280.

PROCEDURE: When a number is rather large, don't be intimidated by it. Identify at least one number (prime or composite) that is a factor and begin the process. The other factors will quickly become smaller and easier to work with.

(1) Is 2 is a factor of 280?
(2) Is 3 is a factor of 280?
(3) Is 5 is a factor of 280?
(4) Is 9 is a factor of 280?
(5) Is 10 is a factor of 280?

10 is a good factor to start with.

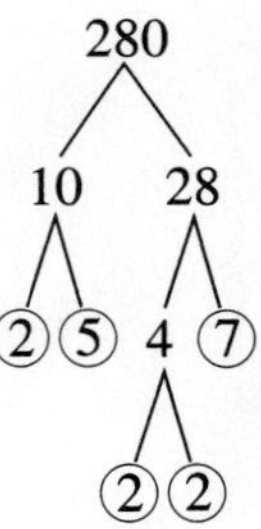

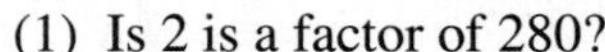

ANSWER: $280 = 2 \cdot 2 \cdot 2 \cdot 5 \cdot 7$ or $2^3 \cdot 5 \cdot 7$.

YOU TRY IT 4 *Find the prime factorization of the following. Write it both with and without exponents. Use Example 4 as a guide.*

a) 260

260 = _______ or _______

(without exponents) or (with exponents)

b) 1,540

1,540 = _______ or _______

(without exponents) or (with exponents)

Factoring Using the Division Method

An alternative to using a factor tree is to repeatedly divide by the lowest possible prime number, generating a new quotient each time. In this division method, the primes we divide by are called **prime divisors**.

The *lowest possible prime number* means divide by 2 if the number is even, and continue to divide by 2 as long as the resulting quotients are even. Once they stop being even, see if you can divide by 3; if not 3, then 5; then try 7, and so on until the final quotient is a prime number. The prime factorization is the product of all prime divisors and the final prime quotient.

EXAMPLE 5 Find the prime factorization of each number using the division method of dividing by the lowest possible prime.

a) 90 b) 189 c) 240

PROCEDURE: If the number is even, we'll divide by 2. We'll then look at the quotient and decide if we can divide by 2 again; if not, we'll see if 3 is a factor using the divisibility test for 3, and so on.

Each new quotient appears *below* the dividend.

ANSWER: a) 90 is even, so the first prime divisor is 2: $90 \div 2 = 45$

45 is not even, but because $4 + 5 = 9$, we know that 3 is a factor: $45 \div 3 = 15$

3 is a factor of 15, giving a quotient of 5.

5 is a prime number, so we won't be able to divide and discover any new primes.

The prime factorization of 90 is the product of all of the prime divisors and the last prime (5).

So, the prime factorization of 90 is $2 \cdot 3 \cdot 3 \cdot 5$ or $2 \cdot 3^2 \cdot 5$.

$$\begin{array}{r|l} 2 & 90 \\ 3 & 45 \\ 3 & 15 \\ & 5 \end{array}$$

b) Because 189 is not even, let's see if 3 works: $1 + 8 + 9 = 18$. Yes. $189 \div 3 = 63$.

If the first number was not even, the next ones won't be either. Try 3 again.

Again, 3 is a factor of 21, giving a quotient of 7, a prime number:

The prime factorization of 189 is the product of all of the prime divisors and the last prime (7).

So, the prime factorization of 189 is $3 \cdot 3 \cdot 3 \cdot 7$ or $3^3 \cdot 7$.

$$\begin{array}{r|l} 3 & 189 \\ 3 & 63 \\ 3 & 21 \\ & 7 \end{array}$$

c) 240 is even, so the first prime divisor is 2: $240 \div 2 = 120$.

120 is also even, so we'll divide by 2 again: $120 \div 2 = 60$.

60 is even, so we divide by 2 again: $60 \div 2 = 30$.

30 is also even, so we divide by 2 again: $30 \div 2 = 15$.

Finally, no more even quotients; we know that 3 is a factor of 15, giving a quotient of 5, which is prime.

$$\begin{array}{r|l} 2 & 240 \\ 2 & 120 \\ 2 & 60 \\ 2 & 30 \\ 3 & 15 \\ & 5 \end{array}$$

The prime factorization of 240 is the product of all of the prime divisors and the last prime (5).

So, the prime factorization of 240 is $2 \cdot 2 \cdot 2 \cdot 2 \cdot 3 \cdot 5$ or $2^4 \cdot 3 \cdot 5$.

YOU TRY IT 5 *Find the prime factorization of the following. Use the division method outlined in Example 5.*

a) 24
24 = ______ or ______
(without exponents) or (with exponents)

b) 60
60 = ______ or ______
(without exponents) or (with exponents)

c) 175
175 = ______ or ______
(without exponents) or (with exponents)

d) 252
252 = ______ or ______
(without exponents) or (with exponents)

e) 405
405 = ______ or ______
(without exponents) or (with exponents)

f) 660
660 = ______ or ______
(without exponents) or (with exponents)

For additional practice with the division method, go back to YTI 3 and 4 and use the division method there. You will come up with the same prime factorizations if everything is done correctly.

You Try It Answers: Section 2.5

YTI 1 a) $3 \cdot 7$ b) $2 \cdot 11$ c) $5 \cdot 7$ d) $7 \cdot 11$

YTI 2 a) $2 \cdot 3 \cdot 7$ b) $2 \cdot 3 \cdot 3 \cdot 3$ c) $2 \cdot 5 \cdot 7$

YTI 3 a) $2 \cdot 2 \cdot 3 \cdot 3$ or $2^2 \cdot 3^2$
b) $2 \cdot 5 \cdot 5$ or $2 \cdot 5^2$

YTI 4 a) $2 \cdot 2 \cdot 5 \cdot 13$ b) $2 \cdot 2 \cdot 5 \cdot 7 \cdot 11$
$2^2 \cdot 5 \cdot 13$ $2^2 \cdot 5 \cdot 7 \cdot 11$

YTI 5 a) $2 \cdot 2 \cdot 2 \cdot 3$ b) $2 \cdot 2 \cdot 3 \cdot 5$
$2^3 \cdot 3$ $2^2 \cdot 3 \cdot 5$
c) $5 \cdot 5 \cdot 7$ d) $2 \cdot 2 \cdot 3 \cdot 3 \cdot 7$
$5^2 \cdot 7$ $2^2 \cdot 3^2 \cdot 7$
e) $3 \cdot 3 \cdot 3 \cdot 3 \cdot 5$ f) $2 \cdot 2 \cdot 3 \cdot 5 \cdot 11$
$3^4 \cdot 5$ $2^2 \cdot 3 \cdot 5 \cdot 11$

Focus Exercises: Section 2.5

Find the prime factorization of the following using a factor tree. Write the answers two ways: with and without exponents.

1. 18 **2.** 48 **3.** 63 **4.** 75
5. 105 **6.** 256 **7.** 496 **8.** 588
9. 720 **10.** 735 **11.** 945 **12.** 1,050

Find the prime factorization of the following using the division method. Write the answers two ways: with and without exponents.

13. 20 **14.** 45 **15.** 52 **16.** 72
17. 76 **18.** 88 **19.** 98 **20.** 111
21. 124 **22.** 135 **23.** 200 **24.** 224

Objectives

In this section, you will learn to:

- Find the Greatest Common Factor (GCF) of two numbers.
- Identify relatively prime numbers.

To successfully complete this section, you need to understand:

- Factors of numbers (2.4)
- Prime factorization (2.5)
- Division of whole numbers (1.5)

SECTION 2.6 Common Factors

Introduction

Thus far, we have looked at individual factors of a number as well as the prime factorization of a number. Next we to consider *common factors* of two numbers. The **common factors** of two numbers are all of the numbers that are factors of both numbers. To best understand what this means, we'll start with an example.

EXAMPLE 1 Find the common factors of 24 and 36.

PROCEDURE: Consider all of the factors of both 24 and 36, and then make a list of the factors that are common to both.

Factors of 24: 1, 2, 3, 4, 6, 8, 12, 24

Factors of 36: 1, 2, 3, 4, 6, 9, 12, 18, 36

ANSWER: Factors that are common to both 24 and 36: 1, 2, 3, 4, 6, 12

YOU TRY IT 1 *Find the common factors of 12 and 30. Use Example 1 as a guide.*

Factors of 12: ____________

Factors of 30: ____________

Factors that are common to both 12 and 30: ____________

Finding the Greatest Common Factor Using Prime Factorization

Refer back to Example 1. Clearly, the highest, or *greatest*, of the common factors of 24 and 36 is 12; so we say 12 is the **greatest common factor (GCF)** of 24 and 36.

It's difficult to make a list of common factors for every pair of numbers that may come along. Is there an easier way to find the GCF of two numbers?

There are actually several methods of finding the GCF of two numbers, but we will use only three. The first involves recognizing the prime factors of each number.

For example, if you were to find the common prime factors of 20 and 30, you could start by using the divisibility tests from Section 2.4. Ask yourself these questions:

(1) Is 2 a common factor of both 20 and 30? Yes, because they are both even numbers.

(2) Is 5 a common factor of both 20 and 30? Yes, because they both have 0 in the ones place.

(3) Is 3 a common factor of 20 and 30? No. Its a factor of 30 but not a factor of 20.

(4) Both 2 and 5 are common prime factors of 20 and 30. Is there a composite number that is a factor of both? Yes, 10 is a common factor (because $2 \cdot 5 = 10$).

Because 1 is a factor of every number, it is also a common factor of 20 and 30, so …

The common factors of 20 and 30 are 1, 2, 5 and 10.

So, as you can see, the GCF is 10.

Notice that, in finding the GCF, we look at common prime factors. The method we used in Section 2.5 for finding prime factors, prime factorization, is useful in recognizing common prime factors of two numbers.

Let's find the GCF of 20 and 30 using prime factorization.

EXAMPLE 2 Find the GCF of 20 and 30.

PROCEDURE: Find the prime factorization of each number, then look for common prime factors. Their product will be the GCF.

ANSWER:

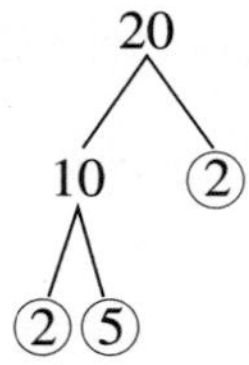

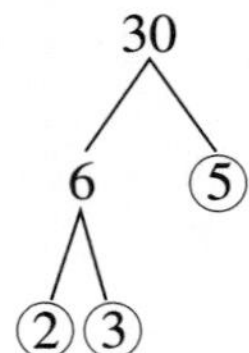

$20 = \mathbf{2} \cdot 2 \cdot \mathbf{5}$

$30 = \mathbf{2} \cdot 3 \cdot \mathbf{5}$

$\text{GCF} = \mathbf{2} \cdot \mathbf{5} = \boxed{10}$

Now, match up the common prime factors, 2 and 5. The GCF is the product of all of the common prime factors.

Notice that in the example above, in the prime factorization of 20, the second factor of 2 does not match up with any prime factors of 30; the factor of 2 (in 30) is already matched up with the first 2 (in 20) and is no longer available for matching.

Let's use prime factorization to find the GCF of 24 and 36. (We already found it to be 12 in Example 1.)

EXAMPLE 3 Find the greatest common factor of 36 and 24.

PROCEDURE: Find the prime factorization of each number:

ANSWER:

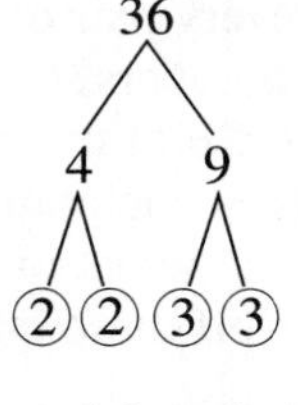

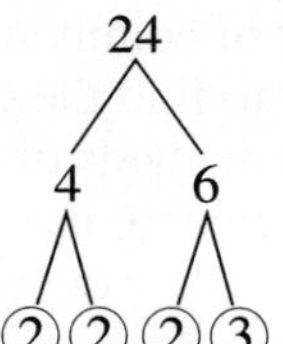

$36 = \mathbf{2} \cdot \mathbf{2} \cdot \mathbf{3} \cdot 3$

$24 = \mathbf{2} \cdot \mathbf{2} \cdot 2 \cdot \mathbf{3}$

$\text{GCF} = \mathbf{2} \cdot \mathbf{2} \cdot \mathbf{3} = \boxed{12}$

A lot of matches! Notice that when writing all of the matching prime factors for the GCF, we write only one prime number from each match; we do *not* write both numbers in the same match.

YOU TRY IT 2

Use prime factorization, as in Examples 2 and 3, to find the GCF of each pair of numbers.

a) 30 and 45   b) 24 and 40   c) 40 and 60

If the prime factorization of each number is written with exponents, then we can look for common bases to find matches for the GCF.

Consider, again, the GCF of 36 and 24. When we match up the common prime factors, we match up two 2's and one 3.

$$36 = 2 \cdot 2 \cdot 3 \cdot 3 = 2^2 \cdot 3^2$$

$$24 = 2 \cdot 2 \cdot 2 \cdot 3 = 2^3 \cdot 3^1$$

$$\text{GCF} = 2 \cdot 2 \cdot \quad 3 = 2^2 \cdot 3^1$$

Notice that the GCF has prime bases of 2 and 3. The exponents of the prime bases in the GCF are the *smallest* of the exponents of each matched pair.

EXAMPLE 4

Given the prime factorization of each pair of numbers, find the GCF.

a) $120 = 2^3 \cdot 3^1 \cdot 5^1$
$100 = 2^2 \cdot 5^2$

b) $60 = 2^2 \cdot 3^1 \cdot 5^1$
$252 = 2^2 \cdot 3^2 \cdot 7^1$

PROCEDURE: Match up prime bases and use the *smallest* exponent of each matched pair.

ANSWER:

a) The prime bases that match up are 2 and 5.
Of the matched bases of 2, the smallest exponent is ^{2};
of the matched bases of 5, the smallest exponent is ^{1}. $\underline{\text{GCF} = 2^2 \cdot 5^1 = 20.}$

b) The prime bases that match up are 2 and 3.
Of the matched bases of 2, the smallest exponent is ^{2} (they are the same);
of the matched bases of 3, the smallest exponent is ^{1}. $\underline{\text{GCF} = 2^2 \cdot 3^1 = 12.}$

YOU TRY IT 3

Given the prime factorization of each pair of numbers, find the GCF. Use Example 4 as a guide.

a) $18 = 2^1 \cdot 3^2$
$24 = 2^3 \cdot 3^1$

b) $40 = 2^3 \cdot 5^1$
$96 = 2^5 \cdot 3^1$

c) $280 = 2^3 \cdot 5^1 \cdot 7^1$
$700 = 2^2 \cdot 5^2 \cdot 7^1$

Relatively Prime Numbers

What if the two numbers have no prime factors in common? Not to worry, they still have a common factor that isn't prime: namely, 1. Consider the following:

Since 1 is a factor of every number, every pair of numbers will have at least one factor in common, 1. So, if two numbers have no *primes* in common, then their greatest common factor is 1.

When two numbers have no common *prime* factors we say that the two numbers are **relatively prime**. In this case, the GCF is 1.

The strange thing is, it's quite possible for two *composite* numbers to be relatively prime.

Even though two numbers, such as 14 and 15, are composite numbers, if they have no common factor other than 1, then we say that they are prime compared to (or relative to) each other; in other words, they are *relatively prime*.

EXAMPLE 5 List the common factors of 12 and 35. What is the GCF of 12 and 35?

ANSWER: The factors of 12 are 1, 2, 3, 4, 6, and 12.

The factors of 35 are 1, 5, 7, and 35.

Therefore, 12 and 35 have only 1 as a common factor (so 1 is the GCF). They are relatively prime.

Example 6 is the same as Example 5, but this time the prime factorization is shown.

EXAMPLE 6 Find the GCF of 12 and 35.

PROCEDURE: Find the prime factorization of each number:

ANSWER:

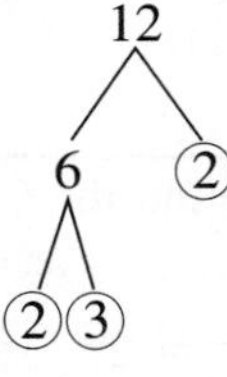

$12 = 2 \cdot 2 \cdot 3 = 2^2 \cdot 3^1$

No matches!

$35 = 5 \cdot 7 = 5^1 \cdot 7^1$

Since there are no prime factor matches, the GCF = 1. 12 and 35 are relatively prime.

YOU TRY IT 4 *For each pair of numbers, identify the GCF. See if you can do these in your head using the divisibility tests for 2, 3, and 5. If the numbers have no common prime factors, then the GCF is 1; write "relatively prime" underneath the numbers.*

a) 6 and 14 b) 9 and 16 c) 15 and 25

d) 12 and 25 e) 8 and 11 f) 18 and 21

Will two different primes numbers always be relatively prime to each other? Explain your answer.

____

____

The next example illustrates a point worth noting. Usually the GCF of two numbers is smaller than the numbers we start with; however, the GCF can actually be one of the numbers itself. The GCF cannot be larger than any of the numbers.

EXAMPLE 7 Find the GCF of 18 and 36.

PROCEDURE: Find the prime factorization of each number:

ANSWER:

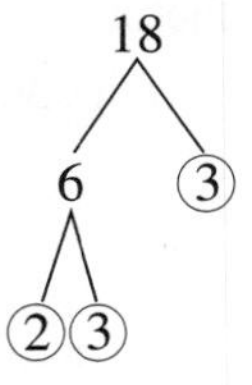

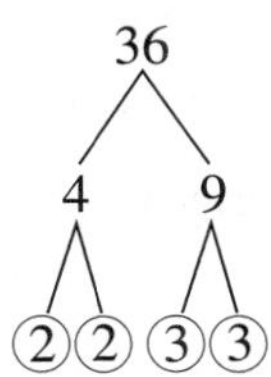

$18 = \mathbf{2 \cdot 3 \cdot 3}$

$36 = \mathbf{2} \cdot 2 \cdot \mathbf{3 \cdot 3}$

$\text{GCF} = \mathbf{2 \cdot 3 \cdot 3} = \mathbf{2^1 \cdot 3^2} = \boxed{\mathbf{18}}$ 18 is one of the numbers.

Example 7 shows us that if one number is a factor of another number, as 18 is a factor of 36, then the GCF of those two numbers will be the smaller of those two numbers.

YOU TRY IT 5

Use prime factorization to find the GCF of each pair of numbers.

a) 12 and 24 b) 16 and 21 c) 18 and 54 d) 35 and 54

Finding the Greatest Common Factor Using the Division Method

This next example—and guidelines—illustrate a different method for finding the GCF. The division method tackles the common factors one at a time without matching them up.

Guidelines for Finding the Greatest Common Factor Using the Division Method

1. Recognize an obvious common *prime* factor.
2. Divide both numbers by that common prime factor to get two quotients.
3. See if the quotients, themselves, have a common prime factor; if they do, divide these quotients by the common prime factor to get newer quotients. Repeat this process until the new quotients are relatively prime.
4. Make a list of all of the common prime factors found. The GCF is the product of all of the common prime factors.

This method is very similar to the division method used to find the prime factorization of a single number (Section 2.5). In this case, we're looking for common prime factors.

EXAMPLE 8 Find the GCF of 60 and 140.

PROCEDURE: Follow the steps outlined above. As in Section 2.5, we'll use an upside-down division symbol to assist us in the process.

ANSWER: Because both numbers are even, 2 is a common prime factor.

Divide both 60 and 140 by 2, then see if the quotients have a common prime factor.

$$\begin{array}{r|rr} 2 & 60 & 140 \\ \hline & 30 & 70 \end{array}$$

⇐ Original numbers

⇐ Quotients (new numbers)

Now find a common prime factor of 30 and 70; again, since they are even, 2 is a common prime factor; repeat the process.

$$\begin{array}{r|rr} 2 & 30 & 70 \\ \hline & 15 & 35 \end{array}$$

⇐ Divide again

⇐ Second pair of quotients

This time, 5 is a common factor:

$$\begin{array}{r|rr} 5 & 15 & 35 \\ \hline & 3 & 7 \end{array}$$

⇐ Divide again

⇐ Third pair of quotients

STOP! 3 and 7 are relatively prime.

Since the third pair of quotients, 3 and 7, have no common prime factors, this part is done. We next pick all the common prime factors (the numbers on the left side) and multiply them to find the GCF:

The common prime factors are 2, 2 and 5.

The GCF of 60 and 140 is $2 \cdot 2 \cdot 5 = 2^2 \cdot 5^1 = \boxed{20}$.

Example 9 shows the steps as you might write them.

EXAMPLE 9 Find the GCF of 54 and 90.

PROCEDURE: Here is the process for finding common factors in its entirety, from beginning to end.

ANSWER:

$$\begin{array}{lr|rr} \text{Prime divisor} \longrightarrow & \mathbf{2} & 54 & 90 \\ \hline \text{Prime divisor} \longrightarrow & \mathbf{3} & 27 & 45 \\ \hline \text{Prime divisor} \longrightarrow & \mathbf{3} & 9 & 15 \\ \hline & & 3 & 5 \end{array}$$

⇐ Divide 54 and 90 by 2.

⇐ Divide 27 and 45 by 3.

⇐ Divide 9 and 15 by 3.

⇐ STOP! 3 and 5 are relatively prime.

The GCF of 54 and 90 is $2 \cdot 3 \cdot 3 = 2^1 \cdot 3^2 = \boxed{18}$

YOU TRY IT 6 *Use the division method to find the GCF of the following pairs of numbers. Use Example 9 as a guide.*

a) 20 and 28 b) 12 and 36 c) 40 and 96

d) 48 and 72 e) 15 and 60 f) 36 and 54

When finding the GCF we don't need to find only common *prime* factors. We can find *any* common factor of the two numbers and start there.

EXAMPLE 10 Find the GCF of 150 and 240.

PROCEDURE: We'll start by finding an obvious common factor between the numbers and divide each by that factor, and so on.

An obvious common factor of 150 and 240 is 10, so we'll first divide by 10:

ANSWER:

10	150	240	⇐ Divide 150 and 240 by **10** (a composite factor).
3	15	24	⇐ Divide 15 and 24 by **3.**
	5	8	⇐ STOP! 5 and 8 are relatively prime.

The greatest common factor is still found by multiplying those two common factors (10 and 3) that were found: GCF $= 10 \cdot 3 = 30$.

EXAMPLE 11 Find the GCF of 21 and 77.

ANSWER: It turns out that these numbers have only one common prime factor.

7	21	77	⇐ Divide 21 and 77 by 7.
	3	11	⇐ STOP! 3 and 11 are relatively prime.

The GCF of 21 and 77 is 7.

EXAMPLE 12 Find the GCF of 25 and 36.

ANSWER: These numbers have no common prime factors; they are relatively prime. When this happens, there is only one answer. The only factor they could possibly have in common is the factor that every pair of numbers shares, namely, 1.

The GCF of 25 and 36 is 1. 25 and 36 are relatively prime.

YOU TRY IT 7 *Find the GCF of the following pairs of numbers. Use Examples 10, 11, and 12 as guides. Remember, you can divide by any obvious common factor, prime or composite; either way is fine.*

a) 80 and 120 b) 42 and 54 c) 150 and 240

d) 16 and 50 e) 56 and 70 f) 35 and 48

g) 55 and 99 h) 64 and 75 i) 28 and 49

You Try It Answers: Section 2.6

YTI 1 Factors of 12: 1, 2, 3, 4, 6, and 12 Factors of 30: 1, 2, 3, 5, 6, 10, 15, and 30
Factors that are common to both 12 and 30: 1, 2, 3, and 6

YTI 2 a) 15 b) 8 c) 20

YTI 3 a) 6 b) 8 c) 140

YTI 4 a) 2 (Both numbers are even.)
b) 1 (The numbers are relatively prime.)
c) 5 (Both numbers end in 5.)
d) 1 (The numbers are relatively prime.)
e) 1 (The numbers are relatively prime.)
f) 3 (Both numbers are divisible by 3.)

YTI 5 a) 12 b) 1 c) 18 d) 1

YTI 6 a) 4 b) 12 c) 8 d) 24
e) 15 f) 18

YTI 7 a) 40 b) 6 c) 30 d) 2
e) 14 f) 1 g) 11 h) 1
i) 7

Focus Exercises: Section 2.6

Use prime factorization to find the GCF of each pair of numbers. If the GCF is 1, write "relatively prime."

1. 15 and 30 **2.** 36 and 48 **3.** 49 and 110 **4.** 35 and 90

5. 30 and 42 **6.** 50 and 125 **7.** 48 and 120 **8.** 60 and 105

Given the prime factorization of each pair of numbers, find the GCF.

9. $108 = 2^2 \cdot 3^3$
$72 = 2^3 \cdot 3^2$

10. $150 = 2^1 \cdot 3^1 \cdot 5^2$
$168 = 2^3 \cdot 3^1 \cdot 7^1$

11. $120 = 2^3 \cdot 3^1 \cdot 5^1$
$180 = 2^2 \cdot 3^2 \cdot 5^1$

12. $525 = 3^1 \cdot 5^2 \cdot 7^1$
$270 = 2^1 \cdot 3^3 \cdot 5^1$

13. $315 = 3^2 \cdot 5^1 \cdot 7^1$
$378 = 2^1 \cdot 3^3 \cdot 7^1$

14. $440 = 2^3 \cdot 5^1 \cdot 11^1$
$1{,}100 = 2^2 \cdot 5^2 \cdot 11^1$

Use the division method to find the GCF of the following pairs of numbers.

15. 45 and 75 **16.** 40 and 72 **17.** 34 and 36 **18.** 50 and 70

19. 20 and 45 **20.** 16 and 24 **21.** 28 and 98 **22.** 42 and 105

23. 100 and 150 **24.** 21 and 32 **25.** 70 and 175 **26.** 105 and 135

27. 90 and 210 **28.** 42 and 154 **29.** 42 and 55 **30.** 120 and 840

31. 45 and 60 **32.** 60 and 96 **33.** 8 and 40 **34.** 24 and 72

35. 270 and 720 **36.** 96 and 144

Chapter 2 Review

Section 2.1 Exponents and Square Roots

CONCEPT	EXAMPLE
Exponents give us a way to abbreviate repeated multiplication using the powers of a whole number. In the notation 2^3, 2 is the **base**, and ^{3} is the **exponent** or **power**. The whole number 2 is raised to the power of 3.	2^3 represents the repeated multiplication $2 \cdot 2 \cdot 2$ and is read "2 to the third power."
The power of 1: If b represents any base, then $b^1 = b$.	$5^1 = 5$
The powers of 10: The exponent of 10 indicates the number of zeros that follows the 1.	10^5 is a 1 followed by five zeros: 100,000. 10,000 can be abbreviated as 10^4, the number of zeros indicating the power of 10.
A **perfect square** is a rectangle with equal side measures, and is a number. The number is equivalent to the area of the square. The **square root** of a perfect square is the length of one side of the square. If $r^2 = p$, then r is a **square root** of p. Also, if r is a square root of p, then $r^2 = p$.	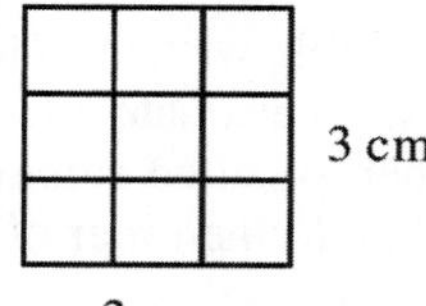 Area = 9 cm^2 A square root of 9 is 3. Because $3^2 = 9$, 3 is a square root of 9.
The square root symbol, a **radical** $\sqrt{}$, represents a square root of a number. The number within the radical is called the **radicand**.	$\sqrt{9} = 3$ 9 is the radicand.

Section 2.2 The Order of Operations

CONCEPT	EXAMPLE
Some grouping symbols form quantities.	( ), [ ], and { }
The radical is both a grouping symbol and an operation.	$\sqrt{25} + 10 = 5 + 10 = 15$

CONCEPT	EXAMPLE
The Order of Operations: 1. Evaluate within all grouping symbols (one at a time), if there are any. 2. Apply any exponents. 3. Apply multiplication and division, reading from left to right. 4. Apply addition and subtraction, reading from left to right.	$(3 + 9) \div 2^2 \cdot 3 - 2$ Evaluate within the parentheses. $= 12 \div 2^2 \cdot 3 - 2$ Apply the exponent. $= 12 \div 4 \cdot 3 - 2$ Apply division. $= 3 \cdot 3 - 2$ Apply multiplication. $= 9 - 2$ Apply subtraction. $= 7$

Section 2.3 Formulas

CONCEPT	EXAMPLE
A **formula** is one variable written in terms of one or more other variables. To evaluate a formula, we replace variables with numbers—called **replacement values**—and evaluate according to the order of operations. **Temperature conversion formulas:** $F = 9 \cdot (C \div 5) + 32$ F = Fahrenheit degrees $C = 5 \cdot (F - 32) \div 9$ C = Celsius degrees	Find the temperature in degrees Fahrenheit for 15° C. Find F when C = 15. Use the formula: $F = 9 \cdot (C \div 5) + 32$ $F = 9 \cdot (15 \div 5) + 32$ Divide. $F = 9 \cdot (3) + 32$ Multiply. $F = 27 + 32$ Add. $F = 59$ 15° C is equivalent to 59° F.
Distance, rate, and time formulas: 1. $d = r \cdot t$ (Distance = rate · time) 2. $r = d \div t$ (Rate = distance ÷ time) 3. $t = d \div r$ (Time = distance ÷ rate)	1. Find the distance traveled when the rate is 18 miles per hour and the time is 3 hours: Distance = 18 miles per hour × 3 hours = 54 miles. 2. Find the rate when the distance is 351 miles and the time is 9 hours: Rate = 351 miles ÷ 9 hours = 59 miles per hour. 3. Find the time when the distance is 85 miles and the rate is 17 miles per hour. Time = 85 miles ÷ 17 miles per hours = 5 hours.

Section 2.4 Factors

CONCEPT	EXAMPLE
A **factor pair** of a number is two factors whose product is the number.	One factor pair of 18 is 2 and 9 because $2 \cdot 9 = 18$. Other factor pairs of 18 are 1 and 18, and 3 and 6.
A whole number is a **prime** number if it has exactly two distinct, whole number factors: 1 and itself. The number 1 is not prime because it has only one factor, 1 itself.	The first ten prime numbers are 2, 3, 5, 7, 11, 13, 17, 19, 23, and 29.
A whole number that has more than two distinct factors is a **composite** number. A composite number is a whole number (greater than 1) that is not prime. The number 1 is neither prime nor composite.	The first ten composite numbers are 4, 6, 8, 9, 10, 12, 14, 15, 16, and 18.
Divisibility Test for 2: 2 is a factor of a whole number if and only if the number is even (it has either 0, 2, 4, 6, or 8 in the ones place).	2 is a factor of each of these numbers: 28, 46, 174, 382, and 590.
Divisibility Test for 5: 5 is a factor of a whole number if and only if the number has either 5 or 0 in the ones place.	5 is a factor of each of these numbers: 35, 70, 105, 230, and 775.
Divisibility Test for 10: 10 is a factor of a whole number if and only if the number has 0 in the ones place.	10 is a factor of each of these numbers: 70, 190, 230, and 900.
Divisibility Test for 3: 3 is a factor of a whole number if and only if the number's digits add to a multiple of 3.	3 is a factor of each of these numbers: 105 because $1 + 0 + 5 = 6$, a multiple of 3 264 because $2 + 6 + 4 = 12$, a multiple of 3
Divisibility Test for 9: 9 is a factor of a whole number if and only if the number's digits add to a multiple of 9.	9 is a factor of each of these numbers: 198 because $1 + 9 + 8 = 18$, a multiple of 9 999 because $9 + 9 + 9 = 27$, a multiple of 9
The Principle of Smaller Factors: If a number, *F*, is a **F**actor of a **L**arger number, *L*, then all of the smaller factors of *F* are also factors of *L*.	21 is a factor of 231. Because 7 and 3 are factors of 21, 7 and 3 are also factors of 231.
The Principle of Composite Factors: If two prime numbers, *P* and *N*, are factors of a larger number *L*, then the product of those prime numbers, $P \cdot N$, is a composite factor of *L*. This principle is also true when there are more than two prime factors.	7 and 3 are prime factors of 189, and $7 \cdot 3 = 21$, so 21 is also a factor of 189. 2, 3, and 5 are prime factors of 90, so $2 \cdot 3 = 6$, $2 \cdot 5 = 10$, $3 \cdot 5 = 15$, and $2 \cdot 3 \cdot 5 = 30$ are also factors of 90.

Section 2.5 Prime Factorization

CONCEPT	EXAMPLE
A **factor tree** shows composite and prime factors of a number. The **prime factorization** of a composite number is the product of the prime factors (including repetitions) of the number.	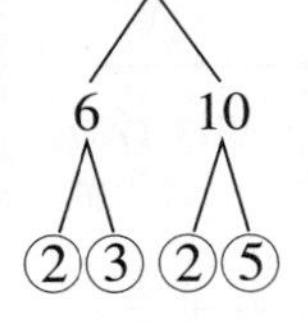 The prime factorization of 60: $60 = 2 \cdot 2 \cdot 3 \cdot 5$ $60 = 2^2 \cdot 3 \cdot 5$
The Division Method: Repeatedly divide by the lowest possible prime number, generating a new quotient each time. The divisibility tests will help determine which prime to use as a divisor. In the division method, the primes we divide by are called **prime divisors.** This process is complete when the new quotient is a prime number.	Find the prime factorization of 60: $60 \div 2 = 30$ 2 | 60 $30 \div 2 = 15$ 2 | 30 New quotient $15 \div 3 = 5$ 3 | 15 New quotient 5 New quotient The prime factorization of 60 is the product of all of the prime divisors and of the last prime (5). So, the prime factorization of 60 is $2 \cdot 2 \cdot 3 \cdot 5$ *or* $2^2 \cdot 3 \cdot 5$.

Section 2.6 Common Factors

CONCEPT	EXAMPLE
The **common factors** of two numbers are all of the numbers that are factors of both numbers. The **greatest common factor (GCF)** of two numbers is the highest, or greatest, of their common factors.	Common factors of 20 and 30: 1, 2, 5, 10 The GCF of 20 and 30: 10
If the only common factor is 1, then the numbers are called **relatively prime**, and the GCF is 1.	Factors of 15: 1, 3, 5 Factors of 16: 1, 2, 4, 8 15 and 16 are relatively prime.
Four methods of finding the GCF of two numbers: 1. List all of the factors of the two numbers, identify which factors are common to both, and then identify which is the greatest of the common factors. 2. Find the prime factorization of each number and match up all common prime factors. 3. Write the prime factorizations with exponents, match common bases, and use the least (smallest) exponent of each common base. 4. Use the division method and divide by common factors (prime or composite) until the quotients are relatively prime.	1. Find the GCF of 54 and 72. Factors of 54: 1, 2, 3, 6, 9, 18, 27, 54 Factors of 72: 1, 2, 3, 4, 6, 8, 9, 12, 18, 24, 36, 72 GCF = 18 2. $72 = 2 \cdot 2 \cdot 2 \cdot 3 \cdot 3$ $54 = 2 \cdot 3 \cdot 3 \cdot 3$ $\text{GCF} = 2 \cdot 3 \cdot 3 = 18$ 3. $72 = 2^3 \cdot 3^2$ $54 = 2^1 \cdot 3^3$ $\text{GCF} = 2^1 \cdot 3^2 = 18$ 4. **2** | 54 72 Divide by 2. **3** | 27 36 Divide by 3. **3** | 9 12 Divide by 3. 3 4 STOP! 3 and 4 are relatively prime.

Chapter 2 Review Exercises

Section 2.1

Expand each and find its value.

1. 1^6 **2.** 2^4 **3.** 3^5 **4.** 4^3

5. 16^1 **6.** 17^2 **7.** 20^3 **8.** 10^7

Express each as a power of 10.

9. 1,000 **10.** 10,000,000 **11.** 100,000 **12.** 10

Rewrite each number as a product using the power of 10 as a factor.

13. 70 **14.** 8,400 **15.** 300,000 **16.** 1,200,000

Evaluate the following square roots.

17. $\sqrt{36}$ **18.** $\sqrt{4}$ **19.** $\sqrt{9}$ **20.** $\sqrt{100}$

Section 2.2

Evaluate each according to the order of operations. Simplify just one step, one operation at a time. Show all work.

21. $3 \cdot 5 - 1$ **22.** $3 \cdot (5 - 1)$ **23.** $(18 - 4) \div 2$ **24.** $18 - 4 \div 2$

25. $54 \div 3^2$ **26.** $2^3 - 2^2$ **27.** $2^3 + 3^2$ **28.** $6^2 - 5 \cdot 3$

29. $8 \div 2^2 + 7$ **30.** $(8 \div 2)^2 + 7$ **31.** $4^2 \cdot 2 - 2$ **32.** $4^2 \cdot (2 - 2)$

33. $(6 - 2) \cdot (12 \div 3)$ **34.** $12 - 30 \div (6 + 4)$ **35.** $24 \div 3 \cdot 4 - 2$ **36.** $24 \div 3 \cdot (4 - 2)$

37. $13 - \sqrt{16}$ **38.** $\sqrt{36} \div 2$ **39.** $\sqrt{4^2 + 9}$ **40.** $\sqrt{3 \cdot 20 + 4}$

Section 2.3

Find the equivalent temperature in either Celsius or Fahrenheit.

$$F = 9 \cdot (C \div 5) + 32 \qquad C = 5 \cdot [(F - 32) \div 9]$$

41. The temperature is 100° C. **42.** The temperature is 15° C.

43. The temperature is 122° F. **44.** The temperature is 77° F.

Evaluate the numerical value of each formula with the given replacement values.

45. $A = (a + b) \div 2$ $a = 77$, $b = 91$

46. $W = A \div L$ $A = 192$, $L = 12$

47. $A = h \cdot (b + c) \div 2$ $h = 5$, $b = 6$, $c = 4$

48. $z = (x - m) \div s$ $x = 53$, $m = 45$, $s = 4$

49. $a = \sqrt{c^2 - b^2}$ $c = 13$, $b = 12$

50. $C = 2 \cdot W \div E^2$ $W = 12$, $E = 2$

Use one of the distance formulas to answer the following.

$$\text{rate} = \frac{\text{distance}}{\text{time}}, \quad \text{time} = \frac{\text{distance}}{\text{rate}}, \quad \text{distance} = \text{rate} \cdot \text{time}$$

51. It took Tracey 4 hours to ride her bike 52 miles to the beach. What was her average rate of speed?

52. When Timara pilots her plane, she usually averages 145 miles per hour. How far can she fly in 6 hours?

53. Charles is planning to drive his car 495 miles from Charleston, West Virginia to Charleston, South Carolina to visit his sisters, Virginia and Caroline. If he is able to average 55 miles per hour, how much time will it take him to get there?

54. Pepito entered his pet snail, Peetey, in a race. The straight race course was 87 cm long and Peetey finished in 3 minutes. What was Peetey's average rate of speed?

Section 2.4

List the first five multiples of each of the following.

55. 3 **56.** 6 **57.** 11 **58.** 12

Use a factor pair table to find all of the factor pairs of the following:

59. 18 **60.** 36 **61.** 45 **62.** 60

Of the following, determine which are prime, which are composite, and which are neither.

63. 15, 17, 29, 0, 81, 45, 11

Prime: ____________

Composite: ____________

Neither: ____________

64. 2, 61, 70, 43, 62, 1, 31, 57

Prime: ____________

Composite: ____________

Neither: ____________

Of the first three prime numbers—2, 3, and 5—which are factors of the following? Use the divisibility tests for 2, 3, and 5.

65. 75 **66.** 91 **67.** 112 **68.** 120

69. 147 **70.** 230 **71.** 625 **72.** 1,782

Determine if 9 is a factor of each number. Verify your answer by dividing each number by 9.

73. 171 **74.** 5,292 **75.** 6,708 **76.** 17,451

Use the Principle of Composite Factors to complete each sentence.

77. Because 3 and 13 are both prime factors of 741, it must be true that …

78. Because 5 and 7 are both prime factors of 1,470, it must be true that …

Section 2.5

Find the prime factorization of the following. Write the answer two ways: with and without exponents.

79. 16 **80.** 44 **81.** 50 **82.** 96

83. 125 **84.** 180 **85.** 325 **86.** 1,225

Section 2.6

Find the GCF of each pair of numbers. If the GCF is 1, write "relatively prime." You may use any method.

87. 15 and 20 **88.** 40 and 48 **89.** 14 and 56 **90.** 36 and 90

91. 35 and 48 **92.** 54 and 96 **93.** 60 and 84 **94.** 75 and 105

95. 90 and 120 **96.** 96 and 72 **97.** 45 and 135 **98.** 81 and 110

Given the prime factorization of each pair of numbers, find their GCF.

99. $40 = 2^3 \cdot 5^1$
$84 = 2^2 \cdot 3^1 \cdot 7^1$

100. $525 = 3^1 \cdot 5^2 \cdot 7^1$
$450 = 2^1 \cdot 3^2 \cdot 5^2$

101. $882 = 2^1 \cdot 3^2 \cdot 7^2$
$252 = 2^2 \cdot 3^2 \cdot 7^1$

Chapter 2 Test

Expand each and find its value.

1. 5^3 **2.** 20^2

Rewrite the number as a product using a power of 10 as a factor.

3. 740,000 **4.** 900

Evaluate the following square roots.

5. $\sqrt{16}$ **6.** $\sqrt{81}$

Evaluate each according to the order of operations. Show all work.

7. $36 \div 4 \cdot 3$ **8.** $2 \cdot 3^2 - 1$ **9.** $2 \cdot (4 + 1)^2$

Find the equivalent temperature in Fahrenheit using this formula: $F = 9 \cdot (C \div 5) + 32$

10. The temperature is 95° C.

Find the equivalent temperature in either Celsius using this formula: $C = 5 \cdot [(F - 32) \div 9]$

11. The temperature is 95° F

Evaluate the numerical value of the formula with the given replacement values.

12. $A = h \cdot (b + c) \div 2$ $h = 8$
$b = 3$
$c = 4$

Use one of the distance formulas to answer the following.

$$r = \frac{d}{t}, \quad t = \frac{d}{r}, \quad d = r \cdot t$$

13. If Rogelio averages 65 miles per hour riding his motorcycle 455 miles from Albuquerque to Denver, how many hours will it take him to get there?

Of the following, determine which are prime, which are composite, and which are neither.

14. 41, 77, 38, 19, 2, 1

Prime: ____________________

Composite: ____________________

Neither: ____________________

Of the first three prime numbers—2, 3, and 5—which are factors of the following?

15. 135 ______

16. 84 ______

17. 149 ______

18. 172 ______

Find the prime factorization of the following. Write the answer two ways: with and without exponents.

19. 84

20. 80

21. 540

Find the GCF of each pair of numbers. If the GCF is 1, write "relatively prime." You may use any method.

22. 16 and 24

23. 27 and 45

24. 70 and 112

Chapters 1 and 2 Cumulative Review

1. Write the value 7 represents in 876,153.

2. Write 500,026 in words.

Round each number to the nearest hundred.

3. 548

4. 7,952

Round each number to the nearest thousand.

5. 8,489

6. 209,607

Which property is being demonstrated?

7. $43 \cdot 6 = 6 \cdot 43$

8. $14 + 0 = 14$

9. $7 \cdot (5 + 8) = 7 \cdot 5 + 7 \cdot 8$

10. $(8 + 5) + 9 = 8 + (5 + 9)$

Align each, then add.

11. 2,549 + 487

12. 1,908 + 93

Align each, then subtract.

13. 1,548 − 673

14. 10,000 − 571

15. Find the perimeter of this figure.

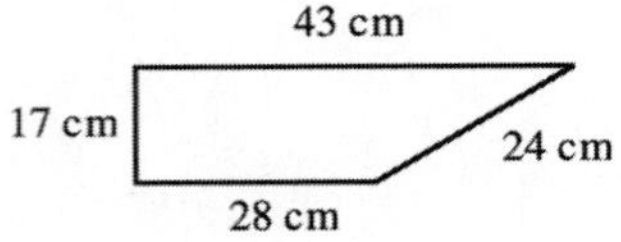

16. Find the perimeter of this rectangle.

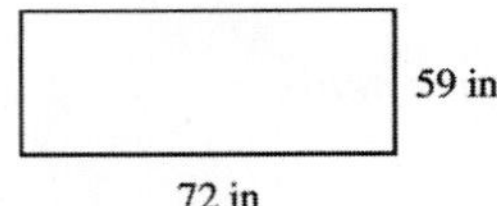

17. Find the area of this rectangle.

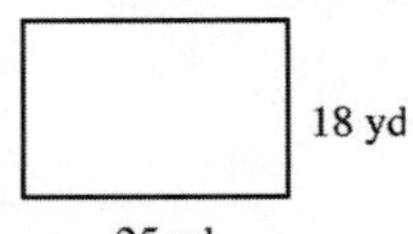

18. In 2000, during the presidential elections, Connecticut voters chose Al Gore—with 816,015 votes—over George W. Bush—with 561,094 votes. How many more votes did Gore receive than Bush?

Source: www.infoplease.com

Multiply.

19. $80 \cdot 700$

20. $165 \cdot 28$

Divide.

21. $379 \div 8$

22. $1{,}456 \div 28$

Work each application and answer it with a complete sentence.

23. Lydia photocopied a packet—containing 34 pages of information—for each of the 15 members attending the annual board meeting. How many pages in total were photocopied?

24. Citrus Hills High School purchased a total of 540 white board markers to be used throughout the semester by 45 teachers. If the markers were evenly distributed to the teachers, how many did each receive?

Solve the following by isolating the variable. Check the answer to show that it is the solution.

25. $n + 45 = 72$

26. $455 = 13 \cdot n$

Work each application and answer it with a complete sentence.

27. Ben and Adrian decided to have a garage sale. Their goal is to raise $500. On Friday, they raised $138. On Saturday, they raised $249. How much do Ben and Adrian need to raise on Sunday to meet their goal?

28. At Amaya's slumber party, a bucket of Red Vines (red licorice) was divided evenly among the 7 girls. If the bucket had 245 Red Vines in it, how many did each girl receive?

Expand each and find its value.

29. 9^3

30. 5^4

Express each as a power of 10.

31. 10,000

32. 1,000,000,000

Rewrite the number as a product using the power of 10 as a factor.

33. 60,000

34. 5,200,000

Evaluate the following square roots.

35. $\sqrt{64}$

36. $\sqrt{121}$

Evaluate each according to the order of operations. Show all work.

37. $36 \div 3^2 + 3$

38. $(36 \div 3)^2 + 3$

39. $\sqrt{36 + 4 \cdot 7}$

40. $\sqrt{36} + 4 \cdot 7$

Find the equivalent temperature in either Celsius or Fahrenheit.

$$F = 9 \cdot (C \div 5) + 32 \qquad C = 5 \cdot [(F - 32) \div 9]$$

41. The temperature is 60° C.

42. The temperature is 113° F.

Evaluate the numerical value of each formula with the given replacement values.

43. $a = \sqrt{c^2 - b^2}$ $\quad c = 10$, $b = 8$

44. $C = 2 \cdot A \div h - b$ $\quad A = 15$, $h = 5$, $b = 2$

Use one of the distance formulas to answer the following. Remember,

$$d = r \cdot t, \quad r = \frac{d}{t}, \text{ and } t = \frac{d}{r}.$$

45. James is a pilot for United Airlines. Recently, it took him 6 hours to fly from Los Angeles to Boston, a 2,610 mile flight. What was the jet's average speed for that flight?

46. Jasper races stock cars. One race in Santa Fe, New Mexico, is a timed race where the racers drive for 3 hours. If Jasper can average 95 miles per hour, how far will he go in that race?

Of the following, determine which are prime, which are composite, and which are neither.

47. 5, 18, 31, 1, 43, 55

Prime: ______________________

Composite: ________________

Neither: ____________________

Of the first three prime numbers—2, 3, and 5—which are factors of the following? Use the divisibility tests for 2, 3, and 5.

48. 150

49. 197

50. 282

51. 765

Determine if 9 is a factor of each number. Verify the answer by dividing each number by 9.

52. 171

53. 5,292

Use the Principle of Composite Factors to finish the sentence.

54. Since 2 and 17 are both prime factors of 816, it must be true that.

Find the prime factorization of the following. Write the answer two ways: with and without exponents.

55. 168

56. 300

Find the GCF of each pair of numbers.

57. 48 and 64

58. 63 and 105

CHAPTER 3

Fractions: Multiplication and Division

Introduction

We use fractions in a variety of occupations and hobbies, some of which might be obvious and some of which you might find surprising. People use fractions on the job—in construction, in the printing industry, in the fashion industry, and in machine repair, to name just a few examples. We also use fractions at home, while cooking, sewing, wood working, and doing home repair. The lists go on and on. Understanding how to work with fractions quickly and effortlessly makes each of these jobs or tasks easier to perform. Understanding fractions can make an employee more efficient, more productive, and more valuable to the employer.

Chapter 3 focuses on multiplying, dividing, and simplifying fractions. Chapter 4 focuses on adding and subtracting fractions. Later in the text we'll see the connections between fractions, decimals, and percents.

Preparation Exercises

Section 1.2, Definitions and Properties: *Fill in the blank.*

1. $15 \times 1 = \_$ **2.** $6 \times \_ = 6$ **3.** $\_ \times 1 = 12$

Section 1.4, Multiplying Whole Numbers: *Multiply.*

4. $6 \cdot 4$ **5.** $8 \cdot 3$ **6.** $4 \cdot 9$ **7.** $6 \cdot 6$

8. $4 \cdot 10$ **9.** $8 \cdot 5$ **10.** $4 \cdot 15$ **11.** $5 \cdot 12$

Section 1.5, Dividing Whole Numbers: *Divide.*

12. $72 \div 4$ **13.** $90 \div 5$ **14.** $42 \div 3$ **15.** $38 \div 2$

Section 1.6, Equations: *Solve by isolating the variable.*

16. $n \cdot 15 = 90$ **17.** $8 \cdot n = 96$ **18.** $54 = 3 \cdot n$

Section 2.2, The Order of Operations: *Evaluate.*

19. $7 + 5 \cdot 3$ **20.** $40 \div 4 \cdot 2$ **21.** $24 \div (8 - 6)$

Section 2.6, Common Factors: *Find the greatest common factor of the two numbers.*

22. 25 and 45 **23.** 24 and 40 **24.** 18 and 36

SECTION 3.1 Introduction to Fractions

Objectives

In this section, you will learn to:

- Identify the numerator and denominator of a fraction.
- Rewrite fractions as division.
- Identify proper fractions, improper fractions, mixed numbers, and complex fractions.
- Write mixed numbers as improper fractions and improper fractions as mixed numbers.
- Use the principles of fractions to evaluate fractions and expressions.
- Identify a unit fraction.

To successfully complete this section, you need to understand:

- The multiplication table (1.4)
- Long division (1.5)

Introduction

A **fraction** is, typically, the comparison of a part of something to its whole, where all of the parts are the same size. For example, a whole week has 7 days, and each day is one-seventh—one equal part—of the week. The weekend includes two of those days, so the weekend is *two-sevenths* of the week.

It is common to express a fraction such as two-sevenths as $\frac{2}{7}$.

Let's take a look at visual representations of some fractions. Each fraction represented below (except for diagram d) is based on $\frac{\textbf{part}}{\textbf{whole}}$, where part of the whole has been shaded. On the small ruler in part d), the whole is represented by 1 inch and the fractions shown are parts of an inch.

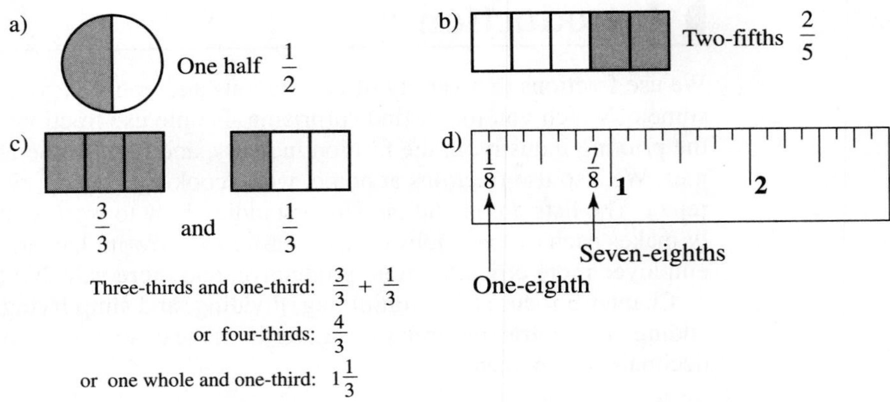

Think about it

Even though one part of two is shaded, does the diagram below represent $\frac{1}{2}$? Explain your answer.

____

____

The Vocabulary of Fractions

> To remember which is the denominator, think that "D" is the first letter of both **D**own and **D**enominator. Once you know which component is the denominator, then the other must be the numerator.

A fraction consists of three components: a **fraction bar**, a number above the fraction bar, and a number below the fraction bar. The number above the fraction bar is called the *numerator*, and the number below is called the *denominator*.

$$\frac{\text{numerator}}{\text{denominator}} \quad \leftarrow \text{the fraction bar}$$

The **numerator** represents the number of equal-sized parts being considered and the **denominator** represents the number of equal-sized parts contained in the whole.

EXAMPLE 1

For the fraction $\frac{5}{7}$, identify the numerator and the denominator.

ANSWER: Numerator: 5 Denominator: 7

YOU TRY IT 1

For each fraction, identify the numerator and the denominator. Use Example 1 as a guide.

a) $\frac{8}{3}$ Numerator:__ Denominator:__

b) $\frac{1}{2}$ Numerator:__ Denominator:__

c) $\frac{0}{5}$ Numerator:__ Denominator:__

YOU TRY IT 2

Write the fraction with the given numerator and denominator. Read each carefully.

a) The numerator is 3, the denominator is 14 b) The numerator is 10, the denominator is 7

c) The denominator is 4, the numerator is 6 d) The denominator is 5, the numerator is 18

Fractions as Division

Fractional notation is another way to indicate the operation of division. For example, $\frac{8}{2}$ can also be written $8 \div 2$. Sometimes the fraction bar is referred to as the division bar.

EXAMPLE 2

Rewrite $\frac{12}{4}$ as a numerical expression with division, and evaluate the expression

ANSWER: $\frac{12}{4} = \underline{12 \div 4} = \underline{3}$

YOU TRY IT 3

Rewrite each fraction as a numerical expression with division, and evaluate the expression. Use Example 2 as a guide.

a) $\frac{20}{4} =$ ________ = ________ b) $\frac{18}{2} =$ ________ = ________

Recall from Section 1.5 the circular (inverse) nature of division and multiplication. In fractional form we can see it as:

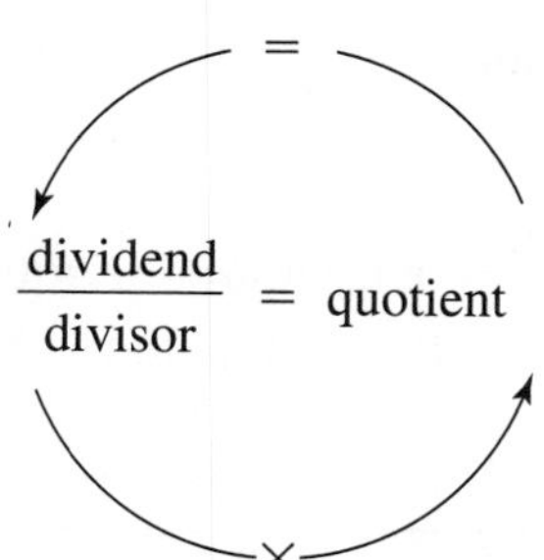

divisor × quotient = divident

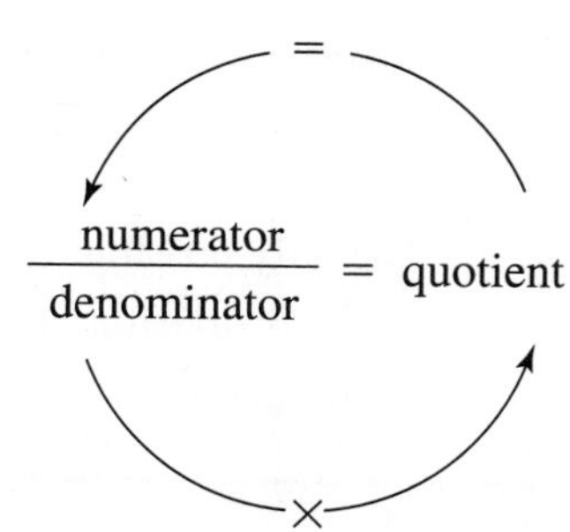

denominator × quotient = numerator

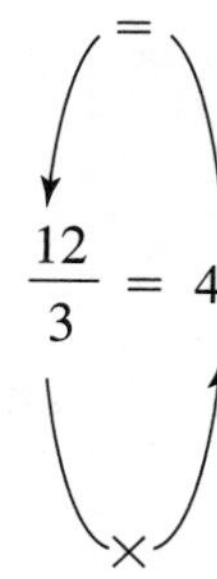

$3 \times 4 = 12$

EXAMPLE 3

Rewrite each division problem as a multiplication problem.

a) $\frac{16}{8} = 2$ $\underline{8 \cdot 2 = 16}$ = b) $\frac{15}{3} = 5$ $\underline{3 \cdot 5 = 15}$

YOU TRY IT 4

Rewrite each division problem as a multiplication problem. Use Example 3 as a guide.

a) $\frac{20}{4} = 5$ ________ b) $\frac{18}{6} = 3$ ________ c) $\frac{35}{5} = 7$ ________

Question: Is there any number that we can write in each box that will make the division and the multiplication true?

(a) $\frac{0}{6} = \square$ $\quad 6 \times \square = 0$ (b) $\frac{4}{0} = \square$ $\quad 0 \times \square = 4$

Answer: For (a), the answer is yes, and the number is 0. For (b), the answer is no: no number times 0 will be 4, since 0 times any number is 0. Thus, $\frac{4}{0}$ doesn't equal any number.

Part (a) shows us that the numerator can be 0, but part (b) shows us that the *denominator may never be 0.* This is consistent with what we learned in Section 1.5: we may never divide by 0.

If you were to use a calculator to evaluate $\frac{4}{0}$ (treating it as $4 \div 0$), you'd get an error message in the display; this means that there is an error in that division, there is no such value. As a fraction, we say that $\frac{4}{0}$ is **undefined**.

Division by Zero

If a stands for *any number*, then $\boldsymbol{a \div 0}$, or $\boldsymbol{\frac{a}{0}}$, is ***undefined***.

Another way to express this is:

the denominator of a fraction can never be zero.

Question: What about the numerator of a fraction? Can it be zero?

We use the equal sign with a slash through it, $\neq$, to represent *is not equal to.* We can express a fraction as $\frac{a}{b}$, $b \neq 0$.

Answer: If we rewrite the fraction $\frac{0}{6} = \boxed{?}$ as a multiplication, it becomes $6 \times \boxed{?} = 0$.

The only possible number for $\boxed{?}$ is 0; try it: $6 \times 0 = 0$, If we treat the fraction $\frac{0}{6}$ as division, it becomes $0 \div 6$. If you were to try this on a calculator you would get 0.

Zero as a Numerator, if $\boldsymbol{a}$ is any number *(except 0)*, then $\boldsymbol{\frac{0}{a} = 0}$.

Think about it

Why does it say "except 0" in the box above? What is another way to write *except 0*?

____

____

Types of Fractions

Let's classify the types of fractions you will work with in this chapter.

A **proper fraction** has a numerator that is *less* than the denominator.

$\frac{1}{7}, \frac{2}{3}, \frac{6}{11}$, and $\frac{23}{24}$ are all examples of proper fractions.

1 is less than 7, 2 is less than 3, 6 is less than 11, and 23 is less than 24.

An **improper fraction** has a numerator that is *equal to* or *greater than* the denominator.

$\frac{7}{7}, \frac{5}{3}, \frac{22}{11}$, and $\frac{24}{24}$ are all examples of improper fractions.

7 is equal to 7, 5 is greater than 3, 22 is greater than 11, and 24 is equal to 24.

A **mixed number** is the *sum* of a whole number and a fraction.

$1\frac{3}{8}$ and $4\frac{1}{5}$ are examples of mixed numbers: $1\frac{3}{8} = 1 + \frac{3}{8}$ and $4\frac{1}{5} = 4 + \frac{1}{5}$

We can say that a mixed number has a whole number part and a fractional part.

A **complex fraction** is a fraction in which either the numerator or denominator (or both) contains a fraction.

$\dfrac{\frac{7}{5}}{2}, \dfrac{1}{\frac{2}{3}}$, and $\dfrac{\frac{2}{5}}{\frac{3}{4}}$ are all examples of complex fractions.

YOU TRY IT 5

Identify each as either a proper fraction, an improper fraction, a mixed number, or a complex fraction.

a) $\frac{5}{8}$ ____________________ b) $\dfrac{1}{\frac{2}{3}}$ ____________________

c) $\frac{13}{4}$ ____________________ d) $5\frac{3}{4}$ ____________________

e) $\frac{3}{3}$ ____________________

Writing Mixed Numbers as Improper Fractions

Recall that two numbers are equivalent when they have the same value. We can write the mixed number $1\frac{2}{3}$ as an improper fraction, $\frac{5}{3}$, so $1\frac{2}{3}$ is equivalent to $\frac{5}{3}$. To see why, let's look at some visual representations of these numbers.

1 + $\frac{2}{3}$

3 thirds and 2 more thirds = 5 thirds: $\frac{5}{3}$, an improper fraction

A mixed number is the sum of a whole number and a fraction. As a sum, $1\frac{2}{3}$ could be written as $1 + \frac{2}{3}$ and be represented by the diagram on the right:

At the same time, recognizing that each shaded rectangle represents one third, we can count up the number of thirds that we see; we get 5 thirds.

This suggests that $1\frac{2}{3}$ is equivalent to $\frac{5}{3}$.

To write a mixed number as an improper fraction, we need to recognize that the whole number 1 can represent a full (complete) set of the fractional part.

For example, if the fractional part is in thirds, then

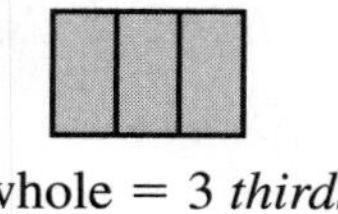

1 whole = 3 *thirds*

$\underline{1 \times 3}$ *thirds*

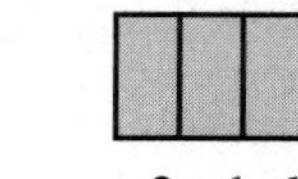

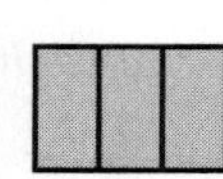

2 whole = 6 *thirds*

$\underline{2 \times 3}$ *thirds*

So, $1\frac{2}{3}$ = 1 whole + 2 thirds
= 1 × 3 thirds + 2 thirds
= 3 thirds + 2 thirds
= 5 thirds

$$1\frac{2}{3} = \frac{5}{3}$$

So, $2\frac{1}{3}$ = 2 wholes + 1 third
= 2 × 3 thirds + 1 third
= 6 thirds + 1 third
= 7 thirds

$$2\frac{1}{3} = \frac{7}{3}$$

Writing a Mixed Number as an Improper Fraction

Every mixed number can be written as an improper fraction according to this conversion formula:

$$\text{Whole} + \frac{\text{numerator}}{\text{denominator}} = \frac{\text{Whole} \times \text{denominator} + \text{numerator}}{\text{denominator}}$$

EXAMPLE 4 Write each mixed number as an improper fraction using the conversion formula.

a) $1\frac{2}{3}$ b) $2\frac{1}{3}$

ANSWER: Check with the results on the previous page to verify that these are accurate.

a) $1\frac{2}{3} = \frac{1 \times 3 + 2}{3} = \frac{3 + 2}{3} = \frac{5}{3}$

b) $2\frac{1}{3} = \frac{2 \times 3 + 1}{3} = \frac{6 + 1}{3} = \frac{7}{3}$

EXAMPLE 5 Write each mixed number as an improper fraction using the conversion formula.

a) $4\frac{7}{9}$ b) $9\frac{3}{10}$ c) $12\frac{1}{5}$

ANSWER:

a) $4\frac{7}{9} = \frac{4 \times 9 + 7}{9} = \frac{36 + 7}{9} = \frac{43}{9}$

b) $9\frac{3}{10} = \frac{9 \times 10 + 3}{10} = \frac{90 + 3}{10} = \frac{93}{10}$

c) $12\frac{1}{5} = \frac{12 \times 5 + 1}{5} = \frac{60 + 1}{5} = \frac{61}{5}$

YOU TRY IT 6 *Write each mixed number as an improper fraction. Use Examples 4 and 5 as guides.*

a) $2\frac{3}{8}$ b) $9\frac{5}{6}$ c) $11\frac{1}{7}$

Writing Improper Fractions as Mixed Numbers

Let's look again at fractions and division. We have seen that, for example, the improper fraction $\frac{45}{5}$ means $45 \div 5$. As you know, 5 divides evenly into 45 and we get $45 \div 5 = 9$.

There are other improper fractions where the denominator does not divide evenly into the numerator, such as $\frac{45}{7}$. In this case, when we divide we'll get a remainder:

$$\begin{array}{r} 6 \text{ r } 3 \\ 7\overline{)45} \\ -\,42 \\ \hline 3 \end{array}$$

This shows us that 7 divides into 45 six whole times with a remainder of 3.

The remainder is a *part* of the whole, not an entire whole; in other words, the remainder is a fractional part of the whole, and we can write the answer as a mixed number, $6\frac{3}{7}$.

Here's a conversion diagram from improper fraction (as long division) to mixed number:

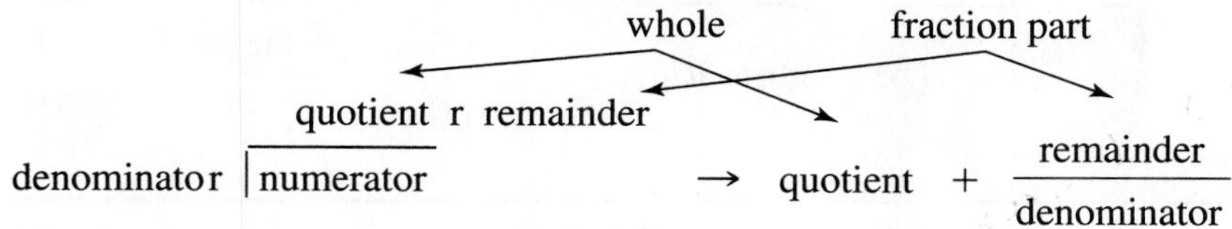

EXAMPLE 6 Write each improper fraction as a mixed number using long division.

a) $\frac{21}{4}$ b) $\frac{38}{5}$ c) $\frac{74}{3}$

PROCEDURE:

a) $\begin{array}{r} 5 \text{ r } 1 \\ 4\overline{)21} \\ -\,20 \\ \hline 1 \end{array}$ b) $\begin{array}{r} 7 \text{ r } 3 \\ 5\overline{)38} \\ -\,35 \\ \hline 3 \end{array}$ c) $\begin{array}{r} 24 \text{ r } 2 \\ 3\overline{)74} \\ -\,6 \\ \hline 14 \\ -\,12 \\ \hline 2 \end{array}$

ANSWER: So, $\frac{21}{4} = 5\frac{1}{4}$ $\frac{38}{5} = 7\frac{3}{5}$ $\frac{74}{3} = 24\frac{2}{3}$

YOU TRY IT 7 *Write each improper fraction as a mixed number. Use Example 6 as a guide.*

a) $\frac{43}{8}$ b) $\frac{25}{6}$ c) $\frac{95}{7}$

The Principles of Fractions

There are certain principles of numbers—first introduced in Chapter 1—that we can now apply to fractions.

1. Recall from Section 1.2, the *multiplicative identity* is 1 because $a \cdot 1 = a$, no matter the value of a.

   For example, $7 \cdot 1 = 7$ and $\frac{3}{10} \cdot 1 = \frac{3}{10}$. Multiplying by 1 doesn't change the value.

2. Recall from Section 1.5 that a natural number divided by itself is 1: $a \div a = 1$.

   For example, $5 \div 5 = 1$. In fraction form $\frac{5}{5} = 1$. $\frac{a}{a} = 1, a \neq 0$.

3. Recall also from Section 1.5 that a number divided by 1 is itself. $a \div 1 = a$.

   For example, $9 \div 1 = 9$. In fraction form $\frac{9}{1} = 9$. $\frac{a}{1} = a$.

YOU TRY IT 8

Evaluate the following.

a) $\frac{9}{9} =$ ____ b) $\frac{6}{1} =$ ____ c) $\frac{3}{5} \cdot 1 =$ ____

A principle new to this section is the **product rule** for multiplying fractions.

> The **Product Rule:** $\frac{a}{b} \cdot \frac{c}{d} = \frac{a \cdot c}{b \cdot d} = \frac{\text{the product of the numerators}}{\text{the product of the denominators}}$

EXAMPLE 7

Multiply the following using the product rule. If the answer is an improper fraction, then write it as a mixed number.

a) $\frac{5}{7} \cdot \frac{2}{3}$ b) $\frac{3}{2} \cdot \frac{5}{4}$ c) $\frac{2}{5} \cdot \frac{3}{3}$ d) $\frac{7}{7} \cdot \frac{8}{3}$

PROCEDURE: Multiply the numerators and multiply the denominators to result in one new fraction.

ANSWER:

a) $\frac{5}{7} \cdot \frac{2}{3} = \frac{5 \cdot 2}{7 \cdot 3} = \frac{10}{21}$ b) $\frac{3}{2} \cdot \frac{5}{4} = \frac{3 \cdot 5}{2 \cdot 4} = \frac{15}{8} = 1\frac{7}{8}$

c) $\frac{2}{5} \cdot \frac{3}{3} = \frac{2 \cdot 3}{5 \cdot 3} = \frac{6}{15}$ d) $\frac{7}{7} \cdot \frac{8}{3} = \frac{7 \cdot 8}{7 \cdot 3} = \frac{56}{21} = 2\frac{14}{21}$

YOU TRY IT 9

Multiply the following using the product rule. If the answer is an improper fraction, then write it as a mixed number. Use Example 7 as a guide.

a) $\frac{7}{6} \cdot \frac{5}{3}$ b) $\frac{8}{3} \cdot \frac{2}{7}$ c) $\frac{1}{4} \cdot \frac{3}{10}$ d) $\frac{5}{8} \cdot \frac{9}{1}$ e) $\frac{4}{4} \cdot \frac{2}{1}$

Unit Fractions

A **unit fraction** is one in which the numerator is 1 and the denominator is any natural number.

EXAMPLE 8

The following are unit fractions: $\frac{1}{7}, \frac{1}{4}, \frac{1}{12}$.

The following are not unit fractions: $\frac{5}{1}, \frac{3}{6}$ ($\frac{5}{1}$ is not a unit fraction because the numerator is not 1.)

YOU TRY IT 10 *Identify which of the following are unit fractions. Circle those that are. Use Example 8 as a guide.*

$$\frac{3}{1} \quad \frac{4}{12} \quad \frac{1}{6} \quad \frac{10}{15} \quad \frac{1}{8} \quad \frac{1}{2}$$

Naming Fractions

Recall from Section 1.4 that *four* 6's means $4 \cdot 6 = 24$. How, then, should we interpret *four* sixths?

Since *one* sixth is $\frac{1}{6}$, a unit fraction, then *four* sixths means $4 \cdot \frac{1}{6}$.

Thinking of 4 as $\frac{4}{1}$ and using the product rule, $4 \cdot \frac{1}{6} = \frac{4}{1} \cdot \frac{1}{6} = \frac{4}{6}$.

Typically, four sixths, as the fraction $\frac{4}{6}$, is spelled with a hyphen, four-sixths.

This example illustrates the idea that we can rewrite the fraction $\frac{a}{b}$ as the product of the numerator, a, and a unit fraction:

$$\frac{a}{b} = a \cdot \frac{1}{b}. \quad \text{For example, } \frac{7}{10} = 7 \cdot \frac{1}{10}.$$

Likewise, we can rewrite the product $a \cdot \frac{1}{b}$ as a single fraction:

$$a \cdot \frac{1}{b} = \frac{a}{b}. \quad \text{For example, } 7 \cdot \frac{1}{10} = \frac{7}{10}.$$

In either case, $7 \cdot \frac{1}{10}$ or $\frac{7}{10}$ is read and written as "seven-tenths." We use this written form to name the fraction.

EXAMPLE 9 Write each of these as either

1. the product of a whole number and a unit fraction, or
2. a single fraction.

Also, name the result.

a) $\frac{7}{8}$ b) $3 \cdot \frac{1}{5}$ c) $\frac{9}{13}$ d) $5 \cdot \frac{1}{4}$

ANSWER:

a) $\frac{7}{8} = 7 \cdot \frac{1}{8}$ seven-eighths

b) $3 \cdot \frac{1}{5} = \frac{3}{5}$ three-fifths

c) $\frac{9}{13} = 9 \cdot \frac{1}{13}$ nine-thirteenths

d) $5 \cdot \frac{1}{4} = \frac{5}{4}$ five-fourths

YOU TRY IT 11 *Write each of these as either (1) the product of a whole number and a unit fraction, or (2) as a single fraction. Also, name the result. Use Example 9 as a guide.*

a) $\frac{4}{7} =$ ____________________

b) $10 \cdot \frac{1}{9} =$ ______________________________

c) $\frac{2}{3} =$ ______________________________

d) $5 \cdot \frac{1}{8} =$ ______________________________

The rest of Chapter 3 is devoted to working with multiplication and division of fractions. At the end of this chapter, we will look at some workplace applications where fractions are commonly used.

You Try It Answers: Section 3.1

YTI 1
a) The numerator is 8, and the denominator is 3
b) The numerator is 1, and the denominator is 2
c) The numerator is 0, and the denominator is 5

YTI 2 a) $\frac{3}{14}$ b) $\frac{10}{7}$ c) $\frac{6}{4}$ d) $\frac{18}{5}$

YTI 3 a) $20 \div 4 = 5$ b) $18 \div 2 = 9$

YTI 4 a) $4 \cdot 5 = 20$ b) $6 \cdot 3 = 18$ c) $5 \cdot 7 = 35$

YTI 5 a) Proper fraction b) Complex fraction c) Improper fraction d) Mixed number e) Improper fraction

YTI 6 a) $\frac{19}{8}$ b) $\frac{59}{6}$ c) $\frac{78}{7}$

YTI 7 a) $5\frac{3}{8}$ b) $4\frac{1}{6}$ c) $13\frac{4}{7}$

YTI 8 a) 1 b) 6 c) $\frac{3}{5}$

YTI 9 a) $\frac{35}{18} = 1\frac{17}{18}$ b) $\frac{16}{21}$ c) $\frac{3}{40}$ d) $\frac{45}{8} = 5\frac{5}{8}$ e) $\frac{8}{4} = 2$

YTI 10 $\frac{1}{6}$, $\frac{1}{8}$, and $\frac{1}{2}$ are all unit fractions.

YTI 11
a) $\boxed{4 \cdot \frac{1}{7}}$ four-sevenths

b) $\boxed{\frac{10}{9}}$ ten-ninths

a) $\boxed{2 \cdot \frac{1}{3}}$ two-thirds

b) $\boxed{\frac{5}{8}}$ five-eighths

Focus Exercises: Section 3.1

Identify each as either a proper fraction, an improper fraction, a mixed number, or a complex fraction.

1. $\frac{7}{3}$ **2.** $\frac{7}{15}$ **3.** $\dfrac{\frac{5}{4}}{6}$ **4.** $\frac{1}{9}$

5. $7\frac{3}{4}$ **6.** $\frac{4}{4}$ **7.** $\frac{6}{1}$ **8.** $\dfrac{3}{\frac{1}{2}}$

Write each mixed number as an improper fraction.

9. $1\frac{4}{9}$ **10.** $1\frac{2}{7}$ **11.** $2\frac{3}{8}$ **12.** $2\frac{2}{3}$

13. $3\frac{1}{3}$ **14.** $3\frac{5}{6}$ **15.** $4\frac{4}{7}$ **16.** $4\frac{5}{9}$

17. $5\frac{1}{4}$ **18.** $5\frac{2}{7}$ **19.** $6\frac{1}{10}$ **20.** $6\frac{4}{11}$

21. $7\frac{1}{3}$ **22.** $8\frac{5}{6}$ **23.** $9\frac{3}{4}$ **24.** $10\frac{2}{3}$

25. $11\frac{7}{8}$ **26.** $12\frac{1}{5}$ **27.** $15\frac{3}{8}$ **28.** $20\frac{3}{4}$

Write each improper fraction as a mixed number.

29. $\frac{11}{5}$ **30.** $\frac{13}{8}$ **31.** $\frac{13}{4}$ **32.** $\frac{9}{2}$

33. $\frac{24}{7}$ **34.** $\frac{17}{6}$ **35.** $\frac{10}{3}$ **36.** $\frac{14}{9}$

37. $\frac{19}{8}$ **38.** $\frac{15}{4}$ **39.** $\frac{32}{5}$ **40.** $\frac{40}{9}$

41. $\frac{37}{5}$ **42.** $\frac{75}{8}$ **43.** $\frac{82}{7}$ **44.** $\frac{97}{4}$

Multiply. If the result is an improper fraction, then write it as a mixed number.

45. $\frac{8}{9}\cdot\frac{1}{5}$ **46.** $\frac{3}{7}\cdot\frac{9}{2}$ **47.** $\frac{3}{5}\cdot\frac{3}{5}$ **48.** $\frac{7}{6}\cdot\frac{1}{4}$

49. $\frac{2}{5}\cdot\frac{4}{3}$ **50.** $\frac{5}{7}\cdot\frac{3}{2}$ **51.** $\frac{7}{8}\cdot\frac{5}{6}$ **52.** $\frac{2}{3}\cdot\frac{11}{5}$

53. $\frac{7}{3}\cdot\frac{1}{2}$ **54.** $\frac{21}{10}\cdot\frac{3}{2}$ **55.** $\frac{9}{4}\cdot\frac{5}{2}$ **56.** $\frac{7}{2}\cdot\frac{11}{6}$

SECTION 3.2 Simplifying Fractions

Objectives

In this section, you will learn to:

- Simplify (reduce) fractions.
- Use the order of operations to evaluate expressions.

To successfully complete this section, you need to understand:

- Division (1.5)
- The order of operations (2.2)
- The greatest common factor (2.6)
- Relatively prime (2.6)
- The principles of fractions (3.1)

Introduction

It is important to recognize that some fractions look different from one another but actually have the same value—they are *equivalent* fractions.

For example, suppose a mechanic needs to loosen a bolt but doesn't know which size wrench to use. She finds that a $\frac{7}{16}$" wrench is too small and a $\frac{9}{16}$" wrench is too big, so she decides to use something in between, an $\frac{8}{16}$" wrench.

The problem is, her wrench set doesn't include an $\frac{8}{16}$" wrench, so what does she do? Knowing that $\frac{8}{16}$" is the same as $\frac{1}{2}$" solves the problem because she *does* have a $\frac{1}{2}$" wrench.

Equivalent Fractions

Recall from Section 3.1 that a fraction is a comparison of a part of something to its whole, where all of the parts are the same size.

Consider this chocolate bar. It has 6 rows of 3 squares each, 18 squares in all. We can treat the whole as having 6 equal parts (each row) or 18 equal parts (each square).

1 whole bar of chocolate

6 rows of chocolate

18 squares of chocolate

one-half of the whole bar

3 rows of chocolate

9 squares of chocolate

If we break off half of the bar, we can say that we have $\frac{1}{2}$ of the bar. In terms of rows, we have 3 of the 6 rows, or $\frac{3}{6}$ of the original rows in the bar; in terms of squares, we have 9 of the 18 squares, or $\frac{9}{18}$ of the original squares in the bar.

Each of these fractions indicates the same amount of chocolate: $\frac{1}{2}$, $\frac{3}{6}$, and $\frac{9}{18}$ of the bar. The fractions are equivalent. Notice that in each fraction, the numerator is half of the denominator.

Of these three fractions $\frac{1}{2}$, $\frac{3}{6}$, and $\frac{9}{18}$, the one that is in *lowest terms* is $\frac{1}{2}$. **Lowest terms** means that the numerator and denominator are relatively prime.

To find an equivalent fraction in lowest terms, we *simplify*, or *reduce*, the fraction.

> To **simplify**, or **reduce**, a fraction means to divide out any factors that are common to both the numerator and denominator.

In other words, if the numerator and the denominator have a common factor (other than 1), then the fraction can be reduced, or simplified.

The Procedure for Simplifying Fractions

Recall, from Section 3.1, the product rule. We can look at it two ways:

1. Multiplying two fractions together: $\frac{a}{b} \cdot \frac{c}{d} = \frac{a \cdot c}{b \cdot d}$ $\quad \frac{5}{7} \cdot \frac{2}{3} = \frac{5 \cdot 2}{7 \cdot 3}$
2. Separating one fraction into two fractions: $\frac{a \cdot c}{b \cdot d} = \frac{a}{b} \cdot \frac{c}{d}$ $\quad \frac{5 \cdot 2}{7 \cdot 3} = \frac{5}{7} \cdot \frac{2}{3}$

We'll use the idea of separating one fraction into two fractions to help us understand how to simplify fractions.

In our example of the wrenches, the mechanic had to simplify the fraction $\frac{8}{16}$. We saw that it is equivalent to $\frac{1}{2}$. A behind-the-scenes look will include some of the principles of numbers. Let's see!

1. First consider common factors of the numerator and denominator; the common factors of 8 and 16 are 2, 4, and 8. $\qquad \frac{8}{16}$ (GCF = 8)
2. Rewrite the numerator and the denominator as a product with 8 as a common factor: $\qquad = \frac{1 \cdot 8}{2 \cdot 8}$
3. Separate this fraction into the product of two fractions: $\qquad = \frac{1}{2} \cdot \frac{8}{8}$
4. Replace $\frac{8}{8}$ with 1: $\qquad = \frac{1}{2} \cdot 1$
5. Multiply $\frac{1}{2}$ by 1; notice the value doesn't change: $\qquad = \frac{1}{2}$

We can say that $\frac{8}{16}$ has been reduced by a factor of 8 to $\frac{1}{2}$. $\frac{8}{16}$ and $\frac{1}{2}$ are equivalent fractions.

In reducing the fraction $\frac{8}{16}$ we have extracted a common factor of 8 from both the numerator and the denominator. In other words, we divided both the numerator and the denominator by 8 to get the equivalent fraction $\frac{1}{2}$:

$$\frac{8}{16} = \frac{8 \div 8}{16 \div 8} = \frac{1}{2}$$

Dividing both the numerator and the denominator by the greatest common factor (GCF) allows us to simplify any fraction in only a few steps.

EXAMPLE 1 Simplify the fraction $\frac{15}{20}$.

PROCEDURE: As defined, simplifying a fraction means *dividing out* a common factor larger than 1. A common factor of 15 and 20 is 5.

ANSWER: $\frac{15}{20} = \frac{15 \div 5}{20 \div 5} = \frac{3}{4}$ Here, we have divided out the common factor of 5.

The fraction $\frac{15}{20}$ has been reduced by a factor of 5.

EXAMPLE 2 Simplify each of the following fractions by dividing both the numerator and denominator by a common factor. If the fraction is improper, write it as a mixed number.

a) $\frac{7}{21}$ b) $\frac{14}{10}$

PROCEDURE: Identify the GCF of the numerator and the denominator, and divide each by that number.

ANSWER: a) $\frac{7}{21}$ The GCF of 7 and 21 is 7. $\qquad \frac{7}{21} = \frac{7 \div 7}{21 \div 7} = \boxed{\frac{1}{3}}$

$\frac{7}{21}$ has been reduced by a factor of 7.

b) $\frac{14}{10}$ The GCF of 14 and 10 is 2.

$\frac{14}{10} = \frac{14 \div 2}{10 \div 2} = \frac{7}{5} = \boxed{1\frac{2}{5}}$

$\frac{14}{10}$ has been reduced by a factor of 2.

YOU TRY IT 1

Simplify each of the following. Use Examples 1 and 2 as guides. If the fraction is improper, write it as a mixed number.

a) $\frac{6}{14} =$

b) $\frac{15}{18} =$

c) $\frac{45}{35} =$

d) $\frac{3}{24} =$

Caution A fraction should always be simplified *completely*—to lowest terms—not just part way. If you simplify a fraction by one factor, you should check to see if the new (equivalent) fraction can, itself, be simplified.

EXAMPLE 3 Simplify $\frac{24}{60}$.

PROCEDURE: Identify a common factor of both the numerator and the denominator, and divide each by that number.

There are many common factors of 24 and 60; one such factor is 3, although it is not the greatest common factor. Let's see what happens.

ANSWER: $\frac{24}{60} = \frac{24 \div 3}{60 \div 3} = \frac{8}{20}$ $\quad \frac{8}{20}$ is equivalent to $\frac{24}{60}$, but $\frac{8}{20}$ can be simplified further by a factor of 4:

Simplifying further, $\frac{8}{20} = \frac{8 \div 4}{20 \div 4} = \boxed{\frac{2}{5}}$

We can say that $\frac{24}{60}$ reduced to lowest terms is $\frac{2}{5}$.

Think about it

In Example 3, the fraction $\frac{24}{60}$ was first reduced by a factor of 3 and then by a factor of 4. Could this fraction have been simplified by a different factor in just one step? If so, by what factor? Explain.

It is best to use the greatest common factor of the numerator and denominator to divide first. Doing so allows us to reduce just once and have the fraction in lowest terms.

We can use one of the techniques introduced in Section 2.6 to help us determine the GCF. For example, in the fraction $\frac{24}{60}$, we can simplify it in one step if we can recognize the GCF of 24 and 60. We could use either the prime factorization method or the division method:

Prime Factorization Method:

$24 = 2 \cdot 2 \cdot 2 \cdot 3 = 2^3 \cdot 3$

$60 = 2 \cdot 2 \cdot 3 \cdot 5 = 2^2 \cdot 3 \cdot 5$

$\text{GCF} = 2 \cdot 2 \cdot 3 = 2^2 \cdot 3 = \mathbf{12}$

Division Method:

$$\begin{array}{r|rr} 2 & 24 & 60 \\ 2 & 12 & 30 \\ 3 & 6 & 15 \\ & 2 & 5 \end{array}$$

$\text{GCF} = 2 \cdot 2 \cdot 3 = \mathbf{12}$

So, since the GCF is 12, we can simplify by a factor of 12: $\frac{24}{60} = \frac{24 \div 12}{60 \div 12} = \frac{2}{5}$.

EXAMPLE 4 Simplify each fraction completely.

a) $\frac{18}{30}$ b) $\frac{56}{84}$

PROCEDURE: Find the GCF of the numerator and denominator. The division method is shown here.

a)
$$\begin{array}{r|rr} 2 & 18 & 30 \\ 3 & 9 & 15 \\ & 3 & 5 \end{array}$$

$\text{GCF} = 2 \cdot 3 = 6$

b)
$$\begin{array}{r|rr} 2 & 56 & 84 \\ 2 & 28 & 42 \\ 7 & 14 & 21 \\ & 2 & 3 \end{array}$$

$\text{GCF} = 2 \cdot 2 \cdot 7 = 28$

ANSWER: $\frac{18}{30} = \frac{18 \div 6}{30 \div 6} = \frac{3}{5}$ $\frac{56}{84} = \frac{56 \div 28}{84 \div 28} = \frac{2}{3}$

You might find that dividing by 28—as in Example 4(b)—is a bit challenging. However, you may have noticed that the end result of the division method gives the reduced fraction's numerator and denominator.

Here, again, is the GCF division method for $\frac{56}{84}$:

$$\begin{array}{r|rr} & \text{N} & \text{D} \\ 2 & \mathbf{56} & \mathbf{84} \\ 2 & 28 & 42 \\ 7 & 14 & 21 \\ & \mathbf{2} & \mathbf{3} \\ & \uparrow & \uparrow \\ & \text{N} & \text{D} \end{array}$$

It's true that the GCF is $2 \cdot 2 \cdot 7 = 28$, but the reduced fraction is found in the bottom two numbers, **2** and **3**: $\frac{56}{84} = \frac{\mathbf{2}}{\mathbf{3}}$.

YOU TRY IT 2 *Simplify each fraction completely. Use Examples 3 and 4 as guides. If the fraction is improper, write it as a mixed number.*

a) $\frac{56}{70} =$ b) $\frac{72}{54} =$

c) $\frac{75}{90} =$ d) $\frac{104}{32} =$

Think about it

If a fraction is improper, should it be written as a mixed number *before* simplifying or *after* simplifying, or does it matter? Explain.

A quicker method of reducing fractions requires mental division. In this method, still called dividing out, we recognize the common factor and cross out the numerator and denominator, writing the reduced values to the side. It's important that we reduce the numerator and denominator by the same factor.

EXAMPLE 5

Reduce the fraction $\frac{6}{15}$.

PROCEDURE: The numerator and denominator have a common factor of 3, so we may divide each by 3. The division is done mentally (we don't actually write " ÷ 3").

ANSWER: $\frac{\not{6}^{2}}{\not{15}_{5}} = \frac{2}{5}$

If, on the first reduction, the fraction is not completely simplified, then this method might need to be performed again.

EXAMPLE 6

Simplify the fraction $\frac{32}{48}$.

PROCEDURE: Sometimes, this process must be performed more than once because the resulting fraction isn't completely simplified. Below is the reducing process for $\frac{32}{48}$.

ANSWER: 1. First in the division format: $\frac{32}{48} = \frac{32 \div 8}{48 \div 8} = \frac{4}{6} = \frac{4 \div 2}{6 \div 2} = \boxed{\frac{2}{3}}$

2. Now in the reducing format:

$$\frac{\not{32}^{4}}{\not{48}_{6}} = \frac{\not{4}^{2}}{\not{6}_{3}} = \frac{2}{3}$$

Reduce by a factor of 8. ↑ ↑ Reduce by a factor of 2.

Either way you choose to reduce is fine, as long as you do it correctly. Also, be sure that you have reduced the fraction completely to lowest terms.

YOU TRY IT 3

Simplify each fraction completely. If the fraction is improper, write it as a mixed number. Use Example 6 as a guide.

a) $\frac{52}{12} =$

b) $\frac{60}{84} =$

c) $\frac{96}{30} =$

d) $\frac{60}{150} =$

The Order of Operations and Fractions

In Section 2.2, we introduced the following grouping symbols in our discussion of the order of operations: parentheses, brackets, braces, and radicals.

It is time to add one more grouping symbol to the list: the fraction bar is also a grouping symbol. It groups the numerator separately from the denominator. We don't often see parentheses used within fractions, but we could write

$$\frac{\text{numerator}}{\text{denominator}} \text{ as } \frac{(\text{numerator})}{(\text{denominator})}.$$

EXAMPLE 7

Evaluate each expression. Simplify the result, if possible.

a) $\dfrac{8 - 2}{11 + 4}$ b) $\dfrac{28 - 2^2}{6 \div \sqrt{4}}$

PROCEDURE: As a grouping symbol, the fraction bar requires we evaluate the numerator separately from the denominator until each is simplified; then we look at the resulting fraction to see if it can be simplified.

ANSWER:

a) $\dfrac{8 - 2}{11 + 4}$ Evaluate the numerator. Evaluate the denominator.

$= \dfrac{6}{15}$ Simplify by a factor of 3.

$= \dfrac{2}{5}$

b) $\dfrac{28 - 2^2}{6 \div \sqrt{4}}$ In the numerator, square the 2. In the denominator, evaluate $\sqrt{4}$.

$= \dfrac{28 - 4}{6 \div 2}$ Evaluate the numerator. Evaluate the denominator.

$= \dfrac{24}{3}$ Simplify by a factor of 3.

$= 8$

YOU TRY IT 4

Evaluate each expression. Simplify completely. Use Example 7 as a guide.

a) $\dfrac{7 + 9}{5 - 1}$ b) $\dfrac{\sqrt{9}}{4^2 + 5}$

c) $\dfrac{12 - 2 \cdot 3}{8 + 4 \div 2}$ d) $\dfrac{9 - \sqrt{25}}{2 \cdot 3^2}$

If there is a fraction within an expression, it must be evaluated first because the fraction bar is a grouping symbol.

EXAMPLE 8

Evaluate each expression. Simplify the result, if possible.

a) $4 + 30 \div \dfrac{12}{2}$ b) $3 \cdot 6 - \dfrac{35}{7}$

PROCEDURE: As a grouping symbol, the fraction bar requires we evaluate the fraction first.

ANSWER:

a) $4 + 30 \div \frac{12}{2}$ Evaluate the fraction first: $\frac{12}{2} = 6$.

$= 4 + 30 \div 6$ Next, apply division.

$= 4 + 5$ Add.

$= 9$

b) $3 \cdot 6 - \frac{35}{7}$ Evaluate the fraction first: $\frac{35}{7} = 5$.

$= 3 \cdot 6 - 5$ Next, apply multiplication.

$= 18 - 5$ Subtract.

$= 13$

YOU TRY IT 5

Evaluate each expression. Simplify completely. Use Example 8 as a guide.

a) $20 - 5 \cdot \frac{12}{4}$ b) $6^2 \div \frac{12}{3}$ c) $16 + \frac{13 + 11}{4}$

Think about it

Write out the steps you took, one at a time, in evaluating the expression in YTI 5 (a).

$20 - 5 \cdot \frac{12}{4}$ ______________________

= ______________________

= ______________________

= ______________________

You Try It Answers: Section 3.2

YTI 1 a) $\frac{3}{7}$ b) $\frac{5}{6}$ c) $\frac{9}{7} = 1\frac{2}{7}$ d) $\frac{1}{8}$

YTI 2 a) $\frac{4}{5}$ (GCF is 14) b) $\frac{4}{3} = 1\frac{1}{3}$ (GCF is 18) c) $\frac{5}{6}$ (GCF is 15) d) $\frac{13}{4} = 3\frac{1}{4}$ (GCF is 8)

YTI 3 a) $\frac{13}{3} = 4\frac{1}{3}$ (GCF is 4) b) $\frac{5}{7}$ (GCF is 12) c) $\frac{16}{5} = 3\frac{1}{5}$ (GCF is 6) d) $\frac{2}{5}$ (GCF is 30.)

YTI 4 a) 4 b) $\frac{1}{7}$ c) $\frac{3}{5}$ d) $\frac{2}{9}$

YTI 5 a) 5 b) 9 c) 22

Focus Exercises: Section 3.2

Simplify completely. If the fraction is improper, write it as a mixed number.

1. $\frac{9}{15}$
2. $\frac{3}{12}$
3. $\frac{18}{8}$
4. $\frac{21}{6}$
5. $\frac{28}{21}$
6. $\frac{60}{20}$
7. $\frac{9}{24}$
8. $\frac{15}{35}$

9. $\frac{8}{32}$ **10.** $\frac{14}{35}$ **11.** $\frac{25}{10}$ **12.** $\frac{77}{22}$

13. $\frac{18}{27}$ **14.** $\frac{42}{46}$ **15.** $\frac{20}{45}$ **16.** $\frac{60}{100}$

17. $\frac{30}{12}$ **18.** $\frac{24}{16}$ **19.** $\frac{10}{45}$ **20.** $\frac{8}{26}$

21. $\frac{15}{3}$ **22.** $\frac{18}{2}$ **23.** $\frac{35}{5}$ **24.** $\frac{42}{7}$

25. $\frac{25}{5}$ **26.** $\frac{14}{7}$ **27.** $\frac{18}{54}$ **28.** $\frac{18}{60}$

29. $\frac{16}{44}$ **30.** $\frac{32}{66}$ **31.** $\frac{28}{42}$ **32.** $\frac{36}{60}$

33. $\frac{52}{20}$ **34.** $\frac{42}{14}$ **35.** $\frac{24}{72}$ **36.** $\frac{96}{120}$

37. $\frac{75}{90}$ **38.** $\frac{24}{96}$ **39.** $\frac{96}{30}$ **40.** $\frac{80}{48}$

Evaluate each expression. Simplify completely.

41. $\frac{8 + 3 \cdot 2}{3 \cdot 5 - 1}$ **42.** $\frac{20 - 4 \cdot 3}{\sqrt{36}}$ **43.** $\frac{5 \cdot (8 - 5)}{4 \cdot (8 + 2)}$ **44.** $\frac{5^2 - 3^2}{3 \cdot (7 + 1)}$

45. $8 + 5 \cdot \frac{9}{3}$ **46.** $12 - 6 \div \frac{10}{5}$ **47.** $\frac{20}{5} \div 2 + 2$ **48.** $6^2 - \frac{32}{8}$

SECTION 3.3 Multiplying Fractions

Objectives

In this section, you will learn to:

- Multiply and simplify fractions.
- Multiply and simplify mixed numbers.
- Solve applications involving multiplying fractions.

To successfully complete this section, you need to understand:

- Multiplying whole numbers (1.4)
- Writing mixed numbers as improper fractions (3.1)
- The product rule (3.1)
- Simplifying fractions (3.2)

Introduction

Recall, from Section 1.4, that multiplication of whole numbers is an abbreviation for repeated addition. For example, if a recipe makes 12 cookies, then we can make twice as many cookies, 24, by doubling the recipe, multiplying all of the ingredients by 2.

However, cutting the recipe in half, that is, multiplying by $\frac{1}{2}$, results in only 6 cookies. This is not repeated addition. In fact, there are fewer cookies than in the original recipe.

When multiplying with fractions, we need to learn different rules, different procedures.

Multiplying Fractions

Recall the product rule from Section 3.1:

The **product rule** is $\frac{a}{b} \cdot \frac{c}{d} = \frac{a \cdot c}{b \cdot d} = \frac{\text{the product of the numerators}}{\text{the product of the denominators}}$

The product rule can be extended to multiplying three fractions, as demonstrated in Example 1.

EXAMPLE 1 Multiply $\frac{3}{4} \cdot \frac{7}{5} \cdot \frac{1}{2}$.

PROCEDURE: The product rule says to multiply the numerators together and then multiply the denominators together:

ANSWER: $\frac{3}{4} \cdot \frac{7}{5} \cdot \frac{1}{2} = \frac{3 \cdot 7 \cdot 1}{4 \cdot 5 \cdot 2} = \boxed{\frac{21}{40}}$

YOU TRY IT 1 *Find the product of the three fractions. Use Example 1 as a guide.*

a) $\frac{1}{3} \cdot \frac{4}{7} \cdot \frac{5}{3}$

b) $\frac{7}{11} \cdot \frac{1}{2} \cdot \frac{5}{3}$

Multiplying and Simplifying Fractions

In Section 3.2, we simplified fractions by dividing out factors that were common to both the numerator and denominator. In this section, we will combine simplifying with multiplying to solve applications involving fractions.

EXAMPLE 2 Find the product. Simplify your answer completely.

a) $\frac{5}{6} \cdot \frac{4}{15}$

b) $\frac{3}{2} \cdot \frac{11}{4}$

PROCEDURE: Apply the product rule to each of these; then, if the result can be simplified, do so. If the result cannot simplify, then leave it as it is.

ANSWER: You might be able to do these in fewer steps; all steps are shown here.

a) $\frac{5}{6}\cdot\frac{4}{15} = \frac{5\cdot 4}{6\cdot 15} = \frac{20}{90} = \frac{20 \div 10}{90 \div 10} = \boxed{\frac{2}{9}}$

This fraction ↑ can be reduced by a factor of 10.

b) $\frac{3}{2}\cdot\frac{11}{4} = \frac{3\cdot 11}{2\cdot 4} = \frac{33}{8}$ This fraction cannot be reduced because 33 and 8 are relatively prime.

The resulting fraction is improper and can be written as a mixed number. → $\frac{33}{8} = 4\frac{1}{8}$

EXAMPLE 3 Find the product of $\frac{9}{6}\cdot\frac{1}{2}\cdot\frac{2}{3}$. Simplify your answer completely.

ANSWER: $\frac{9}{6}\cdot\frac{1}{2}\cdot\frac{2}{3} = \frac{9\cdot 1\cdot 2}{6\cdot 2\cdot 3} = \frac{18}{36} = \frac{18 \div 18}{36 \div 18} = \boxed{\frac{1}{2}}$

This fraction ↑ can be reduced by a factor of 18.

YOU TRY IT 2 *Find the product. Simplify your answer completely. Use Examples 2 and 3 as guides.*

a) $\frac{6}{7}\cdot\frac{2}{3}$

b) $\frac{8}{11}\cdot\frac{3}{4}$

c) $\frac{3}{9}\cdot\frac{10}{5}\cdot\frac{1}{2}$

d) $\frac{7}{4}\cdot\frac{2}{5}\cdot\frac{3}{7}$

Simplifying before Multiplying

Two fractions that cannot be simplified are $\frac{5}{7}$ and $\frac{9}{10}$. Their product, though, can be simplified:

$\frac{5}{7}\cdot\frac{9}{10} = \frac{5\cdot 9}{7\cdot 10} = \frac{45}{70}$, which can be reduced by a factor of 5: $\frac{45 \div 5}{70 \div 5} = \frac{9}{14}$

The method shown above finds the full product before simplifying. It is possible, though, to simplify the fraction before multiplying by first looking at the prime factorization of each number in the numerator and denominator:

$$\frac{5}{7}\cdot\frac{9}{10} = \frac{5\cdot 9}{7\cdot 10} = \frac{5\cdot 3\cdot 3}{7\cdot 2\cdot 5}$$

↑ The product rule

↑ Prime factorization of the numerator and denominator

At this point, we may divide out the common factor of 5 directly, without having to write the actual division:

$$\frac{\cancel{5}^1\cdot 3\cdot 3}{7\cdot 2\cdot \cancel{5}_1} = \frac{9}{14}$$

EXAMPLE 4 Find the product. Simplify before multiplying.

a) $\frac{5}{6}\cdot\frac{4}{15}$ b) $\frac{3}{5}\cdot\frac{4}{3}\cdot\frac{10}{14}$ c) $\frac{6}{8}\cdot\frac{14}{21}$

PROCEDURE: Apply the product rule to each and write it as one fraction. Find the prime factorization of each number and divide out any common factors.

a) $\frac{5}{6}\cdot\frac{4}{15} = \frac{5\cdot4}{6\cdot15} = \frac{\cancel{5}^1\cdot\cancel{2}^1\cdot2}{\cancel{2}_1\cdot3\cdot\cancel{5}_1\cdot3} = \frac{2}{9}$

b) $\frac{3}{5}\cdot\frac{4}{3}\cdot\frac{10}{14} = \frac{3\cdot4\cdot10}{5\cdot3\cdot14} = \frac{\cancel{3}^1\cdot\cancel{2}^1\cdot2\cdot2\cdot\cancel{5}^1}{\cancel{5}_1\cdot\cancel{3}_1\cdot\cancel{2}_1\cdot7} = \frac{4}{7}$

c) $\frac{6}{8}\cdot\frac{14}{21} = \frac{6\cdot14}{8\cdot21} = \frac{\cancel{2}^1\cdot\cancel{3}^1\cdot\cancel{2}^1\cdot\cancel{7}^1}{\cancel{2}_1\cdot2\cdot\cancel{2}_1\cdot\cancel{3}_1\cdot\cancel{7}_1} = \frac{1}{2}$

In part (c), if we multiplied first, we would get $\frac{84}{168}$, and this could take some time to simplify.

Caution

It's important, when dividing out prime factors directly, to write a 1 above and below the common factor being divided out.

In Example 4(c), if we had ***not*** written the 1's, it might appear as though the entire numerator was gone, and we might think that we no longer have a fraction.

A common student error: $\frac{\cancel{2}\cdot\cancel{3}\cdot\cancel{2}\cdot\cancel{7}}{\cancel{2}\cdot2\cdot\cancel{2}\cdot\cancel{3}\cdot\cancel{7}} = \mathbf{2}$ Incorrect!

YOU TRY IT 3 *Find the product. Simplify before multiplying. Use Example 4 as a guide.*

a) $\frac{6}{7}\cdot\frac{4}{9}$ b) $\frac{12}{15}\cdot\frac{5}{7}\cdot\frac{3}{4}$

Another option is to divide out common factors directly instead of first writing a factored form.

EXAMPLE 5 Multiply $\frac{30}{42}\cdot\frac{14}{20}$. Simplify before multiplying.

PROCEDURE: Apply the product rule. Identify some common factors of the numerator and denominator and divide them out. Be sure to simplify completely.

ANSWER: $\frac{30}{42}\cdot\frac{14}{20} = \frac{\cancel{30}^3\cdot\cancel{14}^2}{\cancel{42}_6\cdot\cancel{20}_2} = \frac{6}{12} = \frac{1}{2}$

30 and 20 have a common factor of 10. 42 and 14 have a common factor of 7. ↑ And this fraction can be reduced by a factor of 6.

YOU TRY IT 4

Find the product. Simplify before multiplying. Use Example 5 as a guide.

a) $\frac{9}{16} \cdot \frac{8}{15}$

b) $\frac{14}{21} \cdot \frac{20}{15}$

c) $\frac{4}{15} \cdot \frac{10}{21} \cdot \frac{7}{8}$

Recall from Section 3.1 that a whole number can be written as a fraction with a denominator of 1.

EXAMPLE 6

Multiply by first writing the whole number as a fraction (with a denominator of 1).

$\frac{5}{6} \cdot 8 \cdot \frac{3}{25}$

ANSWER:

$$\frac{5}{6} \cdot 8 \cdot \frac{3}{25} = \frac{5}{6} \cdot \frac{8}{1} \cdot \frac{3}{25} = \frac{\cancel{5}^1 \cdot 8 \cdot \cancel{3}^1}{\cancel{6}_2 \cdot 1 \cdot \cancel{25}_5} = \frac{8}{10} = \frac{4}{5}$$

5 and 25 have a common factor of 5. 6 and 3 have a common factor of 3. ↑ 8 and 10 have a common factor of 2.

YOU TRY IT 5

Find the product. First, rewrite the whole number as a fraction. Simplify your answer completely. Use Example 6 as a guide.

a) $7 \cdot \frac{3}{10} \cdot \frac{5}{21}$

b) $\frac{4}{5} \cdot 10 \cdot \frac{1}{12}$

Multiplying Mixed Numbers

In example 2(b), earlier in this section, we saw the product of two improper fractions resulting in a third improper fraction:

$$\frac{3}{2} \cdot \frac{11}{4} = \frac{33}{8}.$$

If each of these fractions was written as a mixed number, the product would look like this:

$$1\frac{1}{2} \times 2\frac{3}{4} = 4\frac{1}{8}$$

Question: Is there any way that you can see to multiply the mixed numbers $1\frac{1}{2} \times 2\frac{3}{4}$, as they are, to get $4\frac{1}{8}$? Look at the whole numbers, and look at the fractions.

Answer: The whole numbers 1 and 2, by themselves, don't multiply to get 4. Also, the fractions $\frac{1}{2}$ and $\frac{3}{4}$, by themselves, don't multiply to get $\frac{1}{8}$.

The point is this: It is not practical to multiply mixed numbers while they are still mixed numbers. Instead, we must first rewrite them as improper fractions and then multiply.

To Multiply Mixed Numbers

1. Rewrite each mixed number as an improper fraction.
2. Multiply these fractions as you would any others; simplify the result.
3. Rewrite the answer, if appropriate, as a mixed number.

EXAMPLE 7 Multiply. Be sure to simplify completely.

a) $3\frac{1}{2} \times 1\frac{4}{5}$ b) $2\frac{1}{4} \times 3\frac{1}{3}$

PROCEDURE: First rewrite each fraction as an improper fraction, then multiply, simplify, and rewrite the answer as a mixed number.

ANSWER:

a) $3\frac{1}{2} \times 1\frac{4}{5}$

$= \frac{7}{2} \cdot \frac{9}{5}$ ⟵ Rewrite each as an improper fraction and prepare to multiply.

$= \frac{7 \cdot 9}{2 \cdot 5}$ ⟵ The product at left cannot be simplified.

$= \frac{63}{10}$

$= 6\frac{3}{10}$ ⟵ Rewrite the improper fraction as a mixed number.

b) $2\frac{1}{4} \times 3\frac{1}{3}$

$= \frac{9}{4} \cdot \frac{10}{3}$ ⟵ Rewrite each as an improper fraction and prepare to multiply.

$= \frac{\not{9}^{3} \cdot \not{10}^{5}}{\not{4}_{2} \cdot \not{3}_{1}}$

$= \frac{15}{2}$ ⟵ The product at right can be simplified.

$= 7\frac{1}{2}$ ⟵ Rewrite the improper fraction as a mixed number.

A mixed number can also be multiplied by a proper fraction. Also, if one of the factors is a whole number, such as 6, then we can write it as a fraction, $\frac{6}{1}$, before multiplying.

YOU TRY IT 6 *Multiply; simplify completely. Be sure to write the answer as a mixed number, whenever possible. Use Example 7 as a guide.*

a) $1\frac{2}{5} \cdot 3\frac{1}{3}$ b) $6\frac{2}{3} \cdot \frac{3}{8}$ c) $10 \cdot 4\frac{2}{5}$

When *of* Means Multiply

You may have heard this phrase before: "In mathematics, *of* means *multiply*." More appropriately,

A *fraction of* means *multiply.*

For example, if a class has 48 students enrolled, and three-fourths are women, then we could say,

"Three-fourths *of* the students are women."

Mathematically, we can interpret this as $\frac{3}{4} \times$ the number of students = the number of women.

In other words, $\frac{3}{4} \times 48 =$ the number of women.

We can evaluate this to find that the number of women in the class is 36:

$$\frac{3}{4} \cdot \frac{48}{1} = \frac{3 \cdot 48}{4 \cdot 1} = \frac{3 \cdot \not{48}^{12}}{\not{4}_{1} \cdot 1} = \frac{36}{1} = 36$$

Of means ***multiply*** if we are referring to

- *a fraction of,*
- a *decimal* of, or
- *a percent of,* something.

In this section, we'll work only with fractions.

EXAMPLE 8

Evaluate each.

a) $\frac{3}{7}$ of $\frac{5}{4}$ b) half of $\frac{8}{5}$ c) two-thirds of 15 d) three-fourths of $1\frac{7}{9}$

PROCEDURE: Rewrite each as multiplication, evaluate, and simplify, if possible.

ANSWER: a) $\frac{3}{7}$ of $\frac{5}{4}$ means $\frac{3}{7} \cdot \frac{5}{4} = \frac{15}{28}$, which cannot be simplified.

b) half of $\frac{8}{5}$ means $\frac{1}{2} \cdot \frac{8}{5} = \frac{1 \cdot 8}{2 \cdot 5} = \frac{1 \cdot \cancel{8}^4}{\cancel{2}_1 \cdot 5} = \frac{4}{5}$

c) two-thirds of 15 means $\frac{2}{3} \cdot 15 = \frac{2}{3} \cdot \frac{15}{1} = \frac{2 \cdot 15}{3 \cdot 1} = \frac{2 \cdot \cancel{15}^5}{\cancel{3}_1} = \frac{10}{1} = 10$

d) three-fourths of $1\frac{7}{9}$ means $\frac{3}{4} \times 1\frac{7}{9}$. Before we multiply, we must first write the mixed number as an improper fraction:

$$= \frac{3}{4} \cdot \frac{16}{9} = \frac{\cancel{3}^1 \cdot \cancel{16}^4}{\cancel{4}_1 \cdot \cancel{9}_3} = \frac{4}{3} = 1\frac{1}{3}$$

YOU TRY IT 7

Evaluate each by first rewriting it as a product of fractions. Use Example 8 as a guide.

a) $\frac{2}{3}$ of $\frac{4}{5}$ b) $\frac{5}{6}$ of 9 c) three-fourths of $\frac{16}{21}$ d) five-sixths of $4\frac{4}{5}$

Applications Involving Multiplying Fractions

In applications involving multiplying fractions, we look for *a fraction of* something. Sometimes, these situations are straightforward and don't require a variable or an equation. However, a sentence that answers the question is still required.

EXAMPLE 9

A cupcake recipe calls for $5\frac{1}{4}$ cups of flour (among other ingredients). The recipe makes 24 cupcakes. Aisha wants to make two-thirds of this recipe.

a) How many cupcakes will it make? b) How much flour is needed?

PROCEDURE: We see the *fraction of* as **two-thirds of.** This means that we must multiply (a) the number of cupcakes by $\frac{2}{3}$, and (b) the amount of flour by $\frac{2}{3}$.

ANSWER: a) $\frac{2}{3} \times 24$

$= \frac{2}{3} \cdot \frac{24}{1}$

$= \frac{2 \cdot \cancel{24}^{8}}{\cancel{3}_{1} \cdot 1}$

$= \frac{16}{1} = 16$

Sentence:

Two-thirds of the recipe makes 16 cupcakes.

b) $\frac{2}{3} \times 5\frac{1}{4}$

$= \frac{2}{3} \cdot \frac{21}{4}$

$= \frac{\cancel{2}^{1} \cdot \cancel{21}^{7}}{\cancel{3}_{1} \cdot \cancel{4}_{2}}$

$= \frac{7}{2} = 3\frac{1}{2}$

Sentence:

Two-thirds of the recipe requires $3\frac{1}{2}$ cups of flour.

YOU TRY IT 8

A recipe for chili makes 36 servings. The recipe calls for $5\frac{1}{3}$ pounds of ground beef. Willie wants to make three-fourths of the recipe.

a) How many servings will it make?

Sentence:

____

____

b) How many pounds of ground beef are necessary?

Sentence:

____

____

EXAMPLE 10

Andy must find the middle of a piece of wood trim that is $3\frac{1}{4}$ inches wide. How far from the edge must he measure to find the middle of the trimming?

PROCEDURE: Finding the *middle* of any length or width means finding *half* of that measure. Be sure to write the mixed number as an improper fraction.

ANSWER: $\frac{1}{2} \times 3\frac{1}{4} = \frac{1}{2} \cdot \frac{13}{4} = \frac{1 \cdot 13}{2 \cdot 4} = \frac{13}{8} = 1\frac{5}{8}$

SENTENCE: Andy must measure $1\frac{5}{8}$ inches from the edge to find the middle of the wood trim.

YOU TRY IT 9

Carmen must find the middle of the logo she is stitching. It is $2\frac{1}{2}$ inches in height and $3\frac{1}{8}$ inches long. How far from the bottom (height) and how far from the side (length) will she find the middle of the logo?

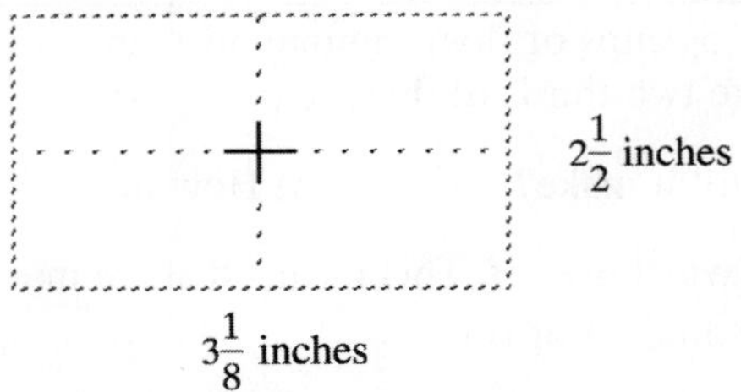

Applications Involving Geometry

Fractions are often used in situations involving geometry. Recall from Section 2.3 that the formula for the area of a rectangle is Area = Length × Width.

EXAMPLE 11 Find the area of the rectangle that is $3\frac{3}{4}$ inches long and $1\frac{2}{3}$ inches wide, as shown.

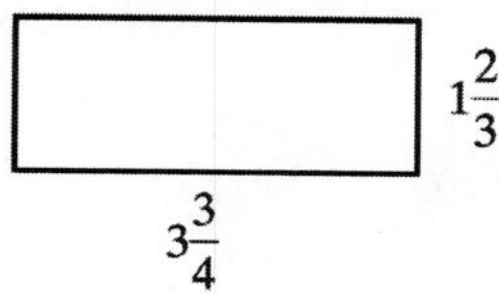

PROCEDURE: Use the formula for the area of a rectangle: Area = Length × Width.

ANSWER: Area $= 3\frac{3}{4} \times 1\frac{2}{3} = \frac{15}{4} \cdot \frac{5}{3} = \frac{\cancel{15}^{5} \cdot 5}{4 \cdot \cancel{3}_{1}} = \frac{25}{4} = 6\frac{1}{4}$

SENTENCE: The area is $6\frac{1}{4}$ in^2.

YOU TRY IT 10 *Find the area of each rectangle. (Each is measured in inches.)*

a) 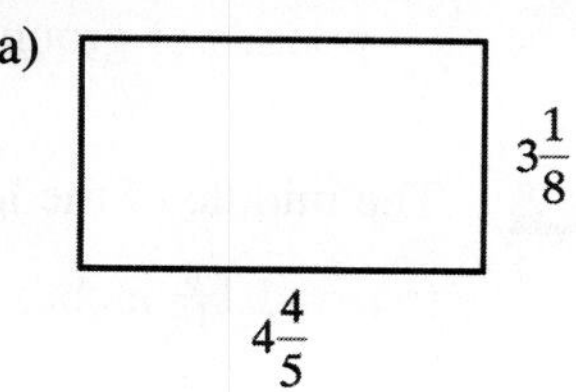

b) 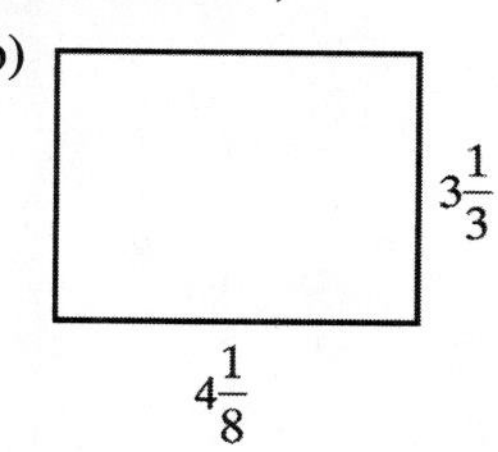

The area formula for a triangle is

$$\text{Area} = \frac{1}{2} \times \text{Base} \times \text{Height}.$$

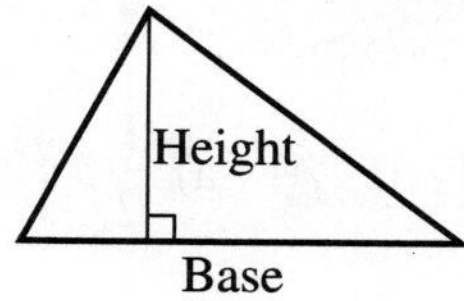

EXAMPLE 12 Find the area of the triangle with base $3\frac{3}{4}$ feet and height $1\frac{2}{3}$ feet, as shown.

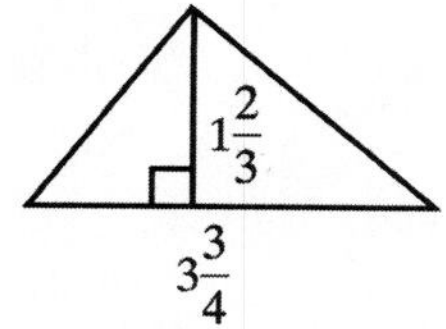

PROCEDURE: Use the formula for the area of a triangle: Area $= \frac{1}{2} \times$ Base × Height.

ANSWER: Area $= \frac{1}{2} \cdot 3\frac{3}{4} \cdot 1\frac{2}{3} = \frac{1}{2} \cdot \frac{15}{4} \cdot \frac{5}{3} = \frac{1 \cdot \cancel{15}^{5} \cdot 5}{2 \cdot 4 \cdot \cancel{3}_{1}} = \frac{25}{8} = 3\frac{1}{8}$

SENTENCE: The area is $3\frac{1}{8}$ ft^2.

YOU TRY IT 11 *Find the area of each triangle. (Each is measured in feet.)*

a)

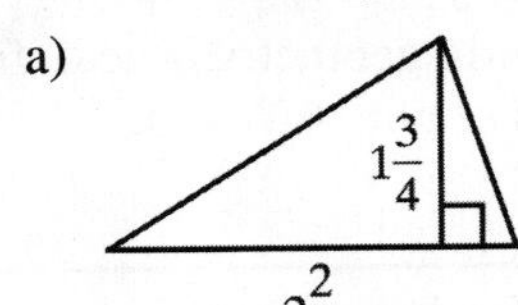

b)

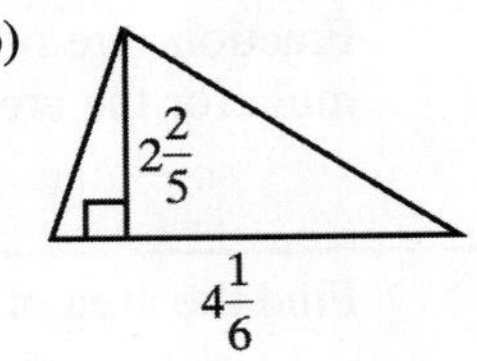

You Try It Answers: Section 3.3

YTI 1 a) $\frac{20}{63}$ b) $\frac{35}{66}$

YTI 2 a) $\frac{4}{7}$ b) $\frac{6}{11}$ c) $\frac{1}{3}$ d) $\frac{3}{10}$

YTI 3 a) $\frac{8}{21}$ b) $\frac{3}{7}$

YTI 4 a) $\frac{3}{10}$ b) $\frac{8}{9}$ c) $\frac{1}{9}$

YTI 5 a) $\frac{1}{2}$ b) $\frac{2}{3}$

YTI 6 a) $4\frac{2}{3}$ b) $2\frac{1}{2}$ c) 44

YTI 7 a) $\frac{8}{15}$ b) $7\frac{1}{2}$ c) $\frac{4}{7}$ d) 4

YTI 8 a) Three-fourths of the recipe will make 27 servings.
b) Three-fourths of the recipe will require 4 pounds of ground beef.

YTI 9 The middle of the logo is $1\frac{1}{4}$ inches from the bottom and $1\frac{9}{16}$ inches from the side.

YTI 10 a) 15 in^2 b) $13\frac{3}{4}$ in^2

YTI 11 a) $2\frac{1}{3}$ ft^2 b) 5 ft^2

Focus Exercises: Section 3.3

Multiply. Simplify each answer completely.

1. $\frac{4}{9} \cdot \frac{1}{5}$ **2.** $\frac{7}{12} \cdot \frac{1}{3}$ **3.** $\frac{5}{6} \cdot \frac{5}{7}$ **4.** $\frac{3}{11} \cdot \frac{4}{5}$

5. $\frac{5}{8} \cdot \frac{4}{3}$ **6.** $\frac{5}{7} \cdot \frac{2}{15}$ **7.** $\frac{5}{21} \cdot \frac{3}{4}$ **8.** $\frac{8}{9} \cdot \frac{7}{12}$

9. $\frac{7}{10} \cdot \frac{5}{14} \cdot \frac{2}{3}$ **10.** $\frac{5}{8} \cdot \frac{4}{9} \cdot \frac{3}{5}$ **11.** $\frac{10}{9} \cdot \frac{3}{4} \cdot \frac{2}{5}$ **12.** $\frac{2}{3} \cdot \frac{9}{15} \cdot \frac{5}{3}$

13. $\frac{14}{21} \cdot \frac{10}{55}$

14. $\frac{25}{35} \cdot \frac{18}{24}$

15. $\frac{9}{15} \cdot \frac{28}{40}$

16. $\frac{8}{32} \cdot \frac{25}{45}$

17. $10 \cdot \frac{3}{5}$

18. $\frac{2}{3} \cdot 18$

19. $3 \cdot \frac{2}{15}$

20. $\frac{7}{9} \cdot 18$

21. $\frac{8}{5} \cdot \frac{3}{21} \cdot \frac{3}{4}$

22. $\frac{1}{9} \cdot 24 \cdot \frac{5}{4}$

23. $8 \cdot \frac{9}{12} \cdot \frac{2}{15}$

24. $\frac{3}{4} \cdot \frac{12}{45} \cdot \frac{5}{4}$

Multiply; simplify completely. Write each answer as a mixed number, whenever possible.

25. $3\frac{3}{4} \times 2\frac{2}{3}$

26. $\frac{3}{4} \times 2\frac{2}{9}$

27. $1\frac{7}{8} \times 3\frac{1}{5}$

28. $2\frac{2}{5} \times 2\frac{2}{9}$

29. $2\frac{1}{10} \times \frac{5}{6}$

30. $2\frac{3}{4} \times \frac{4}{11}$

31. $11\frac{1}{4} \times 1\frac{7}{9}$

32. $2\frac{4}{7} \times 9\frac{1}{3}$

33. $1\frac{1}{14} \times 4\frac{1}{5}$

34. $4\frac{2}{3} \times 2\frac{1}{10}$

35. $1\frac{5}{16} \times 4\frac{4}{9}$

36. $4\frac{3}{8} \times 1\frac{11}{25}$

37. $5\frac{1}{3} \times 6$

38. $15 \times 3\frac{1}{5}$

39. $2\frac{1}{7} \times 21$

40. $18 \times 2\frac{2}{9}$

41. $15 \times 1\frac{3}{10}$

42. $9 \times 1\frac{1}{15}$

43. $2\frac{3}{4} \times 6$

44. $1\frac{1}{14} \times 7$

Evaluate each by first rewriting it as a product of fractions. Write each answer as a mixed number, whenever possible.

45. One-fourth of $\frac{8}{15}$

46. One-third of $\frac{9}{10}$

47. One-fifth of $\frac{15}{16}$

48. Three-fourths of $\frac{8}{9}$

49. Two-thirds of $\frac{9}{16}$

50. Five-sixths of $\frac{12}{25}$

51. One-third of 18

52. Two-fifths of 30

53. Three-eighths of 48

54. Four-ninths of $\frac{3}{8}$

55. One-tenth of $\frac{1}{100}$

56. One-eighth of $\frac{1}{25}$

57. Two-thirds of $2\frac{5}{8}$

58. Three-fifths of $3\frac{8}{9}$

59. Half of $3\frac{1}{5}$

60. Seven-tenths of $3\frac{1}{3}$

61. Three-sevenths of $4\frac{1}{5}$

62. Half of $1\frac{3}{8}$

For each application problem, write a sentence answering the question.

63. $\frac{2}{3}$ of a cup of laundry detergent washes a full load of laundry. How much detergent would wash $\frac{1}{4}$ of a load?

64. Every day, Janet walks her beagle once around the neighborhood. One day, she measured the route in her car and found it to be $1\frac{3}{10}$ miles. How many miles does Janet walk her dog in 30 days?

65. To pass his history class, Pedro needs to get only three-fifths of the problems on the final exam correct. If there are 60 questions on the final, how many must Pedro get correct to pass the class?

66. Connie owns a $6\frac{1}{9}$-acre plot of land in the country. She decides to split it up so that each smaller plot is one-fifth of the original size. How many acres will each new plot contain?

A company's logo is $3\frac{3}{4}$ inches in height and $4\frac{3}{8}$ inches wide. Carmen's Embroidery has been hired to stitch the logo on baseball caps, jacket backs, and polo shirts.

67. How far from the side and how far from the bottom is the middle of the logo in its original size?

68. On the jackets, Carmen needs to make the logo 2 times its original dimensions. What will the dimensions of the stitched logo on the jacket backs be?

Find the area of each geometric figure. (Each is measured in inches.)

69.

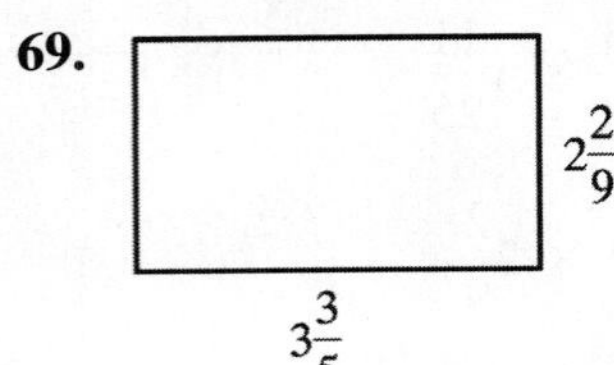

70.

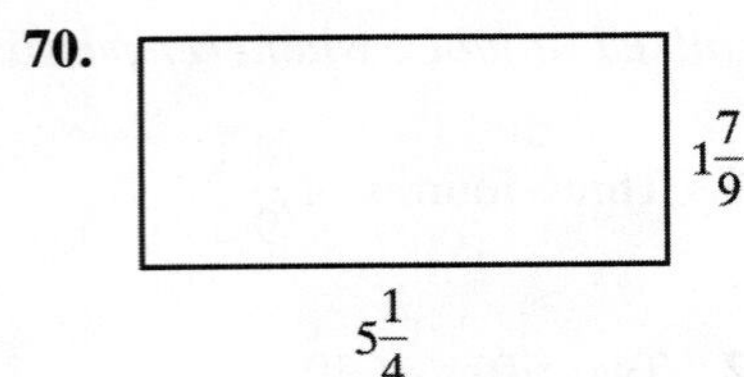

71.

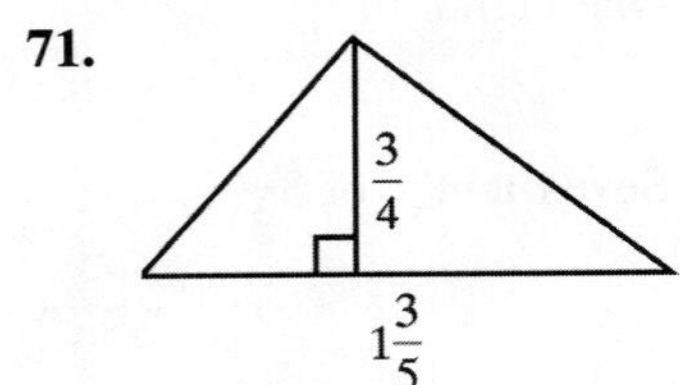

72.

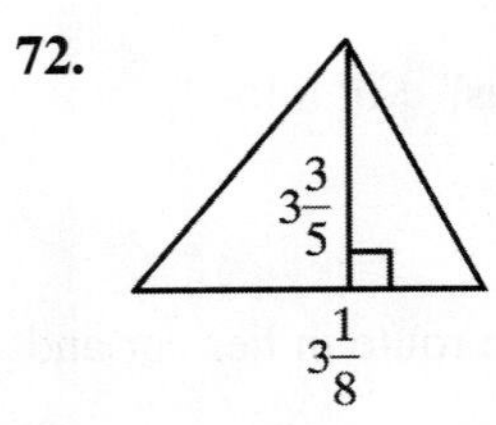

SECTION 3.4 Dividing Fractions

Objectives

In this section, you will learn to:

- Find the reciprocal of a fraction.
- Divide fractions.
- Divide mixed numbers.
- Simplify complex fractions.

To successfully complete this section, you need to understand:

- Rewriting mixed numbers (3.1)
- Simplifying fractions (3.2)
- Multiplying fractions (3.3)

Introduction

Recall, from previous sections in the text, these two ideas about division:

- Section 1.5: Division is *the inverse operation* of multiplication.
- Section 2.2: Multiplication and division have the same rank in the order of operations.

Both of these ideas indicate how much multiplication and division are connected with each other. In this section, we divide one fraction by another by changing the operation from division to multiplication using the Quotient Rule of Fractions.

To prepare ourselves for dividing fractions, we must first learn about the reciprocal of a fraction.

The Reciprocal of a Fraction

Consider this:

> The **reciprocal** of a fraction, $\frac{a}{b}$, is the fraction, $\frac{b}{a}$, as long as a and b are not 0.
>
> That is, the reciprocal of a fraction results from interchanging the numerator and denominator.

Let's use Example 1 to apply this definition to three numbers.

EXAMPLE 1 Identify the reciprocal of each of these numbers: $\frac{2}{3}$, $\frac{1}{4}$, and 7.

PROCEDURE: Interchange the numerator and denominator. First, write any whole number as a fraction before writing its reciprocal.

ANSWER: We'll use the chart at right:

Fraction	Reciprocal
$\frac{2}{3}$	$\frac{3}{2}$
$\frac{1}{4}$	$\frac{4}{1} = 4$
$7 = \frac{7}{1}$	$\frac{1}{7}$

YOU TRY IT 1 *Identify the reciprocal. Use Example 1 as a guide.*

a) The reciprocal of $\frac{6}{7}$ is ____.

b) The reciprocal of $\frac{9}{4}$ is ____.

c) The reciprocal of $\frac{1}{8}$ is ____.

d) The reciprocal of 6 is ____.

Complete the following sentence and explain your answer.

The reciprocal of any improper fraction is ________________________.

Question: Can a fraction that has 0 in the numerator, like $\frac{0}{3}$, have a reciprocal?

Answer: No, because the reciprocal would place a 0 in the denominator, and—as we learned in Sections 1.5 and 3.1—division by 0 is undefined.

The reciprocal of a fraction is also called the multiplicative *inverse* of the fraction. When finding the reciprocal of a fraction, we say that the fraction has been inverted. As an **inverse,** the reciprocal has this special property:

Multiplicative Inverse

The product of a fraction and its reciprocal is 1 (the multiplicative identity):

$$\frac{a}{b} \cdot \frac{b}{a} = 1, \text{ provided } a \neq 0 \text{ and } b \neq 0.$$

EXAMPLE 2 First, identify the reciprocal of the fraction. Second, find the product of the fraction and its reciprocal.

a) $\frac{4}{5}$ b) $\frac{9}{2}$ c) $\frac{1}{7}$ d) 8

ANSWER:

	Fraction	Reciprocal	Product
a)	$\frac{4}{5}$	$\frac{5}{4}$	$\frac{4}{5} \cdot \frac{5}{4} = \frac{20}{20} = 1$
b)	$\frac{9}{2}$	$\frac{2}{9}$	$\frac{9}{2} \cdot \frac{2}{9} = \frac{18}{18} = 1$
c)	$\frac{1}{7}$	$\frac{7}{1}$	$\frac{1}{7} \cdot \frac{7}{1} = \frac{7}{7} = 1$
d)	$8 = \frac{8}{1}$	$\frac{1}{8}$	$\frac{8}{1} \cdot \frac{1}{8} = \frac{8}{8} = 1$

YOU TRY IT 2 *First, identify the reciprocal of each fraction. Second, find the product of each fraction and its reciprocal. Use Example 2 as a guide.*

	Fraction	Reciprocal	Product		Fraction	Reciprocal	Product
a)	$\frac{3}{10}$ ×		___	b)	$\frac{11}{7}$ ×		___
c)	$\frac{1}{5}$ ×		___	d)	9 ×		___

What number is equivalent to its own reciprocal?

Rewriting Division as Multiplication

Because division is the inverse operation of multiplication, and because the reciprocal is the multiplicative inverse, we can rewrite a division problem as multiplication. With fractions, we don't just replace the division sign (÷) with the multiplication sign (×), we must also rewrite the second number as its reciprocal.

This process is called **invert and multiply**:

Writing Division as Multiplication $\frac{a}{b} \div \frac{c}{d} = \frac{a}{b} \cdot \frac{d}{c}$

1. Keep the first number (or fraction) the same.
2. Write the multiplication sign.
3. Invert (write the reciprocal of) the second number (or fraction).

This means, for example, that $8 \div 2$ can be rewritten as $8 \cdot \frac{1}{2}$.

In general, if both numbers are already fractions we can apply the Quotient Rule of Fractions.

Quotient Rule of Fractions

$$\frac{a}{b} \div \frac{d}{c} = \frac{a}{b} \cdot \frac{c}{d}$$

Example: $\frac{5}{7} \div \frac{2}{3} = \frac{5}{7} \cdot \frac{3}{2}$

We have changed the problem from one of division to one of multiplication.

Caution It's best to write the problem as a product before attempting to simplify.

EXAMPLE 3 Divide using the Quotient Rule (invert and multiply). Simplify if possible.

a) $\frac{4}{7} \div \frac{3}{5}$ b) $\frac{4}{9} \div \frac{5}{4}$ c) $3 \div 4$

ANSWER: a) $\frac{4}{7} \div \frac{3}{5}$ Invert and multiply.

$= \frac{4}{7} \cdot \frac{5}{3} = \boxed{\frac{20}{21}}$

b) $\frac{4}{9} \div \frac{5}{4}$ The 4's *cannot* divide out.

$= \frac{4}{9} \cdot \frac{4}{5} = \boxed{\frac{16}{45}}$

c) $3 \div 4$

$\downarrow \quad \downarrow$

$= \frac{3}{1} \cdot \frac{1}{4} = \boxed{\frac{3}{4}}$

YOU TRY IT 3 *Divide using the Quotient Rule. Simplify if possible. Use Example 3 as a guide.*

a) $\frac{4}{3} \div \frac{5}{4}$ b) $\frac{5}{6} \div \frac{7}{12}$ c) $\frac{8}{5} \div \frac{8}{5}$ d) $12 \div 9$

e) $6 \div \frac{4}{5}$ f) $\frac{10}{9} \div 5$

Dividing Mixed Numbers

Just as in multiplying mixed numbers, before dividing with mixed numbers we must first rewrite each as an improper fraction. We may then proceed with the Quotient Rule of Fractions: invert and multiply.

EXAMPLE 4 Divide and simplify.

a) $1\frac{7}{9} \div 2\frac{2}{3}$ b) $3\frac{1}{3} \div \frac{4}{9}$

PROCEDURE: Rewrite each mixed number as an improper fraction. Then, rewrite the division as multiplication: invert and multiply.

ANSWER:

a) $1\frac{7}{9} \div 2\frac{2}{3}$

$= \frac{16}{9} \div \frac{8}{3}$

$= \frac{16}{9} \cdot \frac{3}{8}$

$= \frac{\cancel{16}^2 \cdot \cancel{3}^1}{\cancel{9}_3 \cdot \cancel{8}_1}$

$= \boxed{\frac{2}{3}}$

b) $3\frac{1}{3} \div \frac{4}{9}$

$= \frac{10}{3} \div \frac{4}{9}$

$= \frac{10}{3} \cdot \frac{9}{4}$

$= \frac{\cancel{10}^5 \cdot \cancel{9}^3}{\cancel{3}_1 \cdot \cancel{4}_2}$

$= \frac{15}{2} = \boxed{7\frac{1}{2}}$

YOU TRY IT 4 *Divide; simplify completely. Write each answer as a mixed number, whenever possible. Use Example 4 as a guide.*

a) $4\frac{2}{3} \div 3\frac{1}{2}$ b) $\frac{7}{8} \div 2\frac{1}{10}$

c) $3\frac{3}{4} \div 10$ d) $8 \div 9\frac{1}{3}$

Complex Fractions and Division

The division bar means *divided by*, so we can turn any fraction—including a complex fraction—into a division problem, numerator ÷ denominator.

EXAMPLE 5

Simplify this complex fraction by first rewriting it using the division sign (÷) $\dfrac{\frac{15}{14}}{\frac{20}{21}}$.

ANSWER:

$$\dfrac{\frac{15}{14}}{\frac{20}{21}} = \frac{15}{14} \div \frac{20}{21} = \frac{15}{14} \cdot \frac{21}{20} = \frac{15 \cdot 21}{14 \cdot 20} = \frac{9}{8} = 1\frac{1}{8}$$

Rewrite the fraction as a division problem.

Invert and multiply.

YOU TRY IT 5

Simplify each complex fraction by first rewriting it using the division sign (÷). Use Example 5 as a guide.

a) $\dfrac{\frac{8}{15}}{\frac{16}{35}}$ b) $\dfrac{3}{\frac{5}{2}}$ c) $\dfrac{\frac{8}{9}}{5}$

You Try It Answers: Section 3.4

YTI 1 a) $\frac{7}{6}$ b) $\frac{4}{9}$ c) $\frac{8}{1}$ or 8 d) $\frac{1}{6}$ e) $\frac{15}{2}$ or $7\frac{1}{2}$ f) $\frac{2}{9}$

YTI 2 a) $\frac{3}{10} \times \frac{10}{3} = \frac{30}{30} = 1$ b) $\frac{11}{7} \times \frac{7}{11} = \frac{77}{77} = 1$ c) $\frac{1}{5} \times \frac{5}{1} = \frac{5}{5} = 1$ d) $\frac{9}{1} \times \frac{1}{9} = \frac{9}{9} = 1$

YTI 3 a) $\frac{16}{15}$ or $1\frac{1}{15}$ b) $\frac{10}{7}$ or $1\frac{3}{7}$ c) 1 d) $\frac{4}{3}$ or $1\frac{1}{3}$

YTI 4 a) $\frac{4}{3}$ or $1\frac{1}{3}$ b) $\frac{5}{12}$ c) $\frac{3}{8}$ d) $\frac{6}{7}$

YTI 5 a) $\frac{7}{6}$ or $1\frac{1}{6}$ b) $\frac{6}{5}$ or $1\frac{1}{5}$ c) $\frac{8}{45}$

Focus Exercises: Section 3.4

Identify the reciprocal, if possible.

1. $\frac{3}{5}$
2. $\frac{7}{10}$
3. $\frac{1}{6}$
4. $\frac{0}{5}$
5. 8
6. $\frac{3}{1}$
7. 0
8. $\frac{1}{4}$

Divide. Simplify if possible.

9. $\frac{3}{5} \div \frac{2}{7}$
10. $\frac{2}{9} \div \frac{3}{4}$
11. $\frac{8}{21} \div \frac{4}{7}$
12. $\frac{6}{7} \div \frac{9}{11}$
13. $\frac{8}{15} \div \frac{4}{5}$
14. $\frac{2}{21} \div \frac{6}{9}$
15. $\frac{9}{10} \div \frac{12}{20}$
16. $\frac{14}{15} \div \frac{7}{10}$
17. $\frac{3}{4} \div \frac{15}{16}$
18. $\frac{12}{25} \div \frac{8}{15}$
19. $\frac{8}{35} \div \frac{2}{7}$
20. $\frac{4}{15} \div \frac{16}{20}$
21. $\frac{20}{21} \div \frac{15}{28}$
22. $\frac{3}{8} \div \frac{9}{16}$
23. $\frac{5}{14} \div \frac{10}{21}$
24. $\frac{9}{16} \div \frac{12}{32}$
25. $\frac{27}{28} \div \frac{18}{35}$
26. $\frac{2}{15} \div \frac{8}{9}$
27. $\frac{21}{25} \div \frac{14}{20}$
28. $\frac{18}{35} \div \frac{12}{25}$
29. $\frac{15}{25} \div \frac{9}{10}$
30. $\frac{6}{28} \div \frac{9}{21}$
31. $\frac{21}{30} \div \frac{14}{20}$
32. $\frac{18}{25} \div \frac{27}{40}$

Divide. Simplify if possible. Write the final answer as a mixed number, whenever possible.

33. $2\frac{2}{3} \div 2\frac{1}{2}$
34. $1\frac{4}{5} \div \frac{3}{8}$
35. $3\frac{3}{5} \div \frac{9}{10}$
36. $\frac{4}{15} \div 2\frac{2}{5}$
37. $\frac{8}{15} \div 1\frac{1}{9}$

88. $\frac{7}{9} \div 4\frac{2}{3}$

39. $2\frac{5}{8} \div 1\frac{3}{4}$
40. $\frac{4}{15} \div 3\frac{5}{9}$
41. $6 \div 4\frac{1}{5}$
42. $20 \div 1\frac{1}{3}$
43. $4\frac{2}{7} \div 12$
44. $2\frac{7}{10} \div 9$

First, identify the reciprocal of each fraction. Second, find the product of the fraction and its reciprocal.

	Fraction	Reciprocal	Product		Fraction	Reciprocal	Product
45.	$\frac{4}{5}$	___	___	46.	$\frac{11}{8}$	___	___
47.	7	___	___	48.	$\frac{1}{2}$	___	___

Simplify each complex fraction completely.

49. $\dfrac{\frac{3}{10}}{\frac{7}{9}}$

50. $\dfrac{\frac{21}{40}}{\frac{14}{15}}$

51. $\dfrac{\frac{9}{10}}{\frac{27}{25}}$

52. $\dfrac{\frac{12}{20}}{\frac{9}{5}}$

53. $\dfrac{10}{\frac{5}{4}}$

54. $\dfrac{8}{\frac{4}{7}}$

55. $\dfrac{3}{\frac{18}{4}}$

56. $\dfrac{2}{\frac{18}{5}}$

57. $\dfrac{\frac{15}{25}}{6}$

58. $\dfrac{\frac{20}{9}}{8}$

59. $\dfrac{\frac{25}{8}}{15}$

60. $\dfrac{\frac{12}{7}}{18}$

Divide. Simplify if possible. Write the final answer as a mixed number, whenever possible.

61. $\frac{45}{32} \div \frac{75}{48}$

62. $\frac{60}{49} \div \frac{36}{70}$

63. $\frac{90}{33} \div \frac{54}{55}$

64. $\frac{49}{100} \div \frac{42}{75}$

65. $\frac{72}{25} \div \frac{48}{45}$

66. $\frac{96}{125} \div \frac{32}{50}$

SECTION 3.5 Equations and Applications with Fractions

Objectives

In this section, you will learn to:

- Solve equations and applications involving multiplying and dividing fractions.

To successfully complete this section, you need to understand:

- Solving equations (1.6)
- Multiplying fractions (3.3)
- Dividing fractions (3.4)

Introduction

In Section 1.6, we learned that to solve an equation involving multiplication, such as $6 \cdot n = 18$, we divide each side by the coefficient of n to isolate the variable. This causes the coefficient if n to be just 1, our main goal in isolating the variable.

$6 \cdot n = 18$	Divide each side by 6.
$6 \div 6 \cdot n = 18 \div 6$	$18 \div 6$ can be written as $\frac{18}{6}$.
$1 \cdot n = \frac{18}{6}$	$1 \cdot n$ becomes just n; $\frac{18}{6} = 3$.
$n = 3$	The solution is 3.

The solution for each equation in Section 1.6 was a whole number. This section introduces us to equations in which the solution is a fraction or a mixed number. We'll also solve equations in which the coefficient is a fraction.

Equations with Fractional Solutions

If the coefficient in an equation doesn't divide evenly into the constant on the other side of the equal sign, then the solution is a fraction or a mixed number. We can use the fact that division can be written in the form of a fraction; for example,

$$3 \div 7 = \frac{3}{7}.$$

EXAMPLE 1 Solve the equation $12 = 9 \cdot n$ by dividing by the coefficient so that it isolates the variable.

ANSWER:

$12 = 9 \cdot n$	Divide each side by the coefficient, 9.
$12 \div 9 = 9 \div 9 \cdot n$	$12 \div 9$ can be written as $\frac{12}{9}$.
$\frac{12}{9} = 1 \cdot n$	$\frac{12}{9}$ can be reduced by a factor of 3 to become $\frac{4}{3}$.
$\frac{4}{3} = n$	$\frac{4}{3}$ can be written as a mixed number, $1\frac{1}{3}$.
$n = 1\frac{1}{3}$	Use the improper fraction $\frac{4}{3}$ when doing the check.

Check:

$12 = 9 \cdot \frac{4}{3}$?

$12 = \frac{36}{3}$?

$12 = 12$ ✓

True.

YOU TRY IT 1 *Solve each equation by dividing by the coefficient so that it isolates the variable. If the solution is an improper fraction, write it as a mixed number. Use Example 1 as a guide.*

a) $14 \cdot n = 21$

b) $28 = 42 \cdot n$

Equations Involving Multiplying Fractions

Recall from Section 3.4 that the product of a fraction and its reciprocal is 1; for example,

$$\frac{3}{5}\cdot\frac{5}{3} = 1.$$

So, if the coefficient in an equation is a fraction, we can isolate the variable—get the coefficient of n to be 1—by multiplying each side of the equation by the reciprocal of the coefficient.

EXAMPLE 2

Isolate the variable by multiplying each side by the reciprocal of the coefficient.

a) $n\cdot\frac{2}{3} = 10$ b) $1\frac{3}{5}\cdot n = \frac{16}{3}$

ANSWER: a) $n\cdot\frac{2}{3} = 10$ $\frac{3}{2}$ is the reciprocal of $\frac{2}{3}$, so multiply each side by $\frac{3}{2}$; also, make 10 into a fraction: $\frac{10}{1}$.

$n\cdot\frac{2}{3}\cdot\mathbf{\frac{3}{2}} = \frac{10}{1}\cdot\mathbf{\frac{3}{2}}$

$n\cdot 1 = \frac{30}{2}$ Multiply the fractions together; here $\frac{2}{3}\cdot\frac{3}{2} = 1$.

Simplify: $\frac{30}{2} = 15$.

$n = 15$

Check $n = 15$:

$15\cdot\frac{2}{3} = 10?$

$\frac{15}{1}\cdot\frac{2}{3} = 10?$

$\frac{30}{3} = 10$ ✓

True.

b) $1\frac{3}{5}\cdot n = \frac{16}{3}$ First write $1\frac{3}{5}$ as an improper fraction: $\frac{8}{5}$.

$\frac{8}{5}\cdot n = \frac{16}{3}$ Multiply each side by $\frac{5}{8}$, the reciprocal of $\frac{8}{5}$.

$\frac{8}{5}\cdot\mathbf{\frac{5}{8}}\cdot n = \frac{16}{3}\cdot\mathbf{\frac{5}{8}}$ On the left, $\frac{8}{5}\cdot\frac{5}{8} = 1$.

$1\cdot n = \frac{16\cdot 5}{3\cdot 8}$ On the right, the fraction can be reduced by a factor of 8.

$n = \frac{2\cdot 5}{3\cdot 1}$

$n = \frac{10}{3}$ or $3\frac{1}{3}$

Check $n = \frac{10}{3}$:

$\frac{8}{5}\cdot\frac{10}{3} = \frac{16}{3}?$

$\frac{8\cdot 10}{5\cdot 3} = \frac{16}{3}?$

$\frac{8\cdot 2}{1\cdot 3} = \frac{16}{3}?$

$\frac{16}{3} = \frac{16}{3}$ ✓

True.

YOU TRY IT 2

Isolate the variable by multiplying each side by the reciprocal of the coefficient. Use Example 2 as a guide. Check each answer.

a) $9 = \frac{3}{4}\cdot n$ b) $1\frac{1}{3}\times n = 5$ c) $n\cdot\frac{3}{8} = 2\frac{2}{5}$

Solving Equations Involving Multiplication

- When the coefficient is a whole number, it is easier to divide by the coefficient.
- If the coefficient is a fraction or a mixed number, it is easier to multiply by its reciprocal.

If, in an equation, the coefficient is a whole number, is it possible to isolate the variable by multiplying by its reciprocal? Explain.

Applications Involving Multiplying and Dividing Fractions

In Section 1.7 you were introduced to some situations that require using multiplication. At that time, we explored the formula

(Number of Same Parts) × Part = Whole

Recall that the whole and the part are always of the same unit of measure.

Though this formula involves multiplication, some of the situations you will see here involve dividing the whole into equal parts. Still, this formula can be used consistently for both division and multiplication problems.

In each problem, one of the "pieces" will be unknown. It may be the whole, the part, or the number of repetitions of the part. The key to setting up the formula is recognizing which pieces have the common measure; they will be the whole (larger number) and the part (smaller number).

For example, a dozen (12) cookies can be divided easily among 4 children. The question might be, "How many cookies will each child get?" Let's use this simple situation to illustrate the proper way to approach this problem and others like it.

EXAMPLE 3 If a dozen cookies is to be divided evenly among four children, how many cookies will each child receive?

PROCEDURE: First, determine the common measure, the whole, and the part.

COMMON MEASURE: Cookies. So the part and the whole are the cookies and the part is repeated by the 4 children.

The **whole** is the total number of cookies.

The **part**, the unknown, is how many cookies each child will receive.

Since the part is divided evenly among 4 children, the number of times the part is repeated is 4.

ANSWER: Legend: Let $n =$ the number of cookies each child receives.

$4 \cdot n = 12$ Divide each side by 4.

$4 \div 4 \cdot n = 12 \div 4$

$1 \cdot n = 3$

$n = 3$

SENTENCE: Each child will receive 3 cookies.

It may seem that this example is a bit too easy, especially since it doesn't involve dividing fractions. Consider this next example, though; it is similar, but different.

EXAMPLE 4 Andy has a strip of wood that is $2\frac{1}{4}$ inches wide and needs to be divided into 3 smaller strips of equal width. How wide will each smaller strip be?

PROCEDURE: First, we can write $2\frac{1}{4}$ as an improper fraction: $\frac{9}{4}$.

Next, picture yourself in the situation. You've got a strip of wood that is $\frac{9}{4}$ inches wide. You are going to divide it evenly into smaller pieces.

COMMON MEASURE: Here, we're given a width $\left(\frac{9}{4} \text{ inches}\right)$ and we're asked to find a width. This must mean that the widths (in inches) are the part and the whole.

The larger (original) piece must be the **whole** (total width of $\frac{9}{4}$ inches).

Each smaller strip is a **part**, the width is unknown, and the part is repeated 3 times (there are to be 3 smaller strips).

ANSWER: Legend: Let $n =$ the width of each smaller strip.

$$3 \cdot n = \frac{9}{4} \qquad \text{Divide each side by 3.}$$

$$3 \div 3 \cdot n = \frac{9}{4} \div 3$$

$$\frac{3}{1} \cdot \frac{1}{3} \cdot n = \frac{9}{4} \cdot \frac{1}{3} \qquad \text{Invert and multiply.}$$

$$1 \cdot n = \frac{9}{12} \qquad \text{Reduce } \frac{9}{12} \text{ by a factor of 3.}$$

$$n = \frac{3}{4}$$

SENTENCE: Each smaller strip will be $\frac{3}{4}$ inches wide.

For each application, identify the common measure, the whole, that part, and the number of parts. Write the legend, set up and solve the equation, and write a sentence answering the question.

YOU TRY IT 3 *Gail has a stack of flyers she wants to fold, and she asks Barbara and Jaynelle to help her. They decide to measure the height (thickness) of the stack; it turns out to be $4\frac{1}{8}$ inches high. If they divide the full stack evenly 3 ways, how high would each person's pile be?*

YOU TRY IT 4 *Tadzu works for a landscaper. Their most recent job requires them to prepare, plant, and cultivate $\frac{2}{5}$ of an acre of land. The owner of the company is assigning Tadzu and 3 others (4 workers in all) to the job and wants them to divide the land up evenly among themselves. How much of an acre will each employee be responsible for?*

Sometimes, the number of repetitions is unknown. We can determine this when we identify the common measure: if the known values have the same common measure, then they must be the part and whole, and the unknown value is the number of repetitions.

EXAMPLE 5

Andy needs small strips of wood that are only $\frac{3}{8}$ inches wide. From a board that is $5\frac{1}{4}$ inches wide, how many of these strips of wood can Andy get?

PROCEDURE: First, let's look at the common measure to help us identify the part and the whole. Also, write $5\frac{1}{4}$ as $\frac{21}{4}$.

COMMON MEASURE: Andy has a board that is $\frac{21}{4}$ inches wide and the smaller strips are $\frac{3}{8}$ inches wide. The width of the board is the **whole** $\left(\frac{21}{4}\text{ inches}\right)$ and the width of each strip $\left(\frac{3}{8}\text{ inches}\right)$ is the **part**. Both of these are in inches and are known values, so the unknown value is the number of parts, which is mentioned in the question.

ANSWER: Legend: Let $n =$ the number of strips.

$$n \cdot \frac{3}{8} = \frac{21}{4}$$ Multiply each side by the reciprocal of the coefficient.

$$n \cdot \frac{3}{8} \cdot \frac{8}{3} = \frac{21}{4} \cdot \frac{8}{3}$$ Simplify the right side.

$$n \cdot 1 = \frac{21 \cdot 8}{4 \cdot 3}$$ 21 and 3 have a common factor of 3, and 8 and 4 have a common factor of 4.

$$n = \frac{7 \cdot 2}{1 \cdot 1} = 14$$

SENTENCE: Andy can get 14 smaller strips.

YOU TRY IT 5

At a specialty bicycle shop, Mario can assemble one bicycle in $\frac{2}{3}$ of an hour. If Mario works 8 hours, how many bicycles can he assemble?

YOU TRY IT 6

Marie works in a candy shop that advertises homemade candies. One specialty is a brick of fudge. Marie must cut a 6-inch hunk of fudge into slices each having a width of $\frac{3}{4}$ inches. From the 6-inch brick, how many slices of fudge can Maria cut?

There are some situations in which the whole is unknown. When that occurs, the variable, n, represents the whole.

EXAMPLE 6

At a bookstore, Devra needs to place 32 copies of the new best-selling paperback book tightly together on a shelf. If each book is $1\frac{1}{4}$ inches thick, how many inches of the shelf will the 32 books take up?

COMMON MEASURE: $1\frac{1}{4} = \frac{5}{4}$, so each book is $\frac{5}{4}$ inches thick. The question asks, "How many inches..." so inches of books is the common measure. The **part** is the thickness, in inches, of each book; the whole (the number of inches of books) is unknown; and the number of parts is 32 books.

ANSWER: Legend: Let $n =$ the total number of inches of books.

$$32 \cdot \frac{5}{4} = n$$

$$\frac{32}{1} \cdot \frac{5}{4} = n$$

$$\frac{32 \cdot 5}{1 \cdot 4} = n \qquad \text{Reduce 32 and 4 by a factor of 4.}$$

$$\frac{8 \cdot 5}{1 \cdot 1} = n$$

$$40 = n$$

SENTENCE: The 32 books will take up 40 inches on the shelf.

YOU TRY IT 7

Katie uses $\frac{5}{6}$ yard of fabric for every doll dress she makes. To make 12 doll dresses, how many yards of fabric does Katie need?

YOU TRY IT 8

A cookbook says that a host should plan on $\frac{3}{4}$ pound of turkey for every guest. If Inez buys a $13\frac{1}{2}$ pound turkey for Thanksgiving, how many guests can she serve?

You Try It Answers: Section 3.5

YTI 1 a) $n = \frac{3}{2} = 1\frac{1}{2}$ b) $n = \frac{2}{3}$

YTI 2 a) $n = 12$ b) $n = \frac{15}{4} = 3\frac{3}{4}$ c) $n = \frac{32}{5} = 6\frac{2}{5}$

YTI 3 Each person's pile will be $1\frac{3}{8}$ inches high.

YTI 4 Each employee will be responsible for $\frac{1}{10}$ of an acre.

YTI 5 Mario can assemble 12 bicycles.

YTI 6 Marie can cut 8 slices of fudge.

YTI 7 Katie needs 10 yards of fabric.

YTI 8 Inez can serve 18 guests.

Focus Exercises: Section 3.5

Solve each equation by dividing each side by the coefficient. Simplify.

1. $n \cdot 12 = 8$ **2.** $n \cdot 4 = 14$ **3.** $6 \cdot n = 9$ **4.** $9 \cdot n = 24$

5. $35 \cdot n = 21$ **6.** $45 \cdot n = 20$ **7.** $12 = n \cdot 32$ **8.** $16 = n \cdot 40$

9. $15 = n \cdot 20$ **10.** $12 = 27 \cdot n$ **11.** $18 = 24 \cdot n$ **12.** $18 = n \cdot 30$

Solve each equation. Simplify.

13. $n \cdot \frac{11}{5} = 22$ **14.** $\frac{4}{9} \cdot n = 24$ **15.** $\frac{3}{4} \cdot n = 6$ **16.** $\frac{2}{3} \cdot n = 18$

17. $\frac{1}{2} \cdot n = \frac{5}{9}$ **18.** $\frac{6}{15} \cdot n = \frac{12}{20}$ **19.** $\frac{8}{21} = n \cdot \frac{4}{7}$ **20.** $\frac{25}{42} = n \cdot \frac{10}{7}$

21. $\frac{20}{35} = \frac{8}{7} \cdot n$ **22.** $\frac{4}{15} = n \cdot \frac{16}{9}$ **23.** $\frac{30}{49} = \frac{25}{21} \cdot n$ **24.** $\frac{27}{24} = \frac{45}{16} \cdot n$

Solve each equation. Simplify.

25. $n \cdot 1\frac{2}{3} = 10$ **26.** $n \cdot 2\frac{2}{3} = 8$ **27.** $n \cdot 3\frac{1}{5} = 32$ **28.** $n \cdot 4\frac{1}{2} = 18$

29. $n \cdot 2\frac{2}{5} = 6$ **30.** $n \cdot 3\frac{1}{8} = 5$ **31.** $2 = n \cdot 3\frac{1}{5}$ **32.** $16 = n \cdot 1\frac{1}{15}$

33. $1\frac{1}{9} = n \cdot 1\frac{2}{3}$ **34.** $1\frac{1}{15} = n \cdot 1\frac{1}{3}$ **35.** $10\frac{1}{2} = n \cdot 1\frac{1}{2}$ **36.** $1\frac{1}{4} = n \cdot 1\frac{7}{8}$

37. $3\frac{3}{4} \times n = 3\frac{1}{8}$ **38.** $2\frac{6}{7} \times n = 4\frac{2}{7}$ **39.** $1\frac{1}{8} \times n = 7\frac{1}{2}$ **40.** $2\frac{7}{10} \times n = 3\frac{3}{5}$

For each application, identify the common measure, the whole, the part, and the number of parts. Write the legend, set up and solve the equation, and write a sentence answering the question.

41. Marnay gives guitar lessons $7\frac{1}{2}$ hours each day. Each lesson lasts $\frac{3}{4}$ hour. How many lessons does Marnay give each day?

42. At an amusement park, employees rotate from location to location so that they have a variety of duties to do each day. One location, a hot dog cart, is open for twelve hours. If 8 different employees share evenly the 12 hours that the cart is open, how many hours does each employee spend at the hot dog cart?

43. A mother has a sick child and needs to divide liquid cough medicine into 6 equal doses. If she has $1\frac{1}{2}$ cups of cough syrup, how much cough syrup will each dose contain?

44. Sandra works for the city's Parks and Recreation Department. Each spring, it is her job to mark six soccer playing fields on one large field. The large field is $\frac{3}{8}$ of a mile long, and each of the soccer fields must be of equal length. How long (in miles) will each of the six soccer fields be?

45. At a gift wrapping booth, each package is topped with a ribbon bow made of $2\frac{2}{3}$ feet of ribbon. If a spool has 24 feet of ribbon on it, how many bows can be made from one spool?

46. Joachin, a cross country skier, has fully recovered from a broken leg. His coach has put him on a strict training schedule in which he gradually increases the distance he skis each week. In the third week of this schedule, Joachin must ski a total of 45 miles while skiing the same $7\frac{1}{2}$ mile course each day. To complete all 45 miles, how many days will Joachin need to ski this course?

47. Yuan must complete 45 hours of counseling high school students before she can become a certified educational advisor. Her assignment at Lincoln High School allows her to counsel students in the afternoon for $2\frac{1}{4}$ hours. How many of these afternoon sessions must Yuan complete to receive her certificate?

48. Nate's dog, Banjo, a golden retriever, eats $3\frac{1}{2}$ cups of dog food each day. How many cups of dog food does Banjo eat each month (30 days)?

49. Tim is a janitor for an elementary school. It takes him $\frac{1}{4}$ hour to clean each classroom at the end of the school day. How many hours does it take Tim to clean all 25 classrooms?

50. Ramon has written a book that contains colorful graphs and charts. His printer can print the entire book in $1\frac{1}{3}$ hours. He needs to print out 6 copies for his team of editors. How long will it take to print 6 copies of his book?

Chapter 3 Review

Section 3.1 Introduction to Fractions

CONCEPT	EXAMPLE
A **fraction** is the comparison of a part of something to its whole, where all of the parts are the same size.	$\frac{\text{part}}{\text{whole}}$
A fraction consists of three components: a fraction bar, a number above the fraction bar, and a number below the fraction bar.	$\frac{\text{numerator}}{\text{denominator}}$ ← the fraction bar
The **numerator** represents the number of equal-sized parts being considered and the **denominator** represents the number of equal-sized parts contained in the whole.	There are 8 equally sized rectangles; 3 are shaded. $\frac{3}{8}$ of the rectangles are shaded. 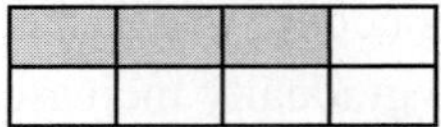
If ***b*** is any number (*except 0*), then $\frac{0}{b} = 0$	$\frac{0}{9} = 0$
The denominator of a fraction can never be zero.	$\frac{a}{0}$ is undefined.
A **proper fraction** has a numerator that is *less than* the denominator.	$\frac{1}{18}, \frac{3}{5}, \frac{7}{19}, \frac{34}{25}$
An **improper fraction** has a numerator that is *equal to* or *greater than* the denominator.	$\frac{4}{4}, \frac{7}{5}, \frac{26}{13}, \frac{42}{42}$
A **mixed number** is the sum of a whole number and a fraction.	$1\frac{4}{5} = 1 + \frac{4}{5}$
In a **complex fraction**, either the numerator or denominator (or both) contains a fraction.	$\frac{\frac{8}{9}}{6}, \frac{4}{\frac{3}{5}}$, and $\frac{\frac{8}{7}}{\frac{1}{2}}$
Every mixed number can be written as an improper fraction: $\text{Whole} + \frac{\text{numerator}}{\text{denominator}} = \frac{\text{Whole} \times \text{denominator} + \text{numerator}}{\text{denominator}}$	$2\frac{3}{8} = \frac{2 \times 8 + 3}{8} = \frac{16 + 3}{8} = \frac{19}{8}$
Every improper fraction can be written as a mixed number using long or short division.	$\frac{36}{5} = 36 \div 5 = 7\frac{1}{5}$ $5\overline{)36}$ = 7 r 1; -35; 1
A natural number divided by itself is 1: $\frac{a}{a} = 1$	$\frac{5}{5} = 1$

CONCEPT	EXAMPLE
A number divided by 1 is itself: $\frac{a}{1} = a$	$\frac{5}{1} = 5$
A **unit fraction** is one in which the numerator is 1 and the denominator is any natural number.	$\frac{1}{2}, \frac{1}{4}, \frac{1}{9}, \frac{1}{17}$

Section 3.2 Simplifying Fractions

CONCEPT	EXAMPLE
Fractions are **equivalent** if they have the same value.	$\frac{1}{2}, \frac{2}{4}, \frac{3}{6}$, and $\frac{5}{10}$ are all equivalent.
To **simplify**, or **reduce**, a fraction, divide out any factors greater than 1 that are common to both the numerator and denominator.	8 and 12 have a common factor of 4, so $\frac{8}{12}$ can be reduced by a factor of 4: $\frac{8 \div 4}{12 \div 4} = \frac{2}{3}$.
A fraction is in **lowest terms** when the numerator and denominator have no common factors other than 1.	$\frac{2}{3}$ is in lowest terms because 2 and 3 have no common factor (other than 1).
A fraction can be reduced by any common factor of the numerator and denominator. To reduce a fraction completely, divide out the greatest common factor (GCF).	The GCF of 24 and 40 is 8; reduce $\frac{24}{40}$ completely by dividing by 8: $\frac{24 \div 8}{40 \div 8} = \frac{3}{5}$
The fraction bar is a grouping symbol. It groups the numerator separately from the denominator. Evaluate the numerator and denominator separately before simplifying the fraction.	Simplify $\frac{12 - 4}{6 + 4}$. $\frac{12 - 4}{6 + 4} = \frac{8}{10}$ Reduce by a factor of 2: $\frac{8 \div 2}{10 \div 2} = \frac{4}{5}$.

Section 3.3 Multiplication of Fractions

CONCEPT	EXAMPLE
The product rule for multiplying fractions: $\frac{a}{b} \cdot \frac{c}{d} = \frac{a \cdot c}{b \cdot d} = \frac{\text{the product of the numerators}}{\text{the product of the denominators}}$	$\frac{5}{3} \cdot \frac{2}{7} = \frac{5 \cdot 2}{3 \cdot 7} = \frac{10}{21}$

CONCEPT

Write a whole number as a fraction, $\dfrac{\text{whole number}}{1}$, before multiplying.

EXAMPLE

$$4\cdot\frac{2}{7}=\frac{4}{1}\cdot\frac{2}{7}=\frac{4\cdot 2}{1\cdot 7}=\frac{8}{7}$$

CONCEPT

It is possible to divide out the common factors directly, without writing the actual division.

EXAMPLE

$$\frac{5}{6}\cdot\frac{9}{10}=\frac{\cancel{5}^{1}\cdot\cancel{9}^{3}}{\cancel{6}_{2}\cdot\cancel{10}_{2}}=\frac{3}{4}$$

CONCEPT

To multiply mixed numbers, first rewrite each mixed number as an improper fraction. If the final product is an improper fraction, rewrite it as a mixed number.

EXAMPLE

$$3\frac{1}{3}\times 2\frac{1}{4}=\frac{10}{3}\cdot\frac{9}{4}=\frac{\cancel{10}^{5}\cdot\cancel{9}^{3}}{\cancel{3}_{1}\cdot\cancel{4}_{2}}=\frac{15}{2}=7\frac{1}{2}$$

CONCEPT

The area of a triangle is $\frac{1}{2}\times$ Base $\times$ Height:

$$A=\frac{1}{2}\cdot b\cdot h$$

EXAMPLE

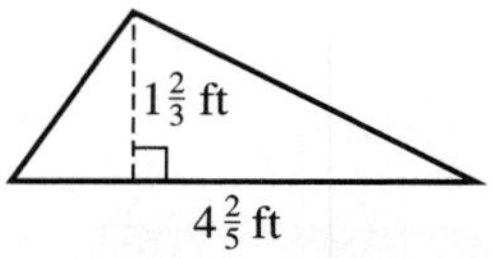

$$A=\frac{1}{2}\times 4\frac{2}{5}\times 1\frac{2}{3}=\frac{1}{2}\cdot\frac{22}{5}\cdot\frac{5}{3}$$

$$=\frac{1\cdot\cancel{22}^{11}\cdot\cancel{5}^{1}}{\cancel{2}_{1}\cdot\cancel{5}_{1}\cdot 3}=\frac{11}{3}=3\frac{2}{3}\text{ ft}^2$$

Section 3.4 Dividing Fractions

CONCEPT

The **reciprocal** of a fraction, $\frac{a}{b}$, is the fraction $\frac{b}{a}$, as long as $a \neq 0$ and $b \neq 0$.

EXAMPLE

The reciprocal of $\frac{5}{3}$ is $\frac{3}{5}$.

CONCEPT

The **reciprocal** of a fraction is also called the *multiplicative inverse*. When finding the reciprocal, we say the fraction has been *inverted*. As an inverse, the reciprocal has this special property:

The product of a fraction and its reciprocal is 1:

$\frac{a}{b}\cdot\frac{b}{a}=1$, provided that $a \neq 0$ and $b \neq 0$.

EXAMPLE

The product of reciprocals $\frac{5}{3}$ and $\frac{3}{5}$ is $\frac{5}{3}\cdot\frac{3}{5}=\frac{15}{15}=1$.

CONCEPT

Quotient Rule of Fractions:

$$\frac{a}{b}\div\frac{d}{c}=\frac{a}{b}\cdot\frac{c}{d}=\frac{a\cdot c}{b\cdot d}$$

To divide by a fraction, $\frac{a}{b}\div\frac{d}{c}$, invert and multiply:

1. Keep the first number (or fraction) the same.
2. Write the multiplication sign.
3. Invert (write the reciprocal of) the second number (or fraction).

EXAMPLE

$$\frac{4}{9}\div\frac{3}{5}=\frac{4}{9}\cdot\frac{5}{3}=\frac{20}{27}$$

CONCEPT	EXAMPLE
To divide mixed numbers, rewrite each mixed number as an improper fraction. Proceed with the Quotient Rule of Fractions: invert and multiply. If the quotient is an improper fraction, rewrite it as a mixed number.	$2\frac{7}{9} \div 3\frac{1}{3} = \frac{25}{9} \div \frac{10}{3} = \frac{25}{9} \cdot \frac{3}{10} = \frac{\cancel{25}^{5} \cdot \cancel{3}^{1}}{\cancel{9}_{3} \cdot \cancel{10}_{2}} = \frac{5}{6}$
A complex fraction can be simplified by treating the main fraction bar as a division bar.	$\frac{\frac{3}{5}}{\frac{7}{2}} = \frac{3}{5} \div \frac{7}{2} = \frac{3}{5} \cdot \frac{2}{7} = \frac{6}{35}$

Section 3.5 Equations and Applications with Fractions

CONCEPT	EXAMPLE
In an equation, if the coefficient of n is a fraction or a mixed number, isolate the variable by multiplying each side by the reciprocal of the coefficient.	$\frac{3}{4} \cdot n = 6$ $\frac{3}{4} \cdot \frac{4}{3} \cdot n = \frac{6}{1} \cdot \frac{4}{3}$ $1 \cdot n = \frac{24}{3}$ $n = 8$
A basic formula involving multiplication and division of fractions is: (Number of same-sized parts) × Part = Whole The whole and the part are always of the same unit of measure.	For a pizza party, Patti has figured that each guest will eat $\frac{3}{8}$ of a pizza. If Patti plans to serve 6 pizzas, how many guests can she invite? Whole = total number of pizzas Part = $\frac{3}{8}$ of a pizza Let n = the number of guest Patti can invite $n \times \frac{3}{8} = 6$ $n \cdot \frac{3}{8} \times \frac{8}{3} = 6 \cdot \frac{8}{3}$ $n \times 1 = 16$ $n = 16$ Patti can invite 16 guests.

Chapter 3 Review Exercises

Section 3.1

Identify each as either a proper fraction, an improper fraction, a mixed number, or a complex fraction.

1. $2\frac{5}{6}$ **2.** $\frac{19}{8}$ **3.** $\frac{\frac{4}{3}}{\frac{7}{2}}$ **4.** $\frac{4}{6}$

Write each mixed number as an improper fraction.

5. $1\frac{7}{8}$ **6.** $3\frac{4}{9}$ **7.** $5\frac{1}{6}$ **8.** $12\frac{3}{4}$

Write each improper fraction as a mixed number.

9. $\frac{23}{5}$ **10.** $\frac{14}{3}$ **11.** $\frac{70}{9}$ **12.** $\frac{17}{2}$

Multiply. If the result is an improper fraction, write it as a mixed number.

13. $\frac{3}{4}\cdot\frac{5}{7}$ **14.** $\frac{9}{5}\cdot\frac{3}{2}$ **15.** $\frac{7}{2}\cdot\frac{9}{4}$ **16.** $\frac{7}{3}\cdot\frac{4}{5}$

Section 3.2

Simplify completely. If the fraction is improper, write it as a mixed number.

17. $\frac{6}{18}$ **18.** $\frac{5}{20}$ **19.** $\frac{8}{36}$ **20.** $\frac{14}{35}$

21. $\frac{9}{33}$ **22.** $\frac{54}{72}$ **23.** $\frac{35}{15}$ **24.** $\frac{99}{44}$

25. $\frac{60}{24}$ **26.** $\frac{75}{60}$ **27.** $\frac{90}{36}$ **28.** $\frac{72}{32}$

Evaluate each expression. Simplify completely.

29. $\frac{12 - 4\cdot 2}{(12 - 4)\cdot 2}$ **30.** $\frac{2^2 + 4^2}{\sqrt{64}}$ **31.** $18 - 4\cdot\frac{21}{7}$ **32.** $12 - 12 \div \frac{12}{4}$

Section 3.3

Multiply. Simplify the answer completely. Write all improper fraction answers as mixed numbers.

33. $\frac{7}{5}\cdot\frac{2}{6}$ **34.** $\frac{4}{3}\cdot\frac{2}{8}$ **35.** $\frac{4}{5}\cdot\frac{3}{4}$ **36.** $\frac{4}{9}\cdot\frac{7}{6}$

37. $\frac{2}{3}\cdot\frac{7}{8}\cdot\frac{4}{3}$ **38.** $\frac{1}{12}\cdot\frac{15}{7}\cdot\frac{6}{5}$ **39.** $\frac{8}{9}\cdot\frac{3}{32}\cdot\frac{3}{5}$ **40.** $\frac{4}{3}\cdot\frac{7}{16}\cdot\frac{9}{5}$

41. $\frac{5}{18}\cdot 3$ **42.** $\frac{21}{14}\cdot 4$ **43.** $8\cdot\frac{9}{24}\cdot\frac{5}{3}$ **44.** $\frac{3}{8}\cdot\frac{6}{25}\cdot 5$

Multiply; simplify completely. Write each answer as a mixed number, whenever possible.

45. $2\frac{1}{2} \times 3\frac{3}{5}$ **46.** $\frac{2}{3} \times 1\frac{1}{4}$ **47.** $4\frac{3}{8} \times 2\frac{4}{5}$ **48.** $3\frac{3}{5} \times 2\frac{1}{9}$

49. $7\frac{1}{2} \times 6$ **50.** $5 \times 2\frac{3}{10}$ **51.** $3\frac{4}{7} \times 14 \times 1\frac{2}{5}$ **52.** $8 \times 3\frac{1}{9} \times 1\frac{2}{7}$

Evaluate each by first rewriting it as a product of fractions. Write each answer as a mixed number, whenever possible.

53. One-fifth of $\frac{2}{3}$ **54.** Two-thirds of $\frac{15}{14}$ **55.** Three-eighths of $\frac{4}{15}$ **56.** Two-thirds of $5\frac{1}{4}$

57. Three-fourths of $2\frac{2}{9}$ **58.** Five-sixths of $4\frac{1}{5}$

For each application problem, write a sentence answering the question.

59. Two-thirds of the students in Ms. Grecu's algebra class are women. If she has 42 students in her class, how many women are in Ms. Grecu's class?

60. Jasper's Meats prepares ready-made hamburger patties that weigh $\frac{2}{3}$ pounds each. How many pounds of meat are there in 12 patties?

Find the area of each geometric figure. (Each is measured in inches.)

61.

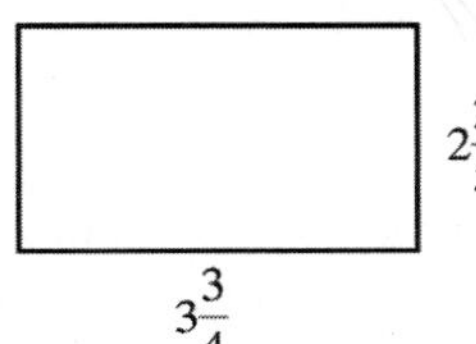

62.

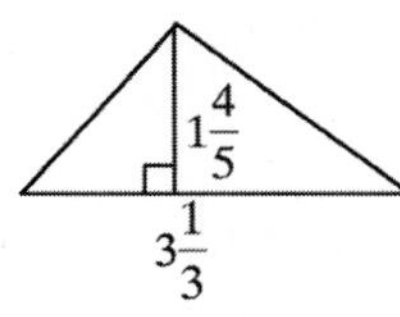

Section 3.4

Identify the reciprocal of the given number, if possible.

63. $\frac{9}{4}$ **64.** $\frac{1}{8}$ **65.** 4 **66.** $\frac{0}{5}$

Divide. Simplify if possible.

67. $\frac{3}{5} \div \frac{6}{11}$ **68.** $\frac{4}{18} \div \frac{2}{9}$ **69.** $\frac{10}{21} \div \frac{5}{3}$ **70.** $\frac{15}{8} \div \frac{5}{16}$

71. $\frac{6}{10} \div \frac{12}{70}$ **72.** $\frac{25}{18} \div \frac{5}{12}$ **73.** $\frac{9}{2} \div \frac{18}{13}$ **74.** $\frac{7}{10} \div \frac{49}{5}$

75. $\frac{16}{45} \div \frac{32}{27}$ **76.** $\frac{40}{81} \div \frac{25}{54}$ **77.** $\frac{77}{42} \div \frac{22}{36}$ **78.** $\frac{60}{49} \div \frac{80}{21}$

Divide. Simplify if possible. Write each final answer as a mixed number, whenever possible.

79. $1\frac{7}{8} \div 3\frac{1}{3}$ **80.** $5\frac{1}{4} \div 3\frac{1}{2}$ **81.** $6\frac{2}{5} \div 5\frac{1}{3}$ **82.** $8\frac{3}{4} \div 2\frac{5}{8}$

Simplify each complex fraction completely.

83. $\dfrac{\frac{7}{5}}{\frac{21}{10}}$ **84.** $\dfrac{\frac{4}{15}}{\frac{8}{25}}$ **85.** $\dfrac{\frac{4}{3}}{6}$ **86.** $\dfrac{20}{\frac{15}{4}}$

Section 3.5

Solve each equation. Simplify any fractions and write each answer as a mixed number, if possible.

87. $n \cdot 12 = 18$

88. $n \cdot 24 = 6$

89. $10 \cdot n = 15$

90. $27 \cdot n = 36$

91. $21 = 30 \cdot n$

92. $32 = 40 \cdot n$

93. $n \cdot \frac{3}{10} = 6$

94. $\frac{5}{7} \cdot n = 15$

95. $\frac{8}{15} = \frac{4}{9} \cdot n$

96. $\frac{9}{7} = n \cdot \frac{12}{35}$

97. $\frac{8}{9} = n \cdot \frac{2}{15}$

98. $\frac{25}{36} = \frac{20}{27} \cdot n$

99. $5\frac{4}{9} \cdot n = 4\frac{2}{3}$

100. $2\frac{7}{10} \cdot n = 3\frac{3}{5}$

101. $7\frac{1}{5} = n \cdot 2\frac{2}{5}$

102. $3\frac{3}{4} = n \cdot 3\frac{1}{8}$

For each application, write out the legend, set up and solve the equation, and write a sentence answering the question.

103. Tanya's fitness goal is to run 20 miles each week, running the same distance each day of the week. As she is planning next week's schedule, she notices that she has only 3 days that allow her time to run. How many miles should Tanya run each day next week?

104. As part of his punishment for painting graffiti on the school wall, Dimitri has to perform 80 hours of community service. Each Saturday, Dimitri spends $3\frac{1}{3}$ hours at a local soup kitchen. How many Saturdays must Dimitri work there to fulfill his 80-hour obligation?

105. Armand was asked to create a "Presidential Wall" of the portraits of United States presidents. The wall is $9\frac{1}{3}$ feet long, and each portrait is $1\frac{1}{3}$- feet wide. How many portraits can fit on the wall side by side?

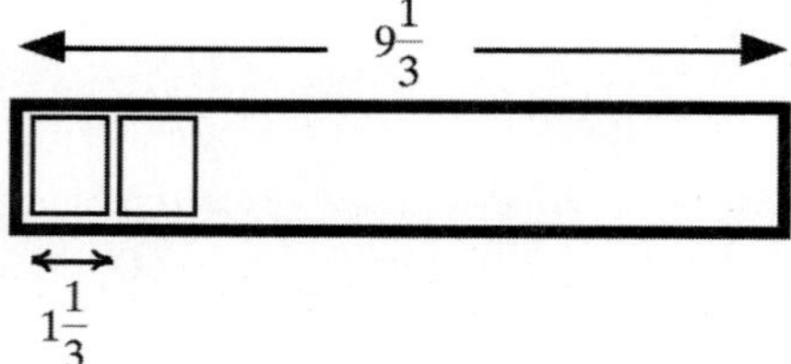

Chapter 3 Test

Write each mixed number as an improper fraction.

1. $7\frac{2}{5}$

2. $2\frac{8}{15}$

Write each improper fraction as a mixed number.

3. $\frac{31}{4}$

4. $\frac{52}{7}$

Evaluate each expression. Simplify completely. If possible, write each answer as a mixed number.

5. $\frac{42}{60}$

6. $\frac{70}{28}$

7. $\frac{3 \cdot 5 - 3}{3 + 3}$

8. $6 + \frac{12}{3} \cdot 5$

Multiply. Simplify each answer completely. If possible, write each answer as a mixed number.

9. $\frac{5}{6} \cdot \frac{9}{10}$ **10.** $\frac{8}{9} \cdot \frac{15}{16} \cdot \frac{3}{5}$ **11.** $5\frac{3}{5} \times 1\frac{7}{8}$ **12.** $5\frac{3}{4} \times 8$

Evaluate each by first rewriting it as a product of fractions.

13. Five-eighths of 12 **14.** Two-ninths of $6\frac{3}{4}$

Find the area of the figure. (Each side is measured in inches.)

15.

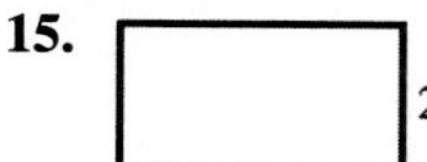

16.

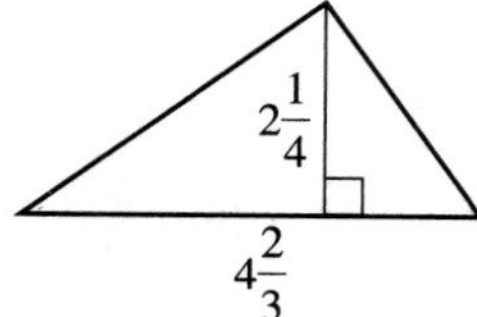

Divide. Simplify. If possible, write each answer as a mixed number.

17. $\frac{14}{15} \div \frac{7}{5}$ **18.** $\frac{18}{25} \div \frac{27}{10}$ **19.** $5\frac{1}{3} \div 2\frac{2}{9}$

Solve each equation. Simplify any fraction answer.

20. $n \cdot 24 = 16$ **21.** $\frac{7}{9} = n \cdot \frac{14}{15}$ **22.** $3\frac{1}{2} = n \cdot 5\frac{1}{4}$

For each application, write out the legend, set up and solve the equation, and write a sentence answering the question.

23. Kareem went to Kinko's to have a photo enlarged into a poster that is 36 inches high. The enlargement is $4\frac{1}{2}$ times the original size of the picture. How high is the original picture?

24. A special gift box contains 18 chocolate bars. If the whole box weighs $22\frac{1}{2}$ pounds, how much does each chocolate bar weigh?

CHAPTER 4

Fractions: Addition and Subtraction

Introduction

Chapter 4 is a continuation of the study of fractions. Whereas Chapter 3 focuses on multiplying and dividing fractions, Chapter 4's topic is on adding and subtracting fractions, including mixed numbers.

As you'll see, the rules for adding and subtracting fractions are very similar to each other, but those rules are very different from the ones for multiplication and division.

To prepare for this chapter, please take some time to do each of these exercises.

Preparation Exercises

Section 1.3, Adding and Subtracting Whole Numbers:

Add.

1. $59 + 267$

2. $8 + 26 + 117$

Subtract.

3. $23 - 18$

4. $136 - 49$

Section 1.4, Multiplying Whole Numbers: *Write the first five multiples of each number.*

5. 6

6. 9

Section 2.5, Prime Factorization: *Find the prime factorization of each number.*

7. 45

8. 60

Section 2.6, Common Factors:

Find the greatest common factor of each pair of numbers.

9. 36 and 60

10. 18 and 54

Determine whether the pair of numbers is relatively prime.

11. 25 and 36

12. 21 and 14

Section 3.1, Introduction to Fractions:

Write each mixed number as an improper fraction.

13. $5\frac{2}{3}$

14. $1\frac{4}{9}$

Write each improper fraction as a mixed number.

15. $\frac{23}{5}$

16. $\frac{29}{18}$

Section 3.2, Simplifying Fractions: *Simplify each fraction completely.*

17. $\frac{8}{20}$

18. $\frac{36}{45}$

Section 3.3, Multiplying Fractions: *Multiply and simplify.*

19. $\frac{3}{8} \cdot \frac{10}{9}$

20. $\frac{4}{15} \cdot \frac{5}{2}$

SECTION 4.1 Common Multiples

Objectives

In this section, you will learn to:

- Identify the Least Common Multiple (LCM).
- Find the LCM by three different methods.

To successfully complete this section, you need to understand:

- Multiples of numbers (1.4)
- Factors of numbers (2.4)
- Prime factorization (2.5)
- The Greatest Common Factor (2.6)
- Relatively prime numbers (2.6)

Introduction

In Section 2.6, we discussed comparing the factors of two numbers and seeing which factors they had in common. Recall, for example, that 12 and 18 have these factors in common: 1, 2, 3, and 6. Each of these factors divides evenly into both 12 and 18. We were able to use the idea of common factors throughout Chapter 3 when reducing fractions and when simplifying before multiplying.

In this section, we learn about common *multiples* between two numbers. The methods we use to find common multiples are similar to the methods you learned for finding common factors. Common multiples are especially important in adding and subtracting fractions with different denominators, as we see in Section 4.4.

Common Multiples

As we learned in Chapter 1, a multiple of a natural number, n, is a product of n and some other natural number. Also, n is a factor of each of those multiples.

Here is a list of the first five multiples of 7 with each number written in a factored form below it:

Multiples:	7	14	21	28	and	35
	$1 \cdot 7$	$2 \cdot 7$	$3 \cdot 7$	$4 \cdot 7$	and	$5 \cdot 7$

We can add 7 each time to get the next multiple

Using the description of multiple above, let's list the multiples of 2 up to (and including) 32:

2, 4, 6, 8, 10, 12, 14, 16, 18, 20, 22, 24, 26, 28, 30, and 32.

Notice that all these multiples of 2 are divisible by 2. In fact, every multiple of 2 is divisible by 2.

Now let's list the multiples of 3 up to (and including) 36.

3, 6, 9, 12, 15, 18, 21, 24, 27, 30, 33, and 36.

All multiplies of 3 are divisible by 3.

Look at our lists of multiples of 2 and of 3. What numbers do they have in common? They have 6, 12, 18, 24, and 30 in common. This is a list of **common multiples** of 2 and 3.

What do you notice about the list of common multiples of 2 and 3? Are they all divisible by the same number(s)? The common multiples are all divisible by 1, 2, 3, and 6.

The multiples of 6 are 6, 12, 18, 24, 30, 36, 42, 48, 54, 60, 66, and so on. Notice that:

- Multiples of 6 are divisible by 6 (they have 6 as a factor).
- Whenever you see a multiple of 6, that number will also be a multiple of both 2 and 3 because 2 and 3 are *factors* of 6.

EXAMPLE 1 Make a list of the first three common multiples of 6 and 15.

PROCEDURE: Let's first take a look at multiples of 6 and of 15.

Multiples of 6: 6, 12, 18, 24, **30**, 36, 42, 48, 54, **60**, 66, 72, 78, 84, **90**,

Multiples of 15: 15, **30**, 45, **60**, 75, **90**, 105, ...

ANSWER: The first three common multiples of 6 and 15 are **30**, **60**, and **90**.

Looking at the results in Example 1, do you think it's possible to find the *greatest* common multiple of 6 and 15? If you answered "no," you are correct. There is no greatest common multiple because the multiples go on forever.

Method 1: Finding the Least Common Multiple by Listing Multiples

Oftentimes, we're not interested in just any common multiple but the ***least* common multiple (LCM)**. Looking back at Example 1, it is possible to find the *least* common multiple of 6 and 15. The least common multiple is the first one that they have in common, 30, also referred to as the *lowest* common multiple or the *first* common multiple.

EXAMPLE 2 Find the LCM of 8 and 12.

PROCEDURE: List the multiples, one at a time for each number, and look for the first match between them. (List the first few multiples of 8, then 12; back to 8, then to 12 again.)

ANSWER: The first few multiples of 8: 8, 16, **24**
The first few multiples of 12: 12, **24**
} We don't need to look any further.

The LCM of 8 and 12 is 24.

YOU TRY IT 1 *Find the LCM of the two given numbers. Use Example 2 as a guide.*

a) 6 and 8

Multiples of 6: ________________

Multiples of 8: ________________

LCM of 6 and 8 is ________________

b) 10 and 12

Multiples of 10: ________________

Multiples of 12: ________________

LCM of 10 and 12 is ________________

c) 4 and 5

Multiples of 4: ________________

Multiples of 5: ________________

LCM of 4 and 5 is ________________

d) 6 and 12

Multiples of 6: ________________

Multiples of 12: ________________

LCM of 6 and 12 is ________________

In your own words, describe the difference between the common multiples of two numbers and their LCM.

____

____

Method 2: Finding the Least Common Multiple Using Prime Factorization

Just as we found the greatest common factor (GCF) using prime factorization (Section 2.6), we can do the same for finding the LCM.

A number is the product of all of its prime factors. We might say that a number is *composed* of its prime factors. For example, 15 isn't 15 without both factors 3 and 5: $15 = 3 \cdot 5$, and 6 isn't 6 without both factors 2 and 3: $6 = 2 \cdot 3$.

This means that every common multiple of 6 and 15 must have prime factors 2 and 3 (for the 6) and prime factors 3 and 5 (for the 15).

We have already seen in Example 1 that the LCM of 6 and 15 is 30, and the prime factorization of $30 = 2 \cdot 3 \cdot 5$.

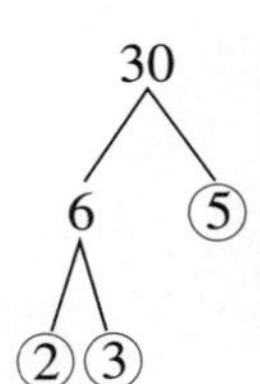

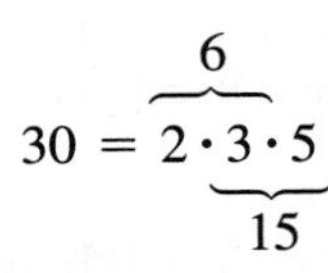

Within 30, we can see the prime factors of 6 (2 and 3) and the prime factors of 15 (3 and 5). The prime factorization of 30 shows us that the 3 is being shared by the 6 and 15. That's okay; sharing is good.

If, in the common multiple, we include *all* of the factors of 6 along with *all* of the factors of 15, we get $(2 \cdot 3) \cdot (3 \cdot 5) = 90$. It is true that 90 is a common multiple of 6 and 15, but it is not the *least* common multiple. In other words, 90 has too many prime factors to be the *least* common multiple of 6 and 15.

$$\overbrace{2 \cdot 3}^{6} \cdot 3 \cdot 5 = 90 \quad\text{where } \underbrace{3 \cdot 5}_{15}$$

Therefore, when finding the *least* common multiple, we need to list as few common prime factors as possible.

Consider another example: 8 isn't 8 without *three* factors of 2: $8 = 2 \cdot 2 \cdot 2$, and 12 isn't 12 without *two* factors of 2 and *one* factor of 3: $12 = 2 \cdot 2 \cdot 3$.

This means that every common multiple of 8 and 12 must have prime factors $\underline{2 \cdot 2 \cdot 2}$ (for the 8) and prime factors $\underline{2 \cdot 2 \cdot 3}$ (for the 12).

We saw in Example 2 that the LCM of 8 and 12 is 24, and the prime factorization of $24 = 2 \cdot 2 \cdot 2 \cdot 3$.

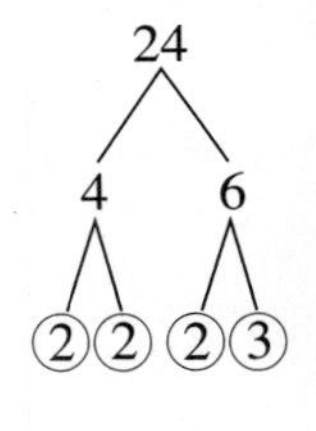

$$24 = \overbrace{2 \cdot 2 \cdot 2}^{8} \cdot 3, \quad \underbrace{2 \cdot 2 \cdot 3}_{12}$$

Within 24, we can see the prime factors of 8 (2 and 2 and 2) and the prime factors of 12 (2 and 2 and 3). The prime factorization of 24 shows us that *two* factors of 2 are being shared by the 8 and 12.

Here are the guidelines for finding the LCM of two natural numbers:

Finding the Least Common Multiple Using Prime Factorization

1. Find the prime factorization of each number (use a factor tree if needed).
2. Write "LCM = ________ = ________"
3. On the line above, write all of the prime factors (with multiplication signs) of the first number.
4. Write in any *prime* factors of the second number that have not yet been written down.
5. Multiply the prime factors together and write that product after the second equal sign.

EXAMPLE 3

Use the guidelines above for finding the LCM of 6 and 15:

1. Find the prime factorization of each number: $6 = 2 \cdot 3$ $\quad 15 = 3 \cdot 5$

You may need to use a factor tree to find the prime factorization.

2. Write: LCM = ______ = ______ (You'll actually do this part on just one line, not on four lines, as shown here.)
3. Write all prime factors of the first number, 6 LCM = $\underline{\mathbf{2 \cdot 3}}$ =
4. Include all primes of the second number, 15, not already included LCM = $\underline{2 \cdot 3 \cdot \mathbf{5}}$ = 15 requires both 3 and 5. Because 3 is already on the line, we need to include only the 5.
5. Multiply: LCM = $\underline{2 \cdot 3 \cdot 5 = \mathbf{30}}$ Be sure to find the LCM by multiplying.

EXAMPLE 4

Use the guidelines on page 206 for finding the LCM of 8 and 12:

1. Find the prime factorization of each number: $8 = 2 \cdot 2 \cdot 2$
   $12 = 2 \cdot 2 \cdot 3$
2. Write: LCM = ______ =
3. Write all prime factors of the first number, 8 LCM = $\underline{\mathbf{2 \cdot 2 \cdot 2}}$ = We start with all of the prime factors of 8.
4. Include all primes of the second number, 12, not already included: LCM = $\underline{2 \cdot 2 \cdot 2 \cdot \mathbf{3}}$ = 12 requires *two* factors of 2 and one factor of 3; because both 2's are already on the line, we need to include only the 3.
5. Multiply: LCM = $\underline{2 \cdot 2 \cdot 2 \cdot 3 = \mathbf{24}}$ Be sure to find the LCM by multiplying.

In practice, lines 2 through 5 are actually written on just one line.

Find the LCM of 8 and 12:

$8 = 2 \cdot 2 \cdot 2$

$12 = 2 \cdot 2 \cdot 3$ LCM = $\underline{2 \cdot 2 \cdot 2 \cdot 3 = 24}$

EXAMPLE 5

Find the LCM of:

a) 4 and 6 b) 12 and 18 c) 5 and 6 d) 4 and 15

ANSWER:

a) The LCM of 4 and 6:
$4 = 2 \cdot 2$
$6 = 2 \cdot 3$
LCM = $\underline{2 \cdot 2 \cdot 3 = 12}$

b) The LCM of 12 and 18:
$12 = 2 \cdot 2 \cdot 3$
$18 = 2 \cdot 3 \cdot 3$
LCM = $\underline{2 \cdot 2 \cdot 3 \cdot 3 = 36}$

c) The LCM of 5 and 6:
$5 = 5$
$6 = 2 \cdot 3$
LCM = $\underline{5 \cdot 2 \cdot 3 = 30}$

5 and 6 are relatively prime and share no prime factors, so the LCM is just their product.

d) The LCM of 4 and 15:
$4 = 2 \cdot 2$
$15 = 3 \cdot 5$
LCM = $\underline{2 \cdot 2 \cdot 3 \cdot 5 = 60}$

4 and 15 are relatively prime and share no prime factors, so the LCM is just their product.

YOU TRY IT 2

Find the LCM of the following pairs of numbers using the given prime factorization of each number. Use Examples 3, 4, and 5 as guides.

a) 10 and 15

$10 = 2 \cdot 5$

$15 = 3 \cdot 5$

LCM = ______ = ______

b) 12 and 20

$12 = 2 \cdot 2 \cdot 3$

$20 = 2 \cdot 2 \cdot 5$

LCM = ______ = ______

c) 4 and 15

$4 = 2 \cdot 2$

$15 = 3 \cdot 5$

LCM = ______ = ______

YOU TRY IT 3

Find the LCM of the following pairs of numbers by first finding each number's prime factorization. Use Examples 3, 4, and 5 as guides.

a) 30 and 40

LCM = ______ = ______

b) 6 and 25

LCM = ______ = ______

c) 8 and 24

LCM = ______ = ______

If the prime factorizations of each number are written with exponents, we can build the LCM by taking the highest exponent of each prime number.

Consider, as we did in Example 4, the LCM of 8 and 12:

$$\left.\begin{aligned} 8 &= 2 \cdot 2 \cdot 2 = 2^3 \\ 12 &= 2 \cdot 2 \cdot 3 = 2^2 \cdot 3^1 \end{aligned}\right\}$$

When we include all of the prime factors of 8, we include all three factors of 2.

To start, list the prime factorization of 8: LCM = $\underline{2 \cdot 2 \cdot 2 \cdot \quad}$ or LCM = $\underline{2^3 \cdot \quad}$

When we next consider the prime factors of 12, the two 2's are already included from the 8, and 12 has only the one factor of 3 to contribute to the LCM.

LCM of 8 and 12 = $\underline{2 \cdot 2 \cdot 2 \cdot 3 = 24}$ or LCM of 8 and 12 = $\underline{2^3 \cdot 3^1 = 24}$

EXAMPLE 6

Given the prime factorization of each pair of numbers, find the LCM.

a) $24 = 2^3 \cdot 3^1$

$18 = 2^1 \cdot 3^2$

b) $90 = 2^1 \cdot 3^2 \cdot 5^1$

$20 = 2^2 \cdot 5^1$

PROCEDURE: For each prime base, use the highest exponent.

ANSWER: a) The prime factors are 2 and 3.

The highest exponent of 2 is ^{3};

The highest exponent of 3 is ^{2}. $\underline{\text{LCM} = 2^3 \cdot 3^2 = 8 \cdot 9 = \mathbf{72}}$

b) The prime factors are 2, 3, and 5.

The highest exponent of 2 is ^{2};

The highest exponent of 3 is ^{2};

The highest exponent of 5 is ^{1}. $\underline{\text{LCM} = 2^2 \cdot 3^2 \cdot 5^1 = 4 \cdot 9 \cdot 5 = \mathbf{180}}$

YOU TRY IT 4

Given the prime factorization of each pair of numbers, find the LCM. Use Example 6 as a guide.

a) $15 = 3^1 \cdot 5^1$

$25 = 5^2$

LCM = ______ = ______

b) $30 = 2^1 \cdot 3^1 \cdot 5^1$

$45 = 3^2 \cdot 5^1$

LCM = ______ = ______

c) $24 = 2^3 \cdot 3^1$

$80 = 2^4 \cdot 5^1$

LCM = ______ = ______

Method 3: Finding the Least Common Multiple Using the Division Method

There is a third method of finding the LCM of two numbers, and you already have experience using it: the division method. In Section 2.6 you were introduced to the division method for finding the GCF of two numbers. We'll use that same method to find their least common multiple as well.

Here's a quick reminder of how to find the GCF using the division method. Recall that the division method stops when the bottom quotients are relatively prime.

EXAMPLE 7 Use the division method to find the GCF of 12 and 30.

PROCEDURE: We'll start by finding a common prime factor and dividing each number by that factor, and so on.

2	12	30	⇐	Divide by 2
3	6	15	⇐	Divide by 3
	2	5	⇐	We can no longer divide; 2 and 5 are relatively prime

ANSWER: The GCF is found by multiplying the two common prime factors: $\mathbf{2 \cdot 3 = 6}$.
The GCF is 6.

Now let's use the division method to find the LCM of two numbers. We'll start with some of the same examples already demonstrated in this section.

From Example 2:
the LCM of 8 and 12 is 24;

From Example 6(b):
the LCM of 90 and 20 is 180.

When using the division method to find the LCM, we begin exactly as we do when using the division method to find the GCF. We identify common factors that can be divided out. These common factors may be prime or composite numbers.

The division method for the LCM, however, requires that we multiply more than just the common factors; we also multiply the numbers across the bottom (the last pair of quotients).

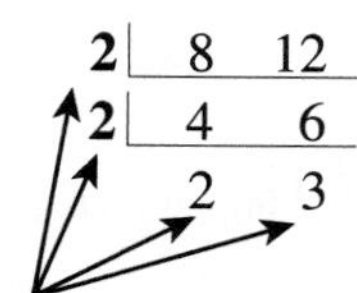

Multiply all of these:

10 | 90 20
9 2

Multiply all of these:

LCM of 8 and 12 $= \mathbf{2 \cdot 2 \cdot 2 \cdot 3} = 24$

LCM of 12 and 18 $= \mathbf{10 \cdot 9 \cdot 2} = 180$

Each of these results is consistent with what we already know from Examples 2 and 6(b).

You might find it helpful to circle all of the factors (as shown), making a large L, indicating the factors of the LCM.

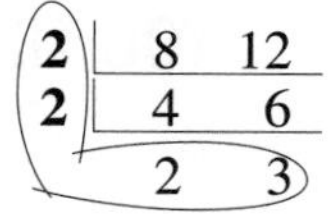

EXAMPLE 8 Find the LCM of each pair of numbers.

a) 12 and 30 b) 18 and 90 c) 21 and 30

PROCEDURE: Use the division method. Please draw the large L around the side primes and bottom quotients.

ANSWER: a) 12 and 30:

2	12	30	⇐ Divide by 2
3	6	15	⇐ Divide by 3
	2	5	⇐ The last pair of quotients is relatively prime.

Multiply the factors along the side with those along the bottom (the last pair of quotients):

LCM = (side factors) × (bottom factors)

LCM = (2 • 3) × (2 • 5) = 60

b) 18 and 90:

2	18	90	⇐ Divide by 2.
3	9	45	⇐ Divide by 3.
3	3	15	⇐ Divide by 3 again.
	1	5	⇐ The last pair of quotients is relatively prime.

LCM = (2 • 3 • 3) • (1 • 5) = 90

c) 21 and 30:

3	21	30	⇐ Divide by 3.
	7	10	⇐ The last pair of quotients is relatively prime.

LCM = 3 • (7 • 10) = 210

Caution

This division method will work for finding the LCM of two numbers only if we complete the division process; in other words, the last pair of quotients must be *relatively* prime.

In Example 8(a) we found the LCM of 12 and 30. If we stopped the division process early, and then multiplied, we would get *a* common multiple, but not the *least* common multiple:

2	12	30
	6	**15**

Multiply all of these?

Does the LCM = 2 • 6 • 15 = 180?

No. It is 3 *times larger* than the real LCM of 60, and 3 is the value of the common factor that we didn't yet divide out.

YOU TRY IT 5

Find the LCM of the following pairs of numbers. Use Example 8 as a guide.

a) 8 and 6

b) 12 and 9

c) 30 and 45

d) 18 and 30

You Try It Answers: Section 4.1

YTI 1 a) 24 b) 60 c) 20 d) 12

YTI 2 a) $2 \cdot 5 \cdot 3 = 30$ b) $2 \cdot 2 \cdot 3 \cdot 5 = 60$
c) $2 \cdot 2 \cdot 3 \cdot 5 = 60$

YTI 3 a) $30 = 2 \cdot 3 \cdot 5$
$40 = 2 \cdot 2 \cdot 2 \cdot 5$
$\text{LCM} = 2 \cdot 3 \cdot 5 \cdot 2 \cdot 2 = 120$

b) $6 = 2 \cdot 3$
$25 = 5 \cdot 5$
$\text{LCM} = 2 \cdot 3 \cdot 5 \cdot 5 = 150$

c) $8 = 2 \cdot 2 \cdot 2$
$24 = 2 \cdot 2 \cdot 2 \cdot 3$
$\text{LCM} = 2 \cdot 2 \cdot 2 \cdot 3 = 24$

YTI 4 a) $\text{LCM} = 3^1 \cdot 5^2 = 75$
b) $\text{LCM} = 2^1 \cdot 3^2 \cdot 5^1 = 90$
c) $\text{LCM} = 2^4 \cdot 3^1 \cdot 5^1 = 240$

YTI 5 a) 24 b) 36 c) 90 d) 90

Focus Exercises: Section 4.1

Find the LCM of each pair of numbers.

1. 4 and 6 **2.** 4 and 10 **3.** 4 and 14 **4.** 4 and 18

5. 6 and 10 **6.** 6 and 15 **7.** 6 and 20 **8.** 6 and 21

9. 8 and 10 **10.** 8 and 18 **11.** 8 and 20 **12.** 8 and 28

13. 4 and 15 **14.** 5 and 12 **15.** 6 and 25 **16.** 8 and 15

17. 4 and 12 **18.** 5 and 35 **19.** 15 and 30 **20.** 12 and 36

21. 14 and 42 **22.** 25 and 30 **23.** 36 and 42 **24.** 36 and 48

25. 32 and 48 **26.** 32 and 80 **27.** 15 and 75 **28.** 15 and 90

29. 6 and 90 **30.** 45 and 60 **31.** 60 and 75 **32.** 80 and 100

33. 60 and 90 **34.** 90 and 120 **35.** 120 and 100 **36.** 80 and 120

SECTION 4.2 Building up Fractions

Objectives

In this section, you will learn to:

- Build up fractions: find equivalent fractions by multiplying by a fractional form of 1.
- Distinguish between like and unlike fractions.

To successfully complete this section, you need to understand:

- The Multiplicative Identity (1.2)
- The multiplication table (1.4)
- The principles of fractions (3.1)
- The product rule of fractions (3.1)
- Equivalent fractions (3.2)

Introduction

With most topics in mathematics, addition and subtraction are introduced before multiplication and division. With fractions, it's different. It's simpler to multiply two fractions than it is to add them.

Though this section is not about addition or subtraction, we're going to use some of the principles of fractions to prepare us for learning about addition and subtraction. We'll start by using multiplication to find equivalent fractions.

In Section 3.2, we learned about simplifying a fraction to an equivalent fraction by dividing out a common factor. For example, $\frac{10}{18}$ can reduce by a factor of 2 to an equivalent fraction $\frac{5}{9}$.

In this section, we learn how to make a single fraction have a specific denominator by multiplying the fraction by a fractional form of 1. We then make two fractions have the same denominator.

Building up Fractions

Recall from Section 3.1 some of the basic principles of fractions:

1. The *Multiplicative Identity* is 1 because $\frac{a}{b} \cdot 1 = \frac{a}{b}$, as long as $b \neq 0$.

   For example, $\frac{3}{10} \cdot 1 = \frac{3}{10}$. Multiplying by 1 doesn't change the value of a number.

2. A number divided by itself is 1: $\frac{a}{a} = 1$, $a \neq 0$. For example, $\frac{5}{5} = 1$.

We can combine these two principles to multiply a fraction by a fractional form of 1, such as $\frac{2}{2}$ and $\frac{5}{5}$, to create an equivalent fraction.

For example, consider $\frac{3}{10} \cdot \frac{2}{2} = \frac{6}{20}$.

Notice that the second fraction, $\frac{2}{2}$, is a fractional form of 1. So, we have multiplied $\frac{3}{10}$ by 1, resulting in an equivalent fraction, $\frac{6}{20}$. Notice also that $\frac{6}{20}$ could be reduced by a factor of 2 to give us the first fraction, $\frac{3}{10}$.

This process of multiplying a fraction by a fractional form of 1 is called **building up** a fraction. This means that both the numerator and the denominator become larger—are built up—but the result is an equivalent fraction.

Caution When we build up a fraction we should not reduce the result. Reducing would undo the building-up process.

EXAMPLE 1 Use the product rule to multiply, but do not simplify. (Notice that the second fraction, in each case, is equivalent to 1.)

a) $\frac{3}{4} \cdot \frac{2}{2} = \frac{6}{8}$ b) $\frac{5}{7} \cdot \frac{4}{4} = \frac{20}{28}$

YOU TRY IT 1

Use the product rule to multiply, but do not simplify. Use Example 1 as a guide.

a) $\frac{5}{6} \cdot \frac{3}{3} =$ b) $\frac{7}{4} \cdot \frac{5}{5} =$ c) $\frac{1}{2} \cdot \frac{6}{6} =$

Think about it

In each case in YTI 1, the resulting fraction is equivalent to the first fraction in the product. Why?

____

____

The process of building up a fraction is especially important in adding and subtracting certain fractions.

Building Up a Fraction

1. Given any fraction, multiply it by a fractional form of 1. Multiplying by 1 guarantees that the value does not change.
2. You can make 1 be any fraction in which the numerator and denominator are the same. The product (the resulting fraction) is equivalent to the first fraction.

EXAMPLE 2

Build up the fractions.

ANSWER:

	Start with		Multiply by 1	Result	
a)	$\frac{2}{3}$	$\times$	$\frac{5}{5}$	$= \frac{10}{15}$;	$\frac{2}{3}$ is equivalent to $\frac{10}{15}$.
b)	$\frac{6}{11}$	$\times$	$\frac{4}{4}$	$= \frac{24}{44}$;	$\frac{6}{11}$ is equivalent to $\frac{24}{44}$.
c)	$\frac{1}{5}$	$\times$	$\frac{10}{10}$	$= \frac{10}{50}$;	$\frac{1}{5}$ is equivalent to $\frac{10}{50}$.
d)	$\frac{5}{4}$	$\times$	$\frac{9}{9}$	$= \frac{45}{36}$;	$\frac{5}{4}$ is equivalent to $\frac{45}{36}$.

YOU TRY IT 2

Build up the fractions. Use Example 2 as a guide.

	Start with		Multiply by 1		Result	
a)	$\frac{1}{8}$	$\times$	$\frac{5}{5}$	$=$	;	______________
b)	$\frac{3}{4}$	$\times$	$\frac{3}{3}$	$=$	;	______________
c)	$\frac{6}{1}$	$\times$	$\frac{2}{2}$	$=$	;	______________

Next, we can build up a fraction so that it has a specific denominator. For example, if we want $\frac{2}{3}$ to be built up to a fraction that has a denominator of 12, we need to find the right fractional form of 1 to multiply times $\frac{2}{3}$.

EXAMPLE 3

Build up $\frac{2}{3}$ to an equivalent fraction that

a) has a denominator of 12.

b) has a denominator of 21.

PROCEDURE: We need to multiply $\frac{2}{3}$ by a fractional form of 1. Look at each denominator to decide by what number to multiply the numerator and denominator of $\frac{2}{3}$.

ANSWER:

a)

Start with		Multiply by 1	Result	
$\frac{2}{3}$	$\times$	$\frac{?}{?}$	$= \frac{?}{12}$	Because $3 \times 4 = 12$, use $\frac{4}{4}$ for 1.
$\frac{2}{3}$	$\times$	$\frac{4}{4}$	$= \frac{8}{12}$	

b)

Start with		Multiply by 1	Result	
$\frac{2}{3}$	$\times$	$\frac{?}{?}$	$= \frac{?}{21}$	Because $3 \times 7 = 21$, use $\frac{7}{7}$ for 1.
$\frac{2}{3}$	$\times$	$\frac{7}{7}$	$= \frac{14}{21}$	

YOU TRY IT 3

Multiply by the appropriate value of 1 to build up each fraction to one with the denominator shown. Use Example 3 as a guide.

	Start with		Multiply by 1	Result		Start with		Multiply by 1	Result
a)	$\frac{3}{4}$	$\times$	$\frac{\ }{\ }$	$= \frac{\ }{24}$	b)	$\frac{5}{8}$	$\times$	$\frac{\ }{\ }$	$= \frac{\ }{24}$
c)	$\frac{2}{5}$	$\times$	$\frac{\ }{\ }$	$= \frac{\ }{35}$	d)	$\frac{8}{9}$	$\times$	$\frac{\ }{\ }$	$= \frac{\ }{45}$
e)	$\frac{9}{7}$	$\times$	$\frac{\ }{\ }$	$= \frac{\ }{28}$	f)	$\frac{3}{1}$	$\times$	$\frac{\ }{\ }$	$= \frac{\ }{8}$

Building up Unlike Fractions

Two or more fractions are **like fractions** if they have the same denominator, often called a **common denominator**. Fractions that don't have the same denominator are ***un*like** fractions.

Like fractions (same denominators)
$\frac{2}{3}$ and $\frac{1}{3}$
$\frac{3}{6}$ and $\frac{7}{6}$

Unlike fractions (different denominators)
$\frac{2}{3}$ and $\frac{1}{2}$
$\frac{5}{8}$ and $\frac{5}{9}$

Caution Don't confuse like fractions with equivalent fractions. Like fractions have the same denominator, as in $\frac{5}{8}$ and $\frac{3}{8}$, but they are equivalent only if they also have the same numerator, as in $\frac{5}{8}$ and $\frac{5}{8}$.

YOU TRY IT 4 *Write the pairs of like fractions on the line below.*

$$\frac{4}{5}, \frac{3}{8}, \frac{9}{4}, \frac{10}{5}, \frac{1}{4}, \frac{7}{10}, \frac{7}{3}, \frac{8}{8}, \frac{1}{10}, \text{ and } \frac{3}{7}$$

Pairs of like fractions: ______________________________

As you will see in this chapter, like fractions are important when adding and subtracting fractions. However, it is not always the case that we are given like fractions from the start. Sometimes, we need to build up unlike fractions so that they have the same denominator and become like fractions.

EXAMPLE 4 Build up the fraction $\frac{2}{3}$ to have the same denominator as $\frac{5}{6}$. Conclude the problem by identifying the (new) like fractions.

PROCEDURE: We must multiply $\frac{2}{3}$ by 1 so that it becomes an equivalent fraction with a denominator of 6. Because $3 \times 2 = 6$, use $\frac{2}{2}$ for 1:

ANSWER: Show work: $\frac{2}{3} \cdot \frac{2}{2} = \frac{4}{6}$

$\frac{4}{6}$ and $\frac{5}{6}$ are like fractions.

YOU TRY IT 5 *Build up the first fraction so that it has the same denominator as the second fraction. Conclude the problem by identifying the (new) like fractions. Use Example 4 as a guide.*

a) Build up $\frac{3}{5}$ to have the same denominator as $\frac{7}{20}$:

Show work:

__________ and __________ are like fractions.

b) Build up $\frac{2}{9}$ to have the same denominator as $\frac{5}{18}$:

Show work:

____

c) Build up $\frac{7}{10}$ to have the same denominator as $\frac{19}{60}$:

Show work:

____

We can also build up each of two fractions so that they both have the same (new) denominator.

EXAMPLE 5 Build up each of the given fractions so that they have the same denominator. Conclude the problem by identifying the (new) like fractions.

Fractions: $\frac{1}{4}$ and $\frac{5}{6}$; Denominator: 12.

PROCEDURE: We must multiply each fraction by 1. The fractions we use for 1 will be different for each one in the pair of fractions.

For $\frac{1}{4}$, use $\frac{3}{3}$ for 1(because $4 \times 3 = 12$).

For $\frac{5}{6}$, use $\frac{2}{2}$ for 1: (because $6 \times 2 = 12$).

ANSWER: $\frac{1}{4} \cdot \frac{3}{3} = \frac{3}{\mathbf{12}}$ $\qquad$ $\frac{5}{6} \cdot \frac{2}{2} = \frac{10}{\mathbf{12}}$

$\frac{3}{12}$ and $\frac{10}{12}$ are like fractions.

YOU TRY IT 6 *Build up each of the given fractions so that they have the same denominator. Conclude the problem by identifying the (new) like fractions. Use Example 5 as a guide.*

a) Fractions: $\frac{1}{4}$ and $\frac{6}{7}$; Denominator: 28.

Show work:

b) Fractions: $\frac{5}{8}$ and $\frac{1}{6}$; Denominator: 24.

Show work:

c) Fractions: $\frac{4}{9}$ and $\frac{7}{12}$; Denominator: 36.

Show work:

You Try It Answers: Section 4.2

YTI 1 a) $\frac{15}{18}$ b) $\frac{35}{20}$ c) $\frac{6}{12}$

YTI 2 a) $\frac{5}{40}$; $\frac{1}{8}$ is equivalent to $\frac{5}{40}$.
b) $\frac{9}{12}$; $\frac{3}{4}$ is equivalent to $\frac{9}{12}$.
c) $\frac{12}{2}$; $\frac{6}{1}$ is equivalent to $\frac{12}{2}$.

YTI 3 a) $\frac{3}{4} \times \frac{6}{6} = \frac{18}{24}$ b) $\frac{5}{8} \times \frac{3}{3} = \frac{15}{24}$ c) $\frac{2}{5} \times \frac{7}{7} = \frac{14}{35}$ d) $\frac{8}{9} \times \frac{5}{5} = \frac{40}{45}$
e) $\frac{9}{7} \times \frac{4}{4} = \frac{36}{28}$ f) $\frac{3}{1} \times \frac{8}{8} = \frac{24}{8}$

YTI 4 $\frac{4}{5}$ and $\frac{10}{5}$, $\frac{3}{8}$ and $\frac{8}{8}$, $\frac{9}{4}$ and $\frac{1}{4}$, $\frac{7}{10}$ and $\frac{1}{10}$

YTI 5 a) $\frac{3}{5} \cdot \frac{4}{4} = \frac{12}{20}$; $\frac{12}{20}$ and $\frac{7}{20}$ are like fractions.
b) $\frac{2}{9} \cdot \frac{2}{2} = \frac{4}{18}$; $\frac{4}{18}$ and $\frac{5}{18}$ are like fractions.

c) $\frac{7}{10} \cdot \frac{6}{6} = \frac{42}{60}$; $\frac{42}{60}$ and $\frac{19}{60}$ are like fractions.

YTI 6 a) $\frac{1}{4} \cdot \frac{7}{7} = \frac{7}{28}$ and $\frac{6}{7} \cdot \frac{4}{4} = \frac{24}{28}$; $\frac{7}{28}$ and $\frac{24}{28}$ are like fractions.

b) $\frac{5}{8} \cdot \frac{3}{3} = \frac{15}{24}$ and $\frac{1}{6} \cdot \frac{4}{4} = \frac{4}{24}$; $\frac{15}{24}$ and $\frac{4}{24}$ are like fractions.

c) $\frac{4}{9} \cdot \frac{4}{4} = \frac{16}{36}$ and $\frac{7}{12} \cdot \frac{3}{3} = \frac{21}{36}$; $\frac{16}{36}$ and $\frac{21}{36}$ are like fractions.

Focus Exercises: Section 4.2

Multiply by the appropriate value of 1 to build up each fraction to one with a denominator shown.

	Start with		Multiply by 1	Result		Start with		Multiply by 1	Result
1.	$\frac{7}{10}$	×	$\frac{}{}$	$= \frac{}{30}$	**2.**	$\frac{5}{12}$	×	$\frac{}{}$	$= \frac{}{24}$
3.	$\frac{4}{9}$	×	$\frac{}{}$	$= \frac{}{18}$	**4.**	$\frac{3}{8}$	×	$\frac{}{}$	$= \frac{}{40}$
5.	$\frac{9}{7}$	×	$\frac{}{}$	$= \frac{}{42}$	**6.**	$\frac{1}{9}$	×	$\frac{}{}$	$= \frac{}{72}$
7.	$\frac{4}{15}$	×	$\frac{}{}$	$= \frac{}{45}$	**8.**	$\frac{6}{1}$	×	$\frac{}{}$	$= \frac{}{9}$
9.	$\frac{3}{20}$	×	$\frac{}{}$	$= \frac{}{100}$	**10.**	$\frac{14}{15}$	×	$\frac{}{}$	$= \frac{}{60}$
11.	$\frac{3}{8}$	×	$\frac{}{}$	$= \frac{}{80}$	**12.**	$\frac{4}{1}$	×	$\frac{}{}$	$= \frac{}{15}$
13.	$\frac{7}{12}$	×	$\frac{}{}$	$= \frac{}{60}$	**14.**	$\frac{5}{6}$	×	$\frac{}{}$	$= \frac{}{66}$
15.	$\frac{8}{25}$	×	$\frac{}{}$	$= \frac{}{100}$	**16.**	$\frac{17}{30}$	×	$\frac{}{}$	$= \frac{}{120}$

Build up each of the given fractions so that they have the same denominator.

17. Fractions: $\frac{2}{5}$ and $\frac{1}{3}$; Denominator: 15

18. Fractions: $\frac{1}{6}$ and $\frac{4}{5}$; Denominator: 30

19. Fractions: $\frac{3}{4}$ and $\frac{2}{3}$; Denominator: 12

20. Fractions: $\frac{5}{9}$ and $\frac{1}{2}$; Denominator: 18

21. Fractions: $\frac{1}{6}$ and $\frac{5}{8}$; Denominator: 24

22. Fractions: $\frac{3}{4}$ and $\frac{9}{10}$; Denominator: 20

23. Fractions: $\frac{2}{9}$ and $\frac{1}{6}$; Denominator: 18

24. Fractions: $\frac{1}{12}$ and $\frac{5}{8}$; Denominator: 24

25. Fractions: $\frac{5}{6}$ and $\frac{1}{12}$; Denominator: 36

26. Fractions: $\frac{7}{8}$ and $\frac{3}{4}$; Denominator: 40

27. Fractions: $\frac{2}{3}$ and $\frac{7}{9}$; Denominator: 18

28. Fractions: $\frac{4}{5}$ and $\frac{8}{15}$; Denominator: 60

29. Fractions: $\frac{4}{9}$ and $\frac{5}{12}$; Denominator: 36

30. Fractions: $\frac{7}{10}$ and $\frac{1}{8}$; Denominator: 40

31. Fractions: $\frac{7}{15}$ and $\frac{1}{12}$; Denominator: 60

32. Fractions: $\frac{4}{15}$ and $\frac{9}{25}$; Denominator: 75

33. Fractions: $\frac{3}{8}$ and $\frac{1}{4}$; Denominator: 8

34. Fractions: $\frac{5}{6}$ and $\frac{7}{12}$; Denominator: 12

35. Fractions: $\frac{3}{5}$ and $\frac{2}{15}$; Denominator: 15

36. Fractions: $\frac{2}{3}$ and $\frac{11}{18}$; Denominator: 18

Write the pairs of like fractions on the lines below.

37. $\frac{5}{2}, \frac{6}{4}, \frac{1}{5}, \frac{9}{2}, \frac{11}{5}, \frac{8}{9}, \frac{8}{6}, \frac{4}{4}, \frac{11}{9},$ and $\frac{6}{8}$

_____ _____ _____ _____ _____

38. $\frac{3}{5}, \frac{10}{4}, \frac{2}{6}, \frac{1}{2}, \frac{11}{4}, \frac{2}{3}, \frac{6}{7}, \frac{3}{2}, \frac{10}{6},$ and $\frac{4}{7}$

_____ _____ _____ _____ _____

SECTION 4.3 Adding and Subtracting Like Fractions

Objectives

In this section, you will learn to:

- Apply rules for adding and subtracting like fractions.

To successfully complete this section, you need to understand:

- Writing mixed numbers (3.1)
- Simplifying fractions (3.2)
- Like fractions (4.2)

Introduction

Checkers and chess are games that are played on the same board, called a checkerboard. Even though they use the same board, the rules for checkers and the rules for chess are completely different.

Likewise, addition and multiplication use the same numbers, including fractions, but the rules for addition and the rules for multiplication are completely different.

We will prepare for the discussion of adding and subtracting fractions by first reviewing how to combine like units.

Combining Like Units of Measure

Recall from our discussion of adding and subtracting whole numbers (Section 1.3) that when units of measure are involved, we can add or subtract only if the units are "like" each other. If units are not like, then we must convert them into like units before they can be combined.

Just as units must be like before combining (adding or subtracting), so must fractions. In other words, two fractions can be added or subtracted as long as they are like fractions, having the same denominator.

To emphasize how we can add like fractions, consider this:

Just as	2 feet	+	3 feet	=	5 feet,
so it is that	2 sevenths	+	3 sevenths	=	5 sevenths.
This means that	$\frac{2}{7}$	+	$\frac{3}{7}$	=	$\frac{5}{7}$.

However, what we really need to know is that $\frac{2}{7} + \frac{3}{7} = \frac{2+3}{7} = \frac{5}{7}$.

Notice that, just as when adding feet, the result is feet; likewise, when adding sevenths, the result is sevenths.

Combining Like Fractions

To combine like fractions means to either add them together or to subtract one from the other.

Adding and Subtracting Like Fractions

Adding Fractions: $\frac{a}{b} + \frac{c}{b} = \frac{a+c}{b}$ **Subtracting Fractions:** $\frac{a}{d} - \frac{c}{d} = \frac{a-c}{d}$

To add (or subtract) two like fractions, add (or subtract) the numerators. The resulting fraction is *like* the original like fractions and has the same denominator.

$$\frac{2}{9} + \frac{5}{9} = \frac{2+5}{9} = \frac{7}{9} \qquad \frac{6}{7} - \frac{4}{7} = \frac{6-4}{7} = \frac{2}{7}$$

Caution

Notice that the denominators are the same throughout each individual problem. The denominators are neither added nor subtracted.

If the result of adding or subtracting two fractions can be simplified, then simplify it at the very end. If the result is an improper fraction, rewrite it as a mixed number.

EXAMPLE 1

Combine these like fractions (add or subtract):

a) $\frac{8}{10} + \frac{1}{10}$ b) $\frac{7}{9} + \frac{4}{9}$

c) $\frac{9}{11} - \frac{3}{11}$ d) $\frac{7}{8} - \frac{5}{8}$

ANSWER:

a) $\frac{8}{10} + \frac{1}{10} = \frac{8+1}{10} = \frac{9}{10}$

b) $\frac{7}{9} + \frac{4}{9} = \frac{7+4}{9} = \frac{11}{9} = 1\frac{2}{9}$ Written as a mixed number

c) $\frac{9}{11} - \frac{3}{11} = \frac{9-3}{11} = \frac{6}{11}$

d) $\frac{7}{8} - \frac{5}{8} = \frac{7-5}{8} = \frac{2}{8} = \frac{1}{4}$ Reduced by a factor of 2

YOU TRY IT 1

Combine these like fractions (add or subtract). Simplify if possible. Use Example 1 as a guide.

a) $\frac{7}{15} + \frac{1}{15}$ b) $\frac{11}{12} + \frac{5}{12}$

c) $\frac{10}{13} - \frac{5}{13}$ d) $\frac{7}{10} - \frac{1}{10}$

Think about it

Take a look again at Example 1a): $\frac{8}{10} + \frac{1}{10}$.

Notice that $\frac{8}{10}$ can be simplified. Would it be a good idea to simplify $\frac{8}{10}$ in problem a)? Why or why not?

Caution

In addition and subtraction: only the *final* answer should be simplified.

EXAMPLE 2

Add or subtract these fractions as indicated. Be sure to maintain like fractions.

a) $\frac{3}{15} + \frac{8}{15}$ b) $\frac{10}{20} - \frac{5}{20}$

PROCEDURE: To add or subtract fractions, the fractions must have the same denominator. Even though at least one of the original fractions can be simplified before combining, don't do it.

ANSWER: a) $\frac{3}{15} + \frac{8}{15} = \frac{3+8}{15} = \frac{11}{15}$ This result can't be simplified.

b) $\frac{10}{20} - \frac{5}{20} = \frac{10 - 5}{20} = \frac{5}{20} = \frac{1}{4}$

YOU TRY IT 2

Combine these fractions. Simplify the result, if possible. Use Example 2 as a guide.

a) $\frac{8}{20} + \frac{2}{20}$ b) $\frac{9}{18} - \frac{5}{18}$ c) $\frac{18}{25} - \frac{3}{25}$

You Try It Answers: Section 4.3

YTI 1 a) $\frac{8}{15}$ b) $\frac{4}{3} = 1\frac{1}{3}$ c) $\frac{5}{13}$ d) $\frac{3}{5}$

YTI 2 a) $\frac{1}{2}$ b) $\frac{2}{9}$ c) $\frac{3}{5}$

Focus Exercises: Section 4.3

Add. Simplify the result whenever possible. Write any answer that contains an improper fraction as a mixed number.

1. $\frac{1}{2} + \frac{1}{2}$ **2.** $\frac{2}{3} + \frac{2}{3}$ **3.** $\frac{2}{3} + \frac{1}{3}$ **4.** $\frac{3}{8} + \frac{7}{8}$

5. $\frac{5}{6} + \frac{4}{6}$ **6.** $\frac{1}{6} + \frac{5}{6}$ **7.** $\frac{4}{9} + \frac{8}{9}$ **8.** $\frac{2}{5} + \frac{1}{5}$

9. $\frac{3}{7} + \frac{1}{7}$ **10.** $\frac{4}{7} + \frac{5}{7}$ **11.** $\frac{4}{7} + \frac{6}{7}$ **12.** $\frac{8}{9} + \frac{7}{9}$

13. $\frac{3}{4} + \frac{3}{4}$ **14.** $\frac{4}{5} + \frac{3}{5}$ **15.** $\frac{3}{10} + \frac{2}{10}$ **16.** $\frac{5}{8} + \frac{7}{8}$

17. $\frac{1}{8} + \frac{3}{8}$ **18.** $\frac{7}{10} + \frac{1}{10}$ **19.** $\frac{3}{11} + \frac{5}{11}$ **20.** $\frac{3}{12} + \frac{8}{12}$

21. $\frac{2}{9} + \frac{7}{9}$ **22.** $\frac{1}{9} + \frac{5}{9}$ **23.** $\frac{7}{10} + \frac{8}{10}$ **24.** $\frac{11}{12} + \frac{7}{12}$

25. $\frac{3}{10} + \frac{1}{10}$

26. $\frac{3}{12} + \frac{1}{12}$

27. $\frac{8}{13} + \frac{5}{13}$

28. $\frac{7}{11} + \frac{9}{11}$

29. $\frac{3}{10} + \frac{7}{10}$

30. $\frac{3}{14} + \frac{4}{14}$

31. $\frac{11}{12} + \frac{5}{12}$

32. $\frac{4}{15} + \frac{1}{15}$

33. $\frac{13}{14} + \frac{9}{14}$

34. $\frac{5}{16} + \frac{11}{16}$

35. $\frac{17}{20} + \frac{13}{20}$

36. $\frac{13}{15} + \frac{14}{15}$

37. $\frac{11}{24} + \frac{7}{24}$

38. $\frac{4}{15} + \frac{2}{15}$

39. $\frac{9}{16} + \frac{3}{16}$

40. $\frac{8}{15} + \frac{2}{15}$

41. $\frac{7}{15} + \frac{2}{15}$

42. $\frac{11}{15} + \frac{7}{15}$

43. $\frac{3}{20} + \frac{11}{20}$

44. $\frac{5}{16} + \frac{3}{16}$

45. $\frac{9}{20} + \frac{3}{20}$

46. $\frac{26}{30} + \frac{9}{30}$

47. $\frac{19}{24} + \frac{13}{24}$

48. $\frac{8}{30} + \frac{12}{30}$

Subtract. Simplify the result whenever possible.

49. $\frac{5}{8} - \frac{3}{8}$

50. $\frac{5}{9} - \frac{1}{9}$

51. $\frac{1}{2} - \frac{1}{2}$

52. $\frac{3}{7} - \frac{2}{7}$

53. $\frac{8}{9} - \frac{7}{9}$

54. $\frac{9}{8} - \frac{5}{8}$

55. $\frac{6}{7} - \frac{3}{7}$

56. $\frac{7}{10} - \frac{3}{10}$

57. $\frac{7}{10} - \frac{1}{10}$

58. $\frac{7}{8} - \frac{1}{8}$

59. $\frac{7}{9} - \frac{4}{9}$

60. $\frac{11}{12} - \frac{5}{12}$

61. $\frac{9}{11} - \frac{3}{11}$

62. $\frac{11}{15} - \frac{8}{15}$

63. $\frac{9}{10} - \frac{7}{10}$

64. $\frac{13}{14} - \frac{9}{14}$

65. $\frac{11}{12} - \frac{2}{12}$

66. $\frac{9}{16} - \frac{5}{16}$

67. $\frac{13}{20} - \frac{7}{20}$

68. $\frac{11}{15} - \frac{4}{15}$

69. $\frac{18}{24} - \frac{4}{24}$

70. $\frac{22}{30} - \frac{7}{30}$

71. $\frac{23}{24} - \frac{7}{24}$

72. $\frac{23}{30} - \frac{11}{30}$

SECTION 4.4 Adding and Subtracting Unlike Fractions

Objectives

In this section, you will learn to:

- Find the Least Common Denominator.
- Add and subtract fractions with different denominators.

To successfully complete this section, you need to understand:

- Simplifying fractions (3.2)
- The Least Common Multiple (4.1)
- Building up fractions (4.2)
- Adding and subtracting like fractions (4.3)

Introduction

In Section 4.2, we learned about building up two fractions to have the same denominator, making them *like* fractions. In Section 4.3, we learned that like fractions can be added or subtracted.

In this section we combine those two ideas and learn to add and subtract *unlike* fractions, fractions with *different* denominators.

Finding the Least Common Denominator

From our work in Section 4.2, we know we can build up two unlike fractions to have the same denominator, a common denominator.

> A **common denominator** of two or more fractions is a common multiple of the given denominators.

For example, $\frac{3}{4}$ and $\frac{1}{6}$ can be built up to many different common denominators because the denominators, 4 and 6, have many multiples in common:

Multiples of 4: 4, 8, **12**, 16, 20, **24**, 28, 32, **36**, 40,...
Multiples of 6: 6, **12**, 18, **24**, 30, **36**, 42, 48, ...

The common multiples of 4 and 6 and are **12**, **24**, **36**, ...

Once two unlike fractions are built up to have the same denominator, they can be combined, either by addition or subtraction. And, no matter which common multiple we use in building up the unlike fractions, the sums (or differences) are equivalent fractions.

So, to make our work most efficient, we could choose the *least common multiple* of the two denominators, also called the **least common denominator**, abbreviated **LCD**.

The LCD of $\frac{3}{4}$ and $\frac{1}{6}$ is the least common multiple of 4 and 6. Here are two methods (from Section 4.1) we can use to find the LCD:

(1) The Prime Factorization Method

$4 = 2 \cdot 2$
$6 = 2 \cdot 3$

$\text{LCD} = 2 \cdot 2 \cdot 3 = 12$

(2) The Division Method (Draw in the ⌊.)

2 | 4 6 ⇐ Divide by 2.
2 3 ⇐ We cant divide any f urther.

$\text{LCD} = 2 \cdot 2 \cdot 3 = 12$

This tells us that we should build up each fraction to have a least common denominator of 12.

EXAMPLE 1 Build up both $\frac{1}{6}$ and $\frac{4}{9}$ to have the least common denominator.

PROCEDURE: The least common denominator is the least common multiple of 6 and 9.

3 | 6 9
2 3 $\text{LCD} = 3 \cdot 2 \cdot 3 = 18$

ANSWER: a) To get a denominator of 18, we need to multiply $\frac{1}{6}$ by $\frac{3}{3}$ and $\frac{4}{9}$ by $\frac{2}{2}$:

$$\frac{1}{6} \cdot \frac{\mathbf{3}}{\mathbf{3}} = \frac{\mathbf{3}}{\mathbf{18}} \quad \text{and} \quad \frac{4}{9} \cdot \frac{\mathbf{2}}{\mathbf{2}} = \frac{\mathbf{8}}{\mathbf{18}}$$

YOU TRY IT 1 *Identify the LCD and build up each pair of fractions to have that denominator. Use Example 1 as a guide.*

a) $\frac{5}{6}$ and $\frac{3}{10}$

b) $\frac{4}{9}$ and $\frac{5}{12}$

c) $\frac{8}{15}$ and $\frac{1}{4}$

d) $\frac{2}{5}$ and $\frac{3}{20}$

Adding and Subtracting Unlike Fractions

The real focus of this section is adding and subtracting fractions when the denominators are not the same. As we've seen, the best common denominator to build up to is the LCD, the least common denominator. Let's put this into practice.

EXAMPLE 2 Evaluate each by first finding the LCD. Completely simplify the result.

a) $\frac{1}{6} + \frac{2}{15}$

b) $\frac{3}{4} + \frac{7}{10}$

PROCEDURE: First find the LCD. Then build up each fraction to have that denominator. Part (a) shows the division method and part (b) shows the prime factorization method.

ANSWER:

a) $\mathbf{3}\,\underline{|\ 6\quad 15}$

$\quad\ \ 2\quad\ 5$

LCD $= 3 \cdot 2 \cdot 5 = 30$

$\frac{1}{6} \cdot \frac{\mathbf{5}}{\mathbf{5}} + \frac{2}{15} \cdot \frac{\mathbf{2}}{\mathbf{2}}$

$= \frac{5}{30} + \frac{4}{30}$

$= \frac{9}{30}$ This simplifies by a factor of 3.

$= \frac{3}{10}$

b) $4 = 2 \cdot 2$

$10 = 2 \cdot 5$

LCD $= 2 \cdot 2 \cdot 5 = 20$

$\frac{3}{4} \cdot \frac{\mathbf{5}}{\mathbf{5}} + \frac{7}{10} \cdot \frac{\mathbf{2}}{\mathbf{2}}$

$= \frac{15}{20} + \frac{14}{20}$

$= \frac{29}{20}$ This is an improper fraction and can be written as a mixed number.

$= 1\frac{9}{20}$

Subtraction works exactly the same way:

EXAMPLE 3 Evaluate $\frac{4}{5} - \frac{7}{15}$.

PROCEDURE: First find the LCD: $\mathbf{5}\,\underline{|\ 5\quad 15}$ LCD $= 5 \cdot 1 \cdot 3 = 15$ The second fraction already has this denominator and does not need to be built up.

$\quad\ \ 1\quad\ 3$

ANSWER: $\frac{4}{5}\cdot\frac{\mathbf{3}}{\mathbf{3}} - \frac{7}{15}$

$= \frac{12}{15} - \frac{7}{15}$

$= \frac{5}{15}$ This can be reduced by a factor of 5.

$= \frac{1}{3}$

YOU TRY IT 2

Evaluate each sum or difference by first finding the LCD and building up the fractions appropriately. Be sure to simplify each answer completely. Use Examples 2 and 3 as guides.

a) $\frac{7}{10} + \frac{1}{8}$

b) $\frac{4}{15} + \frac{9}{10}$

c) $\frac{3}{4} - \frac{2}{5}$

d) $\frac{9}{20} - \frac{4}{15}$

Think about it

Write a set of steps for adding or subtracting unlike fractions.

____

____

If one of the "fractions" happens to be a whole number, it can easily be written as a fraction by making the denominator a 1. From there, the common denominator will just be the denominator of the other fraction.

EXAMPLE 4

Evaluate $3 - \frac{7}{9}$.

PROCEDURE: First write the whole number as a fraction with a denominator of 1.

ANSWER: $3 - \frac{7}{9}$ The LCD is 9; it's the only denominator available.

$= \frac{3}{1}\cdot\frac{9}{9} - \frac{7}{9}$ Multiply $\frac{3}{1}$ by $\frac{9}{9}$.

$= \frac{27}{9} - \frac{7}{9}$ Now the fractions have the same denominator and we can subtract.

$= \frac{20}{9}$ Write this as a mixed number.

$= 2\frac{2}{9}$

EXAMPLE 5 Evaluate $2 + \frac{3}{5}$

ANSWER:

$2 + \dfrac{3}{5}$ The LCD is 5; it's the only denominator available.

$= \dfrac{2}{1} \cdot \dfrac{5}{5} + \dfrac{3}{5}$ Multiply $\frac{2}{1}$ by $\frac{5}{5}$.

$= \dfrac{10}{5} + \dfrac{3}{5}$ Now the fractions have the same denominator and we can add.

$= \dfrac{13}{5}$ Write this as a mixed number.

$= 2\dfrac{3}{5}$

YOU TRY IT 3 *Evaluate each using the techniques learned in this section. Be sure to simplify each answer completely. Use Examples 4 and 5 as guides.*

a) $2 - \dfrac{2}{5}$ b) $4 - \dfrac{7}{8}$ c) $5 + \dfrac{1}{4}$

Think about it What do you notice about the answer for Example 5?

____

____

Is your answer for YTI 3 part c consistent with what you wrote here? _______

Applications

Here are a few applications that involve adding fractions. We'll set these up just as we did in Section 1.7. In each, we'll still:

1. Write the Legend: Let n = _______________,
2. write and solve an equation: "The sum of all of the parts equals the whole," and
3. write the answer in the form of a complete sentence.

EXAMPLE 6 Using a $\frac{3}{8}$-inch drill bit, Marty drilled a hole $\left(\frac{3}{8}\text{ of an inch in diameter}\right)$ that was too small. Instead, he should have drilled a hole that was $\frac{1}{32}$ of an inch bigger. What size drill bit should Marty have originally used?

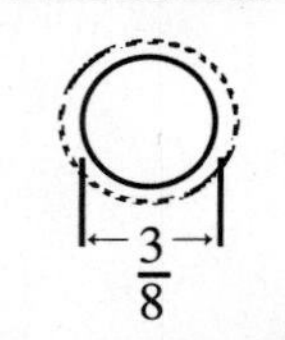

PROCEDURE: The parts are (a) the original drill bit size, and (b) the increase in size (how much bigger the hole should have been).

The whole is the new drill bit size (which is unknown.)

ANSWER: Legend: Let n = The size of the drill bit Marty should have used.

$\frac{3}{8} + \frac{1}{32} = n$ ⟵ First find the LCD. ⟶ LCD:

2	8	32
2	4	16
2	2	8
	1	4

$\frac{3}{8}\cdot\frac{4}{4} + \frac{1}{32} = n$ ⟵ Build up the first fraction only.

$\frac{12}{32} + \frac{1}{32} = n$ ⟵ Add the fractions. LCD $= 2\cdot2\cdot2\cdot1\cdot4 = 32$

$\frac{13}{32} = n$

SENTENCE: Marty should have used a $\frac{13}{32}$-inch drill bit.

YOU TRY IT 4 *To get a light blue shade of paint, Connie mixed $\frac{2}{3}$ gallon of blue paint with $\frac{3}{4}$ gallon of white paint. What is the total, in gallons, of the mixture?*

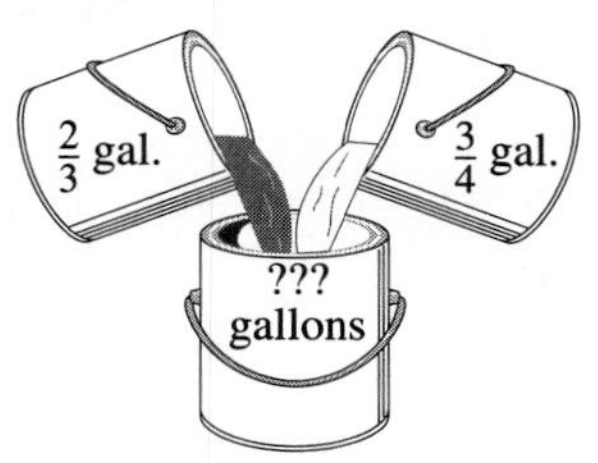

Sentence: ______________________________

You Try It Answers: Section 4.4

YTI 1

a) LCD = 30; so, $\frac{5}{6}\cdot\frac{5}{5} = \frac{25}{30}$; $\frac{3}{10}\cdot\frac{3}{3} = \frac{9}{30}$

b) LCD = 36; so, $\frac{4}{9}\cdot\frac{4}{4} = \frac{16}{36}$; $\frac{5}{12}\cdot\frac{3}{3} = \frac{15}{36}$

c) LCD = 60; so, $\frac{8}{15}\cdot\frac{4}{4} = \frac{32}{60}$; $\frac{1}{4}\cdot\frac{15}{15} = \frac{15}{60}$

d) LCD = 20; so, $\frac{2}{5}\cdot\frac{4}{4} = \frac{8}{20}$; $\frac{3}{20}$ does not need to be built up.

YTI 2

a) $\frac{33}{40}$ b) $\frac{7}{6} = 1\frac{1}{6}$

c) $\frac{7}{20}$ d) $\frac{11}{60}$

YTI 3

a) $1\frac{3}{5}$ b) $3\frac{1}{8}$

c) $5\frac{1}{4}$

YTI 4

The mixture totals $1\frac{5}{12}$ gallons of paint.

Focus Exercises: Section 4.4

Add. Simplify the results, if possible. Also, write any answers that contain improper fractions as mixed numbers.

1. $\frac{3}{5}+\frac{3}{10}$ **2.** $\frac{2}{3}+\frac{4}{5}$ **3.** $\frac{9}{10}+\frac{1}{6}$ **4.** $\frac{1}{12}+\frac{5}{8}$

5. $\frac{1}{12}+\frac{5}{9}$ **6.** $\frac{9}{10}+\frac{4}{5}$ **7.** $\frac{9}{16}+\frac{3}{8}$ **8.** $\frac{3}{10}+\frac{4}{15}$

9. $\frac{1}{6}+\frac{1}{3}$ **10.** $\frac{3}{10}+\frac{1}{5}$ **11.** $\frac{7}{12}+\frac{5}{6}$ **12.** $\frac{4}{9}+\frac{1}{6}$

13. $\frac{3}{7}+\frac{1}{4}$ **14.** $\frac{3}{20}+\frac{7}{30}$ **15.** $\frac{5}{6}+\frac{1}{3}$ **16.** $\frac{3}{4}+\frac{5}{8}$

17. $\frac{1}{2}+\frac{7}{8}$ **18.** $\frac{7}{30}+\frac{3}{10}$ **19.** $\frac{8}{25}+\frac{1}{10}$ **20.** $\frac{4}{15}+\frac{11}{20}$

21. $\frac{4}{5}+\frac{3}{4}$ **22.** $\frac{11}{12}+\frac{1}{3}$ **23.** $\frac{7}{9}+\frac{5}{6}$ **24.** $\frac{13}{18}+\frac{4}{9}$

Subtract. Simplify the results, if possible.

25. $\frac{5}{8}-\frac{1}{3}$ **26.** $\frac{7}{12}-\frac{1}{4}$ **27.** $\frac{5}{9}-\frac{1}{6}$ **28.** $2-\frac{1}{8}$

29. $1-\frac{7}{10}$ **30.** $3-\frac{2}{3}$ **31.** $\frac{13}{15}-\frac{1}{10}$ **32.** $\frac{11}{12}-\frac{4}{9}$

33. $\frac{5}{9}-\frac{1}{3}$ **34.** $\frac{5}{6}-\frac{7}{10}$ **35.** $\frac{15}{8}-\frac{2}{3}$ **36.** $\frac{10}{11}-\frac{2}{3}$

37. $2-\frac{4}{9}$ **38.** $1-\frac{3}{4}$ **39.** $6-\frac{2}{5}$ **40.** $\frac{9}{8}-\frac{1}{2}$

For each application, use the outline described in this section. Write the legend, set up and solve the equation, and write a sentence answering the question.

41. A meatball recipe calls for $\frac{5}{8}$ pound of beef and $\frac{3}{4}$ pound of pork. How much meat is in this recipe?

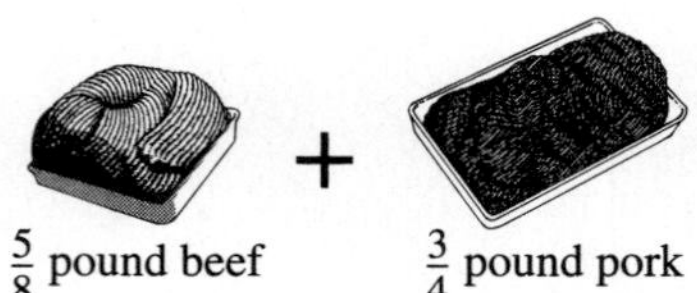

42. Marius is a tile layer, and he is completing the job of laying tile for a new kitchen counter. On top of the cabinets, he is putting down plywood that is $\frac{7}{8}$ inch thick. He is also putting down a $\frac{3}{4}$-inch-thick slate of wonder board. How much total thickness is Marius adding to the top of the cabinets?

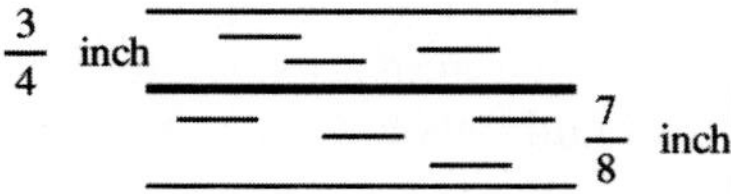

43. Tom is raising a platform by $\frac{7}{4}$ inches by stacking two boards together. The bottom board is $\frac{5}{8}$ inches thick. What must the thickness of the top board be?

$\frac{7}{4}$ inch ??? inch $\frac{5}{8}$ inch

44. Last winter, Rohin started with $\frac{5}{4}$ cord of wood to burn in his fireplace. (A cord is a measure used for a big stack of cut up logs) By the end of winter he had only $\frac{1}{3}$ cord of wood left. How much wood did Rohin burn during the winter?

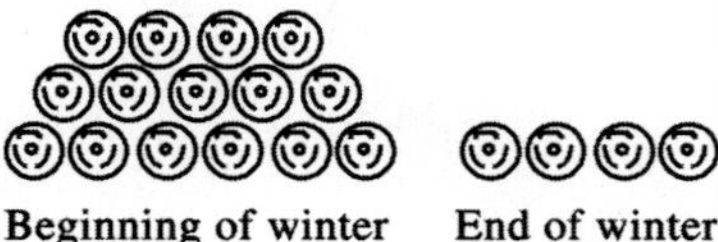

45. Carin needs $\frac{9}{8}$ cups of milk for a pancake recipe. From one carton she was able to pour $\frac{3}{4}$ cup before it was empty. To have enough for the recipe, how much milk must Carin pour from a new carton?

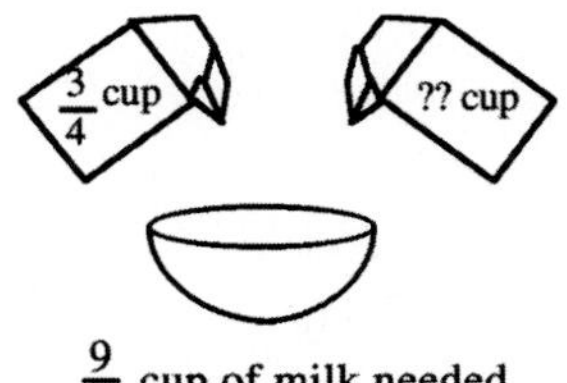

46. Carla owned a $\frac{5}{4}$-acre plot of land before she sold $\frac{3}{5}$ of an acre to a neighbor. How much land (in acres) did she own after the sale?

SECTION 4.5 Adding Mixed Numbers

Objectives

In this section, you will learn to:

- Add mixed numbers.

To successfully complete this section, you need to understand:

- Mixed numbers (3.1)
- Simplifying fractions (3.2)
- Adding fractions (4.3, 4.4)

Introduction

Now that we know how to add fractions with like and unlike denominators, we turn our attention to adding mixed numbers. Knowing how to add mixed numbers allows us to solve problems such as this:

> Henry bought a door for his hallway closet that measured $33\frac{3}{4}$ inches wide. As it turns out, it was not wide enough; in fact, it needs to be $1\frac{7}{16}$ inches wider. How wide is the door that Henry should buy?

Adding Mixed Numbers with Like Denominators

When adding mixed numbers, we add the whole numbers separately from the fractions. We are able to do this because of the Associative and Commutative Properties.

Consider $1\frac{2}{9} + 4\frac{5}{9}$. We could write each as a sum: $\rightarrow$ $\left(1 + \frac{2}{9}\right) + \left(4 + \frac{5}{9}\right)$

The Associative Property allows us to remove the parentheses: $= 1 + \frac{2}{9} + 4 + \frac{5}{9}$

The Commutative Property allows us to change the order of the numbers: $= 1 + 4 + \frac{2}{9} + \frac{5}{9}$

The Associative Property allows us to regroup them: $= (1 + 4) + \left(\frac{2}{9} + \frac{5}{9}\right)$

And the order of operations allows us to add the whole numbers separately from the fractions: $= 5 + \frac{7}{9}$

Giving us a mixed number as an answer: $= 5\frac{7}{9}$

EXAMPLE 1 Add $1\frac{5}{8} + 3\frac{1}{8}$; simplify completely.

PROCEDURE: There are two methods of doing this; either is fine to use.

Method 1:
Write each mixed number as an improper fraction: $1\frac{5}{8} = \frac{13}{8}$ and $3\frac{1}{8} = \frac{25}{8}$

Method 2:
Write the numbers vertically so that the whole numbers are above each other:

ANSWER:

Method 1:

$$1\frac{5}{8} + 3\frac{1}{8}$$
$$= \frac{13}{8} + \frac{25}{8}$$
$$= \frac{38}{8}$$

← The fraction simplifies by a factor of 2. →

$$= \frac{19}{4}$$

→ $\frac{19}{4}$ can be written as a mixed number. →

Method 2:

$$\begin{array}{r} 1\frac{5}{8} \\ +\ 3\frac{1}{8} \\ \hline 4\frac{6}{8} \end{array} = 4\frac{3}{4}$$

$$= 4\frac{3}{4}$$

Think about it

Consider the sum $24\frac{3}{8} + 35\frac{1}{8}$. What might go wrong in using Method 1 in Example 1 to find this sum?

Would you prefer to use Method 1 or Method 2 to find this sum?

YOU TRY IT 1

Evaluate. You may use any method you wish. Simplify the answer, if possible. Use Example 1 as a guide.

a) $1\frac{3}{7} + 4\frac{2}{7}$ b) $3\frac{3}{8} + 1\frac{1}{8}$ c) $15\frac{4}{9} + 23\frac{2}{9}$

Sometimes the fractional parts of mixed numbers add to an improper fraction. In that case, the improper fraction must be rewritten as a mixed number, and we must *adjust* the mixed number.

How do we work with a mixed number within a mixed number? It all goes back to addition.

EXAMPLE 2

This mixed number has a fraction that is improper: $3\frac{5}{4}$. Adjust the mixed number by writing the improper fraction as a mixed number and combining the whole numbers.

PROCEDURE: First separate the whole number from the fraction using a plus sign.

Second, rewrite the improper fraction as a mixed number (with a plus sign)

Third, combine the whole numbers.

ANSWER:

$3\frac{5}{4} = 3 + \frac{5}{4}$ This is a long way to do things, but it shows the thought process behind the work. Some of these steps can be skipped, as we see below.

$= 3 + 1\frac{1}{4}$

$= 3 + 1 + \frac{1}{4}$ $1\frac{1}{4}$ is the same as $1 + \frac{1}{4}$.

$= 4 + \frac{1}{4} = 4\frac{1}{4}$

This time, let's do the same example with some steps left out:

$3\frac{5}{4}$ Separate the whole number and the fraction with a plus sign and at the same time rewrite the fraction as a mixed number.

$= 3 + 1\frac{1}{4}$ Now, simply combine the whole numbers and leave the fraction as it is.

$= 4\frac{1}{4}$ With practice, you may be able to do this in just one step.

EXAMPLE 3 Each mixed number contains a fraction that is improper. Rewrite the improper fraction as a mixed number and combine the whole numbers.

a) $1\frac{8}{5}$ b) $7\frac{6}{6}$

PROCEDURE: Use the shorter method shown after Example 2.

ANSWER:

a) $1\frac{8}{5}$

$= 1 + 1\frac{3}{5}$

$= 2\frac{3}{5}$

b) $7\frac{6}{6}$ This improper fraction simplifies to a whole number with no fraction.

$= 7 + 1$

$= 8$

YOU TRY IT 2 *Use the method shown in Example 3 to rewrite the fraction and adjust the mixed number.*

a) $4\frac{8}{7}$ b) $16\frac{7}{4}$ c) $44\frac{3}{3}$ d) $12\frac{9}{5}$

When adding mixed numbers, if the fractional part becomes improper, we must rewrite the improper fraction and adjust the mixed number.

EXAMPLE 4 Add these fractions. Simplify completely and adjust the mixed number if the fraction is improper.

a) $4\frac{5}{6} + 1\frac{3}{6}$ b) $5\frac{3}{8} + 7\frac{5}{8}$

ANSWER:

a)

$$\begin{array}{r} 4\frac{5}{6} \\ +\ 1\frac{3}{6} \\ \hline 5\frac{8}{6} \end{array}$$

← Adjust the mixed number. →

$= 5 + 1\frac{2}{6}$

$= 6\frac{2}{6}$ ← Simplify the fraction by a factor of 2.

$= 6\frac{1}{3}$

b)

$$\begin{array}{r} 5\frac{3}{8} \\ +\ 7\frac{5}{8} \\ \hline 12\frac{8}{8} \end{array}$$

$12 + 1$

$= 13$

YOU TRY IT 3 *Add these mixed numbers. Simplify completely and adjust the mixed number if the fraction is improper. Use Example 4 as a guide.*

a) $1\frac{3}{4} + \frac{2}{4}$ b) $5\frac{5}{8} + 14\frac{7}{8}$

c) $39\frac{2}{7} + 16\frac{5}{7}$

d) $22\frac{13}{16} + \frac{7}{16}$

Adding Mixed Numbers with Unlike Denominators

If we need to evaluate the sum of two mixed numbers, and the denominators within the fraction parts are different, then we must first find common denominators before combining.

EXAMPLE 5 Evaluate the sum. Be sure to simplify if possible.

a) $4\frac{3}{4} + 5\frac{1}{6}$

b) $3\frac{7}{8} + 1\frac{13}{16}$

PROCEDURE: First, identify a common denominator.

Second, build up each fraction to have that common denominator.

Third, combine the mixed numbers as in the examples presented earlier in this section.

ANSWER: a) For $\frac{3}{4}$ and $\frac{1}{6}$, the LCD is 12:

$$2 \underline{\lfloor\, 4 \quad 6}$$
$$\quad 2 \quad 3$$

$\text{LCD} = 2 \cdot 2 \cdot 3 = 12$

$4\frac{3}{4}$ Build up the fraction. ⟶ $4\frac{3}{4} \cdot \frac{\mathbf{3}}{\mathbf{3}} = \quad 4\frac{9}{12}$

$+\ 5\frac{1}{6}$ Build up the fraction. ⟶ $5\frac{1}{6} \cdot \frac{\mathbf{2}}{\mathbf{2}} = \quad +\ 5\frac{2}{12}$

$$9\frac{11}{12}$$

b) For $\frac{7}{8}$ and $\frac{13}{16}$, the LCD is 16 because 16 is a multiple of 8.

$3\frac{7}{8}$ Build up the fraction. ⟶ $3\frac{7}{8} \cdot \frac{\mathbf{2}}{\mathbf{2}}$ ⟶ $3\frac{14}{16}$

$+\ 1\frac{13}{16}$ Keep this fraction as is. ⟶ $1\frac{13}{16}$ ⟶ $+\ 1\frac{13}{16}$

$$4\frac{27}{16}$$

We must take this one step further by rewriting the improper fraction and adjusting the mixed number:

$$4\frac{27}{16} = 4 + 1\frac{11}{16} = 5\frac{11}{16}$$

YOU TRY IT 4 *Add these mixed numbers. Find a common denominator, simplify completely, and adjust the mixed number if the fraction is improper. Use Example 5 as a guide.*

a) $1\frac{3}{8} + 3\frac{1}{4}$

b) $12\frac{2}{5} + 6\frac{3}{4}$

Applications

Here is a situation that involves adding mixed numbers.

EXAMPLE 6

Joan is a carpenter. She needs one piece of molding that is $28\frac{1}{2}$ inches long and another that is $31\frac{3}{4}$ inches long. How many inches of molding does she need?

$28\frac{1}{2}$ inches

$31\frac{3}{4}$ inches

PROCEDURE: Each of these measures is a part, and we are looking for the whole. We'll set up an equation; however, a lot of the work (like adding mixed numbers) will be done off to the side.

ANSWER: Legend: Let $n =$ the total number of inches of molding needed.

Equation:

$$28\frac{1}{2} + 31\frac{3}{4} = n$$

$$59\frac{5}{4} = n$$

Work off to the side:

$$28\frac{1}{2} \longrightarrow 28\frac{1}{2}\cdot\frac{\mathbf{2}}{\mathbf{2}} \longrightarrow 28\frac{2}{4}$$

$$+\ 31\frac{3}{4} \longrightarrow \quad \longrightarrow +\ 31\frac{3}{4}$$

$$59\frac{5}{4}$$

So, $n = 59\frac{5}{4} \longrightarrow 59 + 1\frac{1}{4} = 60\frac{1}{4}$

$$n = 60\frac{1}{4}$$

SENTENCE: Joan needs a total of $60\frac{1}{4}$ inches of molding.

YOU TRY IT 5

During the weekend, Sharla went hiking in Yellowstone National Park. On Saturday she hiked $5\frac{2}{3}$ miles, and on Sunday, she hiked $4\frac{3}{8}$ miles. How many miles did Sharla hike that weekend?

Sentence: ______________________________

You Try It Answers: Section 4.5

YTI 1 a) $5\frac{5}{7}$ b) $4\frac{1}{2}$ c) $38\frac{2}{3}$

YTI 2 a) $5\frac{1}{7}$ b) $17\frac{3}{4}$ c) 45 d) $13\frac{4}{5}$

YTI 3 a) $2\frac{1}{4}$ b) $20\frac{1}{2}$ c) 56 d) $23\frac{1}{4}$

YTI 4 a) $4\frac{5}{8}$ b) $19\frac{3}{20}$

YTI 5 Sharla hiked $10\frac{1}{24}$ miles that weekend.

Focus Exercises: Section 4.5

Evaluate. If necessary, find common denominators, simplify completely, and adjust the mixed number if the answer contains an improper fraction.

1. $3\frac{7}{10} + 6\frac{1}{10}$

2. $1\frac{5}{12} + 4\frac{1}{12}$

3. $10\frac{2}{9} + 2\frac{5}{9}$

4. $6\frac{1}{5} + 3\frac{2}{5}$

5. $20\frac{1}{4} + 5\frac{3}{8}$

6. $7\frac{1}{6} + 11\frac{3}{4}$

7. $12\frac{1}{6} + 13\frac{2}{9}$

8. $1\frac{7}{10} + 2\frac{1}{5}$

9. $2\frac{3}{8} + 9\frac{5}{8}$

10. $6\frac{3}{7} + 2\frac{4}{7}$

11. $5\frac{1}{10} + 8\frac{9}{10}$

12. $1\frac{2}{5} + 3\frac{3}{5}$

13. $2\frac{3}{4} + 34\frac{3}{4}$

14. $9\frac{5}{6} + 1\frac{3}{6}$

15. $4\frac{5}{8} + \frac{7}{8}$

16. $28\frac{9}{10} + 7\frac{7}{10}$

17. $4\frac{7}{12} + 5\frac{5}{6}$

18. $1\frac{13}{18} + 1\frac{4}{9}$

19. $7\frac{7}{9} + 13\frac{2}{3}$

20. $32\frac{5}{6} + \frac{7}{9}$

21. $17\frac{3}{8} + \frac{11}{12}$

22. $5\frac{2}{3} + 4\frac{1}{2}$

23. $21\frac{2}{3} + 44\frac{3}{4}$

24. $38\frac{5}{8} + 13\frac{5}{6}$

For each application, use the outline described in this section. Write the legend, set up and solve the equation, and write a sentence answering the question.

25. Katie needs $3\frac{1}{4}$ yards of material for a dress she is making for her niece. She also needs $2\frac{3}{8}$ yards of the same fabric to make a skirt for her daughter. How many yards of material in total does Katie need for the two projects?

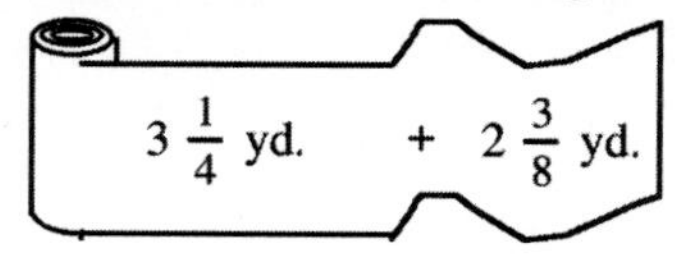

26. Allen purchased two watermelons for a family picnic. One weighed $15\frac{7}{8}$ pounds, and the other weighed $17\frac{3}{4}$ pounds. What is the total weight of the two watermelons?

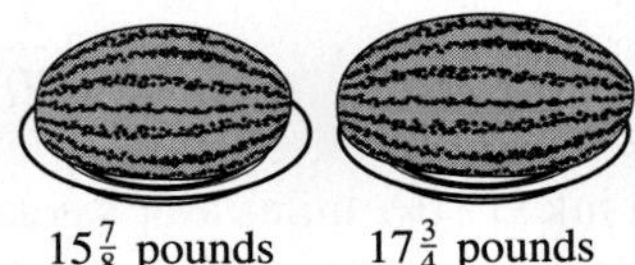

27. Toni combined $2\frac{3}{4}$ cups of flour with $1\frac{1}{3}$ cups of sugar. How many cups of mixture does Toni have?

28. Henry bought a door for his hallway closet that measured $33\frac{3}{4}$ inches wide. As it turns out, the door was not wide enough; in fact, it needs to be $1\frac{7}{16}$ inches wider. How wide is the door that Henry should buy?

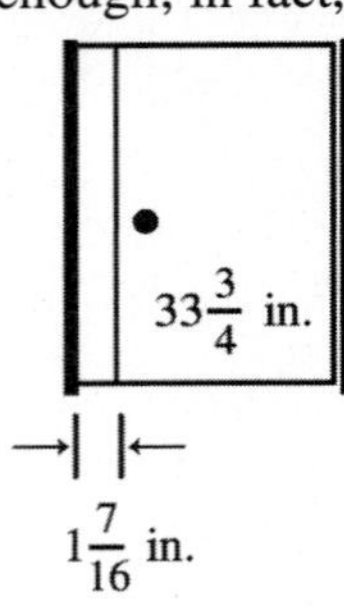

29. Giselle needs to keep track of the number of hours she works on various projects. One day, she spent $4\frac{3}{4}$ hours counting inventory and $2\frac{1}{2}$ hours doing data entry on the computer. How many hours did Giselle work on those projects that day?

Time Sheet	
Giselle Grippen	
inventory	$4\frac{3}{4}$
data entry	$2\frac{1}{2}$
Total	______

30. At birth, Jason measured $19\frac{3}{8}$ inches long. During his first year, he grew $6\frac{3}{4}$ inches. How tall was Jason on his first birthday?

SECTION 4.6 Subtracting Mixed Numbers

Objectives

In this section, you will learn to:

- Regroup mixed numbers.
- Subtract mixed numbers.

To successfully complete this section, you need to understand:

- Subtracting Whole Numbers (1.3)
- Mixed Numbers and Improper Fractions (3.1)
- Simplifying Fractions (3.2)
- Subtracting Fractions (4.3, 4.4)

Introduction

We saw when subtracting whole numbers that sometimes we need to regroup and sometimes we don't. The same is true of subtracting mixed numbers. Just as in addition, when subtracting mixed numbers, we subtract whole number from whole number and fraction from fraction.

Sometimes we can subtract without needing to regroup, as in $8\frac{7}{9} - 2\frac{5}{9}$:

$$\begin{array}{r} 8\frac{7}{9} \\ -\ 2\frac{5}{9} \\ \hline 6\frac{2}{9} \end{array}$$

Other times we'll need to take 1 from the whole number, and put it with the fraction, as in $8\frac{4}{9} - 2\frac{5}{9}$:

$$\begin{array}{r} 8\frac{4}{9} \\ -\ 2\frac{5}{9} \\ \hline \uparrow \end{array}$$

We can't subtract the fractions . . .

Of course, the question is, "So how *do* we subtract those mixed numbers?" We must regroup the first mixed number. To prepare for this type of subtraction, we'll first do a few warm-up exercises about regrouping mixed numbers.

Regrouping with Mixed Numbers

The regrouping process with mixed numbers means taking 1 from the whole number and adding it to the fraction. The fraction becomes an improper fraction, allowing us to subtract directly.

Take 1 from the whole number. Add the 1 to the fraction

$$8\frac{4}{9} \rightarrow 8\frac{4}{9} = (7+1) + \frac{4}{9} \rightarrow 7 + 1 + \frac{4}{9} = 7 + \left(\frac{9}{9} + \frac{4}{9}\right) = 7\frac{13}{9}$$

This is an improper fraction.

EXAMPLE 1

Regroup the mixed number by taking 1 from the whole number, and write it as a sum. Next, combine the 1 and the fraction to get an improper fraction.

ANSWER:

	Mixed number		Taking 1 from the whole number		Combining 1 with the fraction		Regrouped mixed number (add the fractions)
a)	$5\frac{3}{8}$	=	$4 + 1 + \frac{3}{8}$	=	$4 + \frac{8}{8} + \frac{3}{8}$	=	$4\frac{11}{8}$
b)	$1\frac{2}{9}$	=	$0 + 1 + \frac{2}{9}$	=	$0 + \frac{9}{9} + \frac{2}{9}$	=	$\frac{11}{9}$

YOU TRY IT 1

Regroup the mixed number by taking 1 from the whole number and combining it with the fraction, just as in Example 1.

Mixed number	Taking 1 from the whole number	Combining 1 with the fraction	Regrouped mixed number (add the fractions)
a) $4\frac{5}{9} =$	________	________	________
b) $10\frac{1}{6} =$	________	________	________
c) $2\frac{5}{8} =$	________	________	________

Now that we've gone through the warm-up exercises, let's get to what this section is really about.

Subtracting Mixed Numbers with Like Fractions

Subtracting mixed numbers is similar to adding mixed numbers in that we combine the whole numbers together and the fractions together. Sometimes, we can subtract directly (without regrouping) and sometimes we must regroup.

EXAMPLE 2

Subtract; simplify completely.

a) $6\frac{5}{9} - 1\frac{2}{9}$ b) $3\frac{4}{7} - 2$ c) $5\frac{5}{8} - \frac{1}{8}$

PROCEDURE: Rewrite this subtraction *vertically* so that the first mixed number is above the other. In each of these we will be able to subtract directly, without needing to regroup.

ANSWER: a) $6\frac{5}{9} - 1\frac{2}{9}$ Rewrite this so that the first number is above the other.

$$\begin{array}{r} 6\frac{5}{9} \\ -\ 1\frac{2}{9} \\ \hline 5\frac{3}{9} \end{array} = 5\frac{1}{3}$$

Here, we can subtract directly because the numerator in the first fraction is larger than the numerator in the second fraction.

$\frac{3}{9}$ can be reduced by a factor of 3.

b) $3\frac{4}{7} - 2$

$$\begin{array}{r} 3\frac{4}{7} \\ -\ 2 \\ \hline 1\frac{4}{7} \end{array}$$

$\frac{4}{7}$ can't be reduced.

c) $5\frac{5}{8} - \frac{1}{8}$

$$\begin{array}{r} 5\frac{5}{8} \\ -\ \frac{1}{8} \\ \hline 5\frac{4}{8} \end{array} = 5\frac{1}{2}$$

$\frac{4}{8}$ can be reduced by a factor of 4.

YOU TRY IT 2

Evaluate. Simplify whenever possible. Use Example 2 as a guide.

a) $\begin{array}{r} 4\frac{3}{7} \\ -\ 1\frac{2}{7} \\ \hline \end{array}$

b) $\begin{array}{r} 7\frac{3}{8} \\ -\ 1\frac{1}{8} \\ \hline \end{array}$

c) $\begin{array}{r} 17\frac{5}{12} \\ -\ 13 \\ \hline \end{array}$

d) $\begin{array}{r} 20\frac{7}{9} \\ -\ \frac{5}{9} \\ \hline \end{array}$

When working with like fractions, we must regroup when the first fraction's numerator is less than the second fraction's numerator.

EXAMPLE 3 Subtract $8\frac{1}{4} - 6\frac{3}{4}$.

PROCEDURE: First, write the problem vertically.

Second, notice that the first numerator is less than the second numerator; this means that you'll need to regroup the mixed number.

Third, after the problem has been rewritten, subtract as in Example 2.

ANSWER: We must take 1 from the whole number. 1 will be written as $\frac{4}{4}$.

$$\begin{array}{r} 8\frac{1}{4} \\ -\ 6\frac{3}{4} \\ \hline \end{array} \longrightarrow 8\frac{1}{4} = 7 + \frac{4}{4} + \frac{1}{4} \longrightarrow \begin{array}{r} 7\frac{5}{4} \\ -\ 6\frac{3}{4} \\ \hline 1\frac{2}{4} \end{array}$$

(This allows us to subtract directly.)

This answer's fraction can be simplified by a factor of 2: $1\frac{2}{4} = 1\frac{1}{2}$

YOU TRY IT 3

Evaluate. Simplify whenever possible. Use Example 3 as a guide.

a) $\begin{array}{r} 4\frac{3}{7} \\ -\ 1\frac{5}{7} \\ \hline \end{array}$

b) $\begin{array}{r} 7\frac{3}{8} \\ -\ 1\frac{7}{8} \\ \hline \end{array}$

Subtracting Mixed Numbers with Unlike Fractions

When subtracting two mixed numbers with unlike denominators, we must first find common denominators before combining.

EXAMPLE 4 Evaluate. Simplify the answer if possible. $8\frac{3}{4} - 5\frac{1}{6}$

PROCEDURE: First, identify the LCD: $2 \underline{|\ 4 \quad 6\ }$ LCD $= 2 \cdot 2 \cdot 3 = 12$

$\quad\quad 2 \quad 3$

Second, build up each fraction to have a denominator of 12.

Third, combine the mixed numbers as in the examples presented earlier in this section.

Let's rewrite this difference, $8\frac{3}{4} - 5\frac{1}{6}$, vertically. It is easier to work with the fractions that way.

ANSWER:

$8\frac{3}{4}$ Build up the fraction → $8\frac{3}{4} \times \frac{\mathbf{3}}{\mathbf{3}} =$ $8\frac{9}{12}$

$-\ 5\frac{1}{6}$ Build up the fraction → $5\frac{1}{6} \times \frac{\mathbf{2}}{\mathbf{2}} =$ $-\ 5\frac{2}{12}$ We can subtract directly without regrouping.

$3\frac{7}{12}$

YOU TRY IT 4

Evaluate. Simplify the answer if possible. Use Example 4 as a guide.

a) $10\frac{4}{9} - 6\frac{5}{18}$

b) $12\frac{5}{6} - 4\frac{3}{4}$

EXAMPLE 5

Evaluate the difference: $3\frac{5}{12} - 1\frac{2}{3}$. Simplify the answer if possible.

PROCEDURE: At first glance, it may look as though we won't need to regroup, but that can't be decided until after we find the common denominator.

First identify the LCD: 12 is a multiple of 3, so LCD = 12.

Second, build up each fraction to have a denominator of 12.

Third, combine the mixed numbers as in the examples presented earlier in this section.

ANSWER: Write the problem vertically. It is easier to work with the fractions that way.

$3\frac{5}{12}$ Keep this fraction → $3\frac{5}{12}$ = $3\frac{5}{12}$

$-\ 1\frac{2}{3}$ Build up this fraction → $1\frac{2}{3} \times \frac{\mathbf{4}}{\mathbf{4}} =$ $-\ 1\frac{8}{12}$

Now we must regroup before we can subtract:

$3\frac{5}{12}$ → $3\frac{5}{12} = 2 + \frac{12}{12} + \frac{5}{12}$ → $2\frac{17}{12}$

$-\ 1\frac{8}{12}$ ← Keep this mixed number the same → $-\ 1\frac{8}{12}$

$1\frac{9}{12}$

Last, the fraction can reduce by a factor of 3: $1\frac{9}{12} = 1\frac{3}{4}$.

YOU TRY IT 5

Evaluate. Find a common denominator, and regroup if needed. Simplify the answer if possible. Use Example 5 as a guide.

a) $\begin{array}{r} 11\frac{5}{8} \\ -\ 6\frac{3}{4} \\ \hline \end{array}$

b) $\begin{array}{r} 8\frac{1}{3} \\ -\ 4\frac{1}{2} \\ \hline \end{array}$

EXAMPLE 6 Evaluate the difference. Simplify the answer if possible. $7 - 1\frac{2}{3}$

PROCEDURE: Because the first number has no fraction, we will need to take 1 from the 7 and make a fraction. It is a simple matter of choosing 1 to be $\frac{3}{3}$ in order to subtract like fractions.

We must regroup in order to subtract:

ANSWER:

$\begin{array}{r} 7 \\ -\ 1\frac{2}{3} \\ \hline \end{array} \quad \rightarrow \quad 7 = 6 + \frac{3}{3} \quad \rightarrow \quad \begin{array}{r} 6\frac{3}{3} \\ -\ 1\frac{2}{3} \\ \hline 5\frac{1}{3} \end{array}$

This allows us to subtract directly.

YOU TRY IT 6

Evaluate the difference. Take 1 from the whole number, and choose an appropriate denominator. Simplify the answer if possible. Use Example 6 as a guide.

a) $\begin{array}{r} 12 \\ -\ 9\frac{7}{12} \\ \hline \end{array}$

b) $\begin{array}{r} 15 \\ -\ 10\frac{3}{7} \\ \hline \end{array}$

Applications

Here are a few applications that involve subtracting mixed numbers. Most, if not all, of these ask you to find the missing part.

For each, be sure to simplify whenever possible, and write the answer in a complete sentence, using a mixed number.

EXAMPLE 7 Pamela is at her job for $8\frac{1}{2}$ hours each day. During that time she takes a total of $1\frac{1}{4}$ hours for breaks. How many hours of actual work does Pamela do each day?

PROCEDURE: As always, write the legend and the equation; then solve the equation and write a sentence answering the question.

ANSWER: Legend: Let n = the number of actual hours of work. (This is a part.)

The whole is the total number of hours at her job.

Equation: $n + 1\frac{1}{4} = 8\frac{1}{2}$ Isolate the variable by subtracting.

$$n + 1\frac{1}{4} - 1\frac{1}{4} = 8\frac{1}{2} - 1\frac{1}{4}$$

Evaluate this difference off to the side: $8\frac{1}{2} \rightarrow 8 + \frac{1}{2} \times \frac{\mathbf{2}}{\mathbf{2}} \rightarrow 8\frac{2}{4}$

Find a common denominator, if needed: $-\ 1\frac{1}{4} \rightarrow \rightarrow -\ 1\frac{1}{4}$

$$7\frac{1}{4}$$

The equation then becomes:

$$n + 0 = 7\frac{1}{4}$$

$$n = 7\frac{1}{4}$$

SENTENCE: Pamela does $7\frac{1}{4}$ hours of actual work.

Think about it What different method can you think of for solving problems like the one in Example 8?

Demonstrate your method in this space:

YOU TRY IT 7 *Antoinette has a recipe that calls for $3\frac{1}{4}$ cups of flour. Unfortunately, she has only $1\frac{7}{8}$ cups of flour so she'll need to borrow some from her neighbor. How many cups of flour will Antoinette need to borrow to make the recipe?*

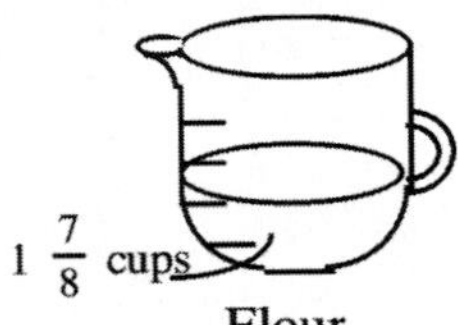

Sentence: ______________________

YOU TRY IT 8 *Amy is a tailor. D'reen brought in a skirt to have the length altered. Currently, the length of the skirt is $34\frac{1}{2}$ inches, but D'reen wants it to be $31\frac{5}{8}$ inches. By how many inches does Amy need to adjust the length of the skirt?*

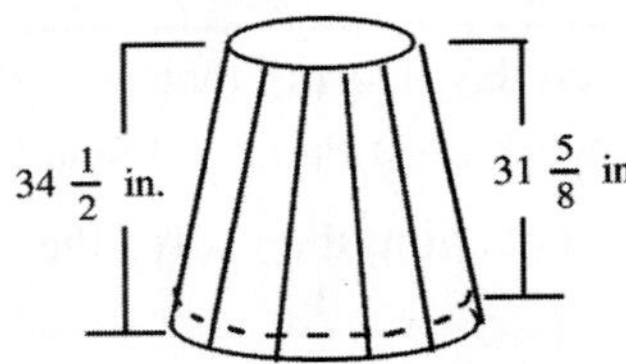

Sentence: ______________________

You Try It Answers: Section 4.6

YTI 1 a) $4\frac{5}{9} = 3 + 1 + \frac{5}{9} = 3 + \frac{9}{9} + \frac{5}{9} = 3\frac{14}{9}$

b) $10\frac{1}{6} = 9 + 1 + \frac{1}{6} = 9 + \frac{6}{6} + \frac{1}{6} = 9\frac{7}{6}$

c) $2\frac{5}{8} = 1 + 1 + \frac{5}{8} = 1 + \frac{8}{8} + \frac{5}{8} = 1\frac{13}{8}$

YTI 2 a) $3\frac{1}{7}$ b) $6\frac{1}{4}$ c) $4\frac{5}{12}$ d) $20\frac{2}{9}$

YTI 3 a) $2\frac{5}{7}$ b) $5\frac{1}{2}$

YTI 4 a) $4\frac{1}{6}$ b) $8\frac{1}{12}$

YTI 5 a) $4\frac{7}{8}$ b) $3\frac{5}{6}$

YTI 6 a) $2\frac{5}{12}$ b) $4\frac{4}{7}$

YTI 7 Legend: Let n = the number of cups of flour to be borrowed; $n + 1\frac{7}{8} = 3\frac{1}{4}$

Antoinette will need to borrow $1\frac{3}{8}$ cups of flour.

YTI 8 Legend: Let n = the number of inches the skirt is to be shortened; $n + 31\frac{5}{8} = 34\frac{1}{2}$

Amy will need to adjust the length of the skirt by $2\frac{7}{8}$ inches.

Focus Exercises: Section 4.6

Subtract. Simplify whenever possible.

1. $5\frac{7}{9} - 3\frac{2}{9}$ **2.** $8\frac{7}{15} - 2\frac{3}{15}$ **3.** $12\frac{5}{7} - 3\frac{1}{7}$

4. $14\frac{7}{11} - 13\frac{5}{11}$ **5.** $4\frac{8}{15} - 3\frac{2}{15}$ **6.** $12\frac{13}{16} - 3\frac{9}{16}$

7. $14\frac{17}{20} - 13\frac{9}{20}$ **8.** $20\frac{13}{18} - 5\frac{7}{18}$ **9.** $6\frac{7}{10} - 3\frac{7}{10}$

10. $9\frac{3}{4} - 2\frac{3}{4}$ **11.** $10\frac{5}{24} - 8\frac{5}{24}$ **12.** $10\frac{6}{25} - 1\frac{6}{25}$

13. $3\frac{7}{10} - 1\frac{1}{4}$ **14.** $5\frac{2}{3} - 3\frac{1}{6}$ **15.** $1\frac{11}{12} - \frac{5}{9}$

16. $6\frac{5}{6} - 5\frac{3}{8}$ **17.** $9 - 6\frac{3}{5}$ **18.** $6 - 3\frac{5}{8}$

19. $9 - 2\frac{4}{9}$ **20.** $4 - 1\frac{5}{12}$ **21.** $7\frac{1}{9} - 2\frac{5}{9}$

22. $1\frac{5}{11} - \frac{9}{11}$ **23.** $12\frac{4}{15} - 4\frac{8}{15}$ **24.** $12\frac{1}{5} - 4\frac{3}{5}$

25. $10\frac{1}{6} - 5\frac{5}{6}$ **26.** $16\frac{1}{10} - 6\frac{7}{10}$ **27.** $13\frac{4}{15} - 9\frac{7}{15}$

28. $4\frac{1}{12} - 2\frac{7}{12}$

29. $5\frac{1}{10} - 3\frac{7}{20}$

30. $12\frac{1}{6} - 6\frac{2}{3}$

31. $12\frac{3}{8} - 4\frac{3}{4}$

32. $1\frac{3}{10} - \frac{1}{2}$

33. $10\frac{3}{8} - 4\frac{5}{6}$

34. $11\frac{4}{15} - 9\frac{7}{10}$

35. $25\frac{5}{6} - 13\frac{11}{12}$

36. $38\frac{5}{9} - 13\frac{5}{6}$

For each application, use the outline described in this section. Write the legend, set up and solve the equation, and write a sentence answering the question.

37. Sanjeer took his aluminum cans to be recycled. After placing them in the wire-framed bin, he had the bin of aluminum cans weighed. The total weight came to $21\frac{1}{4}$ pounds. The empty bin weighs $9\frac{7}{8}$ pounds. How many pounds of aluminum cans did Sanjeer take to be recycled?

38. Jim wanted to know how much coffee his favorite large mug could hold. He took a measuring cup with 3 cups of water and poured as much water as he could into the mug. He then looked at the measuring cup and found it still had $1\frac{2}{3}$ cups of water in it. How much water did Jim pour into the mug?

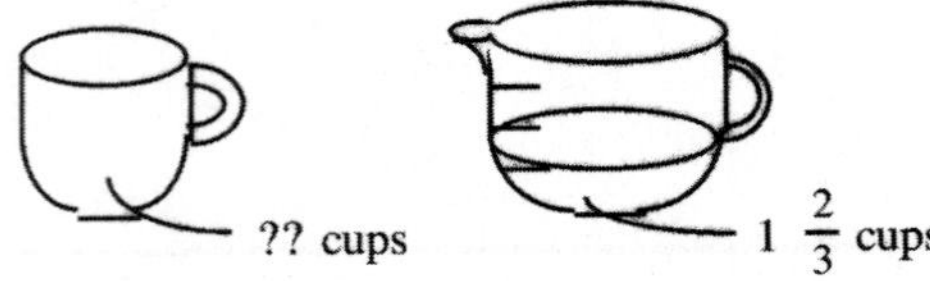

39. Ann works in a fabric store. A new bolt of fabric has 20 yards on it, and a customer buys $5\frac{3}{8}$ yards from that bolt. How many yards of fabric are left on the bolt?

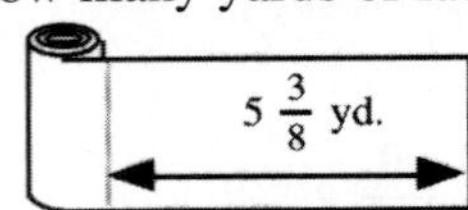

40. When Malatsi was born, he was $18\frac{5}{16}$ inches long. He was measured again when he was three months old and was $22\frac{1}{8}$ inches long. How many inches did Malatsi grow in those three months?

41. To ride on the new Angel's Flight roller coaster, riders must be at least $63\frac{1}{2}$ inches tall. Kaitlin is only $61\frac{3}{4}$ inches tall. To meet the minimum height requirement for the ride, how many inches taller does Kaitlin need to be?

42. Last winter, Larry's Wood Farm started with $8\frac{1}{3}$ cords of wood. By the end of winter, he had only $2\frac{5}{12}$ cords of wood left. How much wood did Larry sell during the winter?

43. Qeesha owned a $6\frac{1}{9}$-acre plot of land in the country. She decided to sell $2\frac{1}{3}$-acres to a real estate office for future home development. How many acres did Qeesha own after the sale?

44. Bob bought a set of new golf clubs, but they were too short for him. The driver was $34\frac{11}{16}$ inches long, but the golf pro at the shop determined that Bob's ideal driver length is $36\frac{1}{8}$ inches. To meet Bob's ideal driver length, how many more inches should be added to the length of the driver?

Chapter 4 Review

Section 4.1 Common Multiples

CONCEPT	EXAMPLE
A **multiple** of a natural number, n, is a product of n and some other natural number. Also, n is a factor of each of those multiples.	The first five multiples of 6 and their factored forms: 6 12 18 24 30 $1 \cdot 6$ $2 \cdot 6$ $3 \cdot 6$ $4 \cdot 6$ $5 \cdot 6$
A **common multiple** between two numbers is any multiple that each of those numbers has in common.	Multiples of 4: 4, 8, 12, 16, 20, 24, 28, 32, 36, 40, 44, 48, 52, ... Multiples of 6: 6, 12, 18, 24, 30, 36, 42, 48, 54, ... Common multiples of 4 and 6 are: 12, 24, 36, and 48, and the list goes on.
The **least common multiple** (LCM) is the lowest common multiple or the first common multiple.	The LCM of 4 and 6 is 12.
We can find the LCM of two numbers by making a list of the multiples of each number. The smallest number common to both lists is the LCM.	Multiples of 2: 2, 4, 6, 8, 10, 12, 14, … Multiples of 3: 3, 6, 9, 12, 15, 18, … The LCM of 2 and 3 is 6.
We can find the LCM using prime factorization: 1. Find the prime factorization of each number. 2. Write "LCM = ________ = ___." 3. On the line above, write all of the prime factors (with multiplication signs) of the first number. 4. Write in any prime factors of the second number that have not yet been written down. 5. Multiply the prime factors together (and write that product after the second equal sign).	Find the LCM of 12 and 40. $12 = 2 \cdot 2 \cdot 3$ $40 = 2 \cdot 2 \cdot 2 \cdot 5$ $\text{LCM} = \underline{2 \cdot 2 \cdot 3 \cdot 2 \cdot 5 = 120}$
Using prime factorizations written with exponents, we can build the LCM by taking the highest exponent of each prime factor in either prime factorization.	Find the LCM of 30 and 40. $30 = 2^1 \cdot 3^1 \cdot 5^1$ $40 = 2^3 \cdot 5^1$ $\text{LCM} = \underline{2^3 \cdot 3^1 \cdot 5^1 = 120}$
We can find the LCM using the Division Method: 1. Divide out any common factor of the two numbers, getting a new pair of numbers, called quotients. The common factors may be prime or composite numbers. 2. Continue dividing until the new quotients are relatively prime. 3. Multiply each factor that was divided out and each number in the relatively prime quotients.	Find the LCM of 12 and 40. 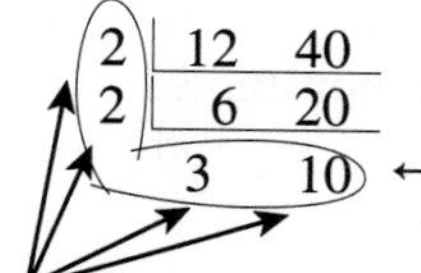 This last pair of quotients is relatively prime. Multiply all of these: $2 \cdot 2 \cdot 3 \cdot 10 = 120$

Section 4.2 Building up Fractions

CONCEPT	EXAMPLE
Multiplying a fraction by a fractional form of 1, such as $\frac{3}{3}$, is called **building up** a fraction. This means that both the numerator and the denominator become larger—are built up—but the result is an equivalent fraction.	To build up $\frac{3}{5}$ to be an equivalent fraction with a denominator of 20, multiply $\frac{3}{5}$ by a fractional form of 1, $\frac{4}{4}$: $\frac{3}{5}\cdot\frac{4}{4} = \frac{12}{20}$. $\frac{12}{20}$ is equivalent to $\frac{3}{5}$.
Two or more fractions are **like fractions** if they have the same denominator.	$\frac{2}{9}, \frac{6}{9}, \frac{7}{9}$ are like fractions.
Two fractions with different denominators are **unlike fractions**.	$\frac{3}{4}$ and $\frac{3}{5}$ are unlike fractions.

Section 4.3 Adding and Subtracting Like Fractions

CONCEPT	EXAMPLE
To add any two like fractions, add the numerators: $\frac{a}{b} + \frac{c}{b} = \frac{a+c}{b}$.	$\frac{2}{9} + \frac{5}{9} = \frac{2+5}{9} = \frac{7}{9}$
To subtract any two like fractions, subtract the numerators: $\frac{a}{b} - \frac{c}{b} = \frac{a-c}{b}$.	$\frac{8}{15} - \frac{5}{15} = \frac{8-5}{15} = \frac{3}{15}$, which can be reduced to $\frac{1}{5}$.

Section 4.4 Adding and Subtracting Unlike Fractions

CONCEPT	EXAMPLE
We can build up two unlike fractions to have the same denominator, called a **common denominator**. A common denominator is a common multiple of the given denominators.	Build up $\frac{1}{4}$ and $\frac{5}{6}$ to have a common denominator of 36. $\frac{1}{4}\cdot\frac{\mathbf{9}}{\mathbf{9}} = \frac{9}{36}$ and $\frac{5}{6}\cdot\frac{\mathbf{6}}{\mathbf{6}} = \frac{30}{36}$
The **least common denominator** (LCD) is the least common multiple of the denominators.	The LCM of 4 and 6 is 12, so the LCD of $\frac{1}{4}$ and $\frac{5}{6}$ is 12 and each fraction can be built up to have 12 as a denominator. $\frac{1}{4}\cdot\frac{\mathbf{3}}{\mathbf{3}} = \frac{3}{12}$ and $\frac{5}{6}\cdot\frac{\mathbf{2}}{\mathbf{2}} = \frac{10}{12}$

CONCEPT	EXAMPLE
Once two unlike fractions are built up to have the same denominator they can be combined, either by addition or subtraction.	Add: $\frac{1}{4}+\frac{1}{6}$ $=\frac{1}{4}\cdot\frac{\mathbf{3}}{\mathbf{3}}+\frac{1}{6}\cdot\frac{\mathbf{2}}{\mathbf{2}}$ $=\frac{3}{12}+\frac{2}{12}=\frac{3+2}{12}=\frac{5}{12}$ Subtract: $\frac{2}{3}-\frac{1}{6}=\frac{2}{3}\cdot\frac{\mathbf{2}}{\mathbf{2}}-\frac{1}{6}$ $=\frac{4}{6}-\frac{1}{6}=\frac{4-1}{6}=\frac{3}{6}$, which can be reduced by a factor of 3 to $\frac{1}{2}$.

Section 4.5 Adding Mixed Numbers

CONCEPT	EXAMPLE
When adding mixed numbers, add the whole numbers separately from the fractions. The sum will be another mixed number. If the fractions are like fractions, then they can be added directly. If not, find a common denominator.	$4\frac{3}{8}$ $+\ 2\frac{1}{8}$ $6\frac{4}{8}=6\frac{1}{2}$
If the fractions add to an improper fraction, then adjust the mixed number by rewriting the improper fraction and then adding the whole numbers.	$4\frac{3}{8}$ $+\ 2\frac{7}{8}$ $6\frac{10}{8}=6+1\frac{2}{8}=7\frac{2}{8}=7\frac{1}{4}$

Section 4.6 Subtracting Mixed Numbers

CONCEPT	EXAMPLE
When subtracting mixed numbers, subtract the fractions first, then the whole numbers. The fractions must have a common denominator, and the first fraction cannot be less than the second fraction	$\begin{array}{r} 7\frac{3}{8} \\ -\ 3\frac{1}{8} \\ \hline 4\frac{2}{8} \end{array} = 4\frac{1}{4}$
If the fractions (with a common denominator) cannot subtract directly, then we need to regroup the first number, making its fraction an improper fraction.	$\begin{array}{r} 8\frac{1}{4} \\ -\ 6\frac{3}{4} \\ \hline \end{array} \rightarrow 8\frac{1}{4} = 7 + \frac{4}{4} + \frac{1}{4} = \begin{array}{r} 7\frac{5}{4} \\ -\ 6\frac{3}{4} \\ \hline 1\frac{2}{4} \end{array} = 1\frac{1}{2}$

Chapter 4 Review Exercises

Section 4.1

Find the LCM of each pair of numbers.

1. 6 and 9 **2.** 14 and 21 **3.** 18 and 24 **4.** 15 and 25

5. 18 and 54 **6.** 20 and 45 **7.** 24 and 60 **8.** 60 and 80

Section 4.2

Multiply by the appropriate form of 1 to build up each fraction to have the denominator shown.

	Start with		Multiply by 1	Result		Start with		Multiply by 1	Result
9.	$\frac{3}{4}$	$\times$	—	$= \frac{}{28}$	**10.**	$\frac{5}{8}$	$\times$	—	$= \frac{}{24}$
11.	$\frac{4}{5}$	$\times$	—	$= \frac{}{45}$	**12.**	$\frac{4}{3}$	$\times$	—	$= \frac{}{60}$

Build up the individual fractions so that each pair has the same given denominator.

13. Fractions: $\frac{1}{4}$ and $\frac{2}{5}$; Denominator: 20

14. Fractions: $\frac{7}{10}$ and $\frac{5}{8}$; Denominator: 40

15. Fractions: $\frac{4}{9}$ and $\frac{7}{15}$; Denominator: 45

16. Fractions: $\frac{2}{15}$ and $\frac{13}{20}$; Denominator: 60

Identify the pairs of like fractions.

17. $\frac{6}{5}, \frac{2}{6}, \frac{5}{7}, \frac{7}{5}$, and $\frac{9}{6}$

18. $\frac{9}{11}, \frac{9}{8}, \frac{11}{9}, \frac{8}{8}$, and $\frac{6}{9}$

Section 4.3

Add. Simplify the result whenever possible. Write any answers that contain improper fractions as mixed numbers.

19. $\frac{1}{5} + \frac{3}{5}$ **20.** $\frac{7}{11} + \frac{3}{11}$ **21.** $\frac{4}{15} + \frac{7}{15}$ **22.** $\frac{4}{9} + \frac{8}{9}$

23. $\frac{10}{28} + \frac{11}{28}$ **24.** $\frac{1}{12} + \frac{7}{12}$ **25.** $\frac{19}{45} + \frac{17}{45}$ **26.** $\frac{13}{60} + \frac{35}{60}$

27. $\frac{17}{25} + \frac{18}{25}$ **28.** $\frac{7}{10} + \frac{9}{10}$ **29.** $\frac{13}{15} + \frac{17}{15}$ **30.** $\frac{11}{18} + \frac{16}{18}$

Subtract. Simplify the result whenever possible.

31. $\frac{4}{5} - \frac{3}{5}$ **32.** $\frac{7}{9} - \frac{2}{9}$ **33.** $\frac{3}{4} - \frac{3}{4}$ **34.** $\frac{13}{12} - \frac{8}{12}$

35. $\frac{16}{15} - \frac{4}{15}$ **36.** $\frac{13}{18} - \frac{7}{18}$ **37.** $\frac{11}{20} - \frac{7}{20}$ **38.** $\frac{17}{21} - \frac{3}{21}$

39. $\frac{17}{24} - \frac{5}{24}$

40. $\frac{31}{25} - \frac{16}{25}$

41. $\frac{17}{30} - \frac{12}{30}$

42. $\frac{31}{36} - \frac{11}{36}$

Section 4.4

Add. Simplify the results, if possible. Write any answers that contain improper fractions as mixed numbers.

43. $\frac{1}{2} + \frac{1}{6}$

44. $\frac{7}{8} + \frac{1}{12}$

45. $\frac{1}{6} + \frac{2}{15}$

46. $\frac{9}{20} + \frac{7}{15}$

47. $\frac{5}{6} + \frac{7}{30}$

48. $\frac{3}{4} + \frac{5}{8}$

49. $\frac{8}{15} + \frac{4}{9}$

50. $\frac{7}{9} + \frac{5}{12}$

Subtract. Simplify the results, if possible.

51. $\frac{4}{9} - \frac{1}{3}$

52. $\frac{11}{18} - \frac{4}{9}$

53. $\frac{5}{6} - \frac{4}{9}$

54. $\frac{11}{12} - \frac{3}{4}$

55. $\frac{13}{15} - \frac{7}{10}$

56. $\frac{7}{8} - \frac{1}{6}$

57. $\frac{17}{20} - \frac{1}{4}$

58. $\frac{13}{20} - \frac{5}{12}$

For each application, write the legend, set up and solve the equation, and write a sentence answering the question.

59. D'Neice invited three friends over to her apartment last Saturday night, and she had two large pizzas delivered. After dinner, there was $\frac{1}{3}$ of a pizza left from one box and $\frac{1}{6}$ of a pizza from the other box. When the two boxes were combined, what fraction of a pizza did D'Neice have left over?

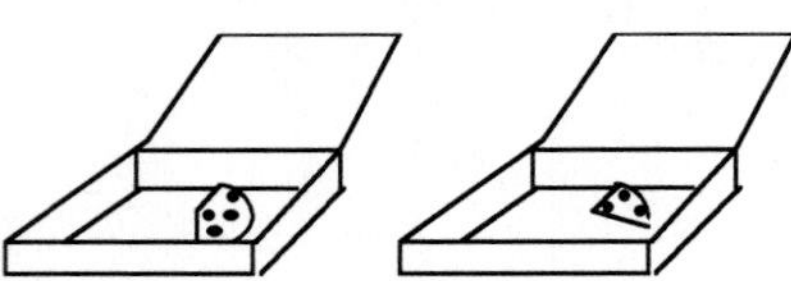

60. Last winter, Mary started with $\frac{5}{6}$ of a cord of wood. At the end of the winter, she had $\frac{2}{15}$ of a cord of wood left. How much wood did Mary burn during the winter?

Beginning of winter

End of winter

Section 4.5

Evaluate. If necessary, find common denominators, simplify completely, and adjust the mixed number if the answer contains an improper fraction.

61. $5\frac{7}{12} + 1\frac{1}{12}$

62. $4\frac{3}{8} + 2\frac{5}{8}$

63. $13\frac{1}{4} + 10\frac{1}{12}$

64. $9\frac{4}{15} + 1\frac{3}{10}$

65. $6\frac{5}{8} + 4\frac{7}{8}$

66. $1\frac{7}{10} + 2\frac{9}{10}$

67. $8\frac{5}{6} + 3\frac{5}{9}$

68. $1\frac{4}{5} + 1\frac{9}{20}$

For each application, write the legend, set up and solve the equation, and write a sentence answering the question.

69. Last weekend, Marco worked $7\frac{11}{12}$ hours on Saturday and $6\frac{3}{4}$ hours on Sunday. How many hours did Marco work that weekend?

70. In Garberville, California, the one-day record rainfall showed $2\frac{3}{4}$ inches before noon and $1\frac{7}{10}$ inches after noon. How many total inches of rain fell in Garberville on that day?

Section 4.6

Subtract. Simplify whenever possible.

71. $6\frac{7}{12} - 1\frac{5}{12}$ **72.** $3\frac{9}{10} - 2\frac{4}{10}$ **73.** $9\frac{3}{4} - 5\frac{4}{9}$ **74.** $10\frac{5}{6} - 2\frac{8}{15}$

75. $7\frac{2}{5} - 4\frac{4}{5}$ **76.** $6\frac{1}{12} - 5\frac{5}{12}$ **77.** $8\frac{1}{3} - 4\frac{11}{15}$ **78.** $12\frac{1}{6} - 3\frac{3}{10}$

Solve the applications.

79. Marika weighed $6\frac{7}{8}$ pounds when she was born. By her first birthday, she weighed $23\frac{1}{4}$ pounds. How much weight did Marika gain during her first year?

80. A bolt of fabric has $8\frac{1}{4}$ yards on it. A customer buys $5\frac{5}{12}$ yards from that bolt. How many yards of fabric are left on the bolt?

Chapter 4 Test

Find the LCM of each pair of numbers.

1. 15 and 20 **2.** 18 and 72

Build up the individual fractions so that each pair has the same given denominator.

3. Fractions: $\frac{1}{8}$ and $\frac{4}{3}$; Denominator: 24 **4.** Fractions: $\frac{7}{10}$ and $\frac{3}{8}$; Denominator: 40

Evaluate. Simplify the result whenever possible. Write any answers that contain improper fractions as mixed numbers.

5. $\frac{8}{15} + \frac{2}{15}$ **6.** $\frac{19}{16} - \frac{13}{16}$

7. $\frac{7}{10} + \frac{3}{4}$ **8.** $\frac{11}{18} - \frac{5}{12}$

9. $3\frac{4}{9} + 1\frac{2}{9}$

10. $3\frac{9}{10} + 6\frac{4}{15}$

11. $7\frac{13}{18} - 4\frac{5}{18}$

12. $5\frac{1}{12} - 4\frac{3}{8}$

For each application, write the legend, set up and solve the equation, and write a sentence answering the question.

13. Last summer, Ricardo went through a teenage growth spurt. In June he grew $\frac{5}{8}$ of an inch taller and in July he grew $\frac{11}{16}$ of an inch taller. How many total inches did Ricardo grow those two months?

14. For her morning workout, Timina walked $2\frac{3}{5}$ miles; for her afternoon workout, she walked $3\frac{2}{3}$ miles. How many total miles did Timina walk that day?

15. On Monday, Digron stock was valued at $22\frac{3}{4}$ points. By Friday, Digron stock was valued at $24\frac{1}{8}$ points. By how many points did Digron's stock value increase that week?

16. In June of last year, Haines, Oregon, recorded its one-day record rainfall of $3\frac{1}{4}$ inches. By noon that day it had rained $1\frac{7}{10}$ inches. How many more inches did it rain that day?

Chapters 3 and 4 Cumulative Review

Evaluate. Simplify completely. Write improper fractions as mixed numbers.

1. $\frac{9}{8} \cdot \frac{4}{15}$

2. $\frac{3}{2} \cdot \frac{5}{6} \cdot \frac{8}{15}$

3. $2\frac{1}{3} \times 9$

4. $\frac{10}{21} \div \frac{15}{14}$

5. $4\frac{1}{6} \div 2\frac{2}{9}$

6. $\frac{13}{24} + \frac{5}{24}$

7. $\frac{38}{45} - \frac{17}{45}$

8. $\frac{3}{10} + \frac{5}{6}$

9. $\frac{29}{35} - \frac{2}{5}$

10. $2\frac{7}{10} + 3\frac{7}{15}$

11. $5\frac{7}{24} - 3\frac{19}{24}$

12. Three-fifths of $3\frac{8}{9}$

Find the area of each geometric figure. (Each is in terms of inches.)

13.

$2\frac{1}{4}$

$4\frac{2}{3}$

14.

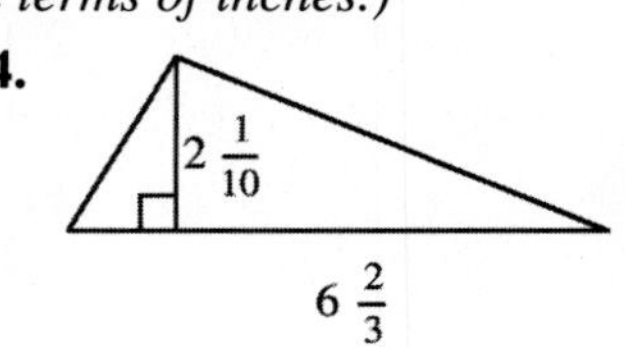

Solve each equation.

15. $28 = 42 \cdot n$

16. $n \cdot \frac{3}{10} = \frac{2}{15}$

Find the LCM of each pair of numbers.

17. 12 and 28

18. 30 and 75

Solve each application.

19. The last event in the Policeman's Olympics is the relay race in which six team members must run an equal portion of the $10\frac{1}{2}$-mile course. How many miles must each team member run in the relay?

20. Looking for a summer activity to keep a group of children busy, Jeannie found an idea in a craft book that required cutting $1\frac{3}{8}$-inch strips from construction paper. Jeannie found a scrap piece of orange construction paper that measured $13\frac{3}{4}$ inches wide. How many strips can Jeannie cut from the piece of construction paper?

21. Kimber has an embroidery design that is rather large and doesn't quite fit the computer screen. It measures $11\frac{1}{4}$ inches across and $9\frac{3}{8}$ inches high. To make it fit, she wants to view it at $\frac{2}{3}$ of its actual size. At what dimensions will the design appear on the screen? (*Hint*: You must consider both dimensions—width and height—separately.)

22. Sun-Yee gets paid \$8 dollars per hour during the week. When he works on the weekends, he gets time-and-a-half. This means that his hourly wage is $1\frac{1}{2}$ times what he normally earns. What is Sun-Yee's weekend hourly wage?

23. Damien is putting new roofing shingles on his house. Each shingle is $1\frac{2}{3}$ feet long. The north part of the house has a roof line that is 60 feet across. How many shingles can be placed (side by side) on the north part of the house?

24. Sondra found two almost empty bags of flour in her pantry. She poured each bag's flour into a large measuring cup. One bag contained $3\frac{2}{3}$ cups of flour and the other contained $2\frac{3}{4}$ cups of flour. How much total flour does Sondra have?

25. Before yesterday, Kahlil's best long jump was 7 feet, $4\frac{5}{8}$ inches. Yesterday, he set a new personal best by jumping 7 feet, $6\frac{1}{16}$ inches. By how many inches did Kahlil surpass his previous best mark?

CHAPTER 5
Decimals

Introduction

We encounter decimals all day long. We see them when dealing with money, such as \$2.349 for a gallon of gas. Decimals are in sports statistics, such as Hank Aaron's lifetime batting average of .305. We also find them in the Nutrition Guide on the side of a cereal box, saying, perhaps, that each serving contains 1.5 grams of fat.

Adding with decimals is the same as adding with whole numbers, and this is true for subtraction, multiplication, and division. The only difference between evaluating with decimals and evaluating with whole numbers is that in Chapter 5 we have a decimal point to keep track of.

Fear not. Every procedure is explained, step by step, and you'll be taught not only *how* to evaluate with decimals but *why* the procedures work the way they do.

Preparation Exercises

Section 1.1, Whole Numbers:

1. Write 1,063 in words.
2. Write *five hundred seven* as a number.
3. Round 71,486 to the nearest thousand.
4. Round 6,952 to the nearest hundred.

Section 1.3, Adding and Subtracting Whole Numbers: *Evaluate.*

5. $75 + 542$
6. $28 + 9 + 672$
7. $926 - 349$
8. $2{,}000 - 153$

Section 1.4, Multiplying Whole Numbers: *Evaluate.*

9. 127×8
10. 24×65

Section 1.5, Dividing Whole Numbers: *Evaluate.*

11. $7\overline{)329}$
12. $23\overline{)805}$

Section 1.6, Equations: *Solve for n.*

13. $326 + n = 509$
14. $25 \cdot n = 475$

Section 3.2, Simplifying Fractions: *Completely simplify each fraction.*

15. $\frac{35}{100}$
16. $\frac{44}{60}$

Section 3.3, Multiplying Fractions: *Multiply and simplify.*

17. $\frac{8}{9} \cdot \frac{15}{4}$
18. $\frac{7}{10} \cdot \frac{9}{10}$

Section 3.4, Dividing Fractions: *Divide and simplify.*

19. $\frac{27}{100} \div \frac{9}{10}$

20. $\frac{7}{10} \div \frac{35}{100}$

Section 4.3, Adding and Subtracting Like Fractions: *Add or subtract. Simplify.*

21. $\frac{11}{18} - \frac{5}{18}$

22. $\frac{43}{100} + \frac{22}{100}$

Section 4.4, Adding and Subtracting Unlike Fractions: *Add or subtract. Simplify.*

23. $\frac{5}{6} - \frac{11}{24}$

24. $\frac{27}{100} + \frac{3}{10}$

Objectives

In this section, you will learn to:

- Identify and define the parts of a decimal.
- Write decimals in word form.
- Write decimals as fractions.
- Write fractions as decimals.
- Abbreviate repeating decimals.

To successfully complete this section, you need to understand:

- Writing whole numbers (1.1)
- Powers of 10 (2.1)
- Mixed numbers (3.1)
- Simplifying fractions (3.2)
- Building up fractions (4.2)

SECTION 5.1 An Introduction to Decimals

Introduction

You've seen decimals used when handling money. "One dollar and fifty-three cents" is represented as \$1.53. The "dot" that separates the dollars from the cents is the **decimal point**, a separator between the whole number and the fractional part of a decimal number.

The whole number is to the *left* of the decimal point, and the fractional part is to the *right* of the decimal point.

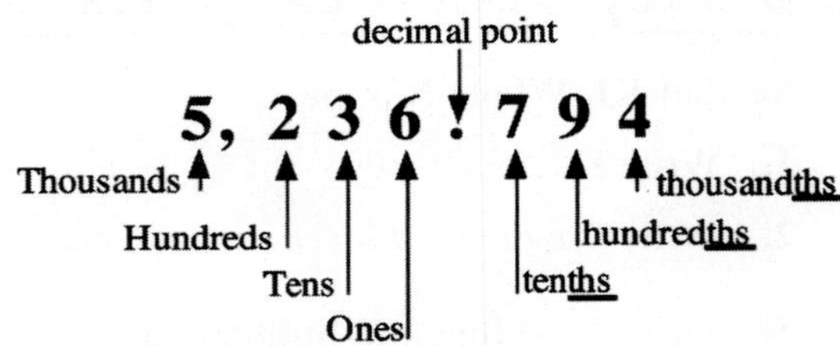

Notice that every place in the fractional part ends in **-ths**.

EXAMPLE 1

In 5,236.794, name the place and the value represented by

a) 5 b) 2 c) 7 d) 9 e) 4

ANSWER:

a) 5 is in the **thousands** place and represents **five thousand.**

b) 2 is in the **hundreds** place and represents **two hundred.**

c) 7 is in the **tenths** place and represents **seven tenths.**

d) 9 is in the **hundredths** place and represents **nine hundredths.**

e) 4 is in the **thousandths** place and represents **four thousandths.**

YOU TRY IT 1

In 213.568, name the place and the value represented by the given digit. Use Example 1 as a guide.

a) 8 b) 5 c) 2

Decimal Fractions

Recall from Section 2.1:
- 100 is the second power of 10: $100 = 10 \times 10 = 10^2$
- 1000 is the third power of 10: $1000 = 10 \times 10 \times 10 = 10^3$

Why is the part *after* the decimal point called the fractional part? To answer that question, consider *seven tenths*:

It can be represented as **.7** or as $\frac{7}{10}$. In other words, **.7** is equivalent to the fraction $\frac{7}{10}$.

Both **.7** and $\frac{7}{10}$ are called *decimal fractions*. Any fraction with a denominator that is a power of 10 (such as 10, 100, 1000, and so on) is called a **decimal fraction.**

For example, $\frac{3}{10}$, $\frac{51}{100}$, and $\frac{92}{1000}$ are decimal fractions because each denominator is a power of 10.

Decimal Mixed Numbers

Consider the number *five and nine tenths*. It can be written two different, but related, ways:

1. As a fraction, five and nine tenths is $5\frac{9}{10}$;
2. as a decimal, five and nine tenths is 5.9.

Interestingly enough, both of these are mixed numbers.

$5\frac{9}{10}$	is a *fractional* mixed number; it has a whole number, 5, and a fractional part, $\frac{9}{10}$.	5.9	is a *decimal* mixed number; it has a whole number, 5, and a decimal part, .9.

When there is no visible whole number, as in .96, it's common to write such a decimal with a whole number of 0, as in 0.96; either way is acceptable, though, and in this text such decimals usually include the 0 whole number.

Naming Decimal Numbers

Consider the decimal 0.73. This is: seven *tenths* and three *hundredths*

$= \frac{7}{10} + \frac{3}{100}$ The common denominator is 100. We must build up the first fraction by multiplying it by $\frac{10}{10}$.

$= \frac{7}{10} \times \frac{10}{10} + \frac{3}{100}$

$= \frac{70}{100} + \frac{3}{100}$ Now the fractions have common denominators, and we can combine them to be one fraction.

$= \frac{73}{100}$

= seventy-three hundredths

Notice that, in naming the fraction $\frac{73}{100}$, there is no mention of the original *tenths*. To name $\frac{73}{100}$, we use the full name of the numerator, seventy-three, and the full name of the denominator, hundredths.

For this reason, when naming decimal numbers, we use only the *right-most place* in the naming.

For example, in 0.73 the right-most digit (3) is in the *hundredths* place, so we would name this *seventy-three hundredths;*

in 0.318 the right-most digit (8) is in the *thousandths* place, so we would name this *three hundred eighteen thousandths.*

If the decimal is a mixed number, then we use the word *and* to represent the decimal point. For example, 8.3 is written *eight and three tenths*.

EXAMPLE 2

Write each of these fractions and decimals in word form.

a) $\frac{3}{10}$ and 0.3 b) $\frac{247}{1,000}$ and 0.247 c) $6\frac{9}{100}$ and 6.09 d) $35\frac{26}{100}$ and 35.26

ANSWER:
a) $\frac{3}{10}$ and 0.3 are both written *three tenths.*

b) $\frac{247}{1,000}$ and 0.247 are both written *two hundred forty-seven thousandths.*

c) $6\frac{9}{100}$ and 6.09 are both written *six and nine hundredths.*

d) $35\frac{26}{100}$ and 35.26 are both written *thirty-five and twenty-six hundredths.*

Caution The word *and* is used between the whole number and the fractional part; the word *and* represents the decimal point in a decimal number.

YOU TRY IT 2

Write each of these in word form. Use Example 2 as a guide.

a) $\frac{6}{10}$ and 0.6 are both written ______________________.

b) $27\frac{4}{100}$ and 27.04 are both written ______________________.

c) $\frac{315}{1,000}$ and 0.315 are both written ______________________.

d) $100\frac{2}{10}$ and 100.2 are both written ______________________.

EXAMPLE 3

Write the underlined number in word form.

A kilometer is about 0.62 miles.

ANSWER: 0.62 is written as sixty-two hundredths.

YOU TRY IT 3

Write the underlined number in word form. Use Example 3 as a guide.

a) The world record in the 100 meter dash is 9.78 seconds.

b) The thermometer showed Joey's temperature to be 101.9 degrees.

When a decimal number is written in words, the place value (such as hundredths) indicates the denominator of the decimal fraction as well as the right-most place value in the decimal. If the word *and* is used, then it is a mixed number with *and* representing the beginning of the fractional or decimal part.

EXAMPLE 4

Write each of these as both a fraction and a decimal.

a) Four tenths

b) Fifty-three hundredths

c) Seven and fifteen thousandths

d) Three hundred and two hundredths

ANSWER:
a) Four tenths is $\frac{4}{10}$ and 0.4.

b) Fifty-three hundredths is $\frac{53}{100}$ and 0.53.

c) Seven and fifteen thousandths is $7\frac{15}{1,000}$ and 7.015.

d) Three hundred and two hundredths is $300\frac{2}{100}$ and 300.02.

YOU TRY IT 4

Write each of these as both a fraction and a decimal. Use Example 4 as a guide.

a) Eight tenths

b) Sixty-one hundredths

c) Three and five hundredths

d) Twenty and forty-two thousandths

e) One hundred ten and four tenths

What is the difference between (a) one hundred twelve thousandths, and (b) one hundred and twelve thousandths?

Write the underlined number in decimal form.

One foot is <u>three hundred four and eight tenths</u> millimeters.

PROCEDURE: Recall that *and* indicates the position of the decimal point in the number.

ANSWER: Three hundred four and eight tenths is written <u>304.8.</u>

YOU TRY IT 5

Write the underlined number in decimal form. Use Example 5 as a guide.

a) Louise Ritter holds the record for the women's high jump at <u>six and seven tenths</u> feet.

b) The distance from downtown Craner to downtown Southwood is <u>ten and three hundredths</u> miles.

Understanding how decimals and decimal fractions are written in words allows us to write decimals as decimal fractions and vice versa.

For example, $\frac{3}{10}$ is three tenths, indicating one decimal place, so $\frac{3}{10} = 0.3$.

Likewise, 0.12 is twelve hundredths, indicating that the denominator is 100, so $0.12 = \frac{12}{100}$.

EXAMPLE 6

Write each fraction as a decimal and each decimal as a fraction.

a) $\dfrac{2}{10}$ b) $\dfrac{361}{1,000}$ c) $\dfrac{28}{100}$ d) 0.982 e) 0.3 f) 0.41

PROCEDURE: Think of what each of these would be if written in words (as in Examples 2 and 3).

ANSWER:

a) $\frac{2}{10} = 0.2$

b) $\frac{361}{1,000} = 0.361$

c) $\frac{28}{100} = 0.28$

d) $0.982 = \frac{982}{1,000}$

e) $0.3 = \frac{3}{10}$

f) $0.41 = \frac{41}{100}$

YOU TRY IT 6

Write each fraction as a decimal and each decimal as a fraction. Use Example 6 as a guide.

a) $\frac{305}{1,000} =$

b) $\frac{9}{10} =$

c) $\frac{67}{100} =$

d) $0.93 =$

e) $0.124 =$

f) $0.1 =$

Writing Mixed Numbers as Decimal Fractions

Consider *one and seven tenths.* As a mixed number, it can be written two different ways.

1. As a fraction: $1\frac{7}{10}$ or $1 + \frac{7}{10}$
2. As a decimal: 1.7 or $1 + .7$

So, $1.7 = 1\frac{7}{10}$.

As an improper fraction $1\frac{7}{10} = \frac{17}{10}$ so it makes sense that $1.7 = \frac{17}{10}$, too.

The point is this: a mixed decimal number can be written as an improper decimal fraction.

For example, Mixed decimal $\rightarrow 2.3 = 2\frac{3}{10} = \frac{23}{10} \leftarrow$ Improper fraction

Mixed decimal $\rightarrow 5.28 = 5\frac{28}{100} = \frac{528}{100} \leftarrow$ Improper fraction

EXAMPLE 7

Write each mixed decimal number as an improper decimal fraction. Do not simplify.

a) 5.4 b) 3.51 c) 14.9

PROCEDURE: First, keep in mind that it's the number of decimal places that determines the power of 10 in the denominator.

Second, the numerator of the fraction will be a whole number that comes from *all* digits in the decimal number.

ANSWER:

a) $5.4 = \frac{54}{10}$ One decimal place, so the denominator is 10; the numerator is the whole number 54.

b) $3.51 = \frac{351}{100}$ Two decimal places, so the denominator is 100; the numerator is 351.

c) $14.9 = \frac{149}{10}$ Again, only one decimal place means a denominator of 10, no matter how many digits are in the whole number.

YOU TRY IT 7

Write each mixed decimal number as an improper decimal fraction. Do not simplify. Use Example 7 as a guide.

a) 2.3 b) 8.61 c) 32.8 d) 4.019

This next example is also a reminder that we may write as many zeros in front of a whole number as we wish and it doesn't change the value; for example, 04 = 4.

Identify the number of decimal places, and then write each as a fraction with a power of 10 in the denominator.

a) 0.04 b) 0.051 c) 2.07

PROCEDURE: Remember, it's the number of decimal places that determines the power of 10 in the denominator.

ANSWER: a) Two decimal places; $0.04 = \dfrac{04}{100} = \dfrac{4}{100}$ In this case, the 0 in the first fraction's numerator is not necessary.

b) Three decimal places; $0.051 = \dfrac{051}{1{,}000} = \dfrac{51}{1{,}000}$ Three decimal places means that the denominator will be 1000 even though the numerator has only two digits.

c) Two decimal places; $2.07 = \dfrac{207}{100}$ Here, the 0 in the numerator is necessary because it is not in front of all of the other digits—it is between them—and there it shall remain.

YOU TRY IT 8

Identify the number of decimal places, and then write each as a fraction with a power of 10 in the denominator. Do not simplify. Use Example 8 as a guide.

a) 0.006 b) 0.00035 c) 5.06

Writing Fractions as Decimals

The preceding examples help us to see that the number of decimal places a number has is tied to the number of zeros in the denominator.

In converting decimal fractions to decimal form, we simply reverse the process in Example 8. Look at the number of zeros in the denominator to determine the number of decimal places needed to the right of the decimal point.

> The number of zeros in the power of 10 (in the denominator) indicates the number of decimal places the decimal number will have.

Still, we must make sure that there are at least as many digits in the numerator as there are zeros in the denominator. One of three situations can happen, based on the number of zeros in the denominator.

1. The numerator has the right amount of digits (the same as the number of zeros in the denominator).
   For example, $\frac{17}{100}$ will have two decimal places because there are two zeros in the denominator. The numerator has two digits to fit into those two decimal places: $\frac{17}{100} = 0.17$.

2. The numerator has fewer digits than the number of zeros in the denominator.
A fraction such as $\frac{3}{100}$ doesn't have enough digits in the numerator to cover the two required decimal places. To compensate, we can rewrite $\frac{3}{100}$ as $\frac{03}{100}$ without changing the value of the fraction. This also allows us to write $\frac{03}{100}$ as 0.03.
3. The numerator has more digits than the number of zeros in the denominator.
The numerator may have more than enough digits, such as $\frac{87}{10}$. In this case, the 7 fits into the one required decimal place, and the 8 is the whole number in the ones place: $\frac{87}{10} = 8.7$.

EXAMPLE 9

Write each fraction as a decimal.

a) $\frac{6}{100}$ b) $\frac{31}{10}$ c) $\frac{8}{1{,}000}$ d) $\frac{513}{100}$ e) $\frac{945}{10}$

PROCEDURE: Write the numerator out completely, then decide how many decimal places it will have by looking at the denominator (as in Example 8).

The number of zeros in the denominator indicates the number of decimal places.

ANSWER:

a) $\frac{6}{100} = 0.06$ The denominator of 100 indicates two decimal places. Think of 6 as 06, making the fraction $\frac{06}{100}$, so that we have two digits to place after the decimal point.

b) $\frac{31}{10} = 3.1$ One zero in the denominator, so one decimal place.

c) $\frac{8}{1{,}000} = 0.008$ Three zeros in the denominator, so three decimal places. This time, think of 8 as 008, giving us $\frac{008}{1000}$.

d) $\frac{513}{100} = 5.13$ Two zeros in the denominator, so two decimal places.

e) $\frac{945}{10} = 94.5$ One zero in the denominator requires us to have only one decimal place.

YOU TRY IT 9

Write each as a decimal number. Use Example 9 as a guide.

a) $\frac{34}{10}$ b) $\frac{512}{100}$ c) $\frac{607}{10}$

d) $\frac{5}{100}$ e) $\frac{23}{1{,}000}$ f) $\frac{6}{1{,}000}$

Place Value and Powers of 10

As you know, we may write as many zeros as we wish in front of any whole number without changing the value of the whole number. Let's see what happens when we add extra zeros to decimals.

Think about "one-half." This can be represented in many ways. In fact, we can build it up to be written with any denominator we choose.

For now, though, let's choose one-half to be written as a decimal fraction.

Decimal fractions that are equivalent to one-half

$$\frac{1}{2} \times \frac{5}{5} = \mathbf{\frac{5}{10}} = .5$$

$$\frac{5}{10} \times \frac{10}{10} = \mathbf{\frac{50}{100}} = .50, \quad \text{which is .5 followed by one zero}$$

$$\frac{50}{100} \times \frac{10}{10} = \mathbf{\frac{500}{1{,}000}} = .500, \quad \text{which is .5 followed by two zeros}$$

$$\frac{500}{1{,}000} \times \frac{10}{10} = \mathbf{\frac{5{,}000}{10{,}000}} = .5000, \quad \text{which is .5 followed by three zeros}$$

Notice that multiplying a decimal fraction by $\frac{10}{10}$ simply places one more zero on the end of the decimal number.

In fact, we can place as many zeros on the *end* of any terminating decimal without changing its value.

Caution We may not place zeros *between* the decimal point and other digits. For example, $1.5 = 1.50$, but $1.5 \neq 1.05$.

EXAMPLE 10 Write each decimal, by including enough zeros at the end, so that it has a total of *three* decimal places.

a) 0.3 b) 4.67 c) 8

ANSWER: a) $0.3 = 0.300$ b) $4.67 = 4.670$ c) $8 = 8.000$

YOU TRY IT 10 *Write each decimal, by including enough zeros at the end, so that it has a total of four decimal places. Use Example 10 as a guide.*

a) 5.78 b) 2.103 c) 0.1 d) 6

If a decimal number has at least one ending zero, then it can be simplified by eliminating that zero (and any other zeros that follow it). To understand *why* we can eliminate those ending zeros, consider 0.30:

$$\text{As it is, } 0.30 = \frac{30}{100}, \text{ which can be reduced by a factor of 10:}$$

$$\frac{30 \div 10}{100 \div 10} = \frac{3}{10} = 0.3 \text{ (three tenths).}$$

This simplifying process is quickened by simply dropping any ending zeros. For example, $3.2100 = 3.21$, and $15.40000 = 15.4$.

Caution Only ending zeros may be eliminated, not those *within* the decimal number:

$$1.80500 = 1.805 \quad \text{and} \quad 0.0070 = 0.007$$

EXAMPLE 11 Simplify each decimal by eliminating any ending zeros.

a) 0.9000 b) 3.580 c) 16.90400

ANSWER: a) 0.9000 = 0.9 b) 3.580 = 3.58 c) 16.90400 = 16.904

Notice that in part c, the 0 that remains in 16.904 is not an ending zero, so it cannot be eliminated.

YOU TRY IT 11 *Simplify each decimal by eliminating any ending zeros. Use Example 11 as a guide.*

a) 5.6000 b) 2.7500 c) 0.109000 d) 0.000300

Terminating and Repeating Decimals

Many decimals end after a few places. We call these **terminating decimals.**

For example, 23.6 terminates after *one* decimal place, 2.589 terminates after *three* decimal places, and 0.12 terminates after *two* decimal places.

Some decimals never terminate, they just go on and on. Such decimal numbers are called **nonterminating decimals**. However, many of these nonterminating decimals repeat a pattern of the same digits over and over, such as 3.656565656565… and so on. Here, the pattern of digits *65* repeats continuously. Such numbers are called **repeating decimals**.

The "block" of repeating digits is called the **repetend**. In the number 3.65656565…, the repetend is 65.

We can't write all of the decimal places if a decimal doesn't terminate. There are a couple of ways to show that a particular pattern of numbers repeats itself.

1. We can use an **ellipsis**, three dots (…), to indicate that a pattern repeats; or
2. we can place a bar over all of the digits that repeat, the repetend.

For example, if a nonterminating decimal number has a repeating pattern of the digits *316*, we can represent it as 0.316316316… or as $0.\overline{316}$.

Repeating decimals can start with more than just the repeated pattern in the decimal places. Using the same repetend of 316 we might have:

1. 7.25316316316 … Once the pattern of 316 is clearly established, the ellipsis indicates that just the digits 316 repeat.
2. $7.25\overline{316}$ The bar goes over the repetend only, not the other digits.

EXAMPLE 12 Write each of these repeating decimals using either the ellipsis or the bar over the repetend, whichever is not shown. *When using the ellipsis, write the repetend at least three times.*

a) 0.28282828 … = $0.\overline{28}$ b) 3.042042042 … = $3.\overline{042}$

c) $19.53\overline{7}$ = 19.5377777 … d) $1.5\overline{63}$ = 1.563636363 …

YOU TRY IT 12 *Write each of these repeating decimals using either the ellipsis or the bar over the repetend, whichever is not shown. When using the ellipsis, write the repetend at least three times. Use Example 12 as a guide.*

a) 0.555555 … = __________ b) 4.2181818 … = __________

c) $3.0\overline{74}$ = __________ d) $0.\overline{206}$ = __________

Pi

There are many decimal numbers that don't terminate and don't repeat. One such number is represented by the Greek letter, π, spelled **pi**, and pronounced "pie."

The first twelve decimal digits of π are shown at right. (In this case, the ellipsis lets us know that there are many more decimal digits not shown, but it does not indicate a pattern of any kind.)

$$\pi \approx 3.141592653589\ldots$$

We will use this number when calculating the perimeter (circumference) of a circle in Section 5.6. At that time, we'll abbreviate the value of π as 3.14. This value for π is an approximate value, shown as $\pi \approx 3.14$.

You Try It Answers: Section 5.1

YTI 1 a) Thousandths; eight thousandths
b) Tenths; five tenths
c) Hundreds; two hundred

YTI 2 a) Six tenths
b) Twenty-seven and four hundredths
c) Three hundred fifteen thousandths
d) One hundred and two tenths

YTI 3 a) Nine and seventy-eight hundredths
b) One hundred one and nine tenths

YTI 4 a) $\frac{8}{10}$ and 0.8 b) $\frac{61}{100}$ and 0.61
c) $3\frac{5}{100}$ and 3.05 d) $20\frac{42}{1{,}000}$ and 20.042
e) $110\frac{4}{10}$ and 110.4

YTI 5 a) 6.7 b) 10.03

YTI 6 a) 0.305 b) 0.9 c) 0.67
d) $\frac{93}{100}$ e) $\frac{124}{1{,}000}$ f) $\frac{1}{10}$

YTI 7 a) $\frac{23}{10}$ b) $\frac{861}{100}$ c) $\frac{328}{10}$ d) $\frac{4{,}019}{1{,}000}$

YTI 8 a) Three decimal places; $\frac{6}{1{,}000}$
b) Five decimal places; $\frac{35}{100{,}000}$
c) Two decimal places; $\frac{506}{100}$

YTI 9 a) 3.4 b) 5.12 c) 60.7
d) 0.05 e) 0.023 f) 0.006

YTI 10 a) 5.7800 b) 2.1030 c) 0.1000 d) 6.0000

YTI 11 a) 5.6 b) 2.75 c) 0.109 d) 0.0003

YTI 12 a) $0.\overline{5}$ b) $4.2\overline{18}$
c) 3.0747474... d) 0.206206206...

Focus Exercises: Section 5.1

Fill in the blanks.

1. Two places to the right of the decimal point is called the ________________ place.
2. The three dots at the end of a repeating decimal are called an ________________.
3. A decimal number that has both a whole number and a decimal part is called a ________________.
4. A decimal number that ends after a few decimal places is called a ________________ decimal.

True or False.

5. The numbers to the left of the decimal point are called whole numbers. ________________

6. The number 1.005 can simplify to 1.5 by eliminating the zeros. ________________

7. It's not possible for a repeating decimal to have a repetend with more than three digits. ________________

8. The number $\pi = 3.14$. ________________

In the given number, name the place value for the digit 3.

9. 12.384 **10.** 1,358.47 **11.** 93.806 **12.** 150.623

Write each of these in word form.

13. $\frac{5}{10} = 0.5$ **14.** $\frac{19}{100} = 0.19$ **15.** $\frac{8}{1{,}000} = 0.008$

16. $5\frac{29}{100} = 5.29$ **17.** $8\frac{2}{10} = 8.2$ **18.** $15\frac{3}{100} = 15.03$

Write the underlined number in word form.

19. Argentina has a population density of <u>37.4</u> people per square mile.

20. A popular hot chocolate drink mix contains <u>0.17</u> grams of sodium per serving.

21. The distance between the first and second frets on a guitar is <u>3.3</u> centimeters.

22. In 2004, the difference in batting averages for the top two National League batters was <u>0.015</u>.

Write each of these as both a fraction and as a decimal.

23. Fifteen hundredths **24.** Two hundredths **25.** Two and three tenths

26. Eleven and one hundredth **27.** Thirty-five thousandths **28.** One hundred and six thousandths

Write the underlined number in fraction and decimal form.

29. Molly caught a trout measuring <u>twenty-nine and fourth tenths</u> centimeters long.

30. At the 2004 Olympics, the difference between first and second place in the men's 100-meter freestyle swim race was <u>six hundredths</u> of a second.

31. In the 1960 presidential election, John F. Kennedy won over Richard M. Nixon by <u>one hundred twenty-three thousandths</u> of a percentage point.

32. The small island country of St. Kitts and Nevis has a total land area of <u>one hundred and nine tenths</u> square miles.

Write each fraction as a decimal.

33. $\frac{4}{10}$ **34.** $\frac{21}{100}$ **35.** $\frac{625}{1{,}000}$ **36.** $\frac{1{,}450}{10{,}000}$

37. $\frac{7}{10}$ **38.** $\frac{5}{100}$ **39.** $\frac{78}{10}$ **40.** $\frac{182}{100}$

41. $\frac{9}{100}$ **42.** $\frac{81}{1{,}000}$ **43.** $\frac{4}{1{,}000}$ **44.** $\frac{229}{10{,}000}$

45. $\frac{409}{100}$ **46.** $\frac{806}{100}$ **47.** $\frac{207}{10}$ **48.** $\frac{508}{10}$

Write each decimal as a fraction. Do not simplify.

49. 0.9 **50.** 0.7 **51.** 0.34 **52.** 0.17

53. 0.593 **54.** 0.708 **55.** 0.2817 **56.** 0.4308

57. 0.08 **58.** 0.03 **59.** 0.04 **60.** 0.09

61. 0.052 **62.** 0.014 **63.** 0.001 **64.** 0.007

65. 2.5 **66.** 1.8 **67.** 9.55 **68.** 15.16

69. 3.08 **70.** 5.06 **71.** 5.284 **72.** 9.309

Write each of these repeating decimals using the bar over the repetend.

73. 0.333333333... **74.** 3.1414141414... **75.** 0.528528528...

76. 0.711111111... **77.** 10.3692929292... **78.** 7.2678967896789...

Write each of these repeating decimals using an ellipsis.

79. $0.\overline{5}$ **80.** $9.\overline{27}$ **81.** $2.\overline{470}$

82. $6.0\overline{4}$ **83.** $0.58\overline{10}$ **84.** $1.62\overline{04}$

SECTION 5.2 Rounding Decimals

Objectives

In this section, you will learn to:

- Round decimals.

To successfully complete this section, you need to understand:

- Rounding whole numbers (1.1)
- Decimal place values (5.1)

Introduction

Money is almost always represented with two decimal places, such as $8.36. There are times, however, when a calculated amount has more than two decimal places.

> For example, the sales tax on a watch costing $29.95 might be $2.321125. The amount beyond $2.32 is a fraction of a penny, but nobody could pay that fraction, so the tax is rounded to just $2.32.

Similarly, gas stations typically charge an extra $\frac{9}{10}$ of a penny per gallon, so you might see the price of gas as $2.169. When this is multiplied by the number of gallons pumped, say 9.381, the total price to pay is $20.347389. When you pay for the gas, though, this number will be rounded to the nearest penny: $20.35. (The gas pump does the rounding automatically.)

In this section, we won't be calculating sales tax and gas prices. Instead, we'll focus only on how to round decimal numbers.

Rounding Decimals to the Nearest Decimal Place

Recall, from Section 1.1, the procedure for rounding whole numbers.

1. Identify the place digit that is to be rounded.
2. Identify the digit to its immediate right, called the rounding digit.
3. a) If the rounding digit is 5 or higher, round *up* (add 1 to the place digit).
   b) If the rounding digit is 4 or lower, round *down* (add 0 to the place digit).
4. Write all digits after the place digit as zeros. Rewrite the number showing the appropriate approximation.

To round decimals, we use the same procedure as for rounding whole numbers, with one major difference: In step 4, we don't write the digits after the place digit as zeros; instead, we *eliminate* those ending digits.

Rounding Decimal Numbers to a Given Decimal Place

1. Identify the place digit that is to be rounded.
2. Identify the digit to its immediate right, called the rounding digit.
3. a) If the rounding digit is 5 or higher, round *up* (add 1 to the place digit).
b) If the rounding digit is 4 or lower, round down (add 0 to the place digit).
4. *Eliminate all digits after the place digit.* Rewrite the number showing the appropriate approximation.

Step 4 of this procedure indicates that the rounded decimal number should terminate at the rounded digit's place. For example, if we are rounding to the nearest *hundredth*, then the rounded number should be a decimal number that terminates in the *hundredths* place.

EXAMPLE 1 Round 0.387 to the nearest tenth.

ANSWER:
Step 1: 0.387: The place digit is in the tenths place: 3.
Step 2: The rounding digit, to the immediate right of the 3, is the number 8.
Step 3: 8 indicates that we must round up (add 1 to 3 to get 4).
Step 4: Everything after the tenths place is eliminated, so the approximation is 0.4.

EXAMPLE 2 Round 3.674921 to the nearest hundredth.

ANSWER:

Step 1: 3.674921: The place digit is in the hundredths place: 7.

Step 2: The rounding digit is the number 4.

Step 3: This indicates that we should round down (add 0 to 7 to get 7)

Step 4: Everything after the hundredths place is eliminated, so the approximation is 3.67.

Think about it If we round a decimal to the nearest thousandth, in what place would the rounding digit be?

____

____

YOU TRY IT 1 *Round each of these decimal numbers to the place shown. Use Examples 1 and 2 as guides.*

Number	To the nearest	Approximation
a) 3.832	tenth	________
b) 0.4258	hundredth	________
c) 0.0509	hundredth	________
d) 5.806427	thousandth	________
e) 0.0047186	thousandth	________

YOU TRY IT 2 *Recall, from Section 5.1, that π (pi) is a decimal number that neither terminates nor repeats. It is used to calculate the area and the circumference of a circle. $\pi \approx 3.141592653589\ldots$. Round this number to the nearest hundredth, and finish this sentence:*

The value of π is approximately _______.

Caution If the place digit is rounded to 0, then we cannot eliminate it with any other ending zeros.

For example, if we round 1.29604 to the nearest hundredth, then the rounding digit, 6, tells us to add 1 to the place digit 9, changing the 29 into 30: $1.29604 \approx 1.30$.

The zero in the hundredths place cannot be eliminated because the rounded approximation must terminate in the hundredths place.

YOU TRY IT 3 *Round each of these numbers to the place shown. Use Examples 1 and 2 as guides. Be sure that the rounding place is represented, even if it is a zero.*

Number	To the nearest	Approximation
a) 7.038	tenth	________
b) 6.19153	hundredth	________

c) 3.0954 hundredth ____________

d) 2.14915 thousandth ____________

e) 0.09982 thousandth ____________

EXAMPLE 3 Round each of these dollar amounts to the nearest penny.

a) $3.12504 b) $78.06198 c) $142.29641 d) $8.99741

PROCEDURE: Rounding to the nearest penny is the same as rounding to the nearest hundredth. Remember, the final result must have two decimal places.

ANSWER: a) $3.13 b) $78.06 c) $142.30 d) $9.00

YOU TRY IT 4 *Round each of these dollar amounts to the nearest penny. Use Example 3 as a guide.*

a) $1.624908 b) $0.69502 c) $251.0523 d) $56.996021

Rounding Decimal Numbers to the Nearest Whole Number

We can also round to the nearest whole number. The rounding digit is in the tenths place. In rounding to the nearest whole number, no decimal or decimal point will be left in the approximation.

EXAMPLE 4 Round each of these numbers to the nearest whole number.

PROCEDURE: In rounding to the nearest whole number, we look at the tenths place to determine whether we should round up or down. The approximation will have no decimal fraction.

Round		Answer
a) 0.83	8 causes it to round up (add 1 to the 0 to get 1).	1
b) 3.524	5 causes it to round up (add 1 to the 3 to get 4).	4
c) 12.096	0 causes it to round down (add 0 to the 2 to get 2).	12
d) 751.6	6 causes it to round up (add 1 to the 1 to get 2).	752

YOU TRY IT 5 *Round each of these numbers to the nearest whole number. Use Example 4 as a guide.*

Number	Approximation	Number	Approximation
a) 1.938	____________	b) 4.2381	____________
c) 3.0954	____________	d) 16.59153	____________
e) 23.4599	____________		

Think about it Sometimes money is rounded to the nearest dollar. What is rounding to the nearest dollar the same as? (*Hint*: Think of what place you would round to.) Explain your answer.

____

____

Applications

As stated at the beginning of this section, we typically round calculations involving money to the nearest penny, the nearest hundredth. If the sales tax on an item is calculated to be \$1.896125, then we would round this up to \$1.90. Even though this is a rounded number, we may state that the sales tax *is* \$1.90 (instead of stating it is *approximately* \$1.90).

EXAMPLE 5 Jerome calculated his car's gas mileage to be 19.628 miles per gallon. Round this number to the nearest tenth.

PROCEDURE: Round the number, and restate the first sentence using the rounded number.

ANSWER: 19.628 rounds down to 19.6 (nearest tenth).

SENTENCE: Jerome's car's gas mileage is 19.6 miles per gallon.

YOU TRY IT 6 *Jenny's grade point average (GPA) is 3.2463. Round this to the nearest hundredth.*

Sentence: ______________________________

YOU TRY IT 7 *Tomás spent \$129.52 on postage for his business last year. When reporting this amount on his tax form, he rounds it to the nearest dollar. How much should Tomás report for postage on his tax form?*

Sentence: ______________________________

YOU TRY IT 8 *Connie calculated her dinner tip to be \$4.57345. Round this number to the nearest dime (tenth), and write the result in dollars and cents.*

Sentence: ______________________________

You Try It Answers: Section 5.2

YTI 1 a) 3.8 b) 0.43 c) 0.05 d) 5.806 e) 0.005

YTI 2 3.14

YTI 3 a) 7.0 b) 6.19 c) 3.10 d) 2.149 e) 0.100
Note: In YTI 3: a) 7.0 may not simplify to 7; 3 c) 3.10 may not simplify to 3.1; and 3 e) 0.100 may not simplify to 0.1.

YTI 4 a) \$1.62 b) \$0.70 c) \$251.05 d) \$57.00

YTI 5 a) 2 b) 4 c) 3 d) 17 e) 23

YTI 6 a) Jenny's GPA is 3.25.

YTI 7 a) Tomás should report \$130 for postage on his tax form.

YTI 8 a) Connie's dinner tip was \$4.60.

Focus Exercises: Section 5.2

Round each of these numbers to the nearest tenth. Each number represents a runner's time in the 100-meter dash.

1. 11.592 **2.** 13.158 **3.** 10.605 **4.** 9.9481

Round each of these numbers to the nearest tenth. Each number represents a student's GPA.

5. 2.036 **6.** 3.027 **7.** 2.958 **8.** 1.962

Round each of these numbers to the nearest hundredth. Each number represents a student's GPA.

9. 1.2618 **10.** 3.5947 **11.** 1.3855 **12.** 2.4092

Round each of these numbers to the nearest hundredth. Each number represents a vehicle's miles per gallon.

13. 14.0737 **14.** 25.0922 **15.** 18.04933 **16.** 31.06509

Round each of these numbers to the nearest hundredth. Each number represents a newborn's weight in kilograms.

17. 4.1983 **18.** 3.4971 **19.** 3.9953 **20.** 2.9982

Round each of these numbers to the nearest hundredth. Each number represents a newborn's length in meters.

21. 0.4618 **22.** 0.4129 **23.** 0.3873 **24.** 0.3984

Round each of these numbers to the nearest thousandth. Each number represents the number of acres a homeowner owns in a rural town.

25. 6.08394 **26.** 12.0407 **27.** 1.0096 **28.** 9.0803

Round each of these numbers to the nearest thousandth. Each number represents a baseball player's batting average.

29. .21618 **30.** .31908 **31.** .3396 **32.** .4099

33. .3165 **34.** .239904 **35.** .29973 **36.** .399185

Round each dollar amount to the nearest penny. Each number represents the amount of sales tax applied to a purchase at a home electronics store.

37. \$5.956 **38.** \$19.0862 **39.** \$14.0381 **40.** \$25.004

41. \$5.99015 **42.** \$21.9935 **43.** \$107.99701 **44.** \$44.99537

Round each dollar amount to the nearest dime (tenth), but express the answer in dollars and cents. Each number represents a 15 percent tip on a restaurant meal.

45. \$6.0085 **46.** \$15.055 **47.** \$3.7735 **48.** \$9.3915

Round each of these numbers to the nearest whole number. Each number represents the average number of SUVs owned, per square mile, in a suburban area.

49. 31.3895 **50.** 48.0892 **51.** 82.5714 **52.** 53.61538

53. 214.9333 **54.** 2.5875 **55.** 0.86375 **56.** 15.02777

Round each of these numbers to the nearest dollar. Each number represents a business expense that is to be entered on a tax form.

57. \$31.08 **58.** \$142.90 **59.** \$20.38 **60.** \$40.08

61. \$29.60 **62.** \$519.73 **63.** \$99.56 **64.** \$139.74

For each, round the number as instructed and restate the first sentence using the rounded number.

65. Yat-Sun's GPA is 3.5256. Round this number to the nearest tenth.

66. Alabama's population density is 88.6953 people per square mile. Round this number to the nearest hundredth.

67. Gabriella's average monthly electric bill is \$53.84666. Round this number to the nearest penny.

68. Tunde calculated that his monthly insurance payment is \$106.52. Round this number to the nearest dollar.

69. Hank Aaron's batting average in 1969 was .2998171. Round this number to the nearest thousandth.

SECTION 5.3 Adding and Subtracting Decimals

Objectives

In this section, you will learn to:

- Add decimals numbers.
- Subtract decimals numbers.

To successfully complete this section, you need to understand:

- Adding whole numbers (1.3)
- Subtracting whole numbers (1.3)
- Solving applications (1.7)

Introduction

Adding decimals is no different than adding whole numbers. If we are given a list of whole numbers to add, then we organize them according to place value.

For example, to add 356 + 1,024 + 17 + 8, we can write the numbers so that the place values are in a line vertically (top to bottom).

We can make the lining up of place values more obvious by including an appropriate number of zeros before each number; doing so allows them to all have the same number of digits.

$$\begin{array}{rcr} 356 & \rightarrow & 0356 \\ 1024 & \rightarrow & 1024 \\ 17 & \rightarrow & 0017 \\ +\quad 8 & \rightarrow & +\ 0008 \\ \hline & & 1405 \end{array}$$

Of course, we don't have to add whole numbers this way. However, placing zeros in front of whole numbers shows the necessity of adding by lining up the place values.

Adding Decimals

Lining up the place values is important in adding decimals as well. With decimals, though, we line up the place values *and* the decimal points. Also, we can place more zeros at the *end* of the number instead of at the beginning.

EXAMPLE 1 Add 4.3 + 1.134 + 7.05 + 0.2861.

PROCEDURE: First, write the sum vertically and align the decimal points. Second, identify the number with the highest number of decimal places. The number 0.2861 has four decimal places, so place enough zeros behind the other numbers to get four decimal places.

$$\begin{array}{lcr} 4.3 & \text{becomes} & 4.3000 \\ 1.134 & \rightarrow & 1.1340 \\ 7.05 & \rightarrow & 7.0500 \\ +\ 0.2861 & \rightarrow & +\quad 0.2861 \\ \hline & & 12.7701 \end{array}$$

Is it necessary to write all of the ending zeros as shown? No, but it's good practice. It *is* necessary, though, to line up the decimal points, and it's important to write your numbers neatly so that all of the decimal place values line up correctly.

ANSWER: 12.7701

YOU TRY IT 1 *Add. Use Example 1 as a guide.*

a) 0.139 + 0.21 + 0.3515 + 0.4

b) 5.09 + 0.3 + 41.38 + 2.005

Subtracting Decimals

Subtracting decimals works exactly the same as subtracting whole numbers. And, just like adding decimals, we must be sure that all of the place values line up properly, especially the decimal point.

EXAMPLE 2

Subtract.

a) $\begin{array}{r} 526 \\ -\ 402 \\ \hline \end{array}$ b) $\begin{array}{r} 85.7 \\ -\ 62.5 \\ \hline \end{array}$ c) $\begin{array}{r} 3.49 \\ -\ 0.34 \\ \hline \end{array}$

ANSWER: a) 124 b) 23.2 c) 3.15

Notice that, in the answers for parts b and c, the decimal point is directly below the other decimal points.

YOU TRY IT 2

Subtract. Use Example 2 as a guide.

a) $\begin{array}{r} 825 \\ -\ 612 \\ \hline \end{array}$ b) $\begin{array}{r} 78.9 \\ -\ 32.8 \\ \hline \end{array}$ c) $\begin{array}{r} 4.38 \\ -\ 1.36 \\ \hline \end{array}$ d) $\begin{array}{r} 86.419 \\ -\ 13.207 \\ \hline \end{array}$

Think about it

Why, when subtracting decimals, is it important to line up the decimal points?

____

____

EXAMPLE 3

Subtract.

a) $\begin{array}{r} 52.43 \\ -\ 21.4 \\ \hline \end{array}$ b) $\begin{array}{r} 1.482 \\ -\ 1.3 \\ \hline \end{array}$ c) $\begin{array}{r} 52.361 \\ -\ 1 \\ \hline \end{array}$

PROCEDURE: Place an appropriate number of zeros behind the decimal numbers so that each number has the same number of decimal places showing. In part c, place the decimal point directly after 1 and then fill in the appropriate number of zeros.

ANSWER:

a) $\begin{array}{r} 52.43 \\ -\ 21.40 \\ \hline 31.03 \end{array}$ b) $\begin{array}{r} 1.482 \\ -\ 1.300 \\ \hline 0.182 \end{array}$ c) $\begin{array}{r} 52.361 \\ -\ 1.000 \\ \hline 51.361 \end{array}$

YOU TRY IT 3

Subtract. This time, place an appropriate number of zeros behind the decimal numbers. Use Example 3 as a guide.

a) $\begin{array}{r} 76.85 \\ -\ 63.5 \\ \hline \end{array}$ b) $\begin{array}{r} 5.596 \\ -\ 3.5 \\ \hline \end{array}$ c) $\begin{array}{r} 26.583 \\ -\ 3 \\ \hline \end{array}$

When written in words, subtraction seems a little bit backwards. For example, **5 − 3** can be written as "Subtract **3** from **5**." In words, the numbers appear in the reverse order of the arithmetic form 5 − 3.

EXAMPLE 4

Evaluate each by first writing it in arithmetic form.

a) Subtract 12 from 32. b) Subtract 8.4 from 9.7.

c) Subtract 3.1 from 5.98. d) Subtract 2.05 from 4.653.

PROCEDURE: First rewrite each in arithmetic form with the "from" number on top. Be sure to line up the decimal points. Also, place zeros after the decimal point, if needed.

ANSWER: a) 32 − 12: $\begin{array}{r} 32 \\ -\ 12 \\ \hline 20 \end{array}$ b) 9.7 − 8.4: $\begin{array}{r} 9.7 \\ -\ 8.4 \\ \hline 1.3 \end{array}$

c) 5.98 − 3.1: $\begin{array}{r} 5.98 \\ -\ 3.10 \\ \hline 2.88 \end{array}$ d) 4.653 − 2.05: $\begin{array}{r} 4.653 \\ -\ 2.050 \\ \hline 2.603 \end{array}$

YOU TRY IT 4

Evaluate each by first writing it in arithmetic form. Use Example 4 as a guide.

a) Subtract 17 from 98. b) Subtract 3.5 from 7.9.

c) Subtract 5.3 from 6.49. d) Subtract 0.5 from 2.801.

Subtracting Decimals Using Regrouping

Subtracting decimals works exactly the same as subtracting whole numbers; sometimes you can subtract directly, and sometimes you'll need to regroup.

Also, when subtracting decimals:

1. The decimal points must line up, one above the other; and
2. you may need to place enough zeros after the last decimal place so that the two numbers have the same number of decimal places.

EXAMPLE 5

Subtract 1.49 from 2.86.

PROCEDURE: First, align them vertically. After placing the decimal point, we treat the subtraction just like whole numbers; we regroup as needed.

ANSWER:

$$\begin{array}{r} 2.86 \\ -\ 1.49 \\ \hline . \end{array}$$

← Place the decimal point directly under the other decimal points.

$$\begin{array}{r} 2.86 \\ -\ 1.49 \\ \hline . \end{array} \rightarrow \begin{array}{r} 2.\not{8}^{7}\not{6}^{16} \\ -\ 1.4\ 9 \\ \hline 1.3\ 7 \end{array}$$

EXAMPLE 6

Subtract 3.56 from 5.7.

PROCEDURE: First, align them vertically. Second, we should place a 0 at the end of 5.7 so that it has the same number of decimal places as 3.56. It is necessary to regrouping in this subtraction.

ANSWER:

$$\begin{array}{r} 5.7 \\ -\ 3.56 \\ \hline . \end{array}$$

← Place the decimal point directly under the other decimal points.

$$\begin{array}{r} 5.7 \\ -\ 3.56 \\ \hline . \end{array} \rightarrow \begin{array}{r} 5.70 \\ -\ 3.56 \\ \hline . \end{array} \rightarrow \begin{array}{r} 5.\not{7}^{6}\not{0}^{10} \\ -\ 3.5\ 6 \\ \hline 2.1\ 4 \end{array}$$

EXAMPLE 7

Subtract 4.62 from 9.

PROCEDURE: Write 9 as 9.00. This way, it has a decimal point and has the same number of decimal places as 4.62. Then regroup as necessary.

ANSWER:

$$\begin{array}{r} 9 \\ -\ 4.62 \\ \hline \end{array} \rightarrow \begin{array}{r} 9.00 \\ -\ 4.62 \\ \hline \end{array} \rightarrow \begin{array}{r} \not{9}^{8}.\not{0}^{10}0 \\ -\ 4\ .6\ \ 2 \\ \hline \end{array} \rightarrow \begin{array}{r} \not{9}^{8}.\not{0}^{\not{10}\,9}\not{0}^{10} \\ -\ 4\ .6\ \ 2 \\ \hline 4\ .3\ \ 8 \end{array}$$

YOU TRY IT 5

Subtract. Some of these require regrouping more than once. Be careful! Use Examples 5, 6, and 7 as guides.

a) $\begin{array}{r} 5.3 \\ -\ 4.8 \\ \hline \end{array}$ b) $\begin{array}{r} 6.8 \\ -\ 4.43 \\ \hline \end{array}$ c) $\begin{array}{r} 11 \\ -\ 4.91 \\ \hline \end{array}$

YOU TRY IT 6

Subtract. Be sure to set up each problem vertically, and line up the decimal points correctly.

a) Subtract 2.6 from 7.95. b) Subtract 5.28 from 6.2. c) Subtract 3.16 from 20.

Applications Involving Adding and Subtracting Decimals

One easy way to demonstrate addition and subtraction of decimals is with money. In each of the following,

1. Decide what operation (addition or subtraction) to use.
2. Set up the problem, one number over another. Be sure to line up the decimals correctly.
3. Place a decimal point and some zeros, if needed, and then apply the operation.

EXAMPLE 8

At the grocery store, Carol is buying the following items: milk at \$1.49, eggs at \$0.95, bacon at \$2.38, and a bag of apples at \$2. What will her total bill be?

PROCEDURE: Decide what operation to use; the word "total" suggests that we'll need to add the items together. As we set up the problem, we'll be sure to line up the decimal points and to include appropriate zeros.

ANSWER:

Milk	\$1.49
Eggs	\$0.95
Bacon	\$2.38
Apples	+ \$2.00
Total	\$6.82

SENTENCE: Carol's total bill will be \$6.82.

EXAMPLE 9

Carol's total grocery bill is \$6.82. She pays for it with a \$10 bill. How much money should she get back?

PROCEDURE: To determine the change Carol will get, means that we subtract \$6.82 from \$10.

ANSWER: Be sure to place a decimal point and two zeros after the 10.

$$\begin{array}{r} \$10.00 \\ -\ 6.82 \\ \hline \$\ 3.18 \end{array}$$

(We must use regrouping here, but it isn't shown.)

SENTENCE: Carol should get \$3.18 back.

YOU TRY IT 7

At Holly's Café, Holly requires the waitresses to add the tabs by hand (it gives an old-fashioned touch to the service). One tab had the items shown at right.

Omelet	\$4.95
Scrambled eggs	3.95
Coffee	0.85
Large juice	1.45
Sales tax	0.88

What is the total tab for this breakfast?

Sentence: ______________________________

YOU TRY IT 8

Yvette bought some school supplies from the college bookstore. The total, with tax, came to \$8.23. Yvette paid with a \$20 bill. How much change did she get back?

Show your work:

Sentence: ______________________________

YOU TRY IT 9

Matt and Jenny drove to Baltimore on their vacation. When they started the trip, their new car's odometer read only 23.6 miles, but when the trip was over it read 718.0 miles. How many miles did they drive on their trip?

Show your work:

Sentence: ______________________________

YOU TRY IT 10

On Monday, the price of Genco stock was $38.625. On Tuesday, it increased $1.825. What was the price of the stock at the end of Tuesday?

Show your work:

Sentence: ______________________________

YOU TRY IT 11

Randy is a senior long jumper at Texas Tech. The Texas Tech record for the long jump is 7.95 meters. Randy's own personal best is 7.47 meters. How much farther does he need to jump to tie the school record?

Show your work:

Sentence: ______________________________

Recall from Section 1.3 that the perimeter of a geometric figure is the sum of the lengths of the sides of that figure.

EXAMPLE 10 Find the perimeter of this triangle:

PROCEDURE: Add the side measures (Be sure to line up the decimal points and place zeros, as needed.)

ANSWER:

$$\begin{array}{r} 2.184 \\ 2.800 \\ +\ 2.650 \\ \hline 7.634 \end{array}$$

2.184 feet
2.8 feet
2.65 feet

SENTENCE: The perimeter of this triangle is 7.634 feet.

YOU TRY IT 12

Find the perimeter of each geometric figure. Use Example 10 as a guide.

a) 2 meters; 1.36 meters; 0.7 meter

b) 4.1 inches; 2.53 inches; 5.79 inches; 3.8 inches

Sentence: ______________________________

Sentence: ______________________________

We can also solve application problems using the formula, "The sum of all of the parts equals the whole" and these problem-solving guidelines:

1. Read the problem through once for general information, then read it through a second time looking for specific information.
2. Identify the parts and whole and decide what is unknown.
3. Write the unknown in a legend (Let $n = \ldots$).
4. Place the known and unknown values into the formula, "The sum of all of the parts equals the whole."
5. Solve the equation, and write a sentence answering the question.

EXAMPLE 11 Patricia embroidered shirts for the high school marching band and charged a flat rate of $25.00 per shirt, including sales tax. If the sales tax on each shirt is $1.74, what is the actual price of the shirt?

PROCEDURE: In this case, the parts are the price of the shirt, which is unknown, and the amount of sales tax, $1.74. The whole is the flat charge $25.00.

ANSWER: Let $n =$ the price of the shirt.

$$n + 1.74 = 25.00$$

$$n + 1.74 - 1.74 = 25.00 - 1.74 \rightarrow \begin{array}{r} 25.00 \\ -\ 1.74 \\ \hline 23.26 \end{array}$$

$$n = 23.26$$

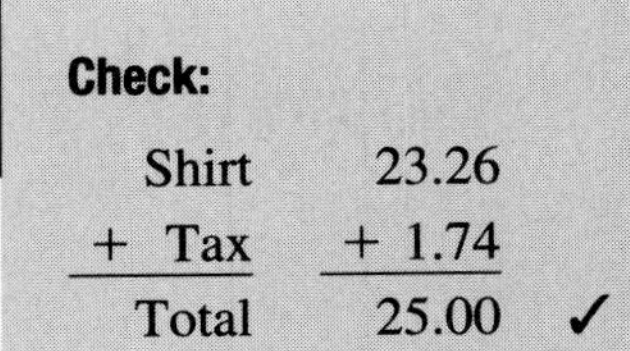

Check:

Shirt	23.26
+ Tax	+ 1.74
Total	25.00 ✓

SENTENCE: The actual price of the shirt is $23.26.

YOU TRY IT 13 *Lyndy owns stock in Klamath Enterprises. She has instructed her stockbroker to sell her stock when the price reaches $25.00 per share. Right now, the stock's value is $22.58 per share. How much will the share value need to increase before Lyndy sells her stock?*

Legend:

Sentence: ______________________________

YOU TRY IT 14 *Find the length of the third side of the triangle, given the information in the diagram.*

Legend:

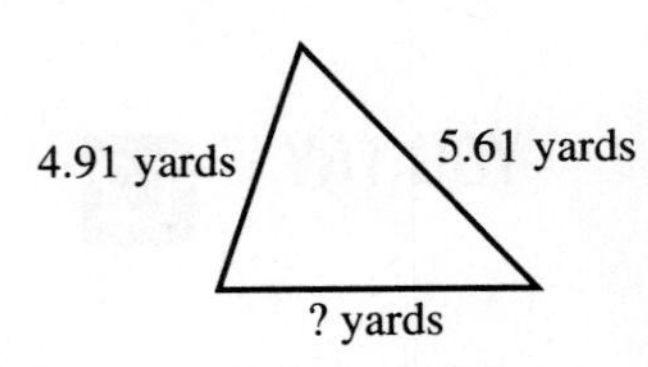

Sentence: ______________________________

You Try It Answers: Section 5.3

YTI 1 a)

0.139	→	0.1390
0.21	→	0.2100
0.3515	→	0.3515
0.4	→	+ 0.4000
		1.1005

b)

5.09	→	5.090
0.3	→	0.300
41.38	→	41.380
2.005	→	+ 2.005
		48.775

YTI 2 a) 213 b) 46.1 c) 3.02 d) 73.212

YTI 3 a) 13.35 b) 2.096 c) 23.583

YTI 4 a) 81 b) 4.4 c) 1.19 d) 2.301

YTI 5 a) 0.5 b) 2.37 c) 6.09

YTI 6 a) 5.35 b) 0.92 c) 16.84

YTI 7 The total tab is $12.08.

YTI 8 Yvette got back $11.77 in change.

YTI 9 Matt and Jenny drove 694.4 miles on their trip.

YTI 10 At the end of Tuesday the price of the stock was $40.45.

YTI 11 Randy needs to jump 0.48 meters farther to tie the school's long jump record.

YTI 12 a) The perimeter is 4.06 meters.
b) The perimeter is 16.22 inches.

YTI 13 **Legend:** Let $n =$ the amount of increase in the share value
Sentence: The share value will need to increase $2.42 before Lyndy sells her stock.

YTI 14 **Legend:** Let $n =$ the length of the third side
Sentence: The third side is 5.48 yards long.

Focus Exercises: Section 5.3

Add. (Place extra zeros behind the decimals as necessary.)

1. 0.308 + 0.52

2. 0.73 + 0.4096

3. 0.1 + 0.96 + 0.441

4. 0.07 + 0.6 + 0.559

Add. (Be sure to line up the decimal points properly.)

5. Add 0.41 and 0.38.

6. Add 1.27 and 3.51.

7. Add 10.73 and 9.68.

8. Add 12.64 and 4.97.

9. Add 0.6 and 0.53.

10. Add 1.8 and 3.56.

11. Add 14.41 and 5.59.

12. Add 0.38 and 0.62.

13. Add 2.59 and 1.426.

14. Add 3.67 and 12.385.

15. Add 4.086 and 5.92.

16. Add 16.239 and 3.77.

17. Add 12.4, 10.018 and 4.36.

18. Add 0.422, 0.06 and 0.9.

19. Add 5, 13.8, 1.047 and 2.59.

20. Add 2.635, 3.84, 25 and 11.7.

Subtract.

21. $\begin{array}{r} 9.38 \\ -\ 2.3 \\ \hline \end{array}$

22. $\begin{array}{r} 48.52 \\ -\ 7 \\ \hline \end{array}$

23. $\begin{array}{r} 7.953 \\ -\ 2.5 \\ \hline \end{array}$

24. $\begin{array}{r} 16.439 \\ -\ 12.31 \\ \hline \end{array}$

25. $\begin{array}{r} 9.1 \\ -\ 3.7 \\ \hline \end{array}$

26. $\begin{array}{r} 7.1 \\ -\ 4.3 \\ \hline \end{array}$

27. $\begin{array}{r} 2.01 \\ -\ 1.46 \\ \hline \end{array}$

28. $\begin{array}{r} 5.21 \\ -\ 2.05 \\ \hline \end{array}$

29. $\begin{array}{r} 6.3 \\ -\ 0.89 \\ \hline \end{array}$

30. $\begin{array}{r} 14.2 \\ -\ 9.82 \\ \hline \end{array}$

31. $\begin{array}{r} 6 \\ -\ 3.028 \\ \hline \end{array}$

32. $\begin{array}{r} 3 \\ -\ 1.408 \\ \hline \end{array}$

Evaluate each by first writing it in arithmetic form.

33. Subtract 2.9 from 4.3.

34. Subtract 14.8 from 16.6.

35. Subtract 0.39 from 6.1.

36. Subtract 1.03 from 5.1.

37. Subtract 5.291 from 14.6.

38. Subtract 8.377 from 12.5.

39. Subtract 9.53 from 15.

40. Subtract 3.26 from 24.

Solve each by adding or subtracting appropriately. Answer the question with a sentence.

41. Juan needed to purchase items for his desk in his office. Looking through the Staples catalog, he came up with the following items and their prices. What is the total (before sales tax)?

Item	Price
Stapler	$25.95
Staples	4.36
Post-it Notes	5.83
Paper clips	0.53

42. At the Summer Olympic trials, Ivana received these scores for her gymnastics floor routine. What was her total score for the event?

Judge	Score
Germany	9.23
France	9.51
Spain	9.66
USA	9.58
Russia	9.47

43. For Thanksgiving dinner, Sharon bought two turkeys. One weighed 15.39 pounds and the other weighed 19.68 pounds. What was the combined weight of the two turkeys?

44. Julie purchased donuts for her office. The total came to $5.83, including tax. She paid with a $10 bill. How much change did Julie get back?

45. At the Summer Olympic trials, Sean's time in the 400-meter race was 43.38 seconds and Torii's time was 45.05 seconds. How many seconds was Torii behind Sean?

46. In January 2005, the price of regular gasoline was $1.979. Two months later, the price was $2.519. What was the increase in the price per gallon of regular gasoline in those two months?

Find the perimeter of each geometric figure.

47.

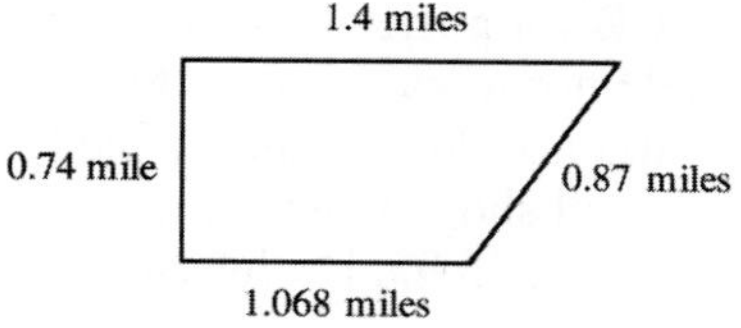

48.

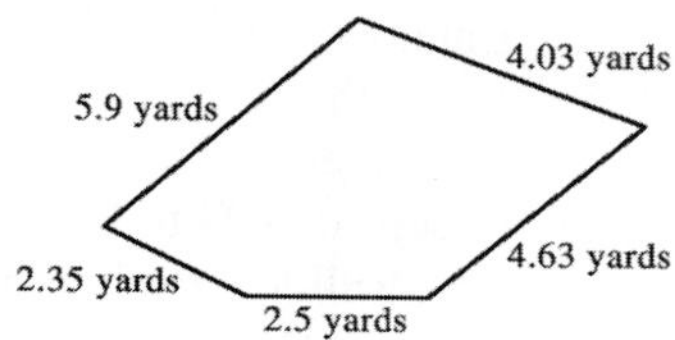

For the following, set up a legend and an equation to answer the question.

49. At the beginning of her diet, Claire wanted to lose 45 pounds. Thanks to good eating habits and exercise she has lost 28.4 pounds so far. How many more pounds does Claire need to lose to reach her goal?

50. Marcia swam two laps in a 50-meter race with an overall time of 40.26 seconds. The time on her first lap was 21.39 seconds. What was the time on Marcia's second lap?

51. Find the length of the third side of the triangle, given the information in the diagram.

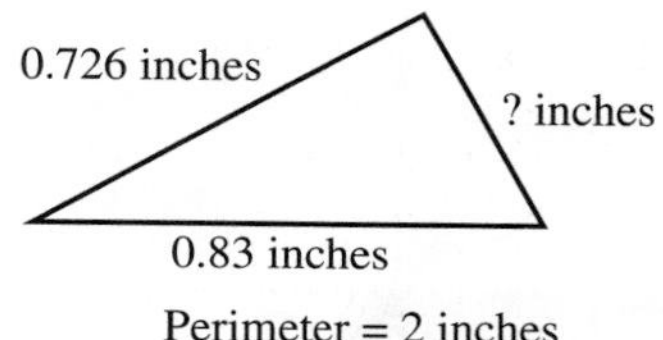

52. Find the length of the third side of the triangle, given the information in the diagram.

? meters

0.97 meters

1.3 meters

Perimeter = 4 meters

SECTION 5.4 Multiplying Decimals

Objectives

In this section, you will learn to:

- Multiply a decimal by a decimal.
- Multiply a decimal by a whole number.
- Multiply a decimal by a power of 10.

To successfully complete this section, you need to understand:

- Multiplying whole numbers (1.4)
- Multiplying fractions (3.3)
- Writing decimals as fractions (5.1)

Introduction

True story, though the names have been changed to protect the innocent.

> Lana went to a small specialty shop to buy a music CD for a friend. While there, the power went out, and the cash register would not work. Neither the employee nor the manager knew how to calculate sales tax, so they didn't want to sell the CD to Lana. Lana, the owner of her own retail shop, showed them how to find sales tax by multiplying the price of the CD, \$15.95, by the sales tax rate, 0.08.

The moral of this story is, don't be totally dependent on machines to do all of the work for you. Learn to know what the machine is doing so that you can do it on your own should you ever need to.

Multiplying Decimal Numbers

A decimal can always be written as a decimal fraction. For example, 0.3 can be written as $\frac{3}{10}$ and 0.07 can be written as $\frac{7}{100}$.

This concept is helpful when we multiply two decimal numbers. The advantage of writing decimals as fractions is that the numerators are whole numbers, and the denominators are powers of 10. We will use this concept to develop a consistent procedure for multiplying decimals.

Consider the product 0.3×0.07. Because each decimal can be written as a fraction, we can multiply using the product rule for fractions:

$$0.3 \times 0.07 = \frac{3}{10} \times \frac{7}{100} = \frac{21}{1{,}000} = 0.021$$

EXAMPLE 1 Multiply 0.06×0.8 by first rewriting each decimal as a fraction.

ANSWER: $0.06 \times 0.8 = \frac{6}{100} \times \frac{8}{10} = \frac{48}{1{,}000} = 0.048$

YOU TRY IT 1 *Multiply by first rewriting each decimal as a fraction. Multiply the fractions, then convert the answer back into a decimal. Use Example 1 as a guide.*

a) $0.5 \times 0.9 =$ ______________________

b) $0.1 \times 0.6 =$ ______________________

c) $0.03 \times 0.8 =$ ______________________

d) $0.11 \times 0.07 =$ ______________________

Consider 0.8×0.21. Let's think about what we see here.

$$0.8 \times 0.21 = \frac{8}{10} \times \frac{21}{100} = \frac{168}{1{,}000} = 0.168$$

In this product, whether we use fractions or decimals, we are multiplying tenths by hundredths and getting thousandths.

In each factor, if we count the number of zeros in each denominator, we will know the number of denominator zeros in the end result:

Fractions:

Tenths × *hundreths* = *thousandths*

$$\frac{8}{10} \times \frac{21}{100} = \frac{168}{1,000}$$

One zero — *Two* zeros — *Three* zeros

Number of zeros: *one* + *two* = *three*

In each factor, if we count the number of decimal places in each number, we will know the number of decimal places in the end result:

Decimals:

Tenths × *hundreths* = *thousandths*

$$0.8 \times 0.21 = 0.168$$

One decimal place — *Two* decimal places — *Three* decimal places

Number of decimal places: *one* + *two* = *three*

The fractions show us we are simply multiplying whole numbers 8 × 21; the decimals show us that the answer is a decimal number. The question is, after we multiply 8 × 21 = 168, where do we place the decimal point?

The diagrams above show that we can count the number of decimal places in the factors, and the result will have that total number of decimal places.

Multiplying Two Decimal Numbers

Multiplying decimals is exactly the same as multiplying whole numbers, but we must:

1. Temporarily ignore the decimal points and multiply the numbers (factors) as if they were both whole numbers; and
2. count up the total number of decimal places in the factors; this total is the number of decimal places in the product (before any simplifying).

Let's practice identifying the number of decimals, as in part 2 of the procedure.

EXAMPLE 2 Given the following multiplication, decide how many decimal places the product (the result) will have. *Do not multiply.*

a) 0.3 × 5 b) 1.2 × 0.4 c) 0.16 × 5.3 d) 1.25 × 0.12

PROCEDURE: Count the total number of decimal places in both numbers. This is the number of decimal places that the answer will have.

ANSWER:

a) 0.3 × 5 0.3 has one decimal place and 5 has none, so their product will have a total of one decimal place.

b) 1.2 × 0.4 1.2 has one decimal place and 0.4 has one, so their product will have a total of two decimal places.

c) 0.16 × 5.3 0.16 has two decimal places and 5.3 has one, so their product will have a total of three decimal places.

d) 1.25 × 0.12 1.25 has two decimal places and 0.12 has two, so their product will have a total of four decimal places.

YOU TRY IT 2

Given the following multiplication, decide how many decimal places the product (the result) will have. Do not multiply. Use Example 2 as a guide.

a) 0.45×1.2 b) 6×4.3 c) 1.08×3.04 d) 4.3×2.6

EXAMPLE 3

Multiply.

a) 13×32 b) 1.3×3.2

ANSWER:

a)
$$\begin{array}{r} 13 \\ \times\ 32 \\ \hline 26 \\ +\ 390 \\ \hline 416 \end{array}$$

b)
$$\begin{array}{r} 1.3 \\ \times\ 3.2 \\ \hline 26 \\ +\ 390 \\ \hline 4.16 \end{array}$$

Temporarily ignore the decimal points and multiply as if the decimals were whole numbers. The two decimal places appear in the end result only.

EXAMPLE 4

Multiply these decimal numbers. (In these, when the whole number is 0, we usually don't multiply it.)

a) 0.3×5 b) 1.2×0.4 c) 0.17×5.1 d) 0.63×2.08

PROCEDURE: Write the numbers with decimals in place. Temporarily ignore the decimal points and multiply as you would with whole numbers. When complete, count up the number of decimals in each product.

ANSWER:

a)
$$\begin{array}{rl} 0.3 & \text{One decimal place} \\ \times\ 5 & \text{No decimal places} \\ \hline 1.5 & \text{One decimal place} \end{array}$$

b)
$$\begin{array}{rl} 1.2 & \text{One decimal place} \\ \times\ 0.4 & \text{One decimal place} \\ \hline 0.48 & \text{Two decimal places} \end{array}$$

c)
$$\begin{array}{rl} 0.17 & \text{Two decimal places} \\ \times\ 5.1 & \text{One decimal place} \\ \hline 17 & \downarrow \\ +\ 850 & \downarrow \\ \hline 0.867 & \text{Three decimal places} \end{array}$$

d)
$$\begin{array}{rl} 0.63 & \text{Two decimal places} \\ \times\ 2.08 & \text{Two decimal places} \\ \hline 504 & \downarrow \\ +\ 12600 & \downarrow \\ \hline 1.3104 & \text{Four decimal places} \end{array}$$

YOU TRY IT 3

Follow the procedure for multiplying decimals to find the product. Use Examples 3 and 4 as guides.

a) 0.6×8 b) 0.7×0.3 c) 0.12×0.9

d) 1.7×0.15 e) 0.27×0.81

Think about it

When adding and subtracting decimals, it is important to line up the decimal points, but it is not necessary to do that when multiplying decimals. Why not?

Caution There are two problems in the next example that involve working with 0 in one way or another. Be careful!

EXAMPLE 5 Multiply.

a) 0.16×0.3 b) 0.25×0.72

PROCEDURE: Follow Example 4, but notice the following:

The first, a), will require three decimal places, but there will be only two digits in the product. A third digit is required before we can place the decimal point in the answer. That third digit is a 0 in front.

The second, b), will have enough decimal places, but there will be a few extra zeros at the end of the number that we can eventually eliminate.

ANSWER:

a)

0.16	Two decimal places
× 0.3	One decimal place
0.048	Three decimal places

$0.16 \times 0.3 = 0.048$

b)

0.25	Two decimal places
× 0.72	Two decimal places
50	↓
+ 1750	↓
0.1800	Four decimal places

We can simplify 0.1800 to 0.18.

$0.25 \times 0.72 = 0.18$

Caution We cannot eliminate any ending zeros until after the decimal point is placed in the end result.

YOU TRY IT 4 *Follow the procedure for multiplying decimals to find the product. Use Example 5 as a guide.*

a) 0.3×0.2 b) 0.96×0.5 c) 0.08×0.35

Multiplying a Decimal by a Power of 10

Multiplying a decimal by 10, or by a larger power of 10—such as 100 or 1,000—has the same effect as changing the position of the decimal point within the number.

In Example 6, pay close attention to the number of decimal places in the factor and to the number of zeros in the power of 10. Based on these examples, and the following You Try It exercises, we'll develop a procedure that can be used consistently.

EXAMPLE 6 Multiply by first rewriting each decimal number as a fraction

a) 3.6 × 10 b) 5.24 × 10 c) 5.9 × 1,000

ANSWER: a) $3.6 \times 10 = \frac{36}{10} \times \frac{10}{1} = \frac{36 \cdot 10}{10 \cdot 1} = \frac{36 \cdot 1}{1 \cdot 1} = 36$ **3.6 × 10 = 36**

Divide out a common factor of 10.

b) $5.24 \times 10 = \frac{524}{100} \times \frac{10}{1} = \frac{524 \cdot 10}{100 \cdot 1} = \frac{524 \cdot 1}{10 \cdot 1} = \frac{524}{10} = 52.4$ **5.24 × 10 = 52.4**

Divide out a common factor of 10.

c) $5.9 \times 1{,}000 = \frac{59}{10} \times \frac{1{,}000}{1} = \frac{59 \cdot 1{,}000}{10 \cdot 1} = \frac{59 \cdot 100}{1 \cdot 1} = \frac{5{,}900}{1} = 5{,}900$

5.9 × 1,000 = 5,900

Divide out a common factor of 10.

YOU TRY IT 5 *Multiply by first writing each number as a fraction, as in Example 6.*

a) 5.9 × 10 b) 3.159 × 1,000

c) 4.28 × 10 d) 1.56 × 100

e) 8.6 × 100

Let's take a second look, carefully, at each resulting product in Example 6:

a) 3.6 × 10 = 36 b) 5.24 × 10 = 52.4 c) 5.9 × 1,000 = 5,900

Question: Do you see a connection between the number of zeros in the power of 10 and the number of places the decimal point was moved to the right in the answers?

Answer: The number of zeros in the power of 10 indicates the number of places the decimal point moves to the right as a result of multiplying.

a) 3.6 × 10 = 36
3 . 6. = 36

Multiplying by 10, which has only one zero, has the effect of moving the decimal point of 3.6 one place to the right; the product becomes the whole number 36 without the need of a decimal point.

b) 5.24 × 10 = 52.4
5 . 2.4 = 52.4

Again, there is one zero in 10, which has the effect of moving the decimal point of 5.24 one place to the right. This time, the decimal point is necessary because 52.4 is still a decimal number.

c) 5.9 × 1,000 = 5,900
↓
5.900 × 1,000 = 5,900
5 . 9 0 0 . = 5,900

Multiplying by 1,000 suggests that we need to move the decimal point in 5.9 three places to the right.

However, there aren't enough decimal places in 5.9, so we must place some zeros at the end of it so that there is someplace to move the decimal point to.

Here is the procedure that results from all of this:

Multiplying a Decimal by a Power of Ten

1. Count the number of zeros in the power of ten.

2. Move the decimal point that many places to the right.

EXAMPLE 7

For each, indicate the number of zeros in the power of ten; to get the product without using fractions, move the decimal point that many places to the right. You may need to place zeros at the end of the decimal number if it doesn't have enough decimal places already.

a) 2.94×10 b) 2.94×100 c) $2.94 \times 1{,}000$

ANSWER:

Multiply	Number of zeros	Move the decimal to the right	Product
a) 2.94×10	one	one	29.4
b) 2.94×100	two	two	294
c) $2.94 \times 1{,}000$	three	three	????

The number 2.94 doesn't have enough decimals to move the decimal point three places to the right, so we need to first place a zero at the end:

c) 2.94**0** $\times$ 1,000	three	three	2,940

YOU TRY IT 6

Multiply by moving the decimal point the appropriate number of places to the right. Use Example 7 as a guide.

a) 3.1×10 b) 0.457×100 c) 17.5×100

d) $0.0094 \times 1{,}000$ e) $0.02 \times 1{,}000$

Applications

Sales tax is calculated by multiplying the price of an item (usually dollars and cents) by the sales tax rate (a decimal). After the sales tax is calculated, it is rounded to the nearest penny (hundredth) and added to the price of the item.

Example 8 refers to the true story at the beginning of this section.

EXAMPLE 8

Lana wants to buy a music CD that costs \$15.95. If the sales tax rate is 0.08, how much total will she pay for the CD?

PROCEDURE: Calculate the sales tax for the CD and round it to the nearest penny. Then, add the sales tax to the cost of the CD to find the amount Lana must pay.

ANSWER:

$$\begin{array}{r} 15.95 \\ \times\ 0.08 \\ \hline 1.2760 \end{array}$$

Round to the nearest penny, $1.2760 \approx 1.28$.

The sales tax is $1.28. Add this to the cost:

$$\begin{array}{r} \$15.95 \\ +\ 1.28 \\ \hline \$17.23 \end{array}$$

SENTENCE: Lana will pay a total of $17.23 for the CD.

YOU TRY IT 7 *JR is buying a baseball glove for his son for little league. The cost of the glove is $27.99, and the tax rate is 0.06. How much total will JR pay for the glove?*

Show your work:

Sentence: ______________________________

Many more applications involving multiplying decimals appear in Section 5.6.

You Try It Answers: Section 5.4

YTI 1
a) $\frac{5}{10} \times \frac{9}{10} = \frac{45}{100} = 0.45$
b) $\frac{1}{10} \times \frac{6}{10} = \frac{6}{100} = 0.06$
c) $\frac{3}{100} \times \frac{8}{10} = \frac{24}{1{,}000} = 0.024$
d) $\frac{11}{100} \times \frac{7}{100} = \frac{77}{10{,}000} = 0.0077$

YTI 2 a) Three b) One c) Four d) Two

YTI 3 a) 4.8 b) 0.21 c) 0.108 d) 0.255 e) 0.2187

YTI 4 a) 0.06 b) 0.480 = 0.48 c) 0.0280 = 0.028

YTI 5 a) 59 b) 3,159 c) 42.8 d) 156 e) 860

YTI 6 a) 31 b) 45.7 c) 1,750 d) 9.4 e) 20

YTI 7 JR must pay a total of $29.67 for the glove.

Focus Exercises: Section 5.4

Multiply by first rewriting each decimal as a fraction. Multiply the fractions, then write the answer as a decimal.

1. 0.8×9 **2.** 0.4×0.7 **3.** 1.2×0.3

4. 1.1×0.6 **5.** 1.4×0.02 **6.** 0.04×9

Follow the procedure for multiplying decimals to find the product.

7. 7×0.3 **8.** 2×0.6 **9.** 0.4×8 **10.** 0.5×5

11. 0.6×0.8 **12.** 0.9×0.7 **13.** 0.4×1.2 **14.** 4.2×0.3

15. 6.1×0.9 **16.** 0.1×8.5 **17.** 1.3×1.1 **18.** 2.4×0.1

19. 0.17×0.2 **20.** 0.12×0.6 **21.** 0.4×0.22 **22.** 0.5×0.13

23. 0.04×0.2 **24.** 0.02×0.3 **25.** 0.01×0.6 **26.** 0.01×0.8

27. 0.15×0.03 **28.** 0.24×0.03 **29.** 0.031×0.08 **30.** 0.045×0.09

31. 0.02×0.04 **32.** 0.01×0.05 **33.** 6.03×0.02 **34.** 5.04×0.02

35. 1.5×0.6 **36.** 2.5×0.2 **37.** 0.5×1.6 **38.** 0.5×2.4

39. 2.5×0.4 **40.** 4.5×0.8 **41.** 6.5×0.08 **42.** 7.5×0.04

43. 1.25×1.2 **44.** 2.25×1.6 **45.** 3.25×2.8 **46.** 4.25×3.2

47. 5×0.034 **48.** 1.9×1.5 **49.** 5.1×3.14 **50.** 14.03×0.18

51. 12.5×1.6 **52.** 6.25×0.8 **53.** 10.4×0.005 **54.** 2.25×0.004

Multiply by moving the decimal point the appropriate number of places to the right.

55. 11.9×10 **56.** 6.1×10 **57.** 0.8×10 **58.** 0.1×10

59. 9.06×10 **60.** 5.07×10 **61.** 3.76×100 **62.** 9.41×100

63. 0.08×100 **64.** 0.09×100 **65.** 1.206×100 **66.** 8.602×100

67. 4.8×100 **68.** 31.5×100 **69.** $0.401 \times 1{,}000$ **70.** $3.159 \times 1{,}000$

71. $8.05 \times 1{,}000$ **72.** $1.56 \times 1{,}000$ **73.** $1.3 \times 1{,}000$ **74.** $6.2 \times 1{,}000$

75. At a hardware store, Steve is buying a pack of batteries priced at \$23.56. If the sales tax rate is 0.07, what is the total amount Steve must pay for the batteries?

76. At a music and video store, JoAn is purchasing a DVD collection priced at \$47.60. If the sales tax rate is 0.065, what is the total amount JoAn must pay for the DVD collection?

77. Tanner wants to buy a Tracy McGrady autographed basketball card priced at \$80.00 If the sales tax rate is 0.0625, what is the total amount Tanner must pay for the card?

78. Renee is buying a used Honda Civic for \$8,500. If the sales tax rate is 0.0775, what is the total amount Renee must pay for the Civic?

SECTION 5.5 Dividing Decimals

Objectives

In this section, you will learn to:

- Divide decimals by whole numbers.
- Divide decimals by decimals.
- Write fractions as decimals.

To successfully complete this section, you need to understand:

- Dividing whole numbers (1.5)
- Repeating decimals (5.1)
- Terminating decimals (5.1)
- Multiplying decimals by powers of 10 (5.4)

Introduction

We know that $40 \div 4 = 10$. What about $36 \div 4$?

If we think about it, 36 is a little bit less than 40, so the quotient of $36 \div 4$ should be a little bit less than 10, and it is: $36 \div 4 = 9$.

Likewise, the quotient of $52 \div 4$ should be a little bit *more* than 10 because 52 is a little bit more than 40. In fact, $52 \div 4 = 13$:

$$\begin{array}{r} 13 \\ 4\overline{)52} \\ -\ 4 \\ \hline 12 \\ -\ 12 \\ \hline 0 \end{array}$$

We can check this by multiplying:

$$\begin{array}{r} 13 \\ \times\ 4 \\ \hline 52 \end{array}$$

We also know that $4 \div 4 = 1$. What could we say about $5.2 \div 4$? Using the same reasoning, since 5.2 is a little bit more than 4, the quotient of $5.2 \div 4$ should be a little bit more than 1, and it is: $5.2 \div 4 = 1.3$.

The point is this: when we divide a decimal number by a whole number, the quotient will also be a decimal number.

$$\begin{array}{r} 1.3 \\ 4\overline{)5.2} \\ -\ 4 \\ \hline 1\ 2 \\ -\ 1\ 2 \\ \hline 0 \end{array}$$

We can check this by multiplying:

$$\begin{array}{r} 1.3 \\ \times\ 4 \\ \hline 5.2 \end{array}$$

Dividing a Decimal by a Whole Number

Dividing a Decimal by a Whole Numbers Using Long Division

1. Place a decimal point in the quotient directly above the decimal point in the dividend.
2. Divide as if each were a whole number.

EXAMPLE 1 Divide using long division: $6.52 \div 4$

PROCEDURE: When the divisor (4) is a whole number and the dividend (6.52) has a decimal point in it:

1. we place a decimal point in the quotient directly above the decimal point in the dividend; and
2. we ignore the decimal point and divide as if each were a whole number.

ANSWER:

$$\begin{array}{r} 1.63 \\ 4\overline{)6.52} \\ -\ 4 \\ \hline 25 \\ -\ 24 \\ \hline 12 \\ -\ 12 \\ \hline 0 \end{array}$$

Notice that the decimal point in the quotient is directly above the decimal point in the dividend.

Check:

By multiplying:

$$\begin{array}{r} 1.63 \\ \times\ 4 \\ \hline 6.52 \end{array}$$

YOU TRY IT 1

Divide using long division. Use Example 1 as a guide.

a) $5.19 \div 3$ b) $8.735 \div 5$ c) $56.7 \div 9$

$\text{divisor}\overline{)\text{dividend}}$ with quotient above

dividend ÷ divisor = quotient

$\frac{\text{dividend}}{\text{divisor}} = \text{quotient}$

When we used long division to divide whole numbers (Section 1.5), we started the quotient at the first possible digit that gave us a nonzero factor. If the divisor doesn't divide into the first digit, we can place a 0 above the first digit and then continued to divide into the first two digits, and so on.

For example, consider $576 \div 9$:

① 9 won't divide into 5, so we usually leave the quotient blank above the 5 and look at 9 dividing into 57.

② 9 does divide into 57 six times, so we start the quotient above the 7.

$$\begin{array}{r} 64 \\ 9\overline{)576} \\ -\,54 \\ \hline 36 \\ -\,36 \\ \hline 0 \end{array}$$

③ We could put a 0 above the 5 and then continue to divide.

$$\begin{array}{r} 064 \\ 9\overline{)576} \\ -\,54 \\ \hline 36 \\ -\,36 \\ \hline 0 \end{array}$$

With decimals, though, it is necessary for us to write the 0 in the quotient. Sometimes we'll need to write more than one 0 before we finally get a nonzero factor.

EXAMPLE 2

Divide using long division.

a) $0.741 \div 3$ b) $\frac{0.354}{6}$

PROCEDURE:

a)
$$\begin{array}{r} 0.247 \\ 3\overline{)0.741} \\ -\,6 \\ \hline 14 \\ -\,12 \\ \hline 21 \\ -\,21 \\ \hline 0 \end{array}$$

b)
$$\begin{array}{r} 0.059 \\ 6\overline{)0.354} \\ -\,0 \\ \hline 35 \\ -\,30 \\ \hline 54 \\ -\,54 \\ \hline 0 \end{array}$$

(b) We place the decimal point in the quotient, along with a 0 in the whole number place.

Because 6 won't divide into 3, this quotient requires a 0 above the 3 as well.

ANSWER: $0.741 \div 3 = 0.247$ $\frac{0.354}{6} = 0.059$

Notice that the answer for part a has a 0 *before* the decimal point—in the whole number position, but the answer for part b has one 0 *before* and one 0 *immediately after* the decimal point.

Caution The quotient should always contain a whole number, even if it is 0. The whole number will be 0 whenever the dividend is less than the divisor.

YOU TRY IT 2

Divide using long division. Use Example 2 as a guide.

a) $1.413 \div 9$ b) $\dfrac{0.035}{5}$ c) $0.8371 \div 11$

Sometimes, there are not enough decimal places in the dividend to divide fully. When that happens, you may place as many zeros as you wish at the end of the dividend. This way, you can continue to divide as long as you need to.

EXAMPLE 3 Divide using long division: $1.37 \div 2$

PROCEDURE: Extend the number of decimal places in the dividend by placing as many zeros at the end of the decimal as needed.

ANSWER:

```
    0.685
 2)1.3700
  - 1 2
    ----
      17
    - 16
    ----
      10
    - 10
    ----
       0
```

We need to place only one extra zero at the end of the dividend. However, it's okay to place more (two extra zeros are shown here). Usually, we don't know ahead of time how many zeros we will actually need. Sometimes, we may need to add more than we originally thought.

Once we get a remainder of zero, we're done.

$1.37 \div 2 = 0.685$

YOU TRY IT 3

Divide using long division. Use Example 3 as a guide. (In each of these, you'll need to place at least one zero at the end of the dividend.)

a) $2.6 \div 5$ b) $\dfrac{0.3}{4}$ c) $0.51 \div 8$

When dividing into a decimal, when is it necessary to add zeros to the end of the dividend?

____

____

Sometimes, we can place as many zeros as we wish but never get a remainder of 0. When this happens, the quotient is a repeating decimal, as you will see in the next example. The repeating pattern will begin to become clear when you get a recurring remainder. Once you see the pattern, you can stop dividing and place a bar over the repeating digits (the repetend), just as you did in Section 5.1.

EXAMPLE 4 Divide using long division: $2.5 \div 3$

PROCEDURE: You can probably see that—temporarily ignoring the decimal—3 will not divide evenly into 25. We will need to extend the number of decimal places in the dividend by placing some zeros at the end.

This time, however, we're going to get a repeating decimal. When you recognize that the pattern is repeating, write the quotient with the bar over the repeating part.

ANSWER:

```
   0.833
 3)2.5000   ←  Place plenty of zeros at the end of 2.5.
 - 2 4
     10     ←  The remainder is 1; bring down the 0.
   -  9
      10    ←  The remainder is 1; bring down the 0.
    -  9
       1    ←  The remainder of 1 is recurring, let's stop.
```

$2.5 \div 3 = 0.8\overline{3}$

Sometimes, the pattern takes a little longer to develop.

EXAMPLE 5 Divide using long division: $1.62 \div 11$

PROCEDURE: This time, the recurring decimal will take two decimal places. Watch!

ANSWER:

```
    0.147272
 11)1.62000   ←  Place plenty of zeros at the end of 1.62.
  - 1 1
      52      ←  The remainder is 5; bring down the 2.
    - 44
       80     ←  The remainder is 8; bring down the 0.
     - 77
        30    ←  The remainder is 3; bring down the 0.
      - 22
         80   ←  The remainder looks familiar; bring down the 0.
       - 77
          3   ←  So does this one; let's stop.
```

The pattern of 72 repeats in the quotient. $1.62 \div 11 = 0.14\overline{72}$

YOU TRY IT 4 *Divide using long division. Use Examples 4 and 5 as guides.*

a) $4.6 \div 9$ b) $0.37 \div 6$ c) $\dfrac{10.42}{22}$

Dividing When the Divisor Contains a Decimal

To this point, you have learned to divide a decimal number by a whole number, such as 6.52 ÷ 4 (as was demonstrated in Example 1). What if we need to divide 6.52 by the decimal number 0.4 instead of the whole number 4?

To answer this question, we will use these three ideas to help us develop a procedure for dividing by a decimal number:

1. Any division can be written as a fraction: $6.52 \div 0.4 = \frac{6.52}{0.4}$
2. We can multiply any decimal number.by a power of 10, moving the decimal point to the right. For example: $\begin{cases} 6.52 \times 10 = 65.2 \\ \text{and } 0.4 \times 10 = 4 \end{cases}$
3. We can multiply any fraction by a form of 1 without changing the value:

$$\frac{6.52}{0.4} \times \frac{10}{10} = \frac{65.2}{4}, \text{ which is } 65.2 \div 4.$$

Notice that we have changed 6.52 ÷ 0.4 into 65.2 ÷ 4 by adjusting the decimal point in *each* number, moving it one place to the right:

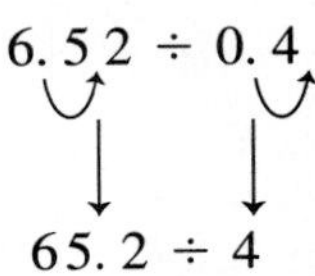

quotient
divisor)dividend

dividend ÷ divisor = quotient

$\frac{\text{dividend}}{\text{divisor}} = \text{quotient}$

The point is this: If the divisor is a decimal number, then we can make it a whole number by moving the decimal point in both the dividend *and* the divisor by the same number of places.

In 6.52 ÷ 0.4, we can move each decimal point one place to the right in one of three settings:

① Fractional Form	② Standard Division	③ Long Division Form
$\frac{6.52}{0.4} \rightarrow \frac{65.2}{4}$	6. 5 2 ÷ 0. 4 → 65. 2 ÷ 4	0. 4.)6.5 .2
Make the denominator a whole number		Make the divisor a whole number.

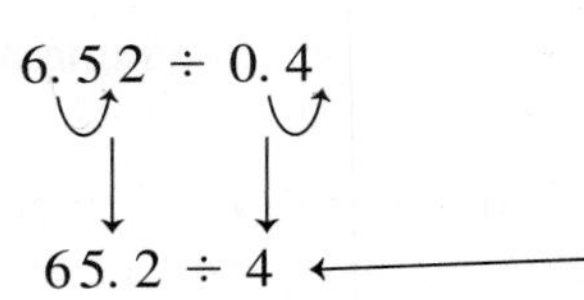

Place the decimal point above the new location right away.

Whichever setting you choose, the actual division should be done using long division.

EXAMPLE 6 Divide.

a) 0.741 ÷ 0.3 b) 0.354 ÷ 0.06

PROCEDURE: First adjust each number so that the divisor is a whole number:

a) Because the divisor has one decimal place, move each decimal point one place to the right:

0. 7 4 1 ÷ 0. 3 → 7.4 1 ÷ 3

b) Because the divisor has two decimal places, move each decimal point two places to the right:

0. 3 5 4 ÷ 0. 0 6 → 35. 4 ÷ 6

Now set up the long division using these adjusted numbers.

ANSWER:

a)
```
   2.47
3)7.41
 - 6
   14
 - 12
    21
  - 21
     0
```

$0.741 \div 0.3 = 2.47$

b)
```
    5.9
6)35.4
 - 30
    5 4
  - 5 4
      0
```

$0.354 \div 0.06 = 5.9$

YOU TRY IT 5

Divide. Adjust the decimal points appropriately to make the divisor into a whole number. Use Example 6 as a guide.

a) $0.45 \div 0.9$ b) $\dfrac{3.95}{0.05}$ c) $0.418 \div 0.0011$

Writing Fractions as Decimals

Any fraction in which both the numerator and denominator are whole numbers can be written as a decimal number, either a terminating decimal or a repeating decimal.

Start by writing the fraction as division, then divide using long division. For example,

$$\frac{3}{4} = 3 \div 4.$$

Because 4 won't divide into 3 directly, it is necessary to write 3 as 3.000 (possibly with more or with fewer ending zeros) in order to divide.

EXAMPLE 7

Find the decimal equivalent of each fraction.

a) $\dfrac{3}{4}$ b) $\dfrac{5}{6}$

PROCEDURE: Write the fraction as division and then divide using long division. Write each numerator with a decimal point followed by some ending zeros.

ANSWER: a) $\frac{3}{4}$ can be thought of as $3 \div 4$

$$\begin{array}{r} 0.75 \\ 4\overline{)3.000} \\ -\ 2\,8 \\ \hline 20 \\ -\ 20 \\ \hline 0 \end{array}$$

$\frac{3}{4} = 0.75$, a terminating decimal

b) $\frac{5}{6}$ can be thought of as $5 \div 6$

$$\begin{array}{r} 0.8333 \\ 6\overline{)5.0000} \\ -\ 4\,8 \\ \hline 20 \\ -\ 18 \\ \hline 20 \\ -\ 18 \\ \hline 20 \end{array}$$

$\frac{5}{6} = 0.8\overline{3}$, a repeating decimal

YOU TRY IT 6

Find the decimal equivalent of each fraction. Use Example 7 as a guide.

a) $\frac{6}{5}$ b) $\frac{4}{9}$ c) $\frac{23}{40}$

A Strategy for Dividing with Decimals

Here is the strategy for dividing with decimals:

1. Divide only by a whole number; if the divisor is a decimal number, then adjust both the dividend and divisor by moving each decimal point an appropriate number of places to the right.
2. If the quotient has no whole number, write 0 in the quotient.
3. Add as many zeros as needed to the end of any decimal dividend to continue to divide. Sometimes the quotient will be a terminating decimal, and other times it will be a repeating decimal.

EXAMPLE 8

Follow the strategy guidelines, above, to divide.

a) $0.375 \div 0.4$ b) $29 \div 0.03$

PROCEDURE: 1. Adjust the dividend and divisor:

a) Move each decimal point one place to the right.

$0.3.75 \div 0.4. \rightarrow 3.75 \div 4$

b) Move each decimal point two places to the right (give 29 a decimal point and some zeros).

$29.00. \div 0.03. \rightarrow 2{,}900 \div 3$

2. Only the quotient in part a requires a zero as the whole number.
3. Add zeros to the end of each dividend for further division.

ANSWER:

a)

$$\begin{array}{r} 0.9375 \\ 4\overline{)3.7500} \\ -\,3\,6 \\ \hline 15 \\ -\,12 \\ \hline 30 \\ -\,28 \\ \hline 20 \\ -\,20 \\ \hline 0 \end{array}$$

$0.375 \div 0.4 = 0.9375$

b)

$$\begin{array}{r} 0966.66 \\ 3\overline{)2900.00} \\ -\,27 \\ \hline 20 \\ -\,18 \\ \hline 20 \\ -\,18 \\ \hline 20 \\ -\,18 \\ \hline 20 \end{array}$$

(repeats...)

$29 \div 0.03 = 966.\overline{6}$

(b) Notice that the recurring remainder, 2, began right away, but we can't abbreviate this repeating digit (with a bar over the 6) until *after* the decimal point in the quotient.

YOU TRY IT 7

Divide. Use Example 8 as a guide.

a) $0.471 \div 8$

b) $\dfrac{9.56}{0.3}$

c) $0.083 \div 0.05$

d) $5 \div 0.004$

e) $3.5908 \div 0.009$

f) $\dfrac{2.58}{1.1}$

You Try It Answers: Section 5.5

YTI 1	a) 1.73	b) 1.747	c) 6.3	YTI 5	a) 0.5	b) 79	c) 380
YTI 2	a) 0.157	b) 0.007	c) 0.0761	YTI 6	a) 1.2	b) $0.\overline{4}$	c) 0.575
YTI 3	a) 0.52	b) 0.075	c) 0.06375	YTI 7	a) 0.058875	b) $31.8\overline{6}$	c) 1.66
					d) 1,250	e) $398.9\overline{7}$	f) $2.\overline{345}$
YTI 4	a) $0.5\overline{1}$	b) $0.061\overline{6}$	c) $0.4\overline{736}$				

Focus Exercises: Section 5.5

Abbreviate any repeating decimals by placing a bar over the repetend.

Divide.

1. $5.4 \div 6$

2. $3.8 \div 2$

3. $\frac{61.5}{5}$

4. $74.1 \div 3$

5. $\frac{87.03}{9}$

6. $51.96 \div 4$

7. $\frac{0.95}{5}$

8. $0.63 \div 7$

9. $1.312 \div 8$

10. $1.737 \div 9$

11. $2.67 \div 5$

12. $\frac{3.09}{5}$

13. $1.62 \div 4$

14. $2.38 \div 4$

15. $0.532 \div 8$

16. $0.676 \div 8$

17. $\frac{4.7}{3}$

18. $\frac{6.5}{3}$

19. $4.8 \div 9$

20. $5.7 \div 9$

21. $3.4 \div 11$

22. $\frac{6.2}{11}$

23. $0.49 \div 15$

24. $0.35 \div 6$

Divide. Be sure to move the decimal points appropriately.

25. $\frac{2.16}{0.6}$

26. $3.42 \div 0.9$

27. $0.468 \div 0.4$

28. $0.736 \div 0.8$

29. $0.198 \div 0.05$

30. $0.267 \div 0.05$

31. $5.6 \div 0.08$

32. $3.6 \div 0.09$

33. $\frac{48}{0.06}$

34. $125 \div 0.05$

35. $0.24 \div 0.012$

36. $0.96 \div 0.032$

37. $0.126 \div 0.3$

38. $\frac{0.535}{0.5}$

39. $0.07128 \div 0.4$

40. $0.0579 \div 0.3$

41. $0.0455 \div 0.09$

42. $0.0316 \div 0.03$

43. $\frac{0.073}{0.11}$

44. $0.038 \div 0.11$

45. $0.0015 \div 0.008$

46. $0.0053 \div 0.004$

47. $0.062 \div 0.25$

48. $\frac{0.021}{0.75}$

Find the decimal equivalent of each fraction.

49. $\frac{5}{2}$

50. $\frac{9}{2}$

51. $\frac{7}{4}$

52. $\frac{13}{4}$

53. $\frac{8}{5}$

54. $\frac{11}{5}$

55. $\frac{3}{8}$

56. $\frac{7}{8}$

57. $\frac{13}{20}$

58. $\frac{29}{20}$

59. $\frac{17}{25}$

60. $\frac{43}{25}$

61. $\frac{5}{6}$

62. $\frac{7}{6}$

63. $\frac{11}{9}$

64. $\frac{23}{9}$

65. $\frac{9}{11}$

66. $\frac{4}{11}$

67. $\frac{8}{15}$

68. $\frac{19}{15}$

69. $\frac{4}{37}$

70. $\frac{5}{37}$

71. $\frac{3}{7}$

72. $\frac{1}{7}$

Objectives

In this section, you will learn to:

- Solve applications involving multiplication and division of decimals.

To successfully complete this section, you need to understand:

- Solving equations (1.6)
- Solving applications (1.7)
- Multiplying decimals (5.4)
- Dividing decimals (5.5)

SECTION 5.6 Applications Involving Decimals

Introduction

There is a variety of situations that involve either multiplying or dividing decimals. If a situation is related to money, or if a formula involves decimals, then we can use the techniques learned in the last two sections to answer questions about the situation.

In each of the following applications you are asked to

- Identify known and unknown values.
- Set up a legend: Let $n = \ldots$.
- Put the values into a formula (equation).
- Solve the equation.
- Write a sentence to answer the question.

Whenever an answer is in terms of dollars and cents, it is necessary that the result has two decimal places. If, in the multiplication process, the answer has fewer than two decimal places, add in the appropriate number of zeros. If, instead, it has more than two decimal places, round it to the nearest penny (hundredth).

Earnings Applications

When a worker is paid the same amount each hour, such as \$7.35 an hour, it is called an hourly wage. To find how much this worker earns in an 8-hour day, we multiply her wage by 8.

Earnings Formula: Number of hours × Hourly wage = Total earnings

EXAMPLE 1 Nancy is paid \$7.35 an hour. What is her wage for an 8-hour day?

PROCEDURE: Use the earnings formula to calculate her total earnings.

ANSWER: *Legend:* Let n = Nancy's wage for an 8-hour day.

number of hours × hourly wage = total earnings

$$8 \times \$7.35 = n$$

You should have found that: Nancy earns \$58.80 for an 8-hour day at work.

You finish it: *Multiply* $8 \times \$7.35$.

EXAMPLE 2 Reza earns \$97.20 for an 8-hour day. How much does he earn per hour?

PROCEDURE: Use the earnings formula. Reza's total earnings are \$97.20. We don't know his hourly wage.

PROCEDURE: *Legend:* Let n = amount Reza earns per hour.

hours worked × hourly wage = total earnings

$$8 \times n = \$97.20$$ To isolate the variable, we must divide each side by 8.

$$8 \div 8 \times n = \$97.20 \div 8$$

$$n = \_\_\_\_\_$$

SENTENCE: Reza earns \$12.15 per hour.

You finish it: *Divide* $\$97.20 \div 8$.

YOU TRY IT 1

For each problem, set up a legend and an equation, and solve. Write the answer as a sentence.

a) Connie is paid \$11.24 per hour at her job. How much will she earn in a day if she works 7.5 hours?

Legend:

Sentence:

b) Hector earned \$435.60 in a week in which he worked 30 hours. How much did Hector earn per hour?

Legend:

Sentence:

Rectangle Applications: Area, Length, and Width

As you know, the area of a rectangle can be found using a formula that involves multiplication:

Length × Width = Area

Remember that area is always represented in square units, such as square inches $\left(\text{in.}^2\right)$ or square centimeters $\left(\text{cm}^2\right)$.

EXAMPLE 3 A rectangular planter is 2.25 feet wide and 9.5 feet long. What is the area of the planter?

ANSWER: *Legend:* Let n = the area

$2.25 \times 9.5 = n$

$\_\_\_\_\_\_ = n$

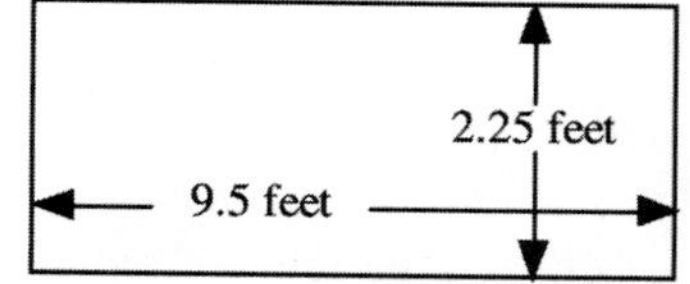

You finish it:

Multiply 2.25×9.5

SENTENCE: The area of the planter is 21.375 square feet.

EXAMPLE 4 A rectangular yard is 10.5 meters long. Its area is 90.3 square meters. What is the width of the yard?

ANSWER: *Legend:* Let n = the width

$n \times 10.5 = 90.3$

$n \times 10.5 \div 10.5 = 90.3 \div 10.5$

$n = \_\_\_$

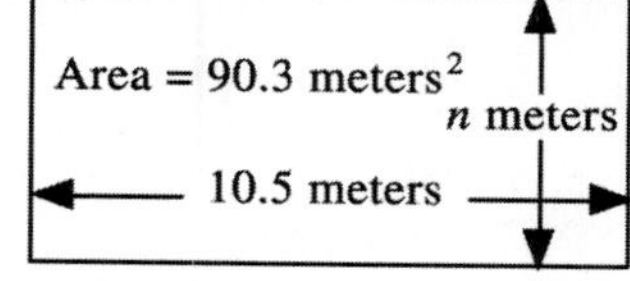

You Finish it:

Divide $90.3 \div 10.5$

SENTENCE: The width of the yard is 8.6 meters.

YOU TRY IT 2

A rectangular bedroom is 12.7 feet long and 9.1 feet long. What is the area of this bedroom? Set up a legend and an equation, and solve.

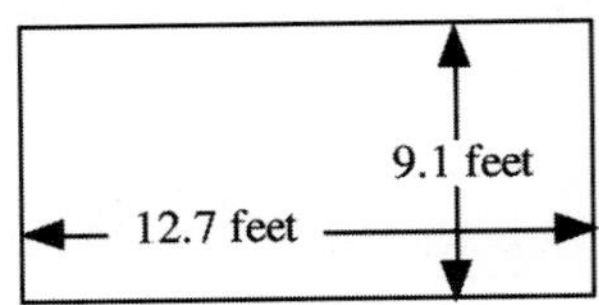

YOU TRY IT 3

A rectangular conference room is covered by 51.3 square yards of carpet. The width of the room is 5.4 yards. What is the length of the conference room? Set up a legend and an equation, and solve.

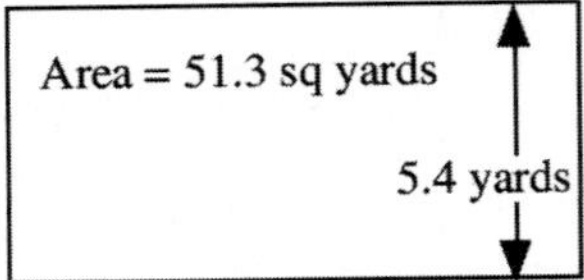

Circle Applications: Radius and Circumference

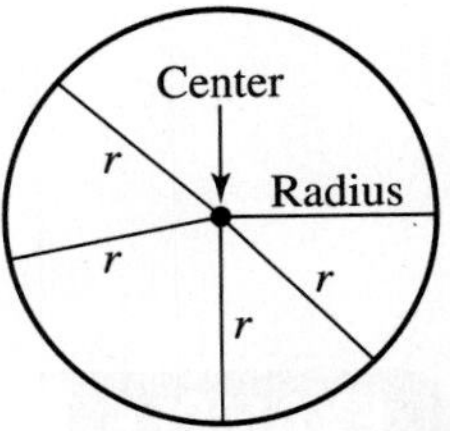

A circle is a round geometric figure with a center point. The center point is the same distance from every point on the circle. This common distance from the center to every point on the circle is called the **radius**, and it is represented in formulas by the letter r.

Recall from Section 5.1 that π is a decimal number that neither terminates nor repeats. Rounded to the nearest hundredth, π is approximately 3.14, written $\pi \approx 3.14$.

The perimeter of a circle is called the **circumference**. It measures the distance around the circle. The formula for the circumference is

$$\boldsymbol{C = 2 \cdot \pi \cdot r} \quad \text{(more commonly read } C = 2\pi r\text{)}$$

$$\boldsymbol{C \approx 2 \times 3.14 \times r.}$$

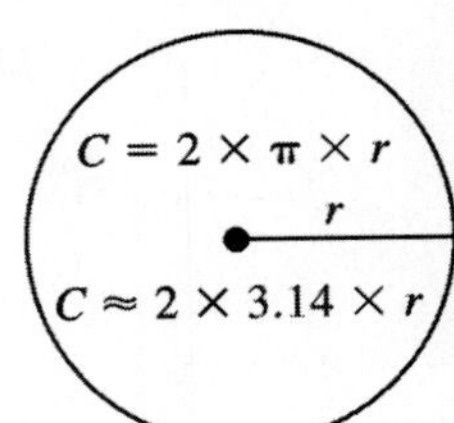

In an equation, we represent this formula with an equal sign, and multiply $2 \times 3.14 = 6.28$, to get

$$C = 6.28 \times r$$

EXAMPLE 5 A circular window has a radius of 1.5 meters. What is the circumference of the window?

ANSWER: *Legend:* Let n = the circumference

$n = 6.28 \times 1.5$

$n =$ ______

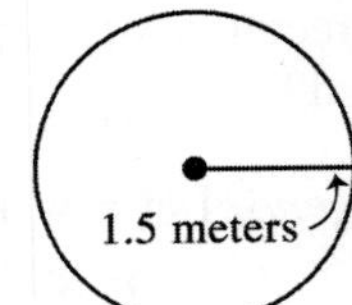

You Finish it:

Multiply 6.28 × 1.5

SENTENCE: The circumference of the window is about 9.42 meters.

EXAMPLE 6 The cover for a circular spa has a circumference of 39.25 feet. What is the radius of the spa cover?

ANSWER: *Legend:* Let $n =$ the radius

$$39.25 = 6.28 \times n$$

$$39.25 \div 6.28 = 6.28 \div 6.28 \times n$$

$$\_\_\_\_\_\_ = n$$

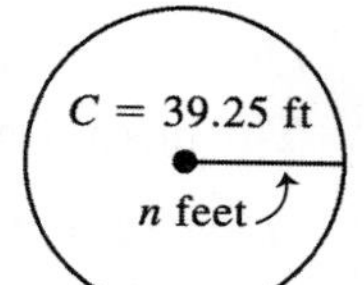

You Finish it:

Divide $39.25 \div 6.28$

SENTENCE: The radius of the spa cover is about 6.25 feet.

Why do the sentence answers to Examples 5 and 6 include the word *about*?

____

____

YOU TRY IT 4 *The center jump circle on a basketball court has a radius of 6 feet. What is the circumference of this jump circle? Set up a legend and an equation, and solve.*

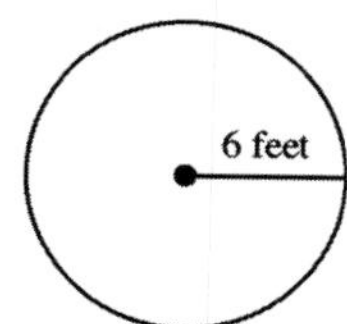

YOU TRY IT 5 *The lens on the end of a telescope is circular and has a circumference of 20.41 centimeters. What is the length of the radius of the lens? Set up a legend and an equation, and solve.*

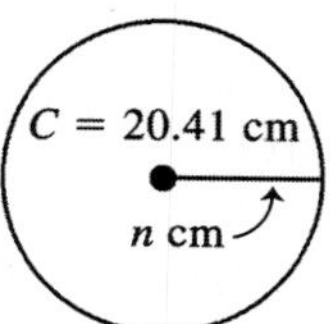

Miles per Gallon Applications

A car is advertised as getting 24 miles per gallon, on average. This means that if the car has 2 gallons of gas, it should be able to go 24 miles on the first gallon and 24 additional miles on the second gallon. In other words, it should go 2×24 miles $= 48$ miles.

Of course, different driving conditions, such as freeway driving or city street driving, can make a difference in the miles per gallon a car gets; this is why we say *average* miles per gallon.

The gas mileage formula (miles per gallon—MPG) is:

Number of gallons $\times$ Average miles per gallon $=$ Total number of miles

or

Gallons $\times$ MPG $=$ Total miles

EXAMPLE 7

On a recent trip, Jim started with a full tank of gas and drove 272 total miles. At the end of the first day, he bought 8.5 gallons to refill his tank. What was his car's average miles per gallon on that first day?

PROCEDURE: Use the gas mileage formula: Gallons × MPG = Total miles.
The unknown is the miles per gallon (MPG)

ANSWER: *Legend:* Let $n =$ the average miles per gallon

$8.5 \times n = 272$ To isolate the variable, we must divide each side by 8.5.

$8.5 \div 8.5 \times n = 272 \div 8.5$

$n =$ _______

You Finish it:

Divide $272 \div 8.5$

SENTENCE: Jim's car averaged 32 miles per gallon on that first day.

YOU TRY IT 6

Su-Ki wanted to check out the gas mileage of her new car. To start, she filled up the tank, set the "trip-o-meter" to 000, then drove as she normally does for a week. At the end of the week she checked the mileage and filled up the tank. She had driven 194.25 miles and her car used 10.5 gallons. What was Su-Ki's car's miles per gallon for that week?

Legend:

Sentence:

Shopping Applications

Two formulas common to shopping are:

1. **Number of items × Price of each item = Total price**

   This is useful if you purchase, for example, 8 apples where each apple has a price of $0.65:

Number of items	×	Price of each item	=	Total price
8	×	$0.65	=	$5.20

We can use this formula if the unknown value is the price of each item, as in **YTI 7a**.

2. **Number of pounds × Price per pound = total price**

   You use this formula to find the total price, for example, of a watermelon that costs $0.38 per pound. If the watermelon weighs 9.4 pounds, then what is the total price of the watermelon?

Number of pounds	×	Price per pound	=	Total price
9.4	×	$0.38	=	$3.572

   This price must be rounded to the nearest penny, so the total price will be $3.57.

We can use this formula if the unknown value is the weight of the item, as in **YTI 7b**.

YOU TRY IT 7

Sara checked her receipt after getting home from shopping. (For each, set up a legend and an equation, then solve.)

a) She noticed that the 12 boxes of macaroni and cheese she purchased cost her a total of \$7.44. What was the price of each box?

b) Sara also noticed that a package of steaks cost her \$7.56. On the package it showed that the total weight was 2.1 pounds but the price per pound was not listed. What was the price per pound of the steak?

Distance, Rate, and Time Applications

The distance someone can travel, whether by car, bicycle, or on foot, is based on the formula

Rate × Time = Distance.

In this formula, rate is another word for speed and is often measured in miles per hour (mph). Time is often measured in hours, and distance is often measured in miles.

The rate is an *average* rate because it's rare to travel the exact same speed for any great length of time. When driving, riding a bike, or jogging, it's common to change speeds for a variety of reasons, such as slowing down to stop at a stop sign.

Someone who rides a bike an average of 12 miles per hour for 3 hours is able to travel a total distance of 36 miles:

Rate	×	Time	=	Distance
12 mph	×	3 hours	=	36 miles

We can use this formula if the unknown value is the rate, as in **YTI 8**, or the time, as in **YTI 9**.

YOU TRY IT 8

Wayne was able to run 11.4 miles in 1.2 hours. What was his average rate?

Legend:

Sentence:

YOU TRY IT 9

Kyla races motorcycles. Normally, she is able to average 35 mph on a winding cross country course. If the course she is racing on Saturday is 80.5 miles long, how many hours should it take her to complete the race?

Legend:

Sentence:

You Try It Answers: Section 5.6

YTI 1 a) Legend: Let n = earnings for the day.
Equation: $7.5 \times 11.24 = n$
Sentence: Connie will earn \$84.30 if she works 7.5 hours.

b) Legend: Let n = Hector's earnings per hour.
Equation: $30 \times n = 435.60$
Sentence: Hector earned \$14.52 per hour.

YTI 2 Legend: Let n = the area of the bedroom.
Equation: $12.7 \times 9.1 = n$
Sentence: The area of the bedroom is 115.57 square feet.

YTI 3 Legend: Let n = the length of the room.
Equation: $n \times 5.4 = 51.3$
Sentence: The length of the room is 9.5 yards.

YTI 4 Legend: Let n = the circumference of the circle.
Equation: $n = 6.28 \times 6$
Sentence: The circumference of the jump circle is about 37.68 feet.

YTI 5 Legend: Let n = the length of the radius.
Equation: $20.41 = 6.28 \times n$
Sentence: The radius of the lens is about 3.25 centimeters.

YTI 6 Legend: Let n = the miles per gallon.
Equation: $10.5 \times n = 194.25$
Sentence: Su-Ki's car averaged 18.5 miles per gallon that week.

YTI 7 a) Legend: Let n = the price of each box.
Equation: $12 \times n = 7.44$
Sentence: The price of each box was \$0.62.

b) Legend: Let n = price per pound.
Equation: $2.1 \times n = 7.56$
Sentence: The price of the steak was \$3.60 per pound.

YTI 8 Legend: Let n = Wayne's rate.
Equation: $n \times 1.2 = 11.4$
Sentence: Wayne's average rate was 9.5 miles per hour.

YTI 9 Legend: Let n = the number of hours.
Equation: $35 \times n = 80.5$
Sentence: Kyla should finish the race in 2.3 hours.

Focus Exercises: Section 5.6

Solve. Answer each question with a complete sentence.

1. Jaime earns \$14.75 per hour working as a mechanic, and she works 8 hours each day. How much does Jaime earn each day?

2. Allison is paid \$10.98 per hour at her job, and she works 6.5 hours each day. How much does Allison earn each day?

3. Andy is paid \$8.25 per hour at his job, and he works 34 hours each week. How much does Andy earn each week?

4. Tom is paid \$11.75 per hour at his job. If he works 152 hours in a month, how much will Tom earn that month?

5. Li worked 7.5 hours yesterday and earned \$64.20. How much does she earn per hour?

6. Shawndra worked 35 hours last week and earned \$341.60. How much does Shawndra earn per hour?

7. Marcus works at an appliance store. He receives a commission on everything he sells. One day he worked 8 hours and earned $154 in commission sales. Regarding his commission, how much did Marcus earn, on average, each hour?

8. Joey works for an electronics superstore. During her 4-hour shift last Saturday, she earned $83.60 in commission sales. Regarding her commission, how much did Joey earn, on average, each hour?

9. The dance floor in a night club is rectangular. It measures 43.5 feet long and 28.5 feet wide. What is the area of the dance floor?

10. A patio is rectangular. It measures 5.2 yards long and 3.5 yards wide. What is the area of the patio?

11. A rectangular pool house has an area of 128.1 square feet. If the length is 12.2 feet, what is the width?

12. A landscaper is designing a yard and wants a small rectangular patch of grass to have an area of 21 square feet. If the width of the patch is 2.4 feet, how long is the length?

13. A circular table top has a radius of 3.5 feet. What is the circumference of the table top? (Round the answer to the nearest tenth.)

14. A circular pond has a radius of 32 meters. What is the circumference of the pond? (Round the answer to the nearest whole number.)

15. The circumference of a lighthouse's circular lobby is 78.5 feet. What is the radius of the lobby?

16. A bicycle wheel has a circumference of 219.8 centimeters. What is the radius of the wheel?

17. Lynn paid $27.60 for a crate of 24 organic oranges. What was the price of each orange?

18. Ron bought a pack of baseball cards for $3.78. The pack contained 6 cards. What was the price of each card?

19. Thom bought 8 cans of gourmet soup for a total of $16.40. What was the price of each can of soup?

20. Laura bought 3.25 yards of linen and paid $20.28. What was the price of a yard of that fabric?

21. Ricky's new car gets 17.8 miles per gallon, and the gas tank holds 13.5 gallons. How many miles can Ricky car travel on a full tank of gas?

22. Dale has a hybrid car that runs on both gasoline and electricity. His car averages 41.5 miles per gallon. How far can Dale drive on 8.4 gallons of gas?

23. On the first day of his road trip, Milo's car traveled 355 miles before he needed to refuel. He refilled the tank with 12.5 gallons of gas. How many miles per gallon did Milo's car average on that day?

24. Beverly drove Dale's hybrid car for one week while Dale was out of town on a business trip. She used it just to get around the city. After a week's time she had driven it 103.8 miles and the car used 2.4 gallons of gas. How many miles per gallon did the car average for that week?

25. During rush hour, it takes Linda 1.5 hours to drive 42 miles. What is Linda's average rate of speed?

26. Jake enjoys cross country skiing and is able to cover a 9.6-mile course in 0.75 hours. For that course, what is Jake's average rate of speed?

27. Kyle rides his bike to the beach. The distance is 24 miles. If he is able to average 15 miles per hour, how long does it take Kyle to reach the beach?

28. Becca loves to go horseback riding. Her favorite trail is 6.5 miles long. If her average rate of speed is 5.2 miles per hour, how long does it take Becca to ride the entire trail?

29. Four friends go out to dinner. They have agreed to split the entire tab (including tax and tip) evenly among themselves. If the total bill is $89.44, how much does each pay?

30. Alan works for a department store that is crazy enough to ask its employees to work on Thanksgiving. Many choose not to, but some will because the store pays 2.25 times their regular hourly wage for the day. If Alan normally earns $7.44 per hour, how much (per hour) will he earn if he works on Thanksgiving?

31. Gabriella works in a department store that pays time and a half (regular pay $\times$ 1.5) for anyone who works on Sunday. Gabriella's regular hourly pay is $8.52. What is Gabriella's hourly pay when she works on Sunday?

32. Maralee is buying a used car from a local dealer. After her $1,000 down payment, she still owes $3,541.44. She made a deal to pay this remaining balance (with no interest!) in 12 equal monthly payments. How much will Maralee pay each month?

Chapter 5 Review

Section 5.1 An Introduction to Decimals

CONCEPT	EXAMPLE
A decimal number is a mixed number with a decimal point that separates the whole number from the fractional part.	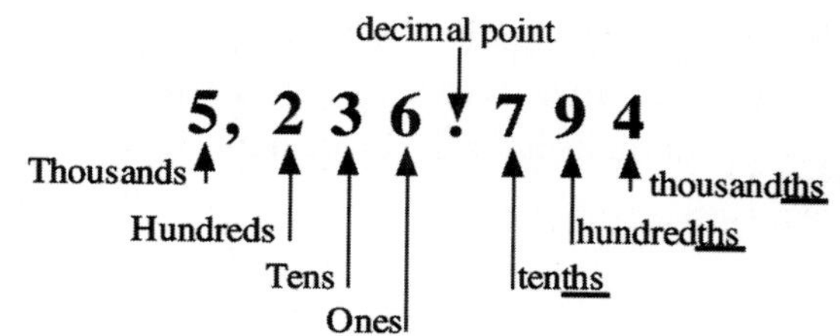
Decimal numbers fit into three categories: 1. Terminating decimals 2. Repeating decimals 3. Non-terminating, nonrepeating decimals	1. 52.9 and 0.625 2. 4.383838383838... and $2.1\overline{7}$ 3. π, which is 3.141592653589...
We can place zeros on the end of any terminating decimal without changing its value. If a decimal number has ending zeros, we may eliminate them, but not those zeros within the decimal number.	$4.7500 = 4.75$ and $0.0030 = 0.003$
Any fraction with a denominator that is a power of 10 (such as 10, 100, 1000, and so on) is called a **decimal fraction**.	0.3 and $\frac{3}{10}$
The number of zeros in the power of 10 (in the denominator) indicates the number of decimal places a decimal number has.	$\frac{893}{1{,}000} = 0.893$
When naming decimals, name the decimal part as you would a whole number, followed by the right-most place in the decimal.	0.46 = forty-six hundredths
If a decimal number has a whole number other than 0, then we use the word *and* to represent the decimal point.	5.9 is written “five and nine tenths.”

Section 5.2 Rounding Decimals

CONCEPT	EXAMPLE
To Round Decimals: 1. Identify the place digit. 2. Identify the rounding digit. a. If the rounding digit is 5 or higher, round up. b. If the rounding digit is 4 or lower, round down. 3. Write all digits after the place digit as zeros. 4. Eliminate all digits after the place digit.	Round 28.714 to the tenths place. 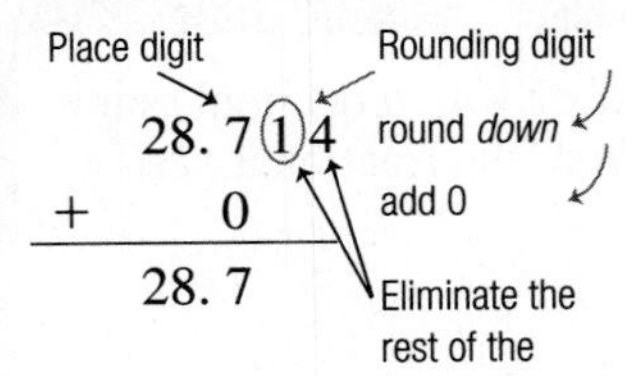 Round 0.3862 to the hundredths place. 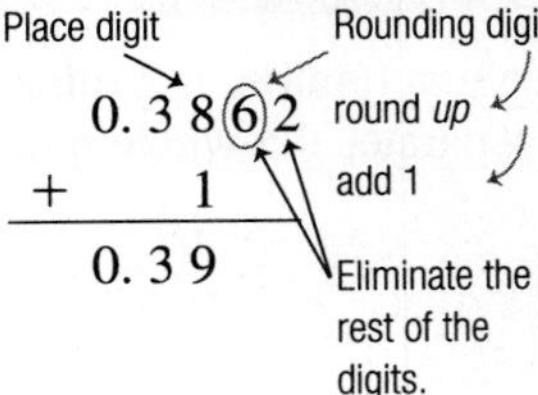

Section 5.3 Adding and Subtracting Decimals

CONCEPT	EXAMPLE
When adding or subtracting decimals, line up the decimal points in each number. It may be necessary to place zeros at the end of some of the numbers to make them all terminate in the same place.	Add 2.03 + 3.1 + 0.528: Place zeros at the end of the first two numbers so that each number has three decimal places. 2.030 3.100 + 0.528 5.658
Subtracting decimals is the same as subtracting whole numbers; sometimes we can subtract directly, and sometimes we must regroup.	Subtract 1.38 from 4.5: 4.50 − 1.38 3.12

Section 5.4 Multiplying Decimals

CONCEPT	EXAMPLE
To multiply decimals: 1. Temporarily inore the decimal points and multiply the numbers (factors) as if they were both whole numbers. 2. Count the total number of decimal places in the factors; this total is the number of decimal places in the product (before any simplifying).	1.3 ← one decimal place + × 0.27 ← two decimal places 91 + 260 0.351 ← three decimal places

CONCEPT	EXAMPLE
If there are not enough decimal places in the answer, then place the appropriate number of zeros to the front of the answer before placing the decimal point.	$0.15 \leftarrow$ two decimal places + $\times\ 0.06 \leftarrow$ two decimal places $0.0090 \leftarrow$ four decimal places We need to place two extra zeros to get four decimal places.
Multiplying a decimal by a power of ten: 1. Count the number of zeros in the power of ten. 2. Move the decimal point that many places to the right.	$3.529 \times 100 = 352.9$ Move the decimal point two places to the right. 3.529

Section 5.5 Dividing Decimals

CONCEPT	EXAMPLE
To divide, the divisor must be a whole number. If the divisor is a decimal number, make it a whole number by moving the decimal points in both the dividend and the divisor the same number of places. 1. Place a decimal point in the quotient directly above the decimal point in the dividend. 2. Divide as if each were a whole number. 3. Place zeros at the end of the dividend if needed.	$$\begin{array}{r} 0.3126 \\ 15\overline{)4.6890} \\ -\underline{45} \\ 18 \\ -\underline{15} \\ 39 \\ -\underline{30} \\ 90 \\ \underline{90} \\ 0 \end{array}$$

Section 5.6 Applications Involving Decimals

CONCEPT	EXAMPLE
Earnings formula	Number of hours × Hourly wage = Total earnings
Area of a rectangle formula	Length × Width = Area
Circumference of a circle formula	$C = 2 \cdot \pi \cdot r \approx 2 \times 3.14 \times r$ $C \approx 6.28 \times r$
Gas mileage formula	Gallons × MPG = Total miles
Formulas common to shopping	1. Number of items × Price of each item = Total price 2. Number of pounds × Price per pound = Total price
Distance traveled formula	Rate × Time = Distance

Chapter 5 Review Exercises

Fill in the blanks.

1. Numbers like $\frac{43}{100}$ and 0.91 are called ______________ fractions. **(5.1)**

2. When rounding to the nearest hundredth, it's the ______________ place that determines whether we round up or round down. **(5.2)**

3. To divide numbers, the divisor must first be a written as a ______________ . **(5.5)**

4. When dividing, the numerator is also called the ______________ . **(5.5)**

Section 5.1

In the given number, name the value of the digit 7.

5. 72.384 **6.** 1,358.47 **7.** 93.706 **8.** 10.6273

Write each of these in word form.

9. $\frac{17}{1000} = 0.017$ **10.** $\frac{3}{100} = 0.03$ **11.** $40\frac{6}{10} = 40.6$ **12.** $200\frac{5}{100} = 200.05$

Write the underlined number in word form.

13. A healthy diet cereal claims to contain only <u>0.006</u> of a gram of sodium per serving.

14. Taiwan's Taipei 101 building is <u>509.1</u> meters high. *Source: www.factmonster.com*

Write each of these as both a fraction and as a decimal.

15. Twenty-three hundredths **16.** Four and four tenths

17. Fifty and eight hundredths **18.** Seventy-six thousandths

Write the underlined number in fraction and decimal form.

19. In early 2005, one Japanese yen was worth <u>twelve thousandths</u> of an Australian dollar.

20. At the 2004 Olympics, the winner of the women's pole vault event, Yelena Isinbayeva of Russia, cleared <u>sixteen and one tenth</u> feet. *Source: 2005 Sports Illustrated Almanac*

Write each fraction as a decimal.

21. $\frac{72}{100}$ **22.** $\frac{3}{100}$ **23.** $\frac{57}{10}$ **24.** $\frac{8}{1000}$

Write each decimal as a fraction. Do not simplify.

25. 0.38 **26.** 1.2 **27.** 0.01 **28.** 2.08

Write each of these repeating decimals using either an ellipsis or a bar over the repetend, whichever is not shown.

29. 1.5555 … **30.** 2.61444 … **31.** 0.232323 …

32. $0.\overline{512}$ **33.** $2.3\overline{8}$ **34.** $4.0\overline{167}$

Section 5.2

Round each of these numbers to the indicated place.

35. 138.65 tenths **36.** 1.5239 hundredths **37.** 26.952 tenths

38. 3.5192 hundredths **39.** 1.499802 thousandths **40.** 24.038 tenths

Round each dollar amount to the nearest penny. Each number represents the amount of sales tax applied to a variety of purchases at a grocery store.

41. $1.5853 **42.** $28.79064 **43.** $0.39526 **44.** $11.99702

Round each dollar amount to the nearest dime (tenth), but express the answer in dollars and cents. Each number represents a 15% tip on a restaurant meal.

45. $8.9235 **46.** $3.582 **47.** $1.2675 **48.** $24.996

Round each of these numbers to the nearest dollar. Each number represents a business expense that is to be entered on a tax form.

49. $128.06 **50.** $49.53 **51.** $267.91 **52.** $1,599.62

For each, round the number as instructed and restate the first sentence using the rounded number.

53. Mariko calculated her GPA to be 3.48953. Round this number to the nearest hundredth.

54. Julia's average daily electricity usage for March was 7.03609 kilowatt-hours. Round this to the nearest thousandth.

Section 5.3

Add, as indicated.

55.
$$\begin{array}{r} 0.351 \\ 0.8 \\ +\ 0.47 \\ \hline \end{array}$$

56.
$$\begin{array}{r} 0.77 \\ 0.065 \\ +\ 0.3 \\ \hline \end{array}$$

57. Add 2.8 and 5.6.

58. Add 1.39 and 2.41.

59. Add 4.7 and 2.38.

60. Add 0.165 and 1.04.

61. Add 6.35, 15.2 and 0.081.

62. Add 3.2, 0.41, 11.907 and 6.

Solve. Answer the question with a sentence.

63. Kelli works in a candy store where customers choose their own quantities and bag the candy themselves. One customer brought four bags of candy to Kelli, and she weighed them one at a time with these results: 1.3 pounds, 0.41 pound, 0.907 pound, and 2 pounds. What was the total weight of the four bags of candy?

64. Zhe-Won, a tax accountant, was working on Samantha's tax return when she came across postage receipts with these totals: $16.32, $20.08, $9.60, $13.41, and $7.45. How much did Samantha pay in postage?

Subtract.

65. $5.74 - 4.2$ **66.** $11.36 - 6$ **67.** $7.2 - 6.51$ **68.** $4 - 1.381$

Evaluate each by first writing it in arithmetic form.

69. Subtract 3.5 from 7.9.

70. Subtract 23.6 from 31.4.

71. Subtract 1.28 from 3.

72. Subtract 0.149 from 1.2.

Solve. Answer the question with a sentence.

73. Brothers Malik and Benjou asked their mother to measure their heights. Their mother found that Malik was 1.28 meters tall and Benjou was 1.55 meters tall. How much taller is Benjou than Malik?

74. Jenny purchased a meal from Burger Basket. The total came to $6.84, including tax, and she paid with a $20 bill. How much change did Jenny receive?

75. Find the perimeter of this geometric figure.

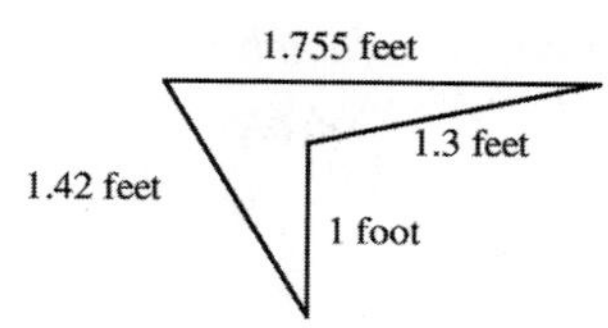

76. Find the length of the third side.

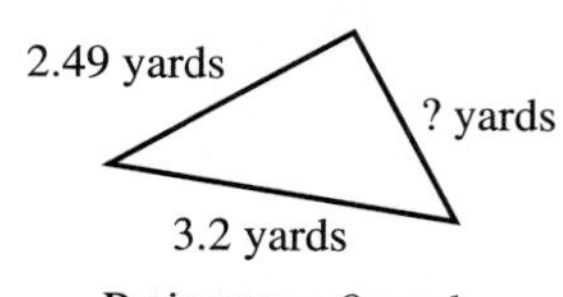

Perimeter = 8 yards

Section 5.4

Multiply by first rewriting each decimal as a fraction. Multiply the fractions, then write the answer as a decimal.

77. 0.3×0.4 **78.** 0.8×0.09 **79.** 0.6×5 **80.** 0.2×0.03

Follow the procedure for multiplying decimals to find the product.

81. 4×2.1 **82.** 0.6×0.73 **83.** 1.2×3.5 **84.** 2.5×5.6

85. 32×0.75 **86.** 1.89×0.06 **87.** 13.4×22.8 **88.** 100.6×0.45

Multiply by moving the decimal point the appropriate number of places to the right.

89. 8.3×10 **90.** 14.12×10 **91.** 2.91×100 **92.** 3.7×100

93. 0.804×100 **94.** $1.691 \times 1{,}000$ **95.** $0.089 \times 1{,}000$ **96.** $0.05 \times 1{,}000$

Solve. Answer the question with a sentence.

97. Carlos is buying a necklace that costs $62.50 for his girlfriend. If the sales tax rate is 0.08, what is the total amount Carlos must pay for the necklace?

98. Jamal is buying a big-screen TV that costs $1,200. If the sales tax rate is 0.075, what is the total amount Jamal must pay for the TV?

Section 5.5

Abbreviate any repeating decimals by placing a bar over the repetend.

Divide.

99. $5.6 \div 7$ **100.** $26.6 \div 4$ **101.** $\dfrac{1.46}{8}$ **102.** $\dfrac{15.7}{6}$

103. $5.2 \div 0.9$ **104.** $0.062 \div 0.11$ **105.** $\dfrac{0.18}{0.025}$ **106.** $\dfrac{0.53}{7.5}$

107. $0.03\overline{)1.058}$ **108.** $0.65\overline{)0.0364}$

Find the decimal equivalent of each fraction.

109. $\frac{4}{5}$

110. $\frac{7}{9}$

111. $\frac{8}{11}$

112. $\frac{1}{8}$

113. $\frac{1}{6}$

114. $\frac{5}{16}$

115. $\frac{13}{25}$

116. $\frac{10}{37}$

Section 5.6

Solve. Answer each question with a complete sentence.

117. Wes earns \$8.75 per hour as a cashier. How much does Wes earn for a 6-hour shift?

118. Sunil is a waiter and worked 5.5 hours yesterday. Including wages and tips, he earned \$93.28. How much did Sunil earn, on average, per hour?

119. The rec room in an apartment complex is rectangular. It measures 62.5 feet long and 33.4 feet wide. What is the area of the rec room?

120. A snare drum has a radius of 6.5 inches. What is the circumference of the snare drum? (Round the answer to the nearest tenth.)

121. Humberto paid \$13.76 for a package of 16 batteries What was the price for each battery?

122. Ruben's truck gets 13.4 miles per gallon, and can hold 24.5 gallons of gas. How far can Ruben's truck travel on a full tank of gas?

123. It took Carmen 3.5 hours to walk 13.3 miles. What was Carmen's average walking rate during that time?

124. Tom and Margaret are financing the purchase of a new bed that costs \$1,872.60, including sales tax. They will pay off the whole amount in 12 months (without interest). How much will Tom and Margaret pay each month?

Chapter 5 Test

1. In 9.6351, name the value of the digit 5.

2. Write 8.03 in word form.

3. Write the underlined number in word form: The pencil is 0.129 meters long.

4. Write fifty and eight hundredths as a decimal.

5. Write the underlined number as a decimal: In 1961, Roberto Clemente won the National League batting title by eight thousandths of a point.

6. Write $\frac{9}{100}$ as a decimal.

7. Write 0.061 as a fraction.

8. Round 49.065 to the nearest whole number.

9. Round 5.9705 to the tenths place.

10. Round \$12.89503 to the nearest penny.

11. Round \$354.53 to the nearest dollar.

Perform the indicated operation. Simplify the answer, if possible. Abbreviate any repeating decimals.

12. Add 1.7 and 3.925.

13. Subtract 2.508 from 3.4.

14. 8.4×2.5

15. 3.8×100

16. $5.3 \div 6$

17. $\frac{0.364}{0.13}$

18. Find the decimal equivalent of $\frac{7}{8}$.

19. Find the decimal equivalent of $\frac{4}{11}$.

Solve. Answer the question with a sentence.

20. JonRey purchased some garden tools for $27.18, including tax, and paid the cashier $40. How much change did JonRey get back?

21. Commuting to and from work last week, Silvia drove her car 189 miles on 8.4 gallons of gas. What was her car's average miles per gallon that week?

22. Donette is making a rectangular crib quilt that has an area of 17.6 square feet. The quilt is 3.2 feet wide. What is the length of the quilt?

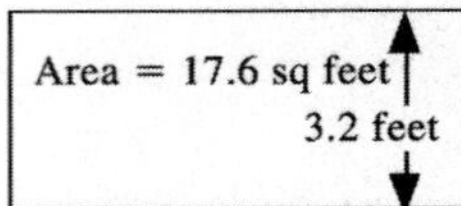

23. The painted circle around a tether ball post has a radius of 5 feet. What is the circumference of this circle?

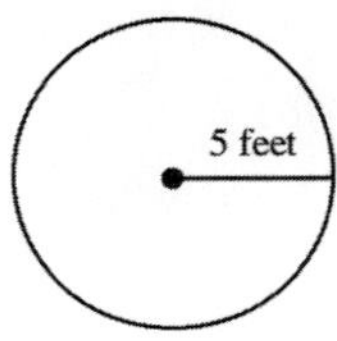

24. Find the length of the third side of this triangle.

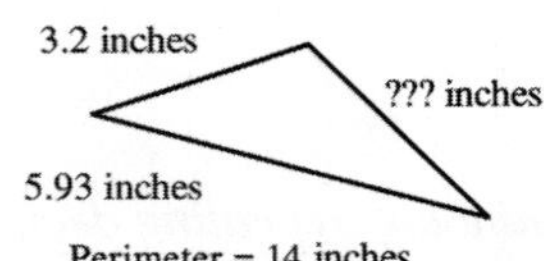

CHAPTER 6

Ratios, Proportions, and Percents

Introduction

In almost every academic and artistic field, both the part and the whole are looked at together.

- In dance, the performer must be aware of, and practice, the smaller steps (part) to be able to perform the entire dance (whole).
- An auto mechanic may look at a car's fuel injection system (the part) and how it affects the engine (the whole) working properly.
- Biologists look at cells (the part) to understand the body (the whole).
- Statisticians ask questions of a small number of people (the part) to predict what the population (the whole) believes.
- Writers must understand *parts* of speech to put a sentence, a paragraph, a chapter, and a *whole* story together.

Where do you use a part of something to better understand the whole?

In our study of ratios, proportions, and percents, we continually compare a part to its whole.

Preparation Exercises

Section 1.6, Equations: *Solve for n.*

1. $6 \cdot n = 114$

2. $185 = n \cdot 5$

Section 3.2, Simplifying Fractions: *Completely simplify.*

3. $\frac{72}{100}$

4. $\frac{32}{80}$

Section 4.2, Building up Fractions: *Build up each to have a denominator of 100.*

5. $\frac{7}{25}$

6. $\frac{3}{5}$

Section 5.1, An Introduction to Decimals: *Write each decimal as a fraction or each fraction as a decmical.*

7. 0.08

8. 1.2

9. $\frac{19}{1000}$

10. $\frac{4}{100}$

Section 5.2, Rounding Decimals: *Round each to the hundredths place.*

11. 3.560914

12. 8.195347

Section 5.4, Multiplying Decimals: *Multiply.*

13. 1.8×6.5 **14.** 0.42×1.03 **15.** 3.7×10 **16.** 0.09×100

17. 71.5×100 **18.** 0.45×10

Section 5.5, Dividing Decimals: *Divide.*

19. $3.43 \div 7$ **20.** $8.5 \div 0.04$ **21.** $0.23 \div 0.6$ **22.** $\frac{7}{8}$

23. $\frac{9}{11}$ **24.** $\frac{2}{15}$

SECTION 6.1 Ratios

Objectives

In this section, you will learn to:

- Define *ratio*, and identify the form in which a ratio is written.
- Simplify ratios.
- Use cross multiplication to determine if two ratios are equivalent.

To successfully complete this section, you need to understand:

- Multiplying whole numbers (1.4)
- Simplifying fractions (3.2)
- Multiplying decimals (5.4)
- Dividing decimals (5.5)

Introduction

Consider this: A father and son went into business together selling collectible sports cards. To start the business, the father, George, invested \$5,000 and the son, Tom, invested \$3,000, a total investment of \$8,000. When they share profits from the income of their sports card shop, George always gets a $\frac{5}{8}$ share and Tom always gets a $\frac{3}{8}$ share. Does this seem like a fair way for them to distribute the profits?

If, in the first month, their profits are \$800, how much of the \$800 should George and Tom receive?

In investment businesses, the greater the amount of the investment, the greater the amount of the *return* when the profits are given out.

We can start to compare George's and Tom's shares by the amount that they originally invested: \$5,000 to \$3,000. However, since not all income will be based in the thousands of dollars, let's look at this in a simplified form: \$5 to \$3.

We can interpret this as for every \$5 that George invested, Tom invested \$3. We can double each amount and the comparison will be consistent: for every \$10 (twice \$5) George invested, Tom invested \$6 (twice \$3).

This type of comparison of numbers is called a *ratio*. A **ratio** is a comparison between two numbers using division. The symbol used to represent a ratio is the colon.

Ratio Forms

The table below shows two ways to write the ratio between two numbers, *A* and *B*. The example next to each compares the amounts of George's and Tom's investments.

1. Standard ratio form	$A : B$	George's amount : Tom's amount	\$5,000 : \$3,000
2. Fractional form	$\frac{A}{B}$	$\frac{\text{George's amount}}{\text{Tom's amount}}$	$\frac{\$5,000}{\$3,000}$
The ratios are read as →	*A* to *B*	George's amount to Tom's amount	\$5,000 to \$3,000

The two numbers forming a ratio are always specific to a certain unit of measure or count.

Examples of units of measure are miles, gallons, pounds, calories and acres. In our example with George and Tom, the unit of measure is *dollars*.

Examples of a count are the number of students, the number of trucks, and the number of candy bars.

Sample ratios are

- 760 calories : 20 candy bars $= \dfrac{\text{760 calories}}{\text{20 candy bars}}$
- 350 miles : 14 gallons $= \dfrac{\text{350 miles}}{\text{14 gallons}}$
- 6 dollars : 100 dollars $= \dfrac{\text{6 dollars}}{\text{100 dollars}}$

A variety of ratios can be written based on known information. In our example with George and Tom's investment, we could create all of these ratios:

Word form	Standard ratio form	Fractional form
George's amount : Tom's amount	\$5,000 : \$3,000	$\dfrac{\$5{,}000}{\$3{,}000}$
George's amount : Total amount	\$5,000 : \$8,000	$\dfrac{\$5{,}000}{\$8{,}000}$
Tom's amount : Total amount	\$3,000 : \$8,000	$\dfrac{\$3{,}000}{\$8{,}000}$

EXAMPLE 1

Ally and Tyra are to receive a total of \$20,000 from their grandfather's will. Of this, Ally will receive \$12,000. According to this situation, write the following ratios in standard ratio form and fractional form.

PROCEDURE: We first need to know how much Tyra will receive, so we subtract: \$20,000 − \$12,000 = \$8,000.

ANSWER:

Word form	Standard ratio form	Fractional form
a) Ally's amount : Tyra's amount	\$12,000 : \$8,000	$\dfrac{\$12{,}000}{\$8{,}000}$
b) Ally's amount : Total amount	\$12,000 : \$20,000	$\dfrac{\$12{,}000}{\$20{,}000}$
c) Tyra's amount : Total amount	\$8,000 : \$20,000	$\dfrac{\$8{,}000}{\$20{,}000}$

YOU TRY IT 1

Dina and Chuck are married, and each contributes to the United Way through their monthly paychecks. Their total monthly contribution is \$150. Each month, Dina contributes \$80 to the United Way. According to this situation, write the following ratios in standard ratio form and fractional form. Use Example 1 as a guide.

Word form	Standard ratio form	Fractional form
a) Dina's amount : Chuck's amount		
b) Dina's amount : Total amount		
c) Chuck's amount : Total amount		

Notice that the simplified ratio is an improper fraction, $\frac{5}{3}$. It is common to leave ratios in *improper fractional form* and not rewrite them as mixed numbers. As a mixed number, it is difficult to build up or to simplify. As a ratio, we must maintain both a numerator and a denominator.

Simplifying Ratios

In fractional form, simplifying a ratio is the same as simplifying a fraction: we divide out any common factors. A ratio of 40 to 24, written as $\frac{40}{24}$, can simplify—by a factor of 8—to $\frac{5}{3}$.

If the unit of measure for each number is the same, then that unit of measure can be divided out as well.

For example, if a rectangular building has a length of 40 feet and a width of 24 feet, then the ratio of length : width is 40 feet : 24 feet, written as $\frac{40 \text{ feet}}{24 \text{ feet}}$. We can simplify the numbers by a factor of 8, and we can simplify the units of measure because they are the same; it is as if we have

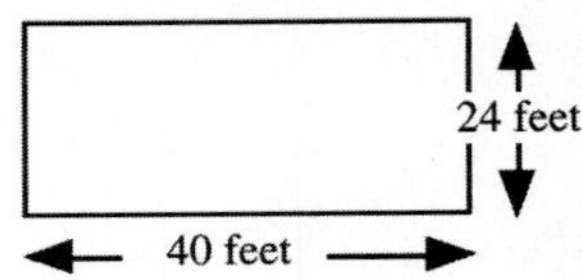

$$\frac{\text{feet}}{\text{feet}} = 1.$$

In other words, $\dfrac{40 \text{ feet}}{24 \text{ feet}} = \dfrac{5 \cdot \cancel{8} \ \cancel{\text{feet}}}{3 \cdot \cancel{8} \ \cancel{\text{feet}}} = \dfrac{5}{3}$

Knowing that this ratio simplifies to $\frac{5}{3}$, an architect can build a model of the building that accurately reflects the building's dimensions.

If the units of measure are not the same, then they may not be divided out. For example, in the ratio 40 dollars : 24 feet, the numbers can be simplified but not the units.

$$\frac{40 \text{ dollars}}{24 \text{ feet}} = \frac{5 \cdot \cancel{8} \text{ dollars}}{3 \cdot \cancel{8} \text{ feet}} = \frac{5 \text{ dollars}}{3 \text{ feet}}$$

Sometimes, the numbers used within the ratio (the numerator and denominator) are decimal numbers. When that happens, we need to multiply by 1, using the same power of 10 in the numerator and denominator, to clear the decimals; then we may simplify the resulting fraction.

For example, Reggie is an experienced waiter and knows how to treat his customers so that he generates, on average, \$3.50 per person in tips. Wayne is relatively new and his average tips are \$2.10 per person. The ratio of Reggie's tips to Wayne's tips can be written as

$$\text{Reggie's tips : Wayne's tips} = \frac{\text{Reggie's tips}}{\text{Wayne's tips}} = \frac{\$3.50}{\$2.10} = \frac{3.5 \text{ dollars}}{2.1 \text{ dollars}} = \frac{3.5}{2.1}$$

To simplify this fraction, we can first multiply both the numerator and denominator by a power of 10 to eliminate the decimals. Because each has one decimal place, we should multiply by 10:

$$\frac{3.5 \times 10}{2.1 \times 10} = \frac{35}{21}$$

Now that the numerator and denominator are whole numbers, we can reduce the fraction by a factor of 7:

$$\frac{35}{21} = \frac{5}{3}$$ This means that for every \$5 that Reggie receives in tips, Wayne receives \$3 in tips.

EXAMPLE 2 Write each ratio in fractional form and then simplify it. Be sure to divide out any common units of measure (or counts) as well.

a) 14 feet : 21 feet b) 45 marbles : 5 marbles c) 3.6 miles : 2.7 liters

PROCEDURE: For part c, first multiply the fraction by $\frac{10}{10}$ to eliminate the decimals.

ANSWER: a) $\frac{14 \text{ feet}}{21 \text{ feet}} = \frac{2 \cdot 7 \text{ feet}}{3 \cdot 7 \text{ feet}} = \frac{2}{3}$ If we want to, we could rewrite this in standard ratio form, 2 : 3.

b) $\frac{45 \text{ marbles}}{5 \text{ marbles}} = \frac{9 \cdot 5 \text{ marbles}}{1 \cdot 5 \text{ marbles}} = \frac{9}{1}$ This fraction cannot simplify to just 9; as a ratio, it must remain in fractional form or be rewritten in standard form.

c) $\frac{3.6 \text{ miles}}{2.7 \text{ liters}} = \frac{3.6 \times 10 \text{ miles}}{2.7 \times 10 \text{ liters}} = \frac{36 \text{ miles}}{27 \text{ liters}} = \frac{4 \cdot 9 \text{ miles}}{3 \cdot 9 \text{ liters}} = \frac{4 \text{ miles}}{3 \text{ liters}}$ In this example, the units of measure are not the same and cannot be divided out.

YOU TRY IT 2

Write each ratio in fractional form and then simplify it. Be sure to divide out any common units of measure (or counts) as well. Use Example 2 as a guide.

a) 18 miles : 24 miles

b) 35 girls : 15 girls

c) 0.3 grams of fat : 1.8 ounces

d) 3.6 feet : 0.4 seconds

Writing Ratios from Phrases

There are some words used in phrases that commonly indicate a ratio:

1. In the context of fractional form, *per* means *divided by*.
2. *For each* means *per 1*, or *divided by 1*.
3. *For every* means *per many*, or *divided by more than 1* (in the denominator).

Typically, when using these words, the units of measure are different, and cannot be divided out.

EXAMPLE 3 Write each of the following comparisons as a ratio in the form of a fraction. Simplify if possible.

ANSWER:

Phrase	Ratio	Simplified
a) 20 miles per gallon (This means "20 miles per 1 gallon.") (The units of measure are miles and gallons.)	$\frac{20 \text{ miles}}{1 \text{ gallon}}$	Already simplified
b) 127 calories for each slice ("For each" means the same as "per 1.") (The unit of measure is calories and the count is the number of slices.)	$\frac{127 \text{ calories}}{1 \text{ slice}}$	Already simplified
c) 2 teachers for every 30 students (The counts are the number of teachers and students.)	$\frac{2 \text{ teachers}}{30 \text{ students}}$	$= \frac{1 \text{ teacher}}{15 \text{ students}}$

YOU TRY IT 3

Write each of the following comparisons as a ratio in the form of a fraction. Simplify if possible. Use Example 3 as a guide.

Phrase	Ratio	Simplified
a) 45 miles per hour		
b) $30 for each ticket (Write $30 as "30 dollars.")		
c) $60 for every 16 pounds		

EXAMPLE 4

Write each ratio as a comparison.

a) $\frac{\text{5 dollars}}{\text{1 ticket}}$ b) $\frac{\text{2 doctors}}{\text{15 patients}}$

ANSWER: a) $\frac{\text{5 dollars}}{\text{1 ticket}}$ <u>$5 per 1 ticket</u> or <u>$5 per ticket</u> or <u>$5 for each ticket</u>

b) $\frac{\text{2 doctors}}{\text{15 patients}}$ <u>2 doctors for every 15 patients</u> Notice that, because the denominator is greater than 1, we use the words *for every* instead of *for each.*

YOU TRY IT 4

Write each ratio as a comparison. Use Example 4 as a guide.

a) $\frac{\text{45 miles}}{\text{1 hour}}$ ______________________

b) $\frac{\text{9 children}}{\text{2 adults}}$ ______________________

c) $\frac{\text{1 winner}}{\text{20 participants}}$ ______________________

Think about it

Where have you heard the word *per* used in every day English? Write some examples.

____

____

Equivalent Ratios

As you know, when two fractions have the same value, such as $\frac{4}{6} = \frac{2}{3}$, we say that they are equivalent fractions. Likewise, if two ratios have the same value, then we say that they are **equivalent ratios**.

If we look at these equivalent fractions, $\frac{4}{6} = \frac{2}{3}$, as two ratios expressed in fractional form (without using any units of measure), then we can rewrite them as $4 : 6 = 2 : 3$.

Using this standard ratio form, we are able to introduce the notion of *extremes* and *means*.

In the ratio form 4 : 6 = 2 : 3, the *outermost* numbers, 4 and 3, are the **extremes**, and the *middle* two numbers, 6 and 2, are the **means**.

Here is a diagram of the extremes and means of both equivalent ratios and equivalent fractions:

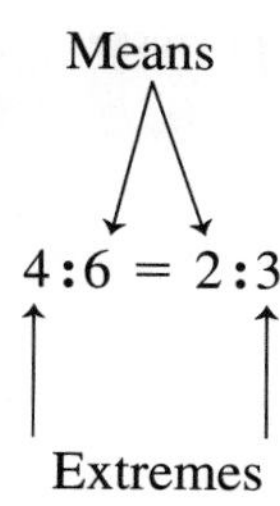

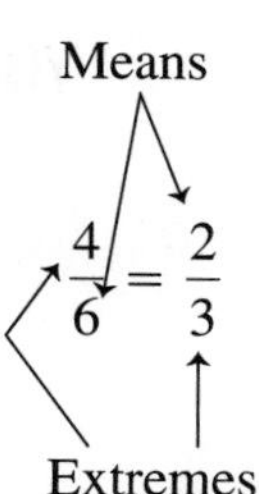

EXAMPLE 5 Identify the extremes and means for the pair of equivalent fractions:

$$\frac{10}{15} = \frac{4}{6}$$

ANSWER: The extremes are 10 and 6.
The means are 15 and 4.

YOU TRY IT 5 *Identify the extremes and means for each pair of equivalent fractions. Use Example 5 as a guide.*

a) $\frac{4}{5} = \frac{20}{25}$ Extremes: ________ Means: ________

b) $\frac{20}{8} = \frac{15}{6}$ Extremes: ________ Means: ______

c) $\frac{9}{15} = \frac{3}{5}$ Extremes: ________ Means: ________

d) $\frac{16}{12} = \frac{4}{3}$ Extremes: ________ Means: ________

We can use the extremes and means to test whether two ratios are equivalent.

The Means-Extremes Product Property: If the product of the extremes = the product of the means, then the two ratios are equivalent.

If the product of the extremes *does not equal* the product of the means, then the two ratios are *not* equivalent.

EXAMPLE 6 Find the products of the extremes and means for each pair of ratios, and determine whether the ratios are equivalent.

a) $\frac{10}{15} \stackrel{?}{=} \frac{4}{6}$

b) $\frac{9}{12} \stackrel{?}{=} \frac{12}{15}$

ANSWER:

a) The product of the extremes is $10 \times 6 = 60$.
The product of the means is $15 \times 4 = 60$.
The ratios $\frac{10}{15}$ and $\frac{4}{6}$ are equivalent.
Note: Both fractions simplify to $\frac{2}{3}$.

b) The product of the extremes is $9 \times 15 = 135$.
The product of the means is $12 \times 12 = 144$.
The ratios $\frac{9}{12}$ and $\frac{12}{15}$ are not equivalent.
Note: $\frac{9}{12}$ simplifies to $\frac{3}{4}$, and $\frac{12}{15}$ simplifies to $\frac{4}{5}$.

YOU TRY IT 6 *Find the products of the means and extremes for each pair of fractions, and determine whether the fractions are equivalent. Use Example 6 as a guide.*

Equivalent ratios?

a) $\frac{4}{5} \overset{?}{=} \frac{20}{25}$ Product of extremes ________ Product of means ________ ________ yes / no

b) $\frac{20}{8} \overset{?}{=} \frac{25}{10}$ Product of extremes ________ Product of means ________ ________ yes / no

c) $\frac{9}{15} \overset{?}{=} \frac{4}{5}$ Product of extremes ________ Product of means ________ ________ yes / no

Cross Multiplication

The direct method for finding the products of the extremes and means is referred to as **cross multiplication**.

Starting with $\frac{4}{3} \overset{?}{=} \frac{8}{6}$

multiply "across" the equal sign,

$$\frac{4}{3} \overset{?}{=} \frac{8}{6}$$

to get

$$4 \times 6 \overset{?}{=} 3 \times 8,$$

and it's true that $24 = 24$. ✓

The product of the extremes = The product of the means.

YOU TRY IT 7 *Determine whether the fractions are equivalent by cross multiplying.*

a) $\frac{2}{3} \overset{?}{=} \frac{8}{12}$ b) $\frac{6}{15} \overset{?}{=} \frac{8}{25}$ c) $\frac{0.4}{1} \overset{?}{=} \frac{0.5}{1.25}$

You Try It Answers: Section 6.1

YTI 1 a) \$80 : \$70; $\frac{\$80}{\$70}$ b) \$80 : \$150; $\frac{\$80}{\$150}$ c) \$70 : \$150; $\frac{\$70}{\$150}$

YTI 2 a) $\frac{3}{4}$ b) $\frac{7}{3}$ c) $\frac{\text{1 gram of fat}}{\text{6 ounces}}$ d) $\frac{\text{9 feet}}{\text{1 second}}$

YTI 3 a) $\frac{\text{45 miles}}{\text{1 hour}}$ b) $\frac{\text{30 dollars}}{\text{1 ticket}}$ c) $\frac{\text{60 dollars}}{\text{16 pounds}} = \frac{\text{15 dollars}}{\text{4 pounds}}$

YTI 4 a) 45 miles per hour or 45 miles for each hour
b) 9 children for every 2 adults
c) 1 winner for every 20 participants

YTI 5
a) The extremes are 4 and 25; the means are 5 and 20.
b) The extremes are 20 and 6; the means are 8 and 15.
c) The extremes are 9 and 5; the means are 15 and 3.
d) The extremes are 16 and 3; the means are 12 and 4.

YTI 6
a) The product of the extremes is $4 \times 25 = 100$; the product of the means is $5 \times 20 = 100$. Yes
b) The product of the extremes is $20 \times 10 = 200$; the product of the means is $8 \times 25 = 200$. Yes
c) The product of the extremes is $9 \times 5 = 45$; the product of the means is $15 \times 4 = 60$. No

YTI 7
a) Yes b) No c) Yes

Focus Exercises: Section 6.1

Fill in the blanks.

1. Feet, meters, ounces, and gallons are examples of ________________.

2. A ratio is a comparison between two numbers using ________________.

3. In the context of fractions, *per* means ________________.

4. If two ratios have the same value, we say that they are ________________ ratios.

Write each of the following comparisons as a ratio in the form of a fraction.

	Phrase	Ratio		Phrase	Ratio
5.	60 miles per gallon		**6.**	\$1.35 for each can	
7.	\$2 for every 3 tickets		**8.**	20 flights per day	
9.	35 miles per hour		**10.**	25 children for every 4 adults	
11.	3 laps every 10 minutes		**12.**	3 autographs for every 25 cards	

Write each fraction as a comparison.

13. $\frac{\text{7 people}}{\text{1 van}}$

14. $\frac{\$8.50}{\text{1 hour}}$

15. $\frac{\text{23.4 miles}}{\text{1 gallon}}$

16. $\frac{\text{8 rooms}}{\text{1 house}}$

17. $\frac{\text{9 lemons}}{\text{5 dollars}}$

18. $\frac{\text{2 coffee shops}}{\text{3 miles}}$

19. $\frac{\text{1 boy}}{\text{2 girls}}$

20. $\frac{\text{5 credits}}{\text{3 members}}$

Write each ratio in fractional form and simplify it completely.

21. 24 feet : 32 feet

22. 20 dollars : 35 dollars

23. 6 hours : 30 hours

24. 9 minutes : 45 minutes

25. 50 miles : 4 hours

26. 45 calories : 6 ounces

27. 120 liters : 30 liters

28. 150 inches : 75 inches

29. 9.6 liters : 0.8 hours

30. 15.6 meters : 1.2 seconds

31. 12.6 degrees : 0.4 degrees

32. 2.8 years : 0.7 years

Write each described ratio in fractional form and simplify it completely.

33. It takes Jupiter about 12 Earth years to orbit the Sun, and it takes Uranus about 84 Earth years to orbit the Sun. Write these orbits as a ratio: Jupiter's time : Uranus's time. *Source: www.windows.ucar.edu*

34. In 2003, the estimated population of Alabama was 4.5 million and the estimated population of Kansas was 2.7 million. Write these populations as a ratio: Alabama's population : Kansas's population

35. In North Carolina, Henderson County has a land area of about 375 square miles and Perquimans County has a land area of about 250 square miles. Write these land areas as a ratio: Henderson's area : Perquimans's area.

36. In 2004, about 52% of high school seniors in both Texas and Washington took the SAT exam. In Texas, the average SAT verbal score was about 490, and in Washington, the SAT verbal score was about 525. Write these SAT verbal scores as a ratio: Texas's scores : Washington's scores.

Write the indicated ratios in standard ratio form, fractional form, and as a simplified fraction.

37. Steve paid \$840 for a pair of season tickets to the Cucamonga Quakes minor league baseball team for both himself and his wife, Lorraine. Steve's seats cost him \$480 and Lorraine's were priced at a discount.

a) Steve's amount : Lorraine's amount **b)** Steve's amount : Total amount **c)** Lorraine's amount : Total amount

38. Paul bought school bonds, issued by the Austin Unified School District, as an investment. He paid \$120 for the Series A bond and \$480 for the Series B bond.

a) Series A amount : Series B amount **b)** Series A amount : Total amount **c)** Series B amount : Total amount

39. Each month, Carmen pays an average utility gas and electric bill of \$120. The electric portion of the bill averages \$90.

a) Electric amount : Gas amount **b)** Electric amount : Total amount **c)** Gas amount : Total amount

40. RaShonda has two children, Zhejan and Leeta, in college. Each semester, she pays a total of \$7,200 in tuition costs. She pays Leeta's college \$2,400 and the rest for Zhejan's college.

a) Zhejan's amount : Leeta's amount **b)** Zhejan's amount : Total amount **c)** Leeta's amount : Total amount

Use cross multiplication to determine whether each pair of fractions is equivalent.

41. $\frac{18}{12} \stackrel{?}{=} \frac{3}{2}$

42. $\frac{15}{6} \stackrel{?}{=} \frac{5}{2}$

43. $\frac{4}{12} \stackrel{?}{=} \frac{5}{10}$

44. $\frac{8}{10} \stackrel{?}{=} \frac{6}{8}$

45. $\frac{12}{30} \stackrel{?}{=} \frac{0.8}{1.5}$

46. $\frac{15}{20} \stackrel{?}{=} \frac{0.2}{0.3}$

47. $\frac{2.5}{1.5} \stackrel{?}{=} \frac{1}{0.6}$

48. $\frac{0.4}{0.6} \stackrel{?}{=} \frac{1.6}{2.4}$

SECTION 6.2 Rates

Objectives

In this section, you will learn to:

- Define and identify *rates*.
- Simplify rates.
- Define and calculate *unit rates*.
- Compare unit prices.

To successfully complete this section, you need to understand:

- Dividing whole numbers (1.5)
- Simplifying fractions (3.2)
- Dividing decimals (5.5)
- Writing ratios from phrases (6.1)
- Simplifying ratios (6.1)

Introduction

Consider this: Gilberto finished the 2004 Baja 1,000 off-road race in 41st place. During the race, he was able to average 50 miles per hour. How many hours did it take him to drive all 1,000 miles?

Recall from Section 6.1 that "50 miles per hour" can be written as a ratio, $\frac{50 \text{ miles}}{1 \text{ hour}}$. This ratio has different units of measure in the numerator and denominator.

A ratio containing different units of measure or counts in the numerator and denominator is called a **rate**. Some of the ratios we saw in Section 6.1 are rates.

$$\frac{760 \text{ calories}}{20 \text{ candy bars}}, \quad \frac{350 \text{ miles}}{14 \text{ gallons}}, \quad \frac{0.3 \text{ grams of fat}}{1.8 \text{ ounces}}, \text{ and } \frac{3.6 \text{ feet}}{0.4 \text{ seconds}} \quad \text{are all rates.}$$

For Gilberto, his racing rate of 50 miles in 1 hour suggests that he will go

- 100 miles in 2 hours; as a rate, this is $\frac{100 \text{ miles}}{2 \text{ hours}}$.
- 500 miles in 10 hours; as a rate, this is $\frac{500 \text{ miles}}{10 \text{ hours}}$.
- 1,000 miles in 20 hours; as a rate, this is $\frac{1{,}000 \text{ miles}}{20 \text{ hours}}$.

By the way, the last rate listed is the answer to the question: It took Gilberto 20 hours to drive all 1,000 miles.

Rates

Rates are best understood when they are completely simplified. For example, the rate of $\frac{760 \text{ calories}}{20 \text{ candy bars}}$ can be simplified by a factor of 20:

$$\frac{760 \text{ calories} \div 20}{20 \text{ candy bars} \div 20} = \frac{38 \text{ calories}}{1 \text{ candy bar}} = 38 \text{ calories per candy bar.}$$

When simplifying a rate, will the units of measure ever divide out? Why or why not?

____

____

EXAMPLE 1 Simplify each rate completely, and write the result in words.

a) $\frac{56 \text{ chairs}}{8 \text{ tables}}$ b) $\frac{4 \text{ counselors}}{30 \text{ campers}}$ c) $\frac{1.5 \text{ miles}}{0.09 \text{ gallons}}$

PROCEDURE: For part (c), we need to first multiply both the numerator and denominator by 100 to eliminate the decimals.

ANSWER:

	Rate		Simplified rate	Word form
a)	$\frac{56 \text{ chairs} \div 8}{8 \text{ tables} \div 8}$	=	$\frac{7 \text{ chairs}}{1 \text{ table}}$	7 chairs per table
b)	$\frac{4 \text{ counselors} \div 2}{30 \text{ campers} \div 2}$	=	$\frac{2 \text{ counselors}}{15 \text{ campers}}$	2 counselors for every 15 campers

	Rate		Simplified rate			Word form
c)	$\dfrac{1.5 \text{ miles} \times 100}{0.09 \text{ gallons} \times 100}$	=	$\dfrac{150 \text{ miles} \div 3}{9 \text{ gallons} \div 3}$	=	$\dfrac{50 \text{ miles}}{3 \text{ gallons}}$	50 miles for every 3 gallons

The answer in Example 1, part c shows multiplying both the numerator and denominator by 100. Why should each be multiplied by 100 and not 10?

____

____

YOU TRY IT 1

Simplify each rate completely, and write the result in words. Use Example 1 as a guide.

	Rate	Simplified rate	Word form
a)	$\dfrac{42 \text{ pounds}}{7 \text{ inches}}$		
b)	$\dfrac{18 \text{ girls}}{12 \text{ boys}}$		
c)	$\dfrac{3 \text{ dollars}}{1.2 \text{ miles}}$		

Unit Rates

In this chapter, we have seen many units of measure, such as ounces, feet, dollars, and gallons. Other types of units include a *single* can of soda in a case of soda, a *single* crayon in a box of crayons, and a *single* apple in a bag of apples. In other words, *unit* often means *one* of something.

A **unit rate** is a rate in which the denominator has been reduced to 1 item. For instance, in Example 1 part a, the rate of $\frac{56 \text{ chairs}}{8 \text{ tables}}$ reduced to a unit rate of $\frac{7 \text{ chairs}}{1 \text{ table}}$. In this case, the single unit is 1 table, and the phrase we can write includes the word *per*, as in 7 chairs per table.

In a rate, the units of measure never divide out, so we may ignore them for the long division process and include them when we write the unit rate. Remember, the unit rate will always have 1 in the denominator.

Sometimes a completely simplified rate is a unit rate, so we don't need to do any other work. For example, a runner who runs at a rate of $\frac{16 \text{ miles}}{2 \text{ hours}}$ has a simplified rate of $\frac{8 \text{ miles}}{1 \text{ hour}}$ or 8 miles per hour.

Other times, long division is necessary. For example, $\frac{55 \text{ miles}}{4 \text{ gallons}}$ cannot simplify directly, but we can divide (using long division, as shown at right.)

We can then write the unit rate as $\frac{13.75 \text{ miles}}{1 \text{ gallon}}$ or 13.75 miles per gallon.

$$
\begin{array}{r}
13.75 \\
4\overline{)55.00} \\
-\ 4 \\
\hline
15 \\
-\ 12 \\
\hline
30 \\
-\ 28 \\
\hline
20 \\
-\ 20 \\
\hline
0
\end{array}
$$

EXAMPLE 2

Simplify each rate to a unit rate, and write the unit rate in words.

a) $\dfrac{80 \text{ people}}{5 \text{ square miles}}$ b) $\dfrac{\$9.00}{12 \text{ cans}}$ c) $\dfrac{0.3 \text{ gallons}}{1.2 \text{ miles}}$

PROCEDURE: For parts a and b use long division. For part c, recall that when dividing decimals, we need to first adjust the decimal points so that the divisor is a whole number.

ANSWER:

	Rate	Long division		Unit rate	Word form
a)	$\frac{80 \text{ people}}{5 \text{ square miles}}$	$5\overline{)80}$ = 16 →		$\frac{16 \text{ people}}{1 \text{ square mile}}$	16 people per square mile
b)	$\frac{9 \text{ dollars}}{12 \text{ cans}}$	$12\overline{)9.00}$ = 0.75 →		$\frac{0.75 \text{ dollar}}{1 \text{ can}}$	\$0.75 per can
c)	$\frac{0.3 \text{ gallon}}{1.2 \text{ miles}}$	$1.2\overline{)0.3}$ →	$12\overline{)3.00}$ = 0.25 →	$\frac{0.25 \text{ gallon}}{1 \text{ mile}}$	0.25 gallon per mile

YOU TRY IT 2

Simplify each rate to a unit rate, and write the unit rate in words. Use Example 2 as a guide.

	Rate	Simplified rate	Word form
a)	$\frac{98 \text{ feet}}{7 \text{ seconds}}$		
b)	$\frac{237 \text{ words}}{5 \text{ minutes}}$		
c)	$\frac{\$6.50}{2.6 \text{ pounds}}$		

When a rate is written within a problem, it is not always written as a phrase that is immediately obvious. In the example below, the pieces of information—the numerator and denominator of the rate—are in two different sentences.

Consider this: Melanie was paid \$120 for removing a dead tree. The project took her 7 hours to complete. Write her earnings as an hourly rate.

From the given information, write a fractional rate. Simplify the rate to a unit rate, and write it as a phrase.

An hourly rate is how much someone earns *per hour*. This suggests that the unit of measure, hours, is in the denominator, $\frac{???}{\text{hours}}$. The other unit of measure is dollars, so from the given information, the rate becomes $\frac{120 \text{ dollars}}{7 \text{ hours}}$.

To write this as a unit rate, we use long division: $7\overline{)120.000}$ = 17.142

Because we are dealing with money, it's good to stop the division after three decimal places and round to the nearest penny: \$17.14. As a unit rate, this can be written as $\frac{17.14 \text{ dollars}}{1 \text{ hour}}$, and then we can answer the question: Melanie earned \$17.14 per hour.

EXAMPLE 3

On a recent trip, Aden drove 147 miles before refilling the gas tank with 8.4 gallons. Write his car's fuel efficiency as a unit rate per gallon.

PROCEDURE: From the given information, write a fractional rate. Simplify the rate to a unit rate, and write it as a phrase.

Per gallon means that the number of gallons is in the denominator.

ANSWER:

Rate	Long division	Unit rate	Word form
$\frac{147 \text{ miles}}{8.4 \text{ gallons}}$	$8.4\overline{)147.0}$ = 17.5 →	$\frac{17.5 \text{ miles}}{1 \text{ gallon}}$	Aden's car's mileage rate was 17.5 miles per gallon.

YOU TRY IT 3

From the given information, write a fractional rate. Simplify the rate to a unit rate, and write it as a phrase. Use Example 3 as a guide.

a) Last week, Nate worked 18 hours and earned a total of $174, including wages and tips, for delivering pizza. Write his earnings as an hourly rate, a unit rate per hour.

b) Last month, Kara's electric bill showed that she used 120 kilowatt-hours, for which she paid $18. Write her average energy charge per kilowatt-hour.

Comparing Unit Prices

When shopping for food, it's common to compare prices of items that are very similar. The unit rate for the price of an item is called **unit price**. For example, the unit price for milk is $2.95 per gallon. This can be written as $\frac{\$2.95}{1\text{ gallon}}$. If we have a choice between two different brands of the same item, then one with the lower unit price is said to be a *better buy*.

It's common to write unit prices as *dollars per unit*. This means that dollars will always be in the numerator.

Consider, for example, two bags of chips that each weigh 28 ounces. If Gorkin's brand costs $2.58 and Byrd's brand costs $2.79, then it's clear that Gorkin's chips are a better buy because those chips cost less.

However, if the bags are different in size and price, it's not as easy to know which bag is the better buy. If, for example, Gorkin's bag of chips weighs 28 ounces and costs $2.46 and Byrd's small bag of chips weighs 16 ounces and costs $1.19, then it's not immediately clear which is the better buy.

We can determine which is the better buy by finding the unit price for each bag of chips:

Gorkin's: $\frac{2.46\text{ dollars}}{28\text{ ounces}}$ $\quad 28\overline{)2.460}$ with quotient 0.088 $\rightarrow \frac{0.088\text{ dollars}}{1\text{ ounce}}$, which rounds to $0.09 per ounce.

Byrd's: $\frac{1.19\text{ dollars}}{16\text{ ounces}}$ $\quad 16\overline{)1.190}$ with quotient 0.074 $\rightarrow \frac{0.074\text{ dollars}}{1\text{ ounce}}$, which rounds to $0.07 per ounce.

This time, Byrd's chips are the better buy.

EXAMPLE 4

A case of 24 cans of Blitz Cola costs $9.60. A case of 16 cans of Zephyr Cola costs $5.60. Which is the better buy?

PROCEDURE: For each, find the unit price of an individual can of cola.

ANSWER:

	Rate	Long division		Unit price	Word form
Blitz:	$\frac{9.60\text{ dollars}}{24\text{ cans}}$	$24\overline{)9.60}$ = 0.40	$\rightarrow$	$\frac{0.40\text{ dollars}}{1\text{ can}}$	$0.40 per can
Zephyr:	$\frac{5.60\text{ dollars}}{16\text{ cans}}$	$16\overline{)5.60}$ = 0.35	$\rightarrow$	$\frac{0.35\text{ dollars}}{1\text{ can}}$	$0.35 per can

SENTENCE: Zephyr Cola is the better buy at $0.35 per can.

YOU TRY IT 4

From the given information, write each rate as a unit price, write it as a phrase, and answer the question. Use Example 4 as a guide.

a) The cost of a box of 64 pens is \$19.20. The cost of a box of 48 pens is \$16.80. Which is the better buy?

b) The cost of 12 donuts at Lucky Donuts is \$5.40. The cost of a box of 15 donuts at Donuts To Go is \$6.30. Which is the better buy?

You Try It Answers: Section 6.2

YTI 1
a) $\frac{6 \text{ pounds}}{1 \text{ inch}}$; 6 pounds per inch.
b) $\frac{3 \text{ girls}}{2 \text{ boys}}$; 3 girls for every 2 boys
c) $\frac{5 \text{ dollars}}{2 \text{ miles}}$; \$5 for every 2 miles

YTI 2
a) $\frac{14 \text{ feet}}{1 \text{ second}}$; 14 feet per second
b) $\frac{47.4 \text{ words}}{1 \text{ minute}}$; 47.4 words per minute
c) $\frac{\$2.50}{1 \text{ pound}}$; \$2.50 per pound

YTI 3
a) $\frac{\$174}{18 \text{ hours}}$; \$9.67 per hour (This number was rounded from 9.666.)
b) $\frac{\$18}{120 \text{ kilowatt-hour}}$; \$0.15 per kilowatt-hour

YTI 4
a) Box of 64 pens: $\frac{0.30 \text{ dollars}}{1 \text{ pen}}$; \$0.30 per pen;box of 48 pens: $\frac{0.35 \text{ dollars}}{1 \text{ pen}}$; \$0.35 per pen. The box of 64 pens is the better buy at \$0.30 per pen.
b) Lucky Donuts: $\frac{0.45 \text{ dollars}}{1 \text{ donut}}$; \$0.45 per donut; Donuts To Go: $\frac{0.42 \text{ dollars}}{1 \text{ donut}}$; \$0.42 per donut. Donuts To Go is the better buy at \$0.42 per donut.

Focus Exercises: Section 6.2

True or False.

1. A rate is a special type of ratio. ____________

2. In a rate, the units of measure in the numerator and denominator are always the same. ____________

Fill in the blanks.

3. In a fractional unit rate, the ________________ is always 1 unit of measure.

4. In a unit price, the numerator's unit of measure is always ________________.

Simplify each rate, and write the result in words.

5. $\frac{390 \text{ stitches}}{6 \text{ inches}}$

6. $\frac{210 \text{ dollars}}{9 \text{ months}}$

7. $\frac{63 \text{ gallons}}{12 \text{ weeks}}$

8. $\frac{\text{45 laps}}{\text{75 minutes}}$

9. $\frac{\text{12 supervisors}}{\text{72 employees}}$

10. $\frac{\text{60 employees}}{\text{24 printers}}$

11. $\frac{\text{90 pounds}}{\text{12 passengers}}$

12. $\frac{\text{108 tourists}}{\text{6 busses}}$

Simplify each rate to a unit rate, and write the unit rate in words.

13. $\frac{\text{256 voters}}{\text{4 precincts}}$

14. $\frac{\text{215 students}}{\text{5 algebra classes}}$

15. $\frac{\text{10 yards of fabric}}{\text{8 doll dresses}}$

16. $\frac{\text{135 dollars}}{\text{18 hours}}$

17. $\frac{\text{1.5 kilowatts}}{\text{0.6 hours}}$

18. $\frac{\text{8.5 pounds}}{\text{3.4 feet}}$

19. $\frac{\text{42.9 miles}}{\text{2.6 gallons}}$

20. $\frac{\text{\$5.40}}{\text{12 tickets}}$

From the given information, write a fractional rate. Simplify the rate to a unit rate, and write it as a phrase.

21. Kevin pays $432 every 6 months for his auto insurance. Write this payment as a unit rate per month.

22. Michelle hit a golf ball 280 yards that, unfortunately, landed in a sand trap. It took 5 full seconds to travel that far. Write how fast the golf ball traveled as a unit rate per second.

23. Paolo figured that he has owned 18 cars over the last 45 years. Write the average length of his car ownership as a unit rate per car.

24. It cost Karin $460 to fly 1,840 miles from Los Angeles, California, to Juneau, Alaska. Write the cost of her flight as a unit rate per mile.

25. Working a total of 45 hours last month as a waitress, Taira earned a total of $558, including wages and tips. Write her earnings as an hourly rate, a unit rate per hour.

26. Marta paid $7.26 for 3.3 pounds of ground beef. Write the price per pound.

27. A box of Raisin Bran has 6.3 grams of sodium in 18 servings. Write the number of grams of sodium per serving.

28. In 1933, Babe Ruth hit 34 home runs in 459 at bats. Write the number of at bats per home run.

From the given information, write each rate as a unit price, write it as a phrase, and answer the question.

29. A tray of 24 Gourmet chocolate chip cookies costs $3.60, and a tray of 30 Savory chocolate chip cookies costs $4.20. Which is the better buy?

30. A bag of 18 mini Goodie candy bars costs $3.78, and a bag of 25 mini Yummie candy bars costs $5.50. Which is the better buy?

31. A box of 8 Lightning energy bars costs $7.36, and a box of 12 Thunder energy bars costs $11.40. Which is the better buy?

32. A 12-pack of Zapper Energy Water costs $13.80, and an 18-pack of Fizzit Energy Water costs $19.80. Which is the better buy?

33. A 42-ounce jug of orange juice costs $2.94, and a 64-ounce jug of orange juice costs $3.84. Which is the better buy?

34. A 13.5-ounce bag of Mayse corn chips costs $2.97, and a 17.5-ounce bag of Bluze corn chips costs $4.20. Which is the better buy?

SECTION 6.3 Proportions

Objectives

In this section, you will learn to:

- Define and identify *proportions.*
- Set up proportions.
- Solve proportions.
- Work applications involving proportions.

To successfully complete this section, you need to understand:

- Solving equations (1.6)
- Simplifying fractions (3.2)
- Ratios (6.1)
- Equivalent ratios (6.1)
- Cross multiplication (6.1)

Introduction

"That's not fair!" cried Alicia. She was complaining to her parents about the number of birthday gifts her sister, Juanita, received. After all, Alicia received 12 presents on her own sixth birthday, just last month, but Juanita received 16 gifts today, on her eighth birthday.

"Yes, it is fair," countered her mother. "On your eighth birthday, you'll get 16 gifts, too."

"Yes," Alicia argued, "but the month after that, Juanita will receive 20 gifts on her tenth birthday. It's just not fair!"

Are Alicia's parents being fair about the number of gifts given on their daughters' birthdays? It seems that the number of gifts each girl receives on her birthday is double the number of years old she is that day. If this plan is consistent then we might see a ratio that expresses it as:

Number of gifts : number of years old or $\frac{\text{Number of gifts}}{\text{Number of years old}}$.

On her 6th birthday, Alicia received 12 gifts: $\frac{12 \text{ gifts}}{6 \text{ years old}}$.

On her 8th birthday, Juanita received 16 gifts: $\frac{16 \text{ gifts}}{8 \text{ years old}}$.

Are these two ratios equivalent? We can cross multiply to find out:

$$\frac{12 \text{ gifts}}{6 \text{ years old}} \stackrel{?}{=} \frac{16 \text{ gifts}}{8 \text{ years old}} \quad \text{Cross multiply.}$$

$$12 \times 8 \stackrel{?}{=} 6 \times 16$$

$$96 = 96 \quad \text{Yes, the ratios are equivalent!}$$

Proportions

When we show that two ratios are equivalent using an equation, that equation is called a *proportion.* A proportion helps keep things consistent, helps keep things fair.

A **proportion** is a statement that two ratios are equivalent:

$$\frac{a}{b} = \frac{c}{d}$$

The product of the extremes is equal to the product of the means:

$$a \cdot d = b \cdot c$$

We often use proportions to answer questions about scale, or size. For example, on a road map you might find that every inch on the map is equivalent to 2 miles of actual road. This could be set up as a ratio

$\frac{1 \text{ inch}}{2 \text{ miles}}$ This is *one set* of information, shown as a ratio.

We might be curious about a certain length of highway that, on the map, is 5 inches long. You probably can see that, in this case, the actual road would be 10 miles long,

$\frac{5 \text{ inches}}{10 \text{ miles}}$ This is *a second set* of information, shown as a ratio.

Let's look at the two sets of information as a proportion: $\frac{1 \text{ inch}}{2 \text{ miles}} = \frac{5 \text{ inches}}{10 \text{ miles}}$

As ratios, we can show that these sets of information are equivalent by cross multiplying:

$$\frac{1}{2} = \frac{5}{10}$$
$$1 \times 10 = 2 \times 5$$
$$10 = 10$$

In working with ratios and proportions, though, consistency is the key. This means that:

1. The numerators of each fraction must be of the same units of measure (or count); and
2. the denominators of each fraction must be of the same units of measure (or count).

In comparing the inches on the map to the actual miles of the road, we can set up two ratios—from the two different sets of information—according to a scheme or plan of approach to a problem.

Here is a possible scheme: inches : miles or $\frac{\text{inches}}{\text{miles}}$

Using this scheme, we can be sure to put inches in the numerator and miles in the denominator for each ratio:

First set of information → $\frac{1 \text{ inch}}{2 \text{ miles}} = \frac{5 \text{ inches}}{10 \text{ miles}}$ ← *Second set of information*

Actually, there's more to being consistent than just getting the inches in the numerator. We need to make sure that each denominator matches up with the correct numerator, that they fit the same set of information.

In other words, we shouldn't write

$$\frac{1 \text{ inch}}{10 \text{ miles}} = \frac{5 \text{ inches}}{2 \text{ miles}},$$

because this is a mix of the two different sets of information. (You can cross multiply to see that the ratios are not equivalent.)

To be consistent, we need to make sure that the smaller units (first set) stay together and the larger units (second set) stay together.

This way, 1 inch will be paired with 2 miles and 5 inches will be paired with 10 miles. We can make sure this happens by setting up a *proportion table*, outlining our scheme, as shown here:

	Small units (or first set)	Large units (or second set)
Inches	1	5
Miles	2	10

With this proportion table, the fractions become clear, and we simply set up the proportion:

$$\frac{1 \text{ inch}}{2 \text{ miles}} = \frac{5 \text{ inches}}{10 \text{ miles}} \text{ or just } \frac{1}{2} = \frac{5}{10}$$

In your own words, explain why it is important that the smaller units always be grouped together and the larger units always be grouped together.

____

____

EXAMPLE 1

It takes 2 trucks to haul away 5 tons of trash in a day. It takes 6 trucks to haul away 15 tons of trash in a day.

a) Set up a proportion table for the problem.

b) Set up the proportion based on that table.

c) Show that the ratios are equivalent using cross multiplication.

PROCEDURE: Draw a proportion table, like the one on the previous page, that helps you line up the small and large units—or the first set and the second set (across the top of the table) and the units of measure (down the side of the table).

ANSWER: a) The first set of information is 2 trucks and 5 tons; the second set is 6 trucks and 15 tons.

	First set	Second Set
Trucks	2	6
Tons	5	15

b) The proportion, according to the table, is $\dfrac{\text{trucks}}{\text{tons}} = \dfrac{\text{trucks}}{\text{tons}}$

$$\frac{2}{5} = \frac{6}{15}.$$

c) Using cross multiplication: $2 \cdot 15 = 5 \cdot 6$

$$30 = 30 \checkmark$$

The ratios are equivalent.

YOU TRY IT 1

Mike earns $93 for 3 days of work. He earns $155 for 5 days of work.

a) Set up a proportion table for the problem.

b) Set up the proportion based on that table.

c) Show that the ratios are equivalent. Use Example 1 as a guide.

a)

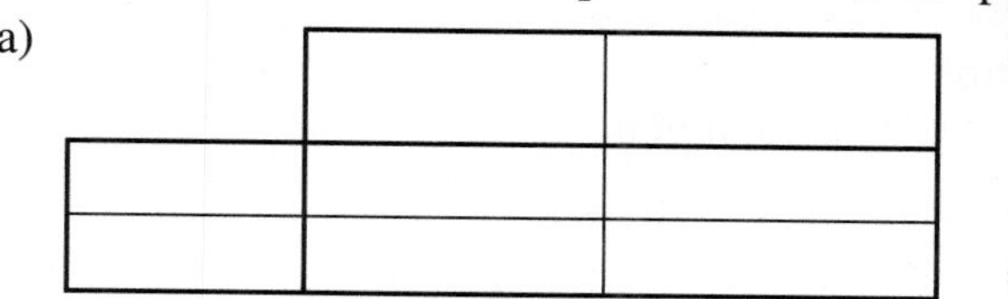

b)

c)

In setting up the proportion table, it's okay to use a different order, as long as the scheme is consistent. For example, the map shows a scale ratio of 1 inch **:** 2 miles, but we could have expressed the scheme's proportion table as miles to inches, instead.

	Large units (second set)	Small units (first set)
Miles	10	2
Inches	5	1

With this table, the proportion is:

$$\frac{10 \text{ miles}}{5 \text{ inches}} = \frac{2 \text{ miles}}{1 \text{ inch}} \text{ or just } \frac{10}{5} = \frac{2}{1}.$$

These are still equivalent ratios because we were consistent in placing the numbers in the proportion table according to the scheme.

In this next exercise, you may set up the proportion table however you wish, but you must be consistent. (Your answer may differ slightly from the answer at the end of this section.)

YOU TRY IT 2

Two adults are needed to supervise 9 children on a field trip. Twelve adults are needed to supervise 54 children on a field trip.

a) Set up a proportion table for the problem.

b) Set up the proportion based on that table.

c) Show that the ratios are equivalent.

a)

b)

c)

Solving Proportions

What if, in a proportion situation, one of the numerical measurements is not given? If one piece of information is not given, we can solve the proportion as an equation to find the value of the missing measurement.

Before we get into actual situations, though, let's look at solving proportions with one of the values unknown.

EXAMPLE 2 Solve for n in each proportion.

a) $\frac{n}{8} = \frac{3}{4}$ b) $\frac{5}{4} = \frac{10}{n}$

PROCEDURE: Use cross multiplication to put the equation into a more familiar form. Then isolate the variable by dividing by the coefficient of n.

ANSWER: a)

$$\frac{n}{8} = \frac{3}{4}$$

$$n \times 4 = 8 \times 3$$

$$n \times 4 = 24$$

$$n \times 4 \div 4 = 24 \div 4$$

$$n = 6$$

Check: $n = 6$

$$\frac{6}{8} = \frac{3}{4}$$

$$6 \times 4 = 8 \times 3$$

$$24 = 24 \checkmark$$

b)

$$\frac{5}{4} = \frac{10}{n}$$

$$5 \times n = 4 \times 10$$

$$5 \times n = 40$$

$$n \times 5 \div 5 = 40 \div 5$$

$$n = 8$$

Check: $n = 8$

$$\frac{5}{4} = \frac{10}{8}$$

$$5 \times 8 = 4 \times 10$$

$$40 = 40 \checkmark$$

YOU TRY IT 3

Solve for n in each proportion. Check each answer. Use Example 2 as a guide.

a) $\frac{n}{12} = \frac{3}{4}$ b) $\frac{5}{3} = \frac{30}{n}$ c) $\frac{24}{n} = \frac{6}{5}$

Sometimes, the fraction that is completely known (the ratio without the variable n) can be simplified before cross multiplying. Simplifying first is helpful because the numbers are then easier to work with.

If we first simplify before cross multiplying, we should check our answer in the *original* proportion, since it's possible a mistake was made in simplifying (before cross multiplying). This will guarantee that our answer is correct for the original problem situation.

EXAMPLE 3

Solve for n in each proportion.

a) $\frac{21}{12} = \frac{n}{8}$ b) $\frac{10}{n} = \frac{25}{30}$

PROCEDURE: First simplify any fraction, if possible. Then use cross multiplication to put the equation into a more familiar form. Isolate the variable by dividing by the coefficient of n.

ANSWER: a)

$$\frac{21}{12} = \frac{n}{8} \quad \text{Simplify } \frac{21}{12} \text{ by a factor of 3.}$$

$$\frac{7}{4} = \frac{n}{8}$$

$$7 \times 8 = 4 \times n$$

$$56 = 4 \times n$$

$$56 \div 4 = n \times 4 \div 4$$

$$14 = n$$

$$n = 14$$

Check: $n = 14$ in the original proportion.

$$\frac{21}{12} = \frac{14}{8}$$

$$21 \times 8 = 12 \times 14$$

$$168 = 168 ✓$$

b)

$$\frac{10}{n} = \frac{25}{30} \quad \text{Simplify } \frac{25}{30} \text{ by a factor of 5.}$$

$$\frac{10}{n} = \frac{5}{6}$$

$$10 \times 6 = n \times 5$$

$$60 = n \times 5$$

$$60 \div 5 = n \times 5 \div 5$$

$$12 = n$$

$$n = 12$$

Check $n = 12$ in the original proportion.

$$\frac{10}{12} = \frac{25}{30}$$

$$10 \times 30 = 12 \times 25$$

$$300 = 300 ✓$$

YOU TRY IT 4

Solve for n in each proportion by first simplifying the known fraction. Check the answer. Use Example 3 as a guide.

a) $\frac{8}{60} = \frac{n}{45}$

b) $\frac{18}{n} = \frac{15}{10}$

c) $\frac{18}{15} = \frac{24}{n}$

Applying Proportions

Consider the following situation. Yusef is a window washer. He can wash 6 windows in 21 minutes. How many minutes will it take him to wash 10 windows?

We are given two sets of information:

One set is complete: 6 windows in 21 minutes.

The other set is incomplete: 10 windows in how many minutes?

We can answer the question by following this strategy:

- Set up a legend and a proportion table.
- Set up the proportion (equation) based on that table.
- Solve the proportion using cross multiplication and other techniques.

EXAMPLE 4

Yusef can wash 6 windows in 21 minutes. How many minutes will it take him to wash 10 windows?

PROCEDURE: Set up a proportion table. From the table, set up a proportion, and solve it.

ANSWER: Legend: Let $n =$ the number of minutes it will take Yusef to wash 10 windows.

Proportion: $\frac{\text{windows}}{\text{minutes}} = \frac{\text{windows}}{\text{minutes}}$

$$\frac{6}{21} = \frac{10}{n}$$
$$6 \cdot n = 10 \cdot 21$$
$$6 \cdot n = 210$$
$$6 \div 6 \cdot n = 210 \div 6$$
$$n = 35$$

	First set	Second Set
Windows	6	10
Minutes	21	n

SENTENCE: It will take Yusef 35 minutes to wash 10 windows.

YOU TRY IT 5

At a candy store, the price of 6 inches of licorice is 15¢. What is the price for 30 inches of licorice?

Legend: Let $n =$

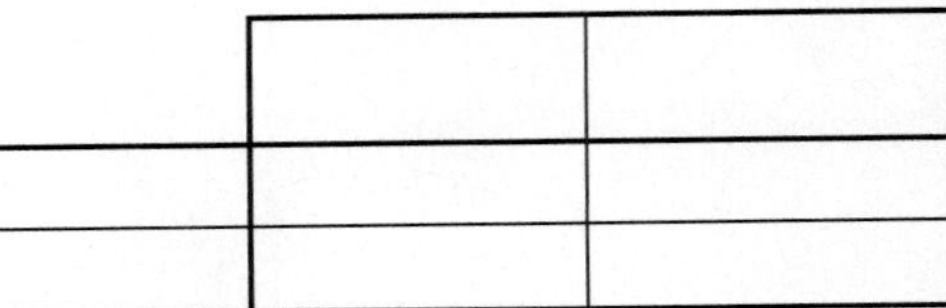

Sentence:

YOU TRY IT 6

Jimi runs 3 miles in 24 minutes. Assuming she can maintain the same rate, how long will it take Jimi to run 5 miles?

Legend: Let n =

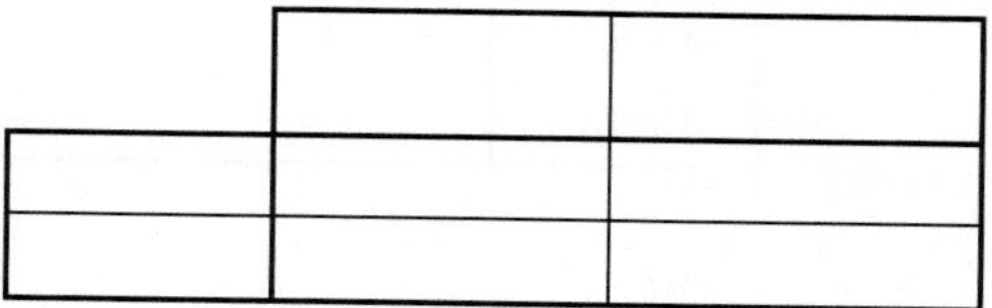

Sentence:

YOU TRY IT 7

To create a living fence, Sari is planting 6 spruce trees every 20 yards. How many spruce trees will Sari need for a 70-yard fence?

Legend: Let n =

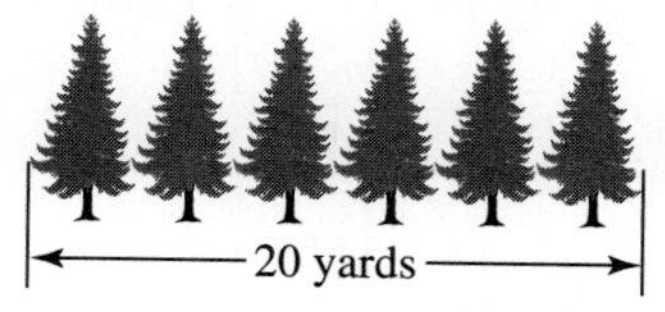

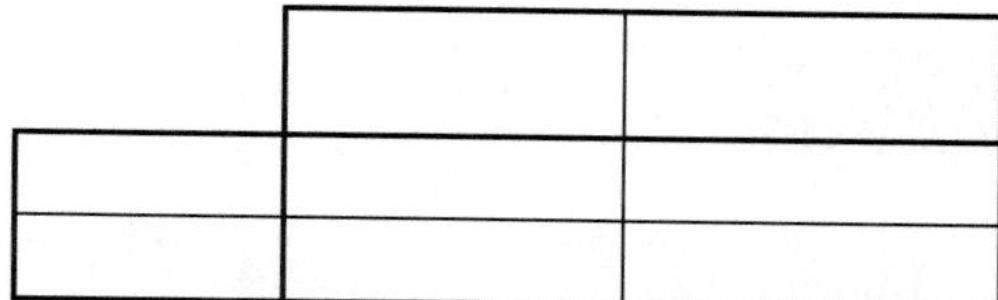

Sentence:

You Try It Answers: Section 6.3

YTI 1 a)

	First set	Second Set
Dollars	93	155
Days	3	5

b) $\dfrac{93}{3} = \dfrac{155}{5}$

c) $93 \times 5 = 3 \times 155$
$465 = 465$

YTI 2 a)

	First set	Second Set
Adults	2	12
Children	9	54

b) $\dfrac{2}{9} = \dfrac{12}{54}$

c) $2 \times 54 = 9 \times 12$
$108 = 108$

YTI 3 a) $n = 9$ b) $n = 18$ c) $n = 20$

YTI 4 a) $n = 6$ b) $n = 12$ c) $n = 20$

YTI 5 Let n = the price for 30 inches of licorice.

	First set	Second Set
Cents	15	n
Inches	6	30

$\dfrac{15}{6} = \dfrac{n}{30}$ The price for 30 inches of licorice is 75¢.

YTI 6 Let $n =$ the number of minutes to run 5 miles.

	First set	Second Set
Miles	3	5
Minutes	24	n

$\frac{3}{24} = \frac{5}{n}$

It will take Jimi 40 minutes to run 5 miles.

YTI 7 Let $n =$ the number of spruce trees needed for 70 yards.

	First set	Second Set
Trees	6	n
Yards	20	70

$\frac{6}{20} = \frac{n}{70}$

Sari will need 21 spruce trees for a 70 yard fence.

Focus Exercises: Section 6.3

Solve for n in each proportion. If possible, first reduce the known fraction.

1. $\frac{3}{7} = \frac{n}{14}$ **2.** $\frac{2}{9} = \frac{n}{45}$ **3.** $\frac{n}{28} = \frac{4}{7}$ **4.** $\frac{n}{18} = \frac{5}{3}$

5. $\frac{11}{5} = \frac{66}{n}$ **6.** $\frac{9}{4} = \frac{54}{n}$ **7.** $\frac{20}{n} = \frac{5}{4}$ **8.** $\frac{36}{n} = \frac{3}{8}$

9. $\frac{n}{15} = \frac{8}{6}$ **10.** $\frac{n}{35} = \frac{12}{15}$ **11.** $\frac{8}{n} = \frac{6}{9}$ **12.** $\frac{50}{n} = \frac{20}{12}$

13. $\frac{30}{6} = \frac{n}{5}$ **14.** $\frac{42}{14} = \frac{n}{8}$ **15.** $\frac{60}{24} = \frac{10}{n}$ **16.** $\frac{36}{48} = \frac{15}{n}$

For each of the following, set up a proportion table. Write a legend and solve the corresponding proportion. Write a sentence answering the question.

17. Tom received 18 votes for every 30 people who voted. If a total of 200 people voted, how many votes did Tom receive?

18. Karen received 15 votes for every 24 people who voted. If she received a total of 300 votes, how many people voted?

19. Cheryl was able to drive 360 miles on 15 gallons of gasoline. At that rate, how many gallons will Cheryl use to drive 120 miles?

20. Cheyenne was able to drive 360 miles on 24 gallons of gasoline. At that rate, how many miles will he be able to drive on 16 gallons?

21. A roofing company sells roofing material for \$12 per square yard. How much will 150 square yards of roofing material cost?

22. A roofing company sells roofing material for \$12 per square yard. How many square yards of roofing material can be purchased for \$900?

23. At a hardware store, the price of 3 feet of rope is \$1.20. What is the price of 8 feet of rope?

24. At a hardware store, the price of 4 feet of chain is \$2.60. What length of chain will \$13.00 buy?

25. Delon can ride his bike an average of 6 miles in 27 minutes. At that rate, how far can he ride in 45 minutes?

26. Delon can ride his bike an average of 6 miles in 27 minutes. At that rate, how many minutes will it take him to ride 16 miles?

27. Hank's Jeep can travel 90 miles on 5 gallons of gas. How many gallons will Hank's Jeep need to travel 54 miles?

28. Sandy's car can travel 84 miles on 4 gallons of gas. How far can her car travel on 15 gallons of gas?

29. Marla works for Kinko's. She needs to make 150 copies of a course pack. Copying the first 30 course packs took 2 hours. How long will it take for the whole job to be complete?

30. Tim can run an average of 6 miles in 40 minutes. How far can he run in 60 minutes?

31. A group of 30 people can fit in 2 boats. How many boats are needed for a group of 75 people?

32. At Charles County Community College, there are 10 math classes for every 15 English classes. If the college offers 28 math classes, how many English classes does it offer?

33. At Essex Community College, there are 9 math classes for every 12 English classes. If the college offers 48 English classes, how many math classes does it offer?

34. There are 3 seniors for every 2 juniors in the concert choir. If there are 21 seniors in all, how many juniors are in the concert choir?

SECTION 6.4 Percents

Objectives

In this section, you will learn to:

- Define *percent*.
- Write a percent as a fraction and a ratio.
- Write a percent as a decimal.
- Write a decimal as a percent.
- Write a fraction as a percent.

To successfully complete this section, you need to understand:

- Writing decimals as fractions (5.1)
- Writing fractions as decimals (5.1)
- Multiplying decimals by powers of 10 (5.4)
- Ratios (6.1)

Introduction

You have, no doubt, seen percents. Oftentimes a sales ad will indicate a discount such as "Save 20%." The symbol % means *percent*, and the number that is written before the percent symbol is called the **percentage**. For example, in 6%, the percentage is 6.

Recall from Section 6.1 that *per* means *divided by*, and indicates a ratio. Percent, or per cent, means *per 100*, or *divided by 100*. Therefore, a **percent** is a ratio in which the denominator is 100.

As a ratio, 32% means 32 : 100,

The diagram at right shows 100 boxes, 32 of which are shaded. As a ratio of shaded box : total boxes, this is 32 : 100 or $\frac{32}{100}$ or 32%. In other words, 32% of the boxes are shaded.

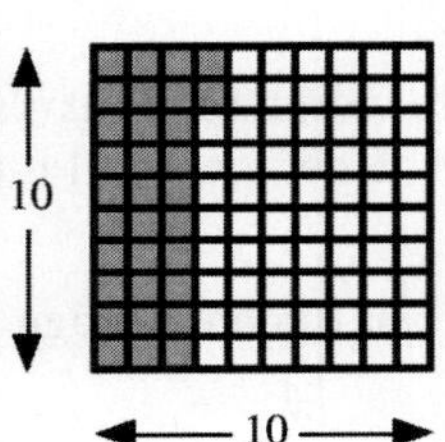

Percents as Fractions

As a fraction, 32% means $\frac{32}{100}$, or "32 out of 100."

EXAMPLE 1 Write each percent as a fraction with 100 in the denominator. Do not simplify.

a) 19% b) 7.75% c) 0.4%

PROCEDURE: The percentage is the numerator, and 100 is the denominator.

ANSWER: a) $19\% = \frac{19}{100}$ b) $7.75\% = \frac{7.75}{100}$ c) $0.4\% = \frac{0.4}{100}$

YOU TRY IT 1 *Write each percent as a fraction with 100 in the denominator. Do not simplify. Use Example 1 as a guide.*

a) 61% b) 3.7% c) 9% d) 0.3%

EXAMPLE 2 Write each percent as a fraction, then simplify the fraction completely.

a) 15% b) 70% c) 100% d) 250%

PROCEDURE: The percentage is the numerator, and 100 is the denominator.

ANSWER:

a) $15\% = \frac{15}{100}$ This simplifies by a factor of 5: $\frac{3}{20}$

b) $70\% = \frac{70}{100}$ This simplifies by a factor of 10: $\frac{7}{10}$

c) $100\% = \frac{100}{100}$ This simplifies to: 1

d) $250\% = \frac{250}{100}$ This simplifies first by a factor of 10: $\frac{25}{10}$ and then by a factor of 5: $\frac{5}{2}$ or $2\frac{1}{2}$

YOU TRY IT 2

Write each percent as a fraction, then simplify the fraction completely. Use Example 2 as a guide.

a) 20% b) 300% c) 150% d) 75%

EXAMPLE 3

Write this sentence with the percent as a simplified fraction.
60% of the students in Mr. DeGuzman's class are women.

PROCEDURE: Write 60% as a fraction and then simplify the fraction: $60\% = \frac{60}{100} = \frac{6}{10} = \frac{3}{5}$

ANSWER: $\frac{3}{5}$ of the students in Mr. DeGuzman's class are women.

YOU TRY IT 3

For each, write the sentence with the percent as a simplified fraction. Use Example 3 as a guide.

a) 65% of the books on Toni's shelf are novels.

b) 25% of the adults in Cypress County have not registered to vote.

If a fraction has a denominator of 100, then the numerator is the percentage and the fraction can be easily written as a percent.

EXAMPLE 4

Write each fraction as a percent.

a) $\frac{28}{100}$ b) $\frac{3}{100}$ c) $\frac{1.8}{100}$ d) $\frac{137}{100}$

PROCEDURE: The numerator is the percentage.

ANSWER: a) $\frac{28}{100} = 28\%$ b) $\frac{3}{100} = 3\%$

c) $\frac{1.8}{100} = 1.8\%$ d) $\frac{137}{100} = 137\%$

YOU TRY IT 4

Write each fraction as a percent. Use Example 4 as a guide.

a) $\frac{2}{100}$ b) $\frac{79}{100}$ c) $\frac{162}{100}$ d) $\frac{1.5}{100}$

EXAMPLE 5 Write this sentence with the suggested fraction as a percent.
72 out of 100 fourth graders prefer ice cream for dessert.

PROCEDURE: Write *72 out of 100* first as a fraction, and then as a percent: $\frac{72}{100} = 72\%$.

When writing the sentence, the words *of all* will follow this new percent.

ANSWER: 72% of all fourth graders prefer ice cream for dessert.

YOU TRY IT 5 *For each, write the sentence with the suggested fraction as a percent. Use Example 5 as a guide.*

a) 13 out of 100 people in the U.S. live below the poverty level.
Source: www.census.gov

b) 62 out of 100 high school students taking an advanced placement exam will pass it.
Source: www.apcentral.collegeboard.com

Writing Percents as Decimals

If the percentage is a whole number, the percent can first be written as a fraction and then as a decimal.

EXAMPLE 6 Write each percent as a decimal by first writing it as a fraction.

a) 29% b) 125% c) 200%

PROCEDURE: Remember, any fraction with a denominator of 100 can be written as a decimal with two decimal places.

ANSWER: a) $29\% = \frac{29}{100} = 0.29$ b) $125\% = \frac{125}{100} = 1.25$

c) $200\% = \frac{200}{100} = 2.00$ or just 2

YOU TRY IT 6 *Write each percent as a decimal by first writing it as a fraction. Use Example 6 as a guide.*

a) 83% b) 4%

c) 300% d) 175%

If the percentage has a decimal in it, then we can first multiply both the numerator and denominator by the same power of 10 to make the numerator into a whole number.

EXAMPLE 7

Write each of these percents as a decimal by first writing it as a fraction. Multiply the fraction by 1 using an appropriate power of 10, and then write it as a decimal.

a) 13.9%   b) 0.65%

PROCEDURE: After writing each as a fraction with a denominator of 100, count the number of decimal places in the numerator.

From that count, decide which power of 10 must be multiplied—in both the numerator and denominator—to make the numerator a whole number.

After the numerator is a whole number, write it as a decimal.

ANSWER: a) $13.9\% = \frac{13.9}{100}$ One decimal place means multiply the numerator and denominator by 10.

$\frac{13.9 \times 10}{100 \times 10} = \frac{139}{1{,}000}$, which can now be written as a decimal.

$= 0.139$

b) $0.65\% = \frac{0.65}{100}$ Two decimal places means multiply the numerator and denominator by 100.

$\frac{0.65 \times 100}{100 \times 100} = \frac{65}{10{,}000}$ The numerator is now a whole number. However, the numerator doesn't have enough digits, so let's place some zeros so that we can write it as a decimal.

$= \frac{0065}{10{,}000}$

$= 0.0065$

Think about it

When writing a percent as a fraction and then a decimal, when do we need to multiply both the numerator and denominator by 10?

____

____

YOU TRY IT 7

Write each of these percents as a fraction, multiply the fraction by 1 using an appropriate power of 10, then write it as a decimal. Use Example 7 as a guide.

a) 6.3%   b) 35.7%

c) 0.04%   d) 8.14%

Is it possible to write percents directly as decimals, without having to use fractions?

Yes it is, and the next example looks closely at doing so. However, it's good to know that we can always refer back to fractions—as we did in Examples 6 and 7—when we need to.

Procedure for Writing Percents as Decimals

Step			
1. Recognize the percentage and notice whether or not it contains a decimal point. If it doesn't, then write one at its end.	9%	→	9.%
	83%	→	83.%
	6.4%	→	6.4%
2. If the percentage doesn't have at least two whole numbers before the decimal point, then place one or two zeros in front of the percentage.	9%	→	**0**9.%
	83%	→	83.%
	6.4%	→	**0**6.4%
3. Rewrite the percentage, without the %, and move the decimal point two places to the left.	09.%	→	.09
	83.%	→	.83
	06.4%	→	.064

Example 8 uses steps 1 and 3 of this procedure.

EXAMPLE 8 Write each percent as a decimal.

a) 29% b) 125% c) 13.9% d) 200%

PROCEDURE: Use step 1 of the procedure above, as necessary, and place a decimal point at the end of each whole number percentage. Then use step 3.

ANSWER: a) 29% or 29.% = .29 or 0.29 b) 125% = 125.% = 1.25

c) 13.9% = .139 or 0.139 d) 200% = 200.% = 2.00 or just 2

NOTE: 13.9% already has two whole number digits in the percentage and has its own decimal point.

Example 9 uses steps 2 and 3 of the procedure above for writing percents as decimals.

EXAMPLE 9 Write each percent as a decimal.

a) 4.9% b) 7.25% c) 0.85% d) 0.06%

PROCEDURE: Use step 2 of the procedure by placing enough zeros in front to get two whole numbers. Then use step 3.

ANSWER: a) 4.9% or **0**4.9% = .049 or 0.049 b) 7.25% = **0**7.25% = .0725 or 0.0725

c) 0.85% = **0**0.85% = .0085 or 0.0085 d) 0.06% = **0**0.06% = .0006 or 0.0006

YOU TRY IT 8 *Write each percent as a decimal. Use Examples 8 and 9 as guides.*

a) 53% b) 35.8% c) 250%

d) 3% e) 7.8% f) 0.58%

Writing Decimals as Percents

Sometimes we need to convert from a decimal to a percent. Knowing how to do this comes in handy, for instance, if you want to write the results of a study—such as 0.126 of all students surveyed are left handed—into a percent: 12.6% of all students surveyed are left handed.

If a decimal number has two decimal places, then it can first be written as fraction with denominator of 100 and then as a percent. If the number has fewer than two decimal places, then we can place one or two ending zeros so that it has two decimal places.

EXAMPLE 10 Write each decimal as a percent by first writing the decimal as a fraction.

a) 0.45 b) 0.07 c) 1.58 d) 0.4 e) 2

PROCEDURE: Remember, any fraction with a denominator of 100 can be written as a decimal with two decimal places. For part d, first place one ending zero, and for part e, first place a decimal point and two ending zeros.

ANSWER:

a) $0.45 = \frac{45}{100} = 45\%$

b) $0.07 = \frac{7}{100} = 7\%$

c) $1.58 = \frac{158}{100} = 158\%$

d) $0.4 = 0.40 = \frac{40}{100} = 40\%$

e) $2 = 2.00 = \frac{200}{100} = 200\%$

YOU TRY IT 9 *Write each decimal as a percent by first writing the decimal as a fraction. Use Example 10 as a guide.*

a) 0.09 b) 2.05 c) 0.76 d) 3 e) 0.9

Below is another technique for writing decimals as percents.

First recall:

- From Section 5.4, that multiplying by 100 has the effect of moving the decimal point two places to the right.
- From Example 2 of this section, that 100% = 1. In other words, 100% is another form of 1, and we can multiply a number by 100% without changing the value of the number.

Putting these ideas together, we can multiply a number such as 0.45 by 100% without changing the value:

$0.45 \times 100\% = 45\%$. Compare this to the answer in Example 10 a).

We multiply 100 by 0.45 to result in 45 (the percentage), and the percent sign is placed after the percentage.

Writing a Decimal as a Percent: Multiply the decimal number by 100%.

EXAMPLE 11 Write each decimal as a percent by multiplying each by 100%.

a) 2.35 b) 3 c) 0.89

d) 0.05 e) 0.6 f) 0.039

PROCEDURE: Multiplying by 100 has the effect of moving the decimal two places to the right.

ANSWER:

a) $2.35 = 2.35 \times 100\% = 235\%$
b) $3 = 3 \times 100\% = 300\%$
c) $0.89 = 0.89 \times 100\% = 89\%$
d) $0.05 = 0.05 \times 100\% = 5\%$
e) $0.6 = 0.6 \times 100\% = 60\%$
f) $0.039 = 0.039 \times 100\% = 3.9\%$

Notice that the percent sign, %, is ignored during the multiplication by 100 and is carried over to the final result.

YOU TRY IT 10

Write each decimal as a percent. Use Example 11 as a guide.

a) 0.18 b) 0.07 c) 0.8

d) 0.091 e) 4 f) 1.75

Writing Fractions as Percents

We have seen, in Example 4, that a fraction with a denominator of 100 can immediately be written as a percent. If the denominator is not 100, then we can convert a fraction into a percent by first writing the fraction as a decimal. Once it is in decimal form, we can multiply it by 100% to find the percent equivalent.

EXAMPLE 12

Write each fraction as a percent.

a) $\frac{3}{20}$ b) $\frac{3}{8}$

PROCEDURE: First use long division to write each fraction as a decimal. The decimal quotient is equivalent to the fraction.

a) $20\overline{)3.00}$ with quotient 0.15 ← **You show the division:** → b) $8\overline{)3.000}$ with quotient 0.375

$\frac{3}{20} = 0.15$ ← The fraction as a decimal. → $\frac{3}{8} = 0.375$

$0.15 \cdot 100\% = 15\%$ ← Now multiply the decimal by 100%. → $0.375 \cdot 100\% = 37.5\%$

ANSWER: a) $\frac{3}{20} = 15\%$ b) $\frac{3}{8} = 37.5\%$

EXAMPLE 13 Write $\frac{4}{7}$ as a percent. Round the percentage to the nearest tenth.

PROCEDURE: Find the decimal equivalent of $\frac{4}{7}$ using long division. Rounding the percentage to the nearest tenth means rounding the quotient to the nearest thousandth. Once in decimal form, multiply the number by 100%.

$$7\overline{)4.0000} = 0.5714$$

At four decimal places, we can round to the nearest thousandth.
The quotient rounds to 0.571.

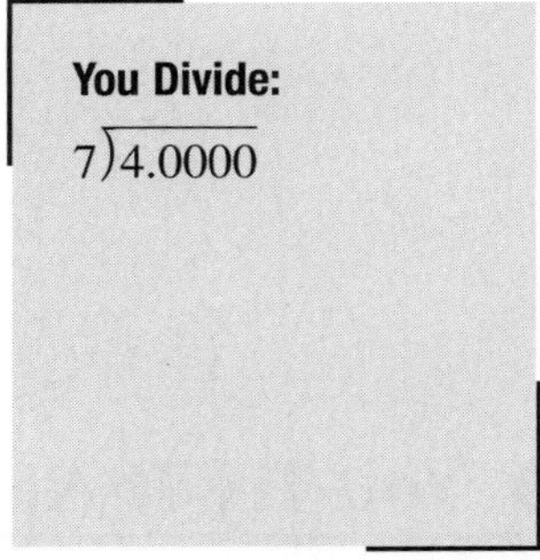

Multiply 0.571 by 100% to find the percent equivalent:
$0.571 \cdot 100\% = 57.1\%$.
Because we rounded, this is an *approximate* value, and we should use the $\approx$ sign to indicate that.
↓

ANSWER: $\frac{4}{7} \approx 57.1\%$

Think about it In the previous example, in rounding the percentage to the nearest tenth, why must we round the quotient to the nearest thousandth?

____

____

YOU TRY IT 11 *Write each fraction as a percent. If necessary, round the percentage to the nearest tenth. Use Examples 12 and 13 as guides.*

a) $\frac{9}{25}$ b) $\frac{7}{40}$ c) $\frac{2}{3}$ d) $\frac{4}{9}$

EXAMPLE 14 Write this sentence with the fraction as a percent. Round the percentage to the nearest tenth.
$\frac{1}{3}$ of all college freshman take English during their first semester.

You divide:
$3\overline{)1.0000}$

$$3\overline{)1.0000} = 0.3333$$

At four decimal places, we can round to the nearest thousandth.
The quotient rounds to 0.333.

Multiply 0.333 by 100% to find the percent equivalent.
$0.333 \cdot 100\% = 33.3\%$

$\frac{1}{3} \approx 33.3\%$

ANSWER: 33.3% of all college freshman take English during their first semester.

Even though 33.3% is an approximation, the word *about* is often excluded from this type of sentence.

YOU TRY IT 12 *For each, write the sentence with the fraction as a percent. Round the percentage to the nearest tenth. Use Example 14 as a guide.*

a) In Nebraska, $\frac{5}{6}$ of the students complete all four years of high school.
Source: www.manhattan-institute.org

b) When reading a newspaper, $\frac{5}{8}$ of all men read the sports section first.

You Try It Answers: Section 6.4

YTI 1 a) $\dfrac{61}{100}$ b) $\dfrac{3.7}{100}$ c) $\dfrac{9}{100}$ d) $\dfrac{0.3}{100}$

YTI 2 a) $\dfrac{1}{5}$ b) 3 c) $\dfrac{3}{2} = 1\dfrac{1}{2}$ d) $\dfrac{3}{4}$

YTI 3 a) $\dfrac{13}{20}$ of the books on Toni's shelf are novels.
b) $\dfrac{1}{4}$ of the adults in Cypress County have not registered to vote.

YTI 4 a) 2% b) 79% c) 162% d) 1.5%

YTI 5 a) 13% of all people in the U.S. live below the poverty level.
b) 62% of all high school students taking an advanced placement exam will pass it.

YTI 6 a) 0.83 b) 0.04 c) 3 d) 1.75

YTI 7 a) 0.063 b) 0.357 c) 0.0004 d) 0.0814

YTI 8 a) .53 or 0.53 b) .358 or 0.358
c) 2.5 d) .03 or 0.03
e) .078 or 0.078 f) .0058 or 0.0058

YTI 9 a) 9% b) 205% c) 76%
d) 300% e) 90%

YTI 10 a) 18% b) 7% c) 80%
d) 9.1% e) 400% f) 175%

YTI 11 a) 36% b) 17.5%
c) $\approx$ 66.7% d) $\approx$ 44.4%

YTI 12 a) In Nebraska, 83.3% of the students complete all four years of high school.
b) When reading a newspaper, 62.5% of all men read the sports section first.

Focus Exercises: Section 6.4

Write each percent as a fraction, then simplify the fraction completely.

1. 45% **2.** 8% **3.** 90% **4.** 125%

Write each sentence with the percent as a simplified fraction.

5. 56% of a school district's budget is for teacher salaries.

6. 35% of all workers in San Francisco use public transportation to commute to and from work.
Source: www.rideshare.511.org

7. 2% of the cars imported into the U.S. come from Sweden.
Source: 2005 World Almanac

8. 12.5% of the book sales at Bookends are romance novels.

Write each percent as a decimal. You may use any method you wish.

9. 16% **10.** 19% **11.** 4.5% **12.** 0.8%

13. 2% **14.** 5% **15.** 184% **16.** 205%

17. 85% **18.** 46% **19.** 260% **20.** 150%

21. 4% **22.** 9% **23.** 3% **24.** 1%

25. 5.2% **26.** 6.8% **27.** 17.2% **28.** 23.9%

29. 7.75% **30.** 1.38% **31.** 0.5% **32.** 0.4%

Write each decimal as a percent.

33. 0.78 **34.** 0.35 **35.** 0.06 **36.** 0.08

37. 0.9 **38.** 0.5 **39.** 2.11 **40.** 1.64

41. 1.4 **42.** 2.3 **43.** 0.128 **44.** 0.875

45. 0.062 **46.** 0.047 **47.** 0.001 **48.** 0.003

Write each fraction as a percent. If necessary, round each percentage to the nearest tenth.

49. $\frac{2}{5}$ **50.** $\frac{1}{10}$ **51.** $\frac{47}{50}$ **52.** $\frac{11}{20}$

53. $\frac{14}{25}$ **54.** $\frac{8}{5}$ **55.** $\frac{5}{4}$ **56.** $\frac{7}{2}$

57. $\frac{5}{8}$ **58.** $\frac{27}{40}$ **59.** $\frac{9}{16}$ **60.** $\frac{13}{80}$

61. $\frac{7}{9}$ **62.** $\frac{5}{11}$ **63.** $\frac{1}{6}$ **64.** $\frac{7}{12}$

65. $\frac{4}{15}$ **66.** $\frac{7}{30}$ **67.** $\frac{9}{22}$ **68.** $\frac{5}{18}$

Write each sentence with the fraction as a percent. Round the percentage to the nearest tenth.

69. $\frac{3}{10}$ of the medals won by South Korean athletes at the 2004 Olympics were gold medals.
Source: www.mapsofworld.com

70. $\frac{1}{40}$ of the U.S. population has a last name of either Smith, Johnson, or Williams.
Source: 2005 World Almanac

71. In May 2005, $\frac{3}{16}$ of all commercial flights either departed late or were canceled.
Source: www.bts.gov

72. By the All-Star break, the Cleveland Cavaliers had won $\frac{5}{9}$ of their games.

SECTION 6.5 Solving Percent Problems Using Proportions

This section may be presented in addition to, or as an alternative to, Section 6.6.

Objectives

In this section, you will learn to:

- Set up a ratio in terms of percentage and base.
- Write a percent equation as a proportion.
- Solve percent proportions.

To successfully complete this section, you need to understand:

- Solving equations (1.6)
- Writing ratios as fractions (6.1)
- Solving proportions (6.3)
- Writing decimals as percents (6.4)

Introduction

100 squares, 80 of which are shaded

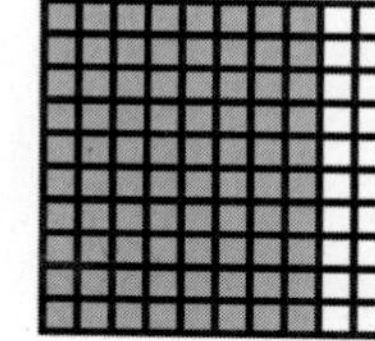

80% of the squares are shaded.

When a ratio is used to compare a part to a whole, we can write the ratio as part : whole or $\frac{\text{part}}{\text{whole}}$.

When the whole is 100, and the part is 80, the ratio of part : whole is 80 : 100 or $\frac{80}{100}$. And, as you know, $\frac{80}{100}$ is the same as 80%. Clearly, more than half of the diagram is shaded (see figure at right).

But, what if there are 200 squares and only 80 are shaded? In that case, less than half of the squares are shaded.

200 squares, 80 of which are shaded.

Less than half of the squares are shaded.

Here, 80 of the 200 squares are shaded, but this amounts to only $\frac{80}{200}$ which reduces (by a factor of 2) to $\frac{40}{100}$, only 40%.

So, knowing that 80 squares are shaded is not enough to determine how much of the whole is shaded. We also need to know how many squares are in the whole.

The whole, then, becomes the basis, or *base*, of our comparison, and this is the denominator of the ratio. In the first diagram, the base is 100, and the ratio $\frac{80}{\text{base}}$ is $\frac{80}{100}$. In the second diagram, the base is 200 and the ratio $\frac{80}{\text{base}}$ is $\frac{80}{200}$.

Recall from Section 6.4 that the number in front of the percent sign (%) is called the *percentage*. As a fraction, 80% becomes $\frac{80}{100}$, or $\frac{\text{percentage}}{100}$. Putting this together with our new word, *base*, $\frac{80}{100}$ becomes $\frac{\text{percentage}}{\text{base}}$, and this is how we may treat all percents.

A ratio that is not a percent can be thought of as $\frac{\text{amount}}{\text{base}}$, where the base is a number other than 100.

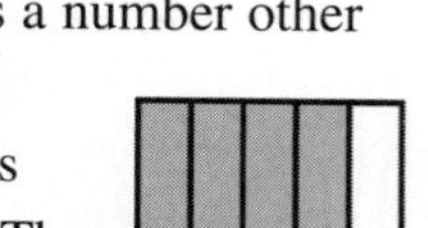

Consider the diagram at right, 4 out of the 5 rectangles are shaded. In this case, the base is 5 and we are interested in the 4 rectangles that are shaded. The shaded to total ratio, $\frac{\text{amount}}{\text{base}}$, is $\frac{4}{5}$.

The Percent Proportion

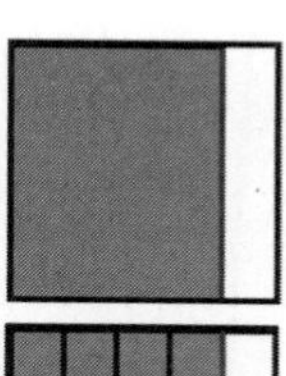

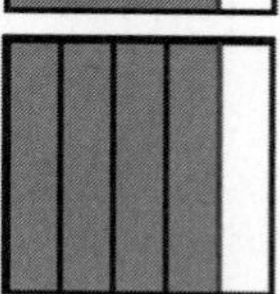

4 of 5 are shaded.

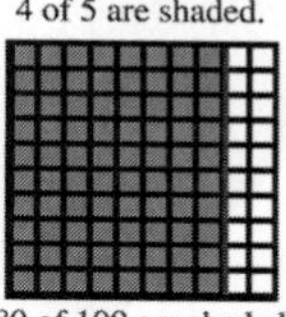

80 of 100 are shaded.

Each of the three squares at right is the same size. The top square is mostly shaded. The middle square shows the top one being divided into 5 long rectangles, 4 of which are shaded, giving a shaded to total ratio of $\frac{4}{5}$. The bottom square is the top one divided into 100 small squares, 80 of which are shaded, giving a shaded to total ratio of $\frac{80}{100}$.

Because the amount of shading in each large square is the same, the shaded to total ratios are the same. In other words, the ratios form a proportion:

$$\frac{80}{100} = \frac{4}{5}$$

This proportion can be treated as $\frac{\text{percentage}}{100} = \frac{\text{amount}}{\text{base}}$. In the proportion table of Section 6.3, the table looks like this:

	Percent	Ratio
Percentage/amount	p	a
Base	100	b

As a general formula, we get: $\frac{p}{100} = \frac{a}{b}$

In the formula $\frac{p}{100} = \frac{a}{b}$, there are three variables:

p, which represents the percentage;
a, which represents the amount; and
b, which represents the base.

For any one problem, two of these variables will be known values, and we can set up and solve a proportion to find the third variable.

When the Percentage Is Unknown

The first two examples demonstrate how to use the formula when the percentage is unknown.

EXAMPLE 1 24 out of the 40 players on the Jefferson High Jaguars varsity football team are seniors. What percent of the players are seniors?

PROCEDURE: The question asks, "What percent…" Since we know that percent always has a base of 100, it's the percentage of 100 that is unknown, and that is reflected in the legend.

	Percent	Ratio
Seniors (Percentage/amount)	p	a
All players (Base)	100	b

ANSWER: Legend: Let p = the unknown percentage

$\frac{p}{100} = \frac{24}{40}$ $\frac{24}{40}$ simplifies by a factor of 8 to $\frac{3}{5}$.

$\frac{p}{100} = \frac{3}{5}$ Cross multiply.

$p \cdot 5 = 100 \cdot 3$

$p \cdot 5 \div 5 = 300 \div 5$

$p = 60$

Check $p = 60$

$\frac{60}{100} = \frac{24}{40}$

$60 \times 40 = 100 \times 24$

$2400 = 2400$ ✓

SENTENCE: 60% of the players are seniors.

YOU TRY IT 1 *18 of the 60 singers in the Tulsa Chorale are sopranos. What percent of the singers are sopranos? Use Example 1 as a guide.*

Legend:

Sentence:

Sometimes, the percentage we seek is a bit unusual, as shown in this next example.

EXAMPLE 2 Of the 24 vehicles sold at Buster Dodge last week, 20 were trucks. What percent of the vehicles sold were trucks?

PROCEDURE: Again, it's the percentage of 100 that is unknown, and that is reflected in the legend.

ANSWER: Legend: Let $p =$ the unknown percentage.

$$\frac{p}{100} = \frac{20}{24}$$

$\frac{20}{24}$ simplifies, by a factor of 4, to $\frac{5}{6}$

	Percent	Ratio
Trucks	p	20
All vehicles	100	24

$$\frac{p}{100} = \frac{5}{6}$$

$$p \cdot 6 = 100 \cdot 5$$

$$p \cdot 6 \div 6 = 500 \div 6 \longrightarrow$$

$6\overline{)500.00}$ = 83.333 We can round this quotient to the nearest tenth to get 83.3. (This is an approximation.)

$$p \approx 83.3$$

SENTENCE: About 83.3% of the vehicles sold were trucks.

The division in Example 2, $500 \div 6$, can be treated in one of three ways:

1. As a fraction, $\frac{500}{6}$, that we write as a mixed number, $83\frac{1}{3}$. Answer: $83\frac{1}{3}$%.
2. As a repeating decimal number: $83.333\ldots = 83.\overline{3}$. Answer: $83.\overline{3}$%.
3. As an approximate value, rounded to the nearest tenth: $83.333\ldots \approx 83.3$. Answer: about 83.3%.

YOU TRY IT 2 *Of the 108 passengers on a flight from Los Angeles to Hawaii, 24 flew first class. What percent of the passengers flew first class? Use Example 2 as a guide.*

Legend:

Sentence:

When the Amount Is Unknown

Example 3 demonstrates how to proceed when we:

1. Know the percent of a situation, and
2. know the whole (base) of a certain set, but
3. don't know the part portion (amount).

EXAMPLE 3 30% of the sixth grade students at Lincoln Elementary School are eligible for the federal school lunch program. If there is a total of 70 sixth graders, how many of them are eligible for the federal school lunch program?

PROCEDURE: In this situation, we know the percent: 30%; we also know the whole (the base of the second set), 70. The unknown is the *amount* of the second set, the number of sixth graders who are eligible for the program.

	Percent	Students
Eligible for program	30	a
All six graders	100	70

ANSWER: Legend: Let $a =$ the number of sixth graders eligible for the program.

$$\frac{30}{100} = \frac{a}{70} \quad \text{Cross multiply and solve.}$$

$$30 \cdot 70 = 100 \cdot a$$

$$2100 \div 100 = 100 \div 100 \cdot a$$

$$21 = a$$

SENTENCE: 21 sixth graders are eligible for the program.

In the answer portion of Example 3, could we first simplify $\frac{30}{100}$, by a factor of 10, to $\frac{3}{10}$? Why or why not?

____

____

YOU TRY IT 3

15% of the seniors at Kraemer High School are eligible for admission to UCLA. If there are 120 seniors at Kraemer High, how many are eligible for admission to UCLA? Use Example 3 as a guide.

Legend:

Sentence:

When the Base Is Unknown

Sometimes it is the base that is unknown.

EXAMPLE 4 15% of the local Kiwanis Club members are employed by the city. If it is known that 6 members of the club work for the city, then how many total members does the club have?

PROCEDURE: In this situation, we know the percent: 15%; we also know the part (the amount of the second set). What is unknown is the base of the second set, the total number of members in the Kiwanis Club?

	Percent	Kiwanis member
Work for city	15	6
All members	100	b

ANSWER: Legend: Let $b =$ the total number of members in the Kiwanis Club.

$$\frac{15}{100} = \frac{6}{b} \quad \text{Cross multiply and solve.}$$

$$15 \cdot b = 100 \cdot 6$$

$$15 \div 15 \cdot b = 600 \div 15$$

$$b = 40$$

SENTENCE: The Kiwanis Club has 40 members.

YOU TRY IT 4 *28% of the University of Virginia Cavaliers baseball team throw left handed. If 7 members of the team throw left handed, how many players are on the team? Use Example 4 as a guide.*

Legend:

Sentence:

You Try It Answers: Section 6.5

YTI 1 Let $p =$ the unknown percentage.

	Percent	Singers
Sopranos	p	18
All singers	100	60

$$\frac{p}{100} = \frac{18}{60}$$

30% of the singers are sopranos.

YTI 2 Let $p =$ the unknown percentage.

	Percent	Passengers
First class	p	24
All passengers	100	108

$$\frac{p}{100} = \frac{24}{108}$$

About 22.2% of the passengers flew first class.

YTI 3 Let $a =$ the number of eligible seniors.

	Percent	Seniors
Eligible for admission	15	a
All seniors	100	120

$$\frac{15}{100} = \frac{a}{120}$$

18 seniors are eligible for admission to UCLA.

YTI 4 Let $b =$ the total number of players on the team.

	Percent	Players
Throw left handed	28	7
All players	100	b

$$\frac{28}{100} = \frac{7}{b}$$

There are 25 players on the University of Virginia Cavaliers baseball team.

Focus Exercises: Section 6.5

For each, use the proportion table outlined in this section. Write a legend, set up and solve the proportion, and write a sentence answering the question.

1. 12% of the packs in a box of baseball cards have an autographed card inside. If the box contains 25 packs, how many of them contain an autographed card?

2. 75% of the faculty at Lemon Valley College are tenured. If there are 72 faculty members in all, how many are tenured?

3. 28% of the female members of a health club attend at least four times a week. If there are 325 female members, how many attend at least four times a week?

4. 45% of the customers at the Gila Bend Starbucks order a frappuccino. If last Saturday, Starbucks served 180 customers, how many ordered a frappuccino?

5. 52% of the voters in Glenn Cove, New York, were in favor of Proposition A on the ballot. If 175 people in total voted, how many voted for Proposition A?

6. 88% of the Fitchberg Annex Post Office mailboxes have been rented. If the post office has 225 mailboxes, how many of them have been rented?

7. 12.5% of the employees in Commandary Publishing Services are managers. If the company has 120 employees, how many are in management?

8. 37.5% of the families in a large neighborhood own three or more cars. If there are 160 families in this neighborhood, how many of them own three or more cars?

9. 12% of the Framingham Post Office mailboxes are extra large. If the post office has 27 extra large mailboxes, how many mailboxes does it have in all?

10. 25% of the basketball cards that Jesse collects are rookie cards. If he has 65 rookie cards, how many cards does he have in all?

11. 32% of the customers at the Wayland Starbucks order a grande-sized drink. Last Sunday, 48 customers ordered a grande-sized drink. What was the total number of customers that day?

12. 68% of the voters in Winooski, Vermont, were in favor of Measure B on the ballot. If 272 people were in favor of Measure B, how many total people voted in this town?

13. 16% of the faculty at Cedar Glen College teach English. If there are 24 English instructors, how many total faculty are there?

14. 15% of the female members of a health club are married. If there are 36 married women members at the club, what is the total number of female members?

15. 87.5% of the families in a neighborhood participate in a huge annual garage sale. If 49 families participate in the garage sale, how many total families live in this neighborhood?

16. 62.5% of the employees in a factory have attained "senior" status (they've worked there at least twenty years). If the factory has 95 senior employees, how many total employees are there?

17. Of the 85 chiropractic patients that Dr. James sees regularly, 34 of them get a weekly massage. What percent of his patients receive a weekly massage?

18. Louie made a record of all of the faculty computers on his campus. Of the 150 computers, 42 of them are Macs. What percent of the faculty computers are Macs?

19. 28 of the 80 football cards that Jermaine owns are memorabilia cards (there is a piece of a player's jersey within the card). What percent of his football card collection is memorabilia cards?

20. 65 of the 250 Woodland Post Office mailbox renters check their mailbox every Sunday. What percent of the renters check their mailbox every Sunday?

21. In a small town, 176 of the 330 voters voted for Becky Kendall for mayor. What percent of the vote did Ms. Kendall get?

22. Karin is the Math and Science Department chair at Quarry Bluffs Community College. Her department has 20 full-time members on a campus that employs 75 full-time faculty. What percentage of the full-time faculty is in Karin's department?

23. Of the 120 employees at Middlesex Community College, 16 ride the bus to work. What percent of the employees ride the bus to work?

24. Of the 90 families in a neighborhood, 32 have children in preschool. What percent of the families have children in preschool?

SECTION 6.6 Solving the Percent Equation

Objectives

In this section, you will learn to:

- Set up and solve a percent equation.

To successfully complete this section, you need to understand:

- Solving equations with fractions (3.5)
- Writing percents as fractions (6.4)
- Writing percents as decimals (6.4)
- Writing decimals as percents (6.4)

This section may be presented in addition to, or as an alternative to, Section 6.5.

Introduction

We've seen percent represented as a fraction, as a decimal, and as a ratio, but still, 25%, in and of itself, doesn't mean very much unless we know, "25% of what?" In other words, percent is almost always *of* something. Furthermore, *percent of* always means *multiply*.

For example, if there are 12 songs on a CD, and 25% of them are love songs, then there are 25% × 12 = 3 love songs.

When multiplying by a percent it is common to write the percent as either a fraction or a decimal:

As a fraction:

$$25\% \times 12 = \frac{25}{100} \times \frac{12}{1} = \frac{1}{4} \times \frac{12}{1} = \frac{12}{4} = 3$$

As a decimal:

$$25\% \times 12 = 0.25 \times 12 = \begin{array}{r} 12 \\ \times\ 0.25 \\ \hline 60 \\ +\ 240 \\ \hline 3.00 \end{array} = 3$$

EXAMPLE 1 Find each product. Write each percent as either a fraction or a decimal.

a) 40% of 45 b) 23% of 45

PROCEDURE: In part a, 40% would simplify nicely as a fraction: $\frac{40}{100} = \frac{4}{10} = \frac{2}{5}$. In part b, 23% would probably work best as a decimal, 0.23. In either case, we need to multiply.

ANSWER:

a) $\frac{40}{100} \times 45$

$= \frac{2}{5} \times \frac{45}{1}$

$= \frac{2 \cdot 45}{5 \cdot 1}$ Reduce by a factor of 5.

$= \frac{2 \cdot 9}{1 \cdot 1}$

$= \frac{18}{1} = 18$

b) 0.23 × 45

$$\begin{array}{r} 45 \\ \times\ 0.23 \\ \hline 135 \\ +\ 900 \\ \hline 10.35 \end{array}$$

SENTENCE: 40% of 45 is 18. 23% of 45 is 10.35.

YOU TRY IT 1 *Find each product. Write each percent as either a fraction or a decimal. Use Example 1 as a guide.*

a) 20% of 75 b) 35% of 24 c) 44% of 125

The Percent Equation

Refer back to Example 1a. The result is that 40% of 45 is 18.

This is an example of the *percent equation.*

40%	of	45	is	18
	↓		↓	
40%	×	45	=	18
	↓		↓	
percent	×	whole	=	part

The Percent Equation: *Percent of whole is part*

$$\text{Percent} \times \text{whole} = \text{part}$$

In a typical percent problem, one of these numbers is unknown, and we can use the percent equation to find its value. For example, we have seen that 40% of 45 is 18. From this, we can generate three different questions, each with a different unknown value and a slightly different equation. (In *this* case, n is easy to find because we already know the whole equation.)

Question	Equation	Answer	Sentence
(a) When the part is unknown, we ask: 40% of 45 is *what number*?	$40\% \times 45 = n$	$n = 18$	40% of 45 is 18.
(b) When the whole is unknown, we ask: 40% of *what number* is 18?	$40\% \times n = 18$	$n = 45$	40% of 45 is 18.
(c) When the percent is unknown, we ask: *What percent* of 45 is 18?	$p \times 45 = 18$	$p = .40$, $p = 40\%$	40% of 45 is 18.

When the Part Is Unknown

This is the simplest type of problem to solve because the part, n, is already isolated.

EXAMPLE 2 Find the missing value. Once the number is found, write a concluding sentence.

a) 15% of 80 is what number? b) 48% of 55 is what number?

PROCEDURE: As in Example 1, we can write the percent as either a fraction or as a decimal. Here, we'll use a fraction in part a and a decimal in part b.

ANSWER: a) Let $n = \textit{what number}$.

$$15\% \times 80 = n$$

$$\frac{15}{100} \times 80 = n \qquad \text{Reduce } \tfrac{15}{100} \text{ by a factor of 5 to } \tfrac{3}{20}.$$

$$\frac{3}{20} \cdot \frac{80}{1} = n$$

$$\frac{3 \cdot 80}{20 \cdot 1} = n \qquad \text{80 and 20 have a common factor of 20.}$$

$$\frac{3 \cdot 4}{1 \cdot 1} = n$$

$$12 = n$$

SENTENCE: 15% of 80 is 12.

b) Let n = *what number*.

$48\% \times 55 = n$

$0.48 \times 55 = n$

$26.40 = n$

$$\begin{array}{r} 55 \\ \times .48 \\ \hline 440 \\ +\ 2200 \\ \hline 26.40 \end{array}$$

SENTENCE: 48% of 55 is 26.4.

YOU TRY IT 2

Find the missing value. Once the number is found, write a conclusion. Use Example 2 as a guide. (You may write the percent as either a fraction or a decimal.)

a) 20% of 35 is what number?

Sentence:

b) 36% of 75 is what number?

Sentence:

When the Whole Is Unknown

When the whole is unknown, the variable, n, will be on the left side with the percent, the coefficient of n. We'll divide by the coefficient to isolate n and solve the equation.

In Example 3 we'll write the percent as a fraction, and in Example 4 we'll write the percent as a decimal.

EXAMPLE 3

Find the missing value. Once the number is found, write a concluding sentence.
15% of what number is 60?

PROCEDURE: This time, we'll write the percent as a fraction.

ANSWER: Let n = *what number*.

$15\% \times n = 60$ — Write 15% as $\frac{15}{100}$.

$\frac{15}{100} \cdot n = 60$ — To isolate n, multiply each side by the reciprocal of the coefficient.

$\frac{15}{100} \cdot \frac{100}{15} \cdot n = 60 \cdot \frac{100}{15}$ — Write 60 as $\frac{60}{1}$.

$1 \cdot n = \frac{60}{1} \cdot \frac{100}{15}$

$n = \frac{60 \cdot 100}{1 \cdot 15}$ — 60 and 15 have a common factor of 15.

$n = \frac{4 \cdot 100}{1 \cdot 1}$

$n = 400$

SENTENCE: 15% of 400 is 60.

Think about it

In Example 3, would it make a difference if we wrote the percent as a decimal instead of a fraction? Why or why not?

EXAMPLE 4 Find the missing value. Once the number is found, write a concluding sentence. 48% of what number is 72?

PROCEDURE: Again, *what number* is the whole.

ANSWER: Let n = *what number*.

$$48\% \times n = 72$$
$$0.48 \times n = 72$$
$$n \times 0.48 \div 0.48 = 72 \div 0.48$$
$$n = 150$$

Long division: $.48\overline{)72.00}$

$$\begin{array}{r} 150 \\ 48\overline{)7200} \\ -\ 48 \\ \hline 240 \\ -\ 240 \\ \hline 00 \end{array}$$

SENTENCE: 48% of <u>150</u> is 72.

YOU TRY IT 3 *Find the missing value. Once the number is found, write a conclusion. Use Examples 3 and 4 as guides. (You may write the percent as either a fraction or a decimal.)*

a) 36% of what number is 9?

b) 75% of what number is 36?

Sentence:

Sentence:

When the Percent Is Unknown

In the percent equation, when the percent is unknown, we'll let p = the unknown percent and solve the equation for p. However, when the concluding sentence is written, we need to express p as a percent.

EXAMPLE 5 Find the missing value. Once the number is found, write a concluding sentence.

a) What percent of 140 is 49? b) What percent of 120 is 9? c) What percent of 12 is 7?

PROCEDURE: When the equation is solved, the value of p will be written as a decimal. Be sure to take one more step to write it as a percent.

ANSWER: For each, Let p = the *percent*.

a) $p \cdot 140 = 49$ Divide each side by 140.

$p \cdot 140 \div 140 = 49 \div 140$

$p = 49 \div 140$ Use long division (at right). →

$p = 0.35$ Since the question is asking what percent, write 0.35 as a percent: 0.35 = 35%.

$p = 35\%$

$$\begin{array}{r} 0.35 \\ 140\overline{)49.00} \\ -\,42\,0 \\ \hline 7\,00 \\ -\,7\,00 \\ \hline 0 \end{array}$$

SENTENCE: 35% of 140 is 49.

b) $p \cdot 120 = 9$ Divide each side by 120.

$p \cdot 120 \div 120 = 9 \div 120$

$p = 9 \div 120$ Use long division (at right). →

$p = 0.075$ Write 0.075 as a percent: 0.075 = 7.5%.

$p = 7.5\%$

$$\begin{array}{r} 0.075 \\ 120\overline{)9.000} \\ -\,8\,40 \\ \hline 600 \\ -\,600 \\ \hline 0 \end{array}$$

SENTENCE: 7.5% of 120 is 9.

c) $p \cdot 12 = 7$ Divide each side by 12.

$p \cdot 12 \div 12 = 7 \div 12$

$p = 7 \div 12$ Use long division (at right). →

$p = 0.58\overline{3}$

$p = 58.\overline{3}\%$

$$\begin{array}{r} 0.5833 \\ 12\overline{)7.0000} \\ -\,6\,0 \\ \hline 1\,00 \\ -\,96 \\ \hline 40 \\ -\,36 \\ \hline 40 \end{array}$$ repeating

SENTENCE: $58.\overline{3}\%$ of 12 is 7.

YOU TRY IT 4

Find the missing value. Once the number is found, write a conclusion. Use Example 5 as a guide. (You may write the percent as either a fraction or a decimal.)

a) What percent of 35 is 14?

Sentence:

b) What percent of 125 is 85?

Sentence:

c) What percent of 56 is 21?

Sentence:

d) What percent of 54 is 45?

Sentence:

Applications Involving the Percent Equation

Typical application situations are not written, in English, in a way that directly asks: "What percent of the whole is the part?" Often it is up to us to analyze and interpret the wording. For example:

> 24% of the shoppers at a grocery store will use the express lane (with only a few items in their carts). If there are 75 people in the store, how many are expected to use the express lane?

In this problem we are given the percent, 24%, and one other number. That other number is either the whole or the part. Let's think about it: only some of the customers use the express lane, not all of them. So, the number of shoppers in the express lane is the *part* and the total number of people in the store, 75, is the *whole*. This is our interpretation:

24% of 75 is what number?

$$24\% \times 75 = n$$

EXAMPLE 6

Identify the percent, whole, and part in each of these situations.

a) In a typical day, 5% of the kindergarten students at Washington Elementary School will be out sick. If there are 80 kindergarten students enrolled, how many are expected to be out sick tomorrow?

b) Lucy made cookies for a bake sale and kept 25% of them at home for her family. If her family got to keep 24 cookies, how many cookies did Lucy make?

c) A local bank's ATM serviced 120 customers one day, and 36 made deposits. What percent of the ATM customers made deposits?

PROCEDURE: For each, identify the percent, the whole, and the part.

ANSWER:

a) Percent: 5%; there are 80 students in total, and they won't all be sick. So, whole: 80 and part: unknown.

b) Percent: 25%; If Lucy gave some cookies (24) to her family, she had to have made many more for the bake sale; so, part: 24, and whole: unknown.

c) We don't see the percent, so it must be the unknown. The other two numbers are the whole (total customers) and the part (customers who made deposits). So, percent: unknown, whole: 120, and part: 36 .

YOU TRY IT 5

Identify the percent, whole, and part in each of these situations. Use Example 6 as a guide.

a) 120 voters were asked whether they would support the local school bond on the upcoming ballot, and 75 people said, "Yes." What percent of the voters said they would support the school bond?

Percent: ____________ Whole: ____________ Part: ____________

b) Paolo works for a computer store and earns 5% commission on everything he sells. On Tuesday, he sold $1,480 worth of computer equipment. How much commission did he earn?

Percent: ____________ Whole: ____________ Part: ____________

c) 18 students in Ms. Chung's algebra classes received an A last semester. This is 15% of all of her algebra students. How many algebra students did Ms. Chung have last semester?

Percent: ____________ Whole: ____________ Part: ____________

d) Oscar was on a business trip to Springfield, Illinois, where he also purchased gifts for his family. On the flight home, Oscar became curious about the sales tax rate in Illinois. His receipt indicated that he paid $120.00 for the gifts and $7.50 in sales tax. What is the sales tax rate in Illinois?

Percent: ____________ Whole: ____________ Part: ____________

YOU TRY IT 6

Solve each by first putting the information you found in YTI 5 into the formula percent × whole = part. *Write a legend and a sentence answering the question.*

a) 120 voters were asked whether they would support the local school bond on the upcoming ballot, and 75 people said, "Yes." What percent of the voters said they would support the school bond?

b) Paolo works for a computer store and earns 5% commission on everything he sells. On Tuesday, he sold $1,480 worth of computer equipment. How much commission did he earn?

c) 18 students in Ms. Chung's algebra classes received an A last semester. This is 15% of all of her algebra students. How many algebra students did Ms. Chung have last semester?

d) Oscar was on a business trip to Springfield, Illinois, where he also purchased gifts for his family. On the flight home, Oscar became curious about the sales tax rate in Illinois. His receipt indicated that he paid $120.00 for the gifts and $7.50 in sales tax. What is the sales tax rate in Illinois?

You Try It Answers: Section 6.6

YTI 1 a) 15 b) 8.4 c) 55

YTI 2 a) 20% of 35 is 7. b) 36% of 75 is 27.

YTI 3 a) 36% of 25 is 9. b) 75% of 48 is 36.

YTI 4 a) 40% of 35 is 14. b) 68% of 125 is 85.
c) 37.5% of 56 is 21. d) $83.\overline{3}\%$ of 54 is 45.

YTI 5 a) Percent: unknown Whole: 120
Part: 75
b) Percent: 5% Whole: $1,480
Part: unknown
c) Percent: 15% Whole: unknown
Part: 18
d) Percent: unknown Whole: $120.00
Part: $7.50

YTI 6 a) Let p = the percent of voters who support the bond.
62.5% of the voters said they would support the school bond.
b) Let n = the amount of his commission.
Paolo earned $74 in commission.
c) Let n = the number of algebra students in Ms. Chung's classes.
Ms. Chung had a total of 120 algebra students last semester.
d) Let p = the percent sales tax.
The sales tax rate in Illinois is 6.25%.

Focus Exercises: Section 6.6

Find the product.

1. 20% of 70
2. 30% of 120
3. 45% of 60
4. 85% of 40
5. 75% of 96
6. 25% of 52
7. 64% of 45
8. 32% of 55
9. 37.5% of 160
10. 12.5% of 240
11. 87.5% of 56
12. 62.5% of 72

For each, find the missing value and write a conclusion.

13. 80% of 95 is what number?
14. 90% of 125 is what number?
15. 35% of 40 is what number?
16. 55% of 60 is what number?
17. 25% of what number is 14?
18. 75% of what number is 63?
19. 45% of what number is 36?
20. 40% of what number is 30?
21. 60% of what number is 48?
22. 30% of what number is 57?
23. What percent of 76 is 38?
24. What percent of 28 is 21?
25. What percent of 65 is 26?
26. What percent of 60 is 48?
27. What percent of 45 is 27?
28. What percent of 96 is 120?

Solve each using the percent equation. Write a sentence answering the question. (You may want to identify the percent, whole, and part before writing the equation.) Use the outline provided with the first problem for the others.

29. Jayne works for a computer store and earns 5% commission on everything she sells. On Wednesday, she made $96 in commissions. How much computer equipment did she sell?
Let n =

To help you think it through:
Percent: ______
Whole: ______
Part: ______

Sentence:

30. 40% of the patrons who went roller skating at Skate-A-Rama last Saturday night rented skates. If 38 people rented skates, how many skaters were there that night?

31. 15% of the cars parked in the college parking lot were in the carpool spaces, reserved for anyone riding in a carpool. If there were 24 cars parked in the carpool spaces, how many total cars were in the parking lot?

32. Last Monday, 7.5% of that day's bank customers needed access to their safe deposit box. If 21 people opened their safe deposit boxes, how many customers did the bank have that day?

33. In a class of 40 students, only 18 brought their books to class on the first day. What percent of the class brought their books on the first day?

34. Last November, it rained 12 days out of 30 at Big Bear Mountain. What percent of the month of November did it rain at Big Bear?

35. Of the 24 deputies in the Sioux Falls Sheriff's Department, 9 are women. What percent of the deputies are women?

36. Of the 250 diners at the King's Grill Buffet, 98 redeemed discount coupons. What percent of the diners used coupons?

SECTION 6.7 Applications Involving Percents

Objectives

In this section, you will learn to:

- Solve percent applications using arithmetic.

To successfully complete this section, you need to understand:

- Rounding decimals (5.2)
- Multiplying decimals (5.4)
- Dividing decimals (5.5)
- Writing percents as decimals (6.4)

Introduction

The percent applications in this section do not require equations to solve. Instead, we will multiply and divide directly *without* using a variable to represent the unknown value.

In each of these, the whole is known, and we'll either:

1. Multiply the percent by the whole to find the part or
2. divide the part by the whole to find the percent.

Let's practice multiplying with percents. In each, it's best to rewrite the percent as a decimal.

EXAMPLE 1 Multiply. For each, round the result to the nearest hundredth.

a) 35% × 70 b) 9% × 26.65 c) 3.2% × 16.95

ANSWER:

a)
$$\begin{array}{r} 70 \\ \times\ 0.35 \\ \hline 350 \\ +\ 2100 \\ \hline 24.50 \end{array}$$
This does not need to be rounded.

b)
$$\begin{array}{r} 26.65 \\ \times\ 0.09 \\ \hline 2.3985 \end{array}$$
This rounds up to 2.40.

c)
$$\begin{array}{r} 16.95 \\ \times\ 0.032 \\ \hline 3390 \\ +\ 50850 \\ \hline 0.54240 \end{array}$$
This rounds down to 0.54.

YOU TRY IT 1 *Multiply. For each, round the result to the nearest hundredth. Use Example 1 as a guide.*

a) 24% × 92 b) 7% × 84.23 c) 4.5% × 49.15

Let's practice dividing to find percents.

EXAMPLE 2 Divide and write the answer as a percent.

a) $\frac{54}{120}$ b) $\frac{36}{96}$ c) $\frac{0.56}{0.9}$

PROCEDURE: Use long division. Add zeros after the decimal point as needed. For part c we'll need to first move each decimal point one place to the right so that the denominator (divisor) is a whole number.

ANSWER:

a)
```
        0.45
120)54.00
   − 48 0
      6 00
    − 6 00
         0
```

b)
```
     0.375
96)36.000
  − 28 8
     7 20
   − 6 72
      480
    − 480
        0
```

c)
```
   0.6222
9)5.6000
 − 5 4
     20
   − 18
     20
   − 18
     20   (repeats)
```

$0.45 = 45\%$ $0.375 = 37.5\%$ $0.62222 \approx 62.2\%$

YOU TRY IT 2

Divide and write the answer as a percent. Use Example 2 as a guide.

a) $\frac{57}{75}$ b) $\frac{42}{125}$ c) $\frac{0.35}{1.8}$

Using Multiplication to Solve Percent Problems

Sales Tax: Sales tax is always a percentage of the purchase price (whole). The amount of sales tax is calculated by multiplying the sales tax rate (%) by the purchase price. This tax is added on to the purchase price at the cash register.

Suppose the price of a new computer keyboard is \$60, and the sales tax rate is 8%. The amount of sales tax is found by multiplying 8% by \$60: $0.08 \times \$60 = \$4.80$. The amount of sales tax, \$4.80, is then added to the price, so the customer ends up paying $\$60.00 + \$4.80 = \$64.80$ for the keyboard.

Caution After you calculate the sales tax, round it to the nearest penny. Then add it to the price to get the total amount to be paid.

EXAMPLE 3 If the sales tax rate is 8%, find the amount of sales tax due on a shirt that has a price of \$23.95. Also, find the total to be paid by the customer.

PROCEDURE: Write the percent as a decimal and multiply it by the price; round that amount to the nearest penny; add the sales tax to the price to find the total amount to be paid.

ANSWER: $8\% = 0.08$, so the sales tax $= 0.08 \times 23.95 = \$1.916$.

Round 1.916 to the nearest penny: \$1.92

Add: Price + sales tax = total to be paid

\$23.95 + \$1.92 = \$25.87

```
  23.95
+  1.92
  25.87
```

SENTENCE: The sales tax is \$1.92, and the customer must pay \$25.87.

You finish it:

Multiply
```
  23.95
× 0.08
```

YOU TRY IT 3

If the sales tax rate is 7%, find the amount of sales tax due on a bicycle that costs $195.99, then find the total paid by the customer. Use Example 3 as a guide.

Sentence:

Commission: The amount of commission that a salesperson earns is always a percentage of the purchase price (whole). The amount of commission is calculated by multiplying the commission rate (%) by the purchase price.

Let's say a furniture salesman earns a 3% commission on everything he sells. In January, he sold $136,000 worth of furniture. His commission for that month is found by multiplying 3% by 136,000: $0.03 \times \$136{,}000 = \$4{,}080$.

Caution The amount of commission is not added to, or subtracted from, anything.

EXAMPLE 4

Connie is a saleswoman at an appliance store and earns a 3.5% commission on everything she sells. Last Saturday she sold appliances totaling $3,946. How much did she earn in commissions that day?

PROCEDURE: Multiply the percent by the total amount sold, and round that amount to the nearest penny.

ANSWER: $3.5\% = 0.035$, so the commission is $0.035 \times 3{,}946$.

You finish it:

Multiply

$$\begin{array}{r} 3946 \\ \times\ 0.035 \\ \hline \end{array}$$

SENTENCE: Connie earned $138.11 in commissions that day.

YOU TRY IT 4

RaeLynn sells stereo and camera equipment at an electronics store and earns 2.5% on everything she sells. Yesterday, she sold electronic gear totaling $4,793. How much did she earn in commissions that day? Use Example 4 as a guide.

Sentence:

Discount: The original price of an item is 100% of that price. When a percent discount is given, it can be directly subtracted from 100% before the discounted price is calculated.

For example, a 25% discount is equal to $100\% - 25\% = 75\%$ of the original price. To find the new price of the item, we multiply the original price by 75%.

Suppose the original price of a new computer keyboard is \$60, but the store is offering a 20% discount. This means that the new price is 100% − 20% = 80% of the price. Multiply 80% by \$60: 0.80 × \$60 = \$48.00.

The new price of the keyboard is \$48.00. (This is before sales tax is added on at the register.)

EXAMPLE 5 This week at Kasey's Department Store, jackets are discounted 15%. Find the new price of a jacket that originally costs \$46.90.

PROCEDURE: 100% − 15% = 85%. Multiply the original price,

ANSWER: \$46.90, by 85% to find the new price.

You finish it:
Multiply 46.90 × 0.85

SENTENCE: The new price is \$39.87.

YOU TRY IT 5 *Diamond Adventure is offering a 30% discount on all of their tents. Find the new price of a tent that originally costs \$148.99. Use Example 5 as a guide.*

Sentence:

Using Division to Solve Percent Problems

Because percent is a ratio, percentage : base, which can be written as a fraction, $\frac{\text{percentage}}{\text{base}}$, there is a *division* relationship between the percentage (part) and the base (whole).

So, to find the comparison—as a percent—between a part and the whole, we divide:

$$\frac{\textbf{Part}}{\textbf{Whole}}, \text{ or } \textbf{part} \div \textbf{whole}, \text{ or } \textbf{whole}\overline{)\textbf{part}}$$

EXAMPLE 6 Carlo, a furniture salesman, sold a total of \$8,500 in merchandise last Monday and earned \$255 in commissions. What is Carlo's commission rate?

PROCEDURE: In this case, we divide $\frac{255}{8,500}$ or 255 ÷ 8,500.

You finish it:
Divide $8,500\overline{)255}$

SENTENCE: Carlo's commission rate is 3%.

YOU TRY IT 6 *Beverly works in a flooring center, selling tile and carpet. Last Tuesday, she sold a total of \$3,800 worth of goods and earned a commission of \$133. What is the her commission rate? Use Example 6 as a guide.*

Sentence:

Determining Percent Increase and Percent Decrease

Many people invest their money in the stock market, hoping that the value of their stock will rise. When a stock rises, investors are interested in its *percent increase*. To find a percent increase we use this ratio:

$$\text{Percent increase} = \frac{\text{Amount of increase}}{\text{Previous amount}}$$

With that in mind, if a company's stock rises \$3 in one day, is that a lot or a little? The answer is: It depends on how much the stock was worth the day before.

For example, if Tuesday's ending price for a stock was \$30.00, and the value increases \$3.00 by the end of Wednesday, then that is a 10% increase:

$$\frac{\text{Amount of increase}}{\text{Previous value}} = \frac{3}{30} = \frac{1}{10} = 0.10 = 10\%$$

However, if Tuesday's ending price for a stock was \$100.00, and the value increases \$3.00 by the end of Wednesday, then that is a 3% increase:

$$\frac{\text{Amount of increase}}{\text{Previous value}} = \frac{3}{100} = 3\%$$

We can also look at the percent of *decrease* if a stock's price is less than the previous day's value.

$$\text{Percent decrease} = \frac{\text{Amount of decrease}}{\text{Previous amount}}$$

For example, if Tuesday's ending price for a different stock was \$40.00, and the value *decreases* \$2.00 by the end of Wednesday, then that is a 5% decrease:

$$\frac{\text{Amount of decrease}}{\text{Previous value}} = \frac{2}{40} = \frac{1}{20} = 0.05 = 5\%$$

When finding a percent increase or decrease, we must know both

1. the amount of increase (or decrease), and
2. the previous amount to which it is compared.

For example, at the end of 2003, a stock was priced at \$24. At the end of 2004, its value had increased to \$30. What was the percent increase?

First, we must identify the amount of increase by subtracting the lower amount from the higher amount:

$$\text{Higher} - \text{lower} = \$30 - \$24 = \$6$$

We must then recognize the previous value, the value that came first according to time. Since the \$24 value was at the end of 2003, and the \$30 value was a year later, we compare the amount of increase (\$6) to \$24, the value that came first:

$$\text{Percent of increase} = \frac{6}{24} = \frac{1}{4} = 25\%$$

EXAMPLE 7 At the end of February, a computer store had \$18,000 in total sales. At the end of March, it had \$20,700 in total sales. What is the percent increase in total sales?

PROCEDURE: First, find the amount of increase. Then, compare that amount to the previous amount, February's sales.

ANSWER: The amount of increase is found by subtracting:
\$20,700 − \$18,000 = \$2,700

This amount is compared to the first total, the total sales in February: $\frac{2{,}700}{18{,}000} = \frac{27}{180}$. This is 27 ÷ 180.

You finish it:
Divide $180\overline{)27}$

SENTENCE: Total sales increased 15% from February to March.

YOU TRY IT 7 *At the end of May, a stock's price was \$32. At the end of June, the price had increased to \$36. What is the percent increase in the price of the stock? Use Example 7 as a guide.*

Sentence:

EXAMPLE 8 In 1999, a top-of-the-line laptop computer was priced at \$4,200. In 2004, a comparable laptop computer was priced at \$3,500. What is the percent decrease in price? (Round the quotient to the nearest thousandth, if necessary.)

PROCEDURE: First, find the amount of decrease. Then, compare that amount to the previous price in 1999.

ANSWER: The amount of decrease is found by subtracting:
\$4,200 − \$3,500 = \$700

$\frac{700}{4{,}200} = \frac{7}{42} = \frac{1}{6}$. This is 1 ÷ 6.

You finish it:
Divide $6\overline{)1}$

SENTENCE: The price for a top-of-the-line laptop decreased 16.7% from 1999 to 2004.

YOU TRY IT 8 *In 2003, the Cyuga Rotary Club had 30 members. In 2004, the club had only 26 members. What is the percent decrease in membership? (Round the quotient to the nearest thousandth, if necessary.) Use Example 8 as a guide.*

Sentence:

You Try It Answers: Section 6.7

YTI 1 a) 22.08 b) 5.90 c) 2.21

YTI 2 a) 76% b) 33.6%

c) $19.\overline{4}\%$ or $\approx$ 19.4%

YTI 3 $7\% \times 195.99 = 13.7193$; 13.7193 rounds up to 13.72.

The sales tax is $13.72, and the customer must pay $209.71.

YTI 4 $2.5\% \times 4{,}793 = 0.025 \times 4{,}793 = 119.825$ which rounds to $119.83.

RaeLynn's commission yesterday was $119.83.

YTI 5 $100\% - 30\% = 70\%$.
$70\% \times 148.99 = 0.70 \times 148.99 = 104.293$, which rounds to $104.29.

The new price of the tent is $104.29.

YTI 6 $133 \div 3{,}800 = 0.035 = 3.5\%$ Beverly's commission rate is 3.5%.

YTI 7 First, the amount of increase is $\$36 - \$32 = \$4$. The percent increase is $4 \div 32 = 0.125 = 12.5\%$.

The price of the stock increased 12.5%.

YTI 8 First, the amount of decrease is $30 - 26 = 4$. The percent decrease is $4 \div 30 = 0.1333\ldots$ which rounds to 0.133 or 13.3%.

The membership decreased 13.3%.

Focus Exercises: Section 6.7

Solve each sales tax and commission application. Write a sentence answering the question.

1. Tanaya bought a jacket that costs $47.70. The sales tax rate in her state is 6%. How much did she pay at the cash register?

2. Sue purchased a portable CD player for $85.60 plus tax. If the sales tax rate in her state is 7%, how much did she pay at the register?

3. Mike is a salesman at a large home electronics store. He receives a 3% commission on everything he sells. One day, he sold $2,850 worth of stereo equipment. How much commission did he make that day?

4. Giorgio is a salesman at a large home appliance store. He earned $98.49 on sales of $2,814. What percent is his commission?

Solve each discount application. Write a sentence answering the question.

5. Ilana saw a sweater that had a discount tag of 40%. The original price of the sweater was $80.00. What is the new price of the sweater?

6. Tessa was shopping for a new MP3 player. She saw an ad for a brand that was 25% off the original price of $180. What was the new price of the MP3 player?

7. Eleazar works at a department store As an employee benefit, he receives a 10% discount on any item he purchases in the store. The suit he chose to buy was originally priced at $183.99. What is the price he'll pay using his employee discount?

8. A car that originally costs $13,599 is discounted 12%. Find the new price of the car.

Find the percent. Write a sentence answering the question.

9. Sarah took a math test and got 34 out of 40 points possible. What is her grade as a percent?

10. Carnell saved $9 on a pair of shoes. The original price was $75. What percent were the shoes discounted?

11. Marcus is raising money to go on the marching band's spring tour. He needs to raise $800. So far, he has raised $680. What percent of his goal has he attained?

12. At the beginning of the month, Traci had 90 jackets in inventory. At the end of the month, she had 27 jackets still in inventory. What percent of the jackets did she sell during the month?

Solve each multistep application. Write a sentence answering the question.

13. Jamal saved $27.00 to buy a gift for his cousin, Amee. He knew he'd have to pay 8% sales tax, so the gift would need to be priced lower than $27.00. He found the perfect gift for her, and it cost $24.50. With the 8% sales tax added on, will he have enough money to buy the gift for Amee, and if so, how much will he pay at the register?

14. Charlene went to the campus bookstore to purchase a textbook and some school supplies. Here is her shopping list and the price of each item:

Item	Price
Textbook	$83.00
Notebook	4.38
3 pencils	1.59
2 pens	3.82

a) Add up the total price.

b) Compute the sales tax if the sales tax rate is 7%.

c) Find the total amount Charlene will pay at the bookstore for these supplies.

15. Bud works for a department store. One fringe benefit the store provides is a 15% discount on all merchandise purchased by employees. Bud found a TV he wants to buy that costs $379.95.

a) What price will Bud pay for the TV set?

b) If the sales tax rate in his city is 8%, how much will Bud pay in sales tax?

c) How much will Bud pay for the TV, including sales tax?

16. Henry took his family out to a nice restaurant to celebrate his daughter's graduation. The meal total came to $126.35.

a) If the sales tax rate is 7.75%, what is the sales tax on the meal?

b) Henry thought the service and the food were good and decided to leave a 15% tip for the server. How much should the tip be? (The tip, by the way, is a percentage of the meal total and should be figured separately from the sales tax.)

c) What was the total amount paid by Henry for dinner that night?

Solve each percent increase and percent decrease application. Write a sentence answering the question.

17. The choir budget was $2,500 last year. This year it is $3,000. What is the percent increase in the choir budget?

18. Last year, Louis was the president of the local Kiwanis Club. During the year, the club grew in membership from 15 to 24. What was the percent increase during his time as club president?

19. During the summer between the tenth and eleventh grade, Nate experienced a growth spurt and grew from 64 inches to 72 inches. By what percent did Nate's height increase?

20. Last year, Daniel and his wife, Sonia, were able to give $450 per month to their synagogue. This year, they have pledged to give $500 a month. What is the percent increase in their monthly gift?

21. Last year, a Chevrolet Marlin was priced at $20,000. This year, its price has dropped to $18,500. What is the percent decrease from last year to this year?

22. At the beginning of the month, Alice weighed 225 pounds. After healthy eating and exercise, she weighed 207 pounds at the end of the month. What was the percent decrease of her weight?

23. For the month of December, sales at Mitch's Sporting Goods were an all-time high at $32,000. As always happens, though, January sales were much lower, at only $20,000. What is the percent decrease in sales from December to January?

24. The Tomlins' house was up for sale for six months before it finally sold. The original asking price was $250,000, but the house sold for only $235,000. What was the percent decrease of the selling price compared to the original asking price?

Chapter 6 Review

Section 6.1 Ratios

CONCEPT	EXAMPLE
A **ratio** is a comparison between two numbers using division. Two numbers forming a ratio are always specific to a certain unit of measure or count.	6 dollars : 10 pounds or $\frac{6 \text{ dollars}}{10 \text{ pounds}}$
To simplify a ratio, divide out any common factors.	$\frac{6 \text{ dollars}}{10 \text{ pounds}}$ simplifies by a factor of 2, to $\frac{3 \text{ dollars}}{5 \text{ pounds}}$
If the unit of measure for each number is the same, then that unit of measure can be divided out as well.	$\frac{24 \text{ dollars}}{30 \text{ dollars}}$ simplifies by a factor of 6, to $\frac{4 \text{ dollars}}{5 \text{ dollars}}$ and the unit of measure, dollars, can divide out as well. $\frac{4 \text{ dollars}}{5 \text{ dollars}} = \frac{4}{5}$, or 4 : 5
If two ratios have the same value, they are **equivalent ratios.**	$\frac{4}{10}$ and $\frac{2}{5}$ are equivalent ratios.
In the equivalence of two ratios, expressed 4 : 6 = 2 : 3, the outermost numbers, 4 and 3, are the **extremes**. The middle two numbers, 6 and 2, are the **means**.	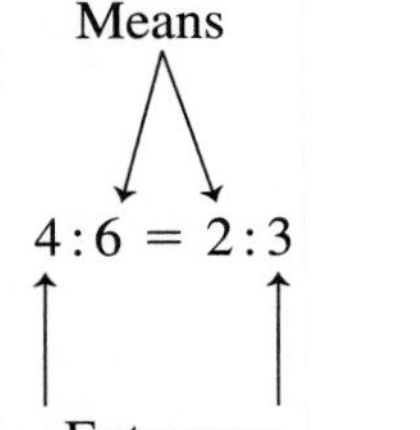 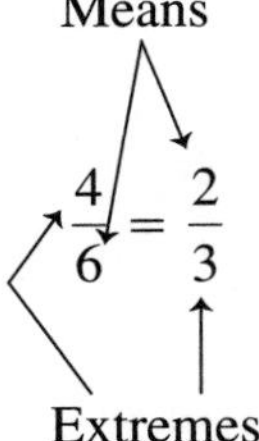
The Means-Extremes Product Property: If the product of extremes = the product of means, then the two ratios are equivalent. This method is called **cross multiplication**, multiplying across the equal sign.	Start with the equality of two ratios: $\frac{2}{3} = \frac{6}{9}$ multiply "across" the equal sign: $\frac{2}{3} \times \frac{6}{9}$ $2 \cdot 9 = 3 \cdot 6$ $18 = 18$

Section 6.2 Rates

CONCEPT	EXAMPLE
In a ratio, when the units of measure—or counts—of the numerator and denominator are different, the ratio is called a **rate**.	$\frac{4.2 \text{ miles}}{0.18 \text{ gallons}}$
Rates are best understood when they are completely simplified.	$\frac{4.2 \text{ miles} \times 100}{0.18 \text{ gallons} \times 100} = \frac{420 \text{ miles} \div 6}{18 \text{ gallons} \div 6}$ $= \frac{70 \text{ miles}}{3 \text{ gallons}} = 70$ miles for every 3 gallons.
A **unit rate** is a rate in which the denominator has been reduced to 1 item. Any rate can be reduced to a unit rate by simplifying the fraction or by using long division.	$\frac{105 \text{ miles}}{6 \text{ gallons}}$ cannot simplify directly, but we can divide $6\overline{)105.0}$ = 17.5 and write the unit fraction as: $\frac{17.5 \text{ miles}}{1 \text{ gallon}}$, or 17.5 miles per gallon.
We can compare prices of two similar items by finding the unit price.	To determine which of two bags of plant food is the better buy, find the unit price of each bag. Bag 1: $\frac{3.48 \text{ dollars}}{24 \text{ ounces}}$ $\quad 24\overline{)3.480}$ = 0.145 $\frac{0.145 \text{ dollars}}{1 \text{ ounce}}$ $0.15 per ounce Bag 2: $\frac{2.10 \text{ dollars}}{12 \text{ ounces}}$ $\quad 12\overline{)2.100}$ = 0.175 $\frac{0.175 \text{ dollars}}{1 \text{ ounce}}$ $0.18 per ounce Bag 1 is the better buy.

Section 6.3 Proportions

CONCEPT	EXAMPLE
A **proportion** is a statement that two ratios are equivalent. In a proportion, the product of the extremes is equal to the product of the means.	$\frac{a}{b} = \frac{c}{d}$ $a \cdot d = b \cdot c$
In setting up a proportion, the numerators of each fraction must be of the same units of measure (or count), and the denominators of each fraction must be of the same units of measure (or count).	$\frac{2 \text{ inches}}{5 \text{ miles}} = \frac{6 \text{ inches}}{15 \text{ miles}}$

CONCEPT	EXAMPLE
To solve a proportion, use cross multiplication. Then divide by the coefficient of the variable. Before cross multiplying, see if one of the fractions can be simplified.	Solve for n in the proportion. $\frac{15}{12} = \frac{20}{n}$ $\frac{15}{12}$ can reduce by a factor of 3 to $\frac{5}{4}$. $\frac{5}{4} = \frac{20}{n}$ Cross multiply. $5 \cdot n = 4 \cdot 20$ $5 \cdot n = 80$ $5 \div 5 \cdot n = 80 \div 5$ $n = 16$

Section 6.4 Percents

CONCEPT	EXAMPLE
The symbol % means *percent*, and the number that is written before the percent symbol is called the **percentage**.	In 12%, the percentage is 12.
Percent, or per cent, means per 100, or divided by 100. A percent is a ratio in which the denominator is 100.	28% means $\frac{28}{100}$, or "28 out of 100."
If the percentage is a whole number, the percent can first be written as a fraction and then as a decimal.	$44\% = \frac{44}{100} = 0.44$
If the percentage is a decimal, multiply the fraction by a form of 1, such as $\frac{10}{10}$ or $\frac{100}{100}$ to make the numerator into a whole number.	$26.5\% = \frac{26.5}{100} \times \frac{10}{10} = \frac{265}{1,000} = 0.265$
If a decimal has two decimal places, it can first be written as a fraction with a denominator of 100 and then as a percent.	$1.05 = \frac{105}{100} = 105\%$
If a decimal has fewer than two decimal places, place one or two ending zeros so that it has two decimal places.	$0.6 = 0.60 = \frac{60}{100} = 60\%$
Procedure for Writing Percents as Decimals:	
1. Recognize the percentage and notice whether or not it contains a decimal point. If it doesn't, then write one at its end.	1. 5% → 5.%
2. If the percentage doesn't have at least two whole numbers before the decimal point, then place one or two zeros in front of the percentage.	2. 5% → 05.%
3. Write the percentage, without the %, and move the decimal point two places to the left.	3. 5% → 05.% → .05 or 0.05

CONCEPT	EXAMPLE
To write a decimal as a percent, multiply the decimal number by 100%.	$0.62 = 0.62 \times 100\% = 62\%$
To write a fraction as a percent, first write it as a decimal (by long division) and then multiply by 100%.	$\frac{3}{4} \rightarrow 4\overline{)3.00}$ (quotient 0.75) $\rightarrow \frac{3}{4} = 0.75 \times 100\% = 75\%$

Section 6.5 Solving Percent Problems Using Proportions

CONCEPT	EXAMPLE
A ratio that is not a percent can be seen as $\frac{\text{amount}}{\text{base}}$, where the base is a number other than 100. The percent proportion is $$\frac{\text{percentage}}{100} = \frac{\text{amount}}{\text{base}},$$ as in the formula $\frac{p}{100} = \frac{a}{b}$. p represents the percentage; a represents the amount; and b represents the base. When two of these variables are known, we can set up and solve a proportion—by first using cross multiplication—to find the third variable.	5 is what percent of 8? $\frac{p}{100} = \frac{5}{8}$ $p \cdot 8 = 100 \cdot 5$ $p \cdot 8 = 500$ $p \cdot 8 \div 8 = 500 \div 8$ $p = 62.5$ 5 is 62.5% of 8.

Section 6.6 Solving the Percent Equation

CONCEPT	EXAMPLE
Percent is always *of* something, and "percent of" indicates multiplication.	If there are 35 candies in a box of chocolates, and 20% of them are caramels, then there are $20\% \times 35 = 7$ caramels.
The percent equation: Percent of whole is part ↓ ↓ Percent × whole = part	$20\% \times 35 = 7$
If the part is unknown, write the legend: Let $n =$ the part.	$20\% \times 35 = n$ $0.20 \times 35 = n$ $7 = n$

CONCEPT	EXAMPLE
If the whole is unknown, write the legend: Let $n =$ the whole.	$20\% \times n = 7$ $0.20 \times n = 7$ $n = 35$
If the percent is unknown, write the legend: Let $p =$ the percent.	$p \times 35 = 7$ $p = 0.20$ $p = 20\%$

Section 6.7 Applications Involving Percents

CONCEPT	EXAMPLE
Sales tax is a percentage of the purchase price (whole). The amount of sales tax is calculated by multiplying the sales tax rate (%) by the purchase price. This tax is added on to the purchase price at the cash register.	If the sales tax rate is 7% and a bookcase costs \$149, how much is the tax on the bookcase? $7\% \times \$149 = \$10.43$. The tax is \$10.43. The amount to be paid at the cash register is $\$149 + \$10.43 = \$159.43$.
The amount of **commission** that a salesperson earns is a percentage of the purchase price (whole); the amount of commission is calculated by multiplying the commission rate (%) by the purchase price.	Joel earns a commission of 4% on the sales he makes, calculated monthly. In August, he made sales totaling \$14,000. What is his commission for that month? $4\% \times \$14{,}000 = \$560$. Joel's commission is \$560.
The original price of an item is 100% of that price. When a percent **discount** is given, it can first be directly subtracted from 100%. This new percent is multiplied by the original price to get the discounted price.	Tyson is shopping for a pair of sneakers, and he finds a pair that originally cost \$95 but is now discounted 30%. What is the new price of the sneakers? $100\% - 30\% = 70\%$ $\$95 \times 70\% = \$66.50$. The new price is \$66.50.
To find a ratio as a percent, divide the part by the whole.	$\frac{\text{part}}{\text{whole}}$, part ÷ whole, $\text{whole}\overline{)\text{part}}$
When finding a percent increase or decrease, we must know both the amount of increase (or decrease), and the previous amount to which it is compared.	$\text{Percent increase} = \frac{\text{amount of increase}}{\text{previous amount}}$ $\text{Percent decrease} = \frac{\text{amount of decrease}}{\text{previous amount}}$
When finding a percent increase or decrease, the comparison value is always the previous value. When given a previous value and a current (or later) value, find the amount of increase (or decrease) by subtracting the lower amount from the higher amount.	In June, a pond was measured to be 80 inches deep. In September, the pond was measured to be 64 inches deep. What was the percent decrease in the depth of the pond? $80 - 64 = 16$ is the amount of decrease. The percent decrease is $\frac{\text{amount of decrease}}{\text{previous amount}} = \frac{16}{80} = \frac{2}{10} = 0.2 = 20\%$

Chapter 6 Review Exercises

Fill in the blanks.

1. A proportion is an equation showing the equivalence of two ______________.
2. In the proportion $\frac{25}{60} = \frac{10}{24}$, the extremes are ______________.
3. We can show that two ratios are equivalent using ______________.
4. The "of" in "percent of" always means ______________.
5. When multiplying by a percent, the percent should first be written as a ______________.
6. The first thing we do with a discount percent is subtract it from ______________.

True or False.

7. The symbol, %, is called the percentage. ________
8. A rate is a unit rate if the denominator value is reduced to 1. ________
9. The sales tax rate is added directly to the price of an item. ________
10. The percent increase compares the amount of increase to the first (previous) amount. ________

Section 6.1

Write each of the following comparisons as a ratio in the form of a fraction.

	Phrase	Ratio		Phrase	Ratio
11.	12 cookies per box		12.	45¢ for each donut	
13.	3 quarts for every 8 children		14.	\$7.00 for every 10 cards	

Write each fraction as a comparison.

	Phrase	Ratio		Phrase	Ratio
15.	$\frac{\text{25 players}}{\text{1 game}}$		16.	$\frac{\$85}{\text{1 week}}$	
17.	$\frac{\text{120 passengers}}{\text{5 cars}}$		18.	$\frac{\text{80 miles}}{\text{3 gallons}}$	

Write each ratio in fractional form and simplify it completely.

19. 72 dollars : 9 shares
20. 18 minutes : 45 minutes
21. 2.4 acres : 3 acres
22. 0.6 calories : 1.5 grams

Write each described ratio in fractional form and simplify it completely.

23. Weekly trash collections in Freemont amount to 12 pounds per household and in Clairhaven, 15 pounds per household. Write these collections as a ratio: Freemont amount : Clairhaven amount.
24. In Montieth, the average yearly rainfall is 20 inches and in Lareno, 32 inches. Write these yearly rainfalls as a ratio: Montieth amount : Lareno amount.
25. Each month, Kendall invests \$120 in mutual funds and \$90 in bonds. According to this situation, write the following ratios in standard ratio form, fractional form, and as a simplified ratio.
    a) Mutual funds amount : Bonds amount
    b) Mutual funds amount : Total amount
    c) Bonds amount : Total amount

26. Each month, Rogelio puts money in a savings account for his daughters' college fund. He puts aside $180 for Maria and $120 for Gloria. According to this situation, write the following ratios in standard ratio form, fractional form, and as a simplified ratio.

a) Maria's amount : Gloria's amount

b) Maria's amount : Total amount

c) Gloria's amount : Total amount

Use cross multiplication to determine whether each pair of fractions is equivalent.

27. $\frac{12}{15} \stackrel{?}{=} \frac{4}{5}$ **28.** $\frac{25}{10} \stackrel{?}{=} \frac{45}{16}$ **29.** $\frac{12}{8} \stackrel{?}{=} \frac{2.5}{1.5}$ **30.** $\frac{5}{12} \stackrel{?}{=} \frac{1.25}{3}$

Section 6.2

Simplify each rate, and write the result in words.

31. $\frac{\text{520 dollars}}{\text{8 days}}$ **32.** $\frac{\text{45 customers}}{\text{6 hours}}$ **33.** $\frac{\text{24 hits}}{\text{72 times at bat}}$ **34.** $\frac{\text{18 repetitions}}{\text{30 minutes}}$

Simplify each rate to a unit rate, and write the unit rate in words.

35. $\frac{\text{48 golf balls}}{\text{12 players}}$ **36.** $\frac{\text{171 students}}{\text{15 tutors}}$ **37.** $\frac{\text{354 phone calls}}{\text{30 days}}$ **38.** $\frac{\text{103.6 miles}}{\text{5.6 gallons}}$

From the given information, write a fractional rate. Simplify the rate as a unit rate, and write it as a phrase.

39. In 2004, the city of Sunnyvale collected $1,350 in sales tax for every 6 residents. Write the amount collected as a unit rate per resident.

40. In 15 games, Carmello scored a total of 339 points. Write his points scored as a unit rate per game.

41. Marcelus trimmed 18 trees and earned $405. Write his earnings as a unit rate per tree.

42. Jenice paid $114 to rent 25 chairs. Write the rental price as a unit rate per chair.

From the given information, simplify each rate to a unit price, write it as a phrase, and answer the question.

43. A 16-ounce jar of Redd's tomato paste costs $1.92, and a 24 ounce jar of Green's tomato paste costs $3.60. Which is the better buy?

44. A pack of 16 AlwaysReady batteries costs $12.96, and a box of 28 LightShine batteries costs $21.00. Which is the better buy?

Section 6.3

Solve for n in each proportion. If possible, first reduce the known fraction.

45. $\frac{9}{6} = \frac{n}{14}$ **46.** $\frac{30}{25} = \frac{18}{n}$ **47.** $\frac{n}{45} = \frac{16}{10}$ **48.** $\frac{21}{n} = \frac{15}{25}$

For each of the following, set up a proportion table (as in Section 6.3). Write a legend and solve the corresponding proportion. Write a sentence answering the question.

49. Kjell's car used 12 gallons of gas to travel 246 miles. How many miles will his car travel on 16 gallons of gas?

50. To paint a wall, Lonnie charges $6.00 for every 4 square feet of wall space. How much will Lonnie charge to paint 82 square feet of wall space?

51. At a walk-a-thon, Karrie raised $13.50 for every 3 laps she walked. If she walked a total of 32 laps, how much money did she raise?

52. Tamra's printer can print 6 pages in 15 seconds. How many seconds will it take to print 22 pages?

Section 6.4

Write each sentence with the percent as a simplified fraction

53. 20% of the homes in Westside Estates are ranch style.

54. 15% of all fruit sold in Bryson's grocery store is organically grown.

55. 8% of all U.S. residents live in Texas. *Source: www.factmonster.com*

56. 2.5% of the medals awarded at the 2004 Summer Olympics went to athletes from Ukraine. *Source: www.biol.org/Athens2004*

Write each percent as a decimal.

57. 47% **58.** 3% **59.** 9.1% **60.** 0.6%

Write each decimal as a percent.

61. 0.26 **62.** 0.02 **63.** 0.175 **64.** 0.7

65. 1.06 **66.** 0.005

Write each sentence with the fraction as a percent. Round the percentage to the nearest tenth.

67. $\frac{3}{20}$ of Sri Lanka's population is Hindu. *Source: www.geohive.com/global/religion*

68. $\frac{16}{25}$ of the shoppers at Lucia's Floristas pay with a credit card.

69. $\frac{7}{8}$ of the students in Ms. Skiba's art class received a passing grade.

70. $\frac{2}{7}$ of all U.S. car sales are small cars. *Source: www.senate.michigan.gov*

Section 6.5

For each, set up a proportion table, write a legend, set up and solve the proportion, and write a sentence answering the question.

71. 15% of the singers in the Lincoln High School choir are tenors. If the choir has 40 members, how many of them are tenors?

72. 37.5% of the engineers at Hudson Dynamic have been with the company for at least ten years. If the company has a total of 32 engineers, how many have been at Hudson Dynamic for at least ten years?

73. 65% of the dinner customers at Chuck's Steakhouse order a salad with their meal. If 91 salads were served last Wednesday night, how many dinner customers were there in all?

74. 2.5% of the teachers in the North Unified High School District have a doctorate degree (Ph.D.). If 8 of the teachers have a Ph.D., how many total teachers are there in the district?

75. Of the 30 days in April last year, it rained for 18 days in the town of Martinville. What percent of the days in April did it rain in Martinville?

76. Of the 18 categories for which it was eligible, the 2002 movie *Chicago* won 6 Oscars at the 2003 Academy Awards. What percent of the Oscars did *Chicago* win? *Source: www.popculturemadness.com*

Section 6.6

Find each number.

77. 40% of 95 **78.** 35% of 140 **79.** 8% of 125 **80.** 2.5% of 240

For each, find the missing value and write a conclusion.

81. 25% of 76 is what number?

82. 60% of 85 is what number?

83. 28% of what number is 35?

84. 55% of what number is 88?

85. What percent of 52 is 39?

86. What percent of 120 is 45?

Solve each using the percent equation. Write a sentence answering the question. (You may want to identify the percent, whole, and part before writing the equation.)

87. A Student Activities report at Cuyama College indicated that only 3% of the student population participate in college clubs. If there are 120 students in college clubs, how many students attend Cuyama College?

88. In 2004, of the 160 National League batters who played regularly, 24 of them hit at least thirty home runs. What percent of these players hit at least thirty home runs? *Source: Sports Illustrated 2005 Almanac*

Section 6.7

Solve each application. Write a sentence answering the question.

89. DuJuan is buying a pair of running shoes that costs $80. The sales tax rate in his state is 7.5%. How much will he pay at the cash register?

90. Sandra is a real estate agent. She receives a 2% commission on every house she sells. One day, she sold a house for $325,000. How much commission did she earn on the sale of that house?

91. Shay's Department Store had an after-Christmas clearance sale with decorations discounted 80%. The original price of a box of bulbs was $24.50. What is the new price of the box of bulbs?

92. Last season, Torraye scored 25 free throws out of 40 attempts. What was his free throw success as a percent?

93. A television at Ed's TVs and Stuff retailed for $1,200. Lorraine was able to bargain with the salesman and save $300 off of the price. What was this savings as a percent of the retail price?

94. Connie has a coupon for 25% off any meal at Don Gordo's Mexican Restaurant. She treated her friend Marjorie to dinner one night and the total food bill came to $48.00.

a) With her 25% coupon, how much was the cost of the meal?

b) If the sales tax rate was 6%, what was the sales tax on the meal?

c) Connie thought the service and the food were outstanding and decided to leave a 20% tip for the server. She knew to base her tip on the un-discounted meal total of $48.00 How much was the tip?

d) What was the total amount paid by Connie for dinner that night?

Solve each percent increase and percent decrease application. Write a sentence answering the question.

95. Last year, the Shoreline Chamber of Commerce had 52 members. This year they have 65 members. What is the percent increase in the Chamber's membership?

96. Last year at this time, Corrine's home was valued at $400,000. Now it is worth $450,000. What is the percent increase in the value of Corrine's home?

97. Gus keeps a large coffee can of water on his porch to check for water evaporation. In one week last August, the water level in the can went from 12 inches to 7.5 inches. What was the percent decrease in the water level for that week?

98. At the beginning of the semester, Dr. Ortega had 45 students in his statistics class. By the end of the semester, he had 33 students. What was the percent decrease in the number of students in Dr. Ortega's statistics class?

Chapter 6 Test

Write the described ratio in fractional form and simplify it completely.

1. Kacey gives a weekly allowance to each of her two daughters, \$60 to Alissa and \$36 to Danita. Write their allowances as a ratio, Alissa's amount **:** Danita's amount, in simplified fractional form.

2. A tractor used 0.8 gallons of diesel to travel 2.8 miles . Write this as a ratio, number of miles **:** number of gallons, in simplified fractional form.

Use cross multiplication to determine whether each pair of fractions is equivalent.

3. $\frac{35}{12} \stackrel{?}{=} \frac{25}{8}$

4. $\frac{2.4}{3.2} \stackrel{?}{=} \frac{15}{20}$

5. Simplify the rate $\frac{63 \text{ seats}}{12 \text{ rows}}$, and write the result in words.

6. A large box of cereal contains 5,200 milligrams of potassium for 25 servings. Write the amount of potassium as a unit rate per serving.

7. Write each item as a unit price, and answer the question: A bag of 15 avocados costs \$8.40, and a box of 12 avocados costs \$7.20. Which is the better buy?

8. Solve for n: $\frac{9}{n} = \frac{12}{32}$

Set up a proportion table. Write a legend and solve the corresponding proportion. Write a sentence answering the question.

9. Carl made a long-distance phone call from a pay phone. He was charged \$6.80 to talk for 4 minutes. How much would he have paid to talk for 9 minutes?

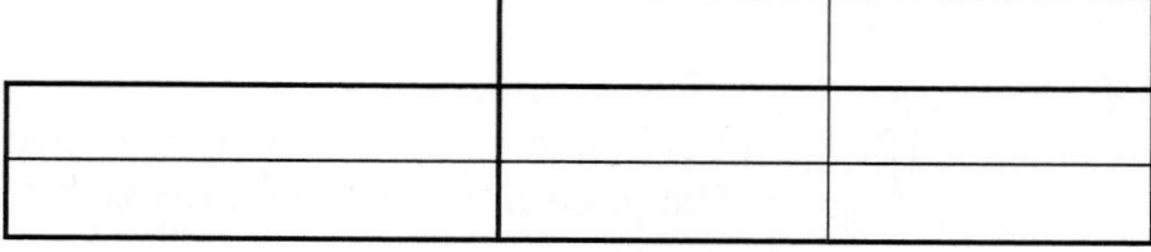

10. Banjo can finish a 16-pound bag of dog food in 40 days. How many days would it take him to finish a 20-pound bag of food?

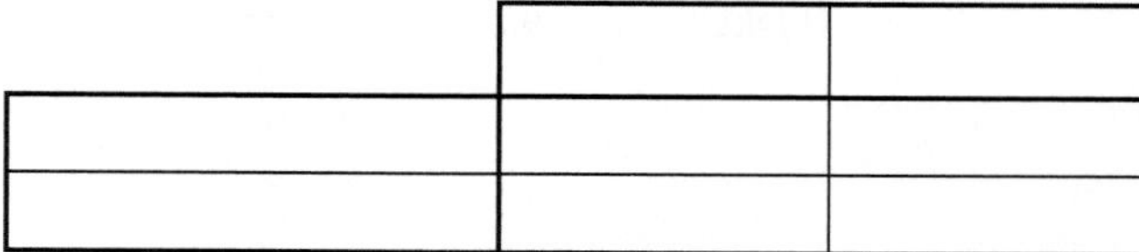

Write each percent as a decimal.

11. 7% **12.** 0.5%

Write each decimal as a percent.

13. 0.57 **14.** 0.2

Write each percent as a simplified fraction.

15. 16% **16.** 45%

Write each fraction as a percent. If necessary, round the percentage to the nearest tenth.

17. $\frac{13}{25}$ **18.** $\frac{4}{11}$

For each, find the missing value and write a conclusion.

19. 14% of what number is 21? **20.** What percent of 80 is 32?

Solve. Write a sentence answering the question.

21. 24% of all students at Riverbend Community College are teenagers. If there are 3,500 students at Riverbend, how many of them are teenagers?

22. Lin-Li bought a textbook that costs $88.00. The sales tax rate in her state is 7.5%. How much will Lin-Li pay for the textbook at the cash register?

23. Yusef is a member of a bicycle club that gives a 15% discount on all bicycle gear he purchases at Cycle-a-Go-Go. The price of a new helmet is $60.00. What will Yusef's discounted price be?

24. Marcus received a raise from $8.00 to $10.00 per hour when he became assistant night manager at Burger Basket. What was the percent increase in his hourly wage?

Chapters 5 and 6 Cumulative Review

Answer as indicated.

1. Write $\frac{43}{1000}$ as a decimal.

2. Write $\frac{91}{10}$ as a decimal.

3. Write 0.71 as a fraction.

4. Round 2.00953 to the nearest thousandth.

5. Round 29.9408 to the tenths place.

6. Round $10.59602 to the nearest penny.

7. Round $532.19 to the nearest dollar.

8. Juan's grade point average is 3.1952708. Round this to the nearest hundredth.

9. Add 5.483 and 4.671.

10. Subtract: $4.1 - 2.974$

11. Subtract 0.149 from 1.2.

12. Beverly paid (including tax) $13.53 for a scarf, and she paid with a $20 bill. How much change will she get back?

13. Find the perimeter of this geometric figure.

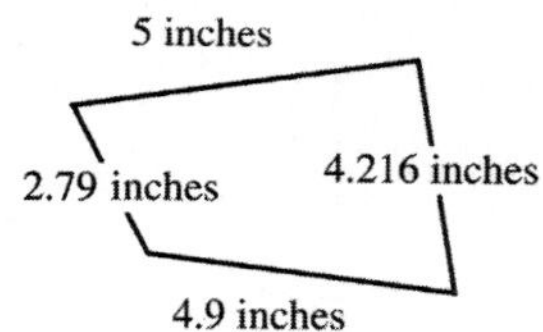

14. Find the length of the third side.

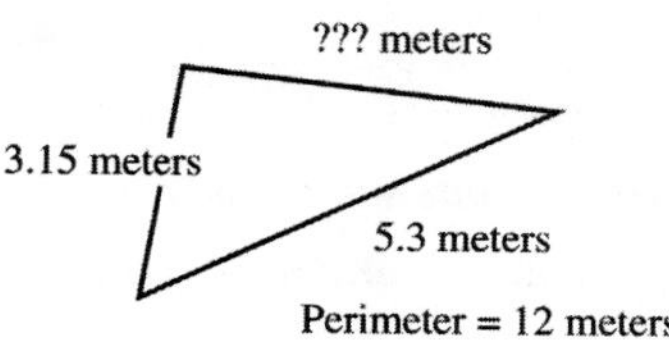

Multiply.

15. 0.2×0.36

16. 4.2×7.5

17. 0.6×100

18. 0.308×100

Divide.

19. $4.92 \div 8$

20. $0.06\overline{)0.104}$

Answer as indicated.

21. Find the decimal equivalent of $\frac{7}{8}$.

22. Petre owns his own cab. Yesterday, in 9.5 hours of driving, he earned $165.30. How much did Petre earn per hour?

23. Allison's pool is rectangular, perfect for swimming laps. It measures 24.5 yards long and 8.4 yards wide. What is the area of the pool?

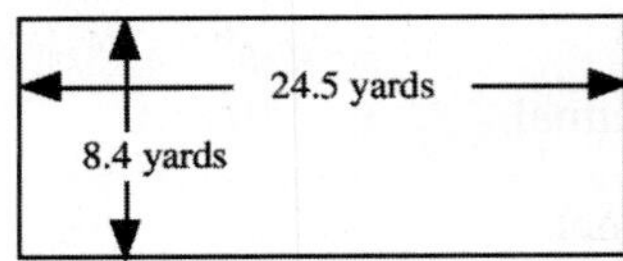

24. A round baking dish has a 4.8 inch radius. What is the circumference of the baking dish? Round the answer to the nearest tenth.

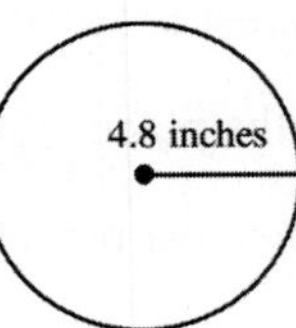

25. Write the ratio 2.7 grams : 0.45 grams in fractional form, and simplify it completely.

26. Simplify $\frac{2.85 \text{ calories}}{1.5 \text{ grams}}$ to a unit rate, and write the unit rate in words.

27. Tomás traveled 195 miles in 4 hours. Write his speed as a unit rate per hour.

28. A 24-ounce cup of Twinklebuck's coffee costs $2.28, and a 20-ounce cup of Sunbuck's coffee costs $1.80. Which has the better value?

Solve for n in each proportion.

29. $\frac{24}{9} = \frac{32}{n}$

30. $\frac{16}{36} = \frac{n}{27}$

Write each percent as a decimal.

31. 5%

32. 3.2%

Write each decimal as a percent.

33. 0.308

34. 0.4

Solve each problem. Write a sentence answering the question.

35. At the fireman's pancake breakfast, Zia can cook 18 pancakes in 4 minutes. How long will it take Zia to cook 90 pancakes?

36. The city of St. Matthew's, in northern Scotland, has a law that no more than 15% of the city employees can live outside of the city limits. If the city has 40 employees, how many may live outside of the city limits?

37. 45% of what number is 63?

38. What percent of 75 is 48?

39. Jolanda has a coupon for a 20% discount at Sidewalk's Shoes. She found a pair of shoes that cost $55.00. What will the discounted price be?

40. The Torres family owns three cars, all financed through their credit union. Last month's car payments totaled $650, but that included the very last payment on their Volvo. This month, they will pay only $390. What is the percent decrease in the Torres' car payment?

CHAPTER 7
Geometry and Units of Measure

Introduction

There are three primary types of learning styles: Visual, Auditory, and Kinesthetic/Tactile. Usually, a person learns using all three styles, but, for each individual, one style is more dominant than the other two.

Visual dominant learners learn through seeing. This may include reading; looking at pictures, diagrams, and graphs; and noticing an instructor's facial expressions.

If you are an auditory-dominant learner, you learn through hearing. You listen to lectures and discussions, you talk about your own ideas and listen to others' ideas, and you notice an instructor's voice pitch or level of loudness.

Kinesthetic/Tactile-dominant learners learn through touching and using their hands. Examples of learning activities for this group are hands-on projects, drawing diagrams and pictures, and dance or other physical activities.

Geometry is about shapes and sizes that can be quickly identified and drawn and is appealing to Visual and Kinesthetic/Tactile learners. Auditory learners will master geometry by verbally explaining the diagram and figures to other learners. It's easy to see geometry in the world around us, in architecture, art, and sports. For example, understanding angles is essential to success in games such as billiards and baseball, where a round ball will bounce off the side of a pool table or a stadium wall.

For more information, go to your favorite Internet search engine and type in "learning styles."

Preparation Exercises

Section 3.1, Introduction to Fractions: *Write each as an improper fraction.*

1. $5\frac{1}{6}$

2. $7\frac{5}{8}$

Section 3.1, Introduction to Fractions: *Write each as a mixed number.*

3. $\frac{95}{12}$

4. $\frac{71}{16}$

Section 3.3, Multiplying Fractions: *Multiply and simplify.*

5. $\frac{3}{8} \cdot \frac{4}{15}$

6. $\frac{8}{9} \cdot \frac{15}{16}$

Section 3.3, Multiplying Fractions: *Multiply and simplify.*

7. $2\frac{1}{4} \cdot 4\frac{2}{3}$

8. $8\frac{1}{3} \cdot 3\frac{3}{5}$

Section 4.3, Adding and Subtracting Like Fractions: *Add and simplify.*

9. $\frac{7}{12} + \frac{11}{12}$

10. $\frac{3}{16} + \frac{9}{16}$

Section 4.4, Adding and Subtracting Unlike Fractions: *Add and simplify.*

11. $\frac{2}{3} + \frac{5}{6}$

12. $\frac{1}{6} + \frac{3}{8}$

Section 5.1, Introduction to Decimals: *Write each decimal as a fraction.*

13. 0.47

14. 0.003

Section 5.1, Introduction to Decimals: *Write each fraction as a decimal.*

15. $\frac{63}{100}$

16. $\frac{2.9}{10}$

Section 5.4, Multiplying Decimals: *Multiply.*

17. 1.25×1.6 **18.** 3.14×3.5 **19.** 5.8×10 **20.** 0.012×100

Section 5.5, Dividing Decimals: *Divide.*

21. $59 \div 4$ **22.** $11.7 \div 6$ **23.** $5.85 \div 1.5$ **24.** $0.86 \div 0.09$

SECTION 7.1 U.S. Measures

Objectives

In this section, you will learn to:

- Identify U.S. measures of length, weight, and capacity.
- Convert one U.S. measure to another.
- Add and subtract feet and inches.
- Add and subtract pounds and ounces.

To successfully complete this section, you need to understand:

- Writing improper fractions as mixed numbers and mixed numbers as improper fractions (3.1)
- Simplifying fractions (3.2)
- Multiplying fractions (3.3)

Introduction

Whenever we seek to measure something—find out how long it is, or how much it weighs, or what its capacity is—we need to use some sort of **unit of measure**, such as feet, pounds, or gallons.

Measures of *length*, for example, are those used to see how long something is. There are both **U.S. measures**, used primarily in the United States, and **metric measures**, used elsewhere in the world. In the fields of science and medicine, however, it is common to use metric measures in the U.S. as well.

In this Section we will concentrate on U.S. measures only. Section 7.2 explores metric measures, and Section 7.3 features a procedure for converting between U.S. and metric measures.

U.S. Measures of Length

Here is a diagram representing a one-foot-long U.S. ruler; it is about half the actual size of a ruler. This ruler indicates that 1 foot is equivalent to 12 inches. To understand the actual length of 1 foot, a standard sheet of paper is 11 inches long, almost 1 foot long.

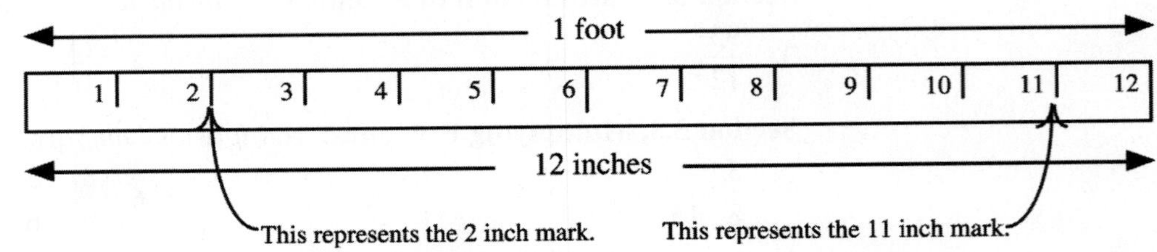

Measures of length are called **linear measures**. Here are some U.S. linear measures and their equivalencies.

U.S. Linear Measures	**Equivalencies**		
inches (in.)	1 ft = 12 in.	and	1 in. $= \frac{1}{12}$ ft
feet (ft)	1 yd = 3 ft	and	1 ft $= \frac{1}{3}$ yd
yards (yd)	1 yd = 36 in.		
miles (mi)	1 mi = 5,280 ft		

Units of measure are actually multiplied by the number that precedes them.

For example, 2 feet means $2 \cdot (1 \text{ foot})$ and 6 inches means $6 \cdot (1 \text{ inch})$

EXAMPLE 1 Write 3 feet in terms of inches.

PROCEDURE: From the chart of equivalencies, 1 foot = 12 inches.

3 feet can be rewritten as $3 \cdot (1 \text{ foot})$.

We can replace 1 foot with 12 inches and multiply:

ANSWER: $3 \text{ feet} = 3 \cdot (1 \text{ foot}) = 3 \cdot (12 \text{ inches}) = 36 \text{ inches}$.

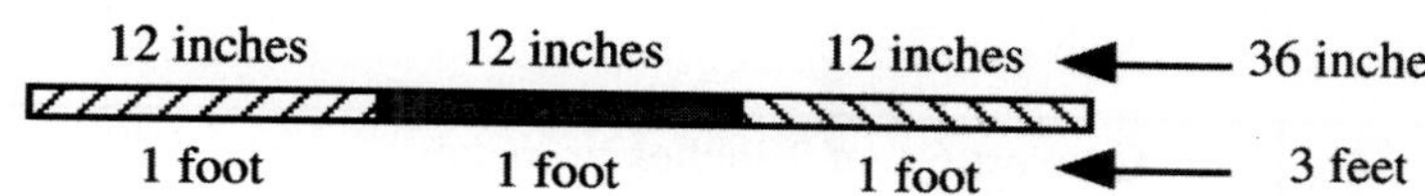

In this case, we have changed from one unit of measure to another, from feet to inches. We say that we have **converted** from feet to inches.

EXAMPLE 2 Convert from one measure to the other.

a) 7 yards to feet b) 8 inches to feet c) $5\frac{1}{4}$ feet to yards

PROCEDURE:
1) Write any mixed number as an improper fraction.
2) Write the given unit of measure as a product.
3) Insert the new unit of measure.
4) Multiply and simplify.

ANSWER: a) $7 \text{ yards} = 7 \cdot (1 \text{ yd}) = 7 \cdot 3 \text{ ft} = 21 \text{ feet}$

b) $8 \text{ inches} = 8 \cdot (1 \text{ in.}) = 8 \cdot \frac{1}{12} \text{ ft} = \frac{8}{12} \text{ ft} = \frac{2}{3} \text{ foot}$

c) $5\frac{1}{4} \text{ feet} = \frac{21}{4} \cdot (1 \text{ ft}) = \frac{21}{4} \cdot \frac{1}{3} \text{ yd} = \frac{21 \cdot 1}{4 \cdot 3} \text{ yd} = \frac{7 \cdot 1}{4 \cdot 1} \text{ yd} = \frac{7}{4} \text{ yd} = 1\frac{3}{4} \text{ yards}$

YOU TRY IT 1 *Convert from one measure to the other. Use Examples 1 and 2 as guides.*

a) $4\frac{1}{2}$ feet to inches b) $6\frac{1}{3}$ yards to feet c) 33 inches to feet

Feet and Inches

Recall that $3\frac{1}{4}$ is a mixed number. It has a whole number, 3, and a fractional part, $\frac{1}{4}$. Also,

$$3\frac{1}{4} \text{ means } 3 + \frac{1}{4}.$$

Units of length can be mixed as well. We can abbreviate 5 ft and 3 in. (which means 5 ft + 3 in.) as 5 ft 3 in. We can also write this in terms of inches only by converting the feet portion to inches:

$$5 \text{ ft} = 5 \cdot (1 \text{ ft}) = 5 \cdot (12 \text{ in.}) = 60 \text{ in.}$$

$$\downarrow$$

So, $$5 \text{ ft } 3 \text{ in.} = 60 \text{ in.} + 3 \text{ in.} = 63 \text{ inches.}$$

This means that a table that is 5 ft 3 in. long is 63 inches long.

12 inches	12 inches	12 inches	12 inches	12 inches	3 in.	← 63 inches
1 foot	1 foot	1 foot	1 foot	1 foot	3 in.	← 5 ft 3 in.

EXAMPLE 3 Convert 6 feet 2 inches to inches.

PROCEDURE: First, convert feet to inches, then add. Use Example 3 as a guide.

ANSWER:

$$6 \text{ ft} = 6 \cdot (1 \text{ ft}) = 6 \cdot (12 \text{ in.}) = 72 \text{ in.}$$

$$72 \text{ in.} + 2 \text{ in.} = 74 \text{ inches}$$

6 ft 2 in. = 74 inches

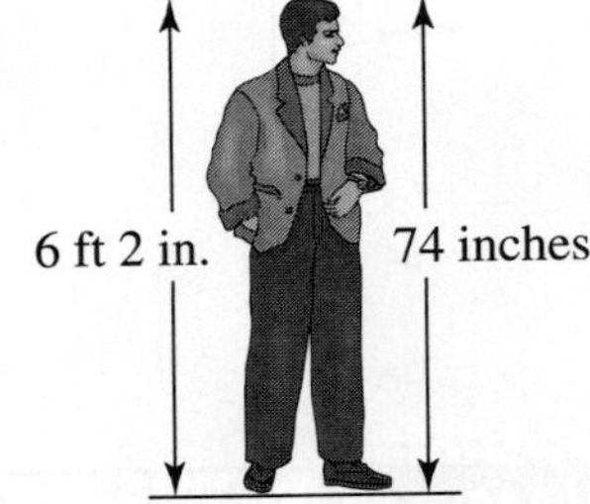

YOU TRY IT 2 *Convert each to inches. Use Example 3 as a guide.*

a) 2 feet 6 inches

b) 10 feet 9 inches

YOU TRY IT 3 *At 7 ft 5 in., Yao Ming is the tallest player in the National Basketball Association. Express this measure in inches.*

Think about it

How tall are you in *feet and inches* and in *inches only*? If you don't know your height, either check your driver's license or compare yourself to someone else in class who is about the same height as you.

Just as 1 foot = 12 inches, 1 inch = $\frac{1}{12}$ foot. This means that we can write 36 inches in terms of feet:

$$36 \text{ inches} = 36 \cdot \frac{1}{12} \text{ foot} = \frac{36}{12} \text{ foot} = 3 \text{ feet}$$

Multiplying the number of inches, 36, by $\frac{1}{12}$ is the same as dividing the number by 12:

$$\begin{array}{r} \mathbf{3} \\ 12\overline{)36} \\ -\ 36 \\ \hline 0 \end{array}$$

← This quotient means that 36 inches = 3 feet.

How does 38 inches compare to 3 feet? 38 inches is 2 inches more than 3 feet:

36 inches + 2 inches
= 3 ft 2 in.

This can also be demonstrated by dividing 12 into 38 inches:

$$\begin{array}{r} \mathbf{3} \\ 12\overline{)38} \\ -\ 36 \\ \hline \mathbf{2} \end{array}$$

← This quotient is the number of feet.

← This remainder is the number of inches. 38 inches = 3 ft 2 in.

EXAMPLE 4 Convert 53 inches to feet and inches.

PROCEDURE: Divide 12 into 53; the quotient is the number of feet and the remainder is the number of inches.

ANSWER:

$$\begin{array}{r} \mathbf{4} \\ 12\overline{)53} \\ -\ 48 \\ \hline \mathbf{5} \end{array}$$

53 inches = 4 ft 5 in.

YOU TRY IT 4 *Convert each to feet and inches. Use Example 4 as a guide.*

a) 70 inches

b) 109 inches

YOU TRY IT 5 *A typical bedroom door frame is 80 inches tall. Express this measure in feet and inches.*

Adding Linear Measures

Recall, from Section 4.3, that we can add like units of measure: 2 feet + 3 feet = 5 feet.

If we have two mixed unit lengths, we can add the feet together and add the inches together. If the sum of the inches is 12 or more, then we can convert 12 of those inches into 1 foot. For example,

$$16 \text{ in.} = 12 \text{ in.} + 4 \text{ in.} = 1 \text{ ft } 4 \text{ in.}$$

EXAMPLE 5 Add:

a) 6 ft 5 in. + 2 ft 10 in. b) 3 ft 8 in. + 1 ft 4 in.

PROCEDURE: Set up each sum vertically and line up the feet and inches. Adjust the number of inches if the total includes 12 or more inches.

ANSWER: a)

$$\begin{array}{rr} 6 \text{ ft} & 5 \text{ in.} \\ + 2 \text{ ft} & 10 \text{ in.} \\ \hline 8 \text{ ft} & 15 \text{ in.} \\ \downarrow & \downarrow \\ 8 \text{ ft} + & 1 \text{ ft} + 3 \text{ in.} \\ = 9 \text{ ft } 3 \text{ in.} & \end{array}$$

Adjust the number of inches: ← 15 inches = 12 in. + 3 in. = 1 ft 3 in.

b)

$$\begin{array}{rr} 3 \text{ ft} & 8 \text{ in.} \\ + 1 \text{ ft} & 4 \text{ in.} \\ \hline 4 \text{ ft} & 12 \text{ in.} \\ \downarrow & \downarrow \\ 4 \text{ ft} + & 1 \text{ ft} \\ = 5 \text{ ft} & \end{array}$$

Adjust the number of inches: ← 12 inches = 1 ft

YOU TRY IT 6 *Add. Use Example 5 as a guide.*

a) 4 ft 6 in. + 7 ft 3 in. b) 2 ft 5 in. + 4 ft 7 in. c) 5 ft 8 in. + 3 ft 10 in.

YOU TRY IT 7 *Standing on the floor, on tiptoes, Ricky can reach 5 feet 9 inches high. How high can Ricky reach if he stands (on tiptoes) on a stool that is 1 foot 6 inches high?*

Subtracting Feet and Inches

Subtracting feet and inches is similar to subtracting whole numbers. Sometimes we can subtract directly, as in

```
  7 ft 9 in.
− 3 ft 2 in.
  4 ft 7 in.
```

and sometimes we need to regroup, as in

```
  6 ft 3 in.
− 4 ft 7 in.
```

Notice that we can't subtract 7 in. directly from 3 in.

We can, however, regroup by changing 1 foot into 12 inches:

```
  5     15
  6̸ ft  3̸ in.
− 4 ft  7 in.
  1 ft  8 in.
```

Notice that we add 12 inches to the 3 inches already there.

EXAMPLE 6

Subtract:

a) 3 ft 6 in. − 2 ft 1 in.

b) 9 ft 4 in. − 5 ft 10 in.

PROCEDURE: Set up each subtraction vertically and line up the feet and inches. If necessary, adjust the number of feet and inches if you can't subtract directly.

ANSWER: a)

```
  3 ft 6 in.
− 2 ft 1 in.
  1 ft 5 in.
```

Subtract directly without regrouping.

b)

```
  9 ft  4 in.     ← Regroup the first number. →      8 ft 16 in.
− 5 ft 10 in.       12 in. + 4 in. = 16 in.        − 5 ft 10 in.
                                                     3 ft  6 in.
```

YOU TRY IT 8

Subtract. Use Example 6 as a guide.

a) 4 ft 6 in. − 1 ft 3 in.

b) 25 ft 8 in. − 18 ft 11 in.

This next example uses the equation Part = Whole − Part. If the whole and one part are known, then we can subtract to find the other part.

EXAMPLE 7

Annie cut 2 feet 10 inches from a board that is 8 feet long. How long is the remaining board?

PROCEDURE: To start, the length of the board is 8 feet 0 inches. From this, we cut 2 feet 10 inches. This means that we subtract: 8 feet 0 inches − 2 feet 10 inches.

ANSWER:

```
  8 ft  0 in.     ← Regroup the first number. →      7 ft 12 in.
− 2 ft 10 in.       12 in. + 0 in. = 12 in.        − 2 ft 10 in.
                                                     5 ft  2 in.
```

SENTENCE: The remaining board is 5 feet 2 inches long.

YOU TRY IT 9 *Taneesha cut a 6-foot-long sub sandwich into two pieces. One of the pieces is 3 feet 8 inches. What is the length of the other piece?*

U.S. Measures of Weight

Weight refers to how heavy something is. The basic units of measure for weight are *ounces*, *pounds*, and *tons*:

U.S. Measures of Weight	Equivalencies
ounces (oz)	1 lb = 16 oz and 1 oz = $\frac{1}{16}$ lb
pounds (lb)	
tons	1 ton = 2,000 lb and 1 lb = $\frac{1}{2000}$ ton

We can convert from one measure of weight to another using multiplication.

EXAMPLE 8 Convert:

a) $1\frac{3}{4}$ pounds to ounces

b) 4,500 pounds to tons

PROCEDURE: Multiply using the equivalency. For part a, use 1 lb = 16 oz. For part b, use 1 lb = $\frac{1}{2000}$ ton. In part a) it may be helpful to write $1\frac{3}{4}$ as $\frac{7}{4}$. Also, we can write 16 as $\frac{16}{1}$.

ANSWER: a) $1\frac{3}{4}\text{ lb} = 1\frac{3}{4} \times 1\text{ lb} = \frac{7}{4} \times \frac{16}{1}\text{ oz} = \frac{7 \times 16}{4 \times 1}\text{ oz} = \frac{7 \times 4}{1 \times 1}\text{ oz} = 28\text{ oz}$

b) $4{,}500\text{ lb} = 4500 \times 1\text{ lb} = 4{,}500 \times \frac{1}{2000}\text{ ton} = \frac{4500}{2000}\text{ tons} = 2\frac{1}{4}\text{ tons}$

YOU TRY IT 10 *Convert one measure to the other. Show all work, as in Example 8.*

a) $5\frac{1}{8}$ pounds to ounces

b) 5,000 pounds to tons

c) $2\frac{3}{10}$ tons to pounds

Pounds and Ounces

If we have a weight measured in both pounds and ounces, then we can convert the weight to only ounces by first converting the pounds to ounces and then adding the ounces already present in the weight.

For example, we can write 5 lb 4 oz in terms of ounces only by converting the pounds portion to ounces:

$$5 \text{ lb} = 5 \cdot (1 \text{ lb}) = 5 \cdot (16 \text{ oz}) = 80 \text{ oz}$$
$$\downarrow$$
So, $5 \text{ lb } 4 \text{ oz} = 80 \text{ oz} + 4 \text{ oz} = 84$ ounces.

This means that a bag of dog food that weighs 5 lb 4 oz also weighs 84 ounces.

EXAMPLE 9 Convert 3 pounds 7 ounces to ounces.

PROCEDURE: Convert 3 pounds to ounces, then add the extra 7 ounces.

ANSWER: $3 \text{ lb} = 3 \cdot (1 \text{ lb}) = 3 \cdot (16 \text{ oz}) = 48 \text{ oz}$

$$\downarrow$$
$$48 \text{ oz} + 7 \text{ oz} = 55 \text{ oz} \longrightarrow 3 \text{ lb } 7 \text{ oz} = 55 \text{ oz}.$$

YOU TRY IT 11 *Convert each to ounces. Use Example 9 as a guide.*

a) 2 pounds 6 ounces

b) 10 pounds 14 ounces

YOU TRY IT 12 *Gladys grew a tomato that weighed 4 pounds 15 ounces. What is the weight of this tomato in ounces?*

To write ounces in terms of pounds and ounces, we divide the number of ounces by 16. For example, to write 100 ounces in terms of pounds and ounces:

$$\begin{array}{r} \mathbf{6} \\ 16\overline{)100} \\ -\ 96 \\ \hline \mathbf{4} \end{array}$$

6 ← This quotient is the number of pounds.

4 ← This remainder is the number of ounces.

100 ounces = 6 lb 4 oz

EXAMPLE 10 Convert 53 ounces to pounds and ounces.

PROCEDURE: Divide 16 into 53; the quotient is the number of pounds and the remainder is the number of ounces.

ANSWER:

$$\begin{array}{r} \mathbf{3} \\ 16\overline{)53} \\ -\ 48 \\ \hline \mathbf{5} \end{array}$$

53 ounces = 3 lb 5 oz

YOU TRY IT 13

Convert each to pounds and ounces. Use Example 10 as a guide.

a) 70 ounces

b) 165 ounces

YOU TRY IT 14

Carla was born prematurely and weighed only 60 ounces at birth. Write her weight in terms of pounds and ounces.

Adding Weight Measures

Adding pounds and ounces is similar to adding feet and inches. If the sum of the ounces is 16 or more, then we can convert 16 of those ounces into 1 pound.

EXAMPLE 11

Add:

a) 6 lb 14 oz + 2 lb 6 oz

b) 3 lb 12 oz + 1 lb 4 oz

PROCEDURE: Set up each sum vertically and line up the pounds and ounces. Adjust the number of ounces if the total includes 16 or more ounces.

ANSWER:

a)

	6 lb	14 oz	
+	2 lb	6 oz	Adjust the number of ounces:
	8 lb	20 oz	← 20 ounces = 16 oz + 4 oz = 1 lb 4 oz
	↓	↓	

8 lb + 1 lb + 4 oz = 9 lb 4 oz

b)

	3 lb	12 oz	
+	1 lb	4 oz	Adjust the number of ounces:
	4 lb	16 oz	← 16 ounces = 1 lb
	↓	↓	

4 lb + 1 lb = 5 lb

YOU TRY IT 15

Add. Use Example 11 as a guide.

a) 4 lb 6 oz + 7 lb 3 oz

b) 2 lb 7 oz + 4 lb 14 oz

c) 5 lb 7 oz + 3 lb 9 oz

YOU TRY IT 16

One watermelon weighs 23 pounds 11 ounces and another watermelon weighs 19 pounds 12 ounces. What is the total weight of the two watermelons?

Subtracting Pounds and Ounces

If regrouping is necessary when subtracting pounds and ounces, then we need to write 1 pound as 16 ounces and add it to the ounces already in the weight measure.

Consider 6 lb 3 oz − 4 lb 7 oz →

$$\begin{array}{r} \overset{5}{\not 6}\text{ lb } \overset{19}{\not 3}\text{ oz} \\ -\ 4\text{ lb } 7\text{ oz} \\ \hline 1\text{ lb } 12\text{ oz} \end{array}$$

Notice that we add 16 ounces to the 3 ounces already there.

EXAMPLE 12

Subtract:

a) 3 lb 6 oz − 2 lb 1 oz b) 9 lb 4 oz − 5 lb 10 oz

PROCEDURE: Set up each difference vertically and line up the pounds and ounces. If necessary, adjust the number of pounds and ounces if you can't subtract directly.

ANSWER:

a)
$$\begin{array}{r} 3\text{ lb } 6\text{ oz} \\ -\ 2\text{ lb } 1\text{ oz} \\ \hline 1\text{ lb } 5\text{ oz} \end{array}$$
Subtract directly without regrouping.

b)
$$\begin{array}{r} 9\text{ lb } 4\text{ oz} \\ -\ 5\text{ lb } 10\text{ oz} \\ \hline \end{array}$$
← Regroup the first number. →
16 oz + 4 oz = 20 oz
$$\begin{array}{r} 8\text{ lb } 20\text{ oz} \\ -\ 5\text{ lb } 10\text{ oz} \\ \hline 3\text{ lb } 10\text{ oz} \end{array}$$

YOU TRY IT 17

Subtract. Use Example 12 as a guide.

a) 4 lb 9 oz − 1 lb 3 oz b) 10 lb 2 oz − 4 lb 7 oz c) 25 lb − 18 lb 10 oz

EXAMPLE 13

Mitch is a butcher for a grocery store. He cut 2 pounds 10 ounces of meat from a ham that weighed 5 pounds 7 ounces. What is the weight of the remaining ham?

PROCEDURE: To start, the ham weighed 5 pounds 7 ounces. From this, Mitch cut 2 pounds 10 ounces. This means that we subtract: 5 pounds 7 ounces − 2 pounds 10 ounces.

ANSWER:

$$\begin{array}{r} 5\text{ lb } 7\text{ oz} \\ -\ 2\text{ lb } 10\text{ oz} \\ \hline \end{array}$$
← Regroup the first number. →
16 oz + 7 oz = 23 oz
$$\begin{array}{r} 4\text{ lb } 23\text{ oz} \\ -\ 2\text{ lb } 10\text{ oz} \\ \hline 2\text{ lb } 13\text{ oz} \end{array}$$

SENTENCE: There are 2 pounds 13 ounces of the ham remaining.

YOU TRY IT 18

Mai's backpack weighs 19 pounds. She took out her history book, which weighs 5 pounds 2 ounces, and left it in her car. How much does her backpack weigh now?

U.S. Measures of Capacity

> Capacity usually refers to a liquid amount, though not always. For example, a pancake recipe includes 1 cup of flour and 1 cup of milk. The flour is dry and the milk is liquid, but a baker can use the same measuring cup, and it will be filled to the same level for each of these two ingredients.

Capacity refers to the amount a container can hold, usually liquid. A *gallon* of milk, a *quart* of orange juice, a *pint* of ice-cream, and a *cup* of sour cream are common grocery items that use measures of capacity.

1 gallon

1 quart

1 pint

An ounce is a unit of measure used in both weight and capacity. To distinguish between the two, we use *fluid ounces* for capacity.

U.S. Measures of Capacity	Equivalencies
fluid ounces (fl oz)	1 cup $=$ 8 fl oz and 1 fl oz $= \frac{1}{8}$ cup
cups	1 pt $=$ 2 cups and 1 cup $= \frac{1}{2}$ pt
pints (pt)	1 qt $=$ 2 pt and 1 pt $= \frac{1}{2}$ qt
quarts (qt)	1 qt $=$ 4 cups and 1 cup $= \frac{1}{4}$ qt
gallons (gal)	1 gal $=$ 4 qt and 1 qt $= \frac{1}{4}$ gal

It is typical to see measures of capacity written in fractional form, such as $1\frac{1}{2}$ cups.

We can convert from one measure of capacity to another using multiplication. When it is known that the measure is a measure of capacity, it is common to refer to *fluid ounces* simply as *ounces*.

EXAMPLE 14 Convert by multiplying:

a) $\frac{5}{16}$ cup into ounces

b) $3\frac{1}{2}$ cups into quarts

PROCEDURE: Use the equivalencies, above, to convert from one measure to another. For part b, convert from cups to pints, then pints to quarts.

ANSWER:

a) $\frac{5}{16}\text{ cup} = \frac{5}{16} \cdot 1\text{ cup} = \frac{5}{16} \cdot \frac{8}{1}\text{ oz} = \frac{5 \cdot 8}{16 \cdot 1}\text{ oz} = \frac{5 \cdot 1}{2 \cdot 1}\text{ oz} = \frac{5}{2}\text{ oz} = 2\frac{1}{2}\text{ oz}$

b) $3\frac{1}{2}\text{ cups} = \frac{7}{2} \cdot 1\text{ cup} = \frac{7}{2} \cdot \frac{1}{4}\text{ qt} = \frac{7}{8}\text{ qt}$

YOU TRY IT 19

Convert by multiplying. Use Example 14 as a guide.

a) 9 quarts into gallons

b) $\frac{3}{8}$ quarts into pints

c) 20 fluid ounces into pints

d) $1\frac{5}{8}$ quarts into cups

You Try It Answers: Section 7.1

YTI 1 a) 54 inches b) 19 feet c) $2\frac{3}{4}$ feet

YTI 2 a) 30 inches b) 129 inches

YTI 3 Yao Ming is 89 inches tall.

YTI 4 a) 5 ft 10 in. b) 9 ft 1 in.

YTI 5 A typical bedroom door frame is 6 feet 8 inches tall. (Yao Ming has to duck!)

YTI 6 a) 11 ft 9 in. b) 7 ft c) 9 ft 6 in.

YTI 7 a) Ricky can reach 7 feet 3 inches high on the stool. (Not even enough to touch the top of Yao Ming's head!)

YTI 8 a) 3 ft 3 in. b) 6 ft 9 in.

YTI 9 The other sandwich piece is 2 feet 4 inches long. (Just the way Yao Ming likes it!)

YTI 10 a) 82 oz b) $2\frac{1}{2}$ tons c) 4,600 lb

YTI 11 a) 38 oz b) 174 oz

YTI 12 The tomato weighs 79 oz. (Just the way Yao Ming likes it, with a little salt.)

YTI 13 a) 4 lb 6 oz b) 10 lb 5 oz

YTI 14 Carla weighed 3 pounds 12 ounces when she was born.

YTI 15 a) 11 lb 9 oz b) 7 lb 5 oz c) 9 lb

YTI 16 The two watermelons weigh a total of 43 pounds 7 ounces.

YTI 17 a) 3 lb 6 oz b) 5 lb 11 oz c) 6 lb 6 oz

YTI 18 Mai's backpack now weighs 13 pounds 14 ounces.

YTI 19 a) $2\frac{1}{4}$ gal b) $\frac{3}{4}$ pt c) $1\frac{1}{4}$ pt d) $6\frac{1}{2}$ cups

Focus Exercises: Section 7.1

Convert from one measure to the other.

1. 4 feet to inches **2.** 8 yards to feet **3.** $\frac{2}{3}$ feet to inches **4.** $4\frac{2}{3}$ yards to feet

5. 16 feet to yards **6.** $5\frac{1}{4}$ feet to yards **7.** 4 inches to feet **8.** 9 inches to feet

Convert each to inches.

9. 12 ft **10.** 2 ft 3 in. **11.** 6 ft 8 in. **12.** 15 ft 6 in.

Convert each to feet and inches.

13. 28 in. **14.** 60 in. **15.** 93 in. **16.** 106 in.

17. The rim of a basketball hoop is 10 feet off of the floor. Express this measure in inches.

18. The record length for a garter snake is 111 inches long. Express this measure in feet and inches.

Add or subtract, as indicated. Express each answer in feet and inches.

19. 4 ft 7 in. + 6 ft 3 in.

20. 5 ft 2 in. + 9 ft 4 in.

21. 1 ft 11 in. + 4 ft 1 in.

22. 13 ft 8 in. + 12 ft 5 in.

23. 8 ft 10 in. − 3 ft 2 in.

24. 12 ft 6 in. − 4 ft 5 in.

25. 12 ft 2 in. − 8 ft 9 in.

26. 15 ft − 6 ft 6 in.

27. Rodney measured 1 foot 9 inches long (tall) at birth. During his first year he grew 1 foot 5 inches. How tall was Rodney on his first birthday?

28. As a workshop is being built, one opening, measuring 3 feet 4 inches high, will include a window on top of an air conditioning unit. If the air conditioning unit measures 1 foot 6 inches high, how high will the window portion be?

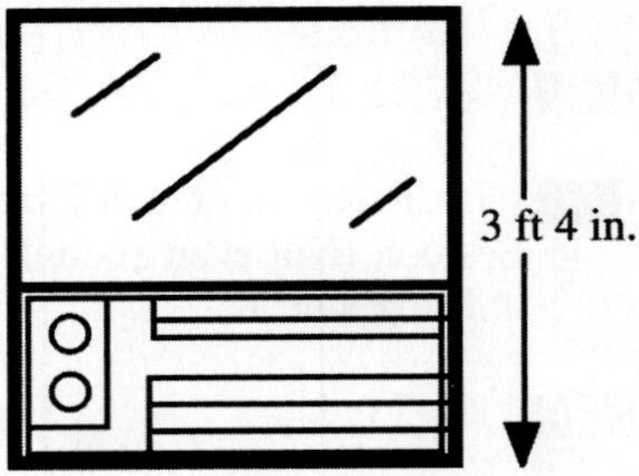

Convert one measure to the other.

29. 5 pounds to ounces

30. $6\frac{2}{5}$ ounces to pounds

31. 4 tons to pounds

32. 1,500 pounds to tons

Convert each to ounces.

33. 9 lb

34. 1 lb 9 oz

35. 6 lb 8 oz

36. 10 lb 6 oz

Convert each to pounds and ounces.

37. 28 oz

38. 60 oz

39. 90 oz

40. 106 oz

41. A home run slugger's baseball bat weighs 2 pounds 2 ounces. Express this measure in ounces.

42. An African bullfrog weighs 95 ounces. Express this measure in pounds and ounces.

Add or subtract, as indicated. Express each answer in pounds and ounces.

43. 4 lb 8 oz + 6 lb 5 oz

44. 5 lb 12 oz + 9 lb 3 oz

45. 0 lb 13 oz + 7 lb 3 oz

46. 13 lb 10 oz + 12 lb 9 oz

47. 8 lb 14 oz − 3 lb 2 oz

48. 12 lb 9 oz − 4 lb 5 oz

49. 12 lb 2 oz − 8 lb 9 oz

50. 16 lb − 7 lb 6 oz

51. Liu is one month old and weighs 9 pounds 12 ounces. His baby carrier weighs 7 pounds 6 ounces. What is the total weight of Liu and his baby carrier?

52. Ginger is a toy poodle. To find her weight she was put on the vet's scale in her carry crate. Together, Ginger and her crate weigh 10 pounds 8 ounces. By itself, the crate weighs 2 pounds 15 ounces. How much does Ginger weigh by herself?

Convert one measure to the other.

53. 5 quarts to pints

54. $3\frac{1}{4}$ cups to fluid ounces

55. $2\frac{3}{8}$ pints to cups

56. $4\frac{1}{2}$ gallons to quarts

57. $2\frac{3}{4}$ quarts to cups

58. $1\frac{1}{2}$ pints to fluid ounces

59. $4\frac{2}{3}$ pints to quarts

60. $5\frac{1}{3}$ quarts to gallons

SECTION 7.2 Metric Measures

Objectives

In this section, you will learn to:

- Identify metric units of measure.
- Identify the prefixes of metric measures.
- Convert between prefixes of metric measures.
- Add and subtract metric measures.

To successfully complete this section, you need to understand:

- Multiplying fractions (3.3)
- Decimal fractions (5.1)
- Adding and subtracting decimals (5.3)
- Multiplying decimals by powers of 10 (5.4)
- U.S. system of measurement (7.1)

Introduction

The metric system of measurement is quite different from the U.S. system presented in Section 7.1. In many ways, the metric system is easier to use because it is based on powers of 10, such as 10, 100, and 1000. This makes converting between measures a simple matter of moving the decimal point to the left or to the right.

The basic metric measurements are as follows:

Length: 1 meter. A **meter** is about $3\frac{3}{8}$ inches longer than a yard. (A yard is three feet, about the height of a doorknob from the floor.)

Weight: 1 gram. A **gram** is about the weight of the contents of a packet of artificial sweetener.

Capacity: 1 liter. A **liter** is a little more than one quart.

Metric Measures and Prefixes

Here is a portion of a metric ruler. It shows both millimeters (the tiny lines) and centimeters (cm). The centimeters are $\frac{1}{100}$, or 0.01, of a meter (m). The millimeters (mm) are $\frac{1}{1000}$, or 0.001, of a meter.

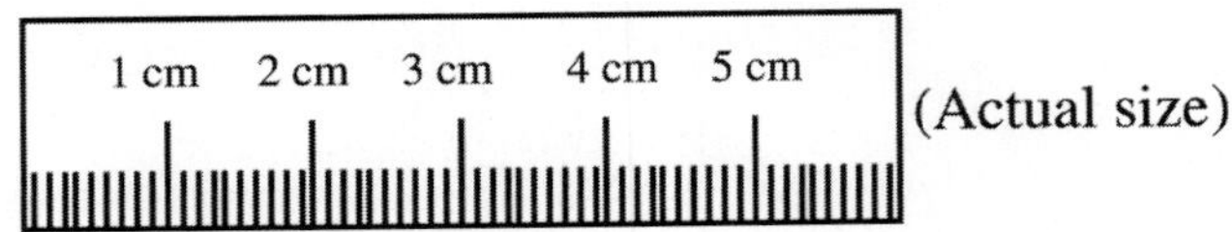

(Actual size)

The great thing about metric measures is that the relationship between two measures is easy to interpret: it's all based on the **prefix** (the part of the word that starts the word) and the **base unit**.

For example, the prefix *kilo-* means *one thousand*, so a kilometer is 1,000 times as long as a meter, its base unit. Similarly, a kilogram is 1,000 grams and a kiloliter is 1,000 liters.

Here is a table of metric prefixes with different base units of measure. Any one of the base units can be used with any of the prefixes.

Prefix	Meaning	Base Unit	Put Together	Meaning
Kilo-	one thousand	gram (g)	kilogram (kg)	1,000 grams
Hecto-	one hundred	liter (L)	hectoliter (hL)	100 liters
Deka-	ten	meter (m)	dekameter (dam)	10 meters
Deci-	one-tenth	liter (L)	deciliter (dL)	$\frac{1}{10}$ or 0.1 of a liter
Centi-	one-hundredth	meter (m)	centimeter (cm)	$\frac{1}{100}$ or 0.01 of a meter
Milli-	one-thousandth	gram (g)	milligram (mg)	$\frac{1}{1{,}000}$ or 0.001 of a gram

One kilometer is 1,000 meters because of the way units, and now prefixes, multiply:

$$1 \text{ kilo-meter} = 1{,}000 \cdot (1 \text{ meter}) = 1{,}000 \text{ meters}$$

$$(1 \text{ km} = 1{,}000 \text{ m})$$

This also means that, for example, 6 kilometers = 6 · 1,000 · (1 meter) = 6,000 meters. Notice that the base units, *meters* (m), *liters* (L), and *grams* (g) have no prefix.

Convert the given unit of measure to its base unit.

a) 7.8 hectometers (hm)
b) 6.3 dekagrams (dag)
c) 219 centimeters (cm)
d) 45 milliliters (mL)

PROCEDURE: Write the given unit of measure as a product based on the prefix, then multiply.

ANSWER:
a) 7.8 hectometers = 7.8 × (100 meters) = 780 m
b) 6.3 dekagrams = 6.3 × (10 grams) = 63 g
c) 219 centimeters = 219 × (0.01 meters) = 2.19 m
d) 45 milliliters = 45 × (0.001 liters) = 0.045 L

YOU TRY IT 1

Convert the given unit of measure to its base unit. Use Example 1 as a guide.

a) 5.21 kilometers
b) 34 deciliters
c) 514 milligrams

The abbreviation for liters is the capital letter L. It is the only metric measure abbreviated with a capital letter. Why do you think it is this way?

The different metric measures are connected to each other in this way: If you were to make a plastic box with a length of 1 decimeter (about 4 inches) all around, it would hold exactly 1 liter of water, and that amount of water would weigh exactly 1 kilogram.

There is a slight connection between U.S. measures: one fluid ounce of water (capacity) weighs about 1 ounce (weight).

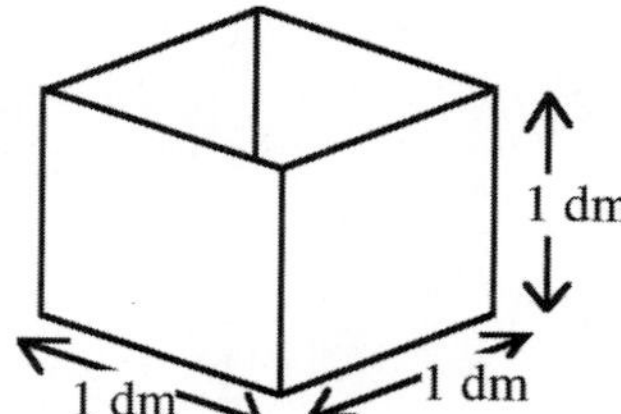

Direct Decimal Conversions of Metric Measures

Another great thing about metric measures is that they are based on a decimal system. This means that a conversion from, say, hectometers to decimeters, is simply a matter of moving the decimal point to the left or to the right. It's all based on the prefix, which represents a power of 10 in one form or another.

For example, we already know that *kilo-* means *1000 times larger*, and that 6 kilometers = 6,000 meters. If we think of 6 as 6**.**000, then converting kilometers to meters has the effect of moving the decimal point *three places to the right:*

6.000 kilometers = 6,000 meters

Similarly, we know that *centi-* means 0.01 meters, and—from Example 1c)—we know that 238 centimeters = 2.38 meters. So, if we think of the decimal point at the end of 238**.**, then converting from centimeters to meters has the effect of moving the decimal point *two places to the left:*

238. centimeters = 2.38 meters

The number of places the decimal point must move is based on the prefix. Whether to move left or right, though, might be hard to remember; here is a diagram that will assist us in knowing which way to move the decimal point.

kilo-	hecto-	deka-	meter	deci-	centi-	milli-
km	hm	dam	m	dm	cm	mm

To use this diagram, locate the starting measure (the "converting from" measure) and count—left or right—to the "converting to" measure, as demonstrated in this next example.

EXAMPLE 2

Convert each according to the diagram.

a) 52 centimeters to dekameters

b) 3.6 hectograms to centigrams

PROCEDURE: Locate the first measure on the chart and count (right or left) the number of spaces it takes to get to the "converting to" measure.

ANSWER: a) Start at centimeters (cm), and move left three places to get to the dekameters (dam) position.

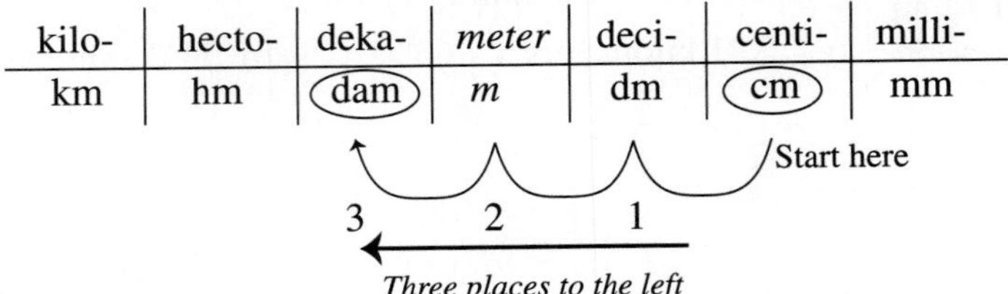

This means that we will move the decimal point three places to the left:

$$0\,52. \text{ centimeters} = 0.052 \text{ dekameter}$$

Moving the decimal point three places to the left requires more digits than we have, so we need to place a 0 in front of the number.

b) Start at hectograms (hg), and move right four places to get to the centigrams (cg) position.

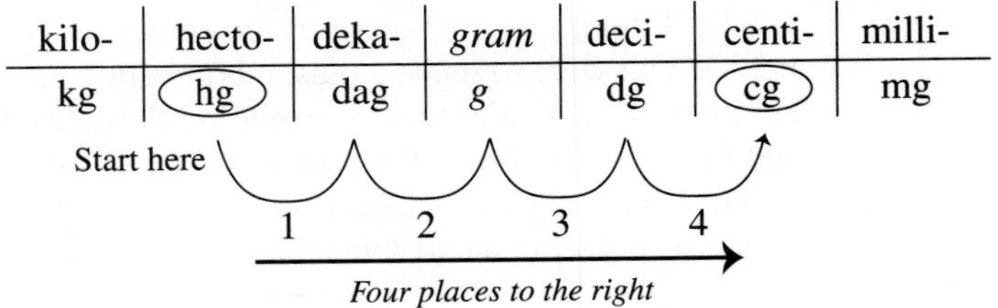

This means that we will move the decimal point four places to the right:

$$3.6000 \text{ hectograms} = 36{,}000. \text{ centigrams}$$

Moving the decimal point four places to the right requires more digits than we have, so we need to place 0's at the end of the number.

YOU TRY IT 2

Convert each measure to its base unit of measure, either meters, grams, or liters. You may use the conversion chart as demonstrated in Example 2.

a) 8 deciliters

b) 18.5 dekagrams

c) 0.59 hectometer

YOU TRY IT 3 *Convert the given unit of measure to the measure shown. You may use the conversion chart as demonstrated in Example 2.*

a) 5.21 kilograms to dekagrams

b) 28 deciliters to milliliters

c) 7.95 hectometers to kilometers

YOU TRY IT 4 *A chewable tablet contains 500 mg of vitamin C. Express this number in grams.*

YOU TRY IT 5 *A soda bottle contains 2.3 L of soda. Express this number in milliliters.*

Adding and Subtracting Metric Measures

Adding and subtracting metric measures is simply a matter of adding and subtracting decimals. We must be sure, though, that the measures are expressed as the same units.

For example, to add 3.56 meters + 2.80 meters, we write them vertically and line up the decimal points:

$$\begin{array}{r} 3.56\text{ m} \\ +\ 2.80\text{ m} \\ \hline 6.36\text{ m} \end{array}$$

← Place a 0 on the end of 2.8 to give each number the same number of decimal places.

However, to add 3.56 meters + 2.8 *decimeters*, we must first write one in terms of the other, then we may add. Let's write 2.8 dm in terms of meters (use the direct method and move the decimal point):

2.8 dm = 0.28 m We can now add 3.56 m + 0.28 m

$$\begin{array}{r} 3.56\text{ m} \\ +\ 0.28\text{ m} \\ \hline 3.84\text{ m} \end{array}$$

EXAMPLE 3 Add or subtract as indicated. Convert each measure to the one that is underlined.

a) 6.4 <u>kilograms</u> + 850 grams

b) 5.1 deciliters − 325 <u>milliliters</u>

PROCEDURE: First convert from one measure to another, then add or subtract.

ANSWER: a) First convert 850 grams to kilograms: 850 g = 0.850 kg

Now add:

$$\begin{array}{r} 6.400\text{ kg} \\ +\ 0.850\text{ kg} \\ \hline 7.250\text{ kg} \end{array}$$

b) First convert 5.1 deciliters to milliliters: 5.1 dL = 510 mL

Now subtract:

$$\begin{array}{r} 510\text{ mL} \\ -\ 325\text{ mL} \\ \hline 185\text{ mL} \end{array}$$

YOU TRY IT 6

Add or subtract as indicated. Convert each measure to the one that is underlined. Use Example 3 as a guide.

a) 48 millimeters + 5.6 centimeters

b) 10.1 kilograms + 540 grams

c) 1.65 liters − 820 milliliters

In the next two examples we'll use the equations

Part + Part = Whole and Part = Whole − Part.

↕ So, if two parts are known, then we can add to find the whole.

↕ If the whole and one part are known, then we can subtract to find the other part.

EXAMPLE 4

When Riley was born she weighed 34 hectograms. During her first week of life she gained 650 grams. How many kilograms did she weigh after the first week?

PROCEDURE: The last sentence indicates that we want everything in terms of kilograms, so we must first convert

1. 34 hectograms to kilograms: 34 hg = 3.4 kg, and
2. 650 grams to kilograms: 650 g = 0.650 kg = 0.65 kg

Next we'll add 3.4 kg + 0.65 kg:

ANSWER:

$$\begin{array}{r} 3.40\text{ kg} \\ +\ 0.65\text{ kg} \\ \hline 4.05\text{ kg} \end{array}$$

SENTENCE: After the first week, Riley weighed 4.05 kilograms.

EXAMPLE 5

Wendy was mixing punch for her son's 8th birthday party. The punch will be a 2 liter mixture of orange juice and grapefruit soda. The first thing she poured into the punch bowl was a 725 milliliter bottle of grapefruit soda. How many milliliters of orange juice must Wendy add?

PROCEDURE: The last sentence indicates that we want everything in terms of milliliters, so we must first convert 2 liters to milliliters: 2 L = 2000 mL

Next, we'll subtract 2000 mL − 725 mL:

ANSWER:

$$\begin{array}{r} 2000\text{ mL} \\ -\ 725\text{ mL} \\ \hline 1275\text{ mL} \end{array}$$

SENTENCE: Wendy must add 1,275 milliliters of orange juice.

YOU TRY IT 7 *A pharmacist is making a single pain pill by combining 45 centigrams of ibuprofen with 325 milligrams of ibuprofen. How many grams of ibuprofen will the pill contain?*

YOU TRY IT 8 *Harvey the snail is in a race to climb a 0.3 meter pole. After one minute he has climbed 1.2 decimeters. How many centimeters does he have left to climb?*

You Try It Answers: Section 7.2

YTI 1 a) 5,210 m b) 3.4 L c) 0.514 g

YTI 2 a) 0.8 L b) 185 g c) 59 m

YTI 3 a) 521 dag b) 2,800 mL c) 0.795 km

YTI 4 The chewable tablet contains 0.5 gram of vitamin C.

YTI 5 The soda bottle contains 2,300 milliliters of soda.

YTI 6 a) 10.4 cm b) 10.64 kg c) 830 mL

YTI 7 The pill will contain 0.775 gram of ibuprofen.

YTI 8 Harvey has 18 centimeters left to climb.

Focus Exercises: Section 7.2

Convert the given unit of measure to its base unit, either meters, grams, or liters.

1. 3.08 km **2.** 28 dL **3.** 0.45 kL **4.** 6.8 dg

5. 870 mg **6.** 2.4 hm **7.** 91 mL **8.** 0.89 hL

9. 365 cm **10.** 3.1 dag **11.** 49 cg **12.** 0.87 dam

13. 6 cL **14.** 27 kL **15.** 4 dm **16.** 40 kg

Convert the given unit of measure to the measure shown.

17. 3.6 kilometers to dekameters

18. 2 decigrams to milligrams

19. 312 milligrams to decigrams

20. 1.2 hectometers to kilometers

21. 0.9 dekaliters to kiloliters

22. 14 centiliters to milliliters

23. 2.5 meters to decimeters

24. 45 meters to kilometers

25. 1,810 milliliters to deciliters

26. 52 centigrams to milligrams

27. 0.83 kilometers to hectometers

28. 3.6 hectometers to centimeters

29. 37 centigrams to decigrams

30. 0.82 kiloliters to deciliters

31. 6 milliliters to centiliters

32. 16 centigrams to decigrams

Write a sentence with the requested measurement.

33. A child weighs 15.6 kilograms. Express this number in grams.

34. Randi's thermos can hold 355 milliliters. Express this number in liters.

35. Veronica's rose bush is 83.5 centimeters high. Express this number in meters.

36. A baseball weighs 155 grams. Express this number in kilograms.

37. A dwarf pygmy goby has a diameter of 0.099 decimeters. Express this number in millimeters. (The dwarf pygmy goby is the smallest known freshwater fish.)

38. A pen holds 8.3 milliliters of ink. Express this number in deciliters.

Add. Convert each measure to the one that is <u>underlined</u>.

39. 1.42 dekagrams + 591 <u>centigrams</u>

40. 745 milliliters + 0.862 <u>liters</u>

41. 3.07 <u>dekaliters</u> + 15 deciliters

42. 28.7 <u>decimeters</u> + 64 millimeters

Subtract. Convert each measure to the one that is <u>underlined</u>.

43. 41 <u>centigrams</u> − 253 milligrams

44. 125 <u>centimeters</u> − 0.72 meters

45. 2 hectoliters − 684 <u>deciliters</u>

46. 1020 milligrams − 0.045 <u>dekagrams</u>

Add or subtract as indicated. Write a sentence answering the question.

47. At a hospital, a fluid drip bag has 1.5 liters of saline solution. A nurse adds 12.5 centiliters of pain medicine to the bag. How many milliliters of fluid are now in the bag?

48. For the first three days of a winter storm, the town of Bedrock received 0.95 decimeters of rain. On the storm's fourth day, the town received 18 millimeters. How many centimeters of rain did Bedrock receive in those four days?

49. Jermaine put 750 milliliters of a fuel additive into his gas tank. He then pumped in 1.265 dekaliters of gas. How many liters in total did he add to his gas tank?

50. In a single serving of a raisin bran cereal, there are 0.35 grams of sodium. With milk, the total amount of sodium is 3.97 decigrams. How many milligrams of sodium are in the serving of milk?

51. On her 10th birthday, Tamayra was 1.15 meters tall. On her 11th birthday, she was 1,237 millimeters tall. How many centimeters did Tamayra grow that year?

52. A small apple weighs 1.42 hectograms, and a large apple weighs 0.22 kilograms. How many grams heavier is the large apple than the small apple?

SECTION 7.3 Converting U.S. and Metric Measures

Objectives

In this section, you will learn to:

- Create and use equivalence fractions to convert between measures.
- Convert between U.S. and metric measures.

To successfully complete this section, you need to understand:

- Writing improper fractions as mixed numbers and mixed numbers as improper fractions (3.1)
- Simplifying fractions (3.2)
- U.S. measures (7.1)
- Metric measures (7.2)

Introduction

One technique for converting measures relies on multiplying by 1. As you know, any fraction in which the numerator and denominator have the same value is equivalent to 1.

Because 1 foot = 12 inches, this is true for the fraction $\frac{1\text{ ft}}{12\text{ in.}}$ and its reciprocal $\frac{12\text{ in.}}{1\text{ ft}}$. Each of these is called an **equivalence fraction**. These equivalence fractions are different ways of expressing the value 1.

Converting Measures Using Equivalence Fractions

Here are a variety of equivalence fractions based on the measures we have used in the past two sections. This is just a sample of the many possible equivalence fractions, with both U.S. and metric measures.

Notice that an equivalence fraction can be expressed two ways. One fraction is the reciprocal of the other.

Equivalency	Equivalence Fractions
1 ft = 12 in.	$\frac{1\text{ ft}}{12\text{ in.}} = 1$ and $\frac{12\text{ in.}}{1\text{ ft}} = 1$
1 gal = 4 qt	$\frac{1\text{ gal}}{4\text{ qt}} = 1$ and $\frac{4\text{ qt}}{1\text{ gal}} = 1$
1 lb = 16 oz	$\frac{1\text{ lb}}{16\text{ oz}} = 1$ and $\frac{16\text{ oz}}{1\text{ lb}} = 1$
1 km = 1,000 m	$\frac{1\text{ km}}{1{,}000\text{ m}} = 1$ and $\frac{1{,}000\text{ m}}{1\text{ km}} = 1$
100 cL = 1 L	$\frac{1\text{ L}}{100\text{ cL}} = 1$ and $\frac{100\text{ cL}}{1\text{ L}} = 1$
1,000 mg = 1 g	$\frac{1\text{ g}}{1{,}000\text{ mg}} = 1$ and $\frac{1{,}000\text{ mg}}{1\text{ g}} = 1$

EXAMPLE 1

Given the following equivalencies, create an equivalence fraction equal to 1. Then write its reciprocal equal to 1.

a) 1 pennyweight = 24 grains b) 8 furlongs = 1 mile

PROCEDURE: Make a fraction from each equivalency and set it equal to 1, then do the same for its reciprocal.

ANSWER:

a) $\frac{1\text{ pennyweight}}{24\text{ grains}} = 1$ and $\frac{24\text{ grains}}{1\text{ pennyweight}} = 1$

b) $\frac{8\text{ furlongs}}{1\text{ mile}} = 1$ and $\frac{1\text{ mile}}{8\text{ furlongs}} = 1$

YOU TRY IT 1

Given the following equivalencies, create an equivalence fraction equal to 1. Then write its reciprocal equal to 1. Use Example 1 as a guide.

a) 1 day = 24 hours b) 1 dekagram = 10 grams c) 2,000 pounds = 1 ton

We can multiply anything by 1 and not change its value. For example, if we need to write 2 feet in terms of inches, we can first write 2 feet as a fraction, $\frac{2\text{ feet}}{1}$, and then multiply $\frac{2\text{ feet}}{1}$ by a special form of 1, namely $\frac{12\text{ inches}}{1\text{ foot}}$.

We are able to divide out common factors, including common units of measure, as shown here:

$$\frac{2\text{ feet}}{1} \times \frac{12\text{ inches}}{1} = \frac{2\text{ \cancel{feet}} \times 12\text{ inches}}{1 \times 1\text{ \cancel{foot}}} = \frac{24\text{ inches}}{1} = 24\text{ inches}$$

Notice that *feet* is in the numerator, and *foot* is in the denominator, so they can be divided out.

Caution

We must choose the correct form of 1 to get the results we seek. Not just any fraction of 1 will do. For example, if we're trying to convert from feet to inches, then we must work with the equivalency 1 foot = 12 inches.

Our choice of fraction should always be $\frac{\text{New unit of measure}}{\text{Original unit of measure}}$.

EXAMPLE 2

Use an equivalence fraction to convert from one measure to another.

Write $11\frac{1}{4}$ feet in terms of yards.

PROCEDURE: First, write $11\frac{1}{4}$ feet as an improper fraction:

$$11\frac{1}{4}\text{ feet} = \frac{45\text{ ft}}{4}.$$ (Notice that the unit of measure is placed in the numerator.)

Second, decide which equivalency to make into 1 so that we can convert properly.

Third, divide out the common units, multiply and simplify.

ANSWER: Multiply $\frac{45\text{ ft}}{4}$ by $\frac{1\text{ yd}}{3\text{ ft}}$ $\frac{\leftarrow\text{New unit}}{\leftarrow\text{Original unit}}$:

$$\frac{45\text{ ft}}{4} \cdot \frac{1\text{ yd}}{3\text{ ft}} = \frac{45\text{ ft} \cdot 1\text{ yd}}{4 \cdot 3\text{ ft}} = \frac{45 \cdot 1\text{ yd}}{4 \cdot 3} = \frac{15 \cdot 1\text{ yd}}{4 \cdot 1} = \frac{15}{4}\text{ yd} = 3\frac{3}{4}\text{ yards}$$

↑ Divide out feet. ↑ Divide out a factor of 3.

EXAMPLE 3

Use an equivalence fraction to convert from one metric measure to another.

Write 3.5 <u>liters</u> in terms of <u>deciliters</u>.

PROCEDURE: First, write 3.5 liters as a fraction over 1.

Second, the equivalency is between liters and deciliter: 10 deciliters = 1 liter.

Use $\frac{\text{New unit}\rightarrow}{\text{Original unit}\rightarrow} = \frac{10\text{ dL}}{1\text{ L}}$.

Third, divide out the common units, multiply and simplify.

ANSWER: $$\frac{3.5\text{ L}}{1} \times \frac{10\text{ dL}}{1\text{ L}} = \frac{3.5\text{ L} \times 10\text{ dL}}{1 \times 1\text{ L}} = \frac{35\text{ dL}}{1} = 35\text{ deciliters}$$

↑ Divide out liters.

YOU TRY IT 2

Use an equivalence fraction to convert from one measure to another. Use Examples 2 and 3 as guides. (You may want to refer back to the equivalencies presented in Section 7.1 and 7.2.)

a) Convert 24 fluid ounces to cups.

b) Convert 350 meters to kilometers.

Converting between U.S. and Metric Linear Measures

We can also convert between U.S. measures and metric measures. Usually, though, these conversions are approximations and not exact. Instead of the equal sign, we use $\approx$ to represent "approximately equal to."

Here is a list of some common U.S. and metric "equivalents." Notice in the first one that 2 inches is *approximately equal to* 5 centimeters. It's appropriate to say that 2 inches is *about* 5 centimeters.

	Approximation	**As a fraction ≈ 1**
Measures of length/distance	2 inches ≈ 5 centimeters	$\frac{2\text{ in.}}{5\text{ cm}} \approx \frac{5\text{ cm}}{2\text{ in.}} \approx 1$
	10 yards ≈ 9 meters	$\frac{10\text{ yd}}{9\text{ m}} \approx \frac{9\text{ m}}{10\text{ yd}} \approx 1$
	5 miles ≈ 8 kilometers	$\frac{5\text{ mi}}{8\text{ km}} \approx \frac{8\text{ km}}{5\text{ mi}} \approx 1$

EXAMPLE 4 Convert 9 miles into kilometers.

PROCEDURE: First, write 9 miles as a fraction over 1.

Second, use an approximate equivalency to make 1; we want to eliminate *miles.*

Third, multiply the fractions. Write the answer as a decimal approximation.

ANSWER:

$9\text{ mi} = \frac{9\text{ mi}}{1}$ We want to eliminate miles, so use $\frac{8\text{ km}}{5\text{ mi}}$ ← New unit / ← Original unit.

$\approx \frac{9\text{ mi}}{1} \cdot \frac{8\text{ km}}{5\text{ mi}}$

$\approx \frac{9\text{ mi} \cdot 8\text{ km}}{1 \cdot 5\text{ mi}}$ Divide out the miles.

$\approx \frac{9 \cdot 8\text{ km}}{1 \cdot 5}$ This is $\frac{72\text{ km}}{5}$, but it is also $\frac{72}{5}$ km.

$\approx \frac{72}{5}\text{ km}$ Divide: $5\overline{)72.0}$ = 14.4

$\approx 14.4\text{ km}$ 9 miles ≈ 14.4 kilometers

The fraction $\frac{72}{5}$ can be written as a mixed number, $14\frac{2}{5}$, or as a decimal, 14.4. In the previous example, we wrote the answer as a decimal. Would it have been better to write the answer as a mixed number, $14\frac{2}{5}$ km? Why or why not?

____

____

EXAMPLE 5 Convert 6 kilometers to miles.

PROCEDURE: First, write 6 km as a fraction over 1.
Second, use an approximate equivalency to make 1; we want to eliminate km.
Third, multiply the fractions and simplify. Write the answer as a mixed number.

ANSWER:

$6 \text{ km} = \dfrac{6 \text{ km}}{1}$ Use $\dfrac{5 \text{ mi}}{8 \text{ km}}$ $\begin{array}{l}\leftarrow \text{New unit} \\ \leftarrow \text{Original unit}\end{array}$.

$\approx \dfrac{6 \text{ km}}{1} \cdot \dfrac{5 \text{ mi}}{8 \text{ km}}$ Multiply the fractions.

$\approx \dfrac{6 \text{ km} \cdot 5 \text{ mi}}{1 \cdot 8 \text{ km}}$ Divide out the kilometers.

$\approx \dfrac{6 \cdot 5 \text{ mi}}{1 \cdot 8}$ This is $\dfrac{30 \text{ mi}}{8} = \dfrac{15 \text{ mi}}{4} = \dfrac{15}{4}$ mi.

$\approx \dfrac{15}{4}$ mi As a mixed number, $\dfrac{15}{4} = 3\dfrac{3}{4} = 3.75$.

6 kilometers $\approx 3\dfrac{3}{4}$ miles

YOU TRY IT 3 *Convert each measure to its alternate U.S. or metric form. Use Examples 4 and 5 as guides. Write a metric measure answer as a decimal approximation and a U.S. measure answer as a mixed number.*

a) Convert 8 inches to centimeters.

b) Convert 15 meters to yards.

c) Convert $17\frac{1}{2}$ miles to kilometers.

EXAMPLE 6 A computer screen is 17 inches wide. Approximately how many centimeters wide is the screen?

PROCEDURE: This problem is simply asking us to convert inches to centimeters. Write the first sentence with the converted measurement.

ANSWER:

$17 \text{ in.} = \dfrac{17 \text{ in.}}{1}$ Use $\dfrac{5 \text{ cm}}{2 \text{ in.}}$ $\begin{array}{l}\leftarrow \text{New unit} \\ \leftarrow \text{Original unit}\end{array}$.

$\approx \dfrac{17 \text{ in.}}{1} \cdot \dfrac{5 \text{ cm}}{2 \text{ in.}}$

$\approx \dfrac{17 \text{ in} \cdot 5 \text{ cm}}{1 \cdot 2 \text{ in.}}$ Divide out the inches.

$\approx \dfrac{17 \cdot 5 \text{ cm}}{1 \cdot 2}$ This is $\dfrac{85 \text{ cm}}{2} = \dfrac{85}{2}$ cm.

$\approx \dfrac{85}{2}$ cm Divide: $2\overline{)85.0}$ = 42.5

≈ 42.5 cm

SENTENCE: The computer screen is approximately 42.5 cm wide.

YOU TRY IT 4 *Soo-Kim jogs 4 kilometers every morning. Approximately how many miles does she jog?*

YOU TRY IT 5 *The longest goldfish in captivity is 37 centimeters long. Express this number in inches.*
Source: Guinness World Records, 2004

Think about it

How tall are you?

a) Write your height in feet and inches.

b) Convert your height to inches only.

c) Write your height in centimeters.

d) Write your height in meters.

Measures of Capacity and Measures of Weight

Here is a list of some common U.S. and metric equivalents for capacity and for weight.

	Approximation	As a fraction ≈ 1
Measures of capacity	20 quarts ≈ 19 liters	$\frac{20\text{ qt}}{19\text{ L}} \approx \frac{19\text{ L}}{20\text{ qt}} \approx 1$
	5 gallons ≈ 19 liters	$\frac{5\text{ gal}}{19\text{ L}} \approx \frac{19\text{ L}}{5\text{ gal}} \approx 1$
Measures of weight	1 ounces ≈ 28 grams	$\frac{1\text{ oz}}{28\text{ g}} \approx \frac{28\text{ g}}{1\text{ oz}} \approx 1$
	11 pounds ≈ 5 kilograms	$\frac{11\text{ lb}}{5\text{ kg}} \approx \frac{5\text{ kg}}{11\text{ lb}} \approx 1$

EXAMPLE 7 Convert 4 kilograms to pounds.

PROCEDURE: First, write 4 kilograms as a fraction over 1.
Second, use an equivalence fraction to make 1.
Third, multiply the fractions and simplify. Write the answer as a mixed number.

ANSWER:

$4\text{ kg} = \frac{4\text{ kg}}{1}$ Use $\frac{11\text{ lb}}{5\text{ kg}}$ ← New unit / ← Original unit

$\approx \frac{4\text{ kg}}{1} \cdot \frac{11\text{ lb}}{5\text{ kg}}$ Multiply the fractions.

$\approx \frac{4\text{ kg} \cdot 11\text{ lb}}{1 \cdot 5\text{ kg}}$ Divide out the kilograms.

$$\approx \frac{4 \cdot 11 \text{ lb}}{1 \cdot 5}$$

$$\approx \frac{44}{5} \text{ lb}$$ Now write the fraction as a mixed number.

$$\approx 8\frac{4}{5} \text{ lb}$$ 4 kilograms $\approx 8\frac{4}{5}$ pounds

YOU TRY IT 6

Convert each measure to its alternate U.S. or metric form. Use Example 7 as a guide. Write improper fractions as mixed numbers for U.S. measures and as decimals for metric measures.

a) Convert 5 ounces to grams.

b) Convert 15 pounds to kilograms.

c) Convert 50 quarts to liters.

YOU TRY IT 7

A prehistoric bird called the teratorn is believed to have weighed about 80 kilograms. Express this number in pounds. Source: Guinness World Records, 2004

YOU TRY IT 8

The largest gelatin dessert ever made contained 35,000 liters of watermelon flavored Jell-O mix. Express this number in gallons. (Round to the nearest whole number.) Source: Guinness World Records, 2004

You Try It Answers: Section 7.3

YTI 1
a) $\frac{1 \text{ day}}{24 \text{ hours}} = 1; \frac{24 \text{ hours}}{1 \text{ day}} = 1$
b) $\frac{1 \text{ dekagram}}{10 \text{ grams}} = 1; \frac{10 \text{ grams}}{1 \text{ dekagram}} = 1$
c) $\frac{2{,}000 \text{ pounds}}{1 \text{ ton}} = 1; \frac{1 \text{ ton}}{2{,}000 \text{ pounds}} = 1$

YTI 2 a) 24 oz = 3 cups b) 350 m = 0.35 km

YTI 3 a) 8 in. $\approx$ 20 cm b) 15 m $\approx 16\frac{2}{3}$ yd c) $17\frac{1}{2}$ mi $\approx$ 28 km

YTI 4 Soo-Kim jogs about $2\frac{1}{2}$ miles every morning.

YTI 5 The longest goldfish in captivity is about $14\frac{4}{5}$ inches long.

YTI 6 a) 5 oz $\approx$ 140 g b) 15 lb $\approx$ 6.82 kg c) 50 qt $\approx$ 47.5 L

YTI 7 The teratorn weighed about 176 pounds.

YTI 8 The Jell-O mix contained about 9,211 gallons.

Focus Exercises: Section 7.3

Use an equivalence fraction to write each in the requested unit of measure. (You may want to refer back to the equivalencies of Sections 7.1 and 7.2.)

1. Convert 42 feet to yards.

2. Convert 60 inches to feet.

3. Convert 28 quarts to gallons.

4. Convert 3000 pounds to tons.

5. Convert 36 fluid ounces to cups.

6. Convert 40 ounces to pounds.

7. Convert 95 centimeters to meters.

8. Convert 86 decimeters to meters.

9. Convert 60 milligrams to grams.

10. Convert 2,850 grams to kilograms.

11. Convert 45 deciliters to liters.

12. Convert 65.4 liters to hectoliters.

Convert each measure to its alternate U.S. or metric form. Write improper fractions as mixed numbers for U.S. measures and as decimals for metric measures.

13. Convert 12 inches to centimeters.

14. Convert 36 meters to yards.

15. Convert 24 kilometers to miles.

16. Convert 25 centimeters to inches.

17. Convert $13\frac{1}{3}$ yards to meters.

18. Convert $22\frac{1}{2}$ miles to kilometers.

19. Convert $12\frac{1}{2}$ gallons to liters.

20. Convert $3\frac{3}{4}$ ounces to grams.

21. Convert $8\frac{1}{4}$ pounds to kilograms.

22. Convert 85.5 liters to gallons.

23. Convert 413 grams to ounces.

24. Convert 45 kilograms to pounds.

Write each sentence using the requested unit of measure. Write improper fractions as mixed numbers for U.S. measures and as decimals for metric measures.

25. A foot race is 10 kilometers. Express this number in miles.

26. An auto race is 120 miles. Express this number in kilometers.

27. A window is 48 inches wide. Express this number in centimeters.

28. A rectangular field is 40 meters long. Express this number in yards.

29. Sammy weighs 27.5 kilograms. Express this number in pounds.

30. A pint of potato salad contains $1\frac{1}{2}$ ounces of fat. Express this number in grams.

31. Papi's pickup truck can hold 30 gallons of gas. Express this number in liters.

32. Tina's fish tank holds 7.6 liters of water. Express this number in quarts.

SECTION 7.4 Lines and Angles

Objectives

In this section, you will learn to:

- Identify the parts of a line.
- Name geometric figures.
- Recognize the different types of angles.
- Find angle measures.

To successfully complete this section, you need to understand:

- Adding and subtracting whole numbers (1.3)
- Adding and subtracting decimals (5.3)
- Adding and subtracting measures (7.1 and 7.2)

Introduction

Geometry is the study of the shapes and sizes of things, such as these:

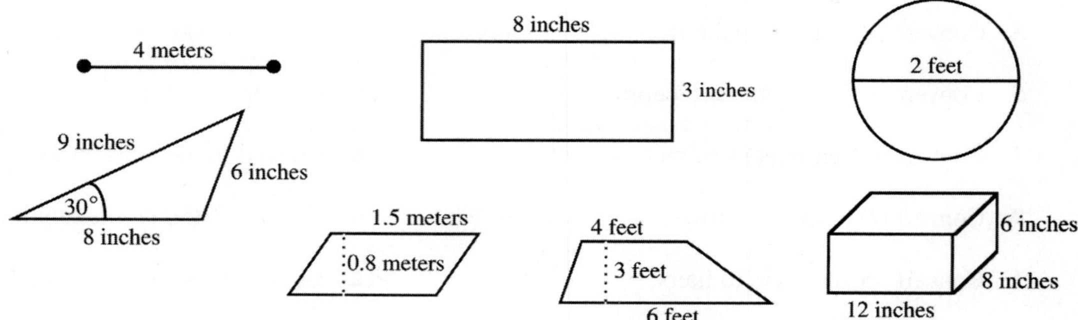

We'll study each of these shapes in this chapter.

Most of the work in this geometry chapter deals with shapes in a *plane*. In geometry, a **plane** is any flat surface that extends forever in each direction.

Though a wall, a floor, and a table top have definite length and width, we might think of those things as part of a plane, as if each went on endlessly.

The Bonneville Salt Flats in Utah might give you a better idea of a geometric plane. It is over 30,000 acres in size, it is flat, and its surface contains (among other minerals) potassium and sodium chloride (table salt).

According to the definition of a plane, is the Bonneville Salt Flats a real plane? Why or why not?

____

____

Lines and Points

There are some highways in America that are straight for miles and miles. Usually, on the side of the highway is a painted line, and this line seems to go on forever.

In geometry, we consider a **line** to be straight, and we say that it goes on forever. To indicate this, we put arrows on each end. We also say that the line has *infinite* length.

At right are four examples of lines:

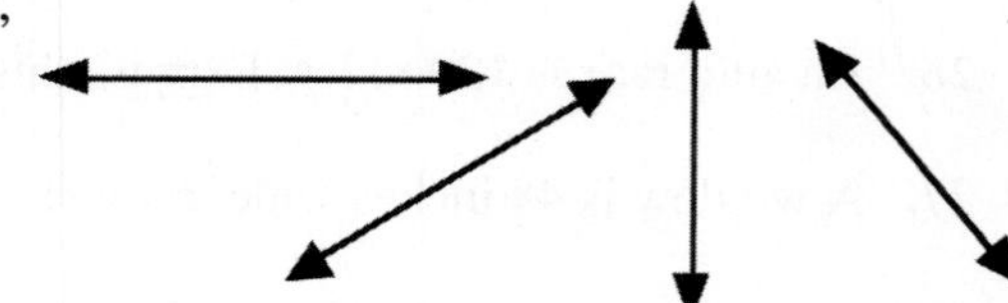

When two lines cross each other they meet in a single **point** of intersection. We say that the lines *intersect* at the point.

A point is very small (it really has no size at all), but we often represent a point with a dot • and label it with a capital letter.

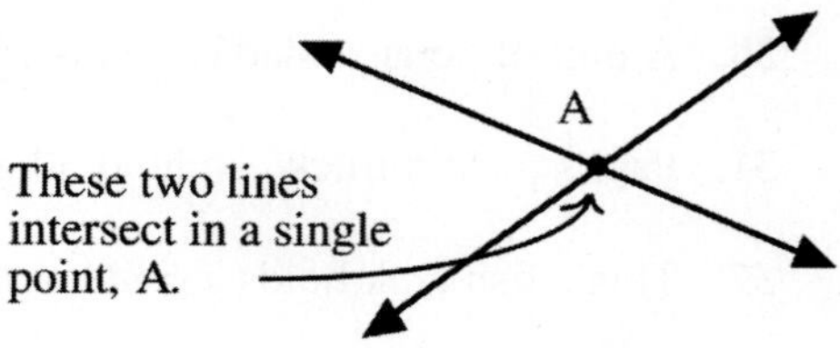

There are actually many points (an *infinite* number of points) on each line, and we might label a few of them. Notice that we can also name a line using any two points on that line, such as this line:

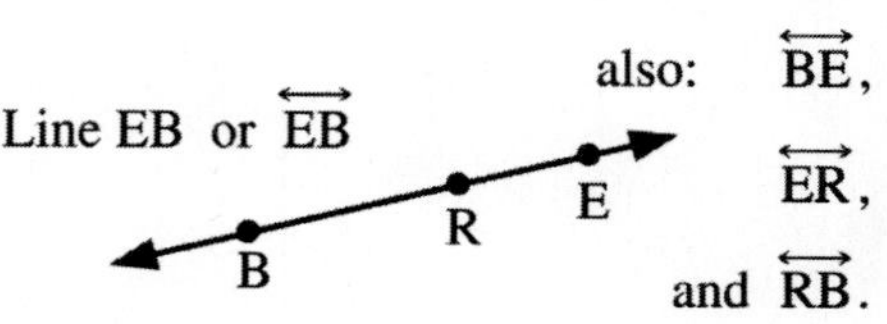

Two lines in the same plane that won't *ever* intersect each other are called **parallel lines**.

In this diagram at right, $\overleftrightarrow{MP}$ and $\overleftrightarrow{QR}$ are parallel to each other:

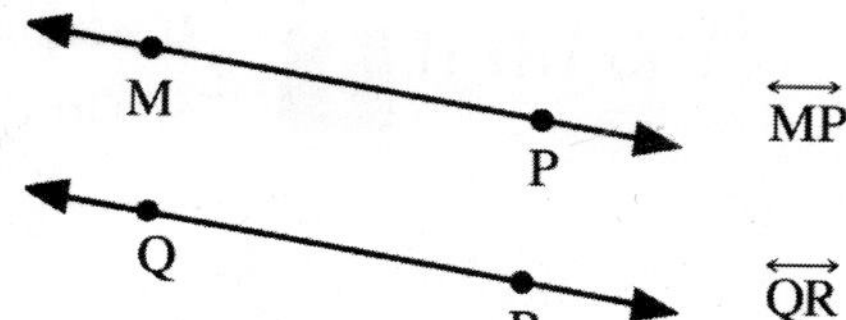

However, $\overleftrightarrow{XY}$ and $\overleftrightarrow{BC}$ are not parallel to each other. (See figure on right.)

Because lines go on forever, we can think of extending each line to see if they'll ever intersect. Even though the lines won't cross on this paper, if our paper were the size of the Bonneville Salt Flats, we'd see that they'd eventually intersect.

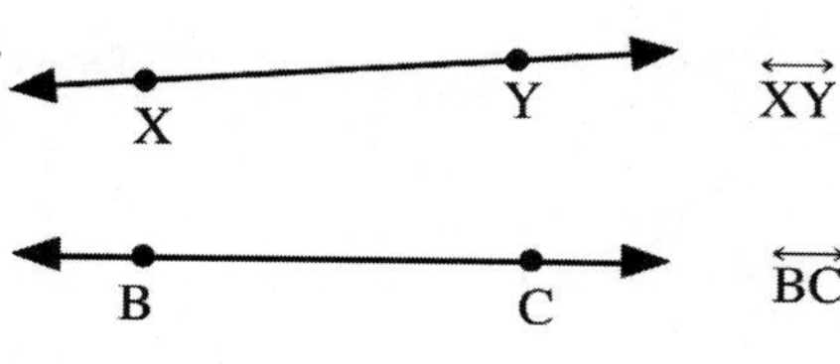

Line Segments

The portion of a line that is drawn between two points is called a **line segment**. A line segment doesn't go on forever in each direction. It has a definite, or *finite*, length. A line segment has definite start and stop points called **endpoints**. We use the two endpoints to name the line segment, and either endpoint can be written first.

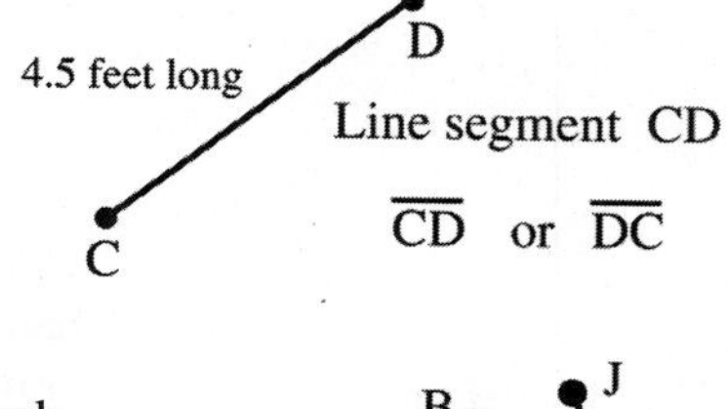

Since line segments don't extend forever, there are many line segments that won't intersect. However, even though they don't intersect, line segments such as $\overline{AB}$ and $\overline{JK}$ are not considered to be parallel.

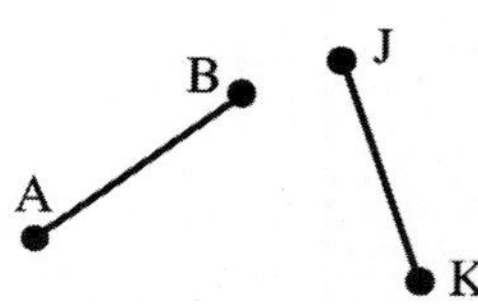

Two line segments are parallel if and only if the lines that contain them are parallel.

So, since *lines* $\overleftrightarrow{AB}$ and $\overleftrightarrow{JK}$ are not parallel, line *segments* $\overline{AB}$ and $\overline{JK}$ are not parallel.

Rays

A piece of a line that starts at one of its points and goes on forever in only one directions is called a **ray**. The starting point of the ray is called the endpoint. The ray will have at least one other point labeled on it indicating the direction of the ray.

Notice that, in naming the ray, *the endpoint is always written first.*

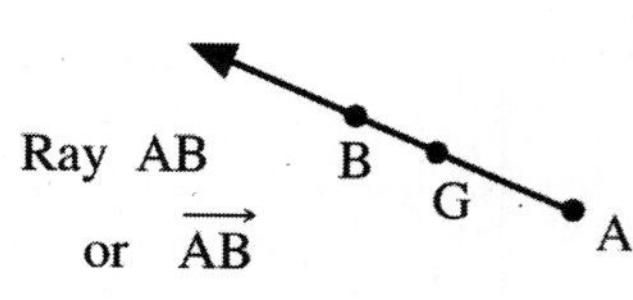

Ray BA

or $\overrightarrow{BA}$

B G A

YOU TRY IT 1 *Use a straightedge (a ruler) to draw the requested figure.*

a) Draw $\overleftrightarrow{PR}$ R W P

b) Draw $\overline{WX}$ X

c) Draw $\overrightarrow{KH}$ K H

Angles

When two rays share the same endpoint they form an **angle**. The common endpoint is called the **vertex** of the angle. The two rays that form the angle are called the sides of the angle.

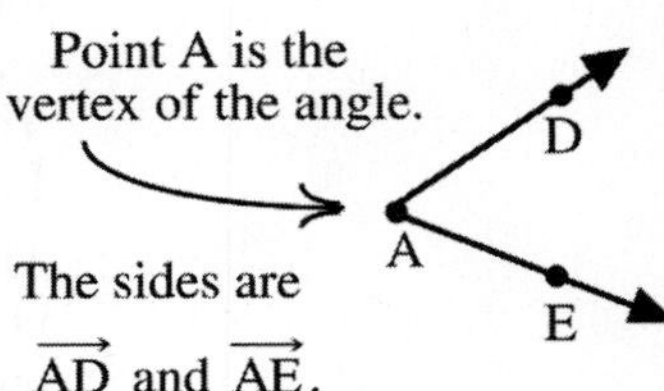

An angle can also be formed when two line segments share the same endpoint. Here, the vertex is G and the sides are line segments, $\overline{GT}$ and $\overline{GM}$.

The angle at the right can be named in a variety of ways using the angle symbol, $\angle$. We can name it $\angle G$, $\angle 1$, $\angle TGM$, or $\angle MGT$. These all name the same angle, according to the diagram. (The number 1 within the angle is only a label; it has nothing to do with the size of the angle.)

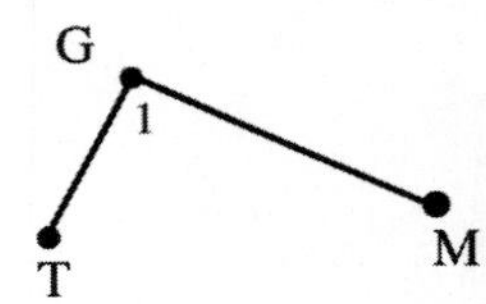

Notice that the last two names, $\angle \boldsymbol{TGM}$ and $\angle \boldsymbol{MGT}$, use the three endpoints of the line segments that define the angle and that the vertex, **G**, is in the middle.

The diagram at left shows what is meant by the *interior* of an angle; it is the shaded portion. Point T is in the interior of the angle.

Just as the rays continue indefinitely, the interior of the angle will continue indefinitely and never cross to the other side of the rays.

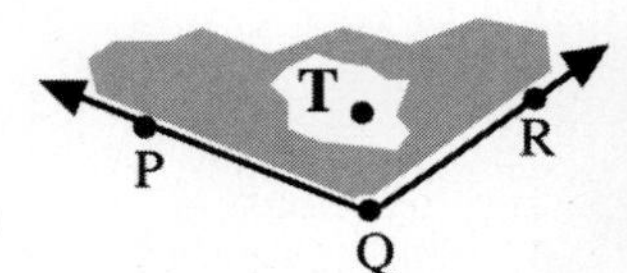

YOU TRY IT 2 *Use a straightedge to draw the angles named. (Keep in mind that the vertex is always in the middle of the name.) You may use line segments for the sides of each angle. Also, lightly shade the interior of the angle.*

a) Draw $\angle PDH$.

b) Draw $\angle PHD$.

H D P

When two lines cross, they form four angles, each with the same vertex, as in the diagram at right. It would not be appropriate to name any of these angles just $\angle \mathbf{G}$ because it would be unclear which of the four angles is being named.

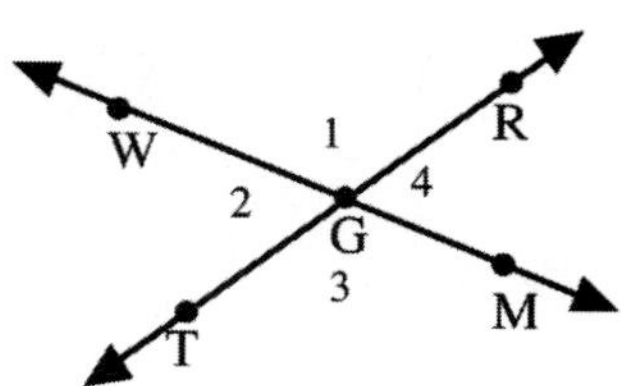

EXAMPLE 1 Identify two other names for each given angle.

ANSWER:

a) $\angle TGW$ can also be named $\underline{\angle 2 \text{ or } \angle WGT.}$

b) $\angle TGM$ can also be named $\underline{\angle 3 \text{ or } \angle MGT.}$

c) $\angle 1$ can also be named $\underline{\angle RGW \text{ or } \angle WGR.}$

d) $\angle 4$ can also be named $\underline{\angle RGM \text{ or } \angle MGR.}$

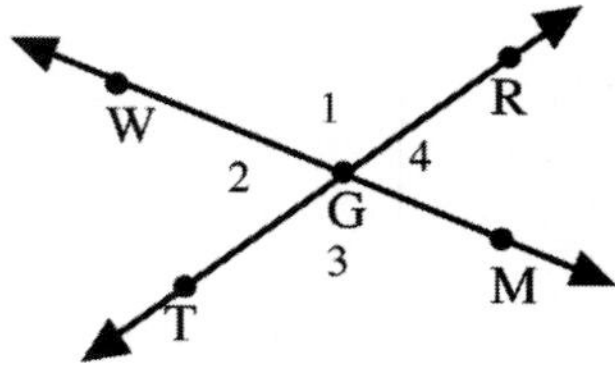

YOU TRY IT 3 *Identify two other names for each given angle. Use Example 1 as a guide.*

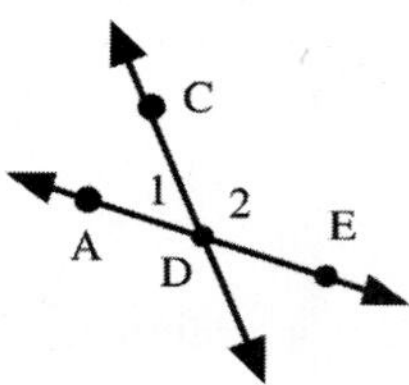

a) $\angle CDE$ can also be named ________

b) $\angle CDA$ can also be named ________

Measurements of Angles

Circles have 360 degrees—instead of 100 degrees or 400 degrees—because 360 has many whole number factors, including 12. This means it can be easily divided into 12 equal parts, the number of months in a year and the number of hours on a standard clock face.

When a ballet dancer performs a pirouette, she is making a complete turn, a complete rotation, so that when the turn is finished, she is facing the same direction as when she started.

A complete turn is also seen as a complete circle, and it is measured in *degrees*.

360°

One full revolution is 360°, read "360 degrees."

This raised little circle is the symbol for *degrees*, the unit used to measure angles.

Half of a turn is 180° and one-fourth of a turn (or a *quarter turn*) is 90°.

The half turn creates a 180° angle in which the two sides, $\overrightarrow{HR}$ and $\overrightarrow{HP}$, form a straight line, so it is called a **straight angle**. Every line forms a straight angle.

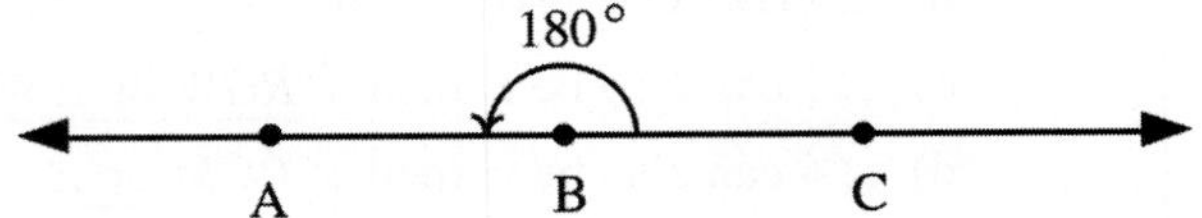

$\angle ABC$ is a straight angle. B is the vertex. It forms $\overleftrightarrow{AC}$.

Any point on a line can be the vertex of a straight angle. Here are just two examples:

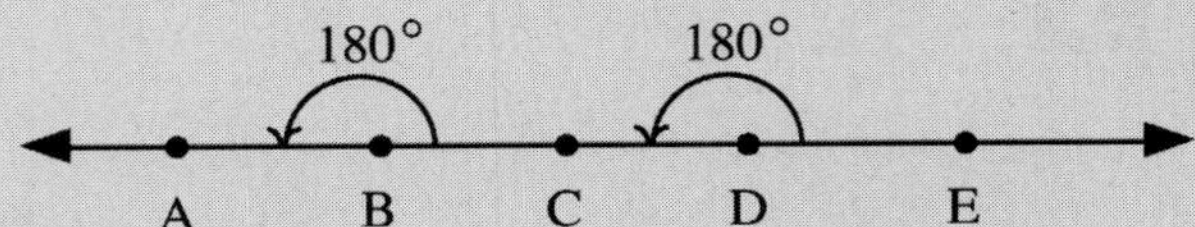

$\angle ABC$ is a straight angle. B is the vertex.

$\angle CDE$ is a straight angle. D is the vertex.

Think about it

What does a 0° angle look like? Does it have another name? (Draw one, if you can.)

____

____

A quarter turn—like making a right turn at an intersection—creates a 90° angle and is called a **right angle**. We use a little square in the angle to show that it is a right angle. (The corner of a page of this textbook fits perfectly into a right angle.)

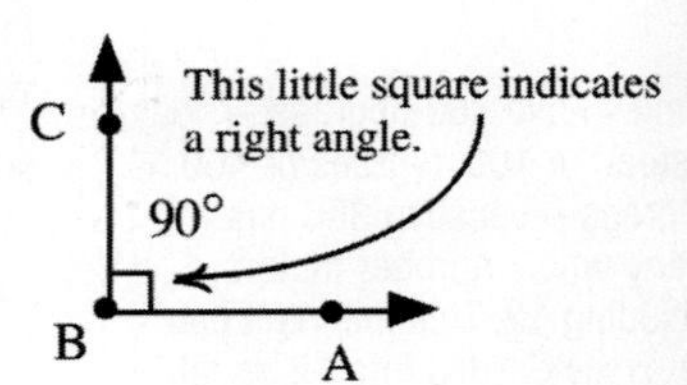

An **acute angle** has a measure greater than 0° and less than 90°.

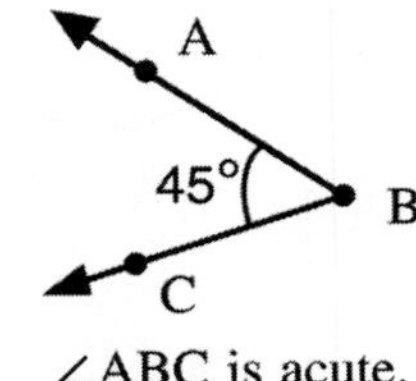

$\angle$ABC is acute.

An **obtuse angle** has a measure greater than 90° and less than 180°.

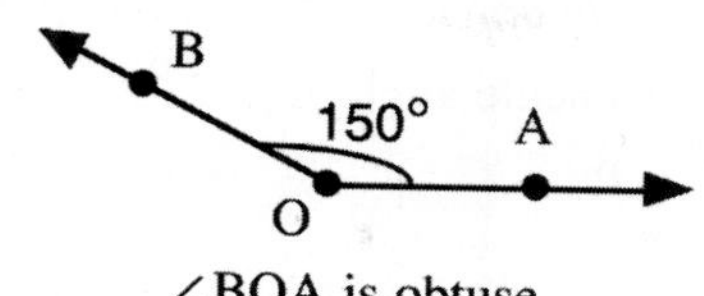

∠BOA is obtuse.

EXAMPLE 2 Use a straightedge to complete the requested angle. Let the point P be the vertex, and be mindful of the interior of the angle.

a) A right angle:

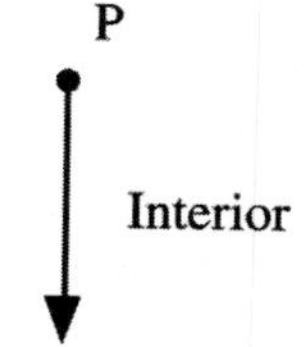

b) An obtuse angle:

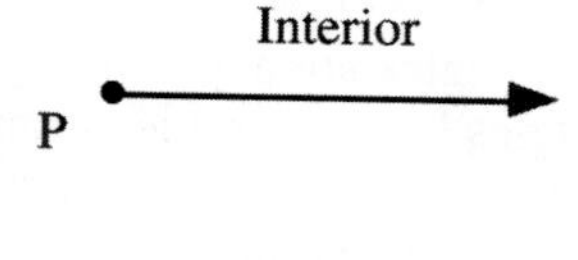

c) An acute angle:

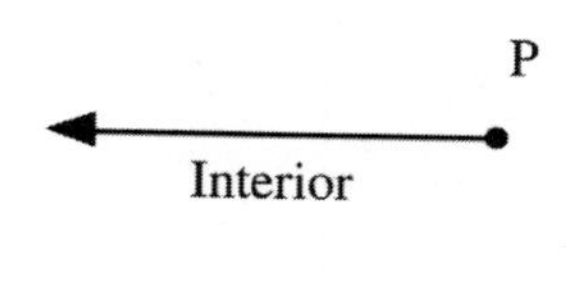

PROCEDURE: Use the definitions of *right, obtuse,* and *acute* to assist you in drawing each angle. The dashed line in b) and c), below, is to show you where a right angle would be for the obtuse and acute angles. The obtuse angle is larger than 90°, and the acute angle is smaller than 90°.

ANSWER: There is only one possible answer for a) but many possible answers for b) and c).

a) A right angle is equal to 90°

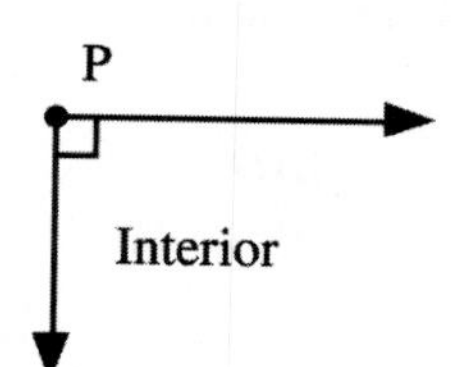

b) An obtuse angle is greater than 90° but less than 180°.

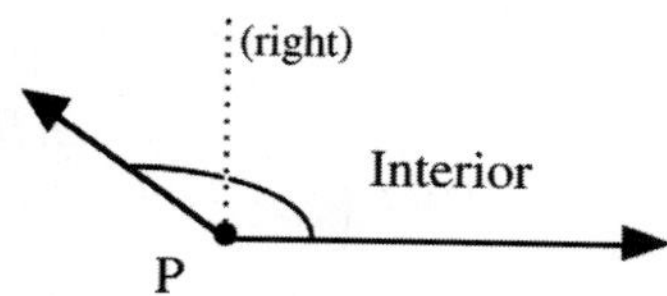

c) An acute angle is less than 90°

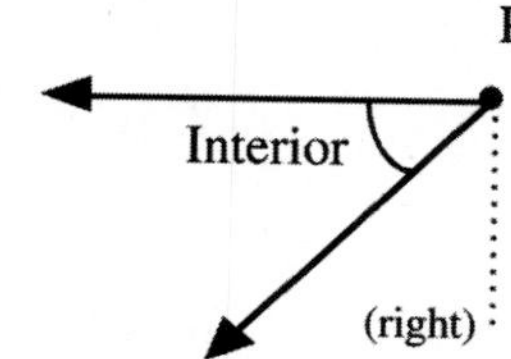

YOU TRY IT 4

Use a straightedge to complete the requested angle. Let the point P be the vertex, and be mindful of the interior of the angle. Use Example 2 as a guide.

a) An acute angle:

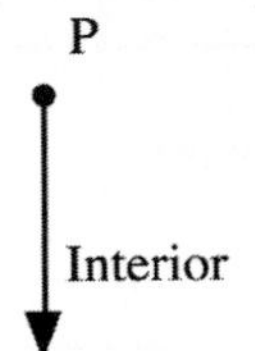

b) A right angle:

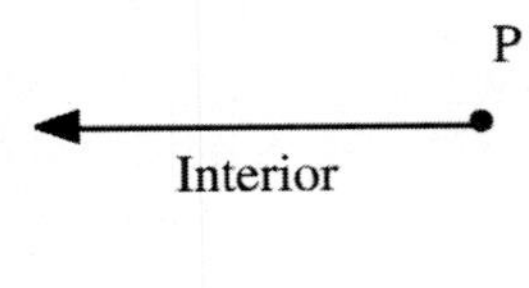

c) An obtuse angle:

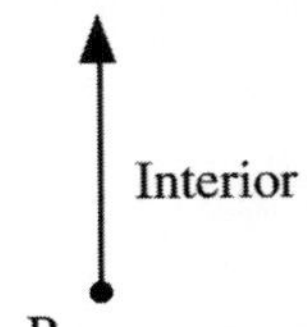

Adjacent Angles

Adjacent angles are any two angles that share a common side, forming an even larger angle; all three angles have the same vertex, and the shared side must be in the interior of the larger angle. In the drawing at right, there are three angles:

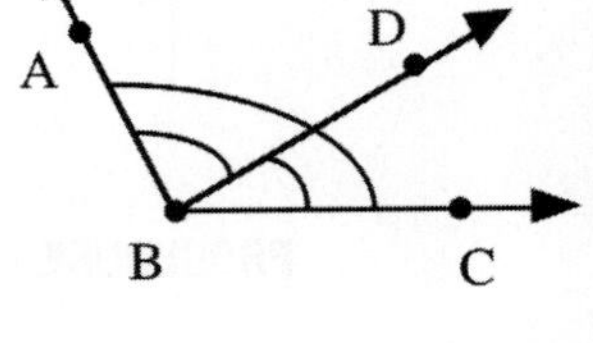

$\angle ABD$ and $\angle DBC$ are adjacent (they share the common side $\overrightarrow{BD}$) and together they form the larger angle, $\angle ABC$.

In fact, the formula, "The sum of the parts equals the whole," applies to adding adjacent angles.

The sum of the measures of the two smaller adjacent angles is equal to the measure of the larger angle:

$$\angle ABD \quad + \quad \angle DBC \quad = \quad \angle ABC$$
$$80° \quad + \quad 40° \quad = \quad 120°$$

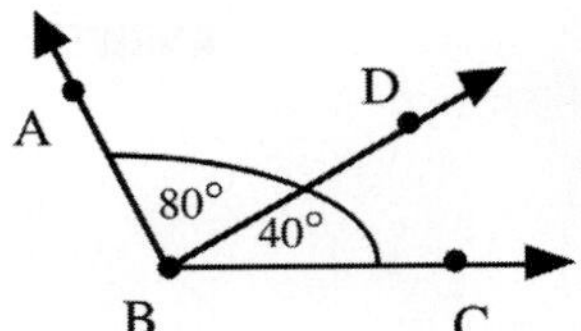

Likewise, the measure of one of the smaller angles is the difference between the measure of the larger angle and the measure of the other smaller angle:

$$\angle DBC \quad = \quad \angle ABC \quad - \quad \angle ABD$$
$$40° \quad = \quad 120° \quad - \quad 80°$$

EXAMPLE 3

Given the measures of two angles, find the measure of the third angle.

a)

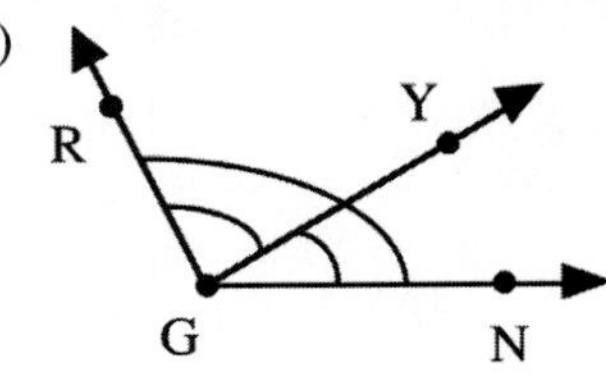

$\angle RGY = 84°$ and $\angle NGY = 39°$

b)

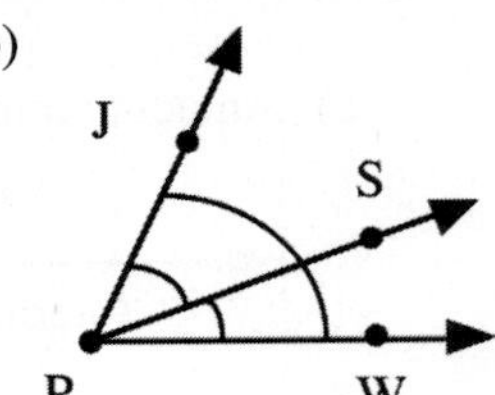

$\angle JPS = 46°$ and $\angle JPW = 74°$

PROCEDURE: Label each diagram with the angle measures given and decide whether you need to:

1. Add to find the measure of the larger angle, or
2. subtract to find the measure of one of the smaller angles.

ANSWER: a)

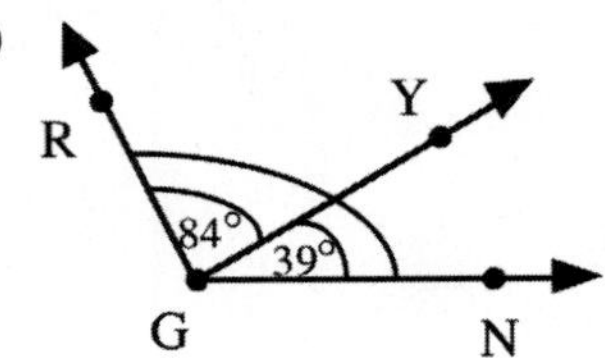

In this diagram we know the measures of the two smaller angles and need to find the measure of the larger angle, $\angle RGN$, so we add:

$$\angle RGN = 84° + 39° = 123°$$

b)

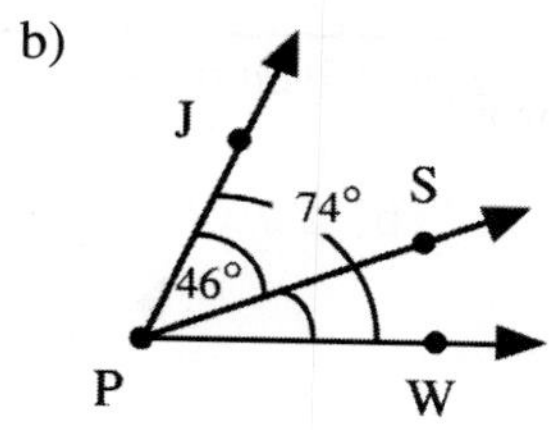

In this diagram, we know the measures of the larger angle and one of the smaller angles, $\angle JPS$, so we subtract to find $\angle SPW$:

$$\angle SPW = 74^\circ - 46^\circ = 28^\circ$$

YOU TRY IT 5

Given the measures of two angles, find the measure of the third angle. Use Example 3 as a guide. (These angles might not be drawn exactly to scale.)

a)

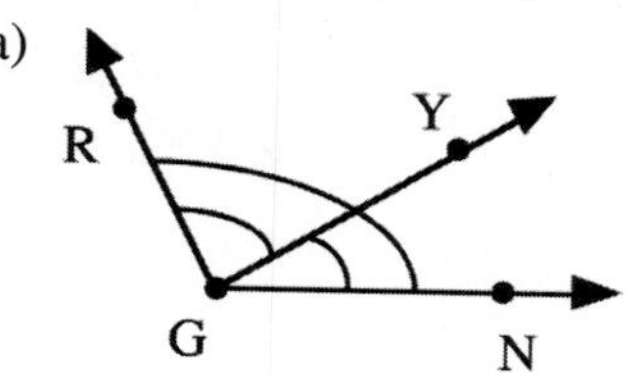

$\angle RGN = 115^\circ$ and

$\angle YGN = 38^\circ$

b)

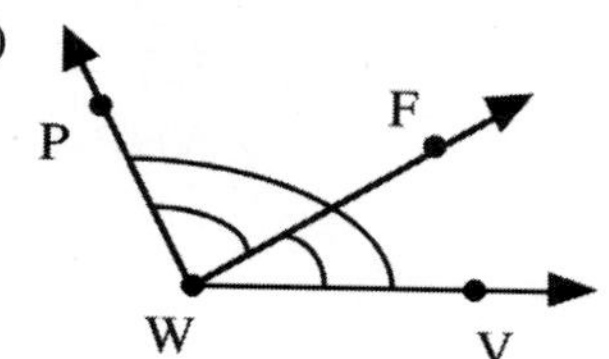

$\angle PWF = 81.6^\circ$ and

$\angle FWV = 35.9^\circ$

Supplementary and Complementary Angles

Supplementary angles are *any* two angles with measures that add to 180°. Supplementary angles can be adjacent, but they don't have to be.

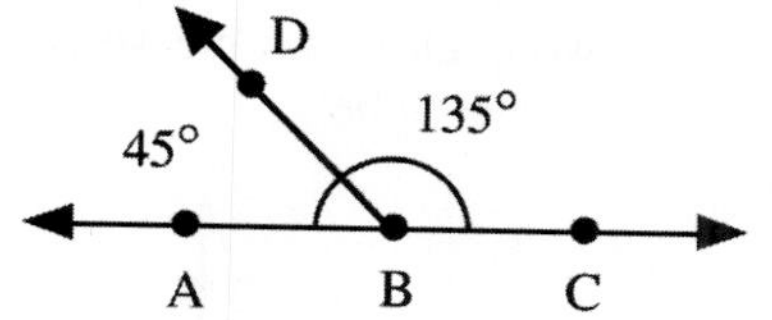

$\angle ABD$ and $\angle DBC$ are supplementary.

$\angle DBC$ is the supplement of $\angle ABD$.

$$\angle ABD + \angle DBC = 180^\circ$$

$\angle ABD$ and $\angle XYZ$ are supplementary.

$\angle XYZ$ is the supplement of $\angle ABD$.

$$\angle ABD + \angle XYZ = 180^\circ$$

If we know that $\angle PQR$ and $\angle STU$ are supplementary angles, and if we know the measure of one of these angles, say $\angle PQR = 70^\circ$, then its supplement, $\angle STU$, can be found by subtracting 70° from 180°:

$$\angle STU = 180^\circ - 70^\circ = 110^\circ$$

EXAMPLE 4 The following pairs of angles are supplementary. Given the measure of one of the angles, find the measure of the other angle.

a) $\angle DEF = 43°$

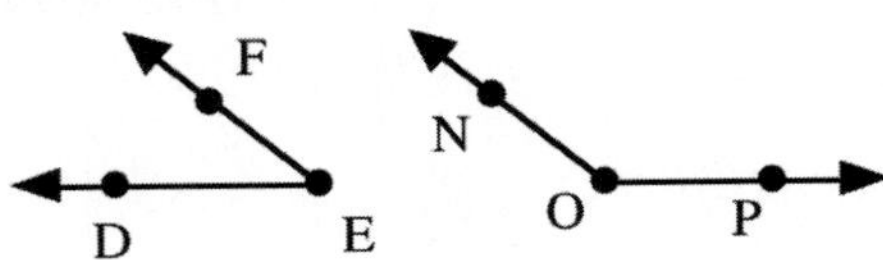

b) $\angle JKL = 112.7°$

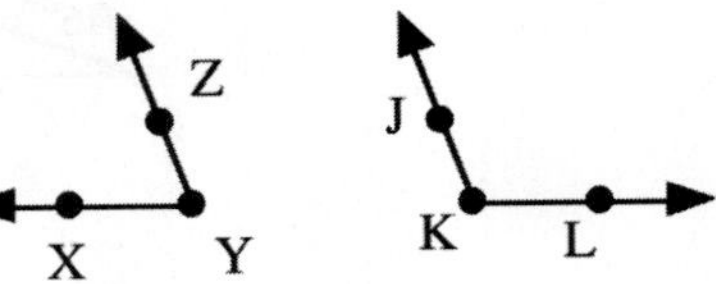

PROCEDURE: Label the known angle measure and subtract it from 180°.

ANSWER:

a) $\angle NOP = 180° - 43°$

$$\begin{array}{r} 180 \\ -\ 43 \\ \hline 137 \end{array}$$

$\angle NOP = 137°$

b) $\angle XYZ = 180° - 112.7°$

$$\begin{array}{r} 180.0 \\ -\ 112.7 \\ \hline 67.3 \end{array}$$

$\angle XYZ = 67.3°$

YOU TRY IT 6 *The following pairs of angles are supplementary. Given the measure of one of the angles, find the measure of the other angle. Use Example 4 as a guide.*

a) $\angle EFG = 146°$

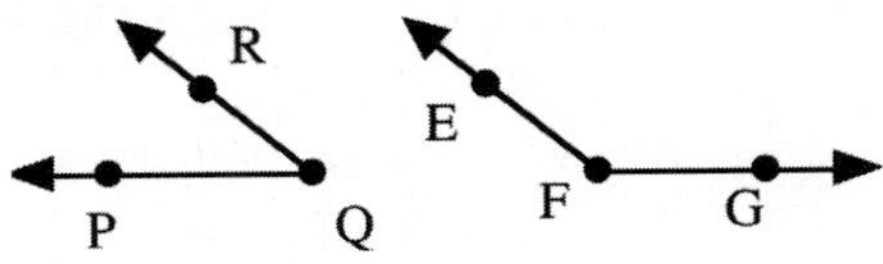

b) $\angle UVW = 78.8°$

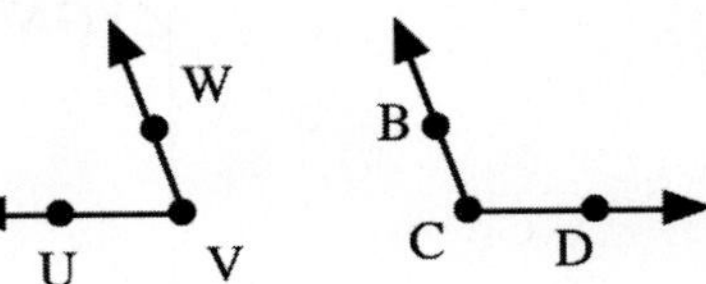

Complementary angles are *any* two angles with measures that add to 90°. Complementary angles can be adjacent, but they don't have to be.

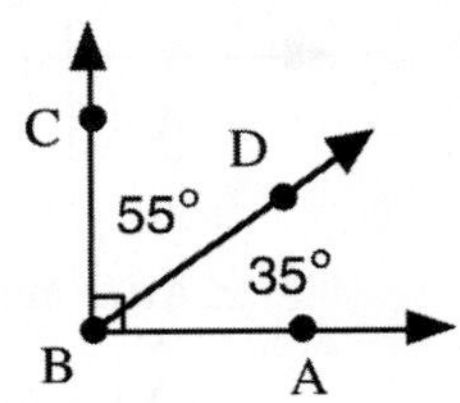

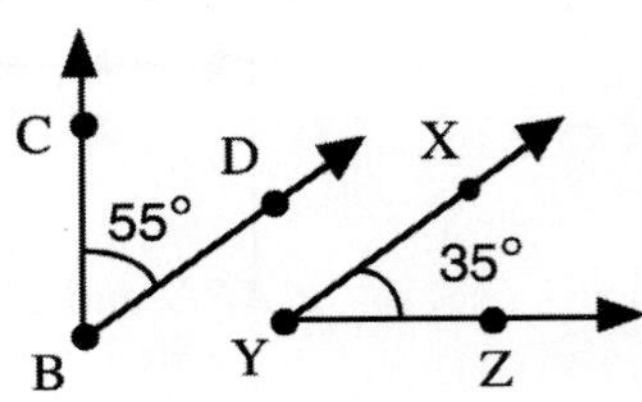

$\angle ABD$ and $\angle DBC$ are complementary.

$\angle DBC$ is the complement of $\angle ABD$.

$\angle ABD + \angle DBC = 90°$

$\angle CBD$ and $\angle XYZ$ are complementary.

$\angle XYZ$ is the complement of $\angle CBD$.

$\angle CBD + \angle XYZ = 90°$

If we know that $\angle PQR$ and $\angle STU$ are complementary angles, and if we know the measure of one of these angles, say $\angle PQR = 70°$, then its complement, $\angle STU$, can be found by subtracting 70° from 90°:

$$\angle STU = 90° - 70° = 20°$$

EXAMPLE 5 The following pairs of angles are complementary. Given the measure of one of the angles, find the measure of the other angle.

a) $\angle DEF = 43°$ b) $\angle XYZ = 22.7°$

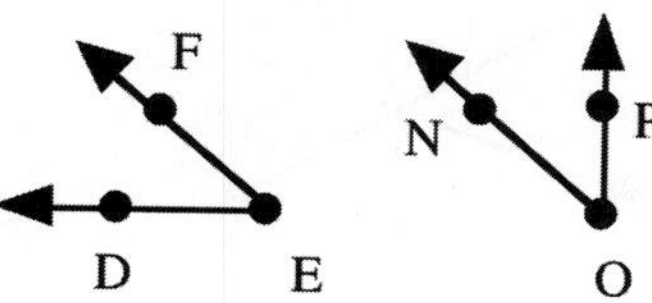

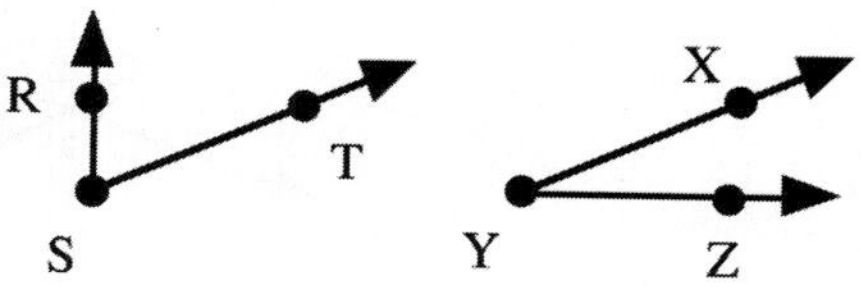

PROCEDURE: Label the known angle measure and subtract it from 90°.

ANSWER: a) $\angle NOP = 90° - 43°$

$$\begin{array}{r} 90 \\ -\ 43 \\ \hline 47 \end{array}$$

$\angle NOP = 47°$

b) $\angle RST = 90° - 22.7°$

$$\begin{array}{r} 90.0 \\ -\ 22.7 \\ \hline 67.3 \end{array}$$

$\angle RST = 67.3°$

YOU TRY IT 7 *The following pairs of angles are complementary. Given the measure of one of the angles, find the measure of the other angle. Use Example 5 as a guide.*

a) $\angle TUV = 48°$ b) $\angle DCB = 59.2°$

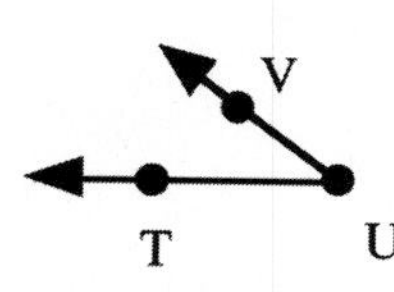

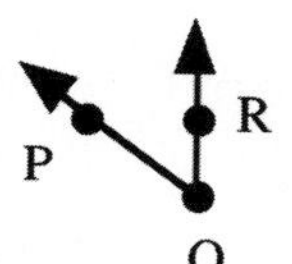

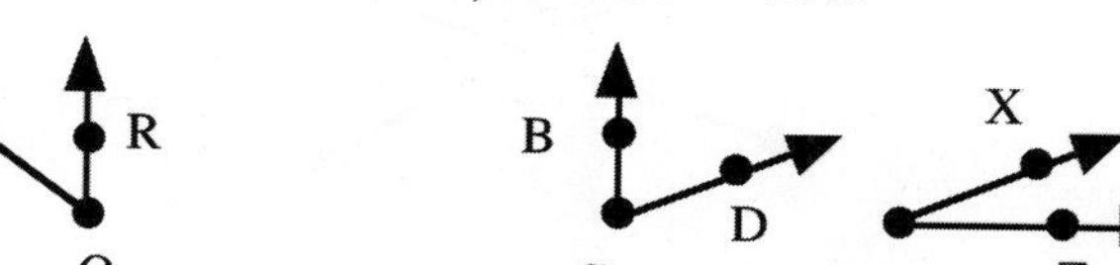

Vertical Angles

When two lines intersect, several pairs of angles are formed, all sharing the same vertex. Some pairs are adjacent and supplementary (forming a straight line), the other pairs are **vertical angles**, angles that are not adjacent to each other.

Pairs of adjacent, supplementary angles:

$\angle 1$ and $\angle 2$ $\angle 2$ and $\angle 3$

$\angle 3$ and $\angle 4$ $\angle 4$ and $\angle 1$

Pairs of vertical angles:

$\angle 1$ and $\angle 3$ $\angle 2$ and $\angle 4$

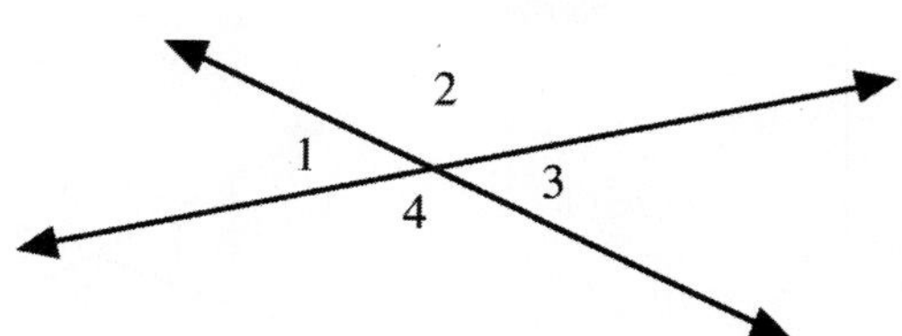

Think about it In the diagram, are $\angle 1$ and $\angle 3$ vertical angles? Why or why not?

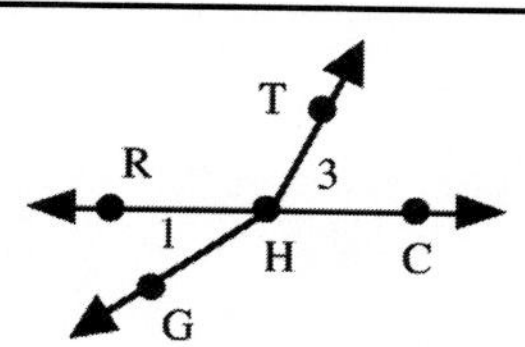

It can easily be shown that *vertical angles have the same measure*. For example, consider the diagram below:

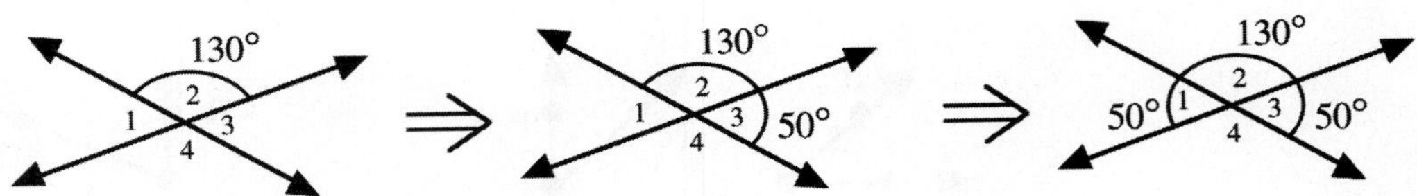

Given: $\angle 2 = 130°$

$\angle 3$ is supplementary to $\angle 2$ so $\angle 3$ is $180° - 130° = 50°$.

Likewise, $\angle 1$ is supplementary to $\angle 2$ so $\angle 1$ is also $50°$.

Notice that vertical angles $\angle 1$ and $\angle 3$ have the same measure; in other words, $\angle 1 = \angle 3$. It follows that $\angle 4$ is also $130°$. So, vertical angles $\angle 4$ and $\angle 2$ have the same measure: $\angle 4 = \angle 2$.

Knowing the measure of one of the angles, it is possible to determine the measures of all four angles.

EXAMPLE 6 Given $\angle 1 = 27°$, find the measures of the other three angles.

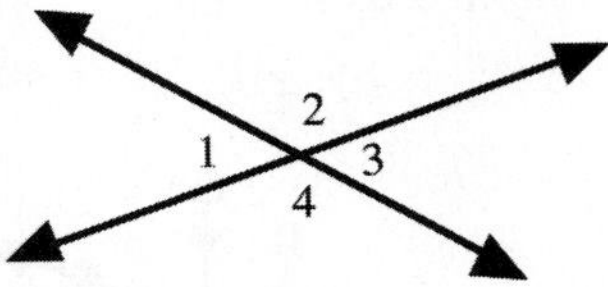

PROCEDURE: Vertical angles have the same measure and the angle vertical with $\angle 1$ is $\angle 3$. Also, $\angle 2$ and $\angle 4$ are both supplementary to $\angle 1$; we can find their value by subtracting $\angle 1$ from $180°$.

ANSWER: $\angle 3 = \angle 1$, so $\angle 3 = 27°$, too.

$\angle 2 = 180° - 27° = 153°$; therefore, $\angle 4 = 153°$, too.

YOU TRY IT 8 *Given the measure of one angle, find the measures of the other three angles. Use Example 6 as a guide.*

a) $\angle 3 = 58°$

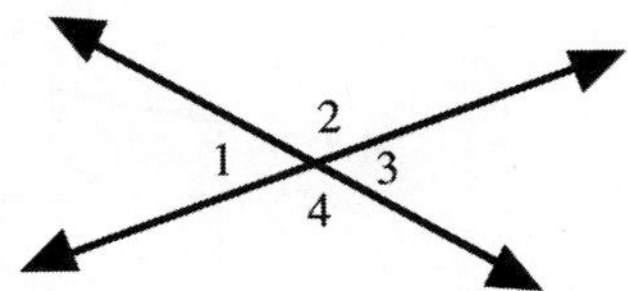

b) $\angle 3 = 142.5°$

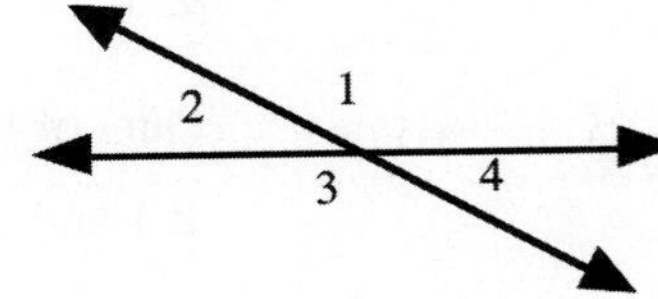

This next exercise leads into the last topic in this section.

YOU TRY IT 9 *Given that $\angle 1 = 90°$, find the measures of the other three angles. Use Example 6 as a guide.*

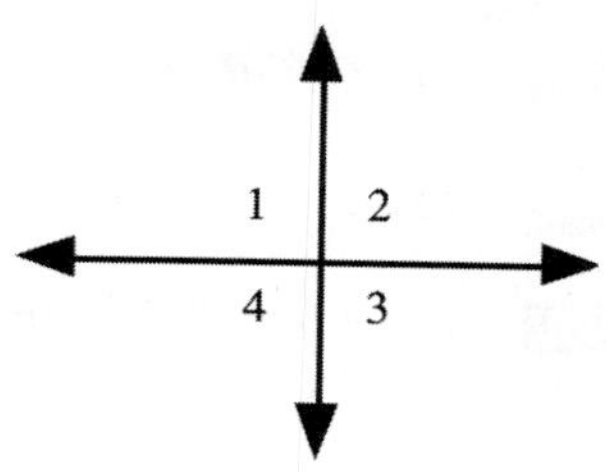

Perpendicular Lines and Line Segments

Two lines are **perpendicular** if they intersect to form four right angles. We use the symbol $\perp$ to indicate that two lines (or line segments) are perpendicular to each other.

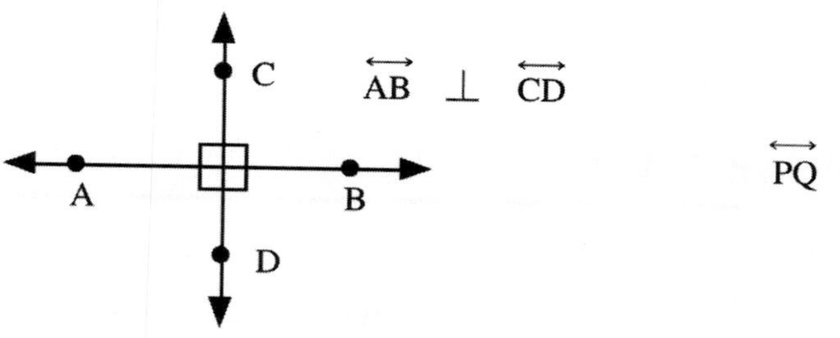

Here, the vertical angles have the same measure as the adjacent, supplementary angles. Two line *segments* that are perpendicular may form *one, two,* or *four* right angles:

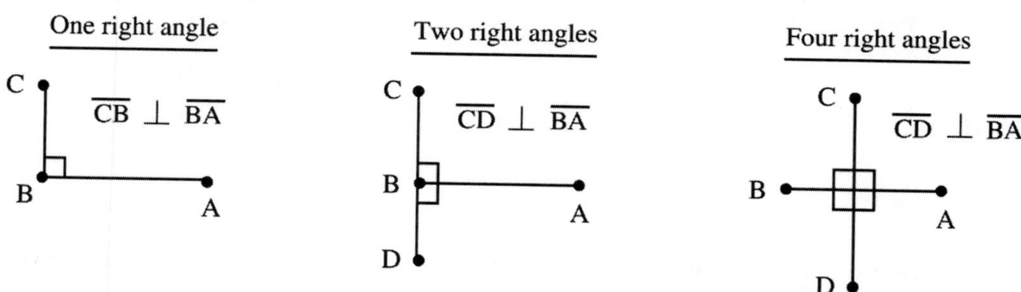

You Try It Answers: Section 7.4

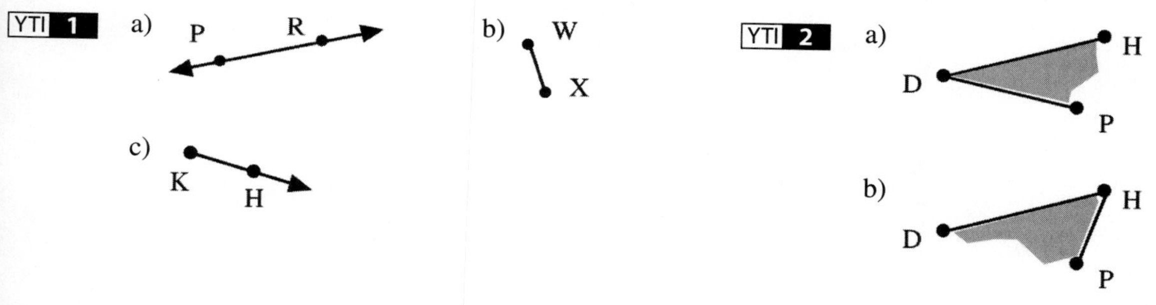

YTI 3 a) $\angle 2$ or $\angle EDC$ b) $\angle 1$ or $\angle ADC$

YTI 4 There are many correct answers for (a) and (c); (b) has only one answer.

a) An acute angle:

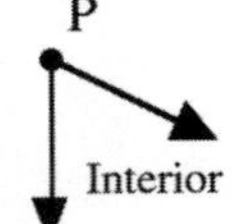

b) A right angle:

P

Interior

c) An obtuse angle:

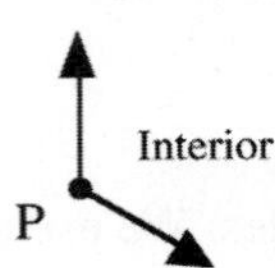

YTI 5 a) $\angle RGY = 77°$ b) $\angle PWV = 117.5°$

YTI 6 a) $\angle PQR = 34°$ b) $\angle BCD = 101.2°$

YTI 7 a) $\angle PQR = 42°$ b) $\angle XYZ = 30.8°$

YTI 8 a) $\angle 1 = 58°$, both $\angle 2$ and $\angle 4 = 122°$
b) $\angle 1 = 142.5°$, both $\angle 2$ and $\angle 4 = 37.5°$

YTI 9 Each of these angles measures 90°.

Focus Exercises: Section 7.4

Answer as indicated.

1. Write four names for this angle:

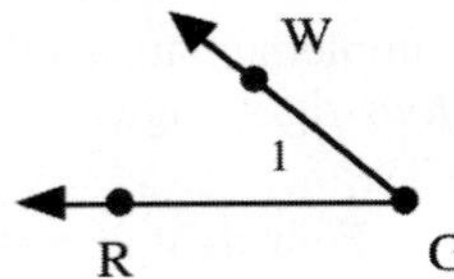

2. What rays form this angle?

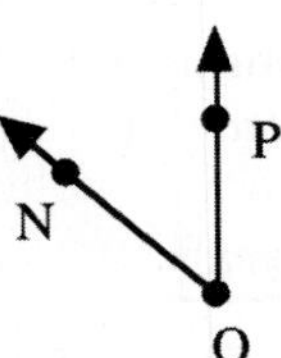

3. Name two lines in this diagram:

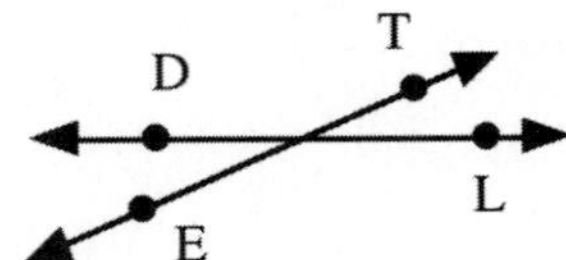

4. Name two acute and two obtuse angles in this diagram:

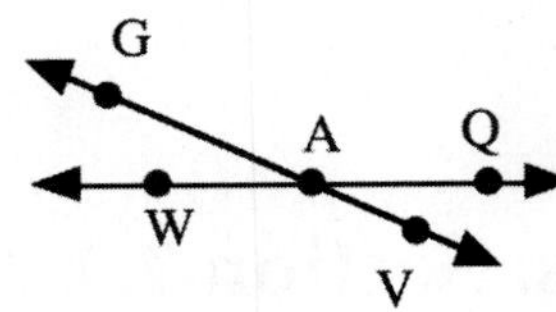

Given the measure of two of the angles, find the measure of the third angle.

5. $\angle FRB = 18°$ and $\angle KRF = 35°$

6. $\angle WTR = 60.8°$ and $\angle VTW = 19.6°$

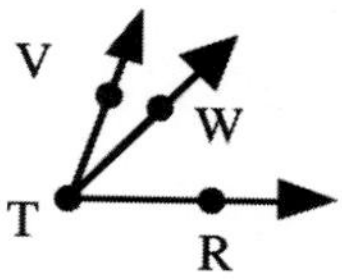

7. $\angle SAX = 153°$ and $\angle PAX = 59°$

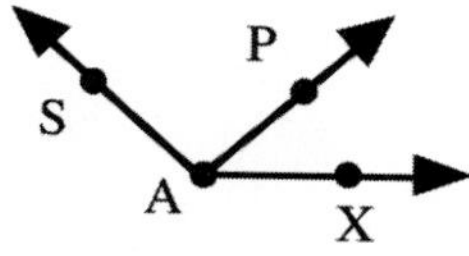

8. $\angle QME = 160.4°$ and $\angle QMD = 62.8°$

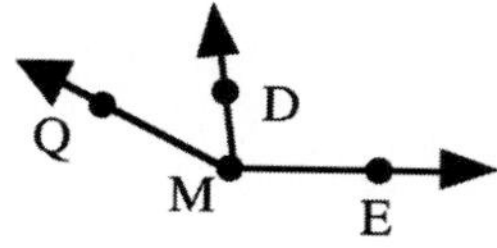

Each pair of angles is supplementary. Given the measure of one of the angles, find the measure of the other angle.

9. $\angle DSZ = 77°$

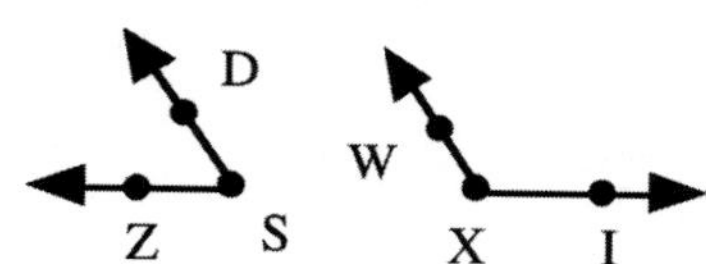

10. $\angle AQP = 72.1°$

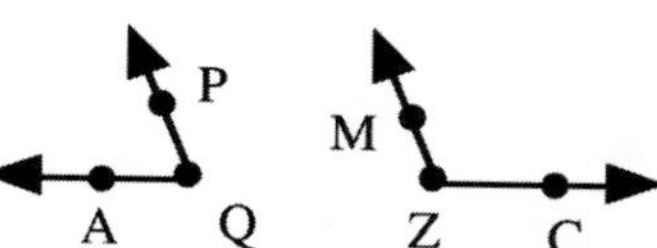

11. $\angle DKH = 132°$

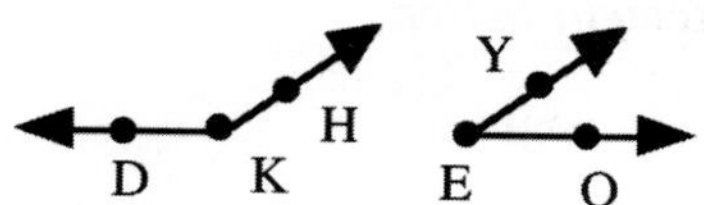

12. $\angle WFZ = 118.4°$

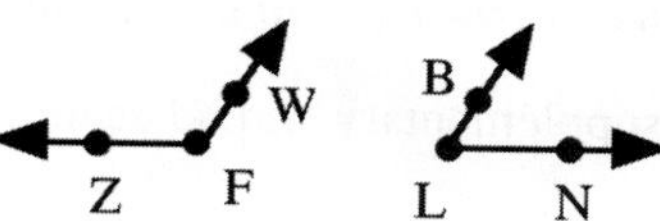

Each pair of angles is complementary. Given the measure of one of the angles, find the measure of the other angle.

13. $\angle RVT = 27°$

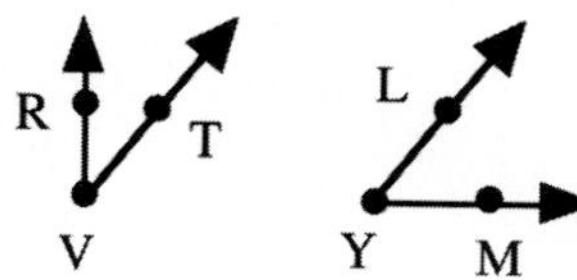

14. $\angle RFX = 29.5°$

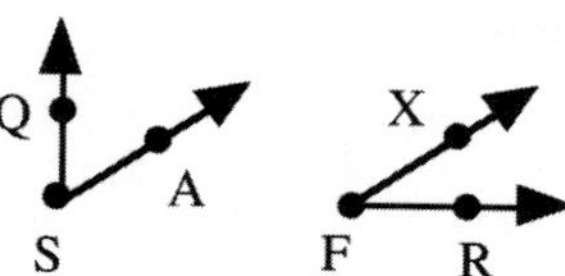

15. $\angle BGY = 72°$

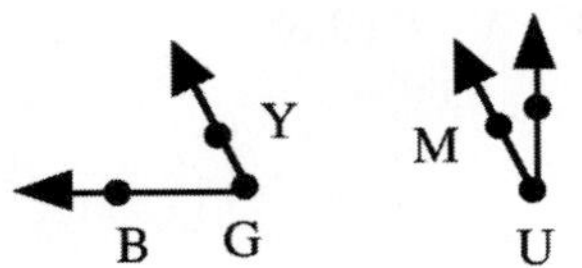

16. $\angle LOP = 49.2°$

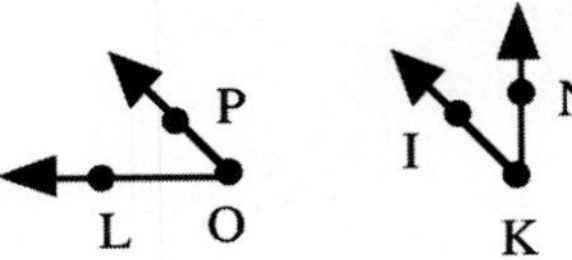

Given the measure of one angle, find the measures of the other three angles.

17. $\angle 3 = 32°$

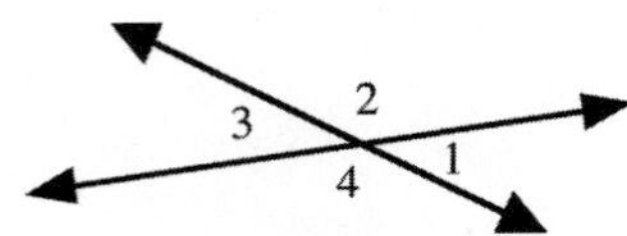

18. $\angle 1 = 47.9°$

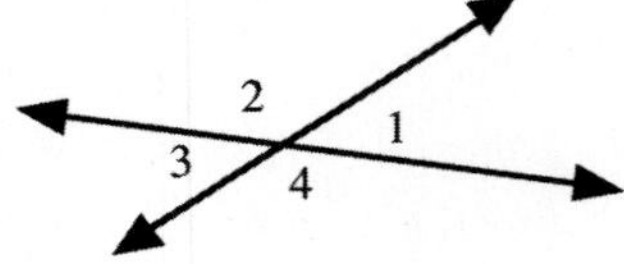

19. $\angle 4 = 111°$

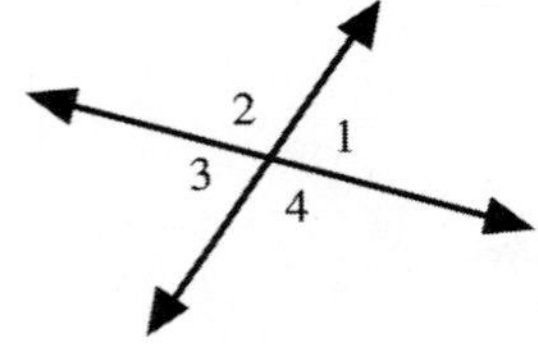

20. $\angle 2 = 127.8°$

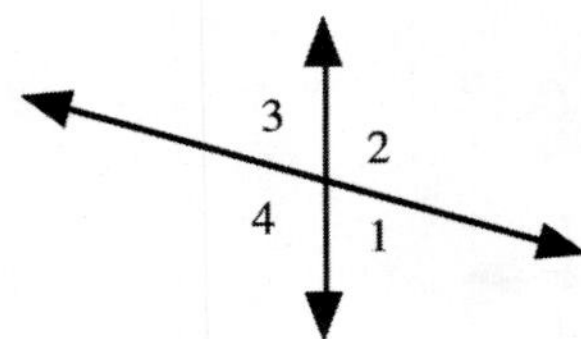

Fill in the blanks. (You are encouraged to draw a picture to help you see the statement better.)

21. Two angles that are supplementary and adjacent form a ____________________ angle.

22. Two angles that are complementary and adjacent form a ____________________ angle.

23. When two lines intersect, the non-adjacent angles are called ____________________ angles.

24. Two perpendicular lines form four ____________________ angles.

True or false:

25. Complementary angles must be adjacent to each other. ___________

26. Vertical angles are never adjacent to each other. ___________

27. Acute angles are always less than 90°. ___________

28. Obtuse angles can be more than 180°. ___________

29. Two line segments that don't intersect must be parallel. ___________

30. Straight angles always measure 180°. ___________

31. If two non-zero angles are complementary to each other, they must both be acute angles. ___________

32. If two lines meet to form a right angle, the lines must be perpendicular. ___________

SECTION 7.5 Geometric Shapes

Objectives

In this section, you will learn to:

- Identify different types of triangles.
- Find the measures of the angles in a triangle.
- Identify some of the types of quadrilaterals (parallelogram, rectangle, square, and trapezoid).
- Find the measures of the angles in quadrilaterals.

To successfully complete this section, you need to understand:

- Solving equations (1.6)
- Complementary angles (7.4)
- Supplementary angles (7.4)
- Right angles (7.4)
- Parallel line segments (7.4)

Introduction

Many geometric shapes are made from connected line segments that form a *polygon*. Each line segment is called a *side*, and every pair of connected sides forms an angle.

In general, a **polygon** is a closed plane figure composed of at least three straight line segments. In a polygon, two line segments meet only at an endpoint, called a **vertex**, and never cross each other. Each vertex is the endpoint of only two sides.

Some examples of polygons are shown below. The type of polygon is based on the number of sides it has. Typically, each vertex is labeled with a capital letter.

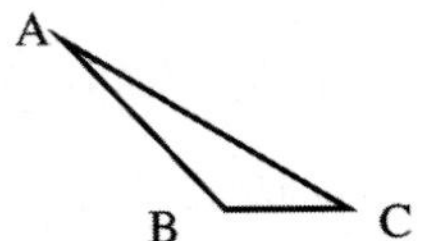

Triangle: *Three* sides

D E F G

Quadrilateral: *Four* sides

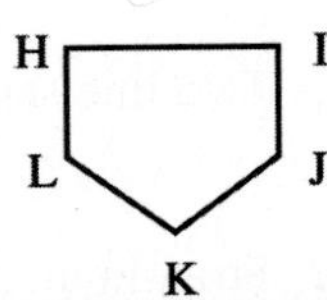

Pentagon: *Five* sides

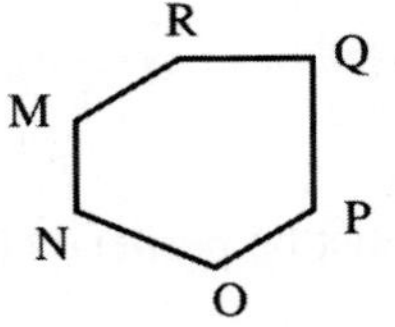

Hexagon: *Six* sides

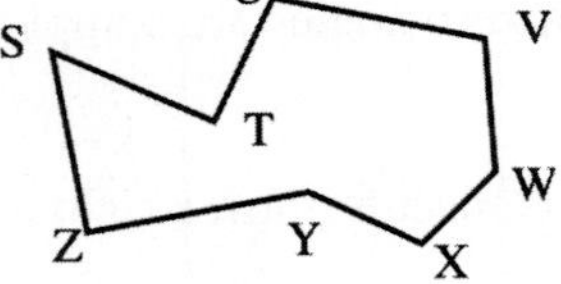

Octagon: *Eight* sides

A polygon must be *closed*: each endpoint of a side must share an endpoint with one other side.

This is *not* a polygon because it is not closed:

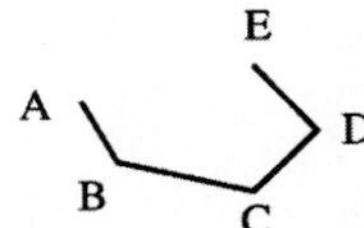

The line segments of a polygon must not cross each other.

This is *not* a polygon because two sides cross each other:

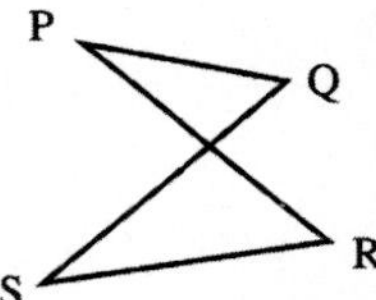

Also, in a polygon, each side must be a line segment and not be curved.

This is *not* a polygon because one of the sides is not a line segment:

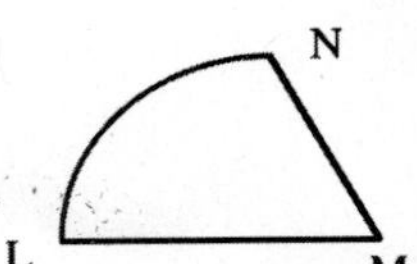

A **triangle** is a polygon that has three sides and three angles. The letters used to label each vertex are also used to name the triangle: ΔABC.

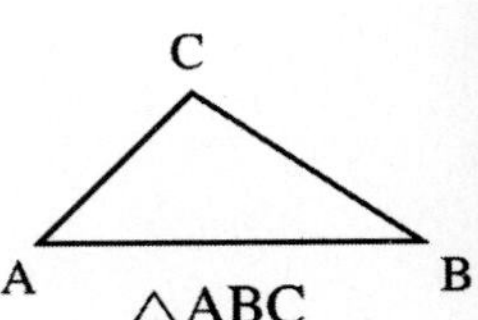

$\triangle ABC$

The Sum of the Angles in a Triangle

The sum of the angles in a triangle is 180°, no matter the shape of the triangle.

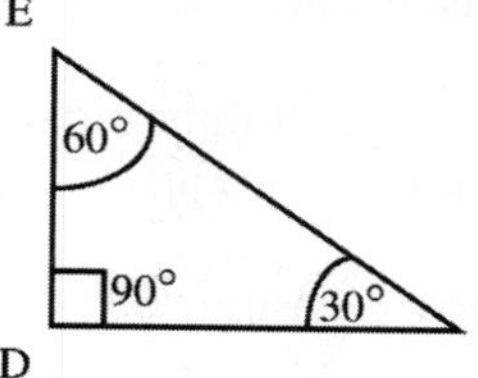

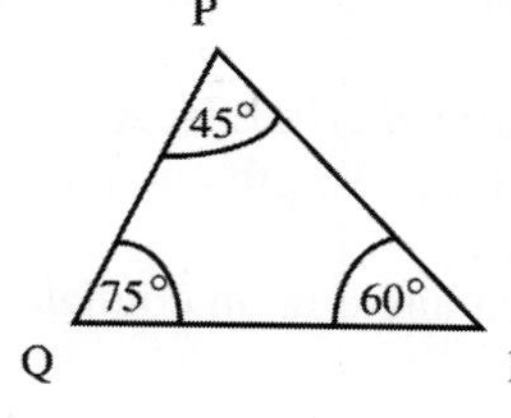

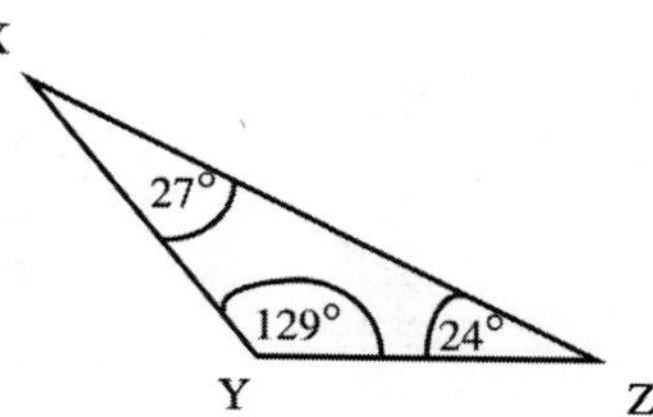

In general, we can say that, in ΔABC, $\angle A + \angle B + \angle C = 180°$.

If the measures of two angles of a triangle are known, then the measure of the third angle can be found, as shown in Example 1.

EXAMPLE 1 In ΔABC, $\angle A = 52°$ and $\angle B = 67°$; find the measure of $\angle C$.

PROCEDURE: One technique is to set up an equation with the measure of $\angle C$ being the unknown value.

ANSWER: Legend: Let $n =$ the measure of $\angle C$. Then use the formula for the sum of the angles in a triangle:

$$52 + 67 + n = 180$$
$$n + 119 = 180$$
$$n + 119 - 119 = 180 - 119$$
$$n = 61$$

The measure of $\angle C$ is 61°. Notice that it's appropriate to write the answer as 61 *degrees*, not just 61.

YOU TRY IT 1 *Given the measures of two angles, find the measure of the third angle. Use Example 1 as a guide.*

a) $\angle J = 60°$
$\angle B = 95°$

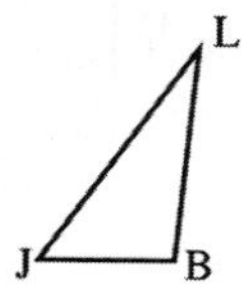

b) $\angle R = 18.9°$
$\angle M = 43.4°$

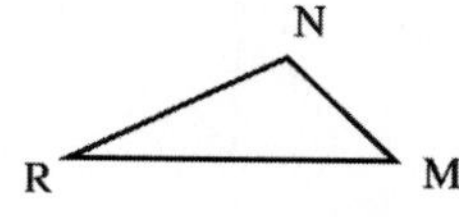

Think about it Is it possible for a triangle to contain two obtuse angles? Why or why not?

(Can you draw a triangle with two obtuse angles?)

____

____

Think about it Is it possible for a triangle to contain two right angles? Why or why not?

(Can you draw a triangle with two right angles?)

____

____

Types of Triangles

We can describe triangles based on (1) their side measures, or (2) their angle measures.

Triangles based on their side measures include:

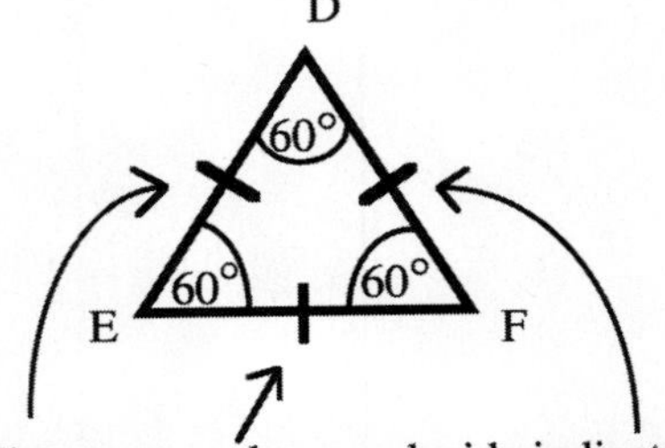

Equilateral triangle: A triangle in which all three sides are of equal length and all three angles are of equal measure.

Each angle in an equilateral triangle measures 60°.

The same mark on each side indicates that each side has the same length.

Isosceles triangle: A triangle in which two (or more) sides are of equal length. The sides with equal length are called **legs**, and the third side is called the **base**.

The angles opposite the legs are called **base angles** and have equal measure.

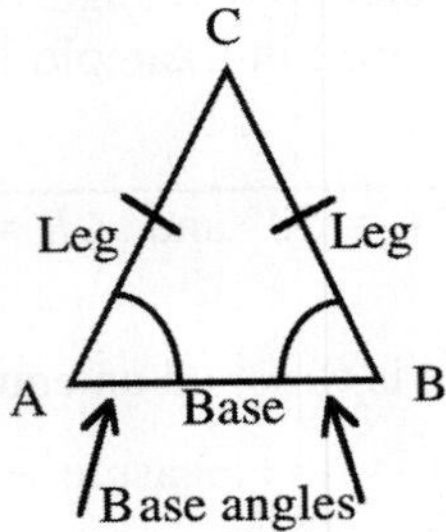

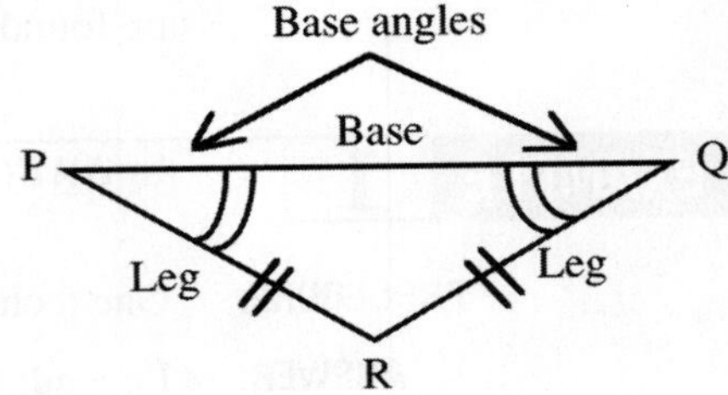

Scalene triangle: A triangle in which no two sides have the same length and no two angles have equal measure.

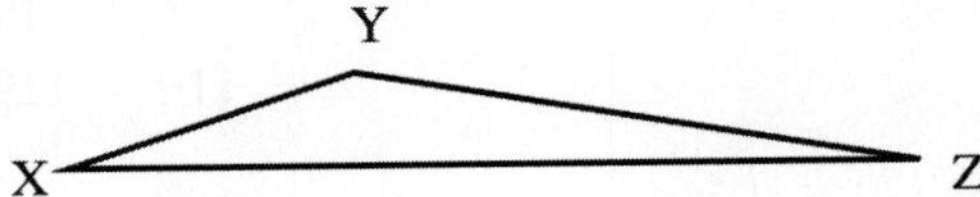

YOU TRY IT 2

For each triangle, based on the side measures given, decide whether it is equilateral, isosceles, or scalene.

a) 3, 6, 8 ______________

b) 10, 21.4, 10 ______________

c) 8, 8, 8 ______________

Think about it

Is an equilateral triangle also isosceles? Why or why not?

____

____

Right Triangles

A type of triangle based on its angle measure is the **right triangle**, in which one angle is a right angle (90°).

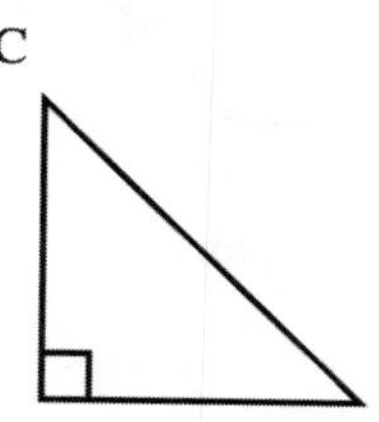

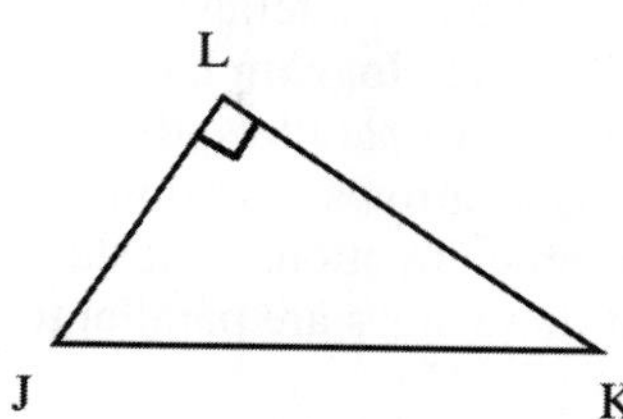

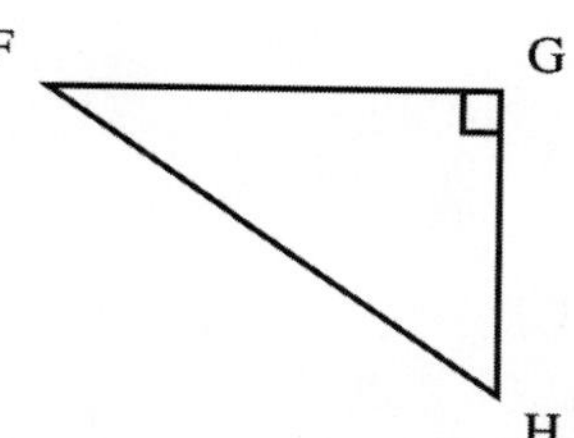

In a right triangle, the other two angles are both acute. In fact:

> The two acute angles in a right triangle are *complementary* to each other.

For example, in ΔABC, if $\angle C$ is the right angle, then we could write the angle equation as

B C A
These two acute angles are complementary

$\angle A + \angle B + 90 = 180$	Subtract 90 from each side.
$\angle A + \angle B + 90 - 90 = 180 - 90$	Simplify each side.
$\angle A + \angle B = 90$	Since the sum of $\angle A + \angle B$ is 90°, it must be that $\angle A$ and $\angle B$ are complementary to each other.

EXAMPLE 2 In ΔABC, $\angle B$ is a right angle. If $\angle C = 67°$, find the measure of $\angle A$.

PROCEDURE: Legend: Let $n =$ the measure of $\angle C$.

We could use all three angles, knowing that $\angle A = 90°$ and $\angle B = 67°$.

ANSWER:

$n + 90 + 67 = 180$

$n + 157 = 180$

$n + 157 - 157 = 180 - 157$

$n = 23$

The measure of $\angle C$ is 23°.

Or, we could use only the two acute angles, knowing that they add to 90°.

$n + 67 = 90$

$n + 67 - 67 = 90 - 67$

$n = 23$

Either way, we get the same result.

YOU TRY IT 3 *Given the measure of one acute angle, find the measure of the other acute angle. Use Example 2 as a guide.*

a) $\angle R = 51°$

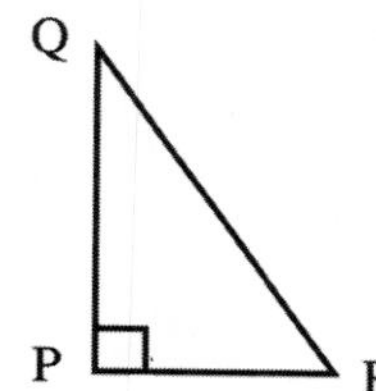

b) $\angle U = 61.8°$

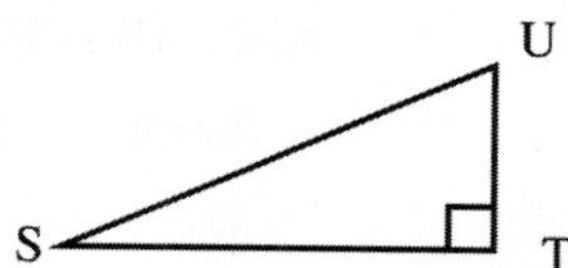

Quadrilaterals

A **quadrilateral** is a four-sided polygon. It also has four angles, and the sum of these angles is 360°.

There are many special types of quadrilaterals:

A **parallelogram** has two pairs of parallel sides.

These arrows, pointing the same direction, indicate that these sides are parallel to each other.

One pair of parallel sides

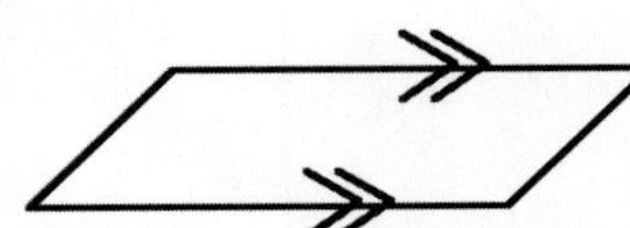

The other pair of parallel sides

The parallel sides are also the same length, as indicated by the number of marks on each side.

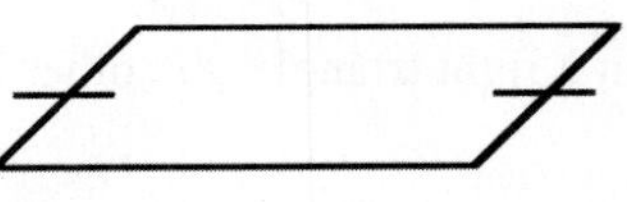

If a parallelogram is not a rectangle, then it has a pair of acute angles and a pair of obtuse angles.

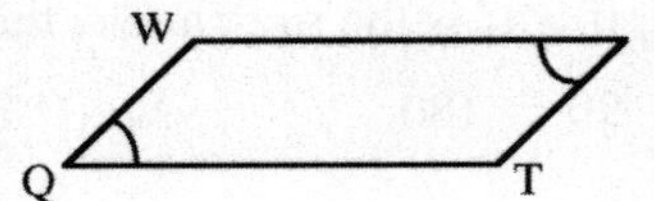

The acute angles are opposite each other.

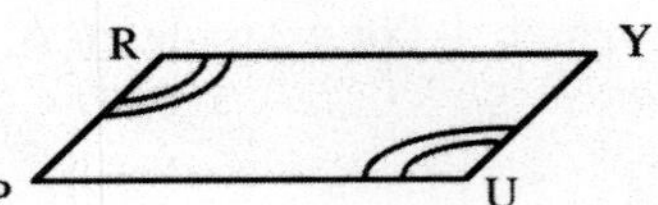

The obtuse angles are opposite each other.

The acute angles are opposite each other and have equal measure. The same is true for the obtuse angles.

Also, an acute angle and an obtuse angle are supplementary.

If you know one angle in a parallelogram, then you can find the others.

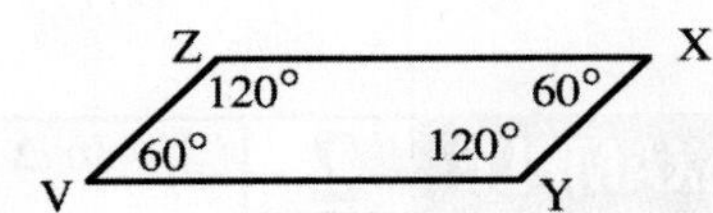

EXAMPLE 3

In this parallelogram, $\overline{CD}$ is 10 centimeters, $\overline{BC}$ is 6 centimeters, and $\angle A = 45°$. Complete this diagram by finding the measures of the other three angles and the lengths of the other two sides.

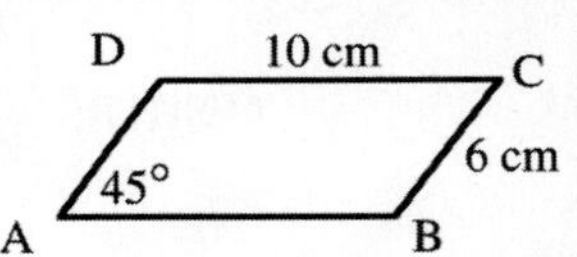

PROCEDURE: Opposite sides of a parallelogram have the same length, and opposite angles have the same measure. $\angle A$ (acute) and $\angle B$ (obtuse) are supplementary.

ANSWER: $\angle A$ and $\angle C$ are both acute, so $\angle C = 45°$, too.

We can find the measure of $\angle B$ by subtracting $\angle A$ from 180°:

$$\begin{array}{r} 180 \\ -\ 45 \\ \hline 135 \end{array}$$

So, $\angle B = 135°$ and that means that $\angle D = 135°$ as well.

Also, $\overline{AB}$ is 10 centimeters, and $\overline{AD}$ is 6 centimeters.

A completed diagram looks like this:

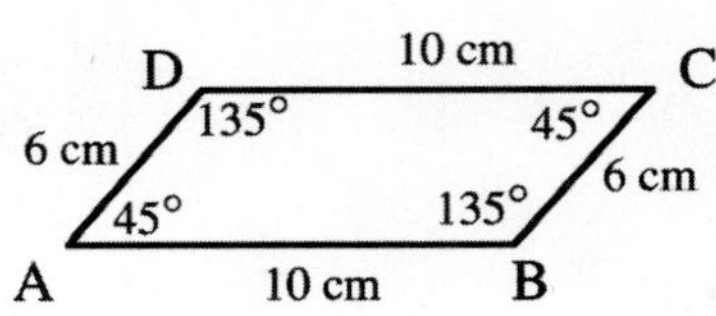

YOU TRY IT 4

For each parallelogram, find the measures of the other three angles and the measures of the other two sides. Use Example 3 as a guide.

a) $\angle D = 127°$, $\overline{AD} = 9$ in. $\overline{DC} = 15$ in.

b) $\angle S = 52.4°$, $\overline{RS} = 3.2$ mm $\overline{RQ} = 5.9$ mm

c) $\angle W = 90°$, $\overline{WZ} = 14$ ft $\overline{XW} = 33$ ft

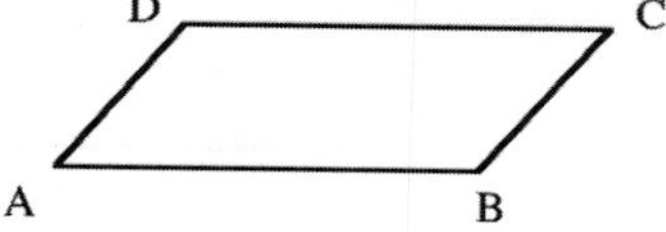

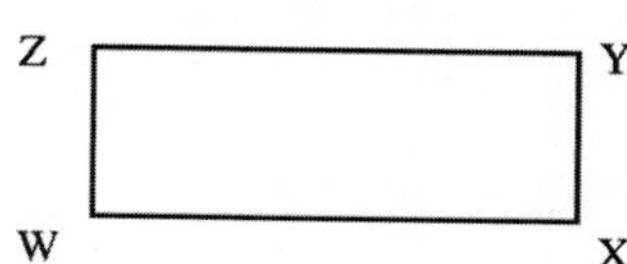

A **rectangle** is a parallelogram with four right angles:

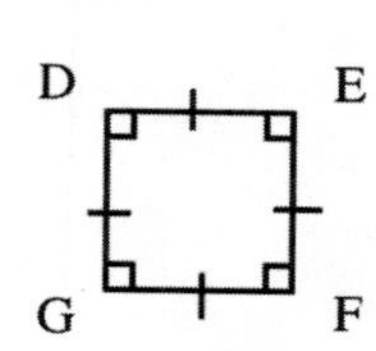

A **square** is a rectangle with four sides of equal length:

D E G F

Is a square also a parallelogram? Why or why not?

____

____

A **trapezoid** is *not* a parallelogram; it is a quadrilateral with only one pair of parallel sides. The parallel sides are called *bases* and have different lengths:

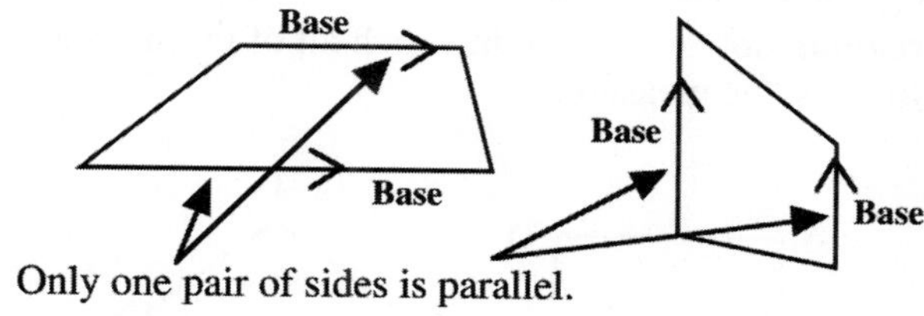

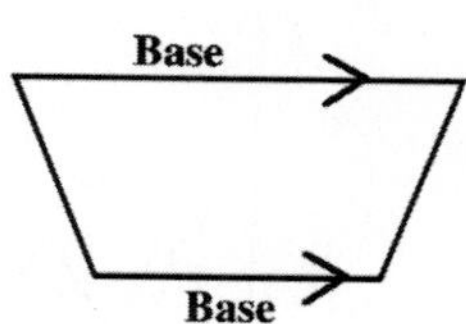

EXAMPLE 4

For each quadrilateral, decide whether it is a parallelogram, rectangle, square, trapezoid, or none of these.

a) 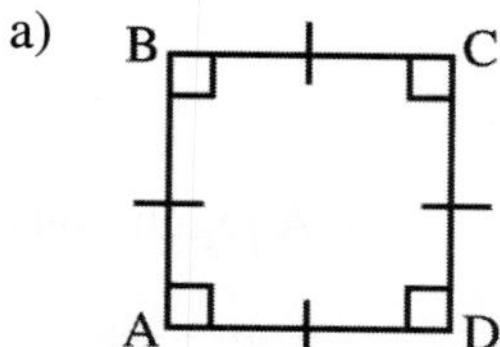

b) 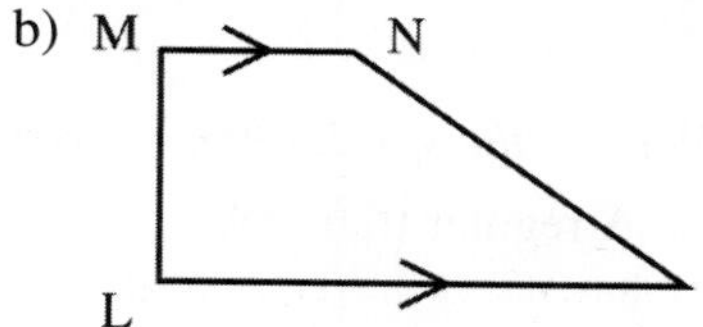

c) 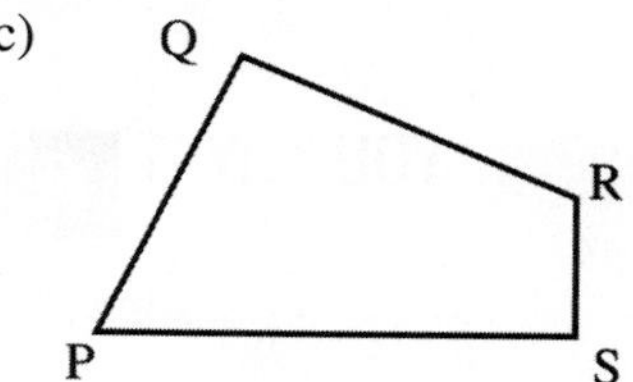

ANSWER:

a) Square, rectangle, and parallelogram

b) Trapezoid (It has only one pair of parallel sides.)

c) None of these (It has no parallel sides.)

YOU TRY IT 5 *For each quadrilateral, decide whether it is a parallelogram, rectangle, square, trapezoid or none of these.*

a) 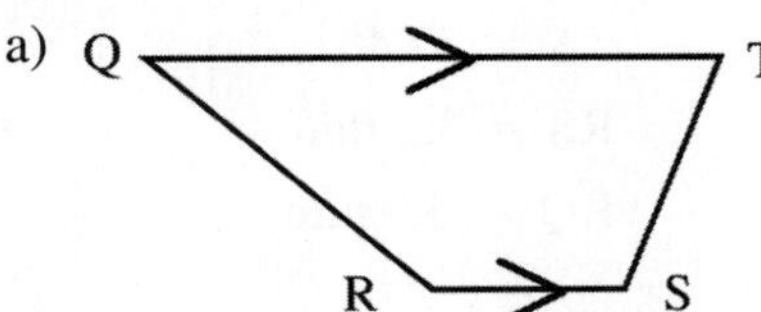

____

b) 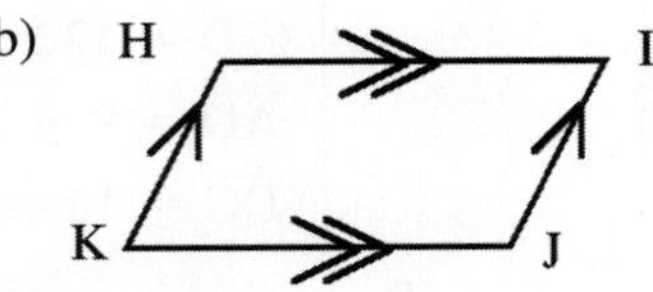

____

c) 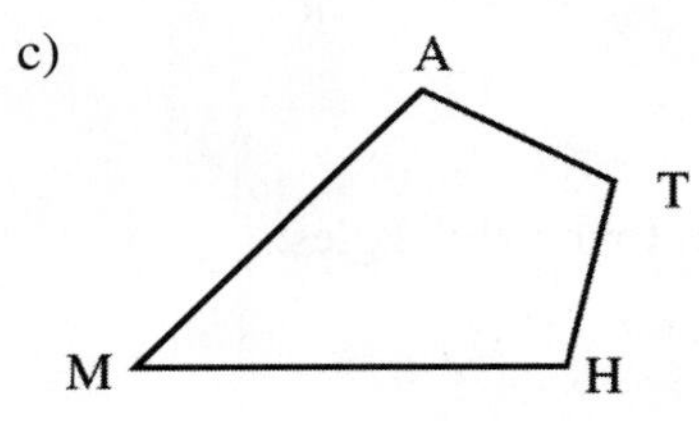

____

d) 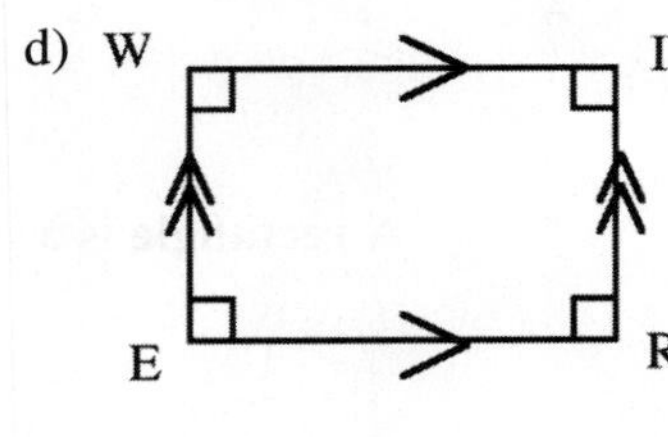

____

e) 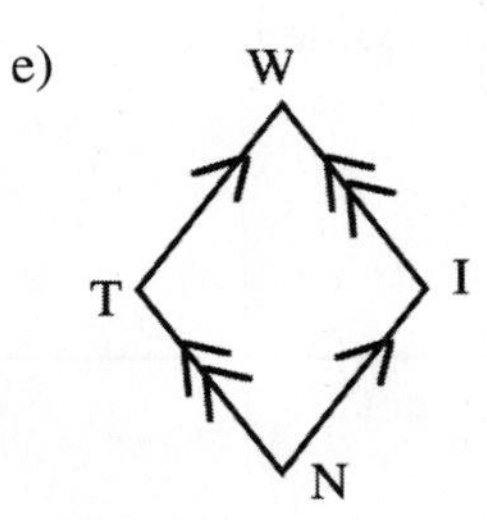

____

Regular Polygons

A **regular polygon** is one in which all of the sides are the same length and all of the angles have the same measure:

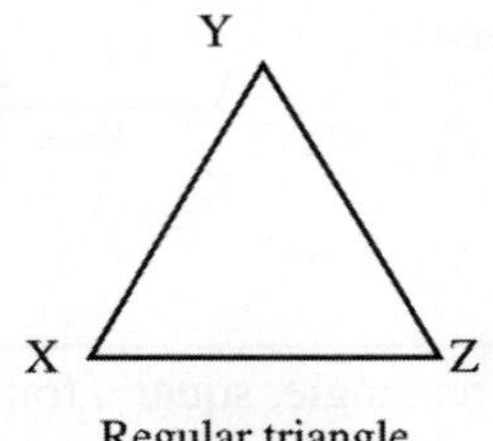

Regular triangle

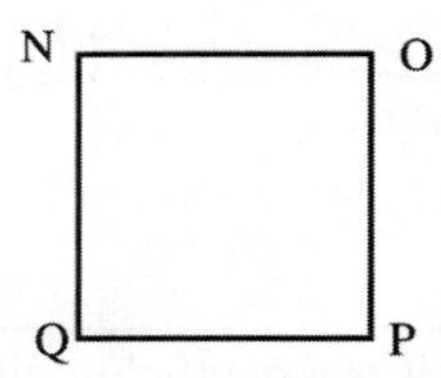

Regular quadrilateral

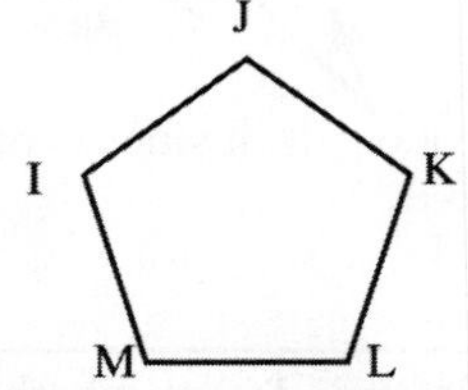

Regular pentagon

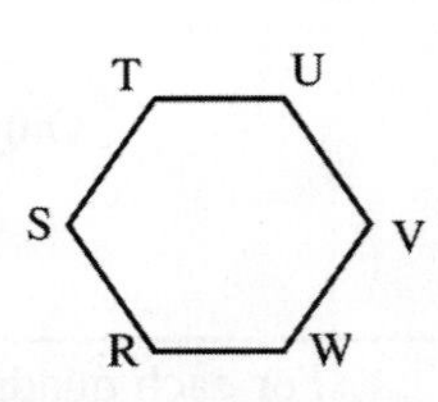

Regular hexagon

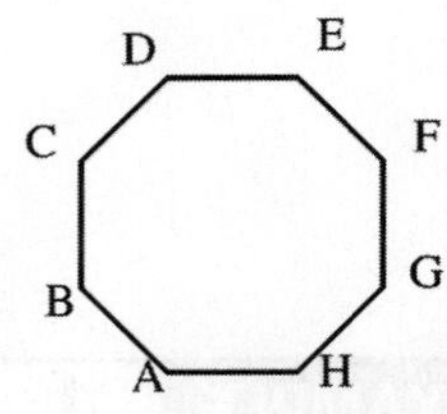

Regular octagon

YOU TRY IT 6 *What is the special name given to:*

a) A regular triangle?

____

b) A regular quadrilateral?

____

YOU TRY IT 7

Complete each regular polygon by filling in the side measures and the angle measures.

a) $\angle M = 108°$,
$\overline{JK} = 9$ m

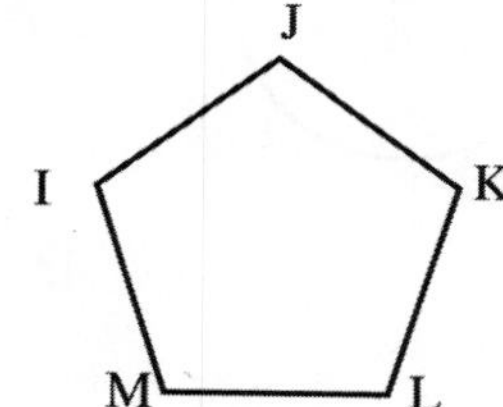

b) $\angle S = 120°$,
$\overline{RS} = 1.2$ yd

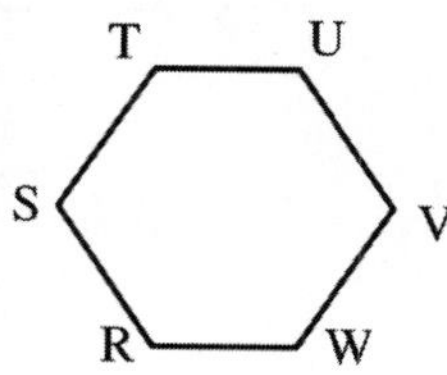

Circles

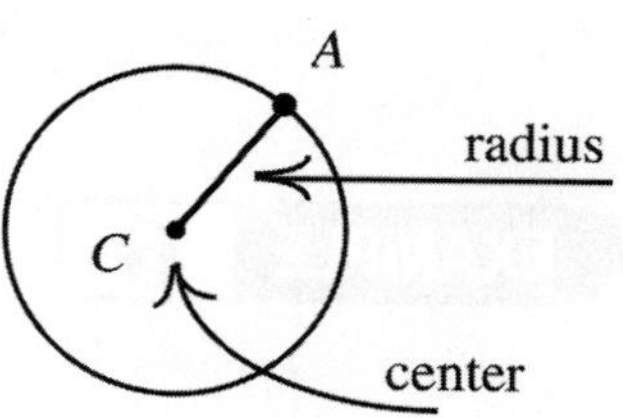

Recall from Section 5.6 that a circle is a round geometric figure with a center point. The center point is the same distance from every point on the circle.

The center names the circle. The circle at right is named *circle C*, or $\odot C$. The center point, C, is not *on* the circle; it is a point that is in the *interior* of the circle.

Recall also that a line segment from the center point to any point on the circle, for example $\overline{CA}$ at right, is called a *radius*. The word *radius* also refers to the length of a radius.

There are many radii (pronounced *ray'−dee−eye*, the plural of radius) in the circle, and each one has the center as one of its endpoints. Here are four radii: $\overline{CG}$, $\overline{CA}$, $\overline{CM}$, and $\overline{CX}$.

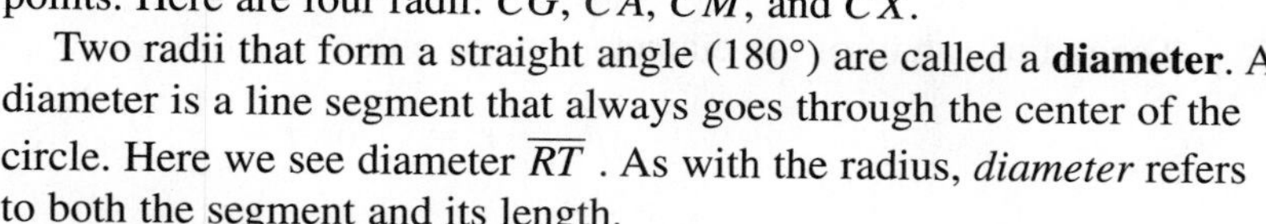

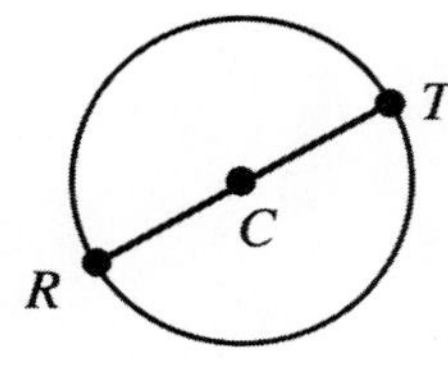

Two radii that form a straight angle (180°) are called a **diameter**. A diameter is a line segment that always goes through the center of the circle. Here we see diameter $\overline{RT}$. As with the radius, *diameter* refers to both the segment and its length.

The length of a diameter, d, is always twice the length of a radius, r: $d = 2 \cdot r$.

EXAMPLE 5 Given the radius of the circle, find the diameter.

a)

b)

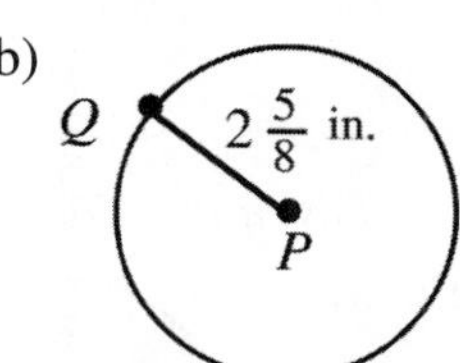

PROCEDURE: The diameter is twice the radius, so use $d = 2 \cdot r$.
For part b, we can write $2\frac{5}{8}$ as $\frac{21}{8}$.

ANSWER:

a) $d = 2 \times 13.7$ cm

$d = 27.4$ cm

b) $d = 2 \cdot \dfrac{21}{8}$ in.

$d = \dfrac{2}{1} \cdot \dfrac{21}{8}$ in.

$d = \dfrac{21}{4}$ in.

$d = 5\dfrac{1}{4}$ in.

YOU TRY IT 8 *Given the radius of the circle, find the diameter. Use Example 5 as a guide.*

a)
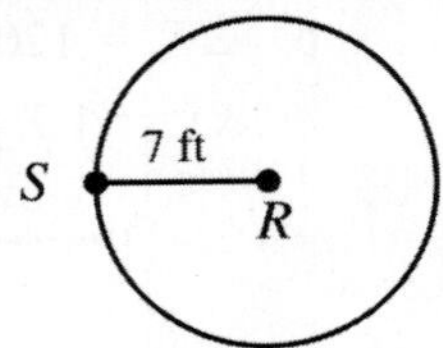

b)
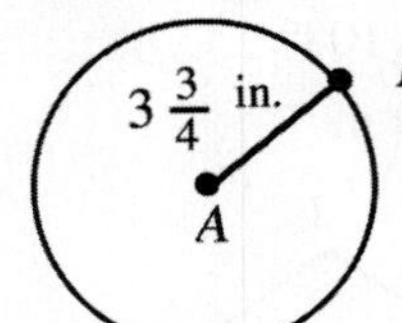

c)
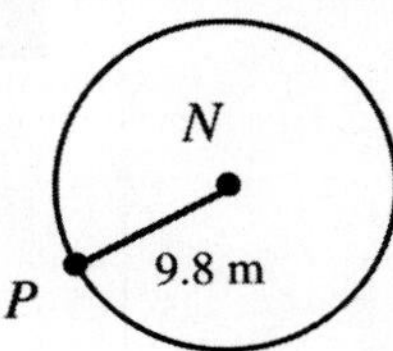

Likewise, the length of a radius, r, is always half the length of the diameter, d.

$$r = \frac{d}{2} \text{ or } r = \frac{1}{2} \cdot d$$

EXAMPLE 6 Given the diameter of the circle, find the radius.

a)
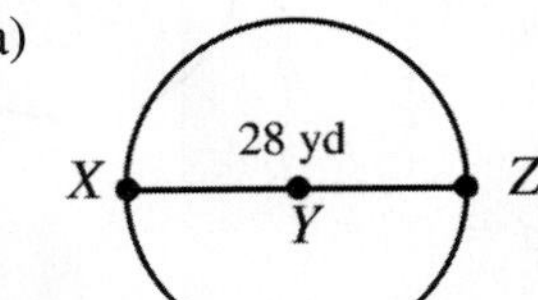

b)
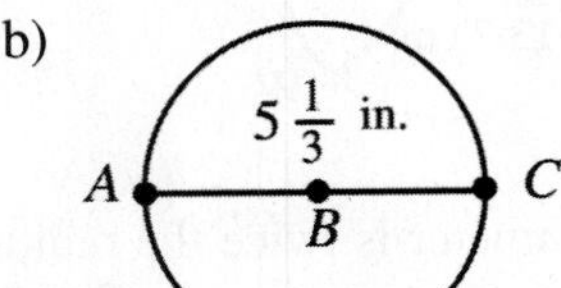

PROCEDURE: The radius is half of the diameter, so use either

$$r = \frac{d}{2} \text{ or } r = \frac{1}{2} \cdot d.$$

For part b, we can write $1\frac{3}{4}$ as $\frac{7}{4}$.

ANSWER: a) $r = \frac{18}{2}$ cm $= 9$ cm b) $r = \frac{1}{2} \cdot \frac{7}{4}$ in. $= \frac{7}{8}$ in.

YOU TRY IT 9 *Given the diameter of the circle, find the radius. Use Example 6 as a guide.*

a)
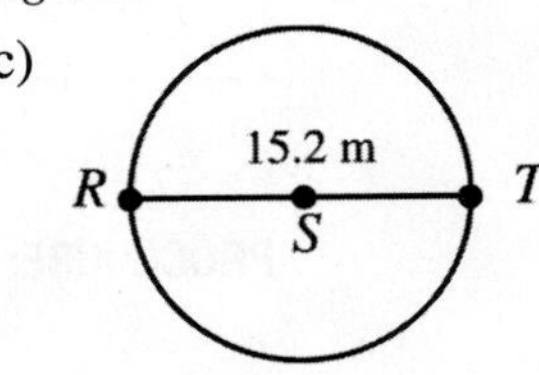

b)

5 1/3 in.
A
B
C

c)

15.2 m
R
S
T

You Try It Answers: Section 7.5

YTI 1 a) The measure of $\angle L$ is 25°.
b) The measure of $\angle N$ is 117.7°.

YTI 2 a) Scalene b) Isosceles c) Equilateral

YTI 3 a) The measure of $\angle Q$ is 39°.
b) The measure of $\angle S$ is 28.2°.

YTI 4 a) $\angle B = 127°$, $\angle A = 53°$ and $\angle C = 53°$; $\overline{BC} = 9$ in. and $\overline{AB} = 15$ in.
b) $\angle Q = 52.4°$, $\angle R = 127.6°$, and $\angle T = 127.6°$; $\overline{TQ} = 3.2$ mm and $\overline{TS} = 5.9$ mm
c) All angles measure 90°; $\overline{XY} = 14$ ft and $\overline{YZ} = 33$ ft

YTI 5 a) Trapezoid
b) Parallelogram
c) None of these
d) Rectangle and parallelogram
e) Parallelogram

YTI 6 a) Equilateral triangle b) Square

YTI 7 a) Each angle measures 108°; each side measures 9 meters.
b) Each angle measures 120°; each side measures 1.2 yards.

YTI 8 a) $d = 14$ ft b) $d = 7\frac{1}{2}$ in. c) $d = 19.6$ m

YTI 9 a) $r = 14$ yd b) $r = 2\frac{2}{3}$ in. c) $r = 7.6$ m

Focus Exercises: Section 7.5

For $\triangle ABC$, given the measures of $\angle A$ and $\angle B$, find the measure of $\angle C$.

1. $\angle A = 30°$ and $\angle B = 70°$
2. $\angle A = 20°$ and $\angle B = 110°$
3. $\angle A = 75°$ and $\angle B = 92°$
4. $\angle A = 61°$ and $\angle B = 48°$
5. $\angle A = 62.9°$ and $\angle B = 41.7°$
6. $\angle A = 119.1°$ and $\angle B = 43.6°$
7. $\angle A = 80°$ and $\angle B = 29.5°$
8. $\angle A = 79.8°$ and $\angle B = 65.4°$

For each, based on the side measures given (in centimeters), decide whether the triangle is equilateral, isosceles or scalene.

9.
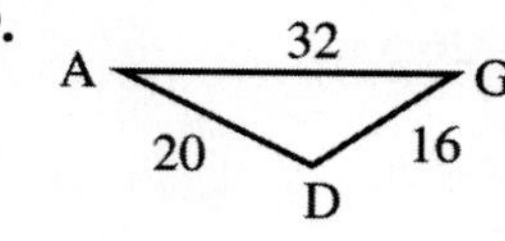

10.
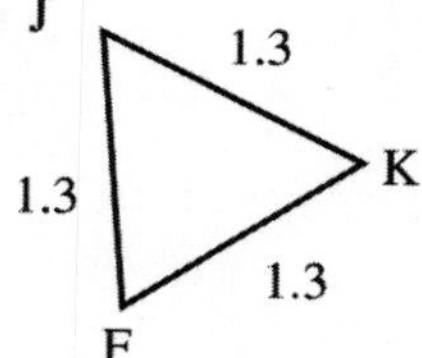

11.
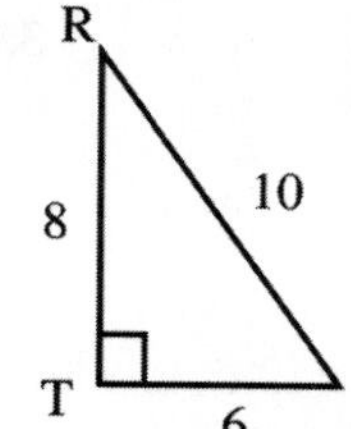

12.
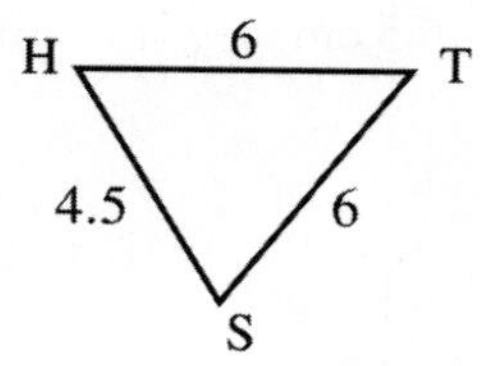

Given the measure of one acute angle, find the measure of the other acute angle.

13. $\angle A = 36°$
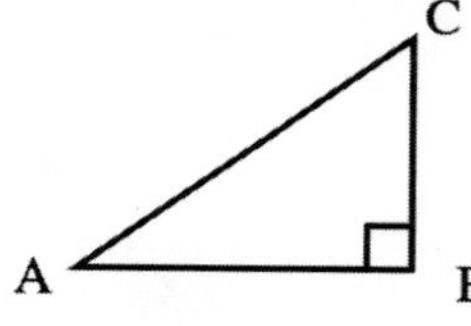

14. $\angle D = 73°$
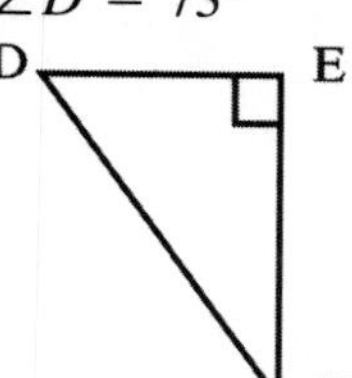

15. $\angle G = 21.5°$
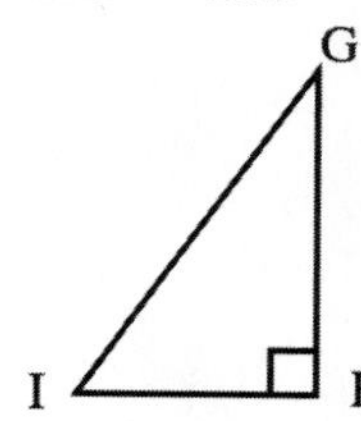

16. $\angle J = 74.6°$
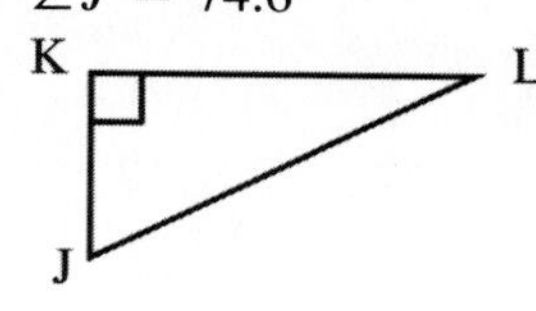

Find the measures of the other three angles and the measures of the other two sides.

17. $\angle N = 35°$
$\overline{NQ} = 3$ in.
$\overline{NO} = 7$ in.

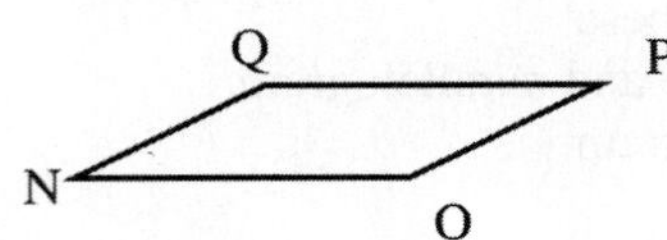

18. $\angle X = 129.1°$
$\overline{WZ} = 3.5$ mi
$\overline{XW} = 5.6$ mi

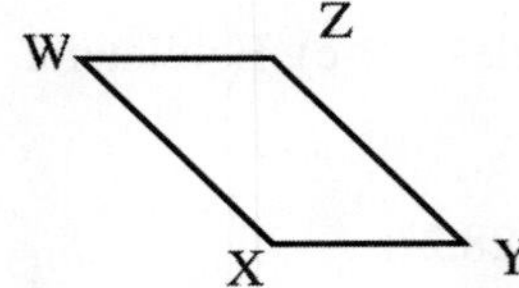

True or false:

19. Some trapezoids are also parallelograms._________

20. Every square is also a parallelogram._________

21. In a trapezoid, it's possible for the two parallel sides (the bases) to be the same length._________

22. If one angle in a parallelogram is a right angle, then the parallelogram is a rectangle._________

23. In a polygon, the number of sides and the number of angles is always the same._________

24. In an equilateral triangle, all three sides are equal in length, but the angles can be of different measures._________

25. A triangle can contain three acute angles._________

26. A regular octagon has eight sides, but an octagon that is not regular can have more than eight sides._________

Answer Yes or No and explain your answer. (You may draw an example that explains your answer.)

27. Is it possible for a right triangle to also be isosceles?_________

28. Is it possible for a right triangle to also be equilateral?_________

Given the radius, r, of a circle, find the diameter; or given the diameter, d, of a circle, find the radius.

29. $r = 6$ in. **30.** $r = 3.8$ m **31.** $d = 20$ in. **32.** $d = 27$ in.

33. $r = 6.5$ cm **34.** $r = 5\frac{3}{4}$ in. **35.** $d = 7\frac{1}{3}$ ft **36.** $d = 26.5$ in.

Objectives

In this section, you will learn to:

- Find the perimeter of a polygon.
- Apply the perimeter formulas for a rectangle and for regular polygons.
- Determine the circumference of a circle.
- Find the perimeter of unusual shapes.

To successfully complete this section, you need to understand:

- Solving equations (1.6)
- Multiplying fractions (3.3)
- Adding and subtracting fractions (4.3, 4.4)
- Adding and subtracting decimals (5.3)
- Multiplying decimals (5.4)
- Geometric shapes (7.5)
- Regular polygons (7.5)

SECTION 7.6 Perimeter

Introduction

Recall from Section 1.3 that we add the lengths of the sides of a figure to find its perimeter:

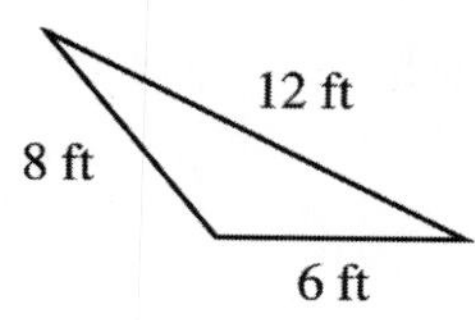

Perimeter: $P = 8 \text{ ft} + 12 \text{ ft} + 6 \text{ ft}$

$P = 26 \text{ ft}$

Recall from Section 2.3 that the formula for the perimeter of a rectangle is $P = 2 \cdot L + 2 \cdot W$:

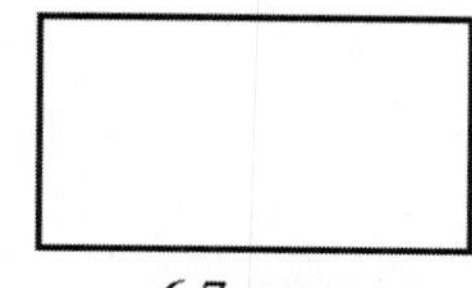

Perimeter: $P = 2 \times 3.5 \text{ cm} + 2 \times 6.7 \text{ cm}$

$P = 7.0 \text{ cm} + 13.4 \text{ cm}$

$P = 20.4 \text{ cm}$

YOU TRY IT 1

Find the perimeter for each polygon.

a)

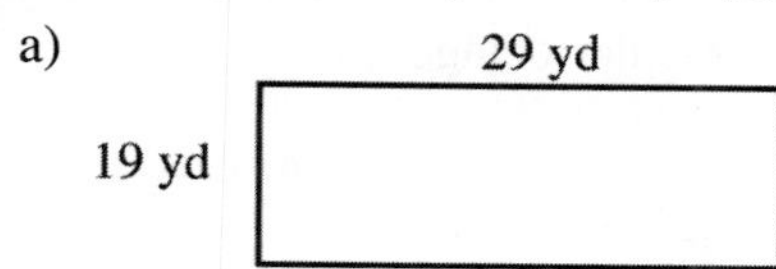

b)

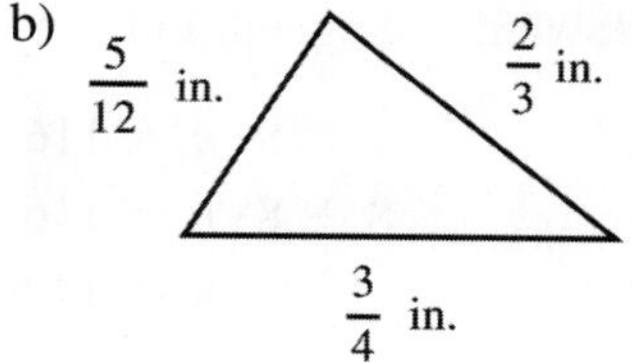

Perimeter of a Regular Polygon

Recall from Section 7.5 that the sides of a regular polygon are all the same length. If a polygon is regular, then knowing the length of one side means you know the length of all of the sides, as demonstrated in this equilateral triangle.

$P = 7 \text{ in.} + 7 \text{ in.} + 7 \text{ in.} = 3 \cdot 7 \text{ in.} = 21 \text{ in.}$

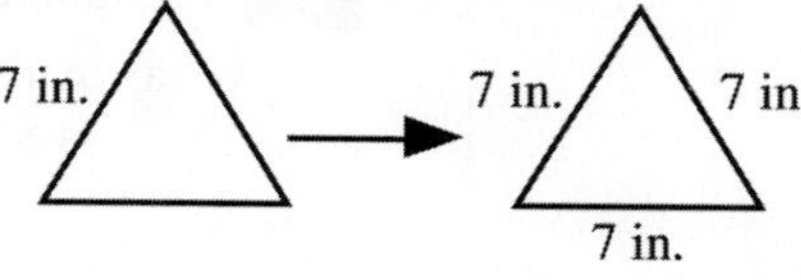

Some perimeter formulas for regular polygons are as follows:

Equilateral Triangle

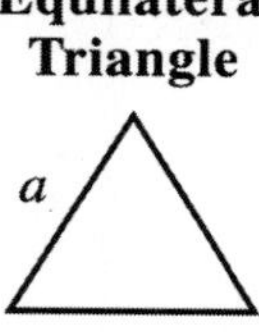

$P = 3 \cdot a$

Square

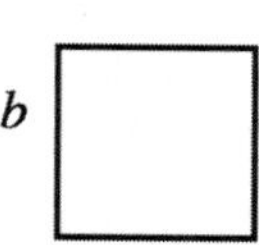

$P = 4 \cdot b$

Regular Pentagon

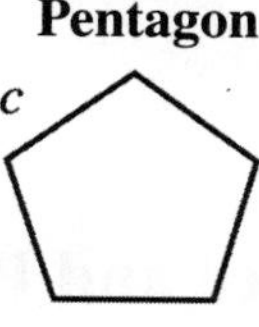

$P = 5 \cdot c$

Regular Hexagon

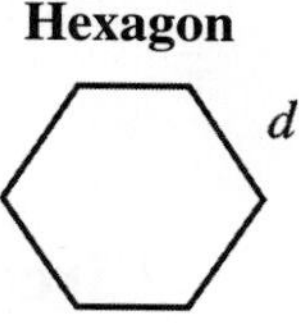

$P = 6 \cdot d$

Regular Octagon

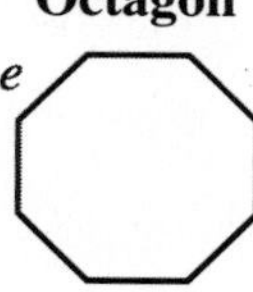

$P = 8 \cdot e$

EXAMPLE 1 Draw a regular hexagon, and label one side as being 5 feet long. What is the perimeter of this hexagon?

PROCEDURE: No one expects you to draw a perfect regular hexagon, so just do your best. Try to copy the one shown previous to this example. Then, label one side as 5 ft.

5 ft

ANSWER: The formula for the perimeter of a regular hexagon (six sides) is $P = 6 \cdot 5\text{ ft} = 30\text{ ft}$.

Draw a regular polygon, and label one side as requested. What is the perimeter of this polygon? Use Example 1 as a guide.

a) An equilateral triangle; one side is 14.8 cm. b) A regular pentagon; one side is $3\frac{1}{2}$ in.

EXAMPLE 2 Draw a regular octagon. Given the perimeter of this octagon is 116 centimeters, find the length of each side.

PROCEDURE: Do your best to draw a regular octagon. If the whole perimeter is 116 cm, and the side value is unknown (n), then we can use the formula to set up an equation to find the length of each side

n

ANSWER: Legend: Let $n =$ one side of the regular octagon.

$$8 \cdot n = 116$$
$$8 \div 8 \cdot n = 116 \div 8$$
$$n = 14.5$$

Divide each side by 8

$$\begin{array}{r} 14.5 \\ 8\overline{)116.0} \\ -\ 8 \\ \hline 36 \\ -\ 32 \\ \hline 40 \\ -\ 40 \\ \hline \end{array}$$

Each side of the octagon is 14.5 centimeters.

Draw a regular polygon. Given the perimeter of the polygon, find the length of each side. Use Example 2 as a guide.

a) A regular hexagon; the perimeter is 84 ft.

b) An equilateral triangle; the perimeter is 73.5 cm.

Circumference and Pi

In finding the perimeter of a polygon, we determine the sum of all of its sides. Because a circle has only one "side", and it isn't straight, the perimeter of the circle—the **circumference**—must be evaluated differently, as we'll soon see.

Imagine a pebble dropped into a pond. A circular ripple is created that grows increasingly larger. As this circle grows, both the diameter and the circumference get larger *proportionally*.

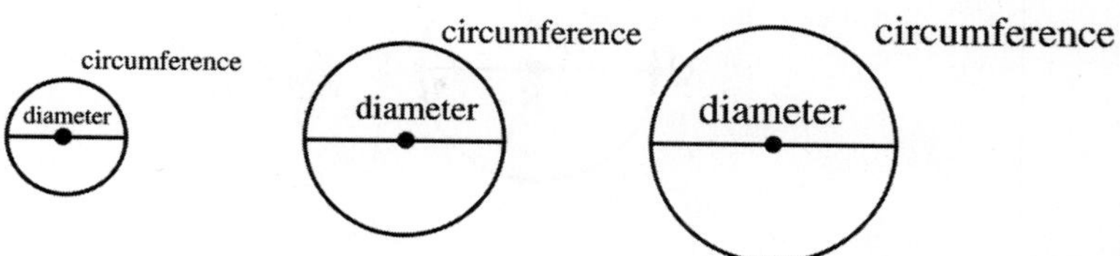

This means that there is a ratio, circumference : diameter or $\frac{\text{circumference}}{\text{diameter}}$, that is the same number no matter how large the circle. This ratio is labeled with the Greek letter pi (π).

If the circumference and diameter of a circle could be precisely measured, we'd find that

$$\pi = \frac{\text{Circumference}}{\text{diameter}} = 3.14159265358979\ldots$$

Recall from Sections 5.1 and 5.6 that π is a decimal number that never terminates and never repeats, so we can never write out an exact decimal value of π.

There are two accepted close approximations to π, one a fraction: $\frac{22}{7} = 3.\overline{142857}$ and the other a rounded decimal, just 3.14. In other words,

$$\boldsymbol{\pi \approx \frac{22}{7} \text{ and } \pi \approx 3.14}$$

The formula for the circumference is: Circumference $= \pi \cdot$ diameter

Abbreviated as: $C = \pi \cdot d$

or as: $C = \pi \cdot 2 \cdot r$ (Because $d = 2 \cdot r$.)

or as: $C = 2 \cdot \pi \cdot r$

To represent an exact value of the circumference, we use the symbol π. For example, if the diameter of a circle is 7 inches, then the exact value of the circumference is written $C = 7 \cdot \pi$ inches or 7π inches.

However, we can't really measure anything if it has the symbol π in it. If we actually want to measure the circumference, then we'll need to use one of the approximate values for π:

$C \approx 7 \cdot \frac{22}{7}$ inches or $C \approx 7 \times 3.14$ inches

$C \approx 22$ inches $\qquad$ $C \approx 21.98$ inches

Notice that the values we found for the circumference, 22 and 21.98, are very close to each other. Why aren't they exactly the same?

____

____

In deciding which approximate value to use for π, it's common to use:

- $\frac{22}{7}$ if the radius or diameter is in a fractional form or is a whole number easily divisible by 7;
- 3.14 if the measure is a decimal or a whole number not divisible by 7.

  Furthermore, when using the decimal approximation, it's common to round the resulting value to an easily measurable amount, usually the tenths place or the hundredths place.

EXAMPLE 3 For each circle, find the circumference. Use an approximate value for π.

a)

3.5 m
Q R S

b)

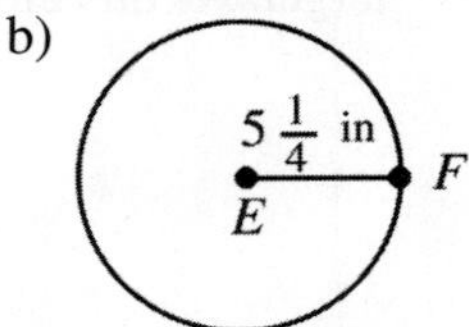

PROCEDURE: For part a) we'll use $C = \pi \cdot d$; For part b) we'll use $C = \pi \cdot 2 \cdot r$. For part a), use $\pi \approx 3.14$ and round the answer to the tenths place.

For part b), use $\pi \approx \frac{22}{7}$. Also, for part b), we can write $5\frac{1}{4}$ as $\frac{21}{4}$.

ANSWER: a) $\overline{QS}$ is a diameter.

$C \approx 3.14 \times 3.5$ m.

$C \approx 10.99$ m.

ROUNDED: $C \approx 11.0$ m.

> **You finish it:** *Multiply*
>
> $$\begin{array}{r} 3.14 \\ \times\ 2.5 \\ \hline \end{array}$$

b) $\overline{EF}$ is a radius (use $C = \pi \cdot 2 \cdot r$).

$$C \approx \frac{22}{7} \cdot 2 \cdot \frac{21}{4} \text{ in.}$$

$$C \approx \frac{22 \cdot 2 \cdot 21}{7 \cdot 1 \cdot 4} \text{ in.}$$ 7 and 21 have a common factor of 7; 2 and 4 have a common factor of 2.

$$C \approx \frac{22 \cdot 1 \cdot 3}{1 \cdot 1 \cdot 2} \textit{ in.}$$

$$C \approx \frac{66}{2} \text{ in.}$$ $\frac{66}{2} = 33$

ROUNDED: $C \approx 33$ in.

YOU TRY IT 4 *For each circle, find an approximate value of the circumference. Use Example 3 as a guide. Round each decimal answer, if necessary, to the nearest tenth.*

a)

$4\frac{3}{8}$ in.
K L

b)

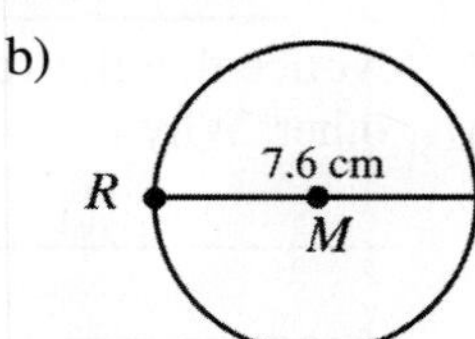

Perimeters of Unusual Shapes

Consider this situation: Arturo and Terry are laying wood flooring in Janet's living room. After laying the flooring, they will place baseboards along each wall. According to the floor plan's dimensions, how many feet of baseboard are needed to complete the room? Assume all angles are right angles.

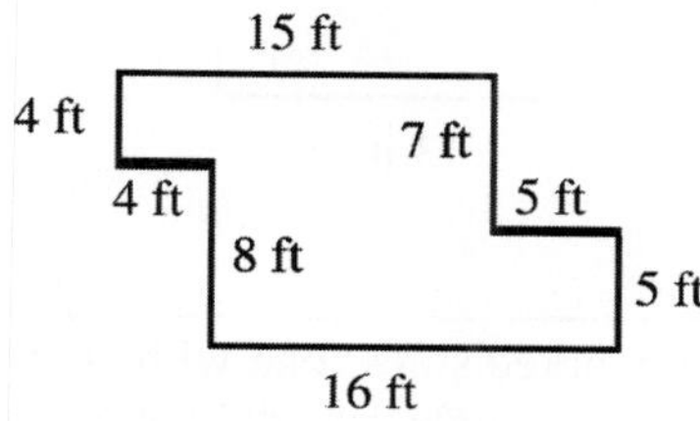

The perimeter is found by adding up all of the side measures:

$$\begin{array}{r} 15 \\ 4 \\ 4 \\ 8 \\ 16 \\ 5 \\ 5 \\ +\ 7 \\ \hline P = 64 \text{ feet} \end{array}$$

Arturo and Terry will need 64 feet of baseboard to complete the room.

As you see from this example, not all geometric shapes are standard shapes, but it doesn't stop us from finding the perimeter. We just need to know all of the dimensions.

Sometimes, though, not all of the dimensions are shown, and we must figure out any missing side measures based on other information in the diagram.

For example, in this diagram, we know the total length to be 18 feet and the total width to be 12 feet. Using other measures in the diagram, fill in the missing side measures, one marked with an x and the other marked with a y.

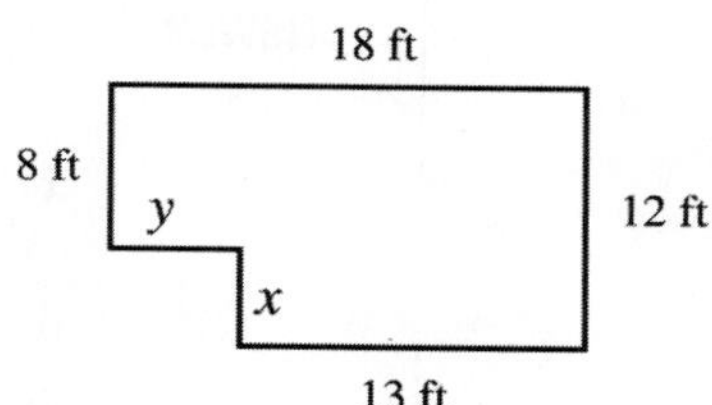

We can label this floor plan, as a polygon, at each vertex. We can even show a point, G, that is not a vertex by creating a rectangle out of the floor plan, rectangle ABCG. In fact, a smaller rectangle is formed by DEFG.

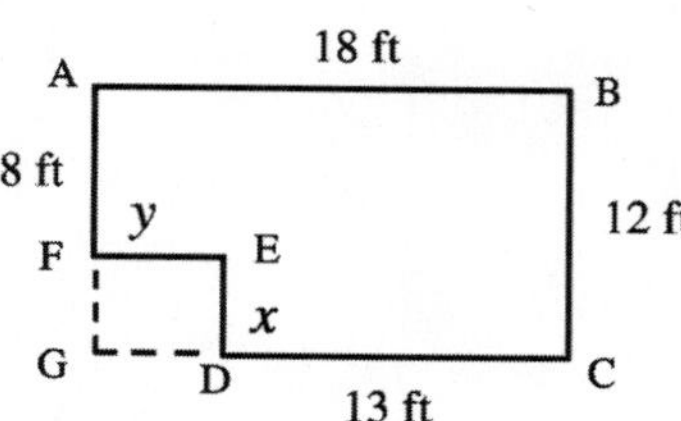

In the larger rectangle, $\overline{GC}$ is the same measure as $\overline{AB}$, and in the smaller rectangle, $\overline{FG}$ is the same measure as $\overline{ED}$. Explain why.

____

____

The two lower measures, $\overline{FE}$ and $\overline{DC}$ add to the total measure of $\overline{AB}$, 18 ft.

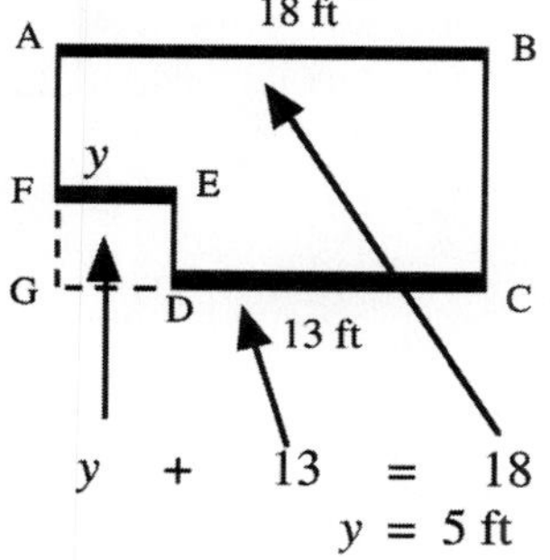

$y + 13 = 18$

$y = 5$ ft

The two left measures, $\overline{AF}$ and $\overline{ED}$ add to the total measure of $\overline{BC}$, 12 ft.

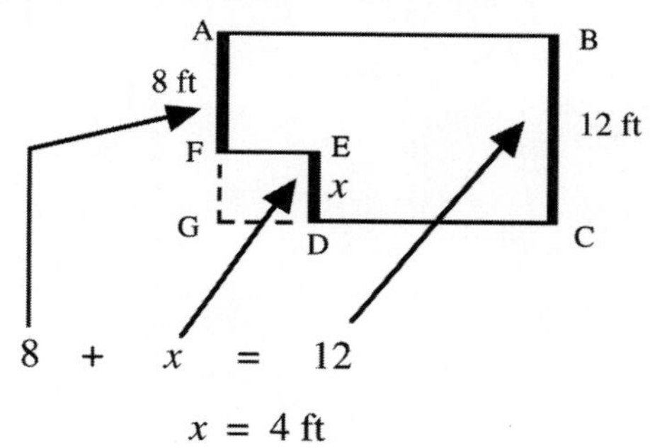

$8 + x = 12$

$x = 4$ ft

We can now put those measures on the diagram and add to find the perimeter.

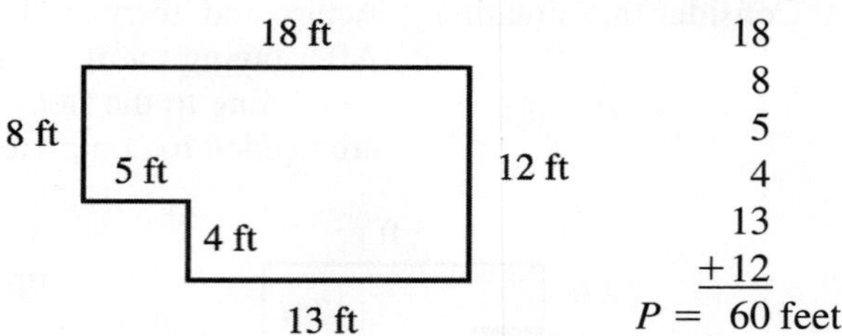

$$\begin{array}{r} 18 \\ 8 \\ 5 \\ 4 \\ 13 \\ +12 \\ \hline P = \ 60 \text{ feet} \end{array}$$

EXAMPLE 4 Find the measures of the marked sides (one with an x, the other with a y); then find the perimeter of the polygon. Assume all angles are right angles.

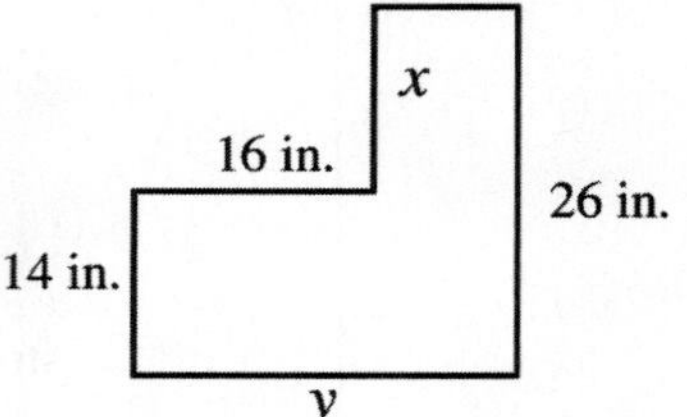

PROCEDURE: Notice that the side marked with a y is across the *whole* width of the figure. The side marked with an x is one of the *parts*, not the whole. (You may want to label each vertex in the polygon, including a point that completes the rectangle.)

ANSWER: Since x is a *part*, we'll use the equation

$$x + 14 = 26$$
$$x + 14 - 14 = 26 - 14$$
$$x = 12$$

Since y is a *whole*, we'll use the equation

$$16 + 7 = y$$
$$23 = y$$

Putting these values into the polygon, we get:

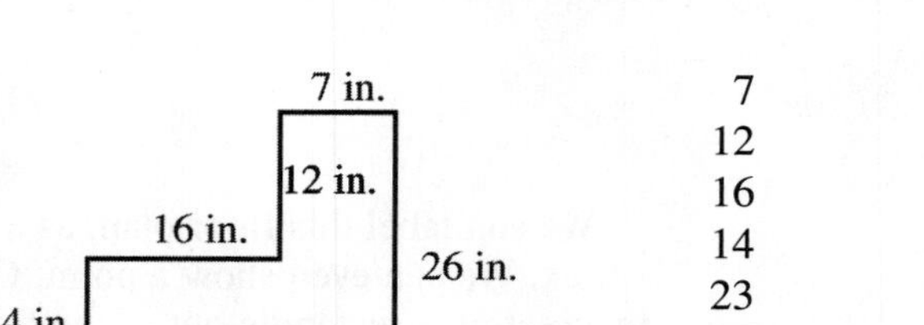

$$\begin{array}{r} 7 \\ 12 \\ 16 \\ 14 \\ 23 \\ +26 \\ \hline P = \ 98 \text{ inches} \end{array}$$

YOU TRY IT 5 *Find the measures of the marked sides (with an x and y) and then find the perimeter of the polygon. Use Example 4 as a guide. Assume all angles are right angles.*

a)

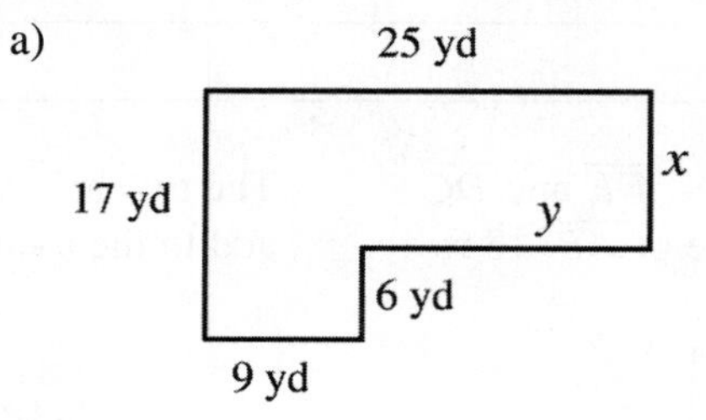

b)

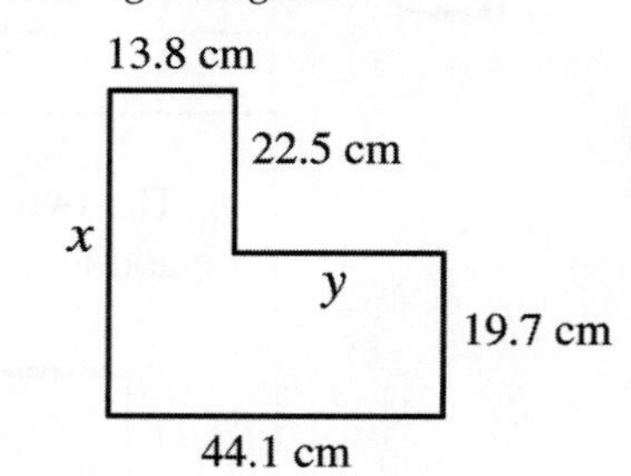

You Try It Answers: Section 7.6

YTI 1 a) $P = 96$ yd b) $P = 1\frac{5}{6}$ in.

YTI 2 a) 14.8 cm $P = 44.4$ cm

b) $3\frac{1}{2}$ in. $P = 17\frac{1}{2}$ in.

YTI 3 a)

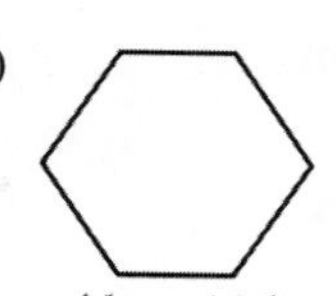

b) side = 24.5 cm

YTI 4 a) $C \approx 27\frac{1}{2}$ in. or $C \approx 27.5$ in.

b) $C \approx 23.9$ cm

YTI 5 a) $x = 11$ yd, $y = 16$ yd, $P = 84$ yd

b) $x = 42.2$ cm, $y = 30.3$ cm, $P = 172.6$ cm

Focus Exercises: Section 7.6

For each, find the perimeter of the polygon described. Answer the question with a sentence.

1. In her design class, Karin created this unusual shape for a lamp stand. What is the perimeter of Karin's lamp stand? (All measures are in inches.)

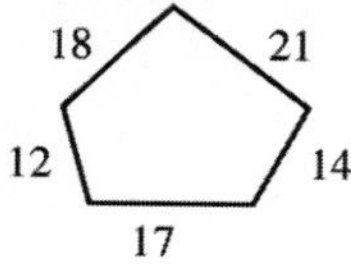

2. Hoi Mai's backyard is in the shape of a trapezoid (at right). What is the perimeter of Hoi Mai's backyard? (All measures are in meters.)

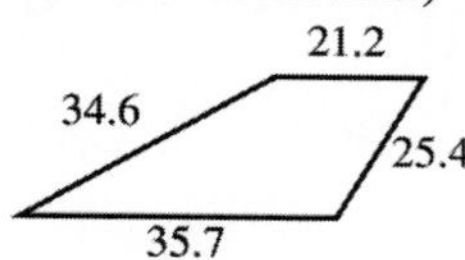

3. The dimensions of home plate for professional baseball are shown at right. What is the perimeter of home plate? (All measures are in inches.)

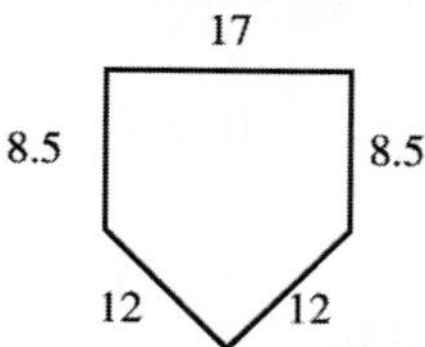

4. A room in a modern home has the unusual shape of a hexagon, as shown at right. What is the perimeter of this room? (All measures are in feet.)

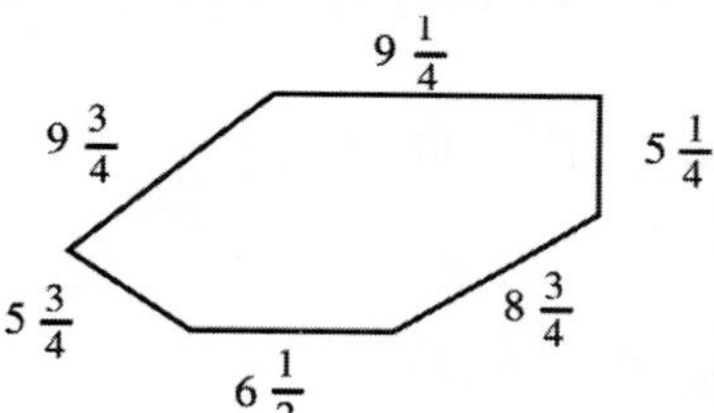

Find the perimeter of each triangle.

5.

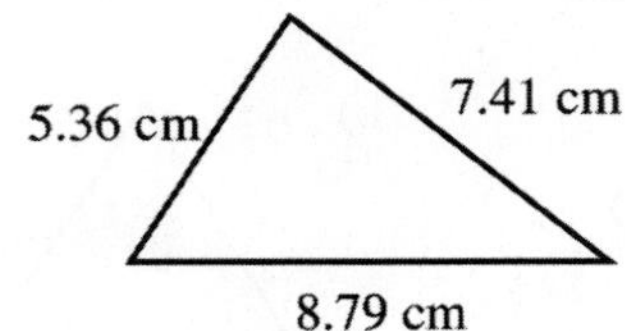

6.

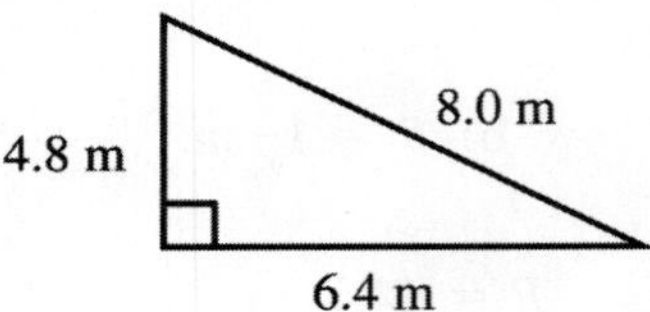

7.

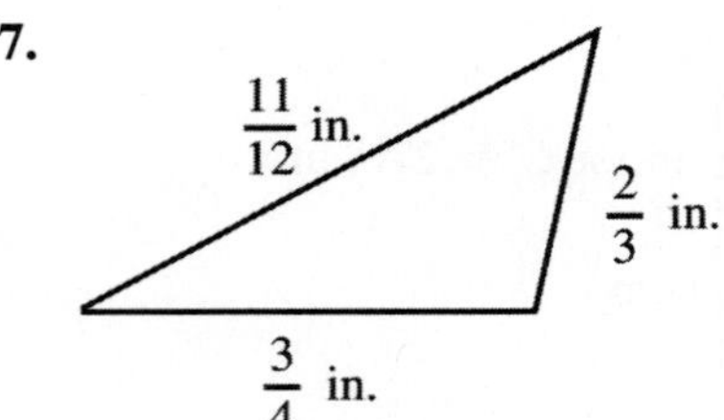

8.

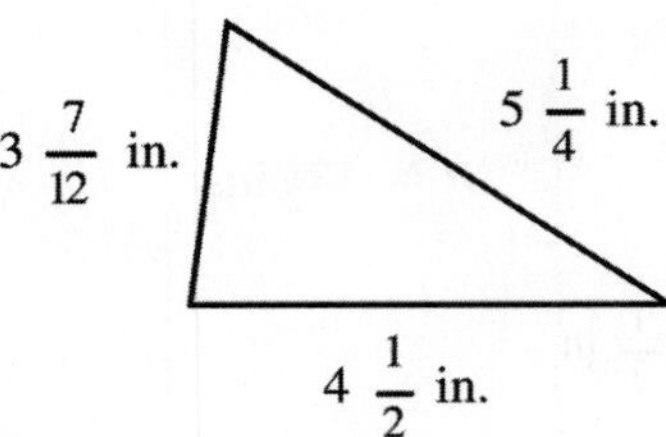

Find the perimeter of each rectangle.

9.

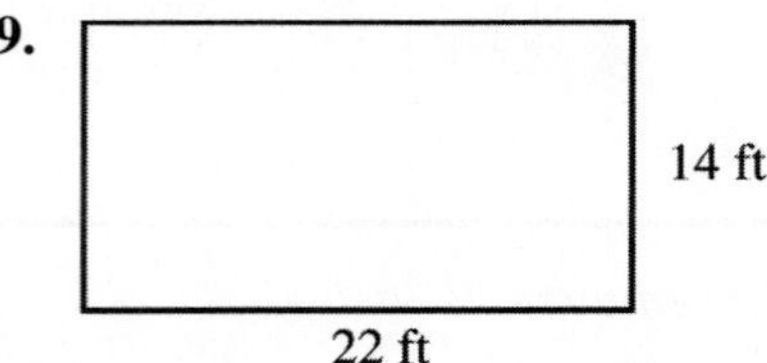

10.

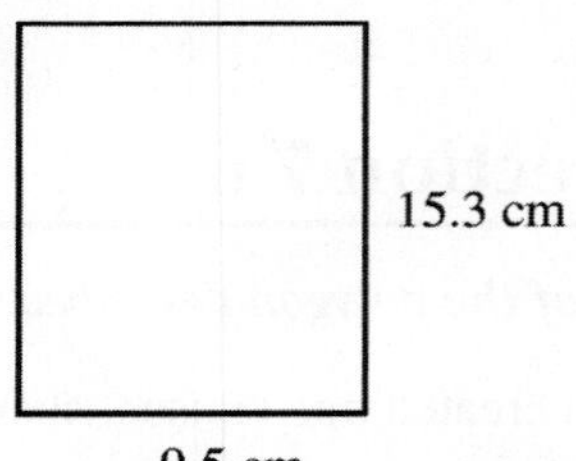

11.

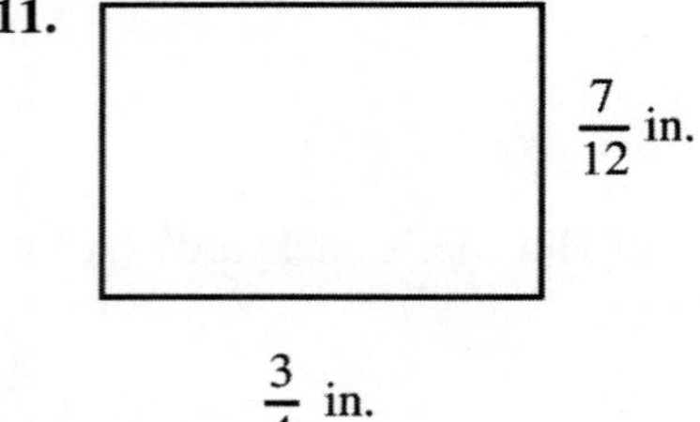

12.

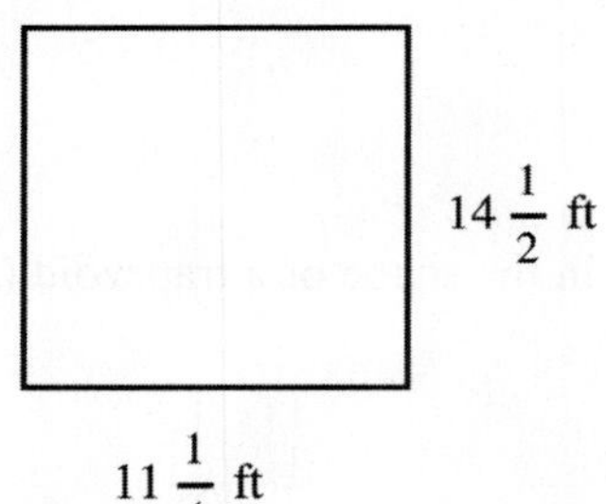

For each, find the perimeter of the polygon described. (Write all improper fraction answers as mixed numbers.)

13. A square; one side is 13 ft.

14. A square; one side is 28.5 m.

15. An equilateral triangle; one side is 31.4 m.

16. An equilateral triangle; one side is $3\frac{5}{12}$ in.

17. A regular pentagon; one side is 148 yd.

18. A regular octagon; one side is 4.65 cm.

19. A regular hexagon; one side is $2\frac{5}{12}$ in.

20. A regular octagon; one side is $6\frac{3}{4}$ in.

Given the perimeter of the regular polygon, find the length of each side. (Write all improper fraction answers as mixed numbers.)

21. An equilateral triangle; $P = 51$ in.

22. An equilateral triangle; $P = 17.25$ m.

23. A square; $P = 71.6$ cm.

24. A square; $P = 55$ ft.

25. A regular hexagon; $P = 105$ yd.

26. A regular pentagon; $P = 16.7$ m.

27. A regular octagon; $P = 10\frac{2}{3}$ ft.

28. A regular octagon; $P = 25\frac{1}{3}$ in.

For each circle with given radius, approximate the circumference using $\pi \approx \frac{22}{7}$.

29. $r = 14$ in.

30. $r = 42$ in.

31. $r = 2.8$ cm

32. $r = 6.3$ cm

33. $r = \frac{7}{8}$ in.

34. $r = 5\frac{1}{4}$ in.

35. $r = 3\frac{1}{2}$ ft

36. $r = 4\frac{2}{3}$ ft

For each circle with given radius, approximate the circumference using $\pi \approx 3.14$; round the result to the tenths place.

37. $r = 5$ yd

38. $r = 6$ yd

39. $r = 4.5$ m

40. $r = 3.2$ m

For each circle with given diameter, approximate the circumference using $\pi \approx 3.14$; round the result to the tenths place.

41. $d = 8$ ft

42. $d = 15$ ft

43. $d = 6.5$ cm

44. $d = 10.5$ cm

Find the measures of the marked sides (with an x and with a y); then find the perimeter of the polygon. Assume all angles are right angles.

45.

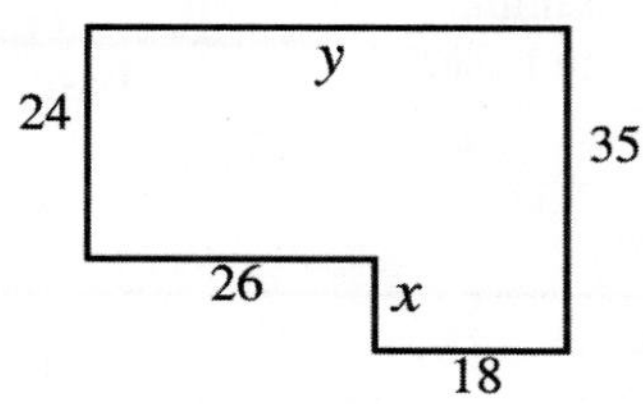

All measures are in inches.

46.

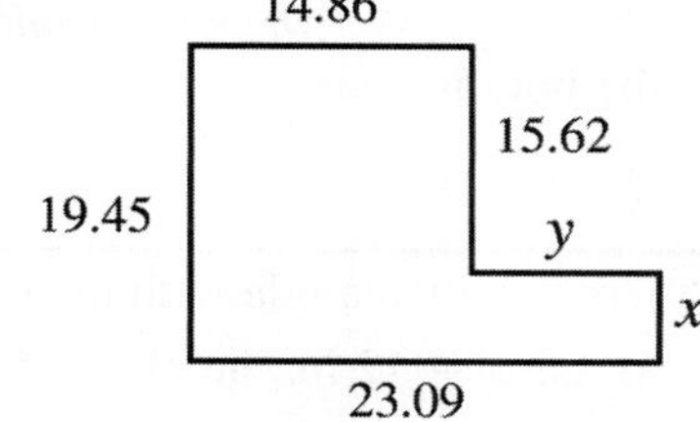

All measures are in meters.

47.

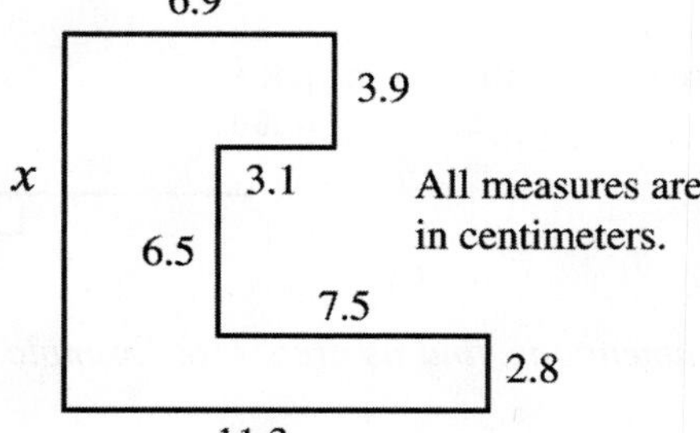

All measures are in centimeters.

48.

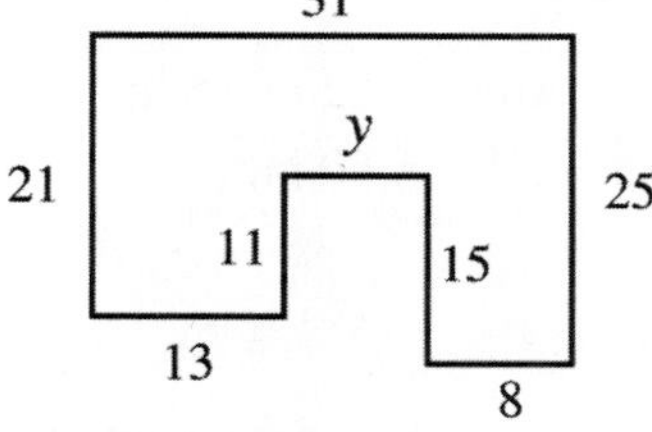

All measures are in feet.

49.

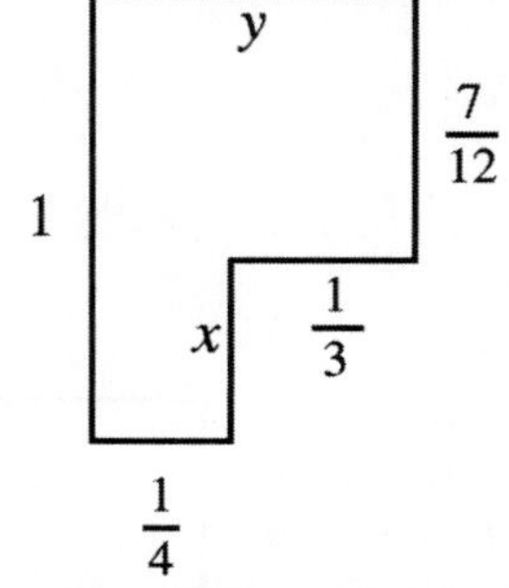

All measures are in inches.

50.

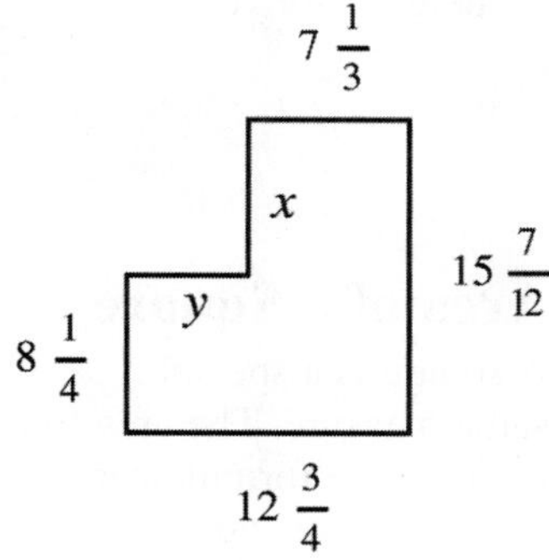

All measures are in feet.

SECTION 7.7 Area

Objectives

In this section, you will learn to:

- Find the area of a rectangle and a square.
- Find the area of a parallelogram.
- Find the area of a triangle.
- Find the area of a trapezoid.
- Find the area of a circle.
- Find the area of unusual shapes.

To successfully complete this section, you need to understand:

- Multiplying Fractions (3.3)
- Multiplying Mixed Numbers (3.3)
- Multiplying Decimals (5.4)
- Perpendicular Lines (7.4)
- Geometric Shapes (7.5)

Introduction

Remember: A plane is a flat surface that extends indefinitely in all directions.

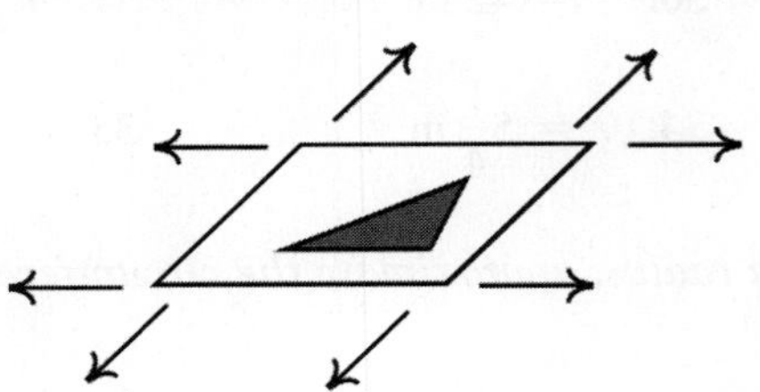

The **area** of a geometric figure is the amount of a region in a plane that the figure covers, measured in square units.

Area of a Rectangle

Recall from Section 1.4 that the area of a rectangle is the product of its length and width: $A = L \times W$.

Sometimes we choose to call the dimensions of a rectangle the *base* and *height*, and **Area** = **base** × **height**.

The height can be measured from anywhere within the rectangle. The height is always *perpendicular* (forms a right angle) to the base, the bottom side.

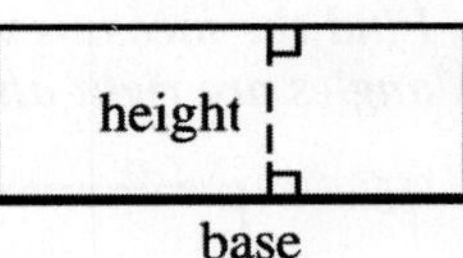

EXAMPLE 1

Draw the rectangle with the given dimensions and find its area.

a) base = 12 in., height = 5 in.

b) base = 6.5 m, height = 4 m

ANSWER:

a) 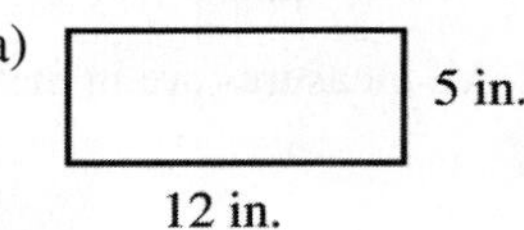

Area = 12 in. · 5 in.
= 60 in.^{2}

b) 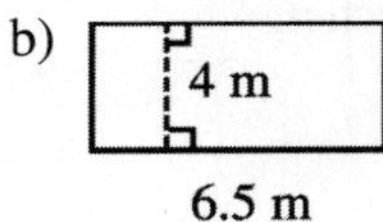

Area = 6.5 m × 4 m
= 26 m^2

$$\begin{array}{r} 6.5 \\ \times\ 4 \\ \hline 26.0 \end{array}$$

YOU TRY IT 1

Sketch a rough drawing of a rectangle with the given dimentions, find its area. Use Example 1 as a guide.

a) base = 15 yd,
height = 9 yd

b) base = 11.25 cm,
height = 9.2 cm

Area of a Square

A square is a special type of rectangle in which all four sides have the same measure. The area formula for a square is the same one for a rectangle, but here the formula can be abbreviated as $A = s \times s = s^2$, where s = the length of each side.

$A = s \times s$

$A = s^2$

s

YOU TRY IT 2

Find the area of a sqare with given side measure.

a) side = 7 ft

b) side = $\frac{5}{8}$ in.

Area of a Parallelogram

The formula for the area of a parallelogram is, just like a rectangle, the product of its base and height. After all, a rectangle is just a special type of parallelogram.

Area of a parallelogram: **Area** = **base** × **height**

However, the height of a parallelogram is perpendicular to both the top side and the bottom side (the base):

height

base

The slanted side measure of a parallelogram is not used in calculating the area.

To demonstrate why a parallelogram has the same area formula as a rectangle, consider this:

We can cut off this triangle and put it on the other side, forming a rectangle.

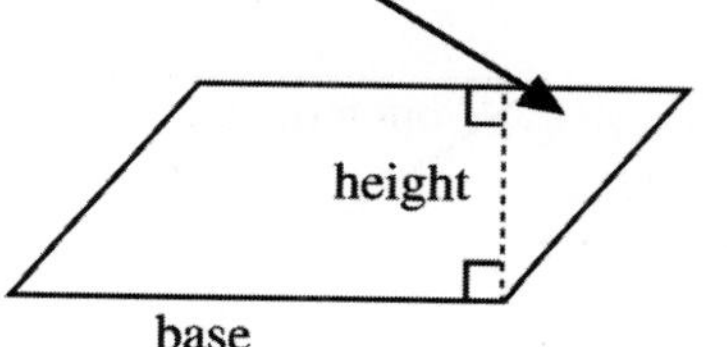

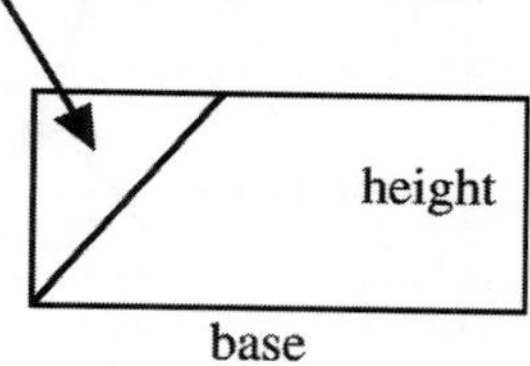

The slanted sides will match up perfectly because they were originally parallel to each other and of the same length. In the rectangle that is formed, the base and height do not change, so

Area of Parallelogram = **base** × **height**

There are some parallelograms where the height needs to be shown outside of the parallelogram. When that happens, imagine extending the base until the height can be drawn perpendicular to it:

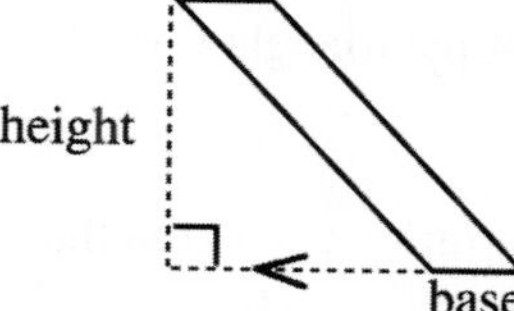

EXAMPLE 2

Find the area of each parallelogram.

a)

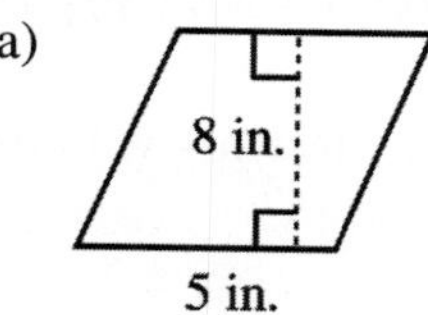

b)

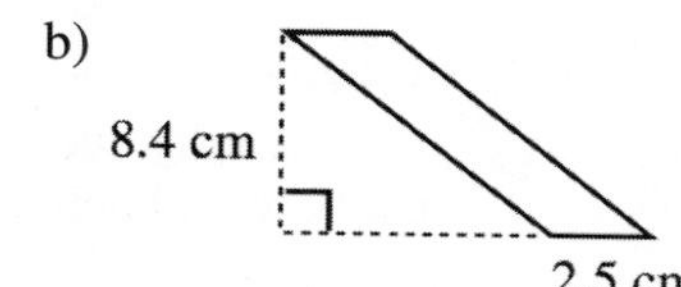

ANSWER: a) Area = 5 in. × 8 in.
= 40 in.^{2}

b) Area = 2.5 cm × 8.4 cm
= 21 cm^2

$$\begin{array}{r} 2.5 \\ \times\ 8.4 \\ \hline 100 \\ +\ 2000 \\ \hline 21.00 \end{array}$$

YOU TRY IT 3

Find the area of each parallelogram. Use Example 2 as a guide.

a) 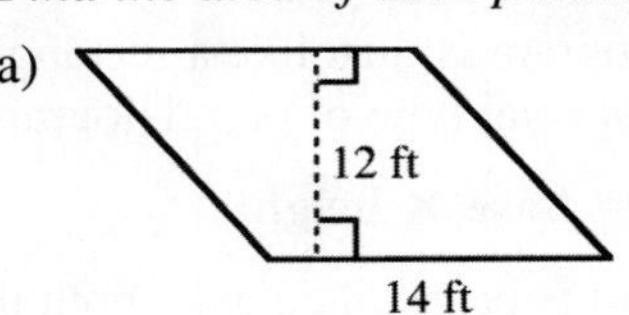

b) 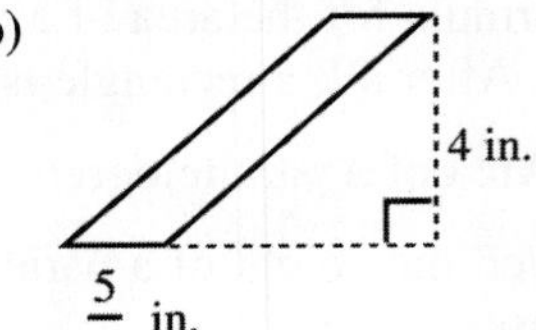

c) 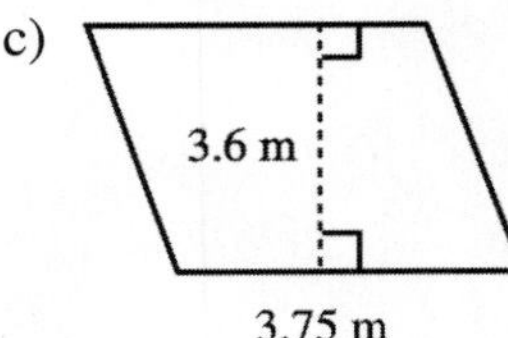

Area of a Triangle

To find the formula for the area of a triangle, we see that two copies of the same triangle can be put together to form a parallelogram.

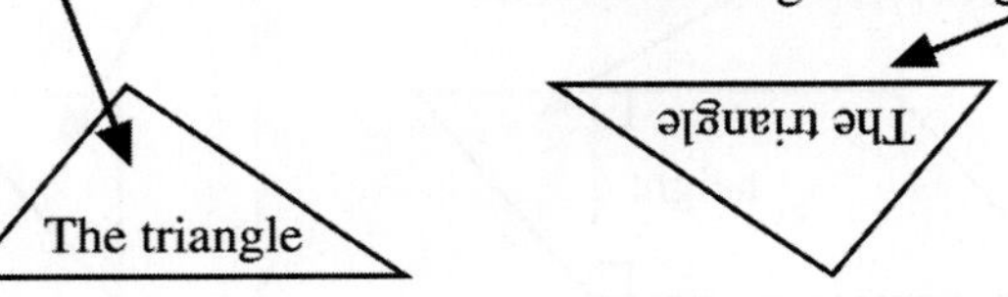

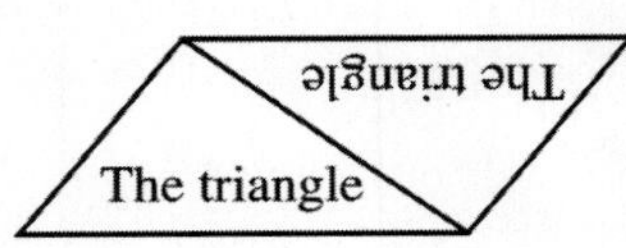

The original triangle has a height, and this is the same height as the new parallelogram.

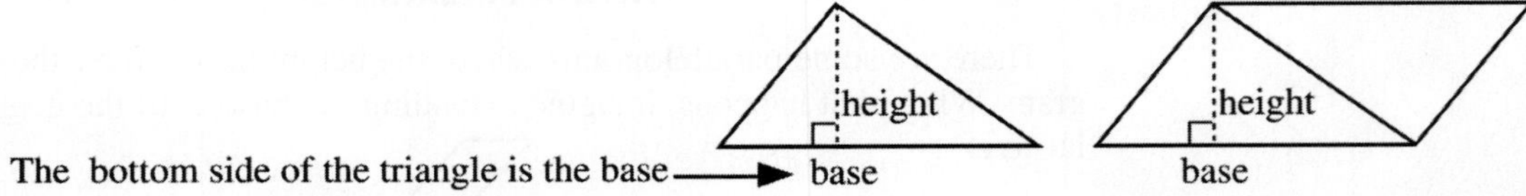

The parallelogram has an area that is base × height, but that parallelogram is twice as large as the original triangle, so the area of the triangle is half of the area of the parallelogram.

Here are two different forms of the formula for the area of a triangle, where b = base and h = height:

(1) $\mathbf{A = \frac{1}{2} \cdot b \cdot h}$ (2) $A = \dfrac{b \cdot h}{2}$

Generally, we choose a form that seems easier to work with based on the numbers given for the base and height.

EXAMPLE 3 Find the area of each triangle.

a)

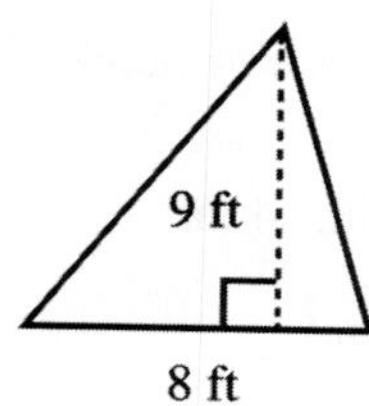

b)

9 m

3 m

PROCEDURE: For each, we need to choose one of the forms of the area of a triangle formula.

ANSWER: a) Let's use form 1:

This is a good form to use because the base is an even number.

$\text{Area} = \frac{1}{2} \cdot 8 \cdot 9$ First, multiply $\frac{1}{2} \cdot 8 = 4$.

$A = 4 \cdot 9$ Now complete the multiplication.

$A = 36 \text{ ft}^2$ The area is stated in square feet.

b) Let's use form 2:

This is a good form to use because neither number is even.

$A = \frac{3 \cdot 9}{2}$ First, multiply the numerator.

$A = \frac{27}{2}$ Simplify this fraction to a mixed number.

$A = 13\frac{1}{2} \text{ m}^2 \text{ or } 13.5 \text{ m}^2$ The area is stated in square meters.

YOU TRY IT 4 *Find the area of each triangle. Use Example 3 as a guide.*

a)

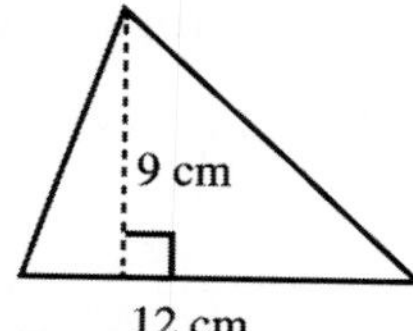

b)

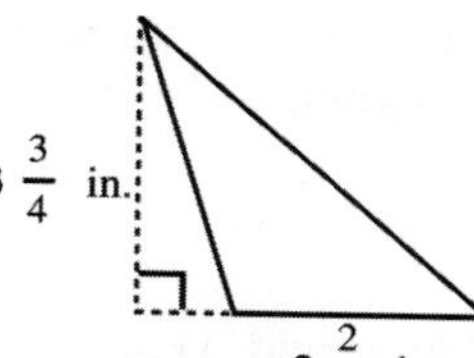

c)

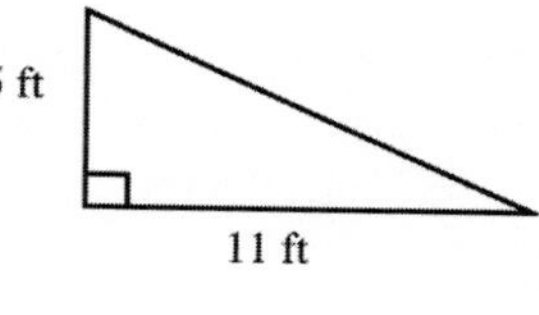

Area of a Right Triangle

The height of a geometric shape is always perpendicular to the base.

In a right triangle, the two sides that form the right angle are perpendicular to each other. This means that one of the sides can be thought of as the base, and the other side can be thought of as the height.

Here is the same triangle rotated in different directions. Notice that we can label either of the perpendicular sides as the base (sometimes it's the 4-inch side, sometimes it's the 6-inch side) and the other as the height.

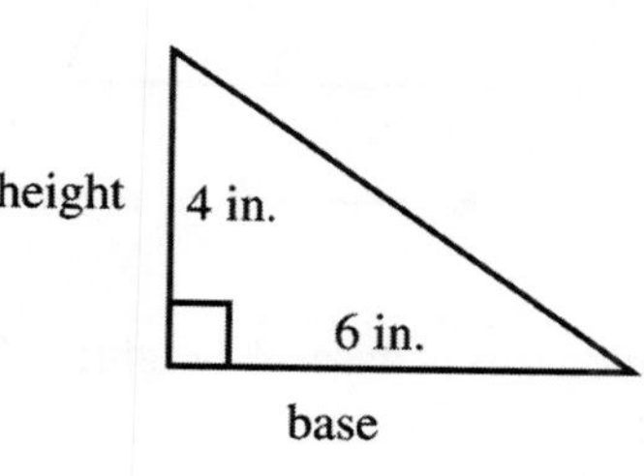

height

6 in.

4 in.

base

height

6 in.

4 in.

base

Since they are the same triangle, they have the same area:

$$A = \frac{1}{2} \times \text{base} \times \text{height}$$

$$A = \frac{1}{2} \cdot 6 \text{ in.} \cdot 4 \text{ in.}$$

$$A = 3 \cdot 4 \text{ in.}^2$$

$$A = 12 \text{ in.}^2$$

YOU TRY IT 5

Find the area of each right triangle.

a)

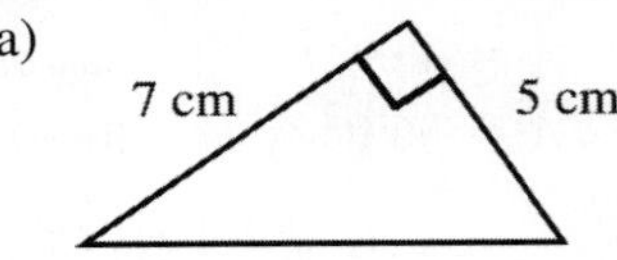

b)

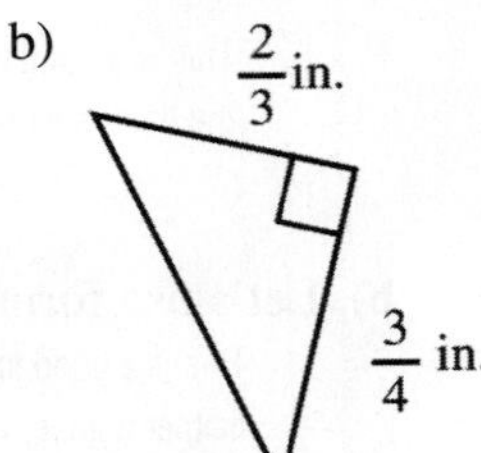

Area of a Trapezoid

Recall that a trapezoid has two bases, a top base, labeled a, and a bottom base, labeled b. A trapezoid also has a height, labeled h.

To find the formula for the area of a trapezoid, we see that two copies of the same trapezoid can be put together to form a parallelogram.

Here is the original trapezoid.

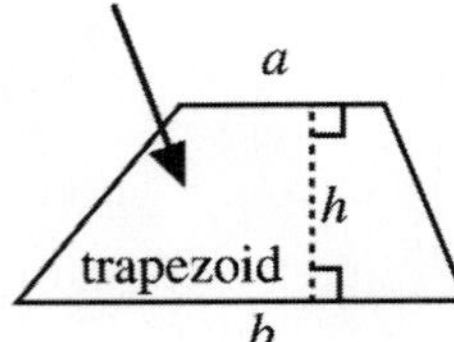

Here is the original trapezoid rotated 180°.

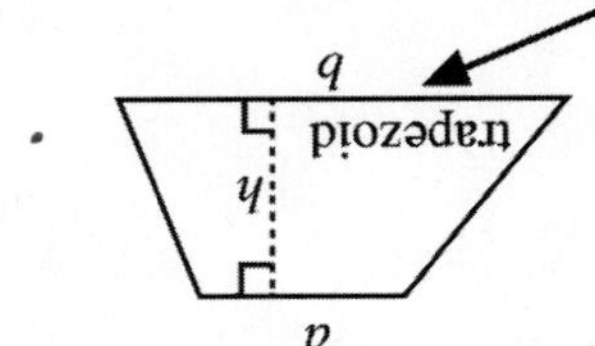

Here are the two trapezoids put together to form a parallelogram.

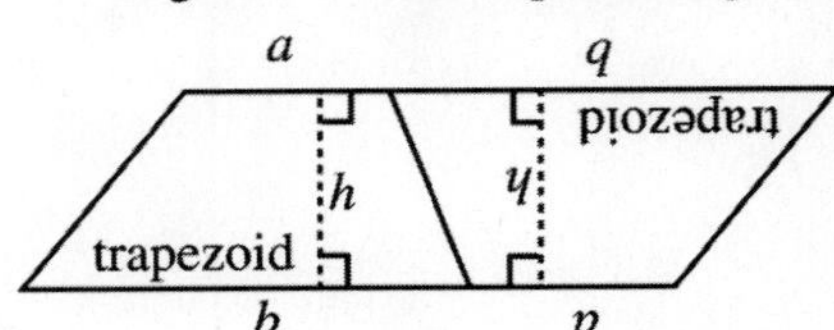

The height of the original trapezoid is the same height as the new parallelogram. Also, the base of the new parallelogram measures $a + b$.

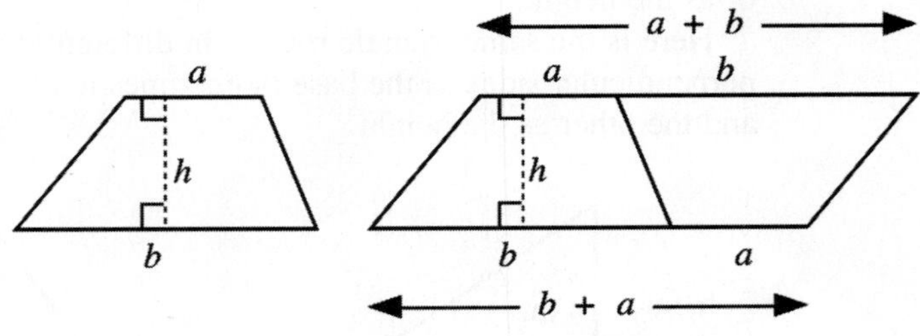

So, the area of this new parallelogram is base × height: $A = (a + b) \cdot h$ or $A = h \cdot (a + b)$.

The parallelogram is, however, twice as large as the original trapezoid, so the area of the trapezoid is half of the area of the new parallelogram.

Here are two different forms of the same formula, Area of a Trapezoid, where a = the top base, b = the bottom base, and h = height.

(1) $A = \frac{1}{2} \cdot h \cdot (a + b)$ (2) $A = \frac{a + b}{2} \cdot h$

EXAMPLE 4 Find the area of the given trapezoid.

a)

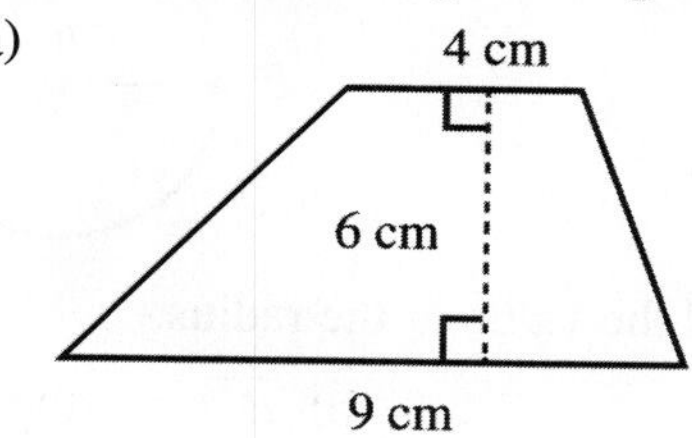

b)

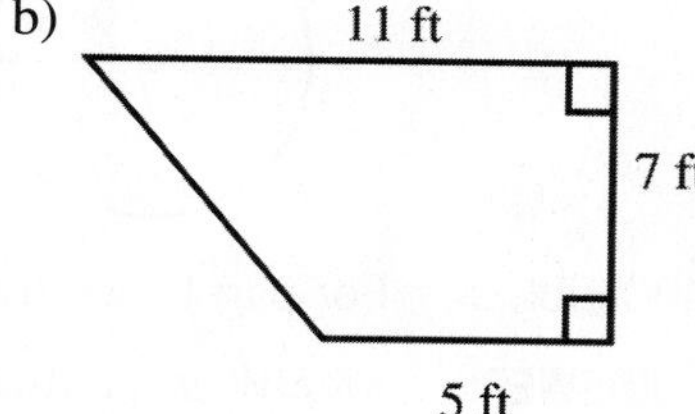

PROCEDURE: For each, we need to choose one of the forms of the area of a trapezoid formula.

In the trapezoid in part b), the right side is perpendicular to both bases (the top *and* the bottom), so that side (which measures 7 ft) is the height.

ANSWER: a) Let's use form (1):

This is a good form to use because h is an even number.

Area $= \frac{1}{2} \cdot 6 \cdot (4 + 9)$ First, add within the parentheses.

$A = \frac{1}{2} \cdot 6 \cdot 13$ Next, multiply $\frac{1}{2} \cdot 6 = 3$.

$A = 3 \cdot 13$

$A = 39 \text{ cm}^2$ The area is stated in square centimeters.

b) Let's use form (2):

This is a good form to use because h is not an even number.

$A = \frac{11 + 5}{2} \cdot 7$ First, add the numerator.

$A = \frac{16}{2} \cdot 7$ Simplify the fraction.

$A = 8 \cdot 7$

$A = 56 \text{ ft}^2$ The area is stated in square feet.

YOU TRY IT 6 *Find the area of each trapezoid. Use Example 4 as a guide.*

a)

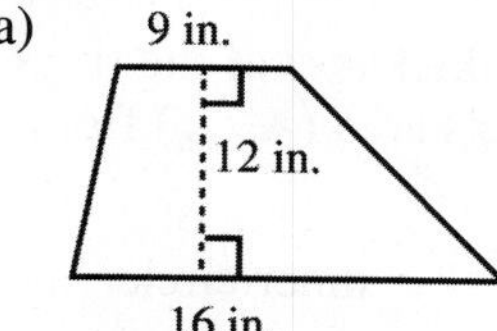

b)

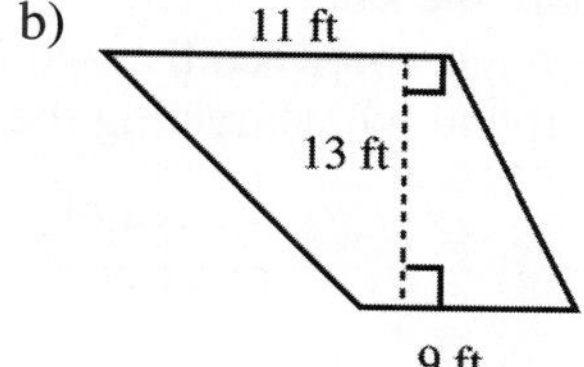

c)

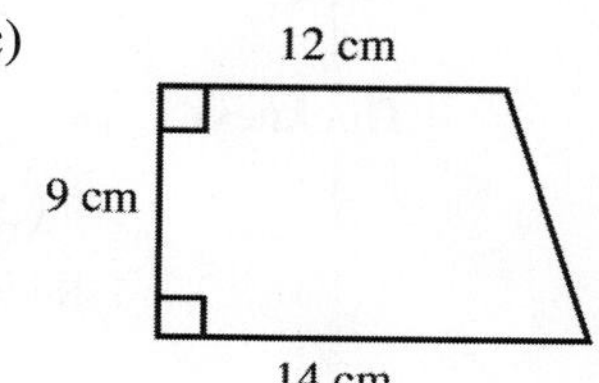

Area of a Circle

It can be shown, using higher level mathematics, that the area of a circle is $A = \pi \cdot r \cdot r$, or $A = \pi \cdot r^2$. Notice that the formula for the area requires the value of the radius, not the diameter; so if you're given the diameter, you must first find the radius before using the area formula.

Also, just as with rectangles and triangles, the area of a circle is stated in square units because when we square the radius, we are also squaring the units of the radius.

For example, if the radius is 2 meters, then

$$A = \pi \cdot (2\text{ m})^2 = \pi \cdot 2\text{ m} \cdot 2\text{ m} = \pi \cdot 4\text{ m}^2.$$

EXAMPLE 5 For each circle, approximate the area. Use $\pi \approx 3.14$ and round the result to the nearest tenth.

a)

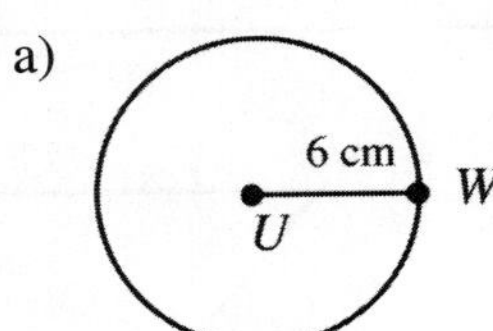

b)

5 ft
B
C
D

PROCEDURE: For part b) we'll need to first find the value of the radius.

ANSWER: a) $\overline{UW}$ is a radius.

$A = \pi \cdot 6^2\text{ cm}^2$

$A \approx 3.14 \times 36\text{ cm}^2$

$A \approx 113.04\text{ cm}^2$

ROUNDED: $A \approx 113.0\text{ cm}^2$

b) $\overline{BD}$ is a diameter. radius $= \frac{5}{2}$ ft $= 2.5$ ft

$A = \pi \cdot (2.5)^2\text{ ft}^2$

$A \approx 3.14 \times 6.25\text{ ft}^2$

$A \approx 19.625\text{ ft}^2$

$A \approx 19.6\text{ ft}^2$

$$\begin{array}{r} 2.5 \\ \times\ 2.5 \\ \hline 125 \\ 500 \\ \hline 6.25 \end{array}$$

YOU TRY IT 7 *For each circle, approximate the area using $\pi \approx 3.14$; round the result to the tenths place. Use Example 5 as a guide.*

a)

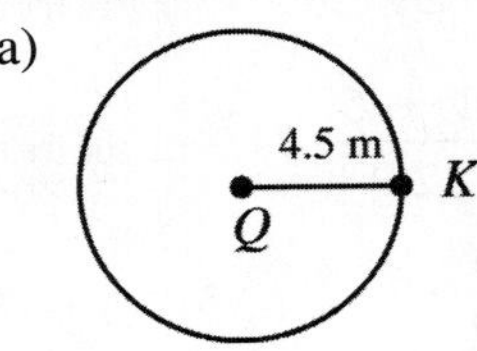

b)

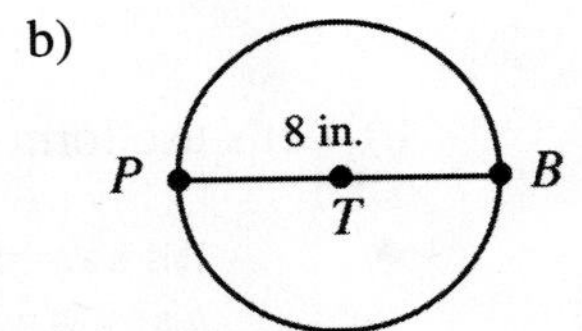

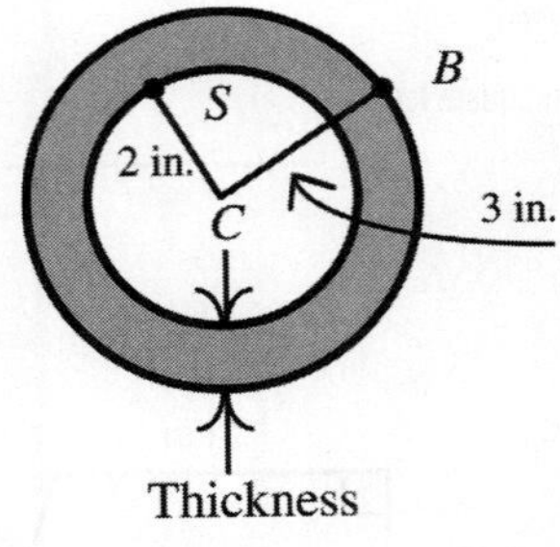

Subtracting Areas

Sometimes the area of interest isn't from a single geometric figure. For example, consider a ring. A ring is, typically, the region between two circles with the same center but different radii.

In the diagram at left, the radius $\overline{CS}$ (2 in.) is shorter than the radius $\overline{CB}$ (3 in.), and the circles share the same center.

The region between the two circles, the thickness of the rings, is shaded, and its area (A_{ring}) can be found by subtracting the inner circle's area (A_{inner}) from the outer circle's area (A_{outer}):

Area of shaded ring	=	Area of outer circle	−	Area of inner circle
		↓		↓
A_{ring}	=	A_{outer}	−	A_{inner}
A_{ring}	=	$\pi \cdot (3)^2$	−	$\pi \cdot (2)^2$
A_{ring}	≈	28.26	−	12.56
A_{ring}	≈	15.7 square inches, or 15.7 in.^{2}		

Outer area:
$\pi \times (3)^2$
$\approx 3.14 \times 9 = 28.26$

Inner area:
$\pi \times (2)^2$
$\approx 3.14 \times 4 = 12.56$

Subtract:
$$\begin{array}{r} 28.26 \\ -\ 12.56 \\ \hline 15.70 \end{array}$$

EXAMPLE 6 Find the area of the shaded region, formed by a circle inside of a square. Use $\pi \approx 3.14$ and round the result to the nearest tenth.

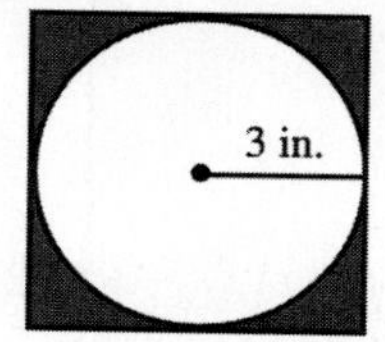

PROCEDURE: Find the area of both the circle and the square and subtract the inner area (circle) from the outer area (square).

Area of shaded region =

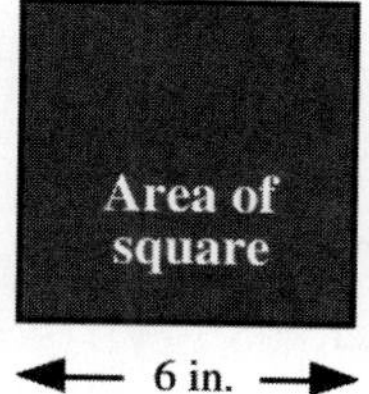

minus
−

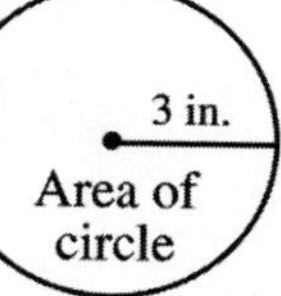

ANSWER: Area of square $= 6^2 = 36$. Area of circle $= \pi \times (3)^2 \approx 3.14 \times 9 = 28.26$.

Subtract: Area $\approx 36 - 28.26 = 7.74$; rounded, Area ≈ 7.7 in.^{2}

Caution Do not round until the last step of the process.

YOU TRY IT 8 *For each figure, approximate the area of the shaded region. Use $\pi \approx 3.14$ and round the result to the tenths place. Use Example 6 as a guide.*

a)

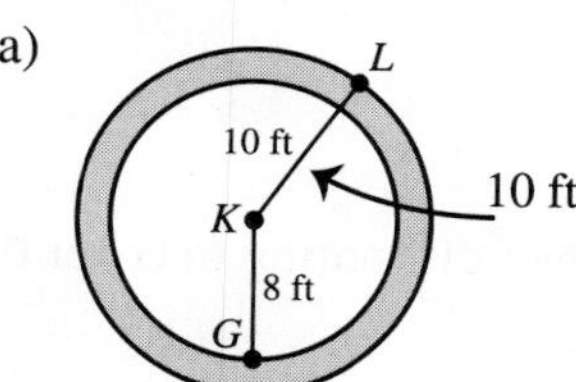

b)

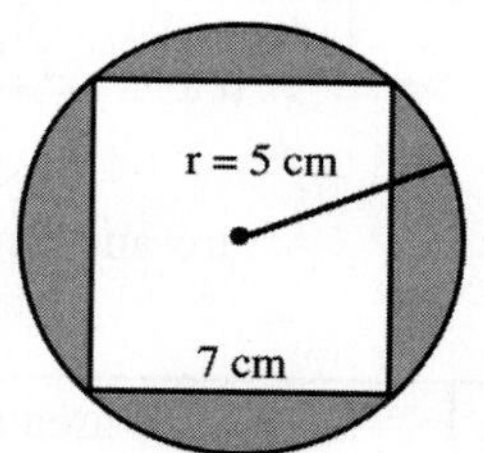

Areas of Unusual Shapes

Consider this situation: Arturo and Terry are laying wood flooring in Janet's living room. They must measure the room (in square feet) to know how much flooring they'll need. According to the diagram and dimensions shown, how many square feet of flooring is needed to cover the whole room?

Here is the original living room floor plan:

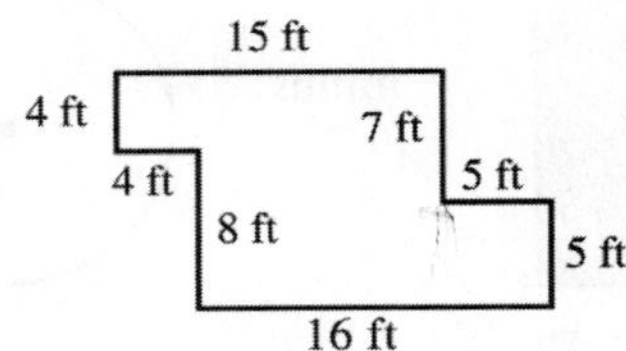

We can break up the room into three rectangles, each having its own dimensions and area.

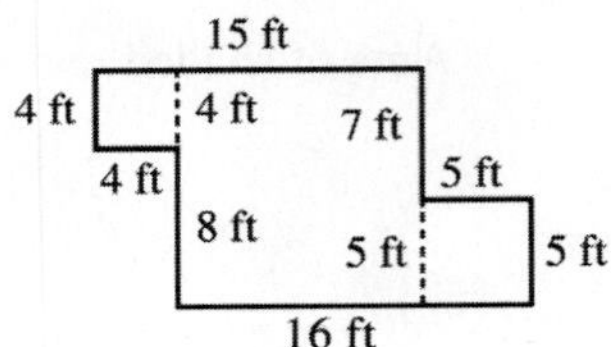

Caution We need to be careful when pulling the rectangles apart. New dimensions will appear that weren't originally shown, such as the 11 ft across the top of the large rectangle and the 12 ft height of the large rectangle.

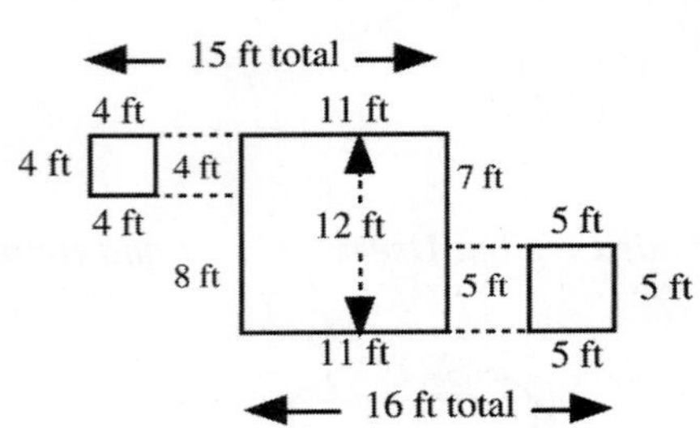

Areas of the rectangles

4 ft by 4 ft rectangle: $A = 4 \times 4 = 16 \text{ ft}^2$

12 ft by 11 ft rectangle: $A = 12 \times 11 = 132 \text{ ft}^2$

5 ft by 5 ft rectangle: $A = 5 \times 5 = 25 \text{ ft}^2$

Total Area:

$$\begin{array}{r} 16 \\ 132 \\ +\ 25 \\ \hline 173 \end{array}$$

Arturo and Terry will need 173 square feet of flooring to cover the whole room.

EXAMPLE 7 Find the area of the polygon with the given dimensions.

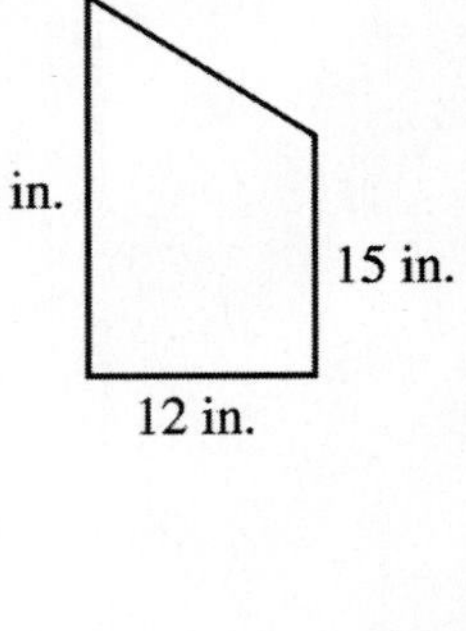

PROCEDURE: Break up the polygon into a rectangle with a triangle on top.

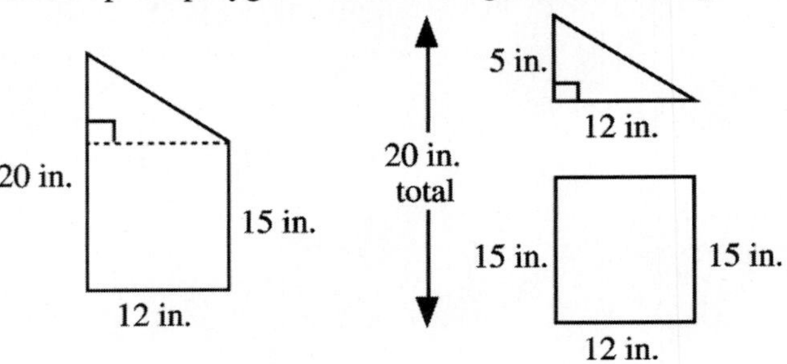

Area of triangle:

$A = \frac{1}{2} \times 12 \times 5 = 30 \text{ in.}^2$

Area of rectangle:

$A = 12 \times 15 = 180 \text{ in.}^2$

Total Area:

$$\begin{array}{r} 30 \\ +\ 180 \\ \hline 210 \end{array}$$

ANSWER: The area of the polygon is 210 square inches.

YOU TRY IT 9 *Find the area of each polygon. Use Example 7 as a guide.*

a)

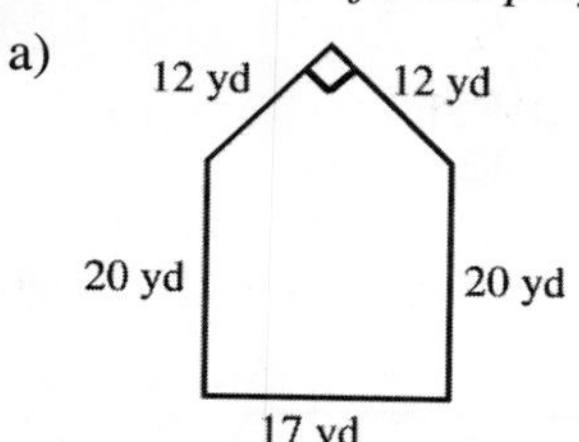

b)

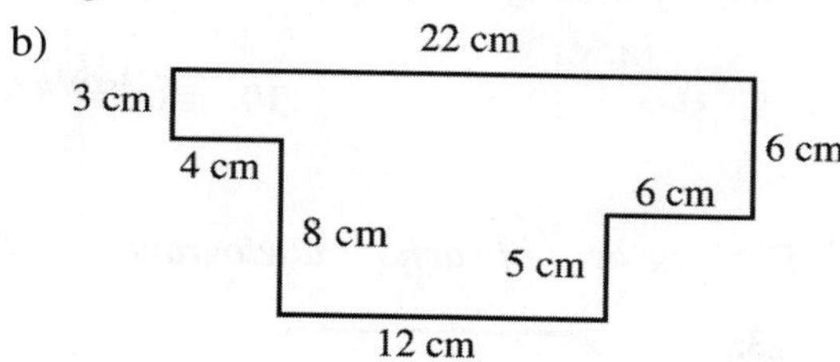

You Try It Answers: Section 7.7

YTI 1 a) 15 yd by 9 yd rectangle; $A = 135 \text{ yd}^2$

b) 11.25 cm by 9.2 cm rectangle; $A = 103.5 \text{ cm}^2$

YTI 2 a) $A = 49 \text{ ft}^2$ b) $A = \frac{25}{64} \text{ in.}^2$

YTI 3 a) $A = 168 \text{ ft}^2$ b) $A = 2\frac{1}{2} \text{ in.}^2$ c) $A = 13.5 \text{ m}^2$

YTI 4 a) $A = 54 \text{ cm}^2$ b) $A = 5 \text{ in.}^2$ c) $A = 27.5 \text{ ft}^2$

YTI 5 a) $A = 17.5 \text{ cm}^2$ b) $A = \frac{1}{4} \text{ in.}^2$

YTI 6 a) $A = 150 \text{ in.}^2$ b) $A = 130 \text{ ft}^2$ c) $A = 117 \text{ cm}^2$

YTI 7 a) $A \approx 63.6 \text{ m}^2$ b) $A \approx 50.2 \text{ in.}^2$

YTI 8 a) $A \approx 113.0 \text{ ft}^2$ b) $A \approx 29.5 \text{ cm}^2$

YTI 9 a) $A = 412 \text{ yd}^2$ b) $A = 180 \text{ cm}^2$

Focus Exercises: Section 7.7

Find the area of each rectangle with given dimensions. h = height and b = base

1. $b = 12$ yd, $h = 8$ yd

2. $h = 9$ yd, $b = 23$ yd

3. $b = \frac{7}{8}$ in., $h = \frac{1}{4}$ in.

4. $b = \frac{3}{4}$ in., $h = \frac{2}{3}$ in.

5. $h = 5.2$ cm, $b = 8.5$ cm

6. $b = 10.25$ m, $h = 5.2$ m

7. $h = 1\frac{1}{3}$ ft, $b = 3\frac{3}{8}$ ft

8. $b = 5\frac{1}{4}$ ft, $h = 2\frac{2}{3}$ ft

Find the area of each square with given side measure.

9. side = 13 ft

10. side = 4.5 cm

11. side = $\frac{7}{12}$ in.

12. side = $2\frac{1}{4}$ ft

Find the area of each parallelogram.

13.

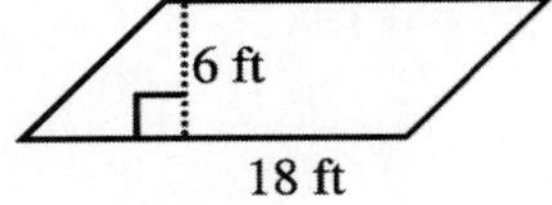

14.

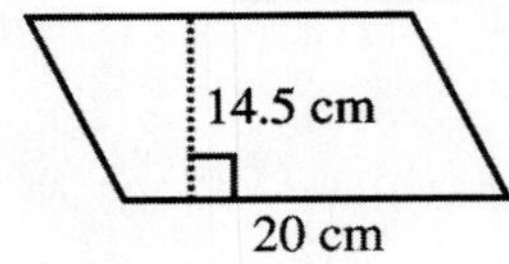

15.

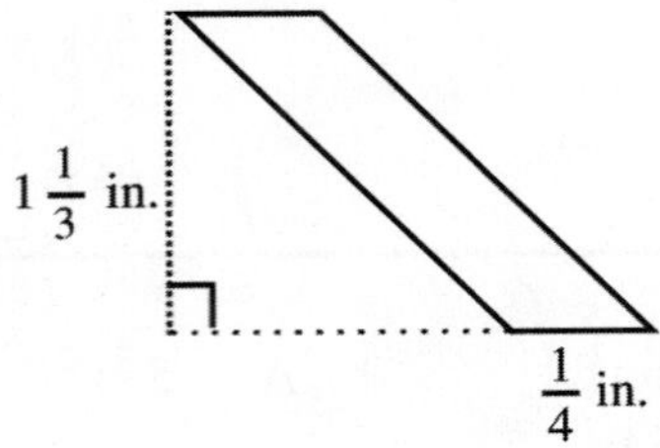

16.

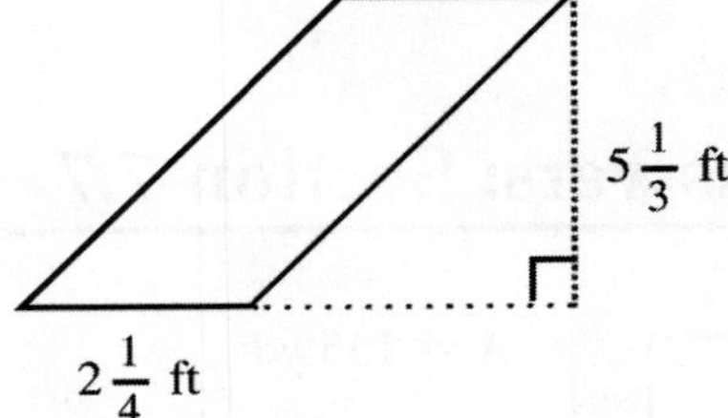

Find the area of each triangle.

17.

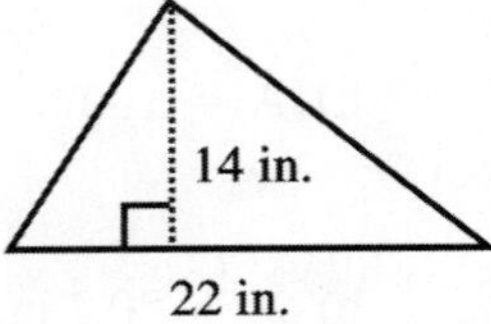

18.

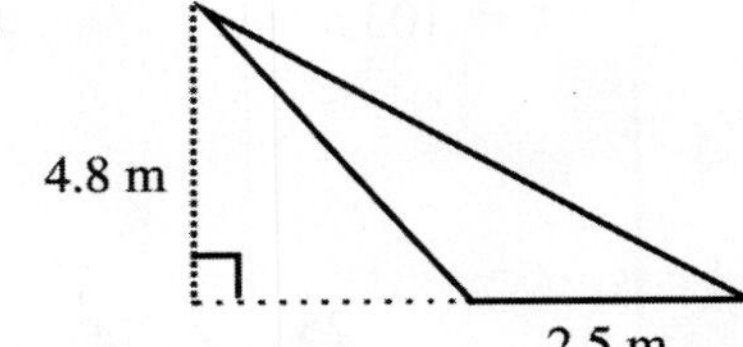

19.

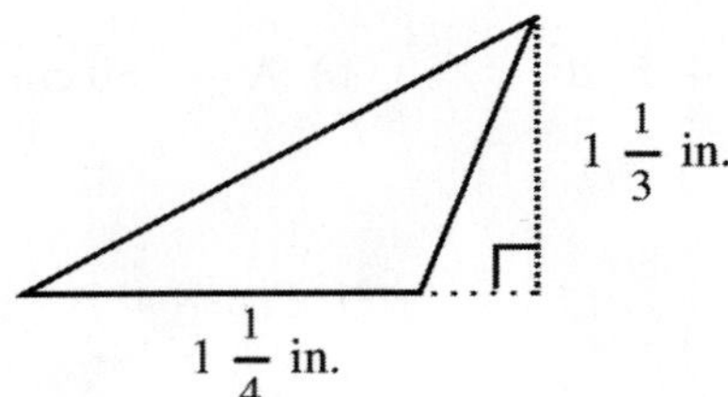

20.

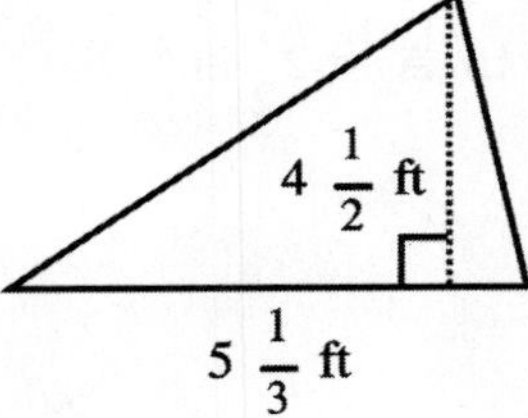

Find the area of each right triangle.

21.

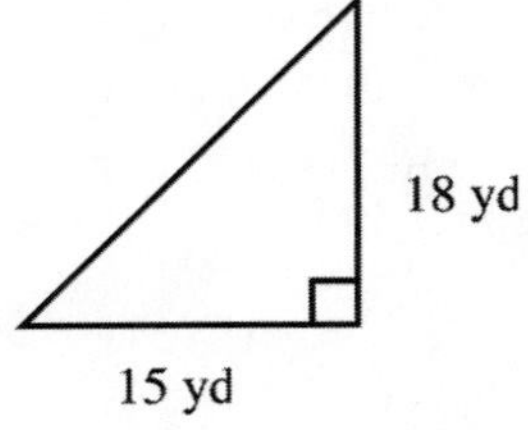

22.

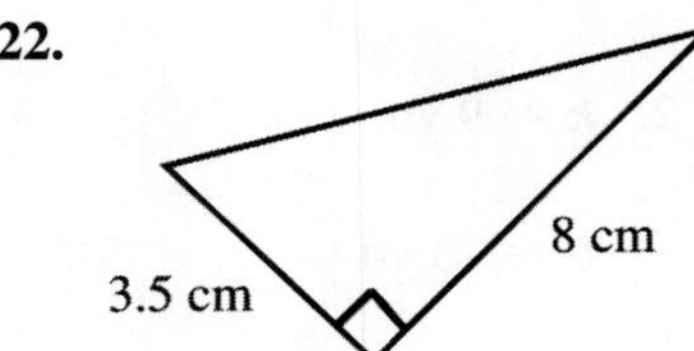

23.

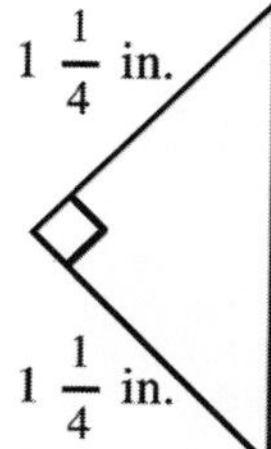

24.

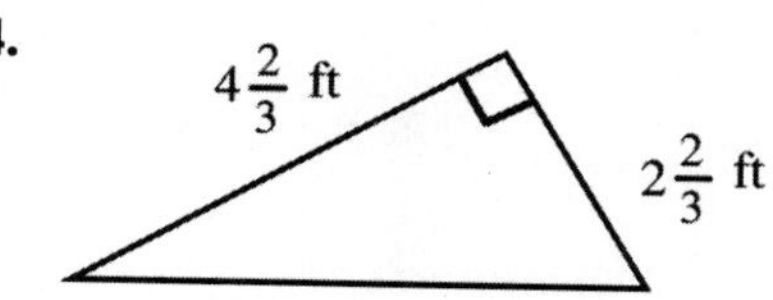

Find the area of each trapezoid.

25.

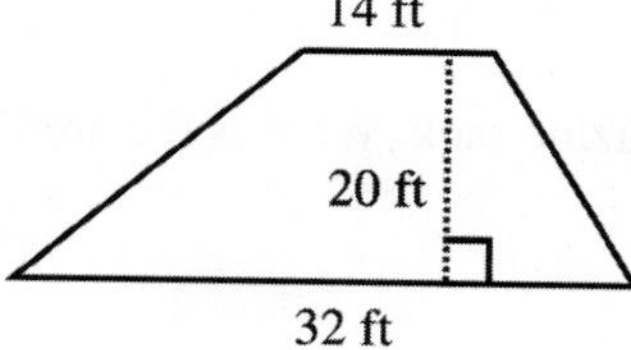

26.

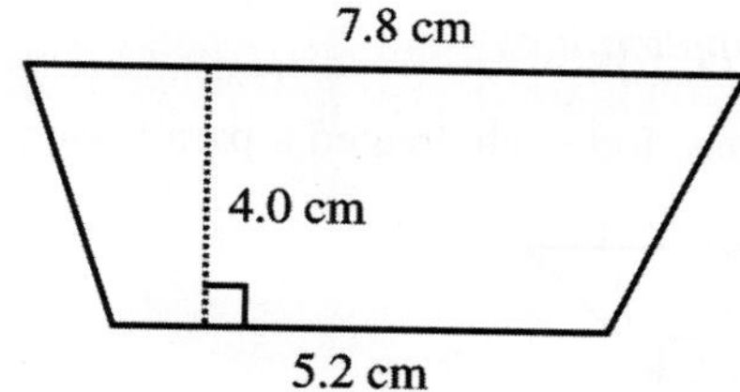

27.

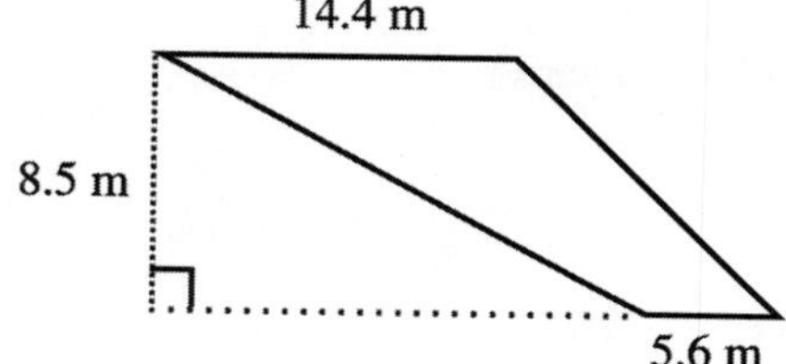

28.

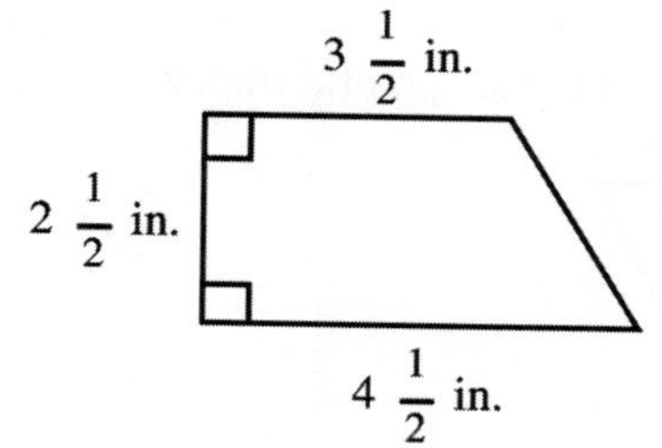

Approximate the area of each circle with given radius. Use $\pi \approx 3.14$ and round the result to the tenths place.

29. $r = 3$ in. **30.** $r = 5$ in. **31.** $r = 1.2$ m **32.** $r = 2.5$ m

Approximate the area of each circle with given diameter. Use $\pi \approx 3.14$ and round the result to the tenths place.

33. $d = 8$ yd **34.** $d = 12$ yd **35.** $d = 2.2$ cm **36.** $d = 3$ cm

Find the area of each polygon.

37.

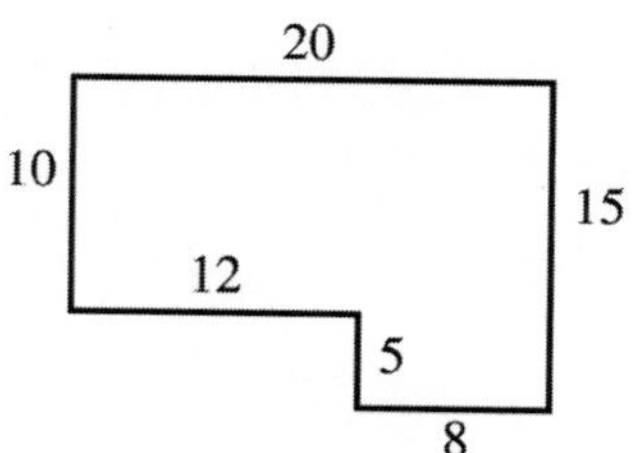

All measures are in inches.

38.

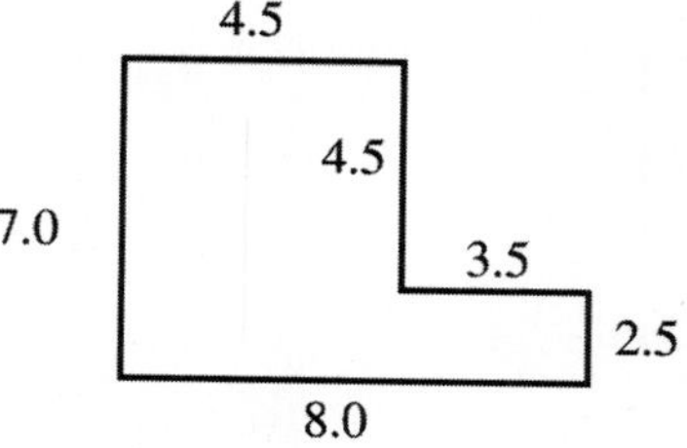

All measures are in meters.

39.

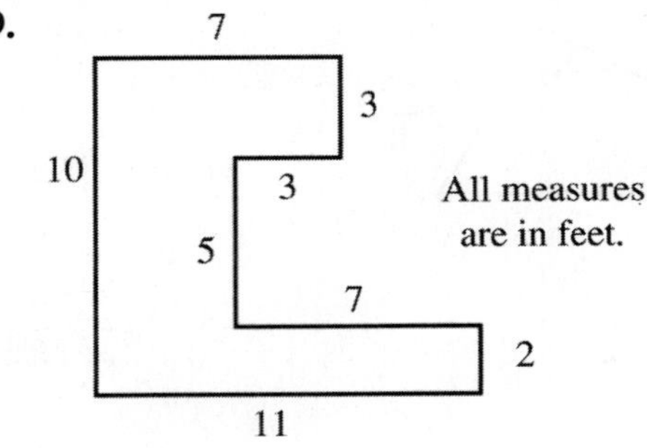

40.

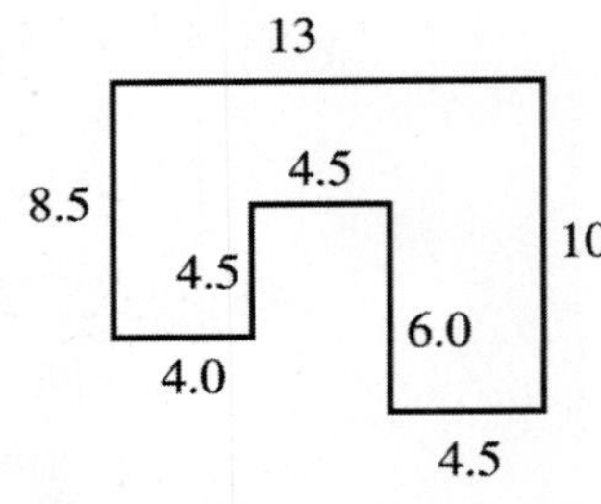

Solve the following applications.

41. In her design class, Rebekah created a parallelogram shape for the side of a magazine rack. What is the area of this side?

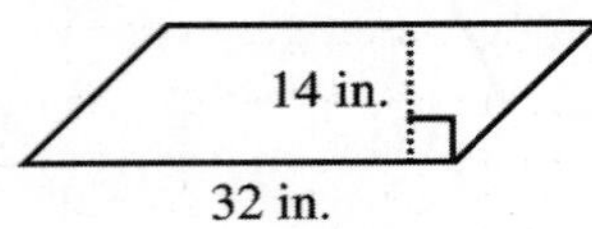

42. Kevin's backyard is in the shape of a trapezoid. What is the area of Kevin's backyard?

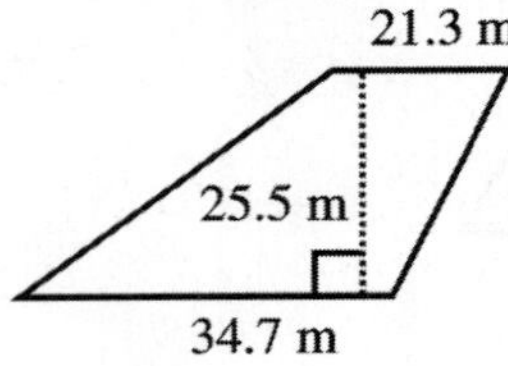

43. A bedroom is in the shape of a rectangle. What is the area of this room?

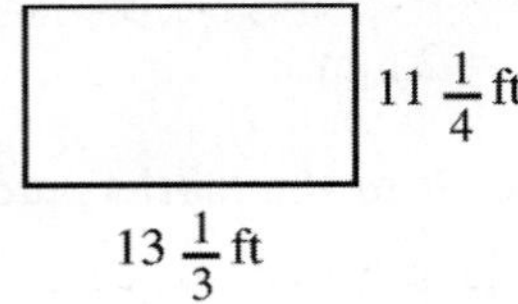

44. The dimensions of home plate for professional baseball are shown here. What is the area of home plate?

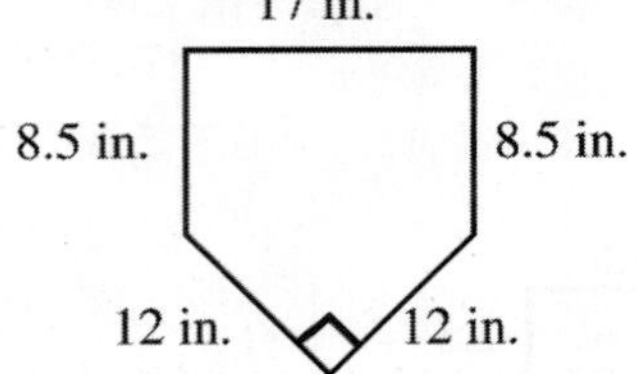

Solve the following applications. Use $\pi \approx 3.14$, and round each result to the nearest whole number.

45. A clock face has a diameter of 20 inches. What is the area of this clock face?

46. A circular table top has a diameter of 2 feet. What is the area of this table top?

47. A hot tub has a circular cover with a diameter of 5 feet. What is the area of this hot tub cover?

48. Nate's drum set contains a drum that is 14 inches in diameter. What is the area of the top of that drum?

Answer as indicated. Round each result to the nearest tenth.

49. Find the area of the ring.

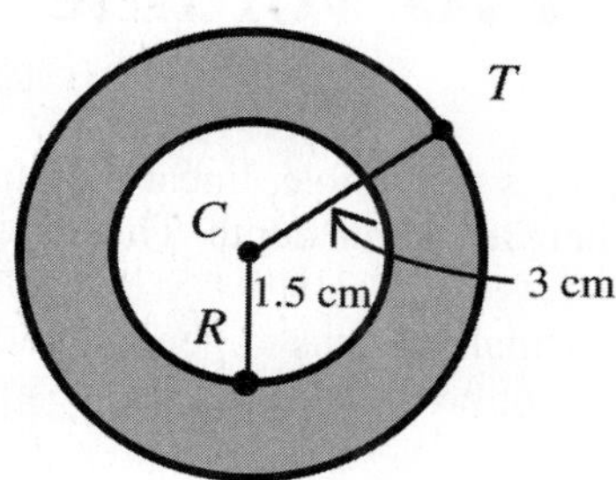

50. Find the area of the shaded region.

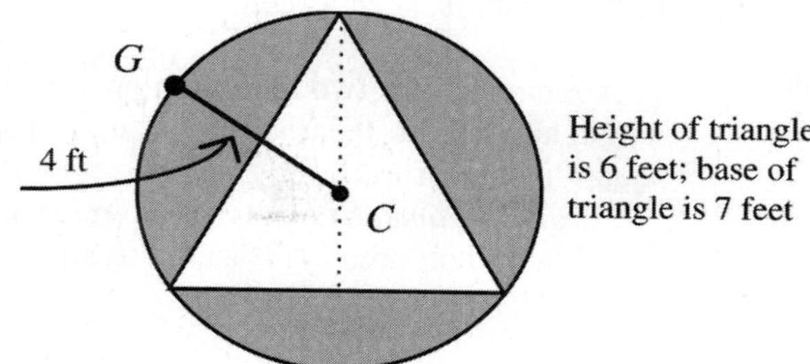

51. A farmer created a small "crop circle," that is a square inside of a circle. The square contains the crop of wheat and the circular part is flat. The circle has a radius of 25 meters and the square has a side length of 35 meters. What is the area of the flat region within this crop circle?

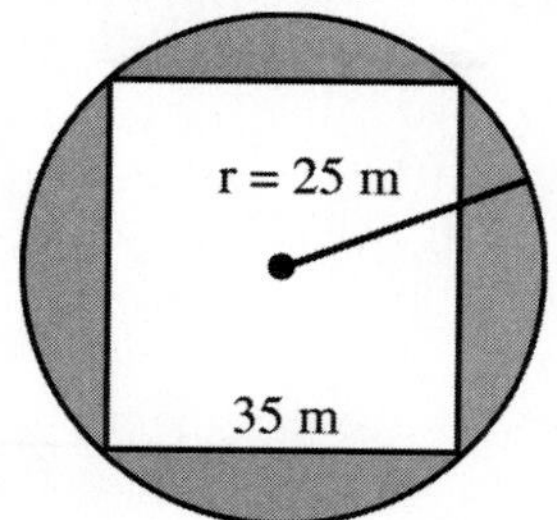

52. LaTanya is building a model of the solar system. To represent the rings of Saturn she is using a single piece of Styrofoam in the shape of a flat ring. The inner radius of the ring is 3 inches and its outer radius is 5 inches. What is the area of the top of the ring?

SECTION 7.8 Volume

Objectives

In this section, you will learn to:

- Recognize different dimensions.
- Find the volume of a rectangular solid.
- Apply the volume formulas for a cylinder, cone, pyramid, and sphere.

To successfully complete this section, you need to understand:

- Multiplying fractions (3.3)
- Multiplying decimals (5.4)
- Parts of a circle (7.5)
- Area (7.7)

Introduction

In geometry, **dimension** is the visible, linear measure of an object, including its length or breadth, its width or height, and its depth. There are a variety of geometric figures that demonstrate dimension:

A *point* is infinitely small and has no length, width, or depth. Points have no dimension; they cannot be measured. •

A *line segment* has length but no height or depth. A line segment has only one measurement, one dimension. Its measure is in simple units, such as centimeters.

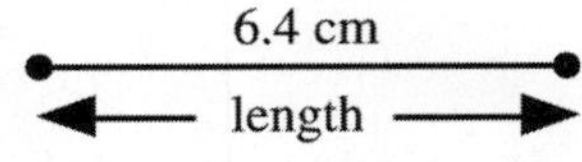

A *rectangle* has two measurements, *two* dimensions, length and height. Its area is measured in square units, such as square inches or in.^{2}

Parallelograms, triangles, and *circles* are also two-dimensional, and their area is measured in square units, or units^2.

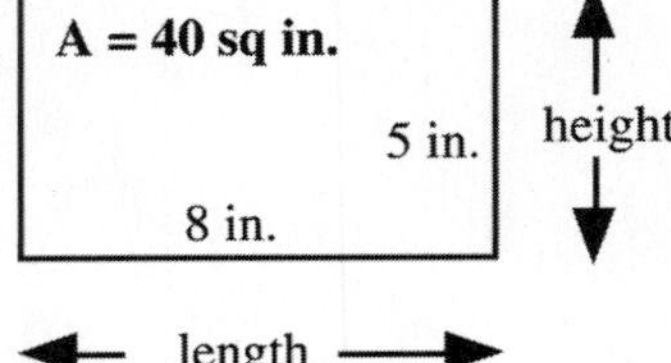

Volume of a Rectangular Solid

A **solid** is a *three-dimensional* object. The box shown here is a solid because it has three distinct measures—three distinct dimensions—length, height, and depth.

Its **volume**—a measure indicating the amount a solid (such as a box) can hold—is the product of those three dimensions:

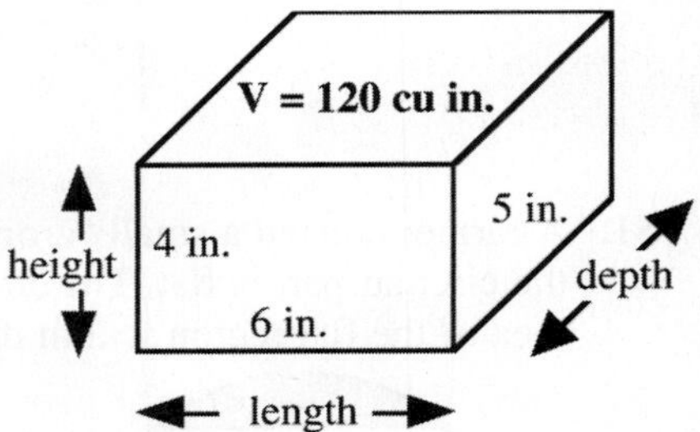

$$\begin{aligned} \text{Volume} &= \text{length} \times \text{depth} \times \text{height} \\ V &= 6 \text{ in.} \times 5 \text{ in.} \times 4 \text{ in.} \\ V &= 6 \times 5 \times 4 \times \text{in.} \times \text{in.} \times \text{in.} \\ V &= 120 \text{ in.}^3 \end{aligned}$$

This is read, "The volume is 120 cubic inches."

For three-dimensional figures, we commonly refer to the flat bottom as the **base**. The base is always two-dimensional. In the case of a box, the base is the rectangle formed by the length and the depth. In some solid figures, the base is the flat surface on the top.

height

base

depth

length

Many of the volume formulas presented in this section require us to find the area of the base. In a volume formula, the **Base** (with a capital B) means the area of the two-dimensional base of the solid figure.

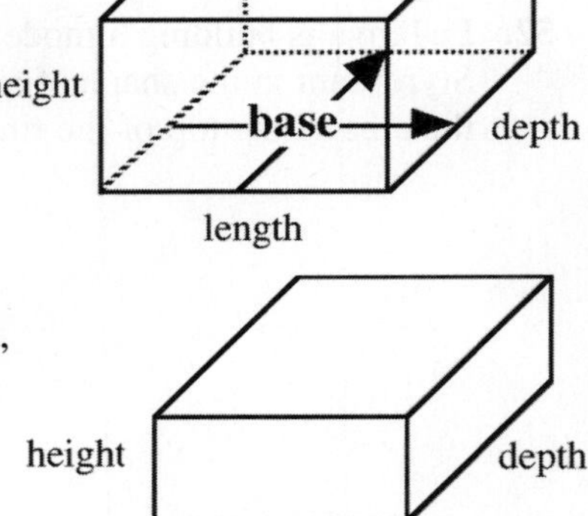

A box in which all three measures are the same is called a **cube**. The cube at right has a volume of one cubic cm. We'll use this cube as a building block to help us visually understand the volume of a box.

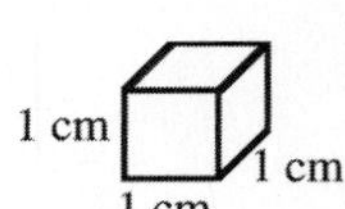

We can put many of these cubes together to form one layer. This layer has a volume of 12 cubic cm:

$V = 4 \text{ cm} \times 3 \text{ cm} \times 1 \text{ cm} = 12 \text{ cm}^3$

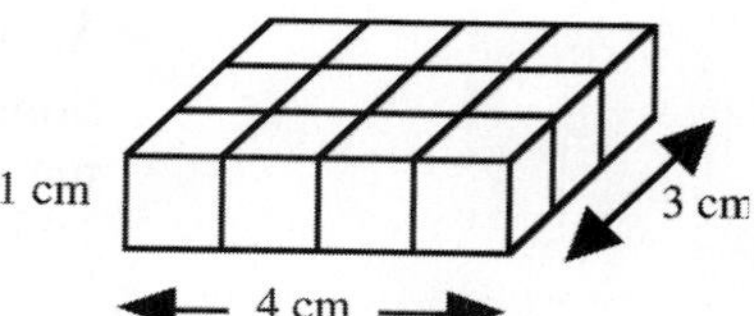

We can stack more cubes on top of this layer to begin to form another layer:

This second layer creates a rectangular solid that has a volume of 24 cubic cm:

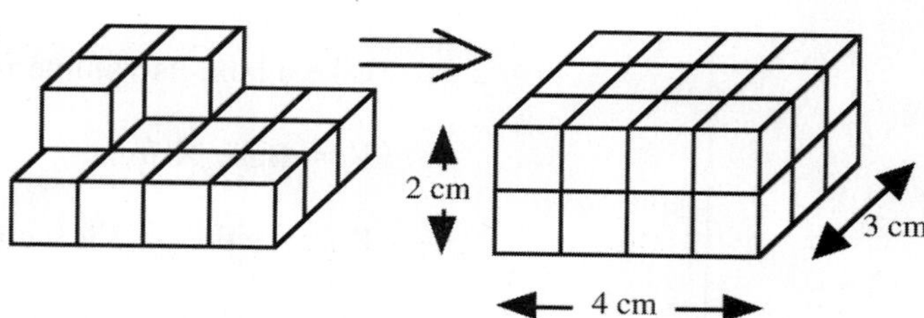

$V = 4 \text{ cm} \times 3 \text{ cm} \times 2 \text{ cm} = 24 \text{ cm}^3$

We could think of the volume of a box as:

Volume	=	(length × depth)	×	height
Volume	=	the area of the base (**Base**)	×	the height (**h**)
V	=	**Base** × ***h***		

EXAMPLE 1

Find the volume of this box:

PROCEDURE: Apply the volume of a box formula.
Remember, the volume will be in cubic inches.
Base = 8 in. × 15 in. = 120 sq in.
height = 6 in.

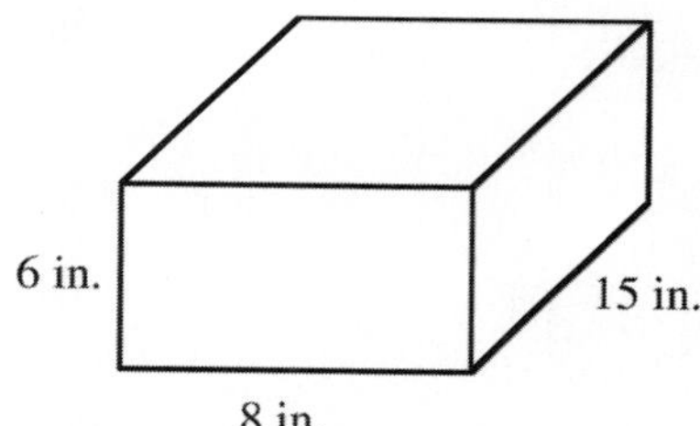

ANSWER: $V = 120 \times 6$ cubic inches

$V = 720 \text{ in.}^3$

The volume of the box is 720 cubic inches.

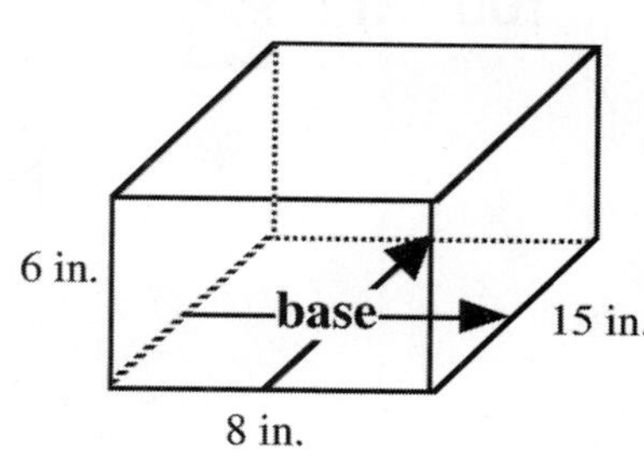

YOU TRY IT 1

Given the dimensions of each box, find the volume. Use Example 1 as a guide. (First find the Base.)

a)

8 cm

25 cm

20 cm

b)

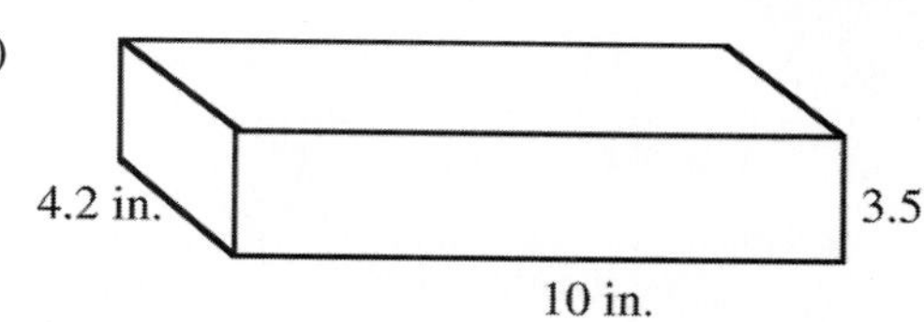

Volumes of Other Solids

Some common solids are the cylinder, cone, pyramid, and sphere. Each has its own volume formula.

The formulas for the cylinder, cone, and pyramid require finding the area of the base.

A **cylinder** is the rounded version of a box, such as a can of soup.

Like a box, its volume is Base × height.

$V = \text{Base} \times h$

Because the base is a circle, the base area is $\pi \times r^2$.

This makes the volume formula $\boxed{V = \pi \times r^2 \times h}$

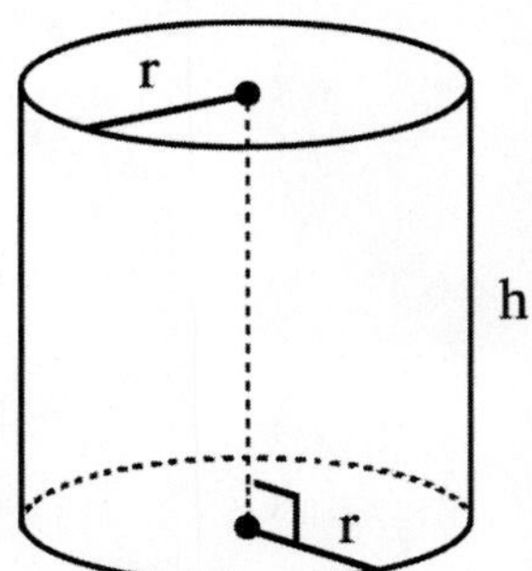

EXAMPLE 2 Find the volume of this cylinder. Use $\pi \approx 3.14$ and round to the nearest tenth.

PROCEDURE: Apply the volume of a cylinder formula. The radius is 3 inches and the height is 8 inches, so the volume will be in cubic inches.

ANSWER: $V = \pi \times 3^2 \times 8 \text{ in.}^3$ Remember the order of operations and apply the exponent to 3 first.

$V \approx 3.14 \times 9 \times 8 \text{ in.}^3$

$V \approx 226.08 \text{ in.}^3$

The volume of the cylinder is about 226.1 cubic inches.

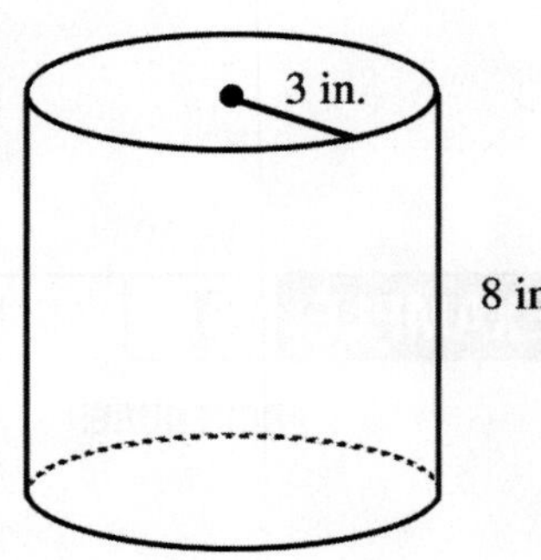

YOU TRY IT 2 *Find the volume of each cylinder. Use $\pi \approx 3.14$ and round the result to the nearest tenth. Use Example 2 as a guide.*

a)

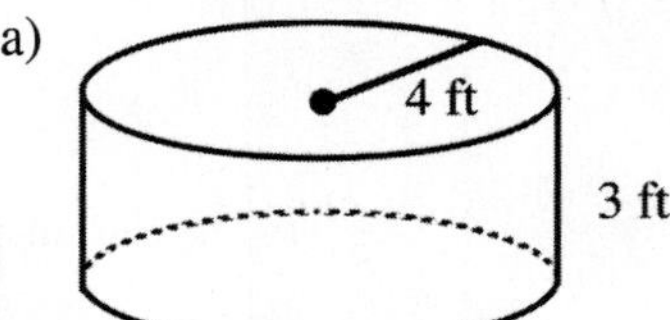

b)

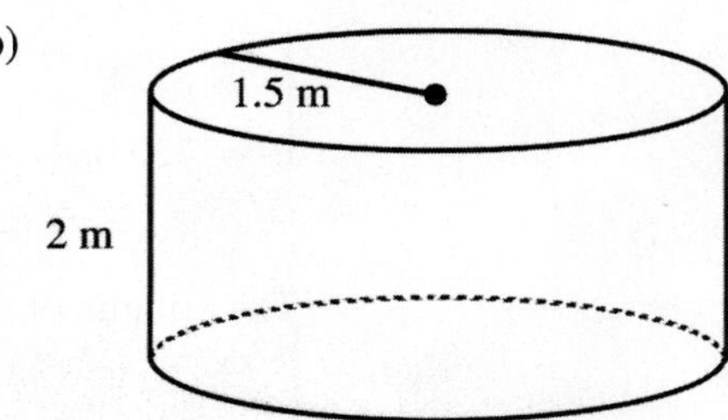

Here are two ways to view a **cone**: like the orange cones used on the highway in a construction zone, or like a snow-cone cup.

Either way, the base is a circle and has base radius r.

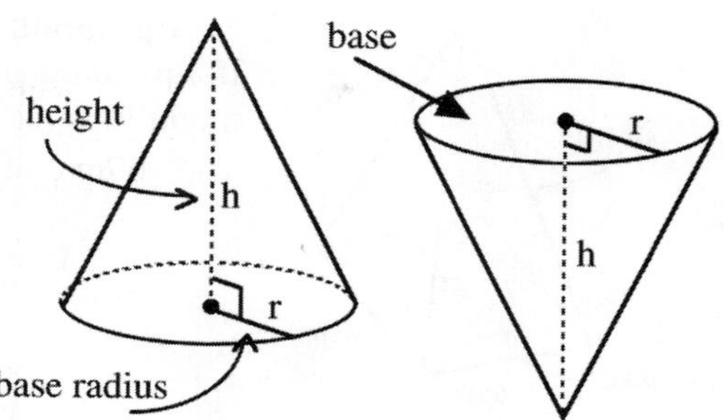

If a cylinder and a cone have the same radius and the same height, then we might imagine the cone fitting inside of the cylinder.

The volume of a cone is $\frac{1}{3}$ of the volume of such a cylinder:

$$V = \frac{1}{3} \times \textbf{Base} \times h \rightarrow \boxed{V = \frac{1}{3} \times \pi \times r^2 \times h}$$

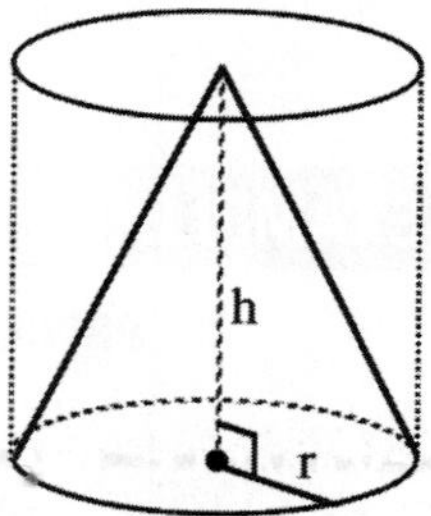

EXAMPLE 3 Find the volume of this cone. Use $\pi \approx 3.14$.

PROCEDURE: Apply the volume of a cone formula. The base radius is 3 centimeters and the height is 8 centimeters, so the volume will be in cubic centimeters.

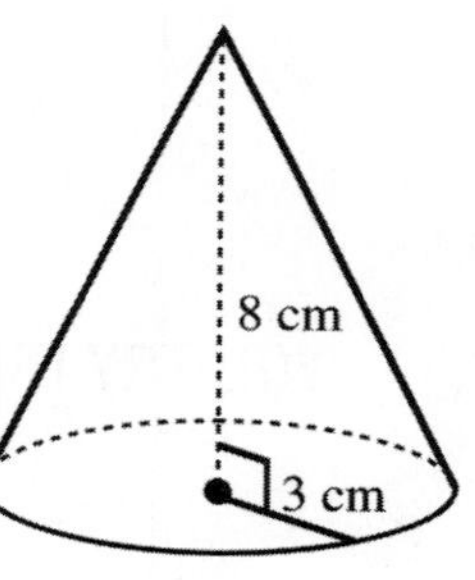

ANSWER:
$V = \frac{1}{3} \times \pi \times 3^2 \times 8 \text{ cm}^3$

$V \approx \frac{1}{3} \times 3.14 \times 9 \times 8 \text{ cm}^3$

$V \approx 3.14 \times 3 \times 8 \text{ cm}^3$ ← $\frac{1}{3} \times 9 = 3$

$V \approx 75.36 \text{ cm}^3 \approx 75.4 \text{ cm}^3$

The volume of the cone is about 75.4 cubic centimeters.

YOU TRY IT 3 *Find the volume of each cone. Use* $\pi \approx 3.14$ *and round the result to the nearest tenth. Use Example 3 as a guide.*

a)

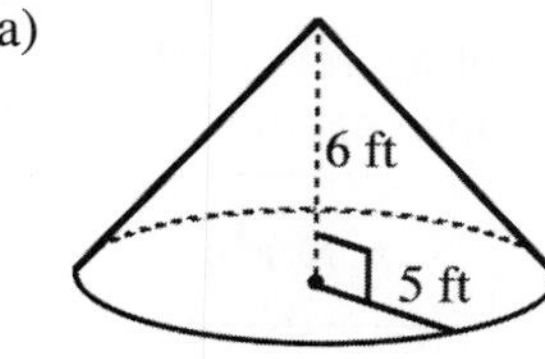

b)

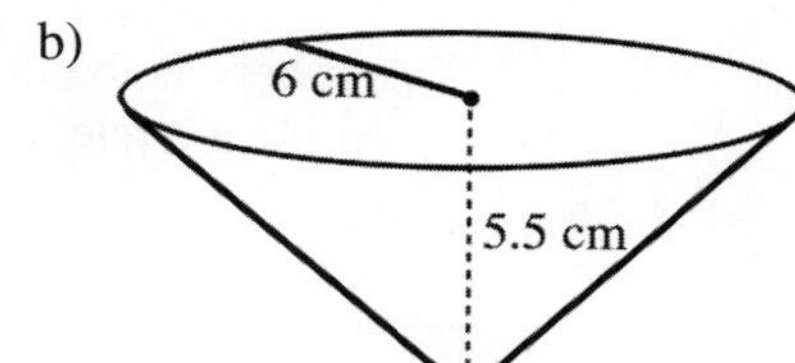

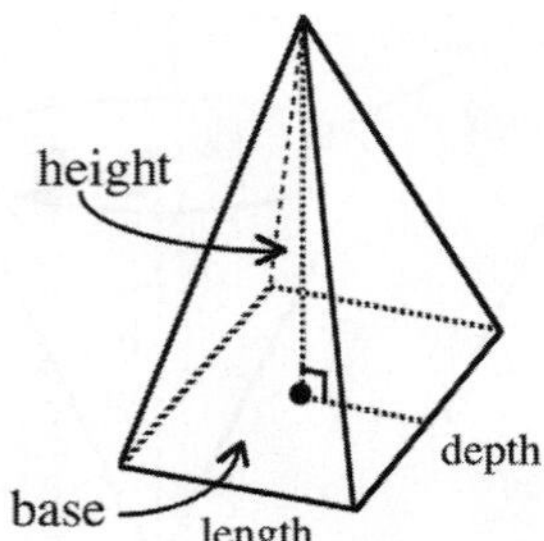

A **pyramid** is like a cone with a rectangular base.
If a pyramid and a box have the same base and same height, then we might imagine the pyramid fitting inside of the box.
The volume of a pyramid is $\frac{1}{3}$ of the volume of such a box:

$$V = \frac{1}{3} \times \textbf{Base} \times \boldsymbol{h} \rightarrow \boxed{\boldsymbol{V = \frac{1}{3} \times l \times d \times h}}$$

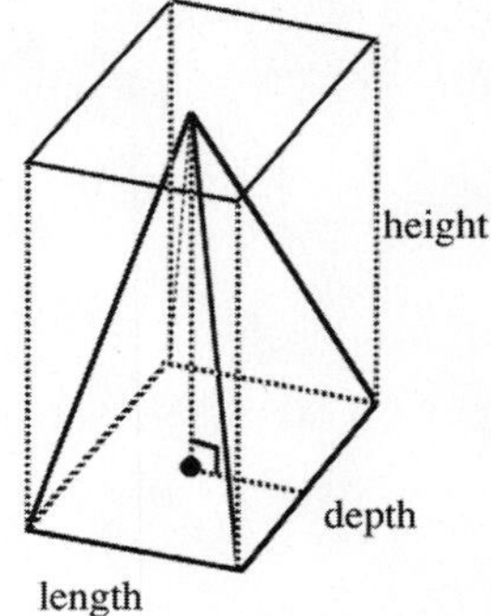

EXAMPLE 4 Find the volume of this pyramid.

PROCEDURE: Apply the volume of a pyramid formula. The base length is 6 feet, its base depth is 8 feet and the height is 10 feet, so the volume will be in cubic feet.

ANSWER: $V = \frac{1}{3} \times 6 \times 8 \times 10 \text{ ft}^3$

$V = 2 \times 8 \times 10 \text{ ft}^3$ $\quad \left(\frac{1}{3} \times 6 = 2\right)$

$V = 160 \text{ ft}^3$

The volume of the pyramid is 160 cubic feet.

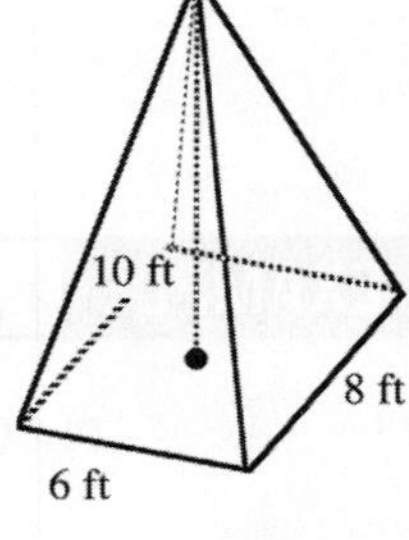

YOU TRY IT 4 *Find the volume of each pyramid. Use Example 4 as a guide.*

a)

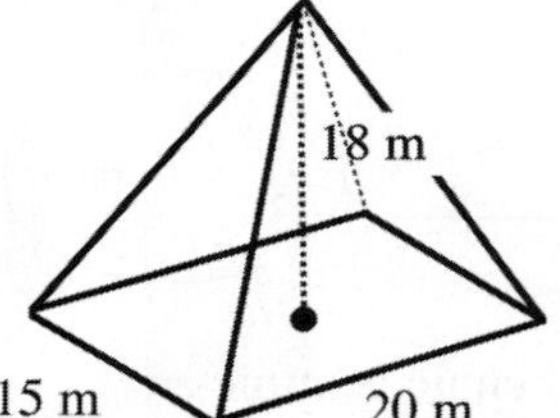

b)

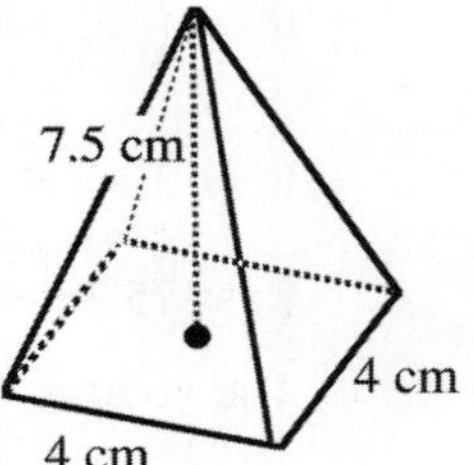

A **sphere** is the three-dimensional version of a circle, such as a ball. Like a circle, it has many radii, all the same length.

Volume of a sphere: $\boxed{V = \frac{4}{3} \times \pi \times r^3}$

We typically use $\pi \approx 3.14$ when finding the volume of a sphere. We can also use a decimal approximation for $\frac{4}{3}$:

$$\frac{4}{3} \approx 1.333.$$

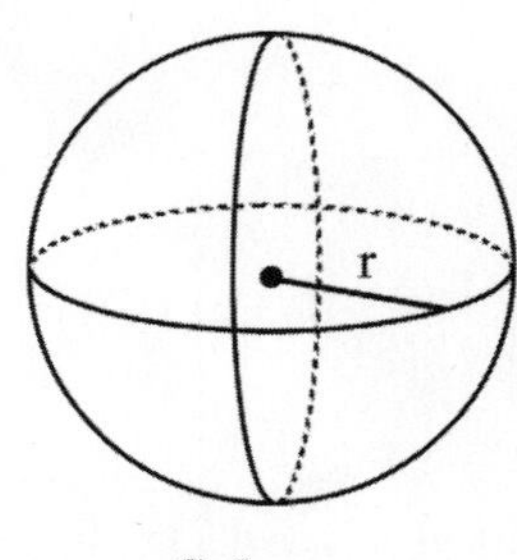

Sphere

EXAMPLE 5 Find the volume of this sphere.
Use $\pi \approx 3.14$ and round the result to the nearest tenth.

PROCEDURE: Use the volume of a sphere formula. The radius is 2 feet, so the volume will be in cubic feet.

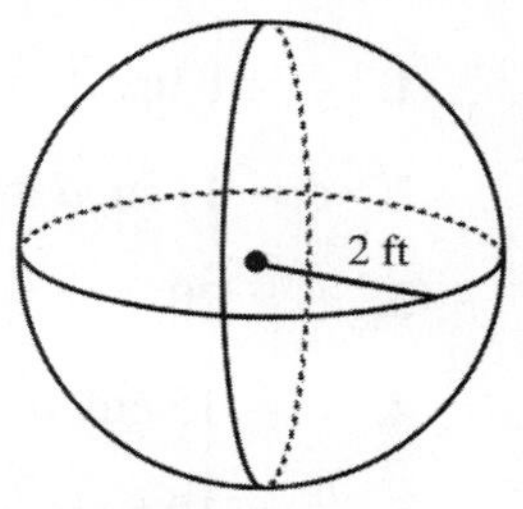

ANSWER: $V = \frac{4}{3} \times \pi \times 2^3 \text{ ft}^3$ Remember the order of operations and apply the exponent to 2 first.

$V \approx 1.333 \times 3.14 \times 8 \text{ ft}^3$

$V \approx 33.4849 \text{ cubic feet} \approx 33.5 \text{ ft}^3$

The volume of the sphere is about 33.5 cubic feet.

YOU TRY IT 5 *Find the volume of each sphere. Use $\pi \approx 3.14$ and round the result to the nearest tenth. Use Example 5 as a guide.*

a)

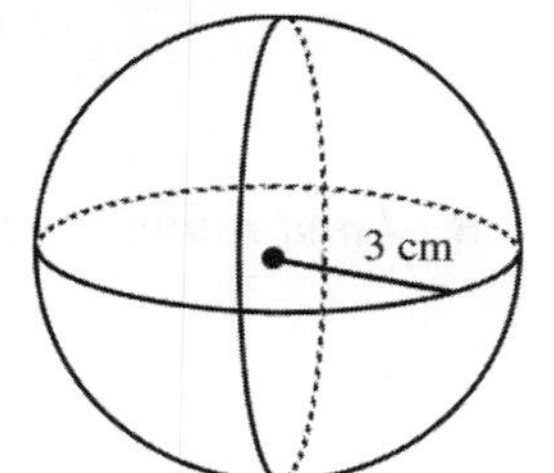

b)

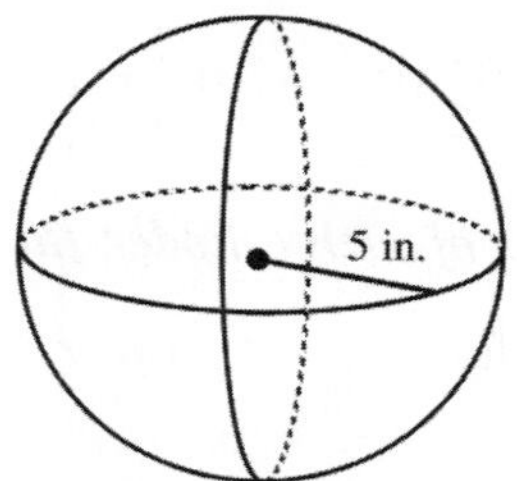

You Try It Answers: Section 7.8

Each decimal answer has been rounded to the nearest tenth.

	a)	b)
YTI 1	a) $V = 4{,}000 \text{ cm}^3$	b) $V = 147 \text{ in.}^3$
YTI 2	a) $V \approx 150.7 \text{ ft}^3$	b) $V \approx 14.1 \text{ m}^3$
YTI 3	a) $V \approx 157 \text{ ft}^3$	b) $V \approx 207.2 \text{ cm}^3$
YTI 4	a) $V = 1{,}800 \text{ m}^3$	b) $V = 40 \text{ cm}^3$
YTI 5	a) $V \approx 113.0 \text{ cm}^3$	b) $V \approx 523.3 \text{ in.}^3$

Focus Exercises: Section 7.8

Given the dimensions of each box, find the volume.

1. $\ell = 8$ in., $d = 6$ in., $h = 5$ in.

2. $\ell = 11$ m, $d = 9$ m, $h = 4$ m

3. $\ell = 20$ ft, $d = 12$ ft, $h = 10$ ft

4. $\ell = 15$ cm, $d = 12$ cm, $h = 8$ cm

5. $\ell = 10.5$ cm, $d = 9.6$ cm, $h = 20$ cm

6. $\ell = 5.2$ m, $d = 6.5$ m, $h = 4.0$ m

7. $\ell = 4$ in., $d = 2\frac{1}{2}$ in., $h = 1\frac{3}{4}$ in.

8. $\ell = 6\frac{1}{4}$ ft, $d = 7\frac{1}{2}$ ft, $h = 10\frac{2}{3}$ ft

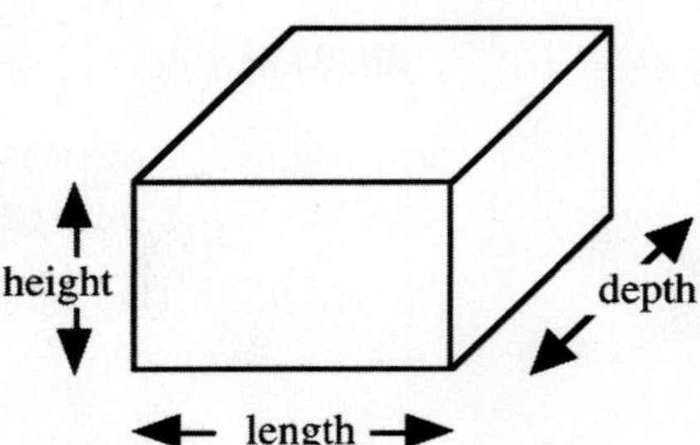

Given the dimensions of each cylinder, find the volume. Use $\pi \approx 3.14$ and round the result to the nearest tenth.

9. $r = 2$ ft, $h = 4$ ft

10. $r = 3$ in., $h = 6$ in.

11. $r = 1.2$ m, $h = 4.5$ m

12. $r = 1.6$ cm, $h = 5.0$ cm

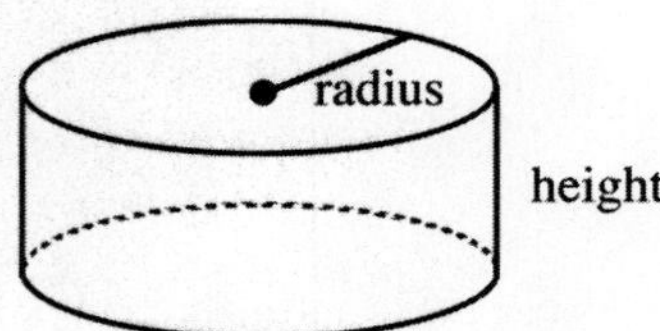

Given the dimensions of each cone, find the volume. Use $\pi \approx 3.14$ and round the result to the nearest tenth.

13. $r = 3$ ft, $h = 5$ ft

14. $r = 5$ in., $h = 6$ in.

15. $r = 2$ m, $h = 3.3$ m

16. $r = 1.5$ cm, $h = 4.0$ cm

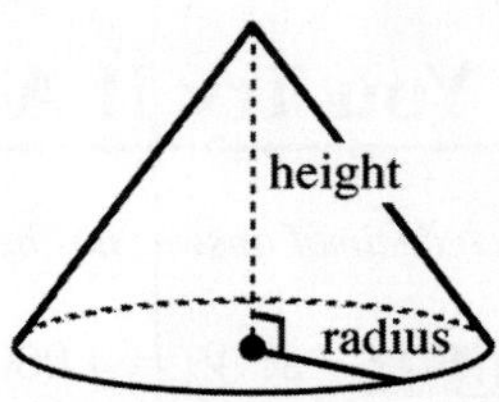

Given the dimensions of each pyramid, find the volume.

17. $\ell = 8$ in., $d = 6$ in., $h = 5$ in.

18. $\ell = 12$ ft, $d = 9$ ft, $h = 7$ ft

19. $\ell = 1.5$ m, $d = 2$ m, $h = 7$ m

20. $\ell = 1.2$ cm, $d = 5$ cm, $h = 4$ cm

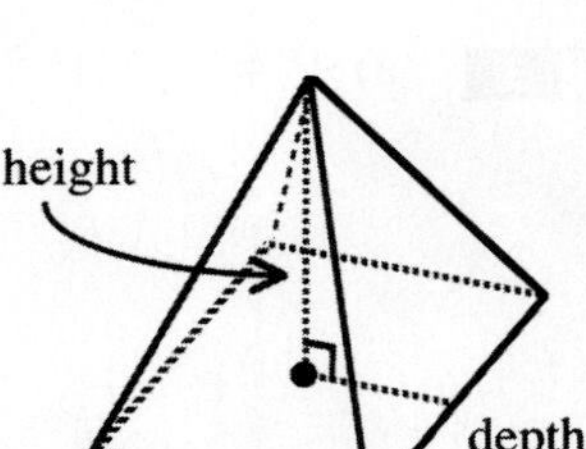

Find the volume of each sphere. Use $\pi \approx 3.14$ and round the result to the nearest tenth.

21. $r = 1$ ft **22.** $r = 3$ in. **23.** $r = 1.2$ m **24.** $r = 2.5$ cm

Solve the following applications. Round each result to the nearest whole number.

25. A storage rental business rents a space that is 8 feet long, 6 feet wide and 12 feet high. What is the volume of this space?

26. An NBA basketball has a radius of 4.7 inches. What is its volume?

27. A soup can has a base radius of 4 centimeters and a height of 12 centimeters. What is the volume of this can?

28. An ice cream sugar cone is in the shape of ... that's right ... a cone! One has a base radius of 3.5 centimeters and a height of 10 centimeters. What is the volume of this cone?

29. Rebecca is building a model of the great pyramids of Egypt. One of her pyramids has a square base with a side length of 6 inches and a height of 3.9 inches. What is the volume of this pyramid?

30. Gregor's above-ground pool is in the shape of a cylinder with a height of six feet and a diameter of 24 feet. If the pool is filled to 5 feet deep, what is the volume of water in Gregor's pool?

Chapter 7 Review

Section 7.1 U.S. Measures

CONCEPT	EXAMPLE
To add feet and inches, set up the addition vertically and line up the feet and inches. When the sum is found, adjust the number of inches if the total includes 12 or more inches.	6 ft 5 in. + 2 ft 10 in. 8 ft 15 in. 8 ft + 1 ft + 3 in. = 9 ft 3 in.
To subtract feet and inches, regroup (if necessary) by changing one foot into 12 inches.	5 15 ~~6~~ ft ~~3~~ in. − 4 ft 7 in. 1 ft 8 in. Notice that we add 12 inches to the 3 inches already there.

Section 7.2 Metric Measures

CONCEPT	EXAMPLE
Converting from one metric measure to another is a matter of moving the decimal point to the left or right.	Convert 83 centimeters to dekameters. 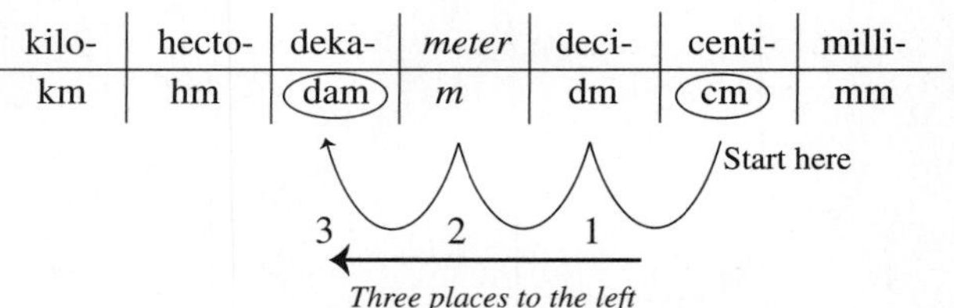 0.83. centimeters = 0.083 dam
Adding and subtracting metric measures is a matter of adding and subtracting decimals. First write one in terms of the other.	Add 7.12 meters + 1.4 decimeters 7.12 m + 0.14 m ← 1.4 dm = 0.14 m 7.26 m

Section 7.3 Converting U.S. and Metric Measures

CONCEPT	EXAMPLE
In an **equivalence fraction**, the numerator and denominator are of equal value but of a different unit measure. Equivalence fractions always have the value 1. We can convert from one measure to another by multiplying by an equivalence fraction.	Convert 4 kilometers to miles using $\frac{5 \text{ mi}}{8 \text{ km}}$. $\frac{4 \text{ km}}{1} \times \frac{5 \text{ mi}}{8 \text{ km}} = \frac{4 \cancel{\text{km}} \times 5 \text{ mi}}{1 \times 8 \cancel{\text{km}}} = \frac{20 \text{ mi}}{8} = 2\frac{1}{2} \text{ miles}$

Section 7.4 Lines and Angles

CONCEPT	EXAMPLE
A **plane** is any flat surface that extends forever in each direction.	
A **line** is straight, and it goes on forever.	
When two distinct lines intersect each other they meet in a single **point**. A point is infinitely small.	
Two lines (in the same plane) that never intersect each other are **parallel lines**.	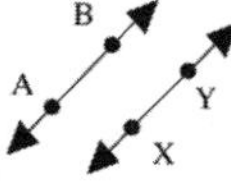
The portion of a line that is drawn between two points (called **endpoints**) is a **line segment**.	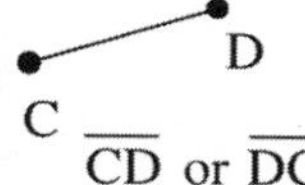 $\overline{CD}$ or $\overline{DC}$
A **ray** is the portion of a line that starts at a point on the line (the endpoint) and goes on forever in only one direction.	 $\overrightarrow{BA}$
When two rays (or line segments) share the same endpoint they form an **angle**. The common endpoint is the **vertex** of the angle. The two rays (line segments) that form the angle are the **sides** of the angle.	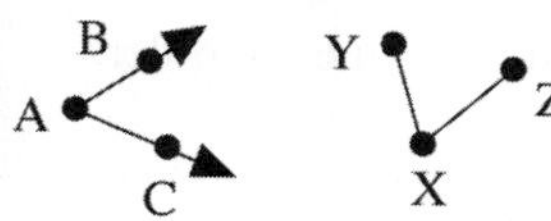
The **interior** of an angle is the portion between the rays that form the angle. Just as the rays continue indefinitely, the interior of the angle continues indefinitely.	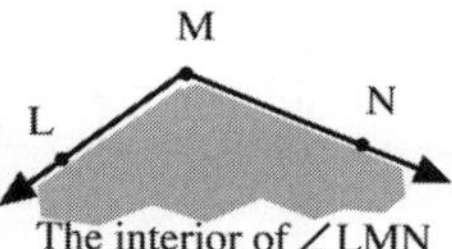 The interior of ∠LMN

CONCEPT	EXAMPLE

If the rays forming an angle go in opposite directions so as to form a line, then the angle is a **straight angle**. A straight angle has a measure of 180°.

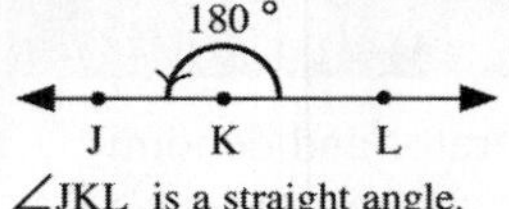

A **right angle** measures 90°.

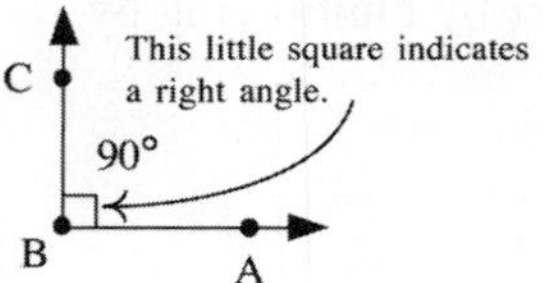

An **acute angle** has a measure greater than 0° and less than 90°.

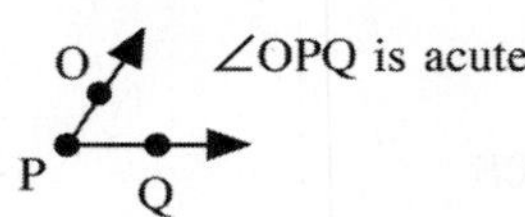

An **obtuse angle** has a measure greater than 90° and less than 180°.

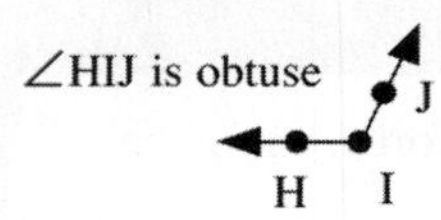

Adjacent angles are any two angles that share a common side, forming an even larger angle; all three angles have the same vertex, and the shared side must be in the interior of the larger angle.

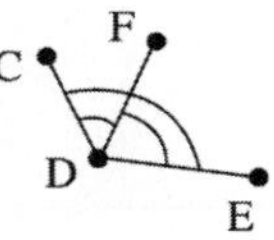

Supplementary angles are any two angles with measures that add to 180°. Supplementary angles can be adjacent, but they don't have to be.

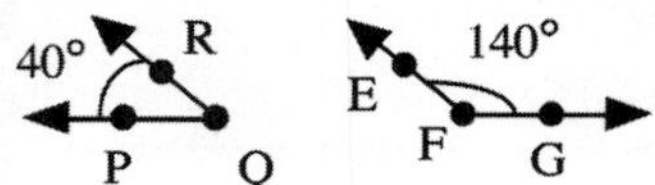

Complementary angles are any two angles with measures that add to 90°. Complementary angles can be adjacent, but they don't have to be.

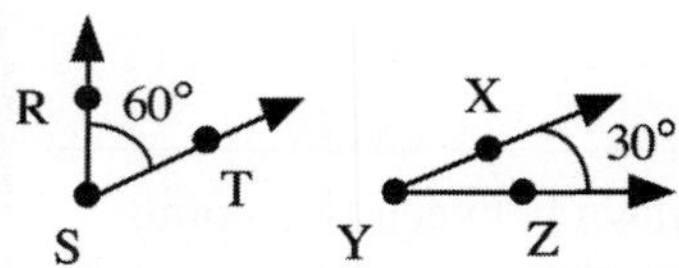

When two lines intersect, several pairs of angles are formed, all sharing the same vertex. Some pairs are adjacent and supplementary (forming a straight line), the other pairs are **vertical angles**, angles that are not adjacent to each other.

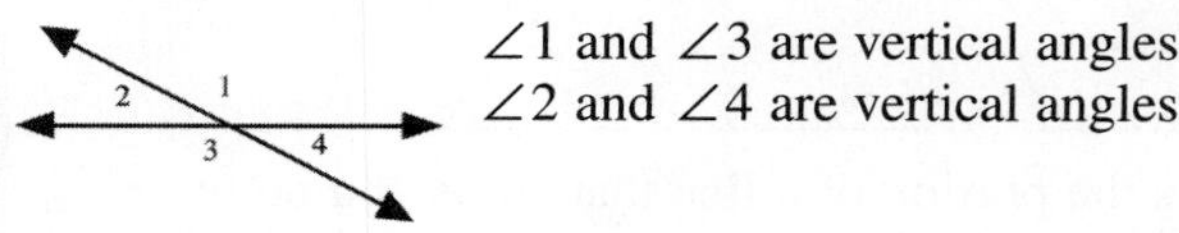

Two lines are **perpendicular** if they intersect to form four right angles. The symbol ⊥ indicates that two lines (or line segments) are perpendicular to each other.

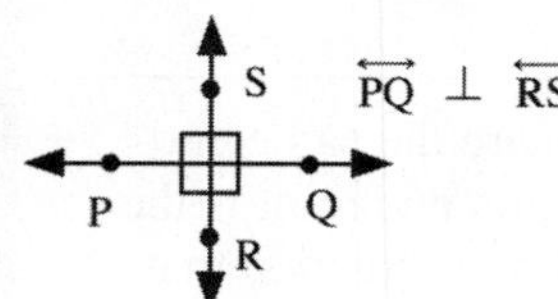

Section 7.5 Geometric Shapes

CONCEPT	EXAMPLE

A **polygon** is a closed plane figure composed of at least three straight line segments. In a polygon, two line segments meet only at an endpoint, called a **vertex**, and never cross each other. Each vertex is the endpoint of only two sides.

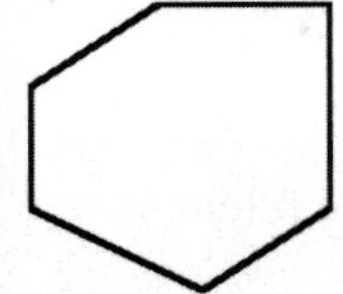

A **triangle** is a polygon that has three sides and three angles. The sum of the angles in a triangle is 180°, no matter the shape of the triangle.

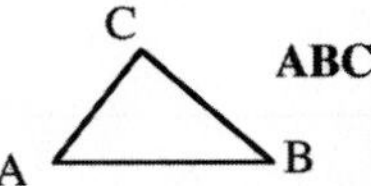

In an **equilateral triangle**, all three sides are of equal length and all three angles are of equal measure. Each angle in an equilateral triangle has a measure of 60°.

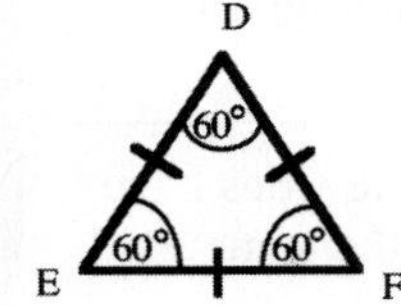

An **isosceles triangle** has two or more sides of equal measure. The angles opposite those sides with equal measure, called **base angles**, also have equal measure.

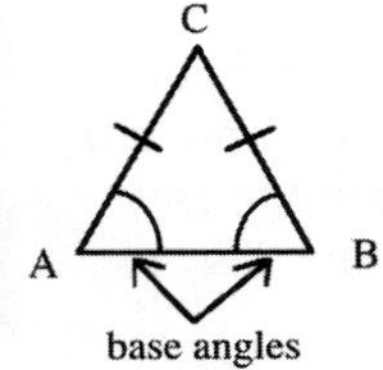

A **scalene triangle** is one in which no two sides have the same length.

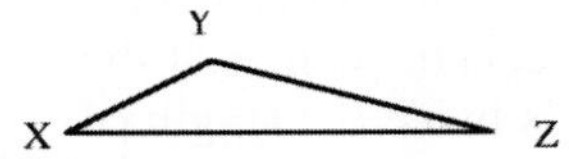

A triangle in which one angle is a right angle (90°) is called a **right triangle.** The other two angles are both acute and are complementary.

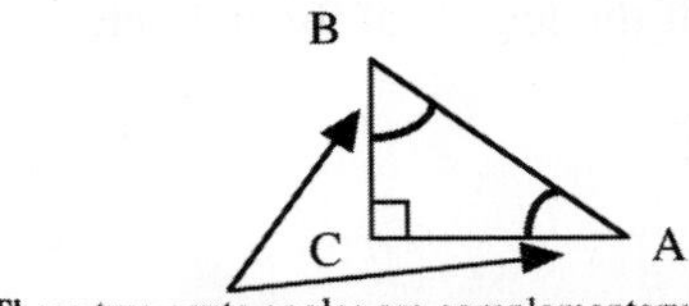

These two acute angles are complementary.

A **quadrilateral** is a four-sided polygon. It has four angles, and the sum of these angles is 360°.

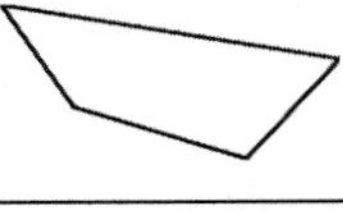

A **parallelogram** has two pairs of parallel sides; each side in a pair has the same length; the angles opposite each other have the same measure. If a parallelogram is not a rectangle, then it has a pair of acute angles and a pair of obtuse angles. Also, in a parallelogram, an acute angle and an obtuse angle are supplementary.

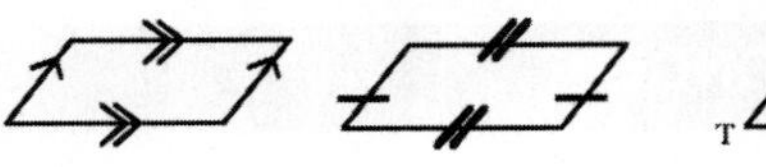

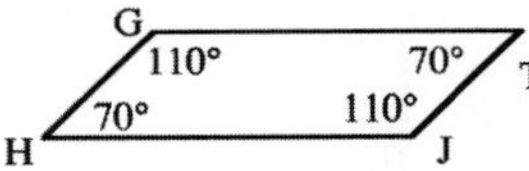

The acute angle is supplementary to the obtuse angle.

CONCEPT	EXAMPLE
A **rectangle** is a parallelogram with four right angles.	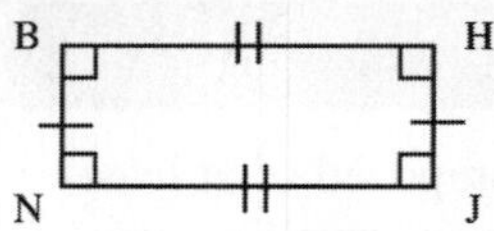
A **square** is a rectangle with four sides of equal length.	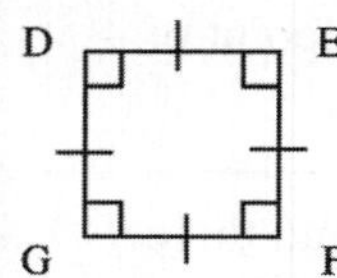
A **trapezoid** is a quadrilateral with only one pair of parallel sides. The parallel sides are called **bases** and have different lengths. A trapezoid is not a parallelogram.	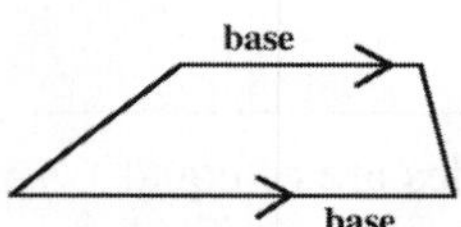
A **regular polygon** is one in which all of the sides have the same length and all of the angles have the same measure.	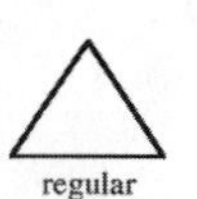 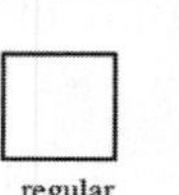 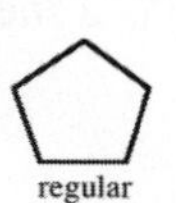 regular hexagon 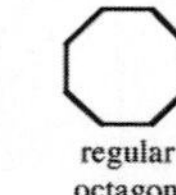
A **circle** is a round geometric figure with a center point. The center point is the same distance from every point on the circle. A line segment from the center point to any point on the circle is a **radius**. The word radius also refers to the length of a radius.	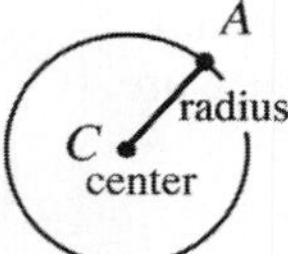
Two radii that form a straight angle (180°) are called a **diameter**. A diameter always intersects the center of the circle. The length of a diameter, d, is twice the length of a radius, r: $d = 2 \cdot r$. The length of a radius is half the length of the diameter: $r = \frac{d}{2}$ or $r = \frac{1}{2} \cdot d$	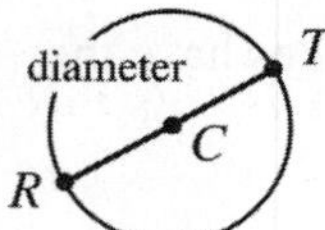

Section 7.6 Perimeter

CONCEPT	EXAMPLE
The **perimeter** of a polygon is the total length (sum) of its side measures: $P = a + b + c$.	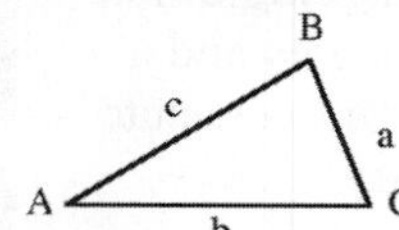

CONCEPT	EXAMPLE
The perimeter formula for a rectangle: $$P = L + W + L + W$$ can be abbreviated as: $$P = 2 \cdot L + 2 \cdot W$$	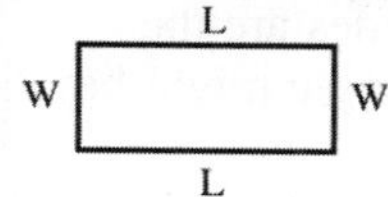
In a regular polygon, the perimeter is the number of sides times the length of one side.	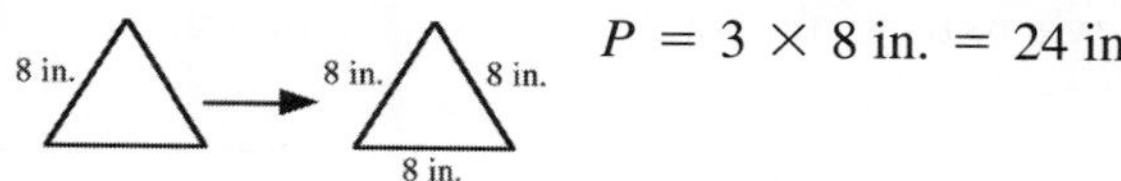 $P = 3 \times 8$ in. $= 24$ in.
The perimeter of a circle—the **circumference**—relies on π. The circumference formula is $C = 2 \cdot \pi \cdot r$, or $C = \pi \cdot d$. We commonly use two approximations for π: $\pi \approx \frac{22}{7}$ and $\pi \approx 3.14$	Find the circumference of a circle with radius 21 centimeters. 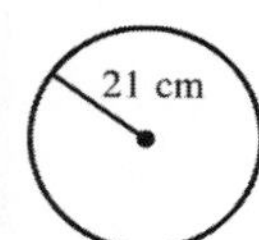 Because the radius is a multiple of 7, use $\pi \approx \frac{22}{7}$. $C \approx 2 \cdot \frac{22}{7} \cdot \frac{21}{1}$ cm ≈ 132 centimeters

Section 7.7 Area

CONCEPT	EXAMPLE
The area of a rectangle is the product of its length and width: $A = L \times W$. The dimensions of a rectangle can also be labeled base and height, in which case the area is base $\times$ height. In a rectangle, the height can be measured from anywhere within the rectangle. The height is always perpendicular to the base.	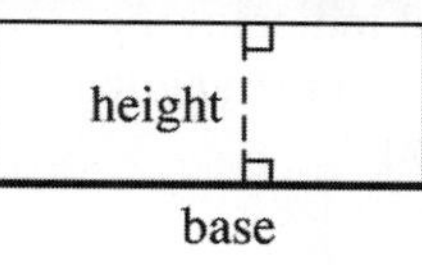
The area of a square with side length s is: $A = s \times s = s^2$.	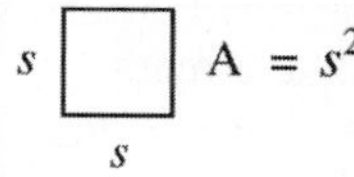 A $= s^2$
The area of a parallelogram is: Area $=$ base $\times$ height. The height of a parallelogram is perpendicular to both the top side and the bottom side (the base):	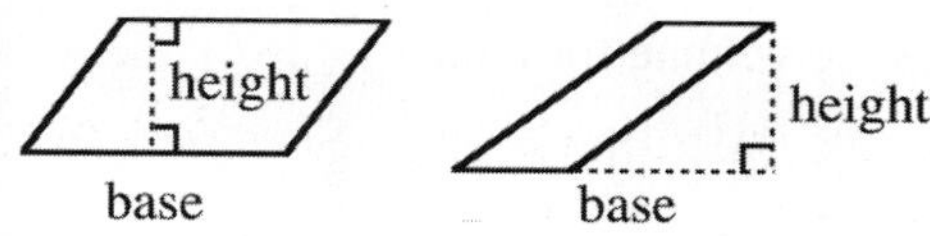
The area of a triangle, where $b =$ base and $h =$ height, can be written as either: $A = \frac{1}{2} \cdot b \cdot h$ or $A = \frac{b \cdot h}{2}$	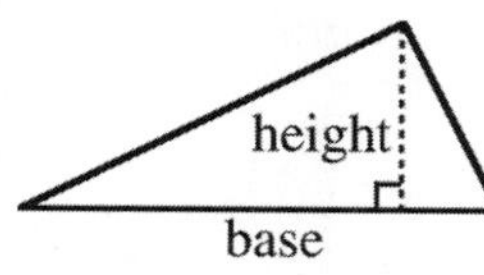

CONCEPT	EXAMPLE
In a right triangle, the two perpendicular sides are the base and the height, no matter how the triangle might be turned.	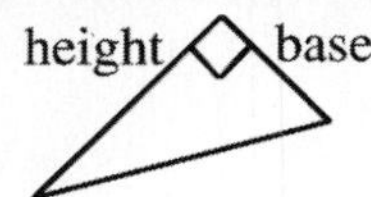
Two different forms of the formula for the area of a trapezoid, where $a =$ the top base, $b =$ the bottom base and $h =$ height are $A = \frac{1}{2} \cdot h \cdot (a + b)$ and $A = \frac{a + b}{2} \cdot h$	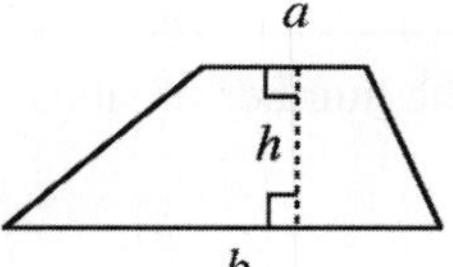
The formula for the area of a circle is $A = \pi \times r^2$.	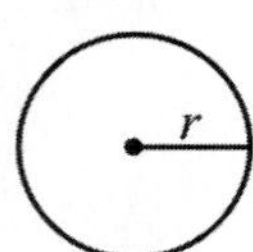

Section 7.8 Volume

CONCEPT	EXAMPLE
A **solid** is a three-dimensional object, having three distinct measures—three distinct dimensions—length, depth, and height. The **volume** of a solid indicates the amount the solid can hold. The volume of a rectangular solid is the product of its three dimensions: Volume = length × depth × height $V = l \times d \times h$ or $V = \text{Base} \times h$	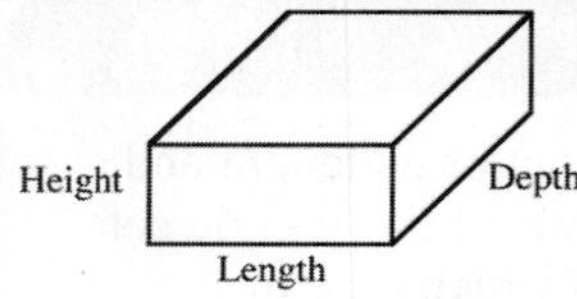
A **cylinder** is the rounded version of a box. Like a rectangular solid, its volume is Base × height: $V = \text{Base} \times h$. Because the base is a circle, the base area is $\pi \times r^2$. This makes the volume formula $V = \pi \times r^2 \times h$	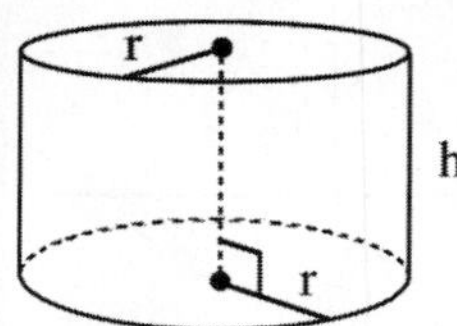 **Cylinder**
A **cone** has a base that is a circle with radius r. The volume of a cone is $\frac{1}{3}$ of the volume of a cylinder: $V = \frac{1}{3} \times \text{Base} \times h$ $V = \frac{1}{3} \times \pi \times r^2 \times h$	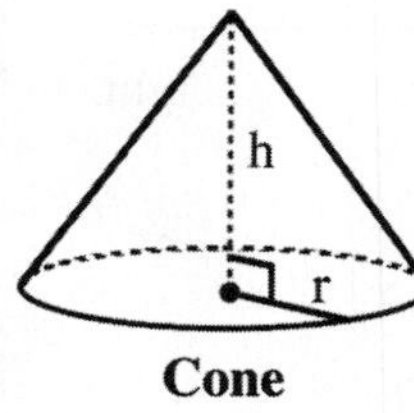 **Cone**

CONCEPT	EXAMPLE
A **pyramid** is like a cone with a rectangular base. The volume of a pyramid is $\frac{1}{3}$ of the volume of a rectangular solid: $V = \frac{1}{3} \times \text{Base} \times h$ $V = \frac{1}{3} \times l \times d \times h$	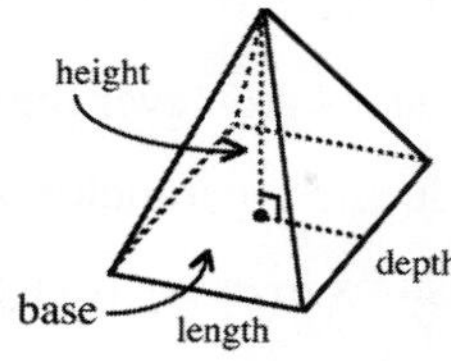 **Pyramid**
A **sphere**, such as a ball, is the three-dimensional version of a circle. Like a circle, it has many radii, all the same length. The volume of a sphere is: $V = \frac{4}{3} \times \pi \times r^3$	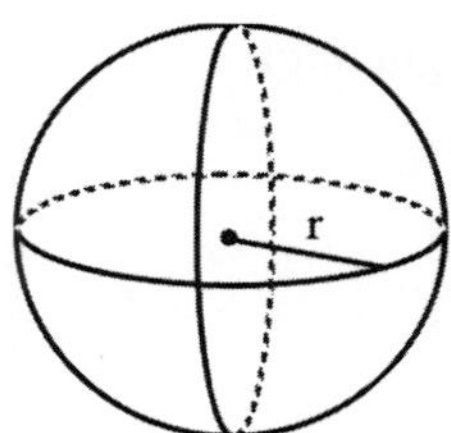

Chapter 7 Review Exercises

True or false:

1. In a trapezoid, the parallel sides are never the same length.______
2. A square is both a rectangle and a parallelogram.______
3. The sum of the angle measures in every triangle is 180°.______
4. A parallelogram contains only one pair of parallel sides.______
5. A straight angle measures 180°.______
6. Two angles that are complementary to each other must be adjacent to each other.______
7. A triangle can have two right angles.______
8. An octagon has eight angles.______

Section 7.1

Convert each to inches.

9. 18 ft
10. 9 ft 11 in.

Convert each to feet and inches.

11. 50 in.
12. 130 in.
13. A tennis racquet is 2 feet 3 inches long. Express this measure in *inches.*
14. At 86 inches tall, Margo Dydek is the tallest woman professional basketball player in the WNBA. Express this measure in feet and inches. *Source: www.tallwomen.org*

Add or subtract, as indicated. Express each answer in feet and inches.

15. 8 ft 4 in. + 3 ft 8 in.
16. 7 ft 4 in. − 5 ft 10 in.
17. In a one-story house, the distance from the floor to the ceiling is 8 feet 3 inches, and the distance from the ceiling to the top of the roof is 4 feet 11 inches. How tall is the house?
18. An alligator measures 17 feet 2 inches from its nose to the tip of its tail. Its tail alone is 8 feet 5 inches long. How long is the rest of its body?

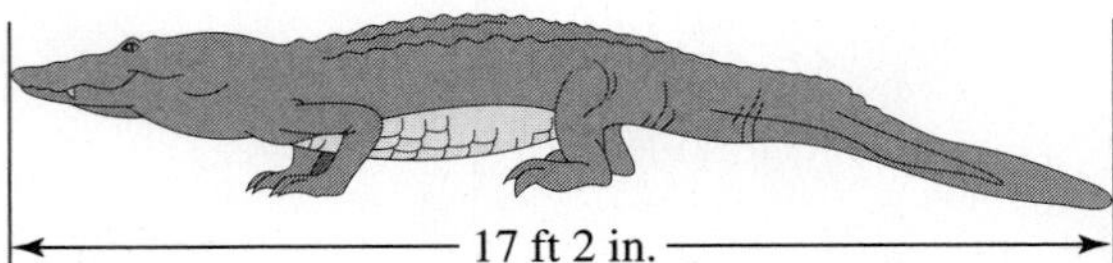

Convert one measure to the other.

19. Convert $15\frac{2}{3}$ yards to feet
20. Convert 51 feet to yards
21. Convert 5 quarts to pints.
22. Convert 12 ounces to pounds.
23. Convert 10 cups to pints.
24. Convert $\frac{7}{16}$ quarts to cups.
25. Convert 3 pints to fluid ounces.
26. Convert 24 pints to gallons.
27. Convert $2\frac{1}{4}$ cups to fluid ounces.
28. Convert $12\frac{4}{5}$ ounces to pounds.
29. Convert $\frac{3}{8}$ pound to ounces.
30. Convert $1\frac{45}{100}$ tons to pounds.

Convert each to ounces.

31. 15 lb

32. 5 lb 2 oz

Convert each to pounds and ounces.

33. 40 oz

34. 142 oz

35. A roasting chicken weighs 3 pounds 13 ounces. Express this measure in ounces.

36. A double box of cereal weighs 76 ounces. Express this measure in pounds and ounces.

Add or subtract, as indicated. Express each answer in pounds and ounces.

37. 8 pounds 9 ounces + 3 pounds 7 ounces

38. 7 pounds 3 ounces − 5 pounds 7 ounces

39. Jena's math book weighs 4 pounds 11 ounces, and her chemistry book weighs 6 pounds 9 ounces. What is the total weight of these two books?

40. A large block of cheese weighs 17 pounds 3 ounces. Ralph cuts off a portion that weighs 3 pounds 12 ounces. How much does the remaining block of cheese weigh?

Section 7.2

Convert the given unit of measure into its base unit, either meters, grams, or liters.

41. 3.08 dag

42. 6.8 kg

43. 870 cm

44. 2.4 dL

Convert the given unit of measure to the measure shown.

45. 2 centigrams to milligrams

46. 0.9 decigrams to centigrams

47. 312 milliliters to deciliters

48. 1.2 hectoliters to kiloliters

49. 3.6 centimeters to dekameters

50. 0.82 kilometers to dekameters

Write a sentence with the requested measurement.

51. Jakhil ran 0.4 kilometers in one minute. Express this number in meters.

52. A hummingbird weighs 1.6 grams. Express this number in milligrams.

Add or subtract as indicated. Convert each measure to the one that is underlined.

53. 14.2 grams + 591 centigrams

54. 52 deciliters − 395 milliliters

Solve each application. Write a sentence answering the question.

55. In preparation for a medical test, Martin had to drink 2.25 liters of a sugary liquid and 850 milliliters of water. How many total liters did Martin drink for his test?

56. Foofi, a toy poodle, weighed 2.95 kilograms on her first birthday. On her second birthday, she weighed 3.43 kilograms. How many grams did she gain during the year?

Section 7.3

Use an equivalence fraction to write each in the terms requested.

57. Convert 14 cups to quarts.

58. Convert $2\frac{1}{4}$ pounds to ounces.

59. Convert 54 inches to feet.

60. Convert 27 kilograms to grams.

61. Convert 95 hectometers to meters.

62. Convert 120 deciliters to liters.

Convert each measure to its alternate U.S. or metric form. Write the answer as a decimal approximation. Write improper fractions as mixed numbers for U.S. measures and as decimals for metric measures.

63. Convert 22 inches to centimeters.

64. Convert 60 centimeters to inches.

65. Convert $9\frac{1}{2}$ liters to quarts.

66. Convert $7\frac{1}{2}$ gallons to liters.

67. Convert 35 grams to ounces.

68. Convert $16\frac{2}{3}$ yards to meters.

Convert each measure to its alternate U.S. or metric form. Write improper fractions as mixed numbers for U.S. measures and as decimals for metric measures.

69. A sack of potatoes weighs 20 pounds. Express this number in kilograms.

70. Jorge is 6 feet tall. (a) How many inches tall is Jorge? (b) Approximately how many centimeters tall is Jorge?

Section 7.4

#71 - 74: Given the measure of two of the angles, find the measure of the third angle.

71. $\angle FRB = 18.6°$ and $\angle KRF = 29.8°$

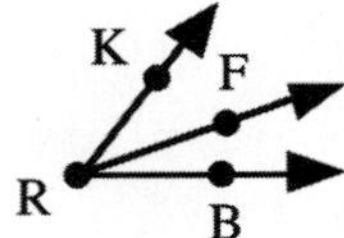

72. $\angle QME = 165.3°$ and $\angle QMD = 67.8°$

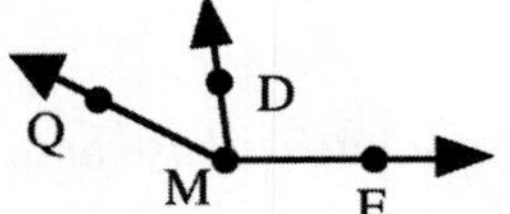

73. ∠WFZ and ∠BLN are supplementary. Given $\angle WFZ = 125.2°$, find $\angle BLN$.

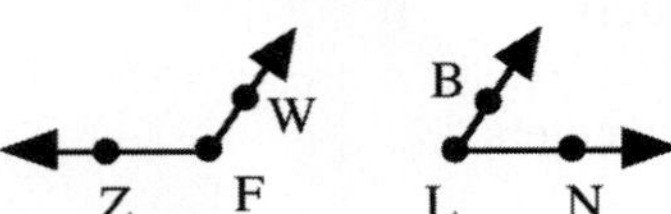

74. $\angle QSA$ and $\angle RFX$ are complementary. Given $\angle QSA = 62.5°$, find $\angle RFX$.

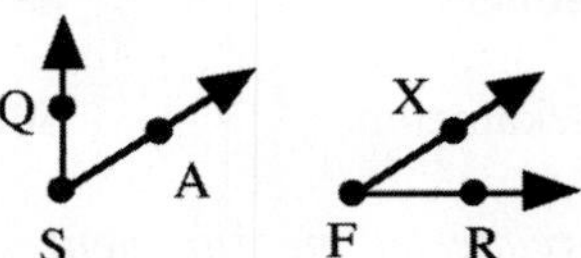

75. Given $\angle 3 = 32°$, find the measures of the other three angles.

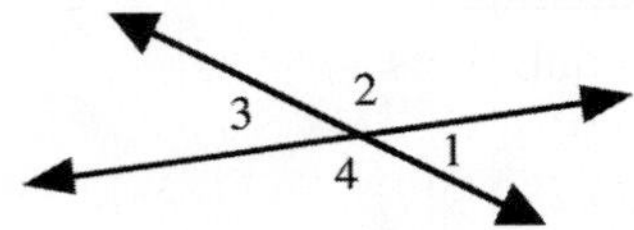

76. ΔABC, given $\angle A = 25°$ and $\angle B = 103°$, find the measure of $\angle C$.

Section 7.5

Based on the side measures given (in centimeters), decide whether the triangle is equilateral, isosceles or scalene.

77. R

8.5

6

T I

6

78.

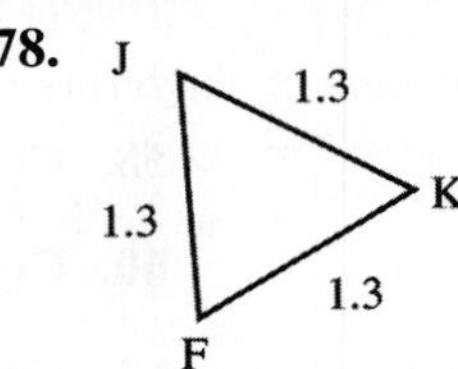

In each right triangle, given the measure of one acute angle, find the measure of the other acute angle.

79. $\angle I = 59.4°$

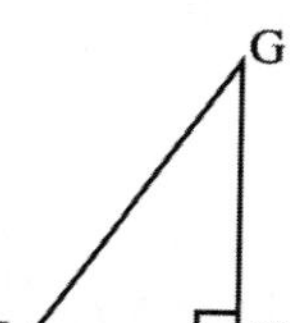

80. $\angle L = 23.8°$

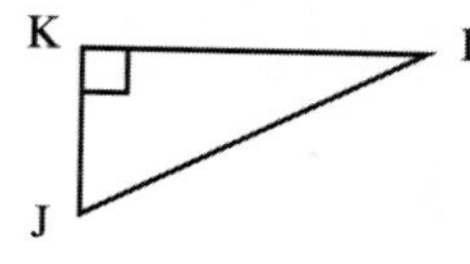

In the parallelogram NOPQ, find the measures of the other three angles and the measures of the other two sides.

81. $\angle N = 40°$; $\overline{NQ} = 5$ cm; $\overline{NO} = 9$ cm

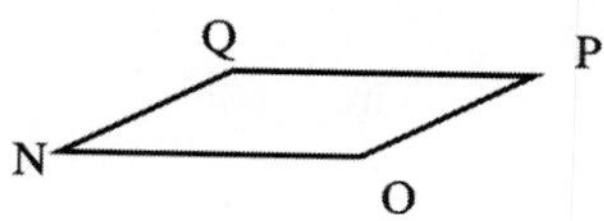

Given the radius, r, of a circle, find the diameter; or given the diameter, d, of a circle, find the radius.

82. $r = 9$ ft

83. $d = 7\frac{1}{3}$ in.

84. $d = 2.3$ m

Section 7.6

Find the perimeter of the polygon described.

85. Leon's pool is in the shape of a trapezoid. What is the perimeter of Leon's pool? (All measures are in yards.)

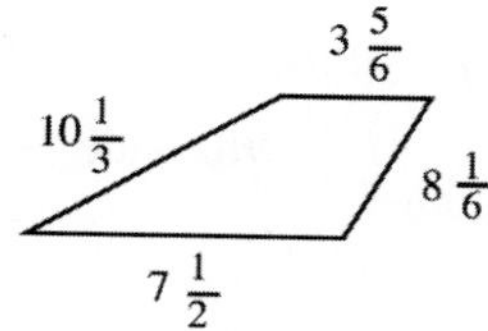

86. The ramp support for model wooden car races is in the shape of a triangle. What is the perimeter of this support structure? (All measures are in meters.)

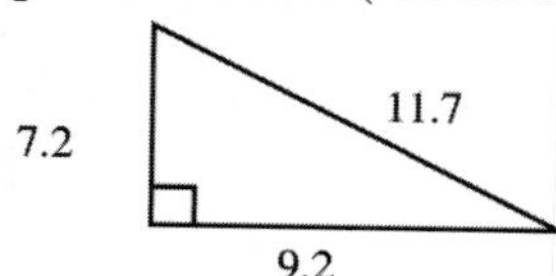

87. Tai's garage is in the shape below. First find the values of x and y and then calculate its perimeter. (All measures are in feet.)

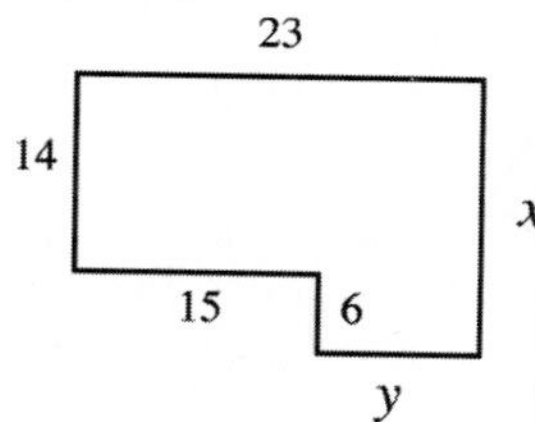

88. The dance floor at the Jitterbug Coffee House is in the shape of a rectangle. What is the perimeter of the dance floor? (All measures are in feet.)

$19\frac{1}{2}$

24

Find the perimeter of the described figure. (Write all improper fraction answers as mixed numbers.)

89. An equilateral triangle; one side is $2\frac{1}{3}$ ft.

90. A regular octagon; one side is 3.75 yd.

Given the perimeter of the regular polygon, find the length of each side.

91. An equilateral triangle; $P = 42$ cm.

92. A regular hexagon; $P = 210$ in.

Solve each application. Write a sentence answering the question.

93. Marcus wants to fence in a circular garden that has a radius of 21 feet. How much fencing is needed to fit around the garden? Use $\pi \approx \frac{22}{7}$.

94. In her living room, Janet has a circular window with a diameter of 30 inches. For better insulation, she wishes to place weather-stripping around the window. How many inches of weather-stripping is needed to go around the window? Use $\pi \approx 3.14$ and round the result to the nearest tenth.

Section 7.7

Find the area of each rectangle.

95. $b = 5$ yd
$h = 4$ yd

96. $h = 2.5$ m
$b = 1.2$ m

Find the area of each square.

97. side $= \frac{3}{8}$ in.

98. side $= 3\frac{1}{2}$ ft

Find the area of each polygon.

99.

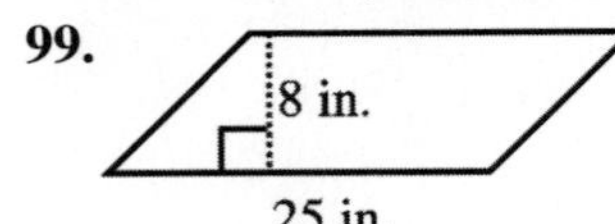

100.

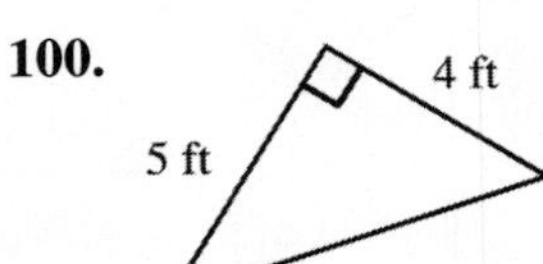

101.

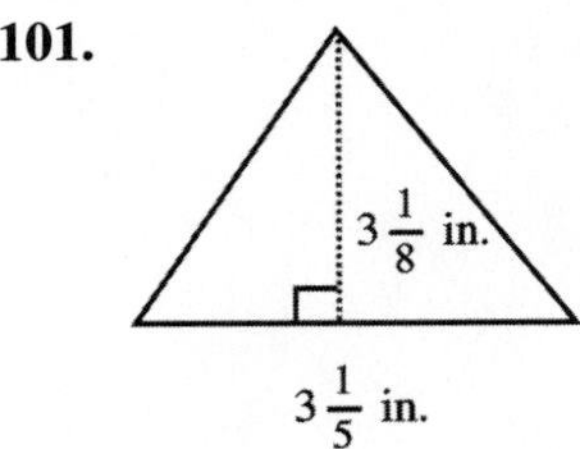

102.

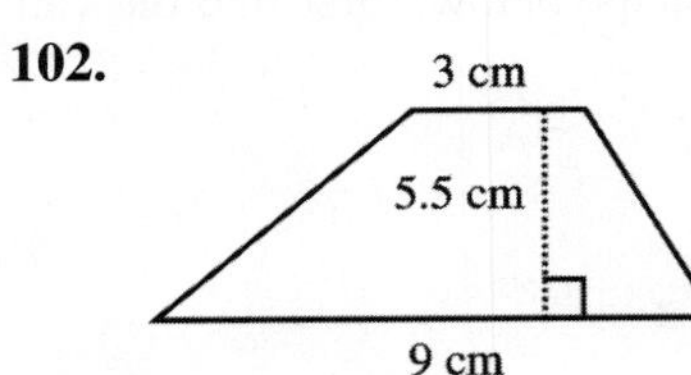

Approximate the area of each circle with given radius or diameter. Use $\pi \approx 3.14$ and round the result to the tenths place.

103. $r = 2$ ft

104. $d = 3.2$ cm

105. A round pond has the basic shape of a circle with a diameter of 60 feet. What is the area of the surface of this pond?

106. Erica's living room is in the shape below. What is the area? (All measures are in feet.)

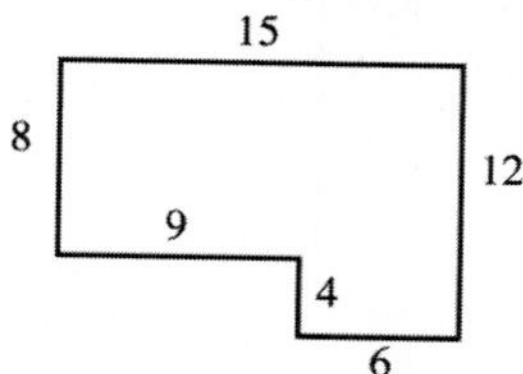

107. This diagram shows a circle within a square. Find the area of the shaded part.

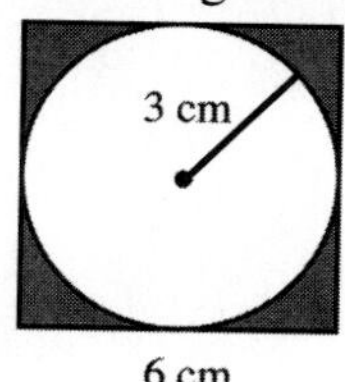

Section 7.8

Find the volume of the box.

108. $l = 9$ in., $d = 12$ in., $h = 5$ in.

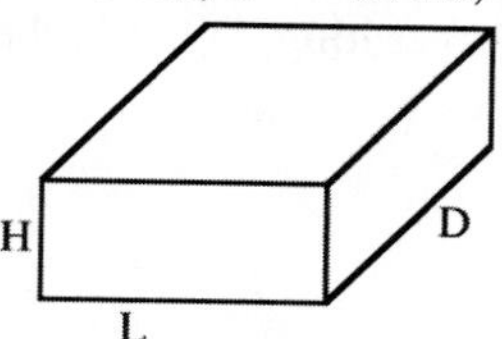

Find the volume of the sphere. Use $\pi \approx 3.14$ and round the result to the nearest tenth.

109. $r = 2$ ft

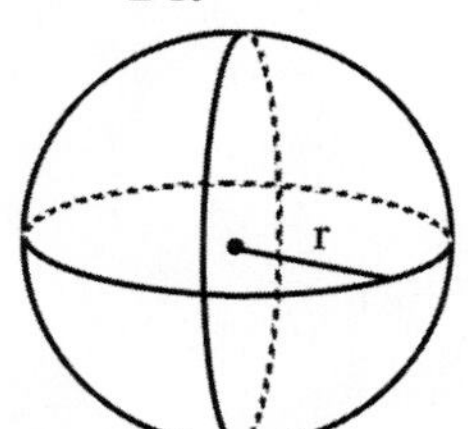

Find the volume of the cylinder. Use $\pi \approx 3.14$ and round the result to the nearest tenth.

110. $r = 5$ in., $h = 4$ in.

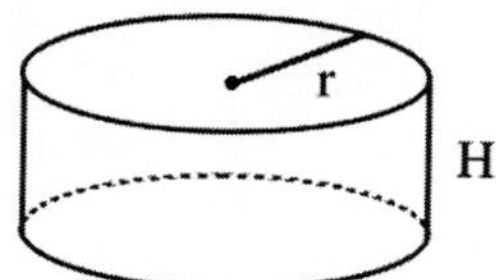

Find the volume of the cone. Use $\pi \approx 3.14$ and round the result to the nearest tenth.

111. $r = 1.5$ ft, $h = 3$ ft

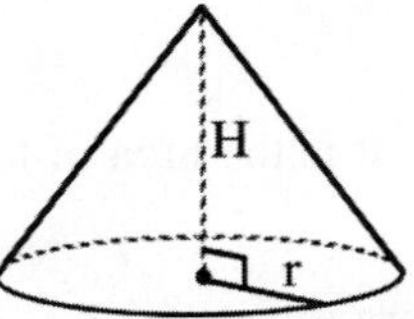

Find the volume of the pyramid.

112. $l = 6$ m, $d = 8$ m, $h = 10$ m

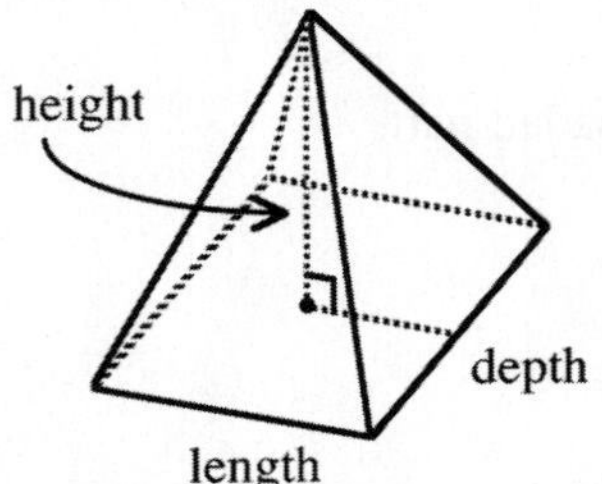

Solve each application. Write a sentence answering the question.

113. An amusement park has a display that is a pyramid with a square base, 20 yards by 20 yards. The pyramid is 15 yards high. What is the volume of this pyramid?

114. The storage area in a U-Drive-It truck is 8 feet wide, 7 feet high, and 12 feet long. What is the volume of this storage area?

Chapter 7 Test

True or false:

1. Two line segments that meet to form a right angle are perpendicular to each other. ______
2. Two angles that are vertical angles always have the same measure. ______
3. In a parallelogram, all four sides are parallel to each other. ______
4. In a right triangle, one of the angles may be obtuse. ______

Add or subtract, as indicated. Express each answer in feet and inches.

5. 9 ft 6 in. + 8 ft 11 in.
6. 20 ft − 6 ft 8 in.

Convert one measure to the other.

7. Convert 6 ft 9 in. to inches.
8. Convert 142 in. to feet and inches.
9. Convert 3 pounds to ounces.
10. Convert $11\frac{1}{4}$ feet to yards.

Convert the given unit of measure into its base unit, either meters, grams, or liters.

11. 28 cL
12. 0.45 hm
13. 91 mm
14. 0.89 kg

Add or subtract as indicated. Convert each measure to the one that is underlined.

15. 28.7 millimeters + 0.64 decimeters
16. 900 dekagrams − 3.75 kilograms

Convert one measure to the other. You may use these equivalencies: 5 mi ≈ 8 km, 11 lb ≈ 5 kg, 5 gal ≈ 19 L

17. Convert 20 miles to kilometers.
18. Convert $6\frac{1}{4}$ kilograms to pounds.
19. Elisa put 9.5 liters of gas into her motorcycle. Convert this to gallons.

Given the measure of two of the angles, find the measure of the third angle.

20. $\angle VTR = 77.6°$ and $\angle VTW = 15.7°$

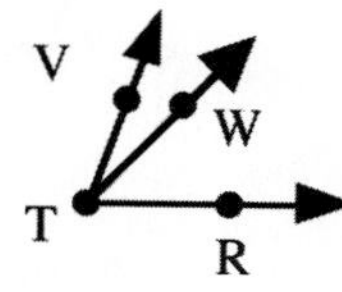

21. $\angle PAS = 92.1°$ and $\angle PAX = 52.4°$

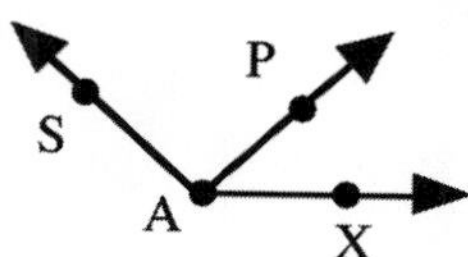

Find the measure of the angle.

22. $\angle DSZ$ and $\angle WXI$ are supplementary. Given $\angle DSZ = 68.3°$, find the measure of $\angle WXI$.

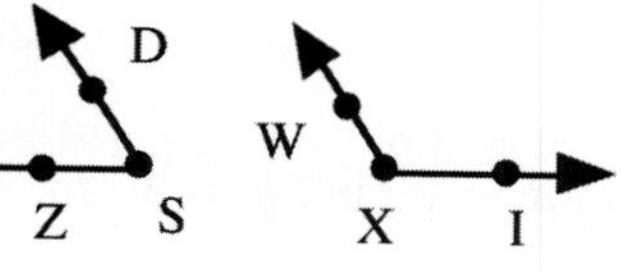

23. $\angle RVT$ and $\angle LYM$ are complementary. Given $\angle RVT = 31.1°$, find the measure of $\angle LYM$.

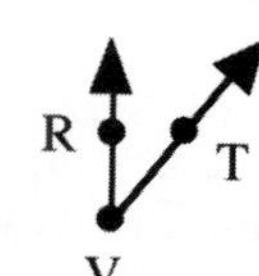

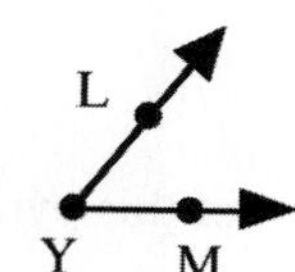

24. In ΔABC, $\angle A = 47.2°$ and $\angle B = 26.9°$. Find the measure of $\angle C$.

B

A C

Solve. Answer the question with a sentence.

25. Siobhán's painted a picture on a canvas in the shape of a parallelogram, as shown. What is the perimeter of the canvas?

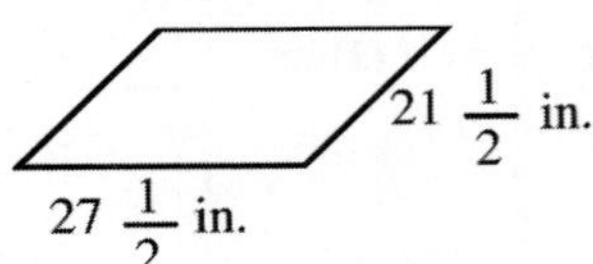

26. Find the perimeter of a square with side measure 7.5 cm.

27. Find the area of a square with side measure $2\frac{1}{3}$ ft.

28. Approximate the circumference of a circle with radius $r = 17\frac{1}{2}$ in.; use $\pi \approx \frac{22}{7}$.

29. A regular octagon has a perimeter of $10\frac{2}{3}$ ft. What is the length of each side?

30. Find the area of this triangle.

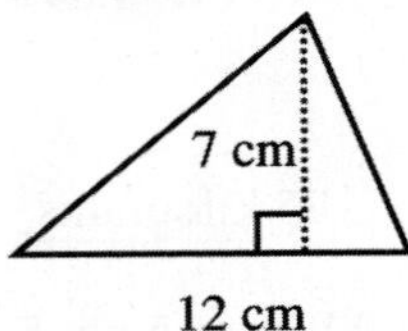

31. The kitchen at the Kountry Folks Restaurant is in the shape shown below. What is its area? (All measures are in feet.)

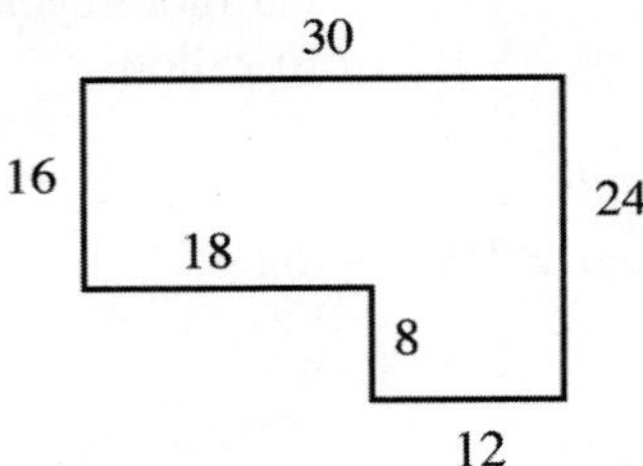

32. Given the dimensions of this cylinder, find its volume. Use $\pi \approx 3.14$. $r = 4$ cm, $h = 7.5$ cm

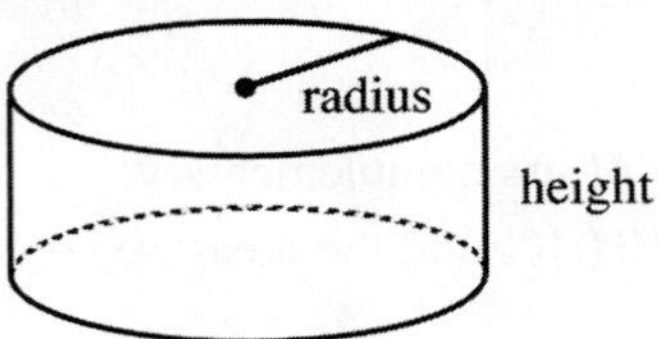

33. Given the dimensions of this pyramid, find its volume. $l = 3$ in., $d = 2\frac{2}{3}$ in., $h = 3\frac{3}{4}$ in.

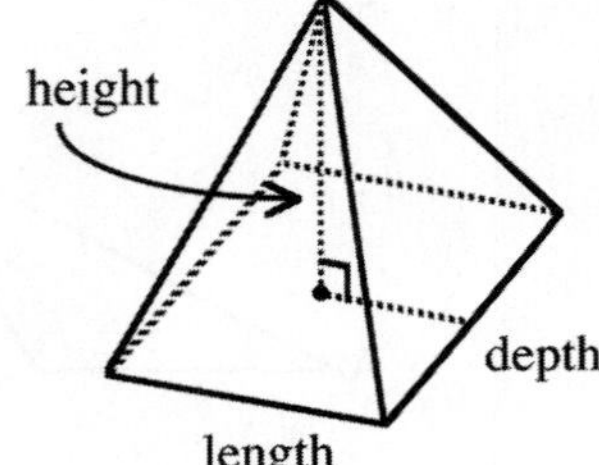

CHAPTER 8
Statistics and Probability

Introduction

Have you ever noticed the Nielsen ratings for television shows? Do your favorite shows make the top 20 list? Are you watching the same shows that "everybody" else is watching? Who determines which television shows stay on the air and which ones will be canceled?

Believe it or not, about 5,000 families all over the nation determine which TV shows are the ones that Americans like to watch. These "Nielsen families" are what make up the Nielsen ratings for TV shows each week. If enough of these families like a particular show, then it is likely to continue to be on the next year.

This is one of many examples of how a smaller group of people, called a *sample*, can represent a whole population, and it is the foundation of statistics. If enough people are asked about their likes and dislikes, the opinions of some will represent the opinions of the rest of us.

Each Nielsen family represents about 60,000 people. Wouldn't it be nice to know which family represents you?

Preparation Exercises

Section 1.5, Whole Numbers: *Divide.*

1. $432 \div 8$

2. $1{,}584 \div 18$

Section 3.2, Simplifying Fractions: *Simplify each fraction.*

3. $\frac{45}{60}$

4. $\frac{18}{90}$

Section 5.2, Rounding Decimals:

Round each to the tenths place.

5. 0.83904

6. 1.9629

Round each to the hundredths place.

7. 0.42639

8. 1.39481

Section 5.3, Adding and Subtracting Decimals:

Add

9. $1.408 + 0.63$

10. $0.49 + 2.357$

Subtract.

11. $2.3 - 1.84$

12. $6 - 3.195$

Section 5.4, Multiplying Decimals: *Multiply.*

13. 3.2×5.6 **14.** 8×9.25 **15.** 0.7×0.3 **16.** 0.25×0.16

Section 5.5, Dividing Decimals: *Divide.*

17. $1.25 \div 5$ **18.** $7.11 \div 0.9$ **19.** $57 \div 0.6$ **20.** $3.83 \div 0.04$

Section 6.4, Percents:

Write each decimal as a percent.

21. 0.47 **22.** 0.03 **23.** 0.279 **24.** 0.005

Write each percent as a decimal.

25. 58% **26.** 9% **27.** 130% **28.** 2.5%

SECTION 8.1 Bar Graphs and Circle Graphs

Objectives

In this section, you will learn to:

- Draw and read bar graphs.
- Draw and read circle graphs.

To successfully complete this section, you need to understand:

- Adding whole numbers (1.3)
- Dividing whole numbers (1.5)
- Multiplying decimals (5.4)
- Writing decimals as percents (6.4)
- Angle measures (7.4)
- Radii in a circle (7.5)

Introduction

Statistics are everywhere: In TV ads, "Four out of five dentists recommend..."
In sports, "Manny Ramirez's batting average is..."
In weather reports, "There is a 30% chance of rain..."
In polling, "The president has a 65% approval rating on his handling of..."
And in many other areas of everyday life.

Often, when a study is conducted, pieces of information—called **data**—are collected, organized into categories, and drawn as a graph. The number of items in a given category is called the **frequency** of the category. (*Frequency* means how frequently—how many times—something occurs.)

For example, Sarah, a newspaper reporter, is interested in knowing about the number of drive-up lunch customers each local fast-food restaurant attracts. She gathers data by asking the managers of each restaurant for their Tuesday count from 12:00 to 2:00 PM. After collecting the data, she puts the numbers into a table, the categories (fast-food restaurants) on the left and the frequency (the number of cars reported) on the right:

Categories → **← Frequency**

Restaurant	Number of Drive-up Customers
Burger King	40
Carl's Jr.	32
Del Taco	28
In-N-Out	36
Jack-in-the-Box	52
KFC	52
McDonald's	64
Taco Bell	36
Wendy's	60

A table is one way to organize information so that it can be easily read. Another way to organize data values is to put them into a graph, giving us a visual representation.

Drawing Bar Graphs

Sarah decides to put the data she collected into a **bar graph.** In a bar graph, the categories in the study are written across the bottom or along the left side. A rectangle, or bar, is drawn for each category indicating the number of data values for that category. The length of the bar indicates the frequency of each category.

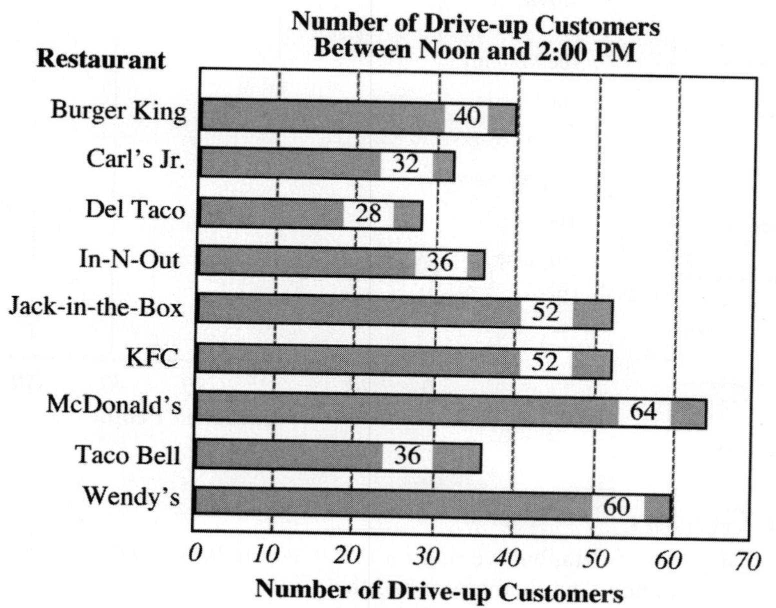

It's also common to see bar graphs with vertical rectangles, as shown below. One way is not any better than the other; each gives you the same information.

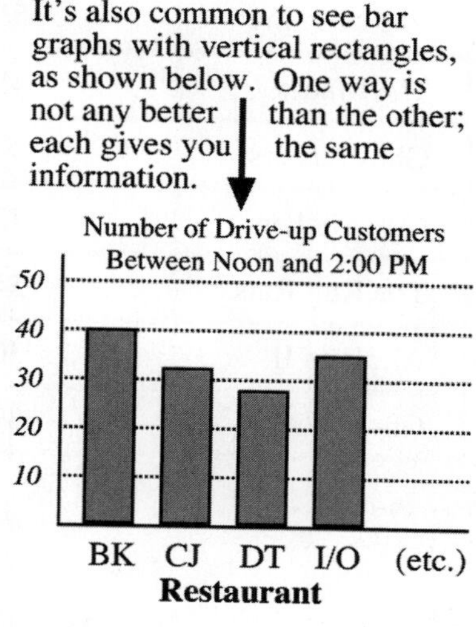

Notice these characteristics of the bar graph:

- The bars are all the same width, and they don't touch each other. The length of each bar is determined by the data for each restaurant—the number of drive-up customers.
- The outline of the graph has numbers on the bottom, a simple standard measure of 10. Two of the bars meet up with the standard measure lines exactly, those of Burger King (40) and Wendy's (60).
- The bars for Jack-in-the-Box and KFC extend a little beyond the 50 line, and the bar for Del Taco falls a little bit short of the 30 line.
- Both In-N-Out and Taco Bell had a total of 36 customers, which is a little more than halfway between 30 and 40. If we were to draw a line at 35, we'd see that the bar for In-N-Out (and Taco Bell) would extend a little beyond the 35 line.

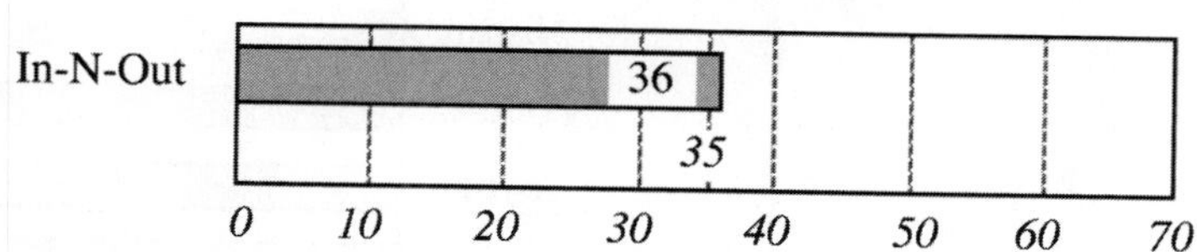

Keep these characteristics in mind when drawing your own bar graph. If possible, use a straightedge and graph paper so that your work is neat and organized.

A local movie center has seven theaters, each of which plays older movies. Last Wednesday, the manager asked Mark to count the number of people in each theater at 5:00. Below is a table showing the data collected.

Draw a bar graph based on the given data. (Be sure to keep in mind the characteristics of a bar graph when you draw it.) A grid is provided to help you draw the bar for each category.

Movie	Number of People
The Mummy	51
The Matrix	45
Ghostbusters	39
City Slickers	42
The Rug Rats	54
Airplane II	30
Ghost	39

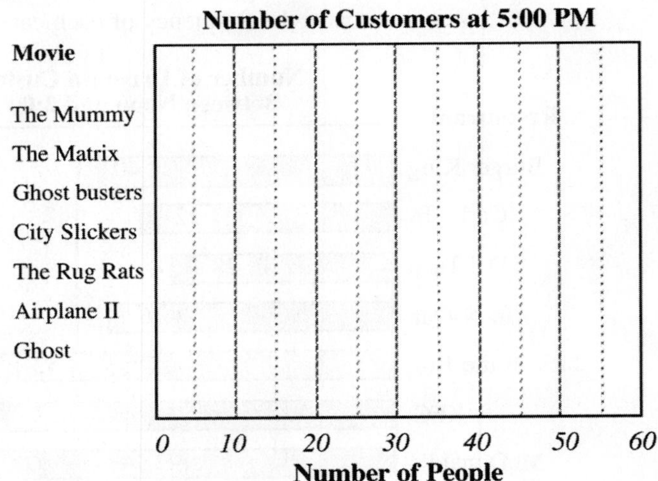

Reading Bar Graphs

If we are shown a bar graph of data, but we don't know what the individual amounts are, we can estimate—using the numbers on the bottom and their lines.

For example, here is the bar graph for the number of new cars sold, during the month of May, at each dealership in the Myriad Mile of Cars. Together, the dealerships sold a total of 180 new cars.

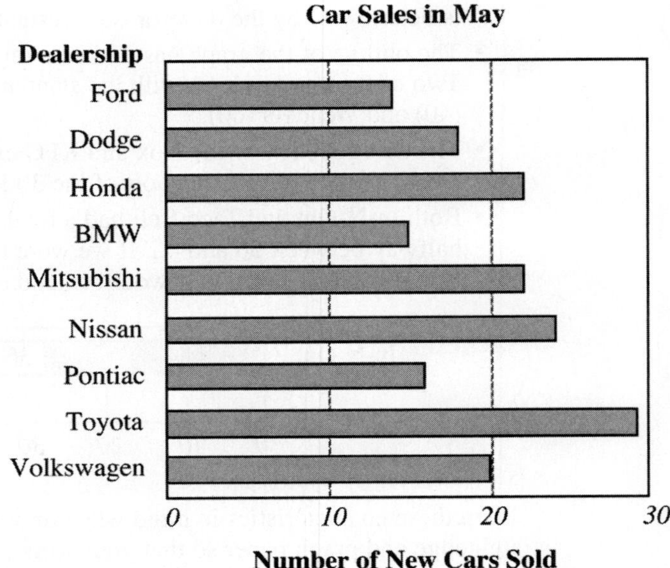

One data value is obvious: There were 20 Volkswagens sold. All of the other values will take some educated visual guessing, called **interpolation**, to determine.

To assist us in this interpolation, we can draw our own lines in the middle between the standard measures. In other words, we can draw lines representing 15 and 25. We can then compare each bar to the lines that we have drawn and see whether a bar is close (or very close) to one of the lines.

Also, a bar may look as though it is in the very middle of, for example, 15 and 20. However, the very middle of 15 and 20 is $17\frac{1}{2}$, and car dealers can't sell half of a car, so the number is either 17 or 18, depending whether it appears closer to 15 or to 20.

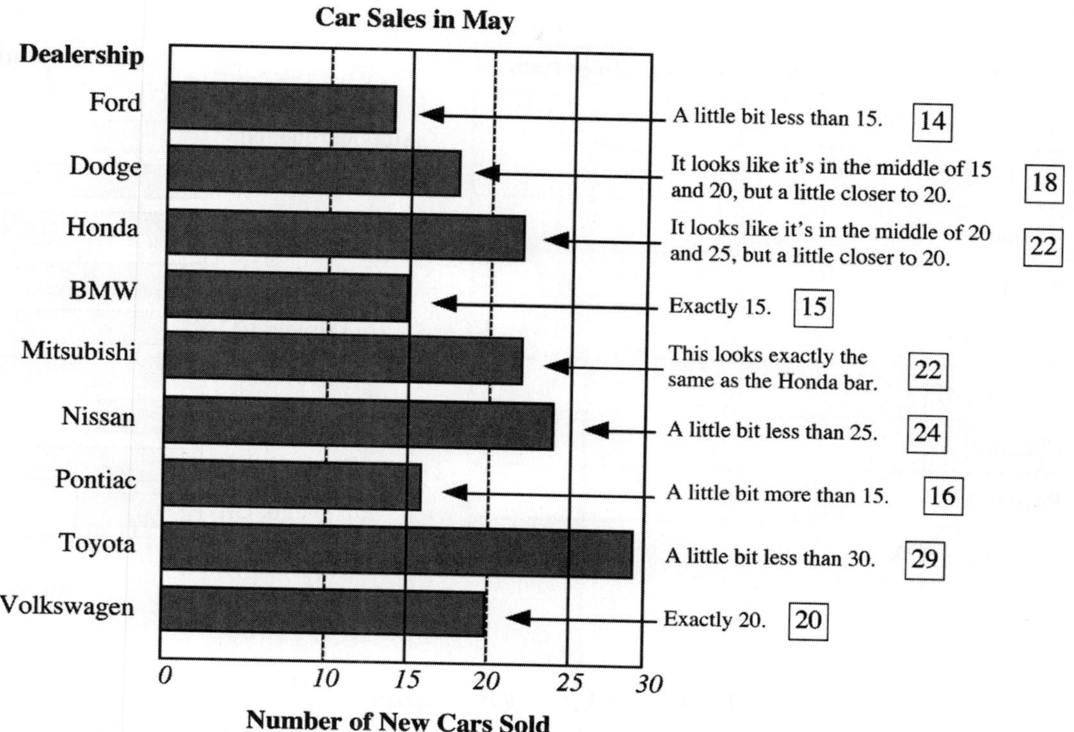

After our interpolation, we can put the values we find into a table.

We can also double check to see if the table is accurate by adding up the column of the number of cars sold. If accurate, it will add to 180.

Do these numbers total 180?

______
Yes or No

Dealership	Number of New Cars Sold
Ford	14
Dodge	18
Honda	22
BMW	15
Mitsubishi	22
Nissan	24
Pontiac	16
Toyota	29
Volkswagen	20

What should you do if the numbers in the table do *not* total 180?

______

______

YOU TRY IT 2

Below is a bar graph of the annual rainfall in selected cities throughout the United States. (Each value has been rounded to the nearest whole number.) Source: The World Almanac, 2005.

Based on the bar graph, complete the data table.

City	Number of Inches of Rain
Albuquerque, NM	
Austin, TX	
Bismarck, ND	
Buffalo, NY	
Denver, CO	
Detroit, MI	
Phoenix, AZ	
Portland, OR	
San Diego, CA	

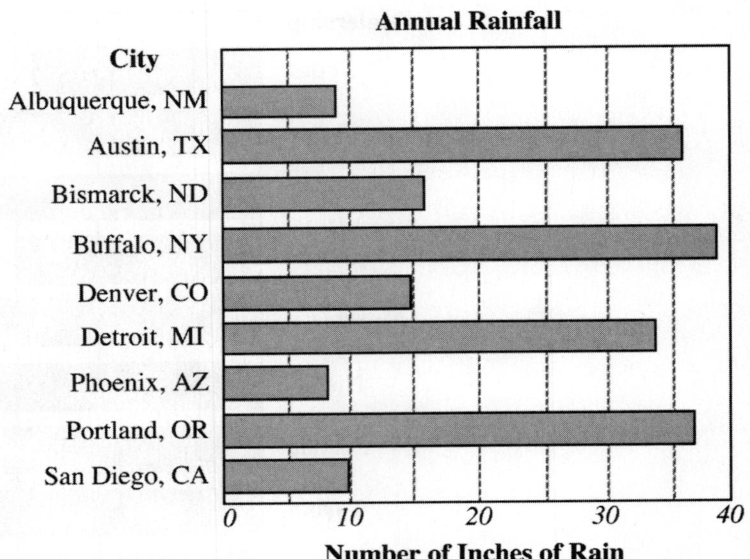

Reading Circle Graphs

Another popular graph is the **circle graph**, sometimes called a *pie chart*. The categories are displayed in a circle, and it is typical to show each category as a percent rather than the actual frequency. Each region in the circle graph, called a **sector**, is defined by two radii.

For example, in a small city, an auto mall offered the following makes of automobiles: Buick, Chrysler, Ford, Mitsubishi, and Toyota. Brian, the city's director of economic development, compiled the following new vehicle sales statistics for the year 2005 and created a circle graph:

Dealership	Percent of Total New Vehicles Sold
Buick	25%
Chrysler	20%
Ford	5%
Mitsubishi	10%
Toyota	40%
Total	**100%**

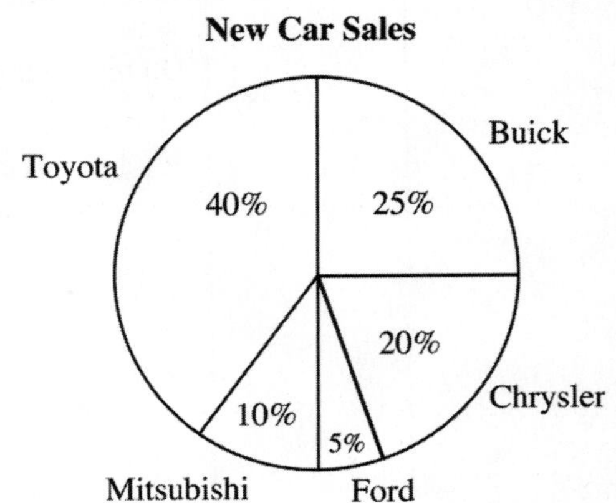

Notice that the total percent of all categories is 100%. Also, the larger the percent, the larger the part of the circle a sector covers. Furthermore, the radii of a 50% sector form a straight angle, and the radii of a 25% sector form a right angle.

Think about it Could the data in YTI 2 be displayed in a circle graph instead of a bar graph? Why or why not?

Because the categories are measured in percents, it's appropriate to use 50% (half the circle) and 25% (one-fourth of the circle) as standards by which to compare other percentages in the circle.

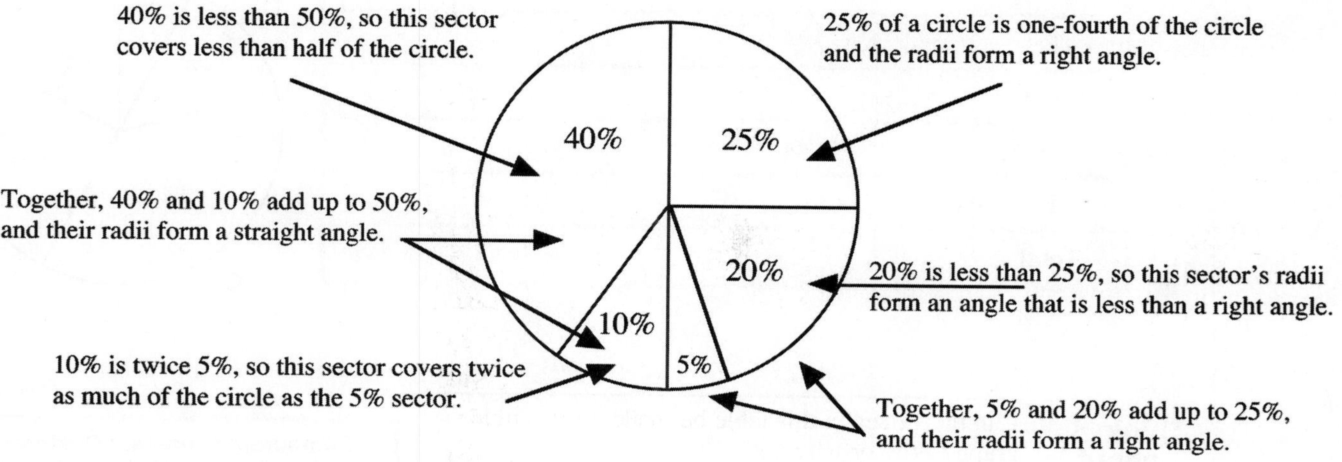

Note: We estimate where we place the radius that divides the 40% and 10% sectors.

If all of the dealerships combined sold 2,400 new cars, how many new cars did each dealership sell?

We can answer this question using the table of percents. Recall from Section 6.6 that, "Percent always needs to be *of* something." For each item in the circle graph, the percent means "of the total number of cars."

Also recall that *percent of* means *percent times*, so when the Ford dealership sold 5%, that is 5% of 2,400 new cars: 5% × 2,400 = 120.

Dealership	Percent of Total New Vehicles Sold	Total New Vehicles Sold (× 2,400)		Write the percent as a decimal and multiply it by 2,400.
Buick	25%	600	←	$0.25 \times 2{,}400 = 600$
Chrysler	20%	480	←	$0.20 \times 2{,}400 = 480$
Ford	5%	120	←	$0.05 \times 2{,}400 = 120$
Mitsubishi	10%	240	←	$0.10 \times 2{,}400 = 240$
Toyota	40%	960	←	$0.40 \times 2{,}400 = 960$
Total	**100%**	**2,400**	←	Make sure this column adds to 2,400.

YOU TRY IT 3

Below is a circle graph with the grade distribution for Dr. Garcia's algebra classes last spring semester. Dr. Garcia had a total of 150 algebra students that semester.

Complete the table by listing both the percent for each grade as well as the number of students receiving that grade.

Grade	Percent of Students Receiving the Grade	Total Number of Students Receiving the Grade
A		
B		
C		
D		
F		
Total		

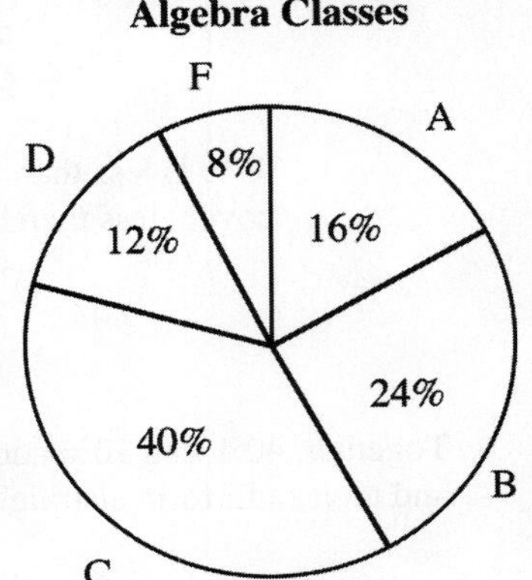

Think about it Can the values in this table be made into a circle graph? Why or why not?

Restaurant Breakfast Customers	
Beverage	**Percent Who Have This Beverage with Breakfast**
Coffee	58%
Juice	34%
Tea	17%
Milk	10%
Other	16%

Drawing Circle Graphs

Sometimes it is our task to make a circle graph from a table of data. Here are some guidelines that we can follow to help us make our circle graph as accurate as possible.

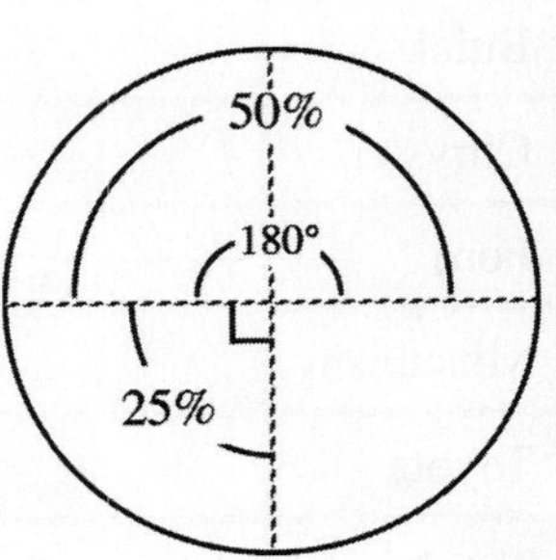

1. We can use the 25% and 50% standards as guidelines. We can first lightly draw in both a horizontal diameter and a vertical diameter, as shown.

   We can use these standards to estimate where a 23% sector (a little less than 25%) and a 42% sector (between 25 and 50%) might fit.

2. It is also helpful to know that 12.5% is halfway between 0 and 25% and forms a 45° angle.

   So, a 12% sector is about halfway between 0 and 25%.

   Furthermore, 37.5% is halfway between 25 and 50%, so a 42% sector (more than halfway between 25 and 50%) can be estimated to be closer to 50% than to 25%.

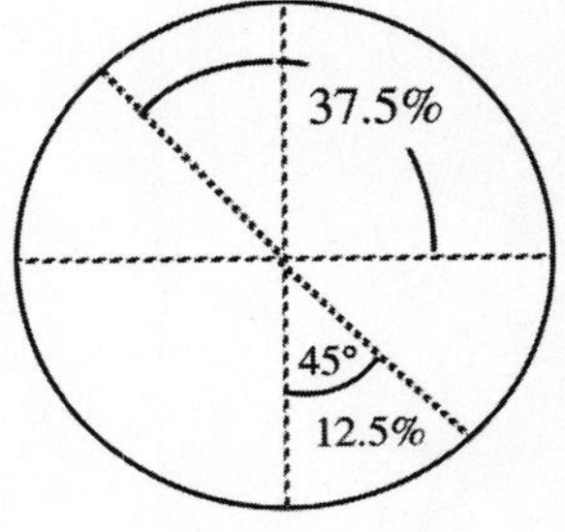

3. If a circle graph has, for example, sectors measuring 12%, 23%, and 42%, then we might place them in the circle first (and erase the diameters that we drew in lightly).

These larger sectors do not need to be adjacent to each other. The other smaller sectors can then fit in next to and around these larger sectors.

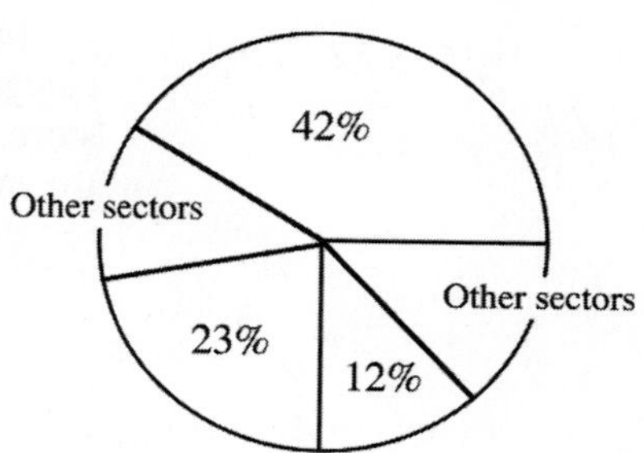

4. Another helpful guideline is to look for two (or more) percents that add up to 25% or 50%.

For example, 17% and 8% add to 25%, so those two sectors can fit into one of the 25% sectors formed by the two lightly drawn diameters.

Also, 39% and 11% add to 50% and can, together, fit into one-half of the circle. The remaining sectors will fit in where they can.

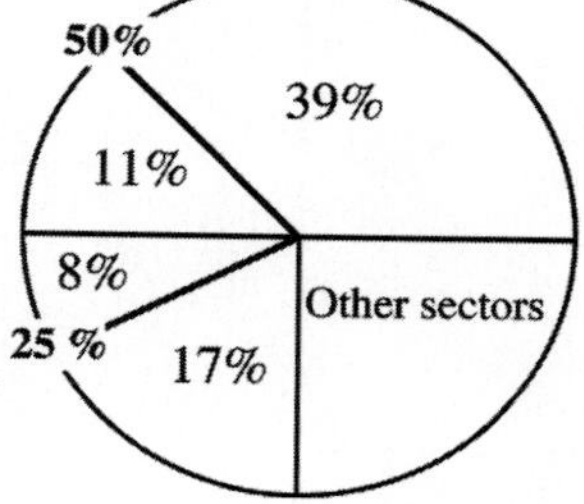

YOU TRY IT 4 *Here is a table of second graders' favorite colors and the percent of those students who favor each color. Fit the percent data into a circle graph.*

Color	Percent of Students Who Favor Each
Black	8%
Blue	35%
Green	9%
Orange	15%
Red	16%
Yellow	12%
Other	5%
Total	**100%**

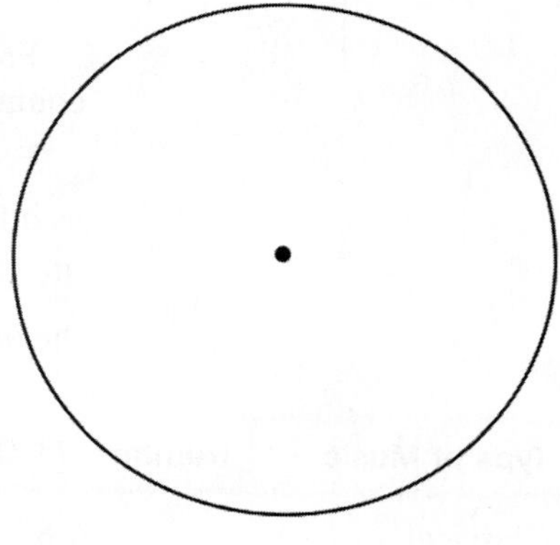

If we are given a table of data values from a study, then we can calculate the percent in each category before drawing its related circle graph. For example, Miko is the manager at a record store. She took the sales data from one weekend and compiled the following information, with the number of CDs sold in parentheses:

> Classical (8); Country (18); Gospel (24); Jazz/Blues (40); Rap/Hip Hop (34); Rock/Soft Rock (60); Other (16). (The Other category includes foreign language and children's CDs.)

Type of Music	Number of CDs Sold
Classical	8
Country	18
Gospel	24
Jazz/Blues	40
Rap/Hip Hop	34
Rock/Soft Rock	60
Other	16
Total	**200**

From the information above we can find the percentage for each category by dividing each count (the number of CDs sold) by the total of 200 CDs sold.

For example, for the Gospel category, the percentage would be $24 \div 200$. This can be seen as a fraction, $\frac{24}{200}$, which simplifies by a factor of 2 to $\frac{12}{100}$, which is 12%. We could also use long division to find the percentage: $200\overline{)24.000}$. Whichever procedure you choose, be sure to write the answer as a percent; don't leave it as a decimal or fraction.

Type of Music	Number of CDs Sold	Percent of Total Sales
Classical	8	4%
Country	18	9%
Gospel	24	12%
Jazz/Blues	40	20%
Rap/Hip Hop	34	17%
Rock/Soft Rock	60	30%
Other	16	8%
Total	**200**	**100%**

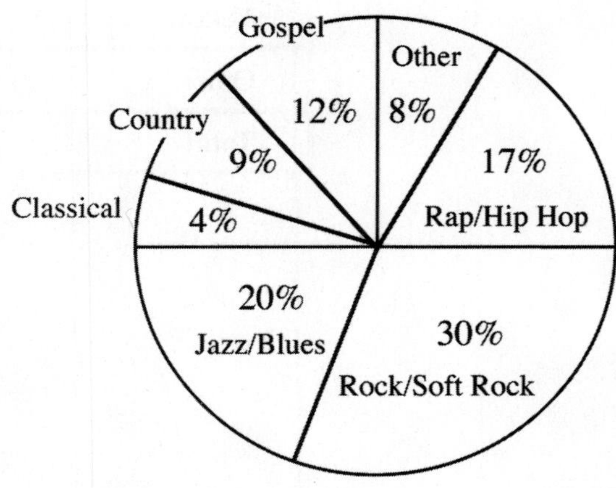

Note: 8% and 17% add to 25%; 20% and 30% add to 50%.

YOU TRY IT 5

Below is a table showing the number of people in Minnesota (in 1,000s) that speak a language other than English. For example, the table shows us that about 16,000 people in Minnesota speak an African language. Source: www.mla.org

Complete the table by listing the percent for each language group, and then place the percent data appropriately to complete the circle graph.

Language Classification	Number of People (in 1,000s)	Percent of Total
Spanish	136	
Asian Languages	100	
Germanic	56	
Russian/Slavic	24	
African Languages	16	
French	24	
Other	44	
Total	**400**	

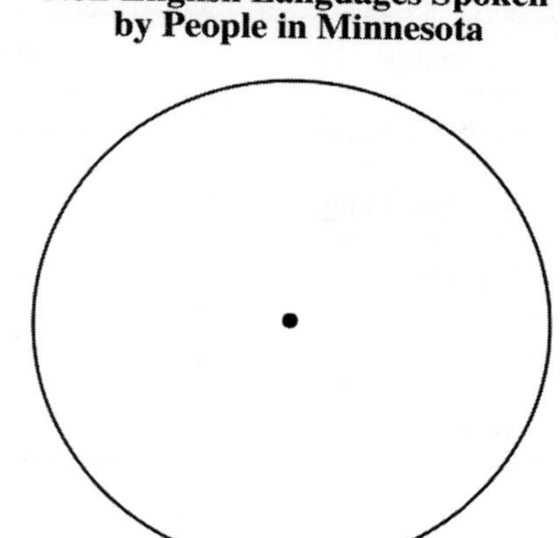

You Try It Answers: Section 8.1

YTI 1

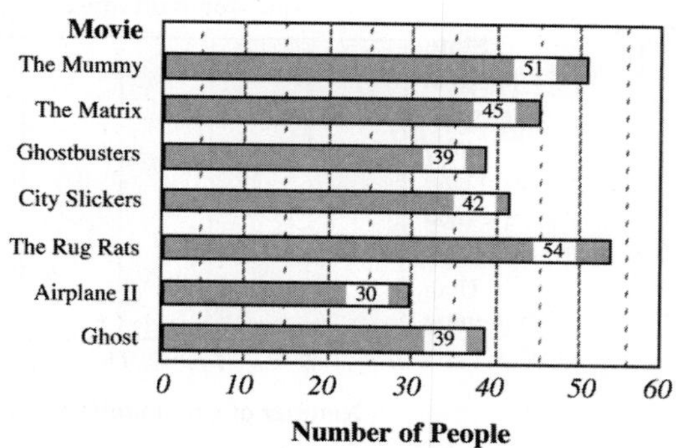

YTI 2

City	Number of Inches of Rain
Albuquerque, NM	9
Austin, TX	36
Bismarck, ND	16
Buffalo, NY	39
Denver, CO	15
Detroit, MI	34
Phoenix, AZ	8
Portland, OR	37
San Diego, CA	10

YTI 3

Grade	Percent of Students Receiving the Grade	Total Number of Students Receiving the Grade
A	16%	24
B	24%	36
C	40%	60
D	12%	18
F	8%	12
Total	**100%**	**150**

YTI 4

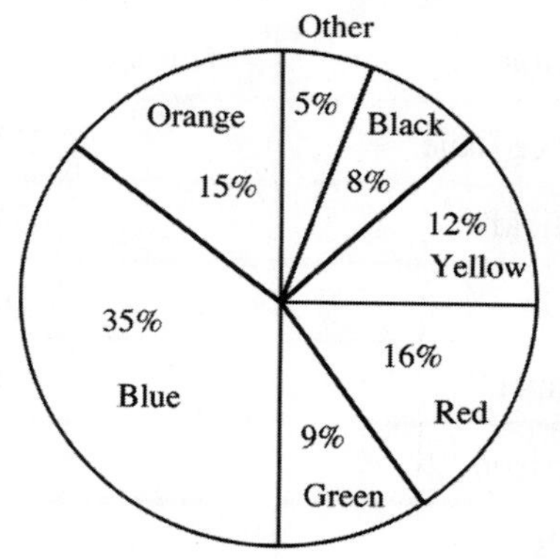

Note: 9% and 16% add to 25% and fit into one-fourth of the circle.

Similarly, 15% and 35% add to 50% and fit into one-half of the circle.

Your placement of the sectors may be different than shown here.

YTI 5

Language Classification	Number of People (in 1,000s)	Percent of Total
Spanish	136	34%
Asian Languages	100	25%
Germanic	56	14%
Russian/Slavic	24	6%
African Languages	16	4%
French	24	6%
Other	44	11%
Total	**400**	**100%**

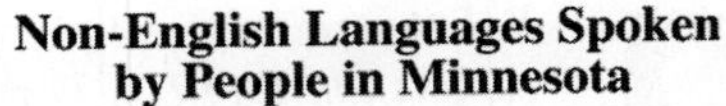

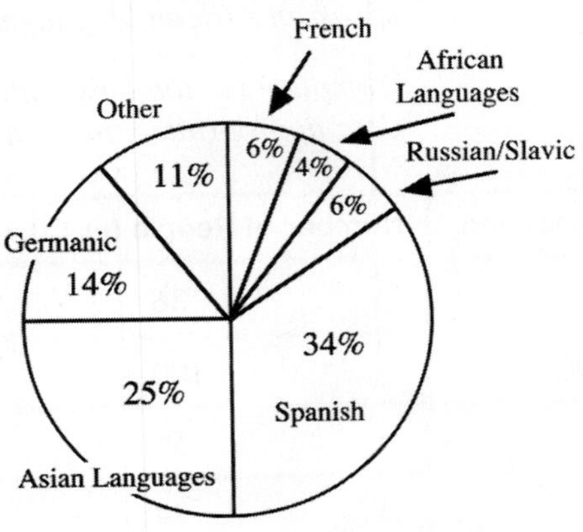

Focus Exercises: Section 8.1

Given a table of values, draw the related bar graph.

1. The number of community colleges in the Rocky Mountain states.

Mountain State	Number of Community Colleges
Arizona	20
Colorado	15
Idaho	3
Montana	14
Nevada	4
New Mexico	19
Utah	4
Wyoming	8

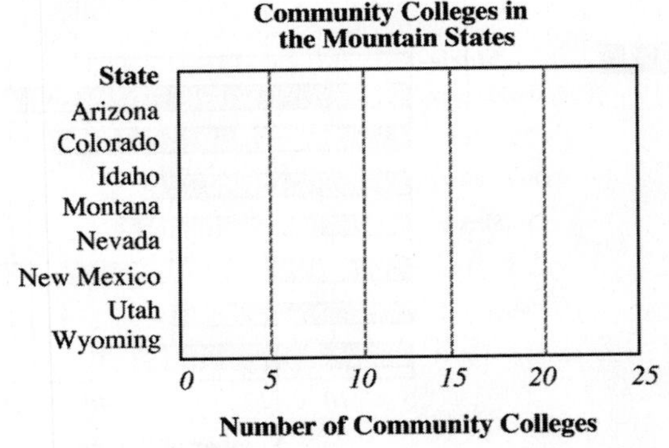

2. The number of student computers at six different elementary schools in the Hartin Unified School District.

Elementary School	Number of Computers
Amber Lane	23
Garfield	34
Hartin	20
Kemper	31
Morrison	27
Wells	25

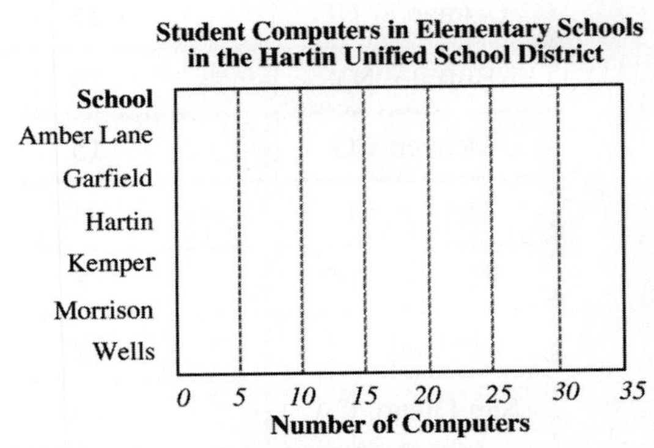

3. The number of athletes representing some South American countries in the 2004 Summer Olympics.

Country	Number of Athletes
Bolivia	7
Chile	22
Colombia	57
Ecuador	17
Paraguay	32
Uruguay	16
Venezuela	51

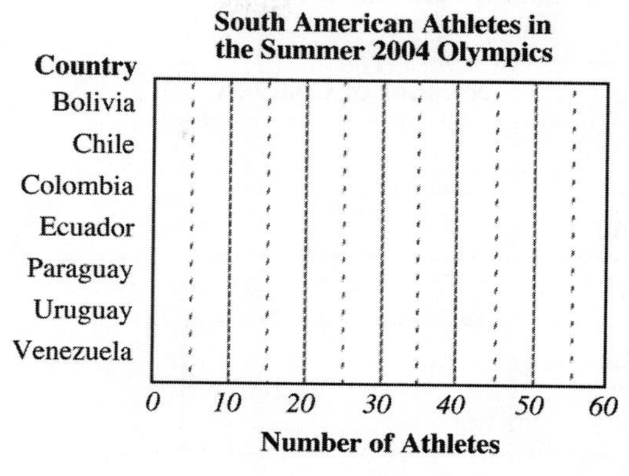

4. The number of votes in the U.S. Electoral College, by geographic region.

U.S. Region	Number of Electoral Votes
New England	34
Mid-Atlantic	83
South	132
Midwest	124
Southwest	56
West	109

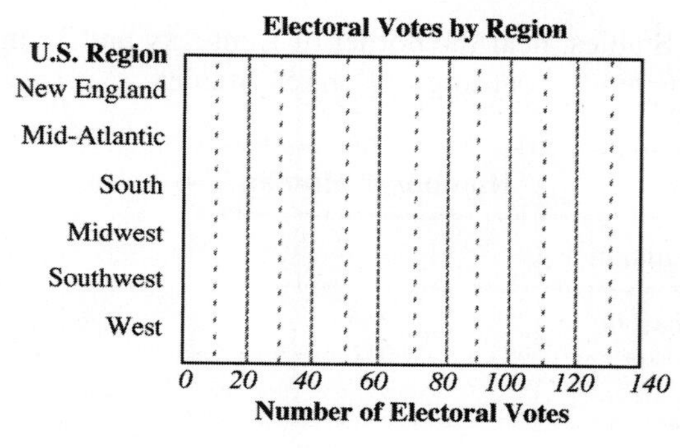

Given a bar graph, write the related table of values. Compare the table values to the total number indicated.

5. The combined age of all five of the charter jets in the Glory Aviators fleet is 33 years. The graph shows the age of each jet.

Jet	Age, in Years
Freedom	
Glory	
Patriot	
Spirit	
Victory	
Total	**33**

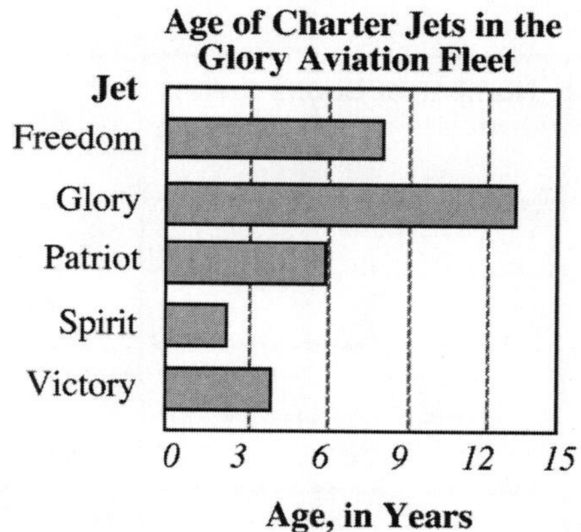

6. At Lincoln Elementary School, a total of 81 children had perfect attendance for the entire school year. Here is a bar graph of the data for each grade level.

Grade	Number of Children
First	
Second	
Third	
Fourth	
Fifth	
Sixth	
Total	**81**

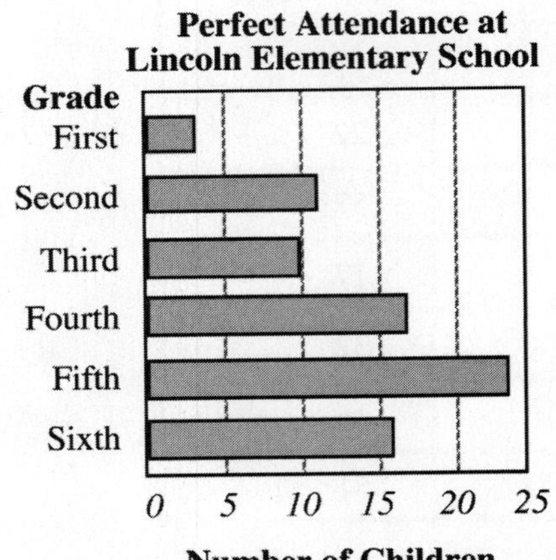

7. KenTen Stables, near the border of Kentucky and Tennessee, boards a variety of horses. Here is a bar graph of the 85 horses currently boarding at KenTen Stables.

Breed	Number of Horses
Andalusian	
Clydesdale	
Friesian	
Paint	
Palomino	
Total	**85**

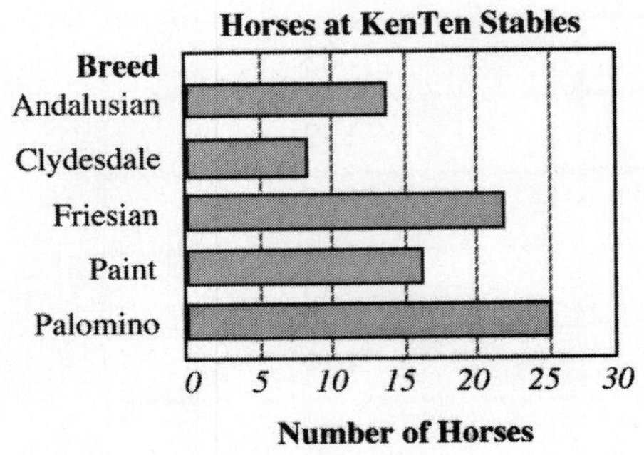

8. Last week, Bargain Book Barn sold a total of 145 of these best-selling authors' books. The bar graph indicates, by author, the number of books sold.

Author	Number of Books Sold
Albom	
Brown	
Crichton	
Grisham	
King	
Steele	
Total	**145**

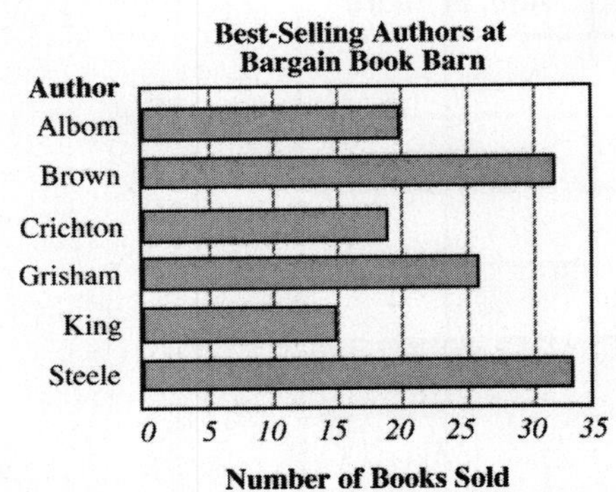

Complete the table by listing both the percent for each category as well as the number of items in that category.

9. The marital status of 120 women who signed up for Rancho College's Sociology 20 class, Marriage and Family, is shown in the circle graph below.

Marital Status	Percent of Women	Total Number of Women
Married		
Divorced		
Widowed		
Legally Separated		
Never Married		
Total		

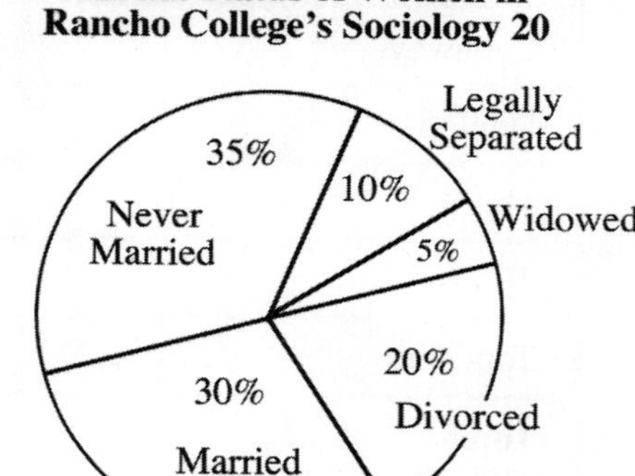

10. Below is a circle graph indicating the education level of the 300 parent members of the PTA at Goodhew Middle School.

Level of Education	Percent of Parents	Total Number of Parents
Less than 12th grade		
High School Diploma		
Some College		
Associate's Degree		
Bachelor's Degree		
Graduate Degree		
Total		

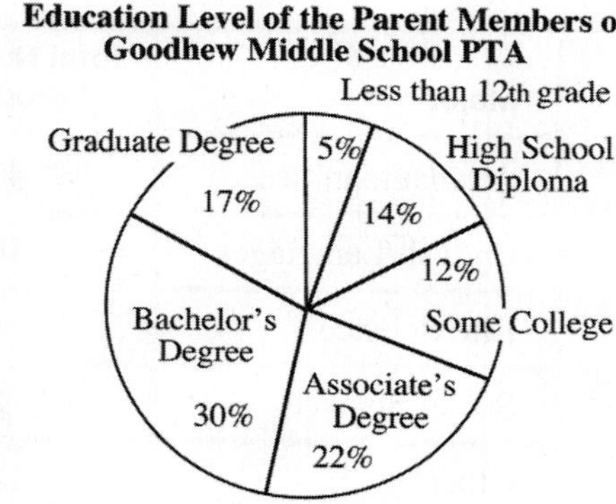

11. Below is a circle graph indicating the type of doctors employed at Vista General Hospital. There are a total of 250 doctors at Vista General.

Type of Doctor	Percent of Doctors	Total Number of Doctors
Anesthesiologists		
General Practitioners		
Gynecologists		
Internists		
Surgeons		
Other		
Total		

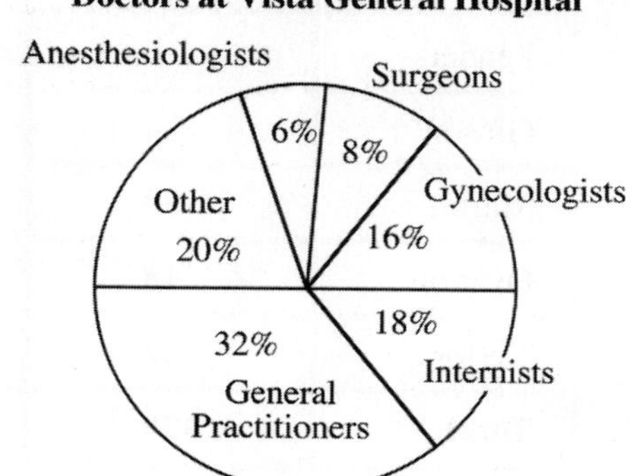

12. Below is a circle graph indicating the brand of golf ball sold at Putt 'N Cup Golf Supplies last week. Putt 'N Cup sold a total of 150 boxes of golf balls.

Golf Ball Brand	Percent of Golf Balls	Total Number of Golf Balls
Callaway		
Dunlop		
Maxfli		
Titleist		
Top-Flite		
Total		

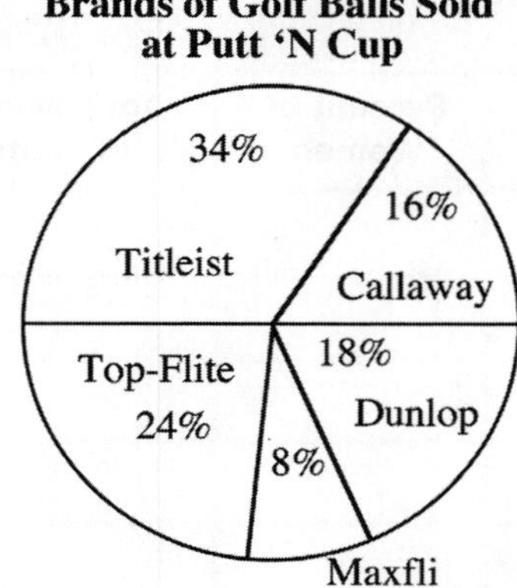

Complete the table by listing the percent of the whole for each category; then place the percent data appropriately in the circle graph.

13. At a liberal arts college, the 80 students living in one dorm had the majors shown in the table.

Major	Total Number of Students	Percent of Students
Arts/Humanities	40	
English/Languages	16	
Life Science	4	
Social Science	8	
Other	12	
Total	**80**	

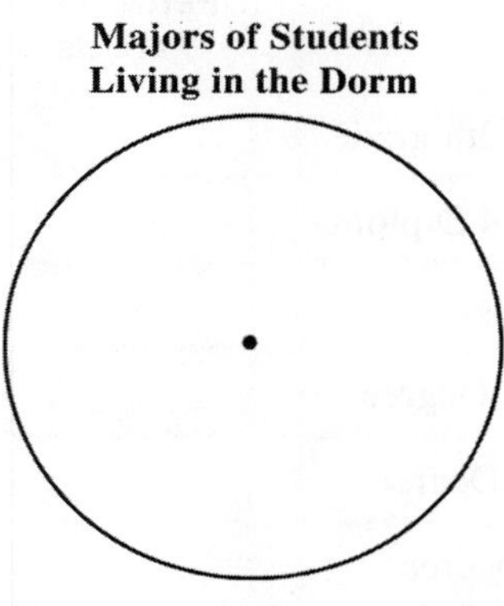

14. At Pick and Strum Guitars, the following acoustic guitar brands were sold last month.

Brand	Total Number of Guitars	Percent of Guitars
Fender	6	
Gibson	24	
Martin	30	
Ovation	18	
Taylor	42	
Total	**120**	

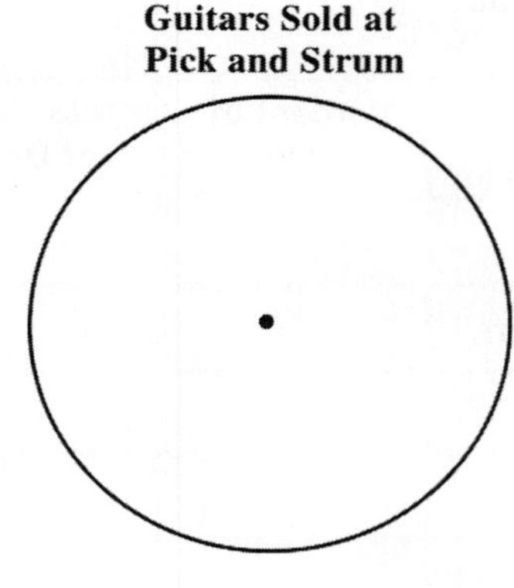

15. A total of 200 children signed up to play Little League in Norco. On the application form, each player was asked to indicate the primary position he would like to try out for: pitcher, catcher, infielder, or outfielder. Some left that answer blank. Below is a table of their responses.

Position	Total Number of Players	Percent of Players
Pitcher	56	
Catcher	10	
Infielder	74	
Outfielder	44	
Left blank	16	
Total	**200**	

Position Indicated on Little League Application Form

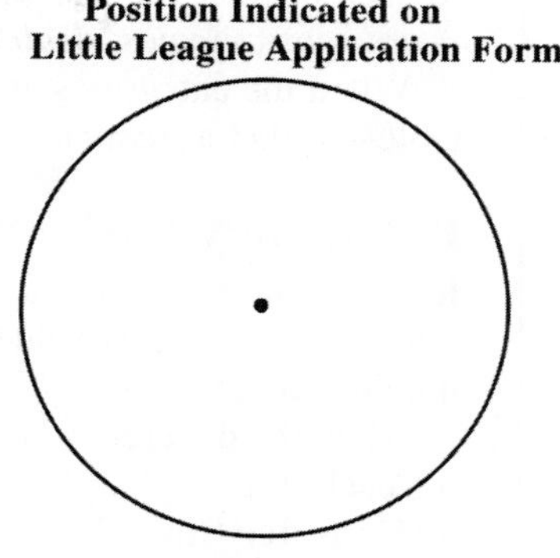

16. At the annual Kiwanis International convention, one session—with 150 delegates—focused on worldwide child hunger. Below is a table of the number of delegates from each of the six continental regions with Kiwanis clubs.

Continental Region	Total Number of Delegates	Percent of Delegates
Oceania	12	
Africa	45	
Asia	21	
Europe	18	
North America	30	
South America	24	
Total	**150**	

Delegates at the Annual Kiwanis International Convention

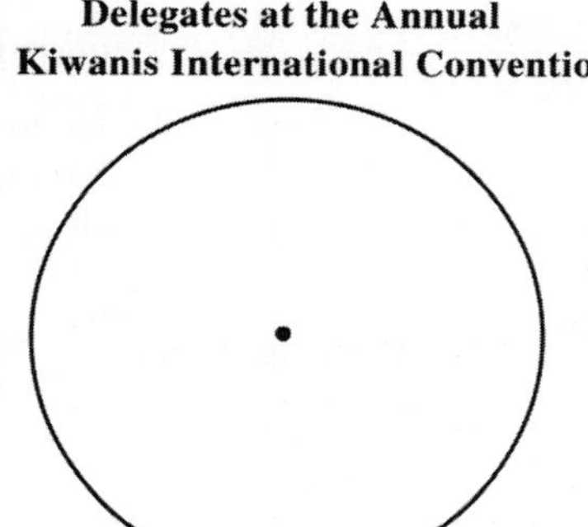

SECTION 8.2 Histograms

Objectives

In this section, you will learn to:

- Read frequency distribution tables.
- Read and draw histograms.

To successfully complete this section, you need to understand:

- Adding whole numbers (1.3)
- Reading and creating bar graphs (8.1)

Introduction

In each of the examples and exercises in the previous section, the categories were *things* like *restaurants*, *movies*, *dealerships*, and *cities*.

When the categories are numbers, we organize the data differently and use a different type of table—called a *frequency distribution table*—and a different type of graph, called a *histogram*.

Frequency Distribution Tables

In the example below, each category is a range of numbers called a **class interval**. Each class interval has a lowest value and a highest value. The class interval also includes every whole number in between.

Also, the difference between the highest and lowest values in each class interval is the same for each one.

Consider this: Nate took a survey of people attending the last game of the Houston Astros 2004 baseball season. He asked 50 Astros fans how many games they had attended that season. For two fans the answer was only one game; others had attended more than 20 games, and one man attended 67 games!

Nate organized the data in numerical order and put each into a class interval; he decided to make the class intervals—representing the number of games a fan had attended—from 1 to 10; from 11 to 20; and so on. The last class interval is from 61 to 70.

He then counted the number of fans that fit into each class interval—called the **class frequency**—and created the **frequency distribution table** below. (Recall that *frequency* means how many times something occurs.)

(Class Interval) Games Attended	(Class Frequency) Number of Fans
1–10	12
11–20	10
21–30	15
31–40	5
41–50	3
51–60	4
61–70	1
Total	**50**

Yes, there were two fans who attended only *one* game, but others attended 3 games, some attended 4 games, and so on.

There were 12 fans in all who fit into this first class interval: 1 – 10 games attended.

From the information above, we know that one man attended 67 games.

Looking at the table only, though, we can't tell how many games he attended, just that he attended anywhere from 61 to 70 games.

Reading Histograms

Nate then displayed these data in a graph called a **histogram**. Notice that the categories (across the bottom) are the class intervals, and the height of each bar shows the corresponding class frequency. (As with a bar graph, the bars in a histogram have the same width.)

Games Attended by Houston Astros Fans

(Frequency) Number of Astros Fans

16
12
8
4

1 – 10 11 – 20 21 – 30 31 – 40 41 – 50 51 – 60 61 – 70

Number of Games Attended

From the frequency distribution table, or from the histogram, we can combine class intervals to answer questions about the distribution. For example,

a) How many fans attended more than 40 games?
'More than 40' includes the last three classes:

3	in the 41–50 class
4	in the 51–60 class
+ 1	in the 61–70 class
← 8	total

8 fans attended more than 40 games.

b) How many fans attended from 11 to 30 games?
'From 11 to 30' includes the 2nd and 3rd classes:

10	in the 11–20 class
+ 15	in the 21–30 class
← 25	total

25 fans attended from 11 to 30 games.

How does a histogram differ from a bar graph?

YOU TRY IT 1

On July 31, Tammy checked the accounts of 50 Hollywood Video customers and looked at how many videos/DVDs they rented that month. Below is a frequency distribution table of the data she collected.

a) Draw a histogram based on the given data. (Use the outline provided, and remember that the width of each bar should be the same.)

Videos Rented	Number of Customers
1–5	14
6–10	10
11–15	12
16–20	5
21–25	6
26–30	3
Total	**50**

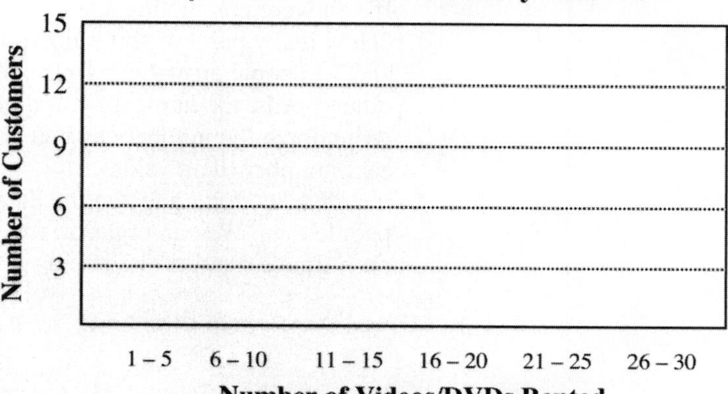

b) How many customers rented from 16 to 25 videos and DVDs?

c) How many customers rented more than 10 videos and DVDs?

d) How many customers rented fewer than 16 videos and DVDs?

YOU TRY IT 2

On September 30, Tanya asked 60 Starbucks customers how many times they visited Starbucks during the month. Below is a histogram of the data she collected.

a) Fill in the frequency distribution table with the data shown in the histogram.

Number of Visits	Number of Customers
Total	**60**

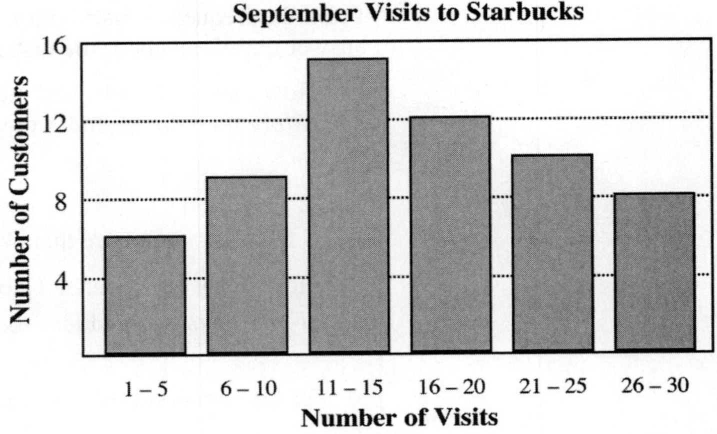

b) How many customers visited more than 20 times?

c) How many customers visited fewer than 11 times?

d) How many customers visited from 11 to 25 times?

Creating Histograms

If you were conducting a survey, you might ask a question that has a numerical answer, such as, "How many pairs of shoes do you own?"

The people answering your question will have answers such as 3, 10, 6, 1, 15, and so on. In other words, the numbers you'd get would not be in numerical order. It would be your job to write down the numbers as you hear them and then later determine into which class interval each number (data value) fits.

Let's say you collected the data shown on page 519 for the number of pairs of shoes thirty people own. We can organize this into a frequency distribution table by making a tally mark each time a number fits into a class interval.

3	10	6	1	15	4
7	6	12	20	13	5
23	4	19	8	2	6
14	20	25	16	9	7
4	12	9	2	8	14

Number of Pairs of Shoes	Tally	Number of People
1–5	~~||||~~ |||	8
6–10	~~||||~~ ~~||||~~	10
11–15	~~||||~~		6
16–20	||||	4
21–25	||	2
Total		**30**

At the end, total the frequency column to make sure that it adds—in this case—to 30, the total number of data values. You can now create a histogram from this table.

YOU TRY IT 3

Ms. Chung wanted to create a histogram of her algebra students' Chapter 5 test results (she has 40 students in this class). Below is the data from her grade book. (Use the discussion above as a guide.)

a) Fill in the frequency distribution table and draw its related histogram.

83	90	76	81	65	87	96
77	96	82	70	53	75	85
93	74	59	88	82	89	79
74	80	75	66	79	70	83
84	92	79	62	58	62	71
71	83	90	68	72		

Scores on Test	Tally	Number of Students
50–59		
60–69		
70–79		
80–89		
90–99		
Total		

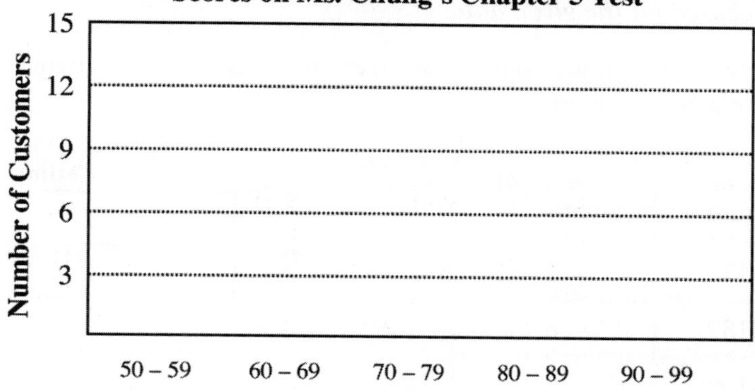

Ms. Chung's grading scale is **A** (90 - 100), **B** (80 - 89), **C** (70 - 79), **D** (60 - 69), **F** (below 60).

b) How many students got an A on the test?

c) How many students got an A or B on the test?

d) How many students got worse than a C on the test?

You Try It Answers: Section 8.2

YTI 1 a)

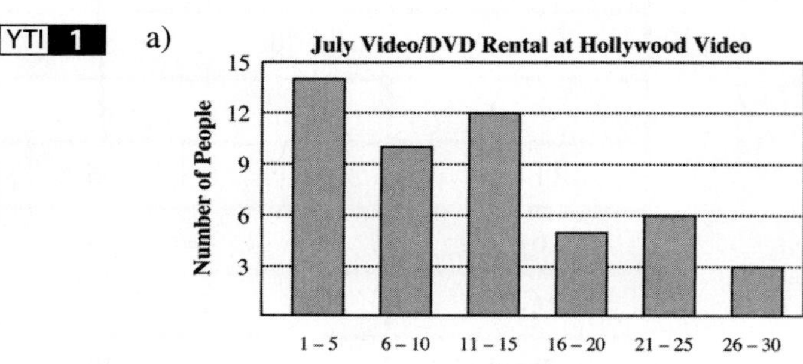

b) 11 c) 26 d) 36

YTI 2 a)

Number of Visits	Number of Customers
1–5	6
6–10	9
11–15	15
16–20	12
21–25	10
26–30	8
Total	**60**

b) 18
c) 15
d) 37

YTI 3 a)

Scores on Test	Tally	Number of Students
50–59	|||	3
60–69	𝍸	5
70–79	𝍸 𝍸 ||||	14
80–89	𝍸 𝍸 ||	12
90–99	𝍸 |	6
Total		**40**

b) 6
c) 18
d) 8

Scores on Ms. Chung's Chapter 5 Test

Number of Students: 15, 12, 9, 6, 3

50 – 59 60 – 69 70 – 79 80 – 89 90 – 99

Focus Exercises: Section 8.2

Draw a histogram based on the given data.

1. 60 night-light bulbs were tested to determine their lifetimes. Below is a frequency distribution table of the data collected.
a) Draw the related histogram.

Number of Hours	Number of Lightbulbs
170–179	2
180–189	8
190–199	15
200–209	19
210–219	13
220–229	3
Total	**60**

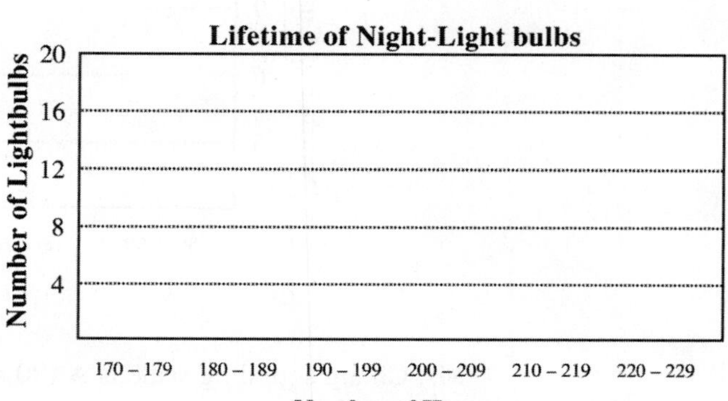

b) How many lightbulbs lasted longer than 189 hours?

c) How many lightbulbs lasted less than 190 hours?

d) How many lightbulbs lasted from 190 to 209 hours?

e) How many lightbulbs lasted at least 200 hours?

2. At the annual *Relay for Life* cancer walk, 40 teams walked for 24 hours straight. (At least one person from each team was on the track throughout the entire 24 hours.) Below is a frequency distribution of the number of miles each team walked.

(a) Draw the related histogram.

Number of Miles	Number of Teams
35–39	4
40–44	3
45–49	12
50–54	9
55–59	5
60–64	7
Total	**40**

b) How many teams walked more than 49 miles?

c) How many teams walked fewer than 50 miles?

d) How many teams walked from 40 to 59 miles?

Fill in the frequency distribution table with the data shown in the histogram.

3. Ms. Mojica's algebra students (90 students in all) were required to do on-line homework. An algebra software package kept track of the number of hours each student spent doing on-line homework. Below is a histogram of the data Ms. Mojica collected at the end of the semester.

a) Fill in the frequency distribution table based on the data in the histogram.

Number of Hours	Number of Students
Total	

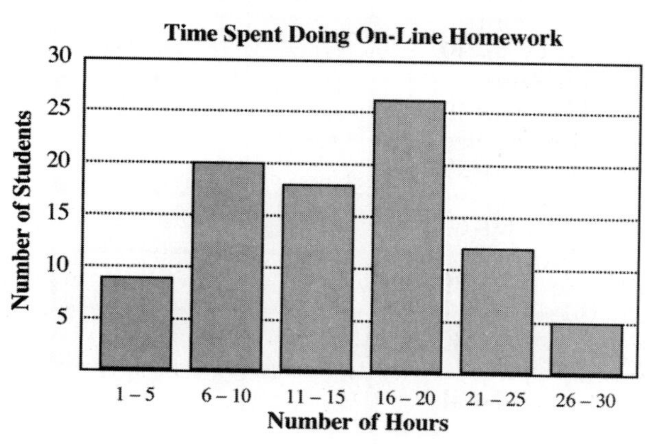

b) How many students spent more than 20 hours on their homework?

c) How many students spent fewer than 11 hours on their homework?

d) How many students spent from 11 to 25 hours on their homework?

4. Leslie's junior bowling league has 40 children in it. Below is a histogram showing the bowlers' best scores of the season.

a) Fill in the frequency distribution table based on the data in the histogram.

Best Score	Number of Bowlers
Total	

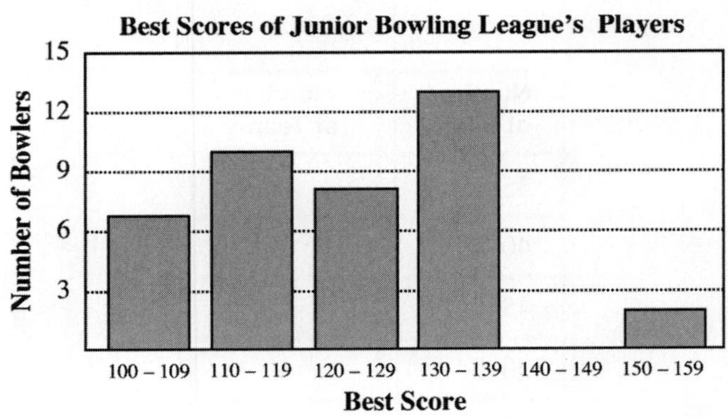

b) How many bowlers' best score was more than 129?

c) How many bowlers' best score was less than 120?

d) How many bowlers' best score was from 130 and 149?

Fill in the frequency distribution table and draw its related histogram.

5. Jane is a manager at 24-hour Fitness. She wanted to know how many minutes clients were spending at the gym each time they visited. Below are the data collected from 50 different clients.

a) Fill in the frequency distribution table and draw the related histogram.

Number of Minutes	Tally	Number of Clients
30–39		
40–49		
50–59		
60–69		
70–79		
80–89		
Total		

52	47	61	80	50	65	73	39
45	56	72	51	62	43	35	67
64	52	49	32	71	58	52	89
70	65	58	42	60	54	33	79
38	46	62	62	51	86	83	48
69	49	75	77	34	59	50	62
40	61						

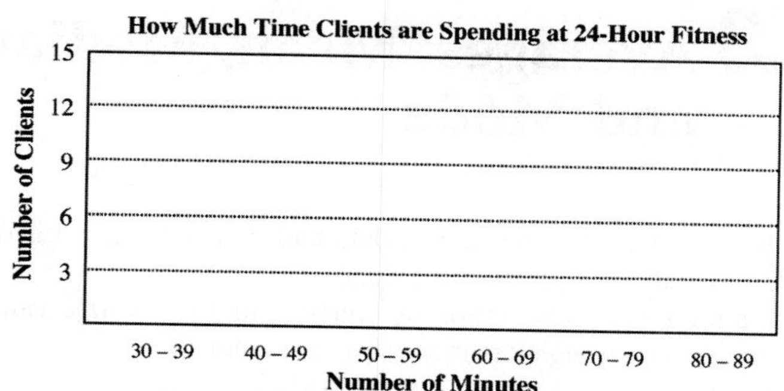

b) How many clients spend less than 50 minutes?

c) How many clients spend from 40 to 69 minutes?

d) How many clients spend at least one hour?

6. Gail, Aldersgate Church's secretary, was asked to compile the 2005 Sunday service and special event attendance for 40 families. (Special events include Ash Wednesday and Christmas Eve services, etc.) Below are the data she collected.

a) Fill in the frequency distribution table and draw the related histogram.

Number of Services	Tally	Number of Families
0–9		
10–19		
20–29		
30–39		
40–49		
50–59		
Total		

38	15	20	5	42	33	29	53
46	21	18	7	35	3	19	42
40	56	25	30	10	12	41	30
29	49	47	26	15	8	27	25
46	32	49	13	41	33	46	28

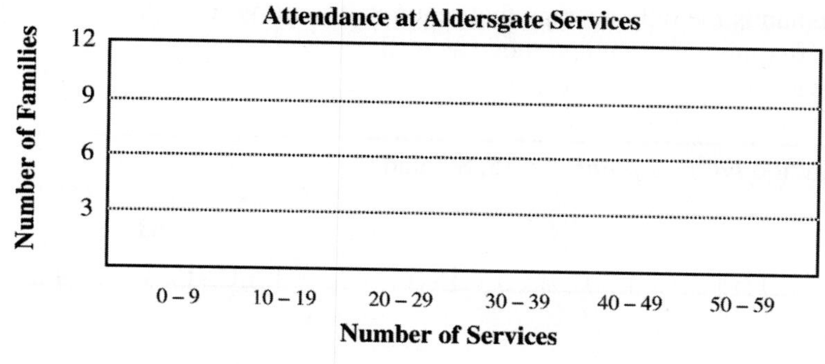

b) How many families attended fewer than 20 services?

c) How many families attended from 40 to 59 services?

d) How many families attended at least 30 services?

SECTION 8.3 Averages: Mean, Median, and Mode

Objectives

In this section, you will learn to:

- Use a formula to find the mean of a set of numerical data values.
- Find the median of a set of numerical data values.
- Find the mode of a set of numerical data values.

To successfully complete this section, you need to understand:

- Adding whole numbers (1.3)
- Rounding decimals (5.2)
- Adding decimals (5.3)
- Dividing decimals (5.5)

Introduction

In the previous section we looked at a set of numerical data and graphed it as a histogram. The histogram provided us with a visual description of the data.

In this section we look at a numerical description by considering the *average* value of the data. And, we will see that the word *average* has more than one interpretation.

As an example, a few years back, there was a newspaper article in the *Cucamonga Community College Chronicle* that described the school's average student as:

- 25 years old;
- having a 3.152 grade point average;
- seeking an AA degree;
- living 5.2 miles from the college; and
- female.

Some young men just out of high school thought, "That doesn't sound anything like me! Am I not a typical student?"

The truth is, they are rather typical, but they don't fit this one description of being *average*. In fact, there might be just one or two students at the whole college that fit that exact description. So what is *average* anyway, and how might we come up with the average community college student?

There are basically three types of averages, the *mean*, the *mode,* and the *median*:

1. The **mean** is the balancing point for all of the data; there is a formula for finding the mean.
2. The **mode** is the data value that occurs the most; this is found by observation.

And, when the data are written in numerical order:

3. The **median** is the very middle number of all of the data; this is found, mostly, by observation.

Though the median is the only average that requires it, writing the data in numerical order can be helpful for finding the mean and mode as well.

We'll explore each average one at a time.

Estimate the mean, the *balance point,* for 75, 89, and 94.

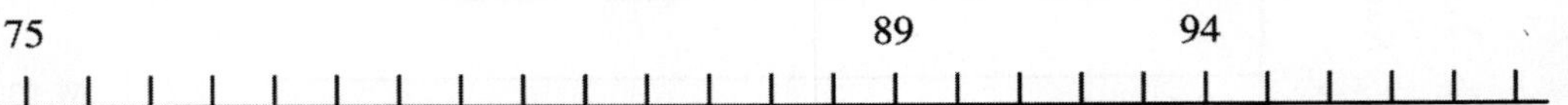

The Mean

Usually when we think of *average*, we're thinking of the mean. The **mean** is a numerical average that is found by addition and division:

$$\text{Mean} = \frac{\text{the sum of all the data values}}{\text{the total number of data values collected}}$$

It is this formula you use to figure out your average score on your math tests. Let's say that, on three 100-point tests, your scores were 89, 75, and 94. Your average score, your *mean* score is:

$$\text{Mean} = \frac{89 + 75 + 94}{3} \begin{array}{l} \leftarrow \text{The sum of the data values: your three scores.} \\ \leftarrow \text{The total number of data values: you had three tests.} \end{array}$$

$$\text{Mean} = \frac{258}{3} = 86 \text{ (the balance point of the three numbers). Your average score is 86.}$$

Think about it

For 75, 89, and 94, the mean is 86. Why do you think the mean is called the *balance point*? (Hint: Find the distance between the mean and each of the three data values.)

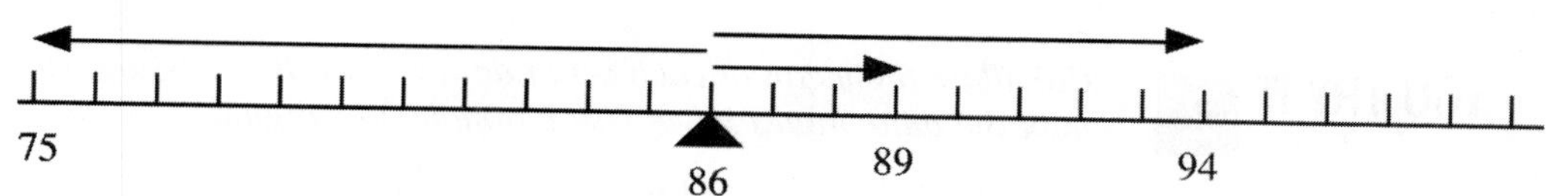

It is common to round the mean to have one more decimal place than the data values have. If the data values are whole numbers, then round to the nearest tenth. If the data values have one decimal place, then round to the nearest hundredth. It's common, though, to round money to the nearest penny.

EXAMPLE 1

Calculate the mean of each of these quiz or test scores. If necessary, round to one more decimal place than the data values have.

a) Four 25-point quizzes: 17, 24, 16, 21

b) Six 50-point tests: 41, 37, 33, 39, 42, 37

PROCEDURE: Add the quiz/test scores and divide by the number of quizzes/tests. Use long division and decimals, if necessary. Because the data values are whole numbers, round the mean to the nearest tenth.

ANSWER: a) $\text{Mean} = \frac{17 + 24 + 16 + 21}{4} = \frac{78}{4} = 19.5$ (Rounding is not necessary.)

b) $\text{Mean} = \frac{41 + 37 + 33 + 39 + 42 + 37}{6} = \frac{229}{6} = 38.166 \approx 38.2$

YOU TRY IT 1

Calculate the mean of each of these quiz or test scores. If necessary, round to one more decimal place than the data values have. Use Example 1 as a guide.

a) Three 20-point quizzes: 17, 20, 15

b) Five 10-point quizzes: 9, 6, 8, 10, 6

The mean can be found for any set of numerical data values in the very same way: add all of the data values together and divide that sum by the number of data values.

EXAMPLE 2

Calculate the mean of each set of data values. If necessary, round to one more decimal place than the data values have.

a) Eight retired men were asked to recall the number of cars they have owned over their lifetimes. Here are their answers: 10, 17, 8, 12, 15, 23, 11, 16.

b) Elton keeps track of the distance (in miles) from his office to his various clients. Here are the distances for six clients: 9.3, 5.2, 7.6, 11.4, 1.9, 8.8.

ANSWER: a) $\text{Mean} = \dfrac{10 + 17 + 8 + 12 + 15 + 23 + 11 + 16}{8} = \dfrac{112}{8} = 14 \text{ or } 14.0$

b) $\text{Mean} = \dfrac{9.3 + 5.2 + 7.6 + 11.4 + 1.9 + 8.8}{6} = \dfrac{44.2}{6} = 7.3666 \approx 7.37$

YOU TRY IT 2

Calculate the mean of each set of data values. If necessary, round to one more decimal place than the data values have. Use Example 2 as a guide.

a) One week of high temperatures in Phoenix:
103°, 105°, 99°, 100°, 106°, 110°, 101°

b) Five runners' times (in seconds) in the 100 meter dash:
11.1, 10.9, 11.2, 10.6, 10.8

c) Tips earned by four servers at Denny's:
$41.20, $38.50, $35.90, $43.70

Knowing how to calculate the mean is helpful in finding a grade point average (GPA). Each grade in college has a point value according to this table:

Grade	A	B	C	D	F
Point Value	4	3	2	1	0

Question: What is the mean between an A, a B, and a C?
Answer: It depends on whether the grades are weighted the same or weighted differently.

Consider these two situations:

1. Trevor is taking a history class and has had to write three term papers so far this semester. His grades on those three papers are C, B, and A; these three grades average to a B:

$$\text{Mean} = \frac{C + A + B}{3} = \frac{2 + 4 + 3}{3} = \frac{9}{3} = 3 = B$$

2. Stacy took three courses last semester: Spanish (5-units), Sociology (3-units), and Yoga (1-unit). Here is a table of her grades:

Course	Spanish	Sociology	Yoga
Grade	C	B	A

It might, at first, look as though Stacy has a B average from these three courses. However, because each class has a different number of units, the grades are weighted differently.

For example, an A in Stacy's Spanish class has 5 times more grade point value than an A in her Yoga class. In other words, we must multiply each grade by the unit value of the class.

Course	Grade	Point Value	Units	Grade Points (Point Value × Units)
Spanish	C	2	5	10
Sociology	B	3	3	9
Yoga	A	4	1	4
		Total:	9	23

Here is how we figure Stacy's grade point average for that semester:

$$\text{Grade point average} = \frac{\text{Total grade points}}{\text{Total units}} = \frac{23}{9} = 2.5555$$

It's common to round the grade point average off to two decimal places: GPA = 2.56.

A GPA of 2.56 is below a B average (which is 3.00). That's because the 5-unit C grade is much stronger than the 1-unit A grade.

YOU TRY IT 3

Calculate the grade point average for this student's spring grade distribution. Round the answer to two decimal places. Use the example above as a guide.

Course	Grade	Point Value	Units	Grade Points (Point Value × Units)
Biology	B		4	
Algebra	A		5	
Guidance	A		1	
History	C		3	
Art	D		2	
		Total:		

Grade Point Average = ________

The Median

After a list of data has been put into numerical order, the **median** is found to be the very middle number of the ordered list. This means that there will be an equal number of data values to its right as to its left.

For example, here are the data collected from 15 art students who were asked their age:

21, 17, 33, 24, 67, 18, 45, 19, 27, 30, 19, 32, 22, 41, 28

When put in numerical order, the list becomes

17, 18, 19, 19, 21, 22, 24, 27, 28, 30, 32, 33, 41, 45, 67

With an odd number of data values (fifteen), once the middle number is found, there is an even number of values (fourteen) remaining to divide equally between the left and the right of the middle number; in this case, there are seven values on each side.

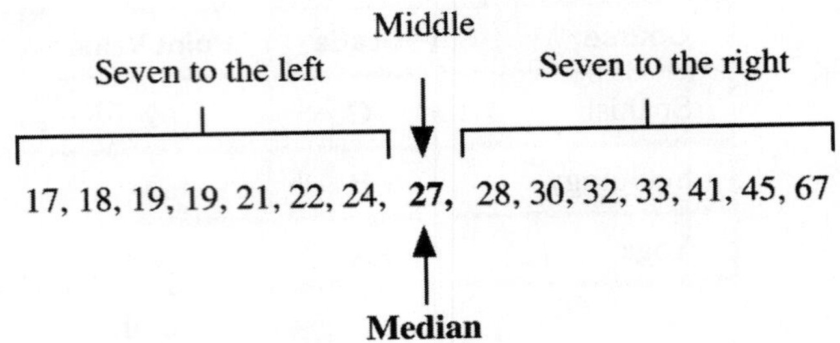

EXAMPLE 3 Put each list in numerical order and identify the median.

a) Nine quiz scores: 8, 5, 9, 10, 4, 5, 2, 9, 6

b) Ages of thirteen students: 18, 26, 39, 22, 19, 23, 21, 18, 42, 21, 25, 28, 22

PROCEDURE: Put the data in numerical order and find the very middle number.

ANSWER: a) Quiz: 2, 4, 5, 5, **6**, 8, 9, 9, 10

Four to the left — Four to the right

Median = 6

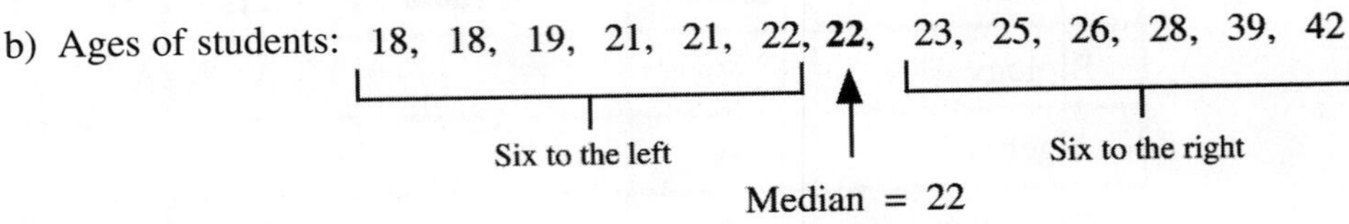

Caution Notice, in part b, that the median is not the only 22 in the list; there is another 22 on the left side of the median, but that doesn't matter when finding the middle number.

YOU TRY IT 4 *Put each list in numerical order and identify the median. Use Example 3 as a guide.*

a) Pairs of shoes owned by eleven people: 10, 9, 1, 4, 18, 12, 7, 5, 4, 15, 2

b) Number of children in fifteen families: 2, 3, 2, 0, 4, 1, 1, 7, 0, 5, 1, 2, 8, 3, 2

In the examples above, the number of data values in each list was odd. This allowed us to identify a single middle number and split the rest of the list equally between the left and the right:

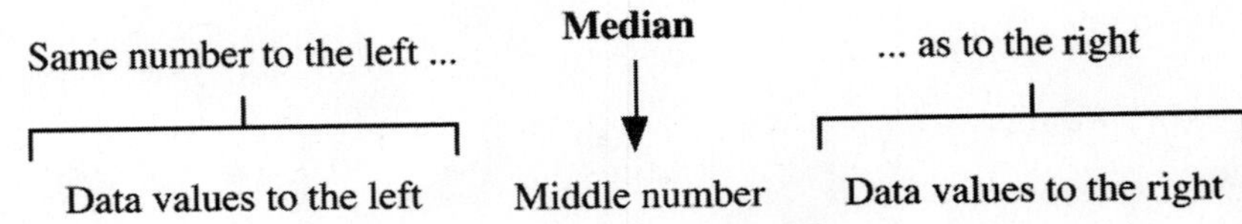

However, when the list has an even number of data values, then the median splits the two middle-most numbers. (Keep in mind that the list of data values must first be put in numerical order.)

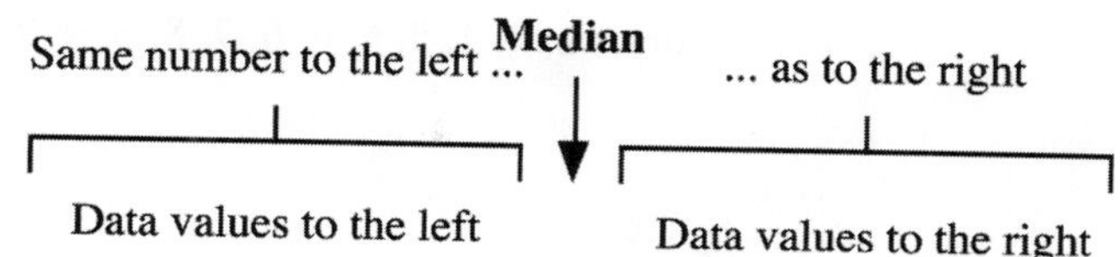

Consider this list of ten numbers representing the ages of cousins at a family gathering (already placed in numerical order):

1, 3, 4, 6, 7, 9, 10, 10, 11, 15

These ten data values can be evenly split with the first five data values on the left and the second five data values on the right. In this case, the median lands between 7 and 9:

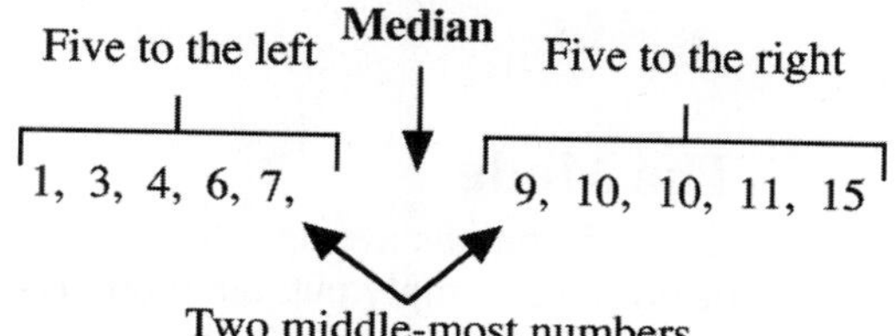

Two middle-most numbers

The median is the number exactly in the middle of **7** and **9**; it is the *mean* of just those *two* middle-most numbers:

$$\text{Median} = \frac{7 + 9}{2} = 8$$

Caution In finding the *mean* of the two middle-most numbers, we're *not* determining the mean of the whole list—just those two numbers—so we divide by 2.

Sometimes the median is a decimal, even though all of the data values are whole numbers. Consider this list of data values representing the number of hours worked by eight members of the Kiwanis Club in preparation for their silent auction: 15, 19, 8, 6, 14, 3, 21, 9.

Put in order, the list is 3, 6, 8, 9, 14, 15, 19, 21. The two middle-most data values are 9 and 14, so

$$\text{Median} = \frac{9 + 14}{2} = \frac{23}{2} = 11.5.$$

Also, it's possible that the two middle-most data values are the same number, as in this list:

2, 6, 9, 11, 11, 14, 19, 23

Here, the two middle-most numbers are both 11, so the median is 11.

EXAMPLE 4 Put each list in numerical order and identify the median.

a) Ten test scores: 77, 81, 63, 92, 82, 88, 75, 95, 60, 71

b) Sixteen quiz scores: 8, 6, 9, 10, 8, 5, 2, 9, 7, 6, 10, 9, 3, 4, 9, 6

PROCEDURE: Put the data in numerical order, underline the two middle-most data values and find the mean of just those two numbers.

ANSWER: a) Test scores: 60, 63, 71, 75, <u>77, 81,</u> 82, 88, 92, 95 Median $= \frac{77 + 81}{2} = \frac{158}{2} = 79$

b) Quiz scores: 2, 3, 4, 5, 6, 6, 6, <u>7, 8,</u> 8, 9, 9, 9, 9, 10, 10 Median $= \frac{7 + 8}{2} = \frac{15}{2} = 7.5$

YOU TRY IT 5 *Put each list in numerical order and identify the median. Use Example 4 as a guide.*

a) High temperatures in San Diego for the first two weeks in July } 86, 85, 82, 75, 72, 77, 86, 81, 75, 76, 75, 86, 83, 77

b) Number of college classes taken by eight students } 14, 9, 23, 17, 6, 11, 5, 20

The Mode

How is it that the average student at a college can be female? This is where the mode is used as the average. Simply put, the **mode** is the value (not necessarily numerical) that occurs most often.

If 3,289 women and 2,956 men are enrolled at Cucamonga College, then there are more women than men, and the mode is *female*. In other words, according to the mode, the average student is a woman.

In a numerical list of data values, we can search out the mode as the number that occurs most often. It's best to put the list in numerical order so that the mode can be easily identified. Sometimes, there is even more than one mode, as shown in the next example.

EXAMPLE 5 Put each list in numerical order and identify the mode.

a) Sixteen quiz scores: 8, 6, 9, 10, 8, 5, 2, 9, 7, 6, 10, 9, 3, 4, 9, 6

b) Ages of fourteen students: 18, 26, 39, 22, 18, 19, 23, 21, 18, 42, 21, 25, 28, 21

c) Fifteen test scores: 95, 46, 77, 81, 63, 92, 80, 88, 75, 93, 60, 71, 82, 90, 79

PROCEDURE: Put the data in numerical order and underline the value(s) that occur most often.

ANSWER: a) Quiz scores: 2, 3, 4, 5, 6, 6, 6, 7, 8, 8, <u>9, 9, 9, 9,</u> 10, 10; Mode = 9

b) Ages of students: <u>18, 18, 18,</u> 19, <u>21, 21, 21,</u> 22, 23, 25, 26, 28, 39, 42;
This list has *two modes*, 18 and 21.

c) Test scores: 46, 60, 63, 71, 75, 77, 79, 80, 81, 82, 88, 90, 92, 93, 95;
Every number on this list occurs only once, so it has *no mode*.

YOU TRY IT 6 *Put each list in numerical order and identify the mode by underlining it. If there is no mode, state so. Use Example 5 as a guide.*

a) Number of daily student absences from Dr. Chavez's weekend class } 0, 2, 1, 5, 6, 2, 4, 1, 5, 3, 4, 6, 5, 2, 5, 0

b) High temperatures in Baltimore for the last two weeks in March } 72, 70, 67, 59, 57, 62, 71, 66, 60, 61, 63, 74, 68, 65

c) Number of pairs of shoes owned by eighteen people } 7, 9, 3, 1, 4, 9, 9, 12, 4, 7, 5, 9, 4, 15, 2, 4, 9, 4

Think about it

Explain in your own words the three mathematical meanings of the word *average*.

YOU TRY IT 7

The following list is the number of quarter-mile laps 12 physical education students completed in 30 minutes. Put this list in numerical order and identify the mean, median, and mode. (If there is no mode, state so.)

12, 5, 9, 4, 9, 20, 14, 18, 6, 9, 15, 16

Numerical Order:

a) Mean: b) Median: c) Mode:

You Try It Answers: Section 8.3

YTI 1 a) 173 b) 7.8

YTI 2 a) 103.4° F b) 10.92 seconds c) \$39.83

YTI 3

Course	Grade	Point Value	Units	Grade Points
Biology	B	3	4	12
Algebra	A	4	5	20
Guidance	A	4	1	4
History	C	2	3	6
Art	D	1	2	2
		Total:	**15**	**44**

Grade Point Average $= \dfrac{44}{15} \approx 2.93$

YTI 4 a) 1, 2, 4, 4, 5, 7, 9, 10, 12, 15, 18; Median = 7
b) 0, 0, 1, 1, 1, 2, 2, 2, 2, 3, 3, 4, 5, 7, 8; Median = 2

YTI 5 a) 72, 75, 75, 75, 76, 77, 77, 81, 82, 83, 85, 86, 86, 86; Median = 79
b) 5, 6, 9, 11, 14, 17, 20, 23; Median = 12.5

YTI 6 a) 0, 0, 1, 1, 2, 2, 2, 3, 4, 4, 5, 5, 5, 5, 6, 6; Mode = 5
b) 57, 59, 60, 61, 62, 63, 65, 66, 67, 68, 70, 71, 72, 74; No Mode
c) 1, 2, 3, 4, 4, 4, 4, 4, 5, 7, 7, 9, 9, 9, 9, 9, 12, 15; Two Modes, 4 and 9

YTI 7 Numerical Order: 4, 5, 6, 9, 9, 9, 12, 14, 15, 16, 18, 20.
a) 11.4 b) 10.5 c) 9

Focus Exercises: Section 8.3

Calculate the mean of each of these quiz or test scores. If necessary, round to one more decimal place than the data values have.

1. Four 100-point tests:
92, 86, 70, 84

2. Five 25-point tests:
23, 20, 18, 22, 17

3. Six 50-point tests:
40, 47, 48, 42, 39, 42

4. Eight 10-point quizzes:
6, 9, 10, 8, 7, 10, 5, 9

5. Five 100-point tests:
72, 81, 86, 75, 83

6. Four 20-point quizzes:
18, 12, 15, 20

7. Three 200-point tests:
157, 172, 174

8. Seven 10-point quizzes:
10, 8, 9, 6, 6, 4, 9

Calculate the mean of each set of data values. If necessary, round to one more decimal place than the data values have.

9. The number of miles eight runners ran in two hours:
15, 19, 23, 17, 17, 20, 19, 22

10. The number of students receiving A's in seven algebra classes:
5, 8, 12, 4, 9, 11, 6

11. The number of cars sold in a 6-month period:
33, 28, 26, 35, 25, 31

12. The number of European cities visited by nine different tourists:
8, 3, 6, 12, 5, 7, 7, 9, 4

13. The number of kilometers five runners ran in two hours:
26.3, 21.8, 22.6, 19.5, 20.1

14. The price of a seedless watermelon at five grocery stores:
$3.80, $4.50, $5.10, $4.20, $4.90

15. The height, in meters, of four children:
1.26, 1.32, 1.41, 1.08

16. The number of miles seven students live from school:
5.7, 6.3, 10.1, 4.2, 0.8, 1.9, 2.4

Calculate the grade point average for each student's fall grade distribution. Round the answer to two decimal places.

17.

Course	Grade	Point Value	Units	Grade Points (Point Value × Units)
Anatomy	C		5	
Guitar	A		1	
English	B		4	
Sociology	A		3	
		Total:		

Grade Point Average = ______

18.

Course	Grade	Point Value	Units	Grade Points (Point Value × Units)
Physics	B		4	
Calculus	A		5	
Political Science	C		3	
Music Theory	B		3	
Art Appreciation	D		2	
		Total:		

Grade Point Average = ______

Identify both the median and the mode.

19. The 18-hole score for thirteen golfers } 82, 71, 75, 73, 80, 69, 71, 78, 76, 71, 79, 81, 77

20. The number of sponsors for eleven people in a walk-a-thon } 23, 18, 25, 36, 24, 17, 41, 32, 19, 38, 14

21. The number of living grandparents of fifteen children } 3, 5, 0, 2, 6, 1, 2, 4, 4, 3, 1, 3, 6, 0, 3

22. The number of cousins of seventeen children: 8, 4, 2, 9, 0, 4, 4, 11, 9, 15, 9, 0, 1, 4, 8, 10, 9

23. The number of rooms in twelve houses: 9, 15, 13, 8, 6, 4, 6, 12, 14, 6, 10, 11

24. The number of strikeouts for eight pitchers in a 40-game season: 20, 32, 40, 26, 52, 49, 29, 41

25. The number of hits for sixteen batters in a 40-game season: 53, 42, 38, 32, 45, 54, 38, 42, 38, 56, 48, 31, 39, 38, 45, 35

26. The number of minutes fourteen students took to finish a final exam: 63, 85, 92, 65, 63, 78, 92, 100, 63, 98, 92, 88, 70, 62

Identify all three averages: the mean, the median, and the mode.

27. The number of push-ups completed by nine sixth-graders:
31, 15, 19, 7, 2, 6, 10, 14, 20

28. The number of reuben sandwiches sold at a deli each day for 15 days:
8, 3, 6, 7, 2, 5, 4, 2, 6, 7, 4, 6, 5, 6, 4

29. The number of hours of flight for 12 novice pilots:
11, 13, 5, 9, 5, 7, 5, 13, 18, 16, 5, 19

30. The number of innings the starting pitcher lasted in 20 consecutive baseball games:
6, 4, 8, 7, 6, 9, 2, 3, 5, 1, 10, 6, 8, 7, 7, 4, 3, 6, 2, 4

SECTION 8.4 Probability

Objectives

In this section, you will learn to:

- Use the vocabulary of probability.
- Use a simple formula to find probabilities.
- Use a bar graph to find probabilities.

To successfully complete this section, you need to understand:

- Simplifying fractions (3.2)
- Writing a fraction as a percent (6.4)
- How to read a bar graph (8.1)

Introduction

Has this ever happened to you?

Tim, a college freshman, wants to take an English class, but it was already full when it was his turn to register for classes. He decides to go to the class the first day to see if the instructor will add him to the class.

There is a total of 4 students who want that class, but the instructor says she will add only 1 student. She takes their add cards and, placing them upside down, chooses a card at random.

Question: What is the probability that Tim's card will be chosen?

Answer: Tim has a 1 out of 4 chance—a 25% chance—of being selected: $\frac{1}{4} = 25\%$.

The Vocabulary of Probability

Situations like the one Tim experienced cause us to think about **probability**—a numerical way to express the likelihood that some particular thing, or *event*, will happen.

Within the probability situation above, let's look at some of the vocabulary related to probability:

- An **experiment** is the act of doing something to create a result.

  In our example, the experiment is the instructor choosing a card at random.
- The **possible outcomes** of an experiment are all of the different results that could occur; usually, only one outcome can occur for each experiment.

  In our example, the possible outcomes are the four different cards the instructor has to choose from; only one card will actually be selected.
- An **event** is an outcome that we're most interested in occurring.

  In our example, the event is that Tim's card is selected; we're not interested in anyone else's card. Choosing Tim's card is considered a **success**.
- The **probability** of an event is a ratio, abbreviated as P(event), and is calculated:

$$\mathbf{P}(\text{event}) = \frac{\text{the number of successes in the event}}{\text{the total number of possible outcomes}}$$

  Probability is commonly written as either a fraction or as a percent. In our example, there's only one way that our event could occur—because Tim has only 1 card in the drawing—and there is a total of 4 possible outcomes:

$$\mathbf{P}(\text{Tim's card}) = \frac{1}{4} = 25\%$$

An important aspect of probability is the idea that the selection is random.

- A **random selection** is the act of choosing something so that each possible outcome has an *equal chance* of being selected and is *equally likely* to be selected.

  In our example, the winning card is selected randomly if there is no way to distinguish between one card or another in the selecting process. Tim's card has just as much chance of being selected as Rey's card, or Amy's card, or Dionne's card.

Two Common Probabilities

Here are two experiments that have simple outcomes. In each, to ensure that a possible outcome has an equal chance of being selected, we assume that the experiment is being conducted fairly.

1. Flip a coin and let it land on the floor. There are only two possible outcomes, *heads* and *tails*. An event could be *landing heads up* or *landing tails up*. Each possible outcome is equally likely if the coin is fair and evenly balanced.

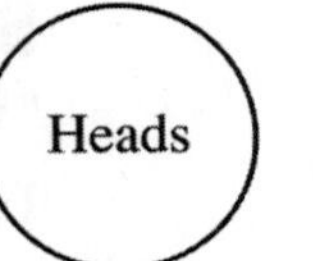

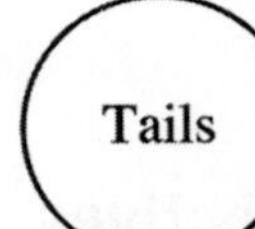

2. Roll a single die (singular of dice). There are six possible outcomes: 1, 2, 3, 4, 5, and 6. An event could be:
   - Rolling a 4 (one success, the number 4), or
   - rolling an even number (three successes, the numbers 2, 4, and 6), or
   - rolling a number higher than 4 (two successes, the numbers 5 and 6).

Each possible outcome is equally likely if the die is evenly balanced.

EXAMPLE 1 A quarter is flipped in the air. What is the probability that it will land tails up?

PROCEDURE: Assume the coin is fair and consider these four things:

1) identify the experiment;
2) identify the total number of possible outcomes;
3) identify the event; and
4) identify the number of successes described in the event.

The experiment is flipping a quarter; there is a total of **2** possible outcomes; the event is the quarter landing tails up; this event has only **1** success.

ANSWER: $\mathbf{P}(\text{tails}) = \dfrac{\text{Number of tails}}{\text{Total possible outcomes}} = \dfrac{1}{2}$ {There's a 1 out of 2 chance of the coin landing tails up.

EXAMPLE 2 Find the probability of each event. Simplify the fraction if possible.

a) A die is rolled. What is the probability of getting a 3?
b) A die is rolled. What is the probability of getting a number greater than 4?

PROCEDURE: Assume the die is fair consider these four things:

1) identify the experiment;
2) identify the total number of possible outcomes;
3) identify the event; and
4) identify the number of successes described in the event.

ANSWER: The experiment is to roll a single die; there are a total of 6 possible outcomes.

a) The event is to roll a 3; this event has only **1** success.

$\mathbf{P}(\text{roll a 3}) = \dfrac{\text{Rolling a 3}}{\text{Total possible outcomes}} = \dfrac{1}{6}$ {There's a 1 out of 6 chance of rolling a 3.

b) The event is to roll a number higher than 4; this event has 2 successes: rolling a 5 or a 6.

$\mathbf{P}(\text{more than 4}) = \dfrac{\text{Rolling a 5 or 6}}{\text{Total possible outcomes}} = \dfrac{2}{6} = \dfrac{1}{3}$ {There is a 1 out of 3 chance of rolling anumber higher than 4.

YOU TRY IT 1

Find the probability of each event. Assume the coin and die are fair. Use Examples 1 and 2 as guides.

a) A nickel is flipped in the air. What is the probability that it will land heads up?

b) A die is rolled. What is the probability of getting a 5?

c) A die is rolled. What is the probability of getting an odd number?

EXAMPLE 3

A bag contains 20 marbles. Four are red, 5 are yellow, 3 are green, and 8 are blue. The experiment is to pick one marble out of the bag.

What is the probability that the chosen marble is a) red? b) green?

PROCEDURE: Assume each marble has an equally likely chance of being selected.

ANSWER: a) There is a total of 20 possible outcomes; the event, *selecting a red marble*, has 4 possible outcomes because there are 4 red marbles.

$$\textbf{P}(\text{red}) = \frac{\text{Number of red marbles}}{\text{Total number of marbles}} = \frac{4}{20} = \frac{1}{5}$$

There's a 1 out of 5 chance of getting a red marble.

b) There is a total of 20 possible outcomes; the event, *selecting a green marble*, has 3 possible outcomes because there are 3 green marbles.

$$\textbf{P}(\text{green}) = \frac{\text{Number of green marbles}}{\text{Total number of marbles}} = \frac{3}{20}$$

There's a 3 out of 20 chance of getting a green marble.

YOU TRY IT 2

A bag has 12 marbles. Two are red, 1 is yellow, 3 are green, and 6 are blue. The experiment is to randomly select one marble from the bag.

What is the probability that the chosen marble is...
(Use Example 3 as a guide.)

a) red?

b) yellow?

c) green?

d) blue?

Bar Graphs and Probability

Consider the bag of marbles in Example 2. The bag has 4 red, 5 yellow, 3 green, and 8 blue marbles, and there is a total of 20 marbles in all.

We could create a bar graph of the bag of marbles:

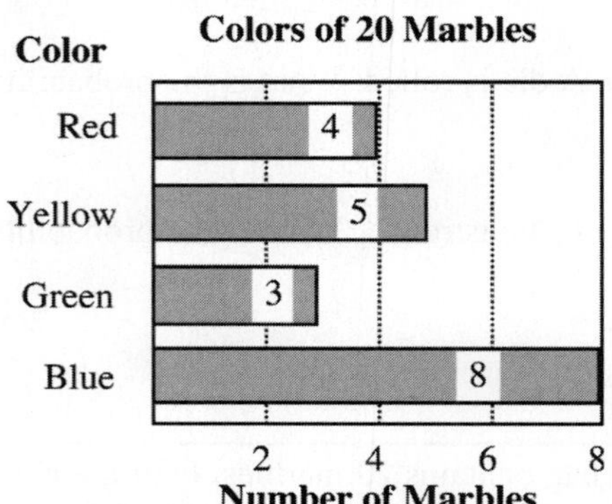

We could ask the same questions as in Example 2 but use the bar graph to help us find the answers. It is important to know that there are 20 marbles in all, as this is the denominator for each probability ratio.

One marble from the bag is randomly chosen.

a) What is the probability that the marble will be red? **P**(red) $= \frac{4}{20} = \frac{1}{5}$

b) What is the probability that the marble will be blue? **P**(blue) $= \frac{8}{20} = \frac{2}{5}$

We can use bar graphs to answer questions of probability that involve a random selection of one kind or another.

EXAMPLE 4

Here is a bar graph representing the number of lunch-hour employees at each restaurant in a shopping mall food court. Use it to answer the probability questions that follow.

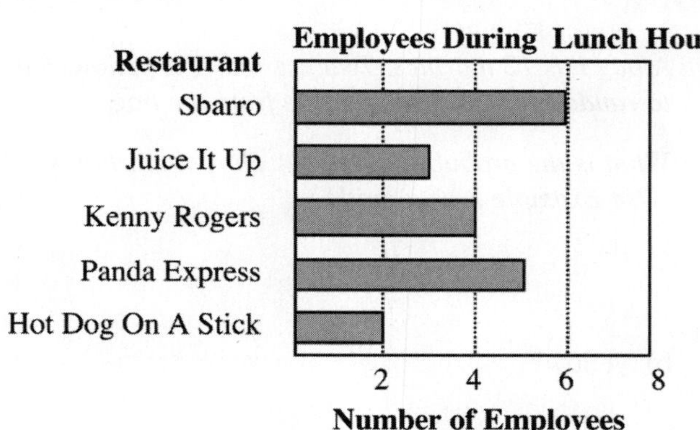

QUESTION: If the mall chooses a food court employee at random to win a mall gift certificate, what is the probability that the employee works for

a) Panda Express?

b) Sbarro?

PROCEDURE: Determine how many employees each bar represents, and determine the total number of employees in the diagram. (This is work that you can do in the original bar graph.)

Employees During Lunch Hour

Restaurant	Number of Employees
Sbarro	6
Juice It Up	3
Kenny Rogers	4
Panda Express	5
Hot Dog On A Stick	2

Number of Employees: 2 4 6 8

Total:
6
3
4
5
+ 2
20

ANSWER: a) $\textbf{P}(\text{Panda Express}) = \dfrac{\text{Number of Panda Express employees}}{\text{Total number of employees}} = \dfrac{5}{20} = \dfrac{1}{4}$

b) $\textbf{P}(\text{Sbarro's}) = \dfrac{\text{Number of Sbarro employees}}{\text{Total number of employees}} = \dfrac{6}{20} = \dfrac{3}{10}$

YOU TRY IT 3

The bar graph below shows the number of singers, by section, in Aldersgate's Chancel Choir. One member is randomly selected to be the guest director for the July 4th patriotic anthem.

What is the probability that the chosen singer is...
(Use Example 4 as a guide.)

a) a soprano?

b) a tenor?

c) an alto?

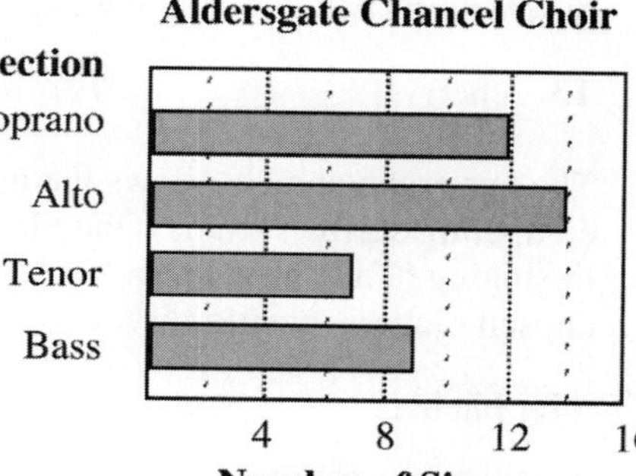

You Try It Answers: Section 8.4

YTI 1 a) $\textbf{P}(\text{heads}) = \dfrac{1}{2}$ b) $\textbf{P}(\text{roll is a 5}) = \dfrac{1}{6}$

c) $\textbf{P}(\text{roll is odd}) = \dfrac{3}{6} = \dfrac{1}{2}$

YTI 2 a) $\textbf{P}(\text{red}) = \dfrac{2}{12} = \dfrac{1}{6}$ b) $\textbf{P}(\text{yellow}) = \dfrac{1}{12}$

c) $\textbf{P}(\text{green}) = \dfrac{3}{12} = \dfrac{1}{4}$ d) $\textbf{P}(\text{blue}) = \dfrac{6}{12} = \dfrac{1}{2}$

YTI 3 a) $\textbf{P}(\text{soprano}) = \dfrac{12}{42} = \dfrac{2}{7}$

b) $\textbf{P}(\text{tenor}) = \dfrac{7}{42} = \dfrac{1}{6}$

c) $\textbf{P}(\text{alto}) = \dfrac{14}{42} = \dfrac{1}{3}$

Focus Exercises: Section 8.4

Find the probability of each event. Simplify all fractions completely.

Experiment: A six-sided die is rolled. What is the probability that it comes up ...

1. 2? **2.** less than 5? **3.** greater than 1?

4. less than 7? **5.** an odd number that is greater than 2? **6.** an even number that is less than 3?

Experiment: The spinner is spun and, when the needle comes to rest, it is pointing toward one of the numbers. What is the probability that it will point toward

7. 3? **8.** an even number?

9. an odd number? **10.** a number greater than 4?

11. a number less than 4? **12.** a number greater than 0?

Spinner

In this diagram, the spinning needle is pointing toward the 5.

Assume each number has an equal chance of being pointed to.

A bag has 20 candies. Eight are cherry, 5 are lemon, 4 are sour apple, and 3 are watermelon. The experiment is to randomly select one candy out of the bag. What is the probability that the chosen candy is

13. cherry? **14.** lemon? **15.** sour apple? **16.** watermelon?

The bar graph at right shows the number of players, by position, on two competing softball teams. One player is randomly selected to lead everyone in singing "Take Me Out to the Ball Game." What is the probability that the chosen player's position is

17. pitcher? **18.** catcher?

19. infielder? **20.** outfielder?

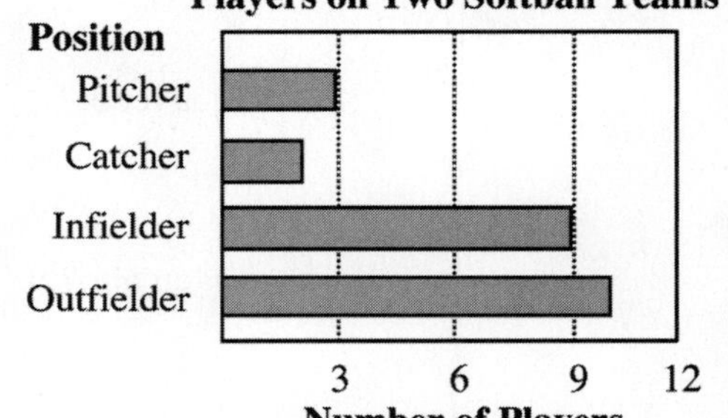

Every year, the Eastvale Rotary Club holds a special dinner to install its new board members. For this event, a member is chosen at random to give a short speech, before the Pledge of Allegiance, about the American Flag and what it represents to that member. The bar graph at right shows the number of members by political party affiliation. What is the probability that the chosen member's political party is

21. Republican? **22.** Green?

23. Libertarian? **24.** Democrat?

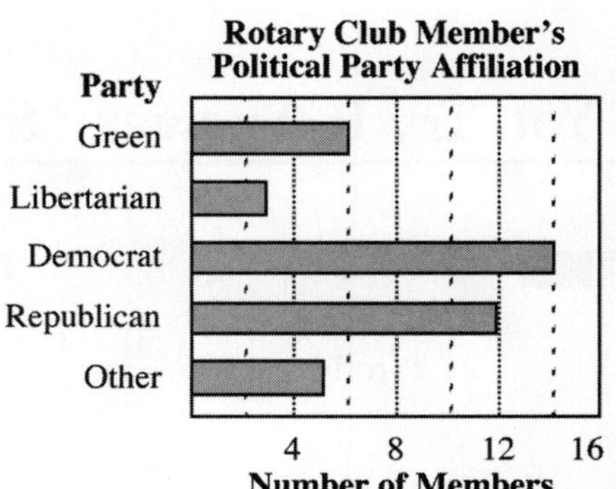

Chapter 8 Review

Section 8.1 Bar Graphs and Circle Graphs

CONCEPT

When a study is conducted, items of information—called **data**—are collected, organized in a table, and drawn as a graph. A **bar graph** uses bars to represent the number of responses to a certain category.

EXAMPLE

Fifty members of the Iowa Association of Birders went bird watching on the first day of spring. Each recorded the first bird he or she saw that day. Kami collected the results, organized them in a table, and drew a bar graph showing the data.

First Bird Spotted	Number of Bird Watchers
Blue Jay	6
Nuthatch	10
Swallow	13
Thrush	7
Wren	14
Total	**50**

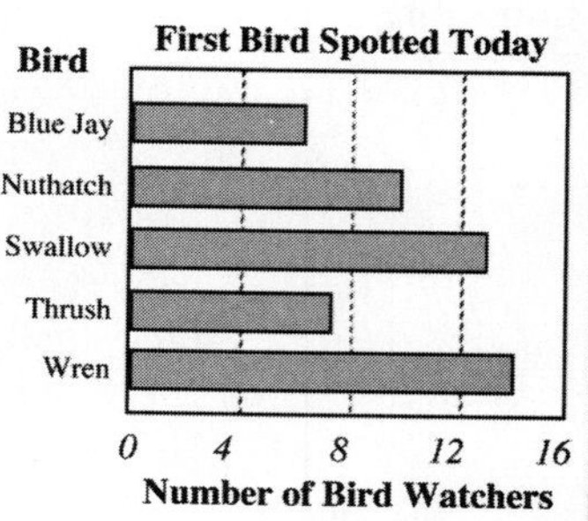

CONCEPT

In a **circle graph**, the categories are displayed in a circle, and we show each category as a percent of the whole, instead of the actual number of data values.

EXAMPLE

First Bird Spotted	Number of Bird Watchers	Percent
Blue Jay	6	12%
Nuthatch	10	20%
Swallow	13	26%
Thrush	7	14%
Wren	14	28%
Total	**50**	**100%**

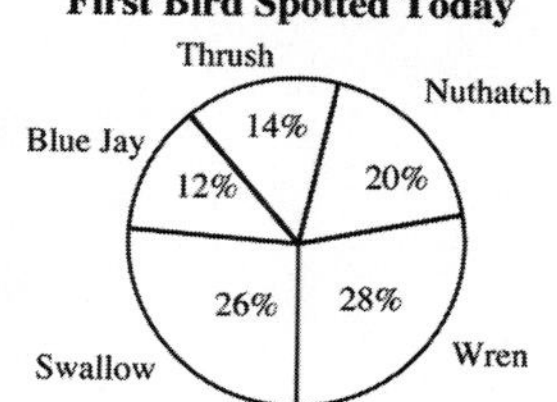

Section 8.2 Histograms

CONCEPT

When the data collected are numerical, the bar graph is called a **histogram**. Each category is a range of numbers called a **class interval**. Each class interval has a lowest value and a highest value. The class interval also includes every whole number in between. The difference between the highest and lowest values in a class interval is the same for each one. The number of data values that fit into each class interval is called the **class frequency**. A table of class frequencies is called a **frequency distribution table**.

EXAMPLE

Fifty members and of the Iowa Association of Birders went bird watching on the second Saturday in April. Each recorded the number of different birds he or she identified that day. Kami collected the results, organized the data in a frequency distribution table, and drew a histogram based on the frequency distribution table.

Number of Birds Identified	Frequency
0–4	2
5–9	8
10–14	13
15–19	10
20–24	6
25–29	11
Total	**50**

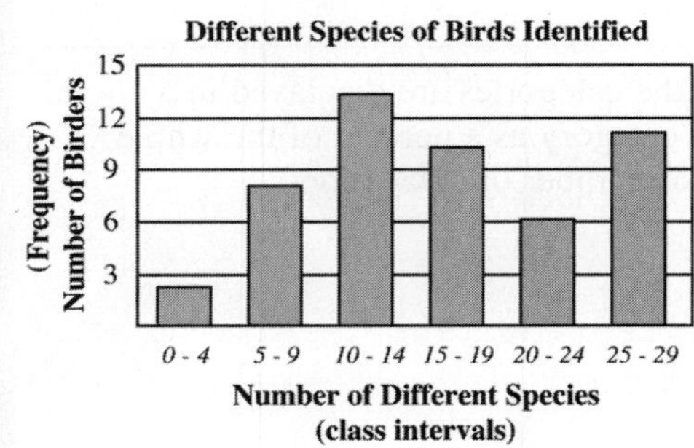

Section 8.3 Averages: Mean, Median, and Mode

CONCEPT	EXAMPLE
The **mean** is the balancing point for all of the data; it is a numerical average that is found by addition and division: $$\text{Mean} = \frac{\text{The sum of all the data values}}{\text{The total number of data values}}$$	**Note: The example presented here runs throughout the review for Section 8.3.** Twelve members of the Ohio Birdwatchers Club went to Crane Creel in Ohio on the 3rd of May. Each recorded the number of different warbler species identified. Stan collected the number of different species and put them in numerical order. The number of different species the 12 members identified: 3, 5, 6, 8, 8, 8, 11, 12, 12, 14, 15, 18. $$\text{Mean} = \frac{3 + 5 + 6 + 8 + 8 + 8 + 11 + 12 + 12 + 14 + 15 + 18}{12} = \frac{120}{12} = \mathbf{10}$$ The birders saw an average (mean) of 10 different species of warblers that day.
When the data values are written in numerical order, the **median** is the middle number. After the median is found to be the middle of the ordered list, there will be an equal number of data values to its right as to its left. With an odd number of data values, the median is the very middle number. With an even number of data values, the median splits the two middle-most numbers; the median is then the mean of the two middle-most data values.	With 12 data values collected, the median will be the mean of the two middle-most data values: 3, 5, 6, 8, 8, 8, 11, 12, 12, 14, 15, 18  $$\text{Median} = \frac{8 + 11}{2} = \frac{19}{2} = 9.5$$ The birders saw an average (median) of 9.5 different species of warblers that day.
The **mode** is the value (not necessarily numerical) that occurs most often.	The data value that occurs the most is 8, so mode = 8. 3, 5, 6, <u>8, 8, 8,</u> 11, 12, 12, 14, 15, 18 The birders saw an average (mode) of 8 different species of warblers that day.

Section 8.4 Probability

CONCEPT	EXAMPLE
Probability is a numerical way to express the likelihood that some particular thing, or event, will happen.	**Note: The example presented here runs throughout the review for Section 8.4.** Elsie is raffling a fruit basket and sells 10 raffle tickets. Carlo bought 1 raffle ticket, Dan bought 2, Ravi bought 3, and Eli bought 4. What is the probability that Ravi will win the raffle?
An **experiment** is the act of doing something to create a result.	The experiment is Elsie choosing a raffle ticket at random.
The **possible outcomes** of an experiment are all of the different results that could occur; usually, only one outcome can occur for each experiment.	The possible outcomes are the 10 different raffle tickets she has to choose from; only one will actually be selected.
An **event** is an outcome that we're most interested in occurring.	The event is that one of Ravi's tickets will be selected.
Each possible outcome within the event, itself, is called a **success**. Within an event, there may be just one success or many successes.	Ravi has three tickets so he has three chances to win, or three successes.
The probability of an event is a ratio, abbreviated as $P(\text{event})$, and is calculated: $P(\text{event}) = \dfrac{\text{The number of successes in the event}}{\text{The total number of possible outcomes}}$ Probability is commonly written as either a fraction or as a percent.	$P(\text{Ravi wins}) = \dfrac{\text{His 3 successes}}{\text{10 total tickets in the drawing}} = \dfrac{3}{10}$ There is a 3 out of 10 chance that Ravi will win the raffle.
A **random selection** is the act of choosing something such that each possible outcome has an equal chance of being selected and is equally likely to be selected.	The winning ticket is selected randomly if there is no way to distinguish between one ticket and another in the selecting process, and if each ticket has an equally likely chance of being selected.

Chapter 8 Review Exercises

Section 8.1

Given a table of values, draw the related bar graph.

1. The New York Yankees have played in the World Series 39 times, winning 26 of them throughout the years. Below is a table of other teams that have a high number of World Series appearances (through the 2005 season). *(Source: www.mistupid.com)*

Team	Number of World Series Appearances
Athletics	14
Cardinals	16
Cubs	10
Dodgers	18
Giants	17
Red Sox	10

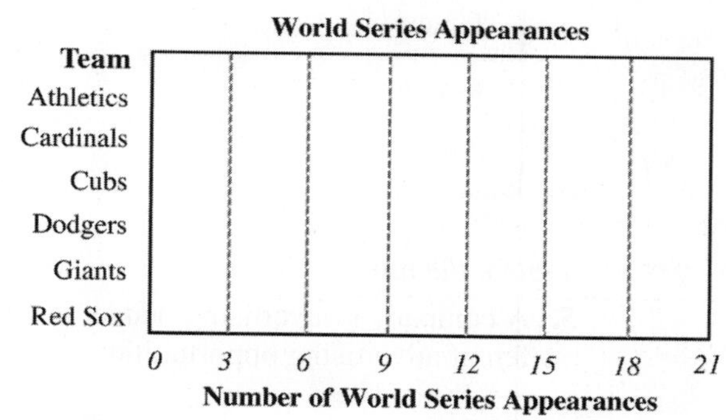

2. Below is a table of the number of teams in the various bowling leagues offered at Pinto Lanes.

Bowling League	Number of Teams
12 and under	10
13 through 17	14
Young Singles	20
Young Couples	16
Young at Heart	18
Seniors	24

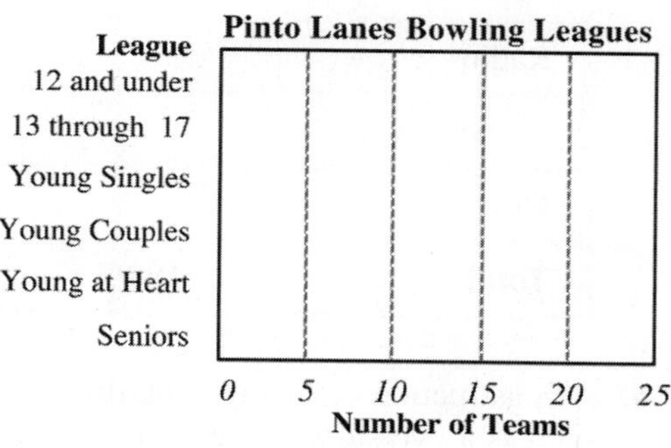

Given a bar graph, write the related table of values.

3. Below is a table of the top six U.S. food companies, which total $96 billion in revenue, based on 2003 revenues (in billions of dollars). *(Source: The World Almanac, 2005)*

Company	Revenue (in $billions)
ConAgra Foods	
General Mills	
H. J. Heinz	
Kellogg	
PepsiCo	
Sara Lee	

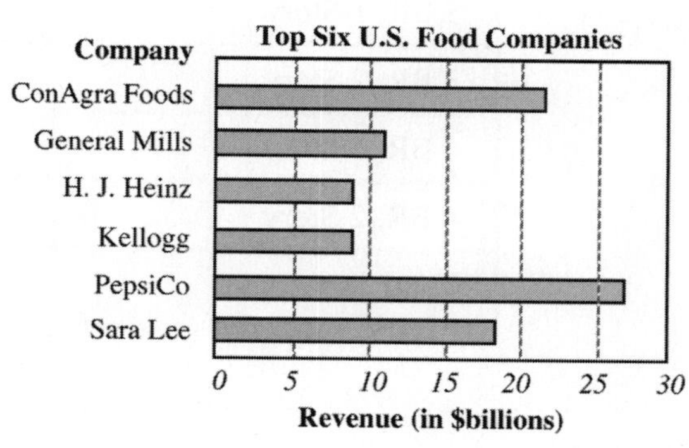

4. There have been 108 runnings of the Boston Marathon, from 1897 to 2004. Of the 108 men's events, a runner outside of the U.S. won it 65 times. Below is a bar graph of the four top foreign countries with winning runners (men's category) as well as all other countries grouped together. *(Source: www.rauzulusstreet.com)*

Country	Number of Winners
Canada	
Great Britain	
Japan	
Kenya	
Other	

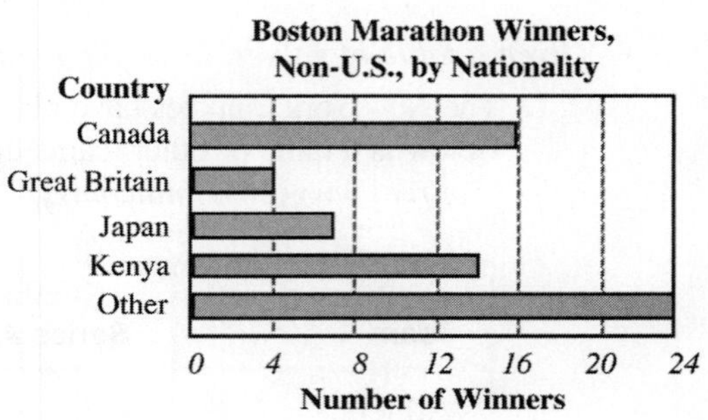

Complete the table

5. A company's advertising budget is $200,000. The circle graph shows the percent of that budget devoted to different advertising opportunities.

Advertising Budget Item	Percent of Budget	Total Amount of Budget
Magazine		
Newspaper		
Radio		
Television		
Other		
Total	**100%**	**$200,000**

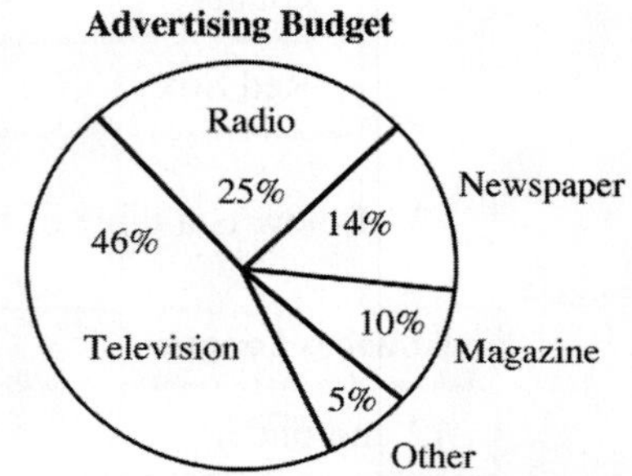

6. A construction company is putting up 500 homes in a new development, offering a variety of home styles, such as a two story, three bedroom house. The circle graph shows the percent of the development for each home style.

Style of New Home	Percent of Development	Total Number of Homes
2 BR, 1 Story		
3 BR, 1 Story		
3 BR, 2 Story		
4 BR, 1 Story		
4 BR, 2 Story		
Total		**100%**

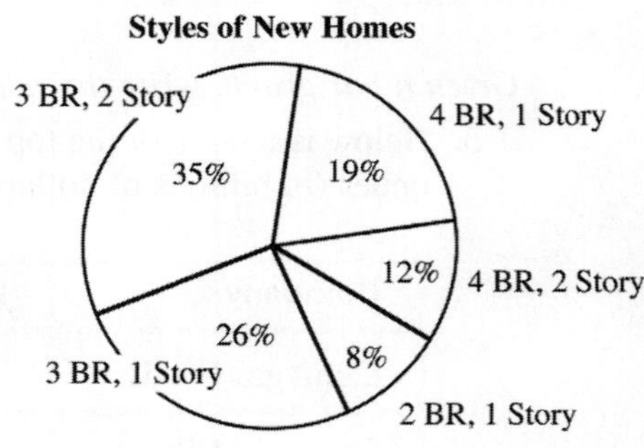

Complete the table by listing the percent of the whole for each category, then place the percent data appropriately in the circle graph.

7. Below is a table of the ethnic diversity of the 120 players in the six-team Connerville High School Baseball League.

Ethnicity	Total Number of Players	Percent of Players
African-American	42	
Asian	18	
Hispanic	30	
White	24	
Other	6	
Total	**120**	

Ethnicity of Ball Players

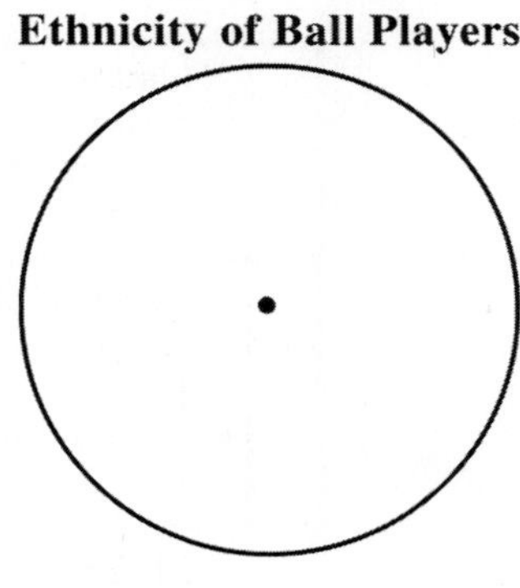

8. Below is a table of the religious affiliations of the attendees at an ecumenical (all-inclusive) Thanksgiving service.

Religion	Total Number of Attendees	Percent of Attendees
Buddhist	8	
Christian	68	
Hindu	24	
Jewish	50	
Muslim	34	
Other	16	
Total	**200**	

Religious Affiliation of Service Attendees

Section 8.2

Fill in the frequency distribution table and/or draw the related histogram, as appropriate.

9. The distance that 75 employees drive to work is recorded in the frequency distribution table below.

a) Draw the related histogram.

Number of Miles	Number of Employees
1–5	12
6–10	15
11–15	19
16–20	14
21–25	9
26–30	6
Total	**75**

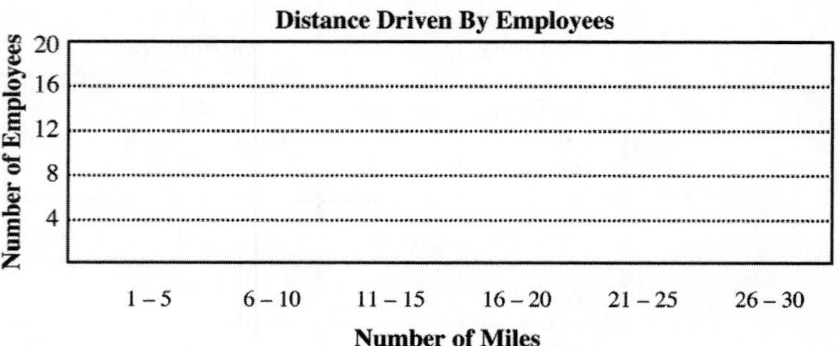

b) How many employees drive less than 11 miles?

c) How many employees drive from 6 to 20 miles?

d) How many employees drive at least 16 miles?

10. Below is the number of years of reign (in numerical order) of the 62 rulers of England and Great Britain before Queen Elizabeth II. (Note: those who are credited with reigning 0 years actually reigned less than 1 year.) *(Source: www.factmonster.com)*

a) Fill in the frequency distribution table and draw its related histogram.

0	3	6	10	16	22	25	39
0	3	6	10	17	22	28	44
0	4	6	12	17	22	33	50
1	5	7	13	19	24	35	56
1	5	9	13	19	24	35	59
2	5	9	13	19	24	35	63
2	5	9	13	20	25	37	
2	6	10	15	21	25	38	

Years	Number of Tally	Number of Rulers
0–9		
10–19		
20–29		
30–39		
40–49		
50–59		
60–69		
Total		

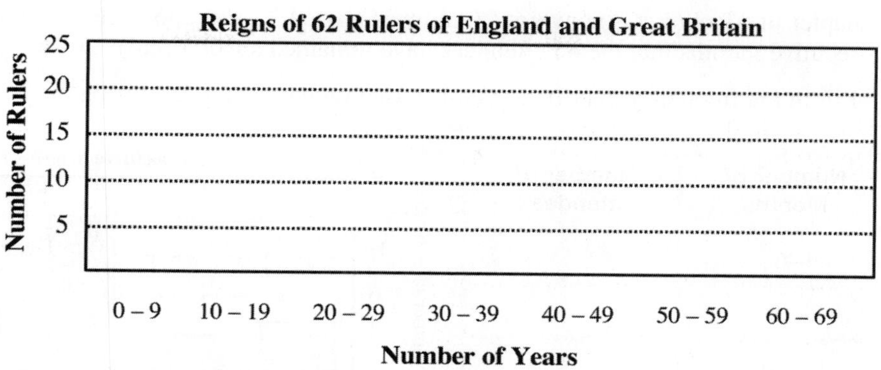

b) How many rulers reigned more than 39 years?

c) How many rulers reigned from 20 to 39 years?

d) How many rulers reigned fewer than 20 years?

11. Below is a histogram of the number of wins for the 30 teams in Major League Baseball in the 2004 season. *(Source: www.nyytrexsky.com)*

a) Fill in the frequency distribution table based on the data in the histogram.

Number of of Wins	Number of Teams
50–57	
58–65	
66–73	
74–81	
82–89	
90–97	
98–105	
Total	**30**

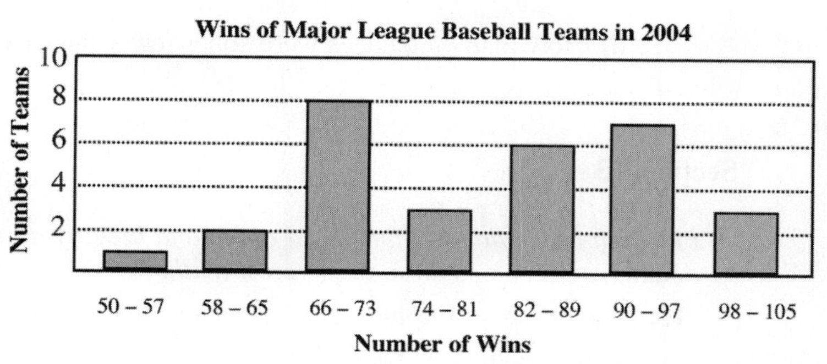

b) How many teams had more than 89 wins?

c) How many teams had from 66 to 89 wins?

d) How many teams had fewer than 74 wins?

12. A chapter of Alcoholics Anonymous (AA) was started 3 years ago. Below is a histogram of the number of consecutive months that the 45 attendees have remained sober. (Yea!)

a) Fill in the frequency distribution table based on the data in the histogram.

Number of Months	Number of Attendees
1–6	
7–12	
13–18	
19–24	
25–30	
31–36	
Total	**45**

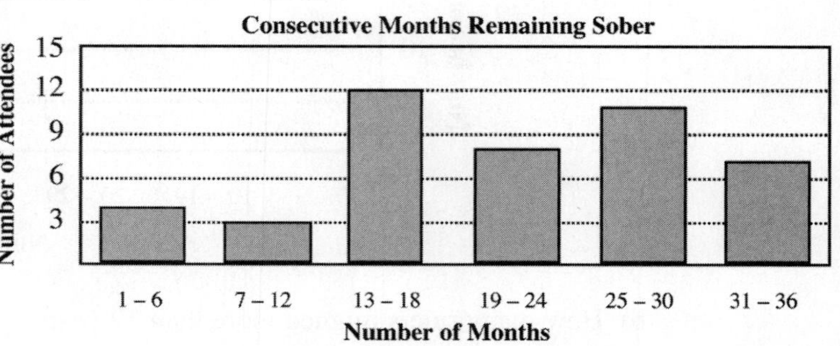

b) How many attendees were sober more than 30 months?

c) How many attendees were sober from 19 to 30 months?

d) How many attendees were sober fewer than 13 months?

Section 8.3

Put each list of data in numerical order and identify all three averages: the mean, the median, and the mode. If necessary, round the mean to the nearest tenth.

13. The number of homes sold by each of the eleven real estate agents at Brooks Realty in 2005:
9, 3, 7, 6, 4, 6, 8, 10, 6, 7, 12

14. The number of minutes it takes Jennifer to get from home to work on nine days in February:
17, 23, 29, 15, 20, 28, 16, 21, 22

15. The number of DVDs rented each month by the Park family in 2005.
6, 2, 3, 0, 4, 3, 5, 6, 7, 4, 5, 6

16. The number of flights 14 business people flew during the month of May:
9, 17, 6, 22, 14, 7, 9, 18, 17, 9, 12, 17, 20, 19

Calculate the grade point average for each student's spring grade distribution. Round the answer to two decimal places.

17.

Course	Grade	Point Value	Units	Grade Points (Point Value × Units)
French	B		5	
Computer Lab	A		1	
CIS	A		3	
Psychology	C		3	
		Total:		

Grade Point Average = ____________

18.

Course	Grade	Point Value	Units	Grade Points (Point Value × Units)
Chemistry	C		4	
Trigonometry	B		4	
History	D		3	
Physical Education	A		1	
Music Appreciation	B		2	
		Total:		

Grade Point Average = ____________

Section 8.4

Find the probability of each event. Simplify all fractions completely.

Experiment: A six-sided die is rolled. What is the probability that it comes up

19. an even number? **20.** less than 3? **21.** greater than 2? **22.** less than 1?

23. an odd number that is greater than 4? **24.** an even number that is less than 5?

Experiment: The spinner has 8 numbers on it. When the needle is spun and comes to rest, it is pointing toward one of the numbers. What is the probability that it will point toward

In this diagram, the spinning needle is pointing toward the 5.

Assume each number has an equal chance of being pointed to.

25. an odd number?

26. a number less than 4?

27. an even number less than 7?

28. a number greater than 6?

29. an odd number less than 4?

30. a number greater than 0?

For questions 31–34: A bag has 30 raffle tickets. Nine are red, 8 are yellow, 2 are green, 5 are pink, and 6 are blue. The experiment is to randomly select one ticket out of the bag. What is the probability that the chosen ticket is

31. pink? **32.** blue? **33.** red? **34.** yellow?

For questions 35–38: At a St. Louis Cardinals baseball game one Friday night, a prize is to be awarded to the ugliest car in the parking lot. Here is a bar graph of the make of the 50 finalists.

Assuming the final car was randomly selected, what is the probability that the chosen car is a

35. Chevy? **36.** Ford?

37. VW? **38.** Dodge?

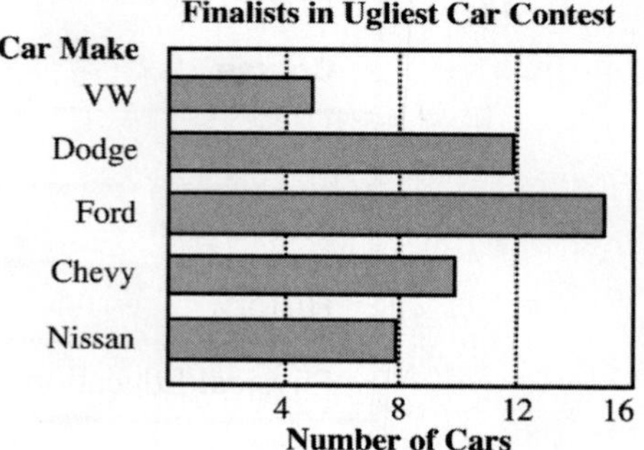

Chapter 8 Test

1. It's not widely known that California is a large farming state. The table shows the amount of some crops (in millions of bushels) produced by California farms in 2003. Draw the bar graph related to this table. *Source: World Almanac, 2005*

Crop	Bushels (in millions)
Barley	4
Corn	27
Hay	9
Oats	3
Wheat	34

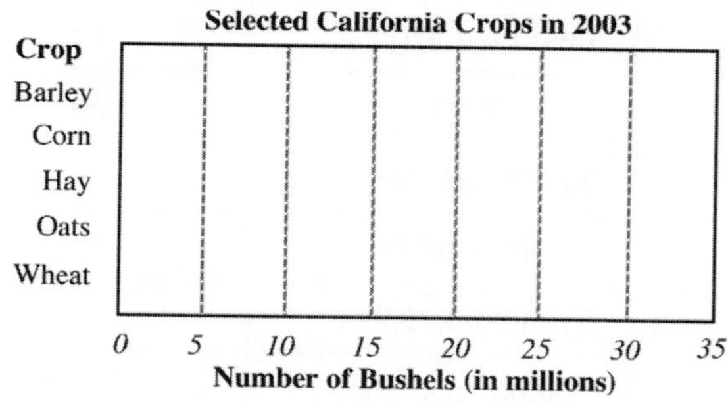

2. Below is a bar graph of the average annual snowfall of six U.S. cities. (These six cities total 85 annual inches of snow.) Write its related table of values. *Source: www.weathertoday.net*

City	Average Snowfall, in Inches
Albuquerque, NM	
Baltimore, MD	
Evansville, IN	
Nashville, TN	
Roanoke, VA	
Wichita Falls, TX	
Total	

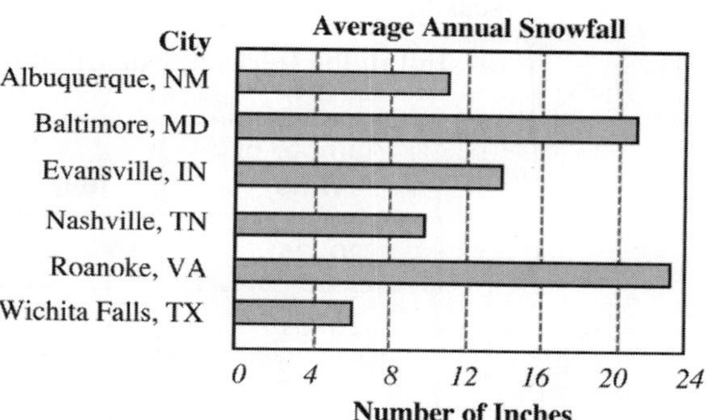

3. A city's economic development plan calls for 150 acres to be set aside for new businesses. Below is a circle graph of the acreage (as a percent) allotted to various types of businesses. Complete the table.

Type of Business	Percent of Acreage	Total Number of Acres
Business Offices		
Grocery		
Restaurants		
Retail		
Services		
Storage		
Total	100%	

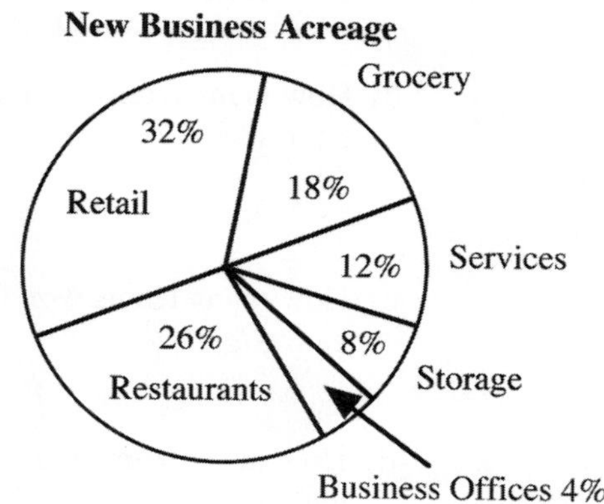

4. Below is a table of the annual giving of the 300 families at the community church. Complete the table by listing the percent of the whole for each category; then place the percent data appropriately around the circle graph.

Annual Giving	Total Number of Families	Percent of Families
Less than $200	12	
$200–$999	36	
$1,000–$4,999	75	
$5,000–$9,999	96	
$10,000–$19,999	54	
$20,000 and above	27	
Total	**300**	

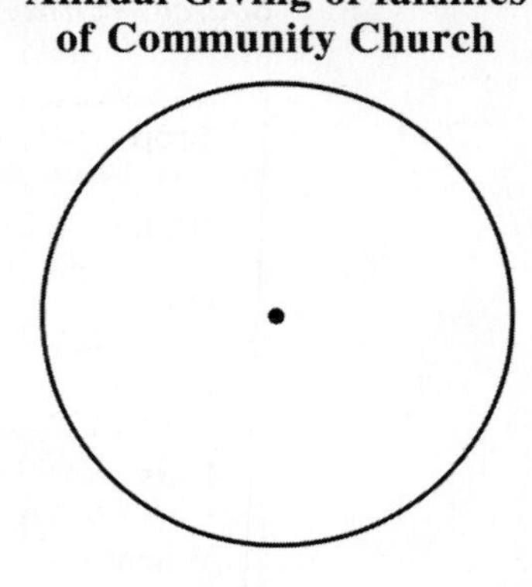

5. Below is the number of wins of the 29 National Basketball Association teams during the 2003 - 2004 regular season.

a) Fill in the frequency distribution table and draw its related histogram.

Number of Wins	Tally	Number of Teams
20–25		
26–31		
32–37		
38–43		
44–49		
50–55		
56–61		
Total		

61	47	58	56
54	42	57	55
41	39	52	41
41	36	50	37
35	33	45	37
33	25	43	29
28	21	42	28
23			

b) How many teams won more than 43 games?

c) How many teams won from 44 to 55 games?

d) How many teams won fewer than 38 games?

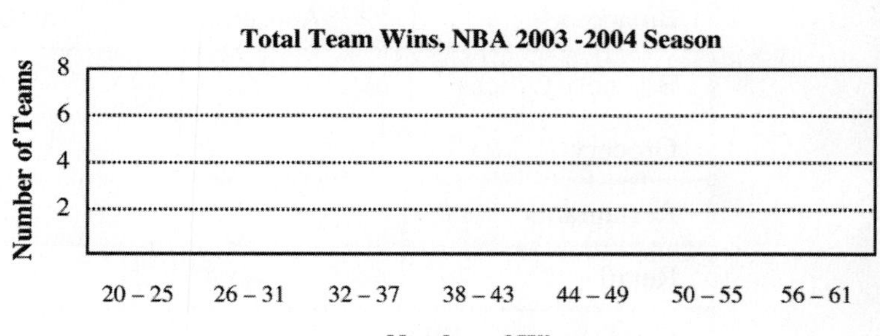

6. Below is a histogram of the grade distribution for all of Ms. Garcia's algebra final exam.
   a) Fill in the frequency distribution table based on the data in the histogram.

Final Exam Score	Number of Students
44–51	
52–59	
60–67	
68–75	
76–83	
84–91	
92–99	
Total	**80**

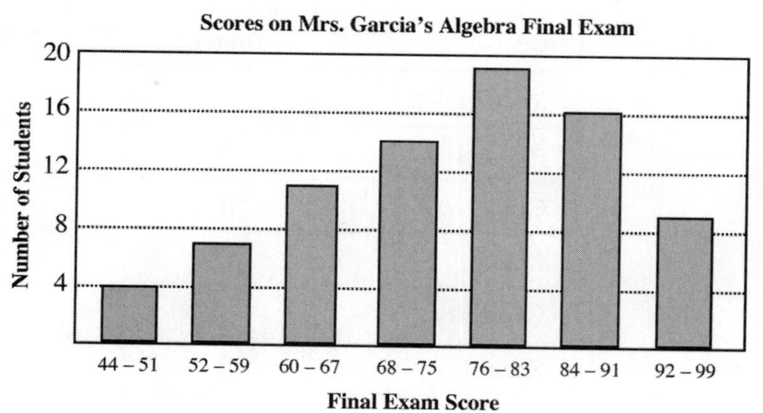

   b) How many students scored more than 75 points?

   c) How many students scored from 60 to 75 points?

   d) How many students scored fewer than 68 points?

Put each list of data in numerical order and identify all three averages: the mean, the median, and the mode. If necessary, round the mean to the nearest tenth.

7. Mr. Singh teaches a sociology class with 75 students in it. Below are the number of absences he had for the 13 class meetings in March:

   5, 8, 2, 6, 8, 10, 4, 1, 11, 8, 3, 8, 6

8. Marci put a grandfather clock up for sale on eBay. Below are the number of hits her auction site generated during each of the ten days the clock was for sale:

   6, 16, 18, 7, 4, 9, 10, 16, 15, 16

Calculate the grade point average for this student's fall and spring grade distribution. Round the answer to two decimal places.

9.

Course	Grade	Point Value	Units	Grade Points (Point Value × Units)
Microbiology	C		5	
Algebra	A		4	
CIS	B		2	
Karate	C		1	
Geometry	C		3	
Spanish	B		5	
Guidance	A		2	
Speech	B		3	
		Total:		

Grade Point Average = ____________

Find the probability of each event. Simplify all fractions completely.

Experiment: The spinner has nine numbers on it. The needle is spun, and when the needle comes to rest, it is pointing toward one of the numbers. What is the probability that it will point toward

In this diagram, the spinning needle is pointing toward the 5.

Assume each number has an equal chance of being pointed to.

10. an even number?

11. a number less than 6?

12. an even number less than 7?

13. a number greater than 6?

14. an odd number less than 4?

15. a number divisible by 3?

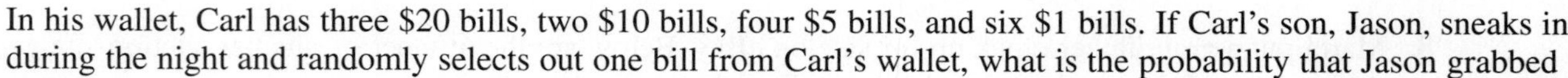

In his wallet, Carl has three $20 bills, two $10 bills, four $5 bills, and six $1 bills. If Carl's son, Jason, sneaks in during the night and randomly selects out one bill from Carl's wallet, what is the probability that Jason grabbed

16. a $5 bill? **17.** a $20 bill? **18.** a $1 bill? **19.** a $10 bill?

In the Smithson household, the family has 40 DVDs. The number of each type of DVD is shown in the bar graph. If a DVD is chosen randomly, what is the probability that it is a (an)

20. comedy? **21.** drama?

22. adventure? **23.** thriller?

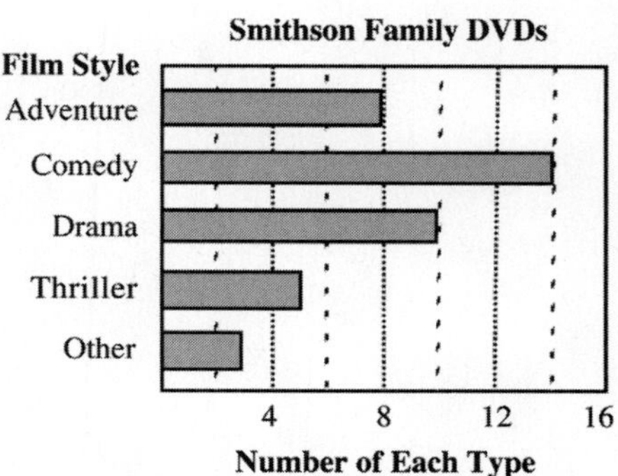

Chapters 7 and 8 Cumulative Review

Convert one measure to the other.

1. $5\frac{1}{6}$ yards to feet
2. $9\frac{3}{5}$ ounces to pounds.
3. 12 cups to quarts.
4. $\frac{7}{16}$ pint to fluid ounces.
5. On Mount Rushmore, in South Dakota, the length of George Washington's nose is said to be 238 inches long. Express this in feet and inches.
6. To understand the health of rainbow trout in the Fall River in Central Oregon, a naturalist studied the length and weight of several fish. One weighed 5 pounds 3 ounces. Express this weight in ounces.
7. The world record for the hammer throw is 284 feet 7 inches. At the 2004 Olympics, Hungarian Adrian Zsolt won the hammer throw with a throw of 272 feet 11 inches. How much longer (in feet and inches) is the world record than Adrian's throw? *(Source: www.trackandfield.com)*

Convert the given unit of measure to the measure shown.

8. 3.1 centimeters to meters
9. 0.05 gram to milligrams
10. 43.5 milliliters to deciliters
11. 1.05 kilograms to grams

Convert each measure to its alternate U.S. or metric form. Write improper fractions as mixed numbers for U.S. measures and as decimals for metric measures.

12. 18 inches to centimeters
13. 54 meters to yards
14. $6\frac{1}{3}$ liters to gallons
15. $\frac{3}{4}$ ounce to grams
16. The distance between Calgary and Edmonton (in the Canadian Province of Alberta) is about 192 kilometers. Express this number in miles.
17. A bag of apples weighs $8\frac{1}{4}$ pounds. Express this number in kilograms.
18. It is believed that the Yeti, the Abominable Snowman of Tibet, is about 5 ft 8 in. tall.
    a) How many inches tall is the Yeti?
    b) Approximately how many centimeters tall is the Yeti?

Find the measures, as indicated.

19. $\angle WFZ$ and $\angle BLN$ are supplementary. Given $\angle WFZ = 118.4°$, find $\angle BLN$.

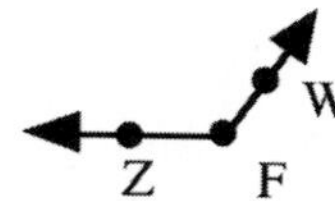

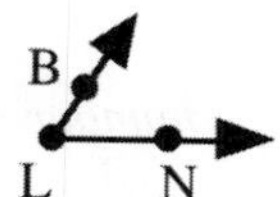

20. In right triangle ΔABC, the measures of $\angle C$ is 63.7°. Find the measure of $\angle B$.

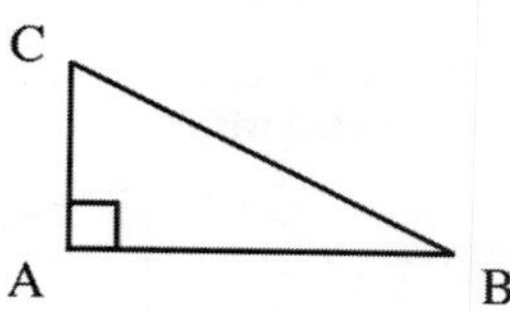

21. The floor in Room 6 at the Community Center is a rectangle. Find both the perimeter and the area of the floor. (All measures are in yards.)

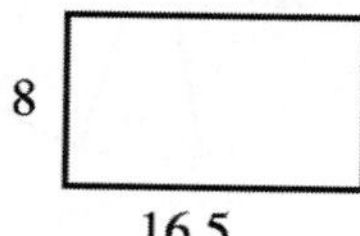

22. Gracie's cabin floor outline is below. Find the values of x and y and then calculate both the perimeter and the area. (All measures are in meters.)

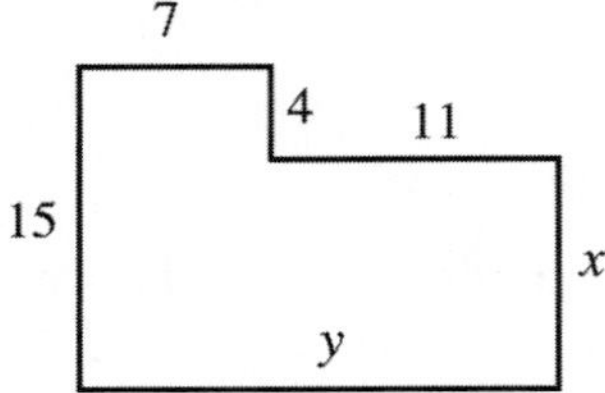

23. Each side of an equilateral triangle is $4\frac{5}{6}$ ft. Find the perimeter of the triangle.

24. A regular octagon has a perimeter of 136 in. Find the length of each side.

25. Find both the perimeter and area of a square with side measure $1\frac{1}{2}$ feet.

26. Approximate both the circumference and the area of a circle with a radius of 5 centimeters. Use $\pi \approx 3.14$, and round each result to the tenths place.

Find the area of each polygon.

27.

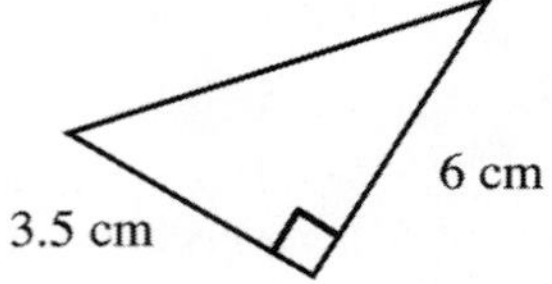

28.

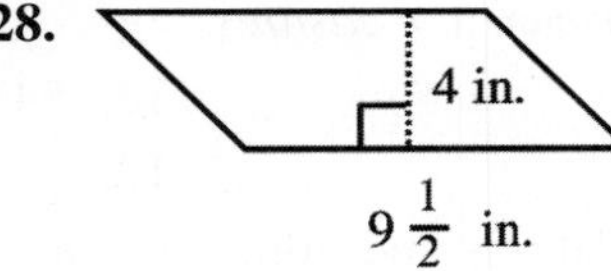

Find the volume.

29. A ball bearing (sphere) has a diameter of 6 millimeters. What is the volume of this ball bearing? Round the volume to the nearest whole number.

30. A 20-foot high water tower has the shape of a cylinder with base radius 10 feet. What is the volume of this water tower?

Complete the table. Round the number of countries to the nearest whole number.

31. There are 190 independent countries in the world. Some of them are island countries that are grouped with nearby continents. The circle graph indicates the approximate percentage of the world's countries within each continental affiliation.

Continental Affiliation	Percent of World's Countries	Total Number of Countries
Asia		
Africa		
Europe		
North America		
Oceania		
South America		
Total	**100%**	**190**

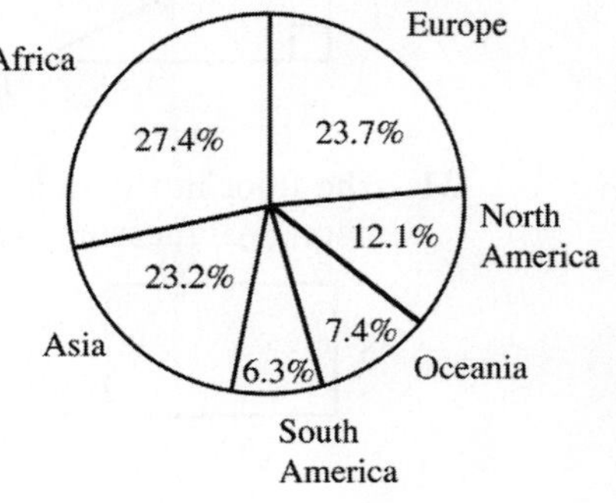

Complete the table by listing the percent of the whole for each category, then place the percent data appropriately in the circle graph.

32. Below is a table of the Athletics Department's equipment budget at Centennial High School for the 2005-06 school year.

Sport	Dollars Budgeted (in $1,000s)	Percent of the Equipment Budget
Aquatics	6	
Baseball	10	
Basketball	4	
Football	20	
Track/Cross Country	5	
Other sports	5	
Total	**50**	

Athletics Department's Equipment Budget

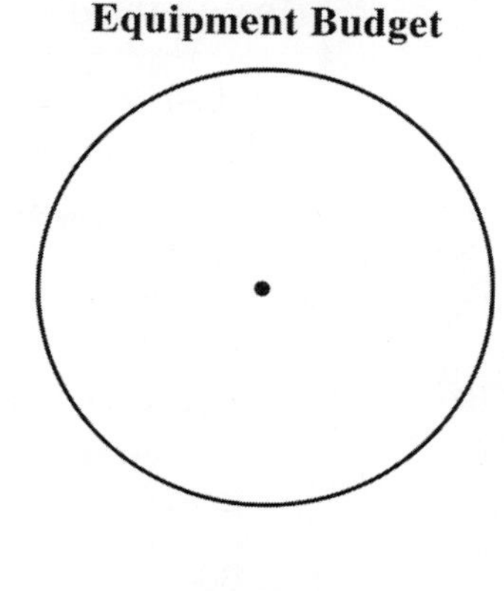

Fill in the frequency distribution table and/or draw the related histogram, as appropriate.

33. The number of units completed by 50 community college students (as of Fall 2005) is recorded in the frequency distribution table below.

a) Draw the related histogram.

Number of Units	Number of Students
0–4	8
5–9	7
10–14	14
15–19	8
20–24	10
25–29	3
Total	**50**

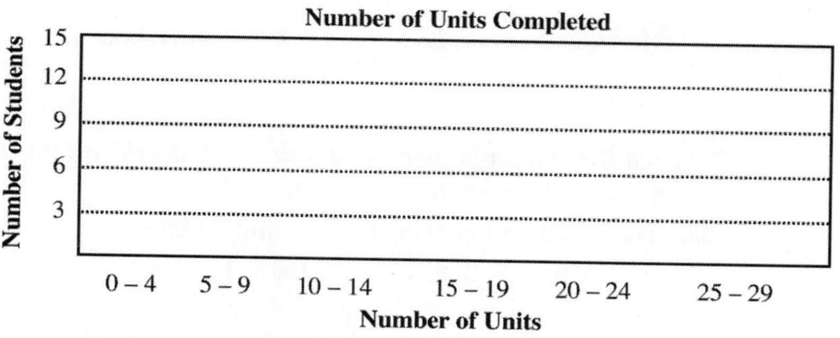

b) How many students completed less than 10 units?

c) How many students completed from 10 to 19 units?

d) How many students completed at least 15 units?

34. Below is a histogram of the number of books the fifth graders at Jefferson Elementary read throughout the school year.

a) Fill in the frequency distribution table based on the data in the histogram.

Number of Books Read	Number of Students
0–4	
5–9	
10–14	
15–19	
20–24	
25–29	
30–34	
Total	**48**

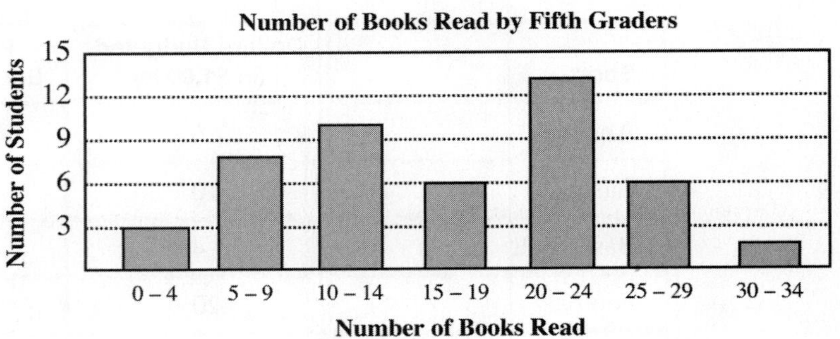

b) How many students read more than 24 books?

c) How many students read from 10 to 19 books?

d) How many students read fewer than 10 books?

Put each list of data in numerical order and identify all three averages: the mean, the median, and the mode. If necessary, round the mean to the nearest tenth.

35. The number of cousins fifteen children have:
2, 8, 4, 0, 1, 5, 6, 8, 12, 7, 3, 15, 8, 1, 10

36. The number of team hits by the Red Sox in twelve straight games:
8, 7, 3, 11, 15, 4, 11, 8, 12, 5, 13, 11

Find the probability of each event. Simplify all fractions completely.

Experiment: The spinner has 5 numbers on it. When the needle is spun and comes to rest, it is pointing toward one of the numbers. What is the probability that it will point toward

In this diagram, the spinning needle is pointing toward the 2.

Assume each number has an equal chance of being pointed to.

37. an odd number?

38. a number less than 5?

39. an even number less than 4?

40. an odd number less than 4?

Experiment: A gum ball machine has 24 gum balls in it. Three are red, 8 are yellow, 6 are pink, 3 are white, and 4 are blue. For a nickel, one random gum ball drops into the holder. What is the probability that the gum ball is

41. yellow? **42.** white? **43.** pink? **44.** blue?

CHAPTER 9

Integers and Algebraic Expressions

Introduction

This chapter introduces you to positive and negative numbers and the beginning elements of algebra. As we step into algebra, it may seem as though we've come to the end of learning arithmetic. Actually, algebra is just arithmetic in a different form, and the rules of arithmetic still apply. The Order of Operations is still the same, and we'll see how it applies to positive and negative numbers.

Starting algebra, though, is not the end of arithmetic. It's actually the beginning of the rest of mathematics. A lot of students want to know how algebra will apply to their everyday lives. It's difficult to make everything you learn in algebra have a practical, everyday purpose. Instead, look at algebra as the gateway to many other areas of study.

Learning algebra opens doors to many opportunities that might otherwise be closed. Understanding algebra allows you to study science, geography, economics, sports conditioning, nursing, fire technology, police investigating, and many other areas. And if your interest is not in any way related to math, then know that learning algebra makes you smarter because it causes you to think more and exercise your brain more.

No, this is not the end of your math study, this is just the beginning.

Preparation Exercises

Section 2.1, Exponents and Square Roots: *Evaluate each.*

1. 2^3

2. 5^2

3. $\sqrt{49}$

4. $\sqrt{81}$

Section 2.2, The Order of Operations: *Evaluate each using the Order of Operations.*

5. $24 \div 6 \cdot 2$

6. $3 + (8 - 2)^2$

Section 3.2, Simplifying Fractions: *Simplify completely.*

7. $\frac{15}{25}$

8. $\frac{27}{36}$

Section 3.3, Multiplying Fractions: *Multiply and simplify.*

9. $\frac{8}{9} \cdot \frac{3}{4}$

10. $\frac{7}{15} \cdot \frac{10}{21}$

Section 3.4, Dividing Fractions: *Divide and simplify.*

11. $\frac{3}{8} \div \frac{9}{4}$

12. $\frac{35}{24} \div \frac{14}{9}$

Section 4.3, Adding and Subtracting Like Fractions: *Add or subtract as indicated. Simplify completely.*

13. $\frac{7}{24} + \frac{11}{24}$

14. $\frac{11}{15} - \frac{8}{15}$

Section 4.4, Adding and Subtracting Unlike Fractions: *Add or subtract as indicated. Simplify completely.*

15. $\frac{5}{12} + \frac{1}{4}$

16. $\frac{5}{6} - \frac{8}{15}$

Objectives

In this section, you will learn to:

- Express ideas through algebraic symbols and abbreviations.
- Translate between English and algebra.
- Identify integers and locate them on the number line.
- Find the absolute value of a number.
- Define *number.*

To successfully complete this section, you need to understand:

- Exponents and square roots (2.1)
- The order of operations (2.2)
- Simplifying fractions (3.2)

The Greek mathematician Diophantus was one of the first to use symbols to *abbreviate* mathematical expressions and thought. Though his symbols were different from what we use today, he is credited with taking the discussion of mathematics and problem solving from sentence form into symbolic form. Could you imagine having to *discuss* everyday mathematics without the use of an addition sign or a multiplication sign?

SECTION 9.1 Introduction to Algebra

Introduction

Algebra is all about symbols and abbreviations, using them and manipulating them. In algebra, we use the same symbols for the five basic operations you've already encountered:

Sum:	addition (+)
Difference:	subtraction (−)
Product:	multiplication (×) and (·)
Quotient:	division (÷ and /) and the fraction bar (—)
Power:	the exponent

Letting symbols represent mathematical ideas allows us to *abbreviate* those ideas. A mathematical sentence written in words can be more easily understood if it is written symbolically, as long as you know what the symbols mean.

For example, the simple English expression "the sum of ten and six" can be easily abbreviated as the numerical expression $10 + 6$.

We also use symbols to represent abbreviations and unknown numbers. Some of these abbreviations are:

1. **Multiplication:** An abbreviation for repeated addition, such as $3 \cdot 5 = 5 + 5 + 5 = 15$.
2. The **exponent:** An abbreviation for repeated factors, such as $2^5 = 2 \cdot 2 \cdot 2 \cdot 2 \cdot 2 = 32$.
3. The **radical:** An abbreviation for the square root, such as $\sqrt{49} = 7$.

Algebra Vocabulary

Recall from Chapter 1 that a variable is a letter that represents a number. A variable, like an operation sign and the radical, is also an algebraic symbol. This leads us to the definition of an *algebraic expression.*

> An **algebraic expression** is a combination of numbers and letters connected by the operations and grouping symbols. At its simplest, an algebraic expression can be just a single variable, such as *y*, or a single number, such as 3.

Because variables represent numbers, an algebraic expression *expresses* a numerical value.

Here are some other examples of algebraic expressions:

$$w + 8 \qquad 5 \cdot x + 6 \cdot y^2 \qquad \sqrt{3 \cdot y - \frac{x}{4}} \qquad \frac{2 \cdot x^2 \cdot y + 4 \cdot w}{1 - 5 \cdot z}$$

Using variables in algebraic expressions gives us a slightly simpler way to represent multiplication. If there is no other operation between a number and a variable, or between two variables, then the operation is automatically assumed to be multiplication.

For example, $5 \cdot x$ can be written as just $5x$.

Likewise, xy means $x \cdot y$

and $6 \cdot x \cdot y^2$ can be abbreviated as $6xy^2$.

As you know, the Commutative Property of Multiplication allows us to write a product in a different order. For example, $5 \cdot y$ can also be written as $y \cdot 5$. Though we might write $5 \cdot y$ as just **5*y***, it's *unusual* to write $y \cdot 5$ as ***y*5**. In other words, when writing the product of a number (coefficient) and a variable, we almost always write the coefficient first. (This is so that we won't think that the 5 is an exponent.)

Variables

Sometimes, we know what number a variable represents, and sometimes we don't. As we saw in Section 2.3, when we are given the numerical value of a variable, that number is called a *replacement value*. We can also say that we *substitute* the value for the variable.

If an expression contains more than one variable, such as $2W + 2L$, then each variable will have its own replacement value, as demonstrated in Example 1.

EXAMPLE 1 Evaluate each expression using the given replacement values.

PROCEDURE: For each, apply the order of operations.

a) $w + y$ Replace ***w*** with 8 and ***y*** with 9: $8 + 9 = 17$

b) $2xy$ Replace ***x*** with 5 and ***y*** with 6: $2 \cdot 5 \cdot 6 = 60$ Remember, $2xy$ means $2 \cdot x \cdot y$.

c) $a^2 - c$ Replace ***a*** with 3 and ***c*** with 7: $3^2 - 7 = 9 - 7 = 2$

d) $2W + 2L$ Replace ***W*** with 5 and ***L*** with 8: $2 \cdot 5 + 2 \cdot 8 = 10 + 16 = 26$

e) $\dfrac{p + 2}{q \div 3}$ Replace ***p*** with 8 and ***q*** with 15: $\dfrac{8 + 2}{15 \div 3} = \dfrac{10}{5} = 2$

YOU TRY IT 1 *Evaluate each expression using the given replacement values. Use Example 1 as a guide.*

a) $2wc$ Replace ***w*** with 5 and ***c*** with 19.

b) $\frac{1}{2} \cdot h \cdot b$ Replace ***h*** with 12 and ***b*** with 9.

c) $(r + n)^2$ Replace ***r*** with 2 and ***n*** with 6.

d) $\dfrac{y + 4}{3k}$ Replace ***y*** with 26 and **k** with 2.

Sometimes, a variable, say w, will appear in more than one part of an expression. When this happens, the replacement value for w is the same for each occurrence of w.

In the expression $3 \cdot w + 20 \div w$, we see two w's. If the replacement value for w is 4, then each w has the value of 4. It is not possible for one w to be 4 and the other w to be, say, 7. If we want the variables to have two different values at the same time, then the expression must contain two different variables.

EXAMPLE 2

Evaluate each expression using the given replacement value(s).

a) $3w + 20 \div w$ Replace w with 4: $3 \cdot 4 + 20 \div 4 = 12 + 5 = 17$

b) $x^2 + 3x - 7$ Replace x with 5: $5^2 + 3 \cdot 5 - 7 = 25 + 15 - 7 = 33$

c) $4x + xy$ Replace x with 3 and y with 2: $4 \cdot 3 + 3 \cdot 2 = 12 + 6 = 18$

YOU TRY IT 2

Evaluate each expression using the given replacement value(s). Use Example 2 as a guide.

a) $y^2 + 5y$ Replace y with 6.

b) $3x + 7x$ Replace x with 5.

c) $w \cdot v + 5w$ Replace w with 4 and v with 9.

d) $P + Pr$ Replace P with 100 and r with 0.06.

Translating between English and Algebra

Variables are particularly helpful when they represent numbers whose values we do not yet know. If we need to represent "the sum of *a number* and 25," we can write this as $x + 25$. We recognize $x + 25$ as a sum, and we have used the x to represent *a number*.

Why would we need to consider writing expressions such as $x + 25$? A simple example is presented here.

Scott just turned 25 when his daughter Jennifer was born. In fact, Jennifer was born on Scott's 25th birthday. As Jennifer grew older, she began to understand how to calculate her dad's age. She realized that her dad's age was the sum of her age and 25.

To think about how old her dad might be at various stages in her life, Jennifer represented her own age as J and was able to write an expression for her dad's age as $J + 25$. Then she thought,

"When I'm 18 and graduate from high school, Dad will be $18 + 25 = 43$;

when I'm 22 and graduate from college, Dad will be $22 + 25 = 47$;

when I'm 30 and start a family of my own, Dad will be $30 + 25 = 55$;

a good age to be a grandpa."

This example also demonstrates that an algebraic expression represents a number; the number represented by $J + 25$ is the age of Jennifer's dad.

In general, if we need to express an unknown number, we can use any variable we choose. A commonly used variable is x.

EXAMPLE 3

Translate each English expression into an algebraic expression. Use any variable of your liking to represent the unknown number. (Here, x is used.)

a) The sum of a number and 18: $x + 18$

b) The difference between a number and 3: $x - 3$ (but *not* $3 - x$)

c) The difference of 17 and a number: $17 - x$ (but *not* $x - 17$)

d) The product of 6 and a number: $6 \cdot x$ or $6x$

e) The quotient of a number and 5: $x \div 5$ or $\frac{x}{5}$

f) The quotient of 20 and a number: $20 \div x$ or $\frac{20}{x}$

g) The square of a number: x^2

h) The square root of a number: $\sqrt{x}$

YOU TRY IT 3

Translate each English expression into an algebraic expression. Use any variable of your liking to represent the unknown number. Use Example 3 as a guide.

a) The product of 5 and a number.

b) The quotient of a number and 4.

c) The difference of 6 and a number.

d) The sum of 11 and a number.

e) The square root of a number.

f) A number squared.

Parentheses as Separators

As you know, parentheses are considered grouping symbols; they group different values together so that they can be treated as one quantity. Parentheses are also used as separators to keep values apart from each other.

Later in this chapter you may see some expressions such as (6) + (3). In this expression, the parentheses are unnecessary because they don't group anything. However, the parentheses do separate the numbers (from each other and from the plus sign), so they are *separators* here. In Section 9.3 it will be more evident why we might use parentheses this way.

Another situation in which parentheses can be used as separators is multiplication. For example, $3 \cdot 5$ can be expressed as $(3) \cdot (5)$, or as (3)(5). Again, what we see are two values with no operation between them; therefore, the operation is *assumed* to be multiplication.

Using parentheses as separators, we can write the product of 3 and 5 in many similar ways:

$$(3)(5) = 15; \quad 3(5) = 15; \quad \text{and } (3)5 = 15.$$

Number Lines

We can represent numbers visually along a horizontal number line.

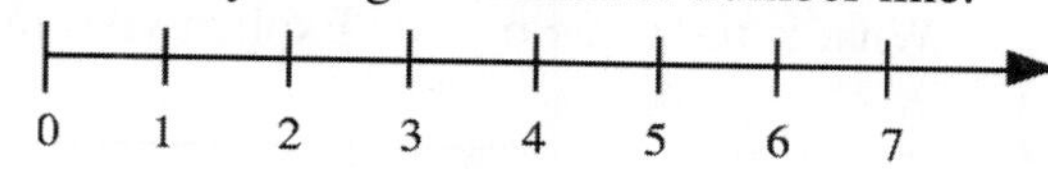

The number zero (0) has a special name on a number line; it is called the **origin**, which means the beginning. The arrowhead on the number line indicates the line goes on in that direction indefinitely.

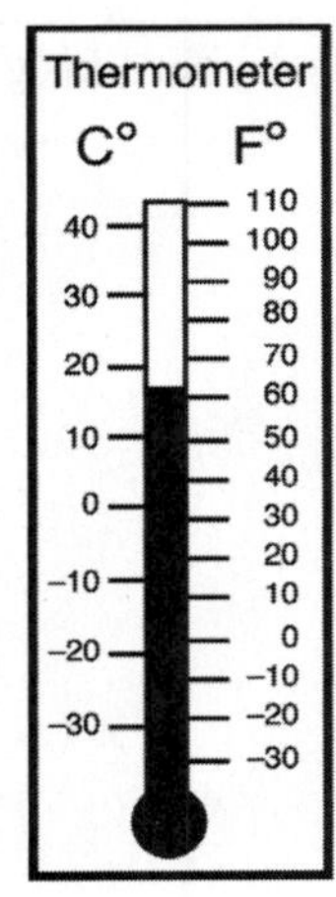

This thermometer has two temperature scales on it: **C** for Celsius and **F** for Fahrenheit.

There are also vertical number lines; one example is a thermometer.

An outdoor thermometer (at left) includes numbers less than zero to indicate temperature below zero.

The numbers less than 0 are called **negative numbers**. Numbers greater than 0 are called **positive numbers**.

On a vertical number line (at right), 0 is still the origin, the positive numbers are above 0, and the negative numbers are below 0.

On a horizontal number line, positive numbers are to the right of 0 and negative numbers are to the left of 0. Even though 0 is in the middle now, it is still referred to as the **origin**.

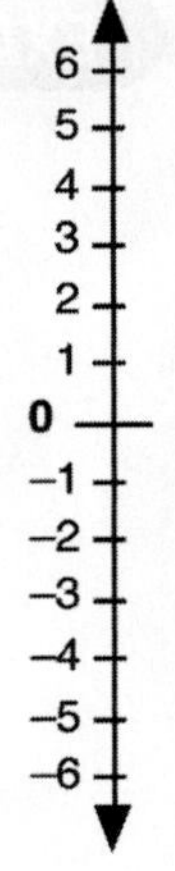

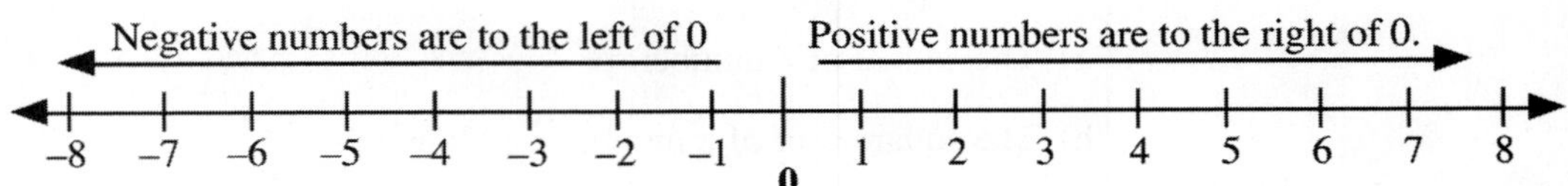

We sometimes write a positive number, such as 6, with a plus sign (+) before the number. The + is not necessary but gives emphasis to the fact that it is a positive number. So, +6 is the same as 6. In this case, the + indicates positive, not addition.

Together, positive and negative numbers are called **signed numbers**.

Two signed numbers, one positive and one negative, with the same numeral are called **opposites**. They are on opposite sides of 0 and are the same distance from 0 on the number line.

For example, + 2 and − 2 are opposites. Each of these is the same distance from 0 on the number line: + 2 is two units to the right of 0 and − 2 is two units to the left of 0.

EXAMPLE 4

Fill in the blanks.

a) The opposite of +15 is ______.
b) The opposite of −16 is ______.
c) ______ is the opposite of 20.
d) ______ is the opposite of −18.
e) 23 is the __________ of −23.
f) −35 is the __________ of 35.

ANSWER: a) −15 b) 16 c) −20 d) 18 e) opposite f) opposite

YOU TRY IT 4

Fill in the blanks. Use Example 4 as a guide.

a) The opposite of +6 is ______.
b) The opposite of −9 is ______.
c) ______ is the opposite of 13.
d) ______ is the opposite of −10.
e) −2 is the __________ of 2.
f) +4 is the __________ of −4.

What is the value of −0? Explain your reasoning.

____

____

The whole numbers and their opposites are called **integers**.

Integers

Each whole number and its opposite is an integer.
The list of integers can be written as $\ldots, -3, -2, -1, 0, 1, 2, 3, \ldots$
0 (zero) is an integer but is neither positive nor negative.

YOU TRY IT 5 *On the blank number line below, write in all of the missing integers.*

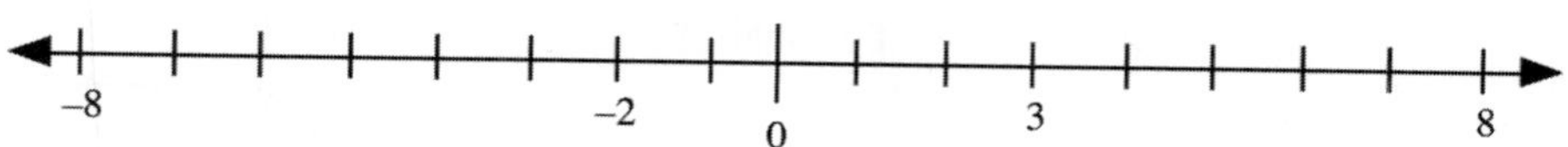

Comparing Signed Numbers

We know that 8 is greater than 3. We can represent this as $8 > 3$. The symbol between the 8 and 3, $>$, is called the **greater than** symbol. (This symbol has the appearance of an arrowhead.)

Similarly, 3 is less than 8. We can represent this as $3 < 8$. The symbol between the 3 and 8, $<$, is called the **less than** symbol.

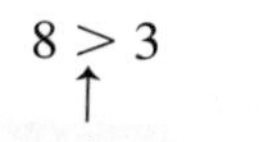

This means *is greater than.*

In each of these, the arrowhead part appears to be pointing toward the lesser number.

$3 < 8$

This means *is less than.*

On a typical horizontal number line, *greater than* means "to the right of," and *less than* means "to the left of." So, 8 is greater than 3 because 8 is to the right of 3 on the number line.

$8 > 3$

8 is greater than 3.

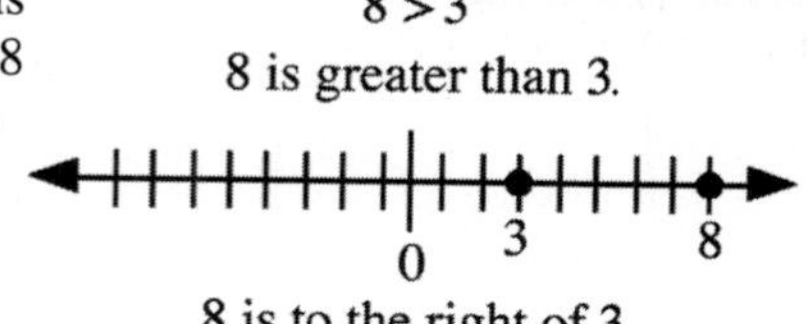

8 is to the right of 3.

Likewise, -5 is less than 2 because -5 is *to the left of* 2 on the number line.

$-5 < 2$

–5 is less than 2.

–5 0 2

–5 is to the left of 2.

EXAMPLE 5 Insert the correct symbol between each pair of numbers, either < (less than) or > (greater than).

a) 1 4 b) 3 −4 c) −8 −5 d) −1 −7

PROCEDURE: Locate each number on the number line and decide whether the first number is to the left of or to the right of the second number.

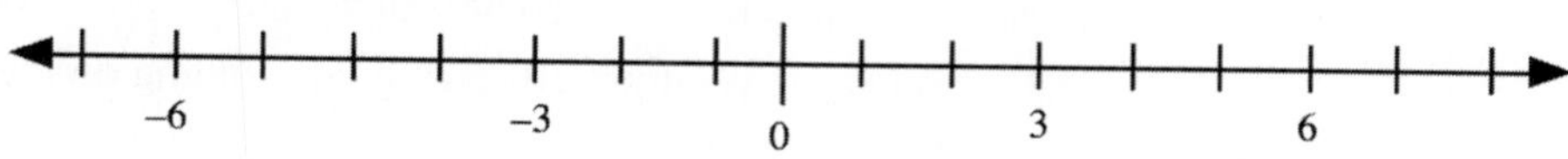

ANSWER: a) $1 < 4$ b) $3 > -4$ c) $-8 < -5$ d) $-1 > -7$

YOU TRY IT 6

Insert the correct symbol between each pair of numbers, either < (less than) or > (greater than). Use Example 5 as a guide.

a) 9 4 b) −6 3 c) −2 −6 d) 4 −8

Absolute Value

The **absolute value** of a number is its distance from 0 on the number line. Whether the number is on the left side of 0 or the right side of 0 doesn't matter, its absolute value is positive.

The symbols we use to represent the absolute value of a number are called *absolute value bars* and look like this: | and |.

For example, both +3 and −3 are three units away from 0.

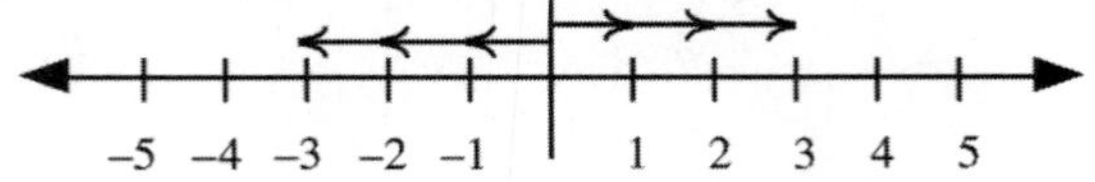

The *absolute value* of 3 is **3** (+3): $|3| = 3$.

The *absolute value* of –3 is also **3** (+3): $|-3| = 3$.

Caution Notice that the absolute value maintains positivity for positive numbers but it becomes the opposite for negative numbers. DO NOT CONFUSE "ABSOLUTE VALUE" WITH "THE OPPOSITE." The absolute value of a positive number is *not* its opposite.

EXAMPLE 6

$|9| = 9$ 9 is a distance of nine units away from the origin.

$|-7| = 7$ −7 is a distance of seven units away from the origin.

$|0| = 0$ 0 is *no* distance away from itself. 0 is the only number without a positive absolute value.

YOU TRY IT 7

Find the absolute value of each number, as indicated. Use Example 6 as a guide.

a) $|12|$ b) $|-5|$ c) $|+24|$ d) $|-1|$ e) $|-0|$

Number Defined

The following definition of the term *number* is extremely helpful in understanding how positive and negative numbers work together.

Non-zero numbers have both a **numerical value** and a **direction**.

- The numerical value is the distance, along the number line, from 0; the numerical value is another name for the absolute value.
- The direction is either left or right, depending on the location on the number line, when compared to 0 (zero):
- Negative numbers are to the left of 0, and positive numbers are to the right of 0.
- Zero has no direction.

EXAMPLE 7

Identify the numerical value and direction of each number.

a) 6 The value is 6 and the direction is to the right.

b) -8 The value is 8 and the direction is to the left.

c) 0 The value is 0 and it has no direction.

d) $+9$ The value is 9 and the direction is to the right.

YOU TRY IT 8

Identify the numerical value and direction of each number. Fill in the blanks. Use Example 7 as a guide.

a) 3 The value is ______, and the direction is ____________.

b) -5 The __________ is ______, and the direction is ____________.

c) $+7$ The __________ is ______, and the direction is ____________.

d) -4 The __________ is ______, and the __________ is __________.

e) $+2$ The ______________________________________.

You Try It Answers: Section 9.1

YTI 1 a) 190 b) 54 c) 64 d) 5

YTI 2 a) 66 b) 50 c) 56 d) 106

YTI 3 a) $5 \cdot x$ or $5x$ b) $x \div 4$ or $\frac{x}{4}$ c) $6 - x$ d) $11 + x$ e) $\sqrt{x}$ f) x^2

YTI 4 a) -6 b) 9 c) -13 d) 10 e) opposite f) opposite

YTI 5 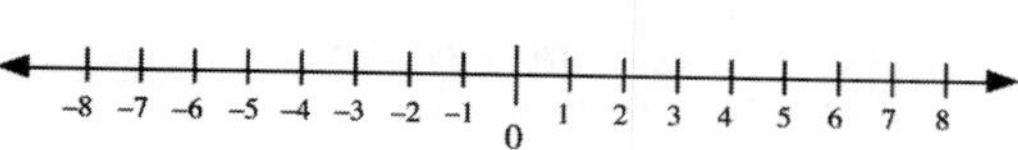

YTI 6 a) $9 > 4$ b) $-6 < 3$ c) $-2 > -6$ d) $4 > -8$

YTI 7 a) 12 b) 5 c) 24 d) 1 e) 0

YTI 8 a) 3, to the right
b) value, 5, to the left
c) value, 7, to the right
d) value, 4, direction, to the left
e) value is 2 and the direction is to the right

Focus Exercises: Section 9.1

Evaluate the following according to the replacement value given.

1. $3x + 4$; replace x with 2.

2. $5x - 4$; replace x with 3.

3. $3v \div 9$; replace v with 6.

4. $\sqrt{w}$; replace w with 36.

5. $19 - 5x$; replace x with 1.

6. $20 - 3m$; replace m with 4.

7. $\frac{b + c}{2}$; replace ***b*** with 29 and ***c*** with 15

8. $h \div c$; replace ***h*** with 36, ***c*** with 12.

9. $y^2 + 3y$; replace ***y*** with 4.

10. $xy + y^2$; replace ***x*** with 8 and ***y*** with 5.

11. $\frac{P + 10}{P}$; replace ***P*** with 5.

12. $\frac{24 - d}{10}$; replace ***d*** with 4.

13. $5u - v$; replace ***u*** with 9 and *v* with 20

14. $3x - 2y$; replace ***x*** with 5, ***y*** with 2.

15. $\frac{p + r}{p - r}$; replace ***p*** with 11 and ***r*** with 9.

16. $\frac{x + 4y}{3x - y}$; replace ***x*** with 2, ***y*** with 3.

Translate each English expression into an algebraic expression. Use any variable to represent the unknown number.

17. The difference of a number and 15.

18. The difference of 12 and a number.

19. The sum of 20 and a number.

20. The sum of a number and five.

21. The quotient of a number and 18.

22. The quotient of 36 and a number.

23. The square of a number.

24. The square root of a number.

25. The product of a number and 9.

26. The product of 7 and a number.

27. The absolute value of a number.

28. The opposite of a number.

Identify the opposite of each number.

29. 8 **30.** -16 **31.** -18 **32.** $+23$

Insert the correct symbol between each pair of numbers, either < (less than) or > (greater than).

33. 0 5 **34.** 3 -9 **35.** -5 4 **36.** -10 -2

37. -1 7 **38.** -6 -13 **39.** -4 0 **40.** 0 -8

Find the absolute value.

41. $|-15|$ **42.** $|7|$ **43.** $|+21|$ **44.** $|-1|$

45. $|0|$ **46.** $|+2.5|$ **47.** $|44|$ **48.** $|-1.8|$

49. $\left|-\frac{1}{2}\right|$ **50.** $|-0|$ **51.** $|-0.65|$ **52.** $\left|+\frac{1}{2}\right|$

Identify the numerica1 value and direction.

53. 6 **54.** $+18$ **55.** -12 **56.** 0

SECTION 9.2 Adding Signed Numbers

Objectives

In this section, you will learn to:

- Represent signed numbers as vectors.
- Add signed numbers using either the number line or rules of addition.

To successfully complete this section, you need to understand:

- Adding and subtracting whole numbers (1.3)
- The integer number line (9.1)
- Absolute value (9.1)

Introduction

At the end of Section 9.1, you were introduced to a definition of *number*:

> Every non-zero number has both value and direction. Zero has value but no direction.

We can represent this notion of number using a linear length—representing the numerical value of the number—and an arrow—representing the direction of the number.

Vectors

Here is a linear length of 5 units. We can identify its length by counting the number marks from either left to right or right to left:

We can give the linear length direction (left or right) by placing an arrowhead at one end or the other. With an arrow, the linear length is called a **vector**.

5 units, counting right to left

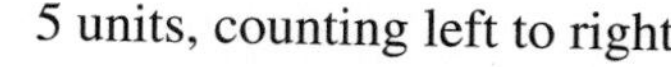

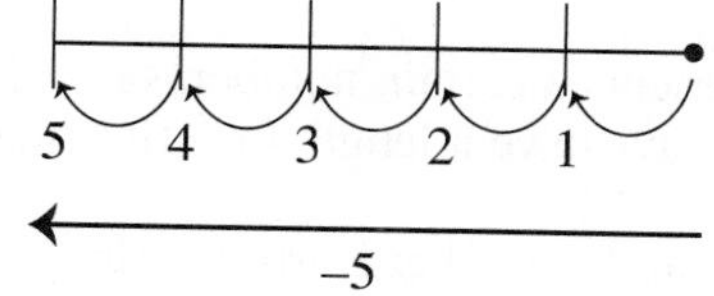

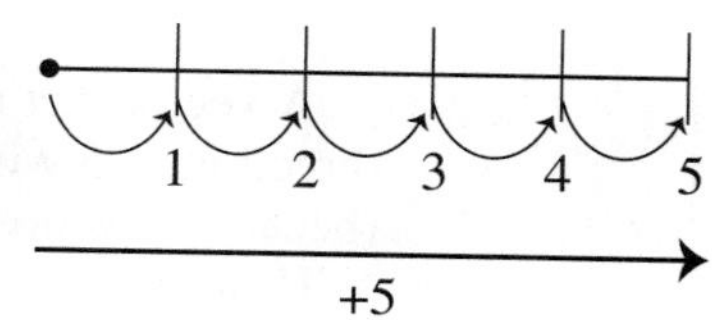

The direction of the vector indicates the sign of the number. A vector pointing left indicates a negative number, and a vector pointing right indicates a positive number.

EXAMPLE 1

To represent the number +5 as a vector, we start at 0 and draw a vector of length 5 units to the right.

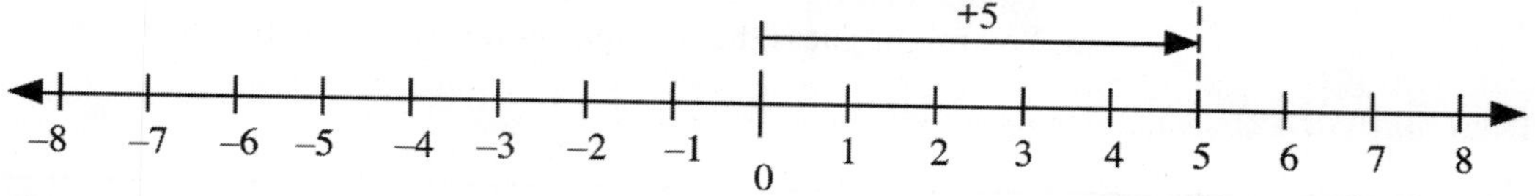

To represent the number +6 as a vector, we start at 0 and draw a vector of length 6 units to the left.

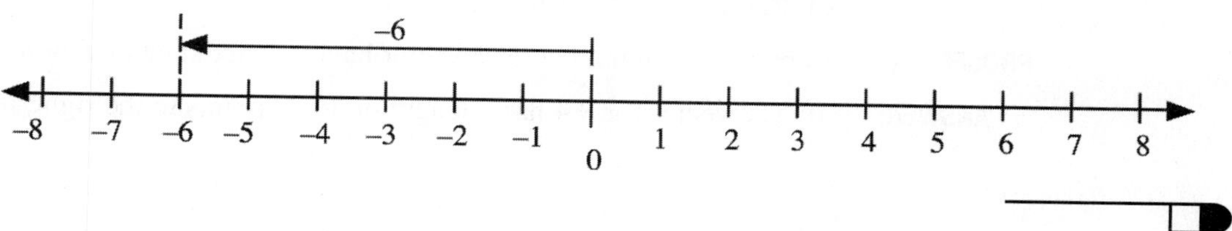

Note: As a vector, zero has no length and no direction. In other words, 0 is neither positive nor negative.

YOU TRY IT 1

Use the number line below to represent the given number as a vector with both a linear length and a direction. For each of these, start the vector at the origin, 0. Use Example 1 as a guide.

a) -3

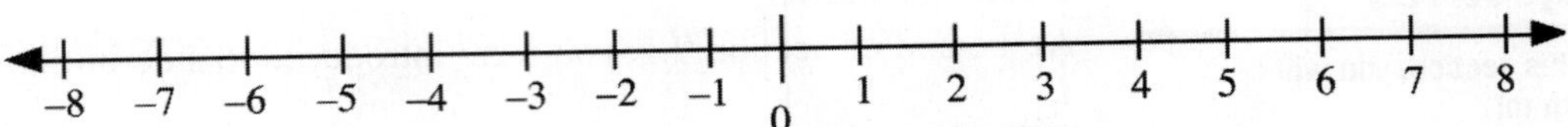

b) $+7$

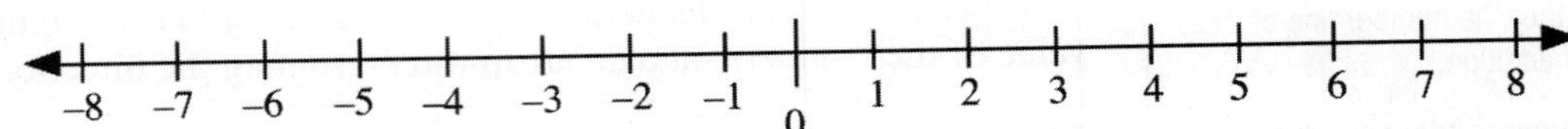

c) -8

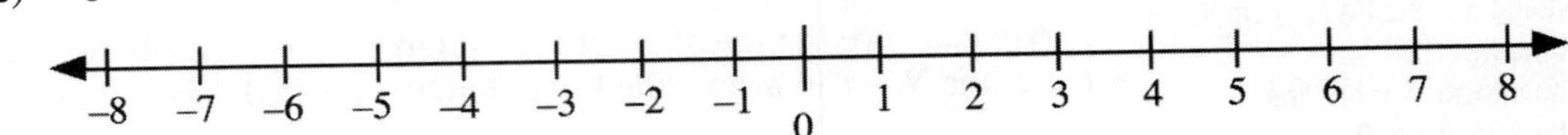

A vector that represents a certain number, say $+5$, must always have the same length and direction. $+5$ will always have a length of 5 (its numerical value) and point to the right (because it is positive).

However, vectors can have other starting points. If the vector representing $+5$ starts at $+3$ on the number line, it will still have a length of 5 and point to the right. It would look like this:

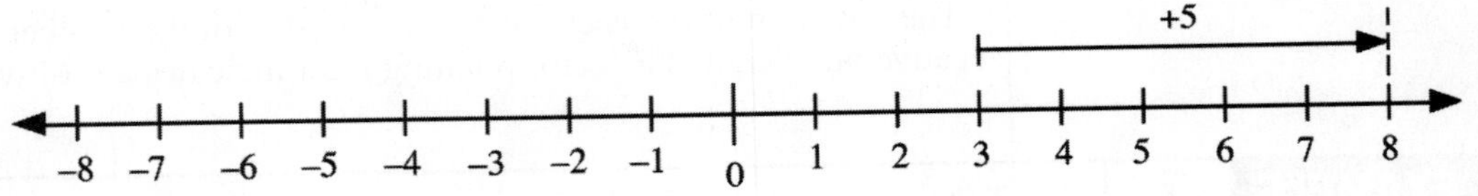

Notice that the vector starts at $+3$ and extends 5 units to the right. Notice, also, that it ends at 8. You might guess that the reason it ends at 8 is because $3 + 5 = 8$, and you'd be right!

EXAMPLE 2

Represent each number as a vector, starting at the given point. State where the vector stops.

a) Represent $+4$ starting at -1

b) Represent -6 starting at $+8$

c) Represent $+3$ starting at -7

PROCEDURE: Represent each number as a vector having length and direction.

ANSWER: a) The vector for $+4$ has a length of 4 and points to the right; here it is, starting at -1.

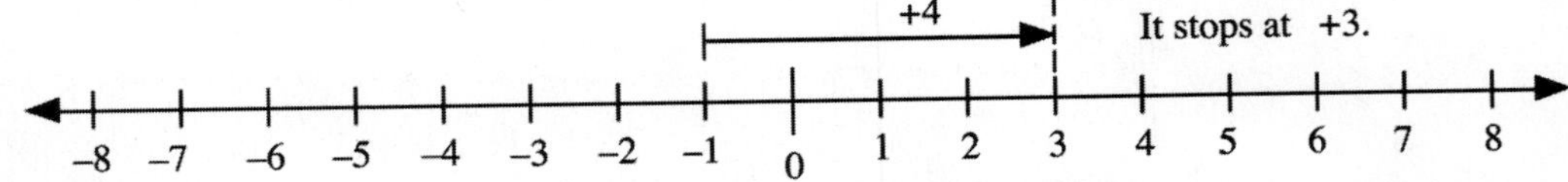

b) The vector for -6 has a length of 6 and points to the left; here it is, starting at $+8$.

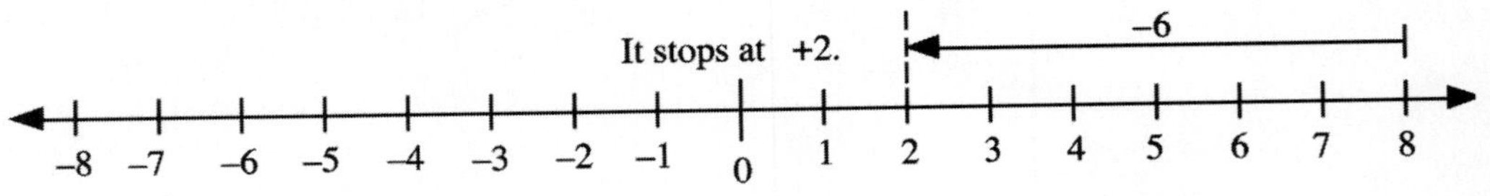

c) The vector for $+3$ has a length of 3 and points to the right; here it is, starting at -7.

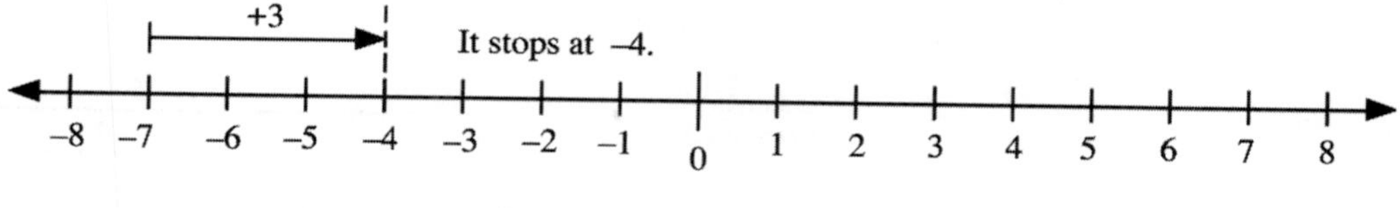

YOU TRY IT 2

Use the number line below to represent the given number as a vector with both a linear length and a direction. Start at the given value, and state where it stops. Use Example 2 as a guide.

a) -3, starting at $+5$.

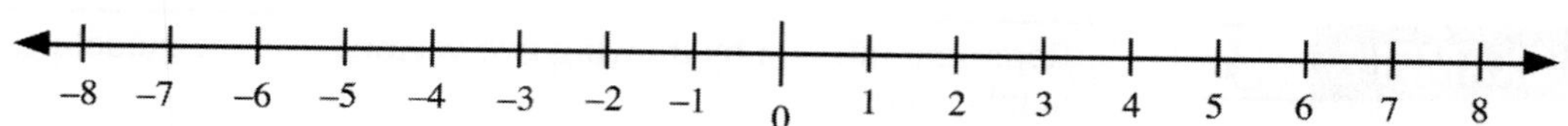

b) $+7$, starting at -4.

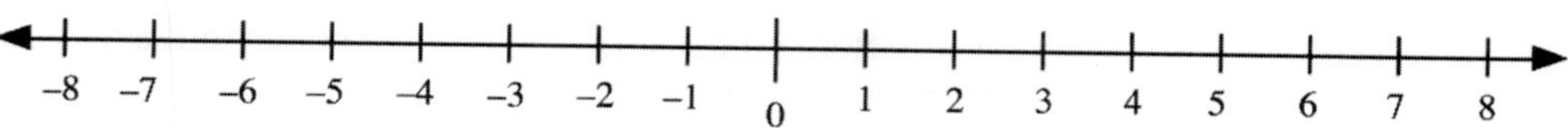

c) -6, starting at -2.

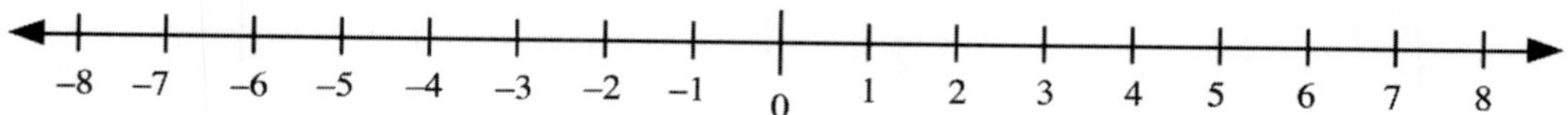

Adding Signed Numbers on the Number Line

We can use the number line to add numbers. For example, to add $3 + 5$ we construct:

1. a vector for $+3$ that starts at the origin, 0, and
2. a vector for $+5$ that *starts at 3* (where the first vector stopped).

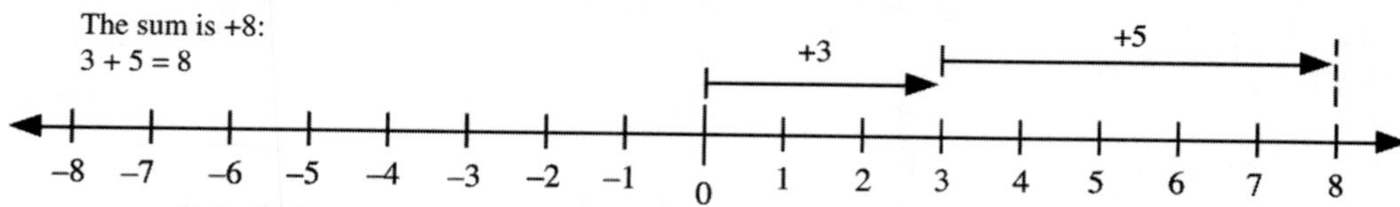

It doesn't matter if the numbers we are adding are positive or negative. Each number can be represented as a vector having a length and a direction. To add them, simply follow these guidelines.

Adding Two Numbers on the Number Line

1. Draw a vector for the first number, starting from the origin, 0.
2. Draw a vector for the second number that starts where the first vector stopped.
3. The number at which the second vector stops is the sum.

We can add +3 and −5, by first showing the vector for +3 (which will start at 0 and stop at +3); then from +3 we can draw the vector for −5 (which points to the left). Where the second vector stops, that is the sum:

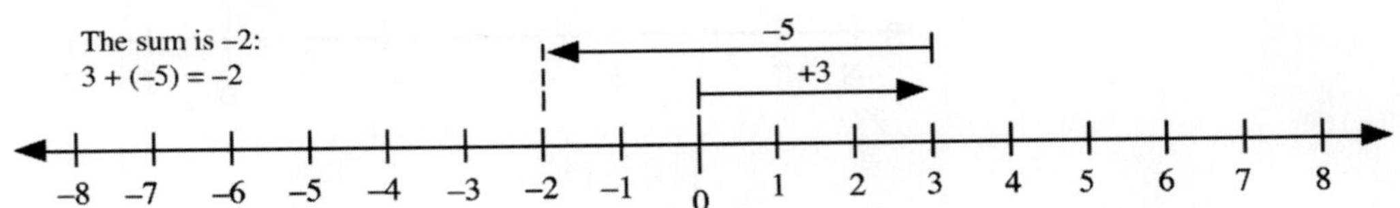

The sum of +3 and −5 is written 3 + (−5). Notice the parentheses around the −5; in this case, the parentheses act as separators, separating the plus sign (+) from the negative sign in −5.

EXAMPLE 3 Represent the sum by drawing two vectors. Use the guidelines for adding two numbers on the number line.

a) 4 + (−1) b) −6 + 8 c) 3 + (−7)

PROCEDURE: Represent each number as a vector having length and direction.

a) As a vector, +4 has a length of 4 and points to the right; as a vector, −1 has a length of 1 and points to the left.

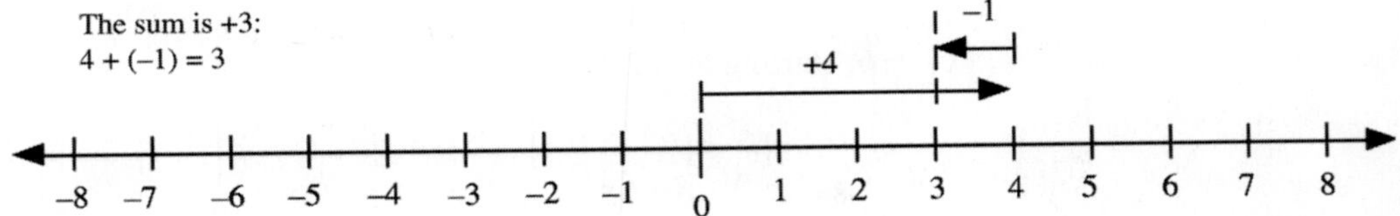

b) As a vector, −6 has a length of 6 and points to the left, and +8 has a length of 8 and points to the right.

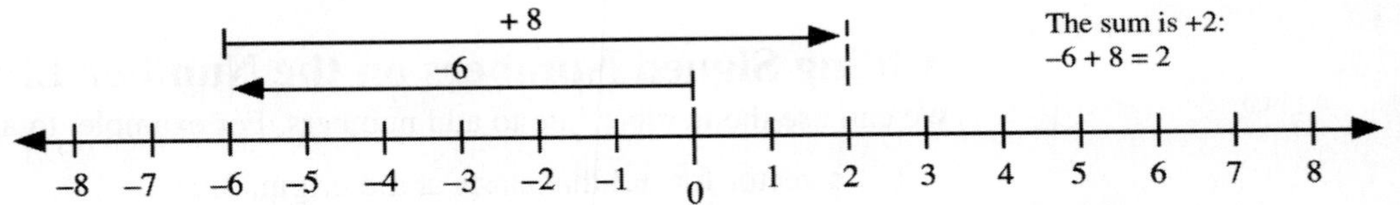

c) As vectors, +3 is 3 to the right; −7 is 7 to the left.

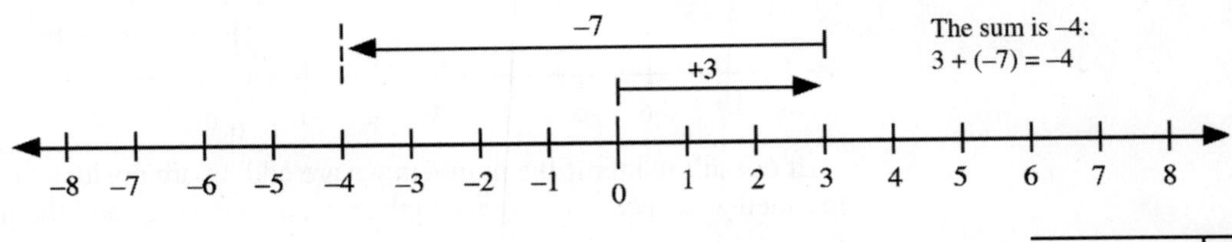

YOU TRY IT 3 *Add. You may use the number line above each pair to help you evaluate the sum. Use Example 3 as a guide.*

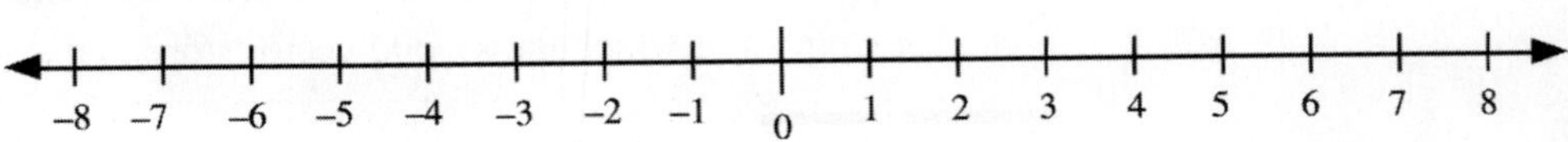

a) $3 + 4 =$ ________ b) $-6 + (-2) =$ ________

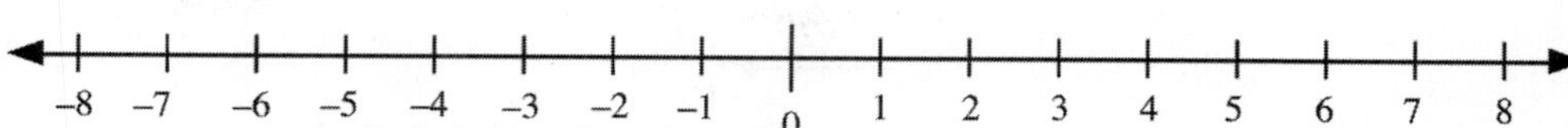

c) $8 + (-3) =$ ________ d) $2 + (-7) =$ ________

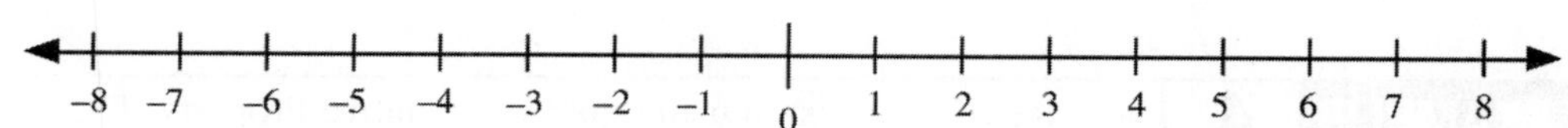

e) $-3 + 6 =$ ________ f) $-8 + 7 =$ ________

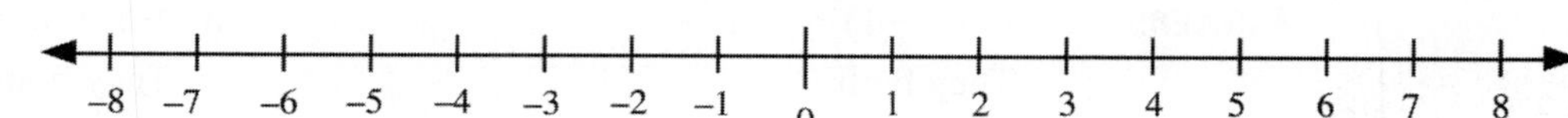

g) $-4 + 4 =$ ________ h) $6 + (-6) =$ ________

As you have seen, the sum of two numbers can be found using the number line and drawing vectors. This time, find these sums mentally by drawing the vector with your mind and not your pencil. Try to visualize the number line and in which direction the vectors would go.

YOU TRY IT 4

Try to do each of these without the aid of a number line. If you need a number line, you may draw one yourself.

a) $-10 + (-6)$ b) $13 + (-4)$ c) $2 + (-10)$

d) $-4 + 11$ e) $-12 + 7$ f) $10 + (-10)$

Recall from Section 1.2 the additive identity: $a + 0 = a$ and $0 + a = a$.

Using a number line and vectors, explain why the sum of any number and zero is always that number.

____

____

Adding Signed Numbers Using the Commutative Property

The Commutative Property of Addition works for integers as well as for whole numbers. You will recall that the Commutative Property of Addition allows the sum $3 + 5$ to be rewritten as $5 + 3$. The same is true for signed numbers.

For example, $2 + (-7)$ can be written as $-7 + 2$. They are both equal to -5:

2 + (−7):

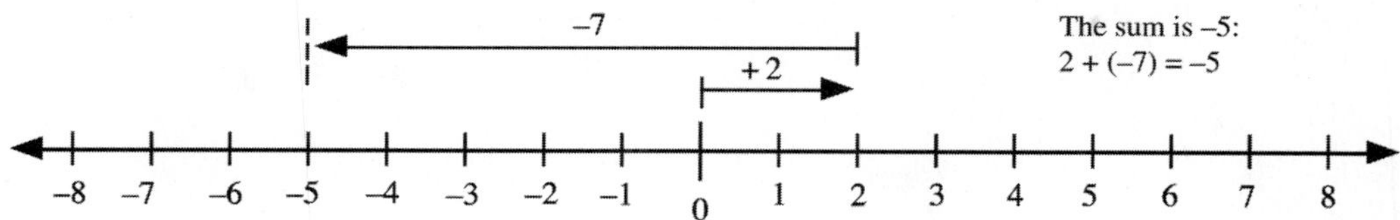

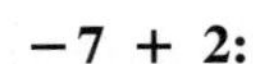

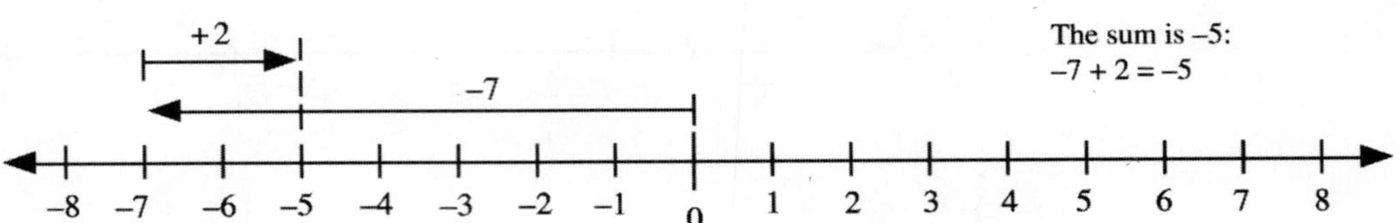

EXAMPLE 4 Rewrite each sum using the Commutative Property. Then, evaluate the original sum and the new sum.

a) $4 + (-1)$ b) $-6 + 0$ c) $3 + (-7)$ d) $-5 + 5$

ANSWER:

a) $4 + (-1) = -1 + 4$
They both $= +3$.

b) $-6 + 0 = 0 + (-6)$
They both $= -6$.

c) $3 + (-7) = -7 + 3$
They both $= -4$.

d) $-5 + 5 = 5 + (-5)$
They both $= 0$.

YOU TRY IT 5 *Rewrite each sum using the Commutative Property. Then, evaluate the original sum and the new sum. Use Example 4 as a guide.*

a) $-10 + 3 =$ _________
They both $=$ _________.

b) $-12 + (-4) =$ _________
They both $=$ _________.

c) $11 + (-8) =$ _________
They both $=$ _________.

d) $0 + (-9) =$ _________
They both $=$ _________.

Adding Numbers: When the Signs Are the Same

By now you should have a sense of how to add integers on the number line. However, some integers are so large in value that placing them on a number line can be a bit difficult. For example, to evaluate the sum $-23 + 48$ would be a challenge on the number line.

We need to develop some rules for adding signed numbers that have large values. These rules, though, must be consistent with our understanding of how to add small-valued integers. We'll develop the rules using smaller numbers and the number line.

The sum of two numbers with the same sign—*same direction*—is a number that has the same direction (same sign), and is either *more positive* or *more negative*.

Consider the sum of two positive numbers. Because the two numbers have the same direction—to the right—their sum will also be in the same direction; it will be farther to the right and will be more positive.

For example, add 8 and 5. The sum of the two right-pointing vectors is even farther to the right, farther away from 0 in the positive direction. The result is a number that is *more positive*.

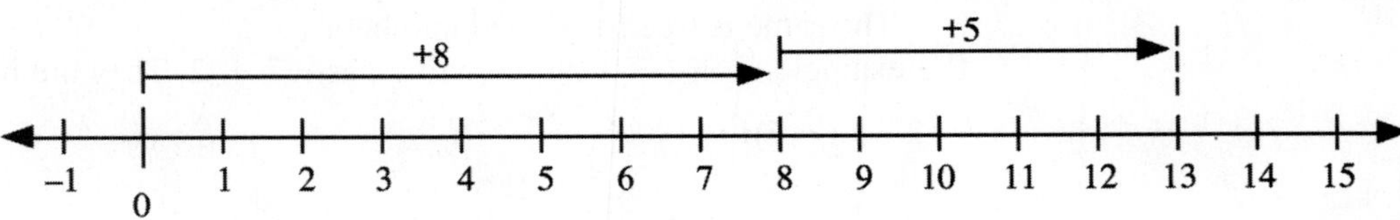

$8 + 5 = 13$

Now consider the sum of two negative numbers. Again, because the two numbers have the same direction—to the left—their sum will also be in the same direction; it will be farther to the left and will be more negative.

For example, add -7 and -8. The sum of the two left-pointing vectors is even farther to the left, farther away from 0 in the negative direction. The result is a number that is *more negative*.

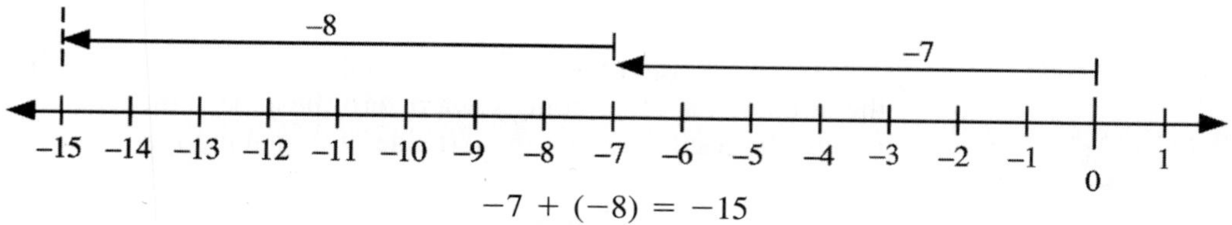

$$-7 + (-8) = -15$$

Because the signs are the same, the vectors go in the same direction. The result has the same sign (+ or −) and is the sum of the two numerical values.

The Sum of Two Numbers with the Same Sign

When finding the sum of two numbers of the same sign,

1. Add their numerical values, and
2. The sign of the sum is the same as the sign of each number.

EXAMPLE 5 Add.

a) $+7 + 4$ b) $-7 + (-3)$ c) $+12 + 26$

d) $-5 + (-8)$ e) $+6 + 9$ f) $-35 + (-52)$

PROCEDURE: Notice that the addends have the same sign, either both positive or both negative.

ANSWER:

a) $+7 + 4 = +11$ b) $-7 + (-3) = -10$ c) $+12 + 26 = +38$

d) $-5 + (-8) = -13$ e) $+6 + 9 = +15$ f) $-35 + (-52) = -87$

YOU TRY IT 6 *Add. Use Example 5 as a guide.*

a) $+2 + 17$ b) $-15 + (-20)$ c) $+43 + 86$

d) $-4 + (-12)$ e) $+15 + 29$ f) $-92 + (-88)$

Adding Numbers: When the Signs Are Different

When adding two numbers of different signs (one positive and the other negative), we can use the Commutative Property and write the sum so that the larger-valued number is first. This is not a requirement, but it will help us develop the rule.

For example, the sum $-5 + 8$ could first be written as $8 + (-5)$. Likewise, the sum $3 + (-7)$ could first be written $-7 + 3$.

When written this way, the first vector will go in the direction of the larger-valued number. The second vector will go in the opposite direction, toward 0.

For example, to find the sum of $8 + (-5)$, we can draw two vectors, one stretching away from 0 (zero) to the right, and the other going toward zero (heading left), but not all the way to 0. In other words, the result stays on the right side of 0, which is a positive number.

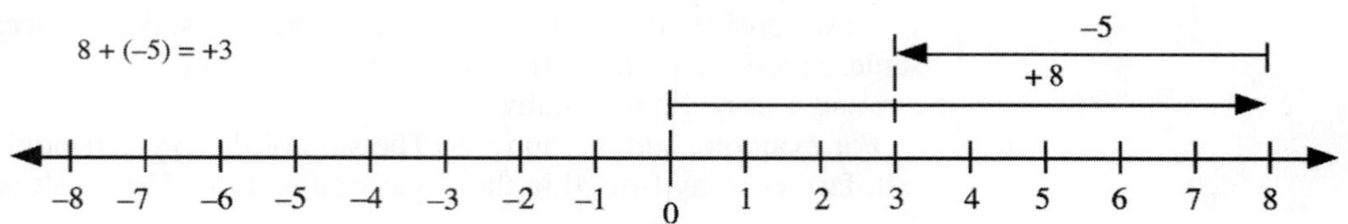

To find the sum of $-7 + 3$, we can draw two vectors, one stretching away from 0 (zero) to the left, and the other going toward zero (heading right), but not all the way to 0. In other words, the result stays on the left side of 0, making it a negative number.

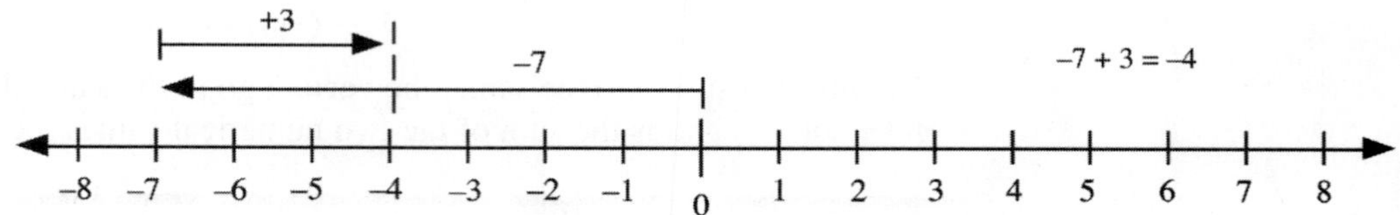

By writing the sum with the larger-valued number first, we get an immediate clue as to whether the result will be positive or negative; the result will have the same sign as the larger-valued number. Also, because the vectors go in opposite directions, one left and one right, the result can be found by subtracting the numerical values.

Here are the guidelines for finding the sum of two numbers with different signs:

The Sum of Two Numbers with Different Signs

When finding the sum of two numbers of the same sign,

1. Subtract the two numerical values: larger value – smaller value, and
2. The sign of the result is the same as the sign of the addend with the larger numerical value.

EXAMPLE 6

Add:

a) $7 + (-5)$ b) $29 + (-35)$ c) $-37 + 49$

PROCEDURE: Notice that the addends have different signs. Follow the guidelines above to find the sum.

ANSWER:

a) $7 + (-5) = +2$ { The larger-valued number is positive, so the result will be positive. The difference: $7 - 5 = 2$, so the result is $+$**2**.

b) $29 + (-35) = -6$ { The larger-valued number is negative, so the result will be negative. The difference: $35 - 29 = 6$, so the result is **−6.**

c) $-37 + 49 = +12$ { The larger-valued number is positive, so the result will be positive. The difference: $49 - 37 = 12$, so the result is $+$**12.**

YOU TRY IT 7

Find each sum. Use Example 6 as a guide.

a) $27 + (-42)$ b) $-38 + 52$ c) $45 + (-29)$ d) $-86 + 42$

Think about it

If two numbers have different signs but have the same numerical value, such as $-3 + 3$, then which sign should be given to the result? Explain.

A number and its opposite have vectors that are the same length but in opposite directions, so when they are added together, the sum is 0.

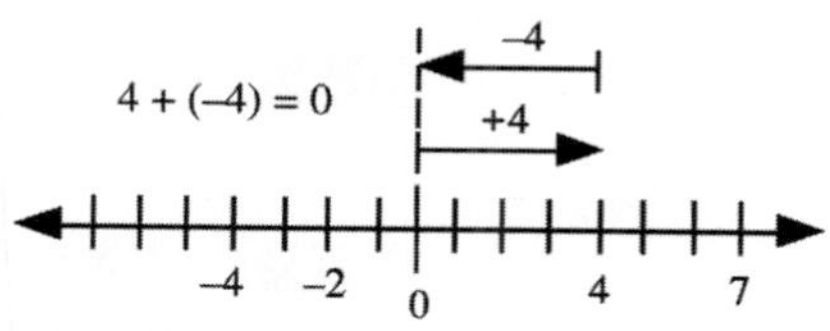

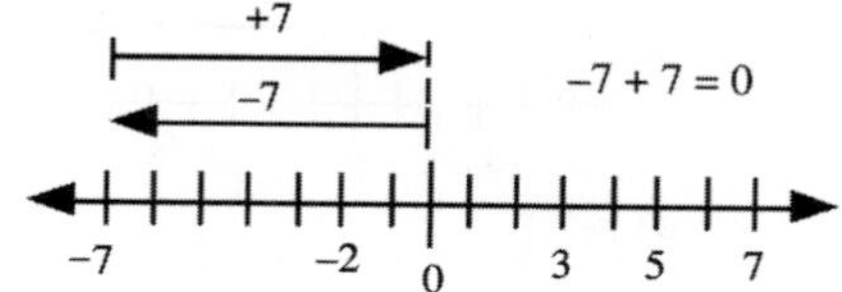

> The sum of a number and its opposite is 0: $a + (-a) = 0$.

EXAMPLE 7 Find the sum:

a) $7 + (-7)$ b) $-6 + 6$

ANSWER: a) $7 + (-7) = 0$ b) $-6 + 6 = 0$

YOU TRY IT 8 *Find each sum. Use Example 7 as a guide.*

a) $12 + (-12)$ b) $-9 + 9$ c) $23 + (-23)$

A sum may contain more than two numbers. If there is more than one positive number, or more than one negative number, we can use the commutative property and add the positive numbers separately from the negative numbers. We can then add the remaining two numbers.

EXAMPLE 8 Find the sum:

$2 + (-3) + (-5) + 4$

PROCEDURE: This sum contains two positive numbers (2 and 4) and two negative numbers (-3 and -5). Use the Commutative Property to write the sum with the two positive numbers first.

ANSWER:

$2 + (-3) + (-5) + 4$ Commute.

$= 2 + 4 + (-3) + (-5)$ Add the positive numbers separately from the negative numbers.

$= 6 + (-8)$ Now add $6 + (-8) = -2$

$= -2$

YOU TRY IT 9 *Find each sum. Use Example 8 as a guide.*

a) $6 + (-4) + (-9) + 1$ b) $-5 + (-6) + 3 + (-7)$

You Try It Answers: Section 9.2

(Note: Positive answers may also be written with a plus sign in front.)

a)

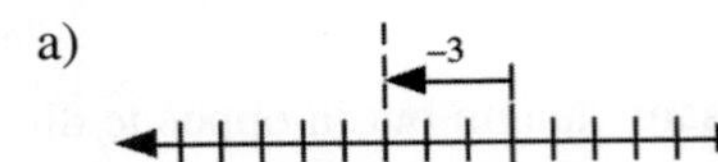

b)

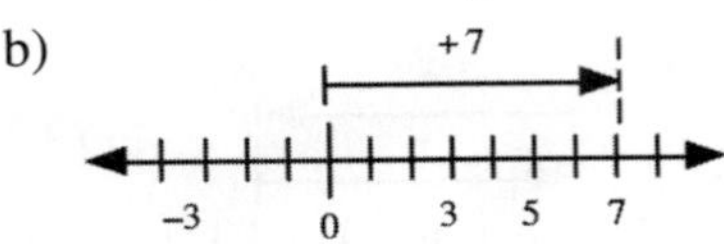

c)

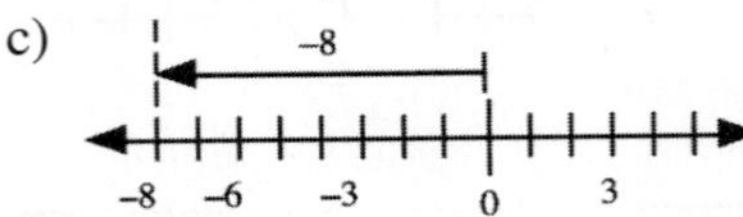

YTI 2 a)

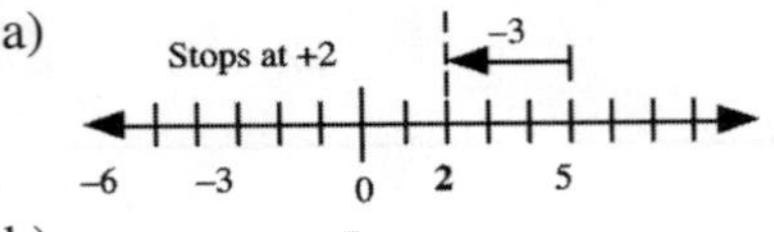

b)

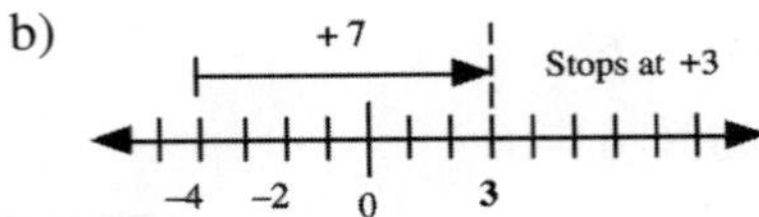

c) –6 Stops at –8.
–8 –2 0 3

YTI 3 a) 7 b) -8 c) 5 d) -5 e) 3 f) -1 g) 0 h) 0

YTI 4 a) -16 b) 9 c) -8 d) 7 e) -5 f) 0

YTI 5
a) $3 + (-10)$; both $= -7$
b) $-4 + (-12)$; both $= -16$
c) $-8 + 11$; both $= 3$
d) $-9 + 0$; both $= -9$

YTI 6 a) 19 b) -35 c) 129 d) -16 e) 44 f) -180

YTI 7 a) -15 b) 14 c) 16 d) -44

YTI 8 a) 0 b) 0 c) 0

YTI 9 a) -6 b) -15

Focus Exercises: Section 9.2

Find the sum.

1. $6 + (-4)$ **2.** $1 + (-9)$ **3.** $-8 + (-5)$ **4.** $-7 + (-6)$

5. $-3 + 8$ **6.** $-10 + 7$ **7.** $-7 + 7$ **8.** $-3 + 3$

9. $6 + (-6)$ **10.** $-1 + 8$ **11.** $-5 + 2$ **12.** $2 + (-7)$

13. $-5 + 4$ **14.** $1 + (-3)$ **15.** $0 + (-1)$ **16.** $0 + 9$

17. $-7 + 0$ **18.** $18 + 0$ **19.** $10 + (-10)$ **20.** $5 + (-5)$

21. $9 + (-8)$ **22.** $+9 + (+15)$ **23.** $-6 + (-11)$ **24.** $-13 + (-5)$

25. $+14 + (-5)$ **26.** $+8 + (-12)$ **27.** $-1 + (+5)$ **28.** $-10 + (+3)$

29. $-7 + 7$ **30.** $-9 + 9$ **31.** $-15 + (-16)$ **32.** $-11 + (-5)$

33. $-3 + 2$ **34.** $+20 + 9$ **35.** $13 + 3$ **36.** $-10 + (-3)$

37. $22 + (-15)$

38. $17 + (-28)$

39. $-22 + (-18)$

40. $-12 + 43$

41. $-31 + 24$

42. $-30 + 14$

43. $-53 + (-33)$

44. $-16 + 42$

45. $28 + (-51)$

46. $-20 + (-32)$

47. $-19 + 19$

48. $25 + (-25)$

Find the sum.

49. $6 + (-14) + 4$

50. $-6 + 3 + (-12) + 4$

51. $-2 + (-5) + (-1)$

52. $5 + (-1) + 3 + (-12)$

53. $-6 + (-4) + 10$

54. $3 + 8 + (-11)$

55. $-9 + 6 + 0 + 5 + (-3) + (-5)$

56. $8 + (-10) + 0 + 13 + (-10) + (-4)$

SECTION 9.3 Subtracting Signed Numbers

Objectives

In this section, you will learn to:

- Subtract signed numbers.
- Write subtraction as addition.
- Solve applications involving signed numbers.

To successfully complete this section, you need to understand:

- The Commutative Property of Addition (1.2)
- Adding signed numbers (9.2)

Introduction

You have been doing subtraction for a long time. In the world of math we call subtraction *finding the difference*. What you might not know is that subtraction is really another form of addition. This section introduces subtraction in a new way, especially as it relates to positive and negative numbers.

The First Three Meanings of the Dash

You have recognized this dash '–' for many years as the subtraction sign, or minus sign. More recently you have seen it used as the negative sign. There is a third meaning that will prove to be very valuable to your understanding of algebra; the dash also means "the opposite of:"

1. The dash means *minus*, as in $9 - 4$ is "9 minus 4."
2. The dash means *negative*, as in -6 is "negative 6."
3. The dash means *the opposite of*, as in -4 is "the opposite of 4."

EXAMPLE 1 Rewrite the outer negative sign as "the opposite of" the number within the parentheses.

ANSWER:
a) $-(+7)$ means the opposite of $+7$, which is -7.

b) $-(-5)$ means the opposite of -5, which is $+5$ (or 5).

c) $-(8)$ means the opposite of 8, which is -8.

YOU TRY IT 1 *Rewrite the outer negative sign as "the opposite of" the number within the parentheses. Also, state its value as we might normally say it. Use Example 1 as a guide.*

a) $-(+3)$ means ____________________, which is ______.

b) $-(-1)$ means ____________________, which is ______.

c) $-(-12)$ means ____________________, which is ______.

d) $-(16)$ means ____________________, which is ______.

The Double Negative

Refer back to Example 1 and YTI 1. What was the result of finding the opposite of a negative number? We may say, "The opposite of a negative number is a positive number." Does that seem accurate? When written algebraically, "the opposite of -5" becomes $-(-5)$, and this has the value of $+5$.

The notation $-(-5)$ is an example of a **double negative**. When two negative signs—two minus signs, two dashes—are next to each other (possibly separated by a parenthesis) then the number can be rewritten as a positive number. In other words, the two negative signs can be replaced by a single positive sign.

In these cases, parentheses are usually quite helpful. For example, it's a little awkward to read $--5$ as anything meaningful, so we always separate the negative signs with parentheses: $-(-5)$.

EXAMPLE 2 Rewrite each double negative as a positive. Be sure to include the + in front of the positive number.

a) $-(-9)$ b) $-(-4)$

ANSWER: a) $-(-9) = +9$ b) $-(-4) = +4$

It's also appropriate to write a double negative with two plus signs, as in $-(-4) = +(+4)$.

YOU TRY IT 2 *Rewrite each double negative as a positive. Be sure to include the + in front of the positive number. Use Example 2 as a guide.*

a) $-(-15)$ b) $-(-59)$ c) $-(-1)$

We'll return to the double negative in a little bit. First, though, let's look at why and how subtraction can be thought of as addition.

Writing Subtraction as Addition

Consider the difference between 7 and 4: $7 - 4$ (which you know is 3). We can see this difference on the number line:

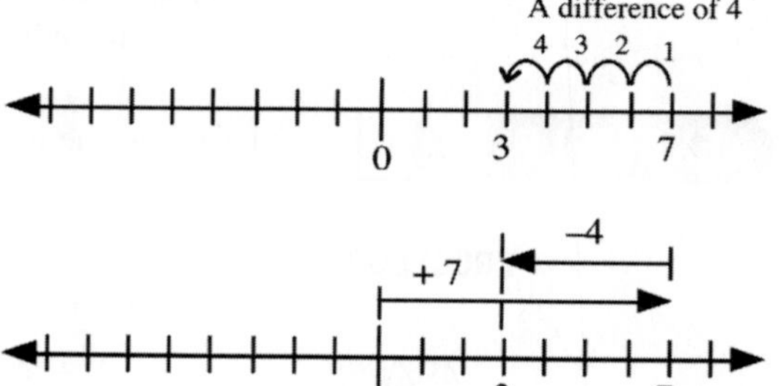

This is the same as $7 + (-4)$ and suggests that $7 - 4 = 7 + (-4)$, or 7 + the *opposite* of 4.

In other words, subtraction can be written as *adding the opposite*.

Similarly, consider the difference between 3 and −2: $3 - (-2)$. We can see this difference on the number line:

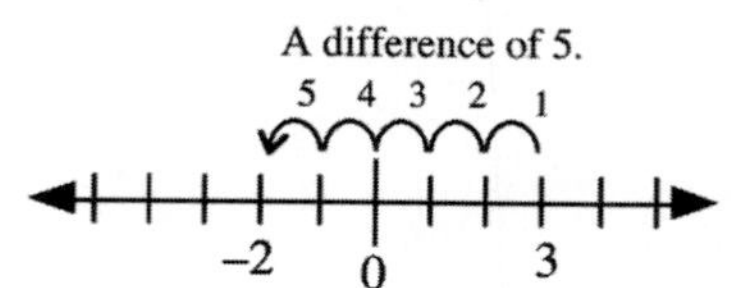

When we rewrite subtraction as *adding the opposite* here, we get $3 + (--2)$, which is—because of the double negative—the same as $3 + (+2)$. This suggests that $3 - (-2) = 3 + (+2)$, which we know to be +5.

> Subtraction can be rewritten as addition, as *adding the opposite*.
>
> Symbolically, this is written: $a - b = a + (-b)$.

The advantage of being able to write subtraction this way is that we do not need to learn new rules; we can use the rules of addition

Let's look at writing subtraction as addition. This means to change two things: change the operation to addition and change the second number to its opposite.

EXAMPLE 3 Rewrite each subtraction as addition and evaluate.

a) $6 - 2$ b) $-1 - 7$ c) $5 - (-6)$ d) $-9 - (-2)$

PROCEDURE: For each of these, the operation will become addition and the second number will become its opposite.

ANSWER: a) $6 - 2 = \underline{6 + (-2)} = \underline{+4}$. b) $-1 - 7 = \underline{-1 + (-7)} = \underline{-8}$.

c) $5 - (-6) = \underline{5 + (+6)} = \underline{+11}$. d) $-9 - (-2) = \underline{-9 + (+2)} = \underline{-7}$.

YOU TRY IT 3 *Rewrite each subtraction as addition. Then, evaluate the sum. Use Example 3 as a guide.*

a) $12 - 5 =$ ______________ = _____. b) $6 - (-4) =$ ______________ = _____.

c) $4 - 10 =$ ______________ = _____. d) $-3 - (-9) =$ ______________ = _____.

e) $-5 - 3 =$ ______________ = _____. f) $-12 - (-2) =$ ______________ = _____.

g) $-6 - (-6) =$ ______________ = _____. h) $0 - 7 =$ ______________ = _____.

If an expression contains more than two integers, then we should keep in mind the order of operations, and add two integers at a time, working from left to right.

EXAMPLE 4 Evaluate the expression:

$2 - 3 + 4 - (-5)$

PROCEDURE: First write each subtraction as addition. Then use the Commutative Property to get the positive number(s) together and the negative number(s) together.

ANSWER:

$2 - 3 + 4 - (-5)$	Change all subtraction to adding the opposite.
$= 2 + (-3) + 4 + (+5)$	Get the three positive numbers together and add.
$= 2 + 4 + 5 + (-3)$	$2 + 4 + 5 = 11$
$= 11 + (-3)$	Add 11 and −3.
$= 8$	

YOU TRY IT 4 *Evaluate each expression. Use Example 4 as a guide.*

a) $6 + (-4) - (-9) - 1$ b) $-5 - (-6) - 7 + 3$

Guidelines for Adding and Subtracting Signed Numbers: A Summary

Our work with signed numbers thus far leads us to these guidelines on how to add and subtract two signed numbers:

1. Change subtraction to addition: add the opposite. $3 - 5 \rightarrow 3 + (-5)$; $-4 - (-7) \rightarrow -4 + (+7)$

2. If the two numbers have the same sign:

	Both positive	Both negative
	$+2 + (+8)$	$-1 + (-6)$
a. Add the numerical values of each number.	↓	↓
b. The resulting sum will have the same sign.	$= +10$	$= -7$

3. If the two numbers have different signs:
   a. Subtract the two numerical values: larger value – smaller value.
   b. The sign of the sum is the same as the sign of the addend with the larger numerical value.

$-8 + 3$	$11 + (-2)$
$8 - 3 = 5$	$11 - 2 = 9$
Larger value is negative $= -5$	Larger value is positive $= +9$

EXAMPLE 5 Evaluate.

a) $29 - 42$ b) $37 + (-25)$ c) $-47 + (-19)$ d) $12 - (-38)$

PROCEDURE: Change all subtraction (if any) to addition. Apply the guidelines in the summary to find the sum.

ANSWER:

a) $29 - 42$ First, rewrite as addition: $29 + (-42)$.
$= 29 + (-42)$ The signs are different; find the difference: $42 - 29 = 13$.
$= -13$ The result is negative: -13.

b) $37 + (-25)$ The signs are different; find the difference: $37 - 25 = 12$.
$= +12$ (or 12) The result is positive: $+12$.

c) $-47 + (-19)$ The signs are the same; they are both negative.
$= -66$ Add the numerical values: $47 + 19 = 66$; the result is negative.

d) $12 - (-38)$ First, rewrite subtraction as addition: $12 + (+38)$.
$= 12 + (+38)$ The signs are the same; they are both positive.
$= +50$ (or 50) Add the numerical values: $12 + 38 = 50$; the result is positive.

YOU TRY IT 5 *Evaluate. Use Example 5 as a guide.*

a) $33 + (-95)$ b) $-21 + 68$ c) $65 - (-15)$ d) $-76 - 48$

Applications with Integers

Here are a few situations in which signed numbers are common:

Finances: Borrowing money represents a debt, a negative amount. Credits and payments are positive amounts; debits and purchases are negative amounts. (The word "debit" is related to "debt.")

Temperature: Even though an outside temperature of only 5° (5 degrees) is cold, −5° is colder by 10°.

Altitude: Below sea level the altitude is negative; above sea level it is positive.

The next few examples and exercises make use of adding and subtracting integers. For each, set up a numerical expression (using addition or subtraction) and then answer the question in a sentence.

EXAMPLE 6 On her Macy's card, Julia has a debit of \$25 and makes a payment of \$14. What is the new balance of her account? Is this new balance a debit or a credit?

PROCEDURE: A debit is a negative number (−\$25), and a payment on an account is a positive number (+\$14) added to the account. Numerically, it looks like this:

ANSWER: Numerical expression: $-25 + 14 = -11$

SENTENCE: The new balance is −\$11; this is a *debit*.

YOU TRY IT 6 *Solve each application. Write a numerical expression, and write the answer in the form of a sentence. Use Example 6 as a guide.*

a) Bonnie has a debit of \$32 on her Sears card. She likes to keep ahead by making larger-than-needed payments. Her most recent payment is for \$50. What is the new balance of her account? Is it a debit or a credit?

Numerical Expression:

Sentence: ______________________________.

b) Art has a credit balance of \$36 on his Visa card. He makes purchases on this card worth \$100. What is the new balance of his account? Is it a debit or a credit?

Numerical Expression:

Sentence: ______________________________.

In the winter, the temperature in some northern states falls below 0°. Such temperatures can be represented by negative numbers.

EXAMPLE 7 If the temperature was 8° at 4:00 PM and then fell 15° by midnight, what was the temperature at midnight?

PROCEDURE: Temperature *falling* means *subtracting* the number of degrees it fell from the starting temperature.

ANSWER: *Numerical expression:* $8 - 15 = -7$

SENTENCE: The temperature at midnight was −7°.

YOU TRY IT 7 *Solve each application. Write a numerical expression, and write the answer in the form of a sentence. Use Example 7 as a guide.*

a) At 2:00 AM the outside temperature was −13°. By noon the temperature had risen 27°. What was the temperature at noon?

Numerical Expression:

Sentence: ______________________________.

b) At noon the outside temperature was −11°. By midnight the temperature had fallen 18°. What was the temperature at midnight?

Numerical Expression:

Sentence: ______________________________.

Finding the Difference between Two Altitudes

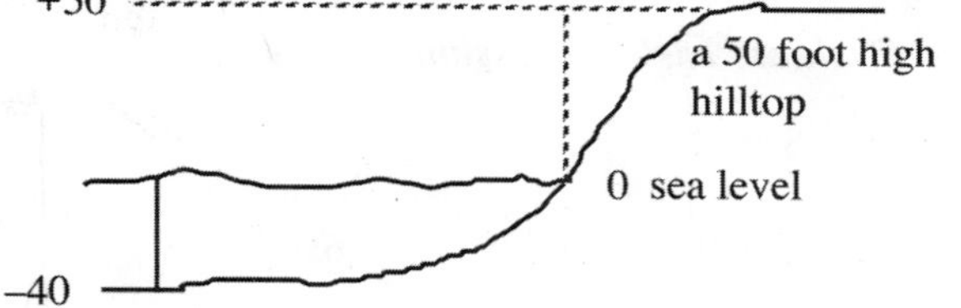

Altitude means how high or how low something is compared to sea level.

If a hilltop is 50 feet above sea level, then it has an altitude of 50 feet, or +50 feet.

If the ocean floor is 40 feet deep, then it is 40 feet below sea level and has an altitude of −40 feet.

Sea level has an altitude of 0 feet.

We use subtraction when finding the difference in altitudes: Higher altitude − Lower altitude.

EXAMPLE 8 Find the difference in altitude between a hill 50 feet above sea level and an ocean floor 40 feet below sea level.

PROCEDURE: When finding difference in altitude, we use the order they are mentioned in the problem: *first altitude – second altitude*. In this case, that is hill − ocean floor.

ANSWER: *Numerical expression:* $+50 - (-40) = 50 + (+40) = +90$

SENTENCE: The difference in altitude is 90 feet.

YOU TRY IT 8 *Solve each application. Write a numerical expression, and write the answer in the form of a sentence. Use Example 8 as a guide.*

a) Find the difference in altitude between an airplane 1,280 feet above sea level and a mountain peak 1,150 feet above sea level.

Numerical Expression:

Sentence: 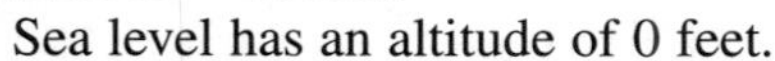

b) Find the difference in altitude between a cliff 45 feet above sea level and an ocean floor 35 feet below sea level.

Numerical Expression:

Sentence: ________________

You Try It Answers: Section 9.3

(Note: Positive answers may also be written with a plus sign in front.)

YTI 1
a) the opposite of +3; −3
b) the opposite of −1; 1
c) the opposite of −12; 12
d) the opposite of 16; −16

YTI 2
a) $-(-15) = +15$ b) $-(-59) = +59$
c) $-(-1) = +1$

YTI 3
a) $12 + (-5)$; 7 b) $6 + (+4)$; 10
c) $4 + (-10)$; −6 d) $-3 + (+9)$; 6
e) $-5 + (-3)$; −8 f) $-12 + (+2)$; −10
g) $-6 + (+6)$; 0 h) $0 + (-7)$; −7

YTI 4
a) 10 b) −3

YTI 5
a) −62 b) 47 c) 80 d) −124

YTI 6
a) $-32 + 50 = 18$; The new balance is \$18. This is a credit.
b) $+36 - 100 = -64$; The new balance is −\$64. This is a debit.

YTI 7
a) $-13 + 27 = 14$; The noon temperature was 14°.
b) $-11 - 18 = -29$; The midnight temperature was −29°.

YTI 8
a) $1{,}280 - 1{,}150 = 130$; The difference in altitude is 130 feet.
b) $45 - (-35) = 45 + (+35) = 80$; The difference in altitude is 80 feet.

Focus Exercises: Section 9.3

Evaluate each expression.

1. 8 − 2	**2.** 3 − 9	**3.** 5 − 11	**4.** 9 − 6
5. 3 − 11	**6.** 7 − 7	**7.** −4 − 4	**8.** −6 − 4
9. 10 − 6	**10.** −7 − 6	**11.** 1 − 8	**12.** −9 − 5
13. 5 − (−2)	**14.** 1 − (−8)	**15.** 7 − (−1)	**16.** 3 − (−6)
17. 8 − (−2)	**18.** 9 − (−3)	**19.** −3 − (−5)	**20.** −2 − (−10)
21. −4 − (−6)	**22.** −11 − (−5)	**23.** −12 − (−2)	**24.** −8 − (−7)
25. −70 − 20	**26.** −26 − 17	**27.** −19 − 35	**28.** 31 − 35
29. 46 − 63	**30.** −21 − 32	**31.** −10 − (−10)	**32.** −34 − (−5)
33. 26 − (−44)	**34.** −28 − (−25)	**35.** 63 − (−28)	**36.** −31 − (−72)
37. 6 + (−2)	**38.** 6 − (−2)	**39.** 2 − 3	**40.** 9 + (−5)
41. −8 + (−9)	**42.** −1 − 8	**43.** −1 − 3	**44.** −28 + (−3)
45. 5 + (−1)	**46.** 9 − 20	**47.** −28 − 7	**48.** −2 + (−1)
49. 4 − (−21)	**50.** −9 + 5	**51.** 3 + (−1)	**52.** 3 − 7
53. 1 − 9	**54.** 6 + (−8)	**55.** −2 + (−6)	**56.** −5 − 2
57. −5 − 9	**58.** −12 + (−9)	**59.** 8 + (−5)	**60.** 6 − 10
61. 2 − (−8) + 5	**62.** 7 − (−3) + 9	**63.** −5 − 6 − (−11)	**64.** 7 − (−2) − (−8)
65. 6 − (−3) − 5	**66.** −16 − (−2) + 4	**67.** −5 + 3 − 8 + 4	**68.** 6 + (−4) − (−3) + 5
69. −1 + 4 − (−10)	**70.** 9 − 3 − 2 − 6	**71.** −12 − 5 − (−13)	**72.** −15 + 9 − (−6) − 8

For each, write a numerical expression and then evaluate. Also, write a sentence answering the question.

Finances:

73. The ATM showed Mike's checking account balance as −$375 at the end of the July. But, on the first day of August, his paycheck of $2,825 was automatically deposited. What was Mike's new account balance?

74. Allison has $25 in her checking account. She wrote a check for $38. What is Allison's new account balance?

75. Joni started the week with a checkbook balance of $58. On Monday, she wrote a check for $72. On Tuesday, she made a deposit of $33. On Wednesday, she wrote a check for $39. On Thursday, she wrote a check for $29, and on Friday she made a deposit of $115. What was Joni's account balance on Saturday?

76. Carter started the week with a checkbook balance of $22. On Monday, he wrote a check for $40. On Tuesday, he made a deposit of $18. On Wednesday, he wrote a check for $26. On Thursday, he wrote a check for $42, and on Friday he made a deposit of $53. What was Carter's account balance on Saturday?

Temperature:

77. At 8:00 AM, the outside temperature was $-16°$. By 10:00 AM, the temperature had warmed up by 7°. What was the temperature at 10:00 AM?

78. This morning, the temperature was $-10°$ F. By the afternoon, the temperature had risen 18° F. What was the new temperature?

79. Last night, the temperature was $-2°$ F. By morning, the temperature had fallen 16° F. What was the new temperature?

80. At 9:00 PM, the outside temperature was 8°. By 3:00 AM the next morning, the temperature had fallen 11°. What was the temperature at 3:00 AM?

Altitude:

81. Find the difference in altitude between a mountain 5,280 feet above sea level and a mountain 1,416 feet above sea level.

82. Find the difference in altitude between a hill 152 feet above sea level and an ocean floor 87 feet below sea level.

83. Find the difference in altitude between a mountain 4,638 feet above sea level and an ocean floor 784 feet below sea level.

84. Find the difference in altitude between an ocean floor 192 feet below sea level and an ocean canyon 397 feet below sea level.

SECTION 9.4 Signed Fractions and Decimals

Objectives

In this section, you will learn to:

- Add and subtract signed decimals.
- Add and subtract signed fractions.

To successfully complete this section, you need to understand:

- Adding and subtracting like fractions (4.3)
- Adding and subtracting unlike fractions (4.4)
- Adding and subtracting decimals (5.3)
- Adding and subtracting integers (9.2 and 9.3)

Introduction

On a number line, between the integers are fractions and decimals, both positive and negative. Let's look at two number lines, one with signed fractions and one with signed decimals.

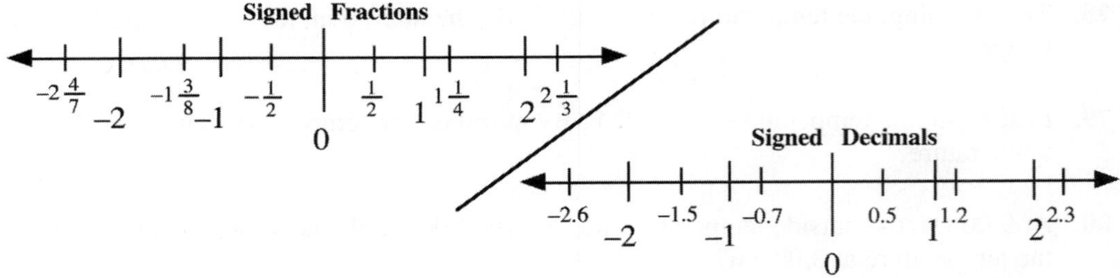

It would be challenging to add signed fractions or signed decimals on the number line using vectors because the spacing is so small. Instead, to add and subtract signed decimals and fractions, we need to rely on the procedures we developed in Sections 9.2 and 9.3.

Adding and Subtracting Signed Numbers

1. Change subtraction to addition: add the opposite.
2. If the two numbers have the same sign:
   a) Add the numerical values of each number.
   b) The resulting sum will have that same sign.
3. If the two numbers have different signs:
   a) Subtract the two numerical values: larger value − smaller value.
   b) The sign of the sum is the same as the sign of the addend with the larger numerical value.

When adding or subtracting signed decimals or signed fractions, keep these guidelines in mind.

Combining Like Fractions

Adding and subtracting signed fractions follows the same rules as above, as long as the fractions are *like* fractions (they have the same denominator). The larger-valued number, then, is determined by the numerator.

Note: In algebra, it is common to leave an improper fraction as it is and not write it as a mixed number.

EXAMPLE 1 Evaluate. Simplify completely.

a) $-\frac{9}{10}+\left(-\frac{7}{10}\right)$ b) $\frac{11}{12}+\left(-\frac{7}{12}\right)$ c) $\frac{7}{21}-\frac{16}{21}$

PROCEDURE: Change subtraction (if any) to addition. Apply the guidelines to find the sum.

ANSWER: a) $-\frac{9}{10} + \left(-\frac{7}{10}\right)$ The signs are the same—they are both negative—so we'll add the fractions but make sure to write the result as negative.

$= -\frac{16}{10}$ Because they are like fractions, adding the fractions means adding the numerators: $9 + 7 = 16$.

$= -\frac{8}{5}$ Simplify, leave the fraction improper.

b) $\frac{11}{12} + \left(-\frac{7}{12}\right)$ The signs are different, so well subtract the numerators: $11 - 7 = 4$. The larger-valued number is positive, so the result is positive as well.

$= +\frac{4}{12} = \frac{1}{3}$ Simplify the fraction.

c) $\frac{7}{21} - \frac{16}{21}$ First, change subtraction to addition: $\frac{7}{21} + \left(-\frac{16}{21}\right)$.

$= \frac{7}{21} + \left(-\frac{16}{21}\right)$ Because the signs are different, well subtract the numerators: $16 - 7 = 9$. The larger-valued number is negative, so the result is negative as well.

$= -\frac{9}{21} = -\frac{3}{7}$ Simplify the fraction.

YOU TRY IT 1

Evaluate. Use Example 1 as a guide.

a) $\frac{11}{30} + \left(-\frac{17}{30}\right)$ b) $-\frac{7}{24} - \left(-\frac{13}{24}\right)$ c) $-\frac{8}{15} - \frac{17}{15}$

Combining Unlike Fractions

If the fractions are not like fractions, then we must build them up to have a common denominator. From there, we follow the guidelines presented at the beginning of this section.

EXAMPLE 2

Evaluate. Simplify completely.

a) $-\frac{3}{5} + \frac{1}{2}$ b) $\frac{7}{8} - \left(-\frac{1}{4}\right)$

PROCEDURE: Change subtraction (if any) to addition. Apply the guidelines to find the sum.

ANSWER: a) $-\frac{3}{5} + \frac{1}{2}$ The LCD is 10: $-\frac{3}{5}\cdot\frac{2}{2} + \frac{1}{2}\cdot\frac{5}{5} = -\frac{6}{10} + \frac{5}{10}$.

$= -\frac{6}{10} + \frac{5}{10}$ The signs are different, so subtract: $6 - 5 = 1$. The larger-valued number is negative, so the result is negative as well.

$= -\frac{1}{10}$ This fraction does not simplify.

b) $\frac{7}{8} - \left(-\frac{1}{4}\right)$ First, change subtraction to addition: $\frac{7}{8} + \left(+\frac{1}{4}\right)$.

$= \frac{7}{8} + \left(+\frac{1}{4}\right)$ The LCD is 8: $\frac{7}{8} + \left(+\frac{1}{4}\right)\cdot\frac{2}{2} = \frac{7}{8} + \frac{2}{8}$.

$= \frac{7}{8} + \frac{2}{8}$ The signs are the same, and they are both positive, so the result is positive.

$= +\frac{9}{8}$ Leave this as an improper fraction.

YOU TRY IT 2

Evaluate. Use Example 2 as a guide.

a) $-\frac{1}{6} + \frac{1}{2}$ b) $-\frac{5}{8} + \left(-\frac{1}{6}\right)$ c) $\frac{1}{15} - \frac{2}{3}$

Adding and Subtracting Signed Decimals

Whether adding or subtracting decimals, it is always best for each decimal to have the same number of decimal places, as we see in Example 3.

EXAMPLE 3

Evaluate.

a) $2.9 - 4.2$ b) $0.37 + (-0.2)$ c) $1.02 - (-0.38)$ d) $-0.047 + (-0.19)$

PROCEDURE: Change all subtraction (if any) to addition. Apply the guidelines to find the sum.

ANSWER:

a) $2.9 - 4.2$ The numbers have the same number of decimal places.

$= 2.9 + (-4.2)$ The signs are different; find the difference. → $4.2 - 2.9 = 1.3$

$= -1.3$ The larger-valued number is negative so the result is negative.

b) $0.37 + (-0.2)$ Write −0.2 as −0.20 so the numbers have the same number of decimal places.

$0.37 + (-0.20)$ The signs are different; find the difference. → $0.37 - 0.20 = 0.17$

$= +0.17$ The larger-valued number is positive so the result is positive.

c) $1.02 - (-0.38)$ The numbers have the same number of decimal places. Change subtraction to addition: 1.02 + (+0.38).

$= 1.02 + (+0.38)$ The signs are the same, and they are both positive. → $1.02 + 0.38 = 1.40$

$= 1.40$ or 1.4

d) $-0.047 + (-0.19)$ Write −0.19 as −0.190 so the numbers have the same number of decimal places.

$= -0.047 + (-0.190)$ The signs are the same, and they are both negative. → $0.047 + 0.190 = 0.237$

$= -0.237$

YOU TRY IT 3

Evaluate. Use Example 3 as a guide.

a) $0.27 + (-1.6)$ b) $-3.8 - 5.2$ c) $0.45 - (-0.29)$ d) $-0.08 + 0.059$

Applications with Signed Decimals

EXAMPLE 4

On her Sears card, Julia has a credit of \$65.17 and makes a purchase of \$103.45. What is the new balance of Julia's account? Is this new balance a debit or a credit?

PROCEDURE: A credit is a positive number (+\$65.17), and a purchase is a negative number (−\$103.45) added to the account.

ANSWER: $65.17 + (-103.45)$ Rearrange this with the larger-valued number in front.

$= -103.45 + 65.17$ The result is negative. Subtract: $\begin{array}{r} 103.45 \\ -\ 65.17 \\ \hline 38.28 \end{array}$

$= -38.28$ (debit)

SENTENCE: Julia's new balance is a debit of \$38.28.

YOU TRY IT 4

Solve this application. Write a numerical expression, and write the answer in the form of a sentence. Use Example 4 as a guide.

On his MasterCard, Marco has a credit balance of \$43.67. He used his MasterCard to buy groceries worth \$90.25. What is the new balance of Marco's account? Is it a debit or a credit?

Numerical Expression:

Sentence: ______________________________.

EXAMPLE 5

Janine was experimenting with a fast freezing technique that her company is developing. She started with water at a Celsius temperature of 15.8°. In the experiment, within one minute the temperature fell 24.65°. What was the water temperature after one minute?

PROCEDURE: Temperature *falling* means *subtracting* the number of degrees it fell from the starting temperature. Apply the techniques used in this section to evaluate.

ANSWER: Numerical expression: $15.8 - 24.65$

SENTENCE: After one minute, the temperature was −8.85°.

Show the work:

Subtract

$15.8 - 24.65$

YOU TRY IT 5

Solve this application. Write a numerical expression, and write the answer in the form of a sentence. Use Example 5 as a guide.

At 2:00 PM, the outside temperature was 3.75°. By 10:00 PM, the temperature fell 5.2°. What was the temperature at 10:00 PM?

Numerical expression:

Sentence: ______________________________

EXAMPLE 6

Find the difference in altitude between a pier that is 2.7 meters above sea level and the ocean floor that is 4.59 meters below sea level.

PROCEDURE: To find the difference in altitude, subtract pier − ocean floor.

ANSWER: Numerical expression: +2.7 − (−4.59)

SENTENCE: The difference in altitude is 7.29 meters.

Show the work:

Subtract
+2.7 − (−4.59)

YOU TRY IT 6

Solve this application. Write a numerical expression, and write the answer in the form of a sentence. Use Example 6 as a guide.

Find the difference in altitude between the top of a lighthouse 23.6 meters above sea level and an undersea reef 40.56 meters below sea level.

Numerical expression:

Sentence: ______________________________

You Try It Answers: Section 9.4

(Note: Positive answers may also be written with a plus sign in front.)

YTI 1 a) $-\frac{1}{5}$ b) $\frac{1}{4}$ c) $-\frac{5}{3}$

YTI 2 a) $\frac{1}{3}$ b) $-\frac{19}{24}$ c) $-\frac{3}{5}$

YTI 3 a) −1.33 b) −9.0 or −9 c) 0.74 d) −0.021

YTI 4 43.67 − 90.25; Marco's new account balance is −\$46.58. This is a debit.

YTI 5 3.75 − 5.2; The temperature at 10:00 PM was −1.45°.

YTI 6 23.6 − (−40.56); The difference in altitude is 64.16 meters.

Focus Exercises: Section 9.4

Evaluate. Simplify, if possible.

1. $\frac{5}{12} - \frac{11}{12}$
2. $\frac{7}{20} - \frac{13}{20}$
3. $-\frac{5}{6} - \frac{1}{6}$
4. $-\frac{1}{8} - \frac{5}{8}$
5. $\frac{7}{18} - \left(-\frac{5}{18}\right)$
6. $\frac{5}{36} - \left(-\frac{13}{36}\right)$
7. $-\frac{1}{4} - \left(-\frac{3}{4}\right)$
8. $-\frac{5}{7} - \left(-\frac{6}{7}\right)$
9. $-\frac{11}{24} - \left(-\frac{5}{24}\right)$
10. $-\frac{13}{30} - \left(-\frac{1}{30}\right)$
11. $\frac{17}{40} - \frac{25}{40}$
12. $-\frac{49}{60} - \frac{17}{60}$
13. $-\frac{11}{18} + \left(-\frac{13}{18}\right)$
14. $-\frac{19}{20} + \left(-\frac{9}{20}\right)$
15. $-\frac{11}{24} + \frac{11}{24}$
16. $\frac{19}{30} + \left(-\frac{19}{30}\right)$
17. $-\frac{41}{36} + \frac{17}{36}$
18. $-\frac{43}{40} + \frac{31}{40}$

Evaluate. First find the least common denominator and build up each fraction as necessary. Simplify, if possible.

19. $\frac{3}{4} + \left(-\frac{5}{8}\right)$
20. $\frac{1}{3} + \left(-\frac{5}{6}\right)$
21. $\frac{2}{3} + \left(-\frac{2}{9}\right)$
22. $\frac{9}{8} + \left(-\frac{3}{10}\right)$
23. $\frac{13}{8} + \left(-\frac{7}{12}\right)$
24. $-\frac{9}{10} + \left(-\frac{3}{4}\right)$
25. $\frac{1}{6} - \left(-\frac{3}{8}\right)$
26. $-\frac{1}{6} - \frac{5}{9}$
27. $-\frac{7}{10} + \frac{8}{15}$
28. $\frac{1}{5} - \frac{3}{4}$
29. $-\frac{4}{15} - \left(-\frac{1}{6}\right)$
30. $-\frac{3}{14} + \frac{11}{21}$

Evaluate.

31. $-2.7 + 3.1$
32. $-3.6 + 6.4$
33. $2.2 + (-3.9)$
34. $4.6 + (-7.8)$
35. $-0.32 + (-0.43)$
36. $-0.53 + (-0.37)$
37. $0.36 + (-0.68)$
38. $0.81 + (-0.75)$
39. $-0.16 + (-0.3)$
40. $-0.52 + (-3.9)$
41. $2.2 + (-0.46)$
42. $-0.34 + 1.2$
43. $4 + (-2.8)$
44. $-6 + 0.52$
45. $-0.9 + (-15)$
46. $-1 + (-.37)$
47. $0.34 + (-0.97)$
48. $-9.1 + 3.5$
49. $5 + (-1.97)$
50. $3 + (-0.15)$
51. $-1.7 + 1.7$
52. $0.35 + (-0.35)$
53. $-2 + (-6.4)$
54. $-1 + (-3.8)$
55. $3.2 - (-2.4)$
56. $-9.1 - (-5.2)$
57. $-5.8 - 3.9$
58. $1.2 - 7.8$
59. $0.19 - (-0.48)$
60. $0.28 - 0.72$
61. $-0.41 - (-0.62)$
62. $-1 - (-3.45)$
63. $3 - (-4.12)$
64. $5 - 9.86$
65. $-0.96 - 0.58$
66. $-6 - 2.58$

For each, write a numerical expression and then evaluate. Also, write a sentence answering the question.

Finances:

67. On her Visa card, Daneice has a debit of \$57.82. She likes to keep ahead by making larger-than-needed payments. Her most recent payment is for \$100. What is Daneice's new account balance? Is this a debit or a credit?

68. Chuck's account had a debit of \$33.16 when he deposited a check for \$55. What is Chuck's new account balance? Is this a debit or a credit?

69. Arnie had \$38.16 in his checking account when he paid his phone bill and wrote a check for \$52.94. What is Arnie's new account balance? Is this a debit or a credit?

70. Charlene was paying bills and her account balance got to −\$15.23 with one more bill left to pay. She decided to write one more check for \$35.89. What is Charlene's new account balance? Is this a debit or a credit?

Temperature:

71. At 2:00 AM, the outside temperature was $-8.4°$. By noon, the temperature had risen $15.25°$. What was the temperature at noon?

72. The temperature of a frozen chicken was $-17.5°$ when George placed it in the microwave to thaw. After two minutes, the chicken's temperature had risen $9.8°$. What was the temperature of the chicken after two minutes?

73. The temperature of a snowball at 10:00 AM was $-3.85°$ Celsius. Manny put the snowball in a freezer and, by noon, its temperature had fallen $5.9°$. What was the temperature of the snowball at noon?

74. At noon, the outside temperature was $5°$. By midnight the temperature had fallen $7.6°$. What was the temperature at midnight?

Altitude:

75. Find the difference in altitude between a lifeguard tower 4.25 meters above sea level and the underwater beach 1.8 meters below sea level.

76. Find the difference in altitude between a fisherman's pole 2.36 meters above sea level and a school of fish 13.4 meters below sea level.

77. Find the difference in altitude between the bottom of a boat 2.65 meters below sea level and a reef 23.9 meters below sea level.

78. Find the difference in altitude between an undersea hill $\frac{1}{4}$ mile below sea level and the ocean floor $\frac{5}{6}$ mile below sea level.

SECTION 9.5 Multiplying and Dividing Signed Numbers

Objectives

In this section, you will learn to:

- Multiply signed numbers.
- Divide signed numbers.

To successfully complete this section, you need to understand:

- Commutative Property of Multiplication (1.2)
- Associative Property of Multiplication (1.2)
- Dividing Whole Numbers (1.5)
- Simplifying Fractions (3.2)
- Multiplying Fractions (3.3)
- Dividing Fractions (3.4)

Introduction

We now turn our attention to multiplication and division of signed numbers. Just as we developed rules for the addition of signed numbers, so shall we develop rules for their multiplication.

The rules for addition and rules for multiplication are different, just like rules for chess and checkers are different, and just like rules for soccer and football are different. These games may be played on the same checkerboard or on the same playing field, but you can't use the rules of one game to play the other.

Likewise, the rules for addition and the rules for multiplication are different; the numbers will look the same, but you can't use the rules of addition to evaluate a problem of multiplication.

The Product of a Positive Number and a Negative Number

As you know, multiplication is an abbreviation for repeated addition. For example, $3 \cdot 4 = 12$ because $3 \cdot 4$ means the sum of *three* 4's: $4 + 4 + 4 = 12$.

With this idea in mind, let's consider what happens when we try to add *two* -5's or $(-5) + (-5)$. We know that the answer is -10, but when we abbreviate this addition problem and turn it into multiplication, it looks like $2 \cdot (-5)$. This introduces us to the idea of multiplying signed numbers.

Positive × Negative:

First: $2 \cdot (-5) = (-5) + (-5) = -10.$

Furthermore,
$3 \cdot (-5) = (-5) + (-5) + (-5) = -15.$

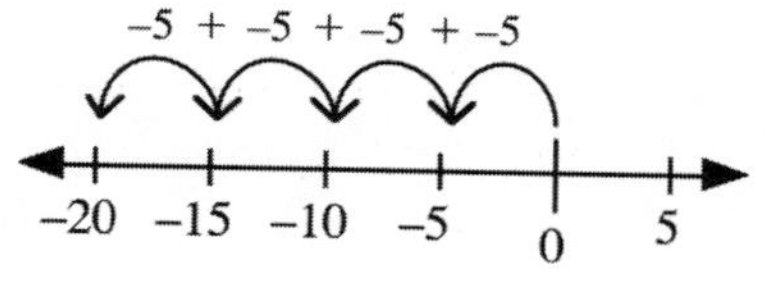

We could add another (-5)—making it $4 \cdot (-5)$—and get -20, a number that is *more* negative, more to the left on the number line.

Think about it

Look carefully at this series of products. What pattern(s) do you see? Complete the final two products.

$3 \cdot 3 = 9$
$3 \cdot 2 = 6$
$3 \cdot 1 = 3$
$3 \cdot 0 = 0$
$3 \cdot (-1) =$ ______
$3 \cdot (-2) =$ ______

The diagram and the Think about It illustrate the first rule for multiplying signed numbers:

> The product of a positive number and a negative number is a negative number.

EXAMPLE 1

Evaluate each product.

a) $6 \cdot (-3)$ b) $12 \cdot (-2)$ c) $7 \cdot (-8)$

d) $4 \cdot (-1)$ e) $0 \cdot (-5)$

PROCEDURE: The product of a positive number and a negative number is negative.

ANSWER: a) $6 \cdot (-3) = -18$ b) $12 \cdot (-2) = -24$ c) $7 \cdot (-8) = -56$
d) $4 \cdot (-1) = -4$ e) $0 \cdot (-5) = 0$ 0 times any number is 0: $0 \times a = 0$.

YOU TRY IT 1

Evaluate each product. Use Example 1 as a guide.

a) $9 \cdot (-4)$ b) $2 \cdot (-11)$ c) $0 \cdot (-8)$ d) $3 \cdot (-10)$ e) $8 \cdot (-1)$

Negative × Positive:

Look carefully at this series of products. What pattern(s) do you see? Complete the final two products.

$3 \cdot 3 = 9$
$2 \cdot 3 = 6$
$1 \cdot 3 = 3$
$0 \cdot 3 = 0$
$-1 \cdot 3 =$ ______
$-2 \cdot 3 =$ ______

Recall the *Commutative Property of Multiplication,* which allows us to write $3 \cdot 4 = 4 \cdot 3$. The Commutative Property is also true for signed numbers, so that we may write $3 \cdot (-5)$ as $(-5) \cdot 3$; the answer, either way we look at it, is -15:

$$3 \cdot (-5) = -15 \text{ and } (-5) \cdot 3 = -15:$$

The Commutative Property and the Think about It illustrate the second rule for multiplying signed numbers:

The product of a negative number and a positive number is a negative number.

EXAMPLE 2

Evaluate each product.

a) $-6 \cdot 4$ b) $-2 \cdot 15$ c) $-5 \cdot 8$
d) $-1 \cdot 4$ e) $-9 \cdot 0$

PROCEDURE: The product of a negative number and a positive number is negative.

ANSWER: a) $-6 \cdot 4 = -24$ b) $-2 \cdot 15 = -30$ c) $-5 \cdot 8 = -40$
d) $-1 \cdot 4 = -4$ e) $-9 \cdot 0 = 0$ Any number times 0 is 0: $a \times 0 = 0$.

YOU TRY IT 2

Evaluate each product. Use Example 2 as a guide.

a) $-7 \cdot 3$ b) $-6 \cdot 0$ c) $-2 \cdot 2$ d) $-1 \cdot 9$ e) $-10 \cdot 5$

The Fourth Meaning of the Dash

Next consider the special number, -1. Notice that -4 is the opposite of 4 and that $(-1) \cdot 4 = -4$.

Therefore, we could think of "multiplication by -1" as the same thing as "the opposite of." So that:

$$(-1) \cdot 3 = -3 \text{ (the opposite of 3)}$$
$$(-1) \cdot 7 = -7 \text{ (the opposite of 7)}$$

By that same reasoning, if we multiply -1 by a negative number, we'll get the opposite of that negative number (a positive number, by the way) as a result:

$$(-1) \cdot (-4) = +4 \text{ (the opposite of } -4\text{).}$$

We now have a fourth interpretation of the dash:

1. Minus $(6 - 2 = 4)$
2. Negative (-5 is "negative 5")
3. "the opposite of" (-8 is "the opposite of" 8)
4. "-1 times" (-4 is $-1 \cdot 4$)

EXAMPLE 3 Evaluate each product.

a) $-1 \cdot 9$ b) $-1 \cdot (-3)$ c) $-1 \cdot 5$ d) $-1 \cdot (-6)$

PROCEDURE: Multiplying a number by -1 results in the opposite of the number.

ANSWER:
a) $-1 \cdot 9 = -9$
b) $-1 \cdot (-3) = +3$ or 3
c) $-1 \cdot 5 = -5$
d) $-1 \cdot (-6) = +6$ or 6

YOU TRY IT 3 *Evaluate each product. Use Example 3 as a guide.*

a) $-1 \cdot 3$ b) $-1 \cdot 7$ c) $-1 \cdot (-8)$ d) $-1 \cdot (-2)$

Likewise, we could think of any negative number as a product of -1 and a positive number, as demonstrated in Example 4.

EXAMPLE 4 Write each negative number two ways as the product of –1 and a positive number.

a) $-9 = \underline{-1 \cdot 9}$ and $\underline{9 \cdot (-1)}$ b) $-3 = \underline{-1 \cdot 3}$ and $\underline{3 \cdot (-1)}$

YOU TRY IT 4 *Write each negative number two ways as the product of -1 and a positive number. Use Example 4 as a guide.*

a) -4 b) -7 c) -15

The Product of Two Negative Numbers

Recall the Associative Property of Multiplication. It says that in a product, we can change the grouping of the factors without affecting the resulting product: $(a \cdot b) \cdot c = a \cdot (b \cdot c)$.

Let's use the Associative Property with the fourth meaning of the dash. Consider, for example, $(-5) \cdot (-4)$. We can think of this as $5 \cdot (-1) \cdot (-4)$.

First, let's group the last two factors:		Second, we'll group the first two factors:
$5 \cdot \underline{(-1) \cdot (-4)}$	← Multiply: $(-1) \cdot (-4) = +4$.	$\underline{5 \cdot (-1)} \cdot (-4)$
$= 5 \cdot (+4)$	← Now, $5 \cdot (+4) = +20$.	$= (-5) \cdot (-4)$
$= +20$	← These products will both be +20. →	$= +20$

This shows us that $(-5) \cdot (-4) = +20$, and suggests that the product of two negative numbers is positive.

Look carefully at this series of products. What pattern(s) do you see? Complete the final two products.

$3 \cdot (-3) = -9$
$2 \cdot (-3) = -6$
$1 \cdot (-3) = -3$
$0 \cdot (-3) = 0$
$-1 \cdot (-3) =$ ______
$-2 \cdot (-3) =$ ______

The product of two negative numbers is a positive number.

EXAMPLE 5 Evaluate each product.

a) $-10 \cdot (-6)$ b) $-5 \cdot (-5)$ c) $(-3) \cdot (-12)$ d) $(-4) \cdot (-7)$

PROCEDURE: The product of two negative numbers is a positive number.

ANSWER: a) $-10 \cdot (-6) = +60$ or 60 b) $-5 \cdot (-5) = +25$ or 25

b) $(-3) \cdot (-12) = +36$ or 36 d) $(-4) \cdot (-7) = +28$ or 28

YOU TRY IT 5 *Evaluate each product. Use Example 5 as a guide.*

a) $-2 \cdot (-8)$ b) $(-5) \cdot (-4)$ c) $(-7) \cdot (-7)$ d) $-6 \cdot (-9)$

The next rule is actually a rule you've been using most of your life, you've just probably never had to think of it this way:

The product of two positive numbers is a positive number.

EXAMPLE 6

Evaluate the product.

a) $6 \cdot 4 = +24$ or 24 b) $2 \cdot 15 = +30$ or 30 c) $5 \cdot 8 = +40$ or 40

The bottom line is that the four rules previously stated can be broken down into just *two* rules:

Multiplying Two Signed Numbers

1. If the signs of the factors are different, the product will be negative.
2. If the signs of the factors are the same, the product will be positive.

If zero is a factor, the product will be 0.

EXAMPLE 7

Find the product of the two given signed numbers.

a) $-8 \cdot 6$ b) $3 \cdot 9$ c) $-4 \cdot (-2)$ d) $5 \cdot (-7)$ e) $-1 \cdot 0$

ANSWER:

	Rule
a) $-8 \cdot 6 = -48$	The signs are different; the product is negative.
b) $3 \cdot 9 = +27$ or 27	The signs are the same; the product is positive.
c) $-4 \cdot (-2) = +8$ or 8	The signs are the same; the product is positive.
d) $5 \cdot (-7) = -35$	The signs are different; the product is negative.
e) $-1 \cdot 0 = 0$	If zero is a factor, then the product is 0.

YOU TRY IT 6

Find the product. Use Examples 6 and 7 as guides.

a) $-7 \cdot (-6)$ b) $-7 \cdot 8$ c) $2 \cdot (-6)$ d) $0 \cdot (-9)$ e) $5 \cdot 4$

The Product of More Than Two Signed Numbers

What if we were to multiply more than two signed numbers? No problem, the Associative Property and the Commutative Property allow us to multiply in any order we choose.

EXAMPLE 8

Find each product.

a) $2 \cdot 3 \cdot 4$ (no negatives) b) $-2 \cdot (-3) \cdot 4$ (two negatives)

PROCEDURE: Notice the number of negatives in the expression.

ANSWER:

a) $2 \cdot 3 \cdot 4$ Nothing special about these; use the Associative Property.

$= (2 \cdot 3) \cdot 4$

$= 6 \cdot 4$

$= 24$

b) $-2 \cdot (-3) \cdot 4$ Two negative factors; the end product is positive.

$= [-2 \cdot (-3)] \cdot 4$

$= +6 \cdot 4$

$= 24$

EXAMPLE 9

Find each product.

a) $-2 \cdot 3 \cdot 4$ (one negative)

b) $-2 \cdot (-3) \cdot (-4)$ (three negatives)

PROCEDURE: Notice the number of negatives in the expression.

ANSWER: a)

$$\begin{aligned} & -2 \cdot 3 \cdot 4 \\ &= (-2 \cdot 3) \cdot 4 \\ &= -6 \cdot 4 \\ &= -24 \end{aligned}$$

One negative; the end product is negative.

b)

$$\begin{aligned} & -2 \cdot (-3) \cdot (-4) \\ &= [-2 \cdot (-3] \cdot (-4) \\ &= +6 \cdot (-4) \\ &= -24 \end{aligned}$$

Three negative factors; two of them make a positive product 6; the third negative factor, though, makes the final product negative.

So, three negative factors gives a negative product. What do you think will happen if there are four negative factors? Let's find out:

$$\begin{aligned} & -1 \cdot (-2) \cdot (-3) \cdot (-4) \\ &= [-1 \cdot (-2)] \cdot [(-3) \cdot (-4)] \\ &= (+2) \cdot (+12) \\ &= 24 \end{aligned}$$

There are two pairs of products, each with two negative factors. Each pair results in a positive product.

Did you expect the answer to be positive? Notice that every *pair* of negative factors produces a positive number. We can actually make rules out of this:

Multiplying Two or More Signed Numbers

If there is no zero factor, then:

1. If there is an odd number of negative factors, the end product will be negative; and
2. if there is an even number of negative factors, then the end product will be positive.

EXAMPLE 10

Multiply. First decide whether the product is positive or negative, then multiply the numerical values of the factors.

a) $(6)(-3)(-2)$

b) $(-5)(4)(10)$

c) $(-2)(-8)(-10)$

d) $(-4)(-3)(5)(-1)$

ANSWER:

	Product of Factors	Number of Negatives	Result is	Product
a)	$(6)(-3)(-2)$	Two (even)	Positive	$(6)(-3)(-2) = +36$
b)	$(-5)(4)(10)$	One (odd)	Negative	$(-5)(4)(10) = -200$
c)	$(-2)(-8)(-10)$	Three (odd)	Negative	$(-2)(-8)(-10) = -160$
d)	$(-4)(-3)(-5)(-1)$	Four (even)	Positive	$(-4)(-3)(-5)(-1) = +60$

YOU TRY IT 7

Multiply. First decide whether the product will be positive or negative, then multiply numerical values. Use Examples 8, 9, and 10 as guides. (You may state the answer directly, without showing all of the work.)

a) $(2)(-4)(-5)$

b) $(-4)(5)(3)(-2)$

c) $(-3)(-1)(-6)$

d) $(-10)(-2)(0)(-3)$

e) $(-1)(-4)(-2)(-3)$

Think about it

The product of two negative numbers is always a positive number. Can the sum of two negative numbers ever be positive? Why or why not?

Dividing Signed Numbers

We have seen the circular connection between multiplication and division (Section 1.5). In a fraction, such as $\frac{15}{3}$, the denominator (divisor) multiplies the quotient to result in the numerator (dividend):

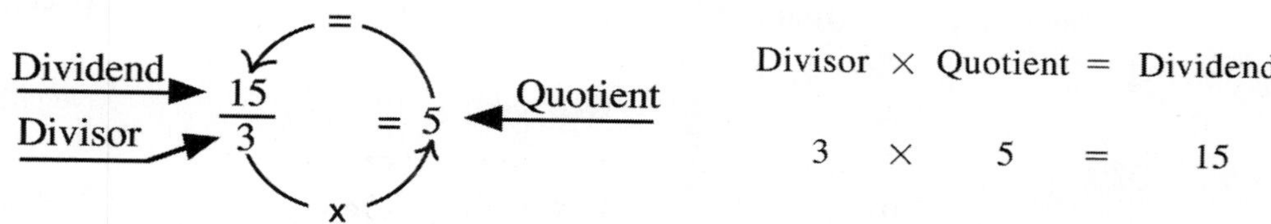

This circular relationship is also seen in standard division: $15 \div 3 = 5$ because $3 \times 5 = 15$.

How would this be different if some negative numbers were included? It would work just the same, but we'd have to put more thought into it.

For example, $15 \div (-3) = -5$, or $\frac{15}{-3} = -5$ because $-3 \times (-5) = +15$

In other words, Positive ÷ Negative = Negative, or $\frac{\text{Positive}}{\text{Negative}}$ = Negative

because Negative × Negative = Positive

YOU TRY IT 8

Use your understanding of the rules for multiplying signed numbers—and the circular relationship between multiplication and division—to fill in the missing quotient.

a) 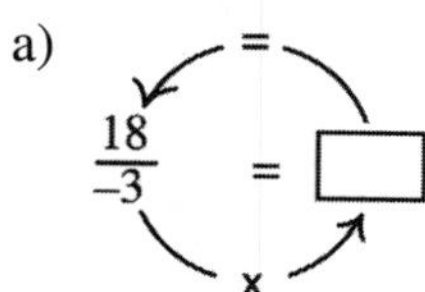

b) 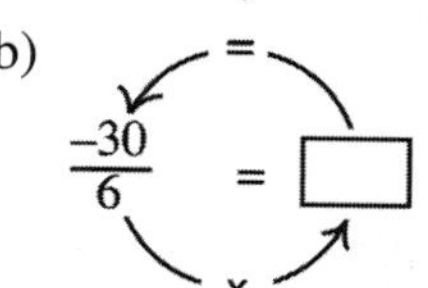

c) 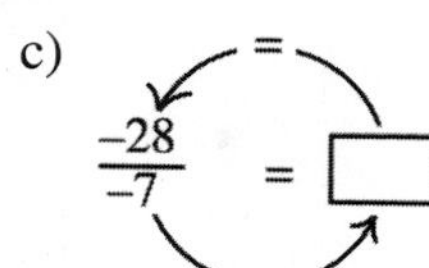

The rules of dividing signed numbers are exactly the same as those for multiplication:

Dividing Signed Numbers

In any division, either by fraction or standard form,

1. If there is odd number of negative factors, the quotient will be negative; and
2. if there is an even number of negative factors, then the quotient will be positive.

Also, recall from Sections 1.5 and 3.1 that we may not divide by 0. Zero may be in the numerator but not the denominator.

Let's do some examples.

EXAMPLE 11 Divide.

a) $\frac{-21}{3}$ b) $\frac{36}{-9}$ c) $-35 \div (-7)$

d) $32 \div 4$ e) $\frac{-4}{0}$ f) $\frac{0}{-2}$

PROCEDURE: First decide whether the quotient is positive or negative (by the number of negatives), then divide the numerical values.

ANSWER:

Quotient	Number of Negatives	Result is	Quotient
a) $\frac{-21}{3}$	One (odd)	Negative	$= -7$
b) $\frac{36}{-9}$	One (odd)	Negative	$= -4$
c) $-35 \div (-7)$	Two (even)	Positive	$= +5$ or 5
d) $32 \div 4$	Zero (even)	Positive	$= +8$ or 8
e) $\frac{-4}{0}$	one, but 0 is in the denominator.	Undefined	None.
f) $\frac{0}{-2}$	One, but 0 is in the numerator.	0	$= 0$

YOU TRY IT 9 *First decide whether the quotient will be positive or negative then divide the numerical values. Use Example 11 as a guide.*

a) $45 \div (-5)$ b) $\frac{-36}{-3}$ c) $-42 \div 0$

d) $-28 \div (-4)$ e) $\frac{0}{-8}$ f) $\frac{-54}{9}$

Multiplying and Dividing Signed Fractions

When multiplying and dividing signed numbers, whether integers or fractions, it's best to decide first whether the result will be positive or negative. Then you can either multiply or divide the numerical values.

EXAMPLE 12 Evaluate.

a) $-3 \cdot \frac{8}{9}$ b) $-\frac{2}{9} \cdot \left(-\frac{3}{4}\right)$ c) $-\frac{7}{8} \div \left(-\frac{7}{12}\right)$ d) $6 \div \left(-\frac{9}{10}\right)$

PROCEDURE: First decide whether the product or quotient is positive or negative (by the number of negatives), then multiply or divide the fractions. Also, if one number is an integer, write it as a fraction with a denominator of 1.

ANSWER:

	Number of Negatives	Result is	Evaluate
a) $-3 \cdot \frac{8}{9}$	One	Negative	$= -\frac{3}{1} \cdot \frac{8}{9} = -\frac{24}{9} = -\frac{8}{3}$
b) $-\frac{2}{9} \cdot \left(-\frac{3}{4}\right)$	Two	Positive	$= +\frac{2}{9} \cdot \frac{3}{4} = \frac{6}{36} = \frac{1}{6}$
c) $-\frac{7}{8} \div \left(-\frac{7}{12}\right)$	Two	Positive	$= +\frac{7}{8} \div \frac{7}{12} = \frac{7}{8} \cdot \frac{12}{7} = \frac{84}{56} = \frac{3}{2}$
d) $6 \div \left(-\frac{9}{10}\right)$	One	Negative	$= -\frac{6}{1} \div \frac{9}{10} = -\frac{6}{1} \cdot \frac{10}{9} = -\frac{60}{9} = -\frac{20}{3}$

YOU TRY IT 10 *Evaluate and simplify by first deciding whether the end result will be positive or negative. Simplify, if possible. Use Example 12 as a guide.*

a) $-\frac{2}{3} \cdot \left(-\frac{4}{5}\right)$ b) $\frac{3}{8} \cdot (-4)$ c) $-\frac{8}{7} \cdot \frac{21}{4}$

d) $-\frac{14}{9} \div \frac{2}{3}$ e) $-\frac{2}{21} \div \left(-\frac{4}{7}\right)$ f) $5 \div \left(-\frac{15}{8}\right)$

You Try It Answers: Section 9.5

(Note: Positive answers may also be written with a plus sign in front.)

YTI 1 a) -36 b) -22 c) 0 d) -30 e) -8

YTI 2 a) -21 b) 0 c) -4 d) -9 e) -50

YTI 3 a) -3 b) -7 c) 8 d) 2

YTI 4 a) $-1 \cdot 4$ and $4 \cdot (-1)$
b) $-1 \cdot 7$ and $7 \cdot (-1)$
c) $-1 \cdot 15$ and $15 \cdot (-1)$

YTI 5 a) 16 b) 20 c) 49 d) 54

YTI 6 a) 42 b) -56 c) -12 d) 0 e) 20

YTI 7 a) 40 b) 120 c) -18 d) 0 e) 24

YTI 8 a) -6 b) -5 c) 4

YTI 9 a) -9 b) 12 c) Undefined d) 7 e) 0 f) -6

YTI 10 a) $\frac{8}{15}$ b) $-\frac{3}{2}$ c) -6 d) $-\frac{7}{3}$ e) $\frac{1}{6}$ f) $-\frac{8}{3}$

Focus Exercises: Section 9.5

Evaluate.

1. $(-5)(-4)$
2. $-11 \cdot (-3)$
3. $9 \cdot (-7)$
4. $(11)(-9)$
5. $6 \cdot 10$
6. $(-2)(0)$
7. $(-4)(-4)$
8. $8 \cdot 8$
9. $0 \cdot (-6)$
10. $(-8)(-8)$
11. $7(-4)$
12. $(-1)(3)$
13. $-20 \cdot 5$
14. $-6 \cdot (-32)$
15. $-3 \cdot 12$
16. $3 \cdot (-5)$
17. $-4 \cdot (-6)$
18. $6 \cdot (-6)$
19. $-8 \cdot 3$
20. $-2 \cdot (-9)$
21. $9 \cdot (-1)$
22. $-4 \cdot 7$
23. $-12 \cdot 5$
24. $-10 \cdot (-3)$
25. $-\frac{1}{8} \cdot \left(\frac{3}{4}\right)$
26. $\frac{7}{9} \cdot \left(-\frac{3}{5}\right)$
27. $14 \cdot \left(-\frac{8}{7}\right)$
28. $\left(-\frac{2}{3}\right) \cdot \left(-\frac{5}{4}\right)$
29. $\left(-\frac{1}{3}\right) \cdot 2$
30. $-3 \cdot \left(-\frac{7}{6}\right)$
31. $\frac{5}{6} \cdot \left(-\frac{8}{15}\right)$
32. $-\frac{3}{10} \cdot \left(-\frac{5}{9}\right)$
33. $-12 \cdot \left(-\frac{5}{3}\right)$
34. $-\frac{15}{4} \cdot \left(-\frac{2}{3}\right)$
35. $\left(-\frac{3}{4}\right) \cdot (-6)$
36. $-8 \cdot -\frac{9}{16}$

37. $-4 \cdot 5 \cdot (-3)$

38. $2 \cdot (-7) \cdot (-1)$

39. $6 \cdot (-2) \cdot 8$

40. $3 \cdot 4 \cdot (-6)$

41. $-1 \cdot (-9) \cdot (-6)$

42. $-4 \cdot (-2) \cdot (-7)$

43. $-4 \cdot 5 \cdot (-3) \cdot 2$

44. $-1 \cdot (-2) \cdot 0 \cdot 11$

45. $-2 \cdot (-1) \cdot 0 \cdot (-4)$

46. $-5 \cdot 6 \cdot (-2) \cdot (-2)$

47. $-4 \cdot (-1) \cdot (-3) \cdot (-5)$

48. $-10 \cdot (-2) \cdot (-2) \cdot (-3)$

49. $-25 \div 5$

50. $-42 \div 7$

51. $-21 \div (-3)$

52. $-28 \div (-4)$

53. $18 \div (-6)$

54. $40 \div (-5)$

55. $-30 \div (-15)$

56. $-42 \div (-6)$

57. $-20 \div 0$

58. $\frac{-36}{-9}$

59. $\frac{-60}{3}$

60. $\frac{-72}{9}$

61. $\frac{0}{-8}$

62. $\frac{16}{-2}$

63. $\frac{-21}{3}$

64. $\frac{-27}{-9}$

65. $\frac{-45}{-5}$

66. $\frac{28}{0}$

67. $-\frac{15}{8} \cdot \left(-\frac{4}{5}\right)$

68. $-\frac{20}{9} \cdot \frac{3}{5}$

69. $-\frac{4}{15} \cdot \left(-\frac{25}{16}\right)$

70. $10 \cdot \left(-\frac{7}{15}\right)$

71. $-6 \cdot \left(-\frac{4}{21}\right)$

72. $-\frac{11}{16} \cdot 8$

73. $\frac{12}{25} \div \left(-\frac{9}{10}\right)$

74. $-\frac{8}{21} \div \frac{36}{7}$

75. $-\frac{5}{28} \div \left(-\frac{25}{21}\right)$

76. $-14 \div \left(-\frac{7}{6}\right)$

77. $-\frac{4}{9} \div (-8)$

78. $12 \div \left(-\frac{18}{5}\right)$

SECTION 9.6 The Order of Operations for Signed Numbers

Objectives

In this section, you will learn to:

- Apply powers to negative numbers.
- Find negative square roots.
- Apply the order of operations to signed numbers.

To successfully complete this section, you need to understand:

- The order of operations (2.2)
- Exponents and square roots (2.1)
- Absolute value (9.1)
- Operations with integers (9.2, 9.3, 9.4, 9.5)

Introduction

You are already quite familiar with the Order of Operations, so why are we looking at it again? We now understand negative numbers and want to see how they work within this system. In this section you will be introduced to a variety of mathematical formulas that use both positive and negative numbers.

The Order of Operations

Recall from Chapter 2 the Order of Operations:

The Order of Operations

1. Evaluate within all grouping symbols, if there are any.
2. Apply any exponents.
3. Apply multiplication and division reading from left to right.
4. Apply addition and subtraction reading from left to right.

Also, remember that we refer to an operation's rank when speaking of which should come first. Because multiplication is applied before addition, multiplication has a higher rank than addition.

Let's practice using the order of operations with a few exercises.

EXAMPLE 1 Evaluate each expression according to the order of operations.

a) $-6 + 12 \div 3$ b) $(4 - 16) \div 2^2$

ANSWER: a) $-6 + 12 \div 3$ Apply division first, then addition.

$= -6 + 4$

$= -2$

b) $(4 - 16) \div 2^2$ Subtraction has the highest rank because it is within the parentheses. $4 - 16 = 4 + (-16) = -12$.

$= -12 \div 2^2$ The exponent has the higher rank, so apply it before applying the division.

$= -12 \div 4$

$= -3$

EXAMPLE 2 Evaluate $\sqrt{24 + 4 \cdot (-2)}$

PROCEDURE: The radical is both a grouping symbol and an operation; as a grouping symbol, we must evaluate within before applying the square root.

ANSWER: $\sqrt{24 + 4 \cdot (-2)}$ Multiply first: $4 \cdot (-2) = -8$.

$= \sqrt{24 + (-8)}$

$= \sqrt{16}$

$= 4$

Caution

The key to successfully applying the order of operations is to do one step at a time. It's very important to show your work every step of the way. This will lead to accurate answers and enable others to read and learn from your work.

YOU TRY IT 1

Evaluate each expression according to the order of operations. Use Examples 1 and 2 as guides.

a) $-24 \div 6 + 2$

b) $(5 - 7) \cdot 2$

c) $-9 \cdot \sqrt{25}$

d) $(6 - 12) \div (-2 \cdot 3)$

Exponents and Negative Numbers

Recall, from Section 2.1, that an exponent is an abbreviation for repeated multiplication. For example, 5^3 means three factors of 5: $5 \cdot 5 \cdot 5 = 125$.

As we know from Section 9.5, an even number of negative factors has a product that is positive, and an odd number of negative factors has a product that is negative.

Let's extend this idea to powers (exponents) of negative numbers. For example, we know that $3^2 = 9$. It's also true that $(-3)^2 = 9$. It's easy to demonstrate this using the definition of exponents:

$$(-3)^2 = (-3)(-3) = +9 = 9.$$

What about $(-3)^3$, $(-3)^4$, and so on? To see their values, let's refer to the definition of exponents:

a) $(-3)^3 = (-3)(-3) \cdot (-3)$ Multiply the first two factors together: $(-3)(-3) = +9$.
$= (+9) \cdot (-3)$
$= -27$

b) $(-3)^4 = (-3)(-3) \cdot (-3)(-3)$ Multiply the first two factors *and* the last two factors.
$= (+9) \cdot (+9)$
$= +81 = 81$

c) $(-3)^5 = (-3)(-3)(-3)(-3) \cdot (-3)$ We already know that the product of the first four factors is $+81$:
$= (+81) \cdot (-3)$
$= -243$

$$\begin{array}{r} 81 \\ \times\ 3 \\ \hline 243 \end{array}$$ ← *But the product is negative.*

Follow the arrows to see the different powers of -3:

1 $(-3)^1 = -3$	→	2 $(-3)^2 = +9 = 9$
	↙	
3 $(-3)^3 = -27$	→	4 $(-3)^4 = +81 = 81$
	↙	
5 $(-3)^5 = -243$	→	6 $(-3)^6 = +729 = 729$

Think about it

What pattern do you notice about the powers of a negative number?

Because the exponent indicates the number of factors of the base, then:

$$(-\text{Base})^{\text{even exponent}} = +\text{number}$$

$$(-\text{Base})^{\text{odd exponent}} = -\text{number}$$

EXAMPLE 3

Evaluate each expression.

a) $(-9)^2$ b) $(-5)^3$ c) $(-2)^4$ d) $(3 - 5)^3$ e) $(-8 + 3)^2$

PROCEDURE: First decide if the result is going to be positive or negative, based on the exponent.

ANSWER:

a) $(-9)^2 = +81 = 81$ The exponent is 2, an even number, so the result is positive; $9 \cdot 9 = 81$.

b) $(-5)^3 = -125$ The exponent is 3 (odd), so the result is negative; $5 \cdot 5 \cdot 5 = 125$.

c) $(-2)^4 = +16 = 16$ The exponent is 4 (even), so the result is positive; $2 \cdot 2 \cdot 2 \cdot 2 = 16$.

For d) and e), evaluate inside the grouping symbols and then decide whether the result will be positive or negative:

d) $(3 - 5)^3 = (-2)^3 = -8$ The exponent is 3 (odd), so the result is negative; $2 \cdot 2 \cdot 2 = 8$.

e) $(-8 + 3)^2 = (-5)^2 = +25 = 25$ The exponent is 2 (even), so the result is positive; $5 \cdot 5 = 25$.

YOU TRY IT 2

Evaluate each expression. Use Example 3 as a guide.

a) $(-7)^2$ b) $(-4)^3$ c) $(-10)^4$ d) $(-1)^5$

e) $(1 - 9)^2$ f) $(-10 + 7)^3$ g) $(-9 - 1)^3$

Negative Square Roots

When you were first introduced to square roots, in Section 2.1, you saw the square root as the "root of a square." It was geometric and quite visual in its description. Now we are going to take an algebraic look at the square root.

We have seen that both $3^2 = 9$ and $(-3)^2 = 9$. This example demonstrates that there are two numbers for which 9 is a perfect square. It's appropriate, therefore, to say that 9 has *two* square roots:

1. a positive square root (+3), and
2. a negative square root (−3).

The **Square Root:** If $r^2 = P$ then r is a square root of P.

Does this change what we've learned about the square root radical? No, $\sqrt{9}$ still means the square root of 9, but now we can say that it refers to only the **principal square root**—the *positive* square root—and $\sqrt{9} = 3$.

We can emphasize, when using the radical, that the square root of a number is the principal, or positive, square root using the plus sign: $\sqrt{9} = +3$.

So, how can we represent -3 as a square root of 9? We simply negate the outside of the radical:

$$-\sqrt{9} = -3.$$

We can also rewrite the expression $-\sqrt{9}$, using the fourth meaning of the dash (Section 9.5), to be $-1 \cdot \sqrt{9}$.

Before we can apply the negative, though, we must first apply the radical—the square root—to 9 because the radical is a grouping symbol and has higher rank.

Think about it

What is $\sqrt{0}$? Does is have a principal square root? Explain your answer.

____

____

EXAMPLE 4 Evaluate each radical expression.

a) $\sqrt{36}$ b) $-\sqrt{36}$ c) $\sqrt{25}$ d) $-\sqrt{25}$

ANSWER: Apply the square roots before negating.

a) $\sqrt{36} = +6$ or 6 b) $-\sqrt{36} = -6$

c) $\sqrt{25} = +5$ or 5 d) $-\sqrt{25} = -5$

YOU TRY IT 3 *Evaluate each radical expression. Use Example 4 as a guide.*

a) $-\sqrt{16}$ b) $\sqrt{49}$ c) $-\sqrt{81}$ d) $-\sqrt{1}$

Double Quantities

Sometimes an expression contains two sets of grouping symbols that are unrelated to each other; in other words, evaluating within one set does not affect the evaluation within the other. This means that some quantities can be evaluated at the same time.

For example, in the expression $(3 - 8) \cdot (12 \div 4)$ we can evaluate within each grouping symbol regardless of what operation each contains:

$(3 - 8) \cdot (12 \div 4)$ Here, there are three operations: subtraction, multiplication, and division. Subtraction and division have EQUAL rank because of the parentheses.

$= (-5) \cdot (3)$ We can evaluate within each grouping separately, yet at the same time.

$= -15$

EXAMPLE 5 Evaluate each according to the *order of operations.*

a) $(5 \cdot 6) \div (4 - 7)$ b) $(-8 + 3) \cdot (-14 \div 2)$

c) $(24 \div 6) - \sqrt{5 + 11}$ d) $\sqrt{4^2} - \sqrt{50 \cdot 2}$

PROCEDURE: Single operations within different grouping symbols have equal rank. They can be applied at the same time.

ANSWER:

a) $(5 \cdot 6) \div (4 - 7)$ — We can apply both the multiplication and the subtraction in the same step.
$= (30) \div (-3)$ — A positive divided by a negative results in a negative.
$= -10$

b) $(-8 + 3) \cdot (-14 \div 2)$ — We can apply both the addition and the division in the same step.
$= (-5) \cdot (-7)$ — A negative multiplied by a negative results in a positive.
$= +35 = 35$

c) $(24 \div 6) - \sqrt{5 + 11}$ — We can apply both the division and the addition in the same step.
$= 4 - \sqrt{16}$ — Now apply the radical, $\sqrt{16} = 4$.
$= 4 - 4$ — Subtract.
$= 0$

d) $\sqrt{4^2} - \sqrt{50 \cdot 2}$ — We can apply both the exponent and the multiplication in the same step.
$= \sqrt{16} - \sqrt{100}$ — Now we can apply both radicals at the same time because they have the same rank.
$= 4 - 10$ — $4 - 10 = 4 + (-10) = -6$.
$= -6$

YOU TRY IT 4

Evaluate each expression according to the order of operations. Use Example 5 as a guide.

a) $(2 \cdot 3) + (-42 \div 6)$

b) $(6 - 13) \cdot (-5 + 2)$

c) $(6 + 3)^2 - \sqrt{-4 + 5}$

d) $\sqrt{12 \cdot 3} - \sqrt{8 + 41}$

Other Grouping Symbols: The Fraction Bar and Absolute Value Bars

As we know, the fraction bar is a grouping symbol. It groups the numerator separately from the denominator. When evaluating an expression that involves a fraction bar, we treat the numerator and denominator as if they were grouped separately and evaluate within them separately.

For example, in the fraction $\frac{3 \cdot 8}{5 + 1}$, the operations multiplication (in the numerator) and addition (in the denominator) have equal rank because of the grouping provided by the fraction bar: $\frac{(3 \cdot 8)}{(5 + 1)}$.

So, we can apply both multiplication and addition at the same time to get $\frac{24}{6}$. This fraction simplifies to 4.

The parentheses shown in $\frac{(3 \cdot 8)}{(5 + 1)}$ are not necessary; they are there to emphasize the grouping nature of the fraction bar.

EXAMPLE 6

Evaluate each completely.

a) $\frac{56 \div 7}{3 - 1}$

b) $\frac{\sqrt{16} - 5}{7 - 2^2}$

PROCEDURE: Remember that the radical is both a grouping symbol and an operation.

ANSWER: a) $\dfrac{56 \div 7}{3 - 1}$ First, apply the division and subtraction individually, but at the same time.

$= \dfrac{8}{2}$ Either consider the result as a fraction that must be reduced (by a factor of 2) or think of it as division: $8 \div 2 = 4$.

$= 4$

b) $\dfrac{\sqrt{16} - 5}{7 - 2^2}$ First, apply the radical in the numerator and square the 2 in the denominator.

$= \dfrac{4 - 5}{7 - 4}$ Next, apply subtraction in the numerator and denominator.

$= \dfrac{-1}{3}$ This fraction cannot simplify, so we're finished.

Caution In Example 5 b) the denominator shows $7 - 2^2$. The order of operations says that we must square the 2 before applying subtraction. Notice that the minus sign is not grouped with the 2.

YOU TRY IT 5 *Evaluate each expression according to the order of operations. Use Example 6 as a guide.*

a) $\dfrac{7 + 3}{9 - 4}$ b) $\dfrac{2 \cdot 3}{-42 \div 7}$ c) $\dfrac{6 - 14}{10 - 4^2}$ d) $\dfrac{3 - 5}{2 - (-4)}$

Absolute value bars are grouping symbols and we must evaluate within them first. However, the absolute value is also an operation, so once the expression within is simplified, we can apply the absolute value to that number.

EXAMPLE 7 Evaluate each completely.

a) $|5| - |-9|$ b) $|4 - 6| + |-3|$

PROCEDURE: Remember, the absolute value bars are both a grouping symbol and an operation.

ANSWER: a) $|5| - |-9|$ Each expression within the absolute value bars is already simplified. We can treat this, though, as a double quantity and evaluate each separately.

$= 5 - 9$ The minus sign is unaffected by the absolute values.

$= 5 + (-9)$ Change subtraction to adding the opposite.

$= -4$

b) $|4 - 6| + |-3|$ Evaluate within the first absolute value only: $|4 - 6| = |-2|$.

$= |-2| + |-3|$ Now we can apply the absolute value, not as a grouping symbol but as an operation.

$= 2 + 3$ Last, apply addition: $2 + 3 = 5$.

$= 5$

YOU TRY IT 6

Evaluate each according to the order of operations. Use Example 7 as a guide.

a) $|-9 + 3|$ b) $|-12| - |-5|$

c) $(6 - 8) \cdot |5 - 10|$ d) $|7 - 4| - |-10|$

You Try It Answers: Section 9.6

(Note: Positive answers may also be written with a plus sign in front.)

YTI 1 a) -2 b) -4 c) -45 d) 1

YTI 2 a) 49 b) -64 c) 10,000 d) -1 e) 64 f) -27 g) $-1{,}000$

YTI 3 a) -4 b) 7 c) -9 d) -1

YTI 4 a) -1 b) 21 c) 80 d) -1

YTI 5 a) 2 b) -1 c) $\frac{4}{3}$ d) $-\frac{1}{3}$

YTI 6 a) 6 b) 7 c) -10 d) -7

Focus Exercises: Section 9.6

Evaluate.

1. $\sqrt{64}$ **2.** $\sqrt{100}$ **3.** $-\sqrt{81}$ **4.** $-\sqrt{1}$

5. $\sqrt{25}$ **6.** $\sqrt{16}$ **7.** $-\sqrt{49}$ **8.** $-\sqrt{36}$

9. $(-1)^2$ **10.** $(-1)^3$ **11.** $(-4)^1$ **12.** $(-4)^2$

13. $(-4)^3$ **14.** $(-8)^2$ **15.** $(-10)^3$ **16.** $(-7)^3$

17. $(-6)^2$ **18.** $(-5)^3$ **19.** $(-3)^4$ **20.** $(-2)^2$

21. $(-2)^3$ **22.** $(-2)^4$ **23.** $(-2)^5$ **24.** $(-2)^6$

Evaluate each expression using the order of operations.

25. $-5 + 6 \cdot 2$ **26.** $8 + 5 \cdot (-3)$ **27.** $6 \cdot 2 - 4 \cdot 8$

28. $-9 + (2 - 5) + 4^2$ **29.** $6 - 2 \cdot (-2) + 2^3$ **30.** $-3(2 - 8)$

31. $2[-6 + 3(7 - 2)]$ **32.** $(-4 + 10) \div (-3)$ **33.** $30 \div 5 \cdot 2 - 5$

34. $6 - 14 \div 2$ **35.** $-24 \div 6 \cdot (-2)$ **36.** $7 - 4^2$

37. $(7-9)^3-6\cdot 3$ **38.** $5^2+|-6|$ **39.** $[-12\div(-3)]^2$

40. $(-3)^2-(4-6)$ **41.** $(5-9)^2$ **42.** $-24\div(6+2)$

43. $-24\div(3-5)$ **44.** $3-4\cdot 5$ **45.** $3-4\cdot(-5)$

46. $(4-10)^2$ **47.** $-2\cdot 3-8\div(-4)$ **48.** $(4-6)^3$

49. $20-(-8)^2$ **50.** $(3-10)^2$ **51.** $-5\cdot(3-4)^2$

52. $-30+(-7)^2$ **53.** $(7+3)\cdot(-9+4)$ **54.** $(-2\cdot 12)\div(-4-2)$

55. $(7+3)^2\div(9-4)^2$ **56.** $(2-3)^3-(-12\div 6)^3$ **57.** $(5-6)^3-4\cdot(-2)$

58. $-\sqrt{81}+24\div(-3)$ **59.** $35\div(-5)+2\cdot(-3)$ **60.** $6-[12\div(-2\cdot 3)]$

61. $|6|-8$ **62.** $|-7|+3$ **63.** $9-|-8|$

64. $-6+|-5|$ **65.** $|9-5|$ **66.** $|1-4|$

67. $|3-9|+8$ **68.** $|2-8|-6$ **69.** $|-3|+|8|$

70. $|-6|-|4|$ **71.** $|11|-|-15|$ **72.** $|-12|-|-18|$

73. $|3+7|+|4-2|$ **74.** $|-4+6|+|-5-1|$

75. $|5-9|-|2-8|$ **76.** $|-7+2|-|-10-1|$

77. $\frac{5-9}{4-2}$ **78.** $\frac{3-11}{7-3}$ **79.** $\frac{-1-3}{6-2}$

80. $\frac{-8+2}{-4-2}$ **81.** $\frac{-3+7}{2-(-3)}$ **82.** $\frac{4-(-6)}{-9-(-4)}$

83. $\frac{-5\cdot 3}{7-3^2}$ **84.** $\frac{2\cdot 5}{8-12}$ **85.** $\frac{\sqrt{4}+8}{5\cdot(-4)}$

86. $\frac{2^2+1}{4^2-6}$ **87.** $\frac{15-3^2}{-12-3\cdot 2}$ **88.** $\frac{2^2}{3^2-3\cdot 7}$

89. $-6+\sqrt{16}$ **90.** $-10\cdot\sqrt{64}$ **91.** $3-\sqrt{81}$

92. $-6-3\sqrt{4}$ **93.** $\sqrt{9}+\sqrt{16}$ **94.** $\sqrt{80\div 5}-9$

95. $18-2\cdot\sqrt{100}$ **96.** $-\sqrt{-4\cdot(-9)}$ **97.** $\sqrt{-1+2\cdot 5}$

98. $\sqrt{(6-2)\cdot 5^2}$ **99.** $-\sqrt{5^2-3^2}$ **100.** $\sqrt{3^2-4(2)}$

SECTION 9.7 Algebraic Expressions: Combining Like Terms

Objectives

In this section, you will learn to:

- Define *coefficient, term,* and *constant.*
- Combine like terms.

To successfully complete this section, you need to understand:

- Adding integers (9.2)
- Subtracting integers (9.3)

Introduction

In algebra, when a number is multiplied by a variable, like $5 \cdot y$, the number, 5, is called a **numerical coefficient**, and the product of a coefficient and a variable creates a **term**. In the term $5y$, the numerical coefficient is 5.

In a term, the variable may have an exponent. For example, $8x^3$ is also a term. Actually, every variable has both a numerical coefficient and an exponent, even if we don't see them.

Consider, for example, the simple term $\boldsymbol{x}$. It *appears* that this term has no coefficient and no exponent. Actually, it has both. In fact,

- x is the same as $1x$ or $1 \cdot x$;
- it's also the same as x^1 (read "x to the first power"); and
- it could even be thought of as $1x^1$.

This may look as if we're getting carried away, but the 1's that you see here are actually very important numbers. In both cases, they are referred to as "the invisible 1." Though it may sound a little like the twilight zone, the "invisible 1" will rush to our aid—and make itself visible—in many situations.

Also, a term can be just a number with no variable: 6, -5, or $\frac{3}{8}$. In this case, as we saw in Chapter 1, the number is called a constant.

EXAMPLE 1

Given the term, identify the coefficient, the variable, and the exponent of the variable.

Term	Coefficient	Variable	Exponent
$8x^2$	8	x	2
$-3a$	-3	a	1
$\frac{2}{3}c^5$	$\frac{2}{3}$	c	5
m^4	1	m	4
$-y$	-1	y	1
7	7*	None	None

* 7 is a term that is really a *constant* term; it is not, itself, a coefficient as defined above.

YOU TRY IT 1

Given the term, identify the coefficient, the variable, and the exponent of the variable. Use Example 1 as a guide.

Term	Coefficient	Variable	Exponent
a) $3y^4$			
b) -4			
c) $-2c$			
d) $-x^2$			
e) $\frac{7}{8}d^5$			
f) w			

Algebraic Expressions

The terms in an algebraic expression are often—though not always—separated by a plus sign and/or a minus sign, and this allows us to distinguish one term from another.

The expression $-2x^3 + 9x + 5$ has three terms, each separated by a plus sign: $-2x^3$, $9x$, and 5.

There are also many algebraic expressions that include subtraction as one of the operations, such as $3x^2 - 8x - 2$. Recall from Section 9.3 that subtraction can be written as *adding the opposite*, so this expression can be rewritten as $3x^2 + (-8x) + (-2)$. Now that it is written in addition only, the individual terms become clearer. The terms are $3x^2$, $-8x$, and -2.

What we see is that the coefficient of the subtracted term takes on the minus sign as a negative. This means that the sign in front of a term—the plus sign or minus sign—belongs to the term and makes it positive or negative.

> The sign in front of a term belongs to that term.

Here are two expressions with their terms separated:

Expression: $7x^2 - 2x - 5$

Term: $+7x^2$ $-2x$ -5

Expression: $-4x^2 + x - 6$

Terms: $-4x^2$ $+1x$ -6

EXAMPLE 2

Identify the terms in each algebraic expression.

	Expression	Terms (separated by commas)
a)	$7x^2 + 6x + 1$	Three terms: $7x^2$, $6x$, 1
b)	$3x^2 - 5x - 2$	Three terms: $3x^2$, $-5x$, -2
c)	$-7w + 8$	Two terms: $-7w$, 8
d)	$3a^5 - 2a^3 - 4a + 9$	Four terms: $3a^5$, $-2a^3$, $-4a$, 9
e)	$-15y$	One term: $-15y$

YOU TRY IT 2

Identify the terms in each algebraic expression. Use Example 2 as a guide.

Expression	Terms
a) $5x^2 - x + 3$	__________
b) $c^3 - 6c^2 - 8c$	__________
c) $-2x - 6y$	__________
d) $-5x^3 + 6x^2 + x - 4$	__________

Like Terms

Two things are "like" each other if they share the same characteristics. For example, *like* fractions have the same denominator (Chapter 4). In algebra, two or more terms are considered to be **like terms** if they have exactly the same variable and exponent, even if the coefficients are different.

For example, $3x^2$ and $9x^2$ are like terms because they have *exactly* the same variable and exponent, x^2.

However, $4c$ and $-7p$ are *not* like terms because the variables are different. Similarly, $3x^2$ and $8x^4$ are *not* like terms because the variables have different exponents.

Furthermore, constants, which have no variable at all, are "like" all other constants. In the example below, carefully examine which terms are "like" and which are *not* like. See if you can decide why some terms are not like others within the same expression.

EXAMPLE 3 In each expression, identify the like terms.

Expression		Like terms
a) $7x - 6x + 1$	One pair of terms is **like:**	$7x$ and $-6x$
b) $5x - 2 + 9$	One pair of terms is **like:**	-2 and 9
c) $3a^2 + 2b^3 + 4a^2 + 9b^3$	Two pairs of terms are **like:**	$3a^2$ and $4a^2$, $2b^3$ and $9b^3$
d) $-15y + 6y - 3y$	All three terms are **like:**	$-15y$ and $6y$ and $-3y$
e) $4x + 6y - 7$	No terms are **like:**	(None)
f) $-2x^3 + 6x^2 + 9x$	No terms are **like:**	(None)

Caution A different exponent on the same variable indicates a different term.

YOU TRY IT 3 *In each expression, identify the like terms. Use Example 3 as a guide.*

Expression	Like Terms
a) $5x - x + 3$	__________
b) $x^2 - 6x - 8x^2$	__________
c) $4 - \frac{2}{3}y - y$	__________
d) $9x^5 + 2x^5 - 6x^5$	__________

Combining Like Terms

In algebra you will be asked to simplify a great deal. Basically, an expression is simplified when it is written in the shortest and least complex form. When working with like terms, an expression is said to be simplified when the like terms are combined. To combine like terms means to find their sum or difference, depending on the operation between the terms.

We can combine like terms because the variable and exponent are the same: $2x + 3x = 5x$.

Notice that the result is "like" the original two terms. In this way, the only change is the coefficient; to get the coefficient of the result, 5, we add the coefficients of the like terms, 3 and 2.

Why is it that combining like terms works this way? Good question. It goes back to the abbreviation called multiplication. Remember that multiplication is just an abbreviation for repeated addition. So, when we wish to find the sum of $4h$ and $3h$, it's like this:

$4h$ means $h + h + h + h$. Likewise, $3h$ means $h + h + h$.

Therefore, $\quad 4h + 3h$

is the same as $(h + h + h + h) + (h + h + h)$

or just $h + h + h + h + h + h + h$

which is abbreviated as … $7h$.

This is also why we *can't* combine $2y + 5x$. It becomes

$$(y + y) + (x + x + x + x + x)$$

In this case, we can't say that we have 7 of anything that is the *same*.

The combining of like terms is not restricted to addition; we can also subtract like terms. In this way it is like eliminating terms. Consider cutting 2 feet off of a 5 foot board.

5 feet − 2 feet = 3 feet.

Or, five x's reduced by two x's leaves three x's: $5x - 2x = 3x$.

Likewise, we can combine like terms with negative coefficients, as demonstrated in these problems:

Dollars: Chuck's account has \$5 in it, but he writes a check for \$8. What is the balance of Chuck's account?

5 dollars − 8 dollars = −3 dollars

Just as: $5y - 8y = -3y$

Temperature: At midnight it was −12° outside; by 10 AM, the temperature has risen by 5°. What is the temperature at 10 AM?

−12 degrees + 5degrees = −7 degrees

Just as: $-12w + 5w = -7w$

To **combine** like terms we need only add or subtract their numerical coefficients.

The resulting term is *like* the original terms.

EXAMPLE 4 Simplify each expression by combining like terms.

a) $7x + 6x$ b) $2h + 3h + 6h$ c) $-2 + 9$

d) $-3a^2 + 4a^2$ e) $4y + 1y$ f) $4p + p$

g) $6w + (-8w)$ h) $-2k + (-3k)$ i) $-2x^3 + 9x^2$

PROCEDURE: If the terms are like terms, then find the sum of the coefficients.

ANSWER:

a) $7x + 6x = 13x$ — Simply add the coefficients together; the result is another like term.

b) $2h + 3h + 6h = 11h$ — Yes, we can combine three terms if they are all like terms.

c) $-2 + 9 = 7$ — All constants are *like* each other and can be combined.

d) $-3a^2 + 4a^2 = 1a^2$ — This can be simplified to just a^2.

e) $4y + 1y = 5y$ — We can see the coefficient of the second term, $1y$, is 1.

f) $4p + p = 5p$ — We can *write* the coefficient of the second term, p, as 1: $4p + 1p$.

g) $6w + (-8w) = -2w$ — Simply add the coefficients together. $6 + (-8) = -2$ (don't forget the w).

h) $-2k + (-3k) = -5k$ — Simply add the coefficients together. $-2 + (-3) = -5$ (don't forget the k).

i) $-2x^3 + 9x^2$ — These terms cannot combine because they are not like terms.

Think about it

In Example 4 i), why aren't $-2x^3$ and $9x^2$ like terms?

YOU TRY IT 4

Simplify each expression by combining like terms. If the terms are not like terms, state so. Use Example 4 as a guide.

a) $3y + 9y$ b) $-6c^2 + 7c^2$ c) $3p + (-4p)$ d) $5p^2 + 6p$

When subtracting terms we can either subtract the coefficients directly or rewrite the subtraction as *adding the opposite*.

EXAMPLE 5

Simplify each expression by combining like terms.

a) $7w - 2w$ b) $3x^2 - 2x^2$ c) $3c - 7c$ d) $5x - 6x$

PROCEDURE: You may subtract directly or change subtraction to *adding the opposite*.

ANSWER:

a) $7w - 2w = 5w$

b) $3x^2 - 2x^2 = 1x^2$ or just x^2 — The coefficient 1 doesn't need to be written.

c) $3c - 7c = 3c + (-7c) = -4c$ — We can rewrite the subtraction as addition.

d) $5x - 6x = -1x$ — This could also be written as $-x$ instead of $-1x$.

YOU TRY IT 5

Simplify each expression by combining like terms. If the terms are not like terms, state so. Use Example 5 as a guide.

a) $11y - 9y$ b) $5w^3 - 8w^3$ c) $-2x - (-6x)$

Remember, if a term has no visible coefficient, then the coefficient is 1 or -1.

EXAMPLE 6

Simplify each expression by combining like terms.

a) $-9y + y$ b) $-c + 7c$ c) $-m - (-6m)$ d) $x - x$

PROCEDURE: You may subtract directly or change subtraction to *adding the opposite*.

ANSWER:

a) $-9y + y = -9y + 1y = -8y$ — We can write the second coefficient as 1.

b) $-c + 7c = -1c + 7c = 6c$ — We can write the first coefficient as -1.

c) $-m - (-6m) = -1m + 6m = 5m$

d) $x - x = 1x + (-1x) = 0x = 0$ — $0x$ means $0 \cdot x = 0$.

In Example 6 d), why does the answer have no variable?

____

____

YOU TRY IT 6

Simplify each expression by combining like terms. If the terms are not like terms, state so. Use Example 6 as a guide.

a) $-c - 8c$ b) $-4x - (-x)$ c) $-6m + 6m$

Expressions with Two Pairs of Like Terms

Because the sign in front of the term belongs to the term, we can move terms around, using the commutative property, within an expression as long as the sign moves with the term.

For example, we can write the terms of the expression $5x + 9 - 2x$ in a different order so that the x-terms are together. Similarly, we can rearrange the terms of the expression $-4y + 8x - 3y$ so that the y-terms are together.

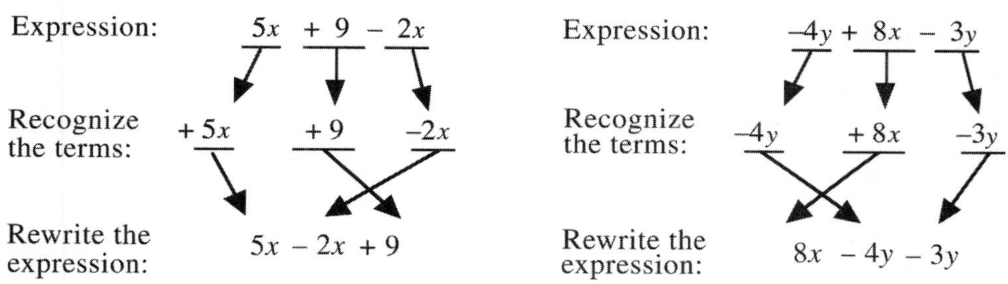

If an expression has more than one pair of like terms, then we can gather each pair separately and combine only those terms that are like each other.

In the expression $3x^2 + 1 + 5x^2 - 6$, we can see that $3x^2$ and $5x^2$ form a pair of like terms; likewise, 1 and -6 form a pair of like terms. We can recognize the terms and rearrange the expression, gathering the like terms together:

$3x^2 + 1 + 5x^2 - 6$ Rearrange the terms so that like terms are together.

$= \underline{3x^2 + 5x^2} + \underline{1 - 6}$ Combine the like terms individually.

$= 8x^2 + (-5)$ This can be written as $8x^2 - 5$. We cannot combine any further.

$= 8x^2 - 5$

EXAMPLE 7

Combine like terms.

a) $5x - 2x + 2 + 8$ b) $2x^2 + 3x + 7x^2 - 5x$ c) $4x - 5 - 6x + 2$

PROCEDURE: First, rearrange the terms by gathering like terms together.

Second, combine any like terms.

ANSWER: a) $5x - 2x + 2 + 8$ The like terms are already gathered together. Lets underline them to see the like terms.

$= \underline{5x - 2x} + \underline{2 + 8}$ Combine like terms.

$= 3x + 10$ We can't combine further.

b) $2x^2 + 3x + 7x^2 - 5x$ — Rearrange the terms to gather the like terms in pairs.
$= 2x^2 + 7x^2 + 3x - 5x$ — Combine the like terms. (Underlining is not necessary.)
$= 9x^2 + (-2x)$ — The final expression has two terms: $9x^2$ and $-2x$, and we can write it as subtraction.
$= 9x^2 - 2x$

c) $4x - 5 - 6x + 2$ — Rearrange the terms to gather the like terms in pairs.
$= 4x - 6x - 5 + 2$ — We can write subtraction as addition.
$= 4x + (-6x) + (-5) + 2$
$= -2x + (-3)$
$= -2x - 3$

YOU TRY IT 7

Simplify each expression by combining like terms. Use Example 7 as a guide.

a) $y + 4y + 6y^2 - 2y^2$ b) $3x^2 - 4x^2 + 2x - 8x$ c) $2c^2 + 3 + c^2 - 8$

d) $3m - 1 + m - 6$ e) $5w - 2 + 1 + 2w$

You Try It Answers: Section 9.7

YTI 1

	Term	Coefficient	Variable	Exponent
a)	$3y^4$	3	y	4
b)	-4	-4	None	None
c)	$-2c$	-2	c	1
d)	$-x^2$	-1	x	2
e)	$\frac{7}{8}d^5$	$\frac{7}{8}$	d	5
f)	w	1	w	1

YTI 2 a) $5x^2, -x, 3$ b) $c^3, -6c^2, -8c$ c) $-2x, -6y$ d) $-5x^3, 6x^2, x, -4$

YTI 3 a) $5x$ and $-x$ b) x^2 and $-8x^2$ c) $-\frac{2}{3}y$ and $-y$ d) $9x^5$, $2x^5$ and $-6x^5$

YTI 4 a) $12y$ b) c^2 c) $-1p$ or $-p$ d) Not like terms

YTI 5 a) $2y$ b) $-3w^3$ c) $4x$

YTI 6 a) $-9c$ b) $-3x$ c) 0

YTI 7 a) $5y + 4y^2$
b) $-1x^2 + (-6x)$ or $-x^2 - 6x$
c) $3c^2 + (-5)$ or $3c^2 - 5$
d) $4m + (-7)$ or $4m - 7$
e) $7w + (-1)$ or $7w - 1$

Focus Exercises: Section 9.7

Given the term, identify the coefficient, the variable, and the exponent of the variable.

	Term	Coefficient	Variable	Exponent
1.	$4m^2$			
2.	$-7x^3$			
3.	$-3y$			
4.	$6c$			
5.	9			
6.	-12			
7.	y^3			
8.	x^2			
9.	$-d^5$			
10.	$-p^4$			
11.	$-\frac{3}{4}n^6$			
12.	$\frac{1}{6}k^5$			

13. Answer each question based on the expression $3x^4 - 5x^3 + x - 9$.

a) What is the first term?

b) What is the second term?

c) What is the coefficient of the third term?

d) What is the constant term?

e) What is the exponent of the first term?

f) What is the exponent of the third term?

14. Answer each question based on the expression $7w^2 - 2 + 4w^3 - w$.

a) What is the first term?

b) What is the third term?

c) What is the coefficient of the fourth term?

d) What is the constant term?

e) What is the exponent of the first term?

f) What is the exponent of the fourth term?

15. Answer each question based on the expression $-8y + y^2 - 3y^4 + 1$.

a) What is the first term?

b) What is the second term?

c) What is the coefficient of the third term?

d) What is the constant term?

e) What is the exponent of the first term?

f) What is the exponent of the third term?

16. Answer each question based on the expression $-\frac{3}{5}y^8 + \frac{1}{5}y^4 - y - \frac{1}{5}$.

a) What is the first term?
b) What is the second term?
c) What is the coefficient of the third term?
d) What is the constant term?
e) What is the exponent of the first term?
f) What is the exponent of the third term?

Simplify. Combine like terms, if possible.

17. $2x + 5x$
18. $6y - 9y$
19. $4x^2 + 9x^2$
20. $7y^3 - 6y^3$
21. $4a - 5a$
22. $-6w^3 + w^3$
23. $-12x^2 - 10x$
24. $b^3 + 6b^3$
25. $-9y^2 - (-11y^2)$
26. $-5x - (-6x)$
27. $3m - 6m$
28. $-3y + (-8y)$
29. $-8r + 8r$
30. $4h^3 - 4h^3$
31. $-p^2 + 9p^2$
32. $-d - 3d$
33. $k + (-7k)$
34. $2x^2 - 9x$
35. $v^2 - 2v^2$
36. $-7a - (-a)$
37. $2s - (-4m)$
38. $3n - 4k$
39. $-3v + 3v$
40. $-v - v$
41. $5y + 7y - 2y$
42. $4w + 3w - 2w$
43. $5x - 3x - 7x$
44. $3p^2 - 9p^2 - p^2$
45. $-8c + 4c + 10c$
46. $-6m + 10m - m$
47. $-13x + 8x - 2x$
48. $-5w^3 + 3w^3 - w^3$
49. $-5y^2 - 6y^2 + 3y^2$
50. $-10c - 5c + c$
51. $-7p - 6p - 15p$
52. $-12b - 8b - b$

Simplify by combining pairs of like terms.

53. $4x + 7x + 8 - 5$
54. $6y + 5y + 7 - 6$
55. $3x - 4x + 4 - 6$
56. $5p - 6p + 3 - 9$
57. $-3a + 7a + 4 - 9$
58. $-5a + 6a + 2 - 7$
59. $3w + 6w^2 + 2w - w^2$
60. $4m^2 + 5m + 3m^2 - m$
61. $-6 - 2x + 5 - x$
62. $-x^2 - 6x + 4x^2 - x$
63. $-5c - 3b + c - b$
64. $-3x - 7y + x - y$

SECTION 9.8 Multiplying Algebraic Expressions

Objectives

In this section, you will learn to:

- Multiply terms.
- Evaluate expressions using the Distributive Property.

To successfully complete this section, you need to understand:

- The Distributive Property (1.4)
- Multiplying integers (9.5)
- Definition of terms (9.7)

Introduction

This section uses ideas that are now familiar to you, such as

- Multiplication is an abbreviation for repeated addition.
- Subtraction can be rewritten as addition: *adding the opposite*.
- The product of a negative number and positive number is negative.
- The product of two negative numbers is positive.
- The sign in front of a term belongs to that term.

Furthermore, algebra is just arithmetic using variables in place of numbers. So, the properties of arithmetic apply to algebra as well. Recall from Chapter 1 the following properties of numbers:

1. The Associative Property of Multiplication (Section 1.2)
   If the only operation is multiplication, then we can change the grouping of the numbers without affecting the resulting product.
2. The Commutative Property of Multiplication (Section 1.2)
   The order in which we multiply two numbers doesn't affect the resulting product.
3. The Distributive Property of Multiplication over Addition (Section 1.4)
   We can distribute a multiplier, say 3, to a sum $(10 + 2)$ so that it multiplies both numbers in the sum.

$$\begin{aligned} \mathbf{3} \cdot (10 + 2) &= 3 \cdot 10 + 3 \cdot 2 \\ &= 30 + 6 \\ &= 36 \end{aligned}$$

3 is a multiplier of both 10 and 2;
3 is being distributed to both the 10 and the 2.

We will explore the role that the Distributive Property plays in algebra a little later in this section. First, we'll apply the Associative Property to find the product of two terms.

Multiplying Terms

Recall from Section 9.7 that a term can be just a number (a constant), or it can be the product of a number and a variable (with an exponent).

Example 1 shows the product of a term that is a constant and a term with a variable.

EXAMPLE 1 Find the product.

a) $3(5x)$ b) $-2(6y^3)$ c) $8 \cdot (-4p^2)$ d) $-5 \cdot (-9m)$

PROCEDURE: Using the Associative Property, we can regroup the multiplication, allowing us to multiply the numbers separately from the variable.

ANSWER:

a) $3(5x)$
$= (3 \cdot 5) \cdot x$
$= 15 \cdot x$
Better written as $15x$

b) $-2(6y^3)$
$= (-2 \cdot 6) \cdot y^3$
$= -12 \cdot y^3$
Better written as $-12y^3$

c) $8 \cdot (-4p^2)$
$= 8 \cdot (-4) \cdot p^2$
$= -32 \cdot p^2$
Better written as $-32p^2$

d) $-5 \cdot (-9m)$
$= (-5) \cdot (-9) \cdot m$
$= +45 \cdot m$
Better written as $45m$

YOU TRY IT 1

Find the product. Use Example 1 as a guide.

a) $(2)(9c)$ b) $-7 \cdot (3x^2)$ c) $(-5)(-2a^5)$ d) $4 \cdot (-3k)$

When multiplying terms, we multiply the coefficients together and include the variable factor in the end result. In other words, we can multiply in just one step:

a) $(-10)(6x^4) = -60x^4$ b) $-5 \cdot (-4y) = 20y$

YOU TRY IT 2

Find the product. Try do these in just one step.

a) $7 \cdot (3c)$ b) $-9 \cdot (-4p)$ c) $6(-4m^5)$ d) $-1(8y)$

Multiplying Algebraic Expressions Using the Distributive Property

In algebra, the Distributive Property works just the same as in arithmetic. The main difference is that we have terms with variables instead of just numbers.

For example, $3(x + y)$ and $3(-2x + 5y)$

$$3 \cdot (x + y) = 3 \cdot x + 3 \cdot y = 3x + 3y$$

$$3 \cdot (-2x + 5y) = 3 \cdot (-2x) + 3 \cdot (5y) = -6x + 15y$$

Here is the general form of the Distributive Property of Multiplication over Addition.

> The **Distributive Property of Multiplication over Addition** is
>
> $$b \cdot (c + d) = b \cdot c + b \cdot d$$

Here's why the Distributive Property works:

Consider the expression $3 \cdot (x + y)$.

Because this is multiplication, and multiplication is an abbreviation for repeated addition, this means	three $(x + y)$'s.
This can be written as:	$= (x + y) + (x + y) + (x + y)$.
The Associative Property allows us to write that expression without parentheses:	$= x + y + x + y + x + y$
We can then use the Commutative Property to reorganize the terms	$= x + x + x + y + y + y$
Let's group the x's separately from the y's:	$= (x + x + x) + (y + y + y)$
Each grouping has *three* of something:	= three x's + three y's $= 3 \cdot x + 3 \cdot y$
So, from the beginning:	$3 \cdot (x + y) = 3 \cdot x + 3 \cdot y$.

EXAMPLE 2 Use the Distributive Property to rewrite $4 \cdot (5y + 6)$.

ANSWER:

$4 \cdot (5y + 6)$ — 4 is the multiplier. Distribute the "4 times" to each term.
$= 4 \cdot 5y + 4 \cdot 6$ — Writing this step isn't necessary, but it shows the multiplication.
$= 20y + 24$

YOU TRY IT 3 *Use the Distributive Property to rewrite each expression. Use Example 2 as a guide.*

a) $3 \cdot (8x + 2)$ b) $6 \cdot (5p + 1)$ c) $4 \cdot (9k + 2)$

If the second term of a quantity is negative, the term is usually written as subtraction. For example, a quantity with terms $5x$ and -3 is written $(5x - 3)$.

If we wish to distribute the multiplier 4 to the quantity $(5x - 3)$, the product, at first, looks like this: $4 \cdot (5x - 3)$. We can, however, think of the quantity $5x - 3$ as $5x + (-3)$, effectively changing the product to $4 \cdot (5x + (- 3))$.

Let's look at it one step at a time:

$4 \cdot (5x - 3)$ — Rewrite subtraction as a sum: "adding the opposite."
$= 4 \cdot (5x + (-3))$ — We can distribute the multiplier to the sum.
$= 4 \cdot 5x + 4 \cdot (-3)$ — $4 \cdot (-3) = -12$.
$= 20x + (-12)$ — This can be rewritten as subtraction.
$= 20x - 12$

We don't need to go through all of that work if we keep in mind that *the sign in front of a number belongs to that number.*

20x −12
4 · (5x − 3)

$4 \cdot (5x - 3)$ Treat $5x$ as $+5x$ and *minus 3* as -3.
$= 20x - 12$ $4 \cdot (+5x) = +20x$; $4 \cdot (-3) = -12$, or *minus 12.*

This leads to a new form of the Distributive Property:

The **Distributive Property of Multiplication over Subtraction** is

$$b \cdot (c - d) = b \cdot c - b \cdot d$$

EXAMPLE 3 Use the Distributive Property to rewrite each expression.

a) $5 \cdot (7y - 3)$ b) $2 \cdot (-4w - 6)$

ANSWER: a) $5 \cdot (7y - 3)$ 5 is the multiplier. Distribute the "5 times" to both terms.

$= 5 \cdot 7y - 5 \cdot 3$ This step isn't necessary, but it shows the multiplication.

$= 35y - 15$

b) $2 \cdot (-4w - 6)$ The multiplier is 2.

$= 2 \cdot (-4w) - 2 \cdot 6$ This step can be done in your head.

$= -8w - 12$ You can distribute and multiply directly without writing down the multiplication step.

YOU TRY IT 4 *Use the Distributive Property to rewrite each expression. Use Example 3 as a guide.*

a) $6 \cdot (4y - 3)$ b) $7 \cdot (9m - 4)$ c) $8 \cdot (-2x - 6)$

The Distributive Property with a Negative Multiplier

We can use the Distributive Property even when the multiplier is negative. We must be more careful when multiplying each term by a negative number, and we need to continually remember that the sign in front of a number belongs to that number.

Consider, for example, the product of the multiplier -2 and the sum $(4x - 3)$. As a product, this looks like $-2 \cdot (4x - 3)$.

$-8x$ $+6$

$-2 \cdot (4x - 3)$ Treat $4x$ as $+4x$ and -3 as -3.

$= -8x + 6$ $-2 \cdot (+4x) = -8x$; $-2 \cdot (-3) = +6$, or *plus 6*.

EXAMPLE 4 Use the Distributive Property to rewrite each expression.

a) $-5 \cdot (7k + 3)$ b) $-2 \cdot (4m - 6)$ c) $-8 \cdot (-5x + 2)$ d) $-3 \cdot (-6w - 1)$

ANSWER: a) $-5 \cdot (7k + 3)$ $-5 \cdot (+7k) = -35k$,

$= -35k - 15$ $-5 \cdot (+3) = -15$.

b) $-2 \cdot (4m - 6)$ $-2 \cdot (+4m) = -8m$,

$= -8m + 12$ $-2 \cdot (-6) = +12$.

c) $-8 \cdot (-5x + 2)$ $-8 \cdot (-5x) = +40x$,

$= 40x - 16$ $-8 \cdot (+2) = -16$.

d) $-3 \cdot (-6w - 1)$ $-3 \cdot (-6w) = +18w$,

$= 18w + 3$ $-3 \cdot (-1) = +3$.

YOU TRY IT 5 *Use the Distributive Property to rewrite these. Use Example 4 as a guide.*

a) $-5 \cdot (6d + 3)$ b) $-2 \cdot (8h - 1)$

c) $-6 \cdot (-10v + 4)$ d) $-4 \cdot (-11k - 5)$

You Try It Answers: Section 9.8

YTI 1 a) 18c b) $-21x^2$ c) $10a^5$ d) $-12k$

YTI 2 a) 21c b) 36p c) $-24m^5$ d) $-8y$

YTI 3 a) $24x + 6$ b) $30p + 6$ c) $36k + 8$

YTI 4 a) $24y - 18$ b) $63m - 28$ c) $-16x - 48$

YTI 5 a) $-30d - 15$ b) $-16h + 2$ c) $60v - 24$ d) $44k + 20$

Focus Exercises: Section 9.8

Find the product.

1. $4(5x)$ **2.** $6(3y)$ **3.** $-2 \cdot (-2y)$ **4.** $-4 \cdot (-5w)$

5. $7 \cdot (-4c^2)$ **6.** $9 \cdot (-2h^3)$ **7.** $-8(6a^4)$ **8.** $-5(9k^5)$

Rewrite each expression using the Distributive Property and simplify the result.

9. $2 \cdot (4w + 5)$ **10.** $3 \cdot (4y + 6)$ **11.** $4 \cdot (5y + 8)$ **12.** $5 \cdot (2x + 9)$

13. $7 \cdot (x^2 + 2)$ **14.** $10 \cdot (w^2 + 6)$ **15.** $2 \cdot (x - 8)$ **16.** $5 \cdot (y - 11)$

17. $7 \cdot (2p - 3)$ **18.** $6 \cdot (10k - 5)$ **19.** $8 \cdot (4x^2 - 1)$ **20.** $12 \cdot (3c^2 - 1)$

21. $2 \cdot (-4c + 3)$ **22.** $6 \cdot (-2m + 5)$ **23.** $5 \cdot (-3x^2 - 1)$ **24.** $9 \cdot (-2w^2 - 1)$

25. $-5 \cdot (2y + 7)$ **26.** $-6 \cdot (3x + 2)$ **27.** $-4 \cdot (9x - 3)$ **28.** $-3 \cdot (2y - 5)$

29. $-4 \cdot (1 - 2b^2)$ **30.** $-5 \cdot (1 - 3p^4)$ **31.** $-6 \cdot (-2x + 5)$ **32.** $-2 \cdot (-2x + 9)$

33. $-2 \cdot (2y + 2)$ **34.** $-4 \cdot (-4x - 4)$ **35.** $-1 \cdot (x + 3)$ **36.** $-7 \cdot (-5x^2 - 1)$

37. $-8 \cdot (-6w^2 - 1)$ **38.** $-1 \cdot (8 - 4y^3)$ **39.** $-1 \cdot (m + 8)$ **40.** $-1 \cdot (3g - 4)$

41. $-1 \cdot (7p - 7)$ **42.** $-1 \cdot (-3m - 2)$ **43.** $-1 \cdot (-9w - 12)$ **44.** $-1 \cdot (5 - 3x^2)$

Chapter 9 Review

Section 9.1 Introduction to Algebra

CONCEPT	EXAMPLE
An **algebraic expression** is a combination of numbers and letters connected by operations and grouping symbols. At its simplest, an algebraic expression can be just a single variable, such as *y*, or a single number, such as 3. Because variables represent numbers, an algebraic expression expresses a numerical value.	$5x + 6y^2$, $\sqrt{3 \cdot y - \frac{x}{4}}$, $\frac{2x^2y + 4w}{1 - 5z}$
When we are given the numerical value of a variable, that number is called a **replacement value**. We replace, or substitute, the variable with the number (the value).	Evaluate the expression $x + x \cdot y$ using the given replacement values. Replace *x* with 2 and *y* with 5: $2 + 2 \cdot 5 = 2 + 10 = 12$
We can represent numbers visually along a **number line**. Numbers less than 0 are **negative** numbers. Numbers greater than 0 are **positive** numbers. On a horizontal number line positive numbers are to the right of 0 and negative numbers are to the left of 0. The number zero (0) is called the **origin**, which means *the beginning*.	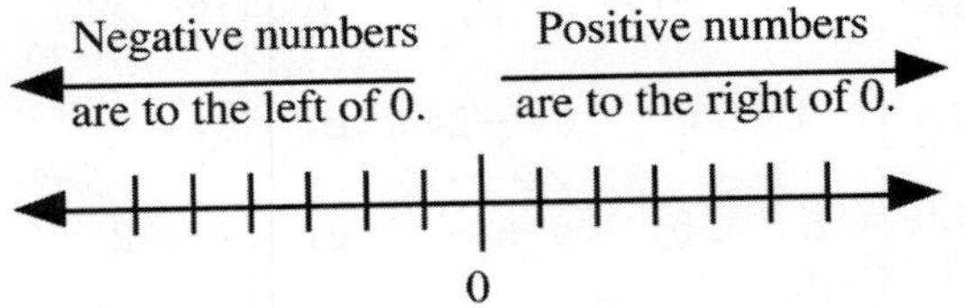
Numbers such as +2 and −2 are called **opposites**, numbers that are the same distance from 0 but on opposite sides of 0. The **integers** include each whole number and its opposite. Zero (0) is an integer but is neither positive nor negative.	Integers: …, −3, −2, −1, 0, 1, 2, 3, …
Two numbers located at different points on the number line are compared to each other based on their location. The number on the left is **less than**, <, the number on the right, and the number on the right is **greater than**, >, the number on the left.	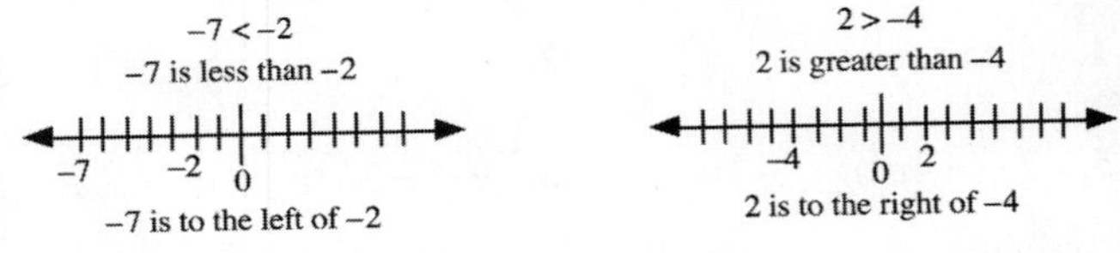
The **absolute value** of a number is its distance from 0 on the number line. For any non-zero number, whether it is on the left side of 0 or the right side of zero doesn't matter; its absolute value is positive. We use **absolute value bars**, | and |, to express the absolute value of a number.	The absolute value of 3 is 3(+3). The absolute value of −3 is also 3(+3). $\|3\| = 3$ and $\|-3\| = 3$. $\|0\| = 0$ because 0 is no distance away from itself.
Non-zero numbers have both a **numerical value** and a **direction**. The numerical value is the distance, along the number line, from 0; the numerical value is another name for the absolute value. The direction is either left or right, depending on the location on the number line, when compared to 0 (zero): 1. Negative numbers are to the left of 0 and positive numbers are to the right of 0. 2. Zero has value but no direction.	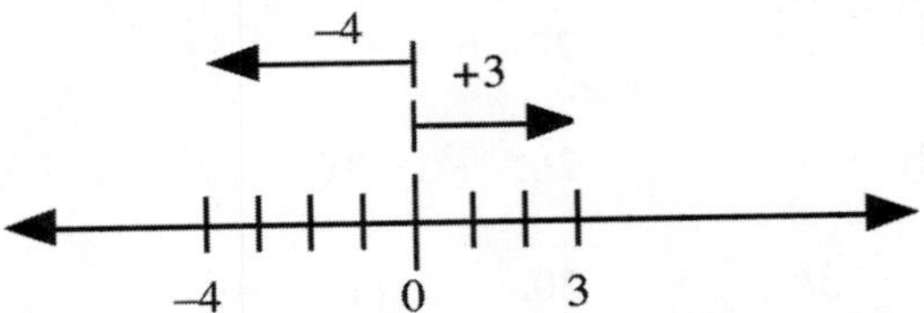 +3; The value is 3; and the direction is to the right. −4; The value is 4; and the direction is to the left.

Section 9.2 Adding Signed Numbers

CONCEPT	EXAMPLE
Each number can be represented on a number line by a **vector**. A vector has a linear length indicating its numerical value and an arrow indicating its direction. As a vector, 0 (zero) has no length and no direction.	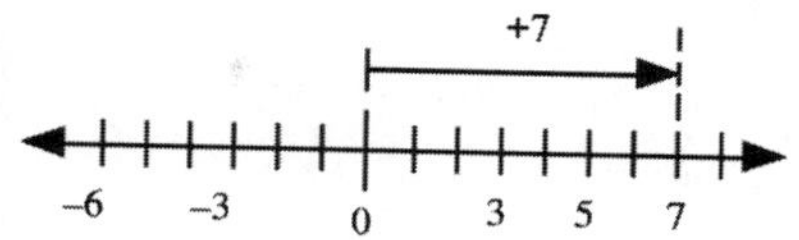
To add two numbers using vectors along the number line: 1. Draw a vector for the first number, starting from the origin, 0. 2. Draw a vector for the second number that starts where the first vector stopped. The number at which the second vector stops is the sum.	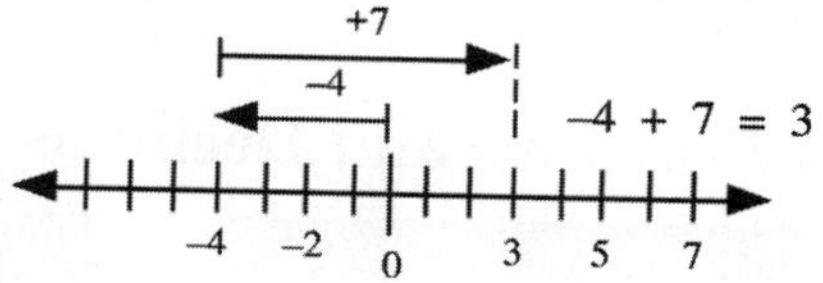
To add two numbers with the same sign: 1. Add the numerical values. 2. The sign of the sum is the same as the sign of each number.	$-18 + (-25)$ 1. The numerical values are 18 and 25; $18 + 25 = 43$ 2. The sign for each number is negative, so $-18 + (-25) = -43$
To add two numbers with different signs: 1. Subtract the numerical values: larger value − smaller value. 2. Give the sum the sign of the addend with the larger numerical value.	$18 + (-25)$ 1. The numerical values are 18 and 25; $25 - 18 = 7$ 2. The larger-valued number is negative, so $18 + (-25) = -7$
The sum of a number and its opposite is 0: $a + (-a) = 0$	$5 + (-5) = 0; \quad -14 + 14 = 0$
If a sum contains more than two integers, use the Commutative and Associative Properties to rewrite the expression to add the positive numbers separately from the negative numbers; then find the sum of those two results.	$8 + (-5) + (-9) + 4$ $= 8 + 4 + (-5) + (-9)$ $= +12 + (-14)$ $= -2$

Section 9.3 Subtracting Signed Numbers

CONCEPT	EXAMPLE
The first three meanings of the dash: 1. Minus 2. Negative 3. "The opposite of"	1. $9 - 5 = 4$ 2. -7 is "negative 7" 3. -3 is "the opposite of" 3
$-(-5)$ is an example of a **double negative.**	$-(-5)$ means the opposite of -5 which is $+5$. $-(-5)$ can be rewritten as $+(+5)$ +5 or just 5.

CONCEPT	EXAMPLE
Write subtraction as addition, as adding the opposite; then follow the rules for addition of signed numbers.	$10 - 17$ $= 10 + (-17)$ $= -7$

Section 9.4 Signed Fractions and Decimals

CONCEPT	EXAMPLE
Whether adding or subtracting signed decimals, it is always best for each decimal to have the same number of decimal places. Then, to evaluate, follow the guidelines for adding and subtracting signed numbers.	$-1.3 + 4.18$ $= -1.30 + 4.18$ $= +2.88$
When signed fractions are like fractions, add or subtract the numerators. It is the numerators that determine which fraction has the larger numerical value.	$\frac{4}{15} - \frac{13}{15}$ $= \frac{4}{15} + -\frac{13}{15}$ $= -\frac{9}{15}$ $= -\frac{3}{5}$
If two fractions are not like fractions, first make them like fractions by building them up to have a common denominator.	$-\frac{3}{4} + \frac{1}{6}$ $= -\frac{3}{4}\cdot\frac{3}{3} + \frac{1}{6}\cdot\frac{2}{2}$ $= -\frac{9}{12} + \frac{2}{12}$ $= -\frac{7}{12}$

Section 9.5 Multiplying and Dividing Signed Numbers

CONCEPT	EXAMPLE
The fourth meaning of the dash: "-1 times"	-6 is $-1 \cdot 6$
Multiplication by -1 is the same as the same "the opposite of."	$(-1)\cdot 7 = -7$ (the opposite of 7) $(-1)\cdot(-4) = +4$ (the opposite of -4)

CONCEPT	EXAMPLE
To multiply two signed numbers: 1. If the signs of the factors are different, the product will be negative. 2. If the signs of the factors are the same, the product will be positive. 3. If one factor is zero, the product is 0.	1. $(6)(-3) = -18$ 2. $(-5)(-4) = +20 = 20$ 3. $(-7)(0) = 0$
When a product has more than non-zero two factors: 1. If there is an even number of negative factors, then the end product will be positive. 2. If there is an odd number of negative factors, the end product will be negative.	1. $(6)(-3)(-2) = +36 = 36$ 2. $(-5)(-4)(-3) = -60$
The rules for dividing two signed numbers are the same as those for multiplication: 1. If the signs of the numbers are different, the quotient will be negative. 2. If the signs of the numbers are the same, the quotient will be positive. 3. The divisor (denominator) can never be 0.	1. $-18 \div 6 = -3$ 2. $-20 \div (-5) = +4 = 4$ 3. $\frac{-5}{0}$ is undefined

Section 9.6 The Order of Operations for Signed Numbers

CONCEPT	EXAMPLE
The Order of Operations: 1. Evaluate within all grouping symbols, if there are any. 2. Apply any exponents. 3. Apply multiplication and division reading from left to right. 4. Apply addition and subtraction reading from left to right.	Evaluate $(4 - 16) \div 2^2$ $= (-12) \div 2^2$ $= -12 \div 4$ $= -3$
We refer to an operation's **rank** when speaking of which should come first. Because multiplication is applied before addition, multiplication has a higher rank than addition.	
If a negative number is the base of an exponent: 1. An odd exponent results in a negative number: $(-\text{base})^{\text{odd exponent}} = -\text{number}$ 2. An even exponent results in a positive number: $(-\text{base})^{\text{even exponent}} = +\text{number}$	1. $(-2)^3 = -8$ 2. $(-7)^2 = +49 = 49$

CONCEPT	EXAMPLE
Because both $3^2 = 9$ and $(-3)^2 = 9$, 9 has two square roots, one positive (+3) and one negative (−3). When using the radical symbol, $\sqrt{9} = +3$ only. This positive square root is called the **principal square root**. To represent the negative square of 9 we must put a negative in front of (outside of) the radical symbol.	Negative square root: $-\sqrt{9} = -3$
If an expression contains two sets of grouping symbols that are unrelated to each other, then each quantity can be evaluated at the same time.	$(2 - 6) \cdot (-10 \div 2)$ $= (-4) \cdot (-5)$ $= +20 = 20$
The fraction bar is a grouping symbol. It groups the numerator separately from the denominator, and each may be evaluated at the same time.	$\dfrac{-2 - 8}{6 \div 3}$ $= \dfrac{-10}{+2}$ $= -5$
Absolute value bars are grouping symbols and we must evaluate within them first. The absolute value is also an operation, so once the expression within is simplified, apply the absolute value to that number.	$\lvert -6 + 2 \rvert - \lvert -7 \rvert$ $= \lvert -4 \rvert - \lvert -7 \rvert$ $= 4 - 7$ $= -3$

Section 9.7 Algebraic Expressions: Combining Like Terms

CONCEPT	EXAMPLE
In algebra, a term can be a constant, or it can be the product of a coefficient and a variable. Also, the variable may have an exponent.	$7, 6x^2, -9w^4$, and $-\frac{2}{3}y$
If a variable has no visible coefficient, then the coefficient is 1. If the variable has no visible exponent, then the exponent is 1.	The coefficient of x^2 is 1: $1x^2$. The coefficient of $-y^3$ is -1: $-1y^3$. The exponent of x in the term $4x$ is 1: $4x^1$.
In algebra, two or more terms are considered to be **like terms** if they have exactly the same variable and exponent, even if the coefficients are different. Caution: a different exponent on the same variable indicates a different term.	$3x^2$ and $9x^2$ are like terms. $5y$ and $5y^2$ are *not* like terms.
To **combine** like terms add or subtract their numerical coefficients.	$-7y + 9y$ $= +2y$ $-4c + c$ $= -4c + 1c$ $= -3c$

CONCEPT	EXAMPLE
The sign in front of a term belongs to that term. Because of the Associative and Commutative Properties, this means that we can move terms around within an expression as long the sign moves with the term.	Rewrite the expression so that the x-terms are together, then combine like terms. $4x + 10 - 7x$ $= 4x - 7x + 10$ $= -3x + 10$

Section 9.8 Multiplying Algebraic Expressions

CONCEPT	EXAMPLE
When a constant is multiplied by a term with a variable, multiply the constant and the coefficient; the variable and its exponent are otherwise unaffected.	$-2(4x) = -8x$ $3(-7y^2) = -21y^2$ $-9 \cdot (-5m) = +45m = 45m$
The Distributive Property of Multiplication over Addition: $b \cdot (c + d) = b \cdot c + b \cdot d$ b is called the *multiplier.*	$3 \cdot (-2y + 1)$ $= 3 \cdot (-2y) + 3 \cdot 1$ $= -6y + 3$
The Distributive Property of Multiplication over Subtraction: $b \cdot (c - d) = b \cdot c - b \cdot d$	$2 \cdot (5x - 9) = 10x - 18$
When the multiplier is negative, remember that the sign in front of a number belongs to that number. This is especially true for the terms within the parentheses.	$-5 \cdot (3p - 4) = -15p + 20$

Chapter 9 Review Exercises

Section 9.1

Evaluate the following according to the replacement value given.

1. $5x + 9$; replace x with 3.
2. $p^2 - 3p$; replace p with 7.
3. $\frac{h + k}{2}$; replace h with 21 and k with 39.
4. $x^2 + xy$; replace x with 3 and y with 8.

Translate each English expression into an algebraic expression. Use any variable to represent the unknown number.

5. The difference of 8 and a number.
6. The sum of a number and 14.

Insert the correct symbol between each pair of numbers, either < (less than) or > (greater than).

7. 9 3
8. −6 0
9. −8 −3
10. 4 −5

Find the absolute value, as indicated.

11. $|+9|$
12. $|-11|$
13. $|-0|$
14. $|21|$

Section 9.2

Find the sum.

15. $2 + (-8)$
16. $1 + (-5)$
17. $-4 + (-9)$
18. $-3 + (-2)$
19. $-3 + 3$
20. $-11 + (-9)$
21. $-13 + 29$
22. $-19 + (-12)$
23. $-16 + 87$
24. $-70 + 18$
25. $-12 + 86$
26. $64 + (-91)$
27. $7 + 4 + (-11) + (-16)$
28. $6 + (-10) + 2 + 17 + (-10) + (-8)$

Section 9.3

Evaluate each expression.

29. $4 - 6$
30. $7 - 11$
31. $0 - 7$
32. $-7 - 5$
33. $6 - (-3)$
34. $-6 - (-10)$
35. $-30 + 60$
36. $-26 + 13$
37. $71 - 79$
38. $82 - 27$
39. $-10 - (-10)$
40. $27 - (-64)$
41. $-9 + 7 - 4 + 8$
42. $-19 + 5 - (-2) - 4$

For each, write a numerical expression and then evaluate. Also, write a sentence answering the question.

43. Find the difference in altitude between a seaside cliff that is 97 feet above sea level and the ocean floor that is 64 feet below sea level.
44. At 3:00 AM, the outside temperature was −13°. By 6:00 AM, the temperature had risen by 8°. What was the temperature at 6:00 AM?
45. Adele has only $10 in her checking account, and she writes a check for $17. What is Adele's new checkbook balance?
46. Adele is being foolish by writing too many checks when she doesn't have enough money. Her check register had a balance of −$26 when she wrote another check for $15. What is Adele's checkbook balance now?

Section 9.4

Evaluate. Simplify, if possible.

47. $\frac{2}{27} - \frac{11}{27}$

48. $-\frac{2}{3} - \frac{1}{3}$

49. $\frac{2}{25} - \left(-\frac{18}{25}\right)$

50. $-\frac{2}{9} - \left(-\frac{8}{9}\right)$

51. $\frac{2}{3} + \left(-\frac{8}{5}\right)$

52. $-\frac{7}{8} + \frac{1}{6}$

Evaluate.

53. $9.3 + (-4.5)$

54. $-0.87 + (-0.98)$

55. $-0.27 + (-8.6)$

56. $7.7 + (-0.93)$

57. $9 - (-7.5)$

58. $-3 - 0.27$

For each, write a numerical expression and then evaluate. Also, write a sentence answering the question.

59. On his American Express card, Clayton has a debit of $57.82. He made a purchase for $25.36. What is the new balance of Clayton's account? Is it a debit or a credit?

60. Find the difference in altitude between the top of an oil derrick's platform that is 10.6 meters above sea level and the ocean floor that is 32.9 meters below sea level.

Section 9.5

Evaluate.

61. $(-3)(-2)$

62. $-11 \cdot (-9)$

63. $(11)(-7)$

64. $4 \cdot 10$

65. $(-2)(-2)$

66. $0 \cdot (-4)$

67. $-\frac{1}{6} \cdot \left(\frac{9}{2}\right)$

68. $\frac{5}{7} \cdot \left(-\frac{9}{10}\right)$

69. $\left(-\frac{8}{9}\right) \cdot \left(-\frac{3}{2}\right)$

70. $\left(-\frac{1}{9}\right) \cdot 6$

71. $-2 \cdot 3 \cdot (-5)$

72. $8 \cdot (-5) \cdot (-1)$

73. $6 \cdot 2 \cdot (-4)$

74. $-1 \cdot (-7) \cdot (-4)$

75. $-33 \div 3$

76. $-48 \div (-8)$

77. $\frac{-42}{-7}$

78. $\frac{-45}{9}$

79. $\frac{14}{25} \div \left(-\frac{7}{10}\right)$

80. $-\frac{9}{20} \div \frac{12}{5}$

Section 9.6

Evaluate.

81. $\sqrt{9}$

82. $-\sqrt{4}$

83. $(-12)^1$

84. $(-9)^2$

Evaluate each expression using the order of operations. Show all steps.

85. $(8 - 14) \div 3$

86. $-36 \div (-9) \cdot (-2)$

87. $(7 - 9)^3$

88. $-20 \div (2 - 6)$

89. $(-18 \div 3) \cdot (2 - 7)$

90. $-\sqrt{-3 \cdot (-12)}$

91. $|-10| - 3$

92. $|1 - 7| + |9 - (-2)|$

93. $\frac{-7 - 1}{2 - 4}$

94. $\frac{-12 + 2}{-9 - (-4)}$

Section 9.7

Answer each question based on the expression $2w - 8w^2 - w^3 + 4$.

95. What is the first term?

96. What is the second term?

97. What is the coefficient of the third term?

98. What is the constant term?

99. What is the exponent of the first term?

100. What is the exponent of the third term?

Simplify. Combine like terms, if possible.

101. $9x + 3x$

102. $2y - 8y$

103. $-5w^2 + w^2$

104. $b^2 + 5b^2$

105. $-4x - (-5x)$

106. $-7r + 7r$

107. $9p - (-3k)$

108. $-12x + 7x - 9x$

109. $4x - 2x - 6x$

110. $-9y + 7y + 4 - 5$

111. $-4c - 8b - c + b$

112. $-5 - 4x - x + 9$

Section 9.8

Find the product.

113. $3(-4x^2)$

114. $-9(-9y)$

115. $7(6p)$

116. $-5(3a^3)$

Rewrite each expression using the Distributive Property.

117. $9 \cdot (y + 2)$

118. $6 \cdot (-2y + 3)$

119. $5 \cdot (3h - 1)$

120. $-2 \cdot (y + 1)$

121. $-3 \cdot (-8y + 7)$

122. $-4 \cdot (2p - 7)$

Chapter 9 Test

Translate each English expression into an algebraic expression.

1. The difference of 15 and a number.

2. The square root of a number.

Insert the correct symbol between each pair of numbers, either < (less than) or > (greater than).

3. $-2 \quad 6$

4. $0 \quad -5$

Evaluate the following according to the replacement value given.

5. $\frac{w + v}{v - 2w}$; replace w with 6, v with 10.

Evaluate each expression.

6. $-5 + 19$

7. $18 + (-20)$

8. $-97 + (-3)$

9. $-3 - 7$

10. $-8 - (-2)$

11. $-61 - (-76)$

12. $-0.6 - (-0.12)$

13. $2 - 6.53$

14. $12(-3)$

15. $4 \cdot (-4)$

16. $-25 \div 5$

17. $28 \div (-4)$

18. $-12 \div 0$

19. $\frac{-30}{-6}$

20. $\left(-\frac{25}{4}\right) \cdot \left(-\frac{8}{15}\right)$

21. $\frac{20}{21} \div \left(-\frac{15}{14}\right)$

22. $-\sqrt{49}$

23. $(-1)^5$

24. $(-4)^2$

25. $(-3)^3$

26. $-5 + 7 - 6 - (-2)$

27. $-3 \cdot (-4) \cdot (-5) \cdot (-2)$

Evaluate. Simplify, if possible.

28. $-\frac{8}{15} + \left(-\frac{2}{15}\right)$

29. $-\frac{3}{10} - \frac{8}{15}$

For each, write a numerical expression and then evaluate. Also, write a sentence answering the question.

30. Son Hee's credit card had a debit of \$145.22 when she made a payment of \$53. What is Son Hee's new account balance? Is it a debit or a credit?

31. Find the difference in altitude between an undersea hilltop that is 162 feet below sea level and the ocean floor that is 458 feet below sea level.

Evaluate each expression using the order of operations. Show all steps.

32. $(-2)^2 - (3 + 5)$

33. $|-6 + 3| - |-2|$

Simplify by combining like terms, if possible.

34. $-p^2 + 8p^2$

35. $-6a - (-a)$

36. $-9x - 6y + y - x$

Find the product.

37. $-4(-8k^4)$

38. $-5(2y)$

Rewrite each expression using the Distributive Property.

39. $3(2w - 5)$

40. $-7(2c - 3)$

CHAPTER 10
Equations

Introduction

Problems! Everybody has them. Some are serious, others are not. Sometimes, problems work themselves out, and other times we need to come up with a creative solution, a strategy that helps us solve the problem.

Here's the story of a woman with a problem. Can you help her find the solution?

Problem: A woman has in her possession a fox, a chicken, and a bag of grain. She must be careful not to leave the fox and chicken alone because the fox will eat the chicken. Likewise, if the chicken and grain are left alone, bye-bye grain. At a river crossing, the water is shallow enough for her to wade across, but she'll be able to carry only one of her possessions at a time. How does she cross the river with her three possessions uneaten?

Solution: She must make seven trips in all. (1) She crosses the river with the chicken only and (2) returns by herself. (3) She crosses back with the fox only, leaves it tied up on shore and (4) returns with the chicken. She leaves the chicken and (5) takes the grain across to be with the fox. (6) She makes one last return trip to pick up the chicken and (7) takes it across to gather up her possessions.

This problem is a bit different than the ones you'll be seeing in this section. There isn't any math involved in this problem, but there is a strategy.

In Chapter 10, you'll be using many of the ideas learned in Chapter 9 to solve equations and applications. For each type of problem that you encounter, a strategy is given so that you will know how to approach a problem with confidence. For some of the problems, the strategy will be to remove something from one side and put it to the other side, just like the woman with the fox, chicken, and bag of grain.

Preparation Exercises

Section 1.6, Equations: *Solve for n.*

1. $n + 19 = 32$

2. $45 = 3 \cdot n$

Section 3.3, Multiply and Simplify: *Multiply and simplify.*

3. $\frac{5}{14} \cdot \frac{21}{10}$

4. $12 \cdot \frac{7}{16}$

Section 3.6, Additional Equations and Applications with Fractions: *Solve for n.*

5. $\frac{2}{5} \cdot n = 8$

6. $\frac{3}{8} = \frac{9}{4} \cdot n$

Section 4.3, Adding and Subtracting Like Fractions: *Add or subtract as indicated.*

7. $\frac{11}{40} + \frac{21}{40}$

8. $\frac{25}{36} - \frac{17}{36}$

Section 9.3, Subtracting Signed Numbers: *Evaluate.*

9. $-7 - 9$

10. $-6 - (-18)$

Section 9.5, Multiplying and Dividing Signed Numbers: *Evaluate.*

11. $\frac{-28}{-7}$

12. $\frac{4}{9} \cdot \left(-\frac{3}{16}\right)$

Section 9.7, Algebraic Expressions: Combining Like Terms: *Combine like terms.*

13. $-4x + 9x$

14. $-5x - 11x$

Section 9.8, Multiplying Algebraic Expressions: *Distribute.*

15. $4(5x - 7)$

16. $-5(3x - 2)$

SECTION 10.1 Solving Equations Involving One Operation

Objectives

In this section, you will learn to:

- Apply the Addition Property of Equations.
- Apply the Division Property of Equations.
- Apply the Multiplication Property of Equations.
- Isolate variables.
- Solve equations involving one operation.

To successfully complete this section, you need to understand:

- Additive identity (1.2)
- Multiplicative identity (1.2)
- Solving equations (1.6 and 3.6)
- Fractions (Chapters 3 and 4)
- Signed numbers and terms (Chapter 9)

Introduction

We first encountered solving equations in Section 1.6. We learned:

- To solve an equation, we must ***isolate the variable*** on one side of the equal sign.

Example:

$$14 = n + 8$$
$$14 - 8 = n + 8 - 8$$
$$6 = n$$
$$n = 6$$

- The **solution** of an equation makes the equation true, and we can check the solution by replacing the variable with that number.

Check $n = 6$: $14 = n + 8$

$$14 = 6 + 8$$
$$14 = 14 \quad \text{True ✓}$$

In Chapter 9, we learned about algebraic expressions, such as $-8x$, $6y - 5$, and $7 - 4w$, and we'll now see those types of expressions in the equations in Chapter 10. In this section, we will solve simple equations, those that have only one operation. In Section 10.2, we'll solve equations that have more than one operation.

The key to solving any equation is to isolate the variable. Once the variable has been correctly isolated, we have the solution to the equation. Isolating the variable is all about having the variable, say x, on one side of the equal sign and a single number (constant) on the other side, as in $x = 5$. This means manipulating the equation so that we get either:

$x + 0 = 5$	or	$1 \cdot x = 5$
$x = 5$	← Each simplifies to $x = 5$. →	$x = 5$
What's special about *plus zero*	and	*one times?*

You may recall from Section 1.2 that

1. 0 is the additive identity, meaning $a + 0 = a$, as in $8 + 0 = 8$.
2. 1 is the multiplicative identity, meaning $1 \cdot a = a$, as in $1 \cdot 7 = 7$.

To solve an equation, then, means that we must achieve $x + 0$ or $1 \cdot x$ on one side of the equation. We will use these three properties to help us isolate the variable:

1. $a + (-a) = 0$ The sum of a number and its opposite is 0 (Section 9.2). For example, $3 + (-3) = 0$ and $-9 + 9 = 0$.
2. $\frac{a}{a} = 1$ Any number (except 0) divided by itself is 1 (Section 3.1). For example, $\frac{6}{6} = 1$ and $\frac{-4}{-4} = 1$.
3. $\frac{a}{b} \cdot \frac{b}{a} = 1$ The product of a number and its reciprocal is 1 (Section 3.5). For example, $\frac{2}{7} \cdot \frac{7}{2} = 1$ and $-\frac{3}{5} \cdot \left(-\frac{5}{3}\right) = 1$.

Last, keep the equation *balanced*:

Whatever we do to modify one side of an equation—by either adding, subtracting, multiplying, or dividing a number or term—we *must do likewise* to the other side.

Isolating the Variable: The Addition Property of Equations

We first look at simple equations in which the only operation is either addition or subtraction, such as $x + 8 = 5$ or $x - 9 = -2$. Each of these equations has a constant on each side of the equal sign. To isolate the variable, we need to "clear" the constant that is on the same side as x. This is done using the Addition Property of Equations:

The Addition Property of Equations

We may add any number, c, to *each side* of an equation.

If $a = b$,
then $a + c = b + c$

This property means that we can add a positive or negative number to each side of the equation. Typically, we'll add the opposite of the constant term that we wish to clear.

Adding the opposite of the constant creates 0. This is called *clearing the constant.*

EXAMPLE 1 Solve each of these equations by clearing the constant. Check each answer to show that it is the solution.

a) $x - 6 = 3$ b) $-9 = y + 4$

PROCEDURE: To clear the constant, *add its opposite* to each side of the equation.

ANSWER: a)

$x - 6 = 3$ Clear the constant, -6, by adding its opposite, $+6$, to each side.

$x - 6 + 6 = 3 + 6$

$x + 0 = 9$ $-6 + 6 = 0$, the additive identity.

$x = 9$ → Check the answer: $9 - 6 = 3$ True ✓

b) $-9 = y + 4$ — Clear the constant, 4, by adding its opposite, -4, to each side.

$-9 + (-4) = y + 4 + (-4)$

$-13 = y + 0$ — $4 + (-4) = 0$, the additive identity.

$-13 = y$

Write the final equation with the variable on the left side. → $y = -13$ → Check the answer: $-9 = -13 + 4$ True ✓

Look back at Example 1 and notice three things:

1. Each step in the solving process is directly below the preceding step.
2. The equal signs are lined up, one below the other.
3. We achieved the additive identity, 0, to isolate the variable.

YOU TRY IT 1

Solve each of these equations by clearing the constant. Show all steps! Also, be sure to check each answer. Use Example 1 as a guide.

a) $a - 4 = 11$ b) $5 = y + 9$ c) $-12 = x - 3$

When the constant is a fraction or decimal, we add the opposite to clear it, just as we would any constant.

EXAMPLE 2

Solve each equation by clearing the constant. Check the answer to show that it is the solution.

a) $w - \frac{2}{5} = \frac{8}{5}$ b) $2 = x + 3.25$

ANSWER: a)

$w - \frac{2}{5} = \frac{8}{5}$ — Clear the constant $-\frac{2}{5}$ by adding its opposite to each side.

$w - \frac{2}{5} + \frac{2}{5} = \frac{8}{5} + \frac{2}{5}$ — The opposite of $-\frac{2}{5}$ is $+\frac{2}{5}$.

$w + 0 = \frac{10}{5}$ — $-\frac{2}{5} + \frac{2}{5} = 0$; this is what we want.

$w = 2$ → Check the answer: $\frac{10}{5} - \frac{2}{5} = \frac{8}{5}$ True ✓

b) $2 = x + 3.25$ — Clear the constant 3.25 by adding its opposite to each side. The opposite of 3.25 is -3.25.

$2 + (-3.25) = x + 3.25 + (-3.25)$

$-1.25 = x + 0$

$-1.25 = x$

$x = -1.25$ → Check the answer: $2 = -1.25 + 3.25$ True ✓

YOU TRY IT 2

Solve each of these equations by clearing the constant. Show all steps! Also, be sure to check each answer. Use Example 2 as a guide.

a) $p - \frac{1}{2} = \frac{5}{2}$

b) $-\frac{8}{15} = x - \frac{11}{15}$

c) $y + 0.75 = -1.5$

Isolating the Variable: The Division Property of Equations

In a simple equation, if the only operation is multiplication, then we need to clear the coefficient. If the coefficient is an integer, as in $4x = -20$ or $-6x = -42$, we can divide each side by the coefficient.

The Division Property of Equations

We may divide each side of an equation by any number, c, $c \neq 0$.

If $a = b$,

then $\frac{a}{c} = \frac{b}{c}$

In the Division Property of Equations, why does it say $c \neq 0$?

____

____

EXAMPLE 3

Solve each of these equations by clearing the coefficient.

a) $5x = -20$

b) $12 = -2w$

PROCEDURE: Divide each side by the coefficient. Remember to keep the equation balanced. Mentally check each answer by using it as a replacement value for the variable in the original equation.

ANSWER:

a) $5x = -20$ — The coefficient is 5; clear it by dividing each side by 5.

$\frac{5x}{5} = \frac{-20}{5}$ — Dividing by 5 makes the coefficient = 1.

$1x = -4$ — We get the new coefficient 1 because $\frac{5}{5} = 1$.

$x = -4$ → Check the answer: $5(-4) = -20$ True ✓

b) $12 = -2w$ — The coefficient is -2; clear it by dividing each side by -2.

$\frac{12}{-2} = \frac{-2w}{-2}$ — Dividing by -2 makes the coefficient = 1.

$-6 = 1w$ — We get the new coefficient 1 because $\frac{-2}{-2} = 1$.

$-6 = w$

$w = -6$ → Check the answer: $12 = -2 \cdot (-6)$ True ✓

Look back at Example 3 and notice three things:

1. Each step in the solving process is directly below the preceding step.
2. The equal signs are lined up, one below the other.
3. We achieved the multiplicative identity, 1, to isolate the variable.

YOU TRY IT 3 *Solve each of these equations by clearing the coefficient. Check each answer. Use Example 3 as a guide.*

a) $3y = -24$ b) $-5x = -20$ c) $18 = -2p$

Isolating the Variable: The Multiplication Property of Equations

The Multiplication Property of Equations

We may multiply each side of an equation by any number, c, $c \neq 0$.

$$\text{If} \quad a = b,$$
$$\text{then} \quad c \cdot a = c \cdot b$$

In the Multiplication Property of Equations, why does it say $c \neq 0$?

____

____

The Multiplication Property of Equations is typically used when the coefficient is a fraction, as in $-\frac{2}{3}y = -8$. In this case, and others like it, we can multiply each side by the reciprocal of the coefficient, as demonstrated in Example 4.

EXAMPLE 4 Solve this equation by clearing the coefficient. $-\dfrac{2}{3}y = -8$

PROCEDURE: Multiply each side by the reciprocal of the coefficient. Check the answer by using it as a replacement value for the variable in the original equation.

ANSWER:

$-\dfrac{2}{3}y = -8$ The coefficient is $-\frac{2}{3}$; clear it by multiplying each side by $-\frac{3}{2}$.

$-\dfrac{3}{2}\cdot\left(-\dfrac{2}{3}\right)y = -\dfrac{8}{1}\cdot\left(-\dfrac{3}{2}\right)$ Multiplying $-\frac{3}{2}\cdot\left(-\frac{2}{3}\right)$ makes the coefficient $= 1$.

$1y = +\dfrac{24}{2}$ The right side simplifies to 12. Check: $-\frac{2}{3}\cdot(12) \stackrel{?}{=} -8$

$y = 12 \rightarrow$

$$-\frac{2}{3}\cdot\frac{12}{1} \stackrel{?}{=} -8$$
$$-\frac{24}{3} = -8 \quad \text{True} ✓$$

YOU TRY IT 4

Solve each equation by clearing the coefficient. Check each answer. Use Example 4 as a guide.

a) $\frac{7}{8}w = -28$ b) $12 = -\frac{3}{5}x$ c) $-\frac{8}{9}y = -\frac{2}{3}$

The reciprocal of -1:
Consider $-1 = \frac{-1}{1}$.
The reciprocal is $\frac{1}{-1} = -1$.

In a simple equation, if the coefficient is -1, we can isolate the variable by either dividing each side by -1 or multiplying each side by the reciprocal of -1, which is -1.

EXAMPLE 5

Solve $-x = 7$ by

a) dividing by -1. b) multiplying by -1.

PROCEDURE: The coefficient is -1. The reciprocal of -1 is -1.

ANSWER:

a) $-x = 7$ Divide each side by -1.

$$\frac{-1x}{-1} = \frac{7}{-1}$$

$$x = -7$$

← We get the same solution. →

b) $-x = 7$ Multiply each side by -1.

$$-1 \cdot (-1x) = -1 \cdot 7$$

$$x = -7$$

YOU TRY IT 5

Solve each equation by clearing the coefficient. Check each answer. Use Example 5 as a guide.

a) $-w = -14$ b) $12 = -y$

Guidelines to Solving Simple Equations

To isolate a variable in a simple equation, we must clear any numerical value—either a constant or coefficient—by applying the appropriate operation to each side of the equation:

1. Clear a constant term by *adding its opposite.*
2. Clear an integer coefficient by *dividing by the coefficient.*
3. Clear a fractional coefficient by *multiplying by its reciprocal.*

Caution

Be sure to keep the equation balanced by modifying each side in the same manner.

You Try It Answers: Section 10.1

YTI 1 a) $a = 15$ b) $y = -4$ c) $x = -9$

YTI 2 a) $p = 3$ b) $x = \frac{1}{5}$ c) $y = -2.25$

YTI 3 a) $y = -8$ b) $x = 4$ c) $p = -9$

YTI 4 a) $w = -32$ b) $x = -20$ c) $y = \frac{3}{4}$

YTI 5 a) $w = 14$ b) $y = -12$

Focus Exercises: Section 10.1

Solve each equation by clearing the constant. Be sure to check each answer.

1. $x - 12 = 6$

2. $p - 2 = 8$

3. $w - 4 = -7$

4. $m - 3 = -10$

5. $y - 9 = -8$

6. $x - 12 = -6$

7. $x + 5 = 8$

8. $h + 4 = 11$

9. $p + 8 = 2$

10. $a + 9 = 6$

11. $m + 6 = -4$

12. $x + 9 = -8$

13. $12 = x + 6$

14. $9 = w + 8$

15. $-4 = c - 7$

16. $-3 = k - 10$

17. $12 = p + 20$

18. $1 = h + 12$

19. $-9 = x + 5$

20. $-6 = y + 1$

21. $-8 = w - 4$

22. $-11 = p - 6$

23. $m - 6 = -6$

24. $x - 8 = -8$

25. $m - 0.3 = -1.2$

26. $y - 2.9 = -3.5$

27. $x + 1.2 = -0.6$

28. $x + 4 = 1.85$

29. $2 = h + 3.6$

30. $1 = p + 4.2$

31. $y - \frac{3}{8} = \frac{5}{8}$

32. $c - \frac{2}{3} = \frac{4}{3}$

33. $k + \frac{3}{12} = \frac{7}{12}$

34. $w + \frac{1}{12} = \frac{7}{12}$

35. $m + \frac{8}{15} = \frac{2}{15}$

36. $y + \frac{9}{10} = \frac{1}{10}$

37. $x - \frac{4}{9} = -\frac{10}{9}$

38. $c - \frac{2}{21} = -\frac{16}{21}$

39. $p + \frac{11}{15} = -\frac{4}{15}$

40. $h + \frac{7}{12} = -\frac{5}{12}$

41. $x + \frac{13}{24} = -\frac{5}{24}$

42. $y + \frac{11}{30} = -\frac{1}{30}$

Solve each equation by clearing the coefficient. Be sure to check each answer.

43. $6n = 42$ **44.** $5x = 20$ **45.** $7y = -42$ **46.** $4m = -28$

47. $-3k = -36$ **48.** $-2x = -18$ **49.** $18 = 9p$ **50.** $35 = 7w$

51. $-16 = 2v$ **52.** $-27 = 3m$ **53.** $-12 = -4y$ **54.** $-36 = -9x$

55. $9y = 12$ **56.** $4p = 18$ **57.** $-21 = 14h$ **58.** $-8 = 6w$

59. $-15c = -24$ **60.** $-12y = -30$ **61.** $\frac{3}{5}y = -21$ **62.** $\frac{2}{3}w = -16$

63. $-\frac{5}{6}x = -10$ **64.** $-\frac{1}{4}m = -6$ **65.** $\frac{9}{10}k = \frac{18}{5}$ **66.** $\frac{3}{8}a = -\frac{9}{4}$

Solve each equation. Be sure to check each answer.

67. $b - 1 = -5$ **68.** $h + 8 = -4$ **69.** $-5 = 20m$ **70.** $-30 = -10x$

71. $-4 + x = -4$ **72.** $7 + y = 7$ **73.** $y - \frac{3}{8} = \frac{3}{4}$ **74.** $c + \frac{2}{3} = \frac{7}{12}$

75. $\frac{3}{8}y = 15$ **76.** $\frac{2}{7}m = 6$ **77.** $-\frac{5}{8}q = \frac{3}{4}$ **78.** $\frac{3}{4}x = -6$

79. $-4x = -60$ **80.** $-42 = -14y$ **81.** $-0.8 + x = -1.2$ **82.** $0.7 = -2.4 + m$

83. $-9 = 13 + w$ **84.** $-\frac{2}{5} = y - \frac{3}{10}$ **85.** $\frac{3}{8} = -\frac{7}{12} + v$ **86.** $-8 = \frac{2}{5}x$

87. $9 = -\frac{3}{4}p$ **88.** $\frac{2}{3}y = 1$ **89.** $\frac{4}{5}w = -1$ **90.** $-\frac{1}{6}x = -1$

SECTION 10.2 Solving Equations Involving Two Operations

Objectives

In this section, you will learn to:

- Solve equations involving more than one operation.
- Solve equations involving more than one variable term.
- Simplify expressions before solving.

To successfully complete this section, you need to understand:

- Signed numbers (Chapter 9)
- Combining like terms (9.7)
- The Distributive Property (9.8)
- Solving equations (10.1)

Introduction

The simple equations we solved in Section 10.1 had only one operation between the variable and a number, either addition, subtraction, or multiplication. To isolate the variable in these equations, we need to clear the constant or the coefficient. Sometimes, however, we need to prepare an equation to be solved by first simplifying one side or the other, by either distributing or combining like terms.

Solving Linear Equations Involving More Than One Operation

Some equations have more than one operation to clear. When this occurs, we must have a consistent method of isolating the variable.

For example, in an equation such as $3x + 5 = -7$, we might ask, "To isolate x, which should we clear first, the *constant* term, 5, or the *coefficient*, 3?"

Because the goal is to isolate the variable, we must prepare this equation—and others like it—by first isolating the variable term. This means that we must clear the constant first. Once the constant has been cleared, we have a simple equation that can be solved by clearing the coefficient.

EXAMPLE 1 Solve $3x + 5 = -7$. Check the answer to show that it is the solution.

PROCEDURE: To isolate the variable term, first clear the constant.

ANSWER:

$3x + 5 = -7$	Prepare the equation for solving by clearing the constant term, +5: add −5 to each side.
$3x + 5 + (-5) = -7 + (-5)$	
$3x + 0 = -12$	Adding 5 + (−5) gives the additive identity, 0.
$3x = -12$	This is now a simple equation. Clear the coefficient by dividing each side by 3.
$\frac{3x}{3} = \frac{-12}{3}$	$\frac{3x}{3}$ reduces to $1x$, or just x.
$x = -4$ →	**Check** the solution, −4: $3(-4) + 5 = -7$ $-12 + 5 = -7$ True ✓

Some equations contain the variable term on the right side, as shown in Example 2.

EXAMPLE 2 Solve $15 = \frac{7}{2}y - 6$. Check the answer to show that it is the solution.

PROCEDURE: To isolate the variable term, first clear the constant.

ANSWER:

$15 = \frac{7}{2}y - 6$ Prepare the equation for solving by clearing the constant term, −6: add +6 to each side.

$15 + 6 = \frac{7}{2}y - 6 + 6$

$21 = \frac{7}{2}y + 0$ Adding $-6 + 6$ gives the additive identity, 0.

$21 = \frac{7}{2}y$ This is now a simple equation. Clear the coefficient by multiplying each side by its reciprocal, $\frac{2}{7}$.

$\frac{2}{7} \cdot 21 = \frac{2}{7} \cdot \frac{7}{2}y$ Left side: $\frac{2}{7} \cdot \frac{21}{1} = \frac{2 \cdot 21}{7 \cdot 1} = \frac{2 \cdot 3}{1 \cdot 1} = \frac{6}{1}$; right side: $\frac{2}{7} \cdot \frac{7}{2} = 1$.

$\frac{6}{1} = 1y$

$6 = y$

$y = 6$

Check the answer: $15 = \frac{7}{2} \cdot 6 - 6$ ← 6 is the same as $\frac{6}{1}$.

$15 = \frac{7}{2} \cdot \frac{6}{1} - 6$ ← $\frac{7}{2} \cdot \frac{6}{1} = 21$.

$15 = 21 - 6$ True ✓

YOU TRY IT 1

Solve each equation. Check the answer to show that it is a solution. Use Examples 1 and 2 as guides.

a) $3x - 5 = 19$

b) $\frac{2}{3}y - 5 = 3$

c) $1 = -2x - 9$

d) $-2 = -\frac{3}{4}p - 8$

Solving Linear Equations Containing More Than One Variable Term

Some equations have more than one variable term, one on each side.

$(4x) + 17 = (6x) + 5$

↑ Should we isolate this variable term... ↑ ...or this variable term?

For example, $4x + 17 = 6x + 5$ has a variable term on each side. You might ask:

"To solve this equation, which variable should we isolate?"

To answer this question, we must remember that any solution we find becomes a replacement value. This replacement value replaces the variable in both variable terms; therefore, the x's are the same variable and must be combined as one term before we can truly isolate the variable.

However, because the variables are in different expressions—on different sides of the equal sign—the only way we can combine them is to clear one of the variable terms by adding its opposite to each side.

Does it really matter which variable term we choose to clear? No. Because the equation has only one solution, clearing either variable term will lead us to the solution.

Example 3 and YTI 2 solve the same equation two different ways.

EXAMPLE 3 Solve: $4x + 17 = 6x + 5$

PROCEDURE: First, combine the variable terms by adding the opposite of one them to each side.

ANSWER: Let's choose to clear the $4x$ term by adding $-4x$ to each side.

$4x + 17 = 6x + 5$ — Prepare the equation for solving by clearing $+4x$: add $-4x$ to each side of the equation.

$4x + (-4x) + 17 = 6x + (-4x) + 5$

$0 + 17 = 2x + 5$ — $4x + (-4x) = 0x$, or just 0.

$17 = 2x + 5$ — Now isolate the variable term by clearing the constant term, $+5$: add -5 to each side.

$17 + (-5) = 2x + 5 + (-5)$

$12 = 2x + 0$ — Now clear the coefficient by dividing each side by 2.

$\frac{12}{2} = \frac{2x}{2}$

$6 = x$

$x = 6$

Check the answer, $x = 6$:

$4(6) + 17 = 6(6) + 5$

$24 + 17 = 36 + 5$

$41 = 41$ True ✓

YOU TRY IT 2 *Solve this equation by clearing the $6x$ term from each side. The first step is shown. Complete the solving process. Use Example 3 as a guide.*

$4x + 17 = 6x + 5$

$4x + (-6x) + 17 = 6x + (-6x) + 5$

Check the answer:

Think about it Comparing the work shown in Example 3 and your own work in YTI 2, which variable term, $4x$ or $6x$, would you likely clear if you had your choice? Why? Share your answer with a classmate.

YOU TRY IT 3 *Solve each equation. Check each answer to show that it is a solution. Use Example 3 as a guide.*

a) $9x - 5 = 10 + 6x$

b) $2p + 5 = -4p + 23$

c) $4w - 5 = 16 + 7w$

d) $x + 10 = 2 - 3x$

Simplifying Expressions before Solving

Sometimes, in preparing the equation for solving, we need to simplify one (or both) of the sides; after all, each side is an expression, and it's common to simplify expressions.

For example,

1. we may need to first distribute a number to a quantity, as in the expression $3(y - 1)$; or
2. we may need to combine like terms, as in the expression $2x + 8 + 4x$.

EXAMPLE 4 Solve $12 - 2y = 3(y - 1)$ by first simplifying each side.

ANSWER:

$12 - 2y = 3(y - 1)$ First distribute on the right side. Do not try to clear any terms just yet.

$12 - 2y = 3y - 3$ Now we can start the process of isolating the variable by getting the variable terms together on the same side. Let's clear $-2y$ by adding its opposite, $+2y$, to each side.

$12 - 2y + 2y = 3y + 2y - 3$

$12 + 0 = 5y - 3$

$12 = 5y - 3$ Now isolate the variable term by clearing the constant. Add the opposite of -3 to each side: $-3 + 3 = 0$.

$12 + 3 = 5y - 3 + 3$

$15 = 5y + 0$

$15 = 5y$ Now clear the coefficient by dividing each side by 5.

$\frac{15}{5} = \frac{5y}{5}$

$3 = y$

$y = 3$

Check the answer by substituting $y = 3$ into the *original* equation:

$12 - 2(3) = 3(3 - 1)$

$12 - 6 = 3(2)$

$6 = 6$ True ✓

EXAMPLE 5 Solve $2x + 8 + 5x = -4 + 3x$ by first simplifying each side.

ANSWER:

$2x + 8 + 5x = -4 + 3x$ First combine like terms on the left side: $2x + 5x = 7x$.

$7x + 8 = -4 + 3x$ Now we can get the variable terms together on the same side. Let's clear $+3x$ by adding its opposite, $-3x$, to each side.

$7x + (-3x) + 8 = -4 + 3x + (-3x)$

$4x + 8 = -4 + 0$

$4x + 8 = -4$ Now isolate the variable term by clearing the constant: add -8 to each side.

$4x + 8 + (-8) = -4 + (-8)$

$4x + 0 = -12$

$4x = -12$ Now clear the coefficient by dividing each side by 4.

$\frac{4x}{4} = \frac{-12}{4}$

$x = -3$

Check the answer by substituting $x = -3$, into the *original* equation:

$2(-3) + 8 + 5(-3) = -4 + 3(-3)$

$-6 + 8 + (-15) = -4 + (-9)$

$-13 = -13$ True ✓

YOU TRY IT 4

Solve each equation by first simplifying each side. Use Examples 4 and 5 as guides.

a) $4(y + 1) = 6y - 6$

b) $-6w + 15 = -3(3w - 4)$

c) $x - 10 = 3x + 6 + 2x$

d) $1 - 2x + 10 = -4x - 9$

You Try It Answers: Section 10.2

YTI 1 a) $x = 8$ b) $y = 12$ c) $x = -5$ d) $p = -8$

YTI 2 $x = 6$

YTI 3 a) $x = 5$ b) $p = 3$ c) $w = -7$ d) $x = -2$

YTI 4 a) $y = 5$ b) $w = -1$ c) $x = -4$ d) $x = -10$

Focus Exercises: Section 10.2

Solve each equation. Check each answer to show that it is a solution.

1. $3x + 8 = 20$

2. $24 = 7w + 3$

3. $5x + 16 = 1$

4. $7 + 3p = -26$

5. $6 - 5w = -34$

6. $13 = -5 - 9c$

7. $43 = 4x + 7$

8. $-23 = 8w + 9$

9. $-7v - 4 = 17$

10. $-2y - 3 = -11$

11. $-y + 5 = 3$

12. $-k - 8 = -1$

13. $-4 = -p + 16$

14. $8 = -m - 3$

15. $-4 = 3x - 4$

16. $6 = 6 - 5m$

17. $2y + 1 = 4$

18. $2 - 5v = 8$

19. $-5 = 4x + 5$

20. $12 = -3 + 6v$

21. $\frac{3}{5}k - 4 = 5$

22. $\frac{1}{4}y + 6 = 1$

23. $-4 = \frac{5}{6}w + 11$

24. $7 = -9 + \frac{4}{3}c$

Solve each equation. Check each answer to show that it is a solution.

25. $4x + 6 = 18 - 2x$

26. $3m + 4 = 7m - 12$

27. $3 - 2y = 9 - 8y$

28. $5 + 2x = -7 + 5x$

29. $2p - 5 = -4p - 23$

30. $3y - 9 = -5y - 41$

31. $3x - 7 = 11 + 5x$

32. $5w + 4 = 9w + 28$

33. $18 + 8y = 7 - 3y$

34. $3 - 2n = 21 + 7n$

35. $14 - 6x = -6 + 4x$

36. $2x - 5 = 12x + 45$

37. $\frac{3}{8}w + 3 = \frac{7}{8}w - 1$

38. $\frac{7}{9}v - 5 = \frac{5}{9}v - 3$

39. $\frac{1}{3}h + 11 = 5 - \frac{1}{3}h$

40. $-\frac{4}{5}c - 3 = 9 - \frac{1}{5}c$

Solve each equation. Check each answer to show that it is a solution.

41. $3 + m + 7 = 19 - 2m$

42. $12 - 8a - 6 = -13a + 21$

43. $-y + 18 + 3y = 6 + 5y$

44. $4x - 2 - 3x = -x + 16$

45. $2(5 - x) = 3x + 6 - x$

46. $4d + 1 - 6d = 3(5 - 3d)$

47. $3(y - 6) = 4y - 8$

48. $4(3c + 2) = 2c - 2$

49. $4x + 15 = 5(x + 4)$

50. $2x + 2 = 6(x + 3)$

51. $-c + 6 + 3c = -2c + 6$

52. $5p + 7 - 3p = 17 - 9p + 12$

53. $2y + 5 - 4y = 6y - 7$

54. $10 - 3w + 1 = 9w + 3 - 6w$

55. $10x + 3 - 20x = 4 - 5x$

56. $15 + 4y - 3 = 12y + 3 - 20y$

57. $\frac{1}{4}k - 4 + \frac{5}{4}k = \frac{3}{4}k + 2$

58. $\frac{2}{3}v + 3 - \frac{4}{3}v = \frac{1}{3}v + 9$

59. $\frac{6}{5}r - 1 = \frac{1}{5}r - 5 + \frac{3}{5}r$

60. $\frac{7}{6}m + 9 = \frac{1}{6}m - 2 - \frac{5}{6}m$

SECTION 10.3 Problem Solving

Objectives

In this section, you will learn to:

- Translate from English to algebra.
- Solve problems with unknown numbers.

To successfully complete this section, you need to understand:

- Solving applications (1.7)
- Translating expressions (9.1)
- Solving equations (10.1 and 10.2)

Introduction

Algebra is more than just putting letters in place of numbers. We can use algebra to answer questions such as, "How long will it take me to earn enough money to put a down payment on a house?" and "How much paint will I need to paint three bedrooms in my house?" and "If Marny is so smart, why do I have 5 cookies and she has only 3?"

Before we begin to explore the problems of algebra, we need to look at how to translate an English problem into an algebraic one.

Translating from English to Algebra: Expressions

In Section 9.1 we first explored how to translate expressions from English to algebra. For example,

The sum of a number and 6 becomes $n + 6$ or $x + 6$.

In every day conversation, we might say instead, "A number *increased by* 6," or "6 *more than* a number." Each of these could also be written as $x + 6$.

Here is a table showing some words that indicate one operation or another. For this, x represents the unknown number.

Word or phrase	Means	Example (expression)	Translation
More than	Addition	"5 more than a number"	$x + 5$
Increased by		"A number increased by 8"	$x + 8$
Less than	Subtraction	"7 less than a number"	$x - 7$
Decreased by		"A number decreased by 4"	$x - 4$
Times		"Four times a number"	$4 \cdot x$ or just $4x$
Twice (two times)	Multiplication	"Twice a number"	$2 \cdot x$ or just $2x$
Fraction of		"Two-thirds of a number"	$\frac{2}{3} \cdot x$ or just $\frac{2}{3}x$

Maybe the most challenging interpretation in the table above is that of "less than," which means subtraction. Why is "7 less than a number" interpreted as $x - 7$? Why isn't it $7 - x$, since that's the order in which the parts were written (7 first, followed by "a number")?

The question is best answered with an example.

Hector's children, Gloria (14 years old) and Tino (10 years old), each receive a weekly allowance. Since Tino is younger and has fewer household responsibilities than Gloria, Hector might say, "Tino's allowance is \$7.00 less than Gloria's." How much does Tino receive for his weekly allowance?

To answer the question we must *first* know how much Gloria receives. If she receives \$12 per week, then Tino receives \$12 − \$7 = \$5 per week; if Gloria receives \$16 per week, then Tino receives \$16 − \$7 = \$9 per week.

In general, if Gloria's amount is unknown (just *a number, x*), then Tino's amount is

7 less than that number, or $x - 7$.

What this means is that we can't always translate an expression word for word, exactly as written. Sometimes, we need to think things through, think about what comes first or what value must be known first. **Thinking is required!**

EXAMPLE 1 Translate each of the following expressions into the language of algebra.

a) A number increased by 3
b) 10 more than a number
c) 6 times a number
d) 9 less than a number
e) Twice a number
f) Three-fifths of a number

PROCEDURE: In each case, we'll let x represent the number.

ANSWER:

a) $x + 3$
b) $x + 10$
c) $6x$
d) $x - 9$
e) $2x$
f) $\frac{3}{5}x$

YOU TRY IT 1 *Translate each of the following expressions into the language of algebra. Here, use the variable x to represent the number. Use Example 1 as a guide.*

a) 12 more than a number
b) Five-fourths of a number
c) 8 less than a number
d) Twice a number
e) A number increased by 8
f) Half of a number
g) A number decreased by 15
h) 10 times a number
i) 20 increased by a number
j) 1 less than a number

Translating from English to Algebra: Equations

Recall that an equation is: one expression = another expression.

The equal sign can be translated, in English, as *equals*, *is*, or *totals*. Each of these words is a verb in the English language, and it is with verbs that we create sentences.

Certain sentences in English can be translated to sentences (equations) in algebra.

For example, the sentence "8 more than a number is 3" can be translated into algebra in this way:

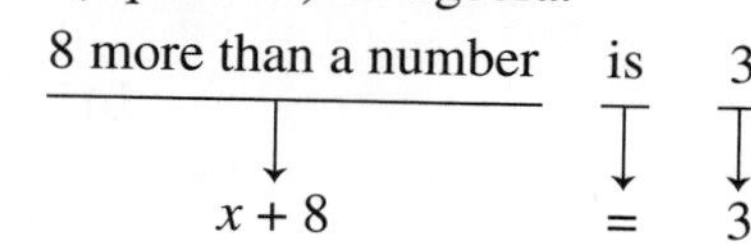

Now that it is an equation, we can solve it:

$$x + 8 = 3$$
$$x + 8 + (-8) = 3 + (-8)$$
$$x = -5$$

Does this answer make sense? Is it true that 8 more than -5 is 3?

It's true visually:

+8
1 2 3 4 5 6 7 8
−5 0 3

It's also true mathematically:

$$-5 + 8 = 3$$
$$3 = 3 \quad \text{True} \checkmark$$

EXAMPLE 2

Translate each of the following sentences into an equation, and find the requested number. Solve and check each answer. Write a sentence answering each question.

a) A number decreased by 8 is -6. What is the number?

b) 10 more than a number totals 3. What is the number?

PROCEDURE: For each, the legend is Let x = the number.

ANSWER: a)

$$x - 8 = -6$$
$$x - 8 + 8 = -6 + 8$$
$$x = 2$$

Isolate the variable by adding $+8$ to each side.

Check $x = 2$: $2 - 8 = -6$

$-6 = -6$ True ✓

SENTENCE: The number is 2.

b)

$$x + 10 = 3$$
$$x + 10 + (-10) = 3 + (-10)$$
$$x = -7$$

Isolate the variable by adding -10 to each side.

Check $x = -7$: $-7 + 10 = 3$

$3 = 3$ True ✓

SENTENCE: The number is –7.

EXAMPLE 3

Translate each of the following sentences into an equation, and find the requested number. Solve and check each answer. Write a sentence answering each question.

a) Four times a number is -18. What is the number?

b) Two-thirds of a number is 10. What is the number?

PROCEDURE: For each, the legend is Let x = the number.

ANSWER: a)

$$4x = -18$$
$$\frac{4x}{4} = \frac{-18}{4}$$
$$x = -\frac{9}{2}$$

Isolate the variable by dividing each side by 4.

Check $x = -\frac{9}{2}$:

$$4 \cdot \left(-\frac{9}{2}\right) = -18$$
$$\frac{4}{1} \cdot \left(-\frac{9}{2}\right) = -18$$
$$-\frac{36}{2} = -18$$
$$-18 = -18 \text{ True ✓}$$

SENTENCE: The number is $-\frac{9}{2}$.

b)

$$\frac{2}{3} \cdot x = 10$$
$$\frac{3}{2} \cdot \frac{2}{3} \cdot x = 10 \cdot \frac{3}{2}$$
$$1 \cdot x = \frac{10}{1} \cdot \frac{3}{2}$$
$$x = 15$$

Isolate the variable by multiplying each side by $\frac{3}{2}$.

Check $x = 15$:

$$\frac{2}{3} \cdot 15 = 10$$
$$\frac{2}{3} \cdot \frac{15}{1} = 10$$
$$\frac{30}{3} = 10$$
$$10 = 10 \text{ True ✓}$$

SENTENCE: The number is 15.

YOU TRY IT 2

Translate each of the following sentences into an equation, and find the requested number. Solve and check each answer, then write a sentence. Use Examples 2 and 3 as guides.

For each, the legend is ______________________________

a) 12 more than a number is –6. What is the number?

Sentence: ____________________

b) Five-fourths of a number is 15. What is the number?

Sentence: ____________________

c) 8 less than a number is –1. What is the number?

Sentence: ____________________

d) Six times a number is 21. What is the number?

Sentence: ____________________

Translating Expressions Containing Two Operations

Some expressions contain more than one operation, as in

"The **sum** of 5 and *twice* a number."

This suggests that we will be adding two terms together, 5 and $2x$: $5 + 2x$. An expression that means the same thing is "5 **more than** *twice* a number," which is written

$$2x + 5.$$

EXAMPLE 4

Translate each of the following expressions into the language of algebra.

a) 7 more than three times a number

b) 8 less than one-half of a number

PROCEDURE: Let $x =$ the number.

ANSWER: a) $3x + 7$ b) $\frac{1}{2}x - 8$

YOU TRY IT 3

Translate each of the following expressions into the language of algebra. Here, use the variable x to represent the unknown number. Use Example 4 as a guide.

a) 6 less than half of a number

b) The sum of four times a number and 9

c) The sum of 10 and one-third of a number

d) 10 more than five times a number

Think about it

Consider this algebraic expression: $2x + 10$.
Try to find more than one way to translate it into English.

____

____

Translating Equations Containing Two Operations

The expressions containing two operations can also be a part of an equation. Remember that the word *is* means *equals.*

EXAMPLE 5

Translate each of the following sentences into an equation, and find the requested number. Solve and check the answer. Write a sentence answering the question.

a) The sum of 3 and twice a number is –9. What is the number?

b) 10 less than one-third of a number is 3. What is the number?

PROCEDURE: For each, the legend is Let $x =$ the number.

ANSWER: a)

$$3 + 2x = -9$$ Isolate the variable by adding -3 to each side.

$$3 + (-3) + 2x = -9 + (-3)$$ The left side becomes $0 + 2x$.

$$2x = -12$$ Divide each side by 2.

$$\frac{2x}{2} = \frac{-12}{2}$$

$$x = -6$$

Check $x = -6$: $3 + 2(-6) = -9$

$3 + (-12) = -9$ True ✓

SENTENCE: The number is -6.

b)

$$\frac{1}{3}x - 10 = 3$$ Isolate the variable by adding $+10$ to each side.

$$\frac{1}{3}x - 10 + 10 = 3 + 10$$ The left side becomes $\frac{1}{3}x + 0$.

$$\frac{1}{3}x = 13$$ Multiply each side by $\frac{3}{1}$.

$$\frac{3}{1} \cdot \frac{1}{3}x = 13 \cdot 3$$

$$1x = 39$$

$$x = 39$$

Check $x = 39$: $\frac{1}{3} \cdot 39 - 10 = 3$

$13 - 10 = 3$ True ✓

SENTENCE: The number is 39.

YOU TRY IT 4

Translate each of the following sentences into an equation, and find the requested number. Solve and check the answer, then write a sentence answering the question. Use Example 5 as a guide.

For each, the legend is ____

a) The sum of three times a number and 8 is 2. What is the number?

b) 2 more than five times a number is -18. What is the number?

c) 3 less than four times a number is 21. What is the number?

d) 6 less than half of a number is -10. What is the number?

You Try It Answers: Section 10.3

YTI 1 a) $x + 12$ b) $\frac{5}{4}x$ c) $x - 8$

d) $2x$ e) $x + 8$ f) $\frac{1}{2}x$

g) $x - 15$ h) $10x$

i) $20 + x$ j) $x - 1$

YTI 2 Legend: Let $x =$ the number.

a) $x + 12 = -6$; The number is -18.

b) $\frac{5}{4}x = 15$; The number is 12.

c) $x - 8 = -1$; The number is 7.

d) $6x = 21$; The number is $\frac{7}{2}$.

YTI 3 a) $\frac{1}{2}x - 6$ b) $4x + 9$

c) $10 + \frac{1}{3}x$ d) $5x + 10$

YTI 4 Legend: Let $x =$ the number.

a) $3x + 8 = 2$; The number is -2.

b) $5x + 2 = -18$; The number is -4.

c) $4x - 3 = 21$; The number is 6.

f) $\frac{1}{2}x - 6 = -10$; The number is -8.

Focus Exercises: Section 10.3

Translate each of the following expressions into the language of algebra. Here, use the variable x to represent the number.

1. 9 more than a number

2. A number increased by 12

3. 5 less than a number

4. A number decreased by 7

5. Three-eighths of a number

6. Seven-sixths of a number

7. Twice a number

8. Five times a number

9. One-fourth of a number

10. Half of a number

11. 18 decreased by a number

12. 12 increased by a number

13. The sum of 9 and a number

14. The difference of a number and 3

15. The product of 8 and a number

16. The product of one-fifth and a number

17. The sum of twice a number and 4

18. The sum of 10 and twice a number

19. The sum of half of a number and 7

20. The sum of 15 and twice a number

21. 1 more than three times a number

22. 3 more than twice a number

23. 8 less than one-third of a number

24. 11 less than half of a number

For each of the following, find the requested number. Use the techniques in this section: write a legend for the unknown value, translate the sentence into an equation, solve and check the answer, and write a sentence that answers the question.

25. 9 more than a number is 6.
What is the number?

26. A number increased by 12 is 5.
What is the number?

27. A number increased by 9 is -5.
What is the number?

28. 6 more than a number is -3.
What is the number?

29. 13 less than a number is -8.
What is the number?

30. A number decreased by 10 is -1.
What is the number?

31. A number decreased by 6 is -12.
What is the number?

32. 5 less than a number is -9
What is the number?

33. Three-eighths of a number is 12.
What is the number?

34. Seven-sixths of a number is 21.
What is the number?

35. Four-ninths of a number is -8.
What is the number?

36. Three-tenths of a number is -24.
What is the number?

37. Twice a number is -5.
What is the number?

38. Four times a number is 18.
What is the number?

39. Six times a number is 14.
What is the number?

40. Eight times a number is -36.
What is the number?

41. The sum of twice a number and 4 is 18.
What is the number?

42. The sum of 10 and twice a number is 34.
What is the number?

43. The sum of half of a number and 7 is 13. What is the number?

44. The sum of $\frac{1}{3}$ of a number and 2 is -5. What is the number?

45. The sum of 5 times a number and 3 is -7. What is the number?

46. The sum of 6 times a number and 9 is -9. What is the number?

47. 1 more than three times a number is 16. What is the number?

48. 3 more than twice a number is 25. What is the number?

49. 8 more than five times a number is -7. What is the number?

50. 9 more than four times a number is 1. What is the number?

51. 1 less than one-third of a number is 9. What is the number?

52. 11 less than half of a number is 2. What is the number?

53. 3 less than one-fourth of a number is -5. What is the number?

54. 10 less than one-fifth of a number is -3. What is the number?

SECTION 10.4 Solving Applications

Objectives

In this section, you will learn to:

- Set up a legend for one or two unknown values.
- Identify a formula for a given situation.
- Solve an application using algebra.

To successfully complete this section, you need to understand:

- Solving applications (1.7)
- Translating expressions (9.1)
- Solving equations (10.2)
- Solving problems (10.3)

Introduction

Here is a typical application situation:

> A rectangle has a perimeter of 44 inches. The length is one inch more than twice the width. What are the dimensions of the rectangle?

If you don't know the answer immediately, that's okay. This section will teach you a step-by-step approach to solving application situations, also known as word problems and story problems.

The following guidelines will help you stay organized because they offer a step-by-step approach.

Guidelines for Mastering an Application Problem

1. Overview: Read the application through once to get a general idea of what it involves (don't be overwhelmed). Then read the application through more carefully, and start identifying key information, such as known and unknown values.

2. Legend: Decide how many unknown values the application is suggesting and use a variable (usually x) to represent each unknown value; use a legend to easily identify the representations.

3. Diagram: If possible, draw a diagram: label the diagram appropriately with both known and unknown values.

4. Formula: Identify a formula that fits the information; from that formula, develop an equation. Solve the equation; check the answer to see if it is a solution to the equation and if it makes sense given the application.

5. Conclusion: Always write the solution in a complete sentence. If possible, be sure to use words that indicate the correct unit of measure, such as feet, miles, hours, pounds, and so forth.

Caution It's important to follow all of these guidelines, but it's not necessary to do them in this exact order. After the overview, it might be appropriate to draw a diagram, then write the formula, and then set up the legend.

Let's take a look at each guideline, one at a time.

Guideline 1: Read the Application Situation

Solving applications is not an instantaneous process. If you tackle solving applications with a step-by-step approach, you can break a large problem into smaller pieces that eventually fit together completely.

Let's consider this typical application situation:

> Ky-lee lives in Los Angeles and every day drives 18 miles through the L.A. traffic to work. She is able to average 24 miles per hour. How much time does it take her to get to work?

Do you know the answer immediately? Most of us do not because we are not able to think quickly enough to know the answer after reading the problem through for the first time. That's why we have these guidelines.

Guideline 2: Determine the Legend for One Unknown Value

In every application situation, there is a lot of information, as well as a question to be answered. In the preceding situation, there is:

1. the information about the distance Ky-lee's drives (18 miles),
2. the fact that she averages 24 miles per hour, and
3. a question asking us to find the amount of time it takes her to get to work.

The question at the end of the problem usually indicates what the unknown value is. The answer to the question is a number. Since we're going to use algebra to find the answer, we will use a variable, typically x, to represent that number.

In the situation presented, there is only one unknown value: the amount of time it takes Ky-lee to get to work. We set up a legend to help us define the variable representation:

Legend: Let x = the time (in hours) it takes Ky-lee to get to work

Notice this about the legend: It defines what the variable x is going to represent.
It says x represents a *number*, an amount of *time*.

The legend is important because it helps you organize your thoughts, and when you finish the problem—by solving an equation—you'll know what the solution means.

For example, if you end the equation with $x = \frac{3}{4}$, then you know that's the amount of time and can answer the question: "It takes Ky-lee $\frac{3}{4}$ of an hour to get to work."

EXAMPLE 1

Identify the unknown value in the last sentence of each of these application problems. Set up a legend to define the variable representation of the unknown value.

a) Two of the angles in a triangle measure 30° and 50°. What is the measure of the third angle?
b) Monica drove 150 miles to get to the Human Resources Trainers Convention. It took her 3 hours to get there. What was her average rate of speed while driving?
c) A rectangle has a perimeter of 54 inches and a length of 20 inches. What is the width of the rectangle?

PROCEDURE: Each of these has only one unknown value. It can be identified from the last sentence:

ANSWER:
a) Legend: Let x = the measure of the third angle.
b) Legend: Let x = Monica's average rate of speed.
c) Legend: Let x = the width of the rectangle.

YOU TRY IT 1

Identify the unknown value in the last sentence of each of these application problems. Set up a legend to define the variable representation of the unknown value. Use Example 1 as a guide.

a) Marjorie took a trip up the East Coast. The total distance she drove was 540 miles, and the total amount of time she spent driving was 12 hours. What was her average rate of speed for the duration of the trip?

Legend: ______________________________

b) A triangle has one angle that measures 47° and another angle that measures 79°. What is the measure of the third angle?

Legend: ______________________________

c) Bette wants to use 60 yards of fencing to enclose a rectangular corral. She wants the width to be 12 yards. What will the length of the corral be?

Legend: ______________________________

Guideline 2: Determine the Legend for Two Unknown Values

Sometimes, a situation has more than one unknown value. In this case, there will always be a statement of comparison between them. The comparison is found in one of the sentences of the situation.

Here are some sentences that compare two unknown values. The comparison phrase is underlined and the unknown values are in bold:

1. The **length** <u>is 3 feet longer than</u> the **width**.
2. Cindy's **score on the second test** <u>was 8 fewer points than</u> her **score on the first test**.
3. It took **Trahn** <u>1 hour longer than</u> **Pam** to complete the bicycle course.
   (Here, the unknown values are **Trahn's *time*** and **Pam's *time***.)
4. **Amy** took <u>twice as long as</u> **Mark** to finish the quiz.
   (Here, the unknown values are **Amy's *time*** and **Mark's *time***.)

Each of these fits this pattern:

The first unknown value <u>compared to</u> **a second unknown value.**

You might ask, "Which unknown do I make x, the first or the second? Does it matter?"

Yes, it matters, and the individual variable, x, will always be the *second* one mentioned. The first unknown is being compared to x.

EXAMPLE 2

Identify the first unknown value, the comparison, and the last unknown value in each of these sentences. Also, decide which one should be represented by *just x* and set up a legend.

a) The length is 3 feet longer than the width.

b) Cindy's score on the second test was 8 fewer points than her score on the first test.

c) It took Trahn 1 hour longer than Pam to complete the bicycle course.

d) Amy took twice as long as Mark to finish the quiz.

e) The height is 4 feet less than twice the length.

ANSWER:

First Unknown	Comparison	Second Unknown	*Part* of the Legend
a) Length	3 longer (more) than	The width	$x =$ **the width**
b) Second test score	8 fewer than	First test score	$x =$ **first test score**
c) Trahn's riding time	1 longer (more) than	Pam's riding time	$x =$ **Pam's riding time**
d) Amy's time	Twice	Mark's time	$x =$ **Mark's time**
e) Height	4 less than twice	The length	$x =$ **the length**

YOU TRY IT 2

Underline the first unknown value, the comparison, and the last unknown value in each of these sentences. Decide which one should be represented by just x and set up a legend. Use Example 2 as a guide.

a) Sarah wants to build a pig pen using 36 feet of fencing. Her design is a simple rectangle in which the width is half of the length. What will the dimensions (length and width) of the pen be?

Legend: ______________________________

b) A new photocopy machine can print twice as many copies as an older machine. If, together, they printed 540 copies, how many copies did each one print?

Legend: ______________________________

c) In a right triangle (in which one of the angles is known to be 90°), the measure of the smallest angle is 10° less than the measure of the middle angle. What are the measures of the smallest and middle angles?

Legend: ______________________________

d) Tom needs to cut a 6-foot board (72 inches) into two pieces. The bigger piece is to be 12 inches longer than the smaller piece. What will be the lengths of the two pieces?

Legend: ______________________________

e) Harry just passed on and left $87,000 for his two grandchildren's college funds. Harry anticipated that the younger grandchild, Nate, would pay more for college (when he is old enough) than would his sister, Katie, since she is already a high school senior. For this reason, Harry's will states that Nate's college fund is to receive $15,000 more than Katie's. How much will each child's college fund receive from their grandfather's gift?

Legend: ______________________________

Think about it

When a problem has two unknowns, why is it better to express both in terms of one variable, x, rather than one in terms of x and the other in terms of y?

____

____

Guideline 2: Interpret the First Unknown in a Comparison

We have just seen how to write the legend for the *second* unknown in a comparison. Now let's look at the legend for the *first* unknown.

If the second unknown is represented by just x, the first unknown will be written in terms of x, based on the statement of comparison.

EXAMPLE 3

Set up a legend for both unknown values based on the comparison given.

a) The length is 3 feet longer than the width.

b) Cindy's score on the second test was 8 points fewer than her score on the first test.

c) It took Trahn 1 hour longer than Pam to complete the bicycle course.

d) Amy took twice as long as Mark to finish the quiz.

e) The height is 4 feet less than twice the length.

PROCEDURE: Let x represent the second unknown value, then use the comparison to decide the first unknown value.

ANSWER:

	First Unknown	Comparison	Second Unknown	Legend
a)	Length	3 longer (more) than	Width	$x =$ width $x + 3 =$ length
b)	Second test score	8 fewer than	First test score	$x =$ first test score $x - 8 =$ second test score
c)	Trahn's riding time	1 longer (more) than	Pam's riding time	$x =$ Pam's time $x + 1 =$ Trahn's time
d)	Amy's time	Twice	Mark's time	$x =$ Mark's time $2x =$ Amy's time
e)	Height	4 less than twice	Length	$x =$ the length $2x - 4 =$ the height

YOU TRY IT 3

Underline the first unknown value, the comparison, and the last unknown value in each of these sentences. Set up a legend for the two unknown values. Use Example 3 as a guide.

a) Sarah wants to build a pig pen using 36 feet of fencing. Her design is a simple rectangle in which the width is half of the length. What will the dimensions (length and width) of the pen be?

Legend: ______________________________

____

b) A new photocopy machine can print twice as many copies as an older machine. If, together, they printed 540 copies, how many copies did each one print?

Legend: ______________________________

____

c) In a right triangle (in which one of the angles is known to be 90°), the measure of the smallest angle is 10° less than the measure of the middle angle. What are the measures of the smallest and middle angles?

Legend: ______________________________

____

d) Tom needs to cut a 6-foot board (72 inches) into two pieces. The bigger piece is to be 12 inches longer than the smaller piece. What will be the lengths of the two pieces?

Legend: ______________________________

____

e) Harry just passed on and left $87,000 for his two grandchildren's college fund. Harry anticipated that the younger grandchild, Nate, would pay more for college (when he is old enough) than would his sister, Katie, since she is already a high school senior. For this reason, Harry's will states that Nate's college fund is to receive $15,000 more than Katie's. How much will each child's college fund receive from their grandfather's gift?

Legend: ______________________________

____

Guideline 3: Draw a Diagram

Some diagrams are easy to draw, such as rectangles and triangles. Sometimes, you can be creative and show a diagram, or picture, with other situations as well. Drawing a diagram, as in Examples 4 and 5, can help organize the information.

EXAMPLE 4 Set up a legend, and draw a diagram for the following application.

Suki's children, Hideko and Mariko, like to help her collate and staple her tests together. This semester, Suki is giving 120 final exams. If Hideko can collate and staple twice as many as Mariko, how many exams will each collate and staple?

PROCEDURE: We can draw two different stacks of tests, one representing Hideko's amount and the other representing Mariko's amount.

Legend: Let x = The number of tests that Mariko can collate and staple;

$2x$ = The number of tests that Hideko can collate and staple.

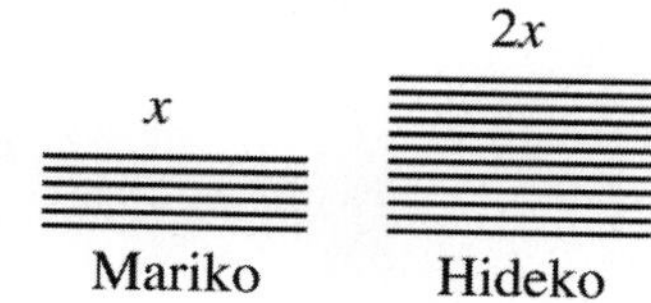

EXAMPLE 5 Set up a legend, and draw a diagram for the following application.

The length of a rectangular patio is 15 feet more than the width. If the perimeter of the patio is 78 feet, what are the length and width?

PROCEDURE: In the legend, length is being compared to width. Draw a diagram and label the known and unknown values.

Legend: Let x = the width of the patio;

$x + 15$ = the length of the patio.

$x + 15$

x Perimeter = 78 x

$x + 15$

YOU TRY IT 4 *Set up a legend, and draw a diagram for the following applications. Use Examples 4 and 5 as guides.*

a) In a right triangle, the measure of the smallest angle is 10° less than the measure of the middle angle. What are the measures of the smallest and middle angles?

b) A 40-inch board is cut into two pieces so that the longer piece is three times the length of the shorter piece. What are the lengths of the two cut pieces?

c) Bette wants to use 60 yards of fencing to enclose a rectangular corral. She wants the width to be 12 yards. What will the length of the corral be?

d) A new photocopy machine can print twice as many copies as an older machine. If, together, they printed 540 copies, how many copies did each one print?

Guideline 4: Identify a Formula and Develop the Equation

To solve any application we must approach the problem in a methodical manner. We need to recognize known values and unknown values. We need to identify an equation—a formula—that will allow us to use our algebraic techniques to answer the question.

The generic formula we'll use is:

The sum of all of the parts equals the whole.

This generic formula is the basis of some of the formulas in geometry. In particular, the generic formula generates the perimeter formulas for both the

Rectangle: Perimeter $= 2 \cdot \text{Length} + 2 \cdot \text{Width}$ and

Triangle: Perimeter $= a + b + c$

Side lengths are a, b, and c,
Angle measures are A, B, and C.

as well as the formula for the sum of the angles in a triangle:

$$A + B + C = 180°.$$

In a right triangle, one angle is known to be 90°:

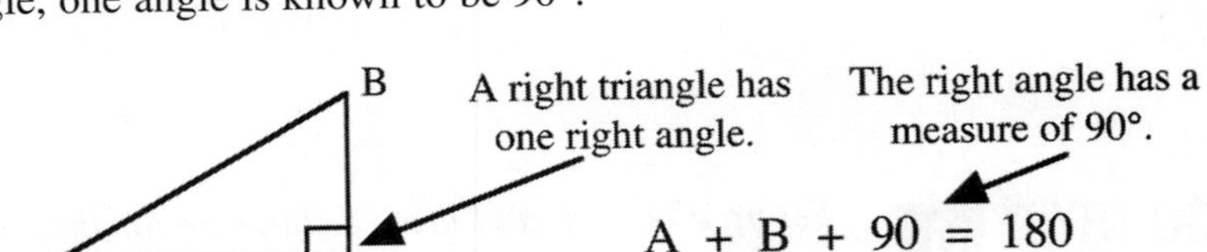

The generic formula—**the sum of all of the parts equals the whole**—is not restricted to just geometric formulas, it relates to other situations, many of which might not have a ready-made formula.

Each of the following situations uses the generic formula.

EXAMPLE 6

For each situation, create an equation using the generic formula. Use words to describe the parts and the whole in the equation.

a) A board is cut into two pieces.
b) An inheritance is split between two people.
c) A photocopying job is split between two machines.

ANSWER: a) Length of shorter piece + length of longer piece = total length of the board

b) First person's share + second person's share = total inheritance

c) Number of copies from first + number of copies from second = total number of copies

In this section, you will also see the motion formula $d = r \cdot t$, distance = rate × time. This one is not based on the generic formula.

EXAMPLE 7 Identify the formula that pertains to each application situation.

a) Two of the angles in a triangle are 30° and 50°. Find the measure of the third angle.

b) Monica drove 150 miles to get to the Human Resources Trainers Convention. It took her 3 hours to get there. What was her average rate of speed while driving?

c) A rectangle has a perimeter of 54 inches and a length of 20 inches. What is the width of the rectangle?

d) In a small town's election for mayor, there was a total of 540 votes cast. If the winner received 70 votes more than the loser, how many votes did each candidate receive?

ANSWER: a) The sum of the angles in a triangle is 180°: $\boldsymbol{A + B + C = 180}$

b) Distance = Rate · Time: $\boldsymbol{D = r \cdot t}$

c) Perimeter = 2 · Length + 2 · Width: $\boldsymbol{P = 2 \cdot L + 2 \cdot W}$

d) Generic: Number of winner's votes + number of loser's votes = total votes: $\boldsymbol{W + L =}$ **Total**

YOU TRY IT 5 *Identify the formula that pertains to each application situation. Use Examples 7 and 8 as guides.*

a) In a right triangle, the measure of the smallest angle is 10° less than the measure of the middle angle. What are the measures of the smallest and middle angles?

b) A 40-inch board is cut into two pieces so that the longer piece is three times the length of the shorter piece. What are the lengths of the two cut pieces?

c) Bette wants to use 60 yards of fencing to enclose a rectangular corral. She wants the width to be 12 yards. What will the length of the corral be?

d) A new photocopy machine can print twice as many copies as an older machine. If, together, they printed 540 copies, how many copies did each one print?

Guideline 5: Write the Solution in Sentence Form

Everything discussed so far leads to an algebraic equation that we must solve to answer the question asked.

Once the equation has been solved, it's important to check to see if the solution makes sense, and then write a complete sentence answering the question. In the sentence, be sure to include the correct units of measure, such as *feet*, *dollars*, *pounds*, *degrees*, and so on.

Solving Application Situations

Let's use the guidelines outlined at the beginning of this section to solve an application situation. Remember, don't try to solve the problem all at once. Also, be neat and organized in your work.

EXAMPLE 8

Tim was disgusted with his performance on his first test and crumpled it up without really paying attention to the grade. Determined to do better on the next test, he studied hard and received a score of 88 points. His instructor also wrote Tim's total score for both tests on the test: Total = 146 points. In light of this, how many points did Tim receive on his first test?

PROCEDURE: Use the following as guidelines to help set up the problem.

ANSWER:

a) How many unknowns are there? There is one unknown value.

b) Set up the legend: Let x = Tim's score on the first test.

c) Draw and label a diagram:

Teacher's Gradebook		
Grades:	Test 1	Test 2
Tim	x	88

d) Identify a formula: The sum of the parts = the whole.

Score on first test + score on second test = total score

$$x + 88 = 146$$ Isolate the variable by adding -88 to each side.

$$x + 88 + (-88) = 146 + (-88)$$

$$x = 58$$

Our legend tells us x = Tim's score on the first test, so his first test score was 58 points.

e) Answer the question with a sentence: Tim received 58 points on the first test.

Does this answer make sense? We can check by adding the two test scores together; they should add to 146:

$$\begin{array}{r} 58 \\ +\ 88 \\ \hline 146 \end{array}$$ Yes!

EXAMPLE 9

In a right triangle, the middle angle is 20° more than the smallest angle. What are the measures of the smallest and middle angles?

PROCEDURE: Use the following as guidelines to help set up the problem. Remember, in a right triangle, the largest angle is 90°.

PROCEDURE:

a) How many unknowns are there? There are two unknown values.

b) Set up the legend: Let x = the measure of the smallest angle;
$x + 20$ = the measure of the middle angle.

c) Draw and label a diagram:

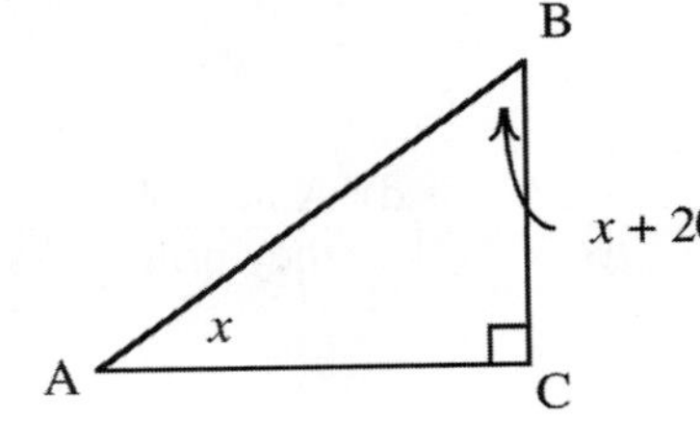

d) Identify a formula: The sum of the angles in a triangle is 180°.

$$A + B + C = 180°$$ Place the angle measures into the formula.

$$(x) + (x + 20) + 90 = 180$$ Remove the parentheses.

$$x + x + 20 + 90 = 180$$ Combine like terms.

$$2x + 110 = 180$$ Isolate the variable by first adding −110 to each side.

$$2x + 110 + (-110) = 180 + (-110)$$

$$2x = 70$$ Divide each side by 2.

$$\frac{2x}{2} = \frac{70}{2}$$ Simplify.

$$x = 35$$

Our legend tells us $x =$ the measure of the smallest angle, so the smallest angle is 35°.

The legend also tells us the middle angle measures $x + 20$, so the middle angle is $35 + 20 = 55°$.

e) Answer the question with a sentence: The smallest angle is 35°, and the middle angle is 55°.

Do these answers make sense? We can check by adding the three angle measures together; they should add to 180°:

$$\begin{array}{r} 35 \\ 55 \\ +\ 90 \\ \hline 180 \end{array}$$ Yes!

Caution In a situation with two unknown values, don't stop after find the value of x; x applies to one unknown value only. Use the legend to find the value of the other unknown.

YOU TRY IT 6

Solve each application situation completely. Write a legend, draw a diagram, identify a formula, solve the equation, and write a sentence answering the question. If necessary, use a separate sheet of paper. Use Examples 9 and 10 as guides.

a) Marjorie took a trip up the East Coast. The total distance she drove was 540 miles, and the total amount of time she spent driving was 12 hours. What was her average rate of speed for the duration of the trip?

b) Bette wants to use 60 yards of fencing to enclose a rectangular corral. She wants the width to be 12 yards. What will the length of the corral be?

c) In a right triangle, the measure of the smallest angle is 10° less than the measure of the middle angle. What are the measures of the smallest and middle angles?

d) A new photocopy machine can print twice as many copies as an older machine. If, together, they printed 540 copies, how many copies did each one

You Try It Answers: Section 10.4

YTI 1

a) **Legend:** Let $x =$ Marjorie's average rate of speed.

b) **Legend:** Let $x =$ the measure of the third angle.

c) **Legend:** Let $x =$ the length of the corral.

YTI 2

a) **Legend:** Let $x =$ the length of the rectangle.

b) **Legend:** Let $x =$ the number of copies from the older machine.

c) **Legend:** Let $x =$ the length of the middle angle.

d) **Legend:** Let $x =$ the measure of the smaller piece.

e) **Legend:** Let $x =$ the amount that Katie's fund receives.

YTI 3

a) **Legend:** Let $x =$ the length of the rectangle;
$\frac{1}{2}x =$ the width of the rectangle.

b) **Legend:** Let $x =$ the number of copies from the older machine;
$2x =$ the number of copies from the newer machine.

c) **Legend:** Let $x =$ the measure of the middle angle;
$x - 10 =$ the measure of the smallest angle.

d) **Legend:** Let $x =$ the length of the smaller piece;
$x + 12 =$ the length of the bigger piece.

e) **Legend:** Let $x =$ the amount that Katie receives;
$x + 15{,}000 =$ the amount that Nathan receives.

YTI 4

a) **Legend:** Let $x =$ the measure of the middle angle;
$x - 10 =$ the measure of the smallest angle.

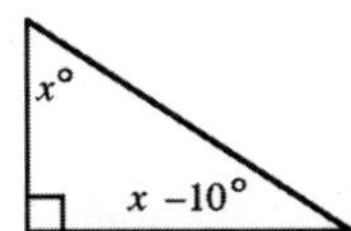

b) **Legend:** Let $x =$ the length of the shorter piece;
$3x =$ the length of the longer piece.

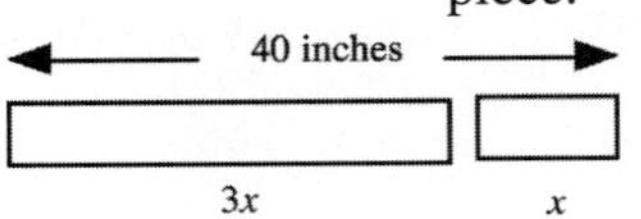

c) **Legend:** Let $x =$ the length of the corral.

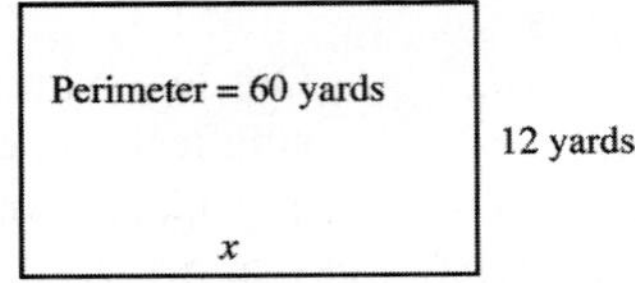

d) **Legend:** Let $x =$ the number of copier, the older machine can print;
$2x =$ the number of copies the newer machine can print.

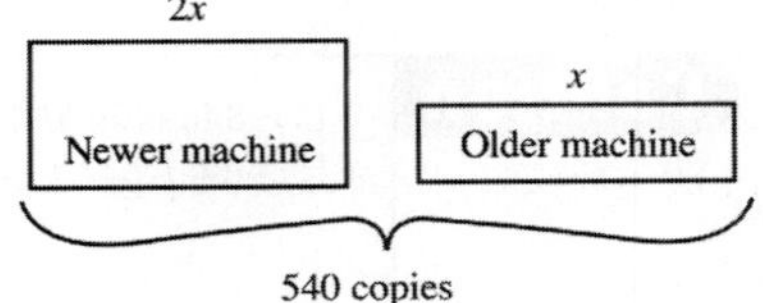

YTI 5

a) Sum of the angles in a triangle is 180:
$A + B + C = 180$

b) Sum of the parts = whole: Length of shorter piece + length of longer piece = total

c) Perimeter = $2 \cdot$ Length + $2 \cdot$ width:
$P = 2 \cdot L + 2 \cdot W$

d) Sum of the parts = whole: New machine's copies + old machine's copies = total copies

YTI 6

a) Marjorie's average rate of speed was 45 miles per hour.

b) The length of the corral will be 18 yards.

c) The smallest angle is 40°, and the middle angle is 50°.

d) The older machine printed 180 copies; the newer one printed 360 copies.

Focus Exercises: Section 10.4

For each, set up the legend, draw a diagram, identify the formula, and create and solve the equation. Be sure to write the answer as a sentence.

1. The perimeter of a rectangle is 178 inches. If the length is 58 inches, what is the width?

2. The perimeter of a square is 152 inches. What is the length of each side of the square?

3. Two of the angles in a triangle measure 108° and 37°. What is the measure of the third angle?

4. Lisa wants to plant a garden in her backyard. Her plan is to make the garden rectangular so that the length is 16 feet. She's planning to use the 58 feet of chicken wire to completely surround the garden (as a perimeter). What should the width of the garden be so that she can use all 58 feet of fencing?

5. Adrienne did not score well on her first test. She studied much harder for her second test and got a score of 95. Her teacher indicated that her two test scores totaled 168 points. What was Adrienne's score on the first test?

6. Anthony received scores of 87 points and 85 points on his first two tests. His goal, by the end of the third test, is to have a total score of 270 points. (This would give him an average score of 90.) How many points will Anthony need to score on his third test to reach his goal?

7. This Saturday, Margo plans to ride her bike 42 miles from her home to the beach. If she is able to average 12 miles per hour, how long will it take her to get there?

8. Every Friday, Andy rides his bike to work. The route he takes is 9 miles long. If he can average 15 miles per hour, how long does it take him to ride to work?

9. In a recent school PTA election, two candidates were running for president. Of the 120 votes cast, Mrs. Jenkins received 16 fewer votes than Mr. Daniels. How many votes did each candidate receive?

10. A 30-inch wire is to be bent into an isosceles triangle so that the longest side is 12 inches, and the other two sides are the same length. What is the length of each shorter side?

11. Jorge and Darush participated in the Boys and Girls Club "Walk for Hunger." Together, the boys walked a total of 58 kilometers. If Darush walked 4 kilometers less than Jorge, how many kilometers did each boy walk?

12. Uncle Jackson has two nieces, Kiesha and Tanya; Tanya is in her first year of college. In his will, he decides to give Tanya $15,000 more than he gives Kiesha so that Tanya can pay for her education. If he leaves them $107,000 in his will, how much will each niece receive?

13. In a triangle, one of the angles is 100°. The measure of the middle angle is 24° more than the measure of the smallest angle. What are the measures of these two angles?

14. In a right triangle, the measure of the middle angle is 18° more than the measure of the smallest angle. What are the measures of these two angles?

15. After two tests, Carol has a total score of 170. The score on her first test was 8 points higher than the score on her second test. How many points did she receive on each test?

16. Omar's score on his third math test was 89. His score on the first test was 5 points higher than his score on the second test. His total for all three tests is 264. What were Omar's scores on the first two tests?

17. A rectangular playground has a perimeter of 180 feet. If the length is 12 feet longer than the width, what are the dimensions of the playground?

18. A 24-foot wire is to be cut into two pieces so that the longer piece is 3 times the length of the shorter piece. What is the length of each piece?

19. A triangle has a perimeter of 38 inches. The longest side is 17 inches. The shortest side is 3 inches less than the middle side. What are the lengths of the shorter and middle sides?

20. A rectangular field has a perimeter of 772 feet. If the length is 8 feet longer than twice the width, what are the dimensions of the field?

Chapter 10 Review

Section 10.1 Solving Equations Containing One Operation

CONCEPT	EXAMPLE
An equation is a mathematical sentence in which one expression = another expression. To solve an equation, we must **isolate the variable** on one side of the equal sign. The **solution** of an equation makes the equation true, and we can check the solution by replacing the variable with that number.	Is 3 the solution to $5x - 4 = 2x + 5$? Check $x = 3$: $5(3) - 4 = 2(3) + 5$ $15 - 4 = 6 + 5$ $11 = 11$ True ✓
The Addition Property of Equations: We may add any number, c, to each side of an equation.	If $a = b$, then $a + c = b + c$ $x - 5 = -9$ $x - 5 + 5 = -9 + 5$
The Division Property of Equations: We may divide each side of an equation by any number, c (as long as $c \neq 0$).	If $a = b$, then $\frac{a}{c} = \frac{b}{c}$ $-3x = 12$ $\frac{-3x}{-3} = \frac{12}{-3}$
The Multiplication Property of Equations: We may multiply each side of an equation by any number, c (as long as $c \neq 0$).	If $a = b$, then $c \cdot a = c \cdot b$ $\frac{5}{2}x = 20$ $\frac{2}{5} \cdot \frac{5}{2}x = \frac{2}{5} \cdot 20$

Section 10.2 Solving Equations Containing Two Operations

CONCEPT	EXAMPLE
When an equation has two operations, first isolate the variable term by clearing the constant; add its opposite to each side of the equation. Then clear any coefficient using the Division or Multiplication Properties of Equations.	$-2x + 9 = 15$ $-2x + 9 + (-9) = 15 + (-9)$ $-2x + 0 = 6$ $-2x = 6$ $\frac{-2x}{-2} = \frac{6}{-2}$ $x = -3$

CONCEPT	EXAMPLE
If an equation has a variable term on each side of the equal sign, add the opposite of one of them to each side of the equation. This will clear the variable term from one side and place all variable terms on the other side.	$5x + 2 = 8x + 11$ $5x + (-5x) + 2 = 8x + (-5x) + 11$ $0 + 2 = 3x + 11$ $2 = 3x + 11$ $2 + (-11) = 3x + 11 + (-11)$ $-9 = 3x + 0$ $-9 = 3x$ $\frac{-9}{3} = \frac{3x}{3}$ $-3 = x$ $x = -3$
Sometimes, in preparing an equation for solving, it is necessary to simplify one (or both) of the sides. We might need to first distribute a number to a quantity, and we might need to combine like terms.	$2x - 10 + 5x = 2(3x - 4)$ $7x - 10 = 6x - 8$ $7x + (-6x) - 10 = 6x + (-6x) - 8$ $x - 10 = 0 - 8$ $x - 10 = -8$ $x - 10 + 10 = -8 + 10$ $x + 0 = 2$ $x = 2$

Section 10.3 Problem Solving

CONCEPT	EXAMPLE
Some expressions contain more than one operation.	"The sum of 5 and twice a number" suggests adding two terms together, 5 and $2x$: $5 + 2x$.
The equal sign can be translated in English as *equals*, *is*, or *totals*.	The sum of 5 and twice a number is 17: $5 + 2x = 17$.

Section 10.4 Solving Applications

CONCEPT	EXAMPLE
When reading through a problem, there will be known and unknown values. We use a **legend** to identify the unknown value(s) in terms of a single variable, such as x. When a problem has one unknown value, the legend is Let $x =$ the unknown value.	The workers at a factory cast 300 ballots in an election for a new union president. Running for the position were Henrietta Howard and Benson Fox. Henrietta received 145 votes. How many votes did Benson receive? **Legend:** Let $x =$ the number of votes Benson received.
When a problem has two unknown values, the problem will have a statement of comparison: the first unknown value compared to a second unknown value. Use this statement of comparison to help set up the legend. In a comparison, x always represents the second unknown mentioned. The other unknown is in terms of x, based on the comparison.	The workers at a factory cast 300 ballots in their election for a new union vice president. Running for the position were Minnie Drover and Abigail Reyes. Minnie received 70 more votes than Abigail received. How many votes did each candidate receive? The comparison: Minnie received 70 more than Abigail received. **Legend:** Let $x =$ the number of votes Abigail received (the second unknown); $x + 70 =$ the number of votes Minnie received (the first unknown).
Guidelines for mastering an application problem: **1.** **Overview**. Read the application through once to get a general idea of what it involves (don't be overwhelmed); then, read the application through more carefully, and start identifying key information, such as known and unknown values.	**1.** The workers at a factory cast 300 ballots in their election for a new union vice president. Running for the position were Minnie Drover and Abigail Reyes. Minnie received 70 more votes than Abigail received. How many votes did each candidate receive?
2. **Legend**. Decide how many unknown values the application is suggesting and use a single variable to represent the unknown value(s); use a legend to easily identify the representations.	**2.** Legend: Let $x =$ the number of votes Abigail received; $x + 70 =$ the number of votes Minnie received.
3. **Diagram**. If possible, draw a diagram and label it with known and unknown values.	**3.** $x + 70$ (Minnie) x (Abigail)
4. **Formula**. Identify a formula that fits the information; from that formula, develop an equation. Solve the equation; check the answer to see if it is a solution to the equation and if it makes sense, given the application.	**4.** Abigail's votes + Minnie's votes = total votes $x + x + 70 = 300$ $x = 115$
5. **Conclusion**. Always write the solution in a complete sentence. If possible, be sure to use words that indicate correct units of measure, such as feet, miles, hours, pounds, and so on.	**5.** Abigail received 115 votes and Minnie received 185 votes.

Chapter 10 Review Exercises

Section 10.1

Determine if the replacement value given is a solution to the equation.

1. $3x - 8 = -2; x = -2$

2. $c + 5 = 2c - 3; c = 8$

Solve. Be sure to check each answer.

3. $m - 7 = -10$

4. $y - 5 = -4$

5. $x - 12 = -2$

6. $-7 = k - 10$

7. $12 = p + 20$

8. $1 = h + 12$

9. $-5 = x + 9$

10. $-2 = y + 1$

11. $-4 = w - 8$

12. $y - \frac{7}{4} = \frac{9}{4}$

13. $c - \frac{2}{7} = \frac{8}{7}$

14. $k + \frac{7}{10} = \frac{3}{10}$

15. $2n = 82$

16. $9x = -45$

17. $-3y = -87$

18. $-28 = 7m$

19. $12 = -8y$

20. $-70 = -5x$

21. $\frac{3}{8}y = -6$

22. $-\frac{2}{5}k = -8$

23. $-\frac{4}{3}a = 6$

24. $\frac{7}{9}y = -21$

25. $-\frac{7}{15}k = -\frac{14}{9}$

26. $-\frac{7}{4}a = \frac{5}{8}$

Section 10.2

Solve. Be sure to check each answer.

27. $6x - 3 = 45$

28. $8x + 19 = 3$

29. $16 = -8 - 4c$

30. $-5y - 6 = -11$

31. $8 = -\frac{5}{8}k - 7$

32. $\frac{1}{7}y + 9 = -1$

33. $6 - 5y = 4 - 3y$

34. $8 + 5x = 2 + 8x$

35. $6y - 2 = 3y + 13$

36. $5p + 8 = -7p + 56$

37. $9x + 17 = 7x - 5$

38. $5x - 82 = 15x + 8$

39. $-y - 12 + 6y = 9 + 8y$

40. $7x - 5 - 6x = -x + 19$

41. $6(y - 5) = 7y - 3$

42. $5x - 7 = 9(x - 3)$

43. $7x + 18 = 8(x + 7)$

44. $8p + 3 - 6p = 12 - 4p + 15$

Section 10.3

Translate each of the following expressions into the language of algebra. Here, use the variable x to represent the number.

45. 12 less than a number

46. Four-ninths of a number

47. 23 decreased by a number

48. 9 increased by a number

49. The sum of half of a number and 16

50. The sum of 5 and twice a number

51. 6 less than twice a number

52. 15 more than half of a number

For each of the following, write a legend for the unknown value, translate the sentence into an equation, solve and check the answer, and write a sentence that answers the question.

53. 7 more than a number is -3. What is the number?

54. A number decreased by 12 is -4. What is the number?

55. Four-fifths of a number is 32. What is the number?

56. Twice a number is 11. What is the number?

57. The sum of $\frac{3}{4}$ of a number and 9 is 3. What is the number?

58. 7 more than twice a number is -15. What is the number?

59. 5 more than four times a number is 41. What is the number?

60. 1 less than one-sixth of a number is -4. What is the number?

Section 10.4

For each problem, set up the legend, draw a diagram, identify the formula, and write and solve the equation. Be sure to write the answer as a sentence.

61. The perimeter of Sufen's rectangular painting canvas is 168 centimeters. If the width is 37 centimeters, what is the length?

62. Enzio drives 245 miles to visit his girlfriend in college. If he is able to average 70 miles per hour, how long should it take him to get there?

63. In her savings account, Auntie Em has set aside a total of $1,200 for Dorothy, toward a college education, and for Toto, to go to dog obedience school. If Toto is to receive $950 less than Dorothy, how much will each receive?

64. Florida's score on her second math test was 15 points higher than her score on the first test. Her total for both tests is 169. What were Florida's scores on her first two math tests?

65. Karl and Kristen are participating in a Relay for Life bicycle event to raise money for cancer research. They agreed before the event that Karl would ride 5 miles more than Kristen. If they rode a total of 63 miles, how many miles did each of them ride?

66. Luigi's triangular garden has a perimeter of 53 yards. The longest side is 24 yards. The shortest side is 7 yards less than the middle side. What are the lengths of the shorter and middle sides?

67. In a triangle, the measure of the largest angle is 100°. The measure of the middle angle is three times the measure of the smallest angle. What are the measures of the middle and smallest angles?

68. The total attendance for the weekend Cucamonga Car Show was 3,400 people. On Sunday there were 850 fewer people in attendance than on Saturday. What was the attendance each day?

Chapter 10 Test

Solve and simplify. Check each answer.

1. $y - 16 = -9$

2. $-9x = 12$

3. $\frac{7}{30} = k + \frac{13}{30}$

4. $\frac{4}{5}x = -8$

5. $6x - 11 = 31$

6. $17 = -13 + \frac{3}{5}x$

7. $16 - 4w = -29 - 9w$

8. $8x - 5 = 25 - 2x$

9. $2x + 5 - 9x = 3x - 15$

10. $30 - y = 4(6 - y)$

For each of the following, the legend is Let x = the number. Translate the sentence into an equation, and solve. Write a sentence that answers the question.

11. 14 more than a number is -11. What is the number?

12. 9 less than twice a number is 13. What is the number?

Write a legend, set up and solve an equation, and write a sentence answering the question.

13. Josh is to receive a total of $450 for trimming the Mr. Elson's trees, a job which will take Josh two days to complete. After the first day, Mr. Elson paid him $185. How much will Mr. Elson pay Josh after the second day?

14. A 72-inch board is to be cut into two pieces so that the longer piece is twice as long as the shorter piece. Find the length of each piece.

15. The perimeter of a triangle is 42 inches. One side is 18 inches long. The second side is 2 inches longer than the third side. What are the lengths of the second and third sides?

16. In a right triangle, the smallest angle is 24° smaller than the middle angle. What are the measures of the smallest and middle angle?

17. Tunde and Marta are married and share their income. Tunde earns $1,500 per year less than Marta. If their total annual income is $47,500, how much does each earn?

18. A rectangular field has a total perimeter of 128 feet. The width is 24 feet less than the length. What are the dimensions of the field?

Chapters 9 and 10 Cumulative Review

Evaluate each expression.

1. $2 + (-2)$

2. $9 - 11$

3. $-8 - 8$

4. $-10 + 7$

5. $9 - (-6)$

6. $-22 + 48$

7. $-15 - 79$

8. $60 + (-76)$

9. $-71 - (-36)$

10. $-0.89 - 1.7$

11. $-\frac{31}{90} + \frac{11}{90}$

12. $-\frac{4}{9} - \frac{1}{6}$

13. $7 \cdot (-5)$

14. $(-6)(-6)$

15. $\frac{30}{-5}$

16. $2 + (-8) - (-7) + 9$

17. $-81 \div (-9)$

Solve. Be sure to write the answer as a sentence.

18. Yesterday, Ajay's checkbook had a balance of −\$123. Fortunately, today he received a check for the \$175 that his brother owed him, and he deposited it in the bank to cover his account. What is the new balance?

Evaluate each expression using the Order of Operations. Show all steps.

19. $(-3)^4$

20. $-3 - \sqrt{25}$

21. $6 - 5^2$

22. $-4 - |-5|$

Simplify by combining like terms, if possible.

23. $2x^3 + 8x^3$

24. $-2y + (-7y)$

25. $3w + 2w - 9w$

26. $-x^4 + 5x - 3x^4 - x$

Find the product.

27. $6(-x^2)$

28. $7(3y)$

Rewrite each expression using the Distributive Property.

29. $4(x - 3)$

30. $-5(9w - 2)$

Solve. Be sure to check each answer.

31. $x - 7 = -3$

32. $24 = -9 - 3c$

33. $-3 - 4y = 15 - 7y$

34. $7x + 16 = 5(2x - 1)$

Translate the sentence into an equation and solve. Write a sentence that answers the question.

35. 5 less than three times a number is -11. What is the number?

For each problem, set up the legend, draw a diagram, identify the formula, and write and solve the equation. Be sure to write the answer as a sentence.

36. The acute angle measures in a right triangle are such that the measure of the larger acute angle is 26° more than the measure of smallest angle. What are the measures of the two acute angles? (Hint: In a right triangle, one angle is 90°.)

37. Two friends, Becca and Andrea, won a lottery worth \$26,500. From their prearranged agreement, Andrea is to receive \$3,500 more than Becca receives. How much of the money will each receive?

Answers

Chapter 1 Focus Exercise Answers

Section 1.1

1. Answers may vary. One possibility is: The whole numbers start at zero, and the counting numbers start at one. **3.** ones ten seventy **5.** thousands hundred seven hundred thousand **7.** 400 + 80 + 6 **9.** 200,000 + 3,000 + 50 + 8 **11.** Four hundred ninety-eight **13.** five hundred seven thousand, ninety-three **15.** 518 **17.** 280,034 **19.** 1,000,426 **21.** 70 **23.** 800 **25.** 600 **27.** 1,700 **29.** 7,000 **31.** 3,000 **33.** 36,000 **35.** 700,000 **37.** 30,000 **39.** 650,000 **41.** 600,000 **43.** 1,000,000 **45.** 4,000,000 **47.** 10,000,000 **49.** The Rialto Unified School District's budget revenue was about $193,000,000. **51.** The total number of gallons of gas used was about 5,000,000,000. **53.** California had about 6,200,000 students enrolled in grades K–12.

Section 1.2

1. Associative Property of Addition **3.** Additive Identity **5.** Commutative Property of Addition **7.** 36 **9.** 28. **11.** 31 **13.** 39

15.	**17.**	**19.**	**21.**	**23.**
= 5 + (5 + 2)	= 8 + (2 + 4)	= 6 + (4 + 5)	= 9 + (1 + 8)	= 7 + (3 + 6)
= (5 + 5) + 2	= (8 + 2) + 4	= (6 + 4) + 5	= (9 + 1) + 8	= (7 + 3) + 6
= 10 + 2	= 10 + 4	= 10 + 5	= 10 + 8	= 10 + 6
= 12	= 14	= 15	= 18	= 16

Section 1.3

1. 59 **3.** 557 **5.** 887 **7.** 6,875 **9.** 62,925 **11.** 757,597 **13.** 104,799 **15.** 1,000,000 **17.** 104 **19.** 817 **21.** 17,011 **23.** 143,900 **25.** 252 **27.** 102 **29.** 3,312 **31.** 25 **33.** 5 **35.** 54 **37.** 57 **39.** 93 **41.** 73 **43.** 293 **45.** 5,425 **47.** 24,835 **49.** 6,731 **51.** 4,293 **53.** 133,343 **55.** 193,422 **57.** Dionne's total contribution to the two charities was $2,133. **59.** Debbie's monthly payment was $79 less in 2004 than in 2003. **61.** The four agents have a combined experience of 80 years. **63. a)** The total attendance for the three-game series was 105,210. **b)** There were 12,777 more fans in attendance on Saturday than on Sunday. **65. a)** 595 meters **b)** 161 inches **c)** 82 feet

Section 1.4

1. 20 **3.** 28 **5.** 36 **7.** 54 **9.** 27 **11.** 35 **13.** 64 **15.** 49 **17.** 240 **19.** 420 **21.** 300 **23.** 2,400 **25.** 6,300 **27.** 2,700 **29.** 36,000 **31.** 480,000 **33.** 342 **35.** 1,849 **37.** 9,810 **39.** 88,825 **41.** 17,136 **43.** 32,768 **45.** Commutative Property of Multiplication **47.** Associative Property of Multiplication **49.** 168 cars can fit in the parking lot. **51.** Ignacio's truck can go 364 miles before it runs out of gas. **53.** The jet will travel 7,872 miles in 16 hours. **55.** Diane earned $414 that first week. **57.** The PTA's field trip program will have a total income of $5,508. **59.** The area of the soccer field is 1,680 square yards. **61.** The area of Wyoming is about 97,200 square miles.

Section 1.5

1. 5 **3.** 0 **5.** 4 **7.** 6 **9.** 9 **11.** 7 **13.** 10 **15.** 4 **17.** 15 **19.** 29 **21.** 37 **23.** 13 **25.** 12 r 7 **27.** 33 r 1 **29.** 118 r 7 **31.** 304 r 2 **33.** 6,009 r 2 **35.** 3,004 **37.** 13,050 **39.** 23 **41.** 73 **43.** 1002 r 6 **45.** 42 **47.** 84 **49.** 2,003 **51.** 1,025 **53.** Each person paid $23 to attend the concert. **55.** Carrie will need 57 boxes for all of the booklets. **57.** Each runner will run 29 miles.

Section 1.6

1. No **3.** Yes **5.** $n = 13$ **7.** $n = 35$ **9.** $n = 198$ **11.** $n = 123$ **13.** $n = 6{,}016$ **15.** $n = 1{,}101$ **17.** $n = 19$ **19.** $n = 14$ **21.** $n = 13$ **23.** $n = 1{,}480$ **25.** $n = 32$ **27.** $n = 47$

Section 1.7

1. Nate needs $89 more to pay for the Xbox. **3.** Adam will have $265 left to spend on other things. **5.** The city must collect $1,371 to equal the costs of operating the pool. **7.** They still need to produce 618 copies. **9.** Ajay pays $21 each month in union dues. **11.** a) He lost an average of 23 pounds each month. b) Lona's total weight loss will be 180 pounds. **13.** Aimee pays $4,500 in rent for a full year. **15.** The top side is 14 inches long. **17.** The length of the rectangle is 121 yards.

Chapter 1 Review Exercise Answers

1. number **2.** numeral **3.** digits **4.** operations **5.** evaluate **6.** perimeter **7.** area **8.** approximation **9.** identity **10.** factors **11.** addition **12.** quotient **13.** remainder **14.** variable **15.** coefficient **16.** constant **17.** solution **18.** legend **19.** multiple **20.** formula **21.** $700 + 20 + 4$ **22.** $6{,}000 + 800 + 7$ **23.** four hundred eight **24.** nine thousand, fifty-one **25.** two hundred six thousand, five **26.** five million, four hundred seventy thousand **27.** 107 **28.** 2,005 **29.** 508,041 **30.** 1,000,652 **31.** 640 **32.** 300 **33.** 1,450 **34.** 3,000 **35.** 600 **36.** 30,300 **37.** 126,500 **38.** 4,900 **39.** 31,000 **40.** 54,000 **41.** 250,000 **42.** 1,000 **43.** In 2003, the total number of full-time airline employees was about 510,000. **44.** In 2004, the U.S. population, was about 294,500,000. **45.** Multiplicative Identity **46.** Associative Property of Addition **47.** Commutative Property of Addition **48.** Additive Identity **49.** 16 **50.** 12 **51.** 60 **52.** 530 **53.** 550 **54.** 2,032 **55.** 1,721 **56.** 10,012 **57.** 110 **58.** 2,865 **59.** Brian burned 682 calories on the exercise bike that morning. **60.** Kaira received a total of 256 points on her first three tests. **61.** 564 centimeters **62.** 98 feet **63.** 24 **64.** 141 **65.** 45 **66.** 74 **67.** 647 **68.** 15,584 **69.** 848 **70.** 178 **71.** 180,207 **72.** 903,795 **73.** On average, there were 18,897 more fans in attendance at Washington home games than Chicago home games. **74.** Nevada is 13,845 square miles larger than Michigan. **75.** 56 **76.** 54 **77.** 28 **78.** 16 **79.** 35 **80.** 12 **81.** 40 **82.** 81 **83.** 120 **84.** 210 **85.** 1,800 **86.** 2,400 **87.** 7,200 **88.** 1,600 **89.** 63,000 **90.** 10,000 **91.** 225 **92.** 376 **93.** 637 **94.** 912 **95.** 1,204 **96.** 4,592 **97.** 2,088 **98.** 58,752 **99.** Associative Property of Multiplication **100.** Multiplication Property of 0 **101.** Distributive Property over Addition **102.** Commutative Property of Multiplication **103.** Marley drove 874 miles to and from work in March. **104.** Colin's basement floor is 646 square feet. **105.** 9 **106.** 7 **107.** 0 **108.** 8 **109.** 8 **110.** 7 **111.** 8 **112.** 9 **113.** 6 r 6 **114.** 6 r 1 **115.** 9 r 2 **116.** 6 r 2 **117.** 14 **118.** 23 **119.** 42 **120.** 86 **121.** 324 **122.** 171 r 1 **123.** 597 r 5 **124.** 314 r 6 **125.** 26 **126.** 64 **127.** 140 **128.** 3,041 **129.** 61 r 1 **130.** 73 r 23 **131.** 72 r 2 **132.** 108 r 45 **133.** Each member contributed $265. **134.** 13 classrooms are needed. **135.** No **136.** Yes **137.** Yes **138.** No **139.** $n = 8$ **140.** $n = 33$ **141.** $n = 453$ **142.** $n = 4{,}390$ **143.** $n = 14$ **144.** $n = 98$ **145.** $n = 1{,}360$ **146.** $n = 36$ **147.** Carlotta's sales need to be $3,160 on Monday to reach the $20,000 goal. **148.** Rhani will pay her parents $125 each month. **149.** On average, Antonio earned $19 in tips from each table. **150.** The length of the carpet is 27 yards.

Chapter 1 Test Answers

1. 700 **2.** 10,000 **3.** 580,000 **4.** Three hundred thousand, forty-five. **5.** 23,604,015 **6.** 8,640 **7.** 4,505 **8.** 558 **9.** 28 **10.** Multiplicative Identity **11.** Distributive Property of Multiplication over Addition **12.** Associative Property of Addition **13.** Commutative Property of Addition **14.** $n = 15$ **15.** $n = 49$ **16.** $n = 19$ **17.** Alfre needs another 126 signatures to reach 500. **18.** The length of the sandbox is 25 yards. **19.** Jerry spent $168 on his team's tickets. **20.** Each member raised an average of $215.

Chapter 2 Preparation Exercise Answers

1. 54 **2.** 32 **3.** 35 **4.** 27 **5.** 80 **6.** 2,400 **7.** 560 **8.** 180 **9.** 4,000 **10.** 12,000 **11.** 336 **12.** 833 **13.** 9 **14.** 9 **15.** 13 **16.** 25 **17.** 24 **18.** 36 **19.** 44 **20.** 106

Chapter 2 Focus Exercise Answers

Section 2.1

1. $6 \cdot 6 \cdot 6 = 216$ **3.** $15 \cdot 15 = 225$ **5.** 12 **7.** $5 \cdot 5 \cdot 5 \cdot 5 = 625$ **9.** $10 \cdot 10 \cdot 10 = 1{,}000$ **11.** 10^5 **13.** 10^4 **15.** $3 \cdot 10^2$ **17.** $48 \cdot 10^3$ **19.** $95 \cdot 10^5$ **21.** 7 **23.** 6 **25.** 9 **27.** 12

Section 2.2

1. 7 **3.** 26 **5.** 10 **7.** 45 **9.** 72 **11.** 8 **13.** 45 **15.** 51 **17.** 93 **19.** 72 **21.** 8 **23.** 18 **25.** 10 **27.** 36 **29.** 45 **31.** 31 **33.** 11 **35.** 12

Section 2.3

1. 41° F **3.** 10° C **5.** $z = 3$ **7.** $a = 8$ **9.** $P = 42$ **11.** $A = 18$ **13.** $W = 8$ **15.** $P = 30$ **17.** Mai's average rate of speed was 67 miles per hour. **19.** Bertie's average rate of speed was 59 miles per hour. **21.** It should take Hank 9 hours to complete the trip. **23.** Padam will need to average 64 miles per hour.

Section 2.4

1. 4, 8, 12, 16, 20, 24, 28, and 32 **3.** 7, 14, 21, 28, 35, 42, 49, and 56 **5.** 1 and 32; 2 and 16; 4 and 8 **7.** 1 and 28; 2 and 14; 4 and 7 **9.** 2 **11.** none of these **13.** 2 **15.** 5 **17.** 3 and 5 **19.** 2 and 3 **21.** 3 **23.** 2, 3, and 5 **25.** No. **27.** Yes. **29.** ... $5 \cdot 13 = 65$ is a composite factor of 715. **31.** ... 6, 14, 21, and 42 are composite factors of 966. **33.** Prime: 7, 23, and 41 Composite: 9, 8, 40, 15, 33, 32, 12, 51, and 50 Neither: 0 and 1

Section 2.5

1. $2 \cdot 3 \cdot 3 = 2 \cdot 3^2$ **3.** $3 \cdot 3 \cdot 7 = 3^2 \cdot 7$ **5.** $3 \cdot 5 \cdot 7$ **7.** $2 \cdot 2 \cdot 2 \cdot 2 \cdot 31 = 2^4 \cdot 31$ **9.** $2 \cdot 2 \cdot 2 \cdot 2 \cdot 3 \cdot 3 \cdot 5 = 2^4 \cdot 3^2 \cdot 5$ **11.** $3 \cdot 3 \cdot 3 \cdot 5 \cdot 7 = 3^3 \cdot 5 \cdot 7$ **13.** $2 \cdot 2 \cdot 5 = 2^2 \cdot 5$ **15.** $2 \cdot 2 \cdot 13 = 2^2 \cdot 13$ **17.** $2 \cdot 2 \cdot 19 = 2^2 \cdot 19$ **19.** $2 \cdot 7 \cdot 7 = 2 \cdot 7^2$ **21.** $2 \cdot 2 \cdot 31 = 2^2 \cdot 31$ **23.** $2 \cdot 2 \cdot 2 \cdot 5 \cdot 5 = 2^3 \cdot 5^2$

Section 2.6

1. $3 \cdot 5 = 15$ **3.** Relatively prime **5.** $2 \cdot 3 = 6$ **7.** $2 \cdot 2 \cdot 2 \cdot 3 = 24$ **9.** $2^2 \cdot 3^2 = 36$ **11.** $2^2 \cdot 3^1 \cdot 5^1 = 60$ **13.** $3^2 \cdot 7^1 = 63$ **15.** 15 **17.** 2 **19.** 5 **21.** 14 **23.** 50 **25.** 35 **27.** 30 **29.** Relatively prime **31.** 15 **33.** 8 **35.** 90

Chapter 2 Review Exercise Answers

1. $1 \cdot 1 \cdot 1 \cdot 1 \cdot 1 \cdot 1 \cdot 1 = 1$ **2.** $2 \cdot 2 \cdot 2 \cdot 2 = 16$ **3.** $3 \cdot 3 \cdot 3 \cdot 3 \cdot 3 = 243$ **4.** $4 \cdot 4 \cdot 4 = 64$ **5.** 16 **6.** $17 \cdot 17 = 289$ **7.** $20 \cdot 20 \cdot 20 = 8{,}000$ **8.** $10 \cdot 10 \cdot 10 \cdot 10 \cdot 10 \cdot 10 \cdot 10 = 10{,}000{,}000$ **9.** 10^3 **10.** 10^7 **11.** 10^5 **12.** 10^1 **13.** $7 \cdot 10^1$ **14.** $84 \cdot 10^2$ **15.** $3 \cdot 10^5$ **16.** $12 \cdot 10^5$ **17.** 6 **18.** 2 **19.** 3 **20.** 10 **21.** 14 **22.** 12 **23.** 7 **24.** 16 **25.** 6 **26.** 4 **27.** 17 **28.** 21 **29.** 9 **30.** 23 **31.** 30 **32.** 0 **33.** 16 **34.** 9 **35.** 30 **36.** 16 **37.** 9 **38.** 3 **39.** 5 **40.** 8 **41.** 212° F **42.** 59° F **43.** 50° C **44.** 25° C **45.** $A = 84$ **46.** $W = 16$ **47.** $A = 25$ **48.** $z = 2$ **49.** $a = 5$ **50.** $C = 6$ **51.** Tracey's average rate of speed was 13 miles per hour. **52.** Timara can fly 870 miles in 6 hours. **53.** It will take Charles 9 hours to get there. **54.** Peetey's average rate of speed was 29 centimeters per minute. **55.** 3, 6, 9, 12, and 15 **56.** 6, 12, 18, 24, and 30 **57.** 11, 22, 33, 44, and 55 **58.** 12, 24, 36, 48, and 60 **59.** 1 and 18; 2 and 9; 3 and 6. **60.** 1 and 36; 2 and 18; 3 and 12; 4 and 9; 6 and 6. **61.** 1 and 45; 3 and 15; 5 and 9. **62.** 1 and 60; 2 and 30; 3 and 20; 4 and 15; 5 and 12; 6 and 10. **63.** Prime: 17, 29, and 11 Composite: 15, 81, and 45 Neither: 0 **64.** Prime: 2, 61, 43, and 31 Composite: 70, 62, and 57 Neither: 1 **65.** 3 and 5 **66.** None of these **67.** 2 **68.** 2, 3, and 5 **69.** 3 **70.** 2 and 5 **71.** 5 **72.** 2 and 3 **73.** Yes. **74.** Yes. **75.** No. **76.** Yes **77.** ... $3 \cdot 13 = 39$ is a composite factor of 741. **78.** ... $5 \cdot 7 = 35$ is a composite factor of 1,470. **79.** $2 \cdot 2 \cdot 2 \cdot 2 = 2^4$ **80.** $2 \cdot 2 \cdot 11 = 2^2 \cdot 11$ **81.** $2 \cdot 5 \cdot 5 = 2 \cdot 5^2$ **82.** $2 \cdot 2 \cdot 2 \cdot 2 \cdot 2 \cdot 3 = 2^5 \cdot 3$ **83.** $5 \cdot 5 \cdot 5 = 5^3$ **84.** $2 \cdot 2 \cdot 3 \cdot 3 \cdot 5 = 2^2 \cdot 3^2 \cdot 5$ **85.** $5 \cdot 5 \cdot 13 = 5^2 \cdot 13$ **86.** $5 \cdot 5 \cdot 7 \cdot 7 = 5^2 \cdot 7^2$ **87.** 5 **88.** 8 **89.** 14 **90.** 18 **91.** Relatively prime **92.** 6 **93.** 12 **94.** 15 **95.** 30 **96.** 24 **97.** 45 **98.** Relatively prime **99.** $2^2 = 4$ **100.** $3^1 \cdot 5^2 = 75$ **101.** $2^1 \cdot 3^2 \cdot 7^1 = 126$

Chapter 2 Test Answers

1. $5 \cdot 5 \cdot 5 = 125$ **2.** $20 \cdot 20 = 400$ **3.** $74 \cdot 10^4$ **4.** $9 \cdot 10^2$ **5.** 4 **6.** 9 **7.** 27 **8.** 17 **9.** 50 **10.** 203° F **11.** 35° C **12.** $A = 28$ **13.** It will take Rogelio 7 hours to get there. **14.** Prime: 41, 19, and 2 Composite: 77 and 38 Neither: 1 **15.** 3 and 5 **16.** 2 and 3 **17.** None of these **18.** 2 **19.** $2 \cdot 2 \cdot 3 \cdot 7 = 2^2 \cdot 3 \cdot 7$ **20.** $2 \cdot 2 \cdot 2 \cdot 2 \cdot 5 = 2^4 \cdot 5$ **21.** $2 \cdot 2 \cdot 3 \cdot 3 \cdot 3 \cdot 5 = 2^2 \cdot 3^3 \cdot 5$ **22.** 8 **23.** 9 **24.** 14

Chapters 1 and 2 Cumulative Review Exercise Answers

1. Seventy thousand **2.** Five hundred thousand, twenty-six **3.** 500 **4.** 8,000 **5.** 8,000 **6.** 210,000 **7.** Commutative Property of Multiplication **8.** Additive Identity **9.** Distributive Property of Multiplication over Addition **10.** Associative Property of Addition **11.** 3,036 **12.** 2,001 **13.** 875 **14.** 9,429 **15.** 112 cm **16.** 262 in **17.** 450 yd^2 **18.** Gore received 254,921 more votes than Bush. **19.** 56,000 **20.** 4,620 **21.** 47 r 3 **22.** 52 **23.** There were a total of 510 photocopied pages made. **24.** Each teacher received 12 white board markers. **25.** $n = 27$ **26.** $n = 35$ **27.** Ben and Adrian need to raise $113 on Sunday to meet their goal. **28.** Each girl received 35 Red Vines. **29.** 729 **30.** 625 **31.** 10^4 **32.** 10^9 **33.** $6 \cdot 10^4$ **34.** $52 \cdot 10^5$ **35.** 8 **36.** 11 **37.** 7 **38.** 147 **39.** 8 **40.** 34 **41.** 140° F **42.** 45° C **43.** $a = 6$ **44.** $C = 4$ **45.** The jet's average speed was 435 miles per hour. **46.** Jasper will go 285 miles. **47.** Prime: 5, 31, and 43 Composite: 18 and 55 Neither: 1 **48.** 2, 3, and 5 **49.** None of these **50.** 2 and 3 **51.** 3 and 5 **52.** Yes. **53.** Yes **54.** ... $2 \cdot 17 = 34$ is a composite factor of 816. **55.** $2 \cdot 2 \cdot 2 \cdot 3 \cdot 7 = 2^3 \cdot 3 \cdot 7$ **56.** $2 \cdot 2 \cdot 3 \cdot 5 \cdot 5 = 2^2 \cdot 3 \cdot 5^2$ **57.** 16 **58.** 21

Chapter 3 Preparation Exercise Answers

1. 15 **2.** 1 **3.** 12 **4.** 24 **5.** 24 **6.** 36 **7.** 36 **8.** 40 **9.** 40 **10.** 60 **11.** 60 **12.** 18 **13.** 18 **14.** 14 **15.** 19 **16.** $n = 6$ **17.** $n = 12$ **18.** $n = 18$ **19.** 22 **20.** 20 **21.** 12 **22.** GCF = 5 **23.** GCF = 8 **24.** GCF = 18

Chapter 3 Focus Exercise Answers

Section 3.1

1. Improper fraction **3.** Complex fraction **5.** Mixed number **7.** Improper fraction **9.** $\frac{13}{9}$ **11.** $\frac{19}{8}$ **13.** $\frac{10}{3}$ **15.** $\frac{32}{7}$ **17.** $\frac{21}{4}$ **19.** $\frac{61}{10}$ **21.** $\frac{22}{3}$ **23.** $\frac{39}{4}$ **25.** $\frac{95}{8}$ **27.** $\frac{123}{8}$ **29.** $2\frac{1}{5}$ **31.** $3\frac{1}{4}$ **33.** $3\frac{3}{7}$ **35.** $3\frac{1}{3}$ **37.** $2\frac{3}{8}$ **39.** $6\frac{2}{5}$ **41.** $7\frac{2}{5}$ **43.** $11\frac{5}{7}$ **45.** $\frac{8}{45}$ **47.** $\frac{9}{25}$ **49.** $\frac{8}{15}$ **51.** $\frac{35}{48}$ **53.** $\frac{7}{6} = 1\frac{1}{6}$ **55.** $\frac{45}{8} = 5\frac{5}{8}$

Section 3.2

1. $\frac{3}{5}$ **3.** $\frac{9}{4} = 2\frac{1}{4}$ **5.** $\frac{4}{3} = 1\frac{1}{3}$ **7.** $\frac{3}{8}$ **9.** $\frac{1}{4}$ **11.** $\frac{5}{2} = 2\frac{1}{2}$ **13.** $\frac{2}{3}$ **15.** $\frac{4}{9}$ **17.** $\frac{5}{2} = 2\frac{1}{2}$ **19.** $\frac{2}{9}$ **21.** 5 **23.** 7 **25.** 5 **27.** $\frac{1}{3}$ **29.** $\frac{4}{11}$ **31.** $\frac{2}{3}$ **33.** $\frac{13}{5} = 2\frac{3}{5}$ **35.** $\frac{1}{3}$ **37.** $\frac{5}{6}$ **39.** $\frac{16}{5} = 3\frac{1}{5}$ **41.** 1 **43.** $\frac{3}{8}$ **45.** 23 **47.** 4

Section 3.3

1. $\frac{4}{45}$ **3.** $\frac{25}{42}$ **5.** $\frac{5}{6}$ **7.** $\frac{5}{28}$ **9.** $\frac{1}{6}$ **11.** $\frac{1}{3}$ **13.** $\frac{4}{33}$ **15.** $\frac{21}{50}$ **17.** 6 **19.** $\frac{2}{5}$ **21.** $\frac{6}{35}$ **23.** $\frac{4}{5}$ **25.** 10 **27.** 6 **29.** $1\frac{3}{4}$ **31.** 20 **33.** $4\frac{1}{2}$ **35.** $5\frac{5}{6}$ **37.** 32 **39.** 45 **41.** $19\frac{1}{2}$ **43.** $16\frac{1}{2}$ **45.** $\frac{2}{15}$ **47.** $\frac{3}{16}$ **49.** $\frac{3}{8}$ **51.** 6 **53.** 18 **55.** $\frac{1}{1000}$ **57.** $1\frac{3}{4}$ **59.** $1\frac{3}{5}$ **61.** $1\frac{4}{5}$ **63.** One-sixth of a cup of laundry detergent washes $\frac{1}{4}$ of a load. **65.** Pedro must get 36 questions correct to pass the class. **67.** The middle of the logo is $2\frac{3}{16}$ inches from the side and $1\frac{7}{8}$ inches from the bottom. **69.** 8 in^2 **71.** $\frac{3}{5}$ in^2

Section 3.4

1. $\frac{5}{3}$ **3.** 6 **5.** $\frac{1}{8}$ **7.** Undefined **9.** $\frac{21}{10} = 2\frac{1}{10}$ **11.** $\frac{2}{3}$ **13.** $\frac{2}{3}$ **15.** $\frac{3}{2} = 1\frac{1}{2}$ **17.** $\frac{4}{5}$ **19.** $\frac{4}{5}$ **21.** $\frac{16}{9} = 1\frac{7}{9}$ **23.** $\frac{3}{4}$ **25.** $\frac{15}{8} = 1\frac{7}{8}$ **27.** $\frac{6}{5} = 1\frac{1}{5}$ **29.** $\frac{2}{3}$ **31.** 1 **33.** $\frac{16}{15} = 1\frac{1}{15}$ **35.** 4 **37.** $\frac{12}{25}$ **39.** $\frac{3}{2} = 1\frac{1}{2}$ **41.** $\frac{10}{7} = 1\frac{3}{7}$ **43.** $\frac{5}{14}$ **45.** $\frac{4}{5} \cdot \frac{5}{4} = 1$ **47.** $7 \cdot \frac{1}{7} = 1$ **49.** $\frac{27}{70}$ **51.** $\frac{5}{6}$ **53.** 8 **55.** $\frac{2}{3}$ **57.** $\frac{1}{10}$ **59.** $\frac{5}{24}$ **61.** $\frac{9}{10}$ **63.** $\frac{25}{9} = 2\frac{7}{9}$ **65.** $\frac{27}{10} = 2\frac{7}{10}$

Section 3.5

1. $n = \frac{2}{3}$ **3.** $n = \frac{3}{2}$ or $1\frac{1}{2}$ **5.** $n = \frac{3}{5}$ **7.** $n = \frac{3}{8}$ **9.** $n = \frac{3}{4}$ **11.** $n = \frac{3}{4}$ **13.** $n = 10$ **15.** $n = 8$ **17.** $n = \frac{10}{9}$ or $1\frac{1}{9}$ **19.** $n = \frac{2}{3}$ **21.** $n = \frac{1}{2}$ **23.** $n = \frac{18}{35}$ **25.** $n = 6$ **27.** $n = 10$ **29.** $n = \frac{5}{2}$ or $2\frac{1}{2}$ **31.** $n = \frac{5}{8}$ **33.** $n = \frac{2}{3}$ **35.** $n = 7$ **37.** $n = \frac{5}{6}$ **39.** $n = \frac{20}{3}$ or $6\frac{2}{3}$ **41.** Marnay gives 10 lessons each day. **43.** Each dose will contain $\frac{1}{4}$ cup of cough syrup. **45.** 9 bows can be made from one spool. **47.** Yuan must complete 20 afternoon sessions to receive her certificate. **49.** It takes Tim $6\frac{1}{4}$ hours to clean all 25 classrooms.

Chapter 3 Review Exercise Answers

1. Mixed number **2.** Improper fraction **3.** Complex fraction **4.** Proper fraction **5.** $\frac{15}{8}$ **6.** $\frac{31}{9}$ **7.** $\frac{31}{6}$ **8.** $\frac{51}{4}$ **9.** $4\frac{3}{5}$ **10.** $4\frac{2}{3}$ **11.** $7\frac{7}{9}$ **12.** $8\frac{1}{2}$ **13.** $\frac{15}{28}$ **14.** $\frac{27}{10} = 2\frac{7}{10}$ **15.** $\frac{63}{8} = 7\frac{7}{8}$ **16.** $\frac{28}{15} = 1\frac{13}{15}$ **17.** $\frac{1}{3}$ **18.** $\frac{1}{4}$ **19.** $\frac{2}{9}$ **20.** $\frac{2}{5}$ **21.** $\frac{3}{11}$ **22.** $\frac{3}{4}$ **23.** $\frac{7}{3} = 2\frac{1}{3}$ **24.** $\frac{9}{4} = 2\frac{1}{4}$ **25.** $\frac{5}{2} = 2\frac{1}{2}$ **26.** $\frac{5}{4} = 1\frac{1}{4}$ **27.** $\frac{5}{2} = 2\frac{1}{2}$ **28.** $\frac{9}{4} = 2\frac{1}{4}$ **29.** $\frac{1}{4}$ **30.** $\frac{5}{2} = 2\frac{1}{2}$ **31.** 6 **32.** 8 **33.** $\frac{7}{15}$ **34.** $\frac{1}{3}$ **35.** $\frac{3}{5}$ **36.** $\frac{14}{27}$ **37.** $\frac{7}{9}$ **38.** $\frac{3}{14}$ **39.** $\frac{1}{20}$ **40.** $\frac{21}{20} = 1\frac{1}{20}$ **41.** $\frac{5}{6}$ **42.** 6 **43.** 5 **44.** $\frac{9}{20}$ **45.** 9 **46.** $\frac{5}{6}$ **47.** $\frac{49}{4} = 12\frac{1}{4}$ **48.** $\frac{38}{5} = 7\frac{3}{5}$ **49.** 45 **50.** $\frac{23}{2} = 11\frac{1}{2}$ **51.** 70 **52.** 32 **53.** $\frac{2}{15}$ **54.** $\frac{5}{7}$ **55.** $\frac{1}{10}$ **56.** $\frac{7}{2} = 3\frac{1}{2}$ **57.** $\frac{5}{3} = 1\frac{2}{3}$ **58.** $\frac{7}{2} = 3\frac{1}{2}$ **59.** There are 28 women in Ms. Grecu's class. **60.** There are 8 pounds of meat in 12 patties. **61.** 9 in^2 **62.** 3 in^2 **63.** $\frac{4}{9}$ **64.** 8 **65.** $\frac{1}{4}$ **66.** Undefined **67.** $\frac{11}{10} = 1\frac{1}{10}$ **68.** 1 **69.** $\frac{2}{7}$ **70.** 6 **71.** $\frac{7}{2} = 3\frac{1}{2}$ **72.** $\frac{10}{3} = 3\frac{1}{3}$ **73.** $\frac{13}{4} = 3\frac{1}{4}$ **74.** $\frac{1}{14}$ **75.** $\frac{3}{10}$ **76.** $\frac{16}{15} = 1\frac{1}{15}$ **77.** 3 **78.** $\frac{9}{28}$ **79.** $\frac{9}{16}$ **80.** $\frac{3}{2} = 1\frac{1}{2}$ **81.** $\frac{6}{5} = 1\frac{1}{5}$ **82.** $\frac{10}{3} = 3\frac{1}{3}$ **83.** $\frac{2}{3}$ **84.** $\frac{5}{6}$ **85.** $\frac{2}{9}$ **86.** $\frac{16}{3} = 5\frac{1}{3}$ **87.** $n = \frac{3}{2} = 1\frac{1}{2}$ **88.** $n = \frac{1}{4}$ **89.** $n = \frac{3}{2} = 1\frac{1}{2}$ **90.** $n = \frac{4}{3} = 1\frac{1}{3}$ **91.** $n = \frac{7}{10}$ **92.** $n = \frac{4}{5}$ **93.** $n = 20$ **94.** $n = 21$ **95.** $n = \frac{6}{5} = 1\frac{1}{5}$ **96.** $n = \frac{15}{4} = 3\frac{3}{4}$ **97.** $n = \frac{20}{3} = 6\frac{2}{3}$ **98.** $n = \frac{15}{16}$ **99.** $n = \frac{6}{7}$ **100.** $n = \frac{4}{3} = 1\frac{1}{3}$ **101.** $n = 3$ **102.** $n = \frac{6}{5} = 1\frac{1}{5}$ **103.** Tanya should run $6\frac{2}{3}$ miles each day next week. **104.** Dimitri must work 24 Saturdays to fulfill his 80-hour obligation. **105.** Seven portraits can fit on the wall side by side.

Chapter 3 Test Answers

1. $\frac{37}{5}$ **2.** $\frac{38}{15}$ **3.** $7\frac{3}{4}$ **4.** $7\frac{3}{7}$ **5.** $\frac{7}{10}$ **6.** $\frac{5}{2} = 2\frac{1}{2}$ **7.** 2 **8.** 26 **9.** $\frac{3}{4}$ **10.** $\frac{1}{2}$ **11.** $\frac{21}{2} = 10\frac{1}{2}$ **12.** 46 **13.** $\frac{15}{2}$ or $7\frac{1}{2}$ **14.** $\frac{3}{2}$ or $1\frac{1}{2}$ **15.** $11\frac{2}{3}$ in^2 **16.** $5\frac{1}{4}$ in^2 **17.** $\frac{2}{3}$ **18.** $\frac{4}{15}$ **19.** $\frac{12}{5} = 2\frac{2}{5}$ **20.** $n = \frac{2}{3}$ **21.** $\frac{5}{6} = n$ **22.** $\frac{2}{3}$ **23.** The original picture is 8 inches high. **24.** Each chocolate bar weighs $1\frac{1}{4}$ pounds.

Chapter 4 Preparation Exercise Answers

1. 326 **2.** 151 **3.** 5 **4.** 87 **5.** 6, 12, 18, 24, and 30 **6.** 9, 18, 27, 36, and 45 **7.** $45 = 3 \cdot 3 \cdot 5$ **8.** $60 = 2 \cdot 2 \cdot 3 \cdot 5$ **9.** 12 **10.** 18 **11.** 25 and 36 are relatively prime. **12.** 21 and 14 are not relatively prime. **13.** $\frac{17}{3}$ **14.** $\frac{13}{9}$ **15.** $4\frac{3}{5}$ **16.** $1\frac{11}{18}$ **17.** $\frac{2}{5}$ **18.** $\frac{4}{5}$ **19.** $\frac{5}{12}$ **20.** $\frac{2}{3}$

Chapter 4 Focus Exercise Answers

Section 4.1

1. 12 **3.** 28 **5.** 30 **7.** 60 **9.** 40 **11.** 40 **13.** 60 **15.** 150 **17.** 12 **19.** 30 **21.** 42 **23.** 252 **25.** 96 **27.** 75 **29.** 90 **31.** 300 **33.** 180 **35.** 600

Section 4.2

1. $\frac{7}{10} \times \frac{3}{3} = \frac{21}{30}$ **3.** $\frac{4}{9} \times \frac{2}{2} = \frac{8}{18}$ **5.** $\frac{9}{7} \times \frac{6}{6} = \frac{54}{42}$ **7.** $\frac{4}{15} \times \frac{3}{3} = \frac{12}{45}$ **9.** $\frac{3}{20} \times \frac{5}{5} = \frac{15}{100}$ **11.** $\frac{3}{8} \times \frac{10}{10} = \frac{30}{80}$ **13.** $\frac{7}{12} \times \frac{5}{5} = \frac{35}{60}$ **15.** $\frac{8}{25} \times \frac{4}{4} = \frac{32}{100}$ **17.** $\frac{6}{15}$ and $\frac{5}{15}$ **19.** $\frac{9}{12}$ and $\frac{8}{12}$ **21.** $\frac{4}{24}$ and $\frac{15}{24}$ **23.** $\frac{4}{18}$ and $\frac{3}{18}$ **25.** $\frac{30}{36}$ and $\frac{3}{36}$ **27.** $\frac{12}{18}$ and $\frac{14}{18}$ **29.** $\frac{16}{36}$ and $\frac{15}{36}$ **31.** $\frac{28}{60}$ and $\frac{5}{60}$

33. $\frac{3}{8}$ and $\frac{2}{8}$ **35.** $\frac{9}{15}$ and $\frac{2}{15}$ **37.** $\frac{5}{2}$ and $\frac{9}{2}$; $\frac{6}{4}$ and $\frac{4}{4}$; $\frac{1}{5}$ and $\frac{11}{5}$; $\frac{8}{9}$ and $\frac{11}{9}$

Section 4.3

1. 1 **3.** 1 **5.** $1\frac{1}{2}$ **7.** $1\frac{1}{3}$ **9.** $\frac{4}{7}$ **11.** $1\frac{3}{7}$ **13.** $1\frac{1}{2}$ **15.** $\frac{1}{2}$ **17.** $\frac{1}{2}$ **19.** $\frac{8}{11}$ **21.** 1 **23.** $1\frac{1}{2}$ **25.** $\frac{2}{5}$ **27.** 1 **29.** 1 **31.** $1\frac{1}{3}$ **33.** $1\frac{4}{7}$ **35.** $1\frac{1}{2}$ **37.** $\frac{3}{4}$ **39.** $\frac{3}{4}$ **41.** $\frac{3}{5}$ **43.** $\frac{7}{10}$ **45.** $\frac{3}{5}$ **47.** $1\frac{1}{3}$ **49.** $\frac{1}{4}$ **51.** 0 **53.** $\frac{1}{9}$ **55.** $\frac{3}{7}$ **57.** $\frac{3}{5}$ **59.** $\frac{1}{3}$ **61.** $\frac{6}{11}$ **63.** $\frac{1}{5}$ **65.** $\frac{3}{4}$ **67.** $\frac{3}{10}$ **69.** $\frac{7}{12}$ **71.** $\frac{2}{3}$

Section 4.4

1. $\frac{9}{10}$ **3.** $1\frac{1}{15}$ **5.** $\frac{23}{36}$ **7.** $\frac{15}{16}$ **9.** $\frac{1}{2}$ **11.** $1\frac{5}{12}$ **13.** $\frac{19}{28}$ **15.** $1\frac{1}{6}$ **17.** $1\frac{3}{8}$ **19.** $\frac{21}{50}$ **21.** $1\frac{11}{20}$ **23.** $1\frac{11}{18}$ **25.** $\frac{7}{24}$ **27.** $\frac{7}{18}$ **29.** $\frac{3}{10}$ **31.** $\frac{23}{30}$ **33.** $\frac{2}{9}$ **35.** $1\frac{5}{24}$ **37.** $1\frac{5}{9}$ **39.** $5\frac{3}{5}$ **41.** There are $1\frac{3}{8}$ pounds of meat in this recipe. **43.** The thickness of the top board is $1\frac{1}{8}$ inches. **45.** Carin must pour $\frac{3}{8}$ of a cup of milk from the new carton.

Section 4.5

1. $9\frac{4}{5}$ **3.** $12\frac{7}{9}$ **5.** $25\frac{5}{8}$ **7.** $25\frac{7}{18}$ **9.** 12 **11.** 14 **13.** $37\frac{1}{2}$ **15.** $5\frac{1}{2}$ **17.** $10\frac{5}{12}$ **19.** $21\frac{4}{9}$ **21.** $18\frac{7}{24}$ **23.** $66\frac{5}{12}$ **25.** Katie needs a total of $5\frac{5}{8}$ yards of material for the two projects. **27.** Toni has $4\frac{1}{12}$ cups of mixture. **29.** Giselle worked $7\frac{1}{4}$ hours on those projects that day.

Section 4.6

1. $2\frac{5}{9}$ **3.** $9\frac{4}{7}$ **5.** $1\frac{2}{5}$ **7.** $1\frac{2}{5}$ **9.** 3 **11.** 2 **13.** $2\frac{9}{20}$ **15.** $1\frac{13}{36}$ **17.** $2\frac{2}{5}$ **19.** $6\frac{5}{9}$ **21.** $4\frac{5}{9}$ **23.** $7\frac{11}{15}$ **25.** $4\frac{1}{3}$ **27.** $3\frac{4}{5}$ **29.** $1\frac{3}{4}$ **31.** $7\frac{5}{8}$ **33.** $5\frac{13}{24}$ **35.** $11\frac{11}{12}$ **37.** Sanjeer took $11\frac{3}{8}$ pounds of aluminum cans to be recycled. **39.** There are $14\frac{5}{8}$ yards of fabric left on the bolt. **41.** Kaitlin needs to be $1\frac{3}{4}$ inches taller. **43.** Qeesha owned $3\frac{7}{9}$ acres after the sale.

Chapter 4 Review Exercise Answers

1. 18 **2.** 42 **3.** 72 **4.** 75 **5.** 54 **6.** 180 **7.** 120 **8.** 240 **9.** $\frac{3}{4} \times \frac{7}{7} = \frac{21}{28}$ **10.** $\frac{5}{8} \times \frac{3}{3} = \frac{15}{24}$ **11.** $\frac{4}{5} \times \frac{9}{9} = \frac{36}{45}$ **12.** $\frac{4}{3} \times \frac{20}{20} = \frac{80}{60}$ **13.** $\frac{5}{20}$ and $\frac{8}{20}$ **14.** $\frac{28}{40}$ and $\frac{25}{40}$ **15.** $\frac{20}{45}$ and $\frac{21}{45}$ **16.** $\frac{8}{60}$ and $\frac{39}{60}$ **17.** $\frac{6}{5}$ and $\frac{7}{5}$; $\frac{2}{6}$ and $\frac{9}{6}$ **18.** $\frac{6}{9}$ and $\frac{11}{9}$; $\frac{9}{8}$ and $\frac{8}{8}$ **19.** $\frac{4}{5}$ **20.** $\frac{10}{11}$ **21.** $\frac{11}{15}$ **22.** $1\frac{1}{3}$ **23.** $\frac{3}{4}$ **24.** $\frac{2}{3}$ **25.** $\frac{4}{5}$ **26.** $\frac{4}{5}$ **27.** $1\frac{2}{5}$ **28.** $1\frac{3}{5}$ **29.** 2 **30.** $1\frac{1}{2}$ **31.** $\frac{1}{5}$ **32.** $\frac{5}{9}$ **33.** 0 **34.** $\frac{5}{12}$ **35.** $\frac{4}{5}$ **36.** $\frac{1}{3}$ **37.** $\frac{1}{5}$ **38.** $\frac{2}{3}$ **39.** $\frac{1}{2}$ **40.** $\frac{3}{5}$ **41.** $\frac{1}{6}$ **42.** $\frac{5}{9}$ **43.** $\frac{2}{3}$ **44.** $\frac{23}{24}$ **45.** $\frac{3}{10}$ **46.** $\frac{11}{12}$ **47.** $1\frac{1}{15}$ **48.** $1\frac{3}{8}$ **49.** $\frac{44}{45}$ **50.** $1\frac{7}{36}$ **51.** $\frac{1}{9}$ **52.** $\frac{1}{6}$ **53.** $\frac{7}{18}$ **54.** $\frac{1}{6}$ **55.** $\frac{1}{6}$ **56.** $\frac{17}{24}$ **57.** $\frac{3}{5}$ **58.** $\frac{7}{30}$ **59.** D'Neice had $\frac{1}{2}$ of a pizza left over. **60.** Mary burned $\frac{7}{10}$ of a cord of wood during the winter. **61.** $6\frac{2}{3}$ **62.** 7 **63.** $23\frac{1}{3}$ **64.** $10\frac{17}{30}$ **65.** $11\frac{1}{2}$ **66.** $4\frac{3}{5}$ **67.** $12\frac{7}{18}$ **68.** $3\frac{1}{4}$ **69.** Marco worked $14\frac{2}{3}$ hours that weekend. **70.** $4\frac{9}{20}$ inches of rain fell in Garberville on that day. **71.** $5\frac{1}{6}$ **72.** $1\frac{1}{2}$ **73.** $4\frac{11}{36}$ **74.** $8\frac{3}{10}$ **75.** $2\frac{3}{5}$ **76.** $\frac{2}{3}$ **77.** $3\frac{3}{5}$ **78.** $8\frac{13}{15}$ **79.** Marika gained $16\frac{3}{8}$ pounds during her first year. **80.** There are $2\frac{5}{6}$ yards of fabric left on the bolt.

Chapter 4 Test Answers

1. 60 **2.** 72 **3.** $\frac{3}{24}$ and $\frac{32}{24}$ **4.** $\frac{28}{40}$ and $\frac{15}{40}$ **5.** $\frac{2}{3}$ **6.** $\frac{3}{8}$ **7.** $1\frac{9}{20}$ **8.** $\frac{7}{36}$ **9.** $4\frac{2}{3}$ **10.** $10\frac{1}{6}$ **11.** $3\frac{4}{9}$ **12.** $\frac{17}{24}$ **13.** Ricardo grew a total of $1\frac{5}{16}$ inches those two months. **14.** Timina walked $6\frac{4}{15}$ miles that day. **15.** Digron's stock value increased $1\frac{3}{8}$ points that week. **16.** It rained $1\frac{11}{20}$ inches more that day.

Chapters 3 and 4 Cumulative Review Answers

1. $\frac{3}{10}$ **2.** $\frac{2}{3}$ **3.** 21 **4.** $\frac{4}{9}$ **5.** $1\frac{7}{8}$ **6.** $\frac{3}{4}$ **7.** $\frac{7}{15}$ **8.** $1\frac{2}{15}$ **9.** $\frac{3}{7}$ **10.** $6\frac{1}{6}$ **11.** $1\frac{1}{2}$ **12.** $2\frac{1}{3}$ **13.** The area is $10\frac{1}{2}$ square inches. **14.** The area is 7 square inches. **15.** $n = \frac{2}{3}$ **16.** $n = \frac{4}{9}$ **17.** 84 **18.** 150 **19.** Each team member must run $1\frac{3}{4}$ miles in the relay. **20.** Jeannie can cut 10 strips from the piece of construction paper. **21.** The design will appear $7\frac{1}{2}$ inches across and $6\frac{1}{4}$ inches high. **22.** Sun-Yee's weekend hourly wage is $12 per hour. **23.** 36 shingles can be placed on the north part of the house. **24.** Sondra has $6\frac{5}{12}$ cups of flour. **25.** Kahlil surpassed his previous best mark by $1\frac{7}{16}$ inches.

Chapter 5 Preparation Exercise Answers

1. One thousand, sixty-three **2.** 507 **3.** 71,000 **4.** 7,000 **5.** 617 **6.** 709 **7.** 577 **8.** 1,847 **9.** 1,016 **10.** 1,560 **11.** 47 **12.** 35 **13.** $n = 183$ **14.** $n = 19$ **15.** $\frac{7}{20}$ **16.** $\frac{11}{15}$ **17.** $\frac{10}{3}$ or $3\frac{1}{3}$ **18.** $\frac{63}{100}$ **19.** $\frac{3}{10}$ **20.** 2 **21.** $\frac{1}{3}$ **22.** $\frac{13}{20}$ **23.** $\frac{3}{8}$ **24.** $\frac{57}{100}$

Chapter 5 Focus Exercise Answers

Section 5.1

1. hundredths **3.** mixed number **5.** True **7.** False **9.** Three tenths **11.** Three **13.** Five tenths **15.** Eight thousandths **17.** Eight and two tenths **19.** Thirty-seven and four tenths **21.** Three and three tenths **23.** $\frac{15}{100}$ and 0.15 **25.** $2\frac{3}{10}$ and 2.3 **27.** $\frac{35}{1000}$ and 0.035 **29.** $29\frac{4}{10}$ and 29.4 **31.** $\frac{123}{1000}$ and 0.123 **33.** 0.4 **35.** 0.625 **37.** 0.7 **39.** 7.8 **41.** 0.09 **43.** 0.004 **45.** 4.09 **47.** 20.7 **49.** $\frac{9}{10}$ **51.** $\frac{34}{100}$ **53.** $\frac{593}{1,000}$ **55.** $\frac{2,817}{10,000}$ **57.** $\frac{8}{100}$ **59.** $\frac{4}{100}$ **61.** $\frac{52}{1,000}$ **63.** $\frac{1}{1,000}$ **65.** $\frac{25}{10}$ or $2\frac{5}{10}$ **67.** $\frac{955}{100}$ or $9\frac{55}{100}$ **69.** $\frac{308}{100}$ or $3\frac{8}{100}$ **71.** $\frac{5,284}{1,000}$ or $5\frac{284}{1,000}$ **73.** $0.\overline{3}$ **75.** $0.\overline{528}$ **77.** $10.3\overline{692}$ **79.** 0.555... **81.** 2.470470470... **83.** 0.58101010...

Section 5.2

1. 11.6 **3.** 10.6 **5.** 2.0 **7.** 3.0 **9.** 1.26 **11.** 1.39 **13.** 14.07 **15.** 18.05 **17.** 4.20 **19.** 4.00 **21.** 0.46 **23.** 0.39 **25.** 6.084 **27.** 1.010 **29.** .216 **31.** .340 **33.** .317 **35.** .300 **37.** $5.96 **39.** $14.04 **41.** $5.99 **43.** $108.00 **45.** $6.00 **47.** $3.80 **49.** 31 **51.** 83 **53.** 215 **55.** 1 **57.** $31 **59.** $20 **61.** $30 **63.** $100 **65.** Yat-Sun's GPA is about 3.5. **67.** Gabriella's average monthly electric bill is $53.85. **69.** Hank Aaron's batting average in 1969 was .300.

Section 5.3

1. 0.828 **3.** 1.501 **5.** 0.79 **7.** 20.41 **9.** 1.13 **11.** 20 **13.** 4.016 **15.** 10.006 **17.** 26.778 **19.** 22.437 **21.** 7.08 **23.** 5.453 **25.** 5.4 **27.** 0.55 **29.** 5.41 **31.** 2.972 **33.** 1.4 **35.** 5.71 **37.** 9.309 **39.** 5.47 **41.** The total is $36.67. **43.** The combined weight of the two turkeys was 35.07 pounds. **45.** Torii was 1.67 seconds behind Sean. **47.** 4.078 miles **49.** Claire needs to lose 16.6 more pounds to reach her goal. **51.** The third side is 0.444 inches long.

Section 5.4

1. 7.2 **3.** 0.36 **5.** 0.028 **7.** 2.1 **9.** 3.2 **11.** 0.48 **13.** 0.48 **15.** 5.49 **17.** 1.43 **19.** 0.034 **21.** 0.088 **23.** 0.008 **25.** 0.006 **27.** 0.0045 2 **29.** 0.00248 **31.** 0.0008 **33.** 0.1206 **35.** 0.90 = 0.9 **37.** 0.80 = 0.8 **39.** 1.00 = 1 **41.** 0.520 = 0.52 **43.** 1.500 = 1.5 **45.** 9.100 = 9.1 **47.** 0.170 = 0.17 **49.** 16.014 **51.** 20.00 = 20 **53.** 0.0520 = 0.052 **55.** 119 **57.** 8 **59.** 90.6 **61.** 376 **63.** 8 **65.** 120.6 **67.** 480 **69.** 401 **71.** 8,050 **73.** 1,300 **75.** Steve must pay a total of $25.21 for the batteries. **77.** Tanner must pay a total of $85.00 for the card.

Section 5.5

1. 0.9 **3.** 12.3 **5.** 9.67 **7.** 0.19 **9.** 0.164 **11.** 0.534 **13.** 0.405 **15.** 0.0665 **17.** $1.5\overline{6}$ **19.** $0.5\overline{3}$ **21.** $0.3\overline{09}$ **23.** $0.032\overline{6}$ **25.** 3.6 **27.** 1.17 **29.** 3.96 **31.** 70 **33.** 800 **35.** 20 **37.** 0.42 **39.** 0.1782 **41.** $0.50\overline{5}$ **43.** $0.\overline{663}$ **45.** 0.1875 **47.** 0.248 **49.** 2.5 **51.** 1.75 **53.** 1.6 **55.** 0.375 **57.** 0.65 **59.** 0.68 **61.** $0.8\overline{3}$ **63.** $1.\overline{2}$ **65.** $0.\overline{81}$ **67.** $0.5\overline{3}$ **69.** $0.\overline{108}$ **71.** $0.\overline{428571}$

Section 5.6

1. Jaime earns \$118.00 each day. **3.** Andy earns \$280.50 each week. **5.** Li earns \$8.56 per hour. **7.** Marcus earned, on average, \$19.25 each hour. **9.** The area of the dance floor is 1,239.75 square feet. **11.** The width of the pool house is 10.5 feet. **13.** The circumference of the table top is about 22.0 feet. **15.** The radius of the lobby is 12.5 feet. **17.** The price of each orange was \$1.15. **19.** The price of each can of soup was \$2.05. **21.** Ricky's car can travel 240.3 miles on a full tank of gas. **23.** Milo's car averaged 28.4 miles per gallon on that day. **25.** Linda's average rate of speed is 28 miles per hour. **27.** It takes Kyle 1.6 hours to get to the beach. **29.** Each pays \$22.36. **31.** On Sunday, Gabriella's hourly pay is \$12.78.

Chapter 5 Review Exercise Answers

1. decimal **2.** thousandths **3.** whole number **4.** dividend **5.** Seventy **6.** Seven hundredths **7.** Seven tenths **8.** Seven thousandths **9.** Seventeen thousandths **10.** Three hundredths **11.** Forty and six tenths **12.** Two hundred and five hundredths **13.** Six thousandths **14.** Five hundred nine and one tenth **15.** $\frac{23}{100}$ and 0.23 **16.** $4\frac{4}{10}$ and 4.4 **17.** $50\frac{8}{100}$ and 50.08 **18.** $\frac{76}{1,000}$ and 0.076 **19.** $\frac{12}{1,000}$ and 0.012 **20.** $16\frac{1}{10}$ and 16.1 **21.** 0.72 **22.** 0.03 **23.** 5.7 **24.** 0.008 **25.** $\frac{38}{100}$ **26.** $\frac{12}{10}$ **or** $1\frac{2}{10}$ **27.** $\frac{1}{100}$ **28.** $\frac{208}{100}$ **or** $2\frac{8}{100}$ **29.** $1.\overline{5}$ **30.** $2.61\overline{4}$ **31.** $0.\overline{23}$ **32.** 0.512512512... **33.** 2.3888... **34.** 4.0167167167... **35.** 138.7 **36.** 1.52 **37.** 27.0 **38.** 3.52 **39.** 1.500 **40.** 24.0 **41.** \$1.59 **42.** \$28.79 **43.** \$0.40 **44.** \$12.00 **45.** \$8.90 **46.** \$3.60 **47.** \$1.30 **48.** \$25.00 **49.** \$128 **50.** \$50 **51.** \$268 **52.** \$1,600 **53.** Mariko calculated her GPA to be 3.49. **54.** Julia's average daily electricity usage for March was 7.036 kilowatt-hours. **55.** 1.621 **56.** 1.135 **57.** 8.4 **58.** 3.80 = 3.8 **59.** 7.08 **60.** 1.205 **61.** 21.631 **62.** 21.517 **63.** The total weight of the four bags of candy was 4.617 pounds. **64.** Samantha paid \$66.86 in postage. **65.** 1.54 **66.** 5.36 **67.** 0.69 **68.** 2.619 **69.** 4.4 **70.** 7.8 **71.** 1.72 **72.** 1.051 **73.** Benjou is 0.27 meter taller than Malik. **74.** Jenny received \$13.16. **75.** The perimeter is 5.475 feet. **76.** The length of the third side is 2.31 yards. **77.** 0.12 **78.** 0.072 **79.** 3 **80.** 0.006 **81.** 8.4 **82.** 0.438 **83.** 4.2 **84.** 14 **85.** 24 **86.** 0.1134 **87.** 305.52 **88.** 45.27 **89.** 83 **90.** 141.2 **91.** 291 **92.** 370 **93.** 80.4 **94.** 1,691 **95.** 89 **96.** 50 **97.** Carlos must pay a total of \$67.50 for the necklace. **98.** Jamal must pay a total of \$1,290.00 for the TV. **99.** 0.8 **100.** 6.65 **101.** 0.1825 **102.** $2.61\overline{6}$ **103.** $5.\overline{7}$ **104.** $0.5\overline{63}$ **105.** 7.2 **106.** $0.070\overline{6}$ **107.** $35.2\overline{6}$ **108.** 0.056 **109.** 0.8 **110.** $0.\overline{7}$ **111.** $0.\overline{72}$ **112.** 0.125 **113.** $0.1\overline{6}$ **114.** 0.3125 **115.** 0.52 **116.** $0.\overline{270}$ **117.** Wes earns \$52.50 for a 6-hour shift. **118.** Sunil earned, on average, \$16.96 per hour. **119.** The area of the rec room is 2,087.5 square feet. **120.** The circumference of the snare drum is about 40.8 inches. **121.** The price of each battery was \$0.86. **122.** Ruben's truck can travel 328.3 miles on a full tank of gas. **123.** Carmen's average walking rate was 3.8 miles per hour. **124.** Tom and Margaret will pay \$156.05 each month.

Chapter 5 Test Answers

1. Five thousandths **2.** Eight and three hundredths **3.** One hundred twenty-nine thousandths **4.** 50.08 **5.** 0.008 **6.** 0.09 **7.** $\frac{61}{1,000}$ **8.** 49 **9.** 6.0 **10.** \$12.90 **11.** \$355 **12.** 5.625 **13.** 0.892 **14.** 21 **15.** 380 **16.** $0.88\overline{3}$ **17.** 2.8 **18.** 0.875 **19.** $0.\overline{36}$ **20.** JonRey got back \$12.82. **21.** Silvia's car averaged 22.5 miles per gallon that week. **22.** The length of the quilt is 5.5 feet. **23.** The circumference of the circle is about 31.4 feet. **24.** The third side of this triangle is 4.87 inches long.

Chapter 6 Preparation Exercise Answers

1. $n = 19$ **2.** $n = 37$ **3.** $\frac{18}{25}$ **4.** $\frac{2}{5}$ **5.** $\frac{28}{100}$ **6.** $\frac{60}{100}$ **7.** $\frac{8}{100} = \frac{2}{25}$ **8.** $\frac{12}{10} = \frac{6}{5}$ **9.** 0.019 **10.** 0.04 **11.** 3.56 **10.** 8.20 **13.** 11.7 **14.** 0.4326 **15.** 37 **16.** 9 **17.** 7,150 **18.** 4.5 **19.** 0.49 **20.** 212.5 **21.** $0.38\overline{3}$ **22.** 0.875 **23.** $0.\overline{81}$ **24.** $0.1\overline{3}$

Chapter 6 Focus Exercise Answers

Section 6.1

1. units of measure **3.** divided by **5.** $\frac{60 \text{ miles}}{1 \text{ gallon}}$ **7.** $\frac{2 \text{ dollars}}{3 \text{ tickets}}$ **9.** $\frac{35 \text{ miles}}{1 \text{ hour}}$ **11.** $\frac{3 \text{ laps}}{10 \text{ minutes}}$ **13.** 7 people per van **15.** 23.4 miles per gallon **17.** 9 lemons for every 5 dollars **19.** 1 boy for every 2 girls **21.** $\frac{24 \text{ feet}}{32 \text{ feet}} = \frac{3}{4}$ **23.** $\frac{6 \text{ hours}}{30 \text{ hours}} = \frac{1}{5}$ **25.** $\frac{50 \text{ miles}}{4 \text{ hours}} = \frac{25 \text{ miles}}{2 \text{ hours}}$ **27.** $\frac{120 \text{ liters}}{30 \text{ liters}} = \frac{4}{1}$ **29.** $\frac{9.6 \text{ liters}}{0.8 \text{ hours}} = \frac{12 \text{ liters}}{1 \text{ hour}}$ **31.** $\frac{12.6 \text{ degrees}}{0.4 \text{ degrees}} = \frac{63}{2}$ **33.** $\frac{12 \text{ years}}{84 \text{ years}} = \frac{1}{7}$ **35.** $\frac{375 \text{ square miles}}{250 \text{ square miles}} = \frac{3}{2}$ **37. a)** \$480 : \$360; $\frac{\$480}{\$360} = \frac{4}{3}$ **b)** \$480 : \$840; $\frac{\$480}{\$840} = \frac{4}{7}$ **c)** \$360 : \$840; $\frac{\$360}{\$840} = \frac{3}{7}$ **39. a)** \$90 : \$30; $\frac{\$90}{\$30} = \frac{3}{1}$ **b)** \$90 : \$120; $\frac{\$90}{\$120} = \frac{3}{4}$ **c)** \$30 : \$120; $\frac{\$30}{\$120} = \frac{1}{4}$ **41.** $36 = 36$; yes **43.** $40 \neq 60$; no **45.** $18 \neq 24$; no **47.** $1.5 = 1.5$; yes

Section 6.2

1. True **3.** denominator **5.** $\frac{65 \text{ stitches}}{1 \text{ inch}}$; 65 stitches per 1 inch **7.** $\frac{21 \text{ gallons}}{4 \text{ weeks}}$; 21 gallons for every 4 weeks **9.** $\frac{1 \text{ supervisor}}{6 \text{ employees}}$; 1 supervisor for every 6 employees **11.** $\frac{15 \text{ pounds}}{2 \text{ passengers}}$; 15 pounds for every 2 passengers **13.** $\frac{64 \text{ voters}}{1 \text{ precinct}}$; 64 voters per precinct **15.** $\frac{1.25 \text{ yards of fabric}}{1 \text{ doll dress}}$; 1.25 yards of fabric per doll dress **17.** $\frac{2.5 \text{ kilowatts}}{1 \text{ hour}}$; 2.5 kilowatts per hour **19.** $\frac{16.5 \text{ miles}}{1 \text{ gallon}}$; 16.5 miles per gallon **21.** $\frac{\$72}{1 \text{ month}}$; \$72 per month **23.** $\frac{2.5 \text{ years}}{1 \text{ car}}$; 2.5 years per car **25.** $\frac{\$12.40}{1 \text{ hour}}$; \$12.40 per hour **27.** $\frac{0.35 \text{ gram of sodium}}{1 \text{ serving}}$; 0.35 gram of sodium per serving **29.** Gourmet: \$0.15 per cookie; Savory: \$0.14 per cookie. Savory is the better buy. **31.** Lightning: \$0.92 per bar; Thunder: \$0.95 per bar. Lightning is the better buy. **33.** 42-ounce jug: \$0.07 per ounce; 64-ounce jug: \$0.06 per ounce. The 64-ounce jug is the better buy.

Section 6.3

1. $n = 6$ **3.** $n = 16$ **5.** $n = 30$ **7.** $n = 16$ **9.** $n = 20$ **11.** $n = 12$ **13.** $n = 25$ **15.** $n = 4$

17. Let $n =$ number of votes Tom received.

	First set	Second set
Tom	18	n
Total	30	200

Tom received a total of 120 votes.

19. Let $n =$ number of gallons.

	First set	Second set
Miles	360	120
Gallons	15	n

Cheryl will use 5 gallons to drive 120 miles.

21. Let $n =$ cost of 150 sq yd of material.

	First set	Second set
Cost	12	n
Square yards	1	150

150 square yards of roofing material will cost \$1,800.

23. Let $n =$ price of 8 feet of rope.

	First set	Second set
Price	1.20	n
Length, feet	3	8

The price of 8 feet of rope is \$3.20.

25. Let $n =$ number of miles in 45 minutes.

	First set	Second set
Miles	6	n
Minutes	27	45

Delon can ride 10 miles in 45 minutes.

27. Let $n =$ number of gallons.

	First set	Second set
Miles	90	54
Gallons	5	n

Hank's Jeep will need 3 gallons of gas to travel 54 miles.

29. Let $n =$ number of hours for 150 copies.

	First set	Second set
Copies	30	150
Hours	2	n

It will take 10 hours for the whole job to be complete.

31. Let $n =$ number of boats for 75 people.

	First set	Second set
People	30	75
Boats	2	n

5 boats are needed for 75 people.

33. Let $n =$ number of math classes.

	First set	Second set
Math	9	n
English	12	48

The college offers 36 math classes.

Section 6.4

1. $\frac{9}{20}$ **3.** $\frac{9}{10}$ **5.** $\frac{14}{25}$ of a school district's budget is for teacher salaries. **7.** $\frac{1}{50}$ of the cars imported into the U.S. come from Sweden. **9.** 0.16 **11.** 0.045 **13.** 0.02 **15.** 1.84 **17.** 0.85 **19.** 2.60 = 2.6 **21.** 0.04 **23.** 0.03 **25.** 0.052 **27.** 0.172 **29.** 0.0775 **31.** 0.005 **33.** 78% **35.** 6% **37.** 90% **39.** 211% **41.** 140% **43.** 12.8% **45.** 6.2% **47.** 0.1% **49.** 40% **51.** 94% **53.** 56% **55.** 125% **57.** 62.5% **59.** ≈ 56.3% **61.** ≈ 77.8% **63.** ≈ 16.7% **65.** ≈ 26.7% **67.** ≈ 40.9% **69.** 30% of the medals won by South Korean athletes at the 2004 Olympics were gold medals. **71.** In May 2005, 18.8% of all commercial flights either departed late or were canceled.

Section 6.5

1. 3 of the packs contain an autographed card. **3.** 91 female members of a health club attend at least four times a week. **5.** 91 voters voted for Proposition A. **7.** 15 employees are in management. **9.** There are 225 mailboxes in all. **11.** There were 150 customers that day. **13.** There are 150 total faculty at Cedar Glen College. **15.** 56 families live in this neighborhood. **17.** 40% of Dr. James' patients receive a weekly massage. **19.** 35% of his football card collection are memorabilia cards. **21.** Ms. Kendall got 53.3% of the vote. **23.** 13.3% of the employees ride the bus to work.

Section 6.6

1. 14 **3.** 27 **5.** 72 **7.** 28.8 **9.** 60 **11.** 49 **13.** 80% of 95 is <u>76</u>. **15.** 35% of 40 is <u>14</u>. **17.** 25% of <u>56</u> is 14. **19.** 45% of <u>80</u> is 36. **21.** 60% of <u>80</u> is 48. **23.** <u>50%</u> of 76 is 38. **25.** <u>40%</u> of 65 is 26. **27.** <u>60%</u> of 45 is 27. **29.** Jayne sold $1,920 in computer equipment. **31.** There were a total of 160 cars in the parking lot. **33.** 45% of the students brought their books on the first day. **35.** 37.5% of the deputies are women.

Section 6.7

1. Tanaya paid $50.56 at the register. **3.** Mike earned $85.50 in commissions that day. **5.** The new price of the sweater is $48.00. **7.** Eleazar will pay $165.59 for the suit. **9.** Sarah's grade is 85%. **11.** Marcus has attained 85% of his goal. **13.** Yes, Jamal will pay $26.46 at the register. **15. a)** Bud's price is $322.96 for the TV set. **b)** Bud will pay $25.84 in sales tax. **c)** Bud will pay $348.80 for the TV set. **17.** The choir budget increased 20%. **19.** Nate's height increased 12.5%. **21.** The price decreased 7.5% from last year to this year. **23.** Sales decreased 37.5% from December to January.

Chapter 6 Review Exercise Answers

1. ratios **2.** 25 and 24 **3.** cross multiplication **4.** multiplication **5.** fraction or decimal **6.** 100% **7.** False **8.** True **9.** False **10.** True **11.** $\frac{\text{12 cookies}}{\text{1 box}}$ **12.** $\frac{\text{45 cents}}{\text{1 donut}}$ **13.** $\frac{\text{3 quarts}}{\text{8 children}}$ **14.** $\frac{\text{\$7.00}}{\text{10 cards}}$ **15.** 25 players per game **16.** $85 per week **17.** 120 passengers for every 5 cars **18.** 80 miles for every 3 gallons **19.** $\frac{\text{72 dollars}}{\text{9 shares}} = \frac{\text{8 dollars}}{\text{1 share}}$ **20.** $\frac{\text{18 minutes}}{\text{45 minutes}} = \frac{2}{5}$ **21.** $\frac{\text{2.4 acres}}{\text{3 acres}} = \frac{4}{5}$ **22.** $\frac{\text{0.6 calories}}{\text{1.5 grams}} = \frac{\text{2 calories}}{\text{5 grams}}$ **23.** $\frac{\text{12 pounds}}{\text{15 pounds}} = \frac{4}{5}$ **24.** $\frac{\text{20 inches}}{\text{32 inches}} = \frac{5}{8}$ **25. a)** \$120 : \$90; $\frac{\$120}{\$90} = \frac{4}{3}$ **b)** \$120 : \$210; $\frac{\$120}{\$210} = \frac{4}{7}$ **c)** \$90 : \$210; $\frac{\$90}{\$210} = \frac{3}{7}$ **26. a)** \$180 : \$120; $\frac{\$180}{\$120} = \frac{3}{2}$ **b)** \$180 : \$300; $\frac{\$180}{\$300} = \frac{3}{5}$ **c)** \$120 : \$300; $\frac{\$120}{\$300} = \frac{2}{5}$ **27.** 60 = 60; yes **28.** 400 ≠ 450; no **29.** 18 ≠ 20; no **30.** 15 = 15; yes **31.** $\frac{\text{65 dollars}}{\text{1 day}}$; $65 per day **32.** $\frac{\text{15 customers}}{\text{2 hours}}$; 15 customers every 2 hours **33.** $\frac{\text{1 hit}}{\text{3 times at bat}}$; 1 hit every 3 times at bat **34.** $\frac{\text{3 repetitions}}{\text{5 minutes}}$; 3 repetitions every 5 minutes **35.** $\frac{\text{4 golf balls}}{\text{1 player}}$; 4 golf balls per player **36.** $\frac{\text{11.4 students}}{\text{1 tutor}}$; 11.4 students per tutor **37.** $\frac{\text{11.8 phone calls}}{\text{1 day}}$; 11.8 phone calls per day **38.** $\frac{\text{18.5 miles}}{\text{1 gallon}}$; 18.5 miles per gallon **39.** $\frac{\text{\$1,350}}{\text{6 residents}} = \frac{\text{\$225}}{\text{1 resident}}$; $225 per resident. **40.** $\frac{\text{339 points}}{\text{15 games}} = \frac{\text{22.6 points}}{\text{1 game}}$; 22.6 points per game. **41.** $\frac{\text{\$405}}{\text{18 trees}} = \frac{\text{\$22.50}}{\text{1 tree}}$; $22.50 per tree. **42.** $\frac{\text{\$114}}{\text{25 chairs}} = \frac{\text{\$4.56}}{\text{1 chair}}$; $4.56 per chair. **43.** Redd's: $0.12 per ounce; Green's: $0.15 per ounce. Redd's is the better buy. **44.** AlwaysReady: $0.81 per battery; LightShine: $0.75 per battery. LightShine is the better buy. **45.** $n = 21$ **46.** $n = 15$ **47.** $n = 72$ **48.** $n = 35$

49. Let $n =$ number of miles.

	First set	Second set
Gallons	12	16
Miles	246	n

Kjell's car can travel 328 miles on 16 gallons of gas.

50. Let $n =$ amount to be charged.

	First set	Second set
Dollars	6	n
Square feet	4	82

Lonnie will charge $123 to paint 82 square feet of wall.

51. Let $n =$ amount of money raised.

	First set	Second set
Dollars	13.50	n
Laps	3	32

Karrie raised $144.

52. Let $n =$ the number of seconds.

	First set	Second set
Pages	6	22
Seconds	15	n

It will take 55 seconds to print 22 pages.

53. $\frac{1}{5}$ of the homes in Westside Estates are ranch style. **54.** $\frac{3}{20}$ of all fruit sold in Bryson's grocery store is organically grown. **55.** $\frac{2}{25}$ of all U.S. residents live in Texas. **56.** $\frac{1}{40}$ of the medals awarded at the 2004 Summer Olympics went to athletes from Ukraine. **57.** 0.47 **58.** 0.03 **59.** 0.091 **60.** 0.006 **61.** 26% **62.** 2% **63.** 17.5% **64.** 70% **65.** 106% **66.** 0.5% **67.** 15% of Sri Lanka's population is Hindu. **68.** 64% of the shoppers at Lucia's Floristas pay with a credit card. **69.** 87.5% of the students in Ms. Skiba's art class received a passing grade. **70.** 28.6% of all U.S. car sales are small cars.

71. Let $a =$ the number of tenors.

	First set	Second set
Tenors	15	a
All singers	100	40

6 of the singers are tenors.

72. Let $a =$ the number of engineers with at least 10 years at Hudson Dynamic.

	First set	Second set
At least ten years	37.5	a
All engineers	100	32

12 engineers have been at Hudson Dynamic for at least ten years.

73. Let $b =$ the number of dinner customers.

	First set	Second set
Order a salad	65	91
All customers	100	b

There were 140 dinner customers in all.

74. Let $b =$ the total number of teachers.

	First set	Second set
Doctorate degree	2.5	8
All teachers	100	b

There are 320 teachers in the district.

75. Let $p =$ the unknown percentage.

	First set	Second set
Rain	p	18
All days	100	30

It rained 60% of the days in April.

76. Let $p =$ the unknown percentage.

	First set	Second set
Chicago	p	6
All Oscars	100	18

Chicago won 33.3% of the Oscars.

77. 38 **78.** 49 **79.** 10 **80.** 6 **81.** 25% of 76 is <u>19</u>. **82.** 60% of 85 is <u>51</u>. **83.** 28% of <u>125</u> is 35. **84.** 55% of <u>160</u> is 88. **85.** <u>75%</u> of 52 is 39. **86.** <u>37.5%</u> of 120 is 45. **87.** 4,000 students attend Cuyama College. **88.** 15% of the National League players hit at least thirty home runs in 2004. **89.** DuJuan will pay $86.00 at the cash register. **90.** Sandra earned $6,500 commission on the sale of that house. **91.** The new price of the box of bulbs is $4.90. **92.** Torraye's free throw success was 62.5%. **93.** This savings was 25% of the retail price. **94. a)** The cost of the meal was $36.00. **b)** The sales tax on the meal was $2.16. **c)** The tip was $9.60. **d)** The total amount paid for dinner was $47.76. **95.** The chamber's membership inreased 2.5%. **96.** Corrine's home value increased 12.5%. **97.** The water level decreased 37.5% that week. **98.** The number of students in Dr. Ortega's statistics class decreased 26.7%.

Chapter 6 Test Answers

1. $\frac{\$60}{\$36} = \frac{5}{3}$ **2.** $\frac{2.8 \text{ miles}}{0.8 \text{ gallons}} = \frac{7 \text{ miles}}{2 \text{ gallons}}$ **3.** $280 \neq 300$; no **4.** $48 = 48$; yes **5.** $\frac{21 \text{ seats}}{4 \text{ rows}}$; 21 seats for every 4 rows. **6.** $\frac{208 \text{ milligrams of potassium}}{1 \text{ serving}}$; 208 milligrams of potassium per serving. **7.** bag: $0.56 per avocado; box: $0.60 per avocado. The bag of avocados is the better value. **8.** $n = 24$

9. Let $n =$ amount to be charged.

	First set	Second set
Charge	6.80	n
Minutes	4	9

Carl would have paid $15.30 to talk for 9 minutes.

10. Let $n =$ the number of days.

	First set	Second set
Pounds	16	20
Days	40	n

It would take Banjo 50 days to finish a 20-pound bag of dog food.

11. 0.07 **12.** 0.005 **13.** 57% **14.** 20% **15.** $\frac{4}{25}$ **16.** $\frac{9}{20}$ **17.** 52% **18.** 36.4% **19.** 14% of <u>150</u> is 21. **20.** <u>40%</u> of 80 is 32. **21.** 840 students at Riverbend Community College are teenagers. **22.** Lin-Li will pay $94.60 at the cash register. **23.** Yusef's discounted price will be $51.00. **24.** Marcus received a 25% increase in his hourly wage.

Chapters 5 and 6 Cumulative Review Answers

1. 0.043 **2.** 9.1 **3.** $\frac{71}{100}$ **4.** 2.010 **5.** 29.9 **6.** $10.60 **7.** $532 **8.** 3.20 **9.** 10.154 **10.** 1.126 **11.** 1.051 **12.** Beverly will get back $6.47. **13.** 16.906 inches **14.** 3.55 meters **15.** 0.072 **16.** 31.5 **17.** 60 **18.** 30.8 **19.** 0.615 **20.** $1.7\overline{3}$ **21.** 0.875 **22.** Petre earned $17.40 per hour. **23.** The area of the pool is 205.8 square yards. **24.** The circumference of the baking dish is about 30.1 inches. **25.** $\frac{2.7 \text{ grams}}{0.45 \text{ grams}} = \frac{6}{1}$ **26.** $\frac{1.9 \text{ calories}}{1 \text{ gram}}$; 1.9 calories per gram **27.** Tomás traveled 48.75 miles per hour. **28.** Twinklebuck's: $0.095 per ounce; Sunbuck's: $0.09 per ounce. Sunbuck's is the better buy. **29.** $n = 12$ **30.** $n = 12$ **31.** 0.05 **32.** 0.032 **33.** 30.8% **34.** 40% **35.** It will take Zia 20 minutes to cook 90 pancakes. **36.** 6 employees may live outside the city limits. **37.** 45% of <u>140</u> is 63. **38.** <u>64%</u> of 75 is 48. **39.** The discounted price will be $44.00. **40.** There is a 40% decrease in the Torres' monthly car payment.

Chapter 7 Preparation Exercise Answers

1. $\frac{31}{6}$ **2.** $\frac{61}{8}$ **3.** $7\frac{11}{12}$ **4.** $4\frac{7}{16}$ **5.** $\frac{1}{10}$ **6.** $\frac{5}{6}$ **7.** $\frac{21}{2} = 10\frac{1}{2}$ **8.** 30 **9.** $\frac{3}{2} = 1\frac{1}{2}$ **10.** $\frac{3}{4}$ **11.** $\frac{3}{2} = 1\frac{1}{2}$ **12.** $\frac{13}{24}$ **13.** $\frac{47}{100}$ **14.** $\frac{3}{1,000}$ **15.** 0.63 **16.** 0.29 **17.** 2 **18.** 10.99 **19.** 58 **20.** 1.2 **21.** 14.75 **22.** 1.95 **23.** 3.9 **24.** $9.\overline{5}$

Chapter 7 Focus Exercise Answers

Section 7.1

1. 48 inches **3.** 8 inches **5.** $5\frac{1}{3}$ yards **7.** $\frac{1}{3}$ foot **9.** 144 in. **11.** 80 in. **13.** 2 ft 4 in. **15.** 7 ft 9 in. **17.** The rim of the basketball hoop is 120 inches off of the floor. **19.** 10 ft 10 in. **21.** 6 ft **23.** 5 ft 8 in. **25.** 3 ft 5 in. **27.** Rodney was 3 feet 2 inches tall on his first birthday. **29.** 80 ounces **31.** 8,000 pounds **33.** 144 oz **35.** 104 oz **37.** 1 lb 12 oz **39.** 5 lb 10 oz **41.** The home run slugger's baseball bat weighs 34 ounces. **43.** 10 lb 13 oz **45.** 8 lb **47.** 5 lb 12 oz **49.** 3 lb 9 oz **51.** Liu and his baby carrier weigh 17 pounds 2 ounces. **53.** 10 pints **55.** $4\frac{3}{4}$ cups **57.** 11 cups **59.** $2\frac{1}{3}$ quarts

Section 7.2

1. 3,080 m **3.** 450 L **5.** 0.87 g **7.** 0.091 L **9.** 3.65 m **11.** 0.49 g **13.** 0.06 L **15.** 0.4 m **17.** 360 dekameters **19.** 3.12 decigrams **21.** 0.009 kiloliter **23.** 25 decimeters **25.** 18.1 deciliters **27.** 8.3 hectometers **29.** 3.7 decigrams **31.** 0.6 centiliter **33.** The child weighs 15,600 grams. **35.** Veronica's rose bush is 0.835 meter high. **37.** The dwarf pygmy goby has a diameter of 9.9 millimeters. **39.** 2,011 centigrams **41.** 3.22 dekaliters **43.** 15.7 centigrams **45.** 1,316 deciliters **47.** 1,625 milliliters of fluid are now in the bag. **49.** Jermaine added 13.4 liters in total to his gas tank. **51.** Tamayra grew 8.7 centimeters that year.

Section 7.3

1. 14 yards **3.** 7 gallons **5.** $4\frac{1}{2}$ cups **7.** 0.95 meter **9.** 0.06 gram **11.** 4.5 liters **13.** 30 centimeters **15.** 15 miles **17.** 12 meters **19.** 47.5 liters **21.** 3.75 kilograms **23.** $14\frac{3}{4}$ ounces **25.** The foot race is $6\frac{1}{4}$ miles. **27.** The window is 120 centimeters wide. **29.** Sammy weighs $60\frac{1}{2}$ pounds. **31.** Papi's pickup truck can hold 114 liters of gas.

Section 7.4

1. $\angle 1$, $\angle G$, $\angle RGW$, and $\angle WGR$ **3.** $\overleftrightarrow{ET}$ and $\overleftrightarrow{DL}$ **5.** $\angle KRB = 53°$ **7.** $\angle SAP = 94°$ **9.** $\angle WXI = 103°$ **11.** $\angle YEO = 48°$ **13.** $\angle LYM = 63°$ **15.** $\angle MUJ = 18°$ **17.** $\angle 1 = 32°$, $\angle 2 = \angle 4 = 148°$ **19.** $\angle 2 = 111°$, $\angle 1 = \angle 3 = 69°$ **21.** straight **23.** vertical **25.** False **27.** True **29.** False **31.** True

Section 7.5

1. $\angle C = 80°$ **3.** $\angle C = 13°$ **5.** $\angle C = 75.4°$ **7.** $\angle C = 70.5°$ **9.** Scalene **11.** Scalene **13.** $\angle C = 54°$ **15.** $\angle I = 68.5°$ **17.** $\angle P = 35°$, $\angle Q = \angle O = 145°$, $\overline{OP} = 3$ in., and $\overline{QP} = 7$ in. **19.** False **21.** False (Note: In a quadrilateral, if a pair of parallel sides are the same length, the quadrialteral is a parallelogram, but can't be a trapezoid.) **23.** True **25.** True **27.** Yes. The two sides that form the right angle can be the same length. **29.** $d = 12$ in. **31.** $r = 10$ in. **33.** $d = 13$ cm **35.** $r = 3\frac{2}{3}$ ft

Section 7.6

1. The perimeter of Karin's lamp stand is 82 inches. **3.** The perimeter of home plate is 58 inches. **5.** $P = 21.56$ cm **7.** $P = 2\frac{1}{3}$ in. **9.** $P = 72$ ft **11.** $P = 2\frac{2}{3}$ in. **13.** $P = 52$ ft **15.** $P = 94.2$ m **17.** $P = 740$ yd **19.** $P = 14\frac{1}{2}$ in. **21.** side $= 17$ in. **23.** side $= 17.9$ cm **25.** side $= 17\frac{1}{2}$ yd **27.** side $= 1\frac{1}{3}$ ft **29.** $C \approx 88$ in. **31.** $C \approx 17.6$ cm **33.** $C \approx 5\frac{1}{2}$ in. **35.** $C \approx 22$ ft **37.** $C \approx 31.4$ yd **39.** $C \approx 28.3$ m **41.** $C \approx 25.1$ ft **43.** $C \approx 20.4$ cm **45.** $x = 11$ in., $y = 44$ in., $P = 158$ in. **47.** $x = 13.2$ cm, $P = 55.2$ cm **49.** $x = \frac{5}{12}$ in., $y = \frac{7}{12}$ in., $P = 3\frac{1}{6}$ in.

Section 7.7

1. $A = 96$ yd^2 **3.** $A = \frac{7}{32}$ in.^{2} **5.** $A = 44.2$ cm^2 **7.** $A = 4\frac{1}{2}$ ft^2 **9.** $A = 169$ ft^2 **11.** $A = \frac{49}{144}$ in.^{2} **13.** $A = 108$ ft^2 **15.** $A = \frac{1}{3}$ in.^{2} **17.** $A = 154$ in.^{2} **19.** $A = \frac{5}{6}$ in.^{2} **21.** $A = 135$ yd^2 **23.** $A = \frac{25}{32}$ in.^{2} **25.** $A = 460$ ft^2 **27.** $A = 85$ m^2 **29.** $A \approx 28.3$ in.^{2} **31.** $A \approx 4.5$ m^2 **33.** $A \approx 50.2$ yd^2 **35.** $A \approx 3.8$ cm^2 **37.** $A = 240$ in.^{2} **39.** $A = 63$ ft^2 **41.** The area of the side is 448 square inches. **43.** The area of the room is 150 square feet. **45.** The area of the clock face is about 314 square inches **47.** The area of the hot tub cover is about 20 square feet. **49.** $A \approx 21.2$ cm^2 **51.** The area of the flat region is about 737.5 square meters.

Section 7.8

1. $V = 240$ in.^{3} **3.** $V = 2{,}400$ ft^3 **5.** $V = 2{,}016$ cm^3 **7.** $V = 17\frac{1}{2}$ in.^{3} **9.** $V \approx 50.2$ ft^3 **11.** $V \approx 20.3$ m^3 **13.** $V \approx 47.1$ ft^3 **15.** $V \approx 13.8$ m^3 **17.** $V = 80$ in.^{3} **19.** $V = 7$ m^3 **21.** $V \approx 4.2$ ft^3 **23.** $V \approx 7.2$ m^3 **25.** The volume of the space is 576 cubic feet. **27.** The volume of the can is about 603 cubic centimeters. **29.** The volume of Rebecca's pyramid is about 47 cubic inches.

Chapter 7 Review Exercise Answers

1. True **2.** True **3.** True **4.** False **5.** True **6.** False **7.** False **8.** True **9.** 216 in. **10.** 119 in. **11.** 4 ft 2 in. **12.** 10 ft 10 in. **13.** A tennis racquet is 27 inches long. **14.** At 7 feet 2 inches tall, Margo Dydek is the tallest woman professional basketball player in the WNBA. **15.** 12 ft **16.** 1 ft 6 in. **17.** The house is 13 feet 2 inches tall. **18.** The rest of its body is 8 feet 9 inches long. **19.** 47 feet **20.** 17 yards **21.** 10 pints **22.** $\frac{3}{4}$ pound **23.** 5 pints **24.** $1\frac{3}{4}$ cups **25.** 48 fluid ounces **26.** 3 gallons **27.** 18 fluid ounces **28.** $\frac{4}{5}$ pound **29.** 6 ounces **30.** 2,900 pounds **31.** 240 oz **32.** 82 oz **33.** 2 lb 8 oz **34.** 8 lb 14 oz **35.** The roasting chicken weighs 61 ounces. **36.** The double box of cereal weighs 4 pounds 12 ounces. **37.** 12 pounds **38.** 1 pound 12 ounces **39.** The total weight of these two books is 11 pounds 4 ounces. **40.** The remaining block of cheese weighs 13 pounds 7 ounces. **41.** 30.8 g **42.** 6,800 g **43.** 8.7 m **44.** 0.24 L **45.** 20 mg **46.** 9 cg **47.** 3.12 dL **48.** 0.12 kL **49.** 0.036 dam **50.** 82 dam **51.** Jakhil ran 400 meters in one minute. **52.** A hummingbird weighs 1,600 milligrams. **53.** 2,011 centigrams **54.** 48.05 deciliters **55.** Martin drank 3.1 liters for his test. **56.** Foofi gained 480 grams during the year. **57.** $3\frac{1}{2}$ quarts **58.** 36 ounces **59.** $4\frac{1}{2}$ feet **60.** 27,000 grams **61.** 9,500 meters **62.** 12 liters **63.** 55 centimeters **64.** 24 inches **65.** 10 quarts **66.** 28.5 liters **67.** $1\frac{1}{4}$ ounces **68.** 15 meters **69.** The sack of potatoes weighs about 9.1 kilograms. **70. a)** Jorge is 72 inches tall. **b)** Jorge is about 180 centimeters tall. **71.** $\angle BRK = 48.4°$ **72.** $\angle EMD = 97.5°$ **73.** $\angle BLN = 54.8°$ **74.** $\angle RFX = 27.5°$ **75.** $\angle 1 = 32°$, $\angle 2 = \angle 4 = 148°$ **76.** $\angle C = 52°$ **77.** Isosceles **78.** Equilateral (and isosceles) **79.** $\angle G = 30.6°$ **80.** $\angle J = 66.2°$ **81.** $\angle P = 40°$, $\angle Q = \angle O = 140°$; $\overline{OP} = 5$ cm; $\overline{QP} = 9$ cm **82.** $d = 18$ ft **83.** $r = 3\frac{2}{3}$ in. **84.** $r = 1.15$ m **85.** The perimeter of Leon's pool is $29\frac{5}{6}$ yards. **86.** The perimeter of the support structure is 28.1 meters. **87.** $x = 20$ ft, $y = 8$ ft; the perimeter is 86 feet. **88.** The perimeter of the dance floor is 87 feet. **89.** $P = 7$ ft **90.** $P = 30$ yd **91.** Each side = 14 cm **92.** Each side = 35 in. **93.** Marcus needs about 132 feet of fencing to fit around the garden. **94.** About 94.2 inches of weather-stripping is needed to go around the window. **95.** $A = 20$ yd^2 **96.** $A = 3$ m^2 **97.** $A = \frac{9}{64}$ in.^{2} **98.** $A = 12\frac{1}{4}$ ft^2 **99.** $A = 200$ in.^{2} **100.** $A = 10$ ft^2 **101.** $A = 5$ in.^{2} **102.** $A = 33$ cm^2 **103.** $A \approx 12.6$ ft^2 **104.** $d = 8.0$ cm^2 **105.** The area of the surface of the pond is 2,826 square feet. **106.** The area of Erica's living room is 144 square feet. **107.** $A \approx 7.74$ cm^2 **108.** $V = 540$ in.^{3} **109.** $V \approx 33.5$ ft^3 **110.** $V \approx 314$ in.^{3} **111.** $V \approx 7.1$ ft^3 **112.** $V = 160$ m^3 **113.** The volume of the pyramid is 2,000 cubic yards. **114.** The volume of the storage area is 672 cubic feet.

Chapter 7 Test Answers

1. True **2.** True **3.** False **4.** False **5.** 18 ft 5 in. **6.** 13 ft 4 in. **7.** 81 inches **8.** 11 feet 10 inches **9.** 48 ounces **10.** $3\frac{3}{4}$ yards **11.** 0.28 L **12.** 45 m **13.** 0.091 m **14.** 890 g **15.** 92.7 mm **16.** 5.25 kg **17.** 32 kilometers **18.** $13\frac{3}{4}$ pounds **19.** Elisa put 2.5 gallons into her motorcycle. **20.** $\angle RTW = 61.9°$ **21.** $\angle XAS = 144.5°$ **22.** $\angle WXI = 111.7°$ **23.** $\angle LYM = 58.9°$ **24.** $\angle C = 105.9°$ **25.** The perimeter of the canvas is 98 inches. **26.** $P = 30$ cm **27.** $A = 5\frac{4}{9}$ ft^2 **28.** $C \approx 110$ in. **29.** Each side $= 1\frac{1}{3}$ ft **30.** $A = 42$ cm^2 **31.** The area of the kitchen is 576 square feet. **32.** $V \approx 376.8$ cm^3 **33.** $V = 10$ in.^{3}

Chapter 8 Preparation Exercise Answers

1. 54 **2.** 88 **3.** $\frac{3}{4}$ **4.** $\frac{1}{5}$ **5.** 0.8 **6.** 2.0 (not 2) **7.** 0.43 **8.** 1.39 **9.** 2.038 **10.** 2.847 **11.** 0.46 **12.** 2.805 **13.** 17.92 **14.** 74.00 = 74 **15.** 0.21 **16.** 0.0400 = 0.04 **17.** 0.25 **18.** 7.9 **19.** 95 **20.** 95.75 **21.** 47% **22.** 3% **23.** 27.9% **24.** 0.5% **25.** 0.58 **26.** 0.09 **27.** 1.30 **28.** 0.025

Chapter 8 Focus Exercise Answers

Section 8.1

1.

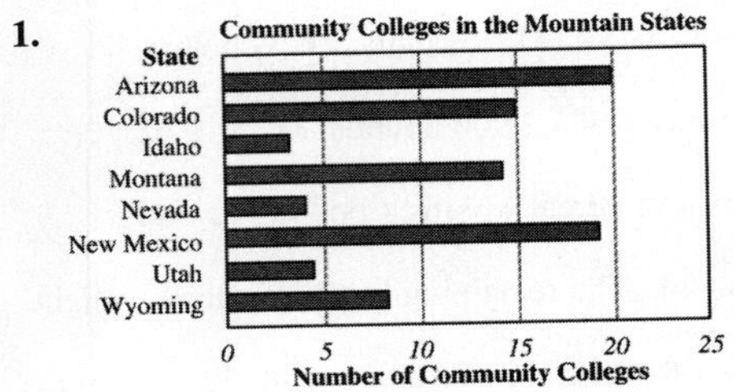

3.

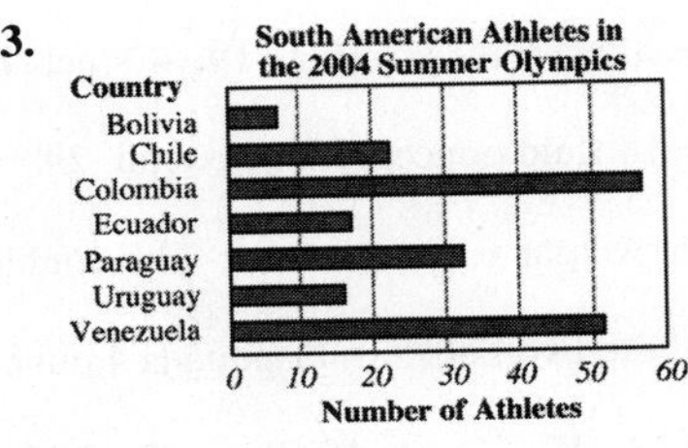

5.

Jet	Age, in Years
Freedom	8
Glory	13
Patriot	6
Spirit	2
Victory	4
Total	**33**

7.

Breed	Number of Horses
Andalusian	14
Clydesdale	8
Friesian	22
Paint	16
Palomino	25
Total	**85**

9.

Marital Status	Percent of Women	Total Number of Women
Married	30%	36
Divorced	20%	24
Widowed	5%	6
Legally Separated	10%	12
Never Married	35%	42
Total	**100%**	**120**

11.

Type of Doctor	Percent of Doctors	Total Number of Doctors
Anesthesiologists	6%	15
General Practitioners	32%	80
Gynecologists	16%	40
Internists	18%	45
Surgeons	8%	20
Others	20%	50
Total	**100%**	**250**

13.

Major	Percent of Students
Arts/Humanities	50%
English/Languages	20%
Life Science	5%
Social Science	10%
Other	15%
Total	**100%**

13. (continued)

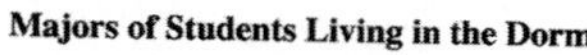

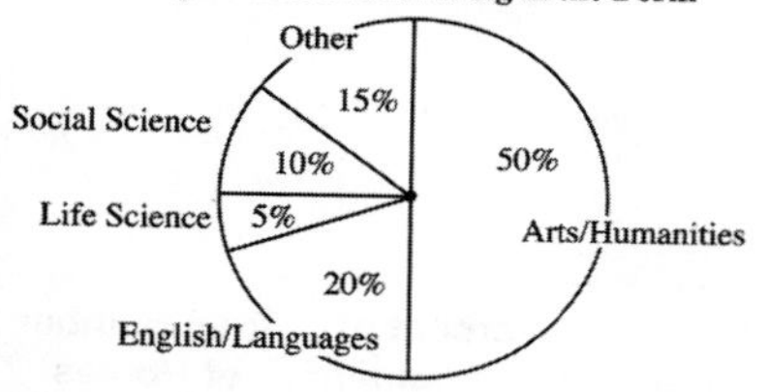

15.

Position	Percent of Players
Pitcher	28%
Catcher	5%
Infielder	37%
Outfielder	22%
Left blank	8%
Total	**100%**

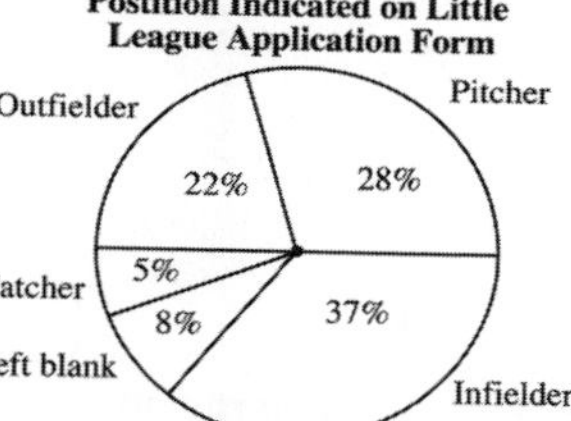

Section 8.2

1. a)

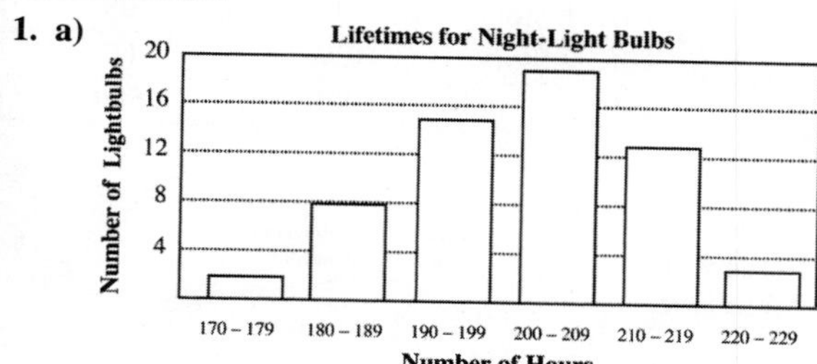

b) 50
c) 10
d) 34
e) 35

3. a)

Number of Hours	Number of Students
1–5	9
6–10	20
11–15	18
16–20	26
21–25	12
26–30	5
Total	**90**

b) 17
c) 29
d) 56

5. a)

Number of Minutes	Tally	Number of Clients
30–39	𝍸 |	6
40–49	𝍸 ||||	9
50–59	𝍸 𝍸 ||	12
60–69	𝍸 𝍸 ||	12
70–79	𝍸 ||	7
80–89	||||	4
Total		**50**

b) 15
c) 33
d) 23

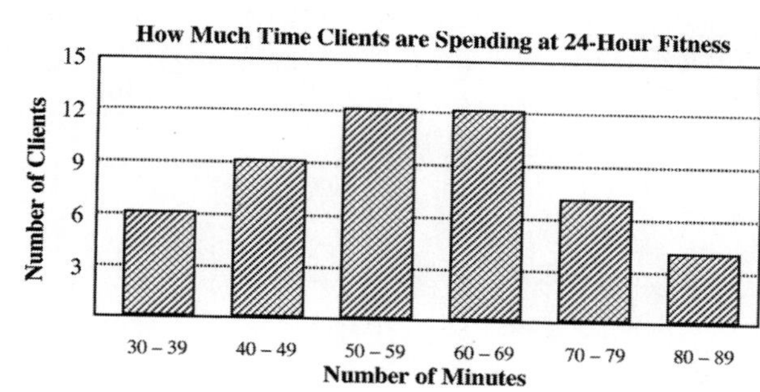

Section 8.3

1. 83 **3.** 43 **5.** 79.4 **7.** 167.7 **9.** 19 miles **11.** 29.7 cars **13.** 22.06 kilometers **15.** 1.268 meters **17.** $\frac{38}{13} \approx 2.92$ **19.** Median: 76; mode: 71 **21.** Median: 3; mode: 3 **23.** Median: 9.5; mode: 6 **25.** Median: 40.5; mode: 38 **27.** Mean: 13.8; median: 14; mode: None **29.** Mean: 10.5; median: 10; mode: 5

Section 8.4

1. $\frac{1}{6}$ **3.** $\frac{5}{6}$ **5.** $\frac{2}{6} = \frac{1}{3}$ **7.** $\frac{1}{5}$ **9.** $\frac{3}{5}$ **11.** $\frac{3}{5}$ **13.** $\frac{8}{20} = \frac{2}{5}$ **15.** $\frac{4}{20} = \frac{1}{5}$ **17.** $\frac{3}{24} = \frac{1}{8}$ **19.** $\frac{9}{24} = \frac{3}{8}$ **21.** $\frac{12}{40} = \frac{3}{10}$ **23.** $\frac{3}{40}$

Chapter 8 Review Exercise Answers

1.

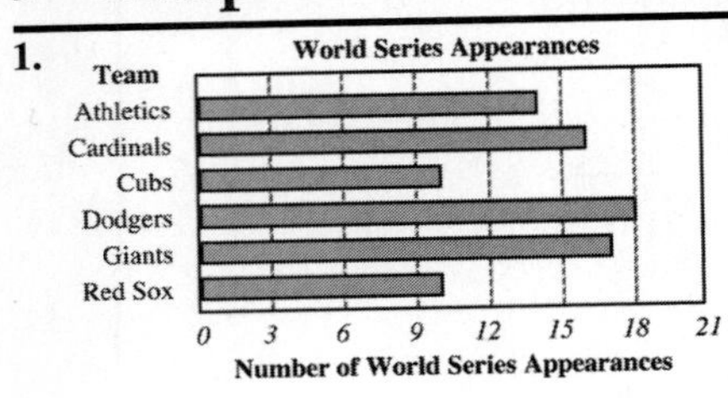

2.

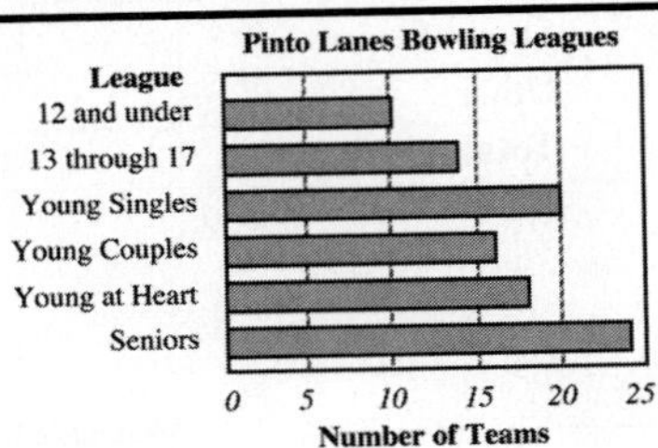

3.

Company	Revenue (in $billions)
ConAgra Foods	22
General Mills	11
H. J. Heinz	9
Kellogg	9
PepsiCo	27
Sara Lee	18
Total	**96**

4.

Country	Number of Winners
Canada	16
Great Britain	4
Japan	7
Kenya	14
Other	24
Total	**65**

5.

Advertising Budget Item	Percent of Budget	Total Amount of Budget
Magazine	10%	$20,000
Newspaper	14%	$28,000
Radio	25%	$50,000
Television	46%	$92,000
Other	5%	$10,000
Total	**100%**	**$200,000**

6.

Style of New Home	Percent of Development	Total Number of Homes
2BR, 1 Story	8%	40
3BR, 1 Story	26%	130
3BR, 2 Story	35%	175
4BR, 1 Story	19%	95
4BR, 2 Story	12%	60
Total	**100%**	**500**

7.

Ethnicity	Percent of Players
African-American	35%
Asian	15%
Hispanic	25%
White	20%
Other	5%
Total	**100%**

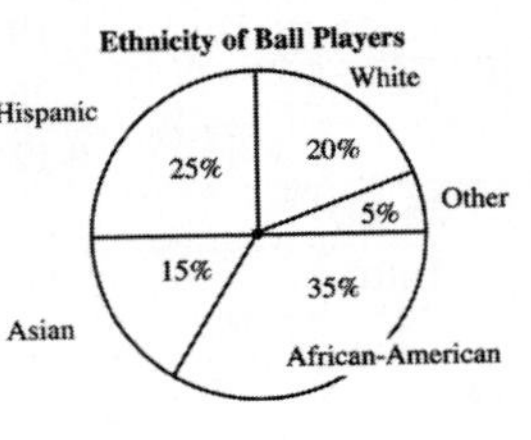

8.

Religion	Percent of Attendees
Buddhist	4%
Christian	34%
Hindu	12%
Jewish	25%
Muslim	17%
Other	8%
Total	**100%**

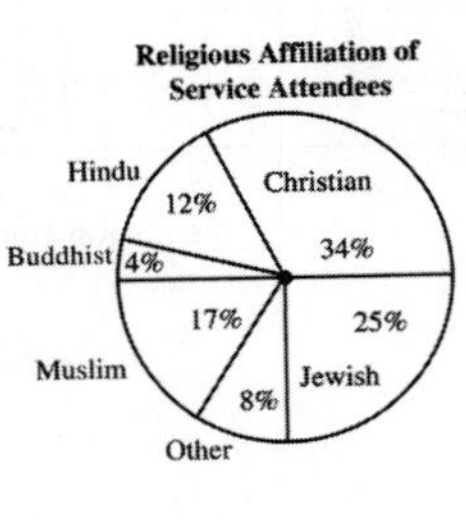

9. a)

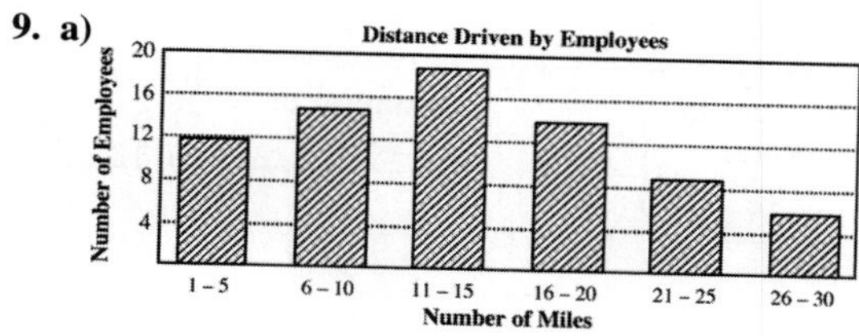

b) 27 **c)** 48 **d)** 29

10. a)

Number of Years	Number of Rulers
0–9	23
10–19	15
20–29	12
30–39	7
40–49	1
50–59	3
60–69	1
Total	**62**

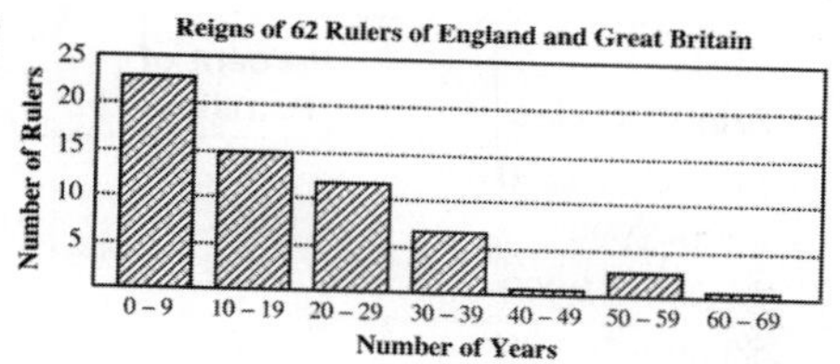

b) 5
c) 19
d) 38

11. a)

Number of Wins	Number of Teams
50–57	1
58–65	2
66–73	8
74–81	3
82–89	6
90–97	7
98–105	3
Total	**30**

b) 10
c) 17
d) 11

12. a)

Number of Months	Number of Attendees
1–6	4
7–12	3
13–18	12
19–24	8
25–30	11
31–36	7
Total	**45**

b) 7
c) 19
d) 7

13. Mean: 7.1; median: 7; mode: 6 **14.** Mean: 21.2; median: 21; mode: None **15.** Mean: 4.3; median: 4.5; mode: 6 **16.** Mean: 14; median: 15.5; modes: 9 and 17 **17.** $\frac{37}{12} \approx 3.08$ **18.** $\frac{33}{14} \approx 2.36$ **19.** $\frac{3}{6} = \frac{1}{2}$ **20.** $\frac{2}{6} = \frac{1}{3}$ **21.** $\frac{4}{6} = \frac{2}{3}$ **22.** $\frac{0}{6} = 0$ **23.** $\frac{1}{6}$ **24.** $\frac{2}{6} = \frac{1}{3}$ **25.** $\frac{4}{8} = \frac{1}{2}$ **26.** $\frac{3}{8}$ **27.** $\frac{3}{8}$ **28.** $\frac{2}{8} = \frac{1}{4}$ **29.** $\frac{2}{8} = \frac{1}{4}$ **30.** $\frac{8}{8} = 1$ **31.** $\frac{5}{30} = \frac{1}{6}$ **32.** $\frac{6}{30} = \frac{1}{5}$ **33.** $\frac{9}{30} = \frac{3}{10}$ **34.** $\frac{8}{30} = \frac{4}{15}$ **35.** $\frac{10}{50} = \frac{1}{5}$ **36.** $\frac{15}{50} = \frac{3}{10}$ **37.** $\frac{5}{50} = \frac{1}{10}$ **38.** $\frac{12}{50} = \frac{6}{25}$

Chapter 8 Test Answers

1.

Selected California Crops in 2003

Crop: Barley, Corn, Hay, Oats, Wheat

0 5 10 15 20 25 30 35

Number of Bushels (in millions)

2.

City	Average Annual Snowfall
Albuquerque, NM	11
Baltimore, MD	21
Evansville, IN	14
Nashville, TN	10
Roanoke, VA	23
Wichita Falls, TX	6
Total	**85**

3.

Type of Business	Percent of Acreage	Total Number of Acres
Business Offices	4%	6
Grocery	18%	27
Restaurants	26%	39
Retail	32%	48
Services	12%	18
Storage	8%	12
Total	**100%**	**150**

4.

Annual Giving	Percent of Families
Less than $200	4%
$200–$999	12%
$1,000–$4,999	25%
$5,000–$9,999	32%
$10,000–$19,999	18%
$20,000 and above	9%
Total	**100%**

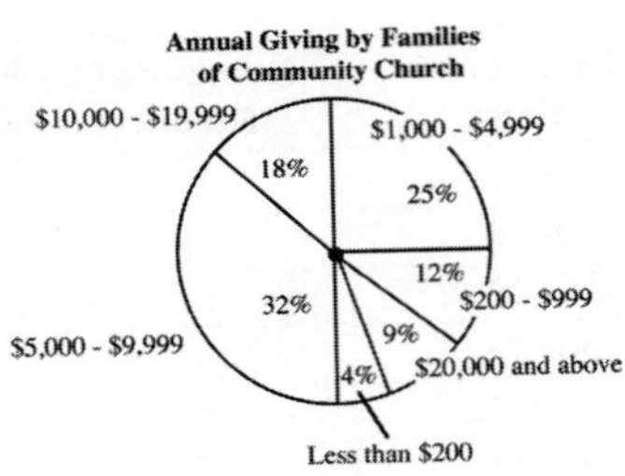

5. a)

Number of Wins	Tally	Number of Teams
20–25	|||	3
26–31	|||	3
32–37	~~||||~~ |	6
38–43	~~||||~~ |	7
44–49	||	2
50–55	||||	4
56–61	||||	4
Total		**29**

b) 10 **c)** 6 **d)** 12

5. (continued)

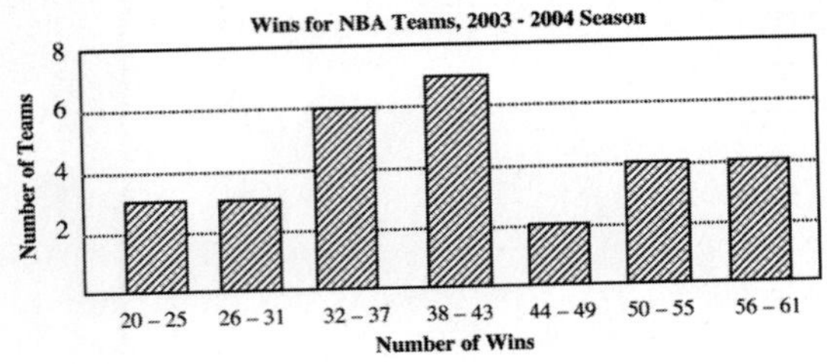

6. a)

Final Exam Score	Number of Students
44–51	4
52–59	7
60–67	11
68–75	14
76–83	19
84–91	16
92–99	9
Total	**80**

b) 44 **c)** 25 **d)** 22

7. Mean: 6.2; median: 6; mode: 8 **8.** Mean: 11.7; median: 12.5; mode: 16 **9.** $\frac{72}{25} = 2.88$ **10.** $\frac{4}{9}$ **11.** $\frac{5}{9}$ **12.** $\frac{3}{9} = \frac{1}{3}$ **13.** $\frac{3}{9} = \frac{1}{3}$ **14.** $\frac{2}{9}$ **15.** $\frac{3}{9} = \frac{1}{3}$ **16.** $\frac{4}{15}$ **17.** $\frac{3}{15} = \frac{1}{5}$ **18.** $\frac{6}{15} = \frac{2}{5}$ **19.** $\frac{2}{15}$ **20.** $\frac{14}{40} = \frac{7}{20}$ **21.** $\frac{10}{40} = \frac{1}{4}$ **22.** $\frac{8}{40} = \frac{1}{5}$ **23.** $\frac{5}{40} = \frac{1}{8}$

Chapters 7 and 8 Cumulative Review Answers

1. $15\frac{1}{2}$ feet **2.** $\frac{3}{5}$ pounds **3.** 3 quarts **4.** 7 fluid ounces **5.** The length of George Washington's nose is said to be 19 feet 10 inches long. **6.** One rainbow trout weighed 83 ounces. **7.** The world record is 11 feet 8 inches longer than Adrian's throw. **8.** 0.031 meter **9.** 50 milligrams **10.** 0.435 deciliter **11.** 1,050 grams **12.** 45 centimeters **13.** 60 yards **14.** $1\frac{2}{3}$ gallons **15.** 21 grams **16.** The distance between Calgary and Edmonton is about 120 miles. **17.** A bag of apples weighs about $3\frac{3}{4}$ (or 3.75) kilograms. **18. a)** The Yeti is about 68 inches tall. **b)** The Yeti is about 170 centimeters tall. **19.** 61.6° **20.** 26.3° **21.** Perimeter: 49 yd; area: 132 yd^2 **22.** $x = 11$; $y = 18$; Perimeter: 66 m; area: 226 m^2 **23.** $14\frac{1}{2}$ ft **24.** 17 in. **25.** Perimeter: 6 ft; area: $2\frac{1}{4}$ ft^2 **26.** Circumference: 31.4 cm; area: 78.5 cm^2 **27.** 10.5 cm^2 **28.** 38 in.^{2} **29.** The volume of this ball bearing is about 113 cubic millimeters. **30.** The volume of the water tower is about 6,280 cubic feet.

31.

Continental Affiliation	Percent of World's Countries	Total Number of Countries
Asia	23.2%	44
Africa	27.4%	52
Europe	23.7%	45
North America	12.1%	23
Oceania	7.4%	14
South America	6.3%	12
Total	**100%**	**190**

Note: The total percent actually adds to 100.1% due to rounding.

32.

Sport	Percent of the Equipment Budget
Aquatics	12%
Baseball	20%
Basketball	8%
Football	40%
Track/Cross Country	10%
Other sports	10%
Total	**100%**

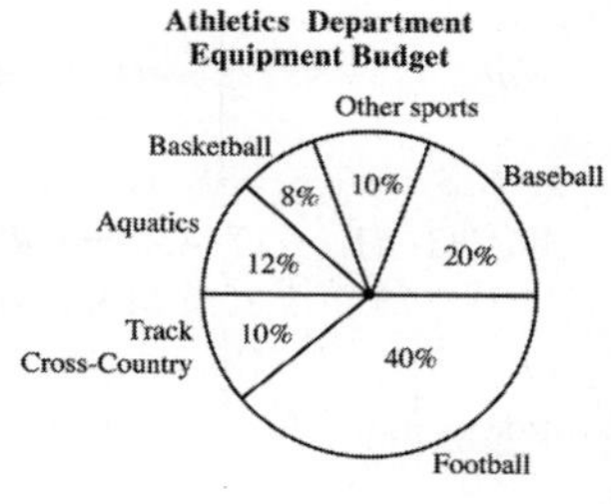

33. a)

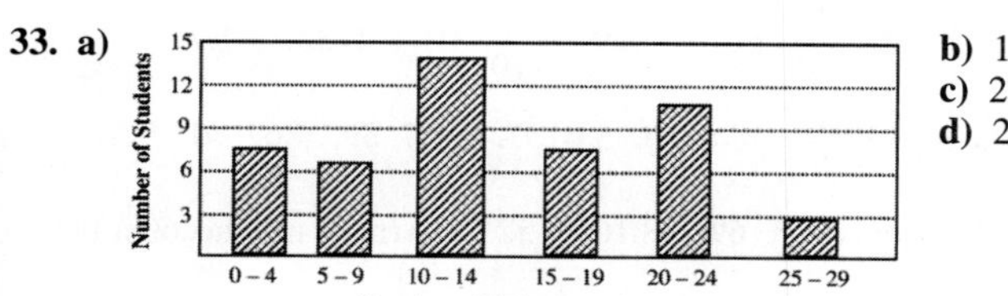

b) 15 **c)** 22 **d)** 21

34. a)

Number of Books Read	Number of Students
0–4	3
5–9	8
10–14	10
15–19	6
20–24	13
25–29	6
30–34	2
Total	**48**

b) 8 **c)** 16 **d)** 11

35. Mean: 6; median: 6; mode: 8 **36.** Mean: 9; median: 9.5; mode: 11 **37.** $\frac{3}{5}$ **38.** $\frac{4}{5}$ **39.** $\frac{1}{5}$ **40.** $\frac{2}{5}$ **41.** $\frac{8}{24} = \frac{1}{3}$ **42.** $\frac{3}{24} = \frac{1}{8}$ **43.** $\frac{6}{24} = \frac{1}{4}$ **44.** $\frac{4}{24} = \frac{1}{6}$

Chapter 9 Preparation Exercise Answers

1. 8 **2.** 25 **3.** 7 **4.** 9 **5.** 8 **6.** 39 **7.** $\frac{3}{5}$ **8.** $\frac{3}{4}$ **9.** $\frac{2}{3}$ **10.** $\frac{2}{9}$ **11.** $\frac{1}{6}$ **12.** $\frac{15}{16}$ **13.** $\frac{3}{4}$ **14.** $\frac{1}{5}$ **15.** $\frac{2}{3}$ **16.** $\frac{3}{10}$

Chapter 9 Focus Exercise Answers

Section 9.1

1. 10 **3.** 2 **5.** 14 **7.** 22 **9.** 28 **11.** 3 **13.** 25 **15.** 10 **17.** $x - 15$ **19.** $20 + x$ **21.** $x \div 18$ or $\frac{x}{18}$ **23.** x^2 **25.** $x \cdot 9$ or $9x$ **27.** $|x|$ **29.** -8 **31.** 18 **33.** $<$ **35.** $>$ **37.** $>$ **39.** $<$ **41.** 15 **43.** 21 **45.** 0 **47.** 44 **49.** $\frac{1}{2}$ **51.** 0.65 **53.** The value is 6 and the direction is to the right. **55.** The value is 12 and the direction is to the left.

Section 9.2

(Note: Positive answers may also be written with a plus sign in front.)

1. 2 **3.** -13 **5.** 5 **7.** 0 **9.** 0 **11.** -3 **13.** -1 **15.** -1 **17.** -7 **19.** 0 **21.** 1 **23.** -17 **25.** 9 **27.** 4 **29.** 0 **31.** -31 **33.** -1 **35.** 16 **37.** 7 **39.** -40 **41.** -7 **43.** -86 **45.** -23 **47.** 0 **49.** -4 **51.** -8 **53.** 0 **55.** -6

Section 9.3

(Note: Positive answers may also be written with a plus sign in front.)

1. 6 **3.** −6 **5.** −8 **7.** −8 **9.** 4 **11.** −7 **13.** 7 **15.** 8 **17.** 10 **19.** 2 **21.** 2 **23.** −10 **25.** −90 **27.** −54 **29.** −17 **31.** 0 **33.** 70 **35.** 91 **37.** 4 **39.** −1 **41.** −17 **43.** −4 **45.** 4 **47.** −35 **49.** 25 **51.** 2 **53.** −8 **55.** −8 **57.** −14 **59.** 3 **61.** 15 **63.** 0 **65.** 4 **67.** −6 **69.** 13 **71.** −8 **73.** −375 + 2,825; Mike's new account balance was $2,450. **75.** 58 − 72 + 33 − 39 − 29 + 115; Joni's account balance on Saturday was $66. **77.** −16 + 7; The temperature at 10:00 AM was −9°. **79.** −2 − 16; The new temperature was −18°. **81.** 5,280 − 1,416; The difference in altitude is 3,864 feet. **83.** 4,638 − (−784); The difference in altitude is 5,422 feet.

Section 9.4

(Note: Positive answers may also be written with a plus sign in front.)

1. $-\frac{1}{2}$ **3.** −1 **5.** $\frac{2}{3}$ **7.** $\frac{1}{2}$ **9.** $-\frac{1}{4}$ **11.** $-\frac{1}{5}$ **13.** $-\frac{4}{3}$ **15.** 0 **17.** $-\frac{2}{3}$ **19.** $\frac{1}{8}$ **21.** $\frac{4}{9}$ **23.** $\frac{25}{24}$ **25.** $\frac{13}{24}$ **27.** $-\frac{1}{6}$ **29.** $-\frac{1}{10}$ **31.** 0.4 **33.** −1.7 **35.** −0.75 **37.** −0.32 **39.** −0.46 **41.** 1.74 **43.** 1.2 **45.** −15.9 **47.** −0.63 **49.** 3.03 **51.** 0 **53.** −8.4 **55.** 5.6 **57.** −9.7 **59.** 0.67 **61.** 0.21 **63.** 7.12 **65.** −1.54 **67.** −57.82 + 100; Daneice's new account balance is $42.18. This is a credit. **69.** 38.16 − 52.94; Arnie's new account balance is −$14.78. This is a debit. **71.** −8.4 + 15.25; The temperature at noon was 6.85°. **73.** −3.85 − 5.9; At noon, the temperature of the snowball was −9.75° Celsius. **75.** 4.25 − (−1.8); The difference in altitude is 6.05 meters. **77.** −2.65 − (−23.9); The difference in altitude is 21.25 meters.

Section 9.5

(Note: Positive answers may also be written with a plus sign in front.)

1. 20 **3.** −63 **5.** 60 **7.** 16 **9.** 0 **11.** −28 **13.** −100 **15.** −36 **17.** 24 **19.** −24 **21.** −9 **23.** −60 **25.** $-\frac{3}{32}$ **27.** −16 **29.** $-\frac{2}{3}$ **31.** $-\frac{4}{9}$ **33.** 20 **35.** $\frac{9}{2}$ **37.** 60 **39.** −96 **41.** −54 **43.** 120 **45.** 0 **47.** 60 **49.** −5 **51.** 7 **53.** −3 **55.** 2 **57.** Undefined **59.** −20 **61.** 0 **63.** −7 **65.** 9 **67.** $\frac{3}{2}$ **69.** $\frac{5}{12}$ **71.** $\frac{8}{7}$ **73.** $-\frac{8}{15}$ **75.** $\frac{3}{20}$ **77.** $\frac{1}{18}$

Section 9.6

(Note: Positive answers may also be written with a plus sign in front.)

1. 8 **3.** 9 **5.** 5 **7.** 7 **9.** 1 **11.** −4 **13.** −64 **15.** −1,000 **17.** 36 **19.** 81 **21.** −8 **23.** −32 **25.** 7 **27.** −20 **29.** 18 **31.** 18 **33.** 7 **35.** 8 **37.** −26 **39.** 16 **41.** 16 **43.** 12 **45.** 23 **47.** −4 **49.** −44 **51.** −5 **53.** −50 **55.** 4 **57.** 7 **59.** −13 **61.** −2 **63.** 1 **65.** 4 **67.** 14 **69.** 11 **71.** −4 **73.** 12 **75.** −2 **77.** −2 **79.** −1 **81.** −2 **83.** $\frac{15}{2}$ **85.** $-\frac{1}{2}$ **87.** $-\frac{1}{3}$ **89.** −2 **91.** −6 **93.** 7 **95.** −2 **97.** 3 **99.** −4

Section 9.7

1. 4, m, 2 **3.** −3, y, 1 **5.** 9, none, none **7.** 1, y, 3 **9.** −1, d, 5 **11.** $-\frac{3}{4}$, n, 6 **13. a)** $3x^4$ **b)** $-5x^3$ **c)** 1 **d)** −9 **e)** 4 **f)** 1 **15. a)** $-8y$ **b)** y^2 **c)** −3 **d)** 1 **e)** 1 **f)** 4 **17.** $7x$ **19.** $13x^2$ **21.** $-1a$ or $-a$ **23.** $-12x^2 - 10x$ (cannot be simplified) **25.** $2y^2$ **27.** $-3m$ **29.** 0 **31.** $8p^2$ **33.** $-6k$ **35.** $-1v^2$ or $-v^2$ **37.** $2s + 4m$ (cannot be simplified) **39.** 0 **41.** $10y$ **43.** $-5x$ **45.** $6c$ **47.** $-7x$ **49.** $-8y^2$ **51.** $-28p$ **53.** $11x + 3$ ... $-x - 2$ **57.** $4a - 5$ **59.** $5w + 5w^2$ **61.** $-1 - 3x$ **63.** $-4c - 4b$

Section 9.8

1. $20x$ **3.** $4y$ **5.** $-28c^2$ **7.** $-48a^4$ **9.** $8w + 10$ **11.** $20y + 32$ **13.** $7x^2 + 14$ **15.** $2x - 16$ **17.** $14p - 21$ **19.** $32x^2 - 8$ **21.** $-8c + 6$ **23.** $-15x^2 - 5$ **25.** $-10y - 35$ **27.** $-36x + 12$ **29.** $-4 + 8b^2$ **31.** $12x - 30$ **33.** $-4y - 4$ **35.** $-1x - 3$ or $-x - 3$ **37.** $48w^2 + 8$ **39.** $-1m - 8$ or $-m - 8$ **41.** $-7p + 7$ **43.** $9w + 12$

Chapter 9 Review Exercise Answers

(Note: Positive answers may also be written with a plus sign in front.)

1. 24 **2.** 28 **3.** 30 **4.** 33 **5.** $8 - x$ **6.** $x + 14$. **7.** $>$ **8.** $<$ **9.** $<$ **10.** $>$ **11.** 9 **12.** 11 **13.** 0 **14.** 21 **15.** -6 **16.** -4 **17.** -13 **18.** -5 **19.** 0 **20.** -20 **21.** 16 **22.** -31 **23.** 71 **24.** -52 **25.** 74 **26.** -27 **27.** -16 **28.** -3 **29.** -2 **30.** -4 **31.** -7 **32.** -12 **33.** 9 **34.** 4 **35.** 30 **36.** -13 **37.** -8 **38.** 55 **39.** 0 **40.** 91 **41.** 2 **42.** -16 **43.** $97 - (-64)$; The difference in altitude is 161 feet. **44.** $-13 + 8$; At 6:00 AM the temperature was $-5°$. **45.** $10 - 17$; Adele's new checkbook balance is $-\$7$. **46.** $-26 - 15$; Adele's new checkbook balance is $-\$41$. **47.** $-\frac{1}{3}$ **48.** -1 **49.** $\frac{4}{5}$ **50.** $\frac{2}{3}$ **51.** $-\frac{14}{15}$ **52.** $-\frac{17}{24}$ **53.** 4.8 **54.** -1.85 **55.** -8.87 **56.** 6.77 **57.** 16.5 **58.** -3.27 **59.** $-57.82 - 25.36$; The new balance of Clayton's account is $-\$83.18$. This is a debit. **60.** $10.6 - (-32.9)$; The difference in altitude is 43.5 meters. **61.** 6 **62.** 99 **63.** -77 **64.** 40 **65.** 4 **66.** 0 **67.** $-\frac{3}{4}$ **68.** $-\frac{9}{14}$ **69.** $\frac{4}{3}$ **70.** $-\frac{2}{3}$ **71.** 30 **72.** 40 &]**73.** -48 **74.** -28 **75.** -11 **76.** 6 **77.** 6 **78.** -5 **79.** $-\frac{4}{5}$ **80.** $-\frac{3}{16}$ **81.** 3 **82.** -2 **83.** -12 **84.** 81 **85.** -2 **86.** -8 **87.** -8 **88.** 5 **89.** 30 **90.** -6 **91.** 7 **92.** 17 **93.** 4 **94.** 2 **95.** $2w$ **96.** $-8w^2$ **97.** -1 **98.** 4 **99.** 1 **100.** 3 **101.** $12x$ **102.** $-6y$ **103.** $-4w^2$ **104.** $6b^2$ **105.** $1x$ or x **106.** 0 **107.** $9p + 3k$ **108.** $-14x$ **109.** $-4x$ **110.** $-2y - 1$ **111.** $-5c - 7b$ **112.** $4 - 5x$ **113.** $-12x^2$ **114.** $81y$ **115.** $42p$ **116.** $-15a^3$ **117.** $9y + 18$ **118.** $-12y + 18$ **119.** $15h - 5$ **120.** $-2y - 2$ **121.** $24y - 21$ **122.** $-8p + 28$

Chapter 9 Test Answers

(Note: Positive answers may also be written with a plus sign in front.)

1. $15 - x$ **2.** $\sqrt{x}$ **3.** $<$ **4.** $>$ **5.** -8 **6.** 14 **7.** 9 **8.** -100 **9.** -10 **10.** -6 **11.** 15 **12.** -0.48 **13.** -4.53 **14.** -36 **15.** -16 **16.** -5 **17.** -7 **18.** Undefined **19.** 5 **20.** $\frac{10}{3}$ **21.** $-\frac{8}{9}$ **22.** -7 **23.** -1 **24.** 16 **25.** -27 **26.** -2 **27.** 120 **28.** $\left(-\frac{2}{3}\right)$ **29.** $-\frac{5}{6}$ **30.** $-145.22 + 53$; Son Hee's new account balance is $-\$92.22$. This is a debit. **31.** $-162 - (-458)$; The difference in altitude is 296 feet. **32.** -4 **33.** 1 **34.** $7p^2$ **35.** $-5a$ **36.** $-10x - 5y$ **37.** $32k^4$ **38.** $-10y$ **39.** $6w - 15$ **40.** $-14c + 21$

Chapter 10 Preparation Exercise Answers

1. $n = 13$ **2.** $n = 15$ **3.** $\frac{3}{4}$ **4.** $\frac{21}{4}$ or $5\frac{1}{4}$ **5.** $n = 20$ **6.** $n = \frac{1}{6}$ **7.** $\frac{4}{5}$ **8.** $\frac{2}{9}$ **9.** -16 **10.** 12 **11.** 4 **12.** $-\frac{1}{12}$ **13.** $5x$ **14.** $-16x$ **15.** $20x - 28$ **16.** $-15x + 10$

apter 10 Focus Exercise Answers

Section 10.1

1. $x = 18$ **3.** $w = -3$ **5.** $y = 1$ **7.** $x = 3$ **9.** $p = -6$ **11.** $m = -10$ **13.** $x = 6$ **15.** $c = 3$ **17.** $p = -8$ **19.** $x = -14$ **21.** $w = -4$ **23.** $m = 0$ **25.** $m = -0.9$ **27.** $x = -1.8$ **29.** $h = -1.6$ **31.** $y = 1$ **33.** $k = \frac{1}{3}$ **35.** $m = -\frac{2}{5}$ **37.** $x = -\frac{2}{3}$ **39.** $p = -1$ **41.** $x = -\frac{3}{4}$ **43.** $n = 7$ **45.** $y = -6$ **47.** $k = 12$ **49.** $p = 2$ **51.** $v = -8$ **53.** $y = 3$ **55.** $y = \frac{4}{3}$ or $y = 1\frac{1}{3}$ **57.** $h = -\frac{3}{2}$ or $h = -1\frac{1}{2}$ **59.** $c = \frac{8}{5}$ or $c = 1\frac{3}{5}$ **61.** $y = -35$ **63.** $x = 12$ **65.** $k = 4$ **67.** $b = -4$ **69.** $m = -\frac{1}{4}$ **71.** $x = 0$ **73.** $y = \frac{9}{8}$ or $y = 1\frac{1}{8}$ **75.** $y = 40$ **77.** $q = -\frac{6}{5}$ or $q = -1\frac{1}{5}$ **79.** $x = 15$ **81.** $x = -0.4$ **83.** $w = -22$ **85.** $v = \frac{23}{24}$ **87.** $p = -12$ **89.** $w = -\frac{5}{4}$

Section 10.2

1. $x = 4$ **3.** $x = -3$ **5.** $w = 8$ **7.** $x = 9$ **9.** $v = -3$ **11.** $y = 2$ **13.** $p = 20$ **15.** $x = 0$ **17.** $y = \frac{3}{2}$ or $y = 1\frac{1}{2}$ **19.** $x = -\frac{5}{2}$ or $x = -2\frac{1}{2}$ **21.** $k = 15$ **23.** $w = -18$ **25.** $x = 2$ **27.** $y = 1$ **29.** $p = -3$ **31.** $x = -9$ **33.** $y = -1$ **35.** $x = 2$ **37.** $w = 8$ **39.** $h = -9$ **41.** $m = 3$ **43.** $y = 4$ **45.** $x = 1$ **47.** $y = -10$ **49.** $x = -5$ **51.** $c = 0$ **53.** $y = \frac{3}{2}$ or $y = 1\frac{1}{2}$ **55.** $x = -\frac{1}{5}$ **57.** $k = 8$ **59.** $r = -10$

Section 10.3

1. $x + 9$ **3.** $x - 5$ **5.** $\frac{3}{8}x$ **7.** $2x$ **9.** $\frac{1}{4}x$ **11.** $18 - x$ **13.** $9 + x$ **15.** $8x$ **17.** $2x + 4$ **19.** $\frac{1}{2}x + 7$ **21.** $3x + 1$ **23.** $\frac{1}{3}x - 8$ **25.** The number is -3. **27.** The number is -14. **29.** The number is 5. **31.** The number is -6. **33.** The number is 32. **35.** The number is -18. **37.** The number is $-\frac{5}{2}$ or $-2\frac{1}{2}$ **39.** The number is $\frac{7}{3}$ or $2\frac{1}{3}$ **41.** The number is 7. **43.** The number is 12. **45.** The number is -2. **47.** The number is 5. **49.** The number is -3. **51.** The number is 30. **53.** The number is -8.

Section 10.4

1. The width is 31 inches. **3.** The measure of the third angle is 35°. **5.** Adrienne's score on the fist test was 73 points. **7.** It will take Margo $3\frac{1}{2}$ hours to get to the beach. **9.** Mr. Daniels received 68 votes, and Mrs. Jenkins received 52 votes. **11.** Jorge walked 31 kilometers, and Darush walked 27 kilometers. **13.** The smallest angle measure is 28°, and the middle angle measure is 52°. **15.** Carol received 89 points on the first test and 81 points on the second test. **17.** The length is 51 feet, and the width is 39 feet. **19.** The shorter side is 9 inches long, and the middle side is 12 inches long.

Chapter 10 Review Exercise Answers

1. No **2.** Yes **3.** $m = -3$ **4.** $y = 1$ **5.** $x = 10$ **6.** $k = 3$ **7.** $p = -8$ **8.** $h = -11$ **9.** $x = -14$ **10.** $y = -3$ **11.** $w = 4$ **12.** $y = 4$ **13.** $c = \frac{10}{7}$ or $c = 1\frac{3}{7}$ **14.** $k = -\frac{2}{5}$ **15.** $n = 41$ **16.** $x = -5$ **17.** $y = 29$ **18.** $m = -4$ **19.** $y = -\frac{3}{2}$ or $y = -1\frac{1}{2}$ **20.** $x = 14$ **21.** $y = -16$ **22.** $k = 20$ **23.** $a = -\frac{9}{2}$ or $a = -4\frac{1}{2}$ **24.** $y = -27$ **25.** $k = \frac{10}{3}$ or $k = 3\frac{1}{3}$ **26.** $a = -\frac{5}{14}$ **27.** $x = 8$ **28.** $x = -2$ **29.** $c = -6$ **30.** $y = 1$ **31.** $k = -24$ **32.** $y = -70$ **33.** $y = 1$ **34.** $x = 2$ **35.** $y = 5$ **36.** $p = 4$ **37.** $x = -11$ **38.** $x = -9$ **39.** $y = -7$ **40.** $x = 12$ **41.** $y = -27$ **42.** $x = 5$ **43.** $x = -38$ **44.** $p = 4$ **45.** $x - 12$ **46.** $\frac{4}{9}x$ **47.** $23 - x$ **48.** $9 + x$ **49.** $\frac{1}{2}x + 16$ **50.** $5 + 2x$ **51.** $2x - 6$ **52.** $\frac{1}{2}x + 15$ **53.** The number is -10. **54.** The number is 8. **55.** The number is 40. **56.** The number is $\frac{11}{2}$. or $5\frac{1}{2}$ **57.** The number is -8. **58.** The number is -11. **59.** The number is 9. **60.** The number is -18. **61.** The length is 47 centimeters. **62.** It should take Enzio $3\frac{1}{2}$ hours to get there. **63.** Toto is to receive \$125 and Dorothy is to receive \$1,075. **64.** Florida's score on her first math test was 77 and the score on her second math test was 92. **65.** Karl rode 34 miles and Kristen rode 29 miles. **66.** The shortest side is 11 yards long and the middle side is 18 yards long. **67.** The measure of the smallest angle is 20°, and the measure of the middle angle is 60°. **68.** The attendance on Saturday was 2,125 and the attendance on Sunday was 1,275.

Chapter 10 Test Answers

1. $y = 7$ **2.** $x = -\frac{4}{3}$ **3.** $k = -\frac{1}{5}$ **4.** $x = -10$ **5.** $x = 7$ **6.** $x = 50$ **7.** $w = -9$ **8.** $x = 3$ **9.** $x = 2$ **10.** $y = -2$ **11.** The number is -25. **12.** The number is 11. **13.** The Elson's will pay Josh \$265 after the second day. **14.** The shorter piece is 24 inches long and the longer piece is 48 inches long. **15.** The second side is 13 inches, and the third side is 11 inches. **16.** The smallest angle measures 33° and the middle angle measures 57°. **17.** Tunde earns \$23,000 and Marta earns \$24,500. **18.** The width is 20 feet and the length is 44 feet.

Chapters 9 and 10 Cumulative Review Answers

1. 0 **2.** -2 **3.** -16 **4.** -3 **5.** 15 **6.** 26 **7.** -94 **8.** -16 **9.** -35 **10.** -2.59 **11.** $-\frac{2}{9}$ **12.** $-\frac{11}{18}$ **13.** -35 **14.** 36 **15.** -6 **16.** 10 **17.** 9 **18.** Ajay's new account balance is $-\$48$. **19.** 81 **20.** -8 **21.** -19 **22.** -9 **23.** $10x^3$ **24.** $-9y$ **25.** $-4w$ **26.** $-4x^4 + 4x$ **27.** $-6x^2$ **28.** $21y$ **29.** $4x - 12$ **30.** $-45w + 10$ **31.** $x = 4$ **32.** $c = -11$ **33.** $y = 6$ **34.** $x = 7$ **35.** The number is -2. **36.** The measure of the smallest angle is 32°, and the measure of the middle angle is 58°. **37.** Becca will receive \$11,500 and Andrea will receive \$15,000.

Index

Student Questionnaire

Basic Mathematics

Preliminary Edition

Robert H. Prior

Dear Student:

Please fill out this form and drop it in the mail. We look forward to hearing what you think and we appreciate the time you take to provide your feedback.

1. Name (print): ______________________ School: ______________________

   City/State: ______________________ Instructor: ______________________

2. Several features are included in this text to make the material more accessible, relevant, and interesting. Please rate this text by circling the appropriate number: 1 = you found it not at all useful/helpful, 5 = you found it very useful/helpful, N/A = you did not cover it.

Feature	**Least Helpful**					**Most Helpful**
Chapter Introductions	1	2	3	4	5	N/A
Preparation Exercises	1	2	3	4	5	N/A
Effectiveness of Explanations	1	2	3	4	5	N/A
Easy to Understand Examples	1	2	3	4	5	N/A
You Try It Exercises after Examples	1	2	3	4	5	N/A
Focus Exercises	1	2	3	4	5	N/A
Accessible/Interesting Writing Style	1	2	3	4	5	N/A
Think about It Exercises	1	2	3	4	5	N/A
Chapter Reviews	1	2	3	4	5	N/A
Chapter Review Exercises	1	2	3	4	5	N/A

3. If you circled a 2 or below on any of the above, please explain why and how we could improve that part of the text.

4. What did you like most about this text?

5. Would you recommend this text to your professor for this course? Why or why not?

   ❑ Yes ❑ No

6. May Addison-Wesley quote you in the promotion of Prior's *Basic Mathematics*?

   ❑ Yes ❑ No

Signature ______________________